The Power of Birthdays, Stars, & Numbers

The Power of Birthdays, Stars, & Numbers

THE COMPLETE PERSONOLOGY
REFERENCE GUIDE

Saffi Crawford and Geraldine Sullivan

BALLANTINE BOOKS · NEW YORK

A Ballantine Book
Published by The Ballantine Publishing Group

http://www.randomhouse.com/BB/

LIBRARY OF CONGRESS CATALOGING-IN-PUBLICATION DATA
Crawford, Saffi.
  The power of birthdays, stars, and numbers : the complete
personology reference guide / Saffi Crawford, Geraldine Sullivan. —
1st ed.
      p.   cm.
  ISBN 0-345-41819-0 (pbk. : alk. paper)
  1. Birthdays—Miscellanea.   2. Astrology and psychology.
3. Numerology.   4. Personality—Miscellanea.   I. Sullivan,
Geraldine.   II. Title.
BF1729.B45C73   1998
133.5—dc21   98-13941
                                                          CIP

Text design by Holly Johnson
Cover design by Dreu Pennington-McNeil and David Stevenson
Cover illustration by Christina Balit

Manufactured in the United States of America

First Edition: November 1998

10   9   8   7   6   5   4   3   2   1

To our families,
who have had to be very patient with us while we completed this book, and for all their support:
our parents, Margaret and Michael Sullivan and Leon and Kristina Grushko,
as well as Melissa Crawford, Ricky Foulcer, and Cleo Foulcer.

Acknowledgments

We would like to thank all those who made this project possible,
in particular, Huw Davies, Jane Laing, Mark Reiner, Chuck Wein, Juliana Doyle, Deirdre Sullivan,
Pat Foster, Tasha Griffiths, Josephine Shannon, Anne Leman, and Alexia Beck.

Contents

Introduction

In the pages of this book, you will find a complete personality profile for people born on each of the 366 days of the year. This book goes far beyond simple Sun sign astrology to provide insight into the unique characteristics of each day. We have drawn on our knowledge of astrology, psychology, numerology, and fixed stars, and only after synthesizing all these disciplines have we created these comprehensive daily profiles. No two days share identical cosmic forces; therefore, each day is uniquely special. Every daily profile provides intriguing information about yourself and your future and will also prove irresistible in checking up on birthdays of friends, lovers, family, and colleagues. You will gain a greater depth of understanding of your own capabilities and potential as well as insight into the character and motivation of the people around you.

Astrology and numerology are languages of symbols that explore the relationship between humankind and the universe. They give us an indication of our place in the greater plan of the cosmos.

Since the earliest days of its history, humankind has always been aware of the forces and cycles of nature. These natural cycles and cosmic rhythms exert an influence on every living organism. Although the fixed stars are situated outside our own solar system, they too have a pull upon us. They have been incorporated into astrology since ancient times. In this book, we introduce modern interpretations of the influence of fixed stars for each day of the Sun's yearly cycle.

Astrology and numerology are ways to interpret these influences, to show how these cycles affect our lives. The many facets of astrological study include astronomy, symbolism, psychology, physics, and geometry, while numerology embodies the theory that numbers possess a duality of quality and quantity. All the powerful interpretive methods have been brought together in this book to give a unique, daily, in-depth profile.

The Power of Birthdays, Stars, and Numbers integrates two different ways of calculating the Sun's yearly cycle. The astrological year begins on March 21, at 0 degrees of Aries, whereas the numerological year based on the Western calendar begins each year on January 1. These two solar year systems, when combined, reveal the holistic vision of astronumerology that can provide deep psychological insight for each birthdate.

Cogent astrological practices are based on a single moment in space and time, making each astrology chart symbolically unique. Although astrologers require the exact year, date, time, and place of birth in order to construct a horoscopic wheel, popular astrology refers only to the twelve basic signs of the zodiac. This division of the year into twelve monthly categories, along with the planets, can be viewed as the ABC of astrological studies.

The Sun is in the center of our solar system, and the planets, including the Earth, orbit around it. The Earth makes two important cycles as it revolves both on its axis and around the Sun in a counterclockwise direction. It is the Earth's rotation on its axis that brings about the cycle of day and night. From the geocentric view (from Earth), the Sun appears to cross the sky from the eastern horizon to the western horizon. The Sun's apparent journey against the backdrop of the fixed stars in the twelve constellations marks a path called the ecliptic around the Earth. The Earth's axis is not only rotating but tilting, with the North Pole facing the Sun and away from the Sun at different times of the year to produce four climate variations called the four seasons. These points are more commonly called spring and autumnal equinoxes and summer and winter solstices. In astrology these four divisions of the year are called the four cardinal points of the 360-degree zodiacal wheel. The astrological year begins in the spring at 0 degrees of Aries; the summer solstice is marked as 0 degrees Cancer; the autumn is at 0 degrees Libra; and the winter solstice is at 0 degrees Capricorn. Since the zodiac wheel is divided into twelve equal parts of 30 degrees arc each, the four cardinal signs of the zodiac wheel are followed by four fixed signs of Taurus, Leo, Scorpio, and Aquarius. The four mutable signs of Gemini, Virgo, Sagittarius, and Pisces complete the twelve signs of the zodiac wheel.

The zodiac is divided into twelve distinct signs. But in advanced astrological practice, those signs are divided further, each division associated with yet other forces. The twelve signs divide into thirds, called decanates. Each decanate describes 10 degrees of the circle of the zodiac, with the three decanates of that sign acting as a subinfluence and complement to the qualities of the sign itself. Each decanate is associated with an additional sign and planet. In this book, you will find not only the sign under which you were born, but also your significant decanate.

As the Sun returns to approximately the same degree every year, astrologers refer to a person's birthday as a solar return. By dividing each of the twelve zodiac signs into thirty individual degrees, and including numerology and fixed stars, *The Power of Birthdays, Stars, and Numbers* creates a link between the twelve zodiac signs and the comprehensive art of astrology.

We also provide a special section that allow readers to further investigate their character and future through the use of numerology. This includes calculating holistic numbers and making predictions through personal year numbers.

The Birthday Profiles

Each birthday profile contains specific insight into the characteristics of each day. The profile provides general knowledge of planetary and numerological configurations along with the Sun sign, degree, and decanate that further individualize the Sun sign by adding the subinfluences of another sign and planet.

We have also included the astrological technique for prediction known as progression. Astrologers regularly use Sun progressions to indicate important years in an individual's life. These turning points for personal development occur approximately three times in a person's life, when the progressed Sun changes signs.

The strengths and weaknesses hidden within each person are revealed in the Secret Self. Suitable career options are featured for each entry, along with a list of the famous personalities born on that day.

In each profile we provide you some insight into the numerology of your birthday. Each day describes the qualities of the numbers, and these numbers are further described through the qualities of the month's numerology. Although your day and month numerology play a significant part in understanding your character, they are secondary to your personal holistic number, which influences your entire life and every aspect of your character. So in order to understand your character you need to read not only your day and month numerology but also your holistic number which is clearly defined in the introduction to this book. If you would like to discover the numerology of how each year applies to you, you may want to calculate your personal year number, which is also provided in the introductory section.

In each daily entry, love and relationships are featured and include specific dates and categories of people with whom the reader is likely to find karmic links, ideal love relationships,

friendships, and partners. Although we have included many suitable dates, these lists are not conclusive; therefore, you may have important relationships with people not listed in this book.

Each birthday profile also provides information regarding the special and powerful influence on each birthday of the fixed stars scattered along the path of the Sun's yearly cycle. Several stars may affect your birthday, or there may be no stars bright and close enough to the Sun's location in the galactic sky that day to exert any Sun-related influence. All the stars that have Sun-related influence for the birthday are listed. And you will also find your primary star's influence. Beginning on p. 795, there is an appendix of all the important fixed stars, so you can look up the influences of all the stars on your list—and if you choose to delve even further into astrological practice, you may find that even if a fixed star is not related to the position of your day's Sun, some stars will nevertheless be linked to the positions of the planets on that day. It is our hope that each of you will want to learn more and delve yet deeper into the rich intricacies of the fixed stars.

Special insights into the characteristics of each day are further described through the qualities of the day's numerology. These are supplemented by interpretations of the month's number. Finally, in each daily entry, love and relationships are featured and include specific dates and categories of people with whom the reader is likely to find karmic links, ideal love relationships, friendships, and partners.

In bringing together in one volume our ranges of expertise, we hope to provide you with the most comprehensive reference tool available in the field of personology. We have worked to synthesize many years of research, complex astrological and chart experience, and thousands of case studies into personology profiles that will give you a greater depth of understanding of your own and others' character, capabilities, and potential. Come with us now into the days of the year. Each day begins as each person begins, unique and full of promise.

Introduction to Astrology

Since the earliest days of our civilizations we have observed the heavens to gain a greater understanding of the relationship between humanity and the universe. To early humans, the impermanence of existence on Earth brought uncertainty. The recurrence of celestial phenomena, however, such as the rising and setting Sun, in contrast brought reassurance. Our ancestors perceived this contrast as the fundamental distinction between celestial and terrestrial domains. Astrology is, therefore, a study of the meaningful interaction between the stars, planetary cycles, and events on Earth.

One of the few remaining philosophies to maintain a holistic perspective, astrology teaches us that everything is interconnected. Nothing stands as a law by itself. Everything is part of a constantly shifting and dynamic relationship with the cycles of the cosmos. We do not stand outside this living system. We affect it, and we are profoundly affected by it. All people are part of a changing and dynamic relationship with other people. The universe is a complex interplay of cycles and forces, as opposite polarities set each other in motion, themselves part of greater systems. Astrologers acknowledge this interplay and try to comprehend it through symbolism.

No person stands alone, for all people are part of shifting and dynamic relationships with other people, and each of these people is involved in shifting and dynamic relationships with the cycles of the cosmos.

All that is organic pulses, is distinguished by periodicity. This cyclic, rhythmic existence is captured by the astrological hypothesis. Astrology embraces complexity, the simultaneity of subjectivity and objectivity. Objectively, astrology measures time by the cycles of the planets, giving a unique perspective on the meaning of duration. Subjectively, astrology operates through deep symbolism and finds knowledge through the study of context.

Astrology maintains that the course of nature is a circle or mandala. In the 360 degrees of the circle we experience each moment of being individually and collectively. Each degree is a separate fragment of the circle, but only with each degree present does the circle exist. The mandala is a symbol of all creation, a self-contained and perfect form with no beginning, no end. The circle stands for both the universe and all human individuals, for the universe within. All of life's activities relate to this circle. Its structure also conveys the cycles of time. By exploring astrology, one can reveal the connections between the external and internal universes, gaining greater psychological and spiritual awareness.

The two major lights in astrology are the Sun and Moon, which correspond to the cycle of day and night. On the basis of this rhythm, solar and lunar calendars were established by early cultures and interpreted as hours, days, months, and years. In psychological terms, the symbolic union of the Sun and Moon is perceived as "the mystical marriage," representing the union of opposites within the individual. In Eastern philosophical terms this union is characterized by the yin/yang, or masculine and feminine, principles.

A personal horoscope is a "map" showing the precise position of the planets in our solar system in relation to Earth at the moment of an individual's birth. In its basic form the astrological birth chart consists of ten planets and twelve zodiac signs.

The Twelve Astrological Roles of the Sun

Common to all of humankind are well-known universal themes such as love, hate, birth, death, childhood, parenthood, and old age. The complete range of these human experiences is symbolized by the astrological wheel as the Sun makes its symbolic journey through the twelve zodiac signs. Astrology maintains that we are all born into life to join this great cycle of existence in order to take on a role within the divine drama. In the words of Shakespeare: "All the world's a stage, and all the men and women merely players."

In the model of wholeness, everything is in relationship with everything else and therefore interconnected. Similarly, in astrology all twelve signs are imbedded in the psyches of individuals and humankind alike, and although a person is born in one particular sign, in order to integrate with the whole, he or she must relate to the other eleven signs. In our daily lives we come to experience all facets of the twelve signs, but our Sun sign can be interpreted as the major role we have come here to learn to play. In psychological terms, Carl Gustav Jung interpreted these universal roles as archetypes.

People often think they are acting out their own role, but through self-realization they come to recognize that individuals are only conduits or channels of the divine and that through them the universe is focused according to the time and place of their performance. The astrologer Dane Rudhyar said in his book *An Astrological Mandala*: "The ego in [an individual] becomes a crystalline lens through which the will of God is concentrated in the individualized act. He does nothing but the One Mind thinks him. His life has become sacred because it is no longer his life but the whole performing with and through the space of his total organism."

The Archetypes and Roles for the Twelve Zodiac Signs

Each zodiac sign takes on and acts out the roles of a particular archetype in order to manifest its own power in the act of creation. In the following list some of the major archetypes and roles are linked to each sign:

ARIES: the Leader, the Enthusiast, the Pioneer, the Warrior, the Daredevil, the Competitor

TAURUS: the Pragmatist, the Sensualist, the Nature Lover, the Singer, the Evaluator

GEMINI: the Communicator, the Interpreter, the Writer, the Speaker, the Storyteller, the Educator

CANCER: the Mother, the Carer, the Psychic, the Counselor, the Protector

LEO: the Performer, the King or Queen, the Child, the Creative Artist, the Lover, the Actor or Actress

VIRGO: the Analyst, the Perfectionist, the Researcher, the Servant, the Refiner, the Critic

LIBRA: the Lover, the Diplomat, the Partner, the Socializer, the Host or Hostess, the Balancer, the Negotiator

SCORPIO: the Controller, the Hypnotist, the Magician, the Detective, the Transformer

SAGITTARIUS: the Traveler, the Philosopher, the Optimist, the Seeker, the Foreigner

CAPRICORN: the Father, the Authority Figure, the Worker, the Disciplinarian, the Traditionalist

AQUARIUS: the Humanitarian, the Detached Observer, the Inventor, the Scientist, the Friend, the Eccentric, the Revolutionary, the Anarchist

PISCES: the Visionary, the Romantic, the Savior, the Mystic, the Healer, the Dreamer, the Poet

The Twelve Astrological Signs

ARIES

FIRST SIGN

CARDINAL FIRE

RULING PLANET: MARS

BODY PART: HEAD

KEYWORDS:

ENERGY, ACTIVITY, LEADERSHIP

Bursting with energy and creative ideas, Arians belong to the first sign of the zodiac. Aries is a fire sign, and Aries people are high-spirited and enthusiastic; they genuinely believe the world is theirs to explore and conquer. Ardent and assertive by nature, these individuals forge ahead with endless projects and activities, which they love to initiate. Arians are the pioneers and leaders of the zodiac, and even the quieter among them secretly want to be number one or first at something. Ruled by the planet Mars, Arians are doers and very rarely sit around twiddling their thumbs. Combining an active body with a daring and enterprising spirit, these personalities eagerly seek to be in the forefront of any activity. Frequently bold and passionate, they can be highly idealistic and fiercely loyal to the people they love. Arians like to talk at length to their partners about their own favorite projects but can be equally supportive of their partners.

As patience is not their strongest point, often you can recognize Aries people by their direct approach, decisive action, and lack of subtlety and tact. This same impatience can also make them intolerant, impulsive, and highly likely to do something rash on a moment's notice. Arians, however, respond well to crises, as they have the ability to meet challenges head-on and to face difficult situations courageously.

Despite opposing public opinion, Arians will usually refuse to compromise their ideals, even if it gets them into trouble. As they get older, however, most will learn humility, but not without first encountering many confrontations. The men of this sign love to play knight-errant and the women may appear forceful and assertive.

Often Arians are quick to anger and eager to express their opinions, but they are just as quick to forgive and forget. Fired by adrenaline and impatient with detail, these individuals are usually in a hurry and work better when launching projects. Nevertheless, Arian personalities may need to guard against a naive, self-centered nature or a tendency to bully others.

Generally, Arians are full of creative energy and inspiration and have great faith in themselves. This often shows in natural leadership ability. It is therefore hardly surprising that they can influence others to follow in their footsteps. Refusing to be put down, dynamic and generous, the Aries spirit lives to fight another day.

TAURUS

SECOND SIGN

FIXED EARTH

RULING PLANET: VENUS

BODY PART: THROAT AND NECK

KEYWORDS:

ENDURANCE, PERSISTENCE, SENSUALITY

Sensible Taureans are quietly determined and very sensible individuals who never give up. Patient and persistent, they will continue when all others have fallen by the wayside. Their warm, seemingly calm and easygoing manner reflects an enjoyment of simplicity in life.

Taureans do not like to rush into things; they make decisions carefully and deliberately, with security and financial issues very much to the fore. With Venus as their ruling planet, Taureans are often magnetic, sensual, and very attractive to the opposite sex. The Venus influence also bestows an enhanced love of beauty, an interest in the arts, and a highly refined sense of touch.

Taurus is a practical Earth sign, and so the basic comforts of life, such as food and home, are very important to these individuals. They often become experts at culinary skills and connoisseurs of wine, and they love entertaining. Taureans are also the symbolic bankers of the zodiac, with the majority of them making careful lists of all their money dealings. Charged with being materialistic, Taureans would reply that they are merely being sensible and looking for value for money. They can be experts at evaluating everything, from money matters to themselves.

Taureans are often generous with their loved ones but may have to avoid being overpossessive. Loyal and devoted friends, they often suffer in silence in order to keep the peace, but if pushed too far, they are notorious for being obstinate and stubborn. Taurean personalities need to feel grounded and stable, and therefore prefer keeping things the way they are. In times of change and instability these individuals may have difficulty adapting to new situations. Happily, they can always find comfort through love of art and creativity, the joys of nature, or music.

Taureans usually have an attractive, calm, and even voice and are often good singers. If stressed, however, illness may affect the throat, although Taureans as a rule tend to be strong and healthy. Taurean personalities love pleasure and comfort but may need to guard against a tendency to overindulge in the good things of life.

Often these individuals are pragmatic and persevering and strive diligently toward their goals. Firm in their desires to build a solid foundation, Taureans can attract and achieve success.

GEMINI

THIRD SIGN

MUTABLE AIR

RULING PLANET: MERCURY

BODY PART: LUNGS, ARMS, HANDS

KEYWORDS:

VERSATILITY, TALKATIVENESS, INGENUITY

Natural communicators with a never-ending thirst for knowledge, Geminis are eternal students. Being an Air sign and very intelligent, Geminis are always on the move, always trying to satisfy their mental curiosity. Extremely quick at picking out the salient points of any subject, they acquire a wide general knowledge, which they love to share with others. Geminis can be bright, multitalented, and enthusiastic but must guard against scattering their energies in too many directions. Through mental discipline and education, Geminis may learn to develop a greater depth of thought.

Linked to Mercury, people of this sign often have an androgynous quality, with a slim and youthful body. Geminis usually have bright, expressive faces and enjoy using their hands when conveying their ideas. Loving to talk, Geminis can chatter on for hours, which often results in extra-large telephone bills. Young in outlook, Geminis are often compared to the eternal child, always in a state of wonder.

Having sensitive nervous systems, Geminis may find it hard to concentrate their full attention on anything or anyone. Like their symbol, the twins, they are renowned for being able to do at least two things at once, as well as being flexible, versatile, and adaptable. Airy, sophisticated Geminis do not like to be pinned down and are determined never to be bored or boring. Not known for their consistency, Geminis appear to have many personalities and changing moods. Gemini individuals are generally intellectual and usually more interested in a stimulating mental challenge than earthly passion.

Light and friendly, Geminis have an easy rapport with others and are often more than willing to share the veritable mine of information they have at their fingertips. With their youthful charm and natural quick wit, is it any wonder that they can be the most delightful friends and companions? Entertaining, with a wealth of ideas, Geminis are highly expressive when they let their mercurial spirits soar.

CANCER

FOURTH SIGN

CARDINAL WATER

RULING PLANET: MOON

BODY PART: BREASTS AND STOMACH

KEYWORDS:

SENSITIVITY, SYMPATHY, AFFECTION

Emotional and sensitive Cancerians are ruled by their feelings. Like their guiding planet, the Moon, they run through the whole gamut of emotions that come with the changing tides. Cancerians have the power of the deepest ocean and the vulnerability of a solitary crab on a lonely beach. Like that crab, they have a protective shell of shyness or reserve to hide their great sensitivity and caution. This should not be interpreted as a weakness, however, as they sometimes withdraw to gather strength.

Sympathetic and kind, Cancerians have a strong need to nurture, so they often take the role of parent, caregiver, or therapist. They can have an extremely strong protective streak and will defend their loved ones against all odds. It is hardly surprising that home and family play a highly important role in their need for security. Generally domestic-oriented, Cancerians are usually connoisseurs of food and good cooks. Many Cancerians go as far as to feel insecure without a full freezer.

Despite their many and changing moods, these personalities are naturally affectionate and may need to avoid smothering others with their protective love and devotion. Cancer is a Water sign, and Cancerians are often shy, with sentimental tendencies, tending to hang on to the past and become avid collectors or hoarders. The objects of this collecting or accumulating can range from family heirlooms and antiques to the memories contained in photos and letters. Cancerians can also have a talent for hanging on to money, which they are likely to store in savings accounts for a rainy day.

Cancerians often have complex personalities. On one hand, they may appear to be a tower of strength, but on the other, they seem to have the vulnerability of a child. Cancerians are masters of the art of passive resistance.

With the Moon coloring their responses, Cancerians are naturally intuitive or mediumistic and can be easily hurt. Their powerful imagination and sensitive understanding may find an avenue of expression through the creative and artistic worlds. Yet above all, once they trust someone enough to show their feelings, they can be strong, loyal, and protective.

LEO

FIFTH SIGN

FIXED FIRE

RULING PLANET: SUN

BODY PART: HEART

KEYWORDS:

VITALITY, CONFIDENCE, SELF-EXPRESSION

Warm, loving, and generous, Leos have big hearts. Their kind and magnanimous gestures come from a love of the dramatic, as Leos play to the crowd and feel happiest with an appreciative audience. Luckily, to compensate for the likelihood of grabbing center stage, Leos can also be attentive to others. They can express bountiful approval for others' projects and shower them with compliments.

Ruled by the Sun, Leos possess a lovable, childlike playfulness and a strong need for creative self-expression. Seeing themselves in leading roles rather than the chorus line, Leos often have trouble with vanity and pride. They find it hard to admit that they are wrong, and flattery leaves them open to manipulation. However, Leos can easily compensate for any failings by their sunny personality, sense of fun, and generosity. These friendly and gregarious people are ideal partners for social events, parties, visits to the theater, and long holidays.

A desire to shine, combined with their royal, commanding air, brings Leos to positions of authority, where they can show their remarkable leadership skills. Leos just take charge naturally. As they sometimes do this without being asked, Leos may be accused of being too bossy. Generally, however, they will work extremely hard to fulfill their responsibilities, and they make excellent managers and leaders. Leos who do not fulfill their natural potential may fall into idleness and lose their spirit.

Lions are known for their courage and would much rather play a strong and protective role for others than be weak and defenseless. Even when the quieter Leos are hiding their pride and greatness under a facade of modesty, their regal dignity shows through. Leos presume that others possess a sense of integrity similar to their own, and they are careful to keep their sense of self-respect in any disagreement. Leos want people to think well of them and are very aware of the impression they make on others.

Belonging to a fixed Fire sign, Leos can be lively and enthusiastic yet somewhat stubborn. Their creativity and sense of drama combine to make them great romantics. Leos love to love and be loved. No matter where you meet them, their sunny personalities will leave a lasting impression.

VIRGO

SIXTH SIGN

MUTABLE EARTH

RULING PLANET: MERCURY

BODY PART: INTESTINES

KEYWORDS:

DISCERNMENT, EFFICIENCY, SERVICE

Analytical and efficient, Virgos have a strong work ethic. They need order in life and want things done in a methodical way. Virgos constantly examine and refine in order to improve existing systems. Unfortunately, this perfectionism may extend to critiquing the people around them, causing their messages to be resisted by others. On the other hand, Virgos do not appreciate your pointing out their faults, as they are already well aware of them and can be their own worst critic. This ability to appreciate their own failings can make Virgos modest and unassuming, and they often validate their own self-worth by being of service to others.

Ruled by Mercury, Virgos are intelligent, articulate, and discriminating, and with the added element of Earth, they can be practical, capable organizers, who can work very hard and pay attention to detail. Economical and prudent with money, Virgos may on occasion keep a tight hold on their purse strings, but they can be more than generous with time and money should anybody need assistance. They will, however, expect the people they help to make an effort to help themselves. Virgos do not usually respond well to stupidity or vulgarity and have logical minds that instinctively want to bring order out of confusion. Virgos usually analyze the smallest of details but must guard against going over and over the same issues and failing to see the big picture.

Possessed of extremely high standards, Virgos can be highly discriminating and extra fastidious in certain areas. Virgos are often interested in cleanliness and nutrition, and they are usually advocates of exercise and a healthy lifestyle. Despite this, at times they may suffer from mental tension, occasionally becoming overanxious or neurotic. This may frequently be due to the pressure of work; because of their strong sense of obligation and duty, Virgos may often take on more than they can handle. Normally wonderful employees, Virgos dislike clutter and are advocates of thoroughness and efficiency.

Dependable and sincere, with a methodical approach to life, Virgos will always be pillars of practical, sensible support. In fact, Virgos will offer their help before you have even asked.

LIBRA

SEVENTH SIGN

CARDINAL AIR

RULING PLANET: VENUS

BODY PART: KIDNEYS

KEYWORDS:

BALANCE, DIPLOMACY, RELATIONSHIP

Librans are the diplomats of the zodiac. To avoid disharmony they will turn on the charm, flash you the most delightful smile, and do everything possible to keep the peace. Affectionate, gracious, and refined, Librans need to be popular. Belonging to an Air sign, they have a lightness about them and are friendly, intelligent, and sociable.

Ruled by Venus and keenly aware of relationships, Librans are always able to see things from another person's point of view. This balancing principle often causes them to need a partner to act as a mirror for a better understanding of themselves. Experts at being just and fair, Libras weigh everything carefully before making a decision. They can discuss the pros and cons of any situation or problem with amazing logic and discernment. This ability ensures their skill at the arts of compromise and negotiation. Unfortunately, this may cause indecisiveness and an inability to arrive at a final conclusion.

Balance is a very powerful keyword for Librans. Although genuinely wanting harmony, they are still prone to difficult periods, when their scales dip down too far on one side. However, as they work on their self-awareness and inner adjustment, they become more self-reliant. This allays their tendency to become dependent on others. Librans may need to learn how to stand up for their beliefs even when it may cause controversy.

Ruled by Venus, Librans are sociable, elegant, and great lovers of beauty and luxury. They usually have an attractive home and are naturally good at some form of artistic expression. Having a natural eye for color, they need to be surrounded by tasteful and harmonious surroundings or they can become unhappy. This love of beauty can also usually be seen from their outward appearance, as they inevitably make an effort to look attractive.

Superb hosts or hostesses, Librans especially love activities that combine sociability with love, such as weddings or small gatherings of friends and family. In fact, they are great romantics who will always appreciate gifts of flowers or chocolate, thus fulfilling their soul's need for beauty and their weakness for anything sweet. With just a little bit of love and affection you can always find your way into a Libran's heart.

SCORPIO

EIGHTH SIGN

FIXED WATER

RULING PLANET: PLUTO

BODY PART: SEX ORGANS

KEYWORDS:

REGENERATION, SECRECY, POWER

Magnetic Scorpios belong to the most passionate sign of the zodiac. Whatever they do, they do powerfully and intensely. There is nothing halfhearted about Scorpios: They are creatures of power, will, and extremes.

Belonging to a Water sign, Scorpios prefer to investigate life at a deeper emotional level. Not for them the frothy language of the dilettante; Scorpios want the real story and probe for the truth. They are experts at receiving subliminal signals, with the namesake of their ruling planet, Pluto, as ruler of the underworld. This results in Scorpios' psychically picking up what others are unconsciously feeling as well as what they are saying. Like a detective or psychologist, they will ask you everything about yourself, yet rarely reveal themselves. This secrecy is usually a cloak of power. As Scorpios feel deeply, they can be painfully hurt and so prefer to be in control.

A major life lesson for Scorpios involves the overcoming of desire through the creative use of the will. As their sign is connected to the very roots of the sex drive, their feelings are strong and intense, sometimes leading to jealousy or possessiveness.

Symbolic death or transformation is a powerful experience that Scorpios are not afraid to undertake. There will be times when they are willing to walk away from everything in order to validate their intense feelings. They cannot be insincere even if that means losing everything; this does, of course, ultimately give them enormous strength, when they are not afraid to let go. Once they have decided to take on something, their will to achieve is tremendous. Belonging to a fixed sign, they have extraordinary staying power and will persevere with a situation until the bitter end.

Scorpios are usually competitive and do not like losing. Once defeated they will often wait until they can prove you wrong or exact revenge, no matter how long they have to wait. On the other hand, when on your side they will be just as passionately loyal and loving, totally giving of themselves regardless of effort or sacrifice.

Scorpio is a sign of regeneration. Scorpios have the potential for enormous strength from connecting with the fundamental creative forces of nature. The magical symbol of the phoenix rising out of the ashes represents their ability to be reborn, to rise again from the depths to the heights with new understanding and power. For Scorpios it is all or nothing; they do not want to live on a superficial level. They need challenge to bring out their power and make them feel alive.

SAGITTARIUS

NINTH SIGN

MUTABLE FIRE

BODY PART: HIPS AND THIGHS

KEYWORDS: HONESTY, EXPLORATION, IDEALISM

Sagittarians are free spirits with a friendly, independent style. They dislike being tied down and are incurable idealists, always looking to expand their horizons and improve their lot. Optimistic and easygoing, they have a love of truth, honesty, and justice that gives them a very philosophical approach to life.

Spirited individuals, Sagittarians think big and see the grander vision. This ability to perceive the "big plan" means that Sagittarians are usually working on some scheme or project for the future. They love to explore and are inveterate travelers of the mind and the world. Placing a high value on knowledge or wisdom, they seek inspiration for themselves and for others, genuinely wishing to uplift people with their amusing, clever words or their big smile. Unfortunately, they often achieve the opposite effect by forgetting to think before they speak. Outspoken and frank, Sagittarians express whatever crosses their mind, with an honesty that is startling in its directness. Buoyantly bouncing back after committing a faux pas is part of the charm of Sagittarius, however, so they can genuinely assure you that they did not mean to offend, and you cannot help but forgive them.

Through their constant need for expansion, Sagittarians often turn to higher learning and enjoy exploring subjects such as philosophy, religion, travel, and law. Some Sagittarians are more sporty than intellectual and get their excitement from playing the game. Usually lucky, they love to take risks in one form or another and may be drawn to gamble or speculate.

Whatever Sagittarians do, they like to do in style. In their need for the good things of life they often indulge in the best. They should be careful, however, not to carry their extravagant streak too far and become greedy or self-indulgent. To compensate, Sagittarians are good-humored and sincere. They love the freedom to move around and thus prefer to leave their options open.

Enthusiastic, warm, and generous, wearing their hearts on their sleeves, Sagittarians, like the archer, aim their arrows far into the distance. They know how to enjoy themselves and are eager for the adventure.

CAPRICORN

TENTH SIGN

CARDINAL EARTH

BODY PART: KNEES, SKELETAL BONES

KEYWORDS: AMBITION, CONSCIENCE, DILIGENCE

The ultimate realists, Capricorns know full well there is no gain without hard work. They have a strong sense of duty and are quite willing to wait patiently to fulfill their ambitions. Like the goat, they will eventually climb to the top of that mountain even if it takes them a whole lifetime.

Hardworking, diligent, and determined, Capricorns need to have a purpose, for without a precise goal they are lost. They desire order and structure to make them feel complete and usually write out daily to-do lists. Security is important to them, and, influenced by their ruling planet, Saturn, they take a cautious and conservative approach to life. They show a great respect for authority and admire the wisdom of age and experience. This extends to their work, for when Capricorns execute a job, they are very conscientious. However, Capricorns can also be stubborn, cold, or calculating, using Saturnine hardness for selfish purposes rather than for self-discipline, normally one of their better qualities.

The economical, practical, and thrifty characteristics of Capricorns' earthy element blend well with their desire for status and prestige, enabling them to rise to positions of power without wasting any effort. They are not frivolous or flighty; they take responsibilities seriously and place home and family at the top of their priorities. Unfortunately, Capricorns can also be pessimistic, feeling they are never good enough, and must guard against depression. When they doubt themselves and their abilities they may give up without even trying, but when given the security of a firm foundation they can be relentless in their drive for success. More than anything else, Capricorns need to develop an optimistic and positive outlook.

Remember that beneath their slightly shy and reserved exterior is a wonderfully dry sense of humor and a tenacity that comes from inner discipline. When others need assistance, they know they can always count on a Capricorn to be reliable and solid.

AQUARIUS

ELEVENTH SIGN

FIXED AIR

BODY PART: ANKLES AND CALVES

KEYWORDS:

DETACHMENT, HUMANITARIANISM, INDEPENDENCE

Original and unconventional, Aquarians are progressive and independent. Aquarians' interest in how the human race operates is an intellectual exercise for them. Always playing the detached observer, they are able to take an impersonal, unemotional viewpoint. This tendency means they can think in terms of group consciousness, realizing that people are separate individuals operating within a larger whole. This humanitarian awareness is a strong characteristic of Aquarians, who often work for universal or philanthropic goals and campaign for just causes. A lack of separatism makes Aquarians friendly and helpful, enabling them to speak to strangers as though they have always known them.

The Aquarian rebel streak originates with their ruling planet, Uranus, which is renowned for endowing the ability to perceive future trends, as well as giving a strong need for freedom. Aquarians do not like to take orders and want to think for themselves, doing things in their own unique way. Too much insistence on following a certain way will certainly cause an Aquarian to do exactly the opposite. The combination of their strong contrary streak with their fixed sign can make them very stubborn. Fortunately, they are always willing to listen to an alternative viewpoint as long as it is presented objectively. The futuristic outlook of Aquarians enables them to embrace technology or new and exciting innovations without being intimidated. Like Uranus, Aquarians have an electric quality, which can manifest as a form of mental intuition. This can often produce the "eureka effect," when Aquarians suddenly know something to be true. Their zany genius can make them volatile and unpredictable but also highly inventive.

Although each Aquarian has an individual look, they all know they are part of a united group that stands for human rights and social reform. Even if the rest of the world does not understand them today, what Aquarians are doing now, others will be doing tomorrow.

Pisceans possess a highly developed feeling nature. Sensitive Pisceans are constantly receiving impressions from their outer environment, yet they are also acutely aware of their inner promptings. They often retreat into a private dream world to enjoy the musings of their powerful, wondrous imagination and sometimes to escape the harsher realities of life. The symbol for Pisces is two fish swimming in opposite directions, indicating a dual personality of extremes. At times they can be tired and lethargic, or just drifting, and at others they can be efficient, precise, and extremely hardworking.

Psychically open to all the more subtle emotions, Pisceans can show generosity and compassion. As they do not always have strong boundaries, they can often dissolve themselves in other people's needs. Pisceans therefore have to be careful not to lose their own sense of self-worth or even martyr themselves. Generally they often need large amounts of reassurance to boost their confidence, and at times they can be quite stubborn, allowing nobody to influence them. The least selfish sign of the zodiac, Pisceans can be extremely patient, but if provoked can become surprisingly aggressive.

Sentimental and kind, with tender emotions, Pisceans are very receptive to environment or the feelings of others. Combined with their remarkable imagination, this facility makes Pisceans excellent for any form of healing, music, art, drama, or photography, and particularly for things of a spiritual nature. Just as the fish swim in opposite directions, Pisceans are also open to mood swings. At times they are extremely optimistic, and at other times they may become vague or suffer a lack of drive and give up too easily. At such times they have to guard against escaping or becoming despondent. It is especially easy for idealistic Pisceans to project their high expectations and dreams onto others and end up being disillusioned.

Fortunately, they use their natural psychic ability to plug directly into the consciousness of all humanity. They are the visionaries who cannot help but uplift those around them with their humor, charm, and sympathy.

The Ten Planets

Each of the planets represents a psychological function and corresponds to aspects of our personality. Character traits are suggested by the positions of the planets and the relationship they have to each other. In astrology, the Sun and Moon, technically named the *luminaries*, are included in the ten planets that make up our solar system. The key issues associated with each planet are listed below.

THE SUN

As the energy center of our solar system, the Sun radiates the power of light and vitality and relates to the life-giving force. In astrology, it represents the energy source of each living thing and gives a forceful assertion of individuality. It signifies the center of our being, our sense of identity and ego. The Sun glyph is a circle with a point in the center, indicating the heart of our physical universe. In esoteric symbolism, this circle represents the totality of infinity or eternity, and the dot in the middle signifies a particular point in time and space within that totality. Willpower, energy, strength, and self-expression are just some of the Sun's attributes. It also stands for ambition and pride, consciousness, and self-confidence, and it is a metaphor for the father or the masculine archetype. In mythology, kings and heroes are frequently associated with Helios or the Sun, which is the planet that rules the zodiac sign of Leo.

• *Positive:* vitality, individuality, creativity, vigor, willpower, inspiration, self-awareness, the ego, identity

• *Negative:* egotism, self-centeredness, pride, arrogance, overbearingness, domination

THE MOON

The Moon receives the reflected light of the Sun and is unique in that it is the only satellite that orbits the Earth. The Moon's influence is essentially receptive and nonrational. The Moon represents our emotional needs and instincts and governs the element of Water, including the oceans and the tides, and nocturnal life.

In mythology Isis, Istar, Artemis, and Diana all represent the many faces of the Moon goddess. Traditionally, the Moon is associated with the feminine, and it is in keeping with the ancient Greek concept of Gaia. Usually associated with intuition and psychic ability, the Moon is also strongly represented in folklore, poetry, and myth. Its divinity is particularly expressed through womanhood and the cycle of fertility, conception, birth, motherhood, and nature's abundance.

In psychological astrology the Moon represents our unconscious reactions and subjective experience. It also corresponds to the unconscious urge to satisfy our basic needs. The Moon reflects our different tensions, and forces us to externalize these feelings. The Moon also influences the fluctuations within these feelings or moods and governs the sign of Cancer.

• *Positive:* sensitivity, nurturing, receptivity, intuition, psychic ability

• *Negative:* moodiness, oversensitivity, overemotional

MERCURY

In mythology Mercury is the messenger of the gods, who gave man language and the capacity to communicate and learn. To the Greeks Mercury was known as Hermes, whose gifts to humankind were writing and language. Mercury has a talent for rhetoric and mental trickery, a reflection of the ability to develop the conscious mind until we become a little too clever for our own good.

Although usually portrayed as a youthful male figure, Mercury is neither male nor female. This is symbolic of its role as a neutral medium for the exchange of information. Mercury represents intellectual, rational thinking and discriminative powers, and is also linked to commerce and the marketplace.

Psychologically, Mercury represents mental ability and the need to comprehend and communicate, whether through speech, writing, teaching, or any other form of mental expression. Mercury rules both Gemini and Virgo.

• *Positive:* cleverness, mental agility, good communication skills, intellectualism

• *Negative:* trickiness, weak intellect or overdevelopment of the intellect, lack of logic

VENUS

In mythology Venus is the goddess of love and beauty, mother of Eros. To the Greeks she was known as Aphrodite. Representing the female principle, Venus harmonizes and creates unity as well as imparting an appreciation of nature and art.

Psychologically, Venus represents the drive to relate to others, the expression of loving feelings, and what brings pleasure. Venus is popular, charming, and alluring, although possibly a little too indulgent or easygoing. Attempting to avoid confrontation at all costs, Venus will attempt to neutralize a threat by captivating or seducing the opposition.

Because Venus's function is to bring union, attraction plays a strong part in its role, with an emphasis on outward appearance, sociability, romantic love, and the opposite sex. The planet Venus imparts a sweetness of character, an appreciation of nature, and strong desires. Venus also "softens" anything it touches, and gives an aesthetic sense or good taste, natural refinement,

and a talent for art and music. Governing what you value, Venus also reveals attitudes toward money and possessions, as well as self-worth. Venus rules the signs of both Taurus and Libra.

• *Positive:* love of beauty and art, warmth, sociability, sense of values, cooperation

• *Negative:* pleasure seeking, overindulgence, idleness, luxury

MARS

In mythology, Mars is the warrior god. Mars governs our survival instinct, whether we fight or flee. The antithesis of Venus, Mars represents the male principle and is competitive, assertive, and ready for action. Mars is full of energy and drive. Showing courage and dynamic forcefulness when facing adversaries, Mars is also associated with the hero archetype. Martian qualities are often associated with acts of bravery and indicate a daredevil mentality. In modern life we may use Mars's energy to push ahead in our careers, accomplish our aims and objectives, or make a stand for our convictions.

As the Mars function concerns our will to survive, it is related to the release of adrenaline in our bodies and the ability to react quickly. In excess, the same energies that provide assertiveness and help us fight can also be expressed through bad temper, anger, aggression, and impatience. Without Mars, however, we would not have dynamism, vigor, initiative, or the driving force to achieve our ambitions through our own efforts. Mars governs the sign of Aries.

• *Positive:* assertiveness, courage, dynamism, action, vigor

• *Negative:* aggression, violence, coarse behavior, anger, restlessness

JUPITER

Jupiter is the largest planet in our solar system. Named after the ruler of the Roman pantheon (known as Zeus to the Greeks), in mythology Jupiter was associated with wisdom, victory, and justice. In keeping with its large size, Jupiter expands or exaggerates. It represents the ability to reach beyond our present horizons and look for the bigger plan or grander vision, and it carries with it the optimism and confidence to carry this through.

The desire to discover meaning and greater truth means Jupiter approaches life philosophically. The desire for greater knowledge inspires higher learning and is linked to universities or spiritual teachers. In addition, as the Lord of Truth, Jupiter is often associated with the judicial system, courts, and law and order.

Along with the urge to expand mentally, emotionally, and spiritually, good fortune and plenty are often associated with Jupiter. Jupiter stimulates a yearning for experience and travel to distant and exotic places. Excessive expansion, however, can bring greed, false optimism, insincerity, and an inflated ego. At its best, Jupiter represents the good-humored and generous idealist who has the faith and wisdom to make his or her large schemes a reality. Jupiter rules Sagittarius.

• *Positive:* desire for truth, generosity, idealism, optimism, long journeys, higher learning

• *Negative:* exaggeration, overexpansion, false optimism, greed

SATURN

In mythology Saturn is Old Father Time, the Reaper. In Greek and Roman times Saturn was the god of social order and was shown as the harvester with a sickle, symbolizing the principle that what we sow, we also reap. Saturn represents perfect justice or the law of cause and effect.

Psychologically, Saturn is the archetype of the wise old man, the teacher. By accepting the responsibility and discipline of self-realization, we become older and wiser. The hard work and training suggested by Saturn's restrictive influence is ultimately worthwhile, because it is the only way to learn. To balance the expansiveness of Jupiter, we have the curtailing influence of Saturn, which can restrain overinflation and maintain order. Saturn's limiting influence, however, can cause pessimism, fear, and excessive seriousness.

Saturn wants definition, form, and structure. It creates boundaries in order to produce control, regulation, and security. Saturn represents anything hard, from our bones and teeth to when we need to be hard with ourselves. As this planet requires us to face up to our responsibilities and duties, its lessons are sometimes uncomfortable. Saturn is totally fair and just: Whatever work has been put in will be repaid exactly. With Saturn you cannot expect to get something for nothing. It provides the determination and the perseverance to succeed. Saturn governs the sign of Capricorn.

• *Positive:* discipline, order, authority, responsibility, wisdom, realism, patience, perseverance

• *Negative:* pessimism, fear, overrestrictiveness

URANUS

The ancient Greek name for Uranus was Heaven or Night Sky, and in mythology Uranus was the father of Saturn. The vastness of the heavens symbolizes our ability to open our minds to the universal. Uranus brings enlightenment and freedom of spirit by breaking away from the restriction and safety of Saturn. This kind of freedom involves leaving a space in our life for the unexpected, or daring to express our own individuality despite the pressures of conformity. If we push this too far, however, we are in danger of becoming rebellious for the sake of rebellion.

Psychologically, through Uranus we can widen our point of view to the universal and comprehend humankind as a family of brothers and sisters. Uranus is willing to fight for human rights and the freedom to express oneself.

Uranus governs electrical energy of all types: television and radio waves, magnetic fields, lasers, computers, and new electronic technology. Always looking to the future and being able to think in a symbolic and abstract way, Uranus represents intuition and inventiveness. This usually means being ahead of society as a whole and expressing oneself in an individualistic or unconventional fashion. Uranus rules the zodiac sign of Aquarius.

• *Positive:* freedom, humanitarianism, detachment, objectivity

• *Negative:* rebellion, eccentricity, revolutionary tendencies, obstinacy

NEPTUNE

In mythology, Neptune is god of the sea, deep, unfathomable, and mysterious. Just as the ocean can dissolve rocks into sand, so Neptune can slowly and subtly dissolve the barriers the ego creates, releasing us into mystical experience. The mists that hang over the seashore are analogous to the mists that surround this planet, where nothing is solid and everything is illusionary and enigmatic.

Psychologically, Neptune's function is to help us transcend our limitations by refining and purifying our emotional nature. Unlike Saturn, it knows no boundaries and feels a sense of oneness with all things. However, this ability to blend with everything can also give a sense of vagueness. The extreme sensitivity to everything, indicated by Neptune's influence, can confer great compassion for the suffering of mankind. It also brings the ability to lose oneself in inspired creative endeavors such as art, music, or drama. Neptune can give an artist the inspiration and imagination for what is possible.

With heightened perception and imagination it can be easy to escape into a world of fantasy, abuse drugs or alcohol, or indulge in self-deception and become lost or confused. Working positively with Neptune means holding the vision of our ideal in order to fulfill our dreams. Neptune rules the zodiac sign of Pisces.

• *Positive:* sensitivity, vision, compassion, inspiration, transcendence

• *Negative:* illusion, deception, escapism, confusion, vagueness

PLUTO

Mythologically, Pluto, god of the underworld, represents transformation, death, and rebirth. Pluto signifies deep change, and its energy is intense and powerful. Under Pluto's influence we can have the ability to penetrate or read the subconscious from the subliminal signals it generates, particularly through body language. This can be used positively in fields such as depth psychology, but it can also be abused to control others.

The discovery of the planet Pluto took place at the same time as the discovery of subatomic particles and the publication of Jung's theory of the unconscious. Whether governing shady underworld characters, fanatics and terrorists, or major transformers of society for good, Pluto's energy can be extreme.

It can also provoke this level of intense reaction within ourselves. Pluto often symbolizes the all-or-nothing response. As part of our continuing efforts toward self-improvement, there will be times when we must leave behind the old with no guarantees for the future. The energy of death and rebirth is powerfully symbolized by Pluto. With Pluto's help, we accept changes in our life, and we learn to let go, when the time is right, of the past or anything we have outgrown. Pluto teaches us that every end is a new beginning and life goes on.

This knowledge assists us in the whole rebuilding process. Pluto governs the sign of Scorpio.

• *Positive:* power, transformation, regeneration, revealing the hidden
• *Negative:* abuse of power, obsession, compulsion

Decanates

A decanate consists of 10 degrees of the 360-degree zodiac circle. Each sign stretches over 30 degrees of that circle, so each sign contains three spatially equivalent, but symbolically different, decanates. Remember that 30 degrees of the zodiac is equivalent to a 30-degree portion of the Earth's path around the sky. As the Sun passes through the zodiac sign (the zodiac constellation in the celestial sky opposite to the position of the Earth in relation to the Sun) over the course of an astrological month, the Sun passes through the three decanates, one after the other. The Sun moves into a new decanate approximately every ten days. Each of the three decanates adds its own associated planet and sign influences to the basic influences of the more general Sun sign. By considering the decanate in addition to the Sun sign, we fine-tune the reading for the individual birthday. For example, a Capricorn born in the second decanate will be under the influence of the Sun sign Capricorn but will also be under the decanate sign of Taurus. The ancient Egyptians considered the meanings of decanates as important as those of the Sun signs themselves.

The influences of the decanates are determined by the element associated with the sign that contains them. Each sign links symbolically with one of the four fundamental elements:

• The element of **fire** rules: Aries, Leo, Sagittarius
  Planetary rulers: Mars, Sun, Jupiter
• The element of **earth** rules: Taurus, Virgo, Capricorn
  Planetary rulers: Venus, Mercury, Saturn
• The element of **air** rules: Gemini, Libra, Aquarius
  Planetary rulers: Mercury, Venus, Uranus
• The element of **water** rules: Cancer, Scorpio, Pisces
  Planetary rulers: Moon, Pluto, Neptune

The sequence of the three decanates follows the same pattern under each of the twelve Sun signs. The decanates under each Sun sign are associated with the three signs associated with the element linked to that Sun sign. For example, as you see above, Aries is linked with fire. All people born under Aries belong to the element of fire. All three decanates under Aries are associated with the signs corresponding with fire. The first Aries decanate is associated with the closest Sun sign in the vicinity of Aries linked with fire, namely, Aries itself. Then, traveling counterclockwise around the circle of the zodiac, the next fire element we come across is Leo. Leo is thus assigned to the second decanate. Traveling further around the circle, we reach the third fire-related sign, Sagittarius. The third decanate of Aries is thus associated with Sagittarius. It works the same way for all the decanates under all the Sun signs.

Each sign, to go one step further, is associated with a planet. Just as each Sun sign has a planetary ruler, so does each decanate sign. The decanate of Aries is ruled by the planet Mars, and the decanate of Sagittarius is ruled by the planet Jupiter.

In the diagram below, you can see clearly how the decanates operate within the different signs.

Following is a list of Sun signs and the influences of the decanates located within them, along with the days associated with each decanate.

ARIES, MARCH 21–APRIL 20

Aries–Aries	Mars decanate: March 20–21 to March 30
Aries–Leo	Sun decanate: March 31 to April 9
Aries–Sagittarius	Jupiter decanate: April 10 to April 20–21

TAURUS, APRIL 21–MAY 21

Taurus–Taurus	Venus decanate: April 20–21 to April 30
Taurus–Virgo	Mercury decanate: May 1 to May 10
Taurus–Capricorn	Saturn decanate: May 11 to May 21–22

GEMINI, MAY 22–JUNE 21

Gemini–Gemini	Mercury decanate: May 21–22 to May 31
Gemini–Libra	Venus decanate: June 1 to June 10
Gemini–Aquarius	Uranus decanate: June 11 to June 21–22

CANCER, JUNE 22–JULY 22

Cancer–Cancer	Moon decanate: June 21–22 to July 1
Cancer–Scorpio	Pluto decanate: July 2 to July 11
Cancer–Pisces	Neptune decanate: July 12 to July 22–23

LEO, JULY 23–AUGUST 22

Leo–Leo	Sun decanate: July 23–24 to August 2
Leo–Sagittarius	Jupiter decanate: August 3 to August 12
Leo–Aries	Mars decanate: August 13 to August 22–23

VIRGO, AUGUST 23–SEPTEMBER 22

Virgo–Virgo	Mercury decanate: August 22–23 to September 2
Virgo–Capricorn	Saturn decanate: September 3 to September 12
Virgo–Taurus	Venus decanate: September 13 to September 22–23

LIBRA, SEPTEMBER 23–OCTOBER 22

Libra–Libra	Venus decanate: September 22–23 to October 3
Libra–Aquarius	Uranus decanate: October 4 to October 13
Libra–Gemini	Mercury decanate: October 14 to October 22–23

SCORPIO, OCTOBER 23–NOVEMBER 21

Scorpio–Scorpio	Pluto decanate: October 22–23 to November 2
Scorpio–Pisces	Neptune decanate: November 3 to November 12
Scorpio–Cancer	Moon decanate: November 13 to November 21–22

SAGITTARIUS, NOVEMBER 22–DECEMBER 21

Sagittarius–Sagittarius	Jupiter decanate: November 21–22 to December 2
Sagittarius–Aries	Mars decanate: December 3 to December 12
Sagittarius–Leo	Sun decanate: December 13 to December 21–22

CAPRICORN, DECEMBER 22–JANUARY 20

Capricorn–Capricorn	Saturn decanate: December 21–22 to December 31
Capricorn–Taurus	Venus decanate: January 1 to January 10
Capricorn–Virgo	Mercury decanate: January 11 to January 20–21

AQUARIUS, JANUARY 21–FEBRUARY 19

Aquarius–Aquarius	Uranus decanate: January 20–21 to January 30
Aquarius–Gemini	Mercury decanate: January 31 to February 9
Aquarius–Libra	Venus decanate: February 10 to February 19–20

PISCES, FEBRUARY 20–MARCH 20

Pisces–Pisces	Neptune decanate: February 19–20 to March 1
Pisces–Cancer	Moon decanate: March 2 to March 11
Pisces–Scorpio	Pluto decanate: March 12 to March 20–21

Progressions

In astrology progressions are widely used as one technique in the system of prediction. The most well known method of progression entails substituting "a day for a year" as a way of symbolically showing our lives in slow motion. In this symbolic system of interpretation, the planetary movements over the course of a day will be translated as the movement of the progressed planets over the course of a year. For example, the positions of the celestial bodies on the twenty-fourth day after birth will correspond to the twenty-fourth year of a person's life.

The Sun is in the sign of the great stellar circle of the zodiac located opposite to the position of the Earth in relation to the Sun. As the Earth orbits around the Sun, the Sun thus moves through the various signs located in the 30-degree intervals of this great stellar circle. In this book, we follow this journey of the Sun through the various signs and we interpret how this affects each individual. With the "day for a year" system of progressions, the Sun takes approximately thirty years, rather than thirty days, to journey through each complete zodiac sign. For example, if you are born at the cusp between two signs, in the "day for a year" system your progressed Sun arrives at the next cusp after thirty years, on your thirtieth birthday. If you are born on the fifteenth day of a particular Sun sign, then your progressed Sun moves into the next Sun sign after fifteen years; on your thirtieth birthday it will have reached the middle of that next sign.

If you are born close to the end of a zodiac sign or born on a cusp, your Sun progresses into the next zodiac sign within a few years. On these occasions you may feel a greater affinity with the following sign than with your own Sun sign. Below are three examples and a corresponding chart of Sun progressions; the turning points are marked with an X.

EXAMPLE 1. If you born at the beginning of the sign of Gemini, that is, on May 23, your Sun progresses through Gemini for twenty-eight years. It moves into the sign of Cancer approximately when you reach the age of twenty-nine. The Sun then takes a further thirty years to complete its journey through the sign of Cancer and moves into Leo as you reach age fifty-nine.

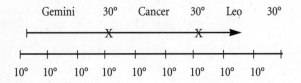

EXAMPLE 2. If you were born in the middle of the sign of Virgo, that is, September 7, your progressed Sun will change zodiac signs and move into Libra when you reach the age of fifteen. The Sun then takes a further thirty years to travel through the sign of Libra before it moves into Scorpio at approximately the time when you reach forty-five. A further change will occur at age seventy-five, when your progressed Sun moves into Sagittarius.

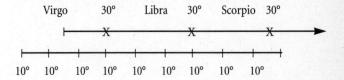

EXAMPLE 3. If you were born in the last few days of Sagittarius, your Sun progresses into Capricorn while you are still a baby. The Sun then takes thirty years to travel through Capricorn. A further change will occur at the age of thirty-one, when your progressed Sun moves into Aquarius. When you reach the age of sixty-one, your progressed Sun changes signs again and enters Pisces.

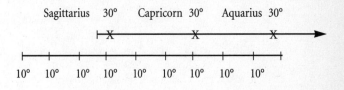

Introduction to Fixed Stars

Fixed stars belong to the great cosmos rather than our solar system. Unlike the planets that orbit our Sun, fixed stars are suns in their own right; in fact, depending on their magnitude, some fixed stars are far larger and brighter than our own Sun. When we discuss fixed stars we use the term "light years" to describe the vast distances that are difficult to calculate or comprehend. Due to these stars' remoteness from Earth they appear to us as stationary, and are therefore called "fixed" stars. The influence of fixed stars is relevant to their strength, which is calculated by their brightness.

Although there are millions of fixed stars in the universe, in astrological practice relatively few are considered—namely, those that are located near the zodiacal ring.

The observation and relationship of fixed stars to world events began thousands of years ago. The naming of fixed stars is recorded in the Mesopotamian and Babylonian eras. Fixed stars are mentioned in the *Epoch of Gilgamesch* and, together with comets, eclipses, and planets, played an important role in the interpretation of weather phenomena. In addition to the Babylonians, the Egyptians believed in the powerful influence of the fixed stars. For example, aware of nature's power and dependent on the river Nile for their survival, Egyptians celebrated their agricultural calendar summer solstice with fertility rites and linked the rising of the star Sirius to the flooding of the river Nile. Recently there has been much evidence to suggest that the Egyptians aligned the majestic pyramids of Giza to the Orion Belt. Although many historians still claim that the great Pyramids are a testimony to the great kings of Egypt, many new archaeological findings reveal a clear connection between the design of the Cheops Pyramids and the circumpolar stars.

In the story of the Nativity, a star guided the three wise men to the stable in Bethlehem. Catalogues of fixed stars were recorded in Greece around 250 B.C. The observation of fixed stars continued throughout history and was incorporated into the celestial understanding of the ancients. Fixed stars were associated with many different aspects of life, and the origin of their interpretation was derived from the symbols with which the constellations were associated. For example, in the constellation of Alpha leonis, or Leo, the brightest fixed star is Regulus (also called the Lion's Heart) and symbolizes strength, power, and authority. This star is one of the most important fixed stars in the sky, associated with royalty and honors. Usually this star appears in the charts of kings, queens, rulers, and high government officials. This star is also linked to people who are favored by the public; it bestows popularity.

The importance of fixed stars derives from the fact that all material bodies in the cosmos are in a state of electrical charge and have a magnetic field surrounding them. Even the weakest emissions can influence life on Earth. This is remarkably akin to the term "butterfly effect" in modern Chaos theory, which argues that even a butterfly's wing stirring the air can create a ripple effect that transforms the weather system at a later date in another part of the world. As the fixed stars are essentially the same as our own Sun, they have similar force fields. The effect of stars is measured by their magnitude or brightness.

Fixed stars offer a fascinating insight into the subconscious mind and the potential or problems an individual might have. This interpretation, however, must be carefully analyzed in relation to a complete natal horoscope; fixed stars are not interpreted separately, but always as a subinfluence on the planets' celestial qualities. Fixed stars must be understood as enhancing or detracting from the planets they are in contact with.

We have listed on the birthday pages the most influential fixed star for that day. Often, other fixed stars exert additional influences, and we have included readings for those stars in the fixed star appendix at the back of the book.

Please note that not all days in this book are associated with a fixed star. We are only discussing Sun-linked stars, and so if there are no major influential stars near the Sun on a particular day, then no fixed stars appear on your birthday's pages. There are, however, most likely other fixed stars associated with the positions of the planets on that day. With a natal chart, you will be able to use the appendix of this book to understand the influences on you of your planet-linked fixed stars. We encourage all our readers to have natal charts done. Our discussion of the fixed stars in this book is intended only as an introduction to their intricate and fascinating realm.

Fixed Stars: Basic Rules of Interpretation

In a year, the Sun travels through the 360 degrees of the zodiacal circle. The twelve astrological signs each span 30 degrees of this circle. The fixed stars themselves occupy single degree points on the circle, but their orbs, or range of influence, can span several degrees. The magnitude of the star affects the potency of its influence. Both the range and the potency must be calculated in order to determine the potential duration and strength of the force that the fixed star will exert. When the Sun or a planet is within the orb of a fixed star, the star's influence is clearly felt, most powerfully at the moment of conjunction, and diminishes as the Sun or planet moves beyond the orb.

FIXED STAR MAGNITUDE

The power of a star is judged by its magnitude.

The highest magnitude approaches 0 to −1.

Magnitude 1: Orb is 2°30'.
Magnitude 2: Orb is 2°10'.
Magnitude 3: Orb is 1°40'.
Magnitude 4: Orb is 1°30'.
Magnitude 5 stars, clusters, and nebulae: Orb is less than 1°.

In this book we illustrate the positive and negative influences of these stars upon your individual birthday. We have attempted not only to provide the classic interpretations but also to suggest modern psychological interpretations of their effects.

We have assigned a strength rating to each star corresponding to its magnitude. A magnitude of −1, the strongest, receives a ten-star strength rating. A magnitude of 5, the weakest, receives a two-star strength rating.

List of Fixed Stars

ARIES

Deneb Kaitos	★★★★★★★★	Baten Kaitos	★★★★★
Algenib	★★★★★★	Al Perg	★★★★★
Sirrah	★★★★★★★★	Vertex	★★★★★

TAURUS

Mirach	★★★★★★★★	Menkar	★★★★★★★
Mira	★★★★★	Zanrak	★★★★★★
El Scheratain	★★★★★★★	Capulus	★★★★
Hamal	★★★★★★★★	Algol	★★★★★★★
Schedir	★★★★★★★	Alcyone	★★★★★★
Alamak	★★★★★★★★		

GEMINI

Alcyone	★★★★★★	Mintaka	★★★★★★★
Prima Hyadum	★★★★	El Nath	★★★★
Ain	★★★★	Ensis	★★★
Aldebaran	★★★★★★★★★★	Alnilam	★★★★★★★★
Rigel	★★★★★★★★★★	Al Hecka	★★★★★★★★
Bellatrix	★★★★★★★★★	Polaris	★★★★★★★★
Capella	★★★★★★★★★★	Betelgeuze	★★★★★★★★★★
Phact	★★★★★★★	Menkalinan	★★★★★★★★

CANCER

Tejat	★★★★★★	Propus	★★★★
Dirah	★★★★★★	Castor	★★★★★★★★
Alhena	★★★★★★★★	Pollux	★★★★★★★★★★
Sirius	★★★★★★★★★★	Procyon	★★★★★★★★★★
Canopus	★★★★★★★★★★	Altarf	★★★★★
Al Wasat	★★★★		

LEO

Altarf	★★★★★	Merak	★★★★★★★★
Praesepe	★★	Al Genubi	★★★★★★
North Asellus	★★★★★	Alphard	★★★★★★★★
South Asellus	★★★★	Adhafera	★★★★★
Kochab	★★★★★★★★	Al Jabhah	★★★★★
Acubens	★★★★	Regulus	★★★★★★★★★★
Dubhe	★★★★★★★★	Phecda	★★★★★★

VIRGO

Phecda	★★★★★★	Copula	★★★★
Alioth	★★★★★★★★	Labrum	★★★★
Zosma	★★★★★★★	Zavijava	★★★★★
Mizar	★★★★★★★	Al Kaid	★★★★★★★★
Denebola	★★★★★★★★	Markeb	★★★★★★★

LIBRA

Zaniah	★★★★	Seginus	★★★★★★
Vindemiatrix	★★★★★★	Foramen	★★★★
Caphir	★★★★★★	Spica	★★★★★★★★★★
Algorab	★★★★★★	Arcturus	★★★★★★★★★★

SCORPIO

Princeps	★★★★★	Al Schemali	★★★★★★★
Khambalia	★★★★	Unukalhai	★★★★★★
Acrux	★★★★★★★★★★	Agena	★★★★★★★★★★
Alphecca	★★★★★★★	Bungula	★★★★★★★★★★
Al Genubi	★★★★★★		

SAGITTARIUS

Yed Prior	★★★★★★	Rasalhague	★★★★★★★★
Isidis	★★★★★★★	Lesuth	★★★★★★
Graffias	★★★★★★	Aculeus	★★★
Han	★★★★★★	Etamin	★★★★★★
Antares	★★★★★★★★★★	Acumen	★★★
Rastaban	★★★★★★★	Sinistra	★★★★★★
Sabik	★★★★★★★		

CAPRICORN

Spiculum	★★	Ascella	★★★★★★
Polis	★★★★	Manubrium	★★★★
Kaus Borealis	★★★★★★	Wega	★★★★★★★★★
Facies	★★	Deneb	★★★★★★
Pelagus	★★★★★★★★	Terebellum	★★

AQUARIUS

Albireo	★★★★★★	Armus	★★
Altair	★★★★★★★★★★	Dorsum	★★★★
Giedi	★★★★	Castra	★★★★
Dabih	★★★★★★	Nashira	★★★★
Oculus	★★	Sad Al Suud	★★★★★★
Bos	★★	Deneb Algedi	★★★★★★

PISCES

Sad Al Melik	★★★★★★	Achernar	★★★★★★★★★★
Fom Al Haut	★★★★★★★★★★	Markab	★★★★★★★★
Deneb Adige	★★★★★★★★★★	Scheat	★★★★★★★★
Skat	★★★★		

Introduction to Numerology

The belief that numbers possess sacred powers has been shared not just by archaic cultures and Greek philosophers, but also by Renaissance scholars and many present-day mathematicians.

Tallying marks and notches carved in groups of bones found in Zaire, dated to between 9000 and 7500 B.C., correspond to records of lunar (Moon) phases, and are one of the earliest signs of mathematical activity.

Numerology is as old as astrology and has its origins in Mesopotamian, Judaic, and ancient Greek civilizations. For example, in the Old Testament numbers and letters are thought to correspond to hidden meanings concerning messages, dreams, and the names of individuals. Each culture developed its own system of interpreting numbers to give meaning to the universe and human nature. The most reputable systems that contain numerology are the Pythagorean, Cabalistic, I Ching, and Mayan theories.

Many Greek philosophers were intrigued by the mystery of numbers. One of the most outstanding thinkers of the early Greek period was Pythagoras, who claimed that numbers were sacred and that "all things are numbers." He was a religious leader, a mystic, and a pure mathematician. Unlike many modern mathematicians, he united theology with rational thinking. Pythagoras provided a unique legacy for Western culture and a starting point for the identification of numbers. By discovering how important was the link between music and numbers, he established a harmonic connection between musical notes and mathematics. Realizing that numbers correspond to shapes, he was the first to describe the oblong, square, and triangle as a set of dots or numbers. His followers, the Pythagoreans, were also among the first to believe that the principles of mathematics were the basis of all existing things, and since, among these principles, numbers are by nature primary archetypes, they, above anything else, establish order in nature and the universe.

Some present-day mathematicians echo these beliefs and argue that the deeper one looks into the way our universe works, the more mathematical one finds the cosmos to be. Numbers and mathematics underline the very precise way in which the universe behaves.

There are three basic patterns to numbers. We can conceive of numbers through mathematical theories, philosophical definitions, and number symbolism. In the early part of the twentieth century, Jung interpreted the number as an archetype of order that has become conscious, and maintained that numbers are instrumental to the creation of order. He believed that a number is both quantitative and qualitative. Indeed, even investigations in particle physics suggest that changes in atomic quantity result in perceptible qualitative differences in the macroscopic world.

Numerology, like astrology, is a symbolic system, one of the many tools we can use to understand ourselves and our life purpose better. Numbers possess a dual nature and can represent either a positive or a negative force. Exploring their meaning can help us discover and develop our personal potential and guide us on life's journey. In this book we will focus particularly on the qualitative interpretations of numbers in relation to a person's day and month of birth, and we show in the following pages how simple it is to discover your holistic number.

How to Calculate Your Holistic Number

Your holistic number represents the total sum of the numbers of your birth day, month, and year. This number reveals your life purpose or challenge with its positive and negative attributes. By understanding your holistic number, you can come to a greater level of self-awareness. Calculating your personal holistic number is a simple process. All you need to do is add all the digits together one by one. For example:

June 28, 1956 (6/28/1956) $= 6 + 2 + 8 + 1 + 9 + 5 + 6 = 37$
$= 3 + 7 = 10 = 1 + 0 = 1$.
Your holistic number is 1, which can also be read as 37/1.

October 20, 1961 (10/20/1961) $= 1 + 0 + 2 + 0 + 1 + 9 + 6 + 1 = 20 = 2 + 0 = 2$.
Your holistic number is 2, which can also be read as 20/2.

The Nine Basic Numbers

The quality of each of the nine basic numbers can have a positive or negative expression in people's personalities, depending on how they approach their life challenges.

NUMBER 1

The number 1 dynamic is conscious. The positive attributes of the number 1 are self-assurance, creativity, singularity, and independence. If your holistic number is 1, it suggests that you are inventive and full of vitality, ambition, and drive. As a pioneer with a daring spirit, you like to take a leading role and express your originality. As you learn about your own creative force and individuality, you need to express yourself and be prepared to stand on your own two feet. Often this can mean thinking differently or acting separately from others. On occasion you can feel isolated from your immediate environment, especially if you are initiating new ideas. Inspiration is the key to your motivation, and developing your intuition will help you decide what to do when you are faced with a number of choices. Your strong willpower and determination urge you to lead rather than follow. Throughout your life you are likely to encounter experiences that will teach you how to overcome your insecurities, whether they are emotional, physical, or mental. Taking responsibility for your own actions is also part of your life lesson. At your best, you are a confident and self-reliant individual who inspires others in a positive way. Developing tolerance, compassion, and patience will help you to achieve your goals. Taking the time to improve your skills will often encourage you to exhibit some of your originality.

The challenges for number 1 individuals include swings from lack of confidence to overconfidence, being demanding, arrogance, selfishness, and a streak of the dictatorial.

NUMBER 2

The number 2 dynamic is sensorial. The positive attributes of the number 2 are sociability, receptivity, and the ability to balance your needs with the needs of others. Number 2 individuals have a flair for people and often learn through cooperative efforts. If your holistic number is 2, you are considerate and sensitive to other people's feelings, with a courteous and romantic nature. You are also diplomatic, friendly, and sociable, with an interest in public relations. Intuitive and adaptable, you thrive on encouragement but can be susceptible to flattery. You may need to learn how to distinguish between being cooperative and of service to others and being subservient and martyring yourself due to emotional insecurities. Your confidence may be undermined if you become overdependent; therefore, you need to constantly give and receive in equal measure. If you are needy or vulnerable, others can easily take advantage of your kind nature. Number 2 individuals need to learn how to be confrontational without being aggressive. Learn when to say no and not feel guilty. You also benefit from accepting help without appearing weak or ineffectual. Self-acceptance is the right path for number 2 individuals. Your positive accomplishments are to achieve inner harmony, develop purposeful goals, and set boundaries.

The challenges for number 2 individuals are dependency, restlessness, insecurity, oversensitivity, becoming discouraged too easily, a habitual mistrust of people, and lack of self-esteem.

NUMBER 3

The number 3 dynamic is expressive or emotional. The positive attributes of the number 3 are creative self-expression, sensitivity, imagination, and versatility. If your holistic number is 3, it suggests that you are enthusiastic, fun-loving, sociable, and friendly. You may choose to display your multitalented nature through a range of artistic endeavors. Making a choice, however, can be one of your challenges. As a number 3, you enjoy interacting with others through entertaining, social gatherings, and intimate conversation. Freedom-loving and emotional, you need to express the joy of living. You are also good at synthesizing knowledge and communicating your ideas. Number 3 people often avoid conflict by staying cheerful and optimistic. As your lessons often relate to emotional growth and self-expression, you may need to develop a deeper understanding of your sentiments, and rather than manipulate situations, you need to state your feelings directly. Number 3 individuals can also experience emotional upheavals or have negative feelings such as jealousy and hate. Although you can be witty and clever with words, if you are shy or insecure, you may become isolated or inhibited, finding it difficult to express your feelings and living in denial. Emotional fulfillment and satisfaction often come from the joy of sharing and learning about love and compassion.

The challenges for number 3 are worry and self-doubt, the tendency to scatter your energy, exaggeration, intolerance, feeling unprepared, indecision, and irresponsibility.

NUMBER 4

The number 4 dynamic is physical. The positive attributes of the number 4 are practicality, organizational skills, and self-discipline. If your holistic number is 4, you are honest, direct, and hardworking, with a desire to create stability. Number 4 individuals are patient, meticulous, and know well that methodology and preparation are essential. Whatever you do in life usually has to have a purpose and a practical application. As a number 4, you have a good sense of form, technical or mechanical skills, and general do-it-yourself ability. Keen on security, number 4 people are drawn to the world of banking or business in general. Although strict and emotionally undemonstrative, you can be loyal and dependable. You tend to be stubborn or rigid, and it is wise for you to learn to be more flexible and adaptable. Your ambition and vitality usually help you to endure when others run out of steam. It may be necessary for you to learn, however, not to take on more than you can master. Although you are protective of those you care for, you need to overcome a tendency to take over situations and be domineering. Number 4 individuals are commonly known as builders and indeed can often be the founders of projects and enterprises.

The challenges for the number 4 are dogmatism, obstinacy, undependability, being either too lazy or a workaholic, having difficulty letting go of the past, and giving in to excess.

NUMBER 5

The number 5 dynamic is instinctive. The positive attributes of the number 5 are ingenuity, quick reactions, and decisive action. Number 5 individuals are enthusiastic and love freedom. If positive, you are self-disciplined and focused, with an alert and astute mind. Although, as a number 5, you can be responsible, you need the autonomy to move freely. Usually versatile and enterprising, you enjoy meeting new people and having different experiences. Liberal and broad-minded, you can easily adapt yourself to new situations or be progressive in your attitude. Often skillful and efficient, you can learn quickly and grasp situations with your no-nonsense approach. Travel and changes are part of a number 5 lifestyle. As you are likely to go with the flow, you welcome reforms and adapt to new environments with little resistance. The negative number 5's are often restless and impatient and lack consistency. Without purpose and perseverance, a number 5 can wander aimlessly through life seeking a true vocation; therefore it is wise not to leave everything to chance. Depth of understanding and greater knowledge help you to utilize your great potential. If you learn to combine your quick thinking with your strong instincts, you can easily outshine others with your swift responses. Witty and audacious, you have a chivalrous or daring personality.

The challenges for number 5 are impetuous behavior, drifting, irresponsible conduct, impatience, lack of consideration, the tendency to scatter your energy, boredom, being too outspoken, and ruthlessness.

NUMBER 6

The number 6 dynamic is emotional and universal. The positive attributes of the number 6 are idealism, creativity, humanitarianism, compassion, and vision. Number 6 individuals are sensitive and responsible, and they often judge life by their feelings. Direct in your response, you mirror your close environment and people's behavior. You can be both home-loving and worldly, and you enjoy being involved in your community. Having strong family ties suggests that you can be a good parent who is supportive and uplifting. As a trustworthy individual and practical advisor, you will have friends who will come to you in times of trouble. Often a perfectionist, you love to be creative or artistic. With your good taste and eye for style, beauty, and form, you like to decorate your surroundings and beautify your home. If you aspire to high ideals, you may separate yourself from the mundane reality of ordinary life. Nevertheless, to make a better world

you should hold on to your utopian ideals and try very hard to live by your high morals. It would be wise, however, to overcome a tendency to be critical and judgmental. By learning to balance your feelings and thoughts, you can create harmony and peace. Accepting your own imperfections and failings helps you to come to terms with the world and its limitations. As a number 6 individual, you need to overcome a tendency to worry or become frustrated. The more you give, the more you will receive.

The challenges for number 6 are a lack of satisfaction, snobbishness, a lack of compassion, being overcritical, being domineering, and being interfering.

NUMBER 7

The number 7 dynamic is intuition and the mental/rational. Some of the positive attributes of the number 7 are honesty and trust, discriminative powers, attention to detail, methodology, and ingenuity. Analytical and thoughtful, number 7 individuals are self-absorbed and reflective, with the ability to perfect and be precise. Your autonomous perspective indicates that you are also self-reliant and assertive. As you prefer to make your own decisions, you frequently learn best through personal experience. If you tend to be oversensitive and insecure, you can become aloof or withdrawn. When you are unable to communicate your feelings, you may also feel misunderstood. An ability to differentiate and refine suggests that although you can easily turn into a fault-finding individual, you can excel in improving on existing systems. Being well informed and meticulous implies that you enjoy gathering information and have an excellent memory. You are good at self-analysis and seek greater self-awareness, which suggests that for you, quality time alone is often important for introspection; however, be careful to avoid isolation. Your interest in reading, writing, or spirituality is usually a source of inspiration and broadens your horizons. This desire to gain understanding may include education and the academic world or research in a specialized field. Although intuitive, number 7 individuals can indulge in overrationalization, which results in becoming lost in details. This in turn often brings lack of faith or creates self-doubt and insecurities. Although you have a tendency to be private, enigmatic, or secretive, you are inquisitive and often ask subtle questions, without letting anyone know what you really think.

The challenges for number 7 are suspicion, insincerity, secretiveness, skepticism, confusion, being too critical, detachment, and being unfeeling.

NUMBER 8

The number 8 dynamic is emotional and material power. The positive attributes of the number 8 are strength and strong convictions. Motivated and determined, you are hardworking and authoritative. The strength or power suggested by the number 8 birthday shows a character with strong values, executive abilities, and sound judgment. As a number 8, you seek security and consistency in permanent situations. Authoritative, with a desire for dominance and material success, number 8's often aspire to great accomplishment and possess an ambitious nature. Usually you get promoted to positions of responsibility and leadership because of your dedication and perseverance. As a number 8 person, you have natural business sense and will benefit greatly from developing your inherent organizational and executive skills. You may have to learn how to delegate your authority or administer in a fair and just way. If you find yourself in positions of influence, you can provide others with practical advice and protection. As a number 8 individual, you need to deal with power, patience, and tolerance by being forgiving, being understanding, and taking others' weaknesses into consideration when making a judgment. The number 8 person seeks security through long-term plans and investments for the future. Usually you possess power to heal yourself as well as others, and you benefit most if you learn how to channel these forces for the betterment of those around you.

The challenges for number 8 are impatience, intolerance, frugality, overwork, being power-hungry, being domineering, and a lack of planning.

NUMBER 9

The number 9 dynamic is the collective or universal. The positive attributes of the number 9 are compassion, tolerance, patience, integrity, sensitivity, and humanitarianism. Number 9 individuals are usually magnetic and charismatic, with perceptive minds and psychic abilities that point to a universal receptivity. If your holistic number is 9, you are usually generous and intuitive, with strong premonitions. Idealistic and impressionable, as a number 9 you usually have foresight and judge life by your feelings and receptivity. This sense of prophetic wisdom implies that as a number 9, you can possess inner wisdom and heightened awareness. Although you can be generous and compassionate, with a great imagination, you may become disillusioned or emotionally frustrated when you or others fail to reach your high expectations. This can result in fluctuating moods or a tendency to indulge in escapism. As a number 9, you need to find inner contentment and avoid losing heart or descending into the depths of melancholy. You may also have to develop understanding, tolerance, and patience as well as learning to become impersonal. As a holistic number 9, you may be destined to be of service to others or contribute to the betterment of humankind. Being universal, you are likely to benefit greatly from world travel and from interacting with people from all walks of life. A need to overcome challenges and a tendency to be oversensitive suggest that you benefit from remaining balanced and

avoiding unrealistic dreams. The combination of inspiration and idealism with an intense inner life and vivid dreams suggests that you may be happiest seeking a spiritual path.

The challenges for number 9 are nervousness, selfishness, stubbornness, impracticality, being easily led, having an inferiority complex, and worry.

How to Calculate Your Personal Year Number

To calculate your personal number for a particular year, simply add your personal month and day of birth to the year in question. For example, if you were born on June 28, 1956, and wished to know what kind of year you would experience in 1999, simply substitute 1999 for your birth year.

For example:
Substitute the 1999 for your year of birth (1956).

June 28, 1999 $= 6 + 2 + 8 + 1 + 9 + 9 + 9 = 44 = 8$.
This vibration would last for only one year, from January 1, 1999 to December 31, 1999.

The Nine Personal Year Interpretations

Personal year numbers fall in cycles of nine years. The following keywords describe the vibrational quality of each personal year:

---

1 YEAR

This is a time for new beginnings. There are numerous opportunities for expanding projects that have already been established or for beginning programs that have the mark of your own individuality. Although taking a new direction can present a risk, and making the right choices takes courage and confidence, listen to your own inner voice, and do not allow yourself to be discouraged by others.

If changes are in the air, this is the time to take action. Self-improvement is genuinely important to you, and the emphasis this year is on being independent, positive, and ambitious; otherwise you might miss the opportunities that a number 1 year has to offer. Any attempts made to go backward either will be denied or are not advisable. Guard against being too lazy or insecure to fulfill your dreams. The most rewarding experience of a number 1 year is to pioneer a new idea or invention that is of benefit to others.

2 YEAR

This is a year of relationships, cooperation, and patience. You are likely to extend your social circle and meet people from a different scene. Learning to be a peacemaker may increase your chances of developing long-lasting relationships or particular partnerships. You may also come across someone who will be a real challenge to you. Do not be put off, as this person has something worthwhile to teach you if you keep an open mind and retain a positive approach. Learning to make agreements, stay balanced and diplomatic, and develop communication skills is possible for you during this year. This is generally a year for improving yourself through self-awareness, and you may learn much about yourself by the way you relate to other people. A number 2 year offers the experience of staying in good company and forming new partnerships that are based on sincerity, while retaining freedom or independence and helping others while you help yourself.

3 YEAR

This is a year of emotional self-expression through creative endeavors, fun, and love. This is also a time of celebration, and you are likely to want more fun out of life. Your creative energies will flow, allowing you to express yourself more fully and freely. It is a time for falling in love, and your cheerful optimism will help you fulfill your need for love and joy. You may also be expanding your social circle. However, guard against jealousy, worry, indecision, and scattering your energy. Number 3 also indicates a year for creativity and expansion: having a baby; traveling for pleasure; bringing art, music, and culture into your home; making your house more pleasant. Social outings, visits to the theater, art exhibitions, or friendly gatherings and entertaining at home are likely to be the sorts of things you want or need this year. If you want to express yourself artistically, this is an excellent time to undertake a hobby or creative pursuit you have always secretly wanted to try, such as amateur dramatics, painting, dancing, singing, or writing. Be confident, try new projects, and remember to have fun. The most rewarding experiences a number 3 year can offer are learning about the joys of life and experiencing emotional growth.

4 YEAR

In a number 4 year good structure is the key. In this year organization, order, patience, and practical application will help you establish a firmer foundation. In this year you can accomplish a great deal, and you will find opportunities to do so. The need to be pragmatic in your outlook suggests that financial or other material challenges can also occur, especially if funds have been mismanaged. Whatever the structure, however, this is the time to review your finances, insurance, or legal affairs and make the necessary arrangements to make everything more simple or efficient.

Number 4 years are good years for business, building and repairing property, or simply moving to a better place. However, guard against making impractical decisions about property or insurance that you might later regret. The most important challenge for this year is to build a strong foundation and not succumb to unwarranted rebelliousness and laziness. The most rewarding experience may be to achieve something you are proud of.

5 YEAR

This is a year of change, which often indicates that circumstances, whether at work or in personal relationships, are in a state of transformation. Opportunities for travel (either short trips or long journeys) or a change of job may create much activity. Your instincts are potent, and a need for variety becomes crucial. You may be looking for new people and new experiences. Expect the unexpected and pleasant surprises.

In a number 5 year adjustment to changes is vital. Exercise calm detachment and guard against impatience, restlessness, and boredom; also be careful about doing things on the spur of the moment that you may regret later. This is a time to move with purpose and determination, so update your image or change your regular routine to avoid feeling as though you're in a rut. The most rewarding elements of a number 5 year are new learning experiences, new faces and new places, and knowing that you can achieve much in a short period of time.

6 YEAR

This is a year of taking responsibilities, either at home or out in the world. Because number 6 is a universal number, you need to become more interested in the wider world and not just your own sphere. This is a time of settling in to a new environment. New responsibilities often concern family members or making your home comfortable and beautiful. Service to others, which may include community work, makes this a year of caring. However, if you work hard, during this year you will reap positive rewards later, as opportunities and unexpected gains arise from helping others. Find time to be with your friends and your nearest and dearest, as they may need your support during this year. A time to bring harmony and beauty into your life, a number 6 year is a good opportunity to make home improvements and to bring some luxury and comfort to your home.

7 YEAR

This is a year for self-improvement, gaining new knowledge, and developing your mind. A desire for new understanding or learning may be high on your list of priorities. This suggests that it will be worthwhile taking stock of your life, a time to reflect on your past effort and achievements and to plan ahead. It is also a good year to learn new skills that build on what you already know or to take up a new subject to study. New opportunities could come through your work, in the form of classes or training that will improve your position or your performance. You might need or want more time on your own, or if alone you might need to find new people with whom you share interests and can easily communicate. A book or an article you read may influence you in a profound way or give you insight into new directions. Writing, reading, or joining an intellectually stimulating group may be the kind of experience you are looking for. Avoid isolating yourself from the world or being overly critical of those around you, as misunderstandings are more likely to occur in a number 7 year. Most rewarding this year is to gain a deeper understanding and communicate your ideas in a new way.

8 YEAR

This is a year for decisive action, establishing and actualizing all the efforts of the past seven years. If you want to succeed, this is not the year for wishful thinking—you must make the effort and push ahead. Achievements or opportunities for advancement are likely to appear through promotions or financial gains. Other plans or investments from the past will bear fruits. This is also a year of hard work and added responsibilities. You may therefore need to guard against overworking yourself.

Making long-term investments, such as buying real estate, will appeal to you, as you feel the need to put down roots and take control of your life or find long-term security. Good business opportunities are also likely this year, and you will be lucky. However, financial management is essential in order to secure good returns. This year consider others and enjoy what the period has to offer without trying to dominate others and without concentrating entirely on personal gains.

9 YEAR

This is the most important and spiritual year in the numerological cycle. It is the year of completion and of tying up a lot of loose ends. A new cycle is not yet born but the preceding one is ending. The fundamental rule of the number 9 is that you shall reap what you have sown. This is also the time to assess where you stand and discard all that is not essential. Avoid holding on to the past; if you have outgrown certain situations or even people, this is the time to say your good-byes and plan for the future, especially in the later part of the year.

The universal symbolism of the number 9 also indicates the achievement of maturity and understanding about the fundamental principles of life in the cycle of death and rebirth, of parting and starting anew. The number 9 represents the basis of the eternal life of change and continuity. The most rewarding experiences for a number 9 year are compassion and forgiveness. Your good deeds are not lost: Charity to others will make a better person out of you and give you the courage to forge ahead.

The Thirty-one Personal Day Interpretations

The personal day number corresponds to the day of the month you were born. It is unchangeable.

DAY 1

The great desire to be first and independent is suggested by your birthdate. As a number 1, you are more inclined to be individual, innovative, and courageous, with plenty of energy. Often there is a need to establish a strong identity and develop self-confidence or assertiveness. The pioneering spirit indicated here encourages you to make your own decisions or strike out alone. These self-starting forces stimulate you to develop executive or leadership abilities. Full of enthusiasm and original ideas, you often show others the way forward. However, a need to be admired and popular may undermine your assurance, and a tendency to depend on others may arise from a lack of confidence. With a number 1 birthday, you may also need to learn that the world does not revolve around you and avoid an inclination to be self-centered or dictatorial. Winning and success are possible through initiating new ideas or inventing various exciting and enterprising ventures.

• *Positive:* leadership, creativity, progressiveness, forcefulness, optimism, strong convictions, competitiveness, independence, gregariousness

• *Negative:* overbearing, jealousy, egotism, pride, antagonism, lack of restraint, selfishness, weakness, instability, impatience

DAY 2

Sensitivity and a strong need to be part of a group are suggested by a number 2 birthday. Often you are adaptable and understanding, and you enjoy cooperative activities where you can experience interaction with others. Receptive and influenced by your surroundings, you possess a friendly and warm personality, with good social skills and a diplomatic approach. A love of harmony and an inclination to work better with others may inspire you to act as a mediator in family matters or become a peacemaker. In your attempt to please others, you may run the risk of becoming overly dependent. By developing confidence, however, you can overcome the tendency to get easily hurt by the actions and criticism of others. In love relationships and associations, learn to trust your intuition. Guard against an inclination to be manipulative.

• *Positive:* good partnerships, gentleness, tact, receptivity, intuition, consideration, harmony, agreeableness, ambassador of goodwill

• *Negative:* suspicion, lack of confidence, subservience, timidity, oversensitivity, selfishness, being too easily hurt, craftiness, deceit

DAY 3

Needs for love, creativity, and emotional expression are all indicated by a number 3 birthday. Often fun-loving, easygoing, and a good companion, you enjoy friendly social activities and many interests. Versatility and a need for self-expression frequently lead you to seek numerous experiences. An inclination to get bored easily may cause you to become indecisive or spread yourself too thin. Although, as a number 3 birthday, you are usually artistic and charming, with a good sense of humor, you may have to develop self-esteem and guard against tendencies toward worry, jealousy, and other emotional insecurities. Personal relationships and a loving atmosphere are of prime importance to you, as they endow you with enthusiasm and inspiration.

• *Positive:* humor, happiness, friendliness, productivity, creativity, artistic ability, power to wish, love of freedom, talent with words

• *Negative:* boredom, vanity, exaggeration, extravagance, self-indulgence, laziness, hypocrisy, worry, indecision, self-doubt

DAY 4

The solid structure and orderly power suggested by the number 4 birthday indicate that you often need stability and like to establish law and order. Endowed with energy, practical skills, and strong determination, you can achieve success through hard work. With a number 4 birthday, you are sensitive to form and composition and are able to create practical systems. Security-conscious, you like to build a strong foundation for yourself and your family. Faithful yet undemonstrative, you are inclined to believe that actions speak louder than words. A pragmatic approach to life confers a good business sense and an ability to achieve material success in life. As a number 4, you are usually honest, frank, and fair. Nevertheless, you may have to learn to be more expressive with your feelings and avoid being stubborn or tactless. The challenges for a number 4 individual may include overcoming periods of instability, financial worry, or ruthlessness.

• *Positive:* organization, self-discipline, steadiness, hard work, craftsmanship, manual ability, pragmatism, trust, exactitude

• *Negative:* destructive behavior, uncommunicativeness, repression, rigidity, laziness, penny pinching, bossiness, strictness

DAY 5

Strong instincts, an adventurous nature, and a desire for freedom are all indicated by the number 5 birthday. The willingness to explore or try anything new and an enthusiastic approach suggest that life will have a lot to offer you. Travel and many opportunities for change, some unexpected, may lead you to undergo a real transformation of views and beliefs. With a number 5 birthday, you need to feel that life is exciting; however, you may also have to develop a responsible attitude and avoid tendencies such as unpredictability, excessiveness, and restlessness. Often having a number 5 birthdate means that you need to learn about patience and attention to detail; you can achieve success by avoiding premature or speculative actions. The natural talent of a number 5 individual is knowing how to go with the flow and staying detached.

• *Positive:* versatility, adaptability, progressiveness, strong instincts, magnetism, luck, daring, love of freedom, quickness, wit, curiosity, mysticism, sociability

• *Negative:* unreliability, changeability, procrastination, inconsistency, undependability, overconfidence, headstrong

DAY 6

Compassion, idealism, and a caring nature are some of the attributes suggested by a number 6 birthday. This is the number of the universal friend, and indicates that you are often a visionary or humanitarian who can be responsible, loving, and supportive.

Although you are often worldly and career-oriented, with a number 6 birthday you are more frequently domestically oriented, a homemaker, and a devoted parent. Intense emotions and a desire to bring universal harmony often encourage you to work hard for what you believe in, whether in the community or via other voluntary service. The more sensitive among you will need to find a form of creative expression and are often drawn to the world of entertaining or art and design. The challenges for some people with number 6 birthdates may include developing more self-confidence and compassion toward their friends and neighbors as well as learning to be more responsible. You may also need to overcome tendencies toward being interfering, worry, discontent, and misplaced sympathy.

• *Positive:* worldliness, universal brotherhood, friendliness, compassion, dependability, understanding, sympathy, idealism, domesticity, humanitarian ideals, poise, artistic talent, balance

• *Negative:* anxiety, shyness, unreasonableness, stubbornness, outspokenness, disharmony, perfectionism, domineering behavior, lack of responsibility, selfishness, suspicion, self-centeredness

DAY 7

Analytical and thoughtful, number 7 individuals are often perfectionistic, critical, and self-absorbed. Often you prefer to make your own decisions, and frequently you learn best through personal experience. With a constant need for greater self-awareness, you enjoy gathering information and may be interested in reading, writing, or spirituality. This desire to learn may also lead you into the academic world or to continuously improve on your existing skills. As a number 7 individual, you may at times overrationalize or get lost in detail. At other times you can become overly sensitive to criticism or feel misunderstood. A tendency to be enigmatic or secretive usually leads you to develop the art of asking subtle questions, without letting anyone know what you really think. Number 7 individuals may also have to avoid being overly critical, opinionated, uncommunicative, and aloof.

• *Positive:* education, trust, meticulousness, idealism, honesty, psychic ability, scientific and rational orientation, reflection

• *Negative:* deceit, loner tendency, secretiveness, skepticism, confusion, detachment, coldness

DAY 8

The strength or power suggested by a number 8 birthday shows a character with strong values and sound judgment. The number 8 often indicates that you aspire to great accomplishment and possess an ambitious nature. A desire for dominance, security, and material success is also indicated by this birthday. As a number 8 person, you have natural business sense and will benefit greatly from developing organizational and executive skills. If you are willing to work hard, you are often given great responsi-

bilities. Nevertheless, you may have to learn how to administer or delegate your authority in a fair and just way. Many people with number 8 birthdays are frequently drawn to occupations linked to justice, law and order, or leadership positions in business management as well as finance and banking. A strong need to feel secure or established urges you to make long-term plans and investments. Many individuals with a number 8 birthday also possess great power to heal themselves as well as others, and benefit most if they learn how to channel these forces for the betterment of humankind.

• *Positive:* leadership, thoroughness, hard work, tradition, authority, protection, power to heal, good judge of values

• *Negative:* impatience, intolerance, miserliness, restlessness, overwork, hunger for power, domineering behavior, being easily discouraged, lack of planning, controlling behavior

DAY 9

Benevolence, compassion, and sentimental sensitivity are all associated with the number 9 birthday. Creative and kind, you are often considered intelligent and generous. Intuitive and psychic abilities point to a universal receptivity, and if channeled positively, they may inspire you to seek a spiritual path. With a number 9 birthday, you usually feel that your life is mapped out for you and does not leave you much room to maneuver. You may also have to develop understanding, tolerance, and patience as well as learn to become impersonal. This birthday may suggest a need to overcome challenges and a tendency to be overly sensitive, with emotional ups and downs. Nevertheless, people with the number 9 birthday are destined to achieve in life and be of service to humankind.

You are likely to benefit greatly from world travel and interaction with people from all walks of life. You may have to avoid unrealistic dreams or an inclination toward escapism.

• *Positive:* idealism, humanitarianism, creativity, sensitivity, generosity, magnetism, poetic nature, charitableness, giving nature, detachment, luck, popularity

• *Negative:* frustration, nervousness, uncertainty, selfishness, impracticality, bitterness, being easily led, inferiority complex, fear, worry, isolation

DAY 10

Like those with a number 1 birthday, you are likely to strive toward accomplishment and achievement. Nevertheless, you may have to overcome many obstacles before you achieve your goals. Usually there is a strong need to establish an identity, and a number 10 birthday indicates that you are likely to be innovative, self-assured, and ambitious. You think big and are usually worldly. Often energetic and original, you stand by your own beliefs even when they differ from others'. At times you may feel alone or unpopular. Your ability to be a self-starter with a pioneering spirit frequently encourages you to travel far afield or strike out on your own. A tendency to depend on others often arises from a lack of confidence, fear, or a need to be admired and recognized. With a number 10 birthday, you may also need to learn that the world does not revolve around you, and should guard against selfishness and being dictatorial. Success and accomplishment are important to all with a number 10 birthday, and frequently you find the way to the top of your profession. Since this usually involves working with larger issues, you may not be domestically inclined.

• *Positive:* leadership, creativity, progressiveness, forcefulness, optimism, strong convictions, competitiveness, independence, gregariousness

• *Negative:* overbearing, jealousy, egotism, pride, antagonism, lack of restraint, selfishness, weakness, instability, impatience

DAY 11

The special vibration of the master number 11 birthday suggests that idealism, inspiration, and innovation are highly important to you. A blend of humility and confidence often challenges you to work toward self-mastery, both materially and spiritually. Through experience you learn how to deal with both sides of your nature and develop a less extremist attitude by trusting your own feelings. Although you possess intuitive powers, you may scatter your energies and often need to find a goal upon which you can focus. Usually you are highly charged and enjoy vitality, but must avoid becoming overly anxious or impractical. At worst, with a number 11 birthday, you may find it hard to distinguish between how you feel and what you want to achieve. At best, you are endowed with qualities of genius that can benefit others.

• *Positive:* balance, focus, objectivity, enthusiasm, inspiration, spirituality, idealism, intuition, intelligence, outgoing character, inventiveness, artistic nature, service orientation, healing ability, humanitarianism, faith, psychic ability

• *Negative:* superiority complex, being overemotional, dishonesty, aimlessness, being easily hurt, being high-strung, selfishness, lack of clarity, domination, meanness

DAY 12

A desire to establish true individuality is often suggested by the number 12 birthday. Usually you are intuitive, helpful, and friendly, and you possess good reasoning power. Innovative, understanding, and sensitive, you also know how to use tact and cooperative methods to achieve your aims and objectives. To others you often appear confident, although self-doubt and suspicion can undermine your usual easygoing personality

and positive outlook. When you achieve the balance between your need for self-expression and your natural inclination to be supportive of others, you can find emotional satisfaction and personal fulfillment. You may nevertheless need to find the courage to stand on your own two feet and develop self-confidence or learn not to get easily discouraged by other people.

• *Positive:* creativity, attractiveness, initiative, discipline, promotion of self or others

• *Negative:* reclusiveness, eccentricity, uncooperativeness, oversensitivity, lack of self-esteem

DAY 13

Emotional sensitivity, enthusiasm, and inspiration are often identified with a number 13 birthday. Numerically, you are associated with ambition and hard work and can accomplish much through creative self-expression. You may, however, need to develop a pragmatic outlook if you want to turn your creative talents into tangible products. Your original and innovative approach inspires new and exciting ideas, which frequently result in work that impresses others. With a number 13 birthday, you are earnest, romantic, charming, and fun-loving, and with dedication you can achieve prosperity. Your powerful emotions and a desire for freedom or emotional self-expression can be your greatest assets. However, learning about partnerships and cooperation will provide you with opportunities to share your great talents with others. Like many individuals who share your birthdate, you may wish to travel or yearn to settle in a new environment to make a better life for yourself. The idealistic among you may choose a career in the entertainment world and seek ways to express your creative talents.

• *Positive:* ambition, creativity, love of freedom, self-expression, initiative

• *Negative:* impulsiveness, indecision, bossiness, unemotional nature, rebelliousness

DAY 14

Intellectual potential, a pragmatic outlook, and strong determination are some of the qualities of the number 14 birthday. Often you possess a strong desire to establish a firm foundation and achieve success through hard work. Indeed, with a number 14 birthday, you frequently put your work first and judge yourself and others upon the basis of career achievements. Although you need stability, the restlessness indicated by the number 14 urges you to forge ahead and take on new challenges in a constant attempt to improve your lot. This innate dissatisfaction may also inspire you to make a great many changes in your life, especially if you are not happy with your working conditions or financial status. Like many individuals associated with this birthday, you can often reach the top of your profession. The hidden characteristics indicated by the number 14 birthday suggest that you will benefit from exploring your creative talents and learning to express your feelings more openly. Love may, at times, be a real test for you, although your versatility, practical good sense, and strong instincts override your tendency to be stubborn. With your perceptive mind, you respond quickly to problems and enjoy solving them. Having a 14 birthdate, you enjoy taking a risk or a gamble and may be lucky enough to gain a windfall.

• *Positive:* decisive actions, hard work, luck, creativity, pragmatism, imagination, industry

• *Negative:* excessive caution or excessive impulsiveness, instability, thoughtlessness, stubbornness

DAY 15

Versatility, generosity, and restlessness are suggested by the number 15 birthday. Usually you are quick and enthusiastic, with a charismatic personality. Your greatest assets are your strong instincts and the ability to learn quickly through combining theory and practice. On many occasions you manage to earn while learning new skills. Often you utilize your intuitive powers and are quick at recognizing opportunities when they arise. With a number 15 birthday, you possess a talent for attracting money and for receiving help and support from others. Habitually carefree and enthusiastic, you welcome the unexpected. Although you are naturally adventurous, you nevertheless need to find a real base or a home that you can call your own. Although full of drive and ambition, at times you can also become stubborn or fixed, and must guard against getting in a rut. Successful conclusions to undertakings can become more frequent if you apply your practical skills to your original ideas and overcome your tendency to be restless or dissatisfied.

• *Positive:* willingness, generosity, responsibility, kindness, cooperation, appreciation, creative ideas

• *Negative:* disruptiveness, restlessness, irresponsibility, self-centeredness, fear of change, loss of faith, worry, indecision, materialism, misuse of power

DAY 16

A number 16 birthday suggests that you are ambitious, yet emotional, caring, and friendly. Your strong desire for self-fulfillment and a need to experience the big world may encourage you to leave your family behind. You often judge life according to how you feel and have a good insight into people and situations. As a number 16 personality, however, you can experience inner tensions when facing friction between a need for self-expression and responsibility to others.

With a number 16 birthday, you may be interested in world affairs and may join international corporations or the media world. Alternatively, you may get involved with charitable organizations and work for worthwhile causes. The creative ones among you have a talent for writing, with sudden flashes of inspiration. The restless undercurrent indicated by the number 16 birthday frequently indicates a spiritual awakening of the self, especially through periods of instability or change. If you have a number 16 birthday, you may need to learn how to balance between being overly confident and being insecure. Although many of you come from a close family, you often choose to live alone or travel extensively.

• *Positive:* higher education, responsibilities to home and family, integrity, intuition, sociability, cooperation, insight

• *Negative:* worry, inability to be satisfied, irresponsibility, self-promotion, being opinionated, skepticism, fussiness, irritability, selfishness, unsympathetic

DAY 17

Having a number 17 birthday, you are often shrewd, with a reserved nature and good analytical abilities. An independent thinker, you are well-educated or skillful, and rely on personal experience. Usually you utilize your knowledge in a specific way in order to develop your expertise and can achieve material success or a prominent position as a specialist or researcher. Private, retrospective, and detached, with a strong interest in facts and figures, you frequently present a serious and thoughtful demeanor and like to take your time. Alternatively, by developing your communication skills you can discover much more about yourself from others. However, once you decide upon a course of action, you can be quite determined and fail to listen to the advice of others, whether the advice is good or bad. Frequently capable of long periods of concentration and endurance, you can learn far more through experience. Nevertheless, the less skeptical you are, the quicker you learn.

• *Positive:* thoughtfulness, expertise, planning, business sense, ability to attract money, individual thinker, painstaking nature, accuracy, research skills, scientific ability

• *Negative:* detachment, loneliness, stubbornness, carelessness, moodiness, oversensitivity, narrow-mindedness, criticism, loner tendency, worry, suspicion

DAY 18

Determination, assertiveness, and ambition are some of the attributes associated with the number 18 birthday. Dynamic and active, you frequently desire power and need constant challenge. Often capable, hardworking, and responsible, you rise to positions of authority and are inclined toward careers in law and order or government. Alternatively, your strong business sense and organizational skills lead you to the world of commerce. With a number 18 birthday, you may be argumentative, critical, or hard to please. You can easily become a workaholic and may need to learn how to relax or slow down from time to time. As a number 18 personality, you may use your power to heal others, give sound advice, or solve other people's problems. However, you may have to learn how to distinguish between the use and misuse of power through learning to live with others.

• *Positive:* progressiveness, assertiveness, intuition, courage, resoluteness, healing ability, efficiency, advisory skills

• *Negative:* uncontrolled emotions, laziness, lack of order, selfishness, callousness, failure to complete work or projects, deceitfulness

DAY 19

Creative, sunny, ambitious, and dynamic, yet humanitarian and sensitive, with a number 19 birthday you are decisive and resourceful. You possess depth of vision, but the dreamer side of your nature is compassionate, idealistic, and sensitive. The need to be someone may be the very thing that pushes you to be dramatic and claim center stage. Often there is a strong desire to establish an individual identity. However, to do so you may first need to overcome the influence of peer group pressure. Only through numerous experiences can you develop self-confidence or leadership abilities. To others you may appear confident, resilient, and resourceful, but inner tensions may cause emotional ups and downs. Although proud, with a need to know that others care and appreciate your efforts, you may also need to learn that the world does not revolve around you. This usually indicates that tendencies to be selfish or arrogant may have to be overcome. You probably also have to learn about courage, planning, and structure, as well as overcoming a fear of being alone. Creative and charismatic, you feel that the world is there for you to explore, and success is more likely if you either go it alone or work within large corporations.

• *Positive:* dynamism, centeredness, creativity, leadership, luck, progressiveness, optimism, strong convictions, competitiveness, independence, gregariousness

• *Negative:* self-centeredness, depression, worry, fear of rejection, ups and downs, materialism, egotism, impatience

DAY 20

With a number 20 birthday, you are intuitive, sensitive, adaptable, and understanding, and often see yourself as a part of a larger group. Usually you enjoy cooperative activities where you can interact, share experiences, or learn from others. Influenced by your surroundings, you can also be artistic or musical. Often

charming and gracious, you develop diplomatic and social skills and can move in different social circles with ease. You may, however, need to develop your confidence or overcome a tendency to be easily hurt by the actions and criticism of others. In relationships and other associations you must guard against an inclination to martyr yourself, be mistrusting, or be overly dependent on others. You are a master at creating a congenial and harmonious atmosphere, and might be called on to act as a mediator in family matters or as a peacemaker at work, where you often assist others.

• *Positive:* good partnerships, gentleness, tact, receptivity, intuition, consideration, harmony, agreeableness, amicableness, ambassador of goodwill

• *Negative:* suspicion, lack of confidence, subservience, timidity, oversensitivity, selfishness, tendency to be easily hurt, deceit

DAY 21

Dynamic drive and an outgoing personality are often present in those with a number 21 birthday. Socially inclined, you have many interests and contacts and are generally fortunate. Usually you show others your friendly and gregarious personality. Highly original and intuitive, you possess an independent spirit. If you have a number 21 birthday, you can be fun-loving, magnetic, and creative, with social charm. Alternatively, you can be shy and reserved, with a need to develop assertiveness, especially in close relationships. In life you often have many opportunities and achieve success with other people. Although you can be inclined toward cooperative relationships or marriage, you always want to be acknowledged for your talents and abilities. Number 21 personalities, however, must guard against being too selfish or seeking their identity in other people's dreams. You can also spend too much time on relationships and thus become codependent.

• *Positive:* inspiration, creativity, love unions, long-lasting relationships

• *Negative:* dependency, nervousness, overemotionalism, lack of vision, disappointment, fear of change

DAY 22

With a number 22 birthdate, you are a proud, practical, disciplined, and highly intuitive individual. This is a master number and can vibrate as both number 22 and number 4. Often honest and hardworking, with natural leadership abilities, you have a charismatic personality and a deep understanding of people and what motivates them. Although undemonstrative, you often show a caring, protective concern for the welfare of others. However, you never lose sight of your pragmatic or realistic stand. Usually cultured and worldly, you have many friends and admirers. Your more obvious attributes are practical skills and executive abilities. Your forthright yet composed personality helps you rise to higher managerial positions. The more competitive among you achieve success and good fortune with help and encouragement from others. Many born on this date have strong links with brothers or sisters and can be protective and supportive of them.

• *Positive:* universality, intuition, pragmatism, practicality, manual ability, skillfulness, building ability, organization, realism, problem solving, achievement

• *Negative:* get-rich-quick attitude, nervousness, inferiority complex, bossiness, materialism, lack of vision, laziness, egotism, self-promotion

---

DAY 23

Intuitive, emotionally sensitive, and creative are some of the attributes of a number 23 birthday. Usually you are versatile, passionate, and a quick thinker, with a professional attitude and a mind full of creative ideas. With the number 23 influence, you can learn new subjects easily but may prefer practice to theory. You may need, however, to overcome a tendency to criticize others or to develop a less selfish attitude. Fond of travel, adventure, and meeting new people, your restlessness urges you to try many different kinds of experiences, and you adapt to make the best of any situation. Generally friendly and fun-loving, with courage and drive, you may need an active life in order to actualize your true potential. Although you are willing to help others, if you are indecisive and frequently change your mind, you can appear irresponsible. Some number 23 individuals may experience numerous short-lived relationships before they find happiness and the perfect mate.

• *Positive:* loyalty, responsibility, travel, communication, intuition, creativity, versatility, trustworthiness, fame

• *Negative:* selfishness, insecurity, stubbornness, uncompromising nature, fault finding, jealousy, withdrawal, restlessness

---

DAY 24

Conscientiousness, responsibility, and enterprise are some of the qualities found in a number 24 birthday. Although you may dislike routine, frequently you are hardworking, with practical abilities and sound judgment. The emotional sensitivity of the number 24 birthday suggests that you may need to establish stability, law, and order. You are also sensitive to form and structure and can easily create a complex yet efficient system. Often honest, dependable, and security-conscious, you need the love and support of a partner and enjoy building a strong foundation for yourself and your family. Faithful, fair, yet undemonstrative, you

are inclined to believe that actions speak louder than words. A pragmatic approach to life also gives you good business sense and an ability to achieve material success in life. With a number 24 birthday, you may have to overcome periods of instability and a tendency to be stubborn or fixed in your ideas. By learning to trust your intuition and develop social skills, you can acquire self-discipline. You must, however, guard against destructive behavior, which can be interpreted by others as ruthlessness and materialism. The main challenge for a number 24 birthday is to learn to get along with people from all walks of life, to overcome suspicious tendencies, and to build a secure home.

• *Positive:* energy, idealism, practical skills, strong determination, honesty, frankness, fairness, generosity, love of home, activity

• *Negative:* ruthlessness, materialism, penny pinching, dislike of routine, laziness, infidelity, domination, stubbornness, vengefulness

---

DAY 25

Intuitive and thoughtful, yet quick and energetic, you need to express yourself through different experiences. These may include new and exciting ideas, people, or locations. A desire for perfection associated with the number 25 birthday often urges you to work hard and be productive. You may, however, need to be less impatient or critical if things do not happen according to plan. Emotional sensitivity and creative, artistic talents are just some of your hidden attributes. You may also need to avoid underestimating yourself, as it can lead to frustration or destructive behavior. A strong need for lasting close personal relationships, love, and affection may be undermined by the restless vibration of the number 25. Usually you are instinctive and alert, and can gain more knowledge through practical application than through mere theory. Good judgment and an eye for detail ensure successful accomplishment. You may have to develop a less skeptical attitude and overcome a tendency to make erratic or impulsive decisions. Fear of change may create emotional tension, moodiness, and jealousy. As a number 25, you possess strong mental energies; when concentrated, they aid you to look at all the facts and arrive at a conclusion faster than anyone else. Success and happiness come when you learn to trust your own instincts and develop perseverance and patience.

• *Positive:* intuition, perfectionism, perception, creativity, people skills

• *Negative:* impulsiveness, impatience, irresponsibility, overemotionalism, jealousy, secrecy, criticism, moodiness, nervousness

---

DAY 26

A number 26 birthday often suggests that you aspire to great accomplishment and possess an ambitious nature. Often you have a pragmatic approach to life, executive ability, and a good business sense. The strength or power suggested by the number 26 birthday shows that you are a cautious character with strong values and sound judgment. If you have a number 26 birthday, you are usually responsible, with a natural aesthetic sense. A love of home and strong parental instincts may also suggest a strong need to build a solid foundation or find real stability. Through stubbornness or lack of self-confidence, however, you may sometimes give up too quickly. Nevertheless, with self-control and careful planning you can achieve success.

An inclination toward idealistic and humanitarian causes may lead you to work in vocations involving people, education, and service to the community. Often a tower of strength for others, you are willing to support friends, family members, and relatives who turn to you in time of need. You may nevertheless need to guard against materialistic tendencies and a desire to control situations or people.

• *Positive:* creativity, practicality, caring, responsibility, pride in family, enthusiasm, courage

• *Negative:* stubbornness, rebelliousness, unenthusiastic, lack of persistence, instability, domination

DAY 27

The number 27 birthdate indicates that your depth of thought can be greatly enhanced by developing patience and self-control. Intuitive yet analytical, you are often forceful, determined, and observant and can pay great attention to details. Often idealistic and sensitive, with a fertile and creative mind, you can impress others with your original thoughts and ideas. Although at times you appear secretive, rational, or detached, in fact you may be hiding inner tensions. These may include tendencies to be impulsive, indecisive, confused, or suspicious about forthcoming changes. In developing good communication skills, you can overcome a reluctance to express your deeper feelings. The key to success is often inspiration, and by developing a more universal outlook, you can refrain from outbursts or worrying about what others may think or say. Education is essential for number 27 persons, and with the proper qualifications you can achieve success through writing, research, or work in large organizations. Naturally versatile and imaginative, with strong instincts or psychic abilities, you can be ambitious and full of ideas. However, restlessness may cause you to be unsettled and impulsive, and you may need to learn how to turn your ideas into tangible results. Although you are often affectionate and considerate, you may occasionally appear overly sensitive and unapproachable. By developing a more detached perspective, you will be able to listen to others and take on board their criticism or ideas.

• *Positive:* versatility, imagination, creativity, resoluteness, bravery, good understanding, mental capabilities, spirituality, inventiveness, mental strength

• *Negative:* disagreeableness, being easily offended, being argumentative, restlessness, nervousness, mistrust, overemotionalism, being highly strung, tension

DAY 28

Independent, idealistic, and unconventional, yet pragmatic and determined, you are often a law unto yourself. An inner conflict between wanting to be independent and wanting to be part of a team is also indicated. Like a number 1 individual, you are ambitious, direct, and enterprising. Always ready for action and new ventures, you courageously take on life's challenges, and with your enthusiasm you can easily inspire others—if not to join you, at least to support you in your latest venture. Among your many attributes are strong conviction, resourcefulness, good judgment, and an ability to accumulate knowledge and use it to refine or solve problems. With a number 28 birthday, you often have leadership abilities and rely on your common sense, logic, and clear thinking. Although you are success-oriented and ambitious, family and home life are very important to you. Finding stability and taking care of your nearest and dearest may at times be a challenge for you. Often you take on responsibilities, but you can also be overly enthusiastic, impatient, or intolerant. You may also have to guard against becoming too bossy, opinionated, or rebellious.

• *Positive:* compassion, progressiveness, daring, artistic ability, creativity, idealism, ambition, hard work, stable home life, strong will

• *Negative:* daydreams, lack of compassion, unrealistic, bossiness, poor judgment, aggressiveness, uncooperative, lack of confidence, dependence on others, pride

DAY 29

Idealistic visionaries with a dynamic and forceful character, number 29 individuals have a powerful personality and extraordinary potential. You are often highly intuitive, sensitive, and emotional. Your compassionate and understanding nature inspires humanitarianism and can encourage others to fulfill their hopes and dreams. Indeed, inspiration is the key to your success story, and without it you may experience lack of purpose. Although you are a true dreamer, often the extreme sides of your nature indicate that you may have to guard against alternating moods. You may go from being very friendly and warm to being cold and uncaring; you may swing between optimism and pessimism. Although with a number 29 birthday you are competitive and ambitious, you need to be popular and care what others think about you. However, you may have to learn how to be less critical, doubtful, shy, or detached and more considerate of those around you. If you trust your innermost feelings and open your heart to others, you can overcome your tendency to worry or use your mind as protective armor. Use your creative thoughts to achieve something special and unique that can inspire or be of service to others.

• *Positive:* inspiration, balance, inner peace, generosity, success, creativity, intuition, mysticism, powerful dreams, worldliness, faith

• *Negative:* unfocused, insecurity, nervousness, moodiness, being difficult, extremism, isolation, oversensitivity

DAY 30

Artistic and creative, friendly and sociable are just some of the ways people with a number 30 birthday are characterized. You enjoy the good life, love socializing, and can be exceptionally charismatic, loyal, and friendly. Emotional and ambitious, with creative potential, you take ideas and expand them in your own dramatic style. Even-tempered and gregarious, with good taste and an eye for style and form, you can achieve success in all types of work concerning art, design, and music. Pride and ambition combined with good opportunities often allow you to climb to the top of your profession. If you have a number 30 birthday, you possess strong feelings, and being in love or contented is a vital requirement. In your pursuit of happiness, avoid being lazy, overindulgent, impatient, or jealous, as these may cause you to experience emotional instability. Among those with a number 30 birthday, many will find recognition or fame, especially musicians, actors, and entertainers, but may have to make some sacrifices for loved ones.

• *Positive:* love of fun, loyalty, friendliness, ability to synthesize, talent with words, creativity, luck

• *Negative:* laziness, obstinacy, erraticism, impatience, overindulgence, indifference, indecision, jealousy

DAY 31

Strong willpower, determination, and an emphasis on self-expression are indicated by the number 31 birthday. You often combine your intuition and practical skill to make the right decisions. Usually you are tireless and determined, with the corresponding need to make material progress; however, you may have to learn to accept the limitations of life, and you therefore may need to build a solid foundation. If you have a number 31 birthday, you have original ideas, a good sense of form, and the ability to succeed in business if you take your time and follow a practical plan of action. Good fortune and lucky opportunities are also suggested by the number 31 birthday, and you can be successful in turning your leisure-time pursuits into profitable ventures. You may, however, have to learn not to be too easily discouraged and to be more considerate of others. Time for love and having fun is crucial to you, as you are likely to be hardworking. Nevertheless, you may have to guard against tendencies to be overindulgent or selfish, as well as being overly optimistic. The weaker individuals associated with the number 31 birthday are insecure and give up too easily on their dreams or indulge in wishful thinking.

• *Positive:* luck, creativity, originality, ability to build and be constructive, persistence, practicality, good conversation, responsibility

• *Negative:* insecurity, impatience, suspicion, tendency to be easily discouraged, lack of ambition, selfishness, stubbornness, materialism

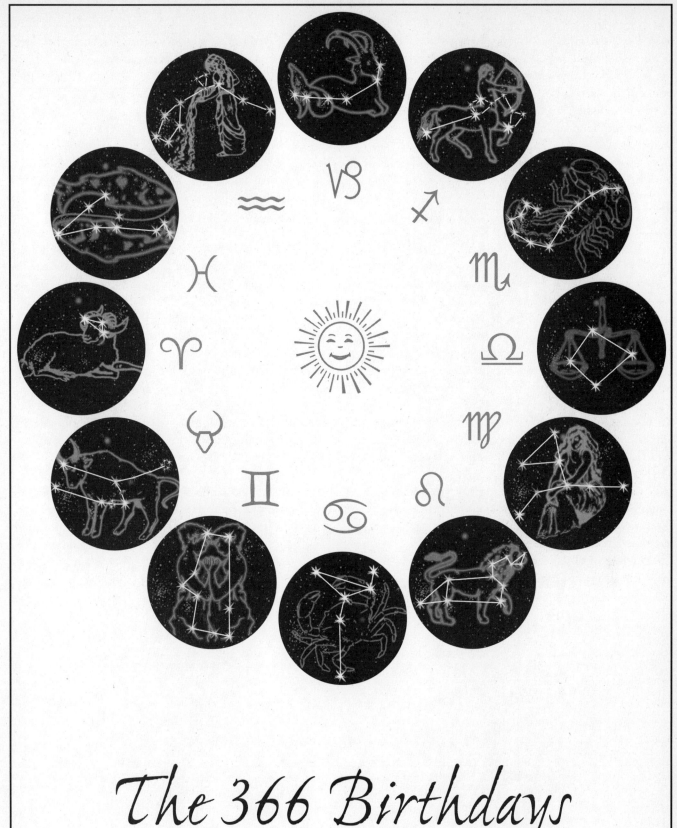

The 366 Birthdays
of the Year

Aries

March 21–April 20

March 21

♈ Determined and assertive, yet friendly and cooperative, you have a natural flair for people-related activities that reveals your need to be part of a team. Born on the cusp, you have an energetic and dynamic personality that is full of drive and ambition. At times you can appear hurried and impatient, driven by a necessity to make real progress in life. The idealistic side of your nature, nevertheless, needs to share and communicate with others, and your splendid ideas often involve you with people from all walks of life.

The double influence of your ruling planet, Mars, gives you courage and an ability to overcome obstacles, while your sharp intuition and common sense instantly recognize good business opportunities. Inspired and imaginative, you frequently have good judgment and know how to impress others with your enthusiasm. An inclination to be stubborn, however, suggests that you may need to overcome a tendency to be argumentative if you do not get your own way. Although you have a natural flair for making money, you may need to learn the art of compromise. If a materialistic streak is evident, you may also need to overcome a fear concerning lack of money, even at times of prosperity and success.

As a good strategist, you learn how to balance your need to succeed and your philanthropic inclinations. Investing in other people may at times bring great rewards; however, you may have to learn whom to trust. Often gregarious, with many contacts, you enjoy mixing your social and professional lives and establishing working partnerships with other hardworking and disciplined individuals.

After you reach the age of thirty, when your progressed Sun moves into Taurus, there is an increased need for stability and financial security. This is likely to be a period when you will concentrate on building a solid foundation for yourself and loved ones. This continues until the beginning of your sixties, when your progressed Sun enters Gemini and starts to transform your way of thinking. As a turning point, it will highlight the growing importance of new interests, learning, and communication.

Your Secret Self

A need for acknowledgment usually drives you to accomplish and succeed. Your potential for material achievement is immense when you combine your vision and your intuition. Since you do not expect something for nothing, you are willing to work hard to achieve results. Often your high ideals are suited for work that would bring in excellent financial rewards while benefiting others.

A blend of opposites within your personality frequently implies that you desire money, power, and status as well as peace and tranquility. One way of achieving harmony may be to find a home that is a haven from the outer world. Another could be to channel some of your desire for power into healing, art, music, or other creative forms. However, you may have to be careful that you do not relax too much and experience inertia or anxiety about lack of achievement.

Work & Vocation

With your excellent ability to make contacts and deal with people on a one-to-one basis, you are perfectly suited for a career such as a negotiator, advisor, public relations specialist, media-

---

FIXED STAR

Star's name: Deneb Kaitos, also called Dipda

Degree position: 1°32'–2°27' Aries between the years 1930 and 2000

Magnitude: 2

Strength: ★★★★★★★

Orb: 2°10'

Constellation: Beta Ceti

Applicable days: March 21, 22, 23, 24, 25, 26

Star qualities: Saturn

Description: a yellow-orange star located at the tail of the Whale

---

PRIMARY STAR'S INFLUENCE

Deneb Kaitos indicates a restrained nature and an ability to move ahead with determination. It also imparts an inherent restlessness, which can lead to spurts of activity followed by periods of recuperation. This star warns against misuse of force and suggests that these individuals should learn how to relax their mind by thinking positively; they may also need to spend time alone.

Linked to your Sun's degree, this star bestows organizational skills and emphasizes duties and responsibilities. With discipline and control it is possible to achieve much. This star may also warn against a tendency to becoming frustrated.

• *Positive:* perseverance, determination

• *Negative:* repression or frustration, doing things on impulse, changing direction without thinking

tor, lawyer, or agent. You also possess an exceptional aptitude for sales, in any form, as long as you believe in what you are selling. Ideally, you are better at using all your enthusiasm and leadership skills to initiate projects, then you can leave others to do the more mundane and routine work. Alternatively, your unique perspective may find expression in the creative world. Nevertheless, whatever career you choose, you are most likely to use your talent for dealing with people. Your natural executive and managerial skills often place you in positions of authority, and you may also do well in mail order businesses or real estate. You may prefer being self-employed, but are likely to benefit more in situations that require cooperative efforts.

Famous people born on your birthday are actors Timothy Dalton and Matthew Broderick, Rosie O'Donnell, and composer Johann Sebastian Bach.

Numerology

With a number 21 birthday, you are fun-loving, magnetic, and creative, with social charm. Usually you show others your amicable and congenial personality. Gregarious and friendly, you have many interests and contacts and are generally fortunate. However, you are highly original and intuitive, with an independent spirit. Alternatively, you can be shy and reserved, with a need to develop assertiveness, especially in close relationships. Although you can be inclined toward cooperative relationships or marriage, you always want to be acknowledged for your talents and abilities. The subinfluence of the number 3 month indicates that you need to express your emotions and show how you really feel. When entertaining, you can be a charming host, and being kind and understanding helps you smooth out difficult situations. You can pay attention to detail, but guard against being critical.

• *Positive:* inspiration, charm, creativity, love unions, long-lasting relationships

• *Negative:* dependency, nervous, loss of emotional control, lack of vision, disappointment, fear of change, envious

Love & Relationships

Your need for mental stimulation often indicates an active social life and many relationships or associations. Attracted to clever and powerful people, you may have to guard against getting caught up in mental power games with partners. When in love you can be very generous and outgoing, but you must learn how to balance your own personal needs with the needs of your partner or lover.

March 22

Strong desires and a dynamic personality are usually present in those born on this day. As an Arian, you are independent, fearless, and daring, with strong instincts and an adventurous nature. Taking the initiative frequently leads you to explore new ideas or proceed in a new direction. Motivation is the key to your success, and usually you rise to the challenges put before you. The double influence of your ruling planet, Mars, gives added vitality, which often assists you to rise above ordinary life.

Broad-minded yet aggressive, you can exhibit leadership abilities, idealism, and a self-assured front in the pursuit of success. Nevertheless, you may have to overcome tendencies to be too blunt or overcritical of people who fail to reach your high expectations. Visionary and independent, you like to think big and are best at initiating new enterprises or being in the forefront of new projects and ideas.

Although you possess a powerful desire to achieve, you may have to overcome a tendency to be overly enthusiastic or dictatorial. Your restlessness may, at times, urge you to change your mind too frequently or become frustrated from lack of activity or procrastination. By avoiding a tendency to magnify little things or exaggerate, you learn how to deal calmly with emotional fluctuations and moodiness.

The more idealistic side of your nature will inspire you to work for the good of others, and with your practical skills, quick grasp of situations, and good strategic abilities you can inspire others with imaginative and creative ideas. A natural humanitarian, your interest in what motivates others often encourages you to develop a good sixth sense about people.

After you reach the age of twenty-nine, when your progressed Sun moves into Taurus, there is an increased determination to acquire wealth and material success. You may desire financial stability or want to be closer to nature from this time onward. This continues until around the age of fifty-nine, when your progressed Sun enters Gemini, a turning point that highlights the growing importance of diversifying your interests and stimulating your desire to learn.

Your Secret Self

At a deep level you possess a strong desire for love and affection, which, if the circumstances are right, you are more than willing to return. When you are positive, this energy just flows from you like a never-ending resource, enhancing your natural leadership with the power of love. When blocked by too much of your own self-interest, it can cause you to become over-emotional or force your will onto others. This same energy can be highly original when directed creatively, whether in the arts, entertainment, or business. Your personal relationships are extremely important to you as a way of communicating and increasing your opportunities for success. Since you usually work best when you stick to your principles rather than doubt yourself, it is better to trust your own instincts and sense of strategy. Usually you are active and hardworking and can win by being direct and to the point, yet not compromising your skills in diplomacy and cooperation.

Work & Vocation

With your courage, commitment, and executive abilities, you may pursue a career in commerce, such as a negotiator, agent, or financial advisor. Alternatively, your individuality may

FIXED STAR

Star's name: Deneb Kaitos, also called Dipda

Degree position: 1°32'–2°27' Aries between the years 1930 and 2000

Magnitude: 2

Strength: ★★★★★★★

Orb: 2°10'

Constellation: Beta Ceti

Applicable days: March 21, 22, 23, 24, 25, 26

Star qualities: Saturn

Description: a yellow-orange star located at the tail of the Whale

PRIMARY STAR'S INFLUENCE

Deneb Kaitos indicates a restrained nature and an ability to move ahead with determination. It also imparts an inherent restlessness, which can lead to spurts of activity followed by periods of recuperation. This star warns against misuse of force and suggests that these individuals should learn how to relax their mind by thinking positively; they may also need to spend time alone.

Linked to your Sun's degree, this star bestows organizational skills and emphasizes duties and responsibilities. With discipline and control it is possible to achieve much. This star may also warn against a tendency to becoming frustrated.

• *Positive:* perseverance, determination

• *Negative:* repression or frustration, doing things on impulse, changing direction without thinking

find expression in the creative world. Motivated by the strong combination of idealism and practicality, you possess natural abilities for leadership. You are likely to thrive on new beginnings or challenges, and in business you have a talent for spotting opportunities. You may often promote others better than you promote yourself; nevertheless, in whatever career you choose, you will benefit from your excellent people skills.

Famous people born on your birthday include composers Andrew Lloyd Webber and Stephen Sondheim, mime Marcel Marceau, Chico Marx, singer George Benson, newsperson Bob Costas, and actors William Shatner and Matthew Modine.

Numerology

The birthdate number 22 is a master number and can vibrate both as itself and as number 4. Often honest and hardworking, with natural leadership abilities, you have a charismatic personality and a deep understanding of people and what motivates them. Although undemonstrative, you often show a caring, protective concern for the welfare of others. Your more obvious attributes are practical skills and executive abilities. Your forthright yet composed personality helps you rise to higher managerial positions. The more competitive among you achieve success and good fortune with help and encouragement from others. The subinfluence of the number 3 month indicates that you grow to be wise and understanding through personal adversity. Introspective and thoughtful, you need to learn to trust your intuition. Avoid pessimism by being realistic yet balanced. Although you need to analyze every situation in great detail, overcome a tendency to be suspicious or critical.

• *Positive:* universality, ability to direct, intuition, pragmatism, practicality, manual ability, building ability, organization, problem-solving skills, achievement, realism

• *Negative:* vulnerability to get-rich-quick schemes, nervousness, inferiority complex, bossiness, materialism, lack of vision, laziness, egotism, self-promotion, greed.

Love & Relationships

Desire for constant change and lack of satisfaction with whatever your current situation is may suggest that you are prone to emotional uncertainty. This may often cause you some confusion as to who you really want. You may need someone who will keep you interested at all times and offer you variety and stimulating ideas. You may also dislike the thought of being restricted in any way and therefore find it hard to commit yourself and settle down. Nevertheless, you are enthusiastic, charming, and friendly, with many acquaintances, and have no problem attracting people. If you take your time in choosing the right friends or partners, you are likely to be less impetuous about love and relationships.

YOUR SPECIAL SOMEONE

You might find emotional fulfillment and that special someone among those born on the following days.

Love & friendship: Jan. 14, 15, 24, 31, Feb. 12, 22, 29, Mar. 10, 20, 27, Apr. 8, 9, 18, 25, May 6, 16, 23, 30, June 4, 14, 21, 28, 30, July 2, 12, 19, 26, 28, 30, Aug. 10, 17, 24, 26, 28, Sept. 8, 15, 22, 24, 26, Oct. 6, 13, 20, 22, 24, 30, Nov. 4, 11, 18, 20, 22, 28, Dec. 2, 9, 16, 18, 20, 26, 29, 30

Beneficial: Jan. 5, 22, 30, Feb. 3, 20, 28, Mar. 1, 18, 26, April, 16, 24, May 14, 22, June 12, 20, July 10, 18, 29, Aug. 8, 16, 27, 31, Sept. 6, 14, 25, 29, Oct. 4, 12, 23, 27, Nov. 2, 10, 21, 25, Dec. 9, 19, 23

Fatal attractions: Jan. 12, Feb. 10, Mar. 8, Apr. 6, May 4, June 2, Sept. 24, 25, 26, 27

Challenging: Jan. 16, 21, Feb. 14, 19, Mar. 12, 17, 30, Apr. 10, 15, 28, May 8, 13, 26, June 6, 11, 24, July 4, 9, 22, Aug. 2, 7, 20, Sept. 5, 18, Oct. 3, 16, Nov. 1, 14, Dec. 12

Soul mates: Jan. 25, Feb. 23, Mar. 21, Apr. 19, May 17, June 15, July 13, Aug. 11, Sept. 9, Oct. 7, Nov. 5, Dec. 3, 4, 30

March 23

FIXED STAR

Star's name: Deneb Kaitos, also called Dipda

Degree position: 1°32'–2°27' Aries between the years 1930 and 2000

Magnitude: 2

Strength: ★★★★★★★

Orb: 2°10'

Constellation: Beta Ceti

Applicable days: March 21, 22, 23, 24, 25, 26

Star qualities: Saturn

Description: a yellow-orange star located at the tail of the Whale

PRIMARY STAR'S INFLUENCE

Deneb Kaitos indicates a restrained nature and an ability to move ahead with determination. It also imparts an inherent restlessness, which can lead to spurts of activity followed by periods of recuperation. This star warns against misuse of force and suggests that these individuals should learn how to relax their mind by thinking positively; they may also need to spend time alone.

Linked to your Sun's degree, this star bestows organizational skills and emphasizes duties and responsibilities. With discipline and control it is possible to achieve much. This star may also warn against a tendency to becoming frustrated.

• *Positive:* perseverance, determination

• *Negative:* repression or frustration, doing things on impulse, changing direction without thinking

Mental power, intelligence, good judgment, and depth of thought are some of your natural attributes. As an Aries, you are forceful and command authority. Your mind is your greatest asset, and if you recognize the power of knowledge and a good education, you can achieve great success. Women of this day often take charge of situations. A natural leader, you are independent and like to be in control or initiate new ideas. Usually you are able to present a unique approach to a problem and give others practical advice and solutions.

Those who know you well see you as a strange mixture of conservatism and radical ideas, but they never think of you as boring or dull. Although you enjoy arguments and debates and often come out on top, you may have to learn that being mentally aggressive or unadaptable does not get you the results you desire.

Frequently you have an insight into other people's rationales, and understanding their needs gives you the ability to delegate work or be a good employer. However, you do not suffer fools gladly and can at times be intolerant of other people's faults. Ironically, one of your own failings is that you think you know it all and can therefore be too domineering. By learning to be more compassionate and tolerant, you increase your chances for success in your dealings and relationships with others. If you disregard your strong need for self-expression, you may be susceptible to moodiness, swinging from optimism to pessimism and experiencing a lack of self-worth. Learning to trust your own intuition enables you to take on challenges such as developing an original artistic talent or your business acumen.

Up until the age of twenty-seven you are likely to be active and adventurous. After the age of twenty-eight, when your progressed Sun moves into Taurus, there is an increased interest in financial affairs and a need for material security. This continues until around age fifty-eight, when your progressed Sun enters Gemini, which will bring into prominence many new interests as well as a stronger desire for communication at all levels.

Your Secret Self

Power is something you usually desire and enjoy, especially when it involves a friendly yet competitive exchange of thoughts. You are willing to work hard, which sometimes involves displaying a relentless determination. As you can also play the diplomat when circumstances warrant, it may take the development of your natural wisdom to decide which one of these two approaches is best in any given situation.

Although you love to discuss ideas and share your opinions with others, you also may have to learn the art of compromise. This suggests that in your desire to be in control, you should not resort to manipulative measures. Outwardly you may at times appear cynical or autocratic, but in your heart you are a crusader fighting injustice, eager to help your fellow man. As you are usually conscientious and responsible, you may have to make sure you do not overtax yourself.

Work & Vocation

Your leadership abilities and your capability to take responsibility and work hard will mark you for advancement, whether in business or in another field. Your acute intellect and good imagination give you a need to express yourself in words, either speaking or writing. You may therefore find yourself being drawn to a career as a lecturer, reformer, or teacher. Alternatively, a natural sense of the dramatic may attract you to some form of the arts or entertainment. Whatever career you choose, your bright intellect makes education of some type essential to realize your exceptional potential.

Famous people born on your birthday include actress Joan Crawford, singers Chaka Khan and Ric Ocasek, astrologer Dane Rudhyar, scientist Werner von Braun, and writer Eric Fromm.

Numerology

Usually you are versatile, passionate, and a quick thinker, with a professional attitude and a mind full of creative ideas. You are fond of travel, adventure, and meeting new people, and the restlessness implied by the number 23 birthdate urges you to try many different kinds of experiences. You adapt to make the best of any situation. With the number 23 influence you can learn new subjects easily but may prefer practice to theory. You may need, however, to overcome a tendency to criticize others; you may also need to develop a less selfish attitude. The subinfluence of the number 3 month indicates that you possess a good memory and a lively imagination, and that you need lots of love and attention. If you learn to express your feelings through a dynamic, creative power, you can overcome emotional insecurities. Generally friendly and fun-loving, with courage and drive, you may need an active life in order to actualize your true potential. It is important to achieve and take on a great deal of responsibility.

• *Positive:* loyalty, responsibility, travel, communication, intuition, creativity, versatility, trustworthy, fame

• *Negative:* selfishness, insecurity, uncompromising nature, fault finding, dullness, withdrawal, prejudice

Love & Relationships

Your need for a secure emotional environment suggests that you want your friends and loved ones around you. Emotionally honest and direct, you are very protective of people in your care and will do anything for those you love. Although others recognize your powers of reasoning, guard against appearing too arrogant. Home and family life are important to you, and you are more likely to form long-lasting and stable relationships where you can find emotional security. Having a strong practical side also assists you to gain some of the comforts of life. You are a passionate person with charisma, however; you must be careful not to let these passions carry you away.

YOUR SPECIAL SOMEONE

You might find a longer-lasting relationship with someone born on one of the following dates.

Love & friendship: Jan. 11, 13, 15, 17, 25, 27, 28, Feb. 9, 11, 13, 15, 23, Mar. 7, 9, 11, 13, 21, Apr. 5, 7, 9, 11, 19, May 3, 5, 7, 9, 17, 31, June 1, 3, 5, 7, 15, 29, July 1, 3, 5, 27, 29, 31, Aug. 1, 2, 3, 11, 25, 27, 29, Sept. 1, 9, 23, 25, 27, Oct. 7, 21, 23, 25, Nov. 5, 19, 21, 23, Dec. 3, 16, 17, 19, 21, 30

Beneficial: Jan. 1, 5, 20, Feb. 3, 18, Mar. 1, 16, Apr. 14, May 12, June 10, July 8, Aug. 6, Sept. 4, Oct. 2

Fatal attractions: Sept. 24, 25, 26, 27

Challenging: Jan. 6, 22, 24, Feb. 4, 20, 22, Mar. 2, 18, 20, Apr. 16, 18, May 14, 16, June 12, 14, July 10, 12, Aug. 8, 10, 31, Sept. 6, 8, 29, Oct. 4, 6, 27, Nov. 2, 4, 25, 30, Dec. 2, 23, 28

Soul mates: Jan. 6, 12, Feb. 4, 10, Mar. 2, 8, Apr. 6, May 4, June 2

March 24

♈ Strong intuition, good judgment, and superior mental talent are often attributed to those born on this day. This combination of wisdom and logic is likely to lead you to positions of authority. As an Arian, you are practical and decisive, with a charming and attractive personality. The double influence of your ruling planet, Mars, urges you to be mentally competitive and ambitious. Nevertheless, it is often the development of your natural intuition and trust in your inner voice that gives you the edge on others.

Self-assured, naturally gifted, honest, and direct is how others usually describe you. However, when you do not feel generous and sympathetic, you can easily turn into a stubborn individual who will not accept interference from others. Intolerant of ignorance, you can also become impatient and mentally restless. Alternatively, in your need to be helpful and kind, be careful not to play the martyr and react too dramatically.

With your powers of determination, you like to put thoughts into action, and your natural curiosity and inquisitive nature always inspire you to explore new territories. When it comes to communication, you are blessed with lightning-fast repartee and impressive eloquence. Socially inclined and highly creative, you may find expression for your talents in artistic pursuits, drama, and humorous writing.

Up to the age of twenty-six you are likely to be independent and bold. After the age of twenty-seven, when your progressed Sun moves into Taurus, there is an emphasis in your life on material success, stability, and security. This more businesslike accent continues until around the age of fifty-seven, when your progressed Sun enters Gemini. As this suggests a turning point for you, you might explore new ideas or learn new skills, as well as emphasize the growing importance of writing, speech, and communication.

FIXED STAR

Star's name: Deneb Kaitos, also called Dipda

Degree position: 1°32'–2°27' Aries between the years 1930 and 2000

Magnitude: 2

Strength: ★★★★★★★

Orb: 2°10'

Constellation: Beta Ceti

Applicable days: March 21, 22, 23, 24, 25, 26

Star qualities: Saturn

Description: a yellow-orange star located at the tail of the Whale

PRIMARY STAR'S INFLUENCE

Deneb Kaitos indicates a restrained nature and an ability to move ahead with determination. It also imparts an inherent restlessness, which can lead to spurts of activity followed by periods of recuperation. This star warns against misuse of force and suggests that these individuals should learn how to relax their mind by thinking positively; they may also need to spend time alone.

Linked to your Sun's degree, this star bestows organizational skills and emphasizes duties and responsibilities. With discipline and control it is possible to achieve much. This star may also warn against a tendency to becoming frustrated.

• *Positive:* perseverance, determination

• *Negative:* repression or frustration, doing things on impulse, changing direction without thinking

Your Secret Self

Although others see you as a highly intelligent person, your birthday suggests that an inner sensitivity underlies your assertive front. This also indicates that you may need to find some creative form of self-expression in order to give voice to your deepest feelings. Since you also seek to fulfill a strong need for recognition, if not in personal terms then in family or ancestral terms, you may be drawn toward ideas that sometimes seem impossible. This should not deter you, however, as the journey toward your dream is often more important than the final destination.

An ability to think big enables you to look far into the distance to see what you can accomplish. By overcoming a tendency to let materialistic considerations rule your life, you come to realize that money or status alone would not be ultimately satisfying, and that there are many rewards that money cannot buy. This emphasizes the need to adhere to life choices that enhance your sense of values and identity.

Work & Vocation

Your humanitarianism could provide you with the impetus to excel as a teacher, counselor, or social worker, or in a job that requires speaking up for others, such as union leader or politician. Other suitable occupations include law, banking, or the ministry. Alternatively, your creativity and quick way with words may lead you to writing, filmmaking, music, or drama. The more practical side of your nature, however, may be attracted to science or business. Whatever career you choose, your greatest fulfillment is most likely to be found through some form of service to others. Since you possess strong leadership qualities, your greatest achievements often put you at the forefront of your chosen profession.

Famous people born on your birthday are actor Steve McQueen, Kelly Le Brock, pre-Raphaelite painter William Morris, and psychologist Wilhelm Reich.

Numerology

Conscientious, responsible, and enterprising are some of the ways people describe someone with a number 24 birthday. Although you may dislike routine, frequently you are hardworking, with practical abilities and sound judgment. Often honest, dependable, and security-conscious, you need the love and support of others and enjoy building a strong foundation for yourself and your family. A pragmatic approach to life also gives you a good business sense and an ability to achieve material success in life. With a number 24 birthday, you may have to overcome a tendency to be stubborn or fixed in your ideas. The main challenges for someone who has a number 24 birthday are to overcome suspicious tendencies and to build a secure home. The subinfluence of the number 3 month indicates that you can be compassionate and broad-minded but need to learn to live up to your ideals by being patient and avoiding petty-mindedness. You can promote harmony and understanding with your thoughtfulness and understanding.

• *Positive:* energy, idealism, practical skills, strong determination, honesty, frankness, fairness, generosity, love of home, activity, energy

• *Negative:* ruthlessness, materialism, instability, dislike of routine, laziness, unfaithfulness, domineering behavior, stubbornness, vengefulness

Love & Relationships

Mentally adventurous and curious, you are intuitive yet practical and can have a sixth sense about people. Friendly and gregarious, you prefer intelligent and active individuals who are ambitious and versatile. Although you usually know what you want out of life, you may have a sudden change of mind and heart due to indecision. You may decide to go in a different direction, leaving others to figure out where they went wrong. You can be loyal and affectionate; however, guard against misplaced sympathy or doing more than your fair share, especially if others take advantage of your kindness. By learning to be patient and by overcoming a tendency to become easily bored, you can build a solid foundation for long-lasting relationships.

YOUR SPECIAL SOMEONE

For that special someone you might want to look among those born on the following dates.

Love & friendship: Jan. 12, 16, 25, Feb. 10, 14, 23, 24, Mar. 8, 12, 22, 23, 31, Apr. 6, 10, 13, 20, 29, May 4, 8, 18, 27, June 2, 6, 16, 25, 30, July 4, 14, 23, 28, Aug. 2, 12, 16, 21, 26, 30, Sept. 10, 19, 24, 28, Oct. 8, 17, 22, 26, Nov. 6, 15, 20, 24, 30, Dec. 4, 13, 17, 18, 22, 28

Beneficial: Jan. 2, 13, 22, 24, Feb. 11, 17, 20, 22, Mar. 9, 15, 18, 20, 28, Apr. 7, 13, 16, 18, 26, May 5, 11, 16, 18, 26, June 3, 9, 12, 14, 22, July 1, 7, 10, 12, 20, Aug. 5, 8, 10, 18, Sept. 3, 6, 8, 16, Oct. 1, 4, 6, 14, Nov. 2, 4, 12, Dec. 2, 10

Fatal attractions: Jan. 25, Feb. 23, Mar. 21, Apr. 19, May 17, June 15, July 13, Aug. 11, Sept. 9, 26, 27, 28, Oct. 7, Nov. 5, Dec. 3

Challenging: Jan. 7, 23, Feb. 5, 21, Mar. 3, 19, 29, Apr. 1, 17, 27, May 15, 25, June 13, 23, July 11, 21, 31, Aug. 9, 19, 29, Sept. 7, 17, 27, 30, Nov. 3, 13, 23, 26, Dec. 1, 11, 21, 24

Soul mates: Jan. 17, Feb. 15, Mar. 13, Apr. 11, 22, May 9, June 7, July 5, Aug. 3, Sept. 1, Nov. 30, Dec. 6, 28

March 25

Personal magnetism, youthfulness, and natural enthusiasm are qualities often linked to those sharing this date of birth. This suggests that in your eagerness to take on life's challenges you are idealistic and naturally optimistic. As an Arian, you are daring and direct, with an active mind and bright ideas. By being too spontaneous, however, you may hype yourself up and become overly zealous or impatient. This may at times influence you to be impulsive or make hasty decisions without proper plans.

Responsibility and taking a more mature reflective attitude are likely to be the keys to your success. Once you have mastered your tendency to be inconsistent or restless, you can indeed show how truly talented and clever you can be. Through education and the pursuit of knowledge you can easily develop your natural flair for the spoken or written word or secure work in research, teaching, or lecturing.

With an accent on individuality, you usually have an original form of artistic or creative expression. More often than not you are inclined to be modern, unconventional, or progressive, with unusual interests or pursuits. Although you are socially inclined and friendly, you like to be carefree and different, and you rarely succumb to peer group pressure. Nevertheless, your characteristic restlessness suggests that you should avoid wasting time or acting in a rebellious way, disregarding the feelings of others.

Up to the age of twenty-five you are likely to be enthusiastic, daring, and carefree. Around the age of twenty-six, when your progressed Sun moves into Taurus, you enter a thirty-year period of increased emphasis on material status, stability, and financial security. The next turning point for you comes after the age of fifty-six, when your progressed Sun moves into Gemini, suggesting that you are liable to become more interested in widening your interests and taking up new areas of study.

Fixed Star

Star's name: Deneb Kaitos, also called Dipda

Degree position: 1°32'–2°27' Aries between the years 1930 and 2000

Magnitude: 2

Strength: ★★★★★★★

Orb: 2°10'

Constellation: Beta Ceti

Applicable days: March 21, 22, 23, 24, 25, 26

Star qualities: Saturn

Description: a yellow-orange star located at the tail of the Whale

PRIMARY STAR'S INFLUENCE

Deneb Kaitos indicates a restrained nature and an ability to move ahead with determination. It also imparts an inherent restlessness, which can lead to spurts of activity followed by periods of recuperation. This star warns against misuse of force and suggests that these individuals should learn how to relax their mind by thinking positively; they may also need to spend time alone.

Linked to your Sun's degree, this star bestows organizational skills and emphasizes duties and responsibilities. With discipline and control it is possible to achieve much. This star may also warn against a tendency to becoming frustrated.

• *Positive:* perseverance, determination

• *Negative:* repression or frustration, doing things on impulse, changing direction without thinking

Your Secret Self

A powerful need for self-expression combined with your vitality supports the need to be at the forefront of activity that will enable you to manifest your powerful feelings and opinions. You may, however, in your strong desire for security, take material considerations too much to heart. Just be careful of wasting your precious energy by worrying unnecessarily about finances.

An inner wealth of feelings can emphasize the importance of love and affection in your life. When you project this outward to the world you can enchant and enrapture others as well as demonstrate your drive to help your fellow human beings. Keeping a balance in your life between money and emotional needs will enable you to display that delightful wit and humor, that can be so uplifting for others.

Work & Vocation

With your talent for communicating in an entertaining and charming way, your aptitudes may lie in lecturing, writing, sales, promotion, public relations, the stock market, or politics. Your strong ideals and dynamism make you an excellent propagandist or fighter for a cause.

Your outstanding potential to acquire knowledge may place you among scholars and academics. Alternatively, with your youthful outlook and creative flair, you are likely to be able to earn your living through art, music, or drama. Since you are willing to work hard for objectives, your fine mind, dramatic flair, and leadership skills could serve you equally well in law or management. Pioneering and exploring are likely to inspire your adventurous nature.

Famous people born on your birthday include singers Elton John and Aretha Franklin, orchestral conductor Arturo Toscanini, director David Lean, feminist writer Gloria Steinem and actress Sarah Jessica Parker.

Numerology

With a number 25 birthdate, you possess strong mental energies; when concentrated, they aid you to look at all the facts and arrive at a conclusion faster then anyone else. Intuitive and thoughtful, yet quick and energetic, you need to express yourself through different experiences. These may include new and exciting ideas, people, or locations. You may, however, need to be less impatient or critical if things do not happen according to plan. Success and happiness come when you learn to trust your own instincts and develop perseverance and patience. The subinfluence of the number 3 month indicates that you can be highly original and confident. Although ambitious, you need to make your own decisions and work independently when possible. Emotional sensitivity and artistic talents are just some of your hidden attributes. Usually you are instinctive and alert, and you can gain more knowledge through practical application than through mere theory.
- *Positive:* intuition, perfectionism, perceptivity, creativity, people skills
- *Negative:* impulsiveness, impatience, irresponsibility, overemotionalism, jealousy, secrecy, criticism, moodiness, nervousness

Love & Relationships

Spontaneous and enthusiastic, you are a daring and passionate individual who loves freedom and likes to remain independent, despite often looking for an ideal love relationship. At times you can be very intense and rush into an emotional involvement without thinking ahead. If your expectations are too high, you can often be let down. You need to learn about responsibilities before you can settle down to a stable relationship. Your tendency to be idealistic also suggests that you need a spiritual bond to overcome issues of being lonely or abandoned. An aura of mystery surrounding love unions often suggests that you may be linked to secret relationships.

YOUR SPECIAL SOMEONE

You might find love and happiness with someone born on the following dates.

Love & friendship: Jan. 7, 10, 17, 18, 27, Feb. 5, 8, 15, 25, Mar. 3, 6, 13, 23, Apr. 1, 4, 11, 21, May 2, 9, 19, June 7, 17, July 5, 15, 29, 31, Aug. 3, 4, 13, 27, 29, 31, Sept. 1, 11, 25, 27, 29, Oct. 9, 23, 25, 27, Nov. 7, 21, 23, 25, Dec. 5, 15, 19, 21, 23

Beneficial: Jan. 3, 5, 20, 25, 27, Feb. 1, 3, 18, 23, 25, Mar. 1, 16, 21, 23, Apr. 14, 19, 21, May 12, 17, 19, June 10, 15, 17, July 8, 13, 15, Aug. 6, 11, 13, Sept. 4, 9, 11, Oct. 2, 7, 9, Nov. 5, 7, Dec. 3, 5

Fatal attractions: Jan. 13, Feb. 11, Mar. 9, Apr. 7, May 5, June 3, July 1, Sept. 27, 28, 29

Challenging: Jan. 16, 24, Feb. 14, 22, Mar. 12, 20, Apr. 10, 18, May 8, 16, 31, June 6, 14, 29, July 4, 12, 27, Aug. 2, 10, 25, Sept. 8, 23, Oct. 6, 21, Nov. 4, 19, Dec. 2, 17

Soul mates: Jan. 16, Feb. 14, Mar. 12, Apr. 10, May 8, June 6, July 4, 31, Aug. 2, 15, 29, Sept. 27, Oct. 25, Nov. 23, Dec. 7, 21

March 26

♈ An astute mind, ambition, and determination are the attributes shared by those born on this day. As an Arian, you are eager for a diversity of experience, but by developing self-discipline, you may be less likely to scatter your mental energies and be more able to focus on important goals.

The double influence of your ruling planet, Mars, indicates that you have the potential to achieve much in life. Yet without inspiration you are likely to feel restless and frustrated, never managing to finish what you have started. Unless you find an objective that can truly fire your imagination, you will continually search for your ultimate goal. One way of overcoming this predicament is through learning self-mastery and introspection.

True satisfaction in life usually comes through achievements based on your own efforts. If you rely on the efforts of others, you can easily become bored and dissatisfied. Success will come from your hard work and single-mindedness. Your visions and inspirations urge you to think independently and on a large scale, rather than pay attention to small details.

You can also be persuasive and encourage others to follow your big dreams. At times you appear unassuming, and your strength or compulsive nature may well be concealed behind a friendly and easygoing personality.

You are likely to experience a strong influence from a male early in life, usually your father. Up to the age of twenty-four you are likely to be active and adventurous. After the age of twenty-five, when your progressed Sun moves into Taurus, you may desire more material security and stability. From your mid-fifties, when the Sun moves into Gemini, there is a shift of emphasis toward knowledge, education, and communication in general. Learning a new skill may make all the difference.

Fixed Star

Star's name: Deneb Kaitos, also called Dipda

Degree position: 1°32'–2°27' Aries between the years 1930 and 2000

Magnitude: 2

Strength: ★★★★★★★

Orb: 2°10'

Constellation: Beta Ceti

Applicable days: March 21, 22, 23, 24, 25, 26

Star qualities: Saturn

Description: a yellow-orange star located at the tail of the Whale

PRIMARY STAR'S INFLUENCE

Deneb Kaitos indicates a restrained nature and an ability to move ahead with determination. It also imparts an inherent restlessness, which can lead to spurts of activity followed by periods of recuperation. This star warns against misuse of force and suggests that these individuals should learn how to relax their mind by thinking positively; they may also need to spend time alone.

Linked to your Sun's degree, this star bestows organizational skills and emphasizes duties and responsibilities. With discipline and control it is possible to achieve much. This star may also warn against a tendency to becoming frustrated.

• *Positive:* perseverance, determination

• *Negative:* repression or frustration, doing things on impulse, changing direction without thinking

Your Secret Self

A desire for honesty is very strong in your makeup and enables you to confront and work through situations that others might avoid. You want a strong foundation to anything you achieve and are willing to work hard in order to accomplish your goals. It is possible for you to synthesize practical common sense with excellent social skills and intuitive insight about people into a formula for success.

A strong creative side to your nature guarantees that both self-expression and people are a vital part of your agenda. You may just have to watch that worry or indecision does not spoil your fun. Your work is an important part of your life and you need to be proud of it. Just be careful that you do not keep yourself so busy that you have no time to listen to that still, small voice of your intuition. However, you can always call on a deeper wisdom when necessary, giving you a philosophical approach to life or a humorous antidote to any social problem.

Work & Vocation

Your dynamic drive, sharp intellect, and outstanding social skills enable you to reach your potential in many different areas of life. Your need for self-expression and a love for the dramatic may lure you to writing or the arts and entertainment worlds. You can also excel in education, research, science, politics, philosophy, and public relations. Since you are never happy being told what to do, it is imperative not to find yourself in a subservient position. In business you will naturally be drawn to large enterprises and are an excellent problem solver. Organizational and managerial abilities often help you rise to positions of prominence. Whatever career you choose, you are likely to love variety and be good at initiating projects with tremendous spirit and enthusiasm.

Famous people born on your birthday include playwright Tennessee Williams, composer Pierre Boulez, psychiatrist Victor Frankl, poet Robert Frost, writer Erica Jong, singer Diana Ross, and actors Martin Short and James Caan.

Numerology

The strength or power suggested by the number 26 birthday shows that you are a cautious character with strong values and sound judgment. You need to acquire a more pragmatic approach to life by developing your executive ability and a good business sense. With a number 26 birthday, you are usually responsible, with a natural aesthetic sense. A love of home and strong parental instincts suggest a need to build a solid foundation or find real stability. Often a tower of strength for others, you are willing to support friends as well as family members who may turn to you in time of need. You may nevertheless need to guard against materialistic tendencies and a desire to control situations or people. The subinfluence of the number 3 month indicates that you are sensitive and idealistic. As a charitable individual with high ideals, you are inclined toward humanitarianism. Although inspiration or other people can get you motivated, let your intuition and personal feelings guide you.

• *Positive:* creativity, practicality, caring, responsibility, pride in family, enthusiasm, courage
• *Negative:* stubbornness, rebelliousness, unstable relationships, lack of enthusiasm, lack of persistence, instability

Love & Relationships

Home-loving and supportive, you are a reliable partner. Nevertheless, you are also independent and ambitious, with firm beliefs, and are often drawn to powerful, assertive individuals who speak their own minds. Although you start everything, including relationships, with great enthusiasm, you can easily lose interest if you find out that your partner is not active, highly ambitious, or intelligent enough. You may need to find friends or lovers who are hardworking or who have a natural sense of authority. Inspired by power and wisdom, you often seek the company of serious and genuine people.

YOUR SPECIAL SOMEONE

If you refrain from being overly domineering yourself, you might find a faithful and reliable lover or partner among those born on the following dates.

Love & friendship: Jan. 1, 14, 19, 28, 31, Feb. 12, 26, 29, Mar. 10, 24, 27, Apr. 8, 13, 22, 25, May 6, 20, 23, June 4, 18, 21, July 2, 16, 19, 30, Aug. 14, 17, 28, 30, Sept. 12, 15, 26, 28, 30, Oct. 10, 13, 24, 26, 28, Nov. 8, 11, 22, 24, 26, Dec. 6, 9, 20, 22, 24

Beneficial: Jan. 26, Feb. 24, Mar. 22, Apr. 20, May 18, June 16, July 14, Aug. 12, Sept. 10, Oct. 8, Nov. 6, Dec. 4

Fatal attractions: Sept. 26, 27, 28, 29

Challenging: Jan. 3, 25, Feb. 1, 23, Mar. 21, Apr. 19, May 17, June 15, July 13, Aug. 11, Sept. 9, Oct. 7, Nov. 5, Dec. 3

Soul mates: Jan. 3, 10, Feb. 1, 8, Mar. 6, Apr. 4, May 2, Aug. 16, Dec. 8

March 27

FIXED STARS

Although your Sun's degree is not linked to a fixed star, some of your other planets' degrees certainly will be. By having an astrological chart calculated, you can find the exact position of the planets on your date of birth. This will tell you which of the fixed stars listed in this book are relevant to you.

Emotional, idealistic, and creative, those born on this day are full of ideas and artistic potential. Although you are highly intuitive and imaginative, an inclination to accept defeat too easily can lead to mental frustration. By mastering self-control and learning to take challenges as a positive learning experience, you develop perseverance. By staying in a constructive frame of mind, you can turn difficult situations to your advantage.

The double influence of your ruling planet, Mars, implies that your pioneering spirit yearns for knowledge, and with a little encouragement you are willing to enthusiastically undertake new and exciting adventures. However, you may have to guard against tendencies to get overly serious or anxious, as these tend to induce restlessness, moodiness, and unnecessary worry.

Kind-hearted and generous to the ones you love, you frequently try to hide your great sensitivity by being friendly and humorous. With your sense of the dramatic and your dynamic personality, you often want excitement out of life and at times can even get caught up in overwhelming situations. Learning to maintain a balance and developing inner peace and harmony can bring truly amazing results. The more universal, broad-minded, or compassionate you are, the more positive and successful you become. Learn to be a doer and not just a dreamer.

Up to the age of twenty-three you are likely to travel or explore and have many interests. After the age of twenty-four, when your progressed Sun moves into Taurus, you may desire material success, security, and financial stability. There may also be a need for contact with nature in some form. From your mid-fifties, when the Sun moves into Gemini, knowledge, education, and communication begin to play a more important part in your life.

Your Secret Self

An inborn dramatic sense that compels you to take center stage exists in a peculiar combination with a desire for peace and contentment. Your need for harmony emphasizes the importance of having a home that you can be proud of and retreat to for security. Usually honest and direct with people, and having a strong call to express your ideas, you may find yourself speaking up for others, often championing the cause of the underdog. Just be careful that when this is combined with your strong sense of responsibility you do not get carried away and start interfering in others' lives.

When positive, you are big-hearted and generous, with an uncanny knack for dealing with people. This can be spoiled, however, if you allow a tendency to be bossy or dictatorial to undermine your warm heart. Keeping a detached viewpoint and having something to believe in can ensure that you always use the remarkable potential available to those born on this day.

Work & Vocation

A need to express your own individual ideas may attract you to occupations such as design, writing, music, art, or drama. Your love of knowledge or your humanitarianism is likely to draw you toward occupations such as teaching, writing, science, social work, or the caring professions. Since you usually enjoy a good debate, your fighting and communication skills could be combined in a career such as lawyer, reformer, or politician, as well as in business. Your ability to raise funds for causes could mean that charity work would also be an excellent structure for your organizational and managerial skills.

Famous people who share your birthday include singers Sarah Vaughan and Mariah Carey, film actress Gloria Swanson, sportsman Randall Cunningham, and actor Michael York.

Numerology

Intuitive yet analytical, people with the number 27 birthdate are often forceful and observant, with an ability to pay attention to details. Although at times you appear secretive, rational, or detached, in fact you may be hiding inner tensions. These may include tendencies to be indecisive or suspicious about forthcoming changes. The key to success is often inspiration; by developing a more universal outlook, you can refrain from emotional outbursts or worrying about what others may think or say. The subinfluence of the number 3 month indicates that you are idealistic and sensitive, with a fertile and creative mind. You can impress others with your original ideas or contribute your knowledge to collective projects. Naturally versatile and imaginative, with strong instincts, you need to stay focused and avoid impulsive actions that may cause you to be unsettled. You may also need to learn how to turn your inspired ideas into tangible concepts.

• *Positive:* versatility, imagination, creativity, resoluteness, bravery, good understanding, mental capability, spirituality, inventiveness, mental strength

• *Negative:* quarrelsomeness, being easily offended or argumentative, restlessness, nervousness, mistrust, overemotionalism, tension

Love & Relationships

Although you can be idealistic and sensitive to the feelings and needs of others, you can also show a determined, self-centered side of your personality. Nevertheless, you are sociable, with many friends and associates. Your intense feelings can at times get the better of you, and you may therefore need time alone to rest, reflect, or meditate. Although relationships are very important to you, guard against a tendency to become too dependent on your partner or live too much by his or her opinions. If you become too idealistic or self-sacrificing, you may feel let down and lose faith in others. Beware of being impatient or temperamental, and learn to communicate your feelings rather than be too reserved or secretive. You need someone with whom you can share your passions, ideas, and beliefs.

YOUR SPECIAL SOMEONE

Among persons born on the following dates, your ideals might be realized more easily.

Love & friendship: Jan. 1, 5, 15, 26, 29, 30, Feb. 13, 24, 27, 28, Mar. 11, 22, 25, 26, Apr. 9, 20, 23, 24, May 7, 18, 21, 22, June 5, 16, 19, 20, July 3, 14, 17, 18, 31, Aug. 1, 12, 15, 16, 29, 31, Sept. 10, 13, 14, 27, 29, Oct. 8, 11, 12, 25, 27, Nov. 6, 9, 10, 23, 25, Dec. 4, 7, 8, 21, 23, 29

Beneficial: Jan. 1, 2, 10, 14, 27, Feb. 8, 12, 25, Mar. 6, 10, 23, Apr. 4, 8, 21, May 2, 6, 19, 30, June 4, 17, 28, July 2, 15, 26, Aug. 13, 24, Sept. 11, 22, Oct. 9, 20, Nov. 7, 18, Dec. 15, 16

Fatal attractions: Sept. 28, 29, 30

Challenging: Jan. 17, 26, Feb. 15, 24, Mar. 13, 22, Apr. 11, 20, May 9, 18, June 7, 16, July 5, 14, Aug. 3, 12, 30, Sept. 1, 10, 28, Oct. 8, 26, 29, Nov. 6, 24, 27, Dec. 4, 22, 25

Soul mates: Jan. 21, Feb. 19, Mar. 17, Apr. 15, May 13, June 11, July 9, 29, Aug. 7, 17, 27, Sept. 5, 25, Oct. 3, 23, Nov. 1, 21, Dec. 9, 19

March 28

♈ The cerebral potential and willpower accessible to those born on this date often indicate that with calm and patience you can achieve great success. Like any true Arian, you have an assertive personality and an aggressive appetite for action, usually of the mental kind.

The double influence of your ruling planet, Mars, encourages you to be independent and direct. Nevertheless, when angry you may have to overcome a tendency to be brutally frank and at times overemotional. Creating a harmonious environment always has a positive influence on you, and developing good communication skills can help you to avoid many misunderstandings.

An ability to excel in all kinds of intellectual activities gives you the edge in debates and discussions, but unless truly inspired, you can become easily bored and waste your great mental power on petty arguments and unnecessary mental tension. Nevertheless, you have a natural sixth sense and can easily detect insincerity in people, especially if they are playing power games.

Although you are quite capable of looking after yourself, at those times when you feel unappreciated and emotionally indecisive, you may have to be careful not to see yourself as a victim of other people's aggression. When you recognize the power in knowledge, your true potential is realized. You can become the master planner and develop a good sense of structure, or become a strategist with a foolproof system. You can also be lucky with investments, and with your multitalented personality, you can be very fortunate materially.

Up to the age of twenty-two you are likely to be enthusiastic, self-determined, and willful. After the age of twenty-three, when your progressed Sun moves into Taurus, you may desire more material success and financial stability. This can be a time when you can become more practical and businesslike, with security in mind. Around the age of fifty-three, when your progressed Sun enters Gemini, you experience a turning point in your life, which will highlight a growing interest in education and communication skills as well as finding new friends.

Fixed Stars

Although your Sun's degree is not linked to a fixed star, some of your other planets' degrees certainly will be. By having an astrological chart calculated, you can find the exact position of the planets on your date of birth. This will tell you which of the fixed stars listed in this book are relevant to you.

Your Secret Self

With your natural luck, you can get by without really trying, but this may be your greatest challenge. Although you are aware of your innate wisdom, you may lack the patience to build on what you already know. It is vital, therefore, to develop the amazing mental potential of those born on this date, through self-discipline and concentration.

Your strong emotional connection to love at a deep level emphasizes the importance of affection in your life and may take you into many different types of experience. Despite the fact that you are usually active, there is also a part of you that needs to retreat from the world and spend time in contemplation, writing, or seeking answers of a more profound nature. With faith and inspiration, you often forge ahead with great determination in pursuit of your objectives.

Work & Vocation

Whatever career you choose, you may find your natural leadership skills bring you to the forefront of your profession, and you are likely to enjoy initiating projects. Your excellent sense of structure and form often suggests that you are a good strategist. Being a visionary may lead you to careers such as architecture, photography, or filmmaking. A natural success with people could be channeled into professions or businesses that involve you with the public. Ideally suited to education, health, social work, or law, you find that your executive abilities are often called upon. The more inspired among you may need to find creative self-expression through the world of art, music, and entertainment.

Famous people who share your birthday include actor Dirk Bogarde, St. Theresa of Avila, composer Petrovich Mussorgsky, singer Cheryl James, and actresses Lucy Lawless and Dianne Wiest.

Numerology

Independent, idealistic, and unconventional, yet pragmatic and determined, you are often a law unto yourself. An inner conflict between wanting to be self-reliant and wanting to be part of a team is also indicated by the number 28 birthdate. Always ready for action and new ventures, you courageously take on life's challenges, and with your enthusiasm you can easily inspire others, if not to join you, at least to support you in your latest venture. Among your many attributes are strong conviction, resourcefulness, good judgment, and common sense. Although you are success-oriented, family and home life are important to you. Finding stability and taking care of your nearest and dearest may, at times, be a challenge for you. The subinfluence of the number 3 month indicates that you are intuitive and creative. You need to have a routine and a practical approach to life. Since proper preparations are essential for good performance, planning helps you to be focused and successful.

• *Positive:* compassion, progressive attitude, daring, artistic bent, creativity, idealism, ambition, hard work, stable home life, strong will

• *Negative:* lack of motivation, lack of compassion, unrealistic, bossiness, lack of judgment, aggression, vacillating, overdependence on others, pride

Love & Relationships

Strong-willed and independent, you are daring and outspoken, yet capable of being loyal and dependable. In your major relationships, it is important that you find someone who can offer you mental stimulation, someone with whom you can share your interests and values. Your relationships are likely to endure if you learn to be fair and less argumentative. By having similar principles or developing a basic level of understanding, you can enjoy a warm and tender relationship with the opposite sex. Often attracted to people who are clever and straightforward, you like to be frank and honest, but you may need to guard against speaking out of turn or impulsive behavior that you may regret later. Nevertheless, you are loyal and hardworking and capable of giving affection and security to those you love.

YOUR SPECIAL SOMEONE

For mental stimulation and love, you might want to begin looking for those born among the following dates.

Love & friendship: Jan. 10, 13, 20, 21, 30, Feb. 8, 11, 18, 19, 28, Mar. 6, 9, 16, 26, Apr. 4, 7, 14, 24, May 2, 5, 12, 22, June 3, 10, 20, July 1, 8, 18, Aug. 6, 16, 30, Sept. 4, 14, 28, 30, Oct. 2, 12, 26, 28, 30, Nov. 10, 24, 26, 28, Dec. 8, 22, 24, 26

Beneficial: Jan. 12, 16, 17, 28, Feb. 10, 14, 15, 26, Mar. 8, 12, 13, 24, Apr. 6, 10, 11, 22, May 4, 8, 9, 20, 29, June 2, 6, 7, 18, 27, July 4, 5, 16, 25, Aug. 2, 3, 14, 23, Sept. 1, 12, 21, Oct. 10, 19, Nov. 8, 17, Dec. 6, 14

Fatal attractions: Mar. 31, Apr. 29, May 27, June 25, July 23, Aug. 21, Sept. 19, 30, Oct. 1, 17, Nov. 15, Dec. 17

Challenging: Jan. 6, 18, 22, 27, Feb. 4, 16, 20, 25, Mar. 2, 14, 18, 23, Apr. 12, 16, 21, May 10, 14, 19, June 8, 12, 17, July 6, 10, 15, Aug. 4, 8, 13, Sept. 2, 6, 11, Oct. 4, 9, Nov. 2, 7, Dec. 5

Soul mates: Mar. 28, Apr. 26, May 24, June 22, July 20, Aug. 18, Sept. 16, Oct. 14, Nov. 12, Dec. 10

March 29

♈ Clever and shrewd, with an ability to quickly assess situations, those born on this date also have potential for a good sixth sense. Although you like to keep yourself well informed, guard against a tendency to be overly critical or opinionated. Often it is the wisdom of your inner voice that really knows the truth.

As an Arian, you are assertive and competitive. However, a strange mixture of skepticism and naïveté leaves others wondering exactly what you are thinking. At times you can be quite stubborn and refuse to listen or be counseled, even when others have your best interests at heart.

With the double influence of your ruling planet, Mars, you need a challenge, and while you like to enjoy great freedom, you usually work hard. Straightforward and direct, you prefer the company of unpretentious people who are honest, frank, and down to earth.

A natural ability to cope with demanding situations allows you never to feel like a victim of destiny. With your willpower and determination, you can achieve material success. Nevertheless, guard against becoming frustrated or worried over money issues, and avoid get-rich-quick schemes.

Up to the age of twenty-one you are likely to be adventurous and independent. After the age of twenty-two, when your progressed Sun moves into Taurus, there is an increased need for financial stability and security. This can be a time when you can become more practical and businesslike. At the age of fifty-two, when your progressed Sun enters Gemini, there are likely to be changes that highlight a growing need for new and exciting areas of interest and learning new skills, such as writing.

Fixed Star

Star's name: Algenib, also called the Carrier or the Wing

Degree position: 8°10'–9°4' Aries between the years 1930 and 2000

Magnitude: 3

Strength: ★★★★★

Orb: 2°

Constellation: Alpha Pegasi

Applicable days: March 29, 30, 31, April 1, 2

Star qualities: Mars/Mercury

Description: a small white star located in the wing on the side of Pegasus

PRIMARY STAR'S INFLUENCE

Algenib imparts powers of thought, a positive and active mind that is capable of great accomplishment through ideas and actions. This star conveys resolution, determination, and enthusiasm, with competitive tendencies. It also enhances the speed of one's mental processes and gives the confidence to retaliate in just the right manner with impressive speech. This star also warns against being quick-tempered and reckless.

Linked to your Sun's degree, this star imparts good business skills, a love of learning, an interest in religious affairs, and a talent for writing. Algenib may also suggest a need for privacy and time alone. It indicates success in dealing with the public.

• *Positive:* decisiveness, spirit of enterprise, strong will, a fighting spirit, verbal repartee

• *Negative:* criticism, sarcasm, headstrong behavior, depressions, augmentative

Your Secret Self

You have an inner power to overcome obstacles, and with determination you can be very successful at creating affluence. Money alone, however, will not totally satisfy you unless you also find a way to express the deeper insight that is part of your mental potential. With a natural talent for understanding the value of things, it is important to use your discrimination in order to be powerful and businesslike with the right people at the right time.

Since you need to feel productive and useful, work is likely to play a prominent role in your life as you get older. With the right inspiration, you are prepared to work hard in order to convert your ideals into something tangible. You may find, however, that you work better when your energy flows, rather than becoming entangled in stops and starts. Despite being spontaneous and having energy and drive, you must guard against being skeptical by having faith and trust in your own intuition.

Work & Vocation

You have a dynamic mental energy that is excellent for business, debating, law, or research. The probability of your possessing technical skills may draw you toward working with computers or engineering. With your leadership ability and fine mind, you could become involved in education, or you may wish to use your talent for communication in writing. This birthday also points to the possibility of your achieving a high position in government service as well as being an instrument for social reform. Your analytical mind may also draw you toward the medical and healing professions, or areas where you can share your knowledge with others.

Famous people who share your birthday include tennis star Jennifer Capriati, singer Pearl Bailey, former British prime minister John Major, and comedian Eric Idle.

Numerology

Idealistic visionaries with a dynamic and a forceful character, individuals with a number 29 birthdate have a powerful personality and remarkable potential. You are often highly intuitive, sensitive, and emotional. Your compassionate and understanding nature inspires humanitarianism and can encourage others to fulfill their hopes and dreams. Although you are competitive and ambitious, you need to be popular, and you care what others think about you. If you trust your innermost feelings and open your heart to others, you can overcome your tendency to worry or use your mind as a protective armor. The subinfluence of the number 3 month indicates that you are intuitive, with a strong sixth sense and creative talents. Restless and energetic, you like your freedom to do as you please and not be accountable to anyone. You need to include discipline and stability in your daily life without getting into a rut. Although you are versatile and imaginative, be practical and thoughtful and avoid being tactless by developing a more cautious attitude.

• *Positive:* inspiration, balance, inner peace, generosity, success, creativity, intuition, mysticism, powerful dreams, worldliness, faith

• *Negative:* lack of focus, insecurity, nervousness, moodiness, difficult personality, extremism, inconsiderate behavior, isolation, oversensitivity

Love & Relationships

Staying positive and determined will help you to overcome a tendency to worry too much about what others think and say. Intuitive and shrewd, yet reticent and secretive, you like to talk about everything except your true feelings. Often your skepticism suggests that you need time to build a trusting, long-term relationship. Nevertheless, you can be passionate and endearing, and if you keep your cool, you can appeal to the opposite sex. You are more likely to be attracted to self-made people or hardworking and ambitious individuals. Finding an inspiring person whom you can trust may make all the difference to your confidence, and you can then be a loyal and faithful partner. Women will prove particularly lucky for you in your career as well as your personal life.

YOUR SPECIAL SOMEONE

For security, mental stimulation, and love, you might want to begin looking for those born among the following dates.

Love & friendship: Jan. 21, 28, 31, Feb. 19, 26, 29, Mar. 17, 24, 27, Apr. 15, 22, 25, May 13, 20, 23, June 11, 18, 21, July 9, 16, 19, Aug. 7, 14, 17, 31, Sept. 15, Oct. 3, 10, 13, 27, 29, 31, Nov. 1, 8, 11, 25, 27, 29, Dec. 6, 9, 23, 25, 27

Beneficial: Jan. 9, 12, 18, 24, 29, Feb. 7, 10, 16, 22, 27, Mar. 5, 8, 14, 20, 25, Apr. 3, 6, 12, 18, 23, May 1, 10, 16, 21, 31, June 2, 8, 14, 19, 29, July 6, 12, 17, 27, Aug. 4, 10, 15, 25, Sept. 2, 8, 13, 23, Oct. 6, 11, 21, Nov. 4, 9, 19, Dec. 2, 7, 17

Fatal attractions: Jan. 3, Feb. 1, Apr. 30, May 28, June 26, July 24, Aug. 22, Sept. 20, Oct. 1, 2, 3, 18, Nov. 16, Dec. 14

Challenging: Jan. 7, 8, 19, 28, Feb. 5, 6, 17, 26, Mar. 3, 4, 15, 24, Apr. 1, 2, 13, 22, May 11, 20, June 9, 18, July 7, 16, Aug. 5, 14, Sept. 3, 12, Oct. 1, 10, Nov. 8, Dec. 6

Soul mates: Jan. 3, 19, Feb. 1, 17, Mar. 15, Apr. 13, May 11, June 9, July 7, Aug. 5, Sept. 3, Oct. 1

March 30

♈ Intuitive and perceptive, you have a creative mind full of ideas and plans. Yet a strange mixture of ambition and inertia may challenge your otherwise great potential. Your birthday reveals you to be a hardworking person with a strong sense of duty and responsibility, but a powerful need for love and emotional satisfaction may hamper your otherwise excellent prospects.

Inspired by many ideas and beliefs, you are often worldly and versatile. However, you can also establish your own unique vision and surprise others with your individual style. Friendly and generous, with a keen mentality, you enjoy sharing your quest for knowledge and are often involved in study groups. Eager to learn, you usually take courses in which you can explore your creative talents, particularly through art or music.

Subtle yet nervous, with a sense for the dramatic, is often the way others describe you. You may have to overcome a tendency to worry unnecessarily, in particular whether you are doing less than is expected of you. By being methodical and not leaving chores until the last minute, you may avoid self-pity or depression. You are often drawn to intelligent people who have made progress in life through their own efforts. Friendly and outgoing, you like to play an important role in your community or be part of a crowd. If lonely or feeling low, you may compensate by escaping or becoming overindulgent. In order to achieve peace of mind and emotional balance, you could try to develop your self-expression.

Up to the age of twenty, you are likely to be lively and experimental. After the age of twenty-one, when your progressed Sun moves into Taurus, you will have a growing interest in acquiring wealth and material security. The quest for financial stability can stimulate a desire to build something solid for yourself, and this continues until your late forties. When the progressed Sun moves into Gemini, heralding a turning point at the age of fifty-one, it highlights an increasing need to communicate and exchange ideas. This can be a time when you can stretch yourself mentally and explore new areas of interest.

Your Secret Self

Although you have natural leadership abilities, you are well aware that you cannot do things without the cooperation of others. Fortunately, you have the skill of dealing with people on a one-to-one basis and a wonderful knack for making the right contacts. Since you possess an inner sense of power and great determination, once you have made up your mind you are a force to be reckoned with. This emphasizes the importance of knowing exactly what are your goals or direction.

At times you may get caught between duties and pleasure. This could also manifest in being powerful at work but being passive at home. It may be necessary to maintain some kind of equilibrium so that you can be sensitive to the feelings of others but not compromise too much in areas of personal power. Make sure that you balance your desires for business and relationships.

Work & Vocation

Although you may be somewhat impatient to develop your skills, your pleasure in mental pursuits could lead to teaching, lecturing, research, or writing. Your easy charm and natural

FIXED STAR

Star's name: Algenib, also called the Carrier or the Wing

Degree position: 8°10'–9°4' Aries between the years 1930 and 2000

Magnitude: 3

Strength: ★★★★★

Orb: 2°

Constellation: Alpha Pegasi

Applicable days: March 29, 30, 31, April 1, 2

Star qualities: Mars/Mercury

Description: a small white star located in the wing on the side of Pegasus

PRIMARY STAR'S INFLUENCE

Algenib imparts powers of thought, a positive and active mind that is capable of great accomplishment through ideas and actions. This star conveys resolution, determination, and enthusiasm, with competitive tendencies. It also enhances the speed of one's mental processes and gives the confidence to retaliate in just the right manner with impressive speech. This star also warns against being quick-tempered and reckless.

Linked to your Sun's degree, this star imparts good business skills, a love of learning, an interest in religious affairs, and a talent for writing. Algenib may also suggest a need for privacy and time alone. It indicates success in dealing with the public.

• *Positive:* decisiveness, spirit of enterprise, strong will, a fighting spirit, verbal repartee

• *Negative:* criticism, sarcasm, headstrong behavior, depressions, argumentative

flair for form and color could draw you to interior design, landscape gardening, the theater, music, or the arts. Having a natural understanding of people, you may be drawn to occupations that involve personal contact or being an advisor, such as therapy, personnel, health, promotions, public relations, sales, or business. This birthday can also produce good managers and executives.

Famous people who share your birthday include actor Warren Beatty, painter Vincent Van Gogh, psychiatrist Melanie Klein, and musicians Eric Clapton and Tracy Chapman.

Numerology

Creative, friendly, and sociable are just some of the attributes associated with the number 30 birthday. You enjoy the good life, love socializing, and can be exceptionally charismatic, loyal, and friendly. Ambitious and versatile, you take ideas and expand them in your own dramatic style. Gregarious, with good taste and an eye for color and form, you enjoy all types of work concerning art, design, and music. In your pursuit of happiness, avoid being lazy, overindulgent, and impatient or jealous, as these may cause you to experience emotional instability. Among those with number 30 birthdays, many will find recognition or fame, especially musicians, actors, and entertainers. The subinfluence of the number 3 month indicates that you are enthusiastic and gifted, with a good memory, and you possess a style of dramatic self-expression that can get you noticed. Although you are generally even-tempered, on occasion you may become temperamental and unreasonable. As a perfectionist, you like everything faultless; if you are unhappy or unsatisfied, you are inclined to complain and criticize.

• *Positive:* love of fun, loyalty, friendliness, ability to synthesize, talent with words, creativity, luck

• *Negative:* laziness, obstinacy, erratic behavior, impatience, insecurity, indifference, tendency to scatter energy

Love & Relationships

Caring and friendly, with great passion, you are a loving and affectionate idealist with dramatic emotions. You need a lot of love and affection, but stability and security may be prerequisites that you cannot give up. Often charming and charismatic, you love socializing and creative pursuits that can fire your imagination. However, guard against tendencies to be emotionally insecure or overly demanding when events do not meet with your approval. You may be drawn to mentally stimulating people with whom you can share your love for knowledge or need for creative self-expression. Through creative outlets, you often release your tension and meet with like-minded people.

YOUR SPECIAL SOMEONE

You might find emotional fulfilment and that special someone among those born on the following days.

Love & friendship: Jan. 8, 18, 22, Feb. 16, 20, Mar. 14, 18, 28, Apr. 12, 16, 26, May 10, 14, 24, June 8, 12, 22, July 6, 10, 20, 29, Aug. 4, 8, 18, 20, 27, 30, Sept. 2, 6, 16, 25, 28, Oct. 4, 14, 23, 26, 30, Nov. 2, 12, 21, 24, 28, Dec. 10, 19, 22, 26, 28

Beneficial: Jan. 6, 10, 25, 30, Feb. 4, 8, 23, 28, Mar. 2, 6, 21, 26, Apr. 4, 19, 24, May 2, 17, 22, June 15, 20, 30, July 13, 18, 28, Aug. 11, 16, 26, Sept. 9, 14, 24, Oct. 7, 12, 22, Nov. 5, 10, 20, Dec. 3, 8, 18

Fatal attractions: May 29, June 27, July 25, Aug. 23, Sept. 21, Oct. 1, 2, 3, 4, 19, Nov. 17, Dec. 15

Challenging: Jan. 13, 29, 31, Feb. 11, 27, 29, Mar. 9, 25, 27, Apr. 7, 23, 25, May 5, 21, 23, June 3, 19, 21, July 1, 17, 19, Aug. 15, 17, Sept. 13, 15, Oct. 11, 13, Nov. 9, 11, Dec. 7, 9

Soul mates: Jan. 6, 25, Feb. 4, 23, Mar. 2, 21, Apr. 19, May 17, June 15, July 13, Aug. 11, 20, Sept. 9, Nov. 7, Dec. 5, 12

March 31

Instinctive, alert, and swift—these are just some of the ways of describing those born on this date. Because of these attributes, you may also be restless or mentally curious and constantly on the move. Although you are continually seeking new experiences, once you have found something worthwhile you can develop a particular line of interest and become a specialist in your chosen field.

As an Arian, you are naturally dynamic, assertive, and daring. However, beware of a tendency to get bored easily, which may cause you to feel unsettled. By developing patience, you can overcome your inclinations to be impulsive. The subinfluence of your decanate ruler, Leo, adds vitality and self-assurance but warns against becoming too arrogant.

The idealistic side of your nature often causes you to see things in black and white, and through lack of satisfaction and a skeptical attitude you may become confused and scatter your energies. If, on the other hand, you realize that through education and learning you can develop methodical concentration and depth of thought, you achieve thoroughness and great skill at problem solving.

Up to the age of nineteen you are likely to be adventurous and unsettled. After the age of twenty, when your progressed Sun moves into Taurus, you develop a more pragmatic mental perspective and have an increased interest in acquiring wealth and security. This desire for material stability continues until the beginning of your fifties, when the progressed Sun enters Gemini. After this turning point the pace of your life is likely to increase, with more of an emphasis on expanding your interests and learning new skills.

Your Secret Self

Your exterior may not show how emotional you are on the inside or that you may need feedback from others more than you are willing to admit. There can also be a dichotomy in your feelings: wanting change, on one hand, and desiring to build something more solid for yourself, on the other. When united positively, these opposites can work together to endow you with a flexible productivity as well as ensure that you educate yourself thoroughly in at least one area of interest.

When in full flow, you may find it hard to give of your time, but when you do stop and give others your full attention and heart, you are likely to do anything for them, to the point of self-sacrifice. A natural charm and spontaneity may lead you to develop some form of creative expression, and if you can do this in some moving or changing situation, so much the better.

Work & Vocation

Your quick intellect and need for mental stimulation necessitate variety in your life and enable you to grasp information very quickly. Your natural leadership qualities could bring success in any field, especially in the business world, philosophy, or the political arena. In your choice of career you may have to guard against boredom, so it is important to select an occupation with constantly changing people or situations, such as working with the public or travel.

Famous people who share your birthday include music composer Joseph Haydn, actress

FIXED STAR

Star's name: Algenib, also called the Carrier or the Wing

Degree position: 8°10'–9°4' Aries between the years 1930 and 2000

Magnitude: 3

Strength: ★★★★★★

Orb: 2°

Constellation: Alpha Pegasi

Applicable days: March 29, 30, 31, April 1, 2

Star qualities: Mars/Mercury

Description: a small white star located in the wing on the side of Pegasus

PRIMARY STAR'S INFLUENCE

Algenib imparts powers of thought, a positive and active mind that is capable of great accomplishment through ideas and actions. This star conveys resolution, determination, and enthusiasm, with competitive tendencies. It also enhances the speed of one's mental processes and gives the confidence to retaliate in just the right manner with impressive speech. This star also warns against being quick-tempered and reckless.

Linked to your Sun's degree, this star imparts good business skills, a love of learning, an interest in religious affairs, and a talent for writing. Algenib may also suggest a need for privacy and time alone. It indicates success in dealing with the public.

• Positive: decisiveness, spirit of enterprise, strong will, a fighting spirit, verbal repartee

• Negative: criticism, sarcasm, headstrong behavior, depressions, argumentative

Rhea Perlman, philosopher René Descartes, film director Nagisa Oshima, U.S. vice president Al Gore, and actors Richard Chamberlain and Christopher Walken.

Numerology

Strong willpower, determination, and an emphasis on self-expression are indicated by the number 31 birthday. You often combine your intuition and practical skills to make the right decisions. Usually you are tireless and determined. With a number 31 birthday, you have original ideas, a good sense of form, and the ability to succeed in business if you take your time and follow a practical plan of action. You can be successful in turning your leisure-time pursuits into profitable ventures. Nevertheless, you may have to guard against tendencies to be overindulgent or selfish, as well as overly optimistic. The subinfluence of the number 3 month indicates that you are creative yet analytical. Your intuitive powers and way with words suggest a particular talent for writing but warn against being oversensitive or cynical. You need a great deal of affection or attention but must avoid being possessive. Introspective and thoughtful, you can at times appear absentminded or aloof.

• *Positive:* luck, creativity, originality, building ability, constructive tendencies, refusal to give up, practicality, good conversation, responsibility

• *Negative:* insecurity, impatience, suspicion, tendency to be easily discouraged, lack of ambition, selfishness, stubbornness

Love & Relationships

Idealistic and highly intuitive, you often possess feelings that can be either deep and concealed or light and on the surface. Emotionally sensitive yet secretive, you prefer to be private about your personal relationships. Take each relationship as a learning experience to keep your spirit of adventure alive. Your career often plays an important role in shaping your personal life. Usually you encounter lessons concerning letting go of the past.

YOUR SPECIAL SOMEONE

To find security, trust, and love, you might begin by looking for someone born on the following days.

Love & friendship: Jan. 13, 19, 23, 24, Feb. 11, 17, 21, Mar. 9, 15, 19, 28, 29, 30, Apr. 7, 13, 17, 26, 27, May 5, 11, 15, 24, 25, 26, June 3, 9, 13, 22, 23, 24, July 1, 7, 11, 20, 21, 22, Aug. 5, 9, 10, 18, 19, 20, Sept. 3, 7, 16, 17, 18, Oct. 1, 5, 14, 15, 16, 29, 31, Nov. 3, 12, 13, 14, 27, 29, Dec. 1, 2, 10, 11, 12, 25, 27, 29

Beneficial: Jan. 7, 15, 20, 31, Feb. 5, 13, 18, 29, Mar. 3, 11, 16, 27, Apr. 1, 9, 14, 25, May 7, 12, 23, June 5, 10, 21, July 3, 8, 19, Aug. 1, 6, 17, 30, Sept. 4, 15, 28, Oct. 2, 13, 26, Nov. 11, 24, Dec. 9, 22

Fatal attractions: Oct. 1, 2, 3, 4

Challenging: Jan. 6, 14, 30, Feb. 4, 12, 28, Mar. 2, 10, 26, Apr. 8, 24, May 6, 22, June 4, 20, July 2, 18, Aug. 16, Sept. 14, Oct. 12, Nov. 10, Dec. 8

Soul mates: Apr. 30, May 28, June 26, July 23, 24, Aug. 22, Sept. 20, Oct. 18, 30, Nov. 16, 28, Dec. 13, 14, 26

April 1

♈ Independent and strong-willed, yet sensitive and aloof, you are pragmatic and mystical, with a unique philosophical point of view. As an Arian, you are keen and ambitious, with strong intuitive powers and leadership abilities. Your inner wisdom frequently suggests that you can gain much knowledge through experience, and you can enhance your chances for success through a good education.

The subinfluence of the Sun contributes to your need for self-expression, and often you want to attain something different and original to take you away from the routine. Your love for freedom or the unusual may also influence you to explore, and traveling may be one of your favorite pastimes.

Finding yourself in a position beneath your true talents may often cause you inner conflict between the visualized ideal and the very different reality of daily life. You may therefore need to overcome a tendency to be bitter or jealous through frustration. To achieve emotional fulfillment, you may also need to find true inner faith or overcome inclinations to be suspicious. Through calmness, patience, and confidence, however, you can actualize your original ideas or dreams.

Up to the age of eighteen you are daring and independent. After the age of nineteen, when your progressed Sun moves into Taurus, there is an increased need for stability and financial security. This continues until around the age of forty-nine, when your progressed Sun enters Gemini. A turning point, this highlights the growing importance of new interests, learning, and communication.

FIXED STAR

Star's name: Algenib, also called the Carrier or the Wing

Degree position: 8°10'–9°4' Aries between the years 1930 and 2000

Magnitude: 3

Strength: ★★★★★

Orb: 2°

Constellation: Alpha Pegasi

Applicable days: March 29, 30, 31, April 1, 2

Star qualities: Mars/Mercury

Description: a small white star located in the wing on the side of Pegasus

PRIMARY STAR'S INFLUENCE

Algenib imparts powers of thought, a positive and active mind that is capable of great accomplishment through ideas and actions. This star conveys resolution, determination, and enthusiasm, with competitive tendencies. It also enhances the speed of one's mental processes and gives the confidence to retaliate in just the right manner with impressive speech. This star also warns against being quick-tempered and reckless.

Linked to your Sun's degree, this star imparts good business skills, a love of learning, an interest in religious affairs, and a talent for writing. Algenib may also suggest a need for privacy and time alone. It indicates success in dealing with the public.

• Positive: decisiveness, spirit of enterprise, strong will, a fighting spirit, verbal repartee

• Negative: criticism, sarcasm, headstrong behavior, depressions, argumentative

Your Secret Self

By recognizing your own inner power, you can place yourself in a leadership role when necessary and challenge yourself to take your abilities to the furthest. When you are offered opportunities, it may be necessary for you to think hard about the possible results and discipline yourself so that you can make the most of your earning potential. Although at times you may find yourself working for people who do not have your level of awareness, your lesson may be to become self-empowered and independent.

A capacity to combine business and pleasure is also part of your makeup and bestows a certain charm. Having a way with people and being active needs to be compensated for by allowing yourself time to be more introspective. These periods can especially inspire you in the areas of art, music, drama, or more mystical interests.

Work & Vocation

Your birthday shows a potential for executive and leadership abilities. These may manifest as becoming a specialist in your field or through management, administration, the military, or politics. Even though you have a sharp business sense, the more creative may be interested in occupations that use your exceptional imagination, such as in art, drama, or music. Since you also have good organizing ability, you are often in a position to handle the financial affairs of others or may excel in merchandising. Your equally strong humanitarian or idealistic streak may draw you toward a career in public-spirited organizations or work as an insightful counselor or teacher.

Famous people who share your birthday include actresses Ali MacGraw and Debbie Reynolds, psychologist Abraham Maslow, and composer Sergei Rachmaninoff.

Numerology

The great desire to be first and independent is suggested by your birthdate. As a number 1, you are more inclined to be individual, innovative, and courageous, with plenty of energy. Often there is a need to establish a strong identity and develop assertiveness. The pioneering spirit indicated here encourages you to strike out alone. These self-starting forces can also stimulate you to develop executive or leadership abilities. Full of enthusiasm and original ideas, you can show others the way forward. With a number 1 birthday, you may also need to learn that the world does not revolve around you, and you may need to avoid an inclination to be self-centered or dictatorial. The subinfluence of the number 4 month indicates that you are practical and hardworking. Energetic and inquisitive, you can be versatile and witty, with strong willpower and high spirits. You may, however, need to overcome a tendency to be headstrong, tactless, or overconfident.

• *Positive:* leadership, creativity, progressive inclinations, forcefulness, optimism, strong convictions, competitiveness, independence, gregariousness

• *Negative:* overbearing behavior, jealousy, egotism, pride, antagonism, lack of restraint, selfishness, weakness, instability, impatience

Love & Relationships

Outgoing and friendly, you are often independent yet practical, with deep emotions and great sensitivity. When you are in the right frame of mind, you can be the life and soul of the party and quite successful socially. Often you are attracted to intelligent people who are well educated. If a woman, you may have to guard against an inclination to be too talkative or domineering. You enjoy learning new things and need mental stimulation. If you join study groups or other educational activities you can do rather well. Romantically, you are charming and witty and have a fun-loving personality.

YOUR SPECIAL SOMEONE

You might find a long-lasting relationship and stability with someone born on one of the following dates.

Love & friendship: Jan. 5, 6, 21, 28, 31, Feb. 19, 26, 29, Mar. 17, 24, 27, Apr. 15, 22, 25, May 13, 20, 23, 30, June 11, 18, 21, July 9, 16, 19, Aug. 7, 14, 17, 31, Sept. 5, 12, 15, 29, Oct. 3, 10, 13, 27, 29, 31, Nov. 1, 8, 11, 25, 27, 29, Dec. 6, 9, 23, 25, 27

Beneficial: Jan. 9, 12, 18, 24, 29, Feb. 7, 10, 16, 22, 27, Mar. 5, 8, 14, 20, 25, Apr. 3, 6, 12, 18, 23, May 1, 4, 10, 16, 21, 31, June 2, 8, 14, 19, 29, July 6, 12, 17, 27, Aug. 4, 10, 15, 25, Sept. 2, 8, 13, 23, Oct. 6, 11, 21, Nov. 4, 9, 19, Dec. 2, 7, 17

Fatal attractions: Jan. 3, Feb. 1, Oct. 4, 5, 6

Challenging: Jan. 7, 8, 19, 28, Feb. 5, 6, 17, 26, Mar. 3, 4, 15, 24, Apr. 1, 2, 13, 22, May 11, 20, June 9, 18, July 7, 16, Aug. 5, 14, Sept. 3, 12, Oct. 1, 10, Nov. 8, Dec. 6

Soul mates: Jan. 3, 19, Feb. 1, 5, 17, Mar. 15, Apr. 13, May 11, June 9, July 7, Aug. 5, Sept. 3, Oct. 1

April 2

♈ Your Aries birthday shows you to be a pioneering and progressive personality. Restless yet original, you possess a subtle power that can motivate you to achieve in your chosen field. Your ruling planet, Mars, inspires you to seek an active and exciting life. With the supporting influence of your decanate ruler, Leo, you have an imaginative and creative sense and a need to be appreciated.

Intuition, charm, and a desire for harmony and peace are also indicated by this date. Although adventurous, you are more likely to be reserved or sensitive, with a refined nature and a need for security in congenial surroundings. The enormous potential accredited to your birthday can be realized through self-discipline. When you find your true strength, you have the willpower and determination to overcome all obstacles. However, you may have to learn to differentiate between stubbornness and perseverance.

Your need for human contact and the subinfluence of the Sun nevertheless can provide you with creative talent and a desire to go out there and accomplish. Often you are friendly and socially inclined, with a strong sense of justice and fair play. Responsible and hardworking, with a serious attitude, is how others often see your personality. Yet behind your subtle front you can be ambitious, with a strong desire to succeed and move forward.

A strong female figure is likely to have an impact on your early years. After the age of eighteen, when your progressed Sun moves into Taurus, there is an increased need for stability and financial security. This continues until around forty-eight, when your progressed Sun enters Gemini and acts as a turning point, highlighting the growing importance of communication and the exploration of more intellectual pursuits.

Fixed Stars

Algenib, also called the Carrier or the Wing; Sirrah, also called Alpheratz and Caput Andromeda

PRIMARY STAR

Star's name: Algenib, also called the Carrier or the Wing
Degree position: 8°10'–9°4' Aries between the years 1930 and 2000
Magnitude: 3
Strength: ★★★★★
Orb: 2°
Constellation: Alpha Pegasi
Applicable days: March 29, 30, 31, April 1, 2
Star qualities: Mars/Mercury
Description: a small white star located in the wing on the side of Pegasus

PRIMARY STAR'S INFLUENCE

Algenib imparts powers of thought, a positive and active mind that is capable of great accomplishment through ideas and actions. This star conveys resolution, determination, and enthusiasm, with competitive tendencies. It also enhances the speed of one's mental processes and gives the confidence to retaliate in just the right manner with impressive speech. This star also warns against being quick-tempered and reckless.

Linked to your Sun's degree, this star imparts good business skills, a love of learning, an interest in religious affairs, and a talent for writing. Algenib may also suggest a need for privacy and

Your Secret Self

Inner vision and trust illuminate your understanding, and it may be necessary for you to learn detachment on a very deep level. This may mean being willing to let go of anything or anyone you may rely on for security. This lesson may not be fully learned until later in life, but when it is, it gives an enormous inner freedom and a desire for things of a more profound nature. In relationships in particular, any tendency to hang on or become dependent is immediately manifested in your becoming too serious. On the other hand, you can also be devoted, caring, and a loyal friend.

You also possess a very humanitarian and generous side that ensures your popularity with others. You are very receptive to other people's needs and can be an excellent asset to any communal or shared project.

Work & Vocation

This birthdate shows that you can be very successful in people-related careers such as media, public relations, psychology, counseling, and liaison or social work. There is also a likelihood of working in partnerships, and advantages can come from learning to collaborate with others. Your original and creative approach can lead to success in acting and the arts as well as in exploring, education, and working for a cause. At times, challenges in terms of work may lead to anxiety, but looking at new alternatives can produce positive results. Attempt to avoid stagnation or monotony. Hardworking, with an instinctive business sense, you are likely to be motivated by a desire for the good things in life.

Famous people born on your birthday include actor Alec Guinness, French author Émile Zola, Hans Christian Andersen, painter William Hunt, and comedian Dana Carvey.

time alone. It indicates success in dealing with the public.

• *Positive:* decisiveness, spirit of enterprise, strong will, a fighting spirit, verbal repartee

• *Negative:* criticism, sarcasm, headstrong behavior, depressions, argumentative

See Appendix for additional fixed star readings.

Numerology

Sensitivity and a strong need to be part of a group are suggested by a number 2 birthday. Adaptable and understanding, you enjoy cooperative activities where you can experience interaction with others. In your attempt to please those you like, you may run the risk of becoming overly dependent. Nevertheless, by developing confidence, you can overcome the tendency to be easily hurt by the action and criticism of others. The subinfluence of the number 4 month indicates that you need the security of a solid base. Often you are inclined toward correctness and perfectionism and like to support or work in collaboration with others. Sociable and a good host, you like to entertain and may be proud of your home. You can be reassuring but not always demonstrative with your feelings. As a perfectionist, you are usually responsible, but you must avoid discontentment or falling into lethargic moods.

• *Positive:* good partnerships, gentleness, tact, receptivity, intuition, consideration, harmony, agreeableness, ambassador of goodwill

• *Negative:* suspicion, lack of confidence, subservience, oversensitivity, selfish, being easily hurt, deceit

YOUR SPECIAL SOMEONE

For security, mental stimulation, and love, you might want to begin looking for those born among the following dates:

Love & friendship: Jan. 6, 10, 20, 22, 24, 30, Feb. 4, 18, 20, 22, 28, Mar. 2, 16, 18, 20, 26, 29, Apr. 14, 16, 18, 24, 27, May 12, 14, 16, 22, 25, June 10, 12, 14, 20, 23, July 8, 10, 12, 18, 21, 29, Aug. 6, 8, 10, 16, 19, Sept. 4, 6, 8, 14, 17, Oct. 2, 4, 6, 12, 15, Nov. 2, 4, 10, 13, Dec. 2, 8, 11, 19

Beneficial: Jan. 1, 3, 4, 14, Feb. 1, 2, 12, Mar. 10, 28, Apr. 8, 26, 30, May 6, 24, 28, June 4, 22, 26, July 2, 20, 24, Aug. 18, 22, Sept. 16, 20, Oct. 14, 18, Nov. 12, 16, Dec. 10, 14

Fatal attractions: Jan. 11, Feb. 9, Mar. 7, Apr. 5, May 3, June 1, Oct. 5, 6, 7

Challenging: Jan. 3, 5, Feb. 1, 3, Mar. 1, July 31, Aug. 29, Sept. 27, 30, Oct. 25, 28, Nov. 23, 26, 30, Dec. 21, 24, 28

Soul mates: Jan. 5, 12, Feb. 3, 6, 10, Mar. 1, 8, Apr. 6, May 4, June 2

Love & Relationships

Intuitive and clever, you are often well informed and have a capacity to learn quickly. Usually you enjoy reading, and your love for knowledge suggests that if you desire true emotional satisfaction, you may need to continue your education or constantly learn new skills. Often you like to be associated with intellectual people who can stimulate your mind. Romantically, you are drawn toward successful people or need a clever partner who is knowledgeable, with a powerful mind. Your personality ensures that you will have many friends and good social contacts. You may, however, have to guard against a tendency to be mistrustful or skeptical in close relationships.

April 3

♈ Your pioneering spirit, versatility, and love of travel ensure that your life will not be dull or uneventful. Your strong motivation and natural talents for communication give you strong powers of persuasion. With your need for self-expression and desire for change, your birthday promises a life of excitement and adventure.

Your ruling planet, Mars, and the element of fire make you enthusiastic, impatient, and dynamic. The subinfluence of your decanate ruler, Leo, implies that you are likely to show others an assertive and daring front. Although your path is paved with challenges, success will be achieved through patience, hard work, and focused determination. Passionate and intense as you are, soul growth will come through learning detachment. Changes are particularly linked to your career, where you may experience some obstacles, but opportunities will present themselves to create new openings and fortunate breaks.

Although you may be prone to moodiness, your determination does not allow you to stay down for very long.

Fun-loving and entertaining, with imagination and enthusiasm, you are friendly and a good companion, with a talent for wit and humor. You may, however, have to guard against a tendency to become easily bored.

In youth you are active, independent, restless, and sometimes reckless. There is also an indication of an influence from a male relative or friend who may need your support. After the age of sixteen or seventeen, you become more practical and financially aware as your progressed Sun enters Taurus. In the middle years, after numerous changes, you are likely to find probable gains through partnerships and cooperative relationships. Your enthusiasm and motivation will ensure that some of your dreams are now being fulfilled. From the age of forty-seven, when your progressed Sun enters Gemini, you will become more mentally curious, which may result in your taking up a totally new interest. Another turning point occurs when you are seventy-seven, when your progressed Sun enters Cancer, making you more sensitive and family-oriented.

Your Secret Self

Your greatest success may come through the power of love. Your strong inner feelings need to be channeled into some practical form, otherwise it is possible that you may get emotionally carried away. Since you have a dramatic side, this could result in your acting out some rather powerful dramas.

Blessed with charm, sensitivity, and a fertile imagination, you may still need to balance these with some form of solid foundation in life. By using your exceptional sense of vision to imagine positive future possibilities and then to organize a plan to achieve them, you can make the most of your outstanding talents. Through diligent and concentrated effort in your work you are able to realize your true potential and connect to the financial protection promised in this birthdate.

Work & Vocation

Careerwise, with your strong persuasive powers and sense of the dramatic, you make an excellent salesperson or promoter. These talents, combined with your need for self-expression, can

FIXED STAR

Star's name: Sirrah, also called Alpheratz and Caput Andromeda
Degree position: 13°11'–14°13' Aries between the years 1930 and 2000
Magnitude: 2
Strength: ★★★★★★★
Orb: 2°10'
Constellation: Alpha Andromedae
Applicable days: April 2, 3, 4, 5, 6, 7
Star qualities: Jupiter/Venus
Description: a blue, white, and purple binary star located in the Head of Andromeda

PRIMARY STAR'S INFLUENCE

Sirrah signifies good relationships with others and popularity. It bestows a harmonious nature and benefits from good social connections. This star can also grant honor and wealth, cheerfulness, optimism, versatility, and sound judgment. It warns, however, against being too outspoken or taking popularity for granted.

Linked to your Sun's degree, this star indicates that usually you can achieve your heart's desire as long as you are clear about your objectives. Sometimes after you obtain what you want, you are at a loss as to what to do next. However, since one of your natural attributes is knowing the right people and being at the right place at the right time, this state does not tend to last long.

• *Positive:* warm heart, joy, popularity, attractive personality
• *Negative:* self-conceit, excess

find you involved in drama, the arts, lecturing, or politics. Careers involving travel and variety, such as couriers, transport, or airline personnel, will ensure job satisfaction. A natural compassion may draw you to the world of health and healing. A major key for people with your birthday may be to keep your spirit of adventure alive and avoid monotonous occupations.

Famous people born on your birthday include actors Marlon Brando, Alec Baldwin, and Eddie Murphy, wildlife researcher Jane Goodall, actress Doris Day, poet George Herbert, and musician Wayne Newton.

Numerology

Having a number 3 birthday, you are sensitive, with a need for creativity and emotional expression. Fun-loving and a good companion, you enjoy friendly social activities and many interests. Although you are versatile and expressive, with a need for different and exciting experiences, an inclination to get bored easily may cause you to become indecisive or spread yourself too thinly. Although, with a number 3 birthday, you are usually artistic and charming, with a good sense of humor, you may have to develop self-esteem and guard against tendencies such as worry and emotional insecurities. The subinfluence of the number 4 month indicates that you like to be well organized. You possess good analytical skills, and by asserting yourself, you can make others take more notice of your opinions. At times you can appear aloof or caught up in your own thoughts. However, when you want to gain others' attention, you can do this with a few words.

• *Positive:* humor, happiness, friendliness, productivity, creativity, artistic inclinations, power to wish, love of freedom, talent with words

• *Negative:* boredom, vanity, overactive imagination, exaggeration, inability to be loving, boastfulness, extravagance, self-indulgence, laziness, hypocrisy

Love & Relationships

Imaginative and visionary, you are a loving, loyal, and devoted individual. Often you are romantic and idealistic about your relationships and seek a partner who can live up to your high ideals. In fact, you can be so idealistic that sometimes you may choose a platonic relationship, as it is hard to find someone who can measure up to your high expectations. It is better to pick a partner who is knowledgeable and has a humanitarian side. When you fall in love, guard against a tendency to put your lover on a pedestal or sacrifice yourself in the role of rescuer, especially if the other person does not want to be saved. Romantically, although you are likely to have a bold front, you may have trouble showing your vulnerability. Develop your communication skills on an intimate level and do not act in haste if you want to find your ideal partner.

YOUR SPECIAL SOMEONE

With persons born on the following dates, your ideals might be realized more easily.

Love & friendship: Jan. 1, 6, 7, 20, 21, 23, 31, Feb. 5, 18, 19, 21, 29, Mar. 3, 17, 19, 27, Apr. 1, 15, 17, 25, May 13, 15, 23, June 11, 13, 21, July 9, 11, 19, Aug. 7, 9, 17, Sept. 5, 7, 15, Oct. 3, 5, 13, Nov. 1, 3, 11, Dec. 1, 9

Beneficial: Jan. 5, 16, 18, Feb. 3, 14, 16, Mar. 1, 12, 14, 29, Apr. 10, 12, 27, May 8, 10, 25, 29, June 6, 8, 23, 27, July 4, 6, 21, 25, Aug. 2, 4, 19, 23, Sept. 2, 17, 21, Oct. 15, 19, Nov. 13, 17, Dec. 11, 15, 29

Fatal attractions: Jan. 6, 30, Feb. 4, 28, Mar. 2, 26, Apr. 24, May 22, June 20, July 18, Aug. 16, Sept. 14, Oct. 5, 6, 12, Nov. 10, Dec 8

Challenging: Jan. 4, Feb. 2, May 29, 31, June 27, 29, 30, July 25, 27, 28, Aug. 23, 25, 26, 30, Sept. 21, 23, 24, 28, Oct. 19, 21, 22, 26, Nov. 17, 19, 20, 24, Dec. 15, 17, 18, 22

Soul mates: Jan. 23, Feb. 21, Mar. 19, Apr. 17, May 15, June 13, July 11, 31, Aug. 6, 9, 29, Sept. 7, 27, Oct. 5, 25, Nov. 3, 23, Dec. 1, 6, 21

April 4

SUN: ARIES
DECANATE: LEO/SUN
DEGREE: 13°30'–14°30' ARIES
MODE: CARDINAL
ELEMENT: FIRE

FIXED STAR

Star's name: Sirrah, also called Alpheratz and Caput Andromeda

Degree position: 13°11'–14°13' Aries between the years 1930 and 2000

Magnitude: 2

Strength: ★★★★★★★

Orb: 2°10'

Constellation: Alpha Andromedae

Applicable days: April 2, 3, 4, 5, 6, 7

Star qualities: Jupiter/Venus

Description: A blue, white, and purple binary star located in the Head of Andromeda

PRIMARY STAR'S INFLUENCE

Sirrah signifies good relationships with others and popularity. It bestows a harmonious nature and benefits from good social connections. This star can also grant honor and wealth, cheerfulness, optimism, versatility, and sound judgment. It warns, however, against being too outspoken or taking popularity for granted.

Linked to your Sun's degree, this star indicates that usually you can achieve your heart's desire as long as you are clear about your objectives. Sometimes after you obtain what you want, you are at a loss as to what to do next. However, since one of your natural attributes is knowing the right people and being at the right place at the right time, this state does not tend to last long.

• *Positive:* warm heart, joy, popularity, attractive personality

• *Negative:* self conceit, excess

With hard work, determination, and a positive attitude, you have the drive to move mountains and impress other people with your knowledge. Usually you seek security and try to build a good foundation for yourself. Through opportunities at work and a sixth sense about business, your strong desires for success can be realized. This suggests that you rarely suffer financial problems, and those that do arise will be short-lived.

Although you are charming, generous, and kind, with the ability to make yourself popular, you may have to learn that by being too direct or overbearing you can also push people away. With your attractiveness and personal magnetism, you know how to enjoy yourself and entertain people; nevertheless, uncertainty in values may cause excess and you may need to moderate your inclination for too much rich living. Alternatively, at times you may become very rigid and display a hard and inflexible front, with little compassion for the needs of others.

As an Arian, you are dynamic and ambitious, yet pragmatic. More often than not, however, it is your great curiosity to explore that brings you an exciting and varied life. The sub-influence of your decanate ruler, Leo, often adds determination and vitality to your already assertive personality. Nevertheless, guard against being too stubborn or strong-willed, as it may lead to destructive behavior.

Up to the age of fifteen you are likely to be daring and rebellious. After the age of sixteen, when your progressed Sun moves into Taurus, there is an increased need for financial stability, material wealth, and security. This continues until around the age of forty-six, when your progressed Sun enters Gemini. A turning point, this highlights the growing importance of new interests, learning, communication, and relations with those around you. At the time you reach age seventy-six, when your progressed Sun enters Cancer, you become more sensitive and home- and family-oriented.

Your Secret Self

To you, knowledge and expertise are power. You respect people who have strong mental abilities and independent thinkers like yourself. Achievement-oriented and ambitious, you have an eye for an opportunity and a creative knack for solving problems.

With your need to be honest and direct with people, you are likely to find success in the constructive use of your willpower and analytical ability. Since you have a naturally inquisitive mind, you will always be finding new and exciting things to explore throughout your life. A major part of your personality is an ability to animate others with your irresistible enthusiasm. Just beware of getting carried away and becoming greedy or overindulgent. Fortunately, you have a very lucky streak, which comes from an open and spirited attitude and which manages to turn any situation your way.

Work & Vocation

When you combine your practical skills and strategic ability, you are excellent at organizing large schemes and projects. This is beneficial for working in management or at an executive level, or possibly also working for yourself. Many entrepreneurs, producers, promoters, and builders are born on your birthday. You may also be attracted toward the arts but are not likely to be interested unless there are also monetary rewards. A good structuralist, you have a good sense of form and are willing to work hard. Often a perfectionist, you are proud of your efforts but may have to guard against expecting excellence from others.

Famous people who share your birthday include blues singer Muddy Waters, actors Anthony Perkins and Robert Downey Jr., film composer Elmer Bernstein, and actress Christine Lahti.

Numerology

The solid structure and orderly power suggested by the number 4 birthday indicates that you need stability and like to establish order. Endowed with energy, practical skills, and strong determination, you can achieve success through hard work. Security-conscious, you like to build a strong foundation for yourself and your family. A pragmatic approach to life confers a good business sense and an ability to achieve material success. With a number 4 birthdate, you are usually honest, frank, and fair. The challenges for a number 4 individual may include overcoming periods of instability or financial worry. The subinfluence of the number 4 month indicates that you are an inquisitive and energetic person who enjoys an active life. Your self-discipline and strong willpower often suggest that you can be self-reliant and commanding, with a taste for power. However, avoid being bossy or controlling. You do not like to be restricted and often object to being told what to do.

• *Positive:* organization, self discipline, steadiness, hard work, organization, craftsmanship, manual ability, pragmatism, trust, exactitude

• *Negative:* inability to communicate, repression, rigidity, laziness, lack of feeling, procrastination, penny pinching, bossiness, hidden affections, resentfulness, strictness

Love & Relationships

Success-oriented, you are ambitious and dynamic, with a strong need for prestige and recognition. Often you like to be associated with professional people or wealthy individuals from an established background. Usually money is an important factor in relationships, and you do not like time wasters or people without potential. Magnanimous and proud, you often have good taste and appreciate quality and beauty. Nevertheless, you may need to overcome some of your materialistic tendencies by learning that emotional fulfillment does not necessarily involve acquiring wealth.

YOUR SPECIAL SOMEONE

For that special someone, you might want to look among those born on one of the following dates.

Love & friendship: Jan. 8, 14, 17, 20, 22, 24, Feb. 6, 15, 18, 20, 22, Mar. 4, 13, 16, 18, 20, Apr. 2, 11, 14, 16, 18, May 9, 12, 14, 16, June 7, 10, 12, 14, July 5, 8, 10, 12, 30, Aug. 3, 6, 8, 10, 28, Sept. 1, 4, 6, 8, 26, Oct. 2, 4, 6, 24, Nov. 2, 4, 22, Dec. 2, 20, 21

Beneficial: Jan. 6, 23, Feb. 4, 21, Mar. 2, 19, 30, Apr. 17, 28, May 15, 26, 30, June 13, 24, 28, July 11, 22, 26, Aug. 9, 20, 24, Sept. 7, 18, 22, Oct. 5, 16, 20, Nov. 3, 14, 18, Dec. 1, 12, 16, 30

Fatal attractions: Jan. 7, Feb. 5, Mar. 3, Apr. 1, Oct. 7, 8

Challenging: Jan. 5, 26, 29, Feb. 3, 24, 27, Mar. 1, 22, 25, Apr. 20, 23, May 18, 21, June 16, 19, 30, July 14, 17, 28, Aug. 12, 15, 26, 31, Sept. 10, 13, 24, 29, Oct 8, 11, 22, 27, Nov. 6, 9, 20, 25, Dec. 4, 7, 18, 23

Soul mates: Jan. 30, Feb. 8, 28, Mar. 26, Apr. 24, May 22, June 20, July 18, Aug. 16, Sept. 14, Oct. 12, 31, Nov. 10, 29, Dec. 8, 27

April 5

FIXED STAR

Star's name: Sirrah, also called
   Alpheratz and Caput Andromeda

Degree position: 13°11'–14°13' Aries
   between the years 1930 and
   2000

Magnitude: 2

Strength: ★★★★★★★

Orb: 2°10'

Constellation: Alpha Andromedae

Applicable days: April 2, 3, 4, 5, 6, 7

Star qualities: Jupiter/Venus

Description: A blue, white, and purple
   binary star located in the Head of
   Andromeda

PRIMARY STAR'S INFLUENCE

Sirrah signifies good relationships with others and popularity. It bestows a harmonious nature and benefits from good social connections. This star can also grant honor and wealth, cheerfulness, optimism, versatility, and sound judgment. It warns, however, against being too outspoken or taking popularity for granted.

Linked to your Sun's degree, this star indicates that usually you can achieve your heart's desire as long as you are clear about your objectives. Sometimes after you obtain what you want, you are at a loss as to what to do next. However, since one of your natural attributes is knowing the right people and being at the right place at the right time, this state does not tend to last long.

• *Positive:* warm heart, joy, popularity, attractive personality

• *Negative:* self-conceit, excess

Your Aries birthday shows you to be a dynamic individual who is persuasive and hardworking. Your versatility and charm, coupled with the competitive spirit of your ruling planet, Mars, contribute toward a bold and self-confident front. The supporting influence of the Sun endows you with a flow of creative energy and the urge for self-expression.

Although you may seem assertive, this may at times conceal an underlying indecisiveness or insecurity. However, your ability to be untiring and relentless in fulfillment of your ambitions can assist you to overcome these obstacles by sheer determination. Your restlessness may mean that you need constant activity. Nevertheless, your strong personality suggests that you are a natural candidate for leadership positions. Just beware that you do not become too bossy or demanding.

With the right attitude, you have the potential to inspire others, but avoid investing your emotional energies in small and unimportant matters, which can strain your sensitive nervous system. Take time to regenerate your energies and look after your health. In later years your varied experiences and the realization of how far you have traveled in your life give you universal understanding and wisdom. Style-wise, your appearance is rather important to you, as you like to make a good impression. A touch of the dramatic ensures that you are not afraid to make a bold statement.

In youth you are inclined to an active life or outdoor activities and are likely to have many friends. After you reach the age of fifteen, when your progressed Sun moves into Taurus, there is a growing need for stability and increased financial security. This continues until around the age of forty-five, when your progressed Sun enters Gemini. This is a turning point, which will emphasize a growing need for knowledge, communication, and learning new skills and is likely to include much travel and change. From the age of seventy-five, when your progressed Sun enters Cancer, your sensitivity increases, with home and family playing a more important part in your life.

Your Secret Self

Life is full of blessings in disguise, and although you crave harmony at a deep level, much of your life is concerned with your attitude toward money, material considerations, and the tests that come with them. It is through facing your doubts and fears that you can truly find faith in yourself and what life has to offer you. Love, friendship, and beauty are yours for the taking, but there is also an emphasis on responsibility. By making yourself accountable for your actions, you will find that life will more than reward you.

You may also have a strong love of art, music, and drama, which you can develop further if you overcome a tendency for restlessness or impatience. When channeled constructively this can give you not only dynamic self-expression but also the ability to entertain others with your youthful charm and charisma.

Work & Vocation

Your progressive, pioneering spirit and need to express your creative potential can lead you to professions such as explorer or politician or to the dramatic world of the theater and cinema.

You may also have an aptitude for research in education, science, law, and philosophy. Your powers of persuasion and natural leadership ability will take you to the fore in any business venture, as well as theological careers, the civil service, or administration. If a career you choose is not profitable, you are highly likely to soon abandon it. Since you possess an ability to access the collective dreams and yearnings of a generation, you may wish to embody this through the arts in some form.

Famous people with your birthday are actors Spencer Tracy and Gregory Peck, educator Booker T. Washington, poet Algernon Swinburne, actress Bette Davis, and General Colin Powell.

Numerology

Strong instincts, an adventurous nature, and a desire for freedom are all indicated by the number 5 birthday. The willingness to explore or try anything new and your enthusiastic approach suggest that life will have a lot to offer you. Travel and many opportunities for change, some unexpected, may lead you to undergo a real transformation of views and beliefs. With a number 5 birthday, you need to feel that life is exciting; however, you may also have to develop a responsible attitude and avoid tendencies such as unpredictability, excessiveness, and restlessness. You can achieve success by avoiding premature or speculative actions and through learning patience. The subinfluence of the number 4 month indicates that you need to feel secure yet free to find your own identity. Intuitive and sensitive, you often want to synthesize your traditional nature with a broad-minded view and think in worldly terms. Avoid being overemotional by staying practical and realistic.

• *Positive:* versatility, adaptability, progressive attitude, strong instincts, magnetism, luck, daring, love of freedom, quickness, wit, curiosity, mysticism, sociability

• *Negative:* unreliability, changeability, procrastination, inconsistency, undependability, overconfidence, headstrong behavior

Love & Relationships

As charm is one of your natural attributes, you have no problems attracting admirers and lovers. Since you draw all types of people, you may need to be selective in your choice of friends. You may also alternate between being very expressive with your thoughts and feelings and experiencing isolation. Nevertheless, you may need time on your own, particularly in nature, to reflect on matters or recharge your energies. You are attracted to active and mentally stimulating people, so some sort of intellectual activity with your mate would prove especially beneficial for you. Your challenge may be to keep your relationships steady and harmonious.

April 6

Daring and ambitious, yet sensitive and charming, people with this birthdate reveal a mixture of idealism and realism. Although you are socially inclined, never far from your mind is the need to balance your high ideals with an inherent practical sense. You are therefore able to utilize opportunities to the best of your abilities.

As an Arian, you are determined and pioneering, with initiative and drive. Although you can be quite independent, you may prefer to work with others rather than work alone. Although at times people and events may cause you to become too intense, avoid becoming overly sensitive and isolating yourself. Usually through partnerships and associations you come to realize your great potential and can benefit financially through team efforts and co-operative endeavors.

The subinfluence of the Sun bestows originality and a love of freedom. However, being boisterous and unruly or going against other people's wishes can also cause you stress. You may have to overcome tendencies such as moodiness, impatience, or stubbornness in order to truly benefit from collaborative work. With your powers of perception and intuition, however, you often develop a humanitarian view and an objective judgment that helps you understand people and what motivates them.

After you reach the age of fourteen, when your progressed Sun moves into Taurus, there is an increasing determination to acquire financial stability and material success in life. You may want to be closer to nature from this time. This influence continues until around the age of forty-four, when your progressed Sun enters Gemini. This is a turning point that accents the growing importance of communication and expanding your mental interests or learning new skills. From the age of seventy-four, when your progressed Sun moves forward into Cancer, you will find a greater awareness of your emotional needs as well as an accent on your family and home.

Your Secret Self

Leading a well-balanced life may be the key to your happiness. Although many lessons revolve around your work, it is also important to avoid becoming stuck in a monotonous routine. Through developing other interests, hobbies, or travel you can expand your horizons and explore other opportunities. Since you are highly imaginative, with a creative flair, one of your challenges may be to put those big dreams of yours into action.

You possess an inner nobility that particularly shows through when you are in positions of leadership or responsibility. You take your work seriously and operate best when given free rein to work in your own individual way. If you become anxious, you may have to overcome a tendency to withdraw rather than share your problems with others. By learning to examine all facets of any difficult situation and compromise rather than play power games, you are more likely to get positive results. Although outwardly sociable, at heart you may be reserved and sensitive, with an unseen inner strength.

Work & Vocation

Whatever career you choose, you will need a balance between your active, pioneering practicality and your sensitivity. Your greatest success may come through working in a partnership

FIXED STAR

Star's name: Sirrah, also called Alpheratz and Caput Andromeda

Degree position: 13°11'–14°13' Aries between the years 1930 and 2000

Magnitude: 2

Strength: ★★★★★★★

Orb: 2°10'

Constellation: Alpha Andromedae

Applicable days: April 2, 3, 4, 5, 6, 7

Star qualities: Jupiter/Venus

Description: A blue, white, and purple binary star located in the Head of Andromeda

PRIMARY STAR'S INFLUENCE

Sirrah signifies good relationships with others and popularity. It bestows a harmonious nature and benefits from good social connections. This star can also grant honor and wealth, cheerfulness, optimism, versatility, and sound judgment. It warns, however, against being too outspoken or taking popularity for granted.

Linked to your Sun's degree, this star indicates that usually you can achieve your heart's desire as long as you are clear about your objectives. Sometimes after you obtain what you want, you are at a loss as to what to do next. However, since one of your natural attributes is knowing the right people and being at the right place at the right time, this state does not tend to last long.

• *Positive:* warm heart, joy, popularity, attractive personality

• *Negative:* self-conceit, excess

or as part of a team and may particularly draw you toward careers such as public relations, diplomacy, negotiation, or representation having to do with foreign places. Alternatively, you may desire activities that benefit others and so be attracted to charity work or working with the disadvantaged. Whatever you choose, you have the ability to work hard, and this will bring its own rewards. You are likely to possess a natural talent for buying and selling and banking, as well as being an excellent agent. If attracted to public life, you may do well in a career in politics or public service. Creative talents and a remarkable visionary sense may particularly manifest in the area of acting and photography as well as writing and other aspects of the arts or the entertainment industry.

Famous people born on your birthday include magician Harry Houdini, artist Raphael, pianist André Previn, writer Baba Ram Dass, musician Peter Tosh, and artist Gustav Moreau.

Numerology

Compassion, idealism, and a caring nature are some of the attributes suggested by a number 6 birthday. This is the number of the perfectionist or the universal friend and frequently indicates that you are a humanitarian who can be responsible, loving, and supportive. Having a number 6 birthday, you are frequently domestically inclined and a devoted parent. The more sensitive among you will need to find a form of creative expression and are drawn to the world of entertaining or art and design. You may need to develop more self-confidence and overcome tendencies such as interfering behavior, worry, and misplaced sympathy. The subinfluence of the number 4 month indicates that you can be ambitious, with an idealistic personality. Original and creative, you can realize your aspiration by developing self-confidence and an independent outlook. Often you may be drawn to travel or work in foreign places. Learning the art of subtle suggestion and being diplomatic help you to make the right contacts.

• *Positive:* worldliness, universal brotherhood, friendliness, compassion, dependability, understanding, sympathy, idealism, domestic orientation, humanitarianism, poise, artistic ability, balance

• *Negative:* discontent, anxiety, shyness, unreasonableness, stubbornness, outspokenness, domineering behavior, lack of responsibility, selfish behavior, suspicion, self-centeredness

Love & Relationships

In love you are a sensual, daring, and romantic charmer, but beneath that enthusiasm a desire for a settled relationship seems particularly important to you. Once the initial honeymoon period of any love affair is over, you usually like to settle down into a more peaceful and harmonious daily pattern. You may have to avoid, however, going too far in the opposite direction and allowing your relationships to become dull or monotonous. This may cause you to become manipulative or moody with the people you love. Fortunately, you possess a friendly charm that usually draws people toward you. This often guarantees you the affection you need.

YOUR SPECIAL SOMEONE

You may have better luck with people born on one of the following dates.

Love & friendship: Jan. 10, 11, 26, 28, Feb. 8, 9, 24, 26, Mar. 6, 22, 24, 30, Apr. 4, 20, 22, 28, May 2, 18, 20, 26, 29, June 16, 18, 24, 27, July 14, 16, 22, 25, Aug. 12,14, 20, 23, 30, Sept. 10,12,18, 21, 28, Oct. 8, 10, 16, 19, 26, Nov. 6, 8, 14, 17, 24, Dec. 4, 6, 12, 15, 22

Beneficial: Jan. 8, Feb. 6, Mar. 4, 28, Apr. 2, 26, May 24, June 22, 30, July 20, 28, 29, Aug. 18, 26, 27, 30, Sept. 16, 24, 25, 28, Oct. 14, 22, 23, 26, 29, Nov. 12, 20, 21, 24, 27, Dec. 10, 18, 19, 22, 25

Fatal attractions: Jan. 15, Feb. 13, Mar. 11, Apr. 9, May 7, June 5, July 3, Aug. 1, Oct. 9, 10

Challenging: Jan. 7, 9, 30, Feb. 5, 7, 28, Mar. 3, 5, 26, Apr. 1, 3, 24, May 1, 22, June 20, July 18, Aug. 16, Sept. 14, Oct. 12, 29, Nov. 10, 27, Dec. 8, 25, 30

Soul mates: Jan. 8, 27, Feb. 6, 10, 25, Mar. 4, 23, Apr. 2, 21, May 19, June 17, July 15, Aug. 13, Sept. 11, Oct. 9, Nov. 7, Dec. 5

April 7

Profound determination and heightened intuitive sensitivity are suggested by this birthdate. With your dynamic personality and love of the new, you are often engaged in the initiation of projects. This suggests that new challenges and beginnings can often bring about real transformation and compensate for periods of procrastination or depression. By developing your inner intuition or sixth sense, however, you can come to understand yourself at a deeper level.

If motivated, you work hard and can be highly dedicated, yet the restlessness indicated by your ruling planet, Mars, does not allow you to stand still. If inspired, you can be quite enthusiastic and creative, with a spontaneous idealism; nevertheless, your tendency to be secretive and uncommunicative may leave others wondering what you are up to next. Although you often project a bold front, you are in fact concealing a shy or sensitive soul. It is usually through learning to let go of the past and overcoming a tendency to torment yourself over emotional issues that you can make real progress and develop self-discipline. You may have to learn to differentiate between inner strength, relentless determination, and stubborn arrogance, which others can perceive as hostility and indifference.

After you reach the age of thirteen, when your progressed Sun moves into Taurus, there is an increased need for stability and material security. This continues until the age of around forty-three, when your progressed Sun enters Gemini. This is a turning point that will bring to prominence many new interests as well as a stronger desire for communication at all levels. This may even involve learning new skills. At the age of seventy-three, when your progressed Sun moves into Cancer, you become more aware of issues concerning your home, family, and emotional sensitivity.

Your Secret Self

Hidden from public view is your sensitive and idealistic emotional nature, which may involve you in reflective contemplation or self-analysis. In your desire for perfection you may find that people do not live up to your high ideals. Guard against an inclination toward becoming suspicious or a fear of being lonely or abandoned. Fortunately, you are blessed with a profound intuition, which when developed ensures that the more spiritual side of your nature protects you and helps you overcome any difficult situations.

Mentally sharp and hardworking, you possess instincts that give you an uncanny ability to assess others' characters. Using this psychological skill with people enables you to avoid becoming nervous and impatient by working diplomatically and amicably. You are able to judge how well you are using this skill in your relationships by assessing whether you have lost your sense of humor and become too serious. When your energy is flowing positively you also have an excellent sense of spontaneity. You can particularly benefit from physical exercise, such as martial arts, sports, or yoga.

Work & Vocation

Your leadership ability and capacity for hard work mark you out for advancement in any field of endeavor. You like to be in control and not subservient to others, so you are likely to prosper in management and executive positions or may prefer to work for yourself. By staying

FIXED STAR

Star's name: Sirrah, also called Alpheratz and Caput Andromeda
Degree position: 13°11'–14°13' Aries between the years 1930 and 2000
Magnitude: 2
Strength: ★★★★★★★
Orb: 2°10'
Constellation: Alpha Andromedae
Applicable days: April 2, 3, 4, 5, 6, 7
Star qualities: Jupiter/Venus
Description: A blue, white, and purple binary star located in the Head of Andromeda

PRIMARY STAR'S INFLUENCE

Sirrah signifies good relationships with others and popularity. It bestows a harmonious nature and benefits from good social connections. This star can also grant honor and wealth, cheerfulness, optimism, versatility, and sound judgment. It warns, however, against being too outspoken or taking popularity for granted.

Linked to your Sun's degree, this star indicates that usually you can achieve your heart's desire as long as you are clear about your objectives. Sometimes after you obtain what you want, you are at a loss as to what to do next. However, since one of your natural attributes is knowing the right people and being at the right place at the right time, this state does not tend to last long.

• *Positive:* warm heart, joy, popularity, attractive personality

• *Negative:* self-conceit, excess

calm under crisis, you show your true strength and gain the admiration of others, which is excellent for a career in a position of authority. Certainly others will value your ability to take charge and your approach to new and original ideas. If drawn to the theater or film, you can be a good actor, producer, or director, and your strong individuality may express itself in writing, art, or music.

Famous people who share your birthday include director Francis Ford Coppola, musician Ravi Shankar, politician Jerry Brown, poet William Wordsworth, actor James Garner, singer Billie Holiday, and martial artist Jackie Chan.

Numerology

Analytical and thoughtful, individuals with a number 7 birthdate are frequently critical and self-absorbed. With a constant need for greater self-awareness, you enjoy gathering information and may be interested in reading, writing, or spirituality. Although shrewd, you may be inclined to be skeptical or to overrationalize issues and become lost in details. A tendency to be spiritual or mystical and aloof suggests that at times you feel misunderstood or out of place. The subinfluence of the number 4 month indicates that you are practical yet highly intuitive and receptive. Because you are a sensitive individual with intense, deep feelings, learn to relax by being cheerful, and avoid overtaxing your mind under stressful situations. A tendency to be enigmatic or secretive usually leads you to develop the art of asking subtle questions, without letting anyone know what you really think.

• *Positive:* education, trust, meticulousness, idealism, honesty, psychic ability, scientific ability, rationality, reflection

• *Negative:* unfriendliness, loner tendency, secretiveness, skepticism, confusion, deceit, detachment, coldness

Love & Relationships

When it comes to love, you are liable to be either highly expressive and spontaneous or withdrawn and emotionally inhibited. As you learn to balance these extremes, you accept people as they are rather than expect them to live up to your high ideals. By channeling this idealism into creative expression, humanitarian endeavors, or spiritual awareness, you become less serious about your personal life. Since you have a wonderful charm that can attract friends and admirers, you are sure to have an active social life. There may, however, be a possible conflict between your own personal desires and your work or duties. You need deep intimacy but may have to guard against becoming too preoccupied with self-interest, which can separate you from others. You are more suited to someone who is as friendly and hardworking as you are.

YOUR SPECIAL SOMEONE

You might find love and a faithful partner among those born on one of the following dates.

Love & friendship: Jan. 11, 20, 21, 25, 27, 29, Feb. 9, 18, 23, 25, 27, Mar. 7, 16, 21, 23, 25, Apr. 5, 14, 19, 21, 23, May 3, 12, 17, 19, 21, June 1, 10, 15, 17, 19, July 8, 13, 15, 17, Aug. 6, 11, 13, 15, Sept. 4, 9, 11, 13, Oct. 2, 7, 9, 11, Nov. 5, 7, 9, Dec. 3, 5, 7

Beneficial: Jan. 9, 26, Feb. 7, 24, Mar. 5, 22, Apr. 3, 20, May 1, 18, 29, June 16, 27, July 14, 25, 29, 30, Aug. 12, 23, 27, 28, 31, Sept. 10, 21, 25, 26, 29, Oct. 8, 19, 23, 24, 27, Nov. 6, 17, 21, 22, 25, Dec. 4, 15, 19, 20, 23

Fatal attractions: Jan. 16, Feb. 14, Mar. 12, Apr. 10, May 8, June 6, July 4, Aug. 2, Oct. 8, 10, 11, 12

Challenging: Jan. 8, 29, 31, Feb. 6, 27, 29, Mar. 4, 25, 27, 28, Apr. 2, 23, 25, 26, May 21, 23, 24, June 19, 21, 22, July 17, 19, 20, Aug. 15, 17, 18, Sept. 13, 15, 16, Oct. 11, 13, 14, 30, Nov. 9, 11, 12, 28, Dec. 7, 9, 10, 26

Soul mates: Feb. 11, May 5, 30, June 28, July 26, Aug. 24, Sept. 22, 30, Oct. 20, 28, Nov. 18, 26, Dec. 16, 24

April 8

SUN: ARIES

DECANATE: LEO/SUN

DEGREE: 17°30'–18°30' ARIES

MODE: CARDINAL

ELEMENT: FIRE

FIXED STARS

Although your Sun's degree is not linked to a fixed star, some of your other planets' degrees certainly will be. By having an astrological chart calculated, you can find the exact position of the planets on your date of birth. This will tell you which of the fixed stars listed in this book are relevant to you.

As an Arian, you are independent and daring, with a need to express yourself in different and original ways. Receptive to new ideas, you are always keen to experience new things. The desire to accomplish much and gain power is often associated with those born on this date. With your forceful personality and pragmatic approach, you usually aim toward a position of authority. The subinfluence of the Sun bestows inexhaustible energy that when added to your natural business sense helps you to take the initiative and make sure your plans have a successful outcome.

In your attempt to reach the top, you are often responsible and hardworking. Although establishing a secure future is especially important to you, from time to time you can make a dramatic move based on a spontaneous decision. You may, however, need to develop self-discipline and overcome a tendency to spring into action without proper planning. You may also have to guard against getting too easily bored or discouraged. Luck, on the other hand, can come out of the blue and take you by surprise. Although you appear to be a traditionalist, you are actually quite progressive, but you need to go through a transformation of values in order to reach true spiritual awareness.

After the age of twelve, when your progressed Sun moves into Taurus, there is an emphasis in your life on material success, stability, and security. This more practical accent continues until around the age of forty-two, when your progressed Sun enters Gemini. This is a turning point for you, when the pace of your life increases, emphasizing the growing importance of new interests, writing, and communication. After the age of seventy-two, when your progressed Sun moves into Cancer, you place a higher priority on your own emotional needs as well as caring for others, home, and family.

Your Secret Self

Your intellectual brightness may lead you to explore many avenues of expression, but this can also be a problem if you attempt to deal with too many projects at one time. More complex than you seem on the outside, you can be subtle, artistic, and extremely clever. Unfortunately, you also may be liable to a quick temper or impatience, but you may conceal this for your own purposes.

Highly creative, you possess a driving force that spurs you on to constantly seek new achievements. Naturally dramatic, but disliking to take orders from others, you may find it hard to accept criticism. You have a wonderful ability with people and are excellent at making contacts, but can alternate between being warm and responsive and being cold and indifferent. Beneath your external self-confidence you are prone to doubts and fears of inadequacy, so it is important to have an emotional support system of warm and loving friends or family.

Work & Vocation

You are hardworking, and your desire for power motivates you to seek leadership positions. Being a natural psychologist, you may be attracted toward counseling or healing in some form, or alternatively may use this gift in the business world, particularly in areas such as personnel and advertising. Being a skilled organizer and not being afraid to think big will aid you in whatever career you choose. Many people of your birthdate are drawn to occupations linked to justice or law and order, or to leadership positions in business management as well as finance and banking. Alternatively, your sharp and clever mind and sense of the dramatic may also draw you to some form of expression through art, drama, or music.

Famous people who share your birthday include singers Carmen McRae and Julian Lennon, Ford Clinic founder Betty Ford, and actress Mary Pickford.

Numerology

The power suggested by the number 8 birthday shows a character with strong values and sound judgment. The number 8 indicates that you aspire to great accomplishment and possess an ambitious nature. Desire for dominance, security, and material success are also indicated by this birthday. As a number 8 person, you have a natural business sense and will benefit greatly from developing organizational and executive skills. A strong need to feel secure or established urges you to make long-term plans and investments. The subinfluence of the number 4 month indicates that you are cautious and pragmatic, with a willingness to take on responsibilities. You can be helpful, friendly, and versatile, with an entertaining and quick wit. Although you can be imaginative and talented, you may have to overcome a tendency to be easily bored. If you are willing to make the effort, you are often given great responsibility. Nevertheless, you may have to learn how to administer or delegate your authority in a fair and just way. Take care you do not overtax yourself through hard work.

• *Positive:* leadership, thoroughness, hard work, tradition, authority, protection, power to heal, good judge of values

• *Negative:* impatience, intolerance, miserliness, restlessness, hunger for power, domineering or controlling behavior, tendency to be easily discouraged, lack of planning

Love & Relationships

In love and friendship you are drawn toward people who are friendly, sociable, and interested in self-improvement. As you are usually optimistic and direct, you expect this level of honesty from others, although at times this may be rather naive. Aware that money is power, you may be particularly attracted to people with the potential for success. Your love of knowledge suggests that you enjoy the company of those who are mentally stimulating or groups where you can learn new information or skills. Since you are also proud, you require respect from others and may have to avoid power games or becoming too controlling and critical with your loved ones. Fortunately, your charm and people skills ensure that you are never without friends.

YOUR SPECIAL SOMEONE

For love and intellectual stimulation, you might want to begin looking among those born on one of the following dates.

Love & friendship: Jan. 3, 4, 11, 12, 26, 28, 30, Feb. 2, 9, 10, 24, 26, 28, Mar. 7, 8, 22, 24, 26, Apr. 5, 6, 20, 22, 24, 30, May 3, 4, 18, 20, 22, 28, 31, June 1, 2, 16, 18, 20, 26, 29, July 14, 16, 18, 24, 27, Aug. 6, 12, 14, 16, 22, 25, Sept. 10, 12, 14, 20, 23, Oct. 8, 10, 12, 18, 21, Nov. 6, 8, 10, 16, 19, Dec. 4, 6, 8, 14, 17

Beneficial: Jan. 10, 29, Feb. 1, 8, 27, Mar. 6, 25, Apr. 4, 23, May 2, 21, June 4, 19, July 17, 30, Aug. 15, 28, Sept. 13, 26, Oct. 11, 24, Nov. 9, 22, Dec. 7, 20

Fatal attractions: Jan. 11, Mar. 7, Apr. 5, May 3, June 1, Oct. 11, 12, 13

Challenging: Jan. 9, Feb. 7, Mar. 5, 28, Apr. 3, 26, May 1, 24, June 22, July 20, Aug 18, Sept. 16, Oct. 14, 30, 31, Nov. 12, 28, 29, Dec. 10, 26, 27

Soul mates: Jan. 7, Feb. 5, Mar. 3, Apr. 1, May 29, June 27, July 25, Aug. 23, Sept. 21, Oct. 19, Nov. 17, Dec. 15

April 9

FIXED STARS

Although your Sun's degree is not linked to a fixed star, some of your other planets' degrees certainly will be. By having an astrological chart calculated, you can find the exact position of the planets on your date of birth. This will tell you which of the fixed stars listed in this book are relevant to you.

Creativity, enterprise, inner strength, and a proud personality are some of the attributes associated with those born on this date. Although receptive, sensitive, and intuitive, you possess a dynamic personality and leadership abilities. You prefer to be part of an association where you can play an important role.

An Arian with a sense of the dramatic, you are also diligent, dependable, and determined, and you take pride in your work. This suggests that a need for security may often override other factors. Generous and philanthropic, with a good judgment of values, is how others often see you. Nevertheless, a preoccupation with material concerns can be a source of worry. Learning how to budget may be one of your challenges.

Because of your strong character, you do not like to be in a subservient position, and although you have charm and a charismatic personality, you may have to guard against being too outspoken or verbally cutting. Your mental curiosity and depth of thought often indicate an inclination toward scientific studies and confirm an ability to come straight to the point of a matter or be exact and precise. Industrious and methodical, you can also organize, define, and clearly explain your ideas or solve problems at a glance.

When you are around age eleven, your progressed Sun moves into Taurus, commencing a thirty-year period of increased emphasis on material stability, status, and financial security. Another turning point occurs around the age of forty-one, when your progressed Sun moves into Gemini, stimulating you to widen your interests and placing more emphasis on knowledge, communication, and study. From the age of seventy-one, when your progressed Sun moves forward into Cancer, you will find a greater awareness of your emotional needs as well as an accent on your family and home.

Your Secret Self

Indecision or worry about material things could block the wonderful creativity at the very core of your being. A challenge to develop this side of you at all costs may mean sacrificing some of those extra material extravagances. However, this sacrifice is likely to prove a key to freeing you from life's burdens and frustrations and opening you to more humanitarian pursuits.

When operating with detachment, you have a lightness about you and are a very good judge of character. This enables you to be very sociable and public-spirited, and you often combine the two by doing something of use for others in a group situation. You can also be very creative and a master of your craft; but beware of holding on to situations past their usefulness. Most of the time, however, you are charitable and generous with your time and energy, often being willing to put in more than your fair share if you really believe in a person or project.

Work & Vocation

You possess energy and enthusiasm and are not afraid to advance into uncharted waters. With your pioneering spirit, courage, and leadership skills, you have a wide variety of choices in your career. Usually you excel in business and like to run your own show. Alternatively, your ability to push through some kind of reform may attract you to leadership in such organizations as trade unions. Those who are not freedom fighters may be interested in education or some other form of public or social interest. Many philanthropists, impresarios, artists, painters, and musicians share your birthdate, along with art dealers and curators. You are likely to shine in positions of authority and can be fair and just; this makes you an excellent manager or administrator.

Famous people who share your birthday are publisher Hugh Hefner, French poet Charles Baudelaire, actor/singer Paul Robeson, and actor Dennis Quaid.

Numerology

Benevolence, thoughtfulness, and sentimental sensitivity are all associated with the number 9 birthday. Tolerant and kind, you are often generous and liberal. Intuitive and psychic abilities point to a universal receptivity and, if channeled positively, may inspire you to seek a spiritual path. This birthday may suggest a need to overcome challenges and a tendency to be overly sensitive, with emotional ups and downs. You benefit greatly from world travel and interaction with people from all walks of life, but may have to avoid unrealistic dreams or an inclination toward escapism. The subinfluence of the number 4 month indicates that you are practical, with good organizational skills. If restricted by limiting circumstances, you are inclined to rebel or become temperamental. You may need to be more flexible and less proud. Adapt to new situations and learn to let go of the past.

• *Positive:* idealism, humanitarianism, creativity, sensitivity, generosity, magnetism, poetic nature, charity, giving nature, detachment, luck, popularity

• *Negative:* frustration, nervousness, uncertainty, selfishness, impracticality, bitterness, unethical behavior, tendency to be easily led, inferiority complex, fear, worry, isolation

Love & Relationships

An amiable nature and a desire for self-expression guarantee you friends and an active social scene. Your original approach to life may draw you toward people who will stimulate your natural creativity. Although you can be very loving, uncertainty or indecisiveness concerning relationships can at times become a source of worry or disappointment. This is not likely to stop you in your quest for the perfect relationship, however, and you are often willing to make sacrifices for those you love. By keeping yourself creative and not dwelling on problems, you will find that you can handle relationship situations in a strong and positive manner.

YOUR SPECIAL SOMEONE

You may find a partner who will understand your need for love among those born on one of the following dates.

Love & friendship: Jan. 13, 14, 21, 29, Feb. 11, 27, 29, Mar. 9, 25, 27, Apr. 7, 23, 25, May 5, 21, 23, 29, June 3, 19, 21, 27, 30, July 1, 17, 19, 25, 28, Aug. 15, 17, 23, 26, Sept. 13, 15, 21, 24, Oct. 11, 13, 19, 22, 29, Nov. 9, 11, 17, 20, 27, Dec. 7, 9, 15, 18, 25

Beneficial: Jan. 11, Feb. 9, Mar. 7, 31, Apr. 5, 29, May 3, 27, 31, June 1, 25, 29, July 23, 27, 31, Aug. 21, 25, 29, 30, Sept. 19, 23, 27, 28, Oct. 17, 21, 25, 26, Nov. 15, 19, 23, 24, 30, Dec. 13, 17, 21, 22, 28

Fatal attractions: Jan. 12, Feb. 10, Mar. 8, Apr. 6, May 4, June 2, Oct. 11, 12, 13, 14

Challenging: Jan. 10, Feb. 8, Mar. 6, 29, Apr. 4, 27, May 2, 25, June 23, July 21, Aug. 19, Sept. 17, Oct. 15, 31, Nov. 13, 29, 30, Dec. 11, 27, 28

Soul mates: Jan. 18, 24, Feb. 16, 22, Mar. 14, 20, Apr. 12, 18, May 10, 16, June 8, 14, July 6, 12, Aug. 1, 4, 10, Sept. 2, 8, Oct. 6, Nov. 4, Dec. 2

April 10

SUN: ARIES

DECANATE: SAGITTARIUS/JUPITER

DEGREE: 19°30'–20°30' ARIES

MODE: CARDINAL

ELEMENT: FIRE

♈ A blend of ambition, drive, and youthful personality are often indicated by this birthdate. You can be high-spirited, charming, and entertaining, with a warm heart, yet your desire for success springs from a strange mixture of materialism and idealism. As an Arian, you are often restless and adventurous. Usually you want life to be exciting and glamorous, and with your enthusiasm and personal magnetism, you often attract many friends and admirers. In your pursuit of achievement, however, you may act impulsively and must guard against tendencies to be inconsistent or irresponsible.

Although you are often mentally sharp, with original forms of artistic or creative expression, you are apt to scatter your energies unless you can find a true direction in life. Nevertheless, before you settle on one particular course of action you will have to overcome the tendency to get sidetracked by other people's ideas.

Although determined, witty, and entertaining, with a sharp mind, you may also show a childlike quality or a reluctance to grow up. Learning to take responsibility may help bring stability into your life, and by adopting a more mature perspective, you can enhance your chances for success.

From the age of ten, when your progressed Sun moves into Taurus, there is an increased need for security. You become particularly aware of affection from others and have a heightened awareness of practical considerations. This continues until around the age of forty, when your progressed Sun enters Gemini. As a turning point, this highlights the growing importance of new interests and communication, and you may possibly learn new skills. From the age of seventy, when your progressed Sun enters Cancer, your sensitivity increases, with home and family playing a more important part in your life.

Your Secret Self

With your bright, personable, expressive qualities, you have many friends, interests, and opportunities. There may be a pull, however, between what really inspires you and what will make money. Since these diverse interests may take you in many directions, it is especially important to have a sense of purpose and not to become too indecisive regarding your life choices.

Although you can be very independent, there is also an accent on relationships. This need for intimate relations points to a positive emphasis on working partnerships in particular, whether personal or professional. When you are off balance you are in danger of becoming anxious, so it is better to turn your wonderful intuitive abilities to work for you. This means allowing them to guide you toward what keeps you truly happy on the inside. As well as being intuitive and creative and having excellent ideas, you also have a natural enthusiasm that will stay with you till the end of your life.

Work & Vocation

Your leadership qualities, organizational skills, and personal charisma indicate a potential to reach the top in your chosen field. The possibility of success is particularly likely in sales, ne-

FIXED STAR

Star's name: Baten Kaitos, also called Cetus or Zeta Ceti

Degree position: 20°57'–21°49' Aries between the years 1930 and 2000

Magnitude: 3.5–4

Strength: ★★★★

Orb: 1°30'

Constellation: Zeta Ceti

Applicable days: April 10, 11, 12, 13

Star qualities: Saturn

Description: a topaz-yellow star located in the body of the Whale

PRIMARY STAR'S INFLUENCE

Baten Kaitos imparts cautiousness, a serious outlook, and sincerity. It also implies responsibility, a straightforward approach, and an ability to overcome great challenges. Often it indicates a preference for working in solitude and a tendency to be impatient if restricted.

Linked to your Sun's degree, this star indicates that you may need to learn how to adjust to changed circumstances, as there is a likelihood of alteration in fortunes and lifestyle. Just when you think that the dust has settled, upheaval occurs. There are, however, also good opportunities for travel or changes of residence due to work.

• *Positive:* thoughtfulness, modesty, dedication, diligence, endurance

• *Negative:* melancholy, selfishness, instability

gotiation, promotion, publishing, advertising, law, or banking. Your ambition is likely to attract you to executive and managerial roles, or it may stimulate you to work for yourself. Whatever field you choose, your people skills are likely to play a large part in your success and give you a competitive edge. Your need for self-expression and a love for the dramatic can also entice you into the art or entertainment world.

Famous people who share your birthday include journalist Joseph Pulitzer, homeopathy founder Samuel Hahnemann, and actors Omar Sharif and Steven Seagal.

Numerology

Like those with a number 1 birthday, you usually strive toward great endeavors, and you are likely to accomplish and achieve. Nevertheless, in order to achieve your goals, you need to develop patience and determination. Energetic and original, you stand by your own beliefs even when they differ from others'. Your ability to be a self-starter with a pioneering spirit encourages you to travel far afield or strike out on your own. You may also learn that the world does not revolve around you, and you should guard against selfishness and being dictatorial. Success and accomplishment are important to you, and you frequently want to reach the top of your profession. The subinfluence of the number 4 month indicates that you are restless and enterprising. Do not give up too easily, but take your responsibilities seriously. Find stability in the midst of change and avoid getting stuck in a monotonous routine.

• *Positive:* leadership, creativity, progressive nature, forcefulness, optimism, strong convictions, competitiveness, independence, gregariousness

• *Negative:* overbearing nature, jealousy, loner tendency, egotism, pride, antagonism, lack of restraint, selfishness, instability, impatience

Love & Relationships

Youthful, lively, and naturally charismatic, you have no problem in attracting friends and admirers. Being enthusiastic and entertaining, you are fun and delightful company at any social event. Adventurous and daring, you are likely to have an active social life. Nevertheless, it may be necessary for you to take your time in choosing your relationships carefully; otherwise you may suffer from rash decisions you may regret later. Usually people with this birthday make good marriages and can benefit from close partnerships.

YOUR SPECIAL SOMEONE

You might find long-lasting relationships and stability with someone born on one of the following dates.

Love & friendship: Jan. 6, 8, 14, 15, 23, 26, 28, Feb. 4, 10, 12, 13, 21, 24, 26, Mar. 2, 10, 12, 19, 22, 24, Apr. 8, 14, 17, 20, 22, May 6, 15, 16, 18, 20, June 4, 13, 16, 18, July 2, 11, 14, 16, 20, Aug. 1, 9, 12, 14, 22, Sept. 7, 10, 12, 24, Oct. 5, 8, 10, 26, Nov. 3, 6, 8, 28, Dec. 1, 4, 6, 30

Beneficial: Jan. 9, 12, Feb. 7, 10, Mar. 5, 8, Apr. 3, 6, May 1, 4, June 2, 30, July 28, Aug. 26, 30, 31, Sept. 24, 28, 29, Oct. 22, 26, 27, Nov. 20, 24, 25, Dec. 18, 22, 23, 29

Fatal attractions: Oct. 12, 13, 14, 15

Challenging: Jan. 11, 13, 29, Feb. 9, 11, Mar. 7, 9, 30, Apr. 5, 7, 28, May 3, 5, 26, 31, June 1, 3, 24, 29, July 1, 22, 27, Aug. 20, 25, Sept. 18, 23, 30, Oct. 16, 21, 28, Nov. 14, 19, 26, Dec. 12, 17, 24

Soul mates: Jan. 12, 29, Feb. 10, 27, Mar. 8, 25, Apr. 6, 23, May 4, 21, June 2, 19, July 17, Aug. 2, 15, Sept. 13, Oct. 11, Nov. 9, Dec. 7

SUN: ARIES

DECANATE: SAGITTARIUS/JUPITER

DEGREE: 20°30'–21°30' ARIES

MODE: CARDINAL

ELEMENT: FIRE

Inspired and success-oriented, you were born on a lucky day, one that promises wealth and achievement. However, in order to receive some of the rewards promised by this birthdate, you will have to master self-discipline and work hard. As an Arian, you are determined and ambitious, with intuition and a good sense of values. Your ruling planet, Mars, endows you with courage, dynamic drive, and an adventurous nature. Others often recognize your leadership abilities as well as your natural potential to materialize ideas and projects.

The subinfluence of your decanate ruler, Sagittarius, often suggests that you are lucky and optimistic and can recognize opportunities well in advance. You may, however, need to avoid taking unnecessary chances or rushing into speculative ventures without thinking.

Material wealth and acquisitions are important to you, and at times you can maintain an extravagant lifestyle. You may, however, need to guard against a tendency to be overly concerned with materialism or to be too ruthless in your attempt to find financial security. If, on the other hand, you become restless, you can create instability by moving from one objective to the next and scattering your energy through lack of purpose.

From the age of nine, when your progressed Sun moves into Taurus, there is an increased desire for material stability and financial security. In the following thirty years, you feel the need to build a strong foundation to what you want to achieve and have a practical approach to life's challenges. There is another shift of emphasis in your life around the end of your thirties, when your progressed Sun enters Gemini. At this point you may recognize a growing interest in relations with others around you as well as realize the importance of communication. After the age of sixty-nine, when your progressed Sun moves into Cancer, you place more emphasis in your life on emotional issues as well as your home and family.

FIXED STAR

Star's name: Baten Kaitos, also called Cetus or Zeta Ceti

Degree position: 20°57'–21°49' Aries between the years 1930 and 2000

Magnitude: 3.5–4

Strength: ★★★★★

Orb: 1°30'

Constellation: Zeta Ceti

Applicable days: April 10, 11, 12, 13

Star qualities: Saturn

Description: a topaz-yellow star located in the body of the Whale

Your Secret Self

You learn very quickly that money is power, and you can be very business-minded. You like to keep yourself busy, and your life is likely to be full all the time. Since you also have excellent organizational potential, you are likely to have recruited others into your plans and schemes by projecting large amounts of positive energy to get them excited. You may have to be careful, though, that keeping yourself busy is not an excuse not to stop and examine the more personal areas of your life.

An inner nobility and a dramatic sense suggest that you should not overload yourself with drudgery but be in some position of power. You have a knack for being a natural liaison or link-up person between people from a variety of groups. People see you as being very confident and rather formidable in your ability to achieve results. You may have to guard against an inadvertent tendency to be selfish. This is not deliberate; it is just that you are so energetically wrapped up in your own projects that you may miss some of the more subtle emotional energy that is happening around you. This is more than compensated for, however, by your exceptional generosity and goodwill.

PRIMARY STAR'S INFLUENCE

Baten Kaitos imparts cautiousness, a serious outlook, and sincerity. It also implies responsibility, a straightforward approach, and an ability to overcome great challenges. Often it indicates a preference for working in solitude and a tendency to be impatient if restricted.

Linked to your Sun's degree, this star indicates that you may need to learn how to adjust to changed circumstances, as there is a likelihood of alteration in fortunes and lifestyle. Just when you think that the dust has settled, upheaval occurs. There are, however, also good opportunities for travel or changes of residence due to work.

• Positive: thoughtfulness, modesty, dedication, diligence, endurance

• Negative: melancholy, selfishness, instability

Work & Vocation

A dislike of taking orders will demand that you become good at delegating, so you are likely to rise to a position of authority. Your natural business acumen and ability to turn on the charm when necessary can bring you many financial rewards, particularly in careers such as sales and marketing, the service industries, and restaurant operation. You are likely to prefer and excel in people-oriented careers rather than solitary employment. Your ability to think on a large scale may draw you toward occupations such as manager, entrepreneur, executive, administrator, official, civil servant, judge, banker, or clergy. A more altruistic side to your nature may attract you to teaching or counseling, and there are many philanthropists and patrons to the arts born on your birthday.

Famous people who share your birthday include Ethel Kennedy, designer Oleg Cassini, politician Dean Acheson, and actor Joel Grey.

Numerology

The special vibration of the master number 11 birthday suggests that idealism, inspiration, and innovation are highly important to you. A blend of humility and confidence challenges you to work toward self-mastery both materially and spiritually. Through experience you learn how to deal with both sides of your nature and develop a less extremist attitude by trusting your own feelings. Usually you are highly charged and enjoy vitality, but must avoid becoming overanxious or impractical. The subinfluence of the number 4 month indicates that you are practical and thoughtful, with a caring and understanding nature. When you synthesize your ideas with your practical skills you can create original concepts. Although generous and cooperative, you may at times be impatient and impulsive. Avoid being self-centered or disruptive by taking time to reflect and analyze situations in the privacy of your own space. Have faith, and do not attempt to solve every problem instantaneously.

• *Positive:* balance, focus, objectivity, enthusiasm, inspiration, spirituality, idealism, intuition, intelligence, outgoing nature, inventiveness, artistic ability, service orientation, healing ability, humanitarianism, faith, psychic ability

• *Negative:* superiority complex, dishonesty, aimlessness, tendency to be easily hurt, highstrung nature, selfishness, lack of clarity, dominating behavior

Love & Relationships

Your charismatic appeal is likely to make you popular and provide you with many social and romantic opportunities. You are a loyal friend who is willing to give generously of yourself to those you love. A tendency to become restless or emotionally dissatisfied indicates that you need variety and excitement in your daily life. Since you possess strong and ardent feelings, you may at times be led by your passions. Do not allow these circumstances to jeopardize your long-term interests. It is possible that you may encounter a pull between your strong need for love and affection and your quest for material security. You may prefer to be associated with people who are ambitious and independent and are therefore less likely to be demanding on an emotional, personal level.

YOUR SPECIAL SOMEONE

For love and friendship, you might just find the right person among those born on the following days.

Love & friendship: Jan. 6, 15, 16, 29, 31, Feb. 4, 13, 14, 27, 29, Mar. 2, 11, 25, 27, Apr. 9, 10, 23, 25, May 7, 21, 23, June 5, 19, 21, July 3, 17, 19, 30, Aug. 1, 10, 15, 17, 28, Sept. 13, 15, 26, Oct. 11, 13, 24, Nov. 9, 11, 22, Dec. 7, 9, 20

Beneficial: Jan. 13, 15, 19, Feb. 11, 13, 17, Mar. 9, 11, 15, Apr. 7, 9, 13, May 5, 7, 11, June 3, 5, 9, July 1, 3, 7, 29, Aug. 1, 5, 27, 31, Sept. 3, 25, 29, Oct. 1, 23, 27, Nov. 21, 25, Dec. 19, 23

Fatal attractions: May 30, June 28, July 26, Aug. 24, Sept. 22, Oct. 13, 14, 15, 20, Nov. 18, Dec. 16

Challenging: Jan. 12, Feb. 10, Mar. 8, Apr. 6, May 4, June 2, Aug. 31, Sept. 29, Oct. 27, 29, 30, Nov. 25, 27, 28, Dec. 23, 25, 26, 30

Soul mates: Jan. 2, 28, Feb. 26, Mar. 24, Apr. 22, May 20, June 18, July 16, Aug. 14, Sept. 12, Oct. 10, Nov. 8, Dec. 6

April 12

♈ Your dynamic personality and an ability to be spontaneous suggest that life is full of action. Although idealistic and optimistic, you nevertheless possess a strong sense of material values. As an Arian, you are ambitious and adventurous, yet generous and kind. With the subinfluence of your decanate ruler, Sagittarius, you are likely to travel and may succeed in foreign places. Constant expansion, whether material or mental, is necessary to keep you inspired or interested.

Although you can easily attract money through self-discipline and hard work, your tendency to make magnanimous gestures can leave you short of money. The irony often linked to your date of birth is that at times you can be incredibly fortunate, and at other times your strong intuitive power fails you and luck simply vanishes.

Clever, broad-minded, and objective, you can use your imagination and individuality to turn hopeless situations into great success stories and should never let others undermine your high spirit. Nevertheless, you might benefit from other people's opinions and may need to guard against being a daredevil or a risk taker. By developing self-restraint and cautiously and slowly attaining your objectives, you can fulfill your plans for success.

From around the time when you reach the age of eight, your progressed Sun moves into the sign of Taurus, commencing a thirty-year period of increased emphasis on practicality, material stability, status, and financial security. Another change of emphasis in your life occurs around the age of thirty-eight, when your progressed Sun moves into Gemini, stimulating you to widen your interests and placing more importance on knowledge, study, and communication with those around you. After the age of sixty-eight, when your progressed Sun moves into Cancer, you place a higher priority on your own emotional needs as well as caring for others, home, and family.

FIXED STAR

Star's name: Baten Kaitos, also called Cetus or Zeta Ceti

Degree position: 20°57'–21°49' Aries between the years 1930 and 2000

Magnitude: 3.5–4

Strength: ★★★★★

Orb: 1°30'

Constellation: Zeta Ceti

Applicable days: April 10, 11, 12, 13

Star qualities: Saturn

Description: a topaz-yellow star located in the body of the Whale

PRIMARY STAR'S INFLUENCE

Baten Kaitos imparts cautiousness, a serious outlook, and sincerity. It also implies responsibility, a straightforward approach, and an ability to overcome great challenges. Often it indicates a preference for working in solitude and a tendency to be impatient if restricted.

Linked to your Sun's degree, this star indicates that you may need to learn how to adjust to changed circumstances, as there is a likelihood of alteration in fortunes and lifestyle. Just when you think that the dust has settled, upheaval occurs. There are, however, also good opportunities for travel or changes of residence due to work.

• Positive: thoughtfulness, modesty, dedication, diligence, and endurance

• Negative: melancholy, selfishness, instability

Your Secret Self

You are a good evaluator with an instinct for money. You may find, however, that your own finances may go through some fluctuations before becoming more settled. By learning how to budget or make long-term investments, you can minimize your financial worries.

Since you have a strong character and do not like to be in a subservient position, you may do well in associations where you can play an important role. It is preferable, though, for your work to involve variety so that you can avoid becoming bored and restless. Since you have excellent brainpower, it is best to trust your abilities and go for new success when the odds are in your favor, but guard against taking unnecessary risks. With all that wonderful authority and leadership, just be wary of becoming bossy or dominating. Others can rely on you, however, when you are diligent and dependable, as you take pride in your work and find fulfilment in your responsibilities.

Work & Vocation

Your intellectual brightness and objectivity ensure that with discipline and determination, you can be successful in any career that you choose. With your ability to command, you will want to be given a position of authority or at least have the freedom to work in your own way, such as in teaching, lecturing, or being your own boss. This date can also indicate possible success in show business and the arts. Being clever, liberal, and humanitarian, you may be drawn to professions such as charity work, image making, the healing professions, or science. Because you are a good evaluator, the more pragmatic side of your nature may be drawn to banking, business, and the stock market.

Famous people who share your birthday include TV star David Letterman, jazz pianist Herbie Hancock, actor/singer David Cassidy, Native American leader Dennis Banks, and actress Clare Danes.

Numerology

Usually you are intuitive, helpful, and friendly, and possess good reasoning power. Since you want to establish true individuality, you are often innovative. Naturally understanding and sensitive, you also know how to use tact and cooperative methods to achieve your aims and objectives. When you achieve a balance between your need for self-expression and the natural inclination to be supportive of others, you can find emotional satisfaction and personal fulfillment. You may nevertheless need to find the courage to stand on your own two feet and develop self-confidence or learn not to get easily discouraged by other people. The subinfluence of the number 4 month indicates that you are hardworking and intelligent. Although often generous and friendly, you may need to be patient and persevering or practical. When positive and confident, you use your analytical skills to solve problems in an ingenious way. Write down your thoughts and ideas to clarify your situation and persist in spite of obstacles. Success can be achieved if you become more compliant and responsible.

• *Positive:* creativity, attractiveness, initiative, discipline, promotion of self or others
• *Negative:* reclusiveness, eccentricity, uncooperativeness, tendency to be overly sensitive, lack of self-esteem

Love & Relationships

You can be a witty and entertaining companion, so you should have no trouble attracting friends and admirers. Since you have a quick mind, you need a partner who is clever and mentally stimulating in order to give you intellectual feedback and keep you on your toes. Although usually understanding and good-hearted, you also encounter periods when you may become disappointed or overly serious, which can bring problems into your relationships. However, by using your natural gifts of diplomacy and psychological insight, you are able to heal troublesome situations. You may be happiest when sharing the company of like-minded people with whom you can enjoy some humorous exchange.

YOUR SPECIAL SOMEONE

You might come closer to finding that special person among those born on one of the following days.

Love & friendship: Jan. 6, 16, 25, Feb. 4, 14, Mar. 2, 12, 28, 30, Apr. 10, 26, 28, May 8, 24, 26, 30, June 6, 22, 24, 28, July 4, 20, 22, 26, 31, Aug. 2, 18, 20, 24, 29, Sept. 16, 18, 22, 27, Oct. 14, 16, 20, 25, Nov. 12, 14, 18, 23, Dec. 3, 10, 12, 16, 21

Beneficial: Jan. 9, 14, 16, Feb. 7, 12, 14, Mar. 5, 10, 12, Apr. 3, 8, 10, May 1, 6, 8, June 4, 6, July 2, 4, Aug. 2, Sept. 30, Oct. 28, Nov. 26, 30, Dec. 24, 28, 29

Fatal attractions: Jan. 21, Feb. 19, Mar. 17, Apr. 15, May 13, June 11, July 9, Aug. 7, Sept. 5, Oct. 3, 14, 15, 16, Nov. 1

Challenging: Jan. 4, 13, 28, Feb. 2, 11, 26, Mar. 9, 24, Apr. 7, 22, May 5, 20, June 3, 18, July 1, 16, Aug. 14, Sept. 12, Oct. 10, 31, Nov. 8, 29, Dec. 6, 27

Soul mates: Jan. 15, 22, Feb. 13, 16, 20, Mar. 11, 18, Apr. 9, 16, May 7, 14, June 5, 12, July 3, 10, Aug. 1, 4, 8, Sept. 6, Oct. 4, Nov. 2

April 13

♈ Determination and a good business sense with strong values are often found in those sharing this birthdate. Your ruling planet, Mars, grants you Arian willpower, vitality, and a commanding personality, with organizational and leadership abilities.

The motivating force of your dynamic nature is the need for security and power or a desire for material success and recognition. Education is also vital for your success, either through passing on knowledge to others or by learning how to use information in a practical and productive way.

In your attempt to build a strong foundation, however, you may have to develop self-control and overcome a tendency to be too manipulative or ruthless or to carry materialism to extremes. If, on the other hand, you put all your energies into a worthwhile project, you have the power and the capacity for record achievements.

Growth and strength come from the ability to overcome difficulties. In your climb to the top, however, you may also need to overcome your inclination to be too extravagant, rebellious, or obstinate, squandering your hard-earned cash on superfluous things. Although others can often describe you as a hard worker, guard against a tendency to be too demanding.

From the age of seven, when your progressed Sun moves into Taurus, there is an increasing desire for material stability and financial security. In the following thirty years you will feel the need to build a strong foundation to what you want to achieve in life. After the age of thirty-seven, when your progressed Sun enters Gemini, you may develop a desire to be more knowledgeable and take up new interests. From the age of sixty-seven, when your progressed Sun enters Cancer, your sensitivity increases, with home and family playing a more important part in your life.

FIXED STAR

Star's name: Baten Kaitos, also called Cetus or Zeta Ceti

Degree position: 20°57'–21°49' Aries between the years 1930 and 2000

Magnitude: 3.5–4

Strength: ★★★★★

Orb: 1°30'

Constellation: Zeta Ceti

Applicable days: April 10, 11, 12, 13

Star qualities: Saturn

Description: a topaz-yellow star located in the body of the Whale

PRIMARY STAR'S INFLUENCE

Baten Kaitos imparts cautiousness, a serious outlook, and sincerity. It also implies responsibility, a straightforward approach, and an ability to overcome great challenges. Often it indicates a preference for working in solitude and a tendency to be impatient if restricted.

Linked to your Sun's degree, this star indicates that you may need to learn how to adjust to changed circumstances, as there is a likelihood of alteration in fortunes and lifestyle. Just when you think that the dust has settled, upheaval occurs. There are, however, also good opportunities for travel or changes of residence due to work.

• *Positive:* thoughtfulness, modesty, dedication, diligence, endurance

• *Negative:* melancholy, selfishness, instability

Your Secret Self

Your natural leadership is revealed through your potential for hard work or spiritual inspiration, and in either case the power here is self-mastery. In the event of your losing faith in either yourself or your abilities to achieve, there is a danger of coldness or isolation. Yet if you spontaneously follow your spirit, your enormous power and strength can uplift both yourself and others.

You possess an innate wisdom that is expressed in a very practical, matter-of-fact way. However, there is also a more hidden part of your nature that can manifest itself as a desire for solitude, self-analysis, or some form of education. This is in contrast to an enjoyment of the dramatic, which stimulates you to express yourself in a fast and competitive way, almost daring others to rise to the occasion.

Work & Vocation

A very dynamic, straightforward, and businesslike style may guarantee that you do not waste time but aim straight for your objectives. You enjoy power, structure, and efficiency, so you will excel as an organizer, manager, supervisor, leader, or pioneer of a new enterprise. People of this birthday may be particularly drawn toward business, law, and politics. Since you do not like taking orders and are very independent, you may prefer being your own boss or delegating to others. Communication, however, in all forms is likely to be part of your natural work experience.

Famous people who share your birthday include U.S. president Thomas Jefferson, playwright Samuel Beckett, chess champion Gary Kasparov, singer Al Green, and actor Jonathan Brandis.

Numerology

Emotional sensitivity, enthusiasm, and inspiration are often identified with the number 13 birthday. Numerically, you are associated with ambition and hard work, and can accomplish much through creative self-expression. You may need to cultivate a pragmatic outlook if you want to turn your creative talents into tangible products. Your original and innovative approach inspires new and exciting ideas, which frequently result in work that impresses others. With a number 13 birthday, you are earnest, romantic, charming, and fun-loving, and with dedication can achieve prosperity. The subinfluence of the number 4 month indicates that you possess sound judgment and a strong individual character. Resourceful and industrious, you are active and energetic. Although often a traditionalist with good business skills and a practical sense, you like to adopt a personal philosophy on life and think independently. A desire for material success and power may at times overshadow other aspects of your personality.
- *Positive:* ambition, creativity, love of freedom, self-expression, initiative
- *Negative:* impulsiveness, indecision, bossiness, unemotionalness, rebellion

Love & Relationships

Very sociable, you have a desire to be popular that should widen your circle of friends and acquaintances. This is helped by an innate creativity or need to express yourself and often adds to your gregarious personality. Usually a loyal friend, you make a real effort to help those you love. Although you are confident about what you want financially, you may find it harder to be certain about how you feel or whom you love. A basic insecurity, jealousy, or indecisiveness is likely to plague you in your close relationships until you learn detachment and decide to let nothing stand in the way of your being happy.

YOUR SPECIAL SOMEONE

You might come closer to finding your true match with someone born on one of the following days.

Love & friendship: Jan. 7, 17, 18, 20, Feb. 5, 15, 18, Mar. 3, 13, 16, 29, 31, Apr. 1, 11, 12, 14, 27, 29, May 9, 12, 25, 27, June 7, 8, 10, 23, 25, July 5, 8, 21, 23, Aug. 3, 4, 6, 19, 21, Sept. 1, 4, 17, 19, Oct. 2, 15, 17, Nov. 13, 15, 30, Dec. 11, 13, 28

Beneficial: Jan. 15, 17, 28, Feb. 13, 15, 26, Mar. 11, 13, 24, Apr. 9, 11, 22, May 7, 9, 20, June 5, 7, 18, July 3, 5, 16, Aug. 1, 3, 14, Sept. 1, 12, Oct. 10, 29, Nov. 8, 27, Dec. 6, 25

Fatal attractions: Jan. 5, Feb. 3, Mar. 1, Oct. 16, 17, 18

Challenging: Jan. 4, 5, 14, Feb. 2, 3, 12, Mar. 1, 10, Apr. 8, 30, May 6, 28, June 4, 26, July 2, 24, Aug. 22, Sept.. 20, Oct. 18, Nov. 16, Dec. 14

Soul mates: Jan. 2, Mar. 29, Apr. 27, May 25, June 23, July 21, Aug. 5, 19, Sept. 17, Oct. 15, Nov. 13, Dec. 11

April 14

FIXED STARS

Although your Sun's degree is not linked to a fixed star, some of your other planets' degrees certainly will be. By having an astrological chart calculated, you can find the exact position of the planets on your date of birth. This will tell you which of the fixed stars listed in this book are relevant to you.

Optimistic and idealistic, yet impatient and restless, you are a dynamic Aries with a magnetic personality and an enthusiasm for life. With the subinfluence of your decanate ruler Sagittarius, you are likely to be direct and outspoken, with an ambitious nature. However, you may have to guard against a tendency to be overly enthusiastic or behave in a compulsive manner. Although you are responsible, with a noble character, and believe in fairness and justice, you may be prone to judge yourself and others on the basis of career achievements. Since you need to accomplish much in life, you often forge ahead and take on new challenges in a constant attempt to improve your lot.

The extreme sides of your personality show, on one hand, a humanitarian nature that is compassionate and caring, and on the other, an overly serious or rigid personality, especially where money is concerned. Nevertheless, with your optimistic outlook and a positive frame of mind, you can achieve great success. At times fortune will smile on you, but beware of taking too much for granted and leaving it all to chance.

A tendency to be restless and impatient often suggests that you are likely to overlook small details and be inaccurate. By learning to be thorough and methodical, you will be able to complete your tasks and overcome a tendency to become frustrated by delays and obstacles.

From the age of six, when your progressed Sun moves into Taurus, there is an increasing desire for material security as well as financial stability. In the following thirty years, you will feel the need to be practical and build something solid in terms of achievement. This influence continues until around the age of thirty-six, when your progressed Sun moves into Gemini and you enter a period of new ideas, with a growing need to understand and communicate. From the age of sixty-six, when your progressed Sun enters Cancer, your sensitivity increases, with home and family playing a more important part in your life.

Your Secret Self

The demonstration of affection can be an important issue for you. Like everybody, you need love and approval, but previously these may have been withheld from you if you have not lived up to other people's expectations. You may be tested as to how far you will compromise your own vitality to get the affection and approval you need and deserve. As you learn in life to value yourself and your feelings, you become more detached emotionally without cutting off your love and becoming cold. This results in your being very generous with others as you expose your vulnerability and allow things to happen spontaneously, without always trying to be in control. By letting go and taking life as it comes, you are immediately rewarded and draw toward you everything you need.

Work & Vocation

An ability to turn on the charm and be very sociable can help you succeed in all people-related careers, especially since you are good at combining business and pleasure. Your dramatic sense and need for self-expression may attract you to a profession in art, drama, music, or writing. With your natural leadership ability, you may gravitate toward positions of authority or being self-employed but may have to be careful that a restless or impatient streak does not prevent you from applying the self-discipline necessary to bring out your potential. You are also likely to need the freedom to work in your own way, and with your good business sense and natural enthusiasm, you should particularly enjoy initiating projects.

Famous people who share your birthday include actors Rod Steiger and John Gielgud, writer Erich von Daniken, actress Julie Christie, Indian musician Ali Akbar Khan, and country singer Loretta Lynn.

Numerology

Intellectual potential, pragmatism, and determination are some of the qualities of the number 14 birthday. Although you need stability, the restlessness indicated by the number 14 urges you to forge ahead or take on new challenges in a constant attempt to improve your lot. This innate dissatisfaction may also inspire you to make a great many changes in your life, especially if you are not happy with your working conditions or financial status. With your perceptive mind, you respond quickly to problems and enjoy solving them. The subinfluence of the number 4 month indicates that you are active, inquisitive, and energetic, with practical skills and a resourceful approach. Since you possess executive abilities and can operate independently, you do not like to be restricted or take orders from others. Your sensitivity and intuition often suggest that you need to balance your idealistic nature with your desire for material success.

- *Positive:* decisive action, hard work, luck, creativity, pragmatism, imagination, industry
- *Negative:* excessive caution or impulsiveness, instability, thoughtlessness, stubbornness

Love & Relationships

Relationships can prove to be a source of both delight and discontent, as you may swing from being loving, warm, and spontaneous to being cold and withdrawn. Nevertheless, your natural charm and sociability indicate that you have a large circle of friends with whom you are generous and giving. A love of beauty and art can stimulate you to express your strong feelings, thus keeping you contented and enthusiastic. This will help you sidestep the occasional inhibition of your emotions, which could cause you to become frustrated or disappointed. Avoid martyring yourself for those who do not deserve your loyalty and affection. It is also possible that you may be attracted to a partner who is of a different age group than yourself.

YOUR SPECIAL SOMEONE

For that someone special, you might want to look among those born on one of the following dates.

Love & friendship: Jan. 4, 8, 18, 19, 23, Feb. 2, 6, 16, 17, 21, Mar. 4, 14, 15, 19, 28, 30, Apr. 2, 12, 13, 17, 26, 28, 30, May 10, 11, 15, 24, 26, 28, June 8, 9, 13, 22, 24, 26, July 6, 7, 11, 20, 22, 24, 30, Aug. 4, 5, 9, 18, 20, 22, 28, Sept. 2, 3, 7, 16, 18, 20, 26, Oct. 1, 5, 14, 16, 18, 24, Nov. 3, 12, 14, 16, 22, Dec. 1, 10, 12, 14, 20

Beneficial: Jan. 5, 16, 27, Feb. 3, 14, 25, Mar. 1, 12, 23, Apr. 10, 21, May 8, 19, June 6, 17, July 4, 15, Aug. 2, 13, Sept. 11, Oct. 9, 30, Nov. 7, 28, Dec. 5, 26, 30

Fatal attractions: Jan. 17, Feb. 15, Mar. 13, Apr. 11, May 9, June 7, July 5, Aug. 3, Sept. 1, Oct. 17, 18, 19

Challenging: Jan. 1, 10, 15, Feb. 8, 13, Mar. 6, 11, Apr. 4, 9, May 2, 7, June 5, July 3, 29, Aug. 1, 27, Sept. 25, Oct. 23, Nov. 21, Dec. 19, 29

Soul mates: Aug. 30, Sept. 28, Oct. 26, Nov. 24, Dec. 22

April 15

SUN: ARIES

DECANATE: SAGITTARIUS/JUPITER

DEGREE: 24°30'–25°30' ARIES

MODE: CARDINAL

ELEMENT: FIRE

You are sensitive and charming, yet ambitious and forceful, and your birthdate reveals a mixture of motivation and inertia. As an Aries, you are often challenged by the desire to achieve success and prosperity. Without the right kind of encouragement, however, you may become easily discouraged and get stuck in a rut or drift aimlessly until something or someone sparks your imagination.

The subinfluence of Jupiter bestows opportunities and luck as well as an open and frank personality. Nevertheless, staying positive and being optimistic are prerequisites if you want to achieve success. Only through hard work, perseverance, and determination will you achieve your objectives.

The confident and compassionate side of your nature also indicates that others often turn to you for support and encouragement, and while you can give good advice, you frequently find it hard to practice what you preach. This suggests that you may need to overcome a tendency to be dogmatic and stubborn, as well as overly proud.

Among your many attributes are your organizational skills and an ability to think in broad terms. Happiness and the promise of success are therefore within your grasp, but you might need to put in a great deal of effort to get your heart's desire.

From around the time you reach the age of five, your progressed Sun moves into Taurus, commencing a thirty-year period of increased emphasis on practical considerations and financial security. Around the age of thirty-five, when your progressed Sun moves into Gemini, there is a change of emphasis in your life; you are likely to be stimulated to widen your interests and place more significance on knowledge, communication, and mental exploration. This may entail taking new courses of study or even learning new skills. After sixty-five, when your progressed Sun moves into Cancer, you become more interested in emotional issues and family life.

FIXED STAR

Star's name: Al Perg, also called Kullat Nuti or Piscium

Degree position: 25°50'–26°46' Aries between the years 1930 and 2000

Magnitude: 3.5–4

Strength: ★★★★★

Orb: 1°30'

Constellation: Eta Piscium

Applicable days: April 15, 16, 17, 18

Star qualities: Saturn and Jupiter

Description: a binary star located in the cord near the tail of the Northern Fish

PRIMARY STAR'S INFLUENCE

Al Perg bestows determination to realize one's objectives. Success comes with patience and steadfastness, but not without struggle. Accomplishment and recognition can be achieved through perseverance and dedication. This star also implies that dissatisfaction with oneself as well as with others may cause irritability.

Linked to your Sun's degree, this star denotes achievement, with a slow and steady rise to greater power, and a preference for work in government and political affairs.

• *Positive:* happiness in solitude, sense of duty, straightforwardness, honesty

• *Negative:* inconstancy, discontent, moodiness, emotional tensions, changing objectives

Your Secret Self

On a deep level you are very creative or intuitive. You may have to be careful, however, that these special qualities are not marred by a tendency to become frustrated. Some of these disappointments may arise because you often attract people who lean on you but are unavailable when you need support yourself. Accept inner change in order to affect your outer circumstances.

When positive, you are highly sociable and possess a very warm interest in people. You are likely to have a wide spectrum of friends who see you as being both broad-minded and generous. In order to avoid a tendency to get caught up in other people's dramas, it may be necessary for you to have a strong sense of your own aims and objectives. Even though part of you is quite content to rest in some fairly easy and predictable routine, a powerful desire for the good things in life is likely to encourage you to make more of an effort.

Work & Vocation

Your excellent mind and ability to speak out directly can attract you to careers such as business, sales, being an agent, or promotion. Whatever field you enter, you may feel a need to pioneer or explore and initiate new projects. Being broad-minded and philosophical may also draw you to the clergy, teaching, or law. Since you are good at dealing with people and are excellent at supporting the underdog, you may wish to fight for good causes. An innate love of color, form, and harmony often prompts you to successfully express yourself in the arts, drama, or music.

Famous people who share your birthday include blues singer Bessie Smith, writer Henry James, artist Leonardo da Vinci, and actresses Claudia Cardinale and Emma Thompson.

Numerology

Versatility and enthusiasm are suggested by the number 15 birthday. Usually you are alert, with a charismatic personality. Your greatest assets are your strong instincts and the ability to learn quickly through combining theory and practice. Often you utilize your intuitive powers and are quick at recognizing opportunities when they arise. You usually possess a talent for attracting money or receiving help and support from others. Although you are naturally adventurous, you nevertheless need to find a real base or a home. The subinfluence of the number 4 month indicates that you are resilient and practical. Although being independent and determined allows you the freedom you want, you need to stay constantly positive and focused. By caring for others you show your strength, but avoid being overbearing. Although to others you may appear confident and self-assured, inner tensions and insecurities may cause fluctuating moods. Nevertheless, you are proud and resolute, with a need to know that others care and appreciate your efforts.

• *Positive:* willingness, generosity, responsibility, kindness, cooperation, appreciation, creative ideas

• *Negative:* disruption, restlessness, irresponsibility, self-centeredness, fear of change, loss of faith, worry, indecision, materialism, misuse of power

Love & Relationships

A friendly warmth and self-awareness ensure that you are popular with others. Since success in dealing with people is a foregone conclusion, it may only be necessary to exercise discrimination as to whom you wish to be close to. Others may become dependent upon you, since you possess an ability to make people feel emotionally comforted. It is therefore necessary to make sure that you keep your relationships on an equal footing. Home and family are liable to play a substantial part in your overall life plan, with material security also being an important issue. Having high expectations from relationships, you may find it especially meaningful to know that you are needed and appreciated.

YOUR SPECIAL SOMEONE

You usually give a great deal to those you love and may find more opportunities for it being reciprocated with those born on one of the following dates.

Love & friendship: Jan. 5, 9, 18, 19, Feb. 3, 7, 16, 17, 18, Mar. 1, 5, 14, 15, 31, Apr. 3, 12, 13, 29, May 1, 10, 11, 27, 29, June 8, 9, 25, 27, July 6, 7, 23, 25, 31, Aug. 4, 5, 6, 21, 23, 29, Sept. 2, 3, 19, 21, 27, 30, Oct. 1, 17, 19, 25, 28, Dec. 13, 15, 21, 24

Beneficial: Jan. 1, 6, 17, Feb. 4, 15, Mar. 2, 13, Apr. 11, May 9, June 7, July 5, Aug. 3, Sept. 1, Oct. 31, Nov. 29, Dec. 27

Fatal attractions: Oct. 17, 18, 19, 20

Challenging: Jan. 2, 16, Feb. 14, Mar. 12, Apr. 10, May 8, June 6, July 4, Aug. 2, Dec. 30

Soul mates: Jan. 11, 31, Feb. 9, 29, Mar. 7, 27, Apr. 5, 25, May 3, 23, June 1, 21, July 19, Aug. 17, Sept. 15, Oct. 13, Nov. 11, Dec. 9

April 16

♈ Love of change and an innate restlessness are often indicated by this birthdate. You are gentle yet ambitious, with a strong desire to take your place in the world. Travel often features prominently in your life, especially in connection with a career move or better job prospects. Alternatively, you may simply enjoy an active life full of excitement and variety.

As an Arian, you are self-confident, ambitious, and daring. The subinfluence of your decanate planet, Jupiter, suggests that you are progressive and enjoy being enterprising. This influence can also indicate a desire to be in a position to inspire others. You possess the power to concentrate upon a particular aim and give it your full attention. Your love of freedom and need for self-expression ensure that if despondent, you do not stay down for long. Through perseverance and determination you are able to overcome difficulties and become more self-assured. By maintaining a methodical order and avoiding impulsive actions, you can minimize fluctuations in financial circumstances.

Informative and communicative, you have an alert mind and can use your intuition to make long-term forecasts. If you can manage to save and consider long-term investments, you can profit handsomely, especially in foreign property.

After you reach the age of four, your progressed Sun moves into Taurus, bringing you over the next thirty years an increasing desire for material stability and financial security. During this time there may be a focus on building a strong foundation to what you want to achieve, as well as an emphasis on your physical needs. There is a turning point in your life around the age of thirty-four, when your progressed Sun enters Gemini, stimulating a growing interest in interpersonal relations and communication skills. This is a time when you may wish to take up a new course of study, whether for business or for pleasure. From age sixty-four, when your progressed Sun enters Cancer, your sensitivity increases, with home and family playing a more important part in your life.

Your Secret Self

At a deep level you may at times experience the insecurity that comes from uncertainty about whether you are making the right decisions. However, using the humanitarian side of your nature, which relates to the "big picture," you can put everything in perspective and stop worrying. You may be better off concentrating on all your wonderful ideas, creative projects, and sense of humor.

Fortunately, you are a quick learner and always have an eye for opportunities that can offer a financial reward. However, with your impatience and desire to fulfill your material needs immediately, you may have to guard against an inclination toward bouts of extravagance or self-indulgence. If you channel your restlessness into something that really interests you, then you are able to become inspired enough to work extremely hard and accept the responsibilities that bring you solid rewards.

Work & Vocation

With your ambition, need for variety, and leadership skills, you are better in a position of authority in a career that does not involve routine. Ideally you need to use both your practical

FIXED STARS

Al Perg, also called Kullat Nuti or Piscium; Vertex, also called Great Nebuli

PRIMARY STAR

Star's name: Al Perg, also called Kullat Nuti or Piscium

Degree position: 25°50'–26°46' Aries between the years 1930 and 2000

Magnitude: 3.5–4

Strength: ★★★★★

Orb: 1°30'

Constellation: Eta Piscium

Applicable days: April 15, 16, 17, 18

Star qualities: Saturn and Jupiter

Description: a binary star located in the cord near the tail of the Northern Fish

PRIMARY STAR'S INFLUENCE

Al Perg bestows determination to realize one's objectives. Success comes with patience and steadfastness, but not without struggle. Accomplishment and recognition can be achieved through perseverance and dedication. This star also implies that dissatisfaction with oneself as well as with others may cause irritability.

Linked to your Sun's degree, this star denotes achievement, with a slow and steady rise to greater power, and a preference for work in government and political affairs.

• *Positive:* happiness in solitude, sense of duty, straightforwardness, honesty

sense and imagination, for example as an actor, writer, photographer, or architect. You may be interested in joining international corporations or the media world. Alternatively, you may get involved with charitable organizations and work for worthwhile causes. Courageously exploring new areas within your work can stimulate and excite you to achieve. You are not likely to stick with any career if you do not reap financial rewards fairly quickly, and you may be particularly attracted to work that involves travel. Alternatively, your desire for action may take you into the area of sports.

You share your birthday with comics Spike Milligan and Charlie Chaplin, musician Henry Mancini, writer Kingsley Amis, actor Peter Ustinov, and basketball player Kareem Abdul-Jabbar.

Numerology

A number 16 birthday suggests that you are thoughtful, sensitive, and friendly. Although analytical, you often judge life and people according to how you feel. As a number 16 personality, however, you can experience inner tensions when facing friction between a need for self-expression and responsibility to others. You may be interested in world affairs and politics. The creative ones among you have a talent for writing with sudden flashes of inspiration. You may need to learn how to balance overconfidence with doubt and insecurity. The subinfluence of the number 4 month indicates that you are practical and hardworking. Socially outgoing and group-oriented, you are sensitive to the feelings of others and can be helpful and friendly. Although you are receptive and value the opinions of others, avoid becoming easily discouraged by the criticism of those you care for. Do not be afraid of change, and learn to be flexible.

• *Positive:* higher education, responsibilities to home and family, integrity, intuition, sociability, cooperation, insight

• *Negative:* worry, inability to be satisfied, irresponsibility, opinionated nature, skepticism, fussiness, irritability, selfishness, lack of sympathy

Love & Relationships

Your quick and observant grasp of people ensures that in sociable situations you can be a lively and amusing companion. Friendships are important to you, and you like to mix with people who can inspire you as well as help you have a good time. Full of ideas and conscious of the image you want to create, you care about the opinion of others. Usually you are willing to work hard to keep the peace in your relationships, but be careful of impatience or occasional argumentative moods that may interfere with your associations. Ideally in relationships you need someone who has a fine mind and with whom you can share your interests. Since you also possess a very youthful and playful side to your personality, it may be necessary to learn about responsibility.

YOUR SPECIAL SOMEONE

You might find greater stability in love and friendship with someone born on one of the following days.

Love & friendship: Jan. 6, 10, 20, 29, Feb. 4, 8, 18, 27, Mar. 2, 6, 16, 25, 28, 30, Apr. 4, 14, 23, 26, 28, 30, May 2, 12, 21, 24, 26, 28, 30, June 10, 19, 22, 24, 26, 28, July 8, 17, 20, 22, 24, 26, Aug. 6, 7, 15, 18, 20, 22, 24, Sept. 4, 13, 16, 18, 20, 22, Oct. 2, 11, 14, 16, 18, 20, Nov. 9, 12, 14, 16, 18, Dec. 7, 10, 12, 14, 16

Beneficial: Jan. 7, 13, 18, 28, Feb. 5, 11, 16, 26, Mar. 3, 9, 14, 24, Apr. 1, 7, 12, 22, May 5, 10, 20, June 3, 8, 18, July 1, 6, 16, Aug. 4, 14, Sept. 2, 12, 30, Oct. 10, 28, Nov. 8, 26, 30, Dec. 6, 24, 28

Fatal attractions: Jan 25, Feb. 23, Mar. 21, Apr. 19, May 17, June 15, July 13, Aug. 11, Sept. 9, Oct. 7, 19, 20, 21, Nov. 5, Dec. 3

Challenging: Jan. 3, 17, Feb. 1, 15, Mar. 13, Apr. 11, May 9, 30, June 7, 28, July 5, 26, 29, Aug. 3, 24, 27, Sept. 1, 22, 25, Oct. 20, 23, Nov. 18, 21, Dec. 16, 19

Soul mates: Jan. 18, Feb. 16, Mar. 14, Apr. 12, May 10, 29, June 8, 27, July 6, 25, Aug. 4, 23, Sept. 2, 21, Oct. 19, Nov. 17, Dec. 15

April 17

♈ Practical and visionary, with an ambitious nature, you are often positive and ready for action. As an Aries, you have the impetus to get up and go, yet in your quest for success you may at times have to overcome a tendency to be restless and change your direction. The subinfluence of Sagittarius, your decanate ruler, suggests that with foresight you can make fortunate decisions. This provides you with natural luck and protects you financially. However, in order to truly profit from this celestial benefactor, you have to put a strong emphasis on values and hard work and develop a responsible attitude. You possess the capacity to cope with challenging situations and solve problems through quick realizations. Although you can overcome obstacles with your determination and vitality, when you complete your tasks you need to stop for a well-earned rest.

Practical skills, strong intuition, and an ability to concentrate on the job at hand are just some of your many talents. The pride you take in your work can also carry the sign of the perfectionist. However, this sense of duty and self-control must not turn you into an individual who is overly concerned with economy. Your efficient and down-to-earth approach often suggests that you are outspoken and direct, but you may have to guard against a tendency to be abrupt as well as stubborn.

Your progressed Sun moves into Taurus where you are age three, commencing a thirty-year period of increased emphasis on security. A turning point occurs around the age of thirty-three, when your progressed Sun moves into Gemini, stimulating you to widen your interests and place more emphasis on knowledge, communication, and study. From your early sixties, when your progressed Sun moves forward into Cancer, you will find a greater awareness of your emotional needs as well as an accent on your family and home.

Your Secret Self

Paradoxically, one part of your personality wants life to be stable, secure, and predictable, while another part of you seeks activity and variety to guard against boredom. Be careful of falling into a rut if your situation becomes congenial and fairly smooth-running, as your opportunities are often away from your usual routine of home and work. If this quest for excitement or new experiences is repressed, you may feel restless and impatient without quite knowing why. This can lead to escapism in order to compensate.

Because you are an active person, you may feel that experience is a better teacher than theory is. You also possess an emotional sensitivity and subtle, intuitive insight that can positively guide you. Rather than rush in different directions, listen to this inner perception, and your life might run more smoothly.

Work & Vocation

Your birthday shows excellent opportunities for commerce and enterprise. With an innate practicality, you like to create method and order, so having a plan for your big visions is vital. In business you are ideally suited for dealing with other people's money, imports and exports, banking, and law; transacting business abroad; and initiating large projects. You are also likely

---

FIXED STARS

Al Perg, also called Kullat Nuti or Piscium; Vertex, also called Great Nebuli

PRIMARY STAR

Star's name: Al Perg, also called Kullat Nuti or Piscium

Degree position: 25°50'–26°46' Aries between the years 1930 and 2000

Magnitude: 3.5–4

Strength: ★★★★★

Orb: 1°30'

Constellation: Eta Piscium

Applicable days: April 15, 16, 17, 18

Star qualities: Saturn and Jupiter

Description: a binary star located in the cord near the tail of the Northern Fish

PRIMARY STAR'S INFLUENCE

Al Perg bestows determination to realize one's objectives. Success comes with patience and steadfastness, but not without struggle. Accomplishment and recognition can be achieved through perseverance and dedication. This star also implies that dissatisfaction with oneself as well as with others may cause irritability.

Linked to your Sun's degree, this star denotes achievement, with a slow and steady rise to greater power, and a preference for work in government and political affairs.

• *Positive:* happiness in solitude, sense of duty, straightforwardness, honesty

to have dexterity and a sense of form. Ambitious, with negotiation skills, you are usually able to strike a good deal and get value for your money. Your birthdate also suggests that you may have an interest in facts or figures and can achieve material success or a prominent position as a specialist or researcher. Alternatively, you may choose to travel and explore, or use your sensitivity and creativity in some form of self-expression through music and the arts.

Famous people who share your birthday include former Russian premier Nikita Khrushchev, actor William Holden, actress Olivia Hussey, banker J. P. Morgan, and musician Jan Hammer.

Numerology

As a shrewd, independent thinker, you benefit from being well educated or skillful. The number 17 birthday means you usually utilize your knowledge in a specific way in order to develop your expertise. With a reserved nature and good analytical abilities, you can rise to a prominent position as a specialist or researcher. Private and introspective, with a strong interest in facts and figures, you frequently present a thoughtful demeanor and like to take your time. By developing your communication skills, you can discover much more about yourself from others. The subinfluence of the number 4 month indicates that you can be friendly and outgoing, with diplomatic skills. By showing your caring and loving nature, you can clear up any misunderstandings. Although you like to resolve problems independently, learn to share your thoughts with others or be part of a team. Avoid a tendency to be greedy or envious. A need for recognition suggests that you are keen to express youself and liberate your creative spirit.

• *Positive:* thoughtfulness, planning, good business sense, financial success, individual thinker, painstaking nature, accuracy, skill at research, scientific ability

• *Negative:* detachment, loneliness, stubbornness, carelessness, moodiness, oversensitivity, narrow-mindedness, criticism, suspicion

Love & Relationships

Warm and sociable, you draw people with your natural charm. With your powerful emotions, you have a great deal of love to give. Nevertheless, if your feelings do not have a positive channel for expression, you may become moody or sulk. The restlessness or impatience associated with your birthday often surfaces if you become too restricted or frustrated with your current situation. Keeping active and adventurous can help you achieve emotional satisfaction. Although at times relationships may be unsettled, you are usually willing to work at keeping the peace, and you rarely give up easily. Your dynamic and emotional energy, however, can ensure that in any company you are able to successfully stand your ground and get the affection or admiration you desire.

YOUR SPECIAL SOMEONE

You might come closer to finding your true match with someone born on one of the following days.

Love & friendship: Jan. 7, 11, 22, 24, Feb. 5, 9, 20, Mar. 3, 7, 18, 31, Apr. 1, 5, 16, 29, May 3, 14, 27, 29, June 1, 12, 25, 27, July 10, 23, 25, Aug. 8, 10, 21, 23, 31, Sept. 6, 19, 21, 29, Oct. 4, 17, 19, 27, 30, Nov. 2, 15, 17, 25, 28, Dec. 13, 15, 23, 26

Beneficial: Jan. 8, 14, 19, Feb. 6, 12, 17, Mar. 4, 10, 15, Apr. 2, 8, 13, May 6, 11, June 4, 9, July 2, 7, Aug. 5, Sept. 3, Oct. 1, 29, Nov. 27, Dec. 25, 29

Fatal attractions: Oct. 20, 21, 22

Challenging: Jan. 9, 18, 20, Feb. 7, 16, 18, Mar. 5, 14, 16, Apr. 3, 12, 14, May 1, 10, 12, June 8, 10, July 6, 8, 29, Aug. 4, 6, 27, Sept. 2, 4, 25, Oct. 2, 23, Nov. 21, Dec. 19

Soul mates: Jan. 9, Feb. 7, Mar. 5, Apr. 3, May 1, Oct. 30, Nov. 28, Dec. 26

April 18

♈ Earnest and serious, yet original and versatile, you often seek ways to express yourself. As an Aries, you are both determined and creative, with charm and an easygoing personality. The subinfluence of your decanate ruler, Sagittarius, encourages you to travel and explore or to seek different experiences and have many interests. This influence, however, also warns against scattering your energies and wasting time.

Although you often rely on your common sense and have the ability to see the numerous sides of every situation, at times you can be indecisive. Nevertheless, you are a natural-born strategist, with strong intuition, and when faced with a problem you can often find a quick yet inventive answer.

Industrious, methodical, and thorough, you like to come straight to the point of a matter. Reliability, shrewdness, and intellectual flexibility often suggest that others are likely to admire your integrity and creative mind. In your enthusiasm to take on life's challenges, beware of a tendency to become overly idealistic or to take reckless chances by believing that new beginnings will solve all your problems.

Since your Sun moves into Taurus at the early age of two, your childhood is likely to have a strong influence of stability, with an emphasis on material security. There is a turning point for you around the age of thirty-two, when your progressed Sun enters Gemini. From this time you may develop a desire to be more knowledgeable and communicative in all areas of your life. Around the age of 62 your Sun moves into the sign of Cancer, bringing a shift that accentuates your emotional needs, home, and family.

Fixed Stars

Mirach, also called Andromeda's girdle; Al Perg, also called Kullat Nuti or Piscium; Vertex, also called Great Nebuli

Primary Star

Star's name: Mirach, also called Andomeda's girdle
Degree position: 29°17' Aries–0°24' Taurus between the years 1930 and 2000
Magnitude: 2
Strength: ★★★★★★★★
Orb: 2°10'
Constellation: Beta Andromedae
Applicable days: April 18, 19, 20, 21, 22, 23
Star qualities: Neptune and Venus
Description: a reddish yellow star located in the side of the girdle of Andromeda

Primary Star's Influence

Mirach bestows sensitivity, a dreamy and idealistic nature, and a refined sense of beauty. Frequently you have a gregarious and cheerful outlook, personal charm, a desire for happiness, and a love of company. The positive influence that this star carries endows you with imaginative power, inspiration, and ideas based on artistic creation. Often you possess mediumistic tendencies and a love of daydreaming. Although adventurous, you can also be devoted and visionary. You have a stimulating influence on others and can make friends easily. Often you are helped in life by others.

Linked to your Sun's degree, this

Your Secret Self

An important part of your makeup may be a constant need for security and affection. This may manifest itself in different ways. For example, when your leadership is challenged you may be prone to prolong situations until you feel safe. Alternatively, when your loved ones seem down, you will want to uplift them with all your devotion.

You are liable to feel anxious or nervous if life seems to become too routine and does not move as fast as you would like. However, it is always only a matter of time before your extremely capable and determined nature moves into action. These temporary static periods may be a prerequisite for finding peace of mind, so utilize these times to stop and reflect in order to recoup your energies and start over.

Work & Vocation

Your excellent mind and communication skills point to a tremendous capacity to achieve. You may just have to guard against taking on too much or a tendency to doubt yourself. When positive, you have a highly creative approach to life, which can manifest in any field of endeavor. If in the arts, you will want to share your original and gifted ideas. Being naturally sociable as well as having shrewd business acumen points you to careers that may incorporate both of these characteristics, such as banking, sales, or real estate. A philosophical or humanitarian leaning may be satisfied through occupations such as the clergy, charity work, or philanthropy. Travel is particularly helpful in opening avenues for expansion.

Famous people born on your birthday include actress Hayley Mills, conductor Leopold Stokowski, philanthropist Huntington Hartford, Queen Frederika of Greece, and T.V. host Conan O'Brien.

Numerology

Determination, assertiveness, and ambition are some of the attributes associated with a number 18 birthday. Active, with a need for challenges, you like to keep busy and are frequently involved in some enterprise. Capable, hardworking, and responsible, you rise to positions of authority. Alternatively, your strong business sense and organizational skills may lead you to the world of commerce. Since you may suffer from overwork, learn how to relax or slow down from time to time. As a number 18 personality, you may use your power to heal others, give sound advice, or solve other people's problems. The subinfluence of the number 4 month indicates that you are efficient, compliant, and imaginative. When in doubt, apply faith and trust your instincts. If at times you become emotionally intense, do not lose your temper or act selfishly; show tolerance and understanding. You are outspoken, so think before you act and avoid being judgmental. When you find yourself in a position of authority, it is important to be truthful, just, and fair.

• *Positive:* progressive attitude, assertiveness, intuition, courage, resoluteness, healing ability, efficiency, advisory skills

• *Negative:* uncontrolled emotions, laziness, lack of order, selfishness, failure to complete work or projects, deceit

Love & Relationships

Versatile and creative, you are likely to have many friends and acquaintances. Your agreeable charm ensures your success in all people-related activities, but particularly those concerning self-expression. If you stay positive in matters of romance, you can be very loving and spontaneous, but if too preoccupied with your own affairs, you may appear cold or indifferent. It is vital that you put aside time for yourself to reflect and listen to your inner, intuitive sensitivity, as this connects you to your high ideals. This is likely to strengthen your faith and help you avoid anxiety in your relationships due to possible worry about financial insecurity.

star bestows a talent for composing or playing music. Your goal may be to create the real out of the ideal. This star also implies that eccentricity might be linked to a lack of self-confidence.

• *Positive:* altruism, brilliant mind, inclination to mysticism, idealism, good taste, artistic talents, wide range of interests

• *Negative:* secret bad habits, romantic preoccupation, excessive idealism, delusion

See Appendix for additional fixed star readings.

YOUR SPECIAL SOMEONE

You are likely to increase your chances of love and romance with those born on one of the following dates.

Love & friendship: Jan. 8, 22, 26, Feb. 6, 20, 21, 24, Mar. 4, 18, 22, Apr. 2, 16, 20, 30, May 14, 18, 28, 30, June 12, 16, 26, 28, July 10, 14, 24, 26, Aug. 8, 9, 12, 22, 24, Sept. 6, 10, 20, 22, 30, Oct. 4, 8, 18, 20, 28, Nov. 2, 6, 16, 18, 26, Dec. 4, 14, 16, 24

Beneficial: Jan. 9, 20, Feb. 7, 18, Mar. 5, 16, 29, Apr. 3, 14, 27, May 1, 12, 25, June 10, 23, July 8, 21, Aug. 6, 19, Sept. 4, 17, Oct. 2, 15, 30, Nov. 13, 28, Dec. 11, 26, 30

Fatal attractions: Jan. 27, Feb. 25, Mar. 23, Apr. 21, May 19, June 17, July 15, Aug. 13, Sept. 11, Oct. 9, 21, 22, 23, Nov. 7, Dec. 5

Challenging: Jan. 2, 10, 19, Feb. 8, 17, Mar. 6, 15, Apr. 4, 13, May 2, 11, June 9, July 7, 30, Aug. 5, 28, Sept. 3, 26, Oct. 1, 24, Nov. 22, Dec. 20, 30

Soul mates: Jan. 15, Feb. 13, Mar. 11, Apr. 9, May 7, June 5, July 3, Aug. 1, Oct. 29, Nov. 27, Dec. 25

April 19

FIXED STARS

Mirach, also called Andromeda's Girdle; Vertex, also called Great Nebulae

PRIMARY STAR

Star's name: Mirach, also called Andromeda's Girdle

Degree position: 29°17' Aries to 0°24' Taurus between the years 1930 and 2000

Magnitude: 2

Strength: ★★★★★★★

Orb: 2°10'

Constellation: Beta Andromedae

Applicable days: April 18, 19, 20, 21, 22, 23

Star qualities: Neptune and Venus

Description: a reddish yellow star located in the side of the girdle of Andromeda

PRIMARY STAR'S INFLUENCE

Mirach bestows sensitivity, a dreamy and idealistic nature, and a refined sense of beauty. Frequently you have a gregarious and cheerful outlook, personal charm, a desire for happiness, and a love of company. The positive influence that this star carries endows you with imaginative power, inspiration, and ideas based on artistic creation. Often you possess mediumistic tendencies and a love of daydreaming. Although adventurous, you can also be devoted and visionary. You have a stimulating influence on others and can make friends easily. Often you are helped in life by others.

Linked to your Sun's degree, this star bestows a talent for composing or

Idealistic and friendly, yet enterprising and with a fondness for material comforts, you often seek associations that can bring you gain and further advancement. As an Arian, you are energetic, assertive, and mentally sharp, with intuitive abilities. This often suggests that you are perceptive and imaginative, with creative talents that encourage you to take the initiative.

The strong emphasis on relationships and partnerships that is linked to your birthday nevertheless implies that although you are a strong and forceful individual, you may have to learn the art of compromise in order to benefit from what others have to offer. The subinfluence of Sagittarius, your decanate ruler, suggests that you are optimistic and resourceful. Frequently you can formulate some exceedingly good ideas that are likely to bring large financial rewards.

Often friendly and generous, you have a visionary perception that leads you to seek work that involves you in the community. If you believe in a cause, you can be quite forceful and persuasive. In business you also have a flair for sales and promotion and can successfully negotiate deals.

When you reach the age of one, your progressed Sun moves into Taurus, commencing a thirty-year period of increased emphasis on security. A turning point occurs around the age of thirty-one, when your progressed Sun moves into Gemini, stimulating you to widen your interests and place more emphasis on knowledge, communication, and new interests. From your early sixties, when your progressed Sun moves forward into Cancer, you will find a greater awareness of your feelings and seek a more harmonious family life.

Your Secret Self

An inner need for recognition drives you to material accomplishments, ensuring that you will not be taken for granted. Embodying a strange mixture of idealism and desire for money and status, you have the energy and determination for substantial achievement, but you may find your greatest fulfillment in satisfying your desire to do something for others. An inherent dream for a haven of peace and harmony may be reflected in your need for a secure home base from which to launch your ambitious plans. It may also lead you to develop skills in music or art, where you can lose yourself in a oneness with your strong universal sense.

With a strong work ethic and an awareness that you do not get anything for nothing, you feel happier when you are clear in your mind about your next goal. Although you may have an unfounded fear of lack of funds, your idealistic nature yearns to accomplish something that will benefit others.

Work & Vocation

Your expertise and enthusiasm for initiating projects may take you into many areas. A propensity for business and being able to sell an idea or product you believe in can take you beyond sales to promoting yourself and your ideals. You are happiest when in charge and able to delegate the more detailed and routine work to others. Your relationship skills and ability to make contacts mean that careers involving people are ideal. These may include public relations, advising, or being a go-between or agent. You may also be drawn toward business negotiations that involve real estate or communications in some form. Although you like to be the boss or work for yourself, you also realize the importance of working cooperatively with others.

Famous people who share your birthday include comedian Dudley Moore, designer Paloma Picasso, statesman Benjamin Disraeli, psychologist Gustav Fechner, and actresses Jayne Mansfield and Ashley Judd.

Numerology

Sunny, ambitious, and humanitarian are some of the ways others describe people with a number 19 birthday. Decisive and resourceful, you possess depth of vision, but the dreamer side of your nature is compassionate, idealistic, and creative. Although you are sensitive, the need to be someone may be the very thing that pushes you to be dramatic and claim center stage. Often there is a strong desire to establish an individual identity. To do so, you may first need to overcome the influence of peer group pressure. To others, you may appear confident, resilient, and resourceful, but inner tensions may cause emotional ups and downs. You are often artistic and charismatic, and the world is there for you to explore. The subinfluence of the number 4 month indicates that although you are practical and hardworking, you have to stay focused and avoid scattering your energies. At times a tendency for premature action may arise from being overly optimistic. By being flexible yet self-assured, you can show your leadership abilities. By applying your practical skills and imagination, you can turn your ideas into tangible products.

• *Positive:* dynamism, centeredness, creativity, leadership, luck, progressive attitude, optimism, strong convictions, competitiveness, independence, gregarious nature

• *Negative:* self-centered, depression, worry, fear of rejection, ups and downs, materialism, egotism, impatience

Love & Relationships

Your dynamic energy indicates that you generally have a busy social life, with many interests. You are likely to be particularly attracted to powerful and intelligent people or those with a strong identity. There is a chance, however, of becoming involved in mental power games or being manipulative if you cannot directly get your way. Nevertheless, you can be generous to and very supportive of others. You also possess the fortunate ability to make friends from all walks of life and can turn some of these new friendships into useful business contacts.

playing music. Your goal may be to create the real out of the ideal. This star also implies that eccentricity might be linked to a lack of self-confidence.

• *Positive:* altruism, brilliant mind, inclination to mysticism, idealism, good taste, artistic talents, wide range of interests

• *Negative:* secret bad habits, romantic preoccupation, excessive idealism, delusion

See Appendix for additional fixed star readings.

YOUR SPECIAL SOMEONE

For love and mental stimulation, you might want to begin looking for those born among the following dates.

Love & friendship: Jan. 3, 23, Feb. 11, 21, 23, Mar. 9, 19, 28, 31, Apr. 7, 17, 26, 29, May 5, 15, 24, 27, 29, 31, June 3, 13, 22, 25, 27, 29, July 1, 11, 20, 23, 25, 27, 29, Aug. 1, 9, 18, 21, 23, 25, 27, Sept. 7, 16, 19, 21, 23, 25, Oct. 5, 14, 17, 19, 21, 23, Nov. 3, 12, 15, 17, 19, 21, Dec. 1, 10, 13, 15, 17, 19

Beneficial: Jan. 3, 4, 10, 21, Feb. 1, 2, 8, 19, Mar. 6, 17, 30, Apr. 4, 15, 28, May 2, 13, 26, June 11, 24, July 9, 22, Aug. 7, 20, Sept. 5, 18, Oct. 3, 16, 31, Nov. 1, 14, 29, Dec. 12, 27

Fatal attractions: Jan. 22, 28, Feb. 20, 26, Mar. 18, 24, Apr. 16, 22, May 14, 20, June 12, 18, July 10, 16, Aug. 8, 14, Sept. 6, 12, Oct. 4, 10, 23, 24, Nov. 2, 8, Dec. 6

Challenging: Jan. 11, 20, Feb. 9, 18, Mar. 7, 16, Apr 5, 14, May 3, 12, 30, June 1, 10, 28, July 8, 26, 31, Aug. 6, 24, 29, Sept. 4, 22, 27, Oct. 2, 20, 25, Nov. 18, 23, Dec. 16, 21

Soul mates: Jan. 26, Feb. 24, Mar. 22, 30, Apr. 20, 28, May 18, 26, June 16, 24, July 14, 22, Aug. 12, 20, Sept. 10, 18, Oct. 8, 16, Nov. 6, 14, Dec. 4, 12

April 20

♈ Being on the cusp of Aries and Taurus, you enjoy both the drive or assertiveness of Aries and the practical determination of Taurus. Ambitious yet sensitive, you possess a strong need for material stability and advancement. This also implies that it may be necessary for you to find a balance between your natural compassion and a tendency to be too self-oriented or authoritarian.

The desire for success and security indicated by your birthday also suggests that you are keen to gain the approval of others and can therefore be friendly and receptive. Your personal magnetism often helps you to overcome early setbacks, and your intuitive power frequently comes to your assistance. These qualities invariably help you grasp a situation quickly and precisely.

Friendly and outgoing, you may nevertheless be sensitive to other people's criticism. By developing a more rational perspective, you can avoid being easily hurt by others.

With your down-to-earth, no-nonsense approach and natural diplomatic skills, you enjoy work involving cooperation with others and are in your element when you can mix business and pleasure or when promoting ideas linked to financial gains.

In your early years there is an especially strong influence from a female figure, usually the mother. Up to the age of thirty, when your progressed Sun is transiting through Taurus, there is an emphasis on material stability, status, and financial security. A turning point occurs at the beginning of your thirties, when the progressed Sun moves into Gemini, stimulating you to widen your interests and placing more significance on knowledge, communication, and study. From around the age of sixty your progressed Sun moves into Cancer, highlighting your emotional needs, home, and family.

FIXED STAR

Star's name: Mirach, also called Andromeda's Girdle

Degree position: 29°17' Aries to 0°24' Taurus between the years 1930 and 2000

Magnitude: 2

Strength: ★★★★★★★

Orb: 2°10'

Constellation: Beta Andromedae

Applicable days: April 18, 19, 20, 21, 22, 23

Star qualities: Neptune and Venus

Description: a reddish yellow star located in the side of the girdle of Andromeda

PRIMARY STAR'S INFLUENCE

Mirach bestows sensitivity, a dreamy and idealistic nature, and a refined sense of beauty. Frequently you have a gregarious and cheerful outlook, personal charm, a desire for happiness, and a love of company. The positive influence that this star carries endows you with imaginative power, inspiration, and ideas based on artistic creation. Often you possess mediumistic tendencies and a love of daydreaming. Although adventurous, you can also be devoted and visionary. You have a stimulating influence on others and can make friends easily. Often you are helped in life by others.

Linked to your Sun's degree, this star bestows a talent for composing or playing music. Your goal may be to create the real out of the ideal. This star also implies that eccentricity might be linked to a lack of self-confidence.

Your Secret Self

A natural instinct for quickly assessing people and situations helps put you one step ahead in getting what you want. Whether using this ability to sell one of your many ideas or to make contacts, you like to initiate projects. When working with others, it is important to avoid using power tactics by developing the art of compromise, diplomacy, and cooperation.

At a deep level you possess extremely strong desires. When these are channeled into selfless love and service, they can be a powerful force for the betterment of others. Be careful of allowing this tremendous force for good to become blocked by fears about money. Since you have the ability to manifest your will on an outer level, it is essential that you know precisely what you want and why.

Work & Vocation

With your enthusiasm, courage, commitment, and executive abilities, you may pursue a career in commerce such as negotiator, agent, or financial advisor. You thrive on new beginnings or challenges, and in business have an ability to spot opportunities. You have the magic capacity to manifest things materially with your strong, focused will and determination. Motivated by a strong combination of idealism and practicality, you possess natural abilities for leadership,

• *Positive:* altruism, brilliant mind, inclination to mysticism, idealism, good taste, artistic talents, wide range of interests

• *Negative:* secret bad habits, romantic preoccupation, excessive idealism, delusion

particularly as a manager, executive, or entrepreneur. A strong dramatic sense and creative ability may attract you to a career in the arts or entertainement.

Famous people born on your birthday include actors Daniel Day Lewis and Ryan O'Neal, painter Joan Miró, singer Luther Vandross, and actress Jessica Lange.

Numerology

As a number 20 birthday, you are intuitive, sensitive, adaptable, and understanding, and you often see yourself as a part of a larger group. Usually you enjoy cooperative activities where you can interact, share experiences, or learn from others. Charming and gracious, you develop diplomatic and social skills and can move in different social circles with ease. You may, however, need to develop your confidence or overcome a tendency to be easily hurt by the actions and criticism of others or to be overly dependent. You are a master at creating a congenial and harmonious atmosphere. The subinfluence of the number 4 month indicates that you can be practical and realistic, yet loving and supportive. Trust your premonitions and avoid becoming worried about others, especially if they cause hurt and mistrust. Since you are often a perfectionist, it is imperative for you to know that you have done your best. You may need to overcome a tendency to criticize or be dissatisfied, and you should learn to make up your own mind rather than listen to the opinions of others.

• *Positive:* good partnerships, gentleness, tact, receptivity, intuition, consideration, harmony, agreeableness, amicable nature, ambassador of goodwill

• *Negative:* suspicion, lack of confidence, timidity, oversensitivity, overemotional reactions, selfishness, deceit

YOUR SPECIAL SOMEONE

You may feel more inspired to share your love and affection with those born on the following days.

Love & friendship: Jan. 14, 24, 31, Feb. 12, 22, 23, 29, Mar. 10, 20, 27, Apr. 8, 18, 25, May 6, 16, 23, 30, June 4, 14, 15, 21, 28, 30, July 2, 12, 19, 26, 28, 30, Aug. 10, 11, 17, 24, 26, 28, Sept. 8, 15, 22, 24, 26, Oct. 6, 13, 20, 22, 24, 30, Nov. 4, 11, 18, 20, 22, 28, Dec. 2, 9, 16, 18, 20, 26, 29

Beneficial: Jan. 5, 22, 30, Feb. 3, 20, 28, Mar. 1, 18, 26, Apr. 16, 24, May 14, 22, June 12, 20, July 10, 18, 29, Aug. 8, 16, 27, 31, Sept. 6, 14, 25, 29, Oct. 4, 12, 23, 27, Nov. 2, 10, 21, 25, Dec. 9, 19, 23

Fatal attractions: Jan. 12, Feb. 10, Mar. 8, Apr. 6, May 4, June 2, Oct. 24, 25

Challenging: Jan. 16, 21, Feb. 14, 19, Mar. 12, 17, 30, Apr. 10, 15, 28, May 8, 13, 26, June 6, 11, 24, July 4, 9, 22, Aug. 2, 7, 20, Sept. 5, 18, Oct. 3, 16, Nov. 1, 14, Dec. 12

Soul mates: Jan. 25, Feb. 23, Mar. 21, Apr. 19, May 17, June 15, July 13, Aug. 11, Sept. 9, Oct. 7, Nov. 5, Dec. 3, 30

Love & Relationships

Friendly and good-hearted, you are likely to experience a busy life and enjoy meeting new people. A tendency to rush into relationships, however, warns that you often change your mind and feel uncertain about long-term commitments. A love of change implies that you may have a great deal of variety and excitement, travel, and adventure in your life. Due to your ambition and determination, ideally you need a partner who is as active and hardworking as you are. Although generally warm and caring, you can at times display selfish and domineering behavior with your loved ones. Through learning patience and impartiality you find balance and emotional stability.

Taurus

April 21–May 21

April 21

The influence of your birthday suggests that you are an intelligent, independent, and competent individual with a straightforward style. Capable of being judicious and careful, as well as inventive and open to new ideas, you like to present a bold and assertive front. Being born on the cusp of both Aries and Taurus, you have the benefits of two zodiac signs. This reveals that you are original and daring, yet sensual, with artistic talents. Unfortunately, this double influence can also make you twice as stubborn and inclined to overindulge.

Since you are very clever, education can be a vital component in utilizing your outstanding potential. Although a pragmatist, you need interests that stimulate your intellectual curiosity and expand your knowledge. You like emotional honesty and strong foundations to what you achieve in life, so it is important to have a secure base to work from. Usually this refers to your home, but it can also relate to business or other areas of your life. Once this is in place you feel able to express your natural authority and realize that you can command a situation through your wisdom. Women of this day often think in a masculine way, but both sexes have to guard against a tendency to become too domineering.

Up to the age of twenty-nine you are likely to be concerned with stability and financial security. After the age of thirty, when your progressed Sun moves into Gemini, there is an emphasis on clear communication as well as new interests. This continues until the beginning of your sixties, when your progressed Sun enters Cancer. After this time you may feel a stronger need for emotional security, and your home and family are likely to play a more important role in your life.

FIXED STARS

Mirach, also called Andromeda's Girdle; Mira, also called Stella Mira

PRIMARY STAR

Star's name: Mirach, also called Andromeda's Girdle

Degree position: 29°17' Aries to 0°24' Taurus between the years 1930 and 2000

Magnitude: 2

Strength: ★★★★★★★★

Orb: 2°10'

Constellation: Beta Andromedae

Applicable days: April 18, 19, 20, 21, 22, 23

Star qualities: Neptune and Venus

Description: a reddish yellow star located in the side of the girdle of Andromeda

Your Secret Self

A combination of inner power and the ability to deal skillfully with people on a personal level suggests that you do not feel happy in a subservient position. You may exert your power by challenging others, either negatively, through becoming hooked into power games, or positively, through friendly rivalry. You love to exchange ideas with others and seem to have an instinct for working or sharing through collective efforts. Your outer appearance may often be a false front to your inner strength and hide your sensitivity and idealism.

Sometimes you may overtax yourself in your desire to fulfill your responsibilities; often you work hard and do not stop until you achieve your objectives. You realize the importance of patience and perseverance in order to realize long-term aims or objectives. Despite your hard work and dedication, you may have to overcome a tendency to be controlling or overly materialistic. Your determination, however, can also be remarkable and uncompromising, even when you are not particularly interested in the job at hand.

PRIMARY STAR'S INFLUENCE

Mirach bestows sensitivity, a dreamy and idealistic nature, and a refined sense of beauty. Frequently you have a gregarious and cheerful outlook, personal charm, a desire for happiness, and a love of company. The positive influence that this star carries endows you with imaginative power, inspiration, and ideas based on artistic creation. Often you possess mediumistic tendencies and a love of daydreaming. Although adventurous, you can also be devoted and visionary. You have a stimulating influence on others and can make friends easily. Often you are helped in life by others.

Work & Vocation

As others will recognize your ability to take command and work hard, you will naturally rise to a position of authority in any career. Your mental powers make education of some description essential to bring out your exceptional potential. Your keen intellect and good imagination can give you a need to express yourself in words, either speaking, writing, singing, or acting. You may therefore find yourself being drawn to a career as a teacher, judge, reformer, or entertainer. If in business, you may be particularly drawn to investments, the stock market, sales, publishing, advertising, real estate, and products of the land.

Famous people who share your birthday include Queen Elizabeth II, writer Charlotte Brontë, musician Iggy Pop, psychologist Rollo May, actress Andie McDowell, and actors Anthony Quinn and Charles Grodin.

Linked to your Sun's degree, this star bestows a talent for composing or playing music. Your goal may be to create the real out of the ideal. This star also implies that eccentricity might be linked to a lack of self-confidence.

• *Positive:* altruism, brilliant mind, inclination to mysticism, idealism, good taste, artistic talents, wide range of interests

• *Negative:* secret bad habits, romantic preoccupation, excessive idealism, delusion

See Appendix for additional fixed star readings.

Numerology

Dynamic drive and an outgoing personality are often present in those with a number 21 birthday. Friendly and gregarious, you have many social contacts and a wide circle of friends. With a number 21 birthday, you can be fun-loving, magnetic, and creative. Alternatively, you can be shy and reserved, with a need to develop assertiveness, especially in close relationships. Although you may be inclined toward cooperative associations or marriage, you always want to be acknowledged for your talents and abilities. The subinfluence of the number 4 month indicates that you are practical and responsible, yet thoughtful and imaginative, with analytical skills. Although you desire the company of others, often you need a private and peaceful environment where you can spend time thinking and reflecting. It may also be necessary to overcome a tendency to be skeptical by developing trust and sincerity. Trusting your intuition helps you to become more assertive and self-disciplined. Overcome the fear of failure by having fun and trying new things. Avoid hasty decisions and learn to accept criticism.

• *Positive:* inspiration, creativity, love unions, long-lasting relationships
• *Negative:* dependency, nervousness, loss of emotional control, lack of vision, disappointment, fear of change

YOUR SPECIAL SOMEONE

For love and a stable relationship, you may want to look out for someone born on one of the following days.

Love & friendship: Jan. 8, 11, 13, 15, 17, 25, Feb. 9, 11, 13, 15, 23, 24, Mar. 7, 9, 11, 13, 21, Apr. 5, 7, 9, 11, 19, May 3, 5, 7, 9, 17, 31, June 1, 3, 5, 7, 15, 29, July 1, 3, 5, 27, 29, 31, Aug. 1, 3, 11, 25, 27, 29, Sept. 1, 9, 23, 25, 27, Oct. 7, 21, 23, 25, Nov. 5, 19, 21, 23, Dec. 3, 17, 19, 21, 30

Beneficial: Jan. 1, 5, 20, Feb. 3, 18, Mar. 1, 16, Apr. 14, May 12, June 10, July 8, Aug. 6, Sept. 4, Oct. 2

Fatal attractions: Oct. 23, 24, 25

Challenging: Jan. 6, 22, 24, Feb. 4, 20, 22, Mar. 2, 18, 20, Apr. 16, 18, May 14, 16, June 12, 14, July 10, 12, Aug. 8, 10, 31, Sept. 6, 8, 29, Oct. 4, 6, 27, Nov. 2, 4, 25, 30, Dec. 2, 23, 28

Soul mates: Jan. 6, 12, Feb. 4, 10, Mar. 2, 8, Apr. 6, May 4, June 2

Love & Relationships

A strong need for emotional stability suggests that while you desire an active and mentally challenging life, you also seek a peaceful home life. With your powers of persuasion, you usually do your utmost to keep relationships on an even keel. However, you may learn that being too critical or arrogant can create tension and unrest. You enjoy mentally stimulating people and need to share a common interest with your partner. You possess a protective nature that safeguards others.

April 22

♉ This birthdate reveals you to be clever and sociable, a confident and charming individual with many natural gifts. Leadership ability comes from being secure in what you know as well as an ability to understand different types of people. You have a quick mind that is likely to enjoy wit, debate, or repartee, and you can be an excellent critic. Usually you possess the courage to speak your mind regardless of the repercussions, and you like to be direct and honest.

With the double influence of your Taurus decanate, you are a strong sensualist who needs to give and receive affection. Appreciating color, art, and beauty, you have a strong creative flair and enjoy luxury. You may have to be careful, however, of enjoying them too much and opening yourself up to indulgence in all its many forms. Nevertheless, you are usually a good evaluator of financial matters and anything concerning material security.

You generally have big plans and an ability to view the whole, which makes you a good organizer or liaison person between different groups. You can be generous and understanding with those you love. However, you may have to guard against a tendency to become too obstinate or self-willed. You set high standards for yourself and generally believe that actions speak louder than words. By applying self-discipline, you can achieve remarkable results.

Up to the age of twenty-eight you are likely to be concerned with values, whether personal or monetary. After the age of twenty-nine, when your progressed Sun moves into Gemini, there is likely to be an emphasis on education and learning new skills. The world of communication in general may play a more important part in your life. This will continue until the end of your fifties, when your progressed Sun enters Cancer. At this point there is a shift of emphasis toward your feelings and the growing importance of emotional security, home, and family.

FIXED STARS

Mirach, also called Andromeda's Girdle; Mira, also called Stella Mira; El Scheratain, also called Sharatan

PRIMARY STAR

Star's name: Mirach, also called Andromeda's Girdle

Degree position: 29°17' Aries to 0°24' Taurus between the years 1930 and 2000

Magnitude: 2

Strength: ★★★★★★★

Orb: 2°10'

Constellation: Beta Andromedae

Applicable days: April 18, 19, 20, 21, 22, 23

Star qualities: Neptune and Venus

Description: a reddish yellow star located in the side of the girdle of Andromeda

PRIMARY STAR'S INFLUENCE

Mirach bestows sensitivity, a dreamy and idealistic nature, and a refined sense of beauty. Frequently you have a gregarious and cheerful outlook, personal charm, a desire for happiness, and a love of company. The positive influence that this star carries endows you with imaginative power, inspiration, and ideas based on artistic creation. Often you possess mediumistic tendencies and a love of daydreaming. Although adventurous, you can also be devoted and visionary. You have a stimulating influence on others and can make friends easily. Often you are helped in life by others.

Your Secret Self

An interesting mixture of materialism and emotional sensitivity, you seek the satisfaction of personal achievement. By overcoming a tendency to let mundane considerations rule your life, you come to realize that money or status alone would not be ultimately satisfying. This often involves discarding the security of the tried and true and totally trusting your own inner faith and intuition. The hard part may be in making the right decisions and allowing yourself fully to trust the creative process. Once decisive and cleared of doubt, you are able to proceed with confidence and determination and often achieve outstanding results. The ability to express yourself will prove most valuable to release your anxieties and prevent you from becoming overly sensitive. This will also stimulate your joy in life and encourage you to be happy and creative.

Work & Vocation

The practical side of your nature may attract you to the financial world, where you are likely to make an excellent banker, economist, or stockbroker. Alternatively, you can become an excellent monetary advisor and accountant or negotiator and dealer. You prefer to be in some leading position, and having excellent organizational skills can guarantee success as a politician, manager, or administrator. You may also be attracted to science, or your quick way with words may lead you to education, social reform, or law. Conversely, the more creative individuals of this birthday may be drawn toward design in all forms, drama, music, and landscape gardening.

Famous people who share your birthday include actor Jack Nicholson, philosopher Immanuel Kant, musicians Charlie Mingus and Yehudi Menuhin, scientist Robert Oppenheimer, and TV producer Aaron Spelling.

• *Positive:* altruism, brilliant mind, inclination to mysticism, idealism, good taste, artistic talents, wide range of interests

• *Negative:* secret bad habits, romantic preoccupation, excessive idealism, delusion

See Appendix for additional fixed star readings.

Numerology

With a number 22 birthdate, you are a practical, disciplined, and highly intuitive individual. This is a master number and can vibrate both as number 22 and as number 4. Often honest and hardworking, with natural leadership abilities, you have a charismatic personality and a deep understanding of people. Although undemonstrative, you often show a caring, protective concern for the welfare of others. However, you never lose sight of your pragmatic or realistic stand. The subinfluence of the number 4 month indicates that you must avoid taking unnecessary risks. By being patient and organized, you can become efficient and constructive. Learn to use your intuition and foresight when dealing with mundane matters. An interest in spirituality helps you to understand the laws and order of the universe and to overcome material tendencies. With determination and hard work you can accomplish much.

• *Positive:* universality, leadership, intuition, pragmatism, practicality, manual ability, building ability, organizational skills, realism, problem-solving ability, achievement

• *Negative:* susceptibility to get-rich-quick schemes, nervousness, inferiority complex, bossiness, materialism, lack of vision, laziness, egotism, greed

YOUR SPECIAL SOMEONE

For security, mental stimulation, and love you might want to begin looking for those born among the following dates.

Love & friendship: Jan. 4, 12, 16, 25, Feb. 10, 14, 23, 24, Mar. 8, 12, 22, 31, Apr. 6, 10, 20, 29, May 4, 8, 18, 27, June 2, 6, 16, 25, 30, July 4, 14, 23, 28, Aug. 2, 12, 21, 26, 30, Sept. 10, 11, 19, 24, 28, Oct. 8, 17, 22, 26, Nov. 6, 15, 20, 24, 30, Dec. 4, 13, 18, 22, 28

Beneficial: Jan. 2, 13, 22, 24, Feb. 11, 17, 20, 22, Mar. 9, 15, 18, 20, 28, Apr. 7, 13, 16, 18, 26, May 5, 11, 16, 18, 26, June 3, 9, 12, 14, 22, July 1, 7, 10, 12, 20, Aug. 5, 8, 10, 18, Sept. 3, 6, 8, 16, Oct. 1, 4, 6, 14, Nov. 2, 4, 12, Dec. 2, 10

Fatal attractions: Jan. 25, Feb. 23, Mar. 21, Apr. 19, May 17, June 15, July 13, Aug. 11, Sept. 9, Oct. 7, 25, 26, 27, Nov. 5, Dec. 3

Challenging: Jan. 7, 23, Feb. 5, 21, Mar. 3, 19, 29, Apr. 1, 17, 27, May 15, 25, June 13, 23, July 11, 21, 31, Aug. 9, 19, 29, Sept. 7, 17, 27, 30, Nov. 3, 13, 23, 26, Dec. 1, 11, 21, 24

Soul mates: Jan. 17, Feb. 15, Mar. 13, Apr. 11, May 9, June 7, July 5, Aug. 3, Sept. 1, Nov. 30, Dec. 28

Love & Relationships

Mentally adventurous and enthusiastic, you enjoy variety and the company of ambitious and highly motivated people. Attractive and sociable, you usually have many opportunities for love and romance. Nevertheless, boredom may creep into your relationships if they do not move fast enough. Often you are attracted to creative individuals with whom you can share your quick wit and sense of humor. However, in your personal relationships guard against a tendency to make too many sacrifices or play the martyr.

April 23

An enthusiastic warmth and charismatic personality are characteristic of those born on this day. Very intelligent, with a gift for communicating ideas, you are sociable and entertaining. Wanting to be honest with your feelings, you often sparkle with individuality and have the ability to make things happen in a big way.

With the influence of your Taurus decanate, you are a lover of beauty, nature, and the arts, and you have a strong need for self-expression. Since you are likely to be gifted in this department, it is excellent if you can combine your talents with your originality. This implies that you resent being pushed and may retaliate by becoming stubborn and obstinate. Nevertheless, you can be led, especially by love. In your overall life plan, material security is a big issue, and you need something solid and stable to rely upon. You are usually good with financial matters and may have the ability to gain resources for yourself or others.

Being very friendly, you can mix with people from different walks of life and like to keep active. You may have to watch a tendency, however, toward nervousness or stress caused by either repressed emotions or taking on too much. You are generally very persuasive, with an ability to organize and lead others in a way that may seem smooth and effortless. However, you may have to guard against being restless or impatient, which can cause you to suddenly become forcefully opinionated. Luckily, your spirit of enterprise does not allow you to stay down for too long, and with your ability to help yourself and others, you look for new ways to expand your horizons.

Leading up to the age of twenty-seven, you are likely to have viewed life from quite a practical and security-conscious angle. After the age of twenty-eight, however, when your progressed Sun moves into Gemini, you start to be more receptive to new ideas and may even want to start studying. This more cerebral influence continues until the end of your fifties, when your progressed Sun enters Cancer. From this time onward there may be more of a shift toward emotional issues, especially those concerning home and family.

Your Secret Self

A strong work ethic and desire to accomplish in life are balanced by an inner playfulness and desire for love and affection. You have a magnetic ability to captivate people when your loving side is given full rein and you feel inspired to express yourself. This ability often suggests that you can be witty, buoyant, and full of enthusiasm. Although you are charismatic and young at heart, you will have to learn some lessons concerning balancing your need for fun with your sense of responsibility. If you feel strongly about certain issues, you are likely to devote your free time to your cause, supporting it with your idealism and ingenuity.

A small hiccup in your enormous drive to succeed is a materialistic streak, which may tempt you to take the safe route of security rather than really challenge yourself. Any fears you may have regarding money are likely to be groundless, as you have an excellent earning capacity. This is increased by your ability to develop your ideas while keeping people interested or entertained.

Work & Vocation

In whatever career you choose, you are willing to work hard to achieve your objectives, and you possess a natural business sense. Your charm, persuasive manner, and communication

FIXED STARS

Mirach, also called Andromeda's Girdle; Mira, also called Stella Mira; El Scheratain, also called Sharatan

PRIMARY STAR

Star's name: Mirach, also called Andromeda's Girdle
Degree position: 29°17' Aries to 0°24' Taurus between the years 1930 and 2000
Magnitude: 2
Strength: ★★★★★★★
Orb: 2°10'
Constellation: Beta Andromedae
Applicable days: April 18, 19, 20, 21, 22, 23
Star qualities: Neptune and Venus
Description: a reddish yellow star located in the side of the girdle of Andromeda

PRIMARY STAR'S INFLUENCE

Mirach bestows sensitivity, a dreamy and idealistic nature, and a refined sense of beauty. Frequently you have a gregarious and cheerful outlook, personal charm, a desire for happiness, and a love of company. The positive influence that this star carries endows you with imaginative power, inspiration, and ideas based on artistic creation. Often you possess mediumistic tendencies and a love of daydreaming. Although adventurous, you can also be devoted and visionary. You have a stimulating influence on others and can make friends easily. Often you are helped in life by others.

skills often point to success in the world of sales, promotion, and negotiation. Alternatively, you may find you are suited for a career in real estate, public relations, law, or politics. Your desire to constantly improve your mind may place you among academics; alternatively, you are likely to be inspired by more creative occupations such as photography, writing, art, music, or drama. You are willing to fight tenaciously for a cause you believe in, which may attract you to work that involves reform. You are also an excellent manager, administrator, or executor.

Famous people born on your birthday include scientist Max Planck, singer Roy Orbison, painter Joseph Turner, entertainer/ambassador Shirley Temple Black, actor Lee Majors, and writer Vladimir Nabokov.

Numerology

Intuition, emotional sensitivity, and creativity are some of the attributes endowed by a number 23 birthday. Usually you are versatile, passionate, and a quick thinker, with a professional attitude and a mind full of creative ideas. With the number 23 influence, you can learn new subjects easily but may prefer practice to theory. Fond of travel, adventure, and meeting new people, you have a restlessness that urges you to try many different kinds of experiences, and you are apt to make the most of any situation. Generally friendly and fun-loving, with courage and drive, you may need an active life in order to actualize your true potential. The subinfluence of the number 4 month indicates that you like order and planning. With the use of your intuition and practical skills, you can often arrive at an inspired idea or plan. A need to stay focused suggests that you must not lose sight of your purpose. This also helps you overcome the feeling of being lonely or isolated. Intelligent and creative, you need to express yourself freely. Compassion and kindness shown to others bring unexpected rewards.

• *Positive:* loyalty, responsibility, travel, communication, intuition, creativity, versatility, trustworthiness, fame

• *Negative:* selfishness, insecurity, stubbornness, uncompromising nature, fault finding, dullness, withdrawal, prejudice

Love & Relationships

Being an ardent lover, you can live for the moment. However, your tendency to be idealistic suggests that you need a spiritual connection, as your conception of love is so high. You can, however, become lonely if your expectations are not met. There may also be a possibility of some unusual relationships or secret affairs. Responsibilities concerning others or burdens concerning members of the family may also influence your relationships. You can, however, be a loyal and supportive partner or friend and attract others with your charismatic personality.

Linked to your Sun's degree, this star bestows a talent for composing or playing music. Your goal may be to create the real out of the ideal. This star also implies that eccentricity might be linked to a lack of self-confidence.

• *Positive:* altruism, brilliant mind, inclination to mysticism, idealism, good taste, artistic talents, wide range of interests

• *Negative:* secret bad habits, romantic preoccupation, excessive idealism, delusion

See Appendix for additional fixed star readings.

YOUR SPECIAL SOMEONE

You might find love and stability with someone born on one of the following dates.

Love & friendship: Jan. 2, 7, 10, 17, 27, Feb. 5, 8, 15, 25, Mar. 3, 6, 13, 23, Apr. 1, 4, 11, 21, May 2, 9, 19, June 7, 17, July 5, 15, 29, 31, Aug. 3, 13, 27, 29, 31, Sept. 1, 11, 25, 27, 29, Oct. 9, 23, 25, 27, Nov. 7, 21, 23, 25, Dec. 5, 19, 21, 23

Beneficial: Jan. 3, 5, 20, 25, 27, Feb. 1, 3, 18, 23, 25, Mar. 1, 16, 21, 23, Apr. 14, 19, 21, May 12, 17, 19, June 10, 15, 17, July 8, 13, 15, Aug. 6, 11, 13, Sept. 4, 9, 11, Oct. 2, 7, 9, Nov. 5, 7, Dec. 3, 5

Fatal attractions: Jan. 13, Feb. 11, Mar. 9, Apr. 7, May 5, June 3, July 1, Oct. 26, 27, 28

Challenging: Jan. 16, 24, Feb. 14, 22, Mar. 12, 20, Apr. 10, 18, May 8, 16, 31, June 6, 14, 29, July 4, 12, 27, Aug. 2, 10, 25, Sept. 8, 23, Oct. 6, 21, Nov. 4, 19, Dec. 2, 17

Soul mates: Jan. 16, Feb. 14, Mar. 12, Apr. 10, May 8, June 6, July 4, 31, Aug. 2, 29, Sept. 27, Oct. 25, Nov. 23, Dec. 21

April 24

Your birthday suggests that you are a warm, intelligent, and determined individual with an independent spirit and the power of attainment. You are likely to become enthusiastic and hardworking when really interested in a project or cause, and you have the potential for extraordinary achievements.

The influence of your Sun in the Taurus decanate indicates that you have a strong sensuality and a love of nature, beauty, and the arts. When necessary, you can turn on the charm and be amusing and sociable. If you do not get your own way, however, you can easily become too self-willed or stubborn.

You usually think on a large scale, and with your executive abilities, you can contribute to group activities by being a natural leader. Although at times you can be arrogant or opinionated, on other occasions you may be strangely lacking in self-confidence. Fortunately, having the ability to make quick decisions and being intuitive help you to overcome these challenges. Your attractive personality and a need to be popular also suggest that you want to be in the limelight. Since you can be highly persuasive, you have only to develop self-discipline in order to make the most of your marvelous potential.

Up to the age of twenty-six, you may be focused on a need for affection and material security, but around the age of twenty-seven, when your progressed Sun moves into Gemini, you may diversify and find many more interests. From this time onward study and communication can become more important to you. There is another turning point after fifty-seven, when your progressed Sun moves into Cancer, making you more sensitive and identifying the importance of a home base.

FIXED STAR

Star's name: El Scheratain, also called Sharatan

Degree position: 2°58'–3°58' Taurus between the years 1930 and 2000

Magnitude: 2.5–3

Strength: ★★★★★★

Orb: 2°

Constellation: Beta Arietis

Applicable days: April 22, 23, 24, 25

Star qualities: Mars/Saturn

Description: a pearl-white star located in the north horn of the Ram

PRIMARY STAR'S INFLUENCE

El Scheratain imparts endurance, the power to overcome by resistance, and energy. Through determination, this star suggests that you can develop leadership abilities and achieve honors and good fortune. The influence of this star also indicates that irritating occurrences need to be addressed with patience. Individuals influenced by this star need to avoid frustration or indecision, as it may deplete their powers.

Linked to your Sun's degree, this star bestows a preference for work requiring endurance and good physical strength. You may achieve distinction in your field. El Scheratain, however, also carries a negative influence, suggesting a tendency to dominate or control situations, thus creating problems.

• *Positive:* persistence, indefatigable strength

• *Negative:* destructive force, stubbornness, lack of energy, lack of vitality

Your Secret Self

An innate understanding that knowledge is power stimulates you to learn constantly. As you also possess a basic practicality and good judgment, you are prepared to put in the groundwork necessary to achieve your big plans. Through perseverance and a realistic appraisal of your goals, you are able to fulfill your remarkable potential. With your advanced social skills and knowing how to organize, you are good at getting others to help you achieve success.

Although you are sociable and love to be spontaneous and free, your work may play a major part in your life. It is also important that you listen to the quiet voice of your intuition, particularly to help you overcome any possible disappointment with others. In your desire to be expansive, just be careful that you do not get carried away and become too greedy or materialistic. You need not worry about money, however, as you have a certain financial protection that will always aid you in your desire for the good things of life.

Work & Vocation

Your fine intellect, dramatic flair, and people skills enable you to reach your potential in many different areas of life. If in business, you are enterprising and can be very protective of people working in positions below you. You have a talent for solving problems and excellent organizational and managerial abilities. Writing is a skill that comes naturally to you, and often this can be used creatively or for business. Attracted to public life, you can become involved in politics, acting, or entertainment. A love of variety and a need to be fairly independent may lead you to employment where you do not have to be in a deferential position. Despite being very practical, some individuals of this birthday are also attracted by philosophy or mysticism.

Famous people born on your birthday include actresses Shirley MacLaine, Barbra Streisand, and Jill Ireland, and guitarist John Williams.

Numerology

The emotional sensitivity of the number 24 birthday suggests that you seek balance and harmony. You are also receptive to form and structure and can easily create a complex yet efficient system. Faithful and fair, you are inclined to be undemonstrative, believing that actions speak louder than words. The main challenge for a number 24 birthday is to learn to associate with people from all walks of life, to overcome suspicious tendencies, and to build a secure home. The subinfluence of the number 4 month indicates that you can be determined, with strong willpower and an inquisitive nature. You may need to overcome a tendency to be impatient, demanding, or controlling. Often you learn that shortcuts lead to longer routes. Being responsible for your actions and paying attention to detail will ultimately save you time. You want recognition but need to work hard in order to receive respect and admiration. Build up your confidence through overcoming a tendency to be defensive.

• *Positive:* energy, idealism, practicality, strong determination, honesty, frankness, fairness, generosity, love of home, activity, energy

• *Negative:* ruthlessness, manipulative tendencies, materialism, instability, dislike of routine, laziness, unfaithfulness, instability, domineering and stubborn

Love & Relationships

A strong influence from an older man, probably your father, may have a strong impact on your perspective. A desire for independence and a busy life may indicate uncertainty about relationships. You may need to find a partner who has a natural sense of authority that you can respect and admire. Inspired by power and wisdom, you are often attracted to serious and hardworking individuals. If you refrain from being autocratic or overly serious yourself, you may find love and happiness in your relationships.

YOUR SPECIAL SOMEONE

You might find a faithful and reliable lover or partner among those born on the following dates.

Love & friendship: Jan. 1, 4, 9, 14, 28, 31, Feb. 12, 26, 29, Mar. 10, 24, 27, Apr. 8, 22, 25, May, 6, 20, 23, June 4, 18, 21, July 2, 16, 19, 30, Aug. 14, 17, 28, 30, Sept. 12, 15, 26, 28, 30, Oct. 10, 13, 24, 26, 28, Nov. 8, 11, 22, 24, 26, Dec. 6, 9, 20, 22, 24

Beneficial: Jan. 26, Feb. 24, Mar. 22, Apr. 20, May 18, June 16, July 14, Aug. 12, Sept. 10, Oct. 8, Nov. 6, Dec. 4

Fatal attractions: Oct. 26, 27, 28, 29

Challenging: Jan. 3, 25, Feb. 1, 23, Mar. 21, Apr. 19, May 17, June 15, July 13, Aug. 11, Sept. 9, Oct. 7, Nov. 5, Dec. 3

Soul mates: Jan. 3, 10, Feb. 1, 8, Mar. 6, Apr. 4, May 2, Sept. 14

April 25

Your birthday suggests that your intellectual brightness marks you out as an individual with something to say. Practical yet idealistic, you have sound common sense and a desire to be open and honest. Broad-minded, you are often a liberal who enjoys debates and acquiring knowledge. You may, however, have to overcome a tendency to think negatively and to guard against being critical or opinionated.

The influence of your Sun in the Taurus decanate suggests that you are reliable and solid, with a strong need for love and affection. There is also a likelihood of your being quite thrifty or economical with money, although you can be very generous with the people that you love. Often a lover of beauty, art, and music, you are likely to possess artistic talents as well as an exceptional voice. With self-discipline, these talents may be developed into a powerful form of self-expression.

In order to overcome a tendency to be obstinate, it may be necessary to ensure that you constantly challenge yourself in new areas rather than sticking with the tried and true. Although generally optimistic, when down you may suffer from impatience, frustration, or lack of self-esteem. Nevertheless, you are likely to be a good organizer and have wonderful ideas, and it may be necessary to put some of them into practice in order to fulfill your remarkable potential.

After the age of twenty-six, when your progressed Sun moves into Gemini, there is an increased need to communicate and exchange ideas. This can be a time when you can stretch yourself mentally through the study of new subjects. After the age of fifty-six, when your progressed Sun enters Cancer, you are likely to experience a major turning point that will highlight your need to feel closer to those you love and care for. There may be possible changes within your family structure.

FIXED STARS

Hamal, also called Al Hamal or the Sheep; El Scheratain, also called Sharatan

PRIMARY STAR

Star's name: Hamal, also called Al Hamal or the Sheep

Degree position: 6°43'–7°38' Taurus between the years 1930 and 2000

Magnitude: 2

Strength: ★★★★★★★

Orb: 2°10'

Constellation: Alpha Arietis

Applicable days: April 25, 26, 27, 28, 29, 30

Star qualities: combined influences of Mars and Saturn

Description: an orange-yellow star located in the forehead of the Ram

PRIMARY STAR'S INFLUENCE

Hamal endows restlessness and a drive to excel, together with an influence of rebelliousness. This star suggests that competitiveness and drive for success may at times challenge you to use unorthodox methods in order to achieve your goals.

Linked to your Sun's degree, this star bestows the power to overcome obstacles with concentration and persistence but warns against being inconsiderate to others or using force to get your own way. Only through patience can you develop your skills, talents, and abilities. Hamal may also suggest a danger of putting money at the top of your priorities.

Your Secret Self

Your relationships and home play an especially important role, as you seek a harmonious setting where you can feel safe and secure. With your creative ability, you often enjoy making your home comfortable and inviting, with a touch of luxury. Another way to express yourself may be through ideas that emphasize the importance of associating with people who are mentally stimulating. Furthering your education can also bring inspiration into your daily routine.

Kind-hearted, you often attract people who need your advice and support. Since you possess great sensitivity and a capacity for dealing with people, you may often find yourself in the role of guide and mentor. By having strong aims and objectives in life, you avoid the danger of becoming too reliant on others. For you, dependency may lead to frustration and disappointment if people do not live up to your expectations. You are a person who is cooperative and likes to play fair and be responsible, so you expect others to be the same.

Work & Vocation

Your creative nature and love of knowledge indicate that you often succeed in education or artistic pursuits. Your humanity and compassion may lead you to be a reformer, social worker,

• *Positive:* patience, discipline, hard work, concentrated energy, leadership
• *Negative:* use of force, unscrupulousness, keeping unsuitable company

See Appendix for additional fixed star readings.

or advisor. You may be gifted as an orator and share your knowledge with others. An interest in business could be explored through many different avenues, such as banking, stockbrokerage, commodities, or real estate. Alternatively, your creative talents suggest that you are good with your hands, and design work may be your forte. Drama and music, singing especially, are areas you may be attracted to. Your ability to raise funds for causes could mean that charity work would be an excellent structure for your organizational and managerial skills.

Famous people born on your birthday include inventor Guglielmo Marconi, singer Ella Fitzgerald, basketball player Meadowlark Lemon, and actor Al Pacino.

Numerology

Intuitive and thoughtful, yet quick and energetic, you need to express yourself through different experiences. A desire for perfection endowed by the number 25 birthdate often urges you to work hard and be productive. Usually you are instinctive and alert and can gain more knowledge through practical application than through mere theory. Good judgment and an eye for detail ensure successful accomplishment. You may have to develop a less skeptical attitude by overcoming a tendency to make erratic or impulsive decisions. With a number 25 birthdate, you possess strong mental energies; when concentrated, they aid you to look at all the facts and arrive at a conclusion faster than anyone else. The subinfluence of the number 4 month indicates that you need to learn patience and be practical in order to channel your creative power. Learn to stay focused by letting your feelings guide you, and trust your intuition. Overcome a tendency to be overanxious or impractical. You may have to develop a less skeptical attitude and overcome an inclination to make erratic or impulsive decisions; learn to think before you act. By using tact and diplomacy, you manage to adapt.

• *Positive:* intuition, perfectionism, perceptivity, creativity, people skills
• *Negative:* impulsiveness, impatience, irresponsibility, overemotionalism, jealousy, secrecy, criticism, moodiness, nervousness

Love & Relationships

For a sensitive and emotional person like you, relationships are very significant. Women of this birthday are usually faithful and dutiful but may have to guard against becoming overly dependent on their partners. Sociable and friendly, you enjoy entertaining, and with your wit or zany humor, you can be good company. Some relationships act as a catalyst or transformer and help you to alter your beliefs and deepen your understanding. Learn to communicate your feelings and not be too reserved or secretive. You need a positive philosophy in life or someone who understands you, as you thrive on encouragement and love.

YOUR SPECIAL SOMEONE

To find long-lasting happiness, security, and a steady environment, you might begin by looking for someone born on one of the following days.

Love & friendship: Jan. 1, 5, 10, 15, 26, 29, 30, Feb. 13, 24, 27, 28, Mar. 11, 22, 25, 26, Apr. 9, 20, 23, 24, May 7, 18, 21, 22, June 5, 16, 19, 20, July 3, 14, 17, 18, 31, Aug. 1, 12, 15, 16, 29, 31, Sept. 10, 13, 14, 27, 29, Oct. 8, 11, 12, 25, 27, Nov. 6, 9, 10, 23, 25, Dec. 4, 7, 8, 21, 23, 29

Beneficial: Jan. 1, 2, 10, 27, Feb. 8, 25, Mar. 6, 23, Apr. 4, 21, May 2, 19, 30, June 17, 28, July 15, 26, Aug. 13, 24, Sept. 11, 22, Oct. 9, 20, Nov. 7, 18, Dec. 5, 16

Fatal attractions: Oct. 28, 29, 30

Challenging: Jan. 17, 26, Feb. 15, 24, Mar. 13, 22, Apr. 11, 20, May 9, 18, June 7, 16, July 5, 14, Aug. 3, 12, 30, Sept. 1, 10, 28, Oct. 8, 26, 29, Nov. 6, 24, 27, Dec. 4, 22, 25

Soul mates: Jan. 21, Feb. 19, Mar. 17, Apr. 15, May 13, June 11, July 9, 29, Aug. 7, 27, Sept. 5, 25, Oct. 3, 23, Nov. 1, 21, Dec. 19

April 26

Your birthday reveals you to be intelligent yet sensitive, a practical visionary who has the potential for tremendous success. Although you are attracted to mental power in all its forms, a dislike of harshness implies that you are sensitive to your environment. You have drive and imagination, and these are ideal when you are inspired and fighting for your dream.

With your Sun in the first decanate of Taurus, you have a very creative side and should deeply appreciate color, form, and sound. This also accents a love of nature, beauty, and luxury, and a strong need for self-expression. Since you are likely to be very affectionate yourself, you are drawn toward people who can be very loving. The subinfluence of your decanate ruler Venus indicates that you have a flair for financial dealings and need only apply self-discipline to manifest your large-scale plans and natural good fortune. Unfortunately, this may also suggest a tendency to overindulge.

Although pragmatic, with a good sense of form, you also possess natural psychic gifts. Your strong instincts give you insight into people's motivations, and suggest that your highly developed perception can lead to universal understanding and a growing sense of compassion.

After the age of twenty-five, when your progressed Sun moves into Gemini, there is an increased desire to express your ideas and interrelate with others in your immediate surroundings. This influence may encourage you to study or mentally diversify in numerous ways, and continues until around the age of fifty-five, when your progressed Sun enters Cancer. As a turning point for you, this will highlight the growing importance of having a secure home base and expressing your feelings, especially in family circles. A strong need to nurture or be nurtured is also indicated.

Fixed Star

PRIMARY STAR'S INFLUENCE

Hamal endows restlessness and a drive to excel, together with an influence of rebelliousness. This star suggests that competitiveness and drive for success may at times challenge you to use unorthodox methods in order to achieve your goals.

Linked to your Sun's degree, this star bestows the power to overcome obstacles with concentration and persistence but warns against being inconsiderate to others or using force to get your own way. Only through patience can you develop your skills, talents, and abilities. Hamal may also suggest a danger of putting money at the top of your priorities.

• Positive: patience, discipline, hard work, concentrated energy, leadership

• Negative: use of force, unscrupulousness, keeping unsuitable company

Your Secret Self

Understanding the value of knowledge and wanting to use it to build for the future, you like to keep yourself productive. This enables you to feel that you are being positive, security-conscious, and true to your strong sense of values. Keeping your amazing mind occupied and living up to your potential are threatened by the danger of falling into escapist tendencies. With your sensitivity and vivid and powerful imagination, it may be too easy sometimes to take the easy way out or tell people what they want to hear. At the other extreme, when you have set your mind on something, your power and determination can be formidable.

Possessing superior organizational skills and being very sociable, you often fare well when involved in group activities. Frequently you like to take a leading role, especially when learning is concerned. When interested in a subject, you are able to learn very quickly and may be drawn toward metaphysical subjects.

Work & Vocation

A practical aptitude together with an organizational flair could suggest that you can achieve success in manufacturing, merchandising, or banking. If business is chosen as a career, you would prefer to be involved in large-scale operations. Your natural creativity could lead you into writing, painting, or music. A flair for relating to people indicates that you can be successful in dealing with the public, especially through education and social welfare. An excellent sense of structure or form combined with your vision may take you into careers such as architecture, photography, or filmmaking. Alternatively, your special insight into psychology and a natural healing ability may draw you toward the medical or alternative health professions.

Famous people born on your birthday include painter Eugene Delacroix, philosopher Ludwig Wittgenstein, entertainer Carol Burnett, and musician Duane Eddy.

Numerology

The strength or power suggested by the number 26 birthday shows that you are a cautious character with strong values and sound judgment. A love of home and parental instincts may also suggest a need to build a solid foundation or find real stability. Often a tower of strength for others, you are willing to support friends, family members, and relatives who may turn to you in time of need. You may nevertheless need to guard against materialistic tendencies and a desire to control people or situations. The subinfluence of the number 4 month indicates that you need to express yourself more freely. You need to develop your inborn talents and be experimental. Avoid being overcritical, lazy, or cynical. If confused, you can become bad-tempered, obstinate, or easily bored. Avoid pessimism by being positive yet realistic, and take time away from your responsibilities to have fun.

• *Positive:* creativity, practicality, caring, responsibility, pride in family, enthusiasm, courage
• *Negative:* stubbornness, rebelliousness, unstable relationships, lack of enthusiasm, lack of persistence, instability

Love & Relationships

In your major partnerships it is important that you find someone who is like-minded, with whom you can share the same values and level of understanding. Your most successful, enduring, and stable social and emotional relationships are likely to be with those who are intellectually stimulating and know their own mind, possibly with those who are concerned with politics, philosophy, spirituality, or education. Work may also play a part in your personal relationships, but guard against a tendency to become involved in power games. Your grasp of subtle emotional changes enables you to enjoy enchanting relationships with the opposite sex.

YOUR SPECIAL SOMEONE

You might just find the inspiring partner you are looking for among those born on the following dates.

Love & friendship: Jan. 10, 13, 20, 30, 31, Feb. 8, 11, 18, 28, Mar. 6, 9, 16, 26, Apr. 4, 7, 14, 24, May 2, 5, 12, 22, June 3, 10, 20, July 1, 8, 18, Aug. 6, 16, 30, Sept. 4, 14, 28, 30, Oct. 2, 12, 26, 28, 30, Nov. 10, 24, 26, 28, Dec. 8, 22, 24, 26, 29

Beneficial: Jan. 12, 16, 17, 28, Feb. 10, 14, 15, 26, Mar. 8, 12, 13, 24, Apr. 6, 10, 11, 22, May 4, 8, 9, 20, 29, June 2, 6, 7, 18, 27, July 4, 5, 16, 25, Aug. 2, 3, 14, 23, Sept. 1, 12, 21, Oct. 10, 19, Nov. 8, 17, Dec. 6, 15

Fatal attractions: Mar. 31, Apr. 29, May 27, June 25, July 23, Aug. 21, Sept. 19, Oct. 17, 29, 30, 31, Nov. 15, Dec. 17

Challenging: Jan. 6, 18, 22, 27, Feb. 4, 16, 20, 25, Mar. 2, 14, 18, 23, Apr. 12, 16, 21, May 10, 14, 19, June 8, 12, 17, July 6, 10, 15, Aug. 4, 8, 13, Sept. 2, 6, 11, Oct. 4, 9, Nov. 2, 7, Dec. 5

Soul mates: Mar. 28, Apr. 26, May 24, June 22, July 20, Aug. 18, Sept. 16, Oct. 14, Nov. 12, Dec. 10

April 27

Your birthday suggests that you are a clever and shrewd Taurean with determination and original ideas. Independent and quick at assessing situations, you can be an interesting mixture of doubt and naïveté. Having a youthful quality, you can inspire people with your exciting and adventurous ideas. You also possess tenacity and persistence and are able to persevere with a project until the very end.

The double influence of your Sun in the Taurus decanate implies that you love the good life and all its little luxuries. If pushed, you are likely to become obstinate and self-willed. However, this may be counterbalanced by a very loving and affectionate side to your nature. A natural sensuality can also bring an appreciation of beauty, color, and form, which may lead to artistic self-expression. There is also an inclination to desire the best that life can offer, with a tendency to overindulge.

It is through the development of your fine mind that your greatest potential can emerge, and by training yourself you can overcome an inclination to negative thinking. It is through worry and anxiety that you may become cold and frustrated, so it is important to have a clear goal and stay positive. When inspired, you are keen and astute, with an ability to act spontaneously and seize the opportunities of the moment.

After the age of twenty-four, when your progressed Sun moves into Gemini, there is an increased need to communicate and exchange ideas. This can be a time when you expand your horizons and learn new skills or take up a new study. At the age of fifty-four, when your progressed Sun enters Cancer, there is another major turning point that highlights the growing emotional need for a strong base or foundation to work from. This places extra emphasis on having a secure home as well as on family ties.

Fixed Stars

Hamal, also called Al Hamal or the Sheep; Schedir, also called Sader

PRIMARY STAR

Star's name: Hamal, also called Al Hamal or the Sheep

Degree position: 6°43'–7°38' Taurus between the years 1930 and 2000

Magnitude: 2

Strength: ★★★★★★★

Orb: 2°10'

Constellation: Alpha Arietis

Applicable days: April 25, 26, 27, 28, 29, 30

Star qualities: combined influences of Mars and Saturn

Description: an orange-yellow star located in the forehead of the Ram

PRIMARY STAR'S INFLUENCE

Hamal endows restlessness and a drive to excel, together with an influence of rebelliousness. This star suggests that competitiveness and drive for success may at times challenge you to use unorthodox methods in order to achieve your goals.

Linked to your Sun's degree, this star bestows the power to overcome obstacles with concentration and persistence but warns against being inconsiderate to others or using force to get your own way. Only through patience can you develop your skills, talents, and abilities. Hamal may also suggest a danger of putting money at the top of your priorities.

Your Secret Self

No matter what difficult situations you encounter in life, deep down you know that you possess the power to triumph over adversity. You have an innate sense of the value of things as well as an inner drive to accomplish materially, which help push you on. You may find the influence of women particularly helpful in achieving your goals. You have the business sense to achieve financially and be successful, but it is important that you believe your work is worthwhile. Education is essential to bring out the best of your gifts.

Since you can be mentally stubborn, you may have to remember to enjoy debating with others without becoming too argumentative. You enjoy friendly battles of wits and take pleasure in asking subtly provocative questions. Although you are sociable, you may need time alone to recoup your energy and give you time to reflect. This develops your natural intuitive sense, which can stand you in good stead and help you overcome a tendency to skepticism.

Work & Vocation

With your mental vitality and love for debate, you can excel in a career such as education or law, or an occupation related to research. You often have good technical skills and can work with computers or various types of engineering. If you share your knowledge with others, you can enjoy work that involves change and social reform. Your fine mind enables you to benefit from higher education, and with your organizational skills, it is possible for you to achieve a high position in government service. Alternatively, you may be interested in psychology, and your analytical mind may draw you toward some areas of the medical profession.

Famous people born on your birthday include inventor Samuel Morse, political activist Coretta Scott King, singer Sheena Easton, feminist writer Mary Wollstonecraft, and actress Sandy Dennis.

Numerology

Intuitive yet inquisitive, the number 27 birthday indicates that your depth of thought can be greatly enhanced by developing patience and self-control. You are often forceful and determined and can pay great attention to detail. Generally idealistic and sensitive, with a fertile and creative mind, you can impress others with your original thought and ideas. Developing good communication skills helps you to overcome a reluctance to express your deeper feelings. Education is beneficial for number 27 persons, and with the proper qualifications you can achieve success through writing, research, and work in large organizations. The subinfluence of the number 4 month indicates that you need direction or control in life. Enthusiastic, you benefit from self-discipline and keeping your life well organized. Naturally versatile and imaginative, with strong instincts or psychic abilities, you are ambitious and full of ideas. However, restlessness may cause you to be unsettled and impulsive, and you may need to learn how to turn your ideas into tangible concepts.

• *Positive:* versatility, imagination, creativity, resoluteness, bravery, good understanding, mental capability, spirituality, inventiveness, mental strength

• *Negative:* disagreeableness, tendency to be easily offended, argumentative nature, restlessness, nervousness, mistrust, tense

YOUR SPECIAL SOMEONE

To keep you interested in a long-term relationship, you might want to look out for those born on the following days.

Love & friendship: Jan. 11, 21, 28, 31, Feb. 19, 26, 29, Mar. 17, 24, 27, Apr. 15, 22, 25, May 13, 20, 23, June 11, 18, 21, July 9, 16, 19, Aug. 7, 14, 17, 31, Sept. 5, 12, 15, 29, Oct. 3, 10, 13, 27, 29, 31, Nov. 1, 8, 11, 25, 27, 29, Dec. 6, 9, 23, 25, 27

Beneficial: Jan. 9, 12, 18, 24, 29, Feb. 7, 10, 16, 22, 27, Mar. 5, 8, 14, 20, 25, Apr. 3, 6, 12, 18, 23, May 1, 10, 16, 21, 31, June 2, 8, 14, 19, 29, July 6, 12, 17, 27, Aug. 4, 10, 15, 25, Sept. 2, 8, 13, 23, Oct. 6, 11, 21, Nov. 4, 9, 19, Dec. 2, 7, 17

Fatal attractions: Jan. 3, Feb. 1, Oct. 30, 31, Nov. 1, 2

Challenging: Jan. 7, 8, 19, 28, Feb. 5, 6, 17, 26, Mar. 3, 4, 15, 24, Apr. 1, 2, 13, 22, May 11, 20, June 9, 18, July 7, 16, Aug. 5, 14, Sept. 3, 12, Oct. 1, 10, Nov. 8, Dec. 6

Soul mates: Jan. 3, 19, Feb. 1, 17, Mar. 15, Apr. 13, May 11, June 9, July 7, Aug. 5, Sept. 3, Oct. 1

Love & Relationships

Intuitive and sensitive, yet enterprising and active, you are drawn toward resourceful individuals. Shrewd and independent, you like to know what motivates others, but it is only when you overcome your tendency to be suspicious that you can open your heart and express your inner feelings. Loyal women may play an important role in your success. Often they can assist you to rise to a position of authority at work or introduce you to people in the right social circles.

April 28

An interesting mixture of mental power, charm, and business acumen mark people who share your birthday as special. With endurance and the ability to advance in life through your own efforts, you have a tenacious approach to fulfilling your own vision. Unfortunately, too strong a love of the good life and a tendency to become too self-absorbed may distract you from accomplishing your big dreams.

The added influence of your Sun in the decanate of Taurus suggests that you have an enhanced appreciation of beauty, color, and sound and a need for creative expression. This may also include a special flair for speaking or singing. With your strong attractions, you need affection from others and are willing to give love in return. You may, however, have to guard against becoming frustrated and channeling your natural sensuality into overindulgence in all its forms.

To avoid a conflict between your sensitive idealism and mundane materialism, it may be necessary for you to get a feel for a situation first before committing yourself to some form of structure. This entails using your excellent intuitive sense in your practical affairs to establish a concrete foundation upon which to build your aspirations.

After the age of twenty-three, when your progressed Sun moves into Gemini, the pace of your life increases and there is more of an emphasis on writing, speech, and communication in general. This continues until around age fifty-three, when your progressed Sun enters Cancer. This is a turning point for you, and it will highlight the growing importance of emotional bonds, security, home, and family.

FIXED STARS

Hamal, also called Al Hamal or the Sheep; Schedir, also called Sader

PRIMARY STAR

Star's name: Hamal, also called Al Hamal or the Sheep

Degree position: 6°43'–7°38' Taurus between the years 1930 and 2000

Magnitude: 2

Strength: ★★★★★★★

Orb: 2°10'

Constellation: Alpha Arietis

Applicable days: April 25, 26, 27, 28, 29, 30

Star qualities: combined influences of Mars and Saturn

Description: an orange-yellow star located in the forehead of the Ram

PRIMARY STAR'S INFLUENCE

Hamal endows restlessness and a drive to excel, together with an influence of rebelliousness. This star suggests that competitiveness and drive for success may at times challenge you to use unorthodox methods in order to achieve your goals.

Linked to your Sun's degree, this star bestows the power to overcome obstacles with concentration and persistence but warns against being inconsiderate to others or using force to get your own way. Only through patience can you develop your skills, talents, and abilities. Hamal may also suggest a danger of putting money at the top of your priorities.

Your Secret Self

A sense of the dramatic, combined with your determination and ability to work cooperatively, points to your leadership ability. You have an innate capacity to commercialize your talents and make contacts but may have to overcome an unfounded fear of a lack of financial reserves.

You maintain a strong protection around the area of your work as long as you are willing to put in the necessary time and effort. It is essential, however, to find a middle course between this area of your life and that of your relationships. You possess the ability to understand concession and compromise with others but may have to be careful of the balance of power in the process. Too much and you may become dominating; too little and you might be left inactive and resigned. You will always have the strength, however, to master any situation with balanced will.

Work & Vocation

Your pleasure in mental pursuits could lead to a career in teaching or writing. An ability to understand human nature indicates that an occupation such as advisor, therapist, or counselor could also be rewarding for you. Your natural flair for form and color could easily inspire you to become a designer or draw you to the theater, music, and the arts. Alternatively, your power of persuasion and bright ideas could motivate you to succeed in the world of advertising, the media, or publishing.

Famous people who share your birthday include writer Harper Lee, dictator Saddam Hussein, actress Ann-Margret, singer Blossom Dearie, actor Lionel Barrymore, and T.V. host Jay Leno.

Numerology

Like a number 1 individual, with a number 28 birthday you are ambitious, direct, and enterprising. Always ready for action and new ventures, you courageously take on life's challenges. With your enthusiasm you can easily inspire others to join or support you in your ventures. Although you are success-oriented and determined, family and home life are very important to you. Finding stability and taking care of your nearest and dearest may, at times, be a challenge for you. The subinfluence of the number 4 month indicates that you are enthusiastic and versatile. Although you need stability and security, you are likely to travel or work away from home. A need to find a balance between duties and a love for freedom suggests that learning self-discipline can help you become determined and assertive. Avoid scattering your energies in all directions. Learn that through process and step-by-step method you can achieve your goals. Your ability to create new structure through a synthesis of old ideas also helps you to use your intuitive powers.

• *Positive:* compassion, progressive attitudes, daring, artistic skill, creativity, idealism, ambition, hard work, stable home life, strong will

• *Negative:* daydreaming, lack of motivation, lack of compassion, unrealistic expectations, bossiness, lack of judgment, aggression, lack of confidence, overdependence on others, excessive pride

Love & Relationships

Emotionally dynamic and dramatic, you need to express your love and creative power. Although you are sensitive and love romance you may need to learn self-discipline and guard against tendencies such as possessiveness, envy, or jealousy. Drawn to people who are creative and friendly, you may prefer theatrical personalities who will bring excitement into your life. Alternatively, in your pursuit of knowledge you may seek like-minded people who share your interests.

YOUR SPECIAL SOMEONE

You might find a partner who will understand your sensitivity and need for love among those born on the following dates.

Love & friendship: Jan. 8, 12, 18, 22, Feb. 10, 16, 20, Mar. 8, 14, 18, 28, Apr. 12, 16, 26, May 10, 14, 24, June 8, 12, 22, July 6, 10, 20, 29, Aug. 4, 8, 18, 27, 30, Sept. 2, 6, 16, 25, 28, Oct. 4, 14, 23, 26, 30, Nov. 2, 12, 21, 24, 28, Dec. 10, 19, 22, 26, 28

Beneficial: Jan. 6, 10, 25, 30, Feb. 4, 8, 23, 28, Mar. 2, 6, 21, 26, Apr. 4, 19, 24, May 2, 17, 22, June 15, 20, 30, July 13, 18, 28, Aug. 11, 16, 26, Sept. 9, 14, 24, Oct. 7, 12, 22, Nov. 5, 10, 20, Dec. 3, 8, 18

Fatal attractions: May 29, June 27, July 25, Aug. 23, Sept. 21, Oct. 19, 31, Nov. 1, 17, Dec. 15

Challenging: Jan. 13, 29, 31, Feb. 11, 27, 29, Mar. 9, 25, 27, Apr. 7, 23, 25, May 5, 21, 23, June 3, 19, 21, July 1, 17, 19, Aug. 15, 17, Sept. 13, 15, Oct. 11, 13, Nov. 9, 11, Dec. 7, 9

Soul mates: Jan. 6, 25, Feb. 4, 23, Mar. 2, 21, Apr. 19, May 17, June 15, July 13, Aug. 11, Sept. 9, Nov. 7, Dec. 5

April 29

FIXED STARS

Hamal, also called Al Hamal or the Sheep; Schedir, also called Sader

PRIMARY STAR

Star's name: Hamal, also called Al Hamal or the Sheep

Degree position: 6°43'–7°38' Taurus between the years 1930 and 2000

Magnitude: 2

Strength: ★★★★★★★

Orb: 2°10'

Constellation: Alpha Arietis

Applicable dates: April 25, 26, 27, 28, 29, 30

Star qualities: combined influences of Mars and Saturn

Description: an orange-yellow star located in the forehead of the Ram

PRIMARY STAR'S INFLUENCE

Hamal endows restlessness and a drive to excel, together with an influence of rebelliousness. This star suggests that competitiveness and drive for success may at times challenge you to use unorthodox methods in order to achieve your goals.

Linked to your Sun's degree, this star bestows the power to overcome obstacles with concentration and persistence but warns against being inconsiderate to others or using force to get your own way. Only through patience can you develop your skills, talents, and abilities. Hamal may also suggest a danger of putting money at the top of your priorities.

The keen intellect and mental quickness available to you ensure that your mind never stops working. Being very instinctive and capable of deep thought, you form instant opinions of people, which are usually right. It may be necessary for you to find an interest and specialize so that you can focus all your mental energy on something worthwhile.

The influence of your Taurus decanate points to a love of beauty and the arts as well as creative self-expression. It indicates a sensual nature that at times can be quite material and security-conscious. The natural business sense that this influence suggests can blend well with your interest in people and helps you make contacts from all different walks of life. Often you are interested in foreign places or meeting new people and are likely to have opportunities to work abroad. Alternatively, in order to avoid boredom you may need to seek new experiences and learn as you earn.

To evade pessimism or cynicism, it may be necessary to give yourself a positive goal that you feel is just within your reach. This stimulates your spirit of enterprise and brings out your optimism and sense of good fortune. Often mentally quick and curious, you are good company and can be very entertaining, with a unique sense of humor.

After the age of twenty-two, when your progressed Sun moves into Gemini, the tempo of your life increases and there is more of an emphasis on writing, speech, and communication. This continues until around age fifty-two, when your progressed Sun enters Cancer. This is a turning point for you, which will highlight the growing importance of emotional intimacy and security.

Your Secret Self

Although an inner restlessness drives you to seek variety in your life, you also have within you a need for order, dependability, and security. With your ingenuity and pragmatic approach, you can skillfully organize your life plans and solve problems. Extremely strong-willed and stubborn when you have made up your mind, you are a force to be reckoned with.

Despite being very practical on the surface, you also possess within you a desire for something deep and meaningful. This may bring secrecy into your relationships or can lead to an interest in subjects of a more profound nature. You also possess emotional sensitivity and can be instinctive or psychic, which enables you to have a good understanding of people. Although you can be loving and caring, guard against a tendency toward fluctuating moods. Nevertheless, when positive, you creatively channel your thoughts and practical skills to achieve your objectives.

Work & Vocation

Your need for mental stimulation and your quick intelligence indicate that you are able to assimilate information very quickly. This gives you a plethora of career choices, though you may have to guard against boredom. Although variety is a key to your success, avoid scattering your energies by having too many irons in the fire. Occupations in the public sphere could well be of interest, as a sense of purpose often comes from people-oriented activities. Those of you who are artistically gifted could perhaps succeed as writers or in journalism, commercial art, advertising, or fashion. Leadership qualities could bring success in the business world or the political arena. Acting or music are also excellent outlets for your imagination and drive.

Famous people who share your birthday include actresses Michelle Pfeiffer and Uma Thurman, musician/composer Duke Ellington, tennis star Andre Agassi, conductors Sir Thomas Beecham and Sir Malcolm Sargent, publishing magnate William Randolph Hearst, and comedian Jerry Seinfeld.

Numerology

With a number 29 birthday, you are often highly intuitive, sensitive, and emotional. Your compassionate and understanding nature inspires humanitarianism and can encourage others to fulfill their hopes and aspirations. Although you are a true dreamer, often the extreme sides of your nature indicate that you may have to guard against alternating moods. Having a number 29 birthdate, you need to be popular and may care what others think about you. The subinfluence of the number 4 month indicates that you need stability and security. Although you can be idealistic and generous, you may benefit from being more aware of others' needs. If restless and unsettled, you can become tactless or disruptive. A need to find a balance among your high ideals, love for freedom, and realism is often achieved through self-discipline and hard work. Accepting limitations and keeping your feet on firm ground help you to achieve some of your goals.

• *Positive:* inspiration, balance, inner peace, generosity, successful, creative, intuitive, mystical, powerful dreams, worldiness, faith

• *Negative:* lack of focus, insecurity, nervousness, moodiness, difficult, extreme, inconsiderate, isolation, oversensitivity

Love & Relationships

Although you are often outspoken and alert, you are emotionally rather secretive about your personal relationships. You may have to overcome a tendency to become overly suspicious about those you love and learn to take each relationship as an enlightening experience. You make a good friend and confidante, however, and your entertaining ways ensure your social success.

YOUR SPECIAL SOMEONE

To find long-lasting happiness and security, you might begin by looking for someone born on one of the following days.

Love & friendship: Jan. 4, 13, 19, 23, Feb. 11, 17, 21, Mar. 9, 15, 19, 28, 29, 30, Apr. 7, 13, 17, 26, 27, May 5, 11, 15, 24, 25, 26, June 3, 9, 13, 22, 23, 24, July 1, 7, 11, 20, 21, 22, Aug. 5, 9, 18, 19, 20, Sept. 3, 7, 16, 17, 18, Oct. 1, 5, 14, 15, 16, 29, 31, Nov. 3, 12, 13, 14, 27, 29, Dec. 1, 10, 11, 12, 25, 27, 29

Beneficial: Jan. 7, 15, 20, 31, Feb. 5, 13, 18, 29, Mar. 3, 11, 16, 27, Apr. 1, 9, 14, 25, May 7, 12, 23, June 5, 10, 21, July 3, 8, 19, Aug. 1, 6, 17, 30, Sept. 4, 15, 28, Oct. 2, 13, 26, Nov. 11, 24, Dec. 9, 22

Fatal attractions: Nov. 1, 2, 3

Challenging: Jan. 6, 14, 30, Feb. 4, 12, 28, Mar. 2, 10, 26, Apr. 8, 24, May 6, 22, June 4, 20, July 2, 18, Aug. 16, Sept. 14, Oct. 12, Nov. 10, Dec. 8

Soul mates: Apr. 30, May 28, June 26, July 24, Aug. 22, Sept. 20, Oct. 18, 30, Nov. 16, 28, Dec. 14, 26

April 30

A sharp practical sense is indicated by your birthday and shows you to be a plain-speaking, hardworking individual. With your pragmatic approach, organizational skills, and loyalty, you may often need to become involved in some kind of large creative project. A rebellious streak, however, may be a deterrent to creating the harmony that you so desire.

The added influence of your Taurus decanate indicates that you are sensual, with strong attractions and a need for love and affection. You have a taste for beauty and luxury but may have to beware of overindulgence in all forms of pleasure. This influence also supplies a love of art, music, and drama as well as an appreciation of nature. Since you have an innate creative streak, you may wish to develop this further into some form of self-expression.

An inborn ability to sense a bargain or make business contacts ensures that you can see opportunities and enjoy a sense of enterprise. Being naturally persuasive yourself, and enjoying a sharp wit, you are usually drawn to people who are clever or successful in their own right. Whatever you do, you like to do it with style and honesty, and you need to feel that you are expanding your knowledge. When enthusiastic and focused, you have the ability to turn your ideas into tangible reality.

Around the age of twenty-one, when your progressed Sun moves into Gemini, you may diversify and find many more interests. At this time study and communication may become more important to you. There is another turning point after fifty-one, when your progressed Sun moves into Cancer, identifying the importance of emotional attachments and a strong home base.

Fixed Star

Star's name: Hamal, also called Al Hamal or the Sheep

Degree position: 6°43'–7°38' Taurus between the years 1930 and 2000

Magnitude: 2

Strength: ★★★★★★★

Orb: 2°10'

Constellation: Alpha Arietis

Applicable days: April 25, 26, 27, 28, 29, 30

Star qualities: combined influences of Mars and Saturn

Description: an orange-yellow star located in the forehead of the Ram

PRIMARY STAR'S INFLUENCE

Hamal endows restlessness and a drive to excel, together with an influence of rebelliousness. This star suggests that competitiveness and drive for success may at times challenge you to use unorthodox methods in order to achieve your goals.

Linked to your Sun's degree, this star bestows the power to overcome obstacles with concentration and persistence but warns against being inconsiderate to others or using force to get your own way. Only through patience can you develop your skills, talents, and abilities. Hamal may also suggest a danger of putting money at the top of your priorities.

• *Positive:* patience, discipline, hard work, concentrated energy, leadership

• *Negative:* use of force, unscrupulousness, keeping unsuitable company

Your Secret Self

The sensitive inner you may find it important to have a safe haven of calm from the rush of the world. Your home may therefore play an important part in your responsibilities and enable you to have a foundation on which to build. Despite a desire for peace and quiet, you are likely to be constantly seeking mental gratification. The stimulus for knowledge as power is likely to drive you to explore new avenues and ideas, whether for financial rewards or to satisfy the idealistic side of your nature.

You are seldom swept off your feet by emotion, even though you feel strongly for your loved ones. When you take on responsibilities, however, you are willing to make the necessary sacrifices. In contrast, your playful side can emerge totally unexpectedly and you can surprise everyone with your spontaneity.

Work & Vocation

You are full of ideas that can make money, and you are a good planner and organizer. It is possible for you to succeed in education, sales, commerce, promotions, or advertising. If in business, you need to be given a lot of space to operate independently and may well be happier being self-employed. Even so, your abilities to plan and implement many worthwhile and financially advantageous schemes make you a valuable member of any team. You are likely to be particularly interested in the study of philosophy, psychology, or religious thought. You may be drawn to professions that use your fine mind, such as those involving selling, information, or education. Alternatively, you may be attracted to the world of entertainment or the arts.

Famous people who share your birthday include singer Willie Nelson, actress Jill Clayburgh, Queen Juliana of Holland, and actress Eve Arden.

Numerology

Creative, friendly, and sociable are just some of the ways people would describe those with a number 30 birthday. With an eye for style and form, you can achieve success in all types of work concerning art, design, and music. Similarly, possessing a need for self-expression and a natural talent for words, you may excel at writing, speaking, or singing. You possess strong feelings, and being in love or secure in your knowledge is a vital requirement. In your pursuit of happiness, avoid being lazy or overindulgent. The subinfluence of the number 4 month indicates that since you possess wonderful ideas, you need a stable and secure place where you can be peaceful and creative. Often you can find yourself deep in thought or inspired by something you observed or read that enables you to see beyond what is obvious. Stay focused and avoid scattering yourself in many activities, which can cause absent-mindedness. Although you can be an extrovert, you look inward to find the answers.

• *Positive:* love of fun, loyalty, friendliness, ability to synthesize, talent with words, creativity, luck

• *Negative:* laziness, obstinacy, erratic behavior, impatience, insecurity, indifference, tendency to scatter energy

Love & Relationships

Although at one stage in your life you may have been drawn to some very unusual relationships, your power of discrimination indicates that you rarely lose your heart. Often you may see relationships as valuable learning experiences that leave you wiser and more knowledgeable about love. Your need for mental challenge suggests that you may be more likely to express your opinions than your feelings, but once you find someone who positively stimulates your mind, then you can be a loyal and supportive partner.

YOUR SPECIAL SOMEONE

For security and love, you might want to begin looking for those born among the following dates.

Love & friendship: Jan. 3, 4, 14, 20, 24, 25, Feb. 2, 12, 18, 22, Mar. 10, 16, 20, 29, 30, Apr. 8, 14, 18, 27, 28, May 6, 12, 16, 25, 26, 31, June 4, 10, 14, 23, 24, 29, July 2, 8, 12, 21, 22, 27, Aug. 6, 10, 19, 20, 25, Sept. 4, 8, 9, 17, 18, 23, Oct. 2, 6, 15, 16, 21, 30, Nov. 4, 13, 14, 19, 28, 30, Dec. 2, 11, 12, 17, 26, 28, 30

Beneficial: Jan. 4, 8, 21, Feb. 2, 6, 19, Mar. 4, 17, 28, Apr. 2, 15, 16, May 13, 24, June 11, 22, July 9, 20, Aug. 7, 18, 31, Sept. 5, 16, 29, Oct. 3, 14, 27, Nov. 1, 12, 25, Dec. 10, 23

Fatal attractions: Jan. 3, Feb. 1, May 31, June 29, July 27, Aug. 25, Sept. 23, Oct. 21, Nov. 2, 3, 4, 19, Dec. 17

Challenging: Jan. 7, 10, 15, 31, Feb. 5, 8, 13, 29, Mar. 3, 6, 11, 27, Apr. 1, 4, 9, 25, May 2, 7, 23, June 5, 21, July 3, 19, Aug. 1, 17, Sept. 15, Oct. 13, Nov. 11, Dec. 9

Soul mates: Mar. 31, Apr. 29, May 27, June 25, July 23, Aug. 21, Sept. 19, Oct. 17, 29, Nov. 15, 27, Dec. 13, 25

May 1

FIXED STARS

Although your Sun's degree is not linked to a fixed star, some of your other planets' degrees certainly will be. By having an astrological chart calculated, you can find the exact position of the planets on your date of birth. This will tell you which of the fixed stars listed in this book are relevant to you.

Your birthday reveals you to be an astute, practical, and creative individual who needs people. You thrive on variety and change, and these may provide you with the excitement you need. Having magnetic charm and being very sociable, you need the approval of others and are generally popular. You have a strong attraction for beauty and the arts, which can be a valuable form of expression for your emotional sensitivity. With an inclination for art, music, or drama, you are likely to use your work as a form of creative self-expression.

The added influence of your Virgo decanate suggests that you have mental agility, discrimination, and enhanced communication skills. Together with your creative abilities, this may manifest as a talent for writing. It also shows an ability to work hard and a desire to be of service, as well as an inclination toward detailed work or research. Since this influence also emphasizes an ability to gain money and material resources, it can help you to realize your ideals.

Having the added advantage of being both practical and analytical as well as emotional and sensitive, you have a wide range to your personality and are therefore in a better position than most to achieve on a grand scale. You may just have to be careful of becoming discouraged or distracting yourself from your high objectives through overindulgence and too great a desire for the good life.

In youth you are sensitive, versatile, and sociable. After the age of twenty, when your progressed Sun moves into Gemini, there is an increased desire to express your ideas and interrelate more with your immediate environment. This may encourage you to study or mentally diversify in some way. In your middle years, after numerous changes, you are likely to find probable gains through partnerships and cooperative relationships. Around the age of fifty, there is another turning point when your progressed Sun enters Cancer. This will highlight the growing importance of needing emotional stability and the security of home.

Your Secret Self

You possess powerful emotions and an ability to give and receive love. It is therefore important to find a form of expression for your feelings rather than seeking fulfillment in financial interests. If drifting, you may find yourself getting caught up in other people's emotional dramas as a way of acting out your own sensitivity. A desire for order and method is generally helpful to you, although a definite life plan is a prerequisite for making good use of all your tremendous potential.

By having a strong sense of values, you can build something worthwhile for the future. Through being diligent, you will be able to convert your excellent vision into a practical reality, and you will find that work opportunities will be offered to you just when you need them. Perseverance is therefore a powerful key to your success, and by being steady you will be able to curb an impatient side to your nature that wants instant gratification.

Work & Vocation

Those of you with creative and musical talents may be drawn toward writing or singing. You are likely to be blessed with a fine voice and a good ear. Travel or work involving change and variety is also liable to interest you. Intuitive and sensitive, you often have an interest in metaphysics, philosophy, or spirituality. Careerwise, you may be a good salesperson with an ability to promote ideas, people, or products. Other suitable professions include banking, real estate, garden centers, dealing in products of the land, or creative cooking and catering. You may also be drawn to the entertainment world, and you have the potential to succeed in any creative pursuit.

Famous people who share your birthday include singers Judy Collins and Rita Coolidge, actor Glenn Ford, astrologer William Lilly, and writers Terry Southern and Joseph Heller.

Numerology

The great desire to be first and autonomous is suggested by your birthdate. As a number 1, you are inclined to be individual, innovative, and courageous, with plenty of energy. The pioneering spirit indicated here encourages you to make your own decisions or strike out alone. Full of enthusiasm and original ideas, you often show others the way forward. With a number 1 birthday, you may also need to learn that the world does not revolve around you. The subinfluence of the number 5 month indicates that you need a steady pace and a purpose. Self-discipline allows you to take control over your life. Since you are versatile and a practical strategist, busy turning your thoughts into deeds, having a routine or a specialty is advantageous. You benefit from being aware of others' needs, and being responsible brings freedom from worry. Strong instincts can guide and inspire you; uplifted, you see new possibilities and a brighter future. Be patient and work within what is possible.

• *Positive:* leadership, creativity, progressive attitudes, forcefulness, optimism, strong convictions, competitiveness, independence, gregariousness

• *Negative:* overbearingness, jealousy, egotism, antagonism, lack of restraint, selfishness, weakness, instability, impatience

Love & Relationships

Romantic and idealistic about relationships, you are likely to take your time finding your true partner. You may sometimes choose platonic friendships, as it is hard to find a relationship that measures up to your high ideals. It is better to pick a partner who is clever and enthusiastic, with a strong humanitarian side. When you fall in love, you love deeply and remain loyal even through periods of difficulty. By developing flexibility and detachment, you can avoid emotional frustration and make your relationships smoother, happier, and more rewarding.

YOUR SPECIAL SOMEONE

You may be lucky in love with a person born on one of the following dates.

Love & friendship: Jan. 1, 7, 8, 21, 23, 31, Feb. 5, 19, 21, 29, Mar. 3, 4, 17, 19, 27, Apr. 1, 15, 17, 25, May 13, 15, 23, June 11, 13, 21, July 9, 11, 19, Aug. 7, 9, 17, Sept. 5, 7, 15, Oct. 3, 5, 13, Nov. 1, 3, 11, Dec. 1, 9

Beneficial: Jan. 5, 16, 18, Feb. 3, 14, 16, Mar. 1, 12, 14, 29, Apr. 10, 12, 27, May 8, 10, 25, 29, June 6, 8, 23, 27, July 4, 6, 21, 25, Aug. 2, 4, 19, 23, Sept. 2, 17, 21, Oct. 15, 19, Nov. 13, 17, Dec. 11, 15, 29

Fatal attractions: Jan. 6, 30, Feb. 4, 28, Mar. 2, 26, Apr. 24, May 22, June 20, July 18, Aug. 16, Sept. 14, Oct. 12, Nov. 2, 3, 4, 10, Dec. 8

Challenging: Jan. 4, Feb. 2, May 29, 31, June 27, 29, 30, July 25, 27, 28, Aug. 23, 25, 26, 30, Sept. 21, 23, 24, 28, Oct. 19, 21, 22, 26, Nov. 17, 19, 20, 24, Dec. 15, 17, 18, 22

Soul mates: Jan. 23, Feb. 21, Mar. 19, Apr. 17, May 15, June 13, July 11, 31, Aug. 9, 29, Sept. 7, 27, Oct. 5, 25, Nov. 3, 23, Dec. 1, 21

125

May 2

Your Taurus birthday shows you to be a practical, determined, and creative individual who is likely to appreciate beauty and the good things in life. Being both honest and direct as well as possessing natural diplomatic skills, you present a friendly image to the world and can project success.

With the supporting influence of the Sun in the Virgo decanate, you also have a natural flair for gaining material resources. You are likely to be receptive and intuitive, yet analytical and practical, with mental agility. There is also a predilection for precise speech and communication, critical skill, and an ability to be discriminating.

Your magnetic charm and warmth ensure that you are lucky in people-related activities. Since you also seek harmonious relationships with others, you are sensitive to your environment and like to surround yourself with taste and luxury. Your home, therefore, becomes an important part of your life agenda, and you are likely to make efforts to have it attractive and comfortable. Your natural creative talents may lead you to activities such as music, art, writing, or drama, where you are likely to excel. Your love for nature may also entice you into gardening or outdoor activities.

After the age of nineteen, when your progressed Sun moves into Gemini, there is an increased need to communicate and exchange ideas. This can be a time when you stretch yourself mentally and become more interested in learning. The age of forty-nine indicates a turning point, when your progressed Sun enters Cancer. This highlights the growing importance of needing to feel close to others as well as a possible review of your place within the family.

Fixed Star

Star's name: Alamak, also called Almach

Degree position: 13°15'–14°20' Taurus between the years 1930 and 2000

Magnitude: 2

Strength: ★★★★★★★

Orb: 2°10'

Constellation: Gamma Andromedae

Applicable days: May 2, 3, 4, 5, 6, 7

Star qualities: Venus

Description: a binary star, orange, emerald, and blue, located on the left foot of Andromeda

PRIMARY STAR'S INFLUENCE

Alamak bestows artistic and musical talent, a good voice, and social popularity. This star also imparts good fortune and success, and you can achieve honors or receive unexpected gains. If you are industrious and patient, success can be attained, as can love, romance, and happiness in domestic affairs.

Linked to your Sun's degree, this star grants honors through writing and creative pursuits, success in dealing with the public at large, and achievements in public affairs, particularly in affairs connected to the law and legal profession. Alamak also indicates that you can often gain fame and prestige.

• Positive: creative talents, loving nature, ability to attract material success

• Negative: selfishness, indulgence, extravagance

Your Secret Self

Being smart, with strong mental powers, you respect experience and knowledgeable people. Part of your success is that you like to apply your skills and turn theory into practice. This is aided by the fact that you are hardworking, success-oriented, ambitious, and a natural leader. With an eye for detail, you are often inventive and excellent at problem solving. A natural curiosity suggests that you are always seeking answers; combined with your imaginative intellect, this suggests that you are likely to be interested in mysticism or spirituality.

As you are loyal yourself, much of your security is built on love and friendship; good relationships are important to your sense of fulfillment. Although you are usually direct and honest, if you start to fool yourself, then you will become stubborn or avoid dealing with the truth through too much self-indulgence.

Work & Vocation

Practical and enterprising, you usually fare well as an entrepreneur, producer, promoter, or builder. Usually you are willing to work hard to support your strong desire for security and expensive tastes. You are attracted toward the arts but need monetary rewards and are likely to succeed in advertising and media as well as writing and acting. Your easygoing approach and executive abilities often make you a good manager or a kind and understanding employer.

With your positive approach and skillful dexterity, you are often good with your hands and enjoy constructing new projects. Luck and opportunities come through work, and your determination aids your ability to succeed in your chosen field.

Famous people who share your birthday include singer Bing Crosby, film director Satyajit Ray, child expert Benjamin Spock, and Bianca Jagger.

Numerology

Sensitivity and a strong need to be part of a group are suggested by your number 2 birthday. Often you are adaptable and understanding, and enjoy cooperative activities. A love of harmony and a desire to interact with others may inspire you to act as a mediator in family matters or become a peacemaker. In your attempt to please, you may run the risk of becoming overly dependent. The subinfluence of the number 5 month indicates that you need to express your feelings and communicate to others. Being positive and decisive helps you to focus and develop self-confidence. You may need to find a balance between being reserved, aloof, or mistrusting and naively expecting too much from others, only to be let down. Creative yet rational, you need to find a deeper understanding to acquire a more detached philosophy of life.

• *Positive:* good partnerships, gentleness, tact, receptivity, intuition, consideration, harmony, agreeable nature, ambassador of goodwill

• *Negative:* suspicion, lack of confidence, subservience, timidity, oversensitivity, selfishness, tendency to be easily hurt, deceit

Love & Relationships

Often ambitious, you like to be associated with success and prestige. Financial security and money are an important factor in relationships, so you prefer accomplished people or those with potential. Since you often possess good taste and value quality, you appreciate this in others. Although you are usually magnanimous and generous with those you love, there are also occasions when you can become surprisingly overly economical. Avoid judging everything in material terms, and learn that flexibility and understanding will gain you the admiration and affection you need.

YOUR SPECIAL SOMEONE

You might find emotional fulfillment and that special someone among those born on the following days.

Love & friendship: Jan. 8, 12, 17, 20, 22, 24, Feb. 6, 15, 18, 20, 22, Mar. 4, 8, 13, 16, 18, 20, Apr. 2, 11, 14, 16, 18, May 9, 12, 14, 16, June 7, 10, 12, 14, July 5, 8, 10, 12, 30, Aug. 3, 6, 8, 10, 28, Sept. 1, 4, 6, 8, 26, Oct. 2, 4, 6, 24, Nov. 2, 4, 22, Dec. 2, 20

Beneficial: Jan. 6, 23, Feb. 4, 21, Mar. 2, 19, 30, Apr. 17, 28, May 15, 26, 30, June 13, 24, 28, July 11, 22, 26, Aug. 9, 20, 24, Sept. 7, 18, 22, Oct. 5, 16, 20, Nov. 3, 14, 18, Dec. 1, 12, 16, 30

Fatal attractions: Jan. 7, Feb. 5, Mar. 3, Apr. 1, Nov. 3, 4, 5

Challenging: Jan. 5, 26, 29, Feb. 3, 24, 27, Mar. 1, 22, 25, Apr. 20, 23, May 18, 21, June 16, 19, 30, July 14, 17, 28, Aug. 12, 15, 26, 31, Sept. 10, 13, 24, 29, Oct. 8, 11, 22, 27, Nov. 6, 9, 20, 25, Dec. 4, 7, 18, 23

Soul mates: Jan. 30, Feb. 28, Mar. 26, Apr. 24, May 22, June 20, July 18, Aug. 16, Sept. 14, Oct. 12, 31, Nov. 10, 29, Dec. 8, 27

May 3

Your birthday shows you to be a person of remarkable intellectual and creative potential. You may only have to watch that worry or indecision does not distract you from achieving your goals. Friendly and sociable, you can project an alluring charm that draws people toward you and guarantees you success in people-related activities.

The influence of your Sun in the Virgo decanate of Taurus points to a practical nature and the knowledge of how to access material resources. Demonstrating an agile mind that grasps knowledge and ideas quickly, you may also have an ability for analysis, detailed work, or communication. Your appreciation of beauty and the arts, combined with your natural sensuality, is likely to be expressed through some form of art, music, or drama. Developing your innate talents can also have a healing effect if you become oversensitive or frustrated.

You have the potential to inspire others and find joy in the efforts you put into projects. When positive, you are hardworking, and your faith in the eventual outcome of your labors will ensure victory. By being detached and learning to work with constructive criticism, you can easily overcome any tendency to be stubborn or dissatisfied. Although pragmatic, you also possess a natural mystical potential that, if developed, could greatly aid you in your understanding of yourself and your environment.

In youth, you are sociable, imaginative, and versatile, with a love for the outdoor life. After the age of eighteen, when your progressed Sun moves into Gemini for thirty years, there is an increased need to communicate and exchange ideas. This can be a time when you stretch yourself mentally, and you may take up a course of study. At the age of forty-eight, when your progressed Sun enters Cancer, there is a turning point in your life that will bring into prominence the emotional need for a strong base or foundation to work from. This places extra emphasis on having a secure home as well as the importance of family ties.

Your Secret Self

With your fine business sense and willingness to work, you are likely to accumulate material possessions slowly but surely. However, your major soul growth may come through learning the lesson of detachment. You crave harmony on an inner level and may be willing to make sacrifices in order to achieve it. For this reason a safe and secure home base becomes an essential part of your life plan.

You will always have a strong inner-child energy, which can be expressed through creativity and playfulness or through feeling sorry for yourself. There may be times when you may become disappointed by your expectations of others and may have to be careful of escaping into excess to compensate. By accepting the responsibility of your more difficult challenges, you will find that life will more than reward you.

Work & Vocation

Self-expression and mental stimulation should be the foundation to your career. Women may play an important part in your career advancement. Your natural business sense may attract you to professions such as commerce, banking, and real estate. Your inclination for hard work,

FIXED STARS

Alamak, also called Almach; Menkar

PRIMARY STAR

Star's name: Alamak, also called Almach

Degree position: 13°15'–14°20' Taurus between the years 1930 and 2000

Magnitude: 2

Strength: ★★★★★★★★

Orb: 2°10'

Constellation: Gamma Andromedae

Applicable days: May 2, 3, 4, 5, 6, 7

Star qualities: Venus

Description: a binary star, orange, emerald, and blue, located on the left foot of Andromeda

PRIMARY STAR'S INFLUENCE

Alamak bestows artistic and musical talent, a good voice, and social popularity. This star also imparts good fortune and success, and you can achieve honors or receive unexpected gains. If you are industrious and patient, success can be attained, as can love, romance, and happiness in domestic affairs.

Linked to your Sun's degree, this star grants honors through writing and creative pursuits, success in dealing with the public at large, and achievements in public affairs, particularly in affairs connected to the law and legal professions. Alamak also indicates that you can often gain fame and prestige.

• *Positive:* creative talents, loving nature, ability to attract material success together with a fine mind, could also lead you to a career in scientific research or law. Alternatively, you may be drawn to creative pursuits that could include writing, interior designing, decorating, or dealing in antiques and objets d'art. Since you are idealistic, when inspired you are able to work unstintingly for a cause. Alternatively, your affinity with nature may lead you to choose careers in agriculture or horticulture. You can also do well in careers dealing with the public.

Famous people who share your birthday include former Israeli prime minister Golda Meir, actresses Mary Astor and Samantha Eggar, singer Pete Seeger, and boxer Sugar Ray Robinson.

Numerology

Often fun-loving and a good companion, you enjoy friendly social activities. You possess a strong need for self-expression and when positive can radiate the joy of life. An inclination to get bored easily, however, may cause you to become indecisive or spread yourself thin. Nevertheless, you are usually artistic and charming, with a good sense of humor. A talent with words may manifest through speaking, writing, or singing. Since you may need to develop self-esteem, guard against tendencies such as worry and other emotional insecurities. The subinfluence of the number 5 month indicates that you need to learn how to utilize the abundance of your creative power. Since you are both versatile and restless, developing a pragmatic outlook can bring stability. Making a real effort and working hard show your determination to succeed. Learning to endure in spite of challenges and delays allows you to take control.

• *Positive:* humor, happiness, friendliness, productivity, creativity, artistic talent, power to wish, love of freedom, talent with words

• *Negative:* overimagination, exaggeration, tendency to be easily bored, vanity, tendency to be unloving, boastfulness, extravagance, self-indulgence, laziness, hypocrisy

Love & Relationships

Although sociable, you can encounter periods when you wish to withdraw and be alone. You may need this time to reflect and gather your thoughts in a peaceful environment or in nature. Attracted by people of intelligence, you prefer someone with whom you can share intellectual activities or leisure pursuits. As charm is one of your primary attributes, you have no problem attracting friends and lovers, but your true victory comes from overcoming challenges in your long-term relationships.

YOUR SPECIAL SOMEONE

You might find stability in relationships by looking for someone born on one of the following days.

Love & friendship: Jan. 9, 11, 13, 23, 25, 27, Feb. 7, 21, 23, 25, Mar. 5, 19, 21, 23, 29, Apr. 3, 17, 19, 21, 27, 30, May 1, 15, 17, 19, 25, 28, June 13, 15, 17, 23, 26, July 11, 13, 15, 21, 24, Aug. 9, 11, 13, 19, 22, Sept. 7, 9, 11, 17, 20, Oct. 5, 7, 9, 15, 18, Nov. 3, 5, 7, 13, 16, Dec. 1, 3, 5, 11, 14

Beneficial: Jan. 2, 4, 7, Feb. 2, 5, Mar. 3, Apr. 1, May 31, June 29, July 27, 31, Aug. 25, 29, Sept. 23, 27, Oct. 21, 25, Nov. 19, 23, Dec. 17, 21

Fatal attractions: Jan. 8, 14, Feb. 6, 12, Mar. 4, 10, Apr. 2, 8, May 6, June 4, July 2, Nov. 4, 5, 6

Challenging: Jan. 6, 19, 29, Feb. 4, 17, 27, Mar. 2, 15, 25, Apr. 13, 23, May 11, 21, June 9 19, July 7, 17, Aug. 5, 15, Sept. 3, 13, 30, Oct. 1, 11, 28, Nov. 9, 26, Dec. 7, 24, 29

Soul mates: Jan. 16, 21, Feb. 14, 19, Mar. 12, 17, Apr. 10, 15, May 8, 13, June 6, 11, July 4, 9, Aug. 2, 7, Sept. 5, Oct. 3, Nov. 1

May 4

An interesting mixture of practicality, charm, and emotional sensitivity marks people with your birthday. Sharing at work and on a personal level is the key to your success. Ambitious and hardworking, you are responsible and conscientious.

The added influence of your Sun in the Virgo decanate of Taurus suggests that you aim toward high standards in your work and enjoy being of service to others. This also indicates that you possess very practical and down-to-earth qualities and that you seek order and organization so as to feel really secure.

Although you are very independent and do not like to be restricted, you are excellent at relating to others on a one-to-one basis. This may be partially due to your innate understanding of human nature and your good powers of perception. Although you are initially interested in material considerations, your need to gain a deeper insight may lead you later in life to an interest in subjects of a more metaphysical or spiritual nature. Nevertheless, there will be times when you can display an almost egocentric stubbornness or be prone to periods of self-doubt. You may have to guard against tendencies to escapism and self-indulgence as a means to compensate for these feelings. Fortuitously, you have the ability to dispel any possible negative moods by using your powerful imagination to create in your mind the vision of the perfect ideal.

After the age of seventeen, when your progressed Sun moves into Gemini, the pace of your life increases and there is more of an emphasis on writing, speech, and communication in general. This continues until the age of forty-seven, when your progressed Sun enters Cancer. This is a turning point that will highlight the growing importance of emotional intimacy, security, and home ties.

Fixed Stars

Alamak, also called Almach; Menkar

Primary Star

Star's name: Alamak, also called Almach

Degree position: 13°15–14°20' Taurus between the years 1930 and 2000

Magnitude: 2

Strength: ★★★★★★★★

Orb: 2°10'

Constellation: Gamma Andromedae

Applicable days: May 2, 3, 4, 5, 6, 7

Star qualities: Venus

Description: a binary star, orange, emerald, and blue, located on the left foot of Andromeda

Primary Star's Influence

Alamak bestows artistic and musical talent, a good voice, and social popularity. This star also imparts good fortune and success, and you can achieve honors or receive unexpected gains. If you are industrious and patient, success can be attained, as can love, romance, and happiness in domestic affairs.

Linked to your Sun's degree, this star grants honors through writing and creative pursuits, success in dealing with the public at large, and achievements in public affairs, particularly in affairs connected to the law and legal professions. Alamak also indicates that you can often gain fame and prestige.

• *Positive:* creative talents, loving nature, ability to attract material success

Your Secret Self

Your leadership ability is naturally displayed when you take over a job you see being done badly or inefficiently. Occasionally this can manifest itself as being bossy, but generally you have a good sense of working cooperatively with others. Your mental powers and ability to grasp information often suggest that you like to be knowledgeable and make up your own mind. By developing your natural intuitive sense as to which of your excellent ideas should be put into tangible form, you can gain enormous advantages.

Your strong sense of responsibility is likely to be recognized by others and helps you succeed. However, you may have to guard against occasionally becoming moody, anxious, or tense, as this can affect the balance of your relationships with others. You need to be in an environment conducive to harmony. Your home, therefore, is likely to be of particular importance and serve as a place of safety and security.

Work & Vocation

You are likely to possess a natural talent for buying and selling, banking, and commerce as well as being an excellent agent or negotiator. Alternatively, you may desire activities that benefit others and be drawn to charity work, counseling, or working with the disadvantaged. If attracted to public life, you may do well in a career in politics, government service, diplomacy, or public relations. Creative talents may particularly manifest in the area of music, photography, and drama. Some people of this birthday may be drawn to sporting activities. Whatever you choose, you have the ability to work hard, and this will bring its own rewards.

Famous people who share your birthday include actress Audrey Hepburn, Egyptian statesman Hosni Mubarak, country singer Randy Travis, and musician Maynard Ferguson.

Numerology

The solid structure and orderly power suggested by the number 4 birthday indicate that often you need stability and like to establish order. With this birthdate, you are sensitive to form and composition. Security-conscious, you like to build a strong foundation for yourself and your family. Your pragmatic approach to life confers a good business sense and an ability to achieve material success in life. Faithful though undemonstrative, you are usually honest, frank, and fair. Nevertheless, you may have to learn how to express your feelings. The challenges for a number 4 individual may include overcoming periods of instability. The subinfluence of the number 5 month indicates that you are enthusiastic yet emotionally sensitive. You need to be motivated by finding an inspired idea or project. Intuitive, you need to learn to trust your instincts and put them to some practical use. Although you want to be a free agent, you recognize the need for self-discipline and stability.

• *Positive:* organization, self-discipline, steadiness, hard work, craftsmanship, manual ability, pragmatism, trust, exactitude

• *Negative:* destructive behavior, uncommunicativeness, repression, laziness, lack of feeling, procrastination, penny-pinching, bossiness, hidden affections, resentment

Love & Relationships

Marriage, a settled relationship, and a secure home seem particularly important to you. A love for knowledge and a need to communicate suggest that you enjoy exploring new ideas and being mentally creative. If bored, you may have to be careful not to allow things to fall into a rut or become monotonous. Sharing creative pursuits with your partner will help both of you to go out and experiment or have fun. Going out, socializing, or entertaining your friends at home always brings pleasure into your life.

YOUR SPECIAL SOMEONE

You might find stimulating company and the perfect partner among those born on the following dates.

Love & friendship: Jan. 10, 11, 14, 26, 28, Feb. 8, 24, 26, Mar. 6, 22, 24, 30, Apr. 4, 20, 22, 28, May 2, 18, 20, 26, 29, June 16, 18, 24, 27, July 14, 16, 22, 25, Aug. 12, 14, 20, 23, 30, Sept. 10, 12, 18, 21, 28, Oct. 8, 10, 16, 19, 26, Nov. 6, 8, 14, 17, 24, Dec. 4, 6, 12, 15, 22

Beneficial: Jan. 8, Feb. 6, Mar. 4, 28, Apr. 2, 26, May 24, June 22, 30, July 20, 28, 29, Aug. 18, 26, 27, 30, Sept. 16, 24, 25, 28, Oct. 14, 22, 23, 26, 29, Nov. 12, 20, 21, 24, 27, Dec. 10, 18, 19, 22, 25

Fatal attractions: Jan. 15, Feb. 13, Mar. 11, Apr. 9, May 7, June 5, July 3, Aug. 1, Nov. 5, 6, 7

Challenging: Jan. 7, 9, 30, Feb. 5, 7, 28, Mar. 3, 5, 26, Apr. 1, 3, 24, May 1, 22, June 20, July 18, Aug. 16, Sept. 14, Oct. 12, 29, Nov. 10, 27, Dec. 8, 25, 30

Soul mates: Jan. 8, 27, Feb. 6, 25, Mar. 4, 23, Apr. 2, 21, May 19, June 17, July 15, Aug. 13, Sept. 11, Oct. 9, Nov. 7, Dec. 5

May 5

♉ Willpower and determination are suggested by your birthdate. A need for diversity and action is also indicated but implies that you may have to overcome an inner restlessness. Being mentally sharp, you pick up on situations immediately and are likely to be happiest when working hard on a project or cause about which you feel deeply.

The added influence of your Sun in the Virgo decanate of Taurus adds critical ability to your practicality and emphasizes the importance of doing a job well. It can also indicate analytical skills, a desire to be methodical, or possibly the ability to be technical in some way. Being stubborn or self-willed may prove to be one of the major blocks to the use of the tremendous possibilities inherent in this birthdate.

Besides the need for material security, you also have a desire to get to a deeper level, whether of a person or perhaps of life itself. This may lead you to investigate and probe beneath the surface and not take everything at face value. Developing this more intuitive side is likely to help you overcome any possible tendency to self-interest, moodiness or depression, and it will act as a great help to access the enormous power potential available to those born on this date.

Possessing initiative, charm, and the need to keep busy, you have the necessary ingredients to take up positions of leadership. With the ability to think visually as well as practically, your ideal would be to live within a secure structure yet still have new or stimulating experiences.

Around the age of sixteen, when your progressed Sun moves into Gemini, you may diversify and find many more interests. At this time study and communication in all forms may become more important to you. There is another turning point after the age of forty-six, when your progressed Sun moves into Cancer. This is liable to increase your sensitivity, your awareness of family connections, and the importance of a strong home base. From the age of seventy-six, when your progressed Sun moves into Leo, you become stronger and more confident.

Your Secret Self

A highly idealistic individual may be hidden beneath your practical exterior. This can lead to involvement in relationships that may not be able to fulfill your high expectations. It may be important to use your unusual sense of humor to stop yourself from becoming overly serious. This enables you to stay balanced and respond to your astute first impressions of others. By trusting this instinctive reaction and even going as far as challenging people in a friendly way, you can push the boundaries of your own power and stop yourself from becoming emotionally disappointed, withdrawn, or cold. This instant trust in your own sense of power gives you tremendous self-confidence and spontaneity.

Contained within you are strong forces that give you the ability to cope with any situation. This enables you to present new ideas to others in a careful and logical way that will impress them with your unique perception.

Work & Vocation

Your ability to grasp original concepts and situations is likely to be recognized and appreciated by your employers or superiors. Adaptability and knowing how to stay calm in a crisis suggest

---

FIXED STARS

Alamak, also called Almach; Menkar

PRIMARY STAR

Star's name: Alamak, also called Almach
Degree position: 13°15'–14°20' Taurus between the years 1930 and 2000
Magnitude: 2
Strength: ★★★★★★★★
Orb: 2°10'
Constellation: Gamma Andromedae
Applicable days: May 2, 3, 4, 5, 6, 7
Star qualities: Venus
Description: a binary star, orange, emerald, and blue, located on the left foot of Andromeda

PRIMARY STAR'S INFLUENCE

Alamak bestows artistic and musical talent, a good voice, and social popularity. This star also imparts good fortune and success, and you can achieve honors or receive unexpected gains. If you are industrious and patient, success can be attained, as can love, romance, and happiness in domestic affairs.

Linked to your Sun's degree, this star grants honors through writing and creative pursuits, success in dealing with the public at large, and achievements in public affairs, particularly in affairs connected to the law and legal professions. Alamak also indicates that you can often gain fame and prestige.

• Positive: creative talents, loving nature, ability to attract material success

that you can overcome challenging situations. These qualities, combined with the willingness to work hard, often help you develop leadership ability. In fact, as you like to be in control and not subservient to others, you do better working for yourself or as a manager or director. You can excel at problem solving and when necessary be tough and authoritarian. This is particularly applicable to bringing in new reforms and making changes. If drawn to the theater or film, you can be a good actor, producer, or director. With your good sense of form and style, you may be drawn to the image-making industries or work as a designer. Another avenue for your talents may be government service or politics, in which you can utilize your natural authority.

Famous people who share your birthday include philosopher Karl Marx, political leader Ho Chi Minh, singer Tammy Wynette, philosopher Søren Kierkegaard, and comedian Michael Palin.

Numerology

Strong instincts, an adventurous nature, and a desire for freedom are all indicated by the number 5 birthday. Travel and many opportunities for change, some unexpected, may lead you to undergo a real transformation of views and beliefs. Often, having a number 5 birthdate means that you lead an active life and need to learn about patience and attention to detail; you can achieve success by avoiding premature or speculative actions. The natural talent of a number 5 individual is knowing how to go with the flow and staying detached. The subinfluence of the number 5 month indicates that you are ambitious and determined but at times can be overconfident. In your attempt to reach your destination quickly, you may miss some of the spectacular scenery. Strong-willed and shrewd, you do not like any form of restriction. Dissatisfaction with yourself or others and confining circumstances urge you to make changes and start anew. Self-discipline is a must if you want to achieve success.

• *Positive:* versatility, adaptability, progressive attitudes, strong instincts, magnetism, luck, daring, love of freedom, quickness and wit, curiosity, mysticism, sociability

• *Negative:* unreliability, changeability, procrastination, inconsistency, lustfulness, overconfidence

Love & Relationships

Although you need love and affection and can be caring and giving, your need for independence and natural spontaneity suggest that you also love freedom. Due to changing circumstances, you may possibly experience a conflict between love and work or between duty and personal wishes. You need deep intimacy, but at times you can be inhibited in expressing your powerful emotions. Nevertheless, you can be devoted and a stable influence on your partner. You may just have to be careful of becoming too preoccupied with self-interest, which can separate you from others. Often you are more suited to someone who shares your high ideals and aspirations.

• *Negative:* selfishness, indulgence, extravagance

See Appendix for additional fixed star readings.

YOUR SPECIAL SOMEONE

If you are looking for a relationship, you might find a faithful lover or partner among those born on the following dates.

Love & friendship: Jan 11,15, 20, 25, 27, 29, Feb. 9, 18, 23, 25, 27, Mar. 7, 16, 21, 23, 25, Apr. 5, 14, 19, 21, 23, May 3, 12, 17, 19, 21, June 1, 10, 15, 17, 19, July 8, 13, 15, 17, Aug. 1, 6, 11, 13, 15, Sept. 4, 9, 11, 13, Oct. 2, 7, 9, 11, Nov. 5, 7, 9, Dec. 3, 5, 7

Beneficial: Jan. 9, 26, Feb. 7, 24, Mar. 5, 22, Apr. 3, 20, May 1, 18, 29, June 16, 27, July 14, 25, 29, 30, Aug. 12, 23, 27, 28, 31, Sept. 10, 21, 25, 26, 29, Oct. 8, 19, 23, 24, 27, Nov. 6, 17, 21, 22, 25, Dec. 4, 15, 19, 20, 23

Fatal attractions: Jan. 16, Feb. 14, Mar. 12, Apr. 10, May 8, June 6, July 4, Aug. 2, Nov. 6, 7, 8

Challenging: Jan. 8, 29, 31, Feb. 6, 27, 29, Mar. 4, 25, 27, 28, Apr. 2, 23, 25, 26, May 21, 23, 24, June 19, 21, 22, July 17, 19, 20, Aug. 15, 17, 18, Sept. 13, 15, 16, Oct. 11, 13, 14, 30, Nov. 9, 11, 12, 28, Dec. 7, 9, 10, 26

Soul mates: May 30, June 28, July 26, Aug. 24, Sept. 22, 30, Oct. 20, 28, Nov. 18, 26, Dec. 16, 24

133

May 6

This birthdate suggests that you are more complex than you seem. Being a natural actor or actress in life's drama, you project a multitalented and self-confident front. Yet beneath your exterior there can be a sense of worry and indecision. Possessing natural leadership ability and a way with people, you should ideally be in a position that makes the most of your wonderful abilities. There is a danger, however, that you may settle for less or a life of ease and not push yourself to your full capabilities.

With the added influence of your Sun in the second decanate of Taurus, you are likely to possess excellent analytical and critical skills, which should aid you in achieving your goals. There is also an inclination for writing as well as a natural business acumen. Learning quickly, you value knowledge and freedom and are open to inventive or progressive ideas.

Home and security are important issues on your agenda, and you are likely to take your responsibilities seriously. Just be careful of caring so much that you may interfere in others' lives and deny them an opportunity to learn in their own way. Luckily, you can turn on the charm, and you have a wonderful way with people. You are likely to have many acquaintances, but you expressly choose friends who are interesting and mentally stimulating. However, since you take pleasure from the good things of life and know how to enjoy yourself, you may also have to watch a tendency to overindulge.

After the age of fifteen, when your progressed Sun moves into Gemini, the tempo of your life increases and there is more of an emphasis on communication. Over the next thirty years there is a need to extend your mental capabilities and relate through the exchange of ideas. The age of forty-five, when your progressed Sun enters Cancer, signals a turning point that highlights the growing importance of emotional closeness, family, and security. From the age of seventy-five, when your progressed Sun moves into Leo, your power and confidence increase.

Your Secret Self

A creative mentality allows you to combine wit with insight, often reflecting people's characteristics back to them in a most subtle yet challenging way. An interest in human nature generally can take you beyond business and sociability to a humanitarian desire to do something meaningful. This may involve fighting for causes, freedom, or your dream, but it will stop you from becoming restless and give you greater satisfaction. Possible blocks to this process may involve a lack of faith in your own abilities or indecision as to your choices. This doubt may result in your taking a secondary role rather than making full use of the power available to you. Since you respond well to encouragement, you may receive motivation from reading about the lives of those you admire and respect; remember that every step you take toward fulfilling your own dreams also works to inspire others. Give others inspiration rather than unwelcome criticism.

Work & Vocation

Having natural psychological skills will definitely be of great assistance to you in whatever career you choose. In business, this insight will enable you to work well with people and intuit the outcome of financial propositions. This works well with your expertise at evaluating situa-

FIXED STARS

Alamak, also called Almach; Menkar

PRIMARY STAR

Star's name: Alamak, also called Almach

Degree position: 13°15'–14°20' Taurus between the years 1930 and 2000

Magnitude: 2

Strength: ★★★★★★★

Orb: 2°10'

Constellation: Gamma Andromedae

Applicable days: May 2, 3, 4, 5, 6, 7

Star qualities: Venus

Description: a binary star, orange, emerald, and blue, located on the left foot of Andromeda

---

PRIMARY STAR'S INFLUENCE

Alamak bestows artistic and musical talent, a good voice, and social popularity. This star also imparts good fortune and success, and you can achieve honors or receive unexpected gains. If you are industrious and patient, success can be attained, as can love, romance, and happiness in domestic affairs.

Linked to your Sun's degree, this star grants honors through writing and creative pursuits, success in dealing with the public at large, and achievements in public affairs, particularly in affairs connected to the law and legal professions. Alamak also indicates that you can often gain fame and prestige.

• Positive: creative talents, loving nature, ability to attract material success

tions and indicates that you have the prerequisites to rise to a position of authority in your chosen field. Alternatively, you may use these gifts in the therapeutic world, where you can also exercise your natural humanitarianism. Your keen intellect and sense of the dramatic is likely to draw you to a career on the stage, and since you are also likely to be blessed with an exceptional voice, this could serve you well as a singer or politician. A career in music or teaching could also make good use of your talents. Having a strong sense of independence and not liking to take orders may encourage you to work for yourself.

Famous people who share your birthday include actor/director Orson Welles, pioneering psychologist Sigmund Freud, baseball player Willie Mays, and actors Rudolph Valentino and George Clooney.

Numerology

Compassion, idealism, and a caring nature are some of the attributes suggested by a number 6 birthday. Frequently domestically inclined, you are a homemaker and a devoted parent. A desire for universal harmony, combined with your intense emotions, often encourages you to work hard for what you believe in. The more sensitive among you will need to find a form of creative expression and are often drawn to the world of entertaining or art and design. The challenges for some with a number 6 birthdate may include developing more self-confidence and compassion toward friends and neighbors as well as learning to be more responsible. The subinfluence of the number 5 month indicates that you are enthusiastic and restless, yet responsible and proud. Tactful and diplomatic, you can charm others with your easygoing nature. You can alternate between being confident and self-assured, on one hand, and impressionable and uncertain, on the other. Inspired by humanitarian causes, you benefit from cooperative endeavors or collaboration with others.

• *Positive:* worldliness, universal brotherhood, friendliness, compassion, dependability, understanding, sympathy, idealism, domestic inclinations, humanitarianism, poise, artistic talent, balance

• *Negative:* discontent, anxiety, shyness, unreasonableness, stubbornness, tendency to be outspoken, perfectionism, domineering behavior, lack of responsibility, selfishness, cynicism

Love & Relationships

Attracted to people who are interested in self-improvement, you often combine your social activities with learning and are interested in exchanging information and knowledge. A love of harmony may be an essential component in your relationships, and you are drawn to those who are mentally stimulating or well educated. Although you are a person with strong character, avoid becoming overly dominant with your loved ones.

YOUR SPECIAL SOMEONE

For security, mental stimulation, and love, you may begin looking for a partner among those born on the following dates.

Love & friendship: Jan. 4, 11, 12, 16, 26, 28, 30, Feb. 2, 9, 10, 24, 26, 28, Mar. 7, 8, 12, 22, 24, 26, Apr. 5, 6, 20, 22, 24, 30, May 3, 4, 18, 20, 22, 28, 31, June 1, 2, 16, 18, 20, 26, 29, July 4, 14, 16, 18, 24, 27, Aug. 12, 14, 16, 22, 25, Sept. 10, 12, 14, 20, 23, Oct. 8, 10, 12, 18, 21, Nov. 6, 8, 10, 16, 19, Dec. 4, 6, 8, 14, 17

Beneficial: Jan. 3, 10, 29, Feb. 1, 8, 27, Mar. 6, 25, Apr. 4, 23, May 2, 21, June 4, 19, July 17, 30, Aug. 15, 28, Sept. 13, 26, Oct. 11, 24, Nov. 9, 22, Dec. 7, 20

Fatal attractions: Jan. 11, Feb. 9, Mar. 7, Apr. 5, May 3, June 1, Nov. 7, 8, 9

Challenging: Jan. 9, Feb. 7, Mar. 5, 28, Apr. 3, 26, May 1, 24, June 22, July 20, Aug. 18, Sept. 16, Oct. 14, 30, 31, Nov. 12, 28, 29, Dec. 10, 26, 27

Soul mates: Jan. 7, Feb. 5, Mar. 3, Apr. 1, May 29, June 27, July 25, Aug. 23, Sept. 21, Oct. 19, Nov. 17, Dec. 15

May 7

Your birthday suggests that you possess a shrewd practicality combined with a strong character. Diligent and self-willed, you should naturally rise toward positions of authority, but you may have to guard against being verbally cutting or domineering. You possess good judgment in regard to evaluating people or practical situations and may find yourself fighting for other people's rights. Preferring to keep yourself busy, and capable of great surges of energy, you possess the capacity for extraordinary achievements.

With the added influence of your Sun in the Virgo decanate of Taurus, you are inclined to a methodical or analytical approach to dealing with life, and have good mental agility and concentration. This can particularly manifest itself as strong persuasive powers or writing and communication skills. Having a realistic approach to life and an ability to come straight to the point is likely to manifest as business acumen. With your depth of thought, you are inclined toward philosophical insight or skill at problem solving. A possible stumbling block to your great potential may be a tendency to withdraw and become stubborn, arrogant, and uncommunicative.

With a natural know-how for gaining material resources, good organizational skills, and an ability to inspire others, you are automatically equipped for leadership in any situation. By combining self-discipline with your inner strength, you have the potential to translate your inspirations into tangible reality.

Around the age of fourteen, when your progressed Sun moves into Gemini, you may start a period of change by finding many new interests. At this time study and communication can become more important to you. There is another turning point after forty-four, when your progressed Sun moves into Cancer. This commences a period when you are likely to focus on emotional relationships, family, and your instinctual understanding of other people's needs. From the age of seventy-four, when your progressed Sun enters Leo, you become more confident in your self-expression.

Your Secret Self

By applying self-discipline to your natural dramatic ability, you are likely to transform your love of art, music, and drama into some concrete form of self-expression. The inner creativity suggested here can be applied to your life in general, whether doing business or in the home. However, a tendency to worry or be indecisive about money or work may cut you off from the marvelous possibilities inherent in your birthday. These anxieties or frustrations may cause you to play it too safe in your life decisions or remain in unsuitable situations too long. A humanitarian and detached side to your personality can inspire you to great heights and stimulate you to be more joyful and daring. Just be careful that once you are feeling free you do not get carried away in wild extravagances or overindulgence in the good things of life.

Work & Vocation

In the realm of careers, you have a wide variety of choices. You are likely to excel in positions of leadership, and with your evaluating skills, you may succeed in merchandising and advertising. Known for your generosity, you can be a philanthropist who supports people and ideas

FIXED STAR

Star's name: Alamak, also called Almach

Degree position: 13°15'–14°20' Taurus between the years 1930 and 2000

Magnitude: 2

Strength: ★★★★★★★

Orb: 2°10'

Constellation: Gamma Andromedae

Applicable days: May 2, 3, 4, 5, 6, 7

Star qualities: Venus

Description: a binary star, orange, emerald, and blue, located on the left foot of Andromeda

PRIMARY'S STAR'S INFLUENCE

Alamak bestows artistic and musical talent, a good voice, and social popularity. This star also imparts good fortune and success, and you can achieve honors or receive unexpected gains. If you are industrious and patient, success can be attained, as can love, romance, and happiness in domestic affairs.

Linked to your Sun's degree, this star grants honors through writing and creative pursuits, success in dealing with the public at large, and achievements in public affairs, particularly in affairs connected to the law and legal professions. Alamak also indicates that you can often gain fame and prestige.

• Positive: creative talents, loving nature, ability to attract material success

• Negative: selfishness, indulgence, extravagance

you believe in. Alternatively, your creativity may draw you to the world of entertainment, art, or music. Usually you are able to combine your appreciation for beauty and the arts with business as an art dealer, impresario, or curator. Your ability to push through some kind of reform may attract you to leadership in such organizations as trade unions. Those who are not freedom fighters may be interested in education or some other form of public or social interest.

Famous people who share your birthday include singer Jimmy Ruffin, actor Gary Cooper, poets Rabindranath Tagore and Robert Browning, political figure Eva Peron, and composers Johannes Brahms and Peter Ilyitch Tchaikovsky.

Numerology

Analytical and thoughtful, number 7 individuals are often perfectionistic, critical, and self-absorbed. Preferring to make your own decisions, you frequently learn best through personal experience. This desire to learn can lead you into the academic world or to improving your skills. At other times you can become overly sensitive to criticism and feel misunderstood. Your tendency to be enigmatic or secretive leads you to develop the art of asking subtle questions without letting anyone know what you really think. The subinfluence of the number 5 month indicates that you are intelligent, with an ability to grasp ideas quickly. You are witty and articulate and can be entertaining company. Creative yet impressionable, you like to have fun and are prone to have many hobbies. Integrity and cooperation are vital to your success. Helpful and friendly, you can encourage and support ideas and people. A tendency to manipulate rather than be direct suggests that you sometimes find it hard to express your true feelings.

• *Positive:* education, trust, meticulousness, idealism, honesty, psychic ability, scientific aptitude, rationality, reflection

• *Negative:* concealment, deceit, unfriendliness, skepticism, confusion, malicious behavior, detachment

Love & Relationships

A need for mental stimulation and creativity often suggests that you are drawn toward intelligent people from all walks of life. Although you are fun to be with and have many interests, indecision or uncertainty about relationships can cause you confusion and worry. If you are not quite sure where your loyalty lies, you probably prefer to go out and socialize with friends. By keeping yourself creative and not dwelling on this area of your life, you can usually sort out personal issues in time.

YOUR SPECIAL SOMEONE

To keep you interested in a long-term relationship, you might want to look out for those born on the following days.

Love & friendship: Jan. 13, 17, 29, Feb. 11, 27, 29, Mar. 9, 25, 27, Apr. 7, 23, 25, May 5, 9, 21, 23, 29, June 3, 19, 21, 27, 30, July 1, 17, 19, 25, 28, Aug. 15, 17, 23, 26, Sept. 1, 13, 15, 21, 24, Oct. 11, 13, 19, 22, 29, Nov. 9, 11, 17, 20, 27, Dec. 7, 9, 15, 18, 25

Beneficial: Jan. 11, Feb. 9, Mar. 7, 31, Apr. 5, 29, May 3, 27, 31, June 1, 25, 29, July 23, 27, 31, Aug. 21, 25, 29, 30, Sept. 19, 23, 27, 28, Oct. 17, 21, 25, 26, Nov. 15, 19, 23, 24, 30, Dec. 13, 17, 21, 22, 28

Fatal attractions: Jan. 12, Feb. 10, Mar. 8, Apr. 6, May 4, June 2, Nov. 8, 9, 10

Challenging: Jan. 10, Feb. 8, Mar. 6, 29, Apr. 4, 27, May 2, 25, June 23, July 21, Aug. 19, Sept. 17, Oct. 15, 31, Nov. 13, 29, 30, Dec. 11, 27, 28

Soul mates: Jan. 18, 24, Feb. 16, 22, Mar. 14, 20, Apr. 12, 18, May 10, 16, June 8, 14, July 6, 12, Aug. 4, 10, Sept. 2, 8, Oct. 6, Nov. 4, Dec. 2

May 8

FIXED STARS

Although your Sun's degree is not linked to a fixed star, some of your other planets' degrees certainly will be. By having an astrological chart calculated, you can find the exact position of the planets on your date of birth. This will tell you which of the fixed stars listed in this book are relevant to you.

Friendly and spontaneous, those born on this day tend to be mentally sharp individuals with personal charm. Sometimes displaying an interesting blend of idealism and materialism, you need people and are warm and sociable. A youthful quality is likely to stay with you throughout your life; this shows a side of you that is guaranteed to keep others enchanted. Since you are also likely to be ambitious, your people skills can certainly help you in your climb to the top.

With the added influence of the Sun in the Virgo decanate of Taurus, an enhancement of your ability to be articulate and mentally agile is shown, as well as increased communication skills. This can also bring an ability for critical analysis and a desire for service as well as a natural aptitude for business. This endows you with the knowledge to gain material resources.

Image-conscious, you are usually aware of how you project yourself to others and generally want to express a strong sense of individuality and style. A wish to transcend the mundane may manifest as a desire for mystical experience or, at the other extreme, confusion, escapism, or impossible dreams. Invariably, though, you like to be honest and direct, and you have a strong urge for freedom. When combined with your practicality, this can enable you to fulfill the potential for success promised by your birthday.

After the age of thirteen, when your progressed Sun moves into Gemini, there is an increased desire to express your ideas and interrelate more with others in your immediate surroundings. This may encourage you to study or mentally diversify in some way. This continues until around the age of forty-three, when your progressed Sun enters Cancer. As a turning point, this highlights the importance of needing to feel more in touch with your emotions as well as emphasizing your home and family. From the age of seventy-three, when your progressed Sun enters Leo, you become more confident and stronger.

Your Secret Self

Since the bright, personable qualities associated with your birthday suggest that you can be versatile, it may be necessary for you to have very clear aims and objectives. By having precise plans, you can avoid some of the indecision or worry to which you may be prone. A desire for money or life's luxuries may lure you away from some of your ideals, so in order to demonstrate your outstanding talents, you may have to decide where your responsibilities truly lie. Fortunately, as you are likely to be blessed with a good mind and an ability to learn quickly, you will always have material protection.

There is also a strong possibility that education and writing may come to play a part in your advancement, perhaps after you have completed a career or later in life. Either way, it would prove an excellent outlet for your creativity and expertise with communication.

Work & Vocation

An ability to make money, combined with your charisma, indicates that you possess the potential to reach the top in your chosen field. The possibility for success is particularly likely in sales, negotiation, and promotion. Likewise, you may be drawn toward the world of publishing, advertising, and the media, or become involved in law and politics or banking. Your leadership qualities and ambition may place you in executive and managerial roles. The need for self-expression may inspire you to be creative and may position you among the writers, poets, and actors. Alternatively, your artistic talents may draw you to the world of music, entertainment, and the arts. There could also be success in dealing or working with the land, such as real estate, building, or farming.

Famous people who share your birthday include U.S. president Harry S. Truman, mystic Krishnamurti, writer Thomas Pynchon, channeler and writer Jane Roberts, and boxer Sonny Liston.

Numerology

The strength or power suggested by the number 8 birthday shows a character with strong values and sound judgment. The number 8 often indicates that you aspire to great accomplishment and possess an ambitious nature. A desire for dominance, security, and material success is also implied by this birthday. As a number 8 person, you have a natural business sense and will benefit greatly from developing organizational and executive skills. You may have to learn how to administer or delegate your authority in a fair and just way. A strong need to feel secure or established urges you to make long-term plans and investments. The subinfluence of the number 5 month indicates that you are enthusiastic and restless, with strong willpower. Carefree, you benefit from expressing your feelings and learning to communicate exactly how you feel. With self-discipline and a positive outlook, you can make the right impression and gain control. A strong need to feel secure or established urges you to make long-term plans and investments.

• *Positive:* leadership, thoroughness, hard work, tradition, authority, protection, power to heal, good judge of values

• *Negative:* impatience, wastefulness, intolerance, miserliness, restlessness, overwork, domineering, easily discouraged, lack of planning, abusiveness, controlling behavior

Love & Relationships

Your need for stability, security, and the funds to support a certain lifestyle suggest that you are interested in financially helpful people and often get assistance from friends. Idealistic yet practical, you are friendly and sociable and need the security of loyal companions. Affectionate and loving, you can be romantic with those you love, but in order to be happy, make sure you achieve long-term financial stability. Take your time in choosing your relationships carefully; otherwise you can suffer from disillusionment if people do not live up to your high expectations.

May 9

FIXED STARS

Your birthday suggests that you are success-oriented, ambitious, and clever, with the necessary people skills to ensure your happiness. Full of energy and drive, you are motivated by the promise of immediate rewards and usually have a plan or scheme in the pipeline. Very shrewd and quick at assessing people and situations, you are constantly seeking opportunities and like big projects.

The added influence of your Sun in the Virgo decanate suggests that with your mental agility you are quite logical, analytical, or technical. The practical approach indicated gives you a natural business sense, and you may enjoy being of service. As your sensual qualities are enhanced, you are likely to enjoy being amorous, but beware of overindulgence in any form.

Being independent and a good planner or organizer, you may be put in charge of all types of projects. Generosity and optimism endear you to others and increase your fortune. However, you need to guard against a resolute obstinacy that may emerge occasionally. Since you have all the ingredients for success, you need only apply self-discipline to bring out the remarkable possibilities associated with your birthday.

After the age of twelve, when your progressed Sun moves into Gemini, the tempo of your life increases, and there is more of an emphasis on your interrelationships with others, as well as learning and communication in general. This continues until the age of forty-two, when you experience a turning point as your progressed Sun enters Cancer. The following years will highlight the growing importance of emotional intimacy and security. From the age of seventy-two, when your progressed Sun enters Leo, the accent of your life may change from home to creativity and greater self-expression.

Your Secret Self

Although you probably have learned early in life that money is power, you may also come to realize that material success does not always bring happiness. You have a natural ability to make money if you are really determined and hardworking, yet you may find that fulfillment and satisfaction come from expression of your inner idealistic nature. With your intellectual flexibility and inventive thinking, you are often ahead of your time and may be interested in changing attitudes in society. This can manifest as a humanitarian or philanthropic interest that can accent your ability to shine when in a leading position. Since you are a natural liaison person, you may know people from many different groups or walks of life and are able to provide them with information that can be beneficial or uplifting.

Work & Vocation

Enterprising and ambitious, you have a natural business acumen that could bring you many rewards, though self-discipline is paramount. Your undoubted charm can lead you to excel in the service industries and you are likely to prefer people-oriented careers rather than solitary employment. With your optimism and big plans, you like to initiate new projects where you have a leading position. A dislike of taking orders may encourage you to work for yourself. Among your many talents, you possess executive abilities and organizational skills that can lead to promotion in posts such as official, civil servant, judge, or banker. If you desire fame, you may be drawn to explore your creative talents as an actor or politician.

Famous people who share your birthday include actress/politician Glenda Jackson, singer Billy Joel, Scottish writer Sir James Barrie, abolitionist John Brown, actor Albert Finney, and actress Candice Bergen.

Numerology

Benevolence, compassion, and sensitivity are all associated with the number 9 birthday. You are often considered intelligent and intuitive, with psychic abilities that point to a universal receptivity. As well as learning to become impersonal, you may have to develop understanding, tolerance, and patience. You are likely to benefit greatly from world travel and interaction with people from all walks of life. Avoid unrealistic dreams or an inclination toward escapism. The subinfluence of the number 5 month indicates that you are enthusiastic and adventurous and like to be busy and active. You may prefer to work for yourself, since you dislike taking orders from others. Through hard work and self-discipline, you can develop a more creative approach. As you need both freedom and stability, you benefit from having order and a practical routine, but guard against getting into a comfortable rut.

• *Positive:* idealism, humanitarianism, creativity, sensitivity, generosity, magnetism, poetic outlook, charitableness, giving nature, detachment, luck, popularity

• *Negative:* frustration, nervousness, uncertainty, selfishness, impracticality, bitterness, tendency to be easily led, inferiority complex, fear

Love & Relationships

Creative and highly charged with powerful desires, you are a charismatic individual with strong convictions. As a loyal friend, you give generously to those you love. Gregarious and sociable, you are likely to be flirtatious and attract many social and romantic opportunities. When you find someone new, you can become inspired and reveal your dramatic and passionate nature. Nevertheless, you probably need to take into consideration your partner's feelings and avoid being too domineering. Alternatively, when inspired you may wish to dedicate your life to some higher vision and can become a staunch supporter of a cause.

YOUR SPECIAL SOMEONE

For that special someone, you might want to look among those born on the following dates.

Love & friendship: Jan. 6, 15, 19, 29, 31, Feb. 4, 13, 27, 29, Mar. 2, 11, 25, 27, Apr. 9, 23, 25, May 7, 21, 23, June 5, 19, 21, July 3, 17, 19, 30, Aug. 1, 15, 17, 28, Sept. 13, 15, 26, Oct. 11, 13, 24, Nov. 9, 11, 22, Dec. 7, 9, 20

Beneficial: Jan. 13, 15, 19, Feb. 11, 13, 17, Mar. 9, 11, 15, Apr. 7, 9, 13, May 5, 7, 11, June 3, 5, 9, July 1, 3, 7, 29, Aug. 1, 5, 27, 31, Sept. 3, 25, 29, Oct. 1, 23, 27, Nov. 21, 25, Dec. 19, 23

Fatal attractions: May 30, June 28, July 26, Aug. 24, Sept. 22, Oct. 20, Nov. 10, 11, 12, 18, Dec. 16

Challenging: Jan. 12, Feb. 10, Mar. 8, Apr. 6, May 4, June 2, Aug. 31, Sept. 29, Oct. 27, 29, 30, Nov. 25, 27, 28, Dec. 23, 25, 26, 30

Soul mates: Jan. 2, 28, Feb. 26, Mar. 24, Apr. 22, May 20, June 18, July 16, Aug. 14, Sept. 12, Oct. 10, Nov. 8, Dec. 6

May 10

Practical and independent, as your birthday shows, you are an ambitious and broad-minded individual with a fine mind. Preferring to keep busy, you have vitality and are able to make quick decisions. A tendency to disappointment or frustration may sometimes sap you of your positivity, so having a definite goal or worthy cause is vital.

With the influence of your Sun in the Virgo decanate of Taurus, you are articulate and resourceful and often intellectually endowed. This also suggests a skill with criticism or an ability to deal with detailed, technical, or research work. The practical emphasis of this combination also points to a natural business sense or a capacity for analyzing monetary situations.

Usually you prefer to be given a free hand to make all your own decisions, and you dislike taking orders from others. Your ability to inspire people with your great plans and enthusiasm indicates that you have the potential to organize new and exciting ventures. However, by becoming willful and stubborn, you may lose the admiration you desire and become insecure. Fortunately, you also possess a wonderful sense of humor that can prevent you from becoming too self-obsessed or compulsive.

Around the age of eleven, when your progressed Sun moves into Gemini, you are likely to experience some changes and find new interests. Over the next thirty years, study and relating to others will become more important to you. There is another turning point at the age of forty-one, when your progressed Sun moves into Cancer. This is liable to increase your sensitivity, and you may place more emphasis on family and a secure home base. From the age of seventy-one, when your progressed Sun enters Leo, you become stronger and more confident in your self-expression.

Fixed Stars

Although your Sun's degree is not linked to a fixed star, some of your other planets' degrees certainly will be. By having an astrological chart calculated, you can find the exact position of the planets on your date of birth. This will tell you which of the fixed stars listed in this book are relevant to you.

Your Secret Self

Many of your challenges may concern financial issues. You have an excellent ability to evaluate situations, which gives you a natural sense of authority, but you can also be a person of extremes. On one hand, you are idealistic, generous, extravagant, and daring; on the other, you can be materialistic, selfish, and too security-conscious. It is important to integrate these opposites and find a balance. Have a realistic savings scheme and guard against extravagant impulses.

When you are detached, you are able to view life from a broad perspective and have a humanitarian outlook, wishing to support others. Your objective viewpoint can translate into intuition, which can assist you in your search for enlightenment as well as in more mundane concerns.

Work & Vocation

Since you are very independent and prefer to give orders rather than accept them, you are usually better in some position of authority or, if working within a group, where you have the freedom to operate in your own way. You often enjoy initiating projects, being involved with progressive ideas, or image making. However, the more practical and businesslike side of your nature may draw you to banking, trading, or stock brokerage. Alternatively, your excellent mental capacities and psychological skills may attract you to teaching, science, or some form of community work. Many people born on this date have natural healing ability, which may manifest itself through a career in medicine or alternative health. Your excellent flair for dealing with people will usually play a large part in any career that you choose.

Famous people who share your birthday include dancer Fred Astaire, songwriter Donovan, I-Ching expert Richard Wilhelm, producer David Selznick, and singers Sid Vicious and Bono.

Numerology

Like those with a number 1 birthday, you are ambitious and independent. Although you may have to overcome challenges before you reach your goals, with determination you often achieve your objectives. Your pioneering spirit frequently encourages you to travel far afield or strike out on your own. Having a number 10 birthday, you may also learn that the world does not revolve around you and that you should guard against being domineering. The subinfluence of the number 5 month indicates that you are enthusiastic, with strong instincts. Often idealistic, you can inspire others with your ideas and plans. However, if you feel restricted, you can be rebellious and disruptive. A good strategist, you need to learn how to apply your practical skills and use your imagination. Avoid making hasty decisions or advancing without a proper plan of action. Create harmony in your life and find a balance between your aspirations and the power to make them a reality.

• *Positive:* leadership, creativity, progressive attitudes, forcefulness, optimism, strong convictions, competitiveness, independence, gregariousness

• *Negative:* overbearing nature, jealousy, egotism, excessive pride, antagonism, lack of restraint, selfishness, instability, impatience

Love & Relationships

Although you often seem unemotional, underneath you have a caring and kind nature. You are happy in the company of those with whom you share some type of intellectual activity. Occasionally you may become too serious and need to develop a more impersonal or detached view. As a good communicator, you get along with most people and can mix well with different groups. Hidden insecurity, however, can be expressed in a negative way by argumentativeness or overindulgence. Partnerships can be especially beneficial for you if there is equal give and take.

YOUR SPECIAL SOMEONE

You might just find an inspiring partner among those born on the following dates.

Love & friendship: Jan. 6, 16, 20, Feb. 4, 14, Mar. 2, 12, 28, 30, Apr. 10, 26, 28, May 8, 24, 26, 30, June 6, 22, 24, 28, July 4, 20, 22, 26, 31, Aug. 2, 18, 20, 24, 29, Sept. 4, 16, 18, 22, 27, Oct. 14, 16, 20, 25, Nov. 12, 14, 18, 23, Dec. 10, 12, 16, 21

Beneficial: Jan. 9, 14, 16, Feb. 7, 12, 14, Mar. 5, 10, 12, Apr. 3, 8, 10, May 1, 6, 8, June 4, 6, July 2, 4, Aug. 2, Sept. 30, Oct. 28, Nov. 26, 30, Dec. 24, 28, 29

Fatal attractions: Jan. 21, Feb. 19, Mar. 17, Apr. 15, May 13, June 11, July 9, Aug. 7, Sept. 5, Oct. 3, Nov. 1, 11, 12, 13

Challenging: Jan. 4, 13, 28, Feb. 2, 11, 26, Mar. 9, 24, Apr. 7, 22, May 5, 20, June 3, 18, July 1, 16, Aug. 14, Sept. 12, Oct. 10, 31, Nov. 8, 29, Dec. 6, 27

Soul mates: Jan. 15, 22, Feb. 13, 20, Mar. 11, 18, Apr. 9, 16, May 7, 14, June 5, 12, July 3, 10, Aug. 1, 8, Sept. 6, Oct. 4, Nov. 2

May 11

Ambitious and determined, you have the willpower and capacity to fulfill the wonderful possibilities inherent in your birthday. Pragmatic, active, and productive, you need to feel that you are expanding your horizons and building a solid and secure future. Superior organizational skills, a good sense of timing, and an ability to deal with people ensure that you are an achiever. Although you are sometimes indecisive, once your mind is made up you possess a direct and forthright approach to your goals, which ensures that you do not waste time.

The influence of Capricorn, your decanate ruler, suggests that you are a hard worker and take your responsibilities seriously. A natural ability to deal with money also indicates that you can be prudent when necessary. Since this emphasizes loyalty and reliability, you are likely to have the respect of others. This may be especially important to you, as you value prestige.

Although you have a somewhat conservative side, you can be surprisingly unconventional and have unusual ideas. Generally confident, you can depend on your intuition but may have to guard against a tendency to become irritable or self-willed and obstinate. This can possibly slow you down in your tenacious climb up the ladder of success.

Around the age of ten, when your progressed Sun moves into Gemini, you may find new interests and become more sociable. Over the next thirty years, study and learning new skills can become more important to you. After forty, there is another turning point when your progressed Sun moves into Cancer. This influence accentuates a need to feel emotionally close to others, and frequently there is an increased emphasis on your home and immediate family. After the age of seventy, when your progressed Sun enters Leo, you become stronger and more confident and sociable.

Your Secret Self

An inner sense of the dramatic, combined with your natural business sense, ensures that with hard work you are likely to reach a prominent position. Your love of knowledge and your razor-sharp mind endow you with an ability to deal with any situation. One of the possible hindrances to your achievement is a tendency to overtax your finely tuned mind or become overly skeptical and doubting. Since you are likely to possess a strong personality and voice your opinions regardless of others' feelings, it is important not to overwhelm people with your strong emotions. One way of achieving self-mastery is through trusting your intuitive insight and developing your willpower with goals that seem just beyond your reach. This may help you build your confidence and faith to achieve your inspired dreams.

Work & Vocation

You enjoy power, structure, and effectiveness, yet also possess an emotional perceptiveness and sensitivity. This combination could work effectively for you in all areas, from the handling of material assets to the creative world. An amiable charm can also be of great assistance in your dealings with others and guarantees your success in people-related careers. You may certainly prefer to be in a position of power or self-employed, as you are not content to be in a subordinate position. However, since you are also aware of the importance of working cooperatively with others, you may have to compromise some of your independent attitude if operating within a teamwork situation. This birthdate often suggests musical, creative, or dramatic talent that can be commercialized.

Famous people born on your birthday include artist Salvador Dali, dancer Martha Graham, songwriter Irving Berlin, singer Eric Burden, and comedian Phil Silvers.

Numerology

The special vibration of the master number 11 birthday suggests that idealism, inspiration, and innovation are highly important to you. A blend of humility and confidence often challenges you to work toward self-mastery both materially and spiritually. Although you possess intuitive powers, you may scatter your energies and often need to find a goal upon which you can focus. Take your responsibilities more seriously. Usually you are highly charged and enjoy vitality but must avoid becoming overly anxious or impractical. The subinfluence of the number 5 month indicates that you are enthusiastic and energetic but need time to develop your thoughts and ideas. Truthful and a good confidant, you know how to keep a secret. You may need to establish a balance between your own wishes and your duties to others. Perceptive, you can pay attention to details, but avoid being critical or mistrusting.

• *Positive:* balance, focus, objectivity, enthusiasm, inspiration, spirituality, idealism, intuition, intelligence, outgoing nature, inventiveness, artistic ability, service orientation, healing ability, humanitarianism, faith, psychic ability

• *Negative:* superiority complex, dishonesty, aimlessness, overemotional, tendency to be easily hurt, high-strung nature, selfishness, lack of clarity, cruelty, dominating behavior, meanness

Love & Relationships

Sensitive and creative, you have a wealth of feelings and can be very sociable. Although generally confident, you can be emotionally indecisive in love, especially if you let yourself become involved in more than one relationship. Nevertheless, you are ordinarily loyal and affectionate and should not underestimate the power of love. You are capable of great sacrifice, but do not martyr yourself to unworthy partners, and guard against jealousy or possessiveness. A love of art and an appreciation for beauty and music suggest that you need an avenue for emotional self-expression and enjoy the company of creative people.

YOUR SPECIAL SOMEONE

You might find love, happiness, and that special someone among those born on the following days.

Love & friendship: Jan. 7, 17, 20, 21, Feb. 5, 15, 18, Mar. 3, 13, 16, 17, 29, 31, Apr. 1, 11, 14, 27, 29, May 9, 12, 25, 27, June 7, 10, 23, 25, July 5, 8, 21, 23, Aug. 3, 6, 19, 21, Sept. 1, 4, 5, 17, 19, Oct. 2, 15, 17, Nov. 13, 15, 30, Dec. 11, 13, 28

Beneficial: Jan. 15, 17, 28, Feb. 13, 15, 26, Mar. 11, 13, 24, Apr. 9, 11, 22, May 7, 9, 20, June 5, 7, 18, July 3, 5, 16, Aug. 1, 3, 14, Sept. 1, 12, Oct. 10, 29, Nov. 8, 27, Dec. 6, 25

Fatal attractions: Jan. 5, Feb. 3, Mar. 1, Nov. 12, 13, 14

Challenging: Jan. 4, 5, 14, Feb. 2, 3, 12, Mar. 1, 10, Apr. 8, 30, May 6, 28, June 4, 26, July 2, 24, Aug. 22, Sept. 20, Oct. 18, Nov. 16, Dec. 14

Soul mates: Jan. 2, Mar. 29, Apr. 27, May 25, June 23, July 21, Aug. 19, Sept. 17, Oct. 15, Nov. 13, Dec. 11

May 12

Your birthday reveals you to be a hardworking yet charming, sincere, and sociable individual. Although you can be warm and spontaneous, you also possess an ability to be tough and dutiful. At times this can cause a conflict between your work and your heart's desires. You are likely to have many friends and, with your stoic strength, can be a loyal and faithful friend yourself.

With the added influence of Capricorn, your decanate ruler, you are usually responsible and place importance on prestige and status. Material security is important to you, and generally you like to make long-term plans. This practical influence also suggests good concentration and an ability to be focused and precise about what you want to achieve. A touch of the perfectionist in you implies that if you undertake a job, you would want to do it properly. Although this suggests that you are strong-willed, industrious, and strongly self-controlled, you may have to be careful that this control does not degenerate into stubbornness.

The sociable quality of your birthday suggests that you enjoy sharing with others and are generous and gregarious. You can be a staunch ally, an excellent parent, and very protective of your family members. Because you have a love of beauty and luxury and possess good taste, your home is liable to be warm and attractive.

After the age of nine, when your progressed Sun moves into Gemini, there is an increased desire to interrelate more with others in your immediate surroundings. Over the next thirty years this influence may encourage you to study or develop your communication skills in some way, and this continues until around the age of thirty-nine, when your progressed Sun enters Cancer. As a turning point, this is likely to highlight the growing importance of home and needing to emotionally care both for yourself and for others. After the age of sixty-nine, when your progressed Sun enters Leo, you develop your confidence and self-expression.

FIXED STARS

Although your Sun's degree is not linked to a fixed star, some of your other planets' degrees certainly will be. By having an astrological chart calculated, you can find the exact position of the planets on your date of birth. This will tell you which of the fixed stars listed in this book are relevant to you.

Your Secret Self

Your openness can be expressed through a love of nature, art, or music that, if developed, has the potential to raise you to an almost mystical awareness. When displaying this bigheartedness positively, as a generous, universal love for all, you are able to accept or love without condition and show genuine compassion. Your powerful emotions can also be expressed negatively as disappointment, frustration, and an inability to let go of the past. However, through your experiences, you come to value the power of love.

You are likely to be someone that other people confide in. As an advisor, you are able to make people more detached about their situation while still showing that you care. If you allow yourself to become negative, however, you are in danger of becoming too self-sacrificing, even sliding into self-pity. Luckily, you also possess wonderful, amusing, childlike characteristics that can emerge at unexpected times and amaze and delight others.

Work & Vocation

A sense of responsibility earns you respect from employers; if you are self-employed, it ensures that you fulfill your commitments. Usually you are better when working with people, and with your natural charm, you have an ability to combine business and pleasure. An innate caring side to your nature may draw you to a career that involves service, such as counseling or teaching, and you generally make a protective employer. Often good in the healing world, you are likely to take a firm approach to health rather than being too sentimental. Since you possess a good business sense, you are usually able to turn talents into material rewards. A strong appreciation of beauty, nature, and form may attract you to a creative career, such as an artist, designer, musician, or landscape gardener. People of this birthdate may also often become involved in charity work.

Famous people born on your birthday include actress Katharine Hepburn, pre-Raphaelite painter Dante Gabriel Rossetti, baseball player and manager Yogi Berra, entertainer George Carlin, and nurse Florence Nightingale.

Numerology

Usually you are intuitive and friendly and possess good reasoning power. A desire to establish true individuality is often suggested by the number 12 birthday. Innovative and sensitive, you know how to use tact and cooperative methods to achieve your aims and objectives. To others you often appear confident, although self-doubt and suspicion can undermine your usual easygoing personality and positive outlook. When you achieve the balance between your need to define yourself and an inclination to be supportive of others, you can find emotional satisfaction and personal fulfillment. The subinfluence of the number 5 month indicates that you benefit from having a realistic perspective. A need to be organized and responsible often suggests that you can pay attention to detail. Ambitious and hardworking, you learn through observation or by developing your existing skills. With perseverance, determination, and hard work, you can achieve success. You need time alone to reflect, gather your thoughts, and recoup your energies.

• *Positive:* creativity, attractiveness, initiative, disciplinarian attitude, promotion of self or others

• *Negative:* reclusiveness, eccentricity, uncooperative behavior, oversensitivity, lack of self-esteem

Love & Relationships

Idealistic and romantic, you usually want serious relationships. You are naturally charming and drawn to sensitive or attractive people. Often you are willing to sacrifice a great deal for love. However, you may need to be careful not to martyr yourself to someone before you know their true worth. Your kindness and understanding draw people toward you for advice and comfort, but if you get hurt, you may withdraw and become uncommunicative. On occasion people of this birthdate find close relationships with someone from a different age group.

May 13

A natural charismatic warmth and ability to deal with people are shown by your Taurus birthday. Possessing an easygoing manner while still being frank and honest, you can be courteous and modest, capable and patient.

The influence of your Sun in the Capricorn decanate shows that you are hardworking and can have the Midas touch. Judicious and prudent, you often can make wise long-term investments. Prestige can be important to you, so you usually present yourself with dignity. The strong sense of responsibility indicated by this influence is generally beneficial as long as it does not result in your taking on other people's troubles as your own.

Although appearing pragmatic, you frequently think irrationally and make intuitive decisions. While you are not particularly aggressive for your own needs, you will fight hard to support the underdog or a meaningful cause. With sound common sense and a generally constructive outlook, you can be a solid rock of support for others. However, sometimes dissatisfaction with yourself and others may make you become overly critical. Alternatively, your caring nature can present a problem if too many people start to lean on you, provoking irritability or stubbornness. Luckily, your wonderfully gracious attitude can restore situations back to the harmony that you need.

After the age of eight, when your progressed Sun moves into Gemini, over the next thirty years there is an increased emphasis on interrelating with others in your immediate surroundings, as well as study and communication. At the age of thirty-eight, when your progressed Sun enters Cancer, there is a turning point that highlights the growing importance of your feelings, home, and family. After the age of sixty-eight, when your progressed Sun enters Leo, you become stronger and more confident.

FIXED STAR

Star's name: Zanrak

Degree position: 22°33'–23°32' Taurus between the years 1930 and 2000

Magnitude: 3

Strength: ★★★★★

Orb: 1°40'

Constellation: Gamma Eridani

Applicable days: May 13, 14, 15, 16

Star qualities: Saturn

Description: a red star located in the river Eridanus

PRIMARY STAR'S INFLUENCE

Zanrak imparts seriousness and a pragmatic outlook, together with a tendency to take life too seriously. This star's influence also suggests oversensitivity to other people's opinions and a pessimistic outlook.

Linked to your Sun's degree, this star can impart a preference for writing, business, and dealing with the public. Zanrak also warns that you can become isolated or encounter obstacles. There are also indications that you are strongly influenced by your immediate environment and need support from other family members.

• *Positive:* pragmatism, seriousness, responsibility, sensitivity

• *Negative:* overly serious or somber demeanor

Your Secret Self

Since you possess a natural aesthetic sense, you have an eye for form and color. Your elegance and style are likely to show in your house decor or in your appearance. You have a gentle charm and a successful way of dealing with people, but it is through your self-expression that you really find faith and trust in your own abilities. This confidence in yourself may be endangered by frustration and a quandary over your life choices. It is better to let go of situations that impede your progress rather than hang on to discouragement or disappointment.

Generally this birthday suggests well-being, physical comfort, and economic security. Your home and friends play an especially important part in your life. Often opportunities come through unpredictable sources and may not be noticed in their ordinary, everyday guise. These should not be overlooked, however, as they may secure advantages that will be very important to you later.

Work & Vocation

Being clever, dependable, and loyal will endear you to employers in whatever career you choose, even though you may not be particularly ambitious. However, others find you broadminded, charming, and gracious, and so you are able to excel in occupations that use people skills, such as sales. Being naturally philosophical may also draw you to teaching or law. An innate love of beauty and harmony often prompts you to successfully express yourself in the arts, drama, or music, and particularly in projects that involve the home, such as decorating, cooking, or interior design. You are also likely to be successful in working with the earth, for instance in landscape gardening and building or in property speculation.

Famous people born on your birthday include musicians Stevie Wonder and Gil Evans, writer Daphne du Maurier, composer Sir Arthur Sullivan, actor Harvey Keitel, actress Bea Arthur, and basketball player Dennis Rodman.

Numerology

Emotional sensitivity and inspiration are often identified with the number 13 birthday. Numerically, you are associated with hard work and can accomplish much through determination and being talented. You may, however, need to develop self-discipline if you want to turn your creative gifts into tangible products. With dedication, you can achieve prosperity. Having a number 13 birthday, you can be charming and fun-loving, with a sociable personality. Like many individuals who share your birthdate, you may wish to travel or yearn to settle in a new environment to make a better life for yourself. The subinfluence of the number 5 month indicates that you are intuitive and receptive with a need for material security. When inspired, you become motivated and show a willingness to work hard. Often persuasive and convincing, you can promote humanitarian causes and work for those who need help and support. You benefit from being broad-minded and by keeping a liberal attitude.

• *Positive:* ambition, creativity, love of freedom, self-expression, initiative
• *Negative:* impulsiveness, indecisiveness, bossiness, unemotional nature, rebelliousness

YOUR SPECIAL SOMEONE

You might find that special someone among those who are born on the following dates.

Love & friendship: Jan. 5, 9, 18, 19, 23, Feb. 3, 7, 16, 17, Mar. 1, 5, 14, 15, 19, 31, Apr. 3, 12, 13, 29, May 1, 10, 11, 27, 29, June 8, 9, 25, 27, July 6, 7, 23, 25, 31, Aug. 4, 5, 21, 23, 29, Sept. 2, 3, 7, 19, 21, 27, 30, Oct. 1, 17, 19, 25, 28, Dec. 13, 15, 21, 24

Beneficial: Jan. 1, 6, 17, Feb. 4, 15, Mar. 2, 13, Apr. 11, May 9, June 7, July 5, Aug. 3, Sept. 1, Oct. 31, Nov. 29, Dec. 27

Fatal attractions: Nov. 13, 14, 15, 16

Challenging: Jan. 2, 16, Feb. 14, Mar. 12, Apr. 10, May 8, June 6, July 4, Aug. 2, Dec. 30

Soul mates: Jan. 11, 31, Feb. 9, 29, Mar. 7, 27, Apr. 5, 25, May 3, 23, June 1, 21, July 19, Aug. 17, Sept. 15, Oct. 13, Nov. 11, Dec. 9

Love & Relationships

Full of emotional vitality, you often have high expectations for relationships. Usually very fortunate in attracting the opposite sex, you may have to beware of becoming too demanding or overly emotional in your love life. As you are likely to give everything to the one you love, take your time in choosing the right partner. With your charismatic personality and the power to attract people from all walks of life comes the necessity to exercise a certain amount of discrimination. This will help you to find true friends who will support you in your time of need rather than distract you from your purpose.

May 14

♉ Your birthday suggests that you are a practical visionary with a quick mind and instinctive reactions. Seeking variety and action to curb an inner restlessness, you need to focus and develop determination and self-awareness to overcome limitations. It is important for you to present a good image, and you are likely to seek the company of intelligent people.

The influence of the Sun in the Capricorn decanate indicates that you are hardworking and can be motivated when you find something of interest. The practical influence suggested by your birthday points to good concentration and an ability to be organized. You may have to be careful that your self-control does not degenerate into plain stubbornness. Although material security, status, and prestige may be particularly important, you will fight hard for your principles.

Mental stimulation is an important ingredient in your life, and you may travel far to expand your horizons. This may even include living in a foreign country. However, you may have to be careful that distractions or avoidance do not stop you from achieving your goals. With all your potential, it may be necessary for you to develop perseverance in order to actively fulfill your wonderful dreams.

After the age of seven, when your progressed Sun moves into Gemini, there is an emphasis over the next thirty years on communication, study, and the exchange of ideas. At the age of thirty-seven, when your progressed Sun enters Cancer, there is a turning point that highlights the growing importance of your home, family, and emotional needs. After the age of sixty-seven, when your progressed Sun enters Leo, you become more confident and self-assertive.

Your Secret Self

Your strong opinions and exceptional mental potential may belie the emotional sensitivity of your birthday. This can possibly expose you to worries or frustrations, particularly about fluctuations in your monetary affairs. When you learn detachment, you are able to rise above these insecurities. You acquire knowledge and information very quickly, which can build up your confidence.

A creative and resourceful side of you is indicated by the blending of your ideas and vivid imagination. Sociable, with a nice sense of humor, you are good at entertaining but may have to be careful of an extravagant streak. If indecisive, you can easily scatter your energies on trivial pursuits. Nevertheless, you can become inspired enough to work extremely hard and accept the responsibilities that pay real dividends.

Work & Vocation

Capable and versatile, you often have many interests and are likely to explore many avenues before you settle into a career. With your love of variety, it is important that you choose a career that does not involve routine. Possessing a strong visual sense, you are highly aware of images, and occupations such as media, graphics, or photography would suit you. Generally hardworking, with people skills, you are likely to be successful in merchandising or work con-

---

FIXED STAR

Star's name: Zanrak

Degree position: 22°33'–23°32' Taurus between the years 1930 and 2000

Magnitude: 3

Strength: ★★★★★

Orb: 1°40'

Constellation: Gamma Eridani

Applicable days: May 13, 14, 15, 16

Star qualities: Saturn

Description: a red star located in the river Eridanus

PRIMARY STAR'S INFLUENCE

Zanrak imparts seriousness and a pragmatic outlook, together with a tendency to take life too seriously. This star's influence also suggests oversensitivity to other people's opinions and a pessimistic outlook.

Linked to your Sun's degree, this star can impart a preference for writing, business, and dealing with the public. Zanrak also warns that you can become isolated or encounter obstacles. There are also indications that you are strongly influenced by your immediate environment and need support from other family members.

• *Positive:* pragmatism, seriousness, responsibility, sensitivity

• *Negative:* overly serious or somber demeanor

nected with foreign locations. With your capacity for deep thought, you may also become involved in careers that utilize your mental abilities, such as research, philosophy, or education.

Famous people born on your birthday include musician David Byrne, film director George Lucas, scientist Gabriel Fahrenheit, and painter Thomas Gainsborough.

Numerology

Intellectual potential, a pragmatic outlook, and strong determination are some of the qualities of those with a number 14 birthday. Often you possess a strong desire to establish a firm foundation and achieve success through hard work. Like many individuals associated with this birthday, you can often reach the top of your profession. With your perceptive mind, you respond quickly to problems and enjoy solving them. You like taking a risk or a gamble and may be lucky enough to gain a windfall. The subinfluence of the number 5 month indicates that you are enthusiastic and ambitious. Often independent and resilient, you want to be in control and lead the way. You may have to find a balance between your personal wishes and a need to be unselfish and compassionate. By utilizing your intuitive wisdom and applying it to some practical project, you can inspire others with your foresight. Although you possess a magnetic personality and can attract others, you need to find your strength from within.

• *Positive:* decisive action, hard work, luck, creativity, pragmatism, imagination, industry

• *Negative:* overly cautious or overly impulsive behavior, instability, thoughtlessness, stubbornness

Love & Relationships

Although you are often restless and unsettled, love and friendships are important to you. Socially inclined, with a natural sense of humor, you can be entertaining, especially with those you love. You like to mix with people who can stimulate your mind as well as help you have a good time. In relationships you need someone who can share your interests and keep you mentally active. Carefree and young at heart, you may need to learn about responsibilities before you finally settle down.

YOUR SPECIAL SOMEONE

For security, mental stimulation, and love you might want to begin looking among those who are born on the following dates.

Love & friendship: Jan. 6, 10, 20, 24, 29, Feb. 4, 8, 18, 27, Mar. 2, 6, 16, 20, 25, 28, 30, Apr. 4, 14, 23, 26, 28, 30, May 2, 12, 21, 24, 26, 28, 30, June 10, 19, 22, 24, 26, 28, July 8, 17, 20, 22, 24, 26, Aug. 6, 15, 18, 20, 22, 24, Sept. 4, 8, 13, 16, 18, 20, 22, Oct. 2, 11, 14, 16, 18, 20, Nov. 9, 12, 14, 16, 18, Dec. 7, 10, 12, 14, 16

Beneficial: Jan. 7, 13, 18, 28, Feb. 5, 11, 16, 26, Mar. 3, 9, 14, 24, Apr. 1, 7, 12, 22, May 5, 10, 20, June 3, 8, 18, July 1, 6, 16, Aug. 4, 14, Sept. 2, 12, 30, Oct. 10, 28, Nov. 8, 26, 30, Dec. 6, 24, 28

Fatal attractions: Jan. 25, Feb. 23, Mar. 21, Apr. 19, May 17, June 15, July 13, Aug. 11, Sept. 9, Oct. 7, Nov. 5, 15, 16, 17, Dec. 3

Challenging: Jan. 3, 17, Feb. 1, 15, Mar. 13, Apr. 11, May 9, 30, June 7, 28, July 5, 26, 29, Aug. 3, 24, 27, Sept. 1, 22, 25, Oct. 20, 23, Nov. 18, 21, Dec. 16, 19

Soul mates: Jan. 18, Feb. 16, Mar. 14, Apr. 12, May 10, 29, June 8, 27, July 6, 25, Aug. 4, 23, Sept. 2, 21, Oct. 19, Nov. 17, Dec. 15

May 15

♉ This birthdate reveals you to be a practical and sensible Taurean with a fertile imagination. Friendly and warm, with a strong accent on values, you project stability yet can be surprisingly sensitive. As you need security, you may find that there is an emphasis in your life on the financial protection that comes through work. You are likely to be loyal and reliable. You may also take pride in your work, as it can provide you with an avenue for your creative ideas and sense of responsibility.

With the added influence of your Sun in the Capricorn decanate, you are diligent and methodical, with a love of order, and have innate common sense. However, the wonderful advantages of your being so hardworking may occasionally be spoiled by your vacillating moods or a tendency to become stubborn or obstinate.

Since others respond to your kindness and caring, you are likely to have many good friends. Being sensitive, you do not respond well to a discordant environment and may need a creative outlet for your high ideals and love of nature, art, and music. In your quest for pleasure, however, you may have to beware of escapism or an overindulgence in the good things of life.

When your progressed Sun moves into Gemini at the time you reach the age of six, it coincides with your commencing school years. Over the following thirty years there is an emphasis on education and communication in general. At the age of thirty-six, when your progressed Sun enters Cancer, there is a turning point that highlights the growing importance of emotional security, home, and family. After sixty-six, when your progressed Sun enters Leo, you are likely to become more confident and extroverted.

Fixed Stars

Zanrak; Algol, also called Caput Medusae

PRIMARY STAR

Star's name: Zanrak
Degree position: 22°33'–23°32' Taurus between the years 1930 and 2000
Magnitude: 3
Strength: ★★★★★
Orb: 1°40'
Constellation: Gamma Eridani
Applicable days: May 13, 14, 15, 16
Star qualities: Saturn
Description: a red star located in the river Eridanus

PRIMARY STAR'S INFLUENCE

Zanrak imparts seriousness and a pragmatic outlook, together with a tendency to take life too seriously. This star's influence also suggests oversensitivity to other people's opinions and a pessimistic outlook.

Linked to your Sun's degree, this star can impart a preference for writing, business, and dealing with the public. Zanrak also warns that you can become isolated or encounter obstacles. There are also indications that you are strongly influenced by your immediate environment and need support from other family members.

• *Positive:* pragmatism, seriousness, responsibility, sensitivity

Your Secret Self

Fortunately, a magnetic charm is likely to save you from many difficult situations and draw people toward you. You also possess an emotional power that gives you the ability to intuitively understand others' motives if you trust your first instincts. This fast-moving inner energy can inspire your spirit to break away from rigid limitations and may help you considerably in your success.

Although you will work very hard to be responsible for home and family, there is also a part of you that does not like to be tied down and can become restless. This indicates that you need to keep active in order to give an inner dynamic to your pragmatism. This also stops you from feeling rebellious and impatient with relationships and your environment.

Work & Vocation

Being practical and perceptive, you can succeed in just about every career, from scientific research and business to something more creative. Although not exceptionally ambitious, you do possess a natural business sense, a desire for order, and diplomatic skills. This may draw you to careers that deal with other people's money, such as banking, law, or transacting business abroad. Alternatively, you may choose to work from home. Although clever, you may prefer to gain knowledge through experience rather than from theory. Some of your skills may also involve working with your hands. Your birthdate shows excellent work opportunities and a strong awareness of responsibility, but you may have to avoid becoming stuck in a routine.

Famous people who share your birthday include actors James Mason and Pierce Brosnan, musician Mike Oldfield, and scientist Pierre Curie.

Numerology

Usually you are quick and enthusiastic, with a charismatic personality. Your greatest assets are your strong instincts and the ability to learn through combining theory and practice. On many occasions you manage to earn while learning new skills. Able to recognize opportunities, you possess a talent for attracting money or receiving help and support from others. Successful conclusions to undertakings become more frequent if you apply your practical skills to your original ideas and overcome your tendency to be restless or dissatisfied. The subinfluence of the number 5 month indicates that you possess common sense and can grasp ideas quickly. Although you often want to have your own way and be an individual, you benefit from learning to be cooperative or a part of a team. By being sympathetic and understanding, you can develop a more patient nature. Although you are naturally adventurous, you nevertheless need to find a real base or a home that you can call your own. Having a routine and a plan of action can help you with self-discipline.

• *Positive:* willingness, generosity, responsibility, kindness, cooperation, appreciation, creative ideas

• *Negative:* restlessness, irresponsibility, self-centered behavior, fear of change, loss of faith, worry, indecision, materialism, misuse of power

YOUR SPECIAL SOMEONE

You might find emotional fulfillment and that special someone among those born on the following days.

Love & friendship: Jan. 7, 11, 22, 25, Feb. 5, 9, 20, Mar. 3, 7, 18, 21, 31, Apr. 1, 5, 16, 29, May 3, 14, 27, 29, June 1, 12, 25, 27, July 10, 23, 25, Aug. 8, 21, 23, 31, Sept. 6, 9, 19, 21, 29, Oct. 4, 17, 19, 27, 30, Nov. 2, 15, 17, 25, 28, Dec. 13, 15, 23, 26

Beneficial: Jan. 8, 14, 19, Feb. 6, 12, 17, Mar. 4, 10, 15, Apr. 2, 8, 13, May 6, 11, June 4, 9, July 2, 7, Aug. 5, Sept. 3, Oct. 1, 29, Nov. 27, Dec. 25, 29

Fatal attractions: Nov. 16, 17, 18

Challenging: Jan. 9, 18, 20, Feb. 7, 16, 18, Mar. 5, 14, 16, Apr. 3, 12, 14, May 1, 10, 12, June 8, 10, July 6, 8, 29, Aug. 4, 6, 27, Sept. 2, 4, 25, Oct. 2, 23, Nov. 21, Dec. 19

Soul mates: Jan. 9, Feb. 7, Mar. 5, Apr. 3, May 1, Oct. 30, Nov. 28, Dec. 26

Love & Relationships

With your powerful emotions and generosity, you have a lot to offer others. Yet if this power is not properly channeled through self-expression, you can be subject to moods and frustration. Since there is a possible danger of disillusionment in your relationships, you may have to be careful of becoming involved in emotional power games or sulking. Nevertheless, your charismatic personality and charm often attract many admirers and friends.

May 16

FIXED STARS

Zanrak; Algol, also called Caput Medusae

PRIMARY STAR

Star's name: Zanrak

Degree position: 22°33'–23°32' Taurus between the years 1930 and 2000

Magnitude: 3

Strength: ★★★★★

Orb: 1°40'

Constellation: Gamma Eridani

Applicable days: May 13, 14, 15, 16

Star qualities: Saturn

Description: a red star located in the river Eridanus

PRIMARY STAR'S INFLUENCE

Zanrak imparts seriousness and a pragmatic outlook, together with a tendency to take life too seriously. This star's influence also suggests oversensitivity to other people's opinions and a pessimistic outlook.

Linked to your Sun's degree, this star can impart a preference for writing, business, and dealing with the public. Zanrak also warns that you can become isolated or encounter obstacles. There are also indications that you are strongly influenced by your immediate environment and need support from other family members.

• *Positive:* pragmatism, serious and responsible behavior, sensitivity

A bright, sociable, and creative you is revealed by your birthdate. Appearing light and congenial, you also have a more serious side that can often involve the study of philosophical subjects.

Usually hardworking and intellectually discerning, you can be rational and practical yet open to new, unusual, and inventive ideas. This suggests that you may be ahead of your time or have a quick, dry wit that is very entertaining. When necessary, you have the ability to cut straight through hypocrisy or things left unsaid to suggest alternatives. Since you are independent, freedom is important to you, but avoid becoming too self-willed or contrary, which may spoil your natural charm.

The added influence of your Sun in the decanate of Capricorn gives an ability to be mentally concentrated and methodical as well as a desire to do a job well. It bestows a shrewd business sense and strong sense of ambition, which are likely to take you to the top of your profession. This influence may also indicate that you are likely to be quite economical or good at obtaining a bargain.

You have an interest in people and a natural humanitarian quality, which suggest that you can mix easily in any social circle, but it is through your excellent mind or creative abilities that you are capable of achieving tremendous results.

From around the age of five, when your progressed Sun moves into Gemini, you start a thirty-year period that emphasizes the importance of study, learning new skills, and communication. There is another turning point after thirty-five, when your progressed Sun moves into Cancer, making you likely to become more sensitive and home- and family-oriented. After the age of sixty-five, when your Sun moves into Leo, there is more of an emphasis on leadership, public life, or having fun.

Your Secret Self

As a perfectionist, you are usually willing to make big sacrifices in order to achieve your objectives or for the people you love. You have a strong sense of responsibility and awareness of the work that you need to put in to achieve results. When these are combined with your inner dramatic sense and quickness at evaluating people and situations, you usually find yourself naturally taking the leadership position. However, you may have to be careful of playing it too safe for the sake of security and not taking the risks necessary to fulfill your potential.

Giving yourself some time alone allows you to reconnect to a deeper, more contemplative, if not mystical, side of your nature. Having a harmonious home base therefore becomes more significant to you in your quest for inner peace. A tendency to worry or be indecisive about material concerns can be overcome through faith or creative self-expression. When happy and content, you are able to project a wonderful inner joy that can inspire others.

Work & Vocation

Creativity, sharp intelligence, and a capacity for hard work indicate that you have the possibility of rising to the top of your chosen profession. However, you may have to guard against scattering your energies. Your inquisitive mind wants to understand things down to the last detail and can be quite analytical or technical. With your charm and communication skills, you are likely to be successful in any career involving the general public. Your strong business sense suggests that careers such as negotiating, banking, or property speculation are also strong possibilities. A philosophical or humanitarian leaning may be satisfied through occupations such as the clergy, charity work, or philanthropy. Alternatively, your desire for self-expression and love of beauty and form may manifest through a career in music, writing, or the arts.

Famous people who share your birthday include singer Janet Jackson, jazz drummer Billy Cobham, guitarist Robert Fripp, gymnast Olga Korbut, designer Christian Lacroix, tennis player Gabriela Sabatini, and actresses Tori Spelling and Debra Winger.

Numerology

A number 16 birthday suggests that you are ambitious yet sensitive. Usually outgoing and sociable, you are friendly and thoughtful. You often judge life according to how you feel, and you have good insight and a caring nature. With a number 16 birthday, you may be interested in world affairs and may join international corporations. The creative ones among you have a talent for writing, with sudden flashes of inspiration. Having a number 16 birthday, you may need to learn how to balance between being overconfident and doubtful and insecure. The subinfluence of the number 5 month indicates that you are intuitive and receptive. Socially inclined and versatile, you have many contacts and interests. A need to be creative suggests that you can combine your original ideas with your practical skills and be inventive. You like to make a good impression and pay attention to your appearance. Learn to trust your inner feelings and overcome your tendency to be indecisive or worried.

• *Positive:* higher education, responsibilities to home and family, integrity, intuition, sociability, cooperation, insight

• *Negative:* worry, inability to be satisfied, irresponsibility, self-promotion, opinionated attitude, skepticism, fussiness, selfishness, lack of sympathy

Love & Relationships

Usually you are highly idealistic in your approach to relationships. Occasionally you may need time on your own to reflect, making you appear withdrawn or indifferent. You can be spontaneous, loyal, and giving, but you need to guard against going to extremes by martyring yourself. By staying positive and having faith you can avoid inclinations to be suspicious, jealous, or preoccupied with your own thoughts.

YOUR SPECIAL SOMEONE

To find long-lasting happiness, security, and love, you might begin by looking for someone born on the following days.

Love & friendship: Jan. 8, 13, 22, 26, Feb. 6, 20, 24, Mar. 4, 18, 22, Apr. 2, 16, 20, 30, May 5, 14, 18, 28, 30, June 12, 16, 26, 28, July 10, 14, 24, 26, Aug. 8, 12, 22, 24, Sept. 6, 10, 20, 22, 30, Oct. 4, 8, 18, 20, 28, Nov. 2, 6, 16, 18, 26, Dec. 4, 14, 16, 24

Beneficial: Jan. 9, 20, Feb. 7, 18, Mar. 5, 16, 29, Apr. 3, 14, 27, May 1, 12, 25, June 10, 23, July 8, 21, Aug. 6, 19, Sept. 4, 17, Oct. 2, 15, 30, Nov. 13, 28, Dec. 11, 26, 30

Fatal attractions: Jan. 27, Feb. 25, Mar. 23, Apr. 21, May 19, June 17, July 15, Aug. 13, Sept. 11, Oct. 9, Nov. 7, 17, 18, 19, Dec. 5

Challenging: Jan. 2, 10, 19, Feb. 8, 17, Mar. 6, 15, Apr. 4, 13, May 2, 11, June 9, July 7, 30, Aug. 5, 28, Sept. 3, 26, Oct. 1, 24, Nov. 22, Dec. 20, 30

Soul mates: Jan. 15, Feb. 13, Mar. 11, Apr. 9, May 7, June 5, July 3, Aug. 1, Oct. 29, Nov. 27, Dec. 25

May 17

Your high idealism, determination, and gregarious personality suggest that you can excel in almost anything. When positive, you project charisma, strong enthusiasm, and belief in your own ideas. Your birthday also points to a natural talent for dealing with people on a personal level and an ability to enjoy yourself.

Even though you will never be without money, there will be times when you may have a groundless fear of not having enough. Luckily, being resolute and persistent, you are not likely to sit around and wait for things to come to you. Strong ambition and a desire for prestige and the luxuries of life are liable to motivate you into action.

With the added influence of your Sun in the Capricorn decanate, you work better with a goal, becoming very focused on the task in hand. You possess excellent ideas, good strategic skills, and an ability to provide for yourself materially. Your capacity to be tough with yourself and others when committed to working on a set plan can be most impressive. A contrasting side to your nature is sensitive and idealistic and may find an outlet in helping your family and friends or compassionate causes.

A thirty-year cycle begins at the age of four, when your progressed Sun moves into Gemini. This points to an emphasis on communication and learning in all forms. This continues until the age of thirty-four, when your progressed Sun enters Cancer. As a turning point, this highlights the growing importance of emotional intimacy and security. In your mid-sixties, when your progressed Sun moves into Leo, there is another change of emphasis, as you may start to change from being family-oriented to being more outward-oriented, sociable, and authoritative.

FIXED STAR

Star's name: Algol, also called Caput Medusae
Degree position: 25°13–26°21' Taurus between the years 1930 and 2000
Magnitude: 2.5
Strength: ★★★★★★★
Orb: 2°
Constellation: Beta Perseus
Applicable days: May 15, 16, 17, 18, 19
Star qualities: Saturn/Jupiter
Description: a white binary and variable star located in the Medusa's head held in the hand of Perseus

PRIMARY STAR'S INFLUENCE

This star carries a double meaning: on one hand, it endows high spiritual values, and on the other, it suggests misfortune and lack of satisfaction or spirituality. When positive, you have the potential to become a leader through achievement and outstanding character, or to be of benefit to the community. This star suggests that bereavement may have a strong impact on a person's life and is often prominent for individuals who counsel the bereaved.

Linked to your Sun's degree, Algol bestows victory after struggle or victory over others in conflict and dispute. Yet it also carries a warning about scattering your energy and becoming confused. This star suggests the importance of maintaining correct conduct, thus avoiding legal entanglements and unsuitable company, which may lead to involvement in vendettas, family feuds, or physical conflicts.

Your Secret Self

Even when your outer life is full of plans and action, deep down you seek an inner peace and harmony. This may stimulate you to develop a musical, artistic, or creative skill or, alternatively, be a healing force for those around you. An innate awareness that you accomplish in life only through what you put in ensures that you do not take things for granted. Pride and a strong need for recognition are often your motivating forces and suggest that you will not tolerate being unappreciated for too long.

Increasing social prestige can bring security and financial rewards as you progress through life. You are quite willing to share these with those you love, but may have to be careful of developing a patronizing attitude or of becoming jealous. Getting in touch with your inner spiritual needs may help you develop a balance between your quest for pleasure and the more meaningful aspects of life.

Work & Vocation

Although you like to be in charge or work for yourself, you also realize the importance of working cooperatively with others. This may stimulate you to become involved in working partnerships or projects involving teamwork. You may also be particularly good at selling or promoting an idea or product. With your relationship skills and ability to make contacts, careers involving people are ideal, such as public relations, liaison workers, and agents. Your shrewd business sense and organizational skills also ensure your success in careers such as financial advisor, negotiator, or banker, or in any work concerning property. Alternatively, education, science, and music are career areas that may prove especially meaningful for you.

Famous people who share your birthday include singer Enya, actor Dennis Hopper, pioneering vaccine researcher Edward Jenner, musician Taj Mahal, and boxer Sugar Ray Leonard.

Numerology

With a number 17 birthday, you are often shrewd, with a reserved nature and good rationality. Since you usually utilize your knowledge in a specific way, you can develop your expertise and achieve success or a prominent position as a specialist or researcher. Private, introspective, and detached, with a strong interest in facts and figures, you frequently present a serious and thoughtful demeanor and like to take your time. Capable of long periods of concentration and endurance, you can learn best through experience. Nevertheless, the less skeptical you are, the quicker you learn. The subinfluence of the number 5 month indicates that you are practical and intelligent and like to rely on facts and figures. A natural business sense and analytical approach suggest that you can become a specialist in your field. Gaining knowledge and broadening your horizon help your self-confidence. Develop your sense of responsibility to others or be of service to your community.

• *Positive:* thoughtfulness, specialist ability, good planning, good business sense, ability to attract money, individual thinker, painstaking nature, accuracy, skill at research, scientific ability
• *Negative:* detachment, stubbornness, carelessness, moodiness, narrowmindedness, criticism, worry, suspicion

Love & Relationships

Usually you have a full social life and are popular. All your relationships are very important to you, and although you are a loyal friend, you prefer powerful people with strong opinions and intelligent minds. Be careful, however, not to become involved in power conflicts with partners, as they may cause you unnecessary stress and anxiety. When you feel secure in relationships, you can be very supportive and generous with the people you love. Trust is a prerequisite in close relationships, and mental stimulation often brings out the best in you.

YOUR SPECIAL SOMEONE

For security, mental stimulation, and love, you might want to begin looking for those born among the following dates.

Love & friendship: Jan. 3, 23, 27, Feb. 11, 21, Mar. 9, 19, 28, 31, Apr. 7, 17, 21, 26, 29, May 5, 15, 24, 27, 29, 31, June 3, 13, 22, 25, 27, 29, July 1, 11, 20, 23, 25, 27, 29, Aug. 9, 18, 21, 23, 25, 27, Sept. 7, 11, 16, 19, 21, 23, 25, Oct. 5, 14, 17, 19, 21, 23, Nov. 3, 12, 15, 17, 19, 21, Dec. 1, 10, 13, 15, 17, 19

Beneficial: Jan. 3, 4, 10, 21, Feb. 1, 2, 8, 19, Mar. 6, 17, 30, Apr. 4, 15, 28, May 2, 13, 26, June 11, 24, July 9, 22, Aug. 7, 20, Sept. 5, 18, Oct. 3, 16, 31, Nov. 1, 14, 29, Dec. 12, 27

Fatal attractions: Jan. 22, 28, Feb. 20, 26, Mar. 18, 24, Apr. 16, 22, May 14, 20, June 12, 18, July 10, 16, Aug. 8, 14, Sept. 6, 12, Oct. 4, 10, Nov. 2, 8, 18, 19, 20, Dec. 6

Challenging: Jan. 11, 20, Feb. 9, 18, Mar. 7, 16, Apr. 5, 14, May 3, 12, 30, June 1, 10, 28, July 8, 26, 31, Aug. 6, 24, 29, Sept. 4, 22, 27, Oct. 2, 20, 25, Nov. 18, 23, Dec. 16, 21

Soul mates: Jan. 26, Feb. 24, Mar. 22, 30, Apr. 20, 28, May 18, 26, June 16, 24, July 14, 22, Aug. 12, 20, Sept. 10, 18, Oct. 8, 16, Nov. 6, 14, Dec. 4, 12

May 18

Your friendliness, leadership skills, and strong-willed determination mark you out as a person who was born to succeed. Pragmatic, with a good understanding of values, you appreciate beauty and the good things of life. Quick to see opportunities, you manage to combine materialism with a strong sense of idealism.

The added influence of your Sun in the Capricorn decanate suggests that hard work and responsibility are part of your daily routine and that material concerns and status are important to you. Needing the respect of your peers, you can be a loyal and untiring worker when committed to a project or cause and are likely to give it your all.

Your idealism and need for spirituality or self-awareness may manifest as a strong humanitarian streak. This interest in people can help you develop compassion and give you an understanding of other people's needs. Your sensitivity and active imagination may also find outlets through art, music, or drama. Possessing a strong desire for knowledge, you enjoy debates, are a good organizer, and have a quick grasp of any situation. You may, however, have to beware of a tendency to become obstinately opposed to others just for the sake of it. Luckily, you may compensate for this by unselfish gestures of generosity.

Around the age of three, when your progressed Sun moves into Gemini, you will begin a thirty-year cycle emphasizing the importance of brothers or sisters, learning new skills, or study. At the age of thirty-three, when your progressed Sun moves into Cancer, you experience a turning point that highlights the significance of family and a home base. After your early sixties, when your progressed Sun moves into Leo, the accent in your life may change from your home situation to creativity and greater self-expression.

Your Secret Self

Since your strong will enables you to turn your ideas into concrete reality, it is especially important that you be clear about your motives and desires. By connecting to your inner power of love, you become a force in helping others as well as uniting the extremes within your personality. These may manifest as being either overly sensitive or too domineering. You can eliminate these problems by staying independent yet applying your natural skills in the art of cooperation and diplomacy. Being a practical visionary, you need to be constantly looking to the future and challenging yourself in order to manifest your big plans. This helps you overcome an innate restlessness or impatience, which could drain your resources.

Work & Vocation

Driven by ambition and idealism, you are willing to work hard to achieve your objectives. With your determination and ability to naturally take the lead, you enjoy initiating new projects and are inclined toward careers in law and order or government. Since you are extremely good at promoting people or selling ideas, you may decide to make a career in an area such as marketing, being an agent, or negotiation. With your endurance, commitment, and administrative abilities, you may also pursue a career in commerce, such as financial advisor, manager, stockbroker, or entrepreneur. Travel may prove especially helpful in the achievement of your

FIXED STAR

Star's name: Algol; also called Caput Medusae

Degree position: 25°13'–26°21' Taurus between the years of 1930 and 2000

Magnitude: 2.5

Strength: ★★★★★★★

Orb: 2°

Constellation: Beta Perseus

Applicable days: May 15, 16, 17, 18, 19

Star qualities: Saturn/Jupiter

Description: a white binary and variable star located in the Medusa's head held in the hand of Perseus

PRIMARY STAR'S INFLUENCE

This star carries a double meaning: on one hand, it endows high spiritual values, and on the other, it suggests misfortune and lack of satisfaction or spirituality. When positive, you have the potential to become a leader through achievement and outstanding character, or to be of benefit to the community. This star suggests that bereavement may have a strong impact on your life, and it is often prominent for individuals who counsel the bereaved.

Linked to your Sun's degree, Algol bestows victory after struggle or victory over others in conflict and dispute. Yet it also carries a warning about scattering your energy and becoming confused. This star suggests the importance of maintaining correct conduct, thus avoiding legal entanglements and unsuitable company, which may lead to involvement in vendettas, family feuds, or physical conflicts.

• *Positive:* high spiritual values, correct conduct

• *Negative:* misfortune, impatience, misconduct, keeping bad company

goals. Your appreciation of beauty may lead you to occupations dealing in luxury goods, antiques, or design. You may also possess a skill for charity fund-raising or working with products of the land. Alternatively, your strong individuality may find expression in the creative world.

Famous people who share your birthday include ballet star Margot Fonteyn, Pope John Paul II, and singers Perry Como and Toyah Willcox.

Numerology

Determination, assertiveness, and ambition are some of the attributes associated with the number 18 birthday. Dynamic and active, you frequently desire power and need constant challenge. At times you may be critical, hard to please, or inclined toward controversial issues. As a number 18 personality, you may use your power to help others, give sound advice, or solve other people's problems. Alternatively, your strong business sense and organizational skills lead you to the world of commerce. The subinfluence of the number 5 month indicates that you are energetic and decisive, with practical sense. By reflecting and analyzing, you can pay attention to small details and clear up any misunderstanding. Being in too much of a hurry or leaving projects half done may cause delays later on. At times you can be too demanding, and a tendency to change your feelings toward other people suggests inner discontent. If unsure, you can be reserved and uncommunicative or give in to moodiness.

• *Positive:* progressive attitudes, assertiveness, intuition, courage, resoluteness, healing ability, efficiency, advisory skills

• *Negative:* uncontrolled emotions, laziness, lack of order, selfishness, callousness, failure to complete work or projects, deceit

Love & Relationships

Although many interests capture your heart, you are often searching for a soul mate with whom you can share some of your ideals. This restlessness also indicates that you are sometimes caught between your duties and personal wishes. Ambitious and security-conscious, you may be tempted to marry for reasons other than love. You admire loyalty and faithfulness; but if in doubt, you can become dissatisfied and experience fluctuating moods. On one hand, you can be very warm and generous; on the other, cold and overly serious. Nevertheless, through honesty and learning patience and perseverance you may find happiness, emotional balance, or stability.

YOUR SPECIAL SOMEONE

You might just find the inspiring partner you are looking for among those born on the following dates.

Love & friendship: Jan. 14, 24, 28, 31, Feb. 12, 22, 26, 29, Mar. 10, 20, 24, 27, Apr. 8, 18, 25, May 6, 16, 23, 30, June 4, 14, 21, 28, 30, July 2, 12, 19, 26, 28, 30, Aug. 10, 17, 24, 26, 28, Sept. 8, 12, 15, 22, 24, 26, Oct. 6, 13, 20, 22, 24, 30, Nov. 4, 11, 18, 20, 22, 28, Dec. 2, 9, 16, 18, 20, 26, 29

Beneficial: Jan. 5, 22, 30, Feb. 3, 20, 28, Mar. 1, 18, 26, Apr. 16, 24, May 14, 22, June 12, 20, July 10, 18, 29, Aug. 8, 16, 27, 31, Sept. 6, 14, 25, 29, Oct. 4, 12, 23, 27, Nov. 2, 10, 21, 25, Dec. 9, 19, 23

Fatal attractions: Jan. 12, Feb. 10, Mar. 8, Apr. 6, May 4, June 2, Nov. 19, 20, 21

Challenging: Jan. 16, 21, Feb. 14, 19, Mar. 12, 17, 30, Apr. 10, 15, 28, May 8, 13, 26, June 6, 11, 24, July 4, 9, 22, Aug. 2, 7, 20, Sept. 5, 18, Oct. 3, 16, Nov. 1, 14, Dec. 12

Soul mates: Jan. 25, Feb. 23, Mar. 21, Apr. 19, May 17, June 15, July 13, Aug. 11, Sept. 9, Oct. 7, Nov. 5, Dec. 3, 30.

May 19

♉ The outstanding leadership promised by your birthday is matched by your excellent mental powers and good perception. Careful and prudent, but also possessing a wilder or more independent streak, you appear to others as confident, in control, and self-assured.

With the added influence of your Sun in the Capricorn decanate, you are willing to put in hard work when committed to a project, and you fare better when you have a definite goal. This influence also points to strong ambition and a sense of duty as well as the attainment of long-term plans. Although you can be stubborn, your tenacious staying power and intuitive ability can help you in your climb to success.

Due to a natural interest in people, you are often a humanitarian who believes in the need for freedom and social reform. Inventive and original, you have a progressive philosophy in life and can be a spokesperson for others. Both men and women born on this date may have to beware of becoming overbearing. A love of debate and friendly bantering, however, can lift your spirits and prove to be an enjoyable pastime. Nevertheless, you may have to guard against appearing self-centered or unsympathetic, and watch out for a tendency to overindulge in the good things of life. However, through your depth of knowledge and good judgment, you generally have a most beneficial effect on others. Education in some form may be vital to bring out the best of your marvelous potential.

When you reach the age of two, your progressed Sun moves into Gemini, emphasizing the importance over the next thirty years of learning, writing, speech, and communication. This continues until your early thirties, when your progressed Sun enters Cancer. This is a turning point for you, highlighting the growing importance of emotional intimacy, family, home, and security. After the age of sixty-two, when the Sun moves into Leo, you are likely to become more confident and interested in public life or your own self-expression.

FIXED STARS

Alcyone; Algol, also called Caput Medusae

PRIMARY STAR

Star's name: Alcyone

Degree position: 29° Taurus–0°6' Gemini between the years 1930 and 2000

Magnitude: 3

Strength: ★★★

Orb: 1°40'

Constellation: Eta Taurus

Applicable days: May 19, 20, 21, 22

Star qualities: Moon/Mars

Description: a green and yellow principal star in the Pleiades cluster, located on the shoulder of the Bull (it is the brightest star of the Pleiades)

PRIMARY STAR'S INFLUENCE

Alcyone imparts openness and frankness, honesty, and sincerity. Restlessness and impulsive actions can also be associated with this star. By nature, these persons are forceful and purposeful, yet when feelings intensify they are inclined to act on impulse. This may cause turbulence and bring about changed circumstances. This star also warns against fevers and problems with eyesight.

Linked to your Sun's degree, Alcyone bestows love, eminence, and a talent for leadership. This star often indicates that you can enjoy success in legal and public matters or use your creative mind to develop your writing skills.

Your Secret Self

Although a natural leader, you are very aware of the importance of teamwork or group efforts. In order to avoid dependent situations, it may be necessary to use your strong intuition to strike just the right balance between standing up for your own ideas and being receptive to the opinions of others. Fortunately, possessing a persuasive charm, you are generally able to convince others of the importance of your ideals and gain their assistance.

A desire for honesty and justice can lead to your taking the reins of power in difficult situations. This can often seem as if you are being autocratic. In fact, you have a need to resolve issues rather than leave them unfinished. Your determination, power, and perseverance can ultimately ensure your success. Underneath all that seriousness, however, is a heart that is idealistic and willing to help other people achieve their own individual rise to the top.

Work & Vocation

The combination of your ability to work hard, perceptive leadership, and capacity to take responsibility points to outstanding prospects for success. Your original and exceptional mind has many innovative ideas, which may particularly draw you to careers in education, philosophy, or scientific research. Humanitarianism and possible spiritual aspirations can steer you toward social reform or religion. Alternatively, a natural sense of the dramatic may attract you to some form of art or entertainment. A way with words can also inspire you to express yourself through speaking, writing, or singing. Possessing an innate healing force, you may prefer to choose a career in medicine or alternative health.

Famous people born on your birthday include political leader Malcolm X, musicians Pete Townshend and Joey Ramone, actress Glenn Close, and singer Grace Jones.

Numerology

Your number 19 birthdate suggests that you are decisive and resourceful, with depth of vision, but that the dreamer side of your nature is compassionate and impressionable. The need to be someone may be the very thing that pushes you to be dramatic and claim center stage. To others you may appear confident and resilient, but inner tensions may cause emotional ups and downs. Although proud, you may also need to learn that the world does not revolve around you. The subinfluence of the number 5 month indicates that you are alert and mentally restless. Although you want harmony and peace, you need to develop an awareness of other people's feelings and needs. Creative and imaginative, you benefit from developing your artistic talents. Avoid worry by learning to relax and be detached. By giving encouragement to others and showing patience, you can overcome a tendency to criticize. You may have to find a balance between being self-centered and performing selfless service for others. Being fair and just shows courage and true self-control.

• *Positive:* dynamism, centeredness, creativity, leadership, luck, progressive attitudes, optimism, strong convictions, competitiveness, independence, gregariousness

• *Negative:* self-centeredness, depression, worry, fear of rejection, ups and downs, materialism, egotism, impatience

Love & Relationships

Open and direct, you are vigilant in defense of those you love. Harmony and a peaceful environment are a prerequisite, and you can also help, with your easygoing personality, those who suffer from emotional tension. Nevertheless, guard against being too arrogant or restless yourself, and avoid getting in a rut. Although you are very sociable, home and family play a strong part in your overall life plan.

YOUR SPECIAL SOMEONE

You might find a long-lasting relationship and stability with someone born on one of the following dates.

Love & friendship: Jan. 11, 13, 15, 17, 25, 29, Feb. 9, 11, 13, 15, 23, Mar. 7, 9, 11, 13, 21, 25, Apr. 5, 7, 9, 11, 19, May 3, 5, 7, 9, 17, 31, June 1, 3, 5, 7, 15, 29, July 1, 3, 5, 27, 29, 31, Aug. 1, 3, 11, 25, 27, 29, Sept. 1, 9, 13, 23, 25, 27, Oct. 7, 21, 23, 25, Nov. 5, 19, 21, 23, Dec. 3, 17, 19, 21, 30

Beneficial: Jan. 1, 5, 20, Feb. 3, 18, Mar. 1, 16, Apr. 14, May 12, June 10, July 8, Aug. 6, Sept. 4, Oct. 2

Fatal attractions: Nov. 19, 20, 21, 22

Challenging: Jan. 6, 22, 24, Feb. 4, 20, 22, Mar. 2, 18, 20, Apr. 16, 18, May 14, 16, June 12, 14, July 10, 12, Aug. 8, 10, 31, Sept. 6, 8, 29, Oct. 4, 6, 27, Nov. 2, 4, 25, 30, Dec. 2, 23, 28

Soul mates: Jan. 6, 12, Feb. 4, 10, Mar. 2, 8, Apr. 6, May 4, June 2

May 20

A bright, personable intelligence marks people who share your birthday as something special. Being a natural leader through enthusiasm and ability to shine, you have a way with people and are kind and very sociable. You are naturally gifted, and others see you as possessing common sense, charm, and self-assurance.

The influence of your Sun in the Capricorn decanate of Taurus suggests that prestige and self-respect are important to you. Retaining your dignity and able to work very hard, you usually take your responsibilities seriously. Having a natural understanding of money, you will probably prefer to budget and keep your accounts or business plans in order. Life's luxuries, however, are still attractive to you, so you are likely to spend on beautiful things; just beware of overindulgence.

Having a natural dramatic sense, you like to surround yourself with people who are intelligent and communicative. Since you are verbally skilled, you will probably enjoy a good debate or witty repartee. With the ability to grasp concepts quickly, you like to be honest and direct, but you may have to guard against a tendency to become opinionated or obstinate.

If your big plans occasionally fail, there is a chance that you may end up feeling sorry for yourself, but this will not last long, as you are determined to overcome obstacles and succeed.

Around the second year of life, your progressed Sun passes into the sign of Gemini. This emphasizes that as a child you are a quick learner and have close links with brothers and sisters. Until the age of thirty, you are likely to concentrate on study and learning new skills. A turning point occurs at thirty-one, when your progressed Sun moves into Cancer, identifying the significance of family links and a home base or center from which to build. From your early sixties, when the progressed Sun moves into Leo, your confidence increases and you are liable to become more outgoing and self-expressive.

FIXED STAR

Star's name: Alcyone

Degree position: 29° Taurus–0°6'
Gemini between the years 1930
and 2000

Magnitude: 3

Strength: ★★★★★

Orb: 1°40'

Constellation: Eta Taurus

Applicable days: May 19, 20, 21, 22

Star qualities: Moon/Mars

Description: a green and yellow
principal star in the Pleiades
cluster, located on the shoulder of
the Bull (it is the brightest star of
the Pleiades)

PRIMARY STAR'S INFLUENCE

Alcyone imparts openness and frankness, honesty, and sincerity. Restlessness and impulsive actions can also be associated with this star. By nature, you are forceful and purposeful, yet when feelings intensify you are inclined to act on impulse. This may cause turbulence and bring about changed circumstances. This star also warns against fevers and problems with eyesight.

Linked to your Sun's degree, Alcyone bestows love, eminence, and a talent for leadership. This star often indicates that you can enjoy success in legal and public matters or use your creative mind to develop your writing skills.

• *Positive:* creative mind, honesty, enthusiasm

• *Negative:* cantankerousness, moodiness, temperamental behavior

Your Secret Self

Although you know that you are capable of accomplishing in a big way, you may have to avoid being too materialistic or self-critical. Your creative spirit ensures that you will always be looking for new and exciting ways to occupy your mind and expand your horizons. Since you are not content to rest with what you already have, you are likely to travel far physically or mentally in order to explore all your possibilities.

Although you may not show it, you are also intensely emotional. As this sensitivity needs to be expressed through the joy of life, it is vital that you do not submerge it in worries or anxieties. When you are happy, it seems as if you will always be able to achieve all the goals that your heart desires. Just remember when making choices to choose faith in yourself so that you can keep your big dream alive. You are capable of amazing success in your life through the combination of your determination, inspiration, and generosity.

Work & Vocation

With your intelligence and need for variety, you are likely to be constantly updating your knowledge. As you enjoy large projects or groups and do not like to be subordinate to others, you ideally need a career where you can be self-employed or retain some control or authority. If you apply the necessary self-discipline, a natural flair for business can guarantee your success. It is necessary that your work have some form of mental challenge or diversity to keep you from becoming bored. Your intuitive intellect may draw you to scientific research, education, metaphysics, or philosophy. Being multitalented and having a fine appreciation of art, music, and drama may also lead you to a career in the arts, media, or entertainment world. Alternatively, your caring nature may find a place in the world of counseling, social work, or fighting for the rights of others.

Famous people born on your birthday include singers Cher and Joe Cocker, Greek philosopher Socrates, actor Jimmy Stewart, and writer Honoré de Balzac.

Numerology

With a number 20 birthday, you are intuitive, adaptable, and understanding. Usually you enjoy cooperative activities where you can interact, share experiences, or learn from others. Often charming and gracious, you develop diplomatic skills and can move in different social circles with ease. You may, however, need to overcome a tendency to be hurt easily by the actions and criticism of others. In relationships you must guard against an inclination to martyr yourself, be mistrusting, or be overly dependent on others. The subinfluence of the number 5 month indicates that you are receptive and intelligent, with a need to be creative and self-expressive. Sometimes shy, you need to learn how to disclose your feelings and express yourself clearly to others. Although you are friendly and see yourself as part of a team, you need to spend time alone in order to be quiet and gather your thoughts. Make the time to study or learn new skills and allow others to assist you to make changes in your life. Trust your intuitive power and improve your mind.

- *Positive:* good partnerships, gentleness, tact, receptivity, intuition, consideration, harmony, agreeableness, amicable nature, ambassador of goodwill
- *Negative:* suspicion, lack of confidence, timidity, oversensitivity, overemotionality, selfishness, tendency to be easily hurt, deceit

Love & Relationships

Sensitive and intuitive, yet mentally quick, you need variety and mental stimulation in relationships. Although you like socializing and meeting different people, you prefer the company of intelligent individuals who possess a wealth of knowledge and ideas. Since you can accomplish a great deal by yourself, in your relationships you refuse secondary positions and usually see yourself as an equal. Affectionate, loyal, and understanding, you care about your nearest and dearest. When in love you are often willing to make great sacrifices. The restlessness shared by those born on this date, however, also suggests that you can change your mind or be indecisive.

YOUR SPECIAL SOMEONE

You might start to look for an exciting partner among those born on the following dates.

Love & friendship: Jan. 12, 16, 25, 30, Feb. 10, 14, 23, 24, Mar. 8, 12, 22, 26, 31, Apr. 6, 10, 20, 29, May 4, 8, 18, 27, June 2, 6, 16, 25, 30, July 4, 14, 23, 28, Aug. 2, 12, 21, 26, 30, Sept. 10, 14, 19, 24, 28, Oct. 8, 17, 22, 26, Nov. 6, 15, 20, 24, 30, Dec. 4, 13, 18, 22, 28

Beneficial: Jan. 2, 13, 22, 24, Feb. 11, 17, 20, 22, Mar. 9, 15, 18, 20, 28, Apr. 7, 13, 16, 18, 26, May 5, 11, 16, 18, 26, June 3, 9, 12, 14, 22, July 1, 7, 10, 12, 20, Aug. 5, 8, 10, 18, Sept. 3, 6, 8, 16, Oct. 1, 4, 6, 14, Nov. 2, 4, 12, Dec. 2, 10

Fatal attractions: Jan. 25, Feb. 23, Mar. 21, Apr. 19, May 17, June 15, July 13, Aug. 11, Sept. 9, Oct. 7, Nov. 5, 21, 22, 23, Dec. 3

Challenging: Jan. 7, 23, Feb. 5, 21, Mar. 3, 19, 29, Apr. 1, 17, 27, May 15, 25, June 13, 23, July 11, 21, 31, Aug. 9, 19, 29, Sept. 7, 17, 27, 30, Nov. 3, 13, 23, 26, Dec. 1, 11, 21, 24

Soul mates: Jan. 17, Feb. 15, Mar. 13, Apr. 11, May 9, June 7, July 5, Aug. 3, Sept. 1, Nov. 30, Dec. 28

May 21

Spirited, intelligent, and ambitious, you are revealed by your birthday to be an active individual with personal magnetism. With the special advantage of being born on the cusp, you possess both the sensuality of Taurus and the intellectual power of Gemini. One of your greatest assets is your gift of dealing with people as well as a natural sense of the dramatic. Full of information, you usually love ideas and knowledge and are excellent at getting your ideas across in an entertaining way. Having the ability to make friends with people from all different walks of life, you have a strong sense of individuality and independence.

The added influence of your Sun on the cusp of two decanates implies that you are responsible, loyal, and hardworking as well as an exceptionally good communicator. Business acumen is likely to come naturally to you, and a strong practical sense affirms that you are aware of issues of home and security. A spirit of enterprise can push your ambition into action and ensure that your big plans are successful. However, you may have to guard against a rebellious or stubborn streak, which can undermine your communication with others.

Witty, creative, and outspoken, you can be very persuasive and have a capacity for organization. A love of luxury and pleasure suggests that you want to enjoy all that life has to offer, but an inclination to excess may prove a threat to your overall happiness. By applying self-discipline, you have the capacity for tremendous achievements in all areas of your life.

In the first thirty years of your life, your progressed Sun passes through the sign of Gemini. This suggests that as a child you are alert and a quick learner. Over this period you also develop your mental powers and skills of communication. When your progressed Sun moves into Cancer at the beginning of your thirties, there is likely to be a shift in your perspective toward emotional needs, home, and family. From the age of sixty, when your progressed Sun moves into Leo, your confidence and self-expression increase and you may be more inclined to a public life.

FIXED STAR

Star's name: Alcyone
Degree position: 29° Taurus–0°6'
    Gemini between the years 1930
    and 2000
Magnitude: 3
Strength: ★★★★★
Orb: 1°40'
Constellation: Eta Taurus
Applicable days: May 19, 20, 21, 22
Star qualities: Moon/Mars
Description: a green and yellow
    principal star in the Pleiades
    cluster, located on the shoulder of
    the Bull (it is the brightest star of
    the Pleiades)

PRIMARY STAR'S INFLUENCE

Alcyone imparts openness and frankness, honesty, and sincerity. Restlessness and impulsive actions can also be associated with this star. By nature you are forceful and purposeful, yet when feelings intensify, you are inclined to act on impulse. This may cause turbulence and bring about changed circumstances. This star also warns against fevers and problems with eyesight.

Linked to your Sun's degree, Alcyone bestows love, eminence, and a talent for leadership. This star often indicates that you can enjoy success in legal and public matters or use your creative mind to develop your writing skills.

• Positive: creative mind, honesty, enthusiasm

• Negative: cantankerousness, moodiness, temperamental behavior

Your Secret Self

A strong materialistic streak points to a possible overemphasis on security in your life, but this is balanced by a big heart and compassion for others. The power of love becomes more significant as you move through life, and you may find it especially important to find avenues for your self-expression. This can encourage you to explore writing, drama, art, or music to develop your innate gifts. Among your many talents, you also possess a childlike sense of fun, which can help ease the burdens of others.

When you care, you are willing to give much of yourself and may have to accept that people are not always able to reciprocate on your level. With your caring concern and an ability to solve problems, you may often find yourself sorting out situations for other people, especially your family. In your own instance, you may find yourself worrying unnecessarily about money, but this is generally unfounded, as what you give out will always come back to you in full, and more.

Work & Vocation

Talented and usually hardworking, you also possess the personal charm to ensure your success in all people-related activities. With your quick mind, you are an excellent conversationalist

164

and may possibly use your talent with words in writing, journalism, teaching, politics, or law. Being persuasive and having natural business acumen, you can also make an outstanding career in sales, marketing, or promotion. Ambition and a desire for the good life are likely to stimulate you to achieve your large plans, but education can be especially important in making the most of your remarkable mental potential. Many people born on this date are drawn to work in the worlds of art, music, or entertainment.

Famous people born on your birthday include writer Harold Robbins, musician Fats Waller, artist Albrecht Dürer, Irish political leader Mary Robinson, and actors Raymond Burr and Robert Montgomery.

Numerology

Dynamic drive and an outgoing personality are often present in those with a number 21 birthday. Friendly and gregarious, you have many social contacts and a wide circle of friends. With a number 21 birthday, you can be fun-loving, magnetic, and creative. Alternatively, you can be shy and reserved, with a need to develop assertiveness, especially in close relationships. Although you may be inclined toward cooperative associations or marriage, you always want to be acknowledged for your talents and abilities. The subinfluence of the number 5 month indicates that you are versatile and enthusiastic. Your ability to grasp ideas quickly allows you to acquire new skills. You may need to develop your business sense and establish a solid foundation for yourself. Creative yet practical, you need to express your ideas and thoughts in an individual way. Although you can begin a project with great enthusiasm, make sure you see it through to the end.

• *Positive:* inspiration, creativity, love unions, long-lasting relationships
• *Negative:* dependency, nervousness, loss of emotional control, lack of vision, disappointment, fear of change

Love & Relationships

Spontaneous and optimistic, yet hardworking and perceptive, you are often caught between the need to be free and independent and the desire to be loving and devoted to a partner. Your enthusiasm and friendly personality suggest that you are socially inclined and popular. You may encounter particular relationships that touch a chord with your need for greater inner perception. Try not to have overly high expectations of others; be realistic, and learn that faith and trust pay off at the end. Take your time in choosing your friends and lovers.

YOUR SPECIAL SOMEONE

Among people born on the following dates, your ideals of love might be more easily realized.

Love & friendship: Jan. 7, 10, 17, 21, 27, Feb. 5, 8, 15, 25, 29, Mar. 3, 6, 13, 23, 27, Apr. 1, 4, 11, 21, May 2, 9, 19, June 7, 17, July 5, 15, 29, 31, Aug. 3, 13, 27, 29, 31, Sept. 1, 11, 15, 25, 27, 29, Oct. 9, 23, 25, 27, Nov. 7, 21, 23, 25, Dec. 5, 19, 21, 23

Beneficial: Jan. 3, 5, 20, 25, 27, Feb. 1, 3, 18, 23, 25, Mar. 1, 16, 21, 23, Apr. 14, 19, 21, May 12, 17, 19, June 10, 15, 17, July 8, 13, 15, Aug. 6, 11, 13, Sept. 4, 9, 11, Oct. 2, 7, 9, Nov. 5, 7, Dec. 3, 5

Fatal attractions: Jan. 13, Feb. 11, Mar. 9, Apr. 7, May 5, June 3, July 1, Nov. 22, 23, 24

Challenging: Jan. 16, 24, Feb. 14, 22, Mar. 12, 20, Apr. 10, 18, May 8, 16, 31, June 6, 14, 29, July 4, 12, 27, Aug. 2, 10, 25, Sept. 8, 23, Oct. 6, 21, Nov. 4, 19, Dec. 2, 17

Soul mates: Jan. 16, Feb. 14, Mar. 12, Apr. 10, May 8, June 6, July 4, 31, Aug. 2, 29, Sept. 27, Oct. 25, Nov. 23, Dec. 21

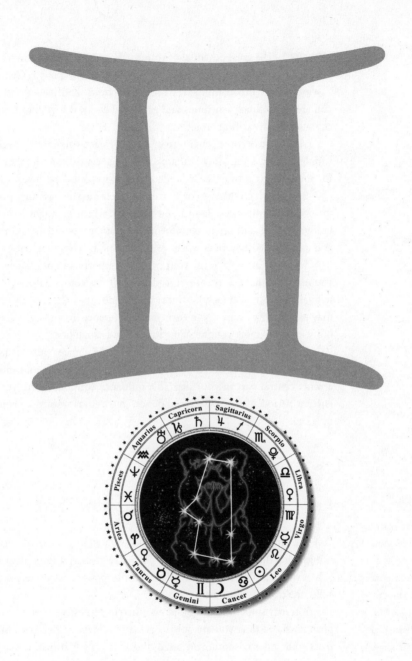

Gemini

May 22–June 21

May 22

Ⅱ The great potential of your birthday is emphasized by your quick intelligence, ambition, and charismatic ability to deal with people. Generally frank and open, you are broad-minded, with liberal views, and have polished common sense. Since you are also a touch rebellious and get bored easily, it is vital to have your remarkable talents channeled into exciting projects.

When you become caught up in a new project, you develop such enthusiasm that you are sure to be successful. Since you are also a person who cannot fake it, finding the right course for your self-expression is absolutely essential to your happiness.

Being born on the cusp of Taurus and Gemini, you have the special advantage of two major decanate influences, Saturn and Mercury, which highlight a practical slant to your mentality as well as a desire to be informed. An ability to understand people's motivations spurs you into exploring avenues where you can combine your pragmatic logic with your big plans.

Since you are able to use your persuasive charm and positive vitality to encourage others, you may find that acceptance of leading positions comes naturally to you. You may just need to guard against obstinacy, hastiness, and a tendency to be too talkative or argumentative. This may particularly occur if you turn your confidence into arrogance rather than take responsibility for developing your amazing insight and capabilities.

In early years there is a strong influence from a male figure, usually the father. After thirty, when your progressed Sun moves into Cancer, home, family, and emotional needs start to play a more central part in your life. This influence continues until your early sixties, when you enter a period of authority, confidence, and self-assurance as your progressed Sun moves into Leo.

Your Secret Self

You have an inner strength that does not want to be associated with failure. You do not take things lying down. This strength of character gives you the potential to achieve in your life. When you combine your determination, your powers of persuasion, and your excellent social skills, the world is your oyster.

You may sometimes find that an inherent restlessness comes from your desire to accomplish far more than you are able to actually achieve. When you listen to your higher self or trust your inner wisdom, you often find that your first instincts are far more accurate than your intellectual rhetoric. Since you need to feel a sense of pride in your achievements, a continual update of knowledge and skill puts you in the most powerful position.

Work & Vocation

Practical and skilled at communication, you are likely to prosper in careers such as sales, writing, promotions, or public relations. Your quick mind and leadership qualities also point to success in business, particularly as an analyst or troubleshooter. Alternatively, you may be drawn to the academic world and find a niche in research or psychology. Your love of wisdom may encourage you to explore the world of metaphysics. You should avoid being in

---

FIXED STAR

Star's name: Alcyone

Degree position: 29° Taurus–0°6' Gemini between the years 1930 and 2000

Magnitude: 3

Strength: ★★★★★

Orb: 1°40'

Constellation: Eta Taurus

Applicable days: May 19, 20, 21, 22

Star qualities: Moon/Mars

Description: a green and yellow principal star in the Pleiades cluster, located on the shoulder of the Bull (it is the brightest star of the Pleiades)

PRIMARY STAR'S INFLUENCE

Alcyone imparts openness and frankness, honesty, and sincerity. Restlessness and impulsive actions can also be associated with this star. By nature you are forceful and purposeful, yet when feelings intensify you are inclined to act on impulse. This may cause turbulence and bring about changed circumstances. This star also warns against fevers and problems with eyesight.

Linked to your Sun's degree, Alcyone bestows love, eminence, and a talent for leadership. This star often indicates that you can enjoy success in legal and public matters or use your creative mind to develop your writing skills.

• *Positive:* creative mind, honesty, enthusiasm

• *Negative:* cantankerousness, moodiness, temperamental behavior

subservient positions, as you do not like being told what to do. Your natural creativity and adventurous spirit may inspire you to a career in the entertainment world. Since you are good with your hands and possess healing ability, you may be drawn into the world of alternative health care.

Famous people who share your birthday include actor Lawrence Olivier, composer Richard Wagner, writer Arthur Conan Doyle, poet Françoise Sagan, and model Naomi Campbell.

Numerology

This is a master number and can vibrate both as number 22 and number 4. Often honest and hardworking, with natural leadership abilities, you have a charismatic personality and a deep understanding of people and what motivates them. Although undemonstrative, you often show a caring, protective concern for the welfare of others, yet you never lose sight of your pragmatic or realistic stand. Usually cultured and worldly, you have many friends and admirers. The more competitive among you achieve success and good fortune with help and encouragement from others. Many born on this date have strong links with brothers or sisters and can be protective and supportive of them. The subinfluence of the number 5 month indicates that you are highly intuitive yet nervous, with creative abilities and imagination. You often assert your individual style without appearing eccentric. Realistic, you can resolve problems with the least of fuss. However, do not overreact to people and situations. Later in life you become more ambitious.

• *Positive:* universal, director, highly intuitive, pragmatic, practical, good with your hands, skillful, builder, good organizer, realist, problem solver, achiever

• *Negative:* get-rich-quick schemes, nervous, inferiority complex, bossy, materialistic, lack of vision, lazy, egotistical

Love & Relationships

Your independent nature and a strong intuitive power suggest that you are drawn to powerful individuals who are determined or self-disciplined. An authoritative older man who is often associated with your date of birth may have a strong impact on your views and convictions. You may need to find a partner who is hardworking or who you can respect. Conversely, you may find yourself trying to emulate self-mastery by bossing around your friends and partners, which ultimately is not what you want to achieve. By gaining wisdom and compassion, however, you can achieve your heart's desire.

YOUR SPECIAL SOMEONE

If you are looking for a partner, you might find stability in a relationship with someone born on one of the following days.

Love & friendship: Jan. 1, 8, 14, 28, 31, Feb. 12, 26, 29, Mar. 10, 24, 27, Apr. 8, 22, 25, 26, May 6, 20, 23, June 4, 18, 21, July 2, 16, 19, 30, Aug. 14, 17, 28, 30, Sept. 12, 15, 16, 26, 28, 30, Oct. 10, 13, 24, 26, 28, Nov. 8, 11, 22, 24, 26, Dec. 6, 9, 20, 22, 24

Beneficial: Jan. 26, Feb. 24, Mar. 22, Apr. 20, May 18, June 16, July 14, Aug. 12, Sept. 10, Oct. 8, Nov. 6, Dec. 4

Fatal attractions: Nov. 22, 23, 24

Challenging: Jan. 3, 25, Feb. 1, 23, Mar. 21, Apr. 19, May 17, June 15, July 13, Aug. 11, Sept. 9, Oct. 7, Nov. 5, Dec. 3

Soul mates: Jan. 3, 10, Feb. 1, 8, Mar. 6, Apr. 4, May 2

May 23

FIXED STARS

Although your Sun's degree is not linked to a fixed star, some of your other planets' degrees certainly will be. By having an astrological chart calculated, you can find the exact position of the planets on your date of birth. This will tell you which of the fixed stars listed in this book are relevant to you.

Ⅱ Friendly and intelligent, you like to communicate your ideas and share your knowledge. You are likely to be young at heart, with an agile mind that allows you to grasp ideas very quickly. Although versatile, you may have to be careful that your desire for speed does not turn into restlessness and impatience.

With the double influence of Mercury in the first decanate of Gemini, you are interested in worldly affairs and may enjoy being on the move. Your general mental outlook is broad-minded, kind, universal, and sincere. You consider it important to tell the truth and be direct and honest with others.

Occasionally you can be prone to disturbing anxieties that can depress or discourage you. At these times it is essential to detach yourself and not become overly sensitive to ordinary misfortunes. Concentrate on your usual bright and optimistic future plans. With your charitable and altruistic approach to life, you are often in the position of supporting the underdog or helping and advising others. Although you can be thrifty and economical, you will be extremely generous with those you care for.

With your innate desire for harmony, your home base is extra important as a foundation for your security, and you may be willing to make sacrifices to keep everything safe. You may, however, also be liable to spiritual or psychic explorations and may have vivid dreams through your close contact with the subconscious. You need clever people around you from whom you can get mental stimulation, as you are interested in a wide range of subjects. As a clever conversationalist, you can talk about your pet subject with great enthusiasm. You may be particularly interested in philosophy, religion, literature, travel, or law.

After the age of twenty-nine, when your progressed Sun moves into Cancer, you are likely to become more sensitive and security-conscious, with a strong accent on your home life. When your progressed Sun moves into Leo, around age fifty-nine, there is a strong need for self-expression and assertiveness, which may inspire you to become more sociable and adventurous.

Your Secret Self

An inner sense of the dramatic points to a strong need to express your creativity and ideas. If this need is not fulfilled, you may become frustrated or disappointed. Having a positive philosophy in life or something to believe in ensures that you do not drift and enables you to be very focused. Discipline of your mind and abilities is a must; education, whether conventional or independent, gives you confidence, encourages you to make the most of your potential, and is a key to your success.

You find it important to be fair, to act responsibly, and to pay your debts, mainly because you have a strong sense of justice and want your surroundings to be as harmonious as possible. Just be careful that in the process of not wanting to rock the boat you do not allow situations to become too much of a predictable routine. Fortunately, you have the capacity to always want to improve yourself.

Work & Vocation

A natural inclination for business combined with good organizational skills is likely to aid you in any career. With your love of knowledge and talent for communication, you could excel in teaching or be drawn to linguistics, science, or journalism. You are likely to be skilled with your hands, especially in creative and artistic pursuits. Alternatively, occupations connected with matters abroad or mixing with people could satisfy your love of variety and keep you from becoming bored. Law, counseling, or psychology could possibly provide an outlet for your talent in offering advice and information. People with this birthday may also succeed in show business or music.

Famous people who share your birthday include actress Joan Collins, hypnotist Anton Mesmer, and actor Douglas Fairbanks.

Numerology

Intuition, emotional sensitivity, and creativity are some of the attributes of a person with a number 23 birthday. Usually you are versatile, passionate, and a quick thinker, with a professional attitude and a mind full of creative ideas. With the number 23 influence, you can learn new subjects easily, but may prefer practice to theory. Fond of travel, adventure, and meeting new people, you may find that restlessness implied by the number 23 urges you to try many different kinds of experiences, and you are apt to make the most of any situation. Generally friendly and fun-loving, with courage and drive, you may need an active life in order to actualize your true potential. The subinfluence of the number 5 month indicates that you are multitalented, with an ambitious and restless nature. You may need to develop your assertiveness and determination by learning to focus on a particular objective. Find your individuality through work and achievement and make your dreams a reality by converting your creative thoughts into decisive action. You need recognition and like to be appreciated for your efforts.

• *Positive:* loyal, responsible, love of travel, communicative, intuitive, creative, versatile, trustworthy, fame

• *Negative:* selfish, insecure, stubborn, uncompromising, fault finding, withdrawn, prejudiced

Love & Relationships

Your home life and finding a partner or soul mate are of prime importance. However, you may have to watch out for becoming overly dependent in your relationships. Although you can be loyal and affectionate, love unions may not always go according to plan. You may need to learn to adapt to changing circumstances. By developing patience, self-discipline, and detachment, you will be able to take on life's challenges and overcome a tendency to give up too easily. If you find your true love early in life, you are likely to settle down and be more content, as you do not like to be on your own.

YOUR SPECIAL SOMEONE

You might find emotional fulfillment and that special someone among those born on the following days.

Love & friendship: Jan. 1, 5, 6, 15, 26, 29, 30, Feb. 13, 24, 27, 28, Mar. 11, 22, 25, 26, 29, Apr. 9, 20, 23, 24, May 7, 18, 21, 22, June 5, 16, 19, 20, July 3, 14, 17, 18, 31, Aug. 1, 12, 15, 16, 29, 31, Sept. 10, 13, 14, 17, 27, 29, Oct. 8, 11, 12, 25, 27, Nov. 6, 9, 10, 23, 25, Dec. 4, 7, 8, 21, 23, 29

Beneficial: Jan. 1, 2, 10, 14, 27, Feb. 8, 12, 25, Mar. 6, 23, Apr. 4, 8, 21, May 2, 6, 19, 30, June 4, 17, 28, July 2, 15, 26, Aug. 13, 24, Sept. 11, 22, Oct. 9, 20, Nov. 7, 18, Dec. 5, 16

Fatal attractions: Nov. 24, 25, 26

Challenging: Jan. 17, 26, Feb. 15, 24, Mar. 13, 22, Apr. 11, 20, May 9, 18, June 7, 16, July 5, 14, Aug. 3, 12, 30, Sept. 1, 10, 28, Oct. 8, 26, 29, Nov. 6, 24, 27, Dec. 4, 22, 25

Soul mates: Jan. 21, Feb. 19, Mar. 17, Apr. 15, May 13, June 11, July 9, 29, Aug. 7, 27, Sept. 5, 25, Oct. 3, 23, Nov. 1, 21, Dec. 19

May 24

FIXED STAR

Star's name: Prima Hyadum

Degree position: 4°41'–5°46' Gemini between the years 1930 and 2000

Magnitude: 4

Strength: ★★★★

Orb: 1°30'

Constellation: Gamma Taurus

Applicable days: May 24, 25, 26, 27, 28

Star qualities: varied interpretations: Saturn/Mercury or Mars/Neptune

Description: an orange star, the chief star of the Hyades, which consists of 132 stars, located at the northern eye and marking the forehead of the Bull

PRIMARY STAR'S INFLUENCE

Prima Hyadum grants energy, ambition, and a desire for prestige, leading to achievement or great success. This star suggests a need for study and education in order to develop clear thinking. Prima Hyadum, however, also carries an influence that implies contradictions in fortunes or times of turbulence.

Linked to your Sun's degree, this star imparts a talent for writing, business, sport, astrology, and success through working with the public. There is also a chance of fame and fortune and opportunities for popularity or notoriety. Prima Hyadum warns against tendencies toward greed and exploitation of others, and suggests refraining from hasty decisions, which may cause upheaval.

• *Positive:* writing, education, communication

• *Negative:* restlessness, lack of knowledge, greed

Ⅱ Intelligence and emotional sensitivity mark this birthday as a special one. Often multitalented, you are curious and mentally expressive, with the ability to grasp the core of any subject extremely quickly. This suggests that you are likely to become bored easily; you need to develop perseverance. Your natural vitality, drive, and keen intellect, however, are likely to keep you constantly investigating new concepts.

The double influence of Mercury in the first decanate of Gemini suggests a sensitivity and a talent for writing or rhetoric. When combining your eloquence and exceptional imagination, you have the potential to be whatever you aspire to. Since you are likely to be of an experimental disposition, you may explore many avenues in your quest to find your true vocation. All that may be necessary is to harness your dormant genius through self-discipline, education, and patience.

An understanding that knowledge is power ensures that you will always have an avid desire for learning. The sensitivity associated with this birthdate implies that you are likely to become a seeker of wisdom. A highly intuitive side to your nature may encourage an interest in mysticism or spirituality and can prove to be a great asset in your dealings with others. Guard against misusing your sensitivity through being deceptive, manipulative, or temperamental, or through becoming involved in escapism.

The cerebral influence of Gemini is emphasized until the age of twenty-eight, when your progressed Sun moves into Cancer. This turning point highlights emotional issues, especially those concerning home and family, as well as creating a base for yourself professionally. This influence continues until the age of fifty-eight, when your progressed Sun moves into Leo and you enter a period of increased authority, strength, and confidence.

Your Secret Self

You are usually able to instinctively understand people's motivations and are quick to judge insincerity. Since mental power is your greatest gift, you are quick to see the opportunities within any situation and turn your excellent ideas into business ventures. As you are clever and witty at times, you may rely on your natural luck. Nevertheless, this may not assist you in finding the responsibility needed to fulfill your high destiny. Although you are likely to have an active social life, do not allow this to scatter your energies and become a further hindrance to your achievement.

Since you have an expansive outlook, you may be tempted to take gambles or risks in the firm belief that you are going to win. This positive viewpoint is likely to be of great help to you in your life as long as you are able to express yourself through a creative pursuit or dedicate yourself to an ideal. You are also very sensitive to your environment, so it is important that your home and workplace are congenial, or you may become discontented and involved in mental power games with others.

Work & Vocation

With your excellent sense of form and structure and your organizational skills, you are likely to take the lead in your chosen field. When inspired and positive, you possess a strong sense of vision, which can assist you in careers such as art and design, photography, or filmmaking. Your communication skills and social awareness can draw you toward a career in education or law but also point to achievement in people-related occupations. Alternatively, your natural business sense may aid you to succeed in commerce, although you are likely to fare better if given free rein to work in your own way. Being sensitive and possessing psychological insight may stimulate your natural healing abilities and attract you to the medical or alternative health care professions. With your drive and ideas, you may wish to pass your inspiration on to others through more creative occupations, such as acting, directing, writing, singing, or composing.

Famous people who share your birthday include singer/songwriter Bob Dylan, Queen Victoria, singers Patti Labelle and Roseanne Cash, and inventor George Washington Carver.

Numerology

With a number 24 birthday, you may dislike routine; however, you are hardworking, with practical abilities and sound judgment. The emotional sensitivity of the number 24 birthday suggests that you need to establish stability and order. Faithful and fair, though sometimes undemonstrative, you are inclined to believe that actions speak louder than words. With this pragmatic approach to life, you develop a good business sense and an ability to overcome obstacles and succeed. Having a number 24 birthday, you may have to overcome a tendency to be stubborn or fixed in your ideas. The subinfluence of the number 5 month indicates that you are receptive and understanding, with spiritual insight. Searching for truth, you can be idealistic and visionary, yet skeptical, demanding material proof. When inspired, you speak from the heart with great sincerity and conviction. Charming and concerned about others, you prefer to be a part of a larger group. Since you usually do not like to be alone, socializing takes a large portion of your time. Trust your intuition and learn to focus on your goals.

• *Positive:* energy, idealism, practical skills, strong determination, honest, frank, fair, generous, love of home, active, energetic

• *Negative:* ruthlessness, materialism, too economical, instability, dislike for routine, lazy, unfaithful, domineering and stubborn, vengeful

Love & Relationships

Finding someone like-minded, with whom you can share the same values and understanding, is a prerequisite in your relationships. Work and home are very important to you, and in a stable environment relationships are more likely to endure. Your most successful social and emotional relationships are likely to be with those who can stimulate you intellectually. Your curiosity about people and what motivates them suggests that at times you can be provocative or argumentative, particularly in discussions of politics, philosophy, or spirituality. Nevertheless, you can enjoy warm and tender relationships with the opposite sex.

YOUR SPECIAL SOMEONE

To find long-lasting happiness, security, and a harmonious environment, you might begin by looking for someone born on one of the following days.

Love & friendship: Jan. 3, 10, 13, 20, 25, 30, Feb. 8, 11, 18, 28, Mar. 6, 9, 16, 26, Apr. 4, 7, 14, 24, 28, May 2, 5, 12, 22, June 3, 10, 20, July 1, 8, 18, Aug. 6, 16, 30, Sept. 4, 14, 18, 28, 30, Oct. 2, 12, 26, 28, 30, Nov. 10, 24, 26, 28, Dec. 8, 22, 24, 26

Beneficial: Jan. 12, 16, 17, 28, Feb. 10, 14, 15, 26, Mar. 8, 12, 13, 24, Apr. 6, 10, 11, 22, May 4, 8, 9, 20, 29, June 2, 6, 7, 18, 27, July 4, 5, 16, 25, Aug. 2, 3, 14, 23, Sept. 1, 12, 21, Oct. 10, 19, Nov. 8, 17, Dec. 6, 14

Fatal attractions: Mar. 31, Apr. 29, May 27, June 25, July 23, Aug. 21, Sept. 19, Oct. 17, Nov. 15, 25, 26, 27, Dec. 17

Challenging: Jan. 6, 18, 22, 27, Feb. 4, 16, 20, 25, Mar. 2, 14, 18, 23, Apr. 12, 16, 21, May 10, 14, 19, June 8, 12, 17, July 6, 10, 15, Aug. 4, 8, 13, Sept. 2, 6, 11, Oct. 4, 9, Nov. 2, 7, Dec. 5

Soul mates: Mar. 28, Apr. 26, May 24, June 22, July 20, Aug. 18, Sept. 16, Oct. 14, Nov. 12, Dec. 10

May 25

♊ The excellent mental potential indicated by this birthdate is likely to be the greatest key to your success. Clever and shrewd, you pick up ideas very quickly and can be innovative and hardworking. Needing independence, you are usually able to react to situations spontaneously, with willpower and determination. A tendency to doubt or lose faith, however, may stop you when you are in full flow and deny you all those wonderful possibilities.

With the double influence of Gemini, your decanate ruler, you like to keep yourself well informed and may enjoy mental excursions of many different types. You are likely to have a gift for writing or debating and need to take responsibility for developing your fine mind. When positive, you are likely to have a quick wit and respond well to intellectual challenges. These are particularly important to provide you with flashes of inspiration and excitement and enable you to feel that you are making progress in life. You may just have to guard against becoming irritable or obstinate, or suffering from nervous tension. Luckily, you can also experience remarkable surges of energy, which can help you attain your goals and inspire others to take positive action.

You find new and interesting developments stimulating, and have the potential to be inventive as well as analytical. You have a most productive work influence, and if you are able to combine this with a humanitarian ideal, so much the better.

After the age of twenty-seven, when your progressed Sun moves into Cancer, you are likely to focus more on your personal emotional life and the people who affect it the most—your family. You become more aware of a need for a foundation or center to build from, which is usually your home. When your progressed Sun moves into Leo, around age fifty-seven, there is a strong need for self-expression and assertiveness, which may inspire you to become more bold and gregarious.

Your Secret Self

You can be very successful at creating wealth. However, money alone will never completely satisfy you. You may need to find a way to explore wisdom and develop and express your capacity for insight. Finding space and time for yourself at regular periods enables you to tune in to this more perceptive part of your character. With a natural talent for understanding the value of things, you also possess an inner power that can add to your tenacity and determination and prove to be a dynamic influence in your overall success.

To overcome a tendency to be too serious, you need outlets for your playful and adventurous spirit. In order to avoid flashes of sudden anger or rebelliousness, you may need to spend time reflecting or relaxing or ensure that your work allows you to express some of your more creative influences. If you believe in a project, you are likely to work extremely hard in order to make it a reality.

Work & Vocation

Being intelligent and eloquent, and enjoying a good debate, you may prefer a career that makes the most of your communication skills, such as salesperson, lawyer, or agent. As well as

---

FIXED STAR

Star's name: Prima Hyadum

Degree position: 4°41'–5°46' Gemini between the years 1930 and 2000

Magnitude: 4

Strength: ★★★★

Orb: 1°30'

Constellation: Gamma Taurus

Applicable days: May 24, 25, 26, 27, 28

Star qualities: varied interpretations: Saturn/Mercury or Mars/Neptune

Description: an orange star, the chief star of the Hyades, which consists of 132 stars, located at the northern eye and marking the forehead of the Bull

---

PRIMARY STAR'S INFLUENCE

Prima Hyadum grants energy, ambition, and a desire for prestige, leading to achievement or great success. This star suggests a need for study and education in order to develop clear thinking. Prima Hyadum, however, also carries an influence that implies contradictions in fortunes or times of turbulence.

Linked to your Sun's degree, this star imparts a talent for writing, business, sport, astrology, and success through working with the public. There is also a chance of fame and fortune and opportunities for popularity or notoriety. Prima Hyadum warns against tendencies toward greed and exploitation of others, and suggests refraining from hasty decisions, which may cause upheaval.

• *Positive:* writing, education, communication

• *Negative:* restlessness, lack of knowledge, greed

being analytical, you possibly possess technical skills, which may find an outlet through working with computers, metals, machinery, or various types of engineering. A humanitarian streak may draw you to careers such as social work, psychology, or the healing professions. Through education you can develop your fine mind to study subjects in depth rather than on a superficial level, and you may become involved in philosophy, metaphysics, or subjects of a more profound nature. A potential for writing or music is particularly emphasized by this birthdate.

Famous people who share your birthday include musician Miles Davis, opera singer Beverly Sills, and writer Ralph Waldo Emerson.

Numerology

Quick and energetic, though intuitive and thoughtful, as a number 25 birthday, you need to express yourself through different experiences. These may include new and exciting ideas, people, or locations. A desire for perfection urges you to work hard and be productive. You may, however, need to be less impatient or critical if things do not happen according to plan. With a number 25 birthdate, you possess strong mental energies that when concentrated aid you to look at all the facts and arrive at a conclusion faster than anyone else. Success and happiness come when you learn to trust your own instincts and develop perseverance and patience. The subinfluence of the number 5 month indicates that you are usually ambitious, well balanced, and confident. Nervousness and restlessness, however, indicate an unwillingness to settle or a certain lack of satisfaction. Although enthusiastic, you can become overconfident or anxious and make mistakes. Avoid worry by being creative and adaptable. Emotionally sensitive, you need to find ways to express yourself freely.

• *Positive:* highly intuitive, perfectionist, perceptive, creative mind, good at dealing with people

• *Negative:* impulsive, impatient, irresponsible, overly emotional, jealous, secretive, critical, moody, nervous

Love & Relationships

Perceptive and shrewd yet reticent and secretive, you like to talk about everything except your true feelings. Because of your skepticism, you need time to develop a trusting long-term relationship. Nevertheless, you can be passionate and endearing, yet with your cool composure, you appeal to the opposite sex. You are more likely to be attracted to industrious individuals, in particular those who are determined, astute, and inventive. By finding an inspiring person you can trust, you can become a loyal and faithful partner.

YOUR SPECIAL SOMEONE

For security, mental stimulation, and love, you might want to begin looking for those born among the following dates.

Love & friendship: Jan. 2, 21, 28, 31, Feb. 19, 26, 29, Mar. 17, 24, 27, Apr. 15, 22, 25, 29, May 13, 20, 23, 27, June 11, 18, 21, July 9, 16, 19, Aug. 7, 14, 17, 31, Sept. 5, 12, 15, 19, 29, Oct. 3, 10, 13, 27, 29, 31, Nov. 1, 8, 11, 25, 27, 29, Dec. 6, 9, 23, 25, 27

Beneficial: Jan. 9, 12, 18, 24, 29, Feb. 7, 10, 16, 22, 27, Mar. 5, 8, 14, 20, 25, Apr. 3, 6, 12, 18, 23, May 1, 10, 16, 21, 31, June 2, 8, 14, 19, 29, July 6, 12, 17, 27, Aug. 4, 10, 15, 25, Sept. 2, 8, 13, 23, Oct. 6, 11, 21, Nov. 4, 9, 19, Dec. 2, 7, 17

Fatal attractions: Jan. 3, Feb. 1, Nov. 26, 27, 28

Challenging: Jan. 7, 8, 19, 28, Feb. 5, 6, 17, 26, Mar. 3, 4, 15, 24, Apr. 1, 2, 13, 22, May 11, 20, June 9, 18, July 7, 16, Aug. 5, 14, Sept. 3, 12, Oct. 1, 10, Nov. 8, Dec. 6

Soul mates: Jan. 3, 19, Feb. 1, 17, Mar. 15, Apr. 13, May 11, June 9, July 7, Aug. 5, Sept. 3, Oct. 1

May 26

FIXED STAR

Star's name: Prima Hyadum

Degree position: 4°41'–5°46' Gemini
between the years 1930 and
2000

Magnitude: 4

Strength:: ★★★★

Orb: 1°30'

Constellation: Gamma Taurus

Applicable days: May 24, 25, 26, 27, 28

Star qualities: varied interpretations:
Saturn/Mercury or Mars/Neptune

Description: an orange star, the chief
star of the Hyades, which consists
of 132 stars, located at the
northern eye and marking the
forehead of the Bull

PRIMARY STAR'S INFLUENCE

Prima Hyadum grants energy, ambition, and a desire for prestige, leading to achievement or great success. This star suggests a need for study and education in order to develop clear thinking. Prima Hyadum, however, also carries an influence that implies contradictions in fortunes or times of turbulence.

Linked to your Sun's degree, this star imparts a talent for writing, business, sport, astrology, and success through working with the public. There is also a chance of fame and fortune and opportunities for popularity or notoriety. Prima Hyadum warns against tendencies toward greed and exploitation of others, and suggests refraining from hasty decisions, which may cause upheaval.

• *Positive:* writing, education, communication

• *Negative:* restlessness, lack of knowledge, greed

Ⅱ Your perceptive mind and easygoing charm add to your multitalented personality. You like to familiarize yourself with situations before pledging a commitment, but once you give your word you are likely to take your responsibilities seriously. Once you have decided on a goal, it is important to find people who can encourage and assist you in your gradual rise to success.

With the influence of Mercury in the first decanate of Gemini, you may enjoy sharing your ideas and unique vision with others and are likely to be curious about many subjects. Since you get straight to the core of issues and enjoy communication, you have the potential to develop innate writing skills as well as possible musical or creative talents. When you synthesize your imaginative and realistic approaches to life, you can make your dreams a reality.

Your home is likely to play a strong part in your life security, and you may be willing to make big sacrifices for those you love. Hampered by a great love of ease and comfort, you must be careful of losing focus or giving up under stress. At the other extreme, once you decide to use your sense of strategy and self-discipline, you can be very determined, hardworking, and tenacious. It is advisable to undertake some form of regular physical exercise to prevent any tendencies toward inertia or a buildup of anger.

Having a strong foundation or home to build from starts to have more importance in your life after the age of twenty-six, when your progressed Sun moves into Cancer. This also highlights your personal emotional needs and continues until around the age of fifty-six, when your progressed Sun enters Leo. This will magnify your confidence and strength and enable you to become more powerful in public situations.

Your Secret Self

A need for recognition may spur you to develop your talents through education. This is excellent for building a foundation for your ambition, as well as adding to your sense of self-confidence. It is important to have a plan of action in order to fully commercialize your skills and abilities, and you may especially benefit from partnerships and cooperative efforts. Do not allow a worrisome attitude about money to undermine your usual determination. If frustrated, do not leave things until later, as you are likely to miss excellent opportunities.

A flair for the dramatic and a need to be in control suggest that you enjoy power or influence. If you find yourself in a position of authority, you have to learn to be just and impartial and avoid being unfair or manipulative. If you choose to help others, you may use your natural healing powers, especially to relieve those with mental stress or emotional anxieties.

Work & Vocation

Although you do not appear particularly ambitious, your quick mind enables you to comprehend situations easily and aids you in whatever career you choose. It may be necessary to discipline yourself to avoid scattering your energies, and when concentrated you are likely to succeed in careers that make the most of your mental potential, such as in teaching or writing. If in business, your ability to be a good conversationalist can help you in the world of sales or customer service. Alternatively, you may prefer a career in the arts, the theater, or music. Since you are likely to be good with your hands, you may be able to use this skill in a creative or practical way. An innate compassion and understanding of human nature may lead you to careers such as counselor or advisor and help you raise money for good causes.

Famous people born on your birthday include musician Stevie Nicks, actors John Wayne and James Arness, and singers Peggy Lee and Hank Williams Jr.

Numerology

With a number 26 birthday, you have a pragmatic approach to life, executive ability, and a good business sense. Usually responsible, with a natural aesthetic sense and a love of home, you need to build a solid foundation or find real stability. Often a tower of strength for others, you are willing to support friends, family members, and relatives who turn to you in time of need. You may nevertheless need to guard against materialistic tendencies and a desire to control situations or people. The subinfluence of the number 5 month indicates that you need stability and security. You should, however, learn to let go of the past and reject what is of no value. You want to express your thoughts and creative ideas in an individual way. Maintaining your standards and being responsible yet flexible help you to overcome obstacles or a tendency to worry. A need to be popular suggests that you have many friends.

• *Positive:* creative, practical, caring, responsible, proud of family, enthusiasm, courage
• *Negative:* stubborn, rebellious, unstable relationships, unenthusiastic, lack of persistence, instability

Love & Relationships

Idealistic and sensitive, with dramatic emotional power, you are romantic with strong feelings. Although you need love and affection, stability and security may be prerequisites that you cannot relinquish. Often charming and friendly, you love socializing and creative pursuits that can fire your imagination. However, guard against tendencies to be overly emotional, insecure, or demanding when events do not meet with your approval. You are attracted by intelligent people who inspire you to use your natural sense of structure to enable you to achieve your goals. Creative outlets release your tension and draw like-minded people toward you.

May 27

Ⅱ The bright, personable nature suggested by your birthday indicates that you are constantly seeking new and exciting things to keep your active mind interested. A fascination for people and change may prompt you to go exploring in your quest for variety and mental challenge. This should keep you active and may even extend to traveling the world.

Since you are in the first decanate of Gemini, you have a double influence of Mercury, the planet of communication. This points to an ability to grasp concepts very quickly, and then you want to move on. This endows you with swiftness of thought but suggests impatience. Often eloquent, you may need to develop the ability to listen rather than talk. Versatile and multitalented, you may need to develop your great mental potential through concentration and thoroughness. When curious about a subject, however, you can apply your practical and serious logic to problem solving. Although you possess depth of thought, guard against becoming too mentally rigid, as you may be stubborn, cynical, or uncommunicative as a result. Alternatively, when assertive, you have the ability to be verbally direct and often go straight to the heart of a matter.

Since you also possess a strong spirit of enterprise, you are usually enthusiastic, optimistic, and adventurous, and may possess a dynamic approach to acquiring money and satisfying your material needs. You may wish to turn the potential of your great spiritual and creative forces to writing or to making your fine ideas into something tangible.

After the age of 25, when your progressed Sun moves into Cancer, issues around emotional security, home, and family start to play a more important part in your life. This influence continues until around the age of fifty-five, when you enter a period of authority, strength, and increased sociability as your progressed Sun moves into Leo.

FIXED STARS

Prima Hyadum, Ain

PRIMARY STAR

Star's name: Prima Hyadum

Degree position: 4°41'–5°46' Gemini between the years 1930 and 2000

Magnitude: 4

Strength: ★★★★

Orb: 1°30'

Constellation: Gamma Taurus

Applicable days: May 24, 25, 26, 27, 28

Star qualities: varied interpretations: Saturn/Mercury or Mars/Neptune

Description: an orange star, the chief star of the Hyades, which consists of 132 stars, located at the northern eye and marking the forehead of the Bull

PRIMARY STAR'S INFLUENCE

Prima Hyadum grants energy, ambition, and a desire for prestige, leading to achievement or great success. This star suggests a need for study and education in order to develop clear thinking. Prima Hyadum, however, also carries an influence that implies contradictions in fortunes or times of turbulence.

Linked to your Sun's degree, this star imparts a talent for writing, business, sport, astrology, and success through working with the public. There is also a chance of fame and fortune and opportunities for popularity or notoriety. Prima Hyadum warns against tendencies toward greed and exploitation of others, and suggests refraining from hasty decisions, which may cause upheaval.

Your Secret Self

Although restlessness may stop you from expressing the dynamic love that is a vital part of your emotional makeup, it is important to channel any tendency to become easily bored into your own self-expression. This can keep life exciting and fast-moving, as well as stop you from wasting your enormous potential in petty diversions. Being instinctive or psychic brings you a good understanding of people, and when this is combined with your spirit of enterprise, it can ensure your success.

In addition to an inner sensitivity that may not be obvious from your bright mental front, you possess a pragmatic outlook that helps keep your feet on the ground. A love of mystery may draw you to metaphysics, and you may find interest in exploring the unknown. Through gaining knowledge and developing your own philosophy or belief system, you will be able to establish stability and feel secure within yourself. Learning to focus may also stop you from scattering your energies.

Work & Vocation

Since you are likely to become bored if your work is too routine, variety is an essential ingredient in any career. Your quick intelligence enables you to learn rapidly, so you need work that is mentally stimulating. Your restless nature and a desire to explore in life could lead to your changing your profession a few times before you settle on something that finally interests you. This influence can suggest the possibility of a second chance at a career later in life or that you may travel in your quest for knowledge and opportunities. Your flair for words and keen insight into people can help you in a career such as sales, writing, promotion, performing, or politics. Shrewd about material considerations, you are likely to fare well in the world of commerce.

Famous people born on your birthday include dancer Isadora Duncan, actors Christopher Lee and Vincent Price, and politician Henry Kissinger.

Numerology

The number 27 birthdate indicates that you are idealistic and sensitive. Intuitive and analytical, with a fertile and creative mind, you can impress others with your original thoughts. Although at times you appear secretive, rational, or detached, in fact you may be hiding inner tensions. These may include tendencies to be impulsive, indecisive, or suspicious about forthcoming changes. In developing good communication skills, you can overcome a reluctance to express your deeper feelings. Education is essential for number 27 persons, and by developing depth of thought you become more patient and self-disciplined. The subinfluence of the number 5 month indicates that you are naturally versatile and imaginative, with strong instincts or psychic abilities. Overcome carelessness by learning to pay attention to details. Give structure to your thoughts, and think before you speak.

• *Positive:* versatile, imaginative, creative, resolute, bravery, good understanding, mentally capable, spiritual, inventive, mental strength

• *Negative:* disagreeable, quarrelsome, easily offended, argumentative, restless, nervous, mistrusting, overly emotional, highly strung, tense

Love & Relationships

Although you are usually articulate and outspoken with your opinions, you are also sensitive and secretive and may prefer to observe and say very little about your personal relationships. This influence suggests that lack of communication may cause you tension or worry about personal relationships. By taking your time and being patient, you are able to approach each relationship as a learning experience and find whom you can grow to love and trust. New beginnings often play an important role in shaping your personal life, and with new opportunities and personal experiences come lessons in letting go of the past.

YOUR SPECIAL SOMEONE

To find security, trust, and love you might begin by looking for someone born on one of the following days.

Love & friendship: Jan. 4, 13, 19, 23, Feb. 11, 17, 21, Mar. 9, 15, 19, 28, 29, 30, Apr. 7, 13, 17, 26, 27, May 5, 11, 15, 24, 25, 26, June 3, 9, 13, 22, 23, 24, July 1, 7, 11, 20, 21, 22, Aug. 5, 9, 18, 19, 20, Sept. 3, 7, 16, 17, 18, Oct. 1, 5, 14, 15, 16, 29, 31, Nov. 3, 12, 13, 14, 27, 29, Dec. 1, 10, 11, 12, 25, 27, 29

Beneficial: Jan. 7, 15, 20, 27, 31, Feb. 5, 13, 18, 29, Mar. 3, 11, 16, 27, Apr. 1, 9, 14, 25, May 7, 12, 23, June 5, 10, 21, July 3, 8, 19, Aug. 1, 6, 17, 30, Sept. 4, 15, 28, Oct. 2, 13, 26, Nov. 11, 24, Dec. 9, 22

Fatal attractions: Nov. 28, 29, 30

Challenging: Jan. 6, 14, 30, Feb. 4, 12, 28, Mar. 2, 10, 26, Apr. 8, 24, May 6, 22, June 4, 20, July 2, 18, Aug. 16, Sept. 14, Oct. 12, Nov. 10, Dec. 8

Soul mates: Apr. 30, May 28, June 26, July 24, Aug. 22, Sept. 20, Oct. 18, 30, Nov. 16, 28, Dec. 14, 26

May 28

FIXED STARS

Aldebaran, also called Al Dabbaran, the Follower; Prima Hyadum; Ain

PRIMARY STAR

Star's name: Aldebaran, also called Al Dabbaran, the Follower

Degree position: 8°48'–9°45' Gemini between the years 1930 and 2000

Magnitude: 1

Strength: ★★★★★★★★★

Orb: 2°30'

Constellation: Alpha Taurus

Applicable days: May 28, 29, 30, 31, June 1, 2

Star qualities: Mars/Mercury/Jupiter

Description: a giant rose-red star, located in the left eye of the Bull

PRIMARY STAR'S INFLUENCE

Aldebaran is one of the four Royal Stars or Watchers of the Heavens and therefore is considered of prime importance. It bestows high aims, honor, intelligence, eloquence, and integrity. You are often courageous and can achieve positions of responsibility and good fortune. In many cases, however, success can be short-lived. This star imparts sharp, impressive speech and the ability to discuss and debate. It also bestows a tendency toward argumentativeness and self-destruction. Other warnings from this star concern jealousy from others, or making enemies, and damage to the eyes.

Linked to your Sun's degree, this star bestows extraordinary mental energy, providing the ability to get on with

With your keen intelligence, idealism, and desire for independence, you are usually happiest when constructively busy and expanding your knowledge. Generally honest and direct, you are shrewd and pragmatic and can be highly intuitive about situations as well as about other people's motives. By cultivating this insight and combining it with your polished common sense, it is possible to become an advisor to others.

Education is usually important to you, whether a formal course or self-study, and you are likely to continue this well into later life. Mercury, the ruler of both your Sun sign and your decanate, highlights your ability to be youthful, with an androgynous sexuality. Articulate and persuasive, you possess quick comprehension; writing or other forms of communication are likely to play a strong part in your success. Although a resourceful strategist, at times you may be too clever for your own good.

As you become inspired by your many ideas, you often have a surge of optimism and energy that enables you to fulfill your dreams and be fortunate in enterprising ventures. Although idealistic, you may need to develop patience and tolerance, particularly when dealing with people less developed than yourself. Possessing an unconventional streak, you may aim for unusual or daring projects; with an ability to see the larger plan, you have a natural aptitude for leadership. Often travel is likely to play a part in feeding your adventurous spirit and inspiring you.

Having a strong foundation or home to build from starts to have more importance in your life after the age of twenty-four, when your progressed Sun moves into Cancer. This also highlights your personal emotional needs and continues until around the age of fifty-four, when your progressed Sun enters Leo. This will magnify your confidence and creativity, enabling you to become more powerful in public situations.

Your Secret Self

You are active and well informed, but what you may really desire is deep peace of mind. This quest for inner serenity will lead you to explore many avenues of knowledge in your life. Even so, you may find the greatest success through learning to slow down and simplify your life. Reflection and learning to focus are what will help keep you calm and able to deal with your inner restlessness. Inside you are extremely sensitive and vulnerable, though on the surface you appear confident and capable. Leading a well-balanced life can be a vital part of your agenda in order to integrate the two sides of your personality.

Working partnerships are likely to play an important part in your life, and you have a happy knack of knowing the right people. Gradually you will discover that the contacts you consider valuable have less to do with material success and more to do with wisdom. Although you can be very responsible, you become more aware of the value of selflessness.

Work & Vocation

Your quick and shrewd mind is likely to be full of money-making ideas. Being very independent, you need the freedom to work in your own way but are still keenly aware of the advantages of working cooperatively with others. This may lead you to partnerships or team efforts that could be very productive for you. As a skillful planner and organizer, you may achieve your potential in sales, commerce, agency work, or promotions. Alternatively, you may prefer to be of service to others and choose a vocation in the worlds of law or education. On the other hand, you can become a specialist in your area as an advisor, whether on a personal level or in business. An ability to articulate your ideas and your love of knowledge or wisdom may draw you to the world of writing, advertising, or publishing. You are also likely to have an interest in the study of philosophy, psychology, or religious thought. Generally, you may find more satisfaction in professions that use your fine mind, but you may have to avoid a tendency to procrastinate or not develop any interest in depth.

Famous people born on your birthday include writer Ian Fleming, singers Gladys Knight and Kylie Minogue, British prime minister William Pitt, and musician John Fogarty.

Numerology

Independent and idealistic, with determination and a pragmatic approach, you are often a law unto yourself. Like a number 1 individual, you are ambitious, direct, and enterprising. An inner conflict between wanting to be independent and wanting to be part of a team is also indicated. Always ready for action and new ventures, you courageously take on life's challenges, and with your enthusiasm you can easily inspire others, if not to join you at least to support you in your latest venture. With a number 28 birthday, you have leadership abilities and rely on your common sense, logic, and clear thinking. Although you can be responsible, avoid being overly enthusiastic, impatient, or intolerant. The subinfluence of the number 5 month indicates that you are shrewd, with strong instincts. You benefit from becoming more supportive or aware of the needs of others. Do not isolate yourself; share your knowledge and expertise by being part of a group or working cooperatively toward the greater good of society.

• *Positive:* compassionate, progressive, daring, artistic, creative, idealistic, ambitious, hardworking, stable home life, strong-willed

• *Negative:* daydreamer, unmotivated, lack of compassion, unrealistic, bossy, lack of judgment, aggressive, lack of confidence, too dependent on others, pride

Love & Relationships

Idealistic yet independent, you often have a clear idea about what you want out of relationships. Yet a certain restlessness or a daring enthusiasm may create problems for you, especially if you are impatient or think you can hurry people along. Wanting someone out of the ordinary also suggests that you can be attracted to unusual relationships, such as with people from foreign countries. Nevertheless, you retreat quickly from unsuitable relationships and with your practical sense seldom truly lose your heart. You may be more likely to express your opinions than your feelings, but once you find someone who positively stimulates your mind, then you can become loving, loyal, and supportive.

life and achieve through considerable determination and persistence. Aldebaran also indicates success, especially in dealing with the public. This star grants the ability to think big and undertake or concentrate on large projects. One important warning about Aldebaran is that fame or success may have a price or sacrifice attached to it. The most beneficial influence of this star is a strong preference for study, writing, and educational reform.

• *Positive:* theological aptitude, love of hermeneutics, expressiveness, popularity

• *Negative:* notoriety, lack of focus, anxiety

See Appendix for additional fixed star readings.

YOUR SPECIAL SOMEONE

For that special someone you might want to look among those born on the following dates.

Love & friendship: Jan. 3, 4, 6, 8, 14, 20, 24, Feb. 1, 2, 12, 18, 22, Mar. 10, 16, 20, 29, 30. Apr. 8, 14, 18, 27, 28, May 6, 12, 16, 25, 26, 31, June 4, 10, 14, 23, 24, 29, July 2, 8, 12, 21, 22, 27, Aug. 6, 10, 19, 20, 25, Sept. 4, 8, 17, 18, 23, Oct. 2, 6, 15, 16, 21, 30, Nov. 4, 13, 14, 19, 28, 30, Dec. 2, 11, 12, 17, 26, 28, 30

Beneficial: Jan. 4, 8, 21, Feb. 1, 2, 6, 19, Mar. 4, 17, 28, Apr. 2, 15, 16, May 13, 24, June 11, 22, July 9, 20, Aug. 7, 18, 31, Sept. 5, 16, 29, Oct. 3, 14, 27, Nov. 1, 12, 25, Dec. 10, 23

Fatal attractions: Jan 3, Feb. 1, May 31, June 29, July 27, Aug. 25, Sept. 23, Oct. 21, Nov. 19, 28, 29, 30, Dec. 1, 11, 17

Challenging: Jan. 7, 10, 15, 31, Feb. 5, 8, 13, 29, Mar. 3, 6, 11, 27, Apr. 1, 4, 9, 25, May 2, 7, 23, June 5, 21, July 3, 19, Aug. 1, 17, Sept. 15, Oct. 13, Nov. 11, Dec. 9

Soul mates: Mar. 31, Apr. 29, May 27, June 25, July 23, Aug. 21, Sept. 19, Oct. 17, 29, Nov. 15, 27, Dec. 13, 25

May 29

FIXED STARS

Aldebaran, also called Al Dabbaran, the Follower; Ain

PRIMARY STAR

Star's name: Aldebaran, also called Al Dabbaran, the Follower

Degree position: 8°48'–9°45' Gemini between the years 1930 and 2000

Magnitude: 1

Strength: ★★★★★★★★

Orb: 2°30'

Constellation: Alpha Taurus

Applicable days: May 28, 29, 30, 31, June 1, 2

Star qualities: Mars/Mercury/Jupiter

Description: a giant rose-red star, located in the left eye of the Bull

PRIMARY STAR'S INFLUENCE

Aldebaran is one of the four Royal Stars or Watchers of the Heavens and therefore is considered of prime importance. It bestows high aims, honor, intelligence, eloquence, and integrity. You are often courageous and can achieve a position of responsibility and good fortune. In many cases, however, success can be short-lived. This star imparts sharp, impressive speech and the ability to discuss and debate. It also bestows a tendency toward argumentativeness and self-destruction. Other warnings from this star concern jealousy from others, or making enemies, and damage to the eyes.

Linked to your Sun's degree, this star bestows extraordinary mental energy, providing the ability to get on with life and achieve through considerable

Ⅱ You project a friendly, easygoing, and magnetic charm, which attracts people to you and may prove to be one of your finest assets. This birthdate implies that you have a way with people and can be very popular, with your wit and astute observations. Nevertheless, the more doubting or indecisive side of your nature may be hidden from others, who may not see your sensitive vulnerability.

A double influence from Mercury, your Sun sign and decanate ruler, highlights your conversational skills and indicates a versatile and expressive personality. Being multitalented, you find yourself interested in different subjects but may scatter yourself in too many directions. You can be determined and single-minded, however, when you have a definite goal that utilizes your strategic skills and enterprise. You need only apply the self-discipline and persistence imparted by this birthdate to bring out your wonderful potential, but there is a danger of distractions too enticing to turn down. Avoid the temptations of overindulgence and guard against a tendency to worry needlessly or scatter your energies.

When positive, you are able to express the joy of life, and this may stimulate an interest in the arts, particularly writing. A natural talent for drama may encourage you to see life as a stage where you can act out your many personalities.

After the age of twenty-three, when your progressed Sun moves into Cancer, you are likely to become more sensitive and security-conscious, with a strong accent on your home life. When your progressed Sun moves into Leo, around the age of fifty-three, there is a strong need for self-expression and assertiveness, which will stimulate your sociability or leadership skills.

Your Secret Self

You possess an inner nobility and pride and have an intrinsic business sense. Money is something that can cause uncertainty in your life, particularly as you may experience fluctuating circumstances having to do with employment or finances. Although you can be very successful, you have an extravagant streak; be careful to budget or make long-term investments and savings plans.

If you feel limited, you may find better opportunities by taking chances or traveling farther afield. This also suggests that variety and change stimulate and inspire you to achieve. Through cultivating faith, you can learn to depend on your own resources and conquer recurring doubt. You can occasionally have a turn of fortunes by trusting your strong instincts. This enables you to take a gamble in life and win.

Work & Vocation

Your versatility and need for change or mental stimulation indicate that you should avoid careers that are too routine. Being naturally charming and socially aware ensures your success in any people-related occupation. Your easy way with words could enable you to be an author or a lecturer, or to excel in sales. If drawn to business, you are likely to take a creative approach and may be successful as an agent or in the world of travel or tourism. The more theatrical side of your nature may find fulfillment through performing or politics, and you are likely to work hard to support a cause that interests you. Similarly, your originality may find successful expression in art or music.

Famous people born on your birthday include former U.S. president John F. Kennedy, comedian Bob Hope, singers Latoya Jackson and Melissa Etheridge, and actress Annette Bening.

Numerology

As a number 29 individual, you have a powerful personality and extraordinary potential. You are highly intuitive, sensitive, and emotional. Inspiration is the key to your success story, and without it you may experience lack of purpose. Although you are a true dreamer, the extreme sides of your nature indicate that you may have to guard against alternating moods. If you trust your innermost feelings and open your heart to others, you can overcome your tendency to worry or use your mind as protective armor. Use your creative thoughts to achieve something special and unique that can motivate or be of service to others. The subinfluence of the number 5 month indicates that you benefit from thinking independently. Knowledge increases your confidence and powers of persuasion. With an eye for detail, you keep your thoughts to yourself and prefer the role of the observer.

• *Positive:* inspirational, balance, inner peace, generous, successful, creative, intuitive, mystical, powerful dreams, worldliness, faith

• *Negative:* unfocused, insecure, nervous, moody, difficult, extremist, inconsiderate, overly sensitive

Love & Relationships

Sensitive and idealistic, you are also charming and romantic, with a poetic heart. You find it easy to make friends and captivate people with your friendly personality and creative talents. Restless and nervous, however, you can be indecisive about how you feel in relationships. As you are likely to become bored easily, you may be interested in different people simultaneously. Although you are able to make great sacrifices in your love life, you can also run cold or become overly serious. Nevertheless, you are very generous with the people you love and when positive can be highly entertaining. You are often looking for a partner who is sensitive and understanding and who has faith in your abilities.

determination and persistence. Aldebaran also indicates success, especially in dealing with the public. This star grants the ability to think big and undertake or concentrate on large projects. One important warning about Aldebaran is that fame or success may have a price or sacrifice attached to it. The most beneficial influence of this star is a strong preference for study, writing, and educational reform.

• *Positive:* theological aptitude, love of hermeneutics, expressiveness, popularity

• *Negative:* notoriety, lack of focus, anxiety

See Appendix for additional fixed star readings.

YOUR SPECIAL SOMEONE

You might find a partner who is caring and loving among those born on the following dates.

Love & friendship: Jan. 21, 25, 30, Feb. 19, 23, Mar. 17, 21, 30, Apr. 15, 19, 28, 29, May 13, 17, 26, 27, 31, June 11, 15, 24, 25, 30, July 9, 13, 22, 23, 28, Aug. 7, 11, 20, 21, 26, 30, Sept. 5, 9, 18, 19, 23, 24, 28, Oct. 3, 7, 16, 17, 22, 26, 29, Nov. 1, 5, 14, 15, 20, 24, 27, Dec. 3, 12, 13, 18, 22, 25, 27, 29

Beneficial: Jan. 5, 13, 16, 22, 28, Feb. 3, 11, 14, 20, 26, Mar. 1, 9, 12, 18, 24, 29, Apr. 7, 10, 16, 22, 27, May 5, 8, 14, 20, 25, June 3, 6, 12, 18, 23, July 1, 4, 10, 16, 21, Aug. 2, 8, 14, 19, Sept. 6, 12, 17, Oct. 4, 10, 15, Nov. 2, 8, 13, Dec. 6, 11

Fatal attractions: June 30, July 28, Aug. 26, Sept. 24, Oct. 22, Nov. 20, 28, 29, 30, Dec. 1, 18

Challenging: Jan. 2, 23, 30, Feb. 21, 28, Mar. 19, 26, 28, Apr. 17, 24, 26, May 15, 22, 24, June 13, 20, 22, July 11, 18, 20, Aug. 16, 18, 19, Sept. 7, 14, 16, Oct. 5, 12, 14, Nov. 3, 10, 12, Dec. 1, 8, 10

Soul mates: Jan 14, 22, Feb. 12, 20, Mar. 10, 18, Apr. 8, 16, May 6, 14, June 4, 12, July 2, 10, Aug. 8, Sept. 6, Oct. 4, Nov. 2

May 30

♊ Your Gemini birthdate shows you to be a versatile, talkative, and sociable individual with a natural sense of humor. Being expressive and mentally quick ensures that you shine in social situations, with a particular emphasis on personal contact. Mercury, ruler of your Sun sign and decanate, endows you with an astute and agile mind and the insight to take advantage of opportunities. Your thirst for knowledge and your sharp intellect may find you involved in many types of activities. However, with your highly tuned nervous system, guard against becoming too restless or scattering your energies with diverse interests.

Relying on your wits gives you the ability to cope with every situation, and with your endurance, you have the determination to succeed. Through perseverance you overcome difficulties and grow in strength. Having a sixth sense about what motivates people, you are a natural psychologist who enjoys friendly yet competitive repartee. You usually speak clearly and enjoy a good discussion or debate, but you need to avoid becoming too provocative or argumentative. By using your diplomatic skills and perceptive awareness, you are able to sense if you are pushing people or situations too far, but you can compensate with your generosity.

In your early years there is a significant influence from a strong male figure, such as a father or uncle. At the age of twenty-two, when your progressed Sun enters Cancer, you are likely to become interested in family life or finding a secure home base. This turning point will also emphasize your growing need for love, understanding, and emotional security. From the age of fifty-two you are likely to receive a strong boost of self-confidence, with a deeper realization of your own personal abilities.

Your Secret Self

A personal sense of nobility and the dramatic ensures that you are warm-hearted and kind, and that you respond well to love and affection. You are often proud, and it is important for you to make a good impression. Although generous with the ones you love, if you sense hostility, you may become irritable or moody. With your speed of thought and quick response, you often protect your extreme sensitivity.

You may possess a desire for something of more depth and substance, which can bring out a more serious and thoughtful side to your character. As you are highly intuitive, you must learn to trust your instincts and develop a way to access your great store of inner wisdom. The need to express yourself indicates that you experience powerful feelings and great creative abilities. If these abilities are developed, you can not only shed your emotional frustrations but reach great creative heights.

Work & Vocation

Your talent with words and shrewd intellect make you an excellent candidate to be a writer, teacher, lecturer, promoter, or negotiator. Equally, with your flair for people, you can excel as an agent, as a salesperson, or in public relations. A natural psychologist, you may find occupations that involve personal contact, such as counseling, therapy, or health care, parti-

FIXED STAR

Star's name: Aldebaran, also called Al Dabbaran, the Follower

Degree position: 8°48'–9°45' Gemini between the years 1930 and 2000

Magnitude: 1

Strength: ★★★★★★★★★

Orb: 2°30'

Constellation: Alpha Taurus

Applicable days: May 28, 29, 30, 31, June 1, 2

Star qualities: Mars/Mercury/Jupiter

Description: a giant rose-red star, located in the left eye of the Bull

PRIMARY STAR'S INFLUENCE

Aldebaran is one of the four Royal Stars or Watchers of the Heavens and therefore is considered of prime importance. It bestows high aims, honor, intelligence, eloquence, and integrity. You are often courageous and can achieve a position of responsibility and good fortune. In many cases, however, success can be short-lived. This star imparts sharp, impressive speech and the ability to discuss and debate. It also bestows a tendency toward argumentativeness and self-destruction. Other warnings from this star concern jealousy from others, or making enemies, and damage to the eyes.

Linked to your Sun's degree, this star bestows extraordinary mental energy, providing the ability to get on with life and achieve through considerable determination and persistence. Aldebaran also indicates success, especially in dealing with the public. This star grants the ability to think big and under-

cularly rewarding. The entertainment and art worlds may appeal to your sense of creative self-expression and love of the dramatic. Alternatively, your leadership abilities, organizational skills, and strategic planning may place you in the world of commerce. Here you can challenge yourself by becoming involved with large projects and sharing your knowledge with others.

Famous people who share your birthday include bandleader Benny Goodman, writer Cornelia Otis Skinner, country singer Wynona Judd, and film director Howard Hawks.

take or concentrate on large projects. One important warning about Aldebaran is that fame or success may have a price or sacrifice attached to it. The most beneficial influence of this star is a strong preference for study, writing, and educational reform.

• *Positive:* theological aptitude, love of hermeneutics, expressiveness, popularity

• *Negative:* notoriety, lack of focus, anxiety

Numerology

Creativity, friendliness, and sociability are just some of the attributes associated with the number 30 birthday. Ambitious, with creative potential, you can take ideas and expand them in your own dramatic style. With a number 30 birthday, you enjoy the good life, and you can be exceptionally charismatic and outgoing. Since you possess strong feelings, being in love or contented is a vital requirement. In your pursuit of happiness, avoid being lazy or overindulgent, as well as the tendency to be impatient or jealous, as these may cause you to experience emotional instability. Among those with number 30 birthdays, many will find recognition or fame, especially as musicians, actors, and entertainers. The subinfluence of the number 5 month indicates that you need to develop a more practical outlook. Use your intelligence, foresight, and creative power constructively and build upon a solid foundation. Complete your tasks and do not abandon projects halfway through. Hard work and cooperation bring great rewards. To get your own way, use tact and diplomacy.

• *Positive:* funloving, loyal, friendly, good synthesizer, talent with words, creative, lucky

• *Negative:* lazy, obstinate, erratic, impatient, insecure, indifferent, scattered energy

YOUR SPECIAL SOMEONE

To find love and long-lasting relationships, look out for someone born on one of the following dates.

Love & friendship: Jan. 6, 7, 16, 18, 22, 26, Feb. 4, 14, 20, 24, Mar. 2, 12, 18, 22, Apr. 10, 16, 20, 30, May 8, 14, 18, 28, June 6, 12, 16, 26, July 4, 10, 14, 24, 31, Aug. 2, 4, 8, 12, 22, 29, Sept. 6. 10, 20, 27, Oct. 4, 8, 18, 25, Nov. 2, 6. 16, 23, 30, Dec. 4, 14, 18, 21, 28, 30

Beneficial: Jan. 6, 17, 23, 31, Feb. 4, 15, 21, 29, Mar. 2, 13, 19, 27, 30, Apr. 11, 17, 25, 28, May 9, 15, 23, 26, June 7, 13, 21, 24, July 5, 11, 19, 22, Aug. 3, 9, 17, 20, Sept. 1, 7, 15, 18, 30, Oct. 5, 13, 16, 28, Nov. 3, 11, 14, 26, Dec. 1, 9, 12, 24

Fatal attractions: Nov. 29, 30, Dec. 1, 2

Challenging: Jan. 24, Feb. 22, Mar. 20, 29, Apr. 18, 27, 29, May 6, 16, 25, 27, 30, June 14, 22, 25, 28, July 12, 21, 23, 26, Aug. 10, 19, 21, 24, Sept. 8, 17, 19, 22, Oct. 6, 15, 17, 20, Nov. 4, 13, 15, 18, Dec. 2, 11, 13, 16

Soul mates: Jan. 13, Feb. 11, Mar. 9, Apr. 7, May 5, June 3, 30, July 1, 28, Aug. 26, Sept. 24, Oct. 22, Nov. 20, Dec. 18

Love & Relationships

Youthful and outgoing, you are likely to have a restless side that will keep you constantly interested in new people and places. Being naturally sociable and discerning, you have no problem attracting friends and admirers. Your need for fun and appreciation makes you a good mixer. Often impulsive in love, you can experience strong attractions. However, a tendency to fluctuating moods indicates that you may need to develop a more mature outlook to overcome difficulties in relationships. You may be drawn to those who can inspire your creativity or help you to touch upon your inner vision.

May 31

Ⅱ A strong-willed, charming, and intelligent character is shown by your Gemini birthday. Being idealistic and practical helps you to turn your many ideas and visions into a reality. Fortunate enough to be blessed with the ability to work well with people, you are usually the initiator or leader of ideas.

The double impact of Mercury, which is your Sun and decanate ruler, highlights your quick and agile mind and points to the importance of education, whether formal or self-directed, to develop your outstanding mental capabilities. A natural teacher yourself, you are usually informative in practical or intellectual matters and can enlighten others with your knowledge. Besides being a creative thinker, you are likely to possess writing ability, diplomatic skills, or an interest in language or literature.

Although idealistic, you can also be quite money-conscious and enjoy beauty and luxury. You may, however, need to guard against excessive vanity or extravagance. Using your fine intellect is an important part of your success, so ideally you need work or other interests that can keep you mentally challenged. Since you can be hardworking, charming, and very intelligent, you need only apply discipline to make the most of your remarkable potential.

After the age of twenty-one, when your progressed Sun moves into Cancer, there is a strong emphasis on home, family, and building a strong foundation. You are likely to have a growing need for personal intimacy and emotional security. This influence continues until the age of fifty-one, when your progressed Sun moves into Leo, commencing a period that highlights creativity, confidence, authority, and strength.

Your Secret Self

Although you appear independent, your need for close relationships suggests that you may even go as far as to feel incomplete without a good partnership. A good friend, you are often willing to make sacrifices for others. Although you can be very giving of your love, time, and commitment, it is also important that you be aware of equal give-and-take. If you compromise too much of yourself for security, there is a danger of being in a fearful or dependent position.

Your inner sensitivity and high ideals may be inspired by peace, and you often find it hard to live with discord or tension. Your longing for love may find expression through dedication to an ideal, art, or music, or you may even be drawn to mystical experience. You are likely to find that people naturally come to you for help because of your competence and understanding.

Work & Vocation

Young at heart, with quick intelligence, you have an exceptional memory that suggests that you can make a valuable contribution in almost any career. A love of facts and a talent with words may attract you to a career in writing, library work, or statistics. With your ability to take the lead and your love of knowledge, you may be drawn to teaching, whether in the classroom or as a trainer in business. An attraction to people-related occupations and activities

FIXED STAR

Star's name: Aldebaran, also called Al Dabbaran, the Follower

Degree position: 8°48'–9°45' Gemini between the years 1930 and 2000

Magnitude: 1

Strength: ★★★★★★★★

Orb: 2°30'

Constellation: Alpha Taurus

Applicable days: May 28, 29, 30, 31, June 1, 2

Star qualities: Mars/Mercury/Jupiter

Description: a giant rose-red star, located in the left eye of the Bull

PRIMARY STAR'S INFLUENCE

Aldebaran is one of the four Royal Stars or Watchers of the Heavens and therefore is considered of prime importance. It bestows high aims, honor, intelligence, eloquence, and integrity. You are often courageous and can achieve a position of responsibility and good fortune. In many cases, however, success can be short-lived. This star imparts sharp, impressive speech and the ability to discuss and debate. It also bestows a tendency toward argumentativeness and self-destruction. Other warnings from this star concern jealousy from others, or making enemies, and damage to the eyes.

Linked to your Sun's degree, this star bestows extraordinary mental energy, providing the ability to get on with life and achieve through considerable determination and persistence. Aldebaran also indicates success, especially in dealing with the public. This star grants the ability to think big and under-

could lead you to a career in public relations as a promoter or propagandist. Since you are likely to be creative, you may achieve fulfillment as an agent in an artistic field, the beauty industry, or musical and artistic pursuits.

Famous people born on your birthday include actor Clint Eastwood, poet Walt Whitman, football player Joe Namath, author/minister Norman Vincent Peale, and actresses Brooke Shields and Lea Thompson.

take or concentrate on large projects. One important warning about Aldebaran is that fame or success may have a price or sacrifice attached to it. The most beneficial influence of this star is a strong preference for study, writing, and educational reform.

• *Positive:* theological aptitude, love of hermeneutics, expressiveness, popularity

• *Negative:* notoriety, lack of focus, anxiety

Numerology

Strong willpower, determination, and an emphasis on self-expression are indicated by the number 31 birthday. You often combine your intuition and practical skill to make the right decisions. With a number 31 birthday, you have original ideas, a good sense of form, and abilities to succeed in business if you take your time and follow a practical plan of action. Good fortune and lucky opportunities are also suggested by this birthday, and you can be successful in turning your leisure-time pursuits into profitable ventures. As you are probably hardworking, time for love and having fun is crucial to you. The subinfluence of the number 5 month indicates that you are idealistic and courageous. Although you are usually easygoing, you possess strong convictions. You appear cool and detached, yet you can be sensitive and nervous. Being patient and focused at all times can help you avoid scattering your energy. Do not give up halfway through a project or a course of study.

• *Positive:* lucky, creative, original, builder, constructive, never gives up, practical, good conversationalist, responsible

• *Negative:* insecure, impatient, suspicious, easily discouraged, lack of ambition, selfish, stubborn

YOUR SPECIAL SOMEONE

You might find a partner who will understand your sensitivity and need for love among those born on the following dates.

Love & friendship: Jan. 1, 4, 9, 27, 29, Feb. 2, 25, 27, Mar. 23, 25, Apr. 21, 23, May 19, 21, 29, June 17, 19, 27, July 15, 17, 25, Aug. 13, 15, 23, Sept. 11, 13, 21, Oct. 9, 11, 19, Nov. 7, 9, 17, Dec. 5, 7, 15, 19

Beneficial: Jan. 3, 10, 15, 18, Feb. 1, 8, 13, 16, Mar. 6, 11, 14, 29, 31, Apr. 4, 9, 12, 27, 29, May 2, 7, 10, 25, 27, June 5, 8, 23, 25, July 3, 6, 21, 23, Aug. 1, 4, 19, 21, Sept. 2, 17, 19, Oct. 15, 17, Nov. 13, 15, Dec. 11, 13

Fatal attractions: Apr. 30, May 28, June 26, July 24, Aug. 22, Sept. 20, Oct. 18, Nov. 16, Dec. 1, 2, 3, 14

Challenging: Jan 9, 14, 16, 25, Feb. 7, 12, 14, 23, Mar. 5, 10, 12, 21, 28, 30, Apr. 3, 8, 10, 19, 26, 28, May 1, 6, 8, 17, 24, 26, June 4, 6, 15, 22, 24, July 2, 4, 13, 20, 22, Aug. 2, 11, 18, 20, Sept. 9, 16, 18, Oct. 7, 14, 16, Nov. 5, 12, 14, Dec. 3, 10, 12

Soul mates: Dec. 29

Love & Relationships

Outgoing and practical, with a forceful poise, you are commanding yet alluring. Often your diplomatic skills keep things harmonious in relationships. Success often comes as a result of your effort or labor, and you prefer hardworking and successful people. Often looking for your soul mate, you believe in unions and can be loyal to the partner you settle with. On occasion, when you do not get the attention or affection you need, guard against becoming temperamental or jealous.

June 1

FIXED STAR

Star's name: Aldebaran, also called Al Dabbaran, the Follower

Degree position: 8°48'–9°45' Gemini between the years 1930 and 2000

Magnitude: 1

Strength: ★★★★★★★★

Orb: 2°30'

Constellation: Alpha Taurus

Applicable days: May 28, 29, 30, 31, June 1, 2

Star qualities: Mars/Mercury/Jupiter

Description: a giant rose-red star, located in the left eye of the Bull

PRIMARY STAR'S INFLUENCE

Aldebaran is one of the four Royal Stars or Watchers of the Heavens and therefore is considered of prime importance. It bestows high aims, honor, intelligence, eloquence, and integrity. You are often courageous and can achieve a position of responsibility and good fortune. In many cases, however, success can be short-lived. This star imparts sharp, impressive speech and the ability to discuss and debate. It also bestows a tendency toward argumentativeness and self-destruction. Other warnings from this star concern jealousy from others, or making enemies, and damage to the eyes.

Linked to your Sun's degree, this star bestows extraordinary mental energy, providing the ability to get on with life and achieve through considerable determination and persistence. Aldebaran also indicates success, especially in dealing with the public. This star grants the ability to think big and under-

Ⅱ Your Gemini birthdate shows you to be mentally quick and intuitive, versatile, and young at heart. As your ruling planet, Mercury, is the messenger of the gods, it gives you good communication skills and a sensitive nervous system. With the subinfluence of your decanate ruler, Libra, you are charismatic, with an ability to be persuasive and charming. This enhances your social and artistic skills and shows that you enjoy a touch of glamour and are attractive.

Personal magnetism and the need for constant variety will bring many new people and experiences into your life, with a possibility of contacts abroad. Although you have many interests and talents, at times you can be extremely focused and single-minded. Your ability to work hard, coupled with faith in the outcome of your labors, will eventually guarantee success. By being detached and learning to work with constructive criticism, you can overcome any tendency to be oversensitive or opinionated. It is especially important that if you have a plan of action, you complete it rather than leave things unfinished. Women may often support you in your efforts and be of considerable help in your enterprises.

Often gifted with perception and sensitivity, you may use your imagination to create art or music or to manifest your idealistic dreams. Alternatively, you can develop your psychic powers and find an interest in spiritual matters.

Your receptive and agile mind enables you to grasp knowledge and ideas very quickly, but after the age of twenty, when your progressed Sun moves into Cancer, you will place more focus on emotional security, home, and family. You may want to establish a base for yourself from which to branch out into other areas. At the age of fifty there is another turning point, when your progressed Sun enters Leo. This enables you to feel stronger, more self-assured, and confident.

Your Secret Self

Although you desire harmony on an inner level, your tests may concern your attitude toward money and material considerations. There can be a vacillation between self-doubt and taking large risks. By facing your fears, you can truly find faith and enjoy what life has to offer. Although you are carefree and adventurous, with maturity comes an emphasis on responsibility. By being accountable for your actions and dealing with matters in a fair and just way, you will find that your life will more than reward you.

You will always have a youthful quality that can be expressed through creativity and playfulness. However, there may be times when you may be disappointed by your expectations of others and may have to be careful of escaping into excess to compensate. Your major soul growth may come through learning the lesson of detachment and when you learn to share or work with others in a spirit of service and cooperation.

Work & Vocation

Your pioneering self-expression and mental agility may be the foundation of your career. With your natural communication skills, you have the ability to be a persuasive salesperson or promoter. Equally, you may be drawn to a career in journalism, lecturing, writing, music, or the theater. The influence of this birthday also suggests that there may be interests or work involving foreign lands. Since you are often in tune with the collective unconscious of your generation, you may wish to embody this through the arts in some way. Fluctuating circumstances in your working environment, however, point to changes in your career.

Famous people born on your birthday include actress Marilyn Monroe, Mormon leader Brigham Young, bandleader Nelson Riddle, poet John Masefield, and singer Alanis Morrissette.

take or concentrate on large projects. One important warning about Aldebaran is that fame or success may have a price or sacrifice attached to it. The most beneficial influence of this star is a strong preference for study, writing, and educational reform.

• *Positive:* theological aptitude, love of hermeneutics, expressiveness, popularity

• *Negative:* notoriety, lack of focus, anxiety

Numerology

As a number 1, you are inclined to be individual, innovative, and courageous, with plenty of energy. Often there is a need to establish a strong identity and develop assertiveness. The pioneering spirit indicated here encourages you to strike out alone. These self-starting forces can also stimulate you to develop executive or leadership abilities. Full of enthusiasm and original ideas, you can show others the way forward. With a number 1 birthday, you may also need to learn that the world does not revolve around you and avoid an inclination to be self-centered or dictatorial. The subinfluence of the number 6 month indicates that you need to be more flexible and receptive to the needs of others. Although self-reliant, you should not neglect family responsibilities. With perseverance and determination, you can develop patience and tolerance. Strong-willed and disciplined, you can be honest or true to yourself and others. Find security in wisdom and knowledge through study and education.

• *Positive:* leadership, creative, progressive, forceful, optimistic, strong convictions, competitive, independent, gregarious

• *Negative:* overbearing, egotistical, too proud, antagonistic, lack of restraint, selfish, weak, vacillating, impatient

YOUR SPECIAL SOMEONE

You are likely to have more luck with someone born on one of the following dates.

Love & friendship: Jan. 9, 13, 23, 25, 27, Feb. 7, 21, 23, 25, Mar. 5, 19, 21, 23, 29, Apr. 3, 17, 19, 21, 27, 30, May 1, 15, 17, 19, 25, 28, June 13, 15, 17, 23, 26, July 11, 13, 15, 21, 24, Aug. 9, 11, 13, 19, 22, Sept. 7, 9, 11, 17, 20, Oct. 5, 7, 9, 15, 18, Nov. 3, 5, 7, 13, 16, Dec. 1, 3, 5, 11, 14

Beneficial: Jan. 2, 4, 7, Feb. 2, 5, Mar. 3, Apr. 1, May 31, June 29, July 27, 31, Aug. 25, 29, Sept. 23, 27, Oct. 21, 25, Nov. 19, 23, Dec. 17, 21

Fatal attractions: Jan. 8, 14, Feb. 6, 12, Mar. 4, 10, Apr. 2, 8, May 6, June 4, July 2, Dec. 2, 3, 4

Challenging: Jan. 6, 19, 29, Feb. 4, 17, 27, Mar. 2, 15, 25, Apr. 13, 23, May 11, 21, June 9, 19, July 7, 17, Aug. 5, 15, Sept. 3, 13, 30, Oct. 1, 11, 28, Nov. 9, 26, Dec. 7, 24, 29

Soul mates: Jan. 16, 21, Feb. 14, 19, Mar. 12, 17, Apr. 10, 15, May 8, 13, June 6, 11, July 4, 9, Aug. 2, 7, Sept. 5, Oct. 3, Nov. 1

Love & Relationships

Although you can attract all types of people, you may need to be discriminating in your choice of friends. Often you alternate between being very expressive of your thoughts and feelings and being emotionally cold and isolated. As charm is likely to be one of your key assets, your charismatic personality ensures that you attract friends and lovers. There may be an air of uncertainty about what you really want, and often your challenge is to maintain harmonious and independent relationships. Since you are drawn to intellectual people, it would be positive to share information and common interests with your friends.

June 2

Ⅱ Your birthday marks you out as a hardworking, amiable, and popular person who can succeed. Although you are independent, with your charm and powers of perception you can work very well with people on a personal level or cooperatively in team situations. Since you also have superior organizational skills, this can particularly aid you in combining business and pleasure.

The subinfluence of your Libra decanate brings innate artistic talent and a love of beauty and luxury. The diplomatic skills that this also confers will certainly help you in your relationships and support your gift for being an articulate negotiator. However, you may just have to guard against misusing your power of speech by offering sharp comments when you become too irritable, stubborn, and self-willed. This more obstinate and rebellious side of your personality is in contrast to an unexpectedly sensitive and compassionate element of your being. As you like to be in control, you may rarely show this side of yourself to others.

Although you possess common sense and the strong vision to make your dreams a reality, beware of diversions that can distract you from your idealistic goals. This suggests that tendencies such as laziness or social excesses may undermine your true potential. When inspired, however, you are willing to work extremely hard, and you certainly have the talents and determination to achieve your objective.

After the age of nineteen, when your progressed Sun moves into Cancer, issues concerning security, home, and family start to have more prominence in your life and suggest that you are likely to be more emotionally aware. This continues until the age of forty-nine, when your progressed Sun moves into Leo and you enter a period of growing vitality and confidence, and develop an increasing interest in personal self-expression.

Fixed Star

Star's name: Aldebaran, also called Al Dabbaran, the Follower

Degree position: 8°48'–9°45' Gemini between the years 1930 and 2000

Magnitude: 1

Strength: ★★★★★★★★

Orb: 2°30'

Constellation: Alpha Taurus

Applicable days: May 28, 29, 30, 31, June 1, 2

Star qualities: Mars/Mercury/Jupiter

Description: a giant rose-red star, located in the left eye of the Bull

PRIMARY STAR'S INFLUENCE

Aldebaran is one of the four Royal Stars or Watchers of the Heavens and therefore is considered of prime importance. It bestows high aims, honor, intelligence, eloquence, and integrity. You are often courageous and can achieve a position of responsibility and good fortune. In many cases, however, success can be short-lived. This star imparts sharp, impressive speech and the ability to discuss and debate. It also bestows a tendency toward argumentativeness and self-destruction. Other warnings from this star concern jealousy from others, or making enemies, and damage to the eyes.

Linked to your Sun's degree, this star bestows extraordinary mental energy, providing the ability to get on with life and achieve through considerable determination and persistence. Aldebaran also indicates success, especially in dealing with the public. This star grants the ability to think big and under-

Your Secret Self

Intelligent and quick to assess people and situations, you recognize the power of knowledge. An inner nobility and sense of the dramatic empowers you with leadership and confidence. Since you can be extremely capable, you can be surprised when you enter periods of self-doubt and experience feelings of inferiority. Fortunately, being highly intuitive, you do realize at a deeper level your own shortcomings and can work on self-improvement. Education in all its forms can therefore benefit you and assist you to achieve your goals and more.

Your responsibilities can particularly extend to your home and family, which are likely to play an important part in your life. Avoid getting into a rut, and don't stick to the same old set routine at the expense of stretching yourself in all areas of your life. Although at times you appear opinionated or bossy, your humanitarian streak suggests that you often volunteer to assist others with your skills and expertise.

Work & Vocation

Your quick understanding of people and easy charm can ensure your success in careers such as sales, promotions, and public relations. If in the world of commerce, you may prefer work that deals with other people's money or, similarly, be an excellent buyer, agent, or negotiator. Your humanitarian streak may also draw you to counseling and other socially responsible occupations. Possessing an inventive and innovative mind may point you toward science and technology. Alternatively, your imagination and visual talents could find expression through photography, drama, or music. Working in partnership or in a group situation may prove particularly profitable for you.

Famous people born on your birthday include writer Thomas Hardy, drummer Charlie Watts, musician/writer Marvin Hamlisch, actors Johnny Weissmuller and Stacy Keach, composer Edward Elgar, and actress Sally Kellerman.

take or concentrate on large projects. One important warning about Aldebaran is that fame or success may have a price or sacrifice attached to it. The most beneficial influence of this star is a strong preference for study, writing, and educational reform.

• *Positive:* theological aptitude, love of hermeneutics, expressiveness, popularity

• *Negative:* notoriety, lack of focus, anxiety

Numerology

Sensitivity and a strong need to be part of a group are suggested by a number 2 birthday. Adaptable and understanding, you enjoy cooperative activities where you can experience interaction with others. In your attempt to please those you like, you may run the risk of becoming overly dependent. Nevertheless, by developing confidence, you can overcome the tendency to be easily hurt by the actions and criticism of others. The subinfluence of the number 6 month indicates that you need to be more responsible for your actions. Take control of life through learning self-discipline and hard work. By being economical and learning to handle money or to budget, you can build a solid foundation and feel secure. Forgiving or being considerate of others' weaknesses and shortcomings can empower you to heal others. Success may be achieved if you persevere in spite of difficulties.

• *Positive:* good partnerships, gentle, tactful, receptive, intuitive, agile, considerate, harmonious, agreeable, ambassador of goodwill

• *Negative:* suspicious, lack of confidence, timid, oversensitive, emotional, selfish, easily hurt, deceitful

YOUR SPECIAL SOMEONE

To find long-lasting happiness, security, and love, you might begin by looking for someone born on one of the following days.

Love & friendship: Jan. 10, 14, 26, 28, Feb. 8, 12, 24, 26, Mar. 6, 22, 24, 30, Apr. 4, 20, 22, 28, May 2, 18, 20, 26, 29, June 16, 18, 24, 27, July 14, 16, 22, 25, Aug. 12, 14, 20, 23, 30, Sept. 10, 12, 18, 21, 28, Oct. 8, 10, 16, 19, 26, Nov. 6, 8, 14, 17, 24, Dec. 4, 6, 12, 15, 22

Beneficial: Jan. 8, Feb. 6, Mar. 4, 28, Apr. 2, 26, May 24, June 22, 30, July 20, 28, 29, Aug. 18, 26, 27, 30, Sept. 16, 24, 25, 28, Oct. 14, 22, 23, 26, 29, Nov. 12, 20, 21, 24, 27, Dec. 10, 18, 19, 22, 25

Fatal attractions: Jan. 15, Feb. 13, Mar. 11, Apr. 9, May 7, June 5, July 3, Aug. 1, Dec. 3, 4, 5

Challenging: Jan. 7, 9, 30, Feb. 5, 7, 28, Mar. 3, 5, 26, Apr. 1, 3, 24, May 1, 22, June 20, July 18, Aug. 16, Sept. 14, Oct. 12, 29, Nov. 10, 27, Dec. 8, 25, 30

Soul mates: Jan. 8, 27, Feb. 6, 25, Mar. 4, 23, Apr. 2, 21, May 19, June 17, July 15, Aug. 13, Sept. 11, Oct. 9, Nov. 7, Dec. 5

Love & Relationships

Although your home is an important part of your life, you may have to guard against allowing relationships to fall into a predictable routine. Highly intuitive, you are sensitive to others' moods and need a harmonious environment. Alternatively, avoid becoming oversensitive or moody yourself. With your understanding and compassion, you can be supportive and encouraging to those you love, and often you are willing to make compromises to keep the peace. Sharing some creative pursuits with your partner can bring you closer. Socializing and entertaining your friends usually lifts your spirit.

June 3

♊ This birthdate shows you to be mentally sharp and determined, sociable and bright, with a strong need for self-expression. With your sensitivity and deep feelings, you are often an idealist. Since you may particularly enjoy initiating new projects, it is vital to keep yourself creatively occupied or actively working to fulfil your great potential.

A strong influence of Venus in the second decanate of Gemini intensifies the importance of dealing with people. You are likely to be creative and have amusing friends, and you may possess a heightened perception of beauty, color, and form. A light-hearted and quick-witted aspect of your personality may suggest that you enthusiastically seek entertainment. Venus's influence also points to the dangers of vanity, indecision, or self-indulgence. When in top form, however, you are able to combine your social and creative skills with the ability to be inventive, hardworking, and persistent in order to succeed.

As well as having skilled powers of communication, you may possess a desire to know yourself at a deeper level. This quest for wisdom implies that you often seek answers to the more profound questions of life, which eventually leads you to explore more spiritual or mystical areas. If these needs are ignored, you may allow the more introspective side of your nature to become too self-involved, making you overly serious, irritable, or even depressed. In contrast, however, you can be extremely charming and idealistic, with a fertile imagination and inspired thinking.

After the age of eighteen, when your progressed Sun moves into Cancer for the next thirty years, you are likely to become more sensitive and security-conscious, with a strong accent on your home life and family. When the progressed sun moves into Leo at the time when you reach the age of forty-eight, there is a strong need for self-expression and assertiveness, which may inspire you to become more gregarious and adventurous.

Your Secret Self

You may seek challenges that can bring about deep transformation within you. This builds up your power to overcome obstacles and gives you inner strength. Your positive qualities of analysis and intuition usually help you in this task, but you may have to beware of jealousy or a fear of being abandoned. Fortunately, you possess a wonderful dark humor that helps alleviate any overly difficult situations in your life.

Responsible and dedicated, you can work extremely hard when you are really interested in a project or idea. With your insight into human nature, you can be understanding and caring. Nevertheless, you also need your own space and time without feeling lonely. Too much isolation, however, could lead to secrecy or moodiness. When you develop your faith and learn to trust your intuition, you are able to handle things on the spot. This can also provide you with a competitive edge that can aid you in your overall plans to succeed.

Work & Vocation

A desire to learn and a tendency to dislike routine imply that you explore many avenues in your quest for a mentally challenging career. A persuasive way with words can ensure your

Star's name: Rigel

Degree position: 15°50'–16°40' Gemini between the years 1930 and 2000

Magnitude: 1

Strength: ★★★★★★★★★

Orb: 2°30'

Constellation: Beta Orionis

Applicable days: June 3, 4, 5, 6, 7, 8, 9

Star qualities: varied influences: Mars/Jupiter or Saturn/Jupiter

Description: a brilliant blue-white double star located on the left foot of Orion

PRIMARY STAR'S INFLUENCE

Rigel confers the ability to rise quickly in life, imparts strong willpower and an ambitious nature, and stimulates the mind to acquire wider general knowledge. A love of action and lucky breaks often stimulate you to be competitive. The ability to develop a scientific mind and even be inventive is linked to this star. Rigel can bestow honor, material riches, and lasting success.

Linked to your Sun's degree, this star suggests that you have a courageous and bold personality, with a broad or liberal outlook. You can also be hardworking, with good business sense and a flair for politics and public affairs. A strong preference for astrology, study, and higher education is also indicated by Rigel. This star indicates that great success can be achieved through assertiveness and a forthright approach, but warns against being too outspoken.

success in the world of communication, sales, writing, or publishing. Others will appreciate your approach to new and original ideas and admire your ability to stay calm under crisis and work hard. With your independent attitude and ability to lead, you can excel in the world of commerce and industry. For a creative or artistic outlet, consider the world of show business, either on the stage or through some kind of musical expression.

Famous people who share your birthday include actor Tony Curtis, singer Curtis Mayfield, entertainer Josephine Baker, and poet Allen Ginsberg.

Numerology

With a number 3 birthday, you are sensitive, with a need for creativity and emotional expression. Fun-loving and a good companion, you enjoy friendly social activities and many interests. Although you are versatile and expressive, with a need for different and exciting experiences, an inclination to get bored easily may cause you to become indecisive or spread yourself too thinly. Although with a number 3 birthday you are usually artistic and charming, with a good sense of humor, you may have to develop self-esteem and guard against tendencies such as worry and emotional insecurities. The subinfluence of the number 6 month indicates that you are idealistic and visionary. Curiosity and a desire to discover a meaning to the broader picture of life suggests a necessity for spiritual development. By showing compassion and understanding, you learn to live up to your ideals. Communicating your thoughts enables you to avoid worry and suspicion.

• *Positive:* humorous, happy, friendly, productive, creative, artistic, power to wish, freedom-loving, a talent with words
• *Negative:* easily bored, vain, tendency to exaggerate, unloving, boastful, extravagant, self-indulgent, lazy, hypocritical, wasteful

Love & Relationships

Being very sociable, you enjoy the company of friends and acquaintances and can be witty and entertaining as well as loyal and compassionate. Although you can be extremely warm and loving, at times there may be conflicts between love and work. This may be overcome by finding a partner who shares your high ideals and aspirations. You need deep intimacy, but if you feel inhibited or insecure, you may become suspicious or jealous and preoccupied with your own interests.

YOUR SPECIAL SOMEONE

At your best you can be extremely spontaneous and flowing, and your high ideals can be more easily met with someone born on one of the following dates.

Love & friendship: Jan. 7, 11, 20, 25, 27, 29, Feb. 9, 18, 23, 25, 27, Mar. 7, 16, 21, 23, 25, Apr. 5, 14, 19, 21, 23, May 3, 12, 17, 19, 21, June 1, 10, 15, 17, 19, July 8, 13, 15, 17, Aug. 6, 11, 13, 15, Sept. 4, 9, 11, 13, Oct. 2, 7, 9, 11, 17, Nov. 5, 7, 9, Dec. 3, 5, 7

Beneficial: Jan. 9, 26, Feb. 7, 24, Mar. 5, 22, Apr. 3, 20, May 1, 18, 29, June 16, 27, July 14, 25, 29, 30, Aug. 12, 23, 27, 28, 31, Sept. 10, 21, 25, 26, 29, Oct. 8, 19, 23, 24, 27, Nov. 6, 17, 21, 22, 25, Dec. 4, 15, 19, 20, 23

Fatal attractions: Jan. 16, Feb. 14, Mar. 12, Apr. 10, May 8, June 6, July 4, Aug. 2, Dec. 4, 5, 6

Challenging: Jan. 8, 29, 31, Feb. 6, 27, 29, Mar. 4, 25, 27, 28, Apr. 2, 23, 25, 26, May 21, 23, 24, June 19, 21, 22, July 17, 19, 20, Aug. 15, 17, 18, Sept. 13, 15, 16, Oct. 11, 13, 14, 30, Nov. 9, 11, 12, 28, Dec. 7, 9, 10, 26

Soul mates: May 30, June 28, July 26, Aug. 24, Sept. 22, 30, Oct. 20, 28, Nov. 18, 26, Dec. 16, 24

June 4

♊ As a clever conversationalist with polished social skills, you are aware of human nature and are able to mix with people from all walks of life. Multitalented, you have the ability to lead in many different areas of life. However, this great attribute can become a hindrance if you spread yourself too thinly and scatter yourself in too many directions. An innate understanding of values enables you to advise others through being an excellent commentator on their situation, whether on a psychological or material level.

With the added influence of Venus in the second decanate of Gemini, you are warm and friendly and attracted to beauty and the creative arts. An easy charm gives you directness without being abrasive and bestows the gift of diplomacy, should you wish to use it. Venus can also emphasize a desire to be popular and make you attractive to the opposite sex.

Possessing an inventive mind and strong individuality, you may find that most of your satisfaction in life comes from fulfilling a need to do something different and original. Stumbling blocks that may arise to stop you in your climb to success are tendencies to become impatient and self-indulgent. This also suggests that taking on too much may cause nervousness and tension. You value knowledge and have the ability to learn fast, and you can usually commercialize this in a practical way. Often broad-minded and an advocate of freedom, you may have an interest in social affairs and human rights.

At the age of seventeen, when your progressed Sun moves into Cancer, you are likely to focus on the importance of harmonious surroundings and have a secure and stable home base. This also highlights your personal emotional needs and continues until around the age of forty-seven, when your progressed Sun enters Leo. This will magnify your confidence and strength and enable you to become more powerful in public situations.

Your Secret Self

Creative and mentally restless, you are inquisitive, with many diverse interests, and you love experimenting with new ideas. However, you may need to learn how to constructively concentrate all your forces and limit yourself to a small number of projects in order to achieve your true potential. Worry and indecision could also prove to be unproductive and drain you of your energy. Although you appear confident, a need to be popular can also suggest that you need the approval of others. If, on the other hand, you discipline yourself to develop your creative ideas, you can succeed in a big way.

Besides a hidden sensitivity, you also have the potential for philosophy or spirituality, which, when developed, allows you to have faith in your own abilities and life in general. Since many people born on this date are found working beneath others with less talent and ability, it is vital to use this faith in accomplishing the goals you are capable of achieving. Spending periods alone in reflection, contemplation, or meditation is particularly good for developing your inner calm. Never underestimate the power of love.

Work & Vocation

Ambitious and determined, you may find that your innate business sense can place you in the world of commerce. Your natural psychological skills could prove helpful in sales, advertising, or any form of therapy. Although people-related occupations are likely to bring you satis-

FIXED STAR

Star's name: Rigel

Degree position: 15°50'–16°40' Gemini between the years 1930 and 2000

Magnitude: 1

Strength: ★★★★★★★★★

Orb: 2°30'

Constellation: Beta Orionis

Applicable days: June 3, 4, 5, 6, 7, 8, 9

Star qualities: varied influences: Mars/Jupiter or Saturn/Jupiter

Description: a brilliant blue-white double star located on the left foot of Orion

PRIMARY STAR'S INFLUENCE

Rigel confers the ability to rise quickly in life, imparts strong willpower and an ambitious nature, and stimulates the mind to acquire wider general knowledge. Love of action and lucky breaks often stimulate you to be competitive. The ability to develop a scientific mind and even be inventive is linked to this star. Rigel can bestow honor, material riches, and lasting success.

Linked to your Sun's degree, this star suggests that you have a courageous and bold personality, with a broad or liberal outlook. You can also be hardworking, with good business sense and a flair for politics and public affairs. A strong preference for astrology, study, and higher education is also indicated by Rigel. This star indicates that great success can be achieved through assertiveness and a forthright approach, but warns against being too outspoken.

faction, you may find teaching or lecturing and sharing your knowledge with others will bring you special rewards. Usually you can collaborate and work well in a team situation; however, as you do not like to take orders from others, you may prefer to work for yourself. Writing and journalism can prove to be very positive outlets for the creative side of your nature. Alternatively, your natural dramatic sense may find release through music, art, dance, or drama.

Famous people who share your birthday include actors Dennis Weaver and Bruce Dern, actress Rosalind Russell, singer Michelle Phillips, and TV personality "Dr. Ruth" Westheimer.

Numerology

The solid structure and orderly power suggested by the number 4 birthday indicate that you need stability and like to establish order. Endowed with energy, practical skills, and strong determination, you can achieve success through hard work. Security-conscious, you like to build a strong foundation for yourself and your family. A pragmatic approach to life confers a good business sense and an ability to achieve material success in life. As a number 4, you are usually honest, frank, and fair. The challenges for a number 4 individual may include overcoming periods of instability or financial worry. The subinfluence of the number 6 month indicate that you are protective and caring. It is important for you to be original, generate your own ideas, and make your own decisions. You may need to learn that being persuasive rather than forceful or bossy brings favorable results. Since you love your freedom, avoid being judgmental or overcritical with others, as they may resent your control.

• *Positive:* well organized, self-discipline, steady, hardworking, craftsmanship, good with your hands, pragmatism, trusting, exact
• *Negative:* destructive behavior, uncommunicative, repressed, rigid, lazy, unfeeling, procrastination, too economical, bossy, hidden affections, resentful

Love & Relationships

Your need for peace and harmony is likely to attract you to intelligent people who practice positive thinking and can provide you with mental stimulation. Your love of knowledge also suggests that you enjoy groups where you can learn new information or skills. In your relationships you prefer people to be direct, and you often see the advantage of using diplomatic methods in order to keep the status quo. Since you are interested in self-improvement, you are often involved with ambitious people who are bettering themselves. Nevertheless, in your attempts to be successful, guard against becoming overly critical or bossy with your spouse or associates.

YOUR SPECIAL SOMEONE

For security, mental stimulation, and love you might want to begin looking for those born among the following dates.

Love & friendship: Jan. 4, 11, 12, 21, 26, 28, 30, Feb. 2, 9, 10, 19, 24, 26, 28, Mar. 7, 8, 22, 24, 26, Apr. 5, 6, 20, 22, 24, 30, May 3, 4, 18, 20, 22, 28, 31, June 1, 2, 16, 18, 20, 26, 29, July 14, 16, 18, 24, 27, Aug. 12, 14, 16, 22, 25, Sept. 10, 12, 14, 20, 23, Oct 3, 8, 10, 12, 18, 21, Nov. 6, 8, 10, 16, 19, Dec. 4, 6, 8, 14, 17

Beneficial: Jan. 3, 10, 29, Feb. 1, 8, 27, Mar. 6, 25, Apr. 4, 23, May 2, 21, June 19, July 17, 30, Aug. 15, 28, Sept. 13, 26, Oct. 11, 24, Nov. 9, 22, Dec. 7, 20

Fatal attractions: Jan. 11, Feb. 9, Mar. 7, Apr. 5, May 3, June 1, Dec. 5, 6, 7, 8

Challenging: Jan. 9, Feb. 7, Mar. 5, 28, Apr. 3, 26, May 1, 24, June 22, July 20, Aug 18, Sept. 16, Oct. 14, 30, 31, Nov. 12, 28, 29, Dec. 10, 26, 27

Soul mates: Jan. 7, Feb. 5, Mar. 3, Apr. 1, May 29, June 27, July 25, Aug. 23, Sept. 21, Oct. 19, Nov. 17, Dec. 15

June 5

♊ Being self-willed, with a strong and determined character, makes you independent and self-reliant. You can be dramatic, yet realistic and pragmatic, an ideal mixture for combining business and pleasure. Since you also have the capacity to be persistent and diligent, success is yours if you do not allow yourself to get overly concerned with materialism.

Libra, your decanate ruler, indicates that you are refined and sociable, with a love of beauty and luxury. This can enhance your creative abilities and may encourage an interest in music, art, or drama. However, it does also point to the importance of money in your overall scheme of things and shows you to have excellent bargaining or negotiating skills. You like to deal with people in a direct and forthright way, but you may have to guard against being bossy or verbally cutting.

At times you can get extraordinary surges of energy and courage that enable you to react quickly to situations and seize opportunities. You have an excellent, precise mind capable of deep thought, and you have a technical or analytical slant. Your independent spirit stimulates you to take an original approach and seek personal freedom. However, you may have to guard against willfulness, sudden temper, obstinacy, or becoming negative and uncommunicative. Fortunately, you are willing to work hard to overcome any obstacles, whether in yourself or in outer situations.

As your progressed Sun moves into Cancer, when you are around age sixteen, security or home issues start to have more importance in your life. This also highlights your concerns regarding your personal emotions and sense of security as well as your family. This continues until the age of forty-six, when your progressed Sun enters Leo and commences a period of growing confidence and strength that enables you to become more outgoing and magnanimous.

Your Secret Self

Tests usually come in the form of worry or indecision about money, and you may have to be careful that the need for material security does not outweigh other important factors. If you do become discouraged and disillusioned, you may be prone to extravagant gestures in order to compensate and make yourself happy. True contentment, however, is more likely to come from your disposition to be generous, light-hearted, and detached.

Appearances are important to you, and in your sure advancement through life you may fare particularly well at public events or in associations where you can play a meaningful role. The wisdom inherent in this birthdate shows that if you channel your restlessness into your fast, progressive spirit of adventure, prosperity follows naturally without your having to worry about it.

Work & Vocation

It is important that you master your chosen craft, as you usually like to do a job well, taking pride in your work. Your natural aptitude for taking a leading role, together with your administrative skills, could lead to your success in the business world, in advertising, or in merchandising. Equally, your verbal skills can ensure your success in law or the world of com-

FIXED STAR

Star's name: Rigel

Degree position: 15°50'–16°40' Gemini between the years 1930 and 2000

Magnitude: I

Strength: ★★★★★★★★★

Orb: 2°30'

Constellation: Beta Orionis

Applicable days: June 3, 4, 5, 6, 7, 8, 9

Star qualities: varied influences: Mars/Jupiter or Saturn/Jupiter

Description: a brilliant blue-white double star located on the left foot of Orion

PRIMARY STAR'S INFLUENCE

Rigel confers the ability to rise quickly in life, imparts strong willpower and an ambitious nature, and stimulates the mind to acquire wider general knowledge. Love of action and lucky breaks often stimulate you to be competitive. The ability to develop a scientific mind and even be inventive is linked to this star. Rigel can bestow honor, material riches, and lasting success.

Linked to your Sun's degree, this star suggests that you have a courageous and bold personality, with a broad or liberal outlook. You can also be hard-working, with good business sense and a flair for politics and public affairs. A strong preference for astrology, study, and higher education is also indicated by Rigel. This star indicates that great success can be achieved through assertiveness and a forthright approach, but warns against being too outspoken.

munication. Your ability to push through some kind of reform may attract you to leadership in organizations such as trade unions and charities or as a freedom fighter. Alternatively, your business sense and artistic talents may be combined in careers such as curator or art administrator. For expression of your creativity and innate dramatic flair, the theater or music is likely to prove a positive outlet. This birthdate often points to success in the world of healthcare. Whatever career you choose, it is important to have variety and change in your working environment to keep you inspired and interested.

Famous people who share your birthday include musicians Marky Mark and Laurie Anderson, broadcaster Bill Moyers, entertainer Spalding Gray, and children's writer Richard Scarry.

Numerology

Strong instincts, an adventurous nature, and a desire for freedom are all indicated by the number 5 birthday. The willingness to explore or try anything new, along with an enthusiastic approach, suggests that life will have a lot to offer you. Travel and many opportunities for change, some unexpected, may lead you to undergo a real transformation of views and beliefs. With a number 5 birthday, you need to feel that life is exciting; however, you may also have to develop a responsible attitude and avoid tendencies such as unpredictability, excessiveness, and restlessness. The natural talent of a number 5 individual is knowing how to go with the flow and staying detached. The subinfluence of the number 6 month indicates that since you are inspired and idealistic, you need to stay focused and single-minded. Learn to trust your intuition and develop a philosophical attitude about life. Usually you are ready to share your thoughts with others; you speak from the heart with sincerity and conviction. Be independent and flexible but guard against selfish motives and hasty actions.

• *Positive:* versatile, adaptable, progressive, strong instincts, magnetic, lucky, daring, freedom-loving, quick and witty, curious, mystical, sociable

• *Negative:* unreliable, changeable, procrastination, inconsistent, undependable, lustful, overconfident, headstrong

Love & Relationships

Friendly and gregarious, with many interests and hobbies, you are likely to have a full social life. Although you can be loving and giving, uncertainty or indecisiveness concerning close relationships can become a source of worry or disappointment. At times you can be extremely generous or make sacrifices for those you love. Guard against becoming overly enthusiastic about people and then losing interest or becoming unsure about how you feel. By expressing yourself diplomatically in your relationships as well making it clear where you stand, you can establish longer-lasting relationships. Enjoying social gatherings, you can be witty and entertaining.

YOUR SPECIAL SOMEONE

You might find a partner who will understand your sensitivity and need for love among those born on the following dates.

Love & friendship: Jan. 13, 22, 29, Feb. 11, 20, 27, 29, Mar. 9, 25, 27, Apr. 7, 23, 25, May 5, 21, 23, 29, June 3, 19, 21, 27, 30, July 1, 17, 19, 25, 28, Aug. 15, 17, 23, 26, Sept. 13, 15, 21, 24, Oct. 11, 13, 19, 22, 29, Nov. 9, 11, 17, 20, 27, Dec. 7, 9, 15, 18, 25

Beneficial: Jan. 11, Feb. 9, Mar. 7, 31, Apr. 5, 29, May 3, 27, 31, June 1, 25, 29, July 23, 27, 31, Aug. 21, 25, 29, 30, Sept. 19, 23, 27, 28, Oct. 4, 17, 21, 25, 26, Nov. 15, 19, 23, 24, 30, Dec. 13, 17, 21, 22, 28

Fatal attractions: Jan. 12, Feb. 10, Mar. 8, Apr. 6, May 4, June 2, Dec. 5, 6, 7, 8

Challenging: Jan. 10, Feb. 8, Mar. 6, 29, Apr. 4, 27, May 2, 25, June 23, July 21, Aug. 19, Sept. 17, Oct. 15, 31, Nov. 13, 29, 30, Dec. 11, 27, 28

Soul mates: Jan. 18, 24, Feb. 16, 22, Mar. 14, 20, Apr. 12, 18, May 10, 16, June 8, 14, July 6, 12, Aug. 4, 10, Sept. 2, 8, Oct. 6, Nov. 4, Dec. 2

June 6

Ⅱ Charismatic and entertaining, you are warm, optimistic, and friendly. The qualities suggested by your birthdate indicate that you need people and are full of inspiration and ideas. With a certain natural grace, you are an expressive communicator and have a strong sense of your own individuality. Although you believe in making a good impression, sincerity is important to you and you like to be direct and honest with others.

With your personal magnetism and the added influence of your decanate ruler, Libra, you have an interest in human relationships and possess good diplomatic skills. You are accomplished at the art of conversation and have a genuine desire for peace. You also have the ability to enchant people and can often use this to your advantage.

Idealism and a desire to transcend the mundane can give you a heightened perception of light, color, form, and sound, as well as an inborn understanding of the dreams and hopes of a whole generation. You may decide to use these talents for artistic or literary creations, mystical or spiritual inclinations, or working for the benefit of others. If undeveloped, however, this same energy is likely to become wasted in escapism, impossible dreams, or a desire for glamour.

Childhood is often a happy experience, and after the age of fifteen, when your progressed Sun moves into Cancer, you are likely to become more sensitive and security-conscious. This brings a strong accent on your family, home, and intimate personal life. When your progressed Sun moves into Leo as you reach the age of forty-five, there is a increased need for self-expression and leadership. This is likely to encourage you to become more assertive and confident and may accent more of a public role. As you reach the age of seventy-five, your progressed Sun moves into Virgo, and you start to develop a more analytical approach by being reflective.

FIXED STAR

Star's name: Rigel
Degree position: 15°50'–16°40 Gemini between the years 1930 and 2000
Magnitude: 1
Strength: ★★★★★★★★★
Orb: 2°30'
Constellation: Beta Orionis
Applicable days: June 3, 4, 5, 6, 7, 8, 9
Star qualities: varied influences: Mars/Jupiter or Saturn/Jupiter
Description: a brilliant blue-white double star located on the left foot of Orion

PRIMARY STAR'S INFLUENCE

Rigel confers the ability to rise quickly in life, imparts strong willpower and an ambitious nature, and stimulates the mind to acquire wider general knowledge. Love of action and lucky breaks often stimulate you to be competitive. The ability to develop a scientific mind and even be inventive is linked to this star. Rigel can bestow honor, material riches, and lasting success.

Linked to your Sun's degree, this star suggests that you have a courageous and bold personality, with a broad or liberal outlook. You can also be hardworking, with good business sense and a flair for politics and public affairs. A strong preference for astrology, study, and higher education is also indicated by Rigel. This star indicates that great success can be achieved through assertiveness and a forthright approach, but warns against being too outspoken.

Your Secret Self

Despite your bright and expressive qualities, you may have difficulties in making choices or decisions. Since many diverse interests often pull you in different directions, it is very important to have a sense of purpose. Without this you are likely to get caught between your ideals and a desire for material satisfaction. One side of you may be particularly drawn toward money, luxury, and an indolent lifestyle, whereas a desire for inspiration can spur you to work hard to fulfill your ideals. Whatever your choice, you are likely to have many opportunities offered to you, and you have an ability to talk or charm your way out of the most difficult situations. A youthful or very playful quality is likely to stay with you until old age and guarantee that you keep people amused and enthralled. As long as this means accepting responsibility and self-discipline, then you are certain of making the most of your outstanding potential.

Work & Vocation

Your magnetism and charisma are likely to be valuable assets in promoting either yourself, a product, or a cause. With excellent social and communication skills, you prosper in all careers that use the personal touch as well as in education, journalism, advertising, or sales. Since you possess strong values, this can be advantageous to you in occupations such as law or politics. Having a naturally creative approach to life, you may find outlets for your emotional expression in the theater or through the arts. Whatever your chosen profession, you are likely to gain particular satisfaction in any occupation that deals with people.

Famous people who share your birthday include tennis player Bjorn Borg, writer Aleksandr Pushkin, actress Billie Whitelaw, Spanish painter Velázquez, and comic Sandra Bernhard.

Numerology

Compassion, idealism, and a caring nature are some of the attributes suggested by a number 6 birthday. This is the number of the perfectionist or the universal friend, and indicates that you are frequently a humanitarian who can be responsible, loving, and supportive. With a number 6 birthday, you are frequently domesticated and a devoted parent. The more sensitive among you will need to find a form of creative expression and are drawn to the world of entertaining or art and design. You may need to develop more self-confidence and overcome tendencies to be interfering, worry, and misplace your sympathy. The subinfluence of the number 6 month indicates that you have compassion toward your friends and neighbors as well as a responsible attitude. You need to develop your assertiveness or self-esteem when confronted by opposition. Popular and friendly, you need the approval of others. However, you need to focus your energies, and do not worry about what others say or do. Learn to say no without being afraid to offend others.

• *Positive:* worldly, friendly, compassionate, dependable, understanding, sympathetic, idealistic, domestic, humanitarian, poised, artistic, balanced

• *Negative:* discontented, anxiety, shy, stubborn, outspoken, perfectionist, domineering, lack of responsibility, selfish, suspicious, cynical, self-centered

Love & Relationships

Enthusiastic and vivacious, you are gregarious and sociable, with an ability to make friends easily. You are more inclined, however, toward people who are hardworking and reliable or those who can provide you with a sense of security. With your charm, you often find that others are willing to help and assist you. Happier when you are financially stable or able to mix business and pleasure, you enjoy entertaining friends or business associates. You are likely to make a good marriage and can benefit from close partnerships.

YOUR SPECIAL SOMEONE

For security, mental stimulation, and love, you might want to begin looking for those born among the following dates.

Love & friendship: Jan. 6, 8, 14, 23, 26, 28, Feb. 4, 10, 12, 21, 24, 26, Mar. 2, 10, 12, 19, 22, 24, Apr. 8, 14, 17, 20, 22, May 6, 15, 16, 18, 20, June 4, 13, 16, 18, July 2, 11, 14, 16, 20, Aug. 9, 12, 14, 22, Sept. 7, 10, 12, 24, Oct. 5, 8, 10, 26, Nov. 3, 6, 8, 28, Dec. 1, 4, 6, 30

Beneficial: Jan. 9, 12, Feb. 7, 10, Mar. 5, 8, Apr. 3, 6, May 1, 4, June 2, 30, July 28, Aug. 26, 30, 31, Sept. 24, 28, 29, Oct. 22, 26, 27, Nov. 20, 24, 25, Dec. 18, 22, 23, 29

Fatal attractions: Dec. 6, 7, 8, 9

Challenging: Jan. 11, 13, 29, Feb. 9, 11, Mar. 7, 9, 30, Apr. 5, 7, 28, May 3, 5, 26, 31, June 1, 3, 24, 29, July 1, 22, 27, Aug. 20, 25, Sept. 18, 23, 30, Oct. 16, 21, 28, Nov. 14, 19, 26, Dec. 12, 17, 24

Soul mates: Jan. 12, 29, Feb. 10, 27, Mar. 8, 25, Apr. 6, 23, May 4, 21, June 2, 19, July 17, Aug. 15, Sept. 13, Oct. 11, Nov. 9, Dec. 7

SUN: GEMINI

DECANATE: LIBRA/VENUS

DEGREE: 15°–16°30' GEMINI

MODE: MUTABLE

ELEMENT: AIR

June 7

♊ Your birthday shows you as a versatile, ambitious, and success-oriented Gemini. Being quick at assessing people and situations as well as having an eye for an opportunity ensure that you are good at materializing your dreams. You may work best when stimulated by the thought of a large reward awaiting you as part of a big plan or project, and you do not like to be small or petty. Generosity, therefore, can be one of your most positive attributes.

Being a charismatic communicator, you get along well with all types of people and have the power to influence them with your ideas. Often ahead of your time, you may be aware of changing attitudes in society before others. With your quick wit and resourcefulness, you are often able to turn this knowledge to your advantage. Although making money may be a preoccupation, you will grow to learn that it does not always bring happiness and be aware of what you may be compromising in your quest for success. With your ability to see the bigger plan, you are an excellent organizer who can delegate work to others. However, guard against scattering your energies or leaving work unfinished.

With the influence of Venus in the second decanate of Gemini, you are likely to be diplomatic and creative in some way. A natural sense of refinement or artistic appreciation may stimulate you to develop your talents, if not for a career, then as a pastime for relaxation. This influence can also point to a love of luxury and the good life, which may particularly stimulate you into action.

After the age of fourteen, when your progressed Sun moves into Cancer, you are likely to focus more on your personal emotional life and the people who affect it the most, your family. You become more aware of a need for security and strong foundations in your life. When your progressed Sun moves into Leo at the age of forty-four, there is a change of emphasis to greater self-expression and assertiveness, which may encourage you to become more prominent in public life. As you reach the age of seventy-four, your progressed Sun moves into Virgo, and you start to develop a more analytical approach by being reflective yet pragmatic.

Your Secret Self

Since you are a natural actor or actress, you are usually able to project confidence. Generally shrewd and intelligent, with a powerful sixth sense, you can swiftly judge people and situations. This enables you to work better in a leading role rather than overexerting yourself in physical labor. Since you also possess an introspective or more serious side to your nature, the choice of wisdom rather than being able to get by extremely well in a material sense is what eventually proves to be your biggest reward.

Although usually generous with your time and money, you may become too expansive or overindulgent. Fortunately, you are open to criticism that enables you to use self-analysis as a valuable tool in your own development. With your strong self-will, you can be very persuasive and have the power to influence people. Often women play an important role in your advancement.

Work & Vocation

Ambitious and friendly, yet independent, you are likely to prefer working alone, whether in a larger organization or for yourself. Career choices such as teaching, lecturing, or writing may provide you with enough space to operate in your own way. As a big planner and excellent delegator, you may excel in commerce or law. Being multitalented, you may find it hard to focus and specialize in one area with the wide variety of choices open to you. Career-wise, your ease in dealing with the public and excellent communication skills can be a big advantage in sales and marketing or publishing. With your natural creativity, you may be drawn to the arts, the theater, or musical entertainment. Possessing an inborn business sense, you can commercialize any talent and usually work better when using your keen intellect.

Famous people who share your birthday include impressionist painter Paul Gauguin, singers Prince and Tom Jones, actor Liam Neeson, and actress Jessica Tandy.

Numerology

Analytical and thoughtful, number 7 individuals are frequently critical and self-absorbed. With a constant need for greater self-awareness, you enjoy gathering information and may be interested in reading, writing, or spirituality. Although shrewd, you may overrationalize or get lost in detail. A tendency to be enigmatic or secretive suggests that at times you feel misunderstood. The subinfluence of the number 6 month indicates that you need order and stability. Take control of your life and first establish a firm foundation. You want to enjoy the best of what life has to offer but must guard against overindulgence. Be responsible for your actions, and think before you speak. Learning from your mistakes enables you to have a more realistic attitude. Success often comes through a willingness to work hard and by developing existing skills and knowledge. Writing your thoughts and ideas down helps you to remember the small details and to be practical, creative, and well organized.

• *Positive:* educated, trusting, meticulous, idealistic, honest, silent thinker, psychic, scientific, rational, reflective

• *Negative:* concealing, deceitful, unfriendly, secretive, skeptical, confused, unfeeling

Love & Relationships

Constantly seeking emotional fulfillment and excitement, you have a passionate nature and strong desires. Since you possess charm and a charismatic personality, you can easily draw friends and admirers. You are attracted to optimistic people who can inspire you with new ideas and opportunities. Your love for freedom suggests that you may prefer to be in relationships that can give you enough space to feel independent. You may need to take your time where love is concerned and not rush or make spur-of-the-moment commitments.

YOUR SPECIAL SOMEONE

To keep you interested in loving relationships, you might want to look out for those born on the following days.

Love & friendship: Jan. 6, 15, 29, 31, Feb. 4, 13, 27, 29, Mar. 2, 11, 25, 27, Apr. 9, 23, 25, May 7, 21, 23, June 5, 19, 21, July 3, 17, 19, 30, Aug. 1, 15, 17, 28, Sept. 13, 15, 26, Oct. 11, 13, 24, Nov. 9, 11, 22, Dec. 7, 9, 20

Beneficial: Jan. 13, 15, 19, Feb. 11, 13, 17, Mar. 9, 11, 15, Apr. 7, 9, 13, May 5, 7, 11, June 3, 5, 9, July 1, 3, 7, 29, Aug. 1, 5, 27, 31, Sept. 3, 25, 29, Oct. 1, 23, 27, Nov. 21, 25, Dec. 19, 23

Fatal attractions: May 30, June 28, July 26, Aug. 24, Sept. 22, Oct. 20, Nov. 18, Dec. 7, 8, 9, 10, 16

Challenging: Jan. 12, Feb. 10, Mar. 8, Apr. 6, May 4, June 2, Aug. 31, Sept. 29, Oct. 27, 29, 30, Nov. 25, 27, 28, Dec. 23, 25, 26, 30

Soul mates: Jan. 2, 28, Feb. 26, Mar. 24, Apr. 22, May 20, June 18, July 16, Aug. 14, Sept. 12, Oct. 10, Nov. 8, Dec. 6

June 8

Ⅱ Your birthday indicates that you are intelligent, generous, and broad-minded, with good communication skills. Independent and resourceful, you generally like to keep busy. Occasionally you may become highly charged yet nervous. By staying as detached as possible, you can remain calm. Fortunately, if frustrated or disappointed, you do not stay down for long, as your quick responses are liable to have you soon back in action.

With the influence of your decanate ruler, Libra, you can be artistic and creative, and have a wonderful charm when dealing with people. Often light-hearted and cheerful, you can be a fun companion and entertain others with your quick repartee. This influence also bestows diplomatic skills and elequence. When you combine your gift of foresight with your inventive or analytical mind, you often create original concepts.

At times you may present a strange and enigmatic mixture of opposites, being sensitive and idealistic yet pragmatic. You can avoid expecting too much of people or situations by keeping a balanced perspective with your natural sense of humor. A tendency to be preoccupied with yourself can lead to positive self-analysis and improvement.

After the age of thirteen, when your progressed Sun moves into Cancer, you are more likely to concentrate on issues concerning your home and emotional life. During the next thirty years you become more aware of family issues. As your progressed Sun moves into Leo, when you are age forty-three, there is a strong need for self-expression and assertiveness that inspires you to become more bold, confident, and gregarious. As you reach the age of seventy-three, your progressed Sun moves into Virgo, and you start to develop a more analytical, practical, and serviceful approach to life.

Your Secret Self

Possessing excellent evaluating skills, you have an instinct for money or material matters. On occasion, you can strike it lucky by combining your sixth sense with unexpected pieces of information. Since there may be periods in your life of fluctuating finances, you may have to solve the problem of how to live well without being extravagant. A natural authority takes you to positions of responsibility where you are able to use your organizational abilities. If this involves some type of creative activity, then so much the better.

If negative, however, you may become too dominant and start spoiling the relationships you have set up. Possessing an inner restlessness, you need variety in all your affairs to keep your spirit of adventure alive. Travel may prove to be an excellent panacea for many of your ills.

Work & Vocation

Your fine mind is always exploring new knowledge that you can turn to your advantage both materially and personally. Careers that use your intellectual skill and excellent powers of communication, such as scientist, lawyer, teacher, or writer, are likely to bring you success. Alternatively, with a natural business sense, you can fare well in banking, treasury, stock brokerage, or

---

FIXED STAR

Star's name: Rigel

Degree position: 15°50'–16°40' Gemini between the years 1930 and 2000

Magnitude: 1

Strength: ★★★★★★★★★

Orb: 2°30'

Constellation: Beta Orionis

Applicable days: June 3, 4, 5, 6, 7, 8, 9

Star qualities: varied influences: Mars/Jupiter or Saturn/Jupiter

Description: a brilliant blue-white double star located on the left foot of Orion

PRIMARY STAR'S INFLUENCE

Rigel confers the ability to rise quickly in life, imparts strong willpower and an ambitious nature, and stimulates the mind to acquire wider general knowledge. Love of action and lucky breaks often stimulate you to be competitive. The ability to develop a scientific mind and even be inventive is linked to this star. Rigel can bestow honor, material riches, and lasting success.

Linked to your Sun's degree, this star suggests that you have a courageous and bold personality, with a broad or liberal outlook. You can also be hardworking, with good business sense and a flair for politics and public affairs. A strong preference for astrology, study, and higher education is also indicated by Rigel. This star indicates that great success can be achieved through assertiveness and a forthright approach, but warns against being too outspoken.

accountancy. A humanitarian side to your nature may find expression through the healing professions or social work. A good sense of structure may manifest through architecture or building. This date also shows the potential for success in show business, art, or music.

Famous people who share your birthday include comedian Joan Rivers, musician Boz Scaggs, painter John Everett Millais, architect Frank Lloyd Wright, astrologer Grant Lewi, and composer Robert Schumann.

Numerology

The power suggested by the number 8 birthday shows a character with strong values and sound judgment. The number 8 indicates that you aspire to great accomplishment and possess an ambitious nature. A desire for dominance, security, and material success is also indicated by this birthday. As a number 8 person, you have natural business sense and will benefit greatly from developing organizational and executive skills. A strong need to feel secure or established urges you to make long-term plans and investments. The subinfluence of the number 6 month indicates that you are caring and loyal, although you may at times act in a thoughtless or unfeeling way. Restless and imaginative, you may need to avoid stubbornness by developing a more flexible attitude. Understanding and spontaneously generous, you can nevertheless overindulge and be careless with your money. Since you are progressive and want to express your feelings freely, avoid monotonous situations or being too rigid. Through cooperation with others you can achieve security and stability.

• *Positive:* leadership, thoroughness, hardworking, tradition, authority, protection, power to heal, good judge of values

• *Negative:* impatient, intolerant, miserly, restless, overwork, domineering, easily discouraged, lack of planning, abusive, controlling

Love & Relationships

A true communicator, you need the company of others and enjoy the personal touch. Although you may often seem cool and unemotional, underneath you have a caring and compassionate heart. You may be happiest when socializing with people with whom you share some type of intellectual activity. Sometimes you tend to become overly serious, and you may need to develop a more detached attitude. Hidden insecurity may also indicate that instead of being your usual diplomatic self, you can sometimes become argumentative or quarrelsome, which can create tension and unrest. Nevertheless, you are loyal, loving, and a supportive friend and partner.

YOUR SPECIAL SOMEONE

To find long-lasting happiness, security, and love, you might begin by looking for someone born on one of the following days.

Love & friendship: Jan. 6, 16, Feb. 4, 14, Mar. 2, 12, 28, 30, Apr. 10, 26, 28, May 8, 24, 26, 30, June 6, 22, 24, 28, July 4, 20, 22, 26, 31, Aug. 2, 18, 20, 24, 29, Sept. 16, 18, 22, 27, Oct. 14, 16, 20, 25, Nov. 12, 14, 18, 23, Dec. 10, 12, 16, 21

Beneficial: Jan. 9, 14, 16, Feb. 7, 12, 14, Mar. 5, 10, 12, Apr. 3, 8, 10, May 1, 6, 8, June 4, 6, July 2, 4, Aug. 2, Sept. 30, Oct. 28, Nov. 26, 30, Dec. 24, 28, 29

Fatal attractions: Jan. 21, Feb. 19, Mar. 17, Apr. 15, May 13, June 11, July 9, Aug. 7, Sept. 5, Oct. 3, Nov. 1, Dec. 8, 9, 10, 11

Challenging: Jan. 4, 13, 28, Feb. 2, 11, 26, Mar. 9, 24, Apr. 7, 22, May 5, 20, June 3, 18, July 1, 16, Aug. 14, Sept. 12, Oct. 10, 31, Nov. 8, 29, Dec. 6, 27

Soul mates: Jan. 15, 22, Feb. 13, 20, Mar. 11, 18, Apr. 9, 16, May 7, 14, June 5, 12, July 3, 10, Aug. 1, 8, Sept. 6, Oct. 4, Nov. 2

June 9

FIXED STARS

Rigel; Bellatrix, also called the Female Warrior; Capella, also called Little She-Goat and Amalthea

PRIMARY STAR

Star's name: Rigel

Degree position: 15°50'–16°40' Gemini between the years 1930 and 2000

Magnitude: 1

Strength: ★★★★★★★★

Orb: 2°30'

Constellation: Beta Orionis

Applicable days: June 3, 4, 5, 6, 7, 8, 9

Star qualities: varied influences: Mars/Jupiter or Saturn/Jupiter

Description: a brilliant blue-white double star located on the left foot of Orion

PRIMARY STAR'S INFLUENCE

Rigel confers the ability to rise quickly in life, imparts strong willpower and an ambitious nature, and stimulates the mind to acquire wider general knowledge. Love of action and lucky breaks often stimulate you to be competitive. The ability to develop a scientific mind and even be inventive is linked to this star. Rigel can bestow honor, material riches, and lasting success.

Linked to your Sun's degree, this star suggests that you have a courageous and bold personality, with a broad or liberal outlook. You can also be hardworking, with good business sense and a flair for politics and public affairs. A strong preference for astrology, study, and higher education is also

♊ A certain willpower and determination suggest that you have the ability to fulfill the great promise of this birthdate. With the desire to expand and to climb up the ladder of success both materially and socially, you are ambitious and tenacious. A setback to your possible achievement, however, may be an obstinate or rebellious attitude. As you like power and authority, at times you can take on responsibility and be quite commanding. You may, however, need to develop patience in order to avoid being too domineering.

With the added influence of your decanate ruler, Libra, you can be very sociable and amusing and are likely to gain from female acquaintances. This also indicates an excellent sense of artistic and creative appreciation and a love of music and dance. Besides money, Venus also brings an interest in human relationships, which may draw you toward creating a better environment for others.

Through self-discipline you are able to bring out the best in yourself, including a capacity to perform record achievements and the ability to overcome obstacles. You can be persistent, with a strong urge for freedom, but may have to avoid kicking against your limitations or getting into trouble with authority figures.

After the age of twelve, when your progressed Sun moves into Cancer, issues concerning security, home, and family start to have more prominence in your life. This influence continues until around the age of forty-two, when you enter a period of energy, power, and confidence as your progressed Sun moves into Leo. As you reach the age of seventy-two, your progressed Sun moves into Virgo, and you will want to become more analytical, practical, and reflective.

Your Secret Self

Inner faith is an important factor in your confidence, and without it you may encounter times of withdrawal, insecurity, or lack of self-esteem. Shrewd and mentally sharp, you grasp information very quickly and use it to your advantage. Although at times you can be very concerned with material issues, it is through the use of your inner wisdom or spiritual insight that you can overcome a cold or skeptical outlook. By daring yourself to live spontaneously and by being fair yet competitive, you challenge yourself and others to feel powerful and alive.

When interested in making things happen, you possess a natural sense of control and can be very focused and patient. At these times you may be willing to work extremely hard and are often drawn to people who are powerful and ambitious. Others recognize your abilities and are usually willing to assist you in your plans.

Work & Vocation

Any people-related activity may prove to be rewarding, and your need for self-expression and a love for the dramatic may lure you to the art and entertainment world. A humanitarian or philanthropic side to your nature may find outlets through counseling or supporting social causes. With organizational skills and potential managerial or executive ability, you can excel in commerce, banking, and industry. Your strong willpower and determination are likely indicated by Rigel. This star indicates that great success can be achieved through assertiveness and a forthright approach, but warns against being too outspoken.

• *Positive:* founder of large enterprises, liberal, education, common sense

• *Negative:* short temper, insolent, unruly, demanding, restless

See Appendix for additional fixed star readings.

to place you in positions of power. You like to act with complete autonomy, so being self-employed may be an attractive option for you. Alternatively, the legal profession and official positions in the public eye can enable you to prosper. Your love of variety and communication skills will hold you in good stead in occupations such as journalism or politics.

Famous people who share your birthday include actors Johnny Depp and Michael J. Fox, composer Cole Porter, politician Robert S. McNamara, and pioneering doctor Elizabeth Garrett Anderson.

Numerology

Benevolence, thoughtfulness, and sentimental sensitivity are all associated with the number 9 birthday. Tolerant and kind, you are often generous and liberal. Intuitive and psychic abilities point to a universal receptivity, and if channeled positively, this may inspire you to seek a spiritual path. This birthday may suggest a need to overcome challenges and a tendency to be overly sensitive, with emotional ups and downs. You benefit greatly from world travel and interaction with people from all walks of life, but may have to avoid unrealistic dreams or an inclination toward escapism. The subinfluence of the number 6 month indicates that you can be responsible and create balance and harmony through good judgment, justice, and fairness. Being generous, cooperative, and caring brings out the humanitarian in you. Avoid being disruptive or vengeful. Try to listen to others' needs and guard against being self-centered or critical; avoid dominating people with your opinions. Compassion and love for others bring ultimate rewards.

• *Positive:* idealistic, humanitarian, creative, sensitive, generous, magnetic, poetic, charitable, giving, detached, lucky, popular

• *Negative:* frustrated, nervous, fragmented, unsure, selfish, impractical, easily led, inferiority complex, fears, worry

Love & Relationships

Often attracted to powerful yet creative individuals, you have a need for love and understanding that is often contrary to your strong and self-assured front. Although you are hardworking, you enjoy having fun and socializing with friends or family. You like to have your own way, but you can be loyal and caring. However, you may need to avoid martyring yourself or being temperamental. The more inspired among you often find self-expression through the love of arts and music or poetry.

YOUR SPECIAL SOMEONE

You might find a partner who will understand your sensitivity and need for love among those born on the following dates.

Love & friendship: Jan. 7, 17, 20, Feb. 5, 15, 18, Mar. 3, 13, 16, 29, 31, Apr. 1, 11, 14, 27, 29, May 9, 12, 25, 27, June 7, 10, 23, 25, July 5, 8, 21, 23, Aug. 3, 6, 19, 21, Sept. 1, 4, 17, 19, Oct. 2, 15, 17, Nov. 13, 15, 30, Dec. 11, 13, 28

Beneficial: Jan. 15, 17, 28, Feb. 13, 15, 26, Mar. 11, 13, 24, Apr. 9, 11, 22, May 7, 9, 20, June 5, 7, 18, July 3, 5, 16, Aug. 1, 3, 14, Sept. 1, 12, Oct. 10, 29, Nov. 8, 27, Dec. 6, 25

Fatal attractions: Jan. 5, Feb. 3, Mar. 1, Dec. 9, 10, 11, 12

Challenging: Jan 4, 5, 14, Feb. 2, 3, 12, Mar. 1, 10, Apr. 8, 30, May 6, 28, June 4, 26, July 2, 24, Aug. 22, Sept. 20, Oct. 18, Nov. 16, Dec. 14

Soul mates: Jan. 2, Mar. 29, Apr. 27, May 25, June 23, July 21, Aug. 19, Sept. 17, Oct. 15, Nov. 13, Dec. 11

June 10

Ⅱ Your birthdate suggests that you have an excellent intellect, with a strong potential for achievement and material success. You are likely to be persuasive and interested in people, as well as having the ability to work with meticulous precision. Wanting independence, you have a capacity to learn from experience and often develop one line of expertise.

With the influence of Venus in the second decanate of Gemini, you have a charismatic personality with a persuasive manner. When positively charged, you are likely to have many creative ideas and be a good conversationalist. Usually sociable, you also possess a feel for beauty and the arts. This can bestow a love of luxury and a skill in working cooperatively with others. Venus also emphasizes the importance of money in your life and shows that you are willing to work hard to acquire it. A challenge may be to balance your desire to work and to be tough, structured, and dutiful with your desire for pleasure, love, and spontaneity.

When you discipline your enormous potential and channel any possible impatience into a creative endeavor, you eventually achieve results in your overall struggle with life's challenges. By learning to stay positive and count your blessings, you realize that gratitude is a special quality that can assist you in your progress and allow your energy to become more free-flowing.

After the age of eleven, when your progressed Sun moves into Cancer, issues around emotional security, home, and family start to play a more important part in your life. This influence continues until the age of forty-one, when your progressed Sun moves into Leo and you enter a thirty-year period of growing confidence, authority, strength, and increased self-expression. When you reach the age of seventy-one, your progressed Sun moves into Virgo, and you develop a more analytical, perfectionist, and pragmatic approach to life.

FIXED STARS

Bellatrix, also called the Female Warrior; Capella, also called Little She-Goat and Amalthea

PRIMARY STAR

Star's name: Capella, also called Little She-Goat and Amalthea

Degree position: 20°52'–21°48' Gemini between the years 1930 and 2000

Magnitude: 1

Strength: ★★★★★★★★★

Orb: 2°30'

Constellation: Alpha Aurigae

Applicable days: June 9, 10, 11, 12, 13, 14

Star qualities: Mercury/Mars

Description: a large bright white star located on the body of the Goat in the arms of Auriga

PRIMARY STAR'S INFLUENCE

Capella grants an energetic nature, inquisitiveness, and a love of learning. This star encourages an interest in research and new inventions. It imparts honor and prominent positions of trust. You may also acquire wealth and success.

Linked to your Sun's degree, this star indicates a tendency to be verbose and suggests that you avoid being too talkative. Capella advises learning to listen to others in order to avoid misunderstandings.

• *Positive:* trustworthy, loyalty, inquisitive mind, comprehensive knowledge

Your Secret Self

Your exterior does not reveal the inner sensitive you. A wealth of feelings indicates a strong need for unconditional love and affection. When you can receive this kind of devotion, you feel you can trust life to take care of you. A need for deep emotional security usually suggests that fear and anxieties may arise if you feel abandoned or unloved, and trust may be a key to your happiness. By holding on to fear or frustration, you may be blocking the one thing you really need.

Often the demonstration of affection can be very important to you. At times you can be all-or-nothing, and although you are forgiving and loving, once you decide you have had enough there is no turning back. Avoid a temptation to be what others expect of you rather than to be true to yourself. When you do open your heart fully, while being detached enough not to care about the results, you can be extremely generous and draw toward you everything you need and desire.

Work & Vocation

Ambition, a good business sense, and the ability to take the lead are likely to help you in your climb to success. Since you are able to combine business with pleasure and can be an excellent conversationalist, you may excel as a diplomat or in public relations. Equally, the worlds of sales, commerce, or communications can be excellent outlets for your talents. Generally, you are likely to fare better in occupations that contain variety and change, as you do not like routine and may become bored. Education, journalism, or the service industries are likely to be areas that can be particularly rewarding for you, or your natural dramatic flair may find expression in the world of entertainment. A talent for dealing with people is likely to be one of your best assets.

Famous people who share your birthday include singer/actress Judy Garland, tycoon Robert Maxwell, musician Howlin' Wolf, and Prince Phillip, the Duke of Edinburgh.

Numerology

Like those with a number 1 birthday, you usually strive toward great endeavors to accomplish and achieve. Nevertheless, you may have to overcome some obstacles before you achieve your goals. Energetic and original, you stand by your own beliefs even when they differ from others'. Your ability to be a self-starter with a pioneering spirit encourages you to travel far afield or strike out on your own. You may also learn that the world does not revolve around you, and you should guard against selfishness and being dictatorial. Success and accomplishment are important to all number 10 birthdays, and frequently you find the way to the top of your profession. The subinfluence of the number 6 month indicates that you possess strong convictions. Observant and with an eye for detail, you like to gather useful information and utilize it in a practical way. If mentally preoccupied, you appear absentminded or restless. Never satisfied with what you know, you may benefit greatly from studies into metaphysics, spirituality, and philosophy. By being flexible and adaptable, you can smooth any misunderstandings.

• *Positive:* leadership, creative, progressive, forceful, optimistic, strong convictions, competitive, independent, gregarious

• *Negative:* overbearing, jealous, egotistical, too proud, antagonistic, selfish, weak, vacillating, impatient

Love & Relationships

With charm, sensitivity, and appreciation for beauty and art, you have a love for the luxuries of life. Often attracted to glamorous people with charismatic personalities, you charm others with your optimism and generosity. Willing to make sacrifices for love, you may nevertheless need to guard against playing the martyr. Although you are usually seeking serious relationships, developing a more realistic attitude to love may minimize your disappointments. You usually work hard to bring stability into a relationship; however, do not neglect your own strong need for creative self-expression. This may include artistic pursuits, as you enjoy music and drama.

YOUR SPECIAL SOMEONE

You might find a partner who will understand your sensitivity and need for love among those born on the following dates.

Love & friendship: Jan. 4, 8, 18, 19, 23, Feb. 2, 6, 16, 17, 21, Mar. 4, 14, 15, 19, 28, 30, Apr. 2, 12, 13, 17, 26, 28, 30, May 10, 11, 15, 24, 26, 28, June 8, 9, 13, 22, 24, 26, July 6, 7, 11, 20, 22, 24, 30, Aug. 4, 5, 9, 18, 20, 22, 28, Sept. 2, 3, 7, 16, 18, 20, 26, Oct. 1, 5, 14, 16, 18, 24, Nov. 3, 12, 14, 16, 22, Dec. 1, 10, 12, 14, 20

Beneficial: Jan. 5, 16, 27, Feb. 3, 14, 25, Mar. 1, 12, 23, Apr. 10, 21, May 8, 19, June 6, 17, July 4, 15, Aug. 2, 13, Sept. 11, Oct. 9, 30, Nov. 7, 28, Dec. 5, 26, 30

Fatal attractions: Jan. 17, Feb. 15, Mar. 13, Apr. 11, May 9, June 7, July 5, Aug. 3, Sept. 1, Dec. 10, 11, 12, 13

Challenging: Jan. 1, 10, 15, Feb. 8, 13, Mar. 6, 11, Apr. 4, 9, May 2, 7, June 5, July 3, 29, Aug. 1, 27, Sept. 25, Oct. 23, Nov. 21, Dec. 19, 29

Soul mates: Aug. 30, Sept. 28, Oct. 26, Nov. 24, Dec. 22

June 11

Ⅱ Your birthdate indicates that idealism and practicality play equal parts in your life story. With your good judgment and reasoning powers, you present an astute yet sensitive front to the world. Possessing a strong desire for honesty, you can manage to be subtle yet direct, and you have discerning common sense.

The influence of Aquarius, your decanate ruler, accents your independence and versatility. This also suggests that you are friendly, outgoing, and people-orientated. Nevertheless, you may also have a more unusual or eccentric side to your nature. Being interested in many different subjects, your excellent mind suggests an original approach and possibly that you are even an inspired thinker. Quickly getting to the heart of a matter, you usually enjoy learning and can be farsighted. You may have to overcome a tendency to be irritable, which can spoil your charms and alienate you from others.

Although charismatic and attractive to many different types of people, you may have to avoid drifting or getting too caught up in other people's dramas. Inspired by many ideas, once you have set a definite goal you can be determined and organized, with a strong sense of purpose. Having the added advantage of natural intuition can be a tremendous benefit, as you are likely to have a sixth sense about people and situations.

After the age of ten, when your progressed Sun moves into Cancer, issues around emotional security, home, and family start to play a more important part in your life. This influence continues until the age of forty, when your progressed Sun moves into Leo. This starts a thirty-year period of confidence, increased self-expression, and increased sociability. When you reach the age of seventy, your progressed Sun moves into Virgo, and you will want to be more analytical, practical, and reflective.

FIXED STARS

Capella, also called Little She-Goat and Amalthea; Bellatrix, also called the Female Warrior; Phact; El Nath

PRIMARY STAR

Star's name: Capella, also called Little She-Goat and Amalthea
Degree position: 20°52'–21°48' Gemini between the years 1930 and 2000
Magnitude: 1
Strength: ★★★★★★★★
Orb: 2°30'
Constellation: Alpha Aurigae
Applicable days: June 9, 10, 11, 12, 13, 14
Star qualities: Mercury/Mars
Description: a large bright white star located on the body of the Goat in the arms of Auriga

PRIMARY STAR'S INFLUENCE

Capella grants an energetic nature, inquisitiveness, and a love of learning. This star encourages an interest in research and new inventions. It imparts honor and prominent positions of trust. You may also acquire wealth and success.

Linked to your Sun's degree, this star indicates a tendency to be verbose and suggests that you avoid being too talkative. Capella advises learning to listen to others in order to avoid misunderstandings.

• *Positive:* trustworthy, loyalty, inquisitive mind, comprehensive knowledge

Your Secret Self

Sensitive and imaginative, you have a mind rich with ideas but might have to avoid a tendency to worry. It is important to build up your confidence, which may be strengthened by your ability to express yourself in all areas in your life, but particularly through music, art, or the written word. Your home is likely to be your safe haven, where you can find peace or security. Although you want harmony, be careful not to compromise too much of yourself in the process

An inner challenge may be an unconscious discontent that springs from frustration or disappointment with your situation or with others. By facing these uncertainties and dealing with them, you are able to make decisions that help you stay detached and positive. Once released of undue worries, you are free to reveal your creative spirit and project the joy of life.

Work & Vocation

Being bright and versatile and possessing excellent communication skills, you are able to adapt to any career opportunity. It may just be necessary to avoid scattering your forces, as you are likely to be multitalented. When interested in a project or cause, however, you are likely to work extremely hard. This will assist you in the worlds of business or social work, or in politics. You may also be drawn to science, law, the civil service, or the clergy. Alternatively, your natural ability to deal with people can aid you in a career in sales or the service industries. Being good with your hands, you may choose to use this skill creatively or practically. By developing your innate artistic talents and expressing your need for inspiration, you may be drawn to film, painting, or music.

Famous people who share your birthday include actor Gene Wilder, marine explorer Jacques Cousteau, composer Richard Strauss, writer Ben Jonson, sportsman Joe Montana, and painter John Constable.

Numerology

The special vibration of the master number 11 birthday suggests that idealism, inspiration, and innovation are highly important to you. A blend of humility and confidence challenges you to work toward self-mastery both materially and spiritually. Through experience you learn how to deal with both sides of your nature and develop a less extremist attitude by trusting your own feelings. Usually you are highly charged and enjoy vitality, but must avoid becoming overly anxious or impractical. The subinfluence of the number 6 month indicates that you are highly intuitive but need to focus on your goals. Although ambitious, you may need to develop a more realistic perspective in order to make your dreams come true. Take your time to build strong foundations. Thoughtful and understanding, you can be an inspiration to others. However, guard against being moody, overly sensitive, or irritable. To turn your ideals into tangible reality, stay with the tried and tested until you know of a better way.

• *Positive:* balanced, focused, objective, enthusiastic, inspirational, spiritual, idealistic, intuitive, intelligent, outgoing, inventive, artistic, service, healing ability, humanitarian, psychic

• *Negative:* superiority complex, dishonest, aimless, overemotional, easily hurt, highly strung, selfish, lack of clarity, dominating

Love & Relationships

Charismatic and charming, you have the power to attract people from all walks of life. With this ability often comes the necessity to exercise a certain amount of discrimination, as you are likely to draw toward you people who will either lean on you or distract you from your purpose. Often you have high expectations from relationships, and if these are not met, you become restless and dissatisfied with yourself and others. A need to be appreciated suggests that you are willing to make sacrifices for the ones you love, yet want a great deal of love and acknowledgment for your efforts. You are generally very fortunate in your dealings with people.

YOUR SPECIAL SOMEONE

You may find longer-lasting relationships and stability with those born on the following dates.

Love & friendship: Jan. 5, 9, 18, 19, Feb. 3, 7, 16, 17, Mar. 1, 5, 14, 15, 31, Apr. 3, 12, 13, 29, May 1, 10, 11, 27, 29, June 8, 9, 25, 27, July 6, 7, 23, 25, 31, Aug. 4, 5, 21, 23, 29, Sept. 2, 3, 19, 21, 27, 30, Oct. 1, 17, 19, 25, 28, Dec. 13, 15, 21, 24

Beneficial: Jan. 1, 6, 17, Feb. 4, 15, Mar. 2, 13, Apr. 11, May 9, June 7, July 5, Aug. 3, Sept. 1, Oct. 31, Nov. 29, Dec. 27

Fatal attractions: Dec. 11, 12, 13, 14

Challenging: Jan. 2, 16, Feb. 14, Mar. 12, Apr. 10, May 8, June 6, July 4, Aug. 2, Dec. 30

Soul mates: Jan. 11, 31, Feb. 9, 29, Mar. 7, 27, Apr. 5, 25, May 3, 23, June 1, 21, July 19, Aug. 17, Sept. 15, Oct. 13, Nov. 11, Dec. 9

June 12

FIXED STARS

Capella, also called Little She-Goat and Amalthea; Bellatrix, also called the Female Warrior; Phact; Mintaka, also called Cingula Orionis; El Nath; Alnilam, also called Al Nitham or the String of Pearls

PRIMARY STAR

Star's name: Capella, also called Little She-Goat and Amalthea

Degree position: 20°52'–21°48' Gemini between the years 1930 and 2000

Magnitude: 1

Strength: ★★★★★★★★★

Orb: 2°30

Constellation: Alpha Aurigae

Applicable days: June 9, 10, 11, 12, 13, 14

Star qualities: Mercury/Mars

Description: a large bright white star located on the body of the Goat in the arms of Auriga

PRIMARY STAR'S INFLUENCE

Capella grants an energetic nature, inquisitiveness, and a love of learning. This star encourages an interest in research and new inventions. It imparts honor and prominent positions of trust. You may also require wealth and success.

Linked to your Sun's degree, this star indicates a tendency to be verbose and suggests that you avoid being too talkative. Capella advises learning to listen to others in order to avoid misunderstandings.

• *Positive:* trustworthy, loyalty, inquisitive mind, comprehensive knowledge

Ⅱ The quick and instinctive qualities suggested by your birthdate blend well with your visionary and versatile personality. You are likely to be constantly on the move, as your inner restlessness has you seeking out new and exciting avenues to explore. Because you can pick up on situations extremely quickly, you may become bored easily and dislike routine. Usually you are drawn to people of keen intelligence who can provide you with mental stimulation. Being friendly and socially inclined, you are generally aware of the image you present to the public and are likely to be popular.

Sensitive, with a powerful imagination, you need to stay focused and have a positive goal. If you become impatient, you are prone to give up too easily, so you may need to develop perseverance in order to attain your great potential.

With the influence of Aquarius, your decanate ruler, you are likely to enjoy debating, and may be drawn to interests of a more unusual nature. This also suggests that although you have a shrewd and resourceful mind, you may encounter a conflict between your idealism and the mundane. This birthdate also implies that travel may strongly influence your life, with the possibility of your working or living in a foreign country.

After the age of nine, when your progressed Sun enters Cancer, you are likely to be more focused on issues of home and family. This turning point brings a growing need for love, understanding, and emotional security. From the age of thirty-nine, when your progressed Sun enters Leo, you are likely to receive a strong boost of self-confidence and a greater recognition of your personal capabilities. When you reach the age of sixty-nine, your progressed Sun moves into Virgo, and you will want to refine your life and be more analytical, practical, and reflective.

Your Secret Self

An uncertainty about finances may cause you unnecessary worry or frustration. Due to an innate impatience, you may need to be careful in money matters not to take the path of expediency rather than the slower route of building for the future. A possible extravagant streak may not help you in this cause. Once you decide to make your vision a reality, however, you can be extremely single-minded and determined.

Your dynamic personality suggests that you need to be purposeful and focused. This will also help you release anxieties or doubts regarding your confidence or self-esteem. You are able to have a highly creative approach to life, which involves rising above any current quandaries to take a larger and more inclusive viewpoint. Although you may have to make sacrifices for others, in the long run this will aid in the development of your finer potentials of compassion and humanitarianism.

Work & Vocation

Your quick mind and ease with communication could particularly benefit you in journalism, customer service, or sales. Although hardworking and ambitious, your love of variety points to a career that involves fast changes and does not entail routine. Occupations such as travel and tourism may suit your adventurous spirit; alternatively, with your love of action, careers involving sport or leisure can be excellent outlets for your energy and drive. You possess a strong sense of vision and structure, which may draw you to photography, graphics, or mathematics, as well as assisting you to become a practical visionary in the business world. Creative expression may be found through drama and music, or if in the healing world, you may utilize your sensitivity by working very intuitively.

Famous people who share your birthday include banker David Rockefeller, diary writer Anne Frank, former U.S. president George Bush, painter Egon Schiele, and musician Chick Corea.

Numerology

People with a number 12 birthday are usually intuitive and friendly. Since you want to establish true individuality, you possess good reasoning and innovative power. Naturally understanding and sensitive, you also know how to use tact and cooperative methods to achieve your aims and objectives. When you achieve the balance between your need for self-expression and the natural inclination to be supportive of others, you can find emotional satisfaction and personal fulfillment. You may nevertheless need to find the courage to stand on your own two feet and develop self-confidence, or learn not to get easily discouraged by other people. The subinfluence of the number 6 month indicates that you need to express your feelings clearly and precisely. To avoid misunderstandings, let others know how you feel and what you are thinking. Keeping an open mind and seeing the bigger plan help you stay optimistic and detached. With a humanitarian attitude and concern for others, you are able to show your true compassion. Avoid worry and indecision by paying attention to what others say without compromising your own beliefs.

- *Positive:* creative, attractive, initiative, disciplinarian, promoting yourself or others
- *Negative:* eccentric, uncooperative, overly sensitive, lack of self-esteem

YOUR SPECIAL SOMEONE

For that someone special, you might want to look among those born on the following dates.

Love & friendship: Jan. 6, 10, 20, 29, Feb. 4, 8, 18, 27, Mar. 2, 6, 16, 25, 28, 30, Apr. 4, 14, 23, 26, 28, 30, May 2, 12, 21, 24, 26, 28, 30, June 10, 19, 22, 24, 26, 28, July 8, 17, 20, 22, 24, 26, Aug. 6, 15, 18, 20, 22, 24, Sept. 4, 13, 16, 18, 20, 22, Oct. 2, 11, 14, 16, 18, 20, Nov. 9, 12, 14, 16, 18, Dec. 7, 10, 12, 14, 16

Beneficial: Jan. 7, 13, 18, 28, Feb. 5, 11, 16, 26, Mar. 3, 9, 14, 24, Apr. 1, 7, 12, 22, May 5, 10, 20, June 3, 8, 18, July 1, 6, 16, Aug. 4, 14, Sept. 2, 12, 30, Oct. 10, 28, Nov. 8, 26, 30, Dec. 6, 24, 28

Fatal attractions: Jan. 25, Feb. 23, Mar. 21, Apr. 19, May 17, June 15, July 13, Aug. 11, Sept. 9, Oct. 7, Nov. 5, Dec. 3, 11, 12, 13, 14

Challenging: Jan. 3, 17, Feb. 1, 15, Mar. 13, Apr. 11, May 9, 30, June 7, 28, July 5, 26, 29, Aug. 3, 24, 27, Sept. 1, 22, 25, Oct. 20, 23, Nov. 18, 21, Dec. 16, 19

Soul mates: Jan. 18, Feb. 16, Mar. 14, Apr. 12, May 10, 29, June 8, 27, July 6, 25, Aug. 4, 23, Sept. 2, 21, Oct. 19, Nov. 17, Dec. 15

Love & Relationships

Intelligent and restless, you are often attracted to people who are original and clever. Friendships are important to you, and socializing or mixing with different types of people suggests that you are often liberal and young at heart. There is a natural entertainer in your makeup, which comes out in the company of those you love. Through education and learning you come to meet people with whom you share common interests. Although you like to have a good time, taking a more mature attitude assures peace and harmony in relationships.

June 13

♊ The bright and practical awareness possessed by those of this birthdate indicates that you are a sociable idealist with a strong sense of values. Since you are likely to be sensible, you may be engaged in building a solid foundation for yourself. There may be a strong emphasis on work in your life, and through diligent and concerted efforts you often establish a secure and prosperous position.

With the added influence of your decanate ruler, Aquarius, you have a wonderfully inventive mind that is able to quickly judge character in others. Since this also suggests that you are articulate, you may need to find avenues for your superior communication skills. Just be careful of becoming too rigid or obstinate in your outlook and spoiling your charms.

When you perform a task, you like to do it well and have a sense of pride in your work. Generally being very loyal, you tend to take your responsibilities seriously, but can also turn from soberness to being very genial and friendly. You are idealistic, and you may feel that your sensitivity is not wasted when you are able to use it to be of help to others. Since you can also be very businesslike, this powerful combination implies that you can be a compassionate pragmatist.

After the age of eight, when your progressed Sun moves into Cancer, you are likely to become more sensitive and security-conscious, with a strong accent on your home life. When the progressed Sun moves into Leo as you reach the age of thirty-eight, there is a strong need for self-expression and assertiveness, encouraging you to become more sociable, bold, and authoritative. Another turning point occurs around the time you reach the age of sixty-eight, when your progressed Sun moves into Virgo and you develop a more analytical, perfectionist, and pragmatic approach to life.

FIXED STARS

Bellatrix, also called the Female Warrior; Phact; Mintaka, also called Cingula Orionis; El Nath; Eusis; Alnilam, also called Al Nitham or the String of Pearls

PRIMARY STAR

Star's name: Capella, also called Little She-Goat and Amalthea

Degree position: 20°52'–21°48' Gemini between the years 1930 and 2000

Magnitude: 1

Strength: ★★★★★★★★

Orb: 2°30'

Constellation: Alpha Aurigae

Applicable days: June 9, 10, 11, 12, 13, 14

Star qualities: Mercury/Mars

Description: a large bright white star located on the body of the Goat in the arms of Auriga

PRIMARY STAR'S INFLUENCE

Capella grants an energetic nature, inquisitiveness, and a love of learning. This star encourages an interest in research and new inventions. It imparts honor and prominent positions of trust. You may also acquire wealth and success.

Linked to your Sun's degree, this star indicates a tendency to be verbose and suggests that you avoid being too talkative. Capella advises learning to listen to others in order to avoid misunderstandings.

• *Positive:* trustworthy, loyalty, inquisitive mind, comprehensive knowledge

Your Secret Self

An inner need for variety and change may not be that obvious on the outside. This adventurous part of your nature may need outlets for the exploration of new and exciting things. As you may sometimes repress your emotions, this same desire could be transferred into restlessness and impatience or could wear away your confidence. In order to compensate for this, you may find yourself experiencing a dissatisfaction with your lot and escaping from this through drink, drugs, TV, or fantasy.

Sympathetic and understanding, you can often sense what others are feeling. Your high ideals bring a desire for love and affection that may find creative outlets through the arts, spirituality, or healing. Through applying this more sensitive awareness to your everyday life, you may find that inspiration comes from positive thinking. However, you may have to protect your delicate nervous system by learning to stay calm and not allowing outside influences to overwhelm you.

Work & Vocation

Practical yet friendly, you may attract many fortunate work opportunities. With your ability to communicate well, careers such as law or education are indicated. With your desire for order and your keen intelligence, you are often drawn to commerce or industry, where you can use your organizational skills to excel. Employers are likely to appreciate your ability to work hard and be dependable and responsible. People of this birthday are often good with their hands and may utilize their skill either creatively or practically. Alternatively, a keen insight into human nature combined with a creative talent may find an outlet in writing, journalism, or the acting profession.

Famous people who share your birthday include writer W. B. Yeats, tennis player Don Budge, actors Basil Rathbone and Malcolm McDowell, and comedian Tim Allen.

Numerology

Emotional sensitivity, enthusiasm, and inspiration are often identified with the number 13 birthday. Numerically, you are associated with ambition and hard work, and can accomplish much through creative self-expression. You may need to develop or cultivate a pragmatic outlook if you want to turn your creative talents into tangible products. Your original and innovative approach inspires new and exciting ideas, which frequently result in work that impresses others. With a number 13 birthday, you are earnest, romantic, charming, and fun-loving, and with dedication can achieve prosperity. The subinfluence of the number 6 month indicates that you are ambitious, resilient, and resourceful, with good reasoning power. Collaborating with others or working in group efforts helps you achieve success. If you lack confidence, you can become dependent on others. Decisive, you like to resolve your problems in your own way. A lack of satisfaction suggests that you can be restless and discontented, but it also urges you to achieve more and move forward.

• *Positive:* ambitious, creative, freedom-loving, self-expressive, initiative
• *Negative:* impulsive, indecisive, bossy, unemotional, rebellious, egotistical

Love & Relationships

Idealistic, with powerful emotions, you are often generous and kind. In your relationships, you can be subject to moods or become dissatisfied or restless. Conversely, you can be charming and gregarious, with a love of socializing, and often have numerous friends and admirers. Nevertheless, beware of being taken advantage of by others or being deceitful. Attracted to powerful people with big plans and strong ambitions, you can benefit from the assistance of influential people.

YOUR SPECIAL SOMEONE

Among people born on the following dates you may find someone with whom you can share your ideals more easily.

Love & friendship: Jan. 7, 11, 22, Feb. 5, 9, 20, Mar. 3, 7, 18, 31, Apr. 1, 5, 16, 29, May 3, 14, 27, 29, June 1, 12, 25, 27, July 10, 23, 25, Aug. 8, 21, 23, 31, Sept. 6, 19, 21, 29, Oct. 4, 17, 19, 27, 30, Nov. 2, 15, 17, 25, 28, Dec. 13, 15, 23, 26

Beneficial: Jan. 8, 14, 19, Feb. 6, 12, 17, Mar. 4, 10, 15, Apr. 2, 8, 13, May 6, 11, June 4, 9, July 2, 7, Aug. 5, Sept. 3, Oct. 1, 29, Nov. 27, Dec. 25, 29

Fatal attractions: Dec. 13, 14, 15

Challenging: Jan. 9, 18, 20, Feb. 7, 16, 18, Mar. 5, 14, 16, Apr. 3, 12, 14, May 1, 10, 12, June 8, 10, July 6, 8, 29, Aug. 4, 6, 27, Sept. 2, 4, 25, Oct. 2, 23, Nov. 21, Dec. 19

Soul mates: Jan. 9, Feb. 7, Mar. 5, Apr. 3, May 1, Oct. 30, Nov. 28, Dec. 26

June 14

Ⅱ This birthdate reveals you to be a congenial and smart communicator with an original approach to life. Although you usually appear bright and friendly, you also have a more serious side that can be positively used for problem solving. Your strong need for self-expression may manifest itself socially or lead to writing or the arts.

With the influence of the third decanate of Gemini, you have an objective and inventive mind that can alternate between flashes of genius and moments of rebelliousness. Luckily, your thinking can be ahead of its time, although sometimes at odds with society. Your quick wit and creative spark can make you very attractive to people, but you may have to beware of a tendency to worry and basic indecisiveness that can subdue your joie de vivre.

As you may be interested in many different and sometimes unusual subjects, it is important not to scatter your energies. You are generally quite forthright in your opinions but on occasion may have to guard against becoming skeptical and uncommunicative. At some point you may develop an interest in philosophical or more spiritual subjects, and since you also possess sharp critical skills, you may be able to turn these toward helping other people rather than being bossy and undermining them. Your versatile personality combined with your creative spark is capable of greatly inspiring others and bringing you lasting and rewarding achievement.

As your progressed Sun moves into Cancer when you are around age seven, security or home issues start to have more importance in your life. This also highlights your emotional needs and security and the people who affect this the most. This continues until around the age of thirty-seven, when your progressed Sun enters Leo, increasing your strength, confidence, and talents. As you reach the age of sixty-seven, your progressed Sun moves into Virgo, and you develop a more analytical, perfectionist, and pragmatic approach to life.

FIXED STARS

Capella, also called Little She-Goat and Amalthea; Phact; Mintaka, also called Cingula Orionis; El Nath; Alnilam, also called Al Nitham or The String of Pearls; Al Hecka

PRIMARY STAR

Star's name: Capella, also called Little She-Goat and Amalthea
Degree position: 20°52'–21°48' Gemini between the years 1930 and 2000
Magnitude: 1
Strength: ★★★★★★★★★
Orb: 2°30'
Constellation: Alpha Aurigae
Applicable days: June 9, 10, 11, 12, 13, 14
Star qualities: Mercury/Mars
Description: a large bright white star located on the body of the Goat in the arms of Auriga

PRIMARY STAR'S INFLUENCE

Capella grants an energetic nature, inquisitiveness, and a love of learning. This star encourages an interest in research and new inventions. It imparts honor and prominent positions of trust. You may also acquire wealth and success.

Linked to your Sun's degree, this star indicates a tendency to be verbose and suggests that you avoid being too talkative. Capella advises learning to listen to others in order to avoid misunderstandings.

• *Positive:* trustworthy, loyalty, inquisitive mind, comprehensive knowledge

Your Secret Self

Reliable and conscientious, you are always available with help and advice, offering your expertise and know-how. You are willing to work very hard and make considerable sacrifices for the people or causes that are close to your heart. Just be careful that this does not become too hard to bear and cause you to become down or depressed. It is important to develop your highly intuitive powers and learn to trust your first instincts.

Your practical side, on the other hand, shows you to be a powerful opponent and a good strategist. Clever and articulate, you can communicate your ideas with compassion and sincerity. This reaching out enables you to move and grow beyond your present capabilities. If you suffer indecision, it may be easy for you to rest on your laurels and keep to the easy path. Usually you know how to enjoy life and find constant amusement in reaching new targets for yourself. Home and a secure base are particularly important for you, as you need harmony and inner peace.

Work & Vocation

Intelligent and articulate, you may need change and variety to keep you constantly inspired. Even if you stay within the same career, you may change or improve the way you operate. With your original ideas and individual approach to life, you are likely to be attracted to writing or careers involving communication. Possessing a shrewd business sense, you are often successful in commerce, or you may use your sharp mind for research and problem solving. Your competitive streak may attract you to the world of sport, or a strong desire for self-expression can bring you success in music or the theater. Although you are attracted to sales and other careers having to do with people, you are also capable of deep, methodical thought and may have an interest in philosophy.

Famous people who share your birthday include revolutionary Che Guevara, writer Harriet Beecher Stowe, tennis player Steffi Graf, singer Boy George, and tycoon Donald Trump.

Numerology

Intellectual potential, pragmatism, and determination are some of the qualities of the number 14 birthday. Indeed, with a number 14 birthday, you frequently put your work first and judge yourself and others upon the basis of career achievements. Although you need stability, the restlessness indicated by the number 14 urges you to forge ahead or take on new challenges in a constant attempt to improve your lot. This innate restlessness and constant lack of satisfaction may also inspire you to make a great many changes in your life, especially if you are not happy with your working conditions or financial status. With your perceptive mind, you respond quickly to problems and enjoy solving them. The subinfluence of the number 6 month indicates that you benefit from trusting your intuition and developing a philosophical attitude to life. Although your versatility and strong instincts override your stubborn tendencies, use your diplomatic skills to avoid becoming anxious or insecure. A need to be recognized for your contributions and efforts suggests that you should not be shy in claiming what is rightfully yours.

• *Positive:* decisive actions, hardworking, lucky, creative, pragmatic, imaginative, industrious
• *Negative:* overly cautious or overly impulsive, unstable, thoughtless, stubborn

Love & Relationships

Usually loving and spontaneous, you are willing to do your utmost for the ones you love. There is, however, also a side to your nature that may come across as being cold or indifferent. As you are more sensitive than you appear, it is vital that you have space for yourself to gather your strength. It might be difficult for anyone to live up to your high expectations for an ideal love. Loyal and caring, however, you seek stability and will remain devoted to your chosen partner.

YOUR SPECIAL SOMEONE

You might find emotional fulfillment and that special someone among those born on the following days.

Love & friendship: Jan. 8, 22, 26, Feb. 6, 20, 24, Mar. 4, 18, 22, Apr. 2, 16, 20, 30, May 14, 18, 28, 30, June 12, 16, 26, 28, July 10, 14, 24, 26, Aug. 8, 12, 22, 24, Sept. 6, 10, 20, 22, 30, Oct. 4, 8, 18, 20, 28, Nov. 2, 6, 16, 18, 26, Dec. 4, 14, 16, 24

Beneficial: Jan. 9, 20, Feb. 7, 18, Mar. 5, 16, 29, Apr. 3, 14, 27, May 1, 12, 25, June 10, 23, July 8, 21, Aug. 6, 19, Sept. 4, 17, Oct. 2, 15, 30, Nov. 13, 28, Dec. 11, 26, 30

Fatal attractions: Jan. 27, Feb. 25, Mar. 23, Apr. 21, May 19, June 17, July 15, Aug. 13, Sept. 11, Oct. 9, Nov. 7, Dec. 5, 14, 15, 16

Challenging: Jan. 2, 10, 19, Feb. 8, 17, Mar. 6, 15, Apr. 4, 13, May 2, 11, June 9, July 7, 30, Aug. 5, 28, Sept. 3, 26, Oct. 1, 24, Nov. 22, Dec. 20, 30

Soul mates: Jan. 15, Feb. 13, Mar. 11, Apr. 9, May 7, June 5, July 3, Aug. 1, Oct. 29, Nov. 27, Dec. 25

June 15

Ⅱ Your birthday suggests that you are a friendly and active Gemini with a quick and perceptive mind. Although independent, you find that your life is oriented to social interaction and developing your communication skills through people-related experiences. Although you are fascinated with original and unusual people, you learn to mix with people from all walks of life. Since you can be very determined, you can be a powerful force when directed toward a goal.

The influence of Uranus from the third decanate of Gemini ensures that your ideas are very original and that you have a good ability to assess people. It also points to a shrewd and creative mentality that may find expression through art, music, or drama, but which can also be drawn toward debating on controversial subjects or writing. One side of your nature is often tough, assertive, and almost dominating, while the other is sensitive, imaginative, and giving. Since they are both a part of you, it is vital to keep a balance. Wanting honesty and directness, you do not feel happy if monetary issues clash with your model for a perfect world. Although you can be very generous with those you love, you may have an unfounded fear of not having enough money. Nevertheless, due to your natural strategic abilities you will always have material protection.

After the age of six, when your progressed Sun moves into Cancer, you are likely to be more aware of all your emotional relationships, particularly with your family. There is more of a need for security and home ties, which is likely to continue until your progressed Sun moves into Leo when you are around age thirty-six. This is a turning point, when there is more of a focus on your personal self-expression and confidence, which may encourage you to use your leadership skills in a more assertive or powerful way. When you are age sixty-six, your progressed Sun moves into Virgo, and you will want to become more analytical, practical, and reflective.

Fixed Stars

Mintaka, also called Cingula Orionis; El Nath; Alnilam, also called Al Nitham or the String of Pearls; Al Hecka

PRIMARY STAR

Star's name: Mintaka, also called Cingula Orionis

Degree position: 21°30'–22°16' Gemini between the years 1930 and 2000

Magnitude: 2.5–3

Strength: ★★★★★★★

Orb: 1°40'

Constellation: Delta Orion

Applicable days: June 12, 13, 14, 15

Star qualities: Mercury/Saturn/Jupiter

Description: A brilliant white and pale violet variable binary star located in the belt of Orion alongside the star Alnilam

PRIMARY STAR'S INFLUENCE

This star imparts good fortune, luck, and dignity. Thinking positively, you can make the best of any situation. Mintaka bestows courage, an industrious nature, and good timing. Executive and managerial capabilities and lasting happiness are also indicated by this star.

Linked to your Sun's degree, this star offers a piercing and sharp mind, good judgment, and memory. You are probably discreet, with a cautious nature, and with patience can bring changes for the better. You have a good sense of timing and a natural talent for turning situations to your advantage. This star gives a strong preference for education.

Your Secret Self

A strong inner need for material security, power, and prestige blends peculiarly with a high idealism. Your ambition and desire for peace and contentment combine well to ensure that when you do succeed, you often are more than willing to give to others from the goodness of your heart. You can also have aspirations for universal understanding. Be alert for a strange form of inertia or anxiety that may stem from your wish to keep the peace.

Always willing to share your knowledge with others, you can make great contributions to partnerships or groups. You possess a strong, constructive inner power that can be turned to influence others, so it is important that you realize the significance of genuine accomplishment rather than just material success. If you believe in a cause, you will give it your full support and use your persuasive ways to convince others.

Work & Vocation

With your quick mind and ability to communicate, you usually fare well in people-related careers. Having a talent for dealing with others on a personal level, you may be particularly drawn to occupations such as public relations or being an agent. Your enthusiasm and ability to sell anything if you really believe in it, whether an idea or a product, can greatly aid you in sales, promotion, or negotiation. With your persuasive and articulate speech, you may be drawn to a career in law or lecturing. People of this birthday often become advisors, whether in business or in counseling. Alternatively, your need for recognition may find expression through drama, art, or music. Your persevering attitude eventually brings you the success you need.

Famous people who share your birthday include Norwegian composer Edvard Grieg, country singer Waylon Jennings, actor Jim Belushi, and actresses Courtney Cox and Helen Hunt.

Numerology

Versatility, enthusiasm, and restlessness are suggested by the number 15 birthday. Your greatest assets are your strong instincts and the ability to learn quickly through combining theory and practice. Often you utilize your intuitive powers and are quick at recognizing opportunities when they arise. With a number 15 birthday, you possess a talent for attracting money or receiving help and support from others. Carefree and resolute, you welcome the unexpected and like to take a gamble. The subinfluence of the number 6 month indicates that you need to balance your own needs and wishes with your obligations to others. Practical and able, you can show your interest without appearing overly enthusiastic. You nevertheless want to be recognized for your talents or efforts and can be ambitious and hardworking. Overcome a sense of limitation by finding ways to express your creativity or feelings more freely. Although you are naturally adventurous, you need to find a real base or a home that you can call your own.

• *Positive:* willing, generous, responsible, kind, cooperative, appreciative, creative ideas

• *Negative:* restless, irresponsible, self-centered, fear of change, loss of faith, worry, indecision, materialistic

YOUR SPECIAL SOMEONE

For security, mental stimulation, and love you might want to begin looking for those born among the following dates.

Love & friendship: Jan. 3, 19, 23, Feb. 11, 21, Mar. 9, 19, 28, 31, Apr. 7, 17, 26, 29, May 5, 15, 24, 27, 29, 31, June 3, 13, 22, 25, 27, 29, July 1, 11, 20, 23, 25, 27, 29, Aug. 9, 18, 21, 23, 25, 27, Sept. 7, 16, 19, 21, 23, 25, Oct. 1, 5, 14, 17, 19, 21, 23, Nov. 3, 12, 15, 17, 19, 21, Dec. 1, 10, 13, 15, 17, 19

Beneficial: Jan. 3, 4, 10, 21, Feb. 1, 2, 8, 19, Mar. 6, 17, 30, Apr. 4, 15, 28, May 2, 13, 26, June 11, 24, July 9, 22, Aug. 7, 20, Sept. 5, 18, Oct. 3, 16, 31, Nov. 1, 14, 29, Dec. 12, 27

Fatal attractions: Jan. 22, 28, Feb. 20, 26, Mar. 18, 24, Apr. 16, 22, May 14, 20, June 12, 18, July 10, 16, Aug. 8, 14, Sept. 6, 12, Oct. 4, 10, Nov. 2, 8, Dec. 6, 14, 15, 16, 17

Challenging: Jan. 11, 20, Feb. 9, 18, Mar. 7, 16, Apr. 5, 14, May 3, 12, 30, June 1, 10, 28, July 8, 26, 31, Aug. 6, 24, 29, Sept. 4, 22, 27, Oct. 2, 20, 25, Nov. 18, 23, Dec. 16, 21

Soul mates: Jan. 26, Feb. 24, Mar. 22, 30, Apr. 20, 28, May 18, 26, June 16, 24, July 14, 22, Aug. 12, 20, Sept. 10, 18, Oct. 8, 16, Nov. 6, 14, Dec. 4, 12

Love & Relationships

Outgoing and gregarious, yet assertive and outspoken, you usually have an active social life. You like to engage in conversations and discussions or meet people from different schools of thought. Usually your relationships are very important, as you test your wits against others and are likely to have firm opinions. Faithful and caring, you make an effort to keep to your promises. Attracted to mentally powerful individuals, you enjoy a good debate. However, guard against getting caught up in arguments or mental power games with partners. Nevertheless, you are very generous with the people you love and are loyal and a reliable friend.

June 16

Ⅱ Quick and down-to-earth, you are revealed by your Gemini birthday to be a shrewd, independent, and strong individual. An interesting combination of sensitive high ideals mixed with a practical desire for money and luxury indicates that you may vacillate between two extremes. On one hand, you desire an expensive and stylish home and a high lifestyle, and on the other hand, you are willing to sacrifice for your ideals. A solution to this may be to find a positive cause that also brings you financial rewards.

With the influence of Aquarius, ruler of your decanate, you are original and broadminded, and you need freedom. Mentally sharp and receptive to new ideas, you are able to make split-second decisions and may have an interest in social reform. With a progressive view of life, you value knowledge, and travel may be one of your favorite pastimes.

At times you are extremely generous and kind with your loved ones. At other times you are likely to be rather domineering or overbearing. You may also need to avoid a tendency to be impatient or restless. If opposed, you obstinately adhere to your own principles from an innate rebelliousness rather than from real conviction.

Ideally you should be in a position where your courage and ability to think big can put you in the forefront as an initiator. Being naturally gregarious, you have an easy way with people and an excellent ability to spot opportunities. As long as you keep faith in yourself, your no-nonsense approach, original ideas, and intuition guarantee you success.

Family and security become more important in your life after the age of five, when your progressed Sun moves into Cancer. This also highlights your personal emotional needs. This continues until around the age of thirty-five, when your progressed Sun enters Leo. This will increase your confidence and strength and enable you to become more assertive and self-expressive. When you reach the age of sixty-five, your progressed Sun moves into Virgo, and you start to develop a more analytical approach by being reflective.

FIXED STARS

El Nath; Alnilam, also called Al Nitham or the String of Pearls; Al Hecka

PRIMARY STAR

Star's name: El Nath

Degree position: 21°36'–22°41' Gemini between the years 1930 and 2000

Magnitude: 2

Strength: ★★★★★★★

Orb: 2°10'

Constellation: Beta Taurus

Applicable days: June 11, 12, 13, 14, 15, 16

Star qualities: Mars/Mercury

Description: a giant brilliant white and pale gray binary star located at the tip of the northern horn of the Bull

PRIMARY STAR'S INFLUENCE

El Nath imparts ambition, determination, and achievement through enterprise. This star also bestows good luck and acclaim. The influence of El Nath endows you with intelligence and a quick grasp of situations. Honors can be attained through research and scientific work or study of philosophy, theology, or history.

Linked to your Sun's degree, this star imparts a good mind, assertive manner, and comprehensive knowledge. El Nath also empowers you through the ability to speak persuasively, and encourages success through work in the legal system and government positions.

Your Secret Self

Your strong emotions usually motivate you to initiate many different involvements or pursuits. You sometimes throw caution to the winds, only to deal with the repercussions at a later date. Because you are constantly evaluating your own self-worth and the advantages to be gained from situations, nobody can bargain or make things happen as well as you. With your enthusiasm, willpower, and determination, you have the power to make your ideas reality. For this reason, it is important that you be sure of what you wish for.

The strength of your desire, when directed into selfless love and helping others, can be a remarkable power for good. When working with this outstanding force, you avoid dominating others with your strong will and can solve any possible concerns about money.

Work & Vocation

The combination of your relationship skills and determination enables you to cooperate with others in a dynamic and positive way. A natural wheeler-dealer and troubleshooter, you thrive on new beginnings or challenges, and in business have a knack for spotting opportunities.

Since you can master the art of persuasion, with your enthusiasm you may often promote ideas, products, or other people. Courageous and committed, with executive abilities, you may pursue a career in commerce, such as negotiator or financial advisor. Your natural communication skills would also enable you to consider a career in teaching and lecturing. Similarly, you may be interested in world affairs and may join international corporations or the media. Alternatively, you may get involved with charitable organizations and work for worthwhile causes. Your individuality may find expression in the creative world, and you are likely to be an original and creative artist or writer.

Famous people who share your birthday include comedian Stan Laurel, theosophist Alice Bailey, writer Erich Segal, economist and writer Adam Smith, actresses Laurie Metcalf and Joan Van Ark, and rapper Tupac Shakur.

Numerology

A number 16 birthday suggests that you are thoughtful, sensitive, and friendly. Although analytical, you often judge life and people according to how you feel. As a number 16 personality, however, you can experience inner tensions when facing friction between a need for self-expression and responsibility to others. Having a number 16 birthday, you may be interested in world affairs and may join international corporations or the media world. The creative ones among you have a talent for writing, with sudden flashes of inspiration. With your number 16 birthday, you may need to learn how to balance between being overly confident or doubtful and insecure. The subinfluence of the number 6 month indicates that you need an secure home life and a congenial environment. Pride and a need to be popular imply that you care about what others think or do. Travel and opportunities to explore and expand will broaden your outlook.

• *Positive:* higher education, responsibilities to home and family, integrity, intuitive, social, cooperative, insightful

• *Negative:* worry, never satisfied, irresponsible, self-promoting, opinionated, skeptical, fussy, irritable, selfish, unsympathetic

Love & Relationships

Intelligent and restless, you need constant emotional stimulation and new and exciting experiences. Your intense feelings are likely to keep you on the lookout for that ideal love, and if you fail you will not be deterred for long. Being practical suggests that although you are idealistic and can easily fall in love, you know how to differentiate between reality and fantasy. You need to know that although you are in a close relationship, you have the freedom to be independent and equal to your partner.

YOUR SPECIAL SOMEONE

For security, whether emotional or financial, you might want to begin looking for those born among the following dates.

Love & friendship: Jan. 3, 5, 14, 24, 31, Feb. 12, 22, 29, Mar. 10, 20, 27, Apr. 8, 18, 25, May 6, 16, 23, 30, June 4, 14, 16, 21, 28, 30, July 2, 12, 19, 26, 28, 30, Aug. 10, 17, 24, 26, 28, Sept. 8, 15, 22, 24, 26, Oct. 6, 13, 20, 22, 24, 30, Nov. 4, 11, 18, 20, 22, 28, Dec. 2, 9, 16, 18, 20, 26, 29

Beneficial: Jan. 5, 22, 30, Feb. 3, 20, 28, Mar. 1, 18, 26, Apr. 16, 24, May 14, 22, June 12, 20, July 10, 18, 29, Aug. 8, 16, 27, 31, Sept. 6, 14, 25, 29, Oct. 4, 12, 23, 27, Nov. 2, 10, 21, 25, Dec. 9, 19, 23

Fatal attractions: Jan. 12, Feb. 10, Mar. 8, Apr. 6, May 4, June 2, Dec. 16, 17, 18

Challenging: Jan. 16, 21, Feb. 14, 19, Mar. 12, 17, 30, Apr. 10, 15, 28, May 8, 13, 26, June 6, 11, 24, July 4, 9, 22, Aug. 2, 7, 20, Sept. 5, 18, Oct. 3, 16, Nov. 1, 14, Dec. 12

Soul mates: Jan. 25, Feb. 23, Mar. 21, Apr. 19, May 17, June 15, July 13, Aug. 11, Sept. 9, Oct. 7, Nov. 5, Dec. 3, 30

June 17

♊ Your birthday suggests that you are a cerebral and dynamic individual who recognizes the power of knowledge and utilizes it to advantage. With an independent mind and a strong character, you like to be in control. Your developed perception makes you quick to assess people and situations.

The added influence of Aquarius, your decanate ruler, indicates that you have an original approach to life and like to be objective in your views. You may just have to be careful of being so detached at times that you even appear cold. With your quick responses and reactions, you are well able to stand up for yourself and may even enjoy a little friendly rivalry or debate. Since you can be responsible and are a good organizer, you are often put in charge of others. Both men and women of this date may have to avoid being bossy.

The good fortune indicated by your birthday is enhanced by a straightforwardness and honesty that others see in you as natural confidence. Your need for order and security suggests that you like to build a base or home that is practical and financially solid, away from the busy life outside. At times you can appear to be quite conservative; at other times, strangely unconventional. You have the potential to use patience and strategy to look at long-term investments and through hard work and discipline can rise to exceptional heights of achievement.

From the age of four, when your progressed Sun moves into Cancer, issues around your emotional relations, security, home, and family have prominence in your life. This influence continues until the age of thirty-four, when you enter a period of strength, power, and confidence as your progressed Sun moves into Leo. Another turning point occurs around the time you are in your mid-sixties, when your progressed Sun moves into Virgo, and you develop a more analytical, perfectionistic, and pragmatic approach to life.

FIXED STARS

Alnilam, also called Al Nitham or the String of Pearls; Al Hecka; Polaris, also known as Al Rukkabah or the Pole Star

PRIMARY STAR

Star's name: Alnilam, also called Al Nitham or the String of Pearls

Degree position: 22°29'–23°22' Gemini between the years 1930 and 2000

Magnitude: 2

Strength: ★★★★★★★

Orb: 2°10'

Constellation: Epsilon Orion

Applicable days: June 12, 13, 14, 15, 16, 17

Star qualities: varied influences: Jupiter/Saturn and Mercury/Saturn

Description: A bright white star located in the center of the belt of Orion

PRIMARY STAR'S INFLUENCE

Alnilam bestows fleeting fame and wealth or public honors. The influence of this star is therefore likely to be of short duration. This star grants a keen and daring personality, but it warns against being headstrong or rash, or changing direction without a suitable strategy.

Linked to your Sun's degree, this star denotes a strong character, full of energy and determination. Alnilam encourages you to undertake large projects or to be enterprising, although it also suggests that you must think before making any statements. Often by avoid-

Your Secret Self

You are a hard worker who has the capability to overcome obstacles. You need to share your knowledge, and through interacting with others you come to learn to evaluate your own power. This may take the form of not letting others get away with things, or even of insisting on doing it your way. However, you may have to learn how to use your power by being just and fair. Ultimately you may find that it is your depth of knowledge that is your true strength. If you couple your inner intuition with your rigorous determination, you are able to accomplish a great deal.

Impressive as you may be in action, you still need others. You can be far more sensitive than you may show on the outside. Since you can be idealistic, with strong opinions, you often fight for what you consider to be of value. You may do this well if you do not lose sight of your sense of humor and manage to stay detached and composed.

Work & Vocation

With your quick mind and ability to lead, you usually have many career opportunities. Although you are independent, others appreciate your capacity for hard work and responsibility, so you often rise to prominent positions. Alternatively, being self-reliant, you may be drawn to work for yourself. You are particularly suited for intellectual professions such as law, interpreting, teaching, science, research, or writing. Your organizational skills and natural communication abilities would be an asset to you in the business world. An inborn humanitarian streak may lure you to be a reformer, whether in society or religion, or to work in the health sector. A desire for creativity and to express your individuality could lead you to the arts, the theater, and particularly music.

Famous people who share your birthday include composer Igor Stravinsky, singer Barry Manilow, church leader John Wesley, and actor Dean Martin.

ing stubbornness and frustration you can use your enormous vitality on something positive and worthwhile.

• *Positive:* daring, energetic, ambitious, gains and victory

• *Negative:* rashness, instability, making sudden changes when convenient to yourself

See Appendix for additional fixed star readings.

Numerology

With a number 17 birthday, you are shrewd, with a reserved nature and good analytical abilities. An independent thinker, you benefit from being well educated or skillful. Usually you utilize your knowledge in a specific way in order to develop your expertise and can achieve material success or a prominent position as a specialist or researcher. Private, introspective, and detached, with a strong interest in facts and figures, you frequently present a serious and thoughtful demeanor and like to take your time. By developing your communication skills, you can discover much more about yourself from others. The subinfluence of the number 6 month indicates that you need to develop a balance between self-reliance and dependence. You benefit from being aware of others' needs and taking responsibility for your words and actions. Practical and supportive, you can help and inspire others. Learn to be flexible and accept changes.

• *Positive:* thoughtful, specialist, good planner, good business sense, attracts money, individual thinker, painstaking, accurate, skilled researcher, scientific

• *Negative:* detached, lonely, stubborn, carelessness, moody, sensitive, narrow-minded, critical, worry

YOUR SPECIAL SOMEONE

For that someone special, you might want to look among those born on the following dates.

Love & friendship: Jan. 11, 13, 15, 17, 22, 25, Feb. 9, 11, 13, 15, 23, Mar. 7, 9, 11, 13, 21, Apr. 5, 7, 9, 11, 19, May 3, 5, 7, 9, 17, 31, June 1, 3, 5, 7, 15, 29, July 1, 3, 5, 27, 29, 31, Aug. 1, 3, 11, 25, 27, 29, Sept. 1, 9, 23, 25, 27, Oct. 4, 7, 21, 23, 25, Nov. 5, 19, 21, 23, Dec. 3, 17, 19, 21, 30

Beneficial: Jan. 1, 5, 20, Feb. 3, 18, Mar. 1, 16, Apr. 14, May 12, June 10, July 8, Aug. 6, Sept. 4, Oct. 2

Fatal attractions: Dec 17, 18, 19

Challenging: Jan. 6, 22, 24, Feb. 4, 20, 22, Mar. 2, 18, 20, Apr. 16, 18, May 14, 16, June 12, 14, July 10, 12, Aug. 8, 10, 31, Sept. 6, 8, 29, Oct. 4, 6, 27, Nov. 2, 4, 25, 30, Dec. 2, 23, 28

Soul mates: Jan. 6, 12, Feb. 4, 10, Mar. 2, 8, Apr. 6, May 4, June 2

Love & Relationships

Sincere and romantic, you are a loyal and reliable partner who can be very protective of those you love. A strong need for a stable relationship means that you are attracted to faithful individuals who are emotionally honest and direct. Nevertheless, guard against being too arrogant or bossy with your partner by learning to be patient and respecting the opinions of others. With your intuitive understanding, knowledge, and sensitivity, you can be very supportive, especially when giving practical help.

June 18

FIXED STARS

Betelgeuze; Polaris, also known as Al Rukkabah or the Pole Star

PRIMARY STAR

Star's name: Betelgeuze

Degree position: 27°46'–28°42' Gemini between the years 1930 and 2000

Magnitude: 1

Strength: ★★★★★★★★★

Orb: 2°30'

Constellation: Alpha Orionis

Applicable days: June 18, 19, 20, 21, 22, 23

Star qualities: Mars/Mercury

Description: a variable orange-red star located on the right shoulder of Orion

PRIMARY STAR'S INFLUENCE

Betelgeuze imparts an ability to judge, an optimistic outlook, a quick mind, and a competitive nature. This star also bestows luck and success through resolution and determination. You may receive honor for outstanding achievement and may also gain material wealth.

Linked to your Sun's degree, this star shows a talent for philosophy and an aptitude for metaphysical studies. Betelgeuze imparts success in sport and legal affairs as well as generally carrying a good influence in all matters dealing with others. Although honor and wealth can be achieved, they are not necessarily long-lasting, for there is an ever-present danger of sudden loss.

• *Positive:* good judgment, problem solving, harmony of action and thought

♊ The fortunate influence of your birthday shows you to be extremely clever, sociable, and self-assured. You are naturally gifted, mentally receptive, generous, and optimistic. Since you have big dreams, you need only apply self-discipline to turn some of them into reality. A quick thinker, you can be witty and assertive and like to be direct and honest.

With the added influence of your decanate ruler, Aquarius, you are self-willed and independent, with original ideas that are often ahead of their time. You have a way with words and are likely to be a good writer. Although you have a touch of the mad genius, you may also have to be wary of being impatient, stubborn, or temperamental. One thing is certain, however—in your life you will always have a desire to be continually learning.

Since you have charisma and a sense of the dramatic, you need to express yourself and feel that life can be fun. You also have a more philosophical bent, which can give you the faculty to survey the whole or can draw you toward things of a more humanitarian nature. The more you develop your intuition, the easier your life decisions become. Although you will not usually accept interference from others, when you are positive about your goals and vision you have the potential to create miracles.

Up to the age of thirty-two you are likely to be occupied by issues regarding your emotional needs, security, and family, with a strong accent on your home life. A turning point around the age of thirty-three occurs when your progressed Sun moves into Leo, starting to stimulate a stronger need for self-expression and assertiveness. This may inspire you to become more confident, brave, and adventurous. From the age of sixty-three, when your progressed Sun moves into Virgo, you develop a more practical, analytical, and perfectionist approach to life.

Your Secret Self

A light and creative core to your being ensures that you will always be able to keep others entertained and find something that can bring happiness into other people's lives. This sensitive and inspiring part of you can get lost if you start to doubt yourself and become indecisive, particularly in affairs of the heart or when dealing with material success.

Although you have the potential to achieve amazing results in concrete terms, especially through the use of your excellent mind, there is a danger that monetary gains will not necessarily bring happiness. To avoid this you need to work on projects that allow you to expand and learn. Luckily, you have a strong sense of purpose and high standards for yourself, which, combined with the ability to think big, ensure that you will not be disheartened by life's challenges for long.

Work & Vocation

Intuitive and creative, you need a career where you can expand your knowledge. Your quick intellect, sharp wit, and talent with words indicate that you can excel in writing and literature, law, education, or the media. Alternatively, you can use your organizational skills in large corporations or government and succeed in the business or manufacturing world. If you are interested in reform, you may be drawn to areas where you can speak up for others, such as union leadership or politics. Similarly, your humanitarian instincts may lead you to counseling or social work. Though you probably prefer something creative, you can be practical and you may express your intuitive mind through science or light engineering. Your need for artistic expression could be most satisfied through music and drama.

Famous people who share your birthday include Beatle Paul McCartney, actresses Isabella Rossellini and Jeanette MacDonald, and singer Alison Moyet.

Numerology

Determination, assertiveness, and ambition are some of the attributes associated with the number 18 birthday. Active, with a need for challenges, you like to keep busy and are frequently involved in some enterprise. Capable, hardworking, and responsible, you rise to positions of authority. Alternatively, your strong business sense and organizational skills lead you to the world of commerce. Since you may suffer from overwork, learn how to relax or slow down from time to time. As a number 18 personality, you may use your power to heal others, give sound advice, or solve other people's problems. The subinfluence of the number 6 month indicates that you need to be less demanding and more caring and compassionate. You benefit from being demonstrative and affectionate and less concerned with yourself. By using your influence or position of authority, you can help those less fortunate than yourself. You need time alone to study or develop your skills. Avoid letting material considerations override other aspects in your life.

• *Positive:* progressive, assertive, intuitive, courageous, resolute, healing ability, efficient, advisory skills

• *Negative:* uncontrolled emotions, lazy, lack of order, selfishness, callousness, failure to complete work or projects, deceitful

Love & Relationships

Clever and witty, you usually have a friendly and cheerful personality. With your love of variety, you enjoy socializing with different people with diverse interests. A certain restlessness, however, implies that you can get bored easily and seek those who can offer you excitement. Traveling and new learning experiences are likely to be some of your favorite pastimes. Alternatively, you may enjoy courses of study where you can learn new skills and meet people who share your interests. The best way of entertaining yourself and having fun can be mentally exploring shared interests.

YOUR SPECIAL SOMEONE

You might start to look for an exciting partner among those born on the following dates.

Love & friendship: Jan. 9, 12, 16, 25, Feb. 10, 14, 23, 24, Mar. 5, 8, 12, 22, 31, Apr. 3, 6, 10, 20, 29, May 4, 8, 18 27, June 2, 6, 16, 25, 30, July 4, 14, 23, 28, Aug. 2, 12, 21, 26, 30, Sept. 10, 19, 24, 28, Oct. 8, 17, 22, 26, Nov. 6, 15, 20, 24, 30, Dec. 4, 13, 18, 22, 28

Beneficial: Jan. 2, 13, 22, 24, Feb. 11, 17, 20, 22, Mar. 9, 15, 18, 20, 28, Apr. 7, 13, 16, 18, 26, May 5, 11, 16, 18, 26, June 3, 9, 12, 14, 22, July 1, 7, 10, 12, 20, Aug. 5, 8, 10, 18, Sept. 3, 6, 8, 16, Oct. 1, 4, 6, 14, Nov. 2, 4, 12, Dec. 2, 10

Fatal attractions: Jan. 25, Feb. 23, Mar. 21, Apr. 19, May 17, June 15, July 13, Aug. 11, Sept. 9, Oct. 7, Nov. 5, Dec. 3, 18, 19, 20

Challenging: Jan. 7, 23, Feb. 5, 21, Mar. 3, 19, 29, Apr. 1, 17, 27, May 15, 25, June 13, 23, July 11, 21, 31, Aug. 9, 19, 29, Sept. 7, 17, 27, 30, Nov. 3, 13, 23, 26, Dec. 1, 11, 21, 24

Soul mates: Jan. 17, Feb. 15, Mar. 13, Apr. 11, May 9, June 7, July 5, Aug. 3, Nov. 30, Dec. 28

223

June 19

Ⅱ The influence of your birthday suggests that you are a popular Gemini with an easygoing charm. Being very intelligent, you possess a wealth of knowledge and have a wonderful ability to pass this on to others. Whether through the spoken or written word, you are likely to be a specialist at communication and manage to convey your ideas with a natural eagerness and excitement.

Always on the move, you love action and often take on more than you can deal with. Having a spirit of free enterprise, you think big and are likely to campaign or fight for your beliefs. Irrepressible and adventurous, you usually speak your mind even if it gets you into trouble; you may need to develop the art of how to listen.

The added influence of your decanate ruler, Aquarius, suggests that you are original and inventive, with good judgment and reasoning power. Since you may sometimes be restless and make hasty decisions, it is important to learn self-discipline and develop your skills. Your persuasive powers and organizational ability can certainly help you in your climb to success. Being ambitious and having a creative outlook on life emphasize the necessity of having projects or causes that you find emotionally and mentally fulfilling rather than just materially rewarding. When you have set your sights on a goal, you are willing to invest a great deal of effort and show how talented and determined you really are.

Up to the age of thirty-one, while your progressed Sun moves through the sign of Cancer, issues around emotional security, home, and family play an important part in your life. At the age of thirty-two, when your progressed Sun moves into Leo, you enter a period of greater self-expression and creativity, with added assertiveness and boldness. At the age of sixty-two, there is another turning point as your progressed Sun moves into Virgo. This points to a desire to be more methodical and orderly as well as to offer practical, helpful service to others.

FIXED STARS

Betelgeuze; Polaris, also known as Al Rukkabah or the Pole Star; Menkalinan, also known as Shoulder of the Rein-Holder

PRIMARY STAR

Star's name: Betelgeuze

Degree position: 27°46'–28°42' Gemini between the years 1930 and 2000

Magnitude: 1

Strength: ★★★★★★★★★

Orb: 2°30'

Constellation: Alpha Orionis

Applicable days: June 18, 19, 20, 21, 22, 23

Star qualities: Mars/Mercury

Description: a variable orange-red star located on the right shoulder of Orion

PRIMARY STAR'S INFLUENCE

Betelgeuze imparts an ability to judge, an optimistic outlook, a quick mind, and a competitive nature. This star also bestows luck and success through resolution and determination. You may receive honor for outstanding achievement and may also gain material wealth.

Linked to your Sun's degree, this star shows a talent for philosophy and an aptitude for metaphysical studies. Belelgeuze imparts success in sport and legal affairs as well as generally carrying a good influence in all matters dealing with others. Although honor and wealth can be achieved, they are not necessarily long-lasting, for there is an ever-present danger of sudden loss.

Your Secret Self

You will always have a youthful and playful quality that, combined with your powerful emotions, enables you to uplift people through your compassion, enthusiasm, and zany humor. You are able to play the court jester with your very amusing and witty conversation. Your humanitarian spirit can often inspire you to help others by giving advice and solving their problems.

Frustration, particularly over money or material situations, is a possible problem for you if you hold on to ideas or feelings for too long. You have a strong desire for material security, but in order to push forward you may need to balance this with the trust that you will always be taken care of and have enough.

Work & Vocation

Creative and intelligent, you are versatile and may have a wide choice of careers. You may be drawn to the world of commerce and use your persuasive charm in sales, promotion, or negotiation. With your positive attitude and easygoing personality, you can succeed in large corporations and gain positions of responsibility. Alternatively, your need for self-expression

• *Positive:* good judgment, problem solving, harmony of action and thought
• *Negative:* obstinate, argumentative, antagonist

See Appendix for additional fixed star readings.

indicates that your artistic talents can lead you to the world of art and design or advertising and media. With your ability to communicate your ideas, you may also be interested in education or training people in business. Equally, you are likely to be attracted to writing, the law, academia, and politics. As a fighter for causes, you can get your ideas across in an entertaining way, which may also be useful in the world of show business.

Famous people who share your birthday include actress Kathleen Turner, singer Paula Abdul, writer Salman Rushdie, former Duchess of Windsor Wallace Simpson, and French philosopher Blaise Pascal.

Numerology

A sunny, ambitious, and humanitarian outlook characterizes a number 19 birthday. Decisive and resourceful, you possess depth of vision, but the dreamer side of your nature is compassionate, idealistic, and creative. Although you are sensitive, the need to be someone may be the very thing that pushes you to be dramatic and claim center stage. Often there is a strong desire to establish an individual identity. To do so, you may first need to overcome the influence of peer group pressure. To others you may appear confident, resilient, and resourceful, but inner tensions may cause emotional ups and downs. The subinfluence of the number 6 month indicates that you need to discipline your imaginative and active thoughts through creativity or inspiration. Have faith and the patience to study and learn new skills, or write down your thoughts and dreams. To avoid misunderstanding with others, be open-minded or frank with your feelings. Develop a philosophical perspective on life so that you do not become too preoccupied with the material world.

• *Positive:* dynamic, centered, creative, leader, lucky, progressive, optimistic, strong convictions, competitive, independent, gregarious

• *Negative:* self-centered, depressive, worry, fear of rejection, ups and downs, materialistic, impatient

Love & Relationships

Young at heart and optimistic, you are likely to be sociable and popular. In personal relationships you are often intuitive and sensitive, yet can also be intense and strong-willed. Although you like to be spontaneous, your feelings may change and you can sometimes appear indifferent. You often seek an ideal love, and if your expectations are too high, you may be prone to disappointments. Attractive to others, you can be a loyal friend and a loving partner when you do find your ideal love.

YOUR SPECIAL SOMEONE

You might find a suitable relationship with someone who will understand your sensitivity and need for love among those born on the following dates.

Love & friendship: Jan. 7, 9, 10, 17, 27, Feb. 5, 8, 15, 25, Mar. 3, 6, 13, 23, Apr. 1, 4, 11, 21, May 2, 9, 19, June 7, 17, July 5, 15, 29, 31, Aug. 3, 13, 27, 29, 31, Sept. 1, 11, 25, 27, 29, Oct. 9, 23, 25, 27, Nov. 7, 21, 23, 25, Dec. 5, 19, 21, 23

Beneficial: Jan. 3, 5, 20, 25, 27, Feb. 1, 3, 18, 23, 25, Mar. 1, 16, 21, 23, Apr. 14, 19, 21, May 12, 17, 19, June 10, 15, 17, July 8, 13, 15, Aug. 6, 11, 13, Sept. 4, 9, 11, Oct. 2, 7, 9, Nov. 5, 7, Dec. 3, 5

Fatal attractions: Jan. 13, Feb. 11, Mar. 9, Apr. 7, May 5, June 3, July 1, Dec. 18, 19, 20, 21

Challenging: Jan. 16, 24, Feb. 14, 22, Mar. 12, 20, Apr. 10, 18, May 8, 16, 31, June 6, 14, 29, July 4, 12, 27, Aug. 2, 10, 25, Sept. 8, 23, Oct. 6, 21, Nov. 4, 19, Dec. 2, 17

Soul mates: Jan. 16, Feb. 14, Mar. 12, Apr. 10, May 8, June 6, July 4, 31, Aug. 2, 29, Sept. 27, Oct. 25, Nov. 23, Dec. 21

June 20

Ⅱ Those born on this date are highly intuitive, with original ideas. You are charismatic and charming, and an important part of your success is an ability to deal with people on a personal level. Having a warm heart and being friendly and sociable, you are often popular and know how to enjoy yourself and keep people entertained. This can help in your desire to be in the limelight, preferably in a leading position. You may have to beware, however, of underachieving through not disciplining yourself and scattering your energies in too many directions.

The influence of Aquarius, your decanate ruler, suggests that you want to explore new and innovative concepts. Your shrewd but restless mind gives you quick responses and reactions and can easily assess people and situations. You may have to avoid being impatient or stubborn, and you can have a tendency to not follow through with the responsibility needed to achieve your outstanding promise.

Usually ambitious, you are likely to be constantly thinking of schemes of how to make money or advance in life. Your desire for creativity often means that you have a strong need for freedom of expression. Since natural enthusiasm is one of your prime assets, the catch is that you need to genuinely believe in an idea in order to throw yourself into a project and get results.

Up to the age of thirty, your progressed Sun is in the sign of Cancer and you may be particularly centered around issues concerning emotional security, home, and family. At the age of thirty-one, when your progressed Sun moves into Leo, you will become more creative and confident. This will endow you with the assertiveness to be more adventurous and enhance your social skills. After sixty, when your progressed Sun moves into Virgo, you are likely to become more practical, discriminating, and orderly.

FIXED STARS

Betelgeuze; Polaris, also known as Al Rukkabah or the Pole Star; Menkalinan, also known as Shoulder of the Rein-Holder

PRIMARY STAR

Star's name: Betelgeuze

Degree position: 27°46'–28°42' Gemini between the years 1930 and 2000

Magnitude: 1

Strength: ★★★★★★★★★

Orb: 2°30'

Constellation: Alpha Orionis

Applicable days: June 18, 19, 20, 21, 22, 23

Star qualities: Mars/Mercury

Description: a variable orange-red star located on the right shoulder of Orion

PRIMARY STAR'S INFLUENCE

Betelgeuze imparts an ability to judge, an optimistic outlook, a quick mind, and a competitive nature. This star also bestows luck and success through resolution and determination. You may receive honor for outstanding achievement and may also gain material wealth.

Linked to your Sun's degree, this star shows a talent for philosophy and an aptitude for metaphysical studies. Belelgeuze imparts success in sport and legal affairs as well as generally carrying a good influence in all matters dealing with others. Although honor and wealth can be achieved, they are not necessarily long-lasting, for there is an ever-present danger of sudden loss.

Your Secret Self

Your desire to understand people and what motivates them suggests that you judge yourself by your relationships with others. In order to establish harmonious unions, you may have to keep a balance between great warmth and cool detachment. Luckily, you have a generous nature and an inner desire for honesty. By using this to acknowledge your own failings, you are able to learn from every situation and move on.

You like power, which, constructively channeled, can be a significant part of your accomplishment. However, misuse of this power may manifest itself as manipulative tactics. Besides a willingness to work hard if you are interested in a project, you can be determined and dedicated. Your innate practicality and organizational skill, when combined with your talent for dealing with people, enable you to attract assistance from others in fulfilling your plans.

Work & Vocation

Your easy charm and organizational skills indicate that you have the potential to succeed in many people-related activities, whether in the business world or in the public sector. You will probably be drawn to areas involving communications and could consider education, person-

• *Positive:* good judgment, problem solving, harmony of action and thought
• *Negative:* obstinate, argumentative, antagonist

See Appendix for additional fixed star readings.

nel, public relations, and politics. Publishing, writing, journalism, and research are also excellent channels for your fine mind. Creative outlets are likely to be through the theater or music, or as a songwriter. If you are talented, people will recognize your unique capabilities and help you reach the limelight.

Famous people who share your birthday include actress Nicole Kidman, actors Errol Flynn and Martin Landau, singers Cyndi Lauper and Lionel Richie, Beach Boys member Brian Wilson, playwright Lillian Hellman, and writer Catherine Cookson.

Numerology

With a number 20 birthday, you are intuitive, sensitive, adaptable, and understanding, and often see yourself as a part of a larger group. Usually you enjoy cooperative activities where you can interact, share experiences, or learn from others. Charming and gracious, you develop diplomatic and social skills and can move in different social circles with ease. You may, however, need to develop your confidence, overcome a tendency to be easily hurt by the actions and criticism of others, and avoid being overly dependent. You are a master at creating a congenial and harmonious atmosphere. The subinfluence of the number 6 month indicates that you need to acquire practical skills and learn to keep a balance between idealism and a desire for material success. Avoid being critical of yourself and others or making unreasonable demands. Determination and willpower are essential keys to your success. Since you are often a perfectionist, counterbalance your failures with your achievements. You need a plan of action and to persevere regardless of the difficulties.
• *Positive:* good partnerships, gentle, tactful, receptive, intuitive, considerate, harmonious, agreeable, amicable, ambassador of goodwill
• *Negative:* suspicious, lack of confidence, timid, oversensitive, emotional, selfish, easily hurt, crafty

Love & Relationships

Sharing and communication are important to you. Your desire to be in the company of people with power or authority suggests that a strong influence from your father or an older man in your youth left a strong mark on your views and beliefs. A need to know and understand about self-mastery suggests that you admire those with a unique approach to life. Although you want to be independent, if you come across exceptional people, you may be tempted to follow them. With your charm and natural authoritative demeanor, you often attract people who believe in you. In close relationships you need to keep light and positive and avoid becoming overly serious, bossy, or critical. A love of knowledge or wisdom may bring you nearer to your ideal partner.

YOUR SPECIAL SOMEONE

Among people born on the following dates, your ideals might be realized more easily.

Love & friendship: Jan. 1, 9, 14, 28, 31, Feb. 7, 12, 26, 29, Mar. 10, 24, 27, Apr. 8, 22, 25, May 6, 20, 23, June 4, 18, 21, July 2, 16, 19, 30, Aug. 14, 17, 28, 30, Sept. 12, 15, 26, 28, 30, Oct. 10, 13, 24, 26, 28, Nov. 8, 11, 22, 24, 26, Dec. 6, 9, 20, 22, 24

Beneficial: Jan. 26, Feb. 24, Mar. 22, Apr. 20, May 18, June 16, July 14, Aug. 12, Sept. 10, Oct. 8, Nov. 6, Dec. 4

Fatal attractions: Dec. 19, 20, 21, 22

Challenging: Jan. 3, 25, Feb. 1, 23, Mar. 21, Apr. 19, May 17, June 15, July 13, Aug. 11, Sept. 9, Oct. 7, Nov. 5, Dec. 3

Soul mates: Jan. 3, 10, Feb. 1, 8, Mar. 6, Apr. 4, May 2

SUN: GEMINI/CANCER CUSP

DECANATE: AQUARIUS/URANUS,
CANCER/MOON

DEGREE: 28°30' GEMINI–0° CANCER

MODE: MUTABLE

ELEMENT: AIR

June 21

FIXED STARS

Betelgeuze; Polaris, also known as Al Rukkabah or the Pole Star; Menkalinan, also known as Shoulder of the Rein-Holder

PRIMARY STAR

Star's name: Betelgeuze

Degree position: 27°46'–28°42' Gemini between the years 1930 and 2000

Magnitude: 1

Strength: ★★★★★★★★

Orb: 2°30'

Constellation: Alpha Orionis

Application days: June 18,19,20,21,22,23

Star qualities: Mars/ Mercury

Description: a variable orange-red star located on the right shoulder of Orion

PRIMARY STAR'S INFLUENCE

Betelgeuze imparts an ability to judge, an optimistic outlook, a quick mind, and a competitive nature. This star also bestows luck and success through resolution and determination. You may receive honor for outstanding achievement and may also gain material wealth.

Linked to your Sun's degree, this star shows a talent for philosophy and an aptitude for metaphysical studies. Belelgeuze imparts success in sport and legal affairs as well as generally carrying a good influence in all matters dealing with others. Although honor and wealth can be achieved, they are not

Ⅱ Your birthday indicates that you are a mentally quick, friendly, and broad-minded individual. Having a creative mind and loving knowledge, you are interested in many subjects but may be particularly drawn to world affairs. Since your image is usually important, in your desire to impress others you generally like the best. Direct with others, you can be kind-hearted and generous.

With the influence of your Sun on the cusp of Gemini and Cancer you are fortunate enough to have two decanate rulers, Aquarius and Cancer, that emphasize your sensitivity and highly intuitive abilities. This influence also endows you with originality, ingenuity, and imagination. Willing to explore new ideas and theories, you may find yourself ahead of your time, and you may desire freedom and independence. This desire may be equaled by a need for home and family. You may, however, have to beware that in your desire for harmony, peace, and security you do not become stuck in a predictable routine.

In your desire to please you may often be unable to say no and may take on too much. This may also mean that you need to guard against scattering your forces. Although you can be responsible and are usually very aware of wanting to pay off your debts, it still takes self-discipline to harness all the outstanding potential of your birthday. Rather than talking about your big plans and knowing a little about everything, it may be necessary to take yourself in hand and make a definite commitment to action and your own self-development.

Before the age of thirty you are likely to be concerned with issues regarding your emotional needs, home, and family. At the age of thirty, when your progressed Sun moves into Leo, you will begin to become more assertive and confident, adding to your independence. At the age of sixty there is another turning point as your progressed Sun moves into Virgo. This is likely to bring a more pragmatic, methodical, and service-oriented approach to life.

Your Secret Self

As optimistic as you can be, there are times when your nervous temperament tends toward depression due to lack of confidence or dissatisfaction. Developing a positive outlook or having something to believe in enables you to channel your strong emotional reactions. This emotional power can be expressed through creativity, whether physical or mental.

Although you are very kind and enjoy helping people, you must be careful of interfering. This also suggests that you may need to listen to others to avoid misunderstandings. It is vital to train or discipline your excellent mind, so education, whether formal or informal, can be a major key to your success. This provides the means to make the most of your potential and puts your focus on positive goals rather than letting you dwell on frustration or disappointment. By learning patience and tolerance, you can present a detached and liberal personality and may find that people are then attracted to your advisory skills.

Work & Vocation

Whatever career you choose, you may have a strong need to express your ideas or creative imagination. Often humanitarian, you have a natural understanding of people and may be

necessarily long-lasting, for there is an ever-present danger of sudden loss.

• *Positive:* good judgment, problem solving, harmony of action and thought

• *Negative:* obstinate, argumentative, antagonist

See Appendix for additional fixed star readings.

drawn to education, counseling, or social work. Alternatively, your organizational and managerial skills may draw you to the world of commerce. A love of knowledge may attract you to philosophy, law, religion, or politics. Creative or artistic and often good with your hands, you may excel in the world of design, particularly items for the home. With your excellent communication skills, you may wish to express yourself through writing, literature, or journalism.

Famous people who share your birthday include writer and philosopher Jean-Paul Sartre, Prince William of England, Pakistani leader Benazir Bhutto, American artist Rockwell Kent, advertising entrepreneur Maurice Saatchi, guitarist Nils Lofgren, and actresses Jane Russell, Juliette Lewis, and Nicole Kidman.

Numerology

Dynamic drive and an outgoing personality are usually present in those with a number 21 birthday. Socially inclined, you have many interests and contacts, and are generally fortunate. Usually you show others your friendly and gregarious personality. Intuitive, with an independent spirit, you are highly inventive and original. With a number 21 birthday, you can be fun-loving and magnetic, with social charm. Alternatively, you can be shy and reserved, with a need to develop assertiveness, especially in close relationships. Although you can be inclined toward cooperative relationships or marriage, you always want to be acknowledged for your talents and abilities. The subinfluence of the number 6 month indicates that you are perceptive and creative. Although you often seek other people's opinions, you must learn to make your own decisions. You demonstrate a caring and compassionate nature but need to express your individuality and feelings by telling others what you think or how you feel. Broaden your views and see the greater plan.

• *Positive:* inspiration, creativity, love unions, long-lasting relationships
• *Negative:* dependency, loss of emotional control, lack of vision, fear of change, nervous

Love & Relationships

Magnetic with social charm, you are cooperative, fun-loving, and creative. Since you need a soul mate, close personal relationships are very important to you. In fact, they are so crucial that you may have to guard against becoming overly dependent on them. You may need to avoid substituting security for love and happiness and settling for second best. You express your true feelings by being caring and generous, but a need to learn to stay detached may help you find a more balanced view on love and relationships. With your tact and diplomatic skills, you make many contacts but need to develop an assertive stand early on in relationships.

YOUR SPECIAL SOMEONE

You might find a partner who will understand your sensitivity and need for love among those born on the following dates.

Love & friendship: Jan. 1, 15, 24, 26, 29, 30, Feb. 13, 24, 27, 28, Mar. 11, 22, 25, 26, Apr. 9, 20, 23, 24, May 7, 18, 21, 22, June 5, 16, 19, 20, July 3, 14, 17, 18, 31, Aug. 1, 12, 15, 16, 29, 31, Sept. 10, 13, 14, 27, 29, Oct. 8, 11, 12, 25, 26, 27, Nov. 6, 9, 10, 23, 25, Dec. 4, 7, 8, 21, 23, 29

Beneficial: Jan. 1, 2, 10, 27, Feb. 8, 25, Mar. 6, 23, Apr. 4, 21, May 2, 19, 30, June 17, 28, July 15, 26, Aug. 13, 24, Sept. 11, 22, Oct. 9, 20, Nov. 7, 18, Dec. 5, 16

Fatal attractions: Dec. 21, 22, 23

Challenging: Jan. 17, 26, Feb. 15, 24, Mar. 13, 22, Apr. 11, 20, May 9, 18, June 7, 16, July 5, 14, Aug. 3, 12, 30, Sept. 1, 10, 28, Oct. 8, 26, 29, Nov. 6, 24, 27, Dec. 4, 22, 25

Soul mates: Jan. 21, Feb. 19, Mar. 17, Apr. 15, May 13, June 11, July 9, 29, Aug. 7, 27, Sept. 5, 25, Oct. 3, 23, Nov. 1, 21, Dec. 19

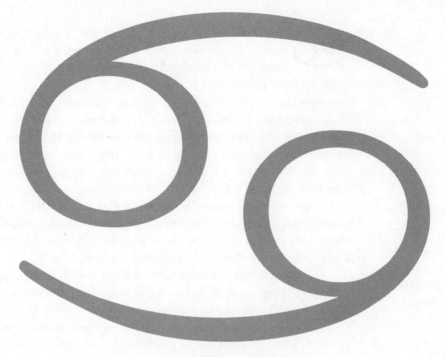

Cancer

June 22–July 22

June 22

Your birthday's unique position on a cusp suggests that you gain from both the signs of Gemini and Cancer. You have mental and intuitive powers second to none, and with your natural receptivity you can be a quick learner with great potential in any field you choose.

Being born in the first decanate of Cancer, you benefit from the double influence of the Moon and possess a sensitive imagination and powerful emotions. Since you are usually multitalented with many interests, you desire knowledge and mental stimulation. If indeed you take on the challenges indicated by your birthday, you can achieve success in any field of study. Alternatively, you may want to use your ingenuity and practical skills by becoming involved in reforms and improving conditions for others.

Clever and caring, you are sympathetic, with a keen mentality. Although you are intelligent and imaginative, without structure or aims you can easily become irritable, stubborn, or involved in power games that cause mental tension. This can often lead to moodiness or self-doubt, especially if you let others undermine your confidence.

The more inspired with this birthday will be drawn to self-expression and the arts, with particular emphasis on music and drama. Often knowing what others want or expect, you use your discerning powers and friendly personality to move with ease in all types of social circles.

You become less security-conscious after the age of thirty, when your progressed Sun moves into Leo. This aids you to positively gain in confidence and perform with skill in your chosen field. If, by middle years, you have not used the powerful energies inherent in your birthday, you will be given another chance to achieve success. From age sixty, when your progressed Sun moves into Virgo, you will have a more pragmatic attitude, with service to others becoming a more prominent focus in your life.

Fixed Stars

Betelgeuze; Polaris, also known as Al Rukkabah or the Pole Star; Menkalinan, also known as Shoulder of the Rein-Holder

Primary Star

Star's name: Betelgeuze
Degree position: 27°46'–28°42' Gemini between the years 1930 and 2000
Magnitude: 1
Strength: ★★★★★★★★★
Orb: 2°30'
Constellation: Alpha Orionis
Applicable days: June 18, 19, 20, 21, 22, 23
Star qualities: Mars/ Mercury
Description: a variable orange-red star located on the right shoulder of Orion

Primary Star's Influence

Betelgeuze imparts an ability to judge, an optimistic outlook, a quick mind, and a competitive nature. This star also bestows luck and success through resolution and determination. You may receive honor for outstanding achievement and may also gain material wealth.

Linked to your Sun's degree, this star shows a talent for philosophy and an aptitude for metaphysical studies. Belelgeuze imparts success in sport and legal affairs as well as generally carrying a good influence in all matters dealing with others. Although honor and wealth can be achieved, they are not necessarily long-lasting, for there is an ever-present danger of sudden loss.

Your Secret Self

The need to feel secure in what you believe may at times be challenged by those you come in contact with. Although you present a confident front, you often wonder if you are in possession of the facts. Frank and outspoken, you like to be direct and expect the same from others. Nevertheless, the strength of your convictions can make you obstinate but persistent. This warns that you perhaps need to learn to differentiate between determination and inflexibility. Objectivity and rational thinking can be one solution if you want to overcome emotional insecurities.

You may enjoy an element of chance or risk and be tempted to fulfill your high aims by speculating. Although it is beneficial for you to think big, you may also need to express yourself creatively or devote yourself to your ideals. However, keeping your remarkable mind productive and living up to your true potential may be endangered by escapist tendencies.

Work and Vocation

Your ambition may lead you to business, where you can excel with your flair for organization and management. This also suggests that you could achieve success in manufacturing, banking, merchandizing, or real estate. Alternatively, your sense of vision and active imagination may take you into careers such as acting, art, photography, music, filmmaking, or interior design. Your natural ability to deal with people could be channeled into professions that involve you with the public, such as communications, education, health, social work, or law. Your special insight and compassion may draw you toward counseling or the healing world, either in the medical or alternative health professions.

Famous people who share your birthday include singer Kris Kristofferson, musician Todd Rundgren, actresses Meryl Streep and Lindsay Wagner, director Billy Wilder, and composer Giacomo Puccini.

Numerology

Having a number 22 birthdate, you are a proud, practical, and highly intuitive individual. Since this is a master number, it can vibrate both as number 22 and number 4. Often honest and hardworking, with natural leadership abilities, you have a charismatic personality and a deep understanding of people. Although undemonstrative, you can show a caring, protective concern for the welfare of others. Many born with this birthdate have strong links with brothers or sisters and can be protective and supportive of them. The subinfluence of the number 6 month indicates that you are security-conscious and like to create harmony. Reliable and responsible, you can be supportive of others and are a sympathetic friend. With your inner gifts of imagination and creativity, you often harbor some idealistic notion, yet your practical side keeps your feet firmly on the ground. Winning is important, and success is often possible through initiating original ideas that can benefit others.

• *Positive:* universal, director, highly intuitive, pragmatic, practical, good with your hands, skillful, builder, good organizer, realist, problem solver, achiever

• *Negative:* get-rich-quick schemes, nervous, bossy, materialistic, lack of vision, lazy, egotistical, self-promoting

Love & Relationships

Your wealth of feelings and strong sixth sense usually suggest that you may need a partner who can understand your sensitivity and share your values and ideas. Although you can be a tower of strength to those you love, you may nevertheless be prone to fluctuating moods. Developing a philosophical perspective and overcoming a tendency to worry can help you establish emotional stability. Your most successful social and loving relationships are likely to be with those who share your many interests or who can intellectually stimulate you.

YOUR SPECIAL SOMEONE

For warm and tender relationships, look out for those born on the following dates.

Love & friendship: Jan. 10, 13, 20, 30, Feb. 8, 11, 18, 28, Mar. 6, 9, 16, 26, Apr. 4, 7, 14, 24, May 2, 5, 12, 22, June 3, 10, 20, July 1, 8, 18, Aug. 6, 16, 30, Sept. 4, 14, 28, 30, Oct. 2, 12, 26, 28, 30, Nov. 10, 24, 26, 28, Dec. 8, 22, 24, 26

Beneficial: Jan. 12, 16, 17, 28, Feb. 10, 14, 15, 26, Mar. 8, 12, 13, 24, Apr. 6, 10, 11, 22, May 4, 8, 9, 20, 29, June 2, 6, 7, 18, 27, July 4, 5, 16, 25, Aug. 2, 3, 14, 23, Sept. 1, 12, 21, Oct. 10, 19, Nov. 8, 17, Dec. 6, 15

Fatal attractions: Mar. 31, Apr. 29, May 27, June 25, July 23, Aug. 21, Sept. 19, Oct. 17, Nov. 15, Dec 17, 21, 22, 23, 24

Challenging: Jan. 6, 18, 22, 27, Feb. 4, 16, 20, 25, Mar. 2, 14, 18, 23, Apr. 12, 16, 21, May 10, 14, 19, June 8, 12, 17, July 6, 10, 15, Aug. 4, 8, 13, Sept. 2, 6, 11, Oct. 4, 9, Nov. 2, 7, Dec. 5

Soul mates: Mar. 28, Apr. 26, May 24, June 22, July 20, Aug. 18, Sept. 16, Oct. 14, Nov. 12, Dec. 10

June 23

♋ Intuitive and receptive, with an ability to quickly grasp ideas, you are revealed by your birthday to be a clever and shrewd individual. As a Cancerian, you are sensitive and shy; however, your great mental potential inspires you to aim high and achieve success. Caring and sympathetic, you are supportive of those around you, usually considering your family to be the most important element in your sense of security and well-being.

As you are mentally alert, you enjoy being occupied and well informed. Although you often trust the way you feel, a tendency to be skeptical implies that you may have to learn that the wisdom of your inner voice is your best asset.

The double influence of Cancer, as both your ruler and decanate planet, indicates that you will benefit from developing your psychic powers. By learning to channel your strong emotions toward a positive goal, you can overcome bouts of frustration and uncertainty.

When positive, you are able to react to situations very spontaneously, with willpower and determination, daring others to keep up with your stream of ideas. A tendency to lose faith, becoming withdrawn and moody, may stop you in full flow, denying you all those wonderful possibilities.

In the years leading up to age twenty-nine you will be very concerned with your sensitivity, home, and family. After this point, when your progressed Sun moves into Leo, you may be drawn more into public situations that require you to be strong and confident. This continues until the age of fifty-nine, when there is another major change of emphasis in your life as your progressed Sun enters Virgo. As this brings more practical issues to prominence in your life, you are likely to become more methodical and businesslike.

Fixed Stars

Betelgeuze; Menkalinan, also known as Shoulder of the Rein-Holder; Tejat, also called Tejat Prior

PRIMARY STAR

Star's name: Betelgeuze

Degree position: 27°46'–28°42' Gemini between the years 1930 and 2000

Magnitude: 1

Strength: ★★★★★★★★★

Orb: 2°30'

Constellation: Alpha Orionis

Applicable days: June 18, 19, 20, 21, 22, 23

Star qualities: Mars/ Mercury

Description: a variable orange-red star located on the right shoulder of Orion

PRIMARY STAR'S INFLUENCE

Betelgeuze imparts an ability to judge, an optimistic outlook, a quick mind, and a competitive nature. This star also bestows luck and success through resolution and determination. You may receive honor for outstanding achievement and may also gain material wealth.

Linked to your Sun's degree, this star shows a talent for philosophy and an aptitude for metaphysical studies. Belelgeuze imparts success in sport and legal affairs as well as generally carrying a good influence in all matters dealing with others. Although honor and wealth can be achieved, they are not necessarily long-lasting, for there is an ever-present danger of sudden loss.

Your Secret Self

With a natural talent for understanding the value of things or making money, you also possess an inner power that adds to your tenacity and determination and proves to be a dynamic influence in your overall success. This gives you the ability to overcome all obstacles no matter how difficult they may seem at the time. Sometimes you may procrastinate and feel like you just cannot get yourself going, but once you believe in a project, you work extremely hard in order to make it become a reality.

Deep within you is a very playful quality that, positively expressed, might have a very creative influence on your life and stop you from becoming too serious. However, you need space and time for yourself at regular periods in order to tune in to the more perceptive part of your character and develop your deeper insight.

Work & Vocation

Your sensitivity and caring nature may attract you to careers working with the underprivileged or to professions such as healing or social reform. With your fine mind, you could also become involved in education or use your talent for communication in writing. Areas where you can share your knowledge with others, such as research, debating, or law, may also appeal to your rational personality. If being technical is your forte, you can be drawn toward working with computers or engineering. Conversely, you may be interested in religion or metaphysics. You may possibly achieve success in government service, in catering, or in commercializing items for the home.

Famous people who share your birthday include England's King Edward VIII (the Duke of Windsor), psychologist and writer Alfred Kinsey, Kinks musician Ray Davies, and Empress Josephine of France.

Numerology

Intuitive, emotionally sensitive, and creative are some of the ways people describe those with a number 23 birthday. Usually you are versatile, passionate, and a quick thinker, with a professional attitude. With a mind full of creative ideas, you are usually multitalented. You are fond of travel, adventure, and meeting new people, and the restlessness implied by the number 23 urges you to try many different kinds of experiences, as you adapt to situations easily. Friendly and fun-loving, with courage and drive, you may need an active life in order to actualize your true potential. The subinfluence of the number 6 month indicates that you are emotional and sensitive, with an idealistic and caring nature. With your strong instincts or psychic abilities, you can feel other people's emotions and thoughts. As you want stability and security, you are frequently domestically inclined and a truly devoted parent. Your challenge may be to develop more self-confidence and to avoid being too dependent.

• *Positive:* loyal, responsible, travel, communicative, intuitive, creative, versatile, trustworthy, fame

• *Negative:* selfish, insecure, stubborn, uncompromising, fault-finding, dull, withdrawn, prejudiced

Love & Relationships

Sensitive, mentally restless, yet highly intuitive, you need to feel emotionally secure and often are supportive and encouraging. Frequently you are attracted to ambitious, strong-willed, and hardworking individuals. This may cause you to seek the company of intelligent people who are self-disciplined and inventive. Although you probably take your time before committing yourself to long-term relationships, once you settle down you have firm convictions and are very loyal.

YOUR SPECIAL SOMEONE

Relationships can be more easily achieved with those born on the following dates.

Love & friendship: Jan. 21, 28, 31, Feb. 19, 26, 29, Mar. 17, 24, 27, Apr. 15, 22, 25, May 13, 20, 23, June 11, 18, 21, July 9, 16, 19, Aug. 7, 14, 17, 31, Sept. 5, 12, 15, 29, Oct. 3, 10, 13, 27, 29, 31, Nov. 1, 8, 11, 25, 27, 29, Dec. 6, 9, 23, 25, 27

Beneficial: Jan. 9, 12, 18, 24, 29, Feb. 7, 10, 16, 22, 27, Mar. 5, 8, 14, 20, 25, Apr. 3, 6, 12, 18, 23, May 1, 10, 16, 21, 31, June 2, 8, 14, 19, 29, July 6, 12, 17, 27, Aug. 4, 10, 15, 25, Sept. 2, 8, 13, 23, Oct. 6, 11, 21, Nov. 4, 9, 19, Dec. 2, 7, 17

Fatal attractions: Jan. 3, Feb. 1, Apr. 30, May 28, Jun. 26, Jul. 24, Aug. 22, Sep. 20, Oct. 18, Nov. 16, Dec. 14, 22, 23, 24, 25

Challenging: Jan 7, 8, 19, 28, Feb. 5, 6, 17, 26, Mar. 3, 4, 15, 24, Apr. 1, 2, 13, 22, May 11, 20, June 9, 18, July 7, 16, Aug. 5, 14, Sept. 3, 12, Oct. 1, 10, Nov. 8, Dec. 6

Soul mates: Jan. 3, 19, Feb. 1, 17, Mar. 15, Apr. 13, May 11, June 9, July 7, Aug. 5, Sept. 3, Oct. 1

June 24

As a Cancerian, you are easygoing, with a friendly though reserved personality. Your conservative approach suggests that you are a good mediator. With your natural flair for people, you prefer to use diplomacy instead of direct confrontation.

The double influence of the Moon often implies that concerns with home and family matters may take a great deal of your time. Should you seek only the security of home comforts, however, you are not likely to realize your true potential.

The necessity for harmony and tranquility implied by your birthdate must not be taken as a sign of weakness, but as an indication of a finely tuned mind. Your clear vision and a natural practical approach make you a good strategist. With your powers of concentration and the willingness to take on difficult and challenging work, you can be hardworking and dedicated. Responsibility and a strong sense of duty can be some of your greatest attributes, and advancement in life comes through your own efforts and fortitude. If inspired, you are willing to work long hours without instant rewards.

Although you can have an exceptionally perceptive mind, your fluctuation between ambition and inertia challenges your otherwise great potential. This warns that only by combining the two sides of your personality are you able to achieve balance and establish equilibrium.

Up to the age of twenty-eight, issues relating to home, security, or family are likely to play a large part in your life. However, after your progressed Sun moves into Leo, you become more daring as your power, creativity, and confidence increase. At the time your progressed Sun moves into Virgo, when you are age fifty-eight, you become more discriminating and efficient in your life, with the likelihood of developing more of an interest in health matters or being of service to others.

Your Secret Self

Although home and family are important, you love power and can be very businesslike and determined. By realizing that you may not operate well alone, you may make cooperative efforts a major part of your life. At times it can be hard to get you out of a comfortable rut, but once you become resolute and goal-oriented, you can be extremely hardworking and skillful at commercializing your talents.

Do not allow anxiety, particularly about money, to undermine your ability to overcome obstacles, as it is generally unfounded. Once anxious, you may be inclined to hide your head in the sand rather than deal with things at the right time. It is therefore important to have a plan of action that can enable you to get moving and make a stand for the recognition you need and deserve.

Work & Vocation

You may be drawn to express the more caring side of your nature through careers such as counseling or raising money for good causes. Interests in mental pursuits could lead to teaching, lecturing, research, or writing. Your easy charm and natural flair for form and color could

FIXED STAR

Star's name: Tejat, also called Tejat Prior

Degree position: 2°27'–3°26' Cancer between the years 1930 and 2000

Magnitude: 3

Strength: ★★★★★

Orb: 1°40'

Constellation: Eta Gemini

Applicable days: June 23, 24, 25, 26

Star qualities: Mercury/Venus

Description: an orange-red binary, variable star located on the left foot of the northern Twin

PRIMARY STAR'S INFLUENCE

Tejat imparts confidence, pride, dignity, and a refined nature. The influence of this star denotes a wealth of feelings, a sense and appreciation of beauty, and artistic and literary abilities. Tejat also grants cheerfulness, a sense of humor, and the knowledge that two heads are better than one. Many benefits can come from cooperation, associative thinking, and developing a diplomatic yet persuasive manner. Tejat, however, warns that this talent can be used negatively to be cunning, overly confident, or inconsistent. It also warns against possible legal difficulties.

Linked to your Sun's degree, this star bestows appreciation for beauty, artistic talent, literary skills, and unusual interests. Tejat bestows a light-hearted nature, yet it also warns against a lack of drive and a tendency to be inconsistent. With this star you may experience some instability or change.

draw you to the theater, music, and the arts. Having a natural understanding of people, you may be attracted to occupations that involve personal contact or being an advisor, such as therapy or personnel. You can excel equally well in business, particularly sales, promotions, and public relations. This birthday can also produce good managers and executives, as well as give you the opportunity to profit from all careers to do with the home.

Famous people who share your birthday include boxer Jack Dempsey, politician Bella Abzug, and aviator Amelia Earhart.

Numerology

The emotional sensitivity associated with the number 24 birthday suggests that you may need to establish harmony and order. Usually honest, dependable, and security-conscious, you need the love and support of a partner and enjoy building a strong foundation for yourself and your family. A pragmatic approach to life also gives you a good business sense and an ability to achieve material success. With a number 24 birthday, you may have to overcome periods of instability and a tendency to be stubborn or fixed in your ideas. The subinfluence of the number 6 month indicates that you are conscientious and responsible. Though often career-oriented, you can also be an excellent homemaker and a devoted parent. Kind and idealistic, you can be determined yet supportive, with a caring nature. Despite your dislike of routine, you seek stability and reassurance. You may also need to overcome a tendency toward discontent, caused by worry and misplaced sympathies.

• *Positive:* energy, idealist, practical skills, strong determination, honest, generous, love of home, active
• *Negative:* materialism, too economical, dislikes routine, lazy, domineering, stubborn, resentful

Love & Relationships

Your strong instincts and passionate nature often reveal a dramatic personality. The parental influence associated with your birthday suggests that you are a devoted parent and a loving partner. The emotional power associated with your birthday implies that you may need to avoid becoming overly sensitive or melodramatic. Nevertheless, you are hospitable, charming, and friendly, with strong links to home and family. Your need for self-expression often suggests that you may be drawn toward creative and theatrical people or can raise funds for some worthwhile cause.

YOUR SPECIAL SOMEONE

For that someone special, you might want to look among those born on the following dates.

Love & friendship: Jan. 18, 22, 28, Feb. 16, 20, 26, Mar. 14, 18, 28, Apr. 12, 16, 26, May 10, 14, 24, June 8, 12, 22, July 6, 10, 20, 29, Aug. 4, 8, 18, 27, 30, Sept. 2, 6, 16, 25, 28, Oct. 4, 14, 23, 26, 30, Nov. 2, 12, 21, 24, 28, Dec. 10, 19, 22, 26, 28

Beneficial; Jan. 6, 10, 25, 30, Feb. 4, 8, 23, 28, Mar. 2, 6, 21, 26, Apr. 4, 19, 24, May 2, 17, 22, June 15, 20, 30, July 13, 18, 28, Aug. 11, 16, 26, Sept. 9, 14, 24, Oct. 7, 12, 22, Nov. 5, 10, 20, Dec. 3, 8, 18

Fatal attractions: May 29, June 27, July 25, Aug. 23, Sept. 21, Oct. 19, Nov. 17, Dec. 14, 23, 24, 25

Challenging: Jan. 13, 29, 31, Feb. 11, 27, 29, Mar. 9, 25, 27, Apr. 7, 23, 25, May 5, 21, 23, June 3, 19, 21, July 1, 17, 19, Aug. 15, 17, Sept. 13, 15, Oct. 11, 13, Nov. 9, 11, Dec. 7, 9

Soul mates: Jan. 6, 25, Feb. 4, 23, Mar. 2, 21, Apr. 19, May 17, June 15, July 13, Aug. 11, Sept. 9, Nov. 7, Dec. 5

June 25

FIXED STARS

Tejat, also called Tejat Prior; Dirah, also called Nuhaiti

PRIMARY STAR

Star's name: Tejat, also called Tejat Prior

Degree position: 2°27'–3°26' Cancer between the years 1930 and 2000

Magnitude: 3

Strength: ★★★★★

Orb: 1°40'

Constellation: Eta Gemini

Applicable days: June 23, 24, 25, 26

Star qualities: Mercury/Venus

Description: an orange-red binary, variable star located on the left foot of the northern Twin

PRIMARY STAR'S INFLUENCE

Tejat imparts confidence, pride, dignity, and a refined nature. The influence of this star denotes a wealth of feelings, a sense and appreciation of beauty, and artistic and literary abilities. Tejat also grants cheerfulness, a sense of humor, and the knowledge that two heads are better than one. Many benefits can come from cooperation, associative thinking, and developing a diplomatic yet persuasive manner. Tejat, however, warns that this talent can be used negatively to be cunning, overly confident, or inconsistent. It also warns against possible legal difficulties.

Linked to your Sun's degree, this star bestows appreciation for beauty, artistic talent, literary skills, and unusual interests. Tejat bestows a light-hearted

Strong instincts, a fine mind, and a need for variety are indicated by your birthday. As a Cancerian, you are sensitive and imaginative, with a caring personality; however, your alert mind and strong intuitive powers urge you to be adventurous. Since you are curious and mentally quick, you are often good company, especially when you use your unique sense of humor to entertain others. Nevertheless, since you are intelligent, you do not suffer fools gladly, and at times can be impatient.

The double influence of the Moon often implies that you are highly intuitive and sensitive. Eager for new experiences and novel things to do, you may have an interest in foreign places and people. This influence, unfortunately, also suggests that you are prone to restlessness and may have to develop self-discipline.

In order to achieve success, you may need to find a subject that can truly capture your imagination, one that will keep you interested and help you develop as a specialist. If you fail to keep yourself mentally challenged, you may run the risk of scattering your energies or could suffer from lack of satisfaction. Conversely, if you develop patience and a responsible attitude and take on obligations, you will soon find out that along with your intuition you also possess depth of thought, an excellent ability to reason, and a good mind for scientific work or research.

Your sensitivity will become less of a problem for you after the age of twenty-seven, when your progressed Sun moves into Leo. This will enable you to become more bold and self-assured in all areas of your life. After the age of fifty-seven, when your progressed Sun moves into Virgo, you are likely to apply more patience and precision to your life skills and take more of a pragmatic approach to life.

Your Secret Self

Practical and enthusiastic, you can inspire others with your ideas. Emotional discontent and the tendency to get bored easily, however, indicate that you need a great deal of variety in your life. This also includes being with many people and experiencing different kinds of friendships or relationships. Mostly friendly, at times you can be secretive about your own emotional needs or involvements.

You have your own philosophy about life, and it often keeps you positive in times of difficulty. An innate common sense and a direct approach help you to simplify issues and resolve problems intuitively, while stating the obvious that others fail to see. When optimistic, you can think in large terms and may be drawn to take risks. The more cautious side to your nature ensures that these are calculated risks rather than simply a matter of acting too hastily.

Work & Vocation

Your quick intelligence and need for mental stimulation necessitate the need for variety in your life and enable you to grasp the facts of any situation very quickly. A need to express your individuality, sensitivity, and wonderful imagination could enable you to succeed as a writer or in journalism, architecture, art, or music. Strong intuition and a desire to investigate may lead you to a career in religion or more mystical areas. In your choice of occupation you may have to guard against boredom, so it is important to select an occupation with constant activity, such as in travel, restaurants, or working with the public.

Famous people who share your birthday include author George Rowel, Spanish architect Antonio Gaudi, singers George Michael and Carly Simon, and artist Peter Blake.

nature, yet it also warns against a lack of drive and a tendency to be inconsistent. With this star you may experience some instability or change.

• *Positive:* thoughts of love, artistic sense, love union, writing skills

• *Negative:* inclination to squander, light-hearted living, vanity, conceit

See Appendix for additional fixed star readings.

Numerology

Usually you are instinctive and alert, with good judgment and an eye for detail. Generally you can gain more knowledge through practical application than mere theory. You may, however, need to be less impatient or discontented if things do not happen according to plan. Emotional sensitivity and artistic talent are just some of your hidden attributes. You possess strong mental energies that, when concentrated, aid you to look at all the facts and arrive at a conclusion faster than anyone else. The subinfluence of the number 6 month indicates that you are usually responsible and enterprising, with practical abilities and sound judgment. As you are interested in self-improvement, the secret to your progress is self-analysis. You may need to learn the art of expressing your feelings more openly and how to communicate your thoughts clearly without being shy or insecure.

• *Positive:* highly intuitive, perfectionist, perceptive, creative mind, good at dealing with people

• *Negative:* impulsive, impatient, irresponsible, overly emotional, jealous, secretive, critical, moody, nervous

YOUR SPECIAL SOMEONE

Relationships can happen more easily with someone born on one of the following days.

Love & friendship: Jan. 13, 19, 23, Feb. 11, 17, 21, Mar. 9, 15, 19, 28, 29, 30, Apr. 7, 13, 17, 26, 27, May 5, 11, 15, 24, 25, 26, June 3, 9, 13, 22, 23, 24, July 1, 7, 11, 20, 21, 22, Aug. 5, 9, 18, 19, 20, Sept. 3, 7, 16, 17, 18, Oct. 1, 5, 14, 15, 16, 29, 31, Nov. 3, 12, 13, 14, 27, 29, Dec. 1, 10, 11, 12, 25, 27, 29

Beneficial: Jan. 7, 15, 20, 31, Feb. 5, 13, 18, 29, Mar. 3, 11, 16, 27, Apr. 1, 9, 14, 25, May 7, 12, 23, June 5, 10, 21, July 3, 8, 19, Aug. 1, 6, 17, 30, Sept. 4, 15, 28, Oct. 2, 13, 26, Nov. 11, 24, Dec. 9, 22

Fatal attractions: Dec. 23, 24, 25, 26

Challenging: Jan. 6, 14, 30, Feb. 4, 12, 28, Mar. 2, 10, 26, Apr. 8, 24, May 6, 22, June 4, 20, July 2, 18, Aug. 16, Sept. 14, Oct. 12, Nov. 10, Dec. 8

Soul mates: Apr. 30, May 28, June 26, July 24, Aug. 22, Sept. 20, Oct. 18, 30, Nov. 16, 28, Dec. 14, 26

Love & Relationships

Social and charming, you usually have many friends. Although you possess great emotional depth, your reluctance to reveal what you feel suggests that you can be aloof. Usually you are highly idealistic; however, at times you may prefer platonic friendships to deep emotional relationships. Occasionally you can become involved with more than one person and may be unable to choose between two loves. When you find the right person, you are likely to be loyal and supportive.

June 26

Your intuition and pragmatic approach to life often indicate that although you are sensitive and caring, you want more out of life. Usually security is important to you, and in your case this is emphasized by the double influence of your ruling planet, the Moon. As a positive thinker with good organizational skills, you like to use your knowledge in some constructive way.

Family life is usually important to every Cancerian, and you have the makings of a good parent and a responsible family member. With your understanding and common sense, you frequently become an advisor to those around you. You have a love of knowledge, and good education is very important to you and helps you establish a firm basis for any career. If you do not enroll in a conventional course of study, you may educate yourself later in life.

The need to communicate your ideas and philosophy of life often involves you in debates on subjects that interest you. You possess a good understanding of buying and selling or negotiating deals, and you know how to use your contacts and diplomacy when it is in your interest. Happy when you are mentally occupied, you enjoy travel and learning about other cultures and habits rather than wasting your energy in the pursuit of trivial pleasures.

Issues around emotion, sensitivity, and family may occupy you well into your mid-twenties. After the age of twenty-six, when your progressed Sun moves into Leo, you are likely to be courageous enough to display your talents and skills in a positive and assured way. After the age of fifty-six, when your progressed Sun moves into Virgo, practical considerations become more prominent, with the likelihood of improvement in your efficiency, competence, and organizational abilities.

Fixed Stars

Tejat, also called Tejat Prior; Dirah, also called Nuhaiti

PRIMARY STAR

Star's name: Tejat, also called Tejat Prior
Degree position: 2°27'–3°26' Cancer between the years 1930 and 2000
Magnitude: 3
Strength: ★★★★★
Orb: 1°40'
Constellation: Eta Gemini
Applicable days: June 23, 24, 25, 26
Star qualities: Mercury/Venus
Description: an orange-red binary, variable star located on the left foot of the northern Twin

PRIMARY STAR'S INFLUENCE

Tejat imparts confidence, pride, dignity, and a refined nature. The influence of this star denotes a wealth of feelings, a sense and appreciation of beauty, and artistic and literary abilities. Tejat also grants cheerfulness, a sense of humor, and the knowledge that two heads are better than one. Many benefits can come from cooperation, associative thinking, and developing a diplomatic yet persuasive manner. Tejat, however, warns that this talent can be used negatively to be cunning, overly confident, or inconsistent. It also warns against possible legal difficulties.

Linked to your Sun's degree, this star bestows appreciation for beauty, artistic talent, literary skills, and unusual interests. Tejat bestows a light-hearted

Your Secret Self

On the surface you appear confident and capable, while inside you are sensitive and security-conscious. With an inner restlessness, you want to be on the move and are not likely to find the happiness you are seeking until you learn to still yourself to reflect or contemplate. When this calmer side is integrated with your love of activity and change, it is most impressive to see you in action.

Highly idealistic, you crave harmony and may be drawn to music, art, or other forms of creativity. This desire for peace may attract you to fight for causes that are close to your heart, or it may be reflected in the significance of your home as a potential haven from the world. Nevertheless, since you constantly want to widen your horizons, you often think of travel or adventures.

Work & Vocation

With your powerful imagination and fast mind, you are full of ideas that are financially advantageous. An interest in food may suggest culinary occupations such as restaurant work. Being a good planner and organizer, you may succeed in sales, commerce, promotions, advertising, sport, or politics. You are likely to be particularly interested in the study of philosophy, psychology, or religious thought. Professions such as teaching, lecturing, politics, and economics can also be excellent outlets for your fine mind. If in business, you need to be given a lot of space to operate independently and may well be happier self-employed. Your abilities to plan and put into operation many worthwhile schemes make you a valuable member of any project.

Famous people who share your birthday include writers Pearl Buck and Colin Wilson, and actors Peter Lorre and Chris O'Donnell.

nature, yet it also warns against a lack of drive and a tendency to be inconsistent. With this star you may experience some instability or change.

• *Positive:* thoughts of love, artistic sense, love union, writing skills

• *Negative:* inclination to squander, light-hearted living, vanity, conceit

See Appendix for additional fixed star readings.

Numerology

The strength or power suggested by the number 26 birthday shows that you are a cautious character with strong values and sound judgment. You have a pragmatic approach to life, executive ability, and a good business sense. With a number 26 birthday, you are usually responsible, with a natural aesthetic sense. Through stubbornness or a lack of self-confidence, however, you may sometimes give up too quickly. The subinfluence of the number 6 month indicates that although you are caring and responsible at times, you can become fussy and overanxious. Often a tower of strength for friends, family members, and relatives, you are usually willing to support those who turn to you in time of need. Since you need to be popular, you go to great lengths to make everyone happy. You may nevertheless need to guard against stretching yourself too thin and in the end pleasing no one.

• *Positive:* creative, practical, caring, responsible, proud of family, enthusiastic, courageous

• *Negative:* stubborn, rebellious, insecure, unenthusiastic, lack of persistence, instability

YOUR SPECIAL SOMEONE

A special relationship is more likely to happen with someone born on the following dates.

Love & friendship: Jan. 3, 4, 14, 20, 24, Feb. 2, 12, 18, 22, Mar. 10, 16, 20, 29, 30, Apr. 8, 14, 18, 27, 28, May 6, 12, 16, 25, 26, 31, June 4, 10, 14, 23, 24, 29, July 2, 8, 12, 21, 22, 27, Aug. 6, 10, 19, 20, 25, Sept. 4, 8, 17, 18, 23, Oct. 2, 6, 15, 16, 21, 30, Nov. 4, 13, 14, 19, 28, 30, Dec. 2, 11, 12, 17, 26, 28, 30

Beneficial: Jan. 4, 8, 21, Feb. 2, 6, 19, Mar. 4, 17, 28, Apr. 2, 15, 16, May 13, 24, June 11, 22, July 9, 20, Aug. 7, 18, 31, Sept. 5, 16, 29, Oct. 3, 14, 27, Nov. 1, 12, 25, Dec. 10, 23

Fatal attractions: Jan. 3, Feb. 1, May 31, June 29, July 27, Aug. 25, Sept. 23, Oct. 21, Nov. 19, Dec. 17, 25, 26, 27, 28

Challenging: Jan. 7, 10, 15, 31, Feb. 5, 8, 13, 29, Mar. 3, 6, 11, 27, Apr. 1, 4, 9, 25, May 2, 7, 23, June 5, 21, July 3, 19, Aug. 1, 17, Sept. 15, Oct. 13, Nov. 11, Dec. 9

Soul mates: Mar. 31, Apr. 29, May 27, June 25, July 23, Aug. 21, Sept. 19, Oct. 17, 29, Nov. 15, 27, Dec. 13, 25

Love & Relationships

Affectionate and sociable, you are likely to have many friends and usually keep in close touch with other family members. Although at one stage in your life you may have been drawn or attracted to some very unusual relationships, your power of discrimination indicates that you very rarely truly fall in love. Once you find someone who positively stimulates your mind, however, you can be very loyal and protective. You prefer to be direct with your partners and offer practical and realistic help and support.

June 27

♋ Imaginative and sensitive, you are a Cancerian with strong intuitive powers. You are often bright, friendly, and versatile, with creative talents; however, a tendency to succumb to emotional fluctuations may reduce the great potential indicated by your birthday.

As a caring and understanding individual, you can show great compassion to those you love. With the subinfluence of your decanate ruler, Cancer, your psychic abilities are doubly reinforced. However, you may also need to guard against a tendency to worry or become stressed and indecisive.

When you feel emotionally insecure, you can perhaps appear to others as too temperamental, talkative, or scattered. At other times, you can be very positive, entertaining, and good company, with an excellent sense of humor.

Versatile and gregarious, you have an intellectual brightness that may lead you to explore many avenues, but it can also be the source of your confusion, as you may try to do too many things. Although you have creative talents and are often full of ideas, you may benefit from learning to focus on a single goal. If, on the other hand, you are already realistic and decisive, your chances for success are there for the taking.

Whether through writing or performing, designing or decorating, you need to learn to express yourself emotionally and mentally. Sociable and friendly, you are fun-loving and need to capture the joy of life.

Although you may appear self-assured, you may find that the solid confidence you seek is not forthcoming until after the age of twenty-five, when your progressed Sun moves into Leo. This increases your strength and creativity and enables you to display more social skills. After the age of 55, when your progressed Sun moves into Virgo, you become more practical and analytical, as well as discriminating.

FIXED STAR

Star's name: Dirah, also called Nuhaiti

Degree position: 4°19'–5°17' Cancer between the years 1930 and 2000

Magnitude: 3

Strength: ★★★★★

Orb: 1°40'

Constellation: Mu Gemini

Applicable days: June 25, 26, 27, 28

Star qualities: Mercury/Venus

Description: a yellow and blue binary star located in the left foot of the northern Twin

PRIMARY STAR'S INFLUENCE

Dirah imparts a sound mind and creative ideas. This star bestows forceful speech accompanied by a witty, sociable, and friendly personality. Often a good communicator, you enjoy discussion, debate, and group popularity. There are also indications that you like music and orderliness and have a flair for making things look elegant and refined. Dirah bestows a talent for writing that, if developed, can bring honor and riches.

Linked to your Sun's degree, this star bestows the ability to make a favorable impression upon those you come into contact with and to gain wide popularity. Dirah's influence suggests prominence in public affairs, academic study, and writing, as well as success in education, literature, and publishing or politics. You may excel in sport, or enjoy studying astrology and esoteric subjects.

Your Secret Self

Travel or change is likely to play a strong part in your life, as you need to find stimulating and challenging experiences. Do not be afraid to take chances and go further afield if promising prospects arise, as these could turn out to be excellent opportunities for you. At times you can be extremely successful, but you may need to make allowances for changing financial circumstances. Although you are generous, a streak of extravagance implies that you may need to avoid overindulgence.

Proud and dignified, you may need faith to build up your confidence and weed out recurring worries. As a good psychologist with an ability to evaluate people, you can quickly detect the strengths and weaknesses of others. Charming and witty, you have the ability to enchant others with your idealism and imagination.

Work & Vocation

Your birthday indicates that you are a good parent or homemaker, and whatever work you are involved with, you like to take a creative approach. Having excellent people skills ensures your

- *Positive:* creativity, wit, communication skills, love of art and beauty
- *Negative:* vanity, conceit, squandering, immature

success in fields such as teaching, counseling, sales, or business. Your need for a changing and stimulating career suggests that you should avoid monotonous occupations. If drawn to business, you are likely to take a positive approach and may be successful as an agent or in real estate. The creative abilities shown by your birthday can bring you successful expression in music, acting, or writing, although the theatrical side of your nature may also lead you to politics.

Famous people who share your birthday include blind educator Helen Keller, politician Ross Perot, revolutionary Emma Goldman, Irish statesman Charles Parnell, and actress Isabelle Adjani.

Numerology

You are intuitive, yet analytical, and the number 27 birthdate indicates that your depth of thought can be greatly enhanced by developing patience and self-control. Determined and observant, you can pay great attention to detail. Although at times you appear secretive, rational, or detached, in fact you may be hiding inner tensions. In developing good communication skills, you can overcome a reluctance to express your deeper feelings. The subinfluence of the number 6 month indicates that you are constantly seeking balance and harmony. Since your strong instincts and feelings may occasionally conflict with your thoughts and beliefs, you can become apprehensive. Although affectionate and considerate, you may sometimes appear overly sensitive and unapproachable. By developing a more detached perspective, you will be able to listen to others and take on board their criticism or ideas.

- *Positive:* versatile, imaginative, creative, resoluteness, bravery, capable, spiritual, inventive, mental strength
- *Negative:* disagreeable, quarrelsome, easily offended, argumentative, mistrusting, highly strung, tense

Love & Relationships

Charming and friendly, with a warm and caring personality, you are often a devoted partner and a loving parent. Family and home life are very important to you. Your willingness to make sacrifices for those you love often suggests that you are very protective of others. Your generous nature and creative talents also imply that you may need to find some way to express your versatility; otherwise you can become frustrated or disappointed. Although you find it easy to make friends and charm people, you can nevertheless have fluctuating moods, and if you are not careful, they can affect your relationships.

YOUR SPECIAL SOMEONE

A special relationship is more likely to happen with those born on the following dates.

Love & friendship: Jan. 21, 25, Feb. 19, 23, Mar. 17, 21, 30, Apr. 15, 19, 28, 29, May 13, 17, 26, 27, June 11, 15, 24, 25, 30, July 9, 13, 22, 23, 28, Aug. 7, 11, 20, 21, 26, 30, Sept. 5, 9, 18, 19, 24, 28, Oct. 3, 7, 16, 17, 22, 26, 29, Nov. 1, 5, 14, 15, 20, 24, 27, Dec. 3, 12, 13, 18, 22, 25, 27, 29

Beneficial: Jan. 5, 13, 16, 22, 28, Feb. 3, 11, 14, 20, 26, Mar. 1, 9, 12, 18, 24, 29, Apr. 7, 10, 16, 22, 27, May 5, 8, 14, 20, 25, June 3, 6, 12, 18, 23, July 1, 4, 10, 16, 21, Aug. 2, 8, 14, 19, Sept. 6, 12, 17, Oct. 4, 10, 15, Nov. 2, 8, 13, Dec. 6, 11

Fatal attractions: June 30, July 28, Aug. 26, Sept. 24, Oct. 22, Nov. 20, Dec. 18, 26, 27, 28, 29

Challenging: Jan. 2, 23, 30, Feb. 28, Mar. 19, 26, 28, Apr. 17, 24, 26, May 15, 22, 24, June 13, 20, 22, July 11, 18, 20, Aug. 16, 18, 19, Sept. 7, 14, 16, Oct. 5, 12, 14, Nov. 3, 10, 12, Dec. 1, 8, 10

Soul mates: Jan. 14, 22, Feb. 12, 20, Mar. 10, 18, Apr. 8, 16, May 6, 14, June 4, 12, July 2, 10, Aug. 8, Sept. 6, Oct. 4, Nov. 2

June 28

Your birthday reveals you to be idealistic yet pragmatic, an astute and highly intuitive individual with a sharp mind and a natural sense of humor. Having keen reasoning powers and being able to quickly grasp ideas and articulate them show an innate talent for language and communication. As a Cancerian, you are both affectionate and impressionable, with a need for the security of strong family ties and home comforts. Your proud, confident, and assertive front often hides a sensitive soul, and although you possess a caring nature, with strong maternal or paternal instincts, the added influence of the Moon may cause fluctuating moods. Keeping yourself constantly occupied may prove to be an antidote to your low boredom threshold. However, your strong convictions and natural ability to quickly assess people and situations, when coupled with an enterprising spirit, can ensure your success.

Being socially oriented, you often mix with people from many different walks of life and thrive on the personal touch. Nevertheless, guard against being too provocative or manipulative, as it can lose you the many benefits that come from collaborative efforts. Learning to balance cooperation with the desire to be independent and self-sufficient can bring great personal satisfaction and increase your feel-good factor.

A strong influence of the Moon in the first decanate of Cancer carries a double impact throughout your childhood and youth. This influence suggests that although in early life you were shy and sensitive, there was still a longing to be at the center of things. After the age of twenty-four, when your progressed Sun moves into Leo, you are likely to receive a much-needed boost of creativity, strength, and confidence. As your progressed Sun moves into Virgo, when you are age fifty-four, you become less dominant, more thoughtful, and analytical. This brings a growing desire for an orderly life.

FIXED STARS

Alhena or Al-Hena, also called the Bright Foot of Gemini; Dirah, also called Nuhaiti

PRIMARY STAR

Star's name: Alhena or Al-Hena, also called the Bright Foot of Gemini

Degree position: 8°7'–9°7' Cancer between the years 1930 and 2000

Magnitude: 2

Strength: ★★★★★★★★

Orb: 2°10'

Constellation: Gamma Gemini

Applicable days: June 28, 29, 30, July 1, 2

Star qualities: Mercury/Venus or Moon/Venus with Jupiter

Description: a brilliant white star in the left foot of the southern Twin

Your Secret Self

With your profound determination and the ability to initiate new projects, you present a proud and dynamic personality. Preferring a direct approach, you usually call a spade a spade; nonetheless, you may need to develop the art of when to keep silent. At your best you serve as an advisor and authority figure whom others admire and respect.

On one hand, you seek depth of understanding, making you serious, security-conscious, reflective, and thoughtful. On the other hand, your satirical wit, spontaneity, and lively repartee allow you to express the theatrical side of your personality, making you the life and soul of the party. With your thirst for knowledge and shrewd intellect, you enjoy a good debate, but guard against becoming too argumentative or sarcastic.

On an inner level, you may reach the lowest depths only to learn to rise up and overcome all obstacles in your path. Your tenacity combined with a strong need for self-awareness can at times result in a desire for total transformation.

PRIMARY STAR'S INFLUENCE

Alhena's influence can bestow prominence in the art world and denotes a refined, lovable, and affable nature. You are often interested in spirituality or art and science. This star also indicates that you take pride in achievement, whether great or small. A love of ease and luxury is also suggested.

Linked to your Sun's degree, this star denotes artistic inclinations, interest in the sciences, and prominence in the study of astrology or metaphysics. You have a charismatic personality and can prosper through social affairs and all dealings with the public. You are motivated by a desire for pleasure and luxury. This star is also associated with

Work & Vocation

Being a natural psychologist, you may be drawn toward occupations that involve personal contacts, such as counseling, personnel, promotions, or public relations. With your brilliant mind, you may also be attracted to professions such as teaching or lecturing, journalism, health, and communications. Your need for self-expression and a love for the dramatic may lure you into the art and entertainment worlds. A desire to be creative in the home may draw you toward careers such as interior design or gourmet cooking. Alternatively, your leadership qualities, organizational skills, and strategic planning abilities may place you in the world of commerce, where you will enjoy the challenge of large projects.

Famous people born on your birthday include film director Mel Brooks, philosopher Jean-Jacques Rousseau, actor John Cusack, painter Peter Paul Rubens, and actress Kathy Bates.

Numerology

Independent, idealistic, and unconventional, yet pragmatic and determined, you are often a law unto yourself. An inner conflict between wanting to be independent and wanting to be part of a team is also indicated. Like a number 1 individual, you are ambitious, direct, and enterprising. Among your many attributes are resourcefulness, good judgment, and an ability to accumulate knowledge and use it to refine or solve problems. With a number 28 birthday, you often have common sense and can think clearly. Although you are success-oriented and ambitious, family and home life are very important to you. The subinfluence of the number 6 month indicates that you possess charm and firm convictions. While you are determined, with a strong sense of purpose, there is a skeptical and suspicious side to your nature. The key to manifesting your dreams into a tangible reality is to show your real generosity and flair for mixing business and pleasure. Your resourcefulness, combined with your managerial ability, is likely to promote you to positions of authority.

• *Positive:* compassionate, progressive, daring, artistic, creative, idealistic, ambitious, hard-working, self-reliant, strong-willed

• *Negative:* daydreamer, unmotivated, lack of compassion, unrealistic, bossy, hasty judgment, aggressive, lack of confidence, too dependent, proud

Love & Relationships

Being friendly, witty, and charming, you have no problem in attracting admirers. Your need for fun and appreciation makes you naturally gregarious, but the tendency to become oversensitive or dwell on the past can present obstacles to the formation of new relationships. Finding someone with whom you can share stimulating intellectual interests is likely to create the ideal relationship.

Achilles' heel and therefore warns against foot injuries.

• *Positive:* tactful, the joy of living, sociability, stylish with film-star mannerisms

• *Negative:* lazy, overindulgent, wasteful, conceited, proud

See Appendix for additional fixed star readings.

YOUR SPECIAL SOMEONE

You may find a greater incentive to build long-lasting relationships with people born on the following dates.

Love & friendship: Jan. 6, 16, 22, 26, Feb. 4, 14, 20, 24, Mar. 2, 12, 18, 22, Apr. 10, 16, 20, 30, May 8, 14, 18, 28, June 6, 12, 16, 26, July 4, 10, 14, 24, 31, Aug. 2, 8, 12, 22, 29, Sept. 6, 10, 20, 27, Oct. 4, 8, 18, 25, Nov. 2, 6, 16, 23, 30, Dec. 4, 14, 21, 28, 30

Beneficial: Jan. 6, 17, 23, 31, Feb. 4, 15, 21, 29, Mar. 2, 13, 19, 27, 30, Apr. 11, 17, 25, 28, May 9, 15, 23, 26, June 7, 13, 21, 24, July 5, 11, 19, 22, Aug. 3, 9, 17, 20, Sept. 1, 7, 15, 18, 30, Oct. 5, 13, 16, 28, Nov. 3, 11, 14, 26, Dec. 1, 9, 12, 24

Fatal attractions: Dec. 26, 27, 28

Challenging: Jan. 24, Feb. 22, Mar. 20, 29, Apr. 18, 27, 29, May 6, 16, 25, 27, 30, June 14, 22, 25, 28, July 12, 21, 23, 26, Aug. 10, 19, 21, 24, Sept. 8, 17, 19, 22, Oct. 6, 15, 17, 20, Nov. 4, 13, 15, 18, Dec. 2, 11, 13, 16

Soul mates: Jan. 13, Feb. 11, Mar. 9, Apr. 7, May 5, June 3, 30, July 1, 28, Aug. 26, Sept. 24, Oct. 22, Nov. 20, Dec. 18

June 29

♋ Inspiration, emotional sensitivity, and a love of knowledge are often part of your personal charm. As a Cancerian, you are idealistic and sensitive, yet dynamic. Frequently your inquisitive mind urges you to be daring and experimental. Being quick on the uptake, you recognize a good idea when you see one. Progressive and innovative, you are usually interested in social and educational reforms or are constantly seeking new and exciting ideas.

Often charming and attractive, with artistic talent, you have a refined nature that presents a light-hearted personality. Nevertheless, when lacking mental stimulation, you are apt to scatter your energies on trivial pursuits. Although you are an idealist, your love of the good things in life implies that money is an important issue, and you do not like to be short of funds. However, since you are capable and informed you can usually find ways of supplementing your income.

With your artistic talents and desire for knowledge, you often gather information, develop good communications skills, and show a natural flair for writing. Agreeable and diplomatic, you can be friendly and stimulating company, though when moody you may appear cold or lose interest.

Being sensitive, you may be inclined to be a touch reserved earlier in your life, but after the age of twenty-three, when your progressed Sun moves into Leo, you are likely to undergo an expansion of your power, creativity, and confidence. At the age of fifty-three, when your progressed Sun moves into Virgo, you tend to use your authoritative abilities to provide helpful, practical service to others.

FIXED STAR

Star's name: Alhena or Al-Hena, also called the Bright Foot of Gemini

Degree position: 8°7'–9°7' Cancer between the years 1930 and 2000

Magnitude: 2

Strength: ★★★★★★★

Orb: 2°10'

Constellation: Gamma Gemini

Applicable days: June 28, 29, 30, July 1, 2

Star qualities: Mercury/Venus or Moon/Venus with Jupiter

Description: a brilliant white star in the left foot of the southern Twin

PRIMARY STAR'S INFLUENCE

Alhena's influence can bestow prominence in the art world and denotes a refined, lovable, and affable nature. You may be interested in spirituality or art and science. This star also indicates that you take pride in achievement, whether great or small. A love of ease and luxury is also suggested.

Linked to your Sun's degree, this star denotes artistic inclinations, interest in the sciences, and prominence in the study of astrology or metaphysics. You have a charismatic personality and can prosper through social affairs and all dealings with the public. You are motivated by a desire for pleasure and luxury. This star is also associated with Achilles' heel and therefore warns against foot injuries.

• *Positive:* tactful, the joy of living, sociability, stylish with film-star mannerisms

• *Negative:* lazy, overindulgent, wasteful, conceited, proud

Your Secret Self

Although appearing clever and self-contained on the outside, at a deep level your relationships with the people you love are vitally important. Your idealistic visions and longing for love may have you searching for that perfect link or may find expression through art, music, or mystical experience. Part of your life lesson may be to learn how to emotionally give of yourself while learning to receive, in order to create a well-balanced you.

Dynamic and dramatic, you are likely to find that people are naturally drawn to you because of your intelligence and understanding. This may lead to giving others practical advice or showing your ability to put yourself in other people's positions. As you can be very protective of those you care for, you are often daring in defending others. Seemingly independent, you are wise enough to realize that you cannot go it alone.

Work & Vocation

Your sensitive intellect combined with your strong memory and leadership abilities can ensure that you make a valuable contribution in many areas. With an attraction to people-related occupations and activities, you may excel in careers such as teacher, trainer, propagandist, or agent, or in public relations. You may also find you have natural skills in promotion or working for a cause. Your imagination and quick intelligence can draw you to science, medicine, alternative healing, or business. Alternatively, it is possible to achieve success in the beauty industry or in careers connected to the home and family. A need for creative expression may draw you to writing, musical, or artistic pursuits.

Famous people who share your birthday include writer Antoine de Saint-Exupéry, surgeon William James Mayo, and fashion designer Claude Montana.

Numerology

Idealistic visionaries with dynamic and forceful characters, number 29 individuals have powerful personalities and extraordinary potential. Inspiration is the key to your success story, and without it you may experience a lack of purpose. Although you are a true dreamer, the extreme sides of your nature indicate that you may have to guard against alternating moods— going from being very friendly and warm to cold and uncaring, or from optimistic to pessimistic. Quite observant, you still may have to learn how to be less critical or doubting and more considerate of those around you. The subinfluence of the number 6 month indicates that you can be responsible, highly intuitive, and receptive. Although you possess good reasoning powers, you usually judge situations by how you feel and need to be in touch with your deep emotions. Once you develop the right set of values and learn to think for yourself, you can become less dependent on others.

• *Positive:* inspirational, balance, inner peace, generous, successful, creative, intuitive, mystical, worldly

• *Negative:* unfocused, insecure, nervous, moody, extremist, inconsiderate

Love & Relationships

You can easily attract people with your wit and social skills, and you usually think in twosomes. A tendency to be changeable and jealous reveals that you may need to develop a more balanced and practical perspective on personal relationships. Once you have found your ideal love, you are willing to make great sacrifices and support your partner in whatever he or she wishes to undertake. With your diplomatic skills, you know how to keep situations harmonious, and can be hospitable and generous. You prefer hardworking, successful people.

June 30

According to your birthday, your greatest power is your emotional strength. This dynamic force is, without a doubt, in search of self-expression. As a Cancerian, you are imaginative and intuitive, with a generous heart. Willing to do anything for the ones you love, you can be a devoted parent, teacher, and friend. This dynamic power, however, can also suggest that you may have to learn self-control and avoid tendencies such as emotional domination, moodiness, or frustration.

The need for love and appreciation often draws you to public life, and with your creative talents and sense of the dramatic, you will soon stand out in the crowd. Many individuals who share your birthday frequently seek positions of authority; like them, you are probably proud and dignified.

Often courageous and direct, you usually want things clear and concise. Passionate and dedicated, you are willing to make great sacrifices and work very hard if you believe in someone or something. Nevertheless, make sure that emotional investments you make are worthwhile.

After the age of twenty-two, when your progressed Sun moves into the sign of Leo, you are exposed to more opportunities to use the theatrical side of your personality. Whether at work or socially, you will be more poised and self-assured. From your early fifties, when your progressed Sun moves into Virgo, you will be more inclined to be practically motivated, becoming more discriminating and orderly.

FIXED STAR

Star's name: Alhena or Al-Hena, also called the Bright Foot of Gemini

Degree position: 8°7'–9°7' Cancer between the years 1930 and 2000

Magnitude: 2

Strength: ★★★★★★★

Orb: 2°10'

Constellation: Gamma Gemini

Applicable days: June 28, 29, 30, July 1, 2

Star qualities: Mercury/Venus or Moon/Venus with Jupiter

Description: a brilliant white star in the left foot of the southern Twin

PRIMARY STAR'S INFLUENCE

Alhena's influence can bestow prominence in the art world and denotes a refined, lovable, and affable nature. You may be interested in spirituality or art and science. This star also indicates that you take pride in achievement, whether great or small. A love of ease and luxury is also suggested.

Linked to your Sun's degree, this star denotes artistic inclinations, interest in the sciences, and prominence in the study of astrology or metaphysics. You have a charismatic personality and can prosper through social affairs and all dealings with the public. You are motivated by desire for pleasure and luxury. This star is also associated with Achilles' heel and therefore warns against foot injuries.

• Positive: tactful, the joy of living, sociability, stylish with film-star mannerisms

• Negative: lazy, overindulgent, wasteful, conceited, proud

Your Secret Self

As you have great dreams and high aspirations, you may also have to learn about patience and perseverance. Hard work and slow advancement can at times be a real challenge to your dynamic personality. Fortunately, with your powers of persuasion and good sense of humor you can usually extricate yourself from difficult situations. Usually ruled by your heart, you can be passionate and loving as well as deeply protective of those you love.

Charming, with a desire for intimacy and the personal touch, you express yourself through spontaneous gestures of generosity. Nevertheless, you may have to guard against displaying your temper through emotional outbursts or being too selfish. As a good psychologist, when need be, you can be very diplomatic and detached and use your insight in a very kindly and altruistic way.

Work & Vocation

With your strong emotions and sense of the dramatic, you may cut a leading figure in any project or career you undertake. Your natural charm, leadership, and communication skills may draw you toward occupations such as teacher, lecturer, or writer. Alternatively, a natural humanitarianism, sympathy, and intuitive ability may lead you to counseling, or to community or charity work. Complementing your highly developed sensitivity is mental expertise, which you may choose to use in the business, science, or entertainment world.

Famous people who share your birthday include actress Susan Hayward, singer Lena Horne, boxer Mike Tyson, French author Georges Duhamel, and jazz drummer Buddy Rich.

Numerology

Friendly and warm-hearted, you enjoy socializing and can be exceptionally charismatic and loyal. Having a number 30 birthday, you possess strong feelings that need to be expressed creatively. Being in love or emotionally contented is a vital requirement, however; in your pursuit of happiness, avoid being overindulgent or impatient. Pride and ambition combined with good opportunities may see you climb to the top of your profession. With good taste and an eye for style and form, you can achieve success in all types of activities concerning art, design, and music. Among those with number 30 birthdays, many will find recognition or fame, especially musicians, actors, and entertainers. The subinfluence of the number 6 month indicates that you are idealistic and sensitive, and often you judge life according to how you feel. You are able to take ideas and expand them in your own dramatic style. Since at times you become disheartened, learn to be decisive and avoid becoming discontented by appreciating what you already achieved.

- *Positive:* fun-loving, loyal, friendly, talent with words, creative, generous
- *Negative:* lazy, obstinate, erratic, impatient, insecure, indifferent, scatters energy

Love & Relationships

The power of love is your greatest asset, and with your romantic nature, passionate temperament, and generosity, people are attracted to your charisma and appeal. Although you are willing to make great sacrifices for the ones you love, you may have to overcome a tendency to let your feelings take control and rule your mind. By learning to give without expecting anything in return, you will achieve self-mastery through compassion.

July 1

♋ Profound determination, sensitivity, and insight indicate that although you are shy and retiring, there is an unyielding nature behind your gentle smile. As a Cancerian, you are impressionable, intuitive, yet hardworking. Caring and protective, you are often a devoted parent and a loyal friend; nevertheless, at times you are likely to be moody or commanding, troubled by conflicting emotions. This indicates that inclinations toward depression or self-torment should be avoided. Nevertheless, your composed and unwavering nature gives you the impetus to overcome great challenges. This power to begin again by initiating new projects and ideas is one of your greatest assets.

The subinfluence of your decanate ruler, Cancer, suggests that although you are ambitious and independent, you need privacy, and a peaceful life is much desired. Although sociable, you attempt to hide some of your movements and resent any interference from others.

Leadership abilities and the need to be active suggest that you do not procrastinate for long periods of time. By developing your natural insight, you grow to learn the value of wisdom gained from life's experiences. If restrictions are imposed on you, you stand your ground by displaying a rebellious streak. An idealist, you can be a force to be reckoned with once you are inspired.

After the age of twenty-one, when your progressed Sun moves into Leo, there are likely to be many opportunities to develop strength, creativity, and self-expression. The emphasis on your growing confidence is likely to continue until around fifty-one, when your progressed Sun moves into Virgo and your focus changes to a more pragmatic and rational desire to be of service.

Your Secret Self

A need for personal or intimate relationships is a vital key to your happiness. You have good communicative skills, and by avoiding suspicion and jealousy you can have many good friends. Learning to stand on your own two feet gives a great boost to your confidence and indicates that you can overcome the fear of being alone or abandoned.

Your leadership ability and capacity for hard work mark you out for advancement in any field of endeavor. A perfectionist with highly idealistic and romantic notions, you have a strong need for love and affection. Since you often set high standards for yourself and others, at times these high expectations are hard to achieve. By having a meaningful cause to support, you are able to successfully channel your high ideals, quick insight, and compassion to help others.

Work & Vocation

With an innate understanding of the general public, you can succeed in people-related careers. You like to be in control rather than subservient to others, so you often excel in management and executive positions or may prefer to work for yourself. You can be sympathetic and intuitive, and yet when necessary be strong and authoritarian—an excellent combination for a career in politics. Certainly others will value your ability to take charge and your approach to

Star's name: Alhena or Al-Hena, also called the Bright Foot of Gemini
Degree position: 8°7'–9°7' Cancer between the years 1930 and 2000
Magnitude: 2
Strength: ★★★★★★★
Orb: 2°10'
Constellation: Gamma Gemini
Applicable days: June 28, 29, 30, July 1, 2
Star qualities: Mercury/Venus or Moon/Venus with Jupiter
Description: a brilliant white star in the left foot of the southern Twin

PRIMARY STAR'S INFLUENCE

Alhena's influence can bestow prominence in the art world and denotes a refined, lovable, and affable nature. You may be interested in spirituality or art and science. This star also indicates that you take pride in achievement, whether great or small. A love of ease and luxury is also suggested.

Linked to your Sun's degree, this star denotes artistic inclinations, interest in the sciences, and prominence in the study of astrology or metaphysics. You have a charismatic personality and can prosper through social affairs and all dealings with the public. You are motivated by a desire for pleasure and luxury. This star is also associated with Achilles' heel and therefore warns against foot injuries.

• *Positive:* tactful, the joy of living, sociability, stylish with film-star mannerisms

• *Negative:* lazy, overindulgent, wasteful, conceited, proud

new and original ideas. If drawn to the theater or film, you can be a good actor and director, or your strong individuality and imagination may seek expression in art, music, or dance. Alternatively, your humanitarian inclinations may attract you to the caring professions or working with children.

Famous people who share your birthday include Princess Diana, sportsman Carl Lewis, actors Dan Aykroyd and Charles Laughton, singer Deborah Harry, actresses Pamela Anderson Lee, Leslie Caron, and Olivia de Havilland, choreographer Twyla Tharp, and cosmetics tycoon Estée Lauder.

Numerology

As a number 1, you are more inclined to be individual, innovative, and courageous, with plenty of energy. Often there is a need to establish a strong identity and develop self-confidence or assertiveness. The pioneering spirit indicated here encourages you to make your own decisions or strike out alone. Full of enthusiasm and original ideas, you often show others the way forward. With a number 1 birthday, you may also need to learn that the world does not revolve around you; avoid an inclination to be self-centered or dictatorial. Winning is important, and initiating new ideas can lead to success. The subinfluence of the number 7 month indicates that you are highly sensitive, with strong intuition and inner wisdom. You need to learn to trust your own instincts and develop faith and understanding. As an individual with strong values and sound judgment, you aspire to great accomplishment. Your ambitious nature and power to heal others suggest that you can work for the betterment of humankind.

• *Positive:* leadership, creative, progressive, forceful, optimistic, strong convictions, competitive, independent, gregarious

• *Negative:* overbearing, jealous, egotistical, too proud, selfish, weak, vacillating, impatient

Love & Relationships

Your desire for security and financial stability often plays an important role in your choice of partners. You may be sympathetic and supportive of those in your care, but often you like to be in charge and take control by making your own decisions. You may prefer a few close friends to many acquaintances, and loyalty and trust play an important role in close friendships. Family life and taking care of your responsibilities may at times clash with your own personal desire for freedom and independence.

YOUR SPECIAL SOMEONE

You may come closer to finding your true partner with people born on the following dates.

Love & friendship: Jan. 11, 20, 25, 27, 29, Feb. 9, 18, 23, 25, 27, Mar. 7, 16, 21, 23, 25, Apr. 5, 14, 19, 21, 23, May 3, 12, 17, 19, 21, June 1, 10, 15, 17, 19, July 8, 13, 15, 17, Aug. 6, 11, 13, 15, Sept. 4, 9, 11, 13, Oct. 2, 7, 9, 11, Nov. 5, 7, 9, Dec. 3, 5, 7

Beneficial: Jan. 9, 26, Feb. 7, 24, Mar. 5, 22, Apr. 3, 20, May 1, 18, 29, June 16, 27, July 14, 25, 29, 30, Aug. 12, 23, 27, 28, 31, Sept. 10, 21, 25, 26, 29, Oct. 8, 19, 23, 24, 27, Nov. 6, 17, 21, 22, 25, Dec. 4, 15, 19, 20, 23

Fatal attractions: Jan. 1, 2, 16, Feb. 14, Mar. 12, Apr. 10, May 8, June 6, July 4, Aug. 2, Dec. 30, 31

Challenging: Jan. 8, 29, 31, Feb. 6, 27, 29, Mar. 4, 25, 27, 28, Apr. 2, 23, 25, 26, May 21, 23, 24, June 19, 21, 22, July 17, 19, 20, Aug. 15, 17, 18, Sept. 13, 15, 16, Oct. 11, 13, 14, 30, Nov. 9, 11, 12, 28, Dec. 7, 9, 10, 26

Soul mates: May 30, June 28, July 26, Aug. 24, Sept. 22, 30, Oct. 20, 28, Nov. 18, 26, Dec. 16, 24

July 2

SUN: CANCER

DECANATE: SCORPIO/PLUTO

DEGREE: 9°45'–11° CANCER

MODE: CARDINAL

ELEMENT: WATER

FIXED STAR

Star's name: Alhena or Al-Hena, also called the Bright Foot of Gemini

Degree position: 8°7'–9°7' Cancer between the years 1930 and 2000

Magnitude: 2

Strength: ★★★★★★★

Orb: 2°10'

Constellation: Gamma Gemini

Applicable days: June 28, 29, 30, July 1, 2

Star qualities: Mercury/Venus or Moon/Venus with Jupiter

Description: a brilliant white star in the left foot of the southern Twin

PRIMARY STAR'S INFLUENCE

Alhena's influence can bestow prominence in the art world and denotes a refined, lovable, and affable nature. You may be interested in spirituality or art and science. This star also indicates that you take pride in achievement whether great or small. A love of ease and luxury is also suggested.

Linked to your Sun's degree, this star denotes artistic inclinations, interest in the sciences, and prominence in the study of astrology or metaphysics. You have a charismatic personality and can prosper through social affairs and all dealings with the public. You are motivated by a desire for pleasure and luxury. This star is also associated with Achilles's heel and therefore warns against foot injuries.

• *Positive:* tactful, the joy of living, sociability, stylish with film-star mannerisms

• *Negative:* lazy, overindulgent, wasteful, conceited, proud

---

Although your birthday is often associated with dynamic and commanding personalities, you are also idealistic, caring, and reserved. The subinfluence of your decanate ruler, Scorpio, makes you naturally assertive, with strong and intense emotions. You frequently possess artistic talent and psychic ability, and need to find ways to express yourself and your originality.

Appearing friendly and unassuming, with a charismatic character, you often draw others to you and benefit from associations and partnerships. A natural psychologist, you want to know exactly what motivates others, and you are often easygoing, with an honest and direct approach. Although a good and loyal friend who enjoys social gatherings, you have a keen material awareness and natural business sense that are subtly concealed behind your warm smile.

It may be your strong desire to enjoy the good things in life that will motivate or inspire you. Nevertheless, an inherent dissatisfaction and a tendency to daydream or get bored easily may undermine your true potential. Guard against restlessly moving from one interest to another or trying to find yourself through other people's dreams. By recognizing that the power of love is greater than the power of money, you become inspired and rich in heart.

After the age of twenty, when your progressed Sun moves into Leo, you are likely to become more dynamic, positive, and self-assured. This influence will last over the next thirty years and will aid you in achieving positions of authority. From the age of fifty, when your progressed Sun moves into Virgo, you become more discriminating and may desire to be practically useful in a more service-oriented way.

Your Secret Self

Insightful, mentally quick, and witty, you have a wonderful ability with people and are excellent at making contacts. Being versatile and multitalented, however, you may have to learn the importance of making decisions. Although intellectually bright, if you lack the confidence to strike out on your own, you may end up working in situations that are below your full capability and talents. By learning to focus on just a few goals, you can avoid worry and indecision and achieve greater success.

Being interested in everything and everyone suggests that you are popular, adaptable, and socially inclined. A need to share your sense of fun with others implies that you are often generous and may find it hard to say no to the people you care about. More often than not, you attempt to keep the peace by using your diplomacy and charm.

Work & Vocation

Career-wise, your people skills, leadership ability, and capacity to grasp values can put you in a position of authority. Not liking to take orders, you are particularly suited for management or executive positions or working for yourself. You may also have a talent for business and do especially well in areas such as real estate, media, or advertising. Being a good psychologist and having natural sympathy, you may be attracted toward therapy, counseling, or healing work. You are a skilled organizer and not afraid to think big, and this will aid you in whatever ca-

252

reer you choose. Alternatively, your sharp mind and sense of the dramatic may draw you to some form of expression through writing, art, drama, or music.

Famous people who share your birthday include writers Franz Kafka and Herman Hesse, comedian Dan Rowan, Phillipine politician Imelda Marcos, and model Jerry Hall.

Numerology

Sensitivity and a strong need to be part of a group are suggested by a number 2 birthday. You are adaptable and understanding, and you enjoy cooperative activities where you can experience interaction with others. Receptive and influenced by your surroundings, you possess a friendly, warm personality with good social skills and a diplomatic approach. In your attempt to please others, you may run the risk of becoming overly dependent. By developing confidence, however, you can overcome the tendency to be easily hurt by the actions of others. The subinfluence of the number 7 month indicates that you are perceptive and reflective. Frequently a perfectionist, you can be critical and self-absorbed. At times, however, you may overrationalize or get lost in detail. By learning to trust your own instincts and developing faith, you can overcome your inclination to be sensitive to criticism by others or to feel misunderstood.

• *Positive:* good partnerships, gentle, tactful, receptive, intuitive, considerate, harmonious, agreeable, ambassador of goodwill

• *Negative:* suspicious, lack of confidence, timid, oversensitive, emotional, easily hurt

Love & Relationships

You may often wish for a simple life with a loyal partner who is intelligent and mentally stimulating. You are attracted to people who are clever and self-aware, as you are interested in your own self-improvement. With a flair for mixing business and pleasure, you are able to socialize and make contacts that can bring you opportunities. Because you are generous with them, your friends come to your aid when you need them.

YOUR SPECIAL SOMEONE

For love and friendship, you might just find the right person among those born on the following days.

Love & friendship: Jan. 4, 11, 12, 26, 28, 30, Feb. 2, 9, 10, 24, 26, 28, Mar. 7, 8, 22, 24, 26, Apr. 5, 6, 20, 22, 24, 30, May 3, 4, 18, 20, 22, 28, 31, June 1, 2, 16, 18, 20, 26, 29, July 14, 16, 18, 24, 27, Aug. 12, 14, 16, 22, 25, Sept. 10, 12, 14, 20, 23, Oct. 8, 10, 12, 18, 21, Nov. 6, 8, 10, 16, 19, Dec. 4, 6, 8, 14, 17

Beneficial: Jan. 3, 10, 29, Feb. 1, 8, 27, Mar. 6, 25, Apr. 4, 23, May 2, 21, June 19, July 17, 30, Aug. 15, 28, Sept. 13, 26, Oct. 11, 24, Nov. 9, 22, Dec. 7, 20

Fatal attractions: Jan. 1, 2, 3, 11, Feb. 9, Mar. 7, Apr. 5, May 3, June 1, Dec. 31

Challenging: Jan. 9, Feb. 7, Mar. 5, 28, Apr. 3, 26, May 1, 24, June 22, July 20, Aug. 18, Sept. 16, Oct. 14, 30, 31, Nov. 12, 28, 29, Dec. 10, 26, 27

Soul mates: Jan. 7, Feb. 5, Mar. 3, Apr. 1, May 29, June 4, 27, July 25, Aug. 23, Sept. 21, Oct. 19, Nov. 17, Dec. 15

July 3

FIXED STAR

Star's name: Sirius

Degree position: 13°6'–14°2' Cancer between the years 1930 and 2000

Magnitude: 1

Strength: ★★★★★★★★★

Orb: 2°30'

Constellation: Alpha Canis Major

Applicable days: July 3, 4, 5, 6, 7, 8

Star qualities: varied interpretations: Moon/Jupiter/Mars

Description: a brilliant white and yellow binary star, located in the mouth of the Great Dog; linked to the Egyptian god Osiris

PRIMARY STAR'S INFLUENCE

Sirius bestows an optimistic, broad outlook and the ability to make loyal friends in high places. With this star's influence, you can enjoy prosperity and success and can act as guardian or have a custodial position. Often, and without much effort, you can receive favors from superiors. Sirius may indicate honor, wealth, and fame as well as an opportunity to exercise power and leadership qualities. Sirius may also encourage rebellious or daredevil behavior, and it thus warns against the danger of pushing ahead prematurely.

Linked to your Sun's degree, this star suggests success in business, domestic happiness, and an inclination toward the arts, astrology, philosophy, or higher learning. If honor comes too early, you might be unprepared and unable to cope with success. Frequently you present a royal demeanor, and you are successful in dealing with the public.

Imaginative and creative, with practical skills, you are a security-conscious Cancerian with powerful feelings. The subinfluence of your decanate ruler, Scorpio, often indicates that since you are a humanitarian with strong emotions, idealism and vision can play an important role in your life. Nevertheless, a preoccupation with material concerns may keep your feet firmly on the ground.

Observant and perceptive, with a good sense of form and style, you are quickly able to turn your interests and creative talents into successful commercial enterprises. With your organizational skills and intuitive powers, you often possess good judgment and have strong material values. With your desire for the good life, however, you may have to avoid overindulgence or extravagance.

Generous, proud, and sensitive, yet critical and all-knowing, is how others may often describe you. This indicates that due to emotional inhibitions you sometimes hide your true feelings and insecurities. Nevertheless, with your dynamic and friendly personality and gift for words, you can be very persuasive.

After the age of nineteen, when your progressed Sun moves into Leo, you become less shy or security-conscious. The Leo influence aids you to gain in confidence and strengthen your performance capacity in your chosen field. From age forty-nine onward, your progressed Sun moves into Virgo and you will have a more practical and discriminating attitude, with service to others becoming a more important part of your life.

Your Secret Self

Although you can be expressive and creative, your greatest challenge may be an inclination to scatter your energies across too many interests. This suggests that indecision and worry, particularly about money matters, may undermine your great potential. Despite a lucky streak, you should avoid speculative ventures or get-rich-quick schemes, as it is through determination and perseverance that you might achieve success. As a rule, you are charitable and generous with your time and energy.

Your potential for greatness arises from your superior intellect and ability to perceive ideas on a grand scale. When inspired, you have the talent to organize big events and work hard for a worthwhile cause. This eventually will bring you the recognition that you deserve.

Work & Vocation

You are likely to shine when in positions of authority, and as you can be fair and just, this makes you an excellent manager or administrator. Altruism and an ability to push through some kind of reform may attract you to leadership in such organizations as trade unions, parental groups, or charity work. Those who are not freedom fighters may be interested in education or some other form of public or social interest. An innate understanding of money and values may draw you to business, where you can do particularly well, especially when using your creative skills, such as being an antiques dealer, chef, restaurant worker, art dealer, or administrator. A need to express your individuality and creativity may draw you to the world of art or entertainment.

Famous people who share your birthday include actor Tom Cruise, director Ken Russell, and playwright Tom Stoppard.

Numerology

A need for love, creativity, and sensitivity are all indicated by the number 3 birthday. Easygoing and a good companion, you enjoy friendly social activities and many interests. Versatility and a need for self-expression lead you to seek numerous experiences. An inclination to get bored easily, however, may cause you to become indecisive or spread yourself too thin. Although with a number 3 birthday you can be enthusiastic and charming, with a good sense of humor, you may have to develop self-esteem to guard against worry and other emotional insecurities. Personal relationships and a loving atmosphere are of prime importance to you, as they endow you with hope and inspiration. The subinfluence of the number 7 month indicates that although you are analytical and intuitive, at times you can be skeptical. You usually have a way with words and develop the art of asking subtle questions without letting anyone know what you really think.

• *Positive:* humorous, happy, friendly, productive, creative, artistic, power to wish, freedom-loving, talent with words

• *Negative:* easily bored, vain, overimaginative, exaggerate, unloving, boastful, self-indulgent, lazy, hypocritical

Love & Relationships

Inclined toward people who are creative and communicative, you often find friendship and love when you can feel at ease with the other person. Generous and proud, you like to display a confident and smart appearance. Your many interests lead you to experience different types of relationships. If insecure, you may find that financial worry and indecision can cause stress in relationships. At times your restlessness and an inability to settle down also suggest that you can have a change of heart, but once you settle down you can be very loyal and caring.

This star also indicates that you are trustworthy and can act as custodian of other people's property.

• *Positive:* faithfulness, important responsibilities, joy of living, love of enterprise, successful, creative activities

• *Negative:* the urge for freedom at any cost, misuse of power and positions of trust

YOUR SPECIAL SOMEONE

To find your ideal partner, you may want to look for someone born on one of the following dates.

Love & friendship: Jan. 13, 29, Feb. 11, 27, 29, Mar. 9, 25, 27, Apr. 7, 23, 25, May 5, 21, 23, 29, June 3, 19, 21, 27, 30, July 1, 17, 19, 25, 28, Aug. 15, 17, 23, 26, Sept. 13, 15, 21, 24, Oct. 11, 13, 19, 22, 29, Nov. 9, 11, 17, 20, 27, Dec. 7, 9, 15, 18, 25

Beneficial: Jan. 11, Feb. 9, Mar. 7, 31, Apr. 5, 29, May 3, 27, 31, June 1, 25, 29, July 23, 27, 31, Aug. 21, 25, 29, 30, Sept. 19, 23, 27, 28, Oct. 17, 21, 25, 26, Nov. 15, 19, 23, 24, 30, Dec. 13, 17, 21, 22, 28

Fatal attractions: Jan. 1, 2, 3, 4, 12, Feb. 10, Mar. 8, Apr. 6, May 4, June 2, Dec. 31

Challenging: Jan. 10, Feb. 8, Mar. 6, 29, Apr. 4, 27, May 2, 25, June 23, July 21, Aug. 19, Sept. 17, Oct. 15, 31, Nov. 13, 29, 30, Dec. 11, 27, 28

Soul mates: Jan. 18, 24, Feb. 16, 22, Mar. 14, 20, Apr. 12, 18, May. 10, 16, June. 8, 14, July 6, 12, Aug. 4, 10, Sept. 2, 8, Oct. 6, Nov. 4, Dec. 2

July 4

♋ Success and determination are often linked to your birthday. Reserved and sensitive, you are also tenacious and ambitious, like other Cancerians. If you find true inspiration, you are often willing to work hard and can achieve prosperity and fame.

Charisma and charm, with a youthful or childlike quality, are some of your natural attributes. Although you can be highly spirited, witty, and entertaining, a more serious side of your nature urges you to accomplish and be ambitious. This unique mixture of materialism and idealism needs a purpose in order to be productive. When you find that special something, you will quickly transform into a responsible and mature individual.

Spontaneous by nature, you have a love of freedom that endows you with enthusiasm. Adaptable, sociable, and aware of your image, you need to feel good and look well groomed, often spending your money on clothes and luxury goods. Wanting excitement, variety, and style, you need the funds that can provide you with the good life. Although you like to be independent, joint efforts and collaboration with others could yield profits and success. With a responsible attitude on your part, you often make excellent contributions to your team.

In the years leading up to age eighteen you are likely to be concerned with home, family, and security. After this point, when your progressed Sun moves into Leo, you may be drawn into public situations that require you to be strong and confident. This continues until the age of forty-eight, when there is another major change of emphasis in your life as your progressed Sun enters Virgo. This brings practical issues to prominence in your life, as you are likely to become more analytical, observant, and orderly.

Fixed Stars

Sirius, Canopus

PRIMARY STAR

Star's name: Sirius

Degree position: 13°6'–14°2' Cancer between the years 1930 and 2000

Magnitude: 1

Strength: ★★★★★★★★★

Orb: 2°30'

Constellation: Alpha Canis Major

Applicable days: July 3, 4, 5, 6, 7, 8

Star qualities: varied interpretations: Moon/Jupiter/Mars

Description: a brilliant white and yellow binary star, located in the mouth of the Great Dog; linked to the Egyptian god Osiris.

PRIMARY STAR'S INFLUENCE

Sirius bestows an optimistic, broad outlook and the ability to make loyal friends in high places. With this star's influence, you can enjoy prosperity and success and can act as guardian or have a custodial position. Often, and without much effort, you can receive favors from superiors. Sirius may indicate honor, wealth, and fame as well as an opportunity to exercise power and leadership qualities. Sirius may also encourage rebellious or daredevil behavior, and it thus warns against the danger of pushing ahead prematurely.

Linked to your Sun's degree, this star suggests success in business, domestic happiness, and an inclination toward the arts, astrology, philosophy, or higher learning. If honor comes too

Your Secret Self

You may feel pulled between what inspires you and what will make money, and often this creates an inner tension. Although you may be creative and skillful, without effort and determination your talents may not be realized. Learning to make the right choices and decisions will be the major challenge you may have to overcome. Since you are gifted with intuition and insight, you have much to gain from listening to your inner voice.

If you recognize the need to challenge yourself mentally, you may understand the value of knowledge and education as a path to success. Since you often have many diverse interests and activities, you may need to develop your powers of discrimination and learn to focus on one particular subject.

Work & Vocation

For your career, any line of activity that involves people will give you the greatest fulfillment. Your personal charisma, leadership qualities, and organizational skills indicate the potential to reach the top in your chosen field. The possibility of success is particularly likely in sales, negotiation, or promotion. Equally, publishing, law, banking, or politics can be a suitable career. Any occupation that deals with items for the home, food, or caring is also a possibility. Your need for self-expression and a love for the dramatic can lure you into the art and entertainment worlds. Independence and ambition are likely to stimulate you to work for yourself.

Famous people who share your birthday include actress Gina Lollobrigida and writer Nathaniel Hawthorne.

Numerology

Endowed with energy, practical skills, and strong determination, you can achieve success through hard work. With a number 4 birthday, you are sensitive to form and composition and are able to create practical systems. Security-conscious, you like to build a strong foundation for yourself and your family. A pragmatic approach to life confers a good business sense and an ability to move forward and achieve material success in life. As a number 4, you are usually honest, frank, and fair. Nevertheless, you may have to learn to be more diplomatic and avoid a tendency to be stubborn or tactless. The subinfluence of the number 7 month indicates that you can be idealistic and intuitive, with inspired and original ideas. A blend of modesty and confidence often challenges you to achieve a more balanced view and overcome a tendency to be easily hurt by others' criticism. This search for balance also implies that you consider how you feel and what you think.

• *Positive:* self-discipline, steady, hardworking, organized, craftsmanship, good with your hands, pragmatic, trusting, exact

• *Negative:* unstable, destructive behavior, uncommunicative, repressed, rigid, lazy, unfeeling, too economical, bossy, resentful, strict

Love & Relationships

Young at heart, you are friendly and sociable, with many interests. Although you have many acquaintances and can make friends easily, you are more inclined toward enterprising and successful people who are determined to succeed. You also have excellent opportunities through friends and associates, and traveling may be one of your many hobbies. Advantages through marriage and partnerships are also indicated, and if there are enough funds, you can be quite content and happy. Nevertheless, take your time in choosing your relationships carefully; otherwise you may encounter short-lived relationships.

early, you might be unprepared and unable to cope with success. Frequently you present a royal demeanor, and you are successful in dealing with the public. This star also indicates that you are trustworthy and can act as custodian of other people's property.

• *Positive:* faithfulness, important responsibilities, joy of living, love of enterprise, successful, creative activities

• *Negative:* the urge for freedom at any cost, misuse of power and positions of trust

See Appendix for additional fixed star readings.

YOUR SPECIAL SOMEONE

You can improve your chances of finding the right partner with someone born on one of the following days.

Love & friendship: Jan. 6, 8, 14, 23, 26, 28, Feb. 4, 10, 12, 21, 24, 26, Mar. 2, 10, 12, 19, 22, 24, Apr. 8, 14, 17, 20, 22, May 6, 15, 16, 18, 20, June 4, 13, 16, 18, July 2, 11, 14, 16, 20. Aug. 9, 12, 14, 22, Sept. 7, 10, 12, 24, Oct. 5, 8, 10, 26, Nov. 3, 6, 8, 28, Dec. 1, 4, 6, 30

Beneficial: Jan. 9, 12, Feb. 7, 10, Mar. 5, 8, Apr. 3, 6, May 1, 4, June 2, 30, July 28, Aug. 26, 30, 31, Sept. 24, 28, 29, Oct. 22, 26, 27, Nov. 20, 24, 25, Dec. 18, 22, 23, 29

Fatal attractions: Jan. 1, 2, 3, 4, 5

Challenging: Jan. 11, 13, 29, Feb. 9, 11, Mar. 7, 9, 30, Apr. 5, 7, 28, May 3, 5, 26, 31, June 1, 3, 24, 29, July 1, 22, 27, Aug. 20, 25, Sept. 18, 23, 30, Oct. 16, 21, 28, Nov. 14, 19, 26, Dec. 12, 17, 24

Soul mates: Jan. 12, 29, Feb. 10, 27, Mar. 8, 25, Apr. 6, 23, May 4, 21, June 2, 19, July 17, Aug. 15, Sept. 13, Oct. 11, Nov. 9, Dec. 7

SUN: CANCER

DECANATE: CANCER/SCORPIO,
MOON/MARS

DEGREE: 12°45'–14° CANCER

MODE: CARDINAL

ELEMENT: WATER

July 5

Optimistic, adventurous, and multitalented, you are revealed by your birthday to be an intuitive Cancerian with a strong desire to achieve and accomplish. Although you are imaginative and have practical skills, without patience and perseverance many of your ideas will remain on the drawing board.

Possessing excellent business sense, you can be a shrewd investor involved in large enterprises and speculations. The subinfluence of your decanate ruler, Cancer, suggests that you seek ways to transform your life. This influence, however, also implies that you may have to overcome an inclination to exploit situations. More often than not, you believe that money is power, and indeed on many occasions it is; however, by seeing only the material benefits you can miss out on the great insight into what is really worthwhile in life.

Even if you are self-disciplined and hardworking, you often have extravagant taste, and acquisitions are important to your sense of worth. As a practical idealist with leadership ability, you do have foresight and vision. With these skills you are frequently able to commercialize your gifts through self-promotion. You have large dreams, and whatever you do in life, you want to do big. This need to expand and extend may indicate, however, that inner restlessness or dissatisfaction with your current situation can encourage you to push yourself even further.

After the age of seventeen, when your progressed Sun moves into Leo, your power, creativity, and confidence increase and you are likely to become more adventurous. At the time your progressed Sun moves into Virgo, when you are age forty-seven, you become more discriminating and efficient. There is a likelihood of a growing interest in health matters or in being of service to others.

FIXED STARS

Sirius, Canopus

PRIMARY STAR

Star's name: Sirius

Degree position: 13°6'–14°2' Cancer between the years 1930 and 2000

Magnitude: 1

Strength: ★★★★★★★★★

Orb: 2°30'

Constellation: Alpha Canis Major

Applicable days: July 3, 4, 5, 6, 7, 8

Star qualities: varied interpretations: Moon/Jupiter/Mars

Description: a brilliant white and yellow binary star, located in the mouth of the Great Dog, linked to the Egyptian god Osiris

Your Secret Self

Spirited yet sensitive, you have the insight and knowledge to quickly evaluate your surroundings. An inner nobility and a sense of dignity or pride suggest that you do not enjoy menial tasks or work that lacks mental challenge. Indeed, it is often your superior mental ability that enables you to achieve recognition and success.

Although you often appear confident and self-assured, it is through education and learning that you may come to realize your true potential. Generous and kind, you are often supportive and caring. Able to comprehend the value of wisdom, you may utilize your skills for humanitarian projects. With good organizational ability and your desire to keep busy, your life is often rich and fulfilling.

PRIMARY STAR'S INFLUENCE

Sirius bestows an optimistic, broad outlook and the ability to make loyal friends in high places. With this star's influence, you can enjoy prosperity and success and can act as guardian or have a custodial position. Often, and without much effort, you can receive favors from superiors. Sirius may indicate honor, wealth, and fame as well as an opportunity to exercise power and leadership qualities. Sirius may also encourage rebellious or daredevil behavior, and it thus warns against the danger of pushing ahead prematurely.

Linked to your Sun's degree, this star suggests success in business, domestic happiness, and an inclination

Work & Vocation

Your natural business acumen, shrewd money sense, and ability to turn on the charm when necessary can bring you many financial rewards. You are inclined to prefer people-oriented careers. A dislike for taking orders often leads you to a position of authority. Multitalented and with an ability to be versatile, you can excel in occupations such as salesperson, promoter, or restaurateur. You can be equally successful as an entrepreneur, administrator, accountant, or banker. Alternatively, a philosophical leaning may draw you to the clergy or metaphysics. As you are likely to be good at delegating and possess a more altruistic side to your nature, you may be drawn to teaching, counseling, or work that will benefit others. Those with creative talents are likely to become writers, actors, filmmakers, or musicians.

Famous people who share your birthday include film director Jean Cocteau, musicians Robbie Robertson and Huey Lewis, former French president George Pompidou, and Sufi leader Hazrath Inayat Khan.

Numerology

Your willingness to explore or try anything new, combined with an enthusiastic approach, suggests that life will have a lot to offer you. Travel and many opportunities for change, some unexpected, may lead you to undergo a real transformation of views and beliefs. With a number 5 birthday, you need to feel that life is exciting. Nevertheless, you may need to develop a responsible attitude and avoid tendencies toward unpredictability and restlessness. The natural talent of a number 5 individual is knowing how to go with the flow and staying detached. The subinfluence of the number 7 month indicates that you are inquisitive, mentally quick, and pragmatic. Usually you rely on your own intuition and prefer to make your own decisions. Strong-willed and confident, you need to feel financially secure. You like to gather useful information that you can utilize in some practical way.

• *Positive:* versatile, adaptable, progressive, strong instincts, magnetic, lucky, daring, freedom-loving, quick and witty, curious, mystical, sociable

• *Negative:* unreliable, changeable, inconsistent, undependable, overconfident, headstrong

Love & Relationships

Sensitive and intuitive, you are passionate, with a strong need to express your feelings in a dramatic way. Friendly and sociable, you find it important to be popular, and usually you are loyal and generous to those you love. Wanting the best of what life can offer, however, can also imply that you can become self-indulgent, especially if you try to compensate for a lack of emotional satisfaction. You prefer to be associated with successful and powerful people who are charismatic and influential, or those who can help you to achieve success.

toward the arts, astrology, philosophy, or higher learning. If honor comes too early, you might be unprepared and unable to cope with success. Frequently you present a royal demeanor, and you are successful in dealing with the public. This star also indicates that you are trustworthy and can act as custodian of other people's property.

• *Positive:* faithfulness, important responsibilities, joy of living, love of enterprise, successful, creative activities

• *Negative:* the urge for freedom at any cost, misuse of power and positions of trust

See Appendix for additional fixed star readings.

YOUR SPECIAL SOMEONE

For love and friendship, you might just find the right person among those born on the following days.

Love & friendship: Jan. 6, 15, 29, 31, Feb. 4, 13, 27, 29, Mar. 2, 11, 25, 27, Apr. 9, 23, 25, May 7, 21, 23, June 5, 19, 21, July 3, 17, 19, 30, Aug. 1, 15, 17, 28, Sept. 13, 15, 26, Oct. 11, 13, 24, Nov. 9, 11, 22, Dec. 7, 9, 20

Beneficial: Jan. 13, 15, 19, Feb. 11, 13, 17, Mar. 9, 11, 15, Apr. 7, 9, 13, May 5, 7, 11, June 3, 5, 9, July 1, 3, 7, 29, Aug. 1, 5, 27, 31, Sept. 3, 25, 29, Oct. 1, 23, 27, Nov. 21, 25, Dec. 19, 23

Fatal attractions: Jan 2, 3, 4, 5, 6, May 30, June 28, July 26, Aug. 24, Sept. 22, Oct. 20, Nov. 18, Dec. 16

Challenging: Jan. 12, Feb. 10, Mar. 8, Apr. 6, May 4, June 2, Aug. 31, Sept. 29, Oct. 27, 29, 30, Nov. 25, 27, 28, Dec. 23, 25, 26, 30

Soul mates: Jan. 2, 28, Feb. 26, Mar. 24, Apr. 22, May 20, June 18, July 16, Aug. 14, Sept. 12, Oct. 10, Nov. 8, Dec. 6

SUN: CANCER

DECANATE: CANCER/SCORPIO,
MOON/MARS

DEGREE: 13°30'–15°30' CANCER

MODE: CARDINAL

ELEMENT: WATER

July 6

♋ Generosity, humanitarianism, and broad-mindedness are some of the qualities associated with your birthday. Often happy and liberal, you can attract people and be popular. Your success, however, very much depends on how well you manage your assets. As a Cancerian, you are sensitive, idealistic, and highly intuitive, with a good sense of humor and satire. Nevertheless, at times you can become overly serious or agitated and may need to learn how to stay detached.

The subinfluence of your decanate ruler, Cancer, indicates that you can also be a person of extremes. By trying to resist your inclinations to be impatient or extravagant, you can minimize your frustrations or sense of uncertainty. This suggests that by developing a balanced and harmonious attitude to life you will be able to avoid many obstacles and disappointments.

Taking a responsible attitude and learning not to take your luck for granted may inspire you to explore your true potential. Although you prefer to deal with the larger picture, in your enthusiasm you may forget about the small yet vital detail. This suggests that by being thorough or methodical, you can enhance your prospects for success.

Your sensitivity will become less of a problem for you after the age of sixteen, when your progressed Sun moves into Leo. This enables you to become bolder and more self-assured in all areas of your life. After the age of forty-six, when your progressed Sun moves into Virgo, you are likely to become health-conscious, precise, and discriminating.

FIXED STARS

Sirius, Canopus

PRIMARY STAR

Star's name: Sirius

Degree position: 13°6'–14°2' Cancer between the years 1930 and 2000

Magnitude: 1

Strength: ★★★★★★★★★

Orb: 2°30'

Constellation: Alpha Canis Major

Applicable days: July 3, 4, 5, 6, 7, 8

Star qualities: varied interpretations: Moon/Jupiter/Mars

Description: a brilliant white and yellow binary star, located in the mouth of the Great Dog; linked to the Egyptian god Osiris

PRIMARY STAR'S INFLUENCE

Sirius bestows an optimistic, broad outlook and the ability to make loyal friends in high places. With this star's influence, you can enjoy prosperity and success and can act as guardian or have a custodial position. Often, and without much effort, you can receive favors from superiors. Sirius may indicate honor, wealth, and fame as well as an opportunity to exercise power and leadership qualities. Sirius may also encourage rebellious or daredevil behavior and it thus warns against the danger of pushing ahead prematurely.

Linked to your Sun's degree, this star suggests success in business, domestic happiness, and an inclination

Your Secret Self

Although you possess a good sense of values, a live-for-the-moment attitude or dissatisfaction with material limitations may result in restlessness. You may wish to travel and explore new opportunities if your situation does not provide you with chances for advancement.

Proud and dramatic, you are conscious of your appearance and attempt to present a favorable image. Although you have a flair for making money, the fact that you are generous and compassionate may mean that you spend it faster than you can make it. This also suggests that fluctuations in finances may limit your aspirations. Learning to budget can be your first lesson on the road to success. Being a good entrepreneur or fighter for a cause, however, means that spectacular opportunities can come to you, since God moves in mysterious ways.

Work & Vocation

An interesting mixture of emotional sensitivity and intellectual insight ensures that with discipline and determination you can be successful in any career you choose. With your leadership ability, you will want to be given positions of authority or at least have the freedom to work in your own way, such as in teaching, lecturing, or self-employment. Being a good evaluator, you may find that the more pragmatic side to your nature draws you to real estate, banking, business, or the stock market. This date can also indicate possible success in show business and the arts. Alternatively, a humanitarian streak may draw you to professions such as charity work, image making, or the healing professions, or to help in the community.

Famous people who share your birthday include the Dalai Lama, painter Frida Kahlo, actor Sylvester Stallone, actress Janet Leigh, former First Lady Nancy Reagan, and musician Bill Haley.

Numerology

Compassion, idealism, and a caring nature are some of the attributes suggested by a number 6 birthday. Often a visionary or a humanitarian, you can be responsible, loving, and supportive. Although you are usually worldly and career-oriented, with a number 6 birthday you can be a homemaker and a devoted parent. The more sensitive among you will need to find a form of creative expression and are often drawn to the world of entertainment or art and design. The challenges for some people with a number 6 birthdate may include developing self-confidence or being more commanding. The subinfluence of the number 7 month indicates that you need to establish your own unique style or be independent and original. Since you are often a perfectionist, you can be critical; however, avoid being overly opinionated or uncommunicative. If you become overly sensitive to criticism yourself, you may feel misunderstood.

• *Positive:* worldly, universal brotherhood, friendly, compassionate, dependable, understanding, sympathetic, idealistic, domestically inclined, humanitarian, poised, artistic, balanced

• *Negative:* discontented, anxious, shy, stubborn, outspoken, disharmonious, lack of responsibility, suspicious, cynical, self-centered

Love & Relationships

Attracted to people who are mentally stimulating, you usually seek some type of intellectual activity. With your quick wit and good sense of humor, you are a natural entertainer and fun to be with. Although you are friendly and sociable, if hidden insecurities come to the surface you may at times resort to arguments and become quarrelsome. This factor can cause you problems in close relationships. Your communication skills, however, can smooth situations.

---

toward the arts, astrology, philosophy, or higher learning. If honor comes too early, you might be unprepared and unable to cope with success. Frequently you present a royal demeanor, and you are successful in dealing with the public. This star also indicates that you are trustworthy and can act as custodian of other people's property.

• *Positive:* faithfulness, important responsibilities, joy of living, love of enterprise, successful, creative activities

• *Negative:* the urge for freedom at any cost, misuse of power and positions of trust

See Appendix for additional fixed star readings.

YOUR SPECIAL SOMEONE

You might come closer to finding that special person among those born on the following days.

Love & friendship: Jan. 6, 16, Feb. 4, 14, Mar. 2, 12, 28, 30, Apr. 10, 26, 28, May 8, 24, 26, 30, June 6, 22, 24, 28, July 4, 20, 22, 26, 31, Aug. 2, 18, 20, 24, 29, Sept. 16, 18, 22, 27, Oct. 14, 16, 20, 25, Nov. 12, 14, 18, 23, Dec. 10, 12, 16, 21

Beneficial: Jan. 9, 14, 16, Feb. 7, 12, 14, Mar. 5, 10, 12, Apr. 3, 8, 10, May 1, 6, 8, June 4, 6, July 2, 4, Aug. 2, Sept. 30, Oct. 28, Nov. 26, 30, Dec. 24, 28, 29

Fatal attractions: Jan. 3, 4, 5, 6, 7, 21, Feb. 19, Mar. 17, Apr. 15, May 13, June 11, July 9, Aug. 7, Sept. 5, Oct. 3, Nov. 1

Challenging: Jan. 4, 13, 28, Feb. 2, 11, 26, Mar. 9, 24, Apr. 7, 22, May 5, 20, June 3, 18, July 1, 16, Aug. 14, Sept. 12, Oct. 10, 31, Nov. 8, 29, Dec. 6, 27

Soul mates: Jan. 15, 22, Feb. 13, 20, Mar. 11, 18, Apr. 9, 16, May 7, 14, June 5, 12, July 3, 10, Aug. 1, 8, Sept. 6, Oct. 4, Nov. 2

July 7

FIXED STARS

Sirius, Canopus

PRIMARY STAR

Star's name: Sirius

Degree position: 13°6'–14°2' Cancer between the years 1930 and 2000

Magnitude: 1

Strength: ★★★★★★★★★

Orb: 2°30'

Constellation: Alpha Canis Major

Applicable days: July 3, 4, 5, 6, 7, 8

Star qualities: varied interpretations: Moon/Jupiter/Mars

Description: a brilliant white and yellow binary star, located in the mouth of the Great Dog; linked to the Egyptian god Osiris

PRIMARY STAR'S INFLUENCE

Sirius bestows an optimistic, broad outlook and the ability to make loyal friends in high places. With this star's influence you can enjoy prosperity and success and can act as guardian or have a custodial position. Often, and without much effort, you can receive favors from superiors. Sirius may indicate honor, wealth, and fame as well as an opportunity to exercise power and leadership qualities. Sirius may also encourage rebellious or daredevil behavior, and it thus warns against the danger of pushing ahead prematurely.

Linked to your Sun's degree, this star suggests success in business, domestic happiness, and an inclination toward the arts, astrology, philosophy, or higher learning. If honor comes too

Strong willpower, determination, and productivity are some of the qualities associated with your birthday. As a Cancerian, you are intuitive and imaginative; however, your sense of values and materialistic inclinations suggest that financial security may play an important part in your overall plan.

The subinfluence of your decanate ruler, Scorpio, suggests that you like to be in a position of influence, and enjoy power or being in control. You may, however, have to guard against a tendency to be too domineering. Hardworking and forceful, with good organizational abilities, you often possess good business sense and a pragmatic approach. Although you often have conservative views and good moral qualities, you want to succeed materially and socially.

Since you want to express your individuality, you do not like to take orders from others; you frequently create your own ethics and moral code of conduct but must guard against being too opinionated. Learning to collaborate with others brings rewarding experiences, and by developing your diplomatic skills, you often enhance your powers of persuasion.

You grow more confident in all areas of your life after the age of fifteen, when your progressed Sun moves into Leo for a thirty-year period. At the age of forty-five there is another change of emphasis in your life, when your progressed Sun moves into Virgo. With this influence you are likely to become more analytical and discriminating. At the age of seventy-five, when your progressed Sun enters Libra, you are likely to want more harmony and beauty in your environment.

Your Secret Self

As a shrewd observer, you are quick on the uptake and able to pay attention to small details. This often helps you capitalize on your talents and make wise investments. Insight, wisdom, and knowledge are some of your natural gifts, but you may need to master self-discipline to bring out your outstanding potential. Although you are highly intuitive, at times you can be mistrusting or full of self-doubt. Nevertheless, you often enjoy a battle of wits with others, enabling you to keep your keen mind finely tuned.

Pride and an inner sense of nobility suggest that you do not like to fail. Occasionally, however, you may become too headstrong and need to develop patience or listen to others' advice. A natural spontaneity stimulates you to be competitive and can help you achieve in creative endeavors.

Work & Vocation

Intuitive, mentally sharp, and hardworking, you have the potential to reach the top in your chosen field. A straightforward and businesslike style may guarantee that you do not waste time but aim straight for your objectives. You enjoy power, structure, and efficiency, so you may succeed in business particularly as an organizer, executive, or supervisor. The possibility of achievement is also likely in sales, negotiation, or publishing. Equally, you can excel in advertising, law, or banking. Alternatively, your need for self-expression and a love for the dramatic can also entice you into the art or entertainment world. Since you do not like taking orders and are very independent, you may prefer being your own boss or delegating to others.

Famous people who share your birthday include designer Pierre Cardin, musician Ringo Starr, film actress Shelley Duvall, painter Marc Chagall, and composer Gustav Mahler.

Numerology

As a number 7 individual, you are analytical and thoughtful. You prefer to make your own decisions, and frequently you learn best through personal experience. With a constant need for greater self-awareness, you enjoy gathering information and may be interested in reading, writing, or spirituality. At times you can become oversensitive to criticism from others and feel misunderstood. A tendency to be enigmatic or secretive leads you to develop the art of asking subtle questions without letting anyone know what you really think. The subinfluence of the number 7 month indicates that you are highly individualistic and proud. Although you are often practical, hardworking, and independent, you can occasionally appear impatient and are easily bored. You often alternate between being misled and impressionable, on one hand, and thinking independently and being skeptical, on the other. A desire for success and money frequently encourages you to learn new skills. By developing your lines of communication to others, you can express your thoughts clearly and precisely.

- *Positive:* trusting, meticulous, idealistic, honest, psychic, scientific, rational, reflective
- *Negative:* concealing, deceitful, unfriendly, secretive, skeptical, confused, too detached

Love & Relationships

Although friendly and sociable, you can be indecisive about your relationships. Since you can easily attract the opposite sex, you may have to beware of becoming too demanding or overly emotional in your love life. As you are likely to give everything to the one you love, take your time in choosing the right partner. Music is often a very good healer if you feel anxious.

early, you might be unprepared and unable to cope with success. Frequently you present a royal demeanor, and you are successful in dealing with the public. This star also indicates that you are trustworthy and can act as custodian of other people's property.

- *Positive:* faithfulness, important responsibilities, joy of living, love of enterprise, successful, creative activities
- *Negative:* the urge for freedom at any cost, misuse of power and positions of trust

See Appendix for additional fixed star readings.

YOUR SPECIAL SOMEONE

You might come closer to finding your true match with someone born on one of the following days.

Love & friendship: Jan. 7, 17, 20, Feb. 5, 15, 18, Mar. 3, 13, 16, 29, 31, Apr. 1, 11, 14, 27, 29, May 9, 12, 25, 27, June 7, 10, 23, 25, July 5, 8, 21, 23, Aug. 3, 6, 19, 21, Sept. 1, 4, 17, 19, Oct. 2, 15, 17, Nov. 13, 15, 30, Dec. 11, 13, 28

Beneficial: Jan. 15, 17, 28, Feb. 13, 15, 26, Mar. 11, 13, 24, Apr. 9, 11, 22, May 7, 9, 20, June 5, 7, 18, July 3, 5, 16, Aug. 1, 3, 14, Sept. 1, 12, Oct. 10, 29, Nov. 8, 27, Dec. 6, 25

Fatal attractions: Jan. 4, 5, 6, 7, 8, Feb. 3, Mar. 1

Challenging: Jan. 4, 5, 14, Feb. 2, 3, 12, Mar. 1, 10, Apr. 8, 30, May 6, 28, June 4, 26, July 2, 24, Aug. 22, Sept. 20, Oct. 18, Nov. 16, Dec. 14

Soul mates: Jan. 2, Mar. 29, Apr. 27, May 25, June 23, July 21, Aug. 19, Sept. 17, Oct. 15, Nov. 13, Dec. 11

July 8

FIXED STARS

Sirius, Canopus

PRIMARY STAR

Star's name: Sirius

Degree position: 13°6'–14°2' Cancer between the years 1930 and 2000

Magnitude: 1

Strength: ★★★★★★★★★

Orb: 2°30'

Constellation: Alpha Canis Major

Applicable days: July 3, 4, 5, 6, 7, 8

Star qualities: varied interpretations: Moon/Jupiter/Mars

Description: a brilliant white and yellow binary star, located in the mouth of the Great Dog; linked to the Egyptian god Osiris

PRIMARY STAR'S INFLUENCE

Sirius bestows an optimistic, broad outlook and the ability to make loyal friends in high places. With this star's influence, you can enjoy prosperity and success and can act as guardian or have a custodial position. Often, and without much effort, you can receive favors from superiors. Sirius may indicate honor, wealth, and fame as well as an opportunity to exercise power and relationship qualities. Sirius may also encourage rebellious or daredevil behavior, and it thus warns against the danger of pushing ahead prematurely.

Linked to your Sun's degree, this star suggests success in business, domestic happiness, and an inclination toward the arts, astrology, philosophy, or higher learning. If honor comes too

You are idealistic and charming, yet practical and skillful, and your birthday suggests that you are a receptive and hardworking individual. Often your gentle and protective nature hides your mental restlessness and ambition. As a Cancerian, you are sensitive and sympathetic and can feel other people's problems as if they were your own. You want to safeguard those you care for, but you need to avoid martyring yourself for the sake of others.

The subinfluence of your decanate ruler, Scorpio, suggests that you possess great inner strength, and since you are persistent, you are often able to rise above crises. Persistent and forceful, with organizational abilities, you often possess good business sense and a pragmatic approach. Although you enjoy power or being in control, a kind and responsible side to your nature shows how caring you often are.

A materialistic element attributed to your birthday indicates that financial security may be an important factor in your decision making. Although you often have conservative views and good moral qualities, you want to succeed materially and socially. Nevertheless, your warmth and need to be emotionally expressive may lead you to pursue your creative talents.

Issues around sensitivity and security may strongly influence you until the age of fourteen, when your progressed Sun moves into Leo. This is likely to give you the strength to display your talents and skills in a more confident way. After the age of forty-four, when your progressed Sun moves into Virgo, practical considerations become more prominent, with the likelihood of improvement in your efficiency, capabilities, and organizational skills. At the age of seventy-four, when your progressed Sun moves into Libra, there is another change of emphasis in your life, highlighting issues of harmony, balance, and relationship.

Your Secret Self

As you learn in life to value your feelings and recognize that they have as much importance as the needs of others, you develop self-confidence. This stops you from becoming disappointed or frustrated by people or situations, as you are able to stay lovingly detached and not take on the projections or expectations of others.

Although you are sociable and spontaneous, with high ideals and morals, you can be a person of extremes. This implies that you can easily go from being light-hearted, generous, and spontaneous one moment to critical and serious the next. By finding a healthy balance between the material and spiritual and no longer needing the approval of others, you are likely to find a wealth of inner love to help you overcome all obstacles.

Work & Vocation

A natural sociability will help you succeed in all people-related careers, especially as you are good at combining business and pleasure. Your dramatic sense and need for self-expression may attract you to a profession in art, drama, or music. With your good business sense, you are likely to need the freedom to work in your own way. Being hardworking, you can gravitate toward positions of authority, or you may prefer being self-employed. With your natural caring and humanitarian streak, you can excel in careers such as teaching, counseling, or working with children. Alternatively, you may be drawn to work that is of benefit to the community.

Famous people who share your birthday include actress Anjelica Huston, industrialist John D. Rockefeller, comedian Marty Feldman, astrologer Alan Leo, actor Kevin Bacon, and writer Marianne Williamson.

early, you might be unprepared and unable to cope with success. Frequently you present a royal demeanor, and you are successful in dealing with the public. This star also indicates that you are trustworthy and can act as custodian of other people's property.

• *Positive:* faithfulness, important responsibilities, joy of living, love of enterprise, successful, creative activities

• *Negative:* the urge for freedom at any cost, misuse of power and positions of trust

See Appendix for additional fixed star readings.

Numerology

The number 8 often indicates that you aspire to great accomplishment and possess an ambitious nature. A desire for dominance, security, and material success is also indicated by this birthday. As a number 8 person, you have a natural business sense and will benefit greatly from developing your organizational and executive skills. If you are willing to work hard, you are often given great responsibility. Nevertheless, you may have to learn how to administer or delegate your authority in a fair and just way. A strong need to feel secure or established urges you to make long-term plans and investments. The subinfluence of the number 7 month indicates that you are quick and enthusiastic, with a charismatic personality. Your greatest assets are your strong instincts and the ability to learn quickly through combining theory and practice. Ambitious, yet emotionally restless and intuitive, you can recognize opportunities when they arise, but without a plan you can lose interest and abandon them.

• *Positive:* leadership, thoroughness, hardworking, traditional, protective, power to heal, good judge of values

• *Negative:* impatient, wasteful, intolerant, overwork, domineering, easily discouraged, lack of planning, controlling behavior

YOUR SPECIAL SOMEONE

If you are looking for your ideal partner, you may have better luck with someone born on one of the following dates.

Love & friendship: Jan. 4, 8, 18, 19, 23, Feb. 2, 6, 16, 17, 21, Mar. 4, 14, 15, 19, 28, 30, Apr. 2, 12, 13, 17, 26, 28, 30, May 10, 11, 15, 24, 26, 28, June 8, 9, 13, 22, 24, 26, July 6, 7, 11, 20, 22, 24, 30, Aug. 4, 5, 9, 18, 20, 22, 28, Sept. 2, 3, 7, 16, 18, 20, 26, Oct. 1, 5, 14, 16, 18, 24, Nov. 3, 12, 14, 16, 22, Dec. 1, 10, 12, 14, 20

Beneficial: Jan. 5, 16, 27, Feb. 3, 14, 25, Mar. 1, 12, 23, Apr. 10, 21, May 8, 19, June 6, 17, July 4, 15, Aug. 2, 13, Sept. 11, Oct. 9, 30, Nov. 7, 28, Dec. 5, 26, 30

Fatal attractions: Jan. 5, 6, 7, 8, 9, 17, Feb. 15, Mar. 13, Apr. 11, May 9, June 7, July 5, Aug. 3, Sept. 1

Challenging: Jan. 1, 10, 15, Feb. 8, 13, Mar. 6, 11, Apr. 4, 9, May 2, 7, June 5, July 3, 29, Aug. 1, 27, Sept. 25, Oct. 23, Nov. 21, Dec. 19, 29

Soul mates: Aug. 30, Sept. 28, Oct. 26, Nov. 24, Dec. 22

Love & Relationships

Caring and unselfish, you are usually a devoted partner and friend to those you love and admire. A need for stability often suggests that you are willing to make great sacrifices for love. Frequently you can end up with someone from a different age group or background. A need to be popular also indicates that you have a large circle of friends and strong links with other family members.

July 9

♋ Charismatic and sociable, you have a flair for people and can make friends easily. Although you are usually outgoing, your birthday shows you to be a person with a sensitive soul and powerful emotions. With your insight, intuitive intellect, and strong sense of justice, you like to speak your mind, and often you have strong convictions. When you stand up for your ideals and fight for others, you show your sympathetic and compassionate nature.

Since you possess sensitive awareness and a strong need for a harmonious environment, you may prefer not to rock the boat. Whether at home with your family or with friends, you can at times be called upon to make important sacrifices in order to please others.

By not harboring resentment, you will find that your good deeds will be rewarded many times over. Guard against the tendency to suffer in silence; this causes emotional outbursts. It is important to form a good foundation in life, progressing at a steady pace, even though you might want to begin making money before you know where your abilities lie.

Endowed with a fertile imagination, you may benefit from channeling your thoughts into constructive pursuits rather than allowing them to develop into anxiety or worry. At your best you are fun-loving, generous, and gregarious, with a good sense of humor.

After the age of thirteen, when your progressed Sun enters into the sign of Leo, you begin to assert yourself and develop more confidence to display your talents and skills. When you are forty-three, your progressed Sun moves into Virgo, there is a change of emphasis in your life, and you are likely to become more discriminating, practical, and perfectionist. At the age of seventy-three, when your progressed Sun moves into Libra, companionship and your relationships in general may start to play a more important part in your life.

FIXED STARS

Canopus, Al Wasat

PRIMARY STAR

Star's name: Canopus

Degree position: 13°58'–15° Cancer between the years 1930 and 2000

Magnitude: 1

Strength: ★★★★★★★★★

Orb: 2°30'

Constellation: Alpha Carinae

Applicable days: July 4, 5, 6, 7, 8, 9, 10

Star qualities: Saturn/Jupiter and Moon/Mars

Description: a yellow-white star located in one of the oars of the ship Argo

PRIMARY STAR'S INFLUENCE

The Egyptian god Canopus, patron of ships and voyages, is linked to this star, which bestows travel and suggests long voyages. This star imparts a kind nature, conservatism, astuteness, and success through education and academic achievements. You have the ability to acquire comprehensive knowledge as well as work for the community. This star also warns about family and relations, domestic afflictions, and troubles with a parent.

Linked to your Sun's degree, this star bestows success in public affairs and attainment of far-reaching objectives through industrious effort. Fame can also be achieved but is not always long-lasting. There may be some minor problems on the domestic front or with

Your Secret Self

Doubt or frustration may pull you away from concentrating on your positive goals, but by enduring, you can fortify your willpower. This can ensure that you will not be controlled by circumstances but rather control them. By challenging yourself to excel, you surprise yourself with what you can achieve.

With the sensitivity and imagination to put yourself in the place of others, you possess an exceptional gift for understanding humanity. You may, however, need to complement this with your own form of self-expression in order to give yourself the power and purpose you need. Being very creative and intuitive, you are likely to find many avenues for your talents.

Work & Vocation

Your gift for dealing with people and a natural empathy make you ideal for working with the public. Your interest in humanity, the community, and social conditions may lead you to the healing professions, law, social work, or counseling. This birthday also indicates possible success in sales and promotions. Your ability to speak out may attract you to be an orator; talented with words, you may wish to be a writer. Alternatively, your imagination may find an outlet through business or artistic pursuits, such as the theater, art and design, or publishing. Your creative side may particularly enjoy work involving the home, such as interior design.

Famous people who share your birthday include actors Tom Hanks and Richard Roundtree, artist David Hockney, writer Barbara Cartland, former British prime minister Edward Heath, and inventor Nicola Tesla.

friends and relatives, although help is there when it is needed most.

• *Positive:* earnestness, commitment, love of travel, perseverance, success in law

• *Negative:* frustration, discontent, most problems are of your own doing, involvement in lawsuits

See Appendix for additional fixed star readings.

Numerology

Benevolence, compassion, and sentimental sensitivity are all associated with the number 9 birthday. Intuitive and psychic abilities point to a universal receptivity; if channeled positively, this may inspire you to seek a spiritual path. With a number 9 birthday, you usually feel that your life is mapped out for you and does not leave you much room to maneuver. You may also have to develop understanding, tolerance, and patience, as well as learning to become impersonal. Learn to trust your own instincts and avoid being dissatisfied with your lot. Success often comes through persistence and a positive outlook. The subinfluence of the number 7 month indicates that you are reserved and thoughtful, with a sensitive nature and a strong desire for self-fulfillment. As a humanitarian, at times you can experience inner tensions when facing friction between a need for self-expression and responsibility to others. You may need to learn how to strike a balance between being overly confident and being doubtful and insecure.

• *Positive:* idealistic, creative, sensitive, generous, magnetic, poetic, charitable, giving, detached, lucky, popular

• *Negative:* frustrated, nervous, fragmented, unsure, selfish, impractical, easily led, worried, isolated

YOUR SPECIAL SOMEONE

For love and happiness, look for a partner among those born on the following dates.

Love & friendship: Jan. 5, 9, 18, 19, Feb. 3, 7, 16, 17, Mar. 1, 5, 14, 15, 31, Apr. 3, 12, 13, 29, May 1, 10, 11, 27, 29, June 8, 9, 25, 27, July 6, 7, 23, 25, 31, Aug. 4, 5, 21, 23, 29, Sept. 2, 3, 19, 21, 27, 30, Oct. 1, 17, 19, 25, 28, Dec. 13, 15, 21, 24

Beneficial: Jan. 1, 6, 17, Feb. 4, 15, Mar. 2, 13, Apr. 11, May 9, June 7, July 5, Aug. 3, Sept. 1, Oct. 31, Nov. 29, Dec. 27

Fatal attractions: Jan. 6, 7, 8, 9

Challenging: Jan. 2, 16, Feb. 14, Mar. 12, Apr. 10, May 8, June 6, July 4, Aug. 2, Dec. 30

Soul mates: Jan. 11, 31, Feb. 9, 29, Mar. 7, 27, Apr. 5, 25, May 3, 23, June 1, 21, July 19, Aug. 17, Sept. 15, Oct. 13, Nov. 11, Dec. 9

Love & Relationships

You make a loyal and reliable friend, and with your natural charm you are often popular with a large circle of acquaintances. Having high expectations from relationships, you often give a lot to those you love, but you need to be loved and appreciated yourself. With the power to attract people from all walks of life comes the necessity to exercise a certain amount of discrimination. Although relationships and marriage are important to you, material security may be a prerequisite.

July 10

♋ Ambitious and restless, yet reflective and reserved, you are a Cancerian with a dynamic personality. Life has a lot in store, for you may want to experience many different activities before you settle down.

Motivation and perseverance are vital keys to your success. With the subinfluence of your decanate ruler, Scorpio, you are full of determination and drive. There is a likelihood, however, that in your search for better prospects you will leave your past behind and move forward to make a fresh start. This inherent restlessness suggests that you need to avoid monotony by being active or seeking variety. Nevertheless, for security, long-term plans and investments may provide peace of mind.

Individual and clever, you learn quickly through direct experience. You are versatile, with a sensitive heart, and your instinctive feelings, which are uncannily right, can often help you assess new possibilities. Self-confidence and a love of freedom are often linked with opportunities for travel or work in foreign countries. By staying open-minded and optimistic, you come to learn that if you do not succeed the first time, you can always try again somewhere else.

When your progressed Sun moves into Leo as you reach the age of twelve, your strength and creativity increase and enable you to display more confidence in your dealings with others. At the age of forty-two, when your progressed Sun moves into Virgo, you begin to be more practical and analytical, as well as developing order and discrimination in all your dealings. At the age of seventy-two, when your progressed Sun moves into Libra, you change your perspective and start to take more of an interest in your relationships. You may also seek more harmony and balance or develop latent artistic or literary interests.

Your Secret Self

Multitalented and adaptable, you are a very quick learner but may on occasion suffer from a lack of self-confidence or from doubt that you can succeed. Invariably this is unfounded, as you possess a highly creative spirit and an ability to view life in a very broad and detached way. This more humanitarian side to your nature is able to look past current problems to a more universal perspective.

Since you may have to learn that responsibilities can bring you solid rewards, you may need to find projects or enterprises that really interest you. If uncertainty about finances causes you unnecessary worry or frustration, it is often due to an innate impatience. Should you avoid the path of instant rewards, you often take the slower route of building a secure and worry-free future.

Work & Vocation

Your natural ability to deal with people may be your best attribute for success in your career. Although you have a strong love of home and its comforts, your need for variety leads you to careers that do not involve routine. Ideally, if you can use both your practical sense and your imagination—for example, as an actor, photographer, artist, or musician—then so much the

---

FIXED STARS

Canopus, Al Wasat, Propus, Castor

PRIMARY STAR

Star's name: Canopus

Degree position: 13°58'–15° Cancer between the years 1930 and 2000

Magnitude: 1

Strength: ★★★★★

Orb: 2°30'

Constellation: Alpha Carinae

Applicable days: July 4, 5, 6, 7, 8, 9, 10

Star qualities: Saturn/Jupiter and Moon/Mars

Description: a yellow-white star located in one of the oars of the ship Argo

PRIMARY STAR'S INFLUENCE

The Egyptian god Canopus, patron of ships and voyages, is linked to this star, which bestows travel and suggests long voyages. This star imparts a kind nature, conservatism, astuteness, and success through education and academic achievements. You have the ability to acquire comprehensive knowledge as well as work for the community. This star also warns about family and relations, domestic afflictions, and troubles with a parent.

Linked to your Sun's degree, this star bestows success in public affairs and attainment of far-reaching objectives through industrious effort. Fame can also be achieved but is not always long-lasting. There may be some minor problems on the domestic front or with

better. You usually do not stick with any career if it does not provide financial rewards fairly quickly, and you may be particularly attracted to work that involves travel. Otherwise, you may be drawn to counseling or the healing world, where you are likely to work very intuitively. Your desire for action can also direct you to the world of sports.

Famous people who share your birthday include writer Marcel Proust, painters James Abbott McNeil Whistler, Camille Pissarro, and Giorgio De Chirico, theologian John Calvin, and tennis champions Virginia Wade and Arthur Ashe.

Numerology

With a number 10 birthday, you have a strong need to establish an identity and achieve. You are likely to be innovative, self-assured, and ambitious. Energetic and original, you stand by your own beliefs even when they differ from others'. Your pioneering spirit frequently encourages you to travel far afield or strike out on your own. Having a number 10 birthday, you may also have to learn that the world does not revolve around you, and you should guard against being selfish and dictatorial. Success and accomplishment are important, and you could find the way to the top of your profession. Since this usually involves working with larger issues, you may not be domestically inclined. The subinfluence of the number 7 month indicates that you are inquisitive and thoughtful. As you prefer to make your own decisions, you dislike interference. Learning best through personal experience, you will find that the key to your success is taking a responsible and mature view.

• *Positive:* leadership, creative, progressive, forceful, optimistic, strong convictions, competitive, independent, gregarious

• *Negative:* overbearing, jealous, egotistical, too proud, antagonistic, lack of restraint, selfish, weak, vacillating, impatient

Love & Relationships

Sensitive, friendly, and intelligent, you need the company of mentally stimulating people. Usually you are attracted to forceful individuals who know their own mind or those who are independent and ambitious. You are sometimes reserved and like to present a smart appearance. Observant and aware, you may nevertheless have to avoid being critical or judgmental if you want relationships to last.

friends and relatives, although help is there when it is needed most.

• *Positive:* earnestness, commitment, love of travel, perseverance, success in law

• *Negative:* frustration, discontent, most problems are of your own doing, involvement in lawsuits

See Appendix for additional fixed star readings.

YOUR SPECIAL SOMEONE

If you are looking for your ideal partner, you might find greater stability in love and friendships with someone born on one of the following dates.

Love & friendship: Jan. 6, 10, 20, 29, Feb. 4, 8, 18, 27, Mar. 2, 6, 16, 25, 28, 30, Apr. 4, 14, 23, 26, 28, 30, May 2, 12, 21, 24, 26, 28, 30, June 10, 19, 22, 24, 26, 28, July 8, 17, 20, 22, 24, 26, Aug. 6, 15, 18, 20, 22, 24, Sept. 4, 13, 16, 18, 20, 22, Oct. 2, 11, 14, 16, 18, 20, Nov. 9, 12, 14, 16, 18, Dec. 7, 10, 12, 14, 16,

Beneficial: Jan. 7, 13, 18, 28, Feb. 5, 11, 16, 26, Mar. 3, 9, 14, 24, Apr. 1, 7, 12, 22, May 5, 10, 20, June 3, 8, 18, July 1, 6, 16, Aug. 4, 14, Sept. 2, 12, 30, Oct. 10, 28, Nov. 8, 26, 30, Dec. 6, 24, 28

Fatal attractions: Jan. 7, 8, 9, 10, 25, Feb. 23, Mar. 21, Apr. 19, May 17, June 15, July 13, Aug. 11, Sept. 9, Oct. 7, Nov. 5, Dec. 3

Challenging: Jan. 3, 17, Feb. 1, 15, Mar. 13, Apr. 11, May 9, 30, June 7, 28, July 5, 26, 29, Aug. 3, 24, 27, Sept. 1, 22, 25, Oct. 20, 23, Nov. 18, 21, Dec. 16, 19

Soul mates: Jan. 18, Feb. 16, Mar. 14, Apr. 12, May 10, 29, June 8, 27, July 6, 25, Aug. 4, 23, Sept. 2, 21, Oct. 19, Nov. 17, Dec. 15

July 11

FIXED STARS

Castor, Al Wasat, Propus

PRIMARY STAR

Star's name: Castor

Degree position: 19°16'–20°13' Cancer between the years 1930 and 2000

Magnitude: 2

Strength: ★★★★★★★

Orb: 2°10'

Constellation: Alpha Gemini

Applicable days: July 10, 11, 12, 13, 14, 15

Star qualities: varied influences of Mercury, Venus, Mars, and Jupiter

Description: a binary star, bright white and pale white, located on the head of the northern Twin

PRIMARY STAR'S INFLUENCE

Castor's influence bestows a quick mind and keen intellect. This star indicates fluctuating circumstances of gains alternating with losses, and sudden rises in fortune that may be followed by a fall.

Linked to your Sun's degree, Castor bestows energetic characteristics and a talent for wit and satire, but also a tendency to cynicism. This star imparts a flair for writing and good communication skills. You are probably interested in public affairs and may choose a career in the media. This star also imparts opportunities in foreign affairs, as well as good intuition and talent for metaphysical studies.

Practical skills, productivity, and a need for security are often identified with your birthday. As a Cancerian, you are sensitive and imaginative, with a forceful and determined personality. Receptive and attuned to form and structure, you can combine your practical skills with your artistic talents. With your ability to establish a workable system, you can often develop your natural technical, organizational, and business skills.

The subinfluence of your decanate ruler, Scorpio, suggests that although you are sensible and practical, you must learn to trust your strong instincts or first impressions and recognize your great inner strength. Your efficient and down-to-earth approach also implies that you are outspoken and direct; nevertheless, you may have to guard against a tendency to be impatient or stubborn.

Though you are often blessed with good fiscal circumstances, if you do find yourself a little short, your troubles are usually short-lived. Although your financial prospects are favorable, a strong emphasis on work implies that through perseverance and concentrated effort you can take advantage of the many opportunities that come your way.

Being able to do a job well, you take pride in your work; as a perfectionist, you are inclined to be thrifty and economical, with a strong sense of duty. A lot may depend, however, on your ability to exercise self-control. This may also suggest that at times a sense of duty dominates the inclinations of your heart.

At the age of eleven your progressed Sun moves into Leo for a thirty-year period. With this influence, your self-confidence and creativity gradually increase. After the age of forty-one, when your progressed Sun moves into Virgo, you are likely to become more patient and analytical. This may include providing helpful practical service to others. There is another turning point at the age of seventy-one, when your progressed Sun moves into Libra. This influence brings an added emphasis to all your relationships and may encourage a greater interest in harmony and beauty.

Your Secret Self

Although stability may be one of your prime objectives, an inner emotional restlessness may urge you to look for new prospects and opportunities. A possible dissatisfaction with your lot may be overcome by developing patience or by finding harmony within yourself. If this need for action and adventure is not recognized, you may turn to escapism to compensate.

Opportunities for work may come out of the blue and could involve a change of residence or travel to new locations. Since you are a perfectionist and multitalented, your versatility suggests that you are capable of applying your skills and producing excellent work in whatever you do. With your strong instincts, you often apply your intuition to your judgment and can successfully use it in your daily routine.

Work & Vocation

Since you are imaginative and practical, what you may need is a plan to manifest your dreams. In business you are ideally suited for dealing with other people's money through banking, law, or foreign transactions. Equally, you may be successful in sales, particularly dealing with items for the home. Interested in people, you can excel at promotions and public relations. You are also likely to be good with your hands; this dexterity may be useful in crafts, carpentry, or cookery. Image-conscious, sensitive, and creative, you may prefer a career in art and design, music, or drama. This birthdate usually shows good opportunities for financial enterprises.

Famous people who share your birthday include actor Yul Brynner, actress Sela Ward, former U.S. president John Quincy Adams, and fashion designer Giorgio Armani.

Numerology

The special vibration of the master number 11 birthday suggests that idealism, inspiration, and innovation are highly important to you. Although you possess intuitive powers, you may scatter your energies and need to find a goal upon which you can focus. Usually you are highly charged and enjoy vitality, but you must avoid becoming overanxious or impractical. A blend of modesty and self-assurance challenges you to work toward finding a balance both materially and spiritually. The subinfluence of the number 7 month indicates that although you are reserved, you can be determined and ambitious, with an active mind. You may have to develop understanding, tolerance, and patience as well as learn to become impersonal. You frequently desire power and recognition, but need to develop your analytical skills.

• *Positive:* balanced, focused, objective, enthusiastic, inspirational, spiritual, idealistic, intelligent, outgoing, inventive, artistic, humanitarian, psychic

• *Negative:* superiority complex, aimless, overemotional, easily hurt, highly strung, selfish, lack of clarity, dominating

Love & Relationships

Romantic and sensitive, you have a lot of powerful love to give. If your strong emotions do not have a positive channel for expression, you can be subject to fluctuating moods. Idealistic and imaginative, you usually look for a devoted partner and have high expectations in love. The restlessness associated with your birthday can surface if you become too restricted, so keeping active is a prerequisite to happiness and emotional satisfaction.

YOUR SPECIAL SOMEONE

You might come closer to finding your true match with someone born on the following days.

Love & friendship: Jan. 7, 11, 22, Feb. 5, 9, 20, Mar. 3, 7, 18, 31, Apr. 1, 5, 16, 29, May 3, 14, 27, 29, June 1, 12, 25, 27, July 10, 23, 25, Aug. 8, 21, 23, 31, Sept. 6, 19, 21, 29, Oct. 4, 17, 19, 27, 30, Nov. 2, 15, 17, 25, 28, Dec. 13, 15, 23, 26

Beneficial: Jan. 8, 14, 19, Feb. 6, 12, 17, Mar. 4, 10, 15, Apr. 2, 8, 13, May 6, 11, June 4, 9, July 2, 7, Aug. 5, Sept. 3, Oct. 1, 29, Nov. 27, Dec. 25, 29

Fatal attractions: Jan. 8, 9, 10, 11

Challenging: Jan. 9, 18, 20, Feb. 7, 16, 18, Mar. 5, 14, 16, Apr. 3, 12, 14, May 1, 10, 12, June 8, 10, July 6, 8, 29, Aug. 4, 6, 27, Sept. 2, 4, 25, Oct. 2, 23, Nov. 21, Dec. 19

Soul mates: Jan. 9, Feb. 7, Mar. 5, Apr. 3, May 1, Oct. 30, Nov. 28, Dec. 26

July 12

Creativity and enterprise, practical skills, and intuitive insight are some of the qualities identified with your birthday. As a Cancerian, you are imaginative and idealistic, yet your natural business sense and an ability to present an unusual and original point of view often suggest that you are an objective thinker. This objectivity, however, can be challenged by your tendency to be indecisive or unpredictable.

The subinfluence of your decanate ruler, Pisces, adds to your receptivity and usually implies that you can easily absorb the atmosphere around you. This influence also suggests that you can be prone to moods and therefore need a harmonious environment.

More often than not, worry and anxiety revolve around money issues and can interfere with your ability to resolve problems and find simple solutions. Nevertheless, your inspirational ideas and a bright outlook frequently give you the edge when the call is for originality.

As a perfectionist, your thoroughness or concentration enables you to pick up on ideas and methods very quickly, and with your communication skills you usually appear light and congenial.

A positive philosophy is essential to your well-being. By avoiding pessimism, you can focus your attention on the matter at hand rather than scatter and diffuse your energies through nervous haste.

After the age of ten, when your progressed Sun moves into Leo, there may be increased opportunities to develop strength, creativity, and self-expression. Your growing confidence is likely to continue to the beginning of your forties, when your progressed Sun enters Virgo. Your focus is then liable to change so that you become more pragmatic and discerning. At the age of seventy, when your progressed Sun enters Libra, you may experience another turning point as your interest turns more to relationships, harmony, and balance.

FIXED STARS

Castor, Al Wasat, Propus

PRIMARY STAR

Star's name: Castor

Degree position: 19°16'–20°13' Cancer between the years 1930 and 2000

Magnitude: 2

Strength: ★★★★★★★

Orb: 2°10'

Constellation: Alpha Gemini

Applicable days: July 10, 11, 12, 13, 14, 15

Star qualities: varied influences of Mercury, Venus, Mars, and Jupiter

Description: a binary star, bright white and pale white, located on the head of the northern Twin

PRIMARY STAR'S INFLUENCE

Castor's influence bestows a quick mind and keen intellect. This star indicates fluctuating circumstances of gains alternating with losses, and sudden rises in fortune that may be followed by a fall.

Linked to your Sun's degree, Castor bestows energetic characteristics and a talent for wit and satire, but also a tendency to cynicism. This star imparts a flair for writing and good communication skills. You are probably interested in public affairs and may choose a career in the media. This star also imparts opportunities in foreign affairs, as well as good intuition and talent for metaphysical studies.

Your Secret Self

Many of your projects may center around home and its responsibilities. This sense of home could stretch out to the planet Earth itself, as you can be a true humanitarian. You feel things keenly and intensely and often have ideas that bring harmony out of chaos. You may feel that at times it seems too hard to achieve your objectives, but you have the dedication and capabilities for outstanding achievement.

Inside you are extremely sensitive and vulnerable, though on the surface you appear confident and capable. A quest for peace of mind may lead you to investigate metaphysics or spirituality as a way to develop inner serenity. Alternatively, you can be highly creative, with a need for emotional self-expression. Possessing high morals, you can be very supportive and often fight for a cause you believe in.

Work & Vocation

You have a creative approach to life that may manifest through writing or the arts, but as you are naturally sociable, it can also come out in business. Shrewd financial acumen points to a career in banking or real estate. Your excellent mind and communication skills indicate a tremendous potential to achieve; you may just have to guard against scattering your energies or overcome a tendency to doubt. A philosophical or humanitarian leaning may be satisfied through occupations such as the clergy or charity work, or becoming a philanthropist. If you stay in the same career, you are likely to be always looking for ways to change or improve the way you work.

Famous people who share your birthday include actor and producer Bill Cosby, artist Amedeo Modigliani, and inventor and theorist Buckminster Fuller.

Numerology

A desire to establish true individuality is often suggested by the number 12 birthday. Usually you are intuitive, helpful, and friendly, and you possess good reasoning power. Innovative, understanding, and sensitive, you also know how to use tact and cooperative methods to achieve your aims and objectives. To others, you often appear confident, although self-doubt and suspicion can undermine your easygoing personality and positive outlook. When you achieve the balance between your need for self-expression and your natural inclination to be supportive of others, you can find emotional satisfaction and personal fulfillment. The subinfluence of the number 7 month indicates that you are intelligent and a creative thinker. You like to make your own decisions, although at times you can be indecisive and unsettled. Since you are full of enthusiasm and original ideas, you need to develop your executive abilities and have the courage to lead others in a new direction.

• *Positive:* creative, attractive, initiative, disciplinarian, promote self or others
• *Negative:* reserved, selfish, eccentric, uncooperative, overly sensitive, shy, lack of self-esteem

YOUR SPECIAL SOMEONE

You are likely to increase your chances of love and romance with those born on the following dates.

Love & friendship: Jan. 8, 22, 26, Feb. 6, 20, 24, Mar. 4, 18, 22, Apr. 2, 16, 20, 30, May 14, 18, 28, 30, June 12, 16, 26, 28, July 10, 14, 24, 26, Aug. 8, 12, 22, 24, Sept. 6, 10, 20, 22, 30, Oct. 4, 8, 18, 20, 28, Nov. 2, 6, 16, 18, 26, Dec. 4, 14, 16, 24

Beneficial: Jan. 9, 20, Feb. 7, 18, Mar. 5, 16, 29, Apr. 3, 14, 27, May 1, 12, 25, June 10, 23, July 8, 21, Aug. 6, 19, Sept. 4, 17, Oct. 2, 15, 30, Nov. 13, 28, Dec. 11, 26, 30

Fatal attractions: Jan. 9, 10, 11, 12, 27, Feb. 25, Mar. 23, Apr. 21, May 19, June 17, July 15, Aug. 13, Sept. 11, Oct. 9, Nov. 7, Dec. 5

Challenging: Jan. 2, 10, 19, Feb. 8, 17, Mar. 6, 15, Apr. 4, 13, May 2, 11, June 9, July 7, 30, Aug. 5, 28, Sept. 3, 26, Oct. 1, 24, Nov. 22, Dec. 20, 30

Soul mates: Jan. 15, Feb. 13, Mar. 11, Apr. 9, May 7, June 5, July 3, Aug. 1, Oct. 29, Nov. 27, Dec. 25

Love & Relationships

Idealistic and sensitive, you have intuitive powers that are at times very accurate, even if your need for security and love causes you to ignore your own instincts and thereby commit yourself to certain relationships whatever the cost. If you find yourself in unsuitable partnerships, guard against martyring yourself to those who fail to recognize your wonderful potential. By staying spontaneous and independent, you can develop your own inner powers and still enjoy loving relationships.

July 13

♋ Receptive and intuitive, with deep convictions and an insight into other people's characters, you are a Cancerian with strong social inclinations and outstanding ideas. Your powerful emotions need some form of expression. An inclination to be involved in financial ventures indicates that you could benefit from and gain success in co-operative endeavors and associations.

The subinfluence of your decanate ruler, Pisces, adds strength to your sensitivity and implies that you are imaginative and idealistic. You easily absorb the atmosphere around you, but shifting between uplifting and depressing moods can influence your inner equilibrium. This also suggests that you are in need of balance and stability.

Extremely generous to people you love and admire, you have a tendency to worry about money, which explains why you might appear materialistic or selfish at times. Your need for personal contacts, however, indicates that through learning to share and communicate, you can inspire others with your idealistic and friendly nature.

An active mind and a natural flair for people-related activities point out that you love a good mental challenge and thrive on new opportunities and contacts. This also suggests that you can excel in salesmanship. However, guard against an inclination to be argumentative and quarrelsome when you do not get your own way.

After the age of nine, when your progressed Sun moves into Leo, you are likely to become more dynamic, positive, and confident. This will give you the advantage of learning to develop social skills early in your life. At the age of thirty-nine, when your progressed Sun moves into Virgo for a thirty-year period, you become more orderly and discriminating, with a desire to be of service. At the age of sixty-nine, when your progressed Sun moves into Libra, there is another change of emphasis. This influence suggests that relationships will play a greater part in your life, and your need for art and beauty will be on the increase.

Your Secret Self

Strong inner forces drive you to initiate projects or create new opportunities for success. You experience more optimism with life when this power to accomplish is combined with your idealism to manifest your lofty objectives. This often places you in positions of leadership, but by uniting your ambition and drive with your awareness of diplomacy and cooperative efforts, you can really achieve success.

An inherent need for harmony within your personality emphasizes the special significance of a secure home that acts as an oasis from the outer world. Alternatively, this may draw you to develop musical or creative gifts. Just be careful that in your desire to keep the peace you do not become a victim to anxiety or inertia. When positive, you possess a lively, vivacious personality that enables you to share your sense of fun with others.

Work & Vocation

Your relationship skills and ability to make contacts ensure that careers involving people are ideal. These may include fields such as public relations or sales, or positions such as advisor,

---

FIXED STARS

Pollux, also known as the Boxing Twin or Hercules; Al Wasat; Propus; Castor

PRIMARY STAR

Star's name: Pollux, also known as the Boxing Twin or Hercules

Degree position: 22°15'–23°11' Cancer between the years 1930 and 2000

Magnitude: 1

Strength: ★★★★★★★★★

Orb: 2°30'

Constellation: Beta Gemini

Applicable days: July 13, 14, 15, 16, 17, 18

Star qualities: varied influences: Mars/Moon/Uranus

Description: a bright orange star located on the head of the southern Twin

PRIMARY STAR'S INFLUENCE

Pollux's influence suggests a subtle yet self-reliant, spirited, and brave nature. This star imparts a love of competitive sports. Pollux's negative influence is in hastiness and oversensitivity, which may create frustration and quarrels, resulting in unpleasant situations.

Linked to your Sun's degree, this star indicates love of adventure and a talent for sport. You are likely to go it alone or attempt to achieve success by your own effort. Pollux also imparts psychic abilities and the courage to pursue personal ideals and goals. Prominence in higher education and interests in philosophy are also indicated by the influence of this star.

go-between, or agent. A propensity for business combined with your ability to sell an idea or product you believe in can stimulate your strong potential for success. There is a likelihood that you may also be interested in the areas of food preparation, things for the home, landscape gardening, or negotiations that involve real estate. Although you like to be the boss or work for yourself, you also realize the importance of working cooperatively with others. A strong idealistic streak may attract you to education, religion, or working to uplift the community.

Famous people who share your birthday include former Ethiopian emperor Haile Selassie, historian Kenneth Clark, actors Harrison Ford and Patrick Stewart, and comedian/actor Cheech Marin.

Numerology

Numerically, you are associated with ambition and hard work and can accomplish much through creative self-expression. Your original and innovative approach inspires new and exciting ideas that result in work that impresses others. With a number 13 birthday, you are earnest, romantic, charming, and fun-loving, and with dedication you can achieve prosperity. Receptive and influenced by your surroundings, you are often inclined to work better with others than on your own. Although friendly and cooperative, you may need to work on issues concerning trust and loyalty. The subinfluence of the number 7 month indicates that you are rational, reflective, and self-absorbed. At times, however, you can become overly sensitive to criticism from others and feel misunderstood. Highly intuitive, you need to take your time to think or make your own judgments. Since you are frequently concerned with stability, you may need to learn that security comes from within through personal experience.

• *Positive:* ambitious, creative, freedom-loving, self-expressive, initiative
• *Negative:* impulsive, indecisive, bossy, unemotional, rebellious

Love & Relationships

Strong convictions and a stubborn streak suggest that you are determined and assertive, with a mind of your own. Nevertheless, you do need intimacy and understanding as well as people who can mentally stimulate you. You are very observant, so little escapes you. When you sense that things are not right, you usually want to confront the situation and clear the air. Having strong principles, you stand your ground, admiring powerful, independent people.

YOUR SPECIAL SOMEONE

You might come close to finding your true match with someone born on one of the following dates.

Love & friendship: Jan. 3, 23, Feb. 11, 21, Mar. 9, 19, 28, 31, Apr. 7, 17, 26, 29, May 5, 15, 24, 27, 29, 31, June 3, 13, 22, 25, 27, 29, July 1, 11, 20, 23, 25, 27, 29, Aug. 9, 18, 21, 23, 25, 27, Sept. 7, 16, 19, 21, 23, 25, Oct. 5, 14, 17, 19, 21, 23, Nov. 3, 12, 15, 17, 19, 21, Dec. 1, 10, 13, 15, 17, 19

Beneficial: Jan. 3, 4, 10, 21, Feb. 1, 2, 8, 19, Mar. 6, 17, 30, Apr. 4, 15, 28, May 2, 13, 26, June 11, 24, July 9, 22, Aug. 7, 20, Sept. 5, 18,. Oct. 3, 16, 31, Nov. 1, 14, 29, Dec. 12, 27

Fatal attractions: Jan. 10, 11, 12, 13, 22, 28, Feb. 20, 26, Mar. 18, 24, Apr. 16, 22, May 14, 20, June 12, 18, July 10, 16, Aug. 8, 14, Sept. 6, 12, Oct. 4, 10, Nov. 2, 8, Dec. 6

Challenging: Jan. 11, 20, Feb. 9, 18, Mar. 7, 16, Apr. 5, 14, May 3, 12, 30, June 1, 10, 28, July 8, 26, 31, Aug. 6, 24, 29, Sept. 4, 22, 27, Oct. 2, 20, 25, Nov. 18, 23, Dec. 16, 21

Soul mates: Jan. 26, Feb. 24, Mar. 22, 30, Apr. 20, 28, May 18, 26, June 16, 24, July 14, 22, Aug. 12, 20, Sept. 10, 18, Oct. 8, 16, Nov. 6, 14, Dec. 4, 12

July 14

A strong-willed individual with a forceful mind and tender heart is suggested by your Cancerian birthday. With a sharp intellect and an excellent ability to deal with people, you show to others a natural leadership ability and a confident front. More sensitive than you seem, your interesting mixture of pragmatism and idealism guarantees you the potential to achieve in a remarkable way.

With the subinfluence of your decanate ruler, Pisces, you are imaginative, with a strong sixth sense as to what the public wants. Your shrewd money sense and an ability to grasp a situation quickly mean that you can usually spot an opportunity for advancement. By seeking happiness more in your mind and less in material things, you will feel more stable and fulfilled.

An attractive and luxurious home is likely to be high on your priority list, and you usually want value for your money. With farsightedness and an ability to organize, you have the potential to back up your big plans. As this could require the assistance of helpers, you may have to guard against a tendency to become obstinately opposed to others just for the sake of it.

After the age of eight, when your progressed Sun moves into Leo, you become less shy or security-conscious. The Leo influence lasts over the next thirty years, assisting you in building confidence and helping you to excel in your chosen field. From age thirty-eight onward, when your progressed Sun moves into Virgo, you will develop a more methodical and discriminating attitude, with a possible desire to be of service to others. At the age of sixty-eight, when your progressed Sun moves into Libra, there is a turning point as you change your focus to relationships and increased awareness of a need for harmony and balance.

FIXED STARS

Pollux, also known as the Boxing Twin or Hercules; Castor

PRIMARY STAR

Star's name: Pollux, also known as the Boxing Twin or Hercules

Degree position: 22°15'–23°11' Cancer between the years 1930 and 2000

Magnitude: 1

Strength: ★★★★★★★★★

Orb: 2°30'

Constellation: Beta Gemini

Applicable days: July 13, 14, 15, 16, 17, 18

Star qualities: varied influences: Mars/Moon/Uranus

Description: a bright orange star located on the head of the southern Twin

PRIMARY STAR'S INFLUENCE

Pollux's influence suggests a subtle yet self-reliant, spirited, and brave nature. This star imparts a love of competitive sports. Pollux's negative influence is in hastiness and oversensitivity, which may create frustration and quarrels, resulting in unpleasant situations.

Linked to your Sun's degree, this star indicates love of adventure and a talent for sport. You are likely to go it alone or attempt to achieve success by your own effort. Pollux also imparts psychic abilities and the courage to pursue personal ideals and goals. Prominence in higher education and interests in philosophy are also indicated by the influence of this star.

Your Secret Self

Although charming, you have powerful emotions and desires, and these are the prime motivators for initiating new pursuits or involvements. In order to succeed, you may need to develop perseverance and allow your intuition to guide you. Active and energetic, you possess the drive and enthusiasm to make things happen. It is important to use your diplomatic and cooperative skills rather than control situations with demanding behavior.

Fortunately, you are blessed with the gift of one-to-one relating and have the ability to mix business and pleasure. Since you possess an eye for a bargain or opportunity, you can see a business angle to almost anything. Alternatively, you can be of practical help to others and can give generously and unstintingly of your time, energy, and love. When you use your positive, dynamic willpower to achieve your objectives, you are a force to be reckoned with.

Work & Vocation

With your good business sense, you may possibly pursue a career in commerce, such as negotiator, agent, or financial advisor. Once you have decided upon something, you have the determination, will, and leadership abilities to succeed, particularly as a manager, executive, director, or entrepreneur. Motivated by a strong combination of idealism and practicality, you possess natural abilities for politics or fighting for a cause. Alternatively, a strong dramatic sense and creative ability may attract you to a career in the arts, entertainment, or working with youth. A humanitarian side to your nature may be particularly interested in education and achieving something of social worth.

Famous people who share your birthday include film director Ingmar Bergman, songwriter Woody Guthrie, painter Gustav Klimt, writer Irving Stone, suffragette Emmeline Pankhurst, and former U.S. president Gerald Ford.

Numerology

Intellectual potential, a pragmatic outlook, and strong determination are some of the qualities of the number 14 birthday. Often you possess a strong desire to establish a firm foundation and achieve success through hard work. Indeed, with a number 14 birthday, you frequently put your work first and judge yourself and others upon the basis of career achievements. Although you need stability, the restlessness indicated by the number 14 urges you to forge ahead and take on new challenges in a constant attempt to improve your lot. The subinfluence of the number 7 month indicates that you are perceptive, mentally creative, and ambitious. Often independent and self-absorbed, you prefer to rely on personal judgment or make your own decisions. Learning about trust and being broad-minded help you to see the need for greater self-awareness.

• *Positive:* decisive actions, hardworking, lucky, creative, pragmatic, imaginative, industrious
• *Negative:* overly cautious or overly impulsive, unstable, thoughtless, stubborn

YOUR SPECIAL SOMEONE

You may feel more inspired to share your love and affection with those born on the following dates.

Love & friendship: Jan. 14, 24, 31, Feb. 12, 22, 29, Mar. 10, 20, 27, Apr. 8, 18, 25, May 6, 16, 23, 30, June 4, 14, 21, 28, 30, July 2, 12, 19, 26, 28, 30, Aug. 10, 17, 24, 26, 28, Sept. 8, 15, 22, 24, 26, Oct. 6, 13, 20, 22, 24, 30, Nov. 4, 11, 18, 20, 22, 28, Dec. 2, 9, 16, 18, 20, 26, 29

Beneficial: Jan. 5, 22, 30, Feb. 3, 20, 28, Mar. 1, 18, 26, Apr. 16, 24, May 14, 22, June 12, 20, July 10, 18, 29, Aug. 8, 16, 27, 31, Sept. 6, 14, 25, 29, Oct. 4, 12, 23, 27, Nov. 2, 10, 21, 25, Dec. 9, 19, 23

Fatal attractions: Jan. 11, 12, 13, 14, Feb. 10, Mar. 8, Apr. 6, May 4, June 2

Challenging: Jan. 16, 21, Feb. 14, 19, Mar. 12, 17, 30, Apr. 10, 15, 28, May 8, 13, 26, June 6, 11, 24, July 4, 9, 22, Aug. 2, 7, 20, Sept. 5, 18, Oct. 3, 16, Nov. 1, 14, Dec. 12

Soul mates: Jan. 25, Feb. 23, Mar. 21, Apr. 19, May 17, June 15, July 13, Aug. 11, Sept. 9, Oct. 7, Nov. 5, Dec. 3, 30

Love & Relationships

A penchant for rushing into relationships implies that you may change your mind and feel uncertain about long-term commitments. Nevertheless, you are sensitive and caring, willing to support those you love and admire. You enjoy an active life, meeting new people and experiencing a variety of relationships before finally settling down. Your ideal partner would be someone who is loving and dynamic, keeping you constantly interested.

July 15

Good reasoning powers, strong intuition, and a commanding disposition are frequently associated with your birthday. As a Cancerian, you are instinctive and sensitive, with good perception, yet are often ruled by your mind rather than your heart. Your intelligence is usually your greatest asset, and in order to truly utilize your potential you may have to recognize the power of knowledge.

The subinfluence of your decanate ruler, Pisces, empowers you with imagination and psychic abilities. Autonomous and goal-oriented, you are an articulate deep thinker and are willing to work hard.

An interesting blend of conservatism and idealism associated with your birthday also suggests that you alternate between being overly confident or insecure and being inclined to self-doubt. A pragmatist by nature, you can be radical or unconventional at times, but you must guard against a tendency to be contrary just for the sake of being difficult. Nevertheless, through patience and perseverance you can endure great challenges and, with hard work, often achieve success.

Knowledgeable and well informed, more often than not you like to make up your own mind and be in control. Women of this day also tend not to allow their heart to rule their mind. As others quickly recognize your strength, you usually rise to positions of authority and power.

You become more confident and able to express yourself after the age of seven, when your progressed Sun moves into Leo for thirty years. At the age of thirty-seven there is another turning point as your progressed Sun moves into Virgo. After this time, your goals are likely to become more pragmatic and realistic, and you may find that your patience and efficiency increase. At the age of sixty-seven, as your progressed Sun moves into Libra, it highlights the area of relationships and a need for widening your social circle.

FIXED STARS

Pollux, also known as the Boxing Twin or Hercules; Castor

PRIMARY STAR

Star's name: Pollux, also known as the Boxing Twin or Hercules

Degree position: 22°15'–23°11' Cancer between the years 1930 and 2000

Magnitude: 1

Strength: ★★★★★★★★★

Orb: 2°30'

Constellation: Beta Gemini

Applicable days: July 13, 14, 15, 16, 17, 18

Star qualities: varied influences: Mars/Moon/Uranus

Description: a bright orange star located on the head of the southern Twin

PRIMARY STAR'S INFLUENCE

Pollux's influence suggests a subtle yet self-reliant, spirited, and brave nature. This star imparts a love of competitive sports. Pollux's negative influence is in hastiness and oversensitivity, which may create frustration and quarrels, resulting in unpleasant situations.

Linked to your Sun's degree, this star indicates love of adventure and a talent for sport. You are likely to go it alone or attempt to achieve success by your own effort. Pollux also imparts psychic abilities and the courage to pursue personal ideals and goals. Prominence in higher education and interests in philosophy are also indicated by the influence of this star.

Your Secret Self

An inner ambition or desire to achieve in a powerful way can extend to all parts of your life. To be motivated, you need to be genuinely enthusiastic. Once inspired, your determination can be relentless and uncompromising. A willingness to work hard helps you in your desire to accomplish. Although you are willing to take on responsibilities and help others, you rarely allow people to take you for granted. This also suggests that if you think others are getting too far out of line, you can become confrontational and challenge them.

Although diplomacy and the art of negotiation can be part of your makeup, you may have to develop the art of trust, as well as work to achieve balance in your personal relationships. With your understanding of the importance of collaboration with others, you may enjoy sharing your knowledge. Usually this occurs at work, but it may include other situations that use your insight or authority in joint efforts.

Work & Vocation

Your sensitive leadership and your capacity to take responsibility ensure your potential for outstanding success. With an exceptional mind, you may also be attracted to professions such

278

as teaching or lecturing, journalism, or health care. Alternatively, a natural sense of the dramatic may attract you to some form of art or entertainment. Your good imagination may find a form of expression in words, either speaking, writing, singing, or acting. Whatever career you choose, education of some type may be important in realizing your exceptional potential. Having an understanding and sympathetic nature may draw you to counseling or some form of the caring professions.

Famous people who share your birthday include singer Linda Ronstadt, Dutch painter Rembrandt van Rijn, novelist Iris Murdoch, and the Sultan of Brunei.

Numerology

Versatility, generosity, and restlessness are suggested by the number 15 birthday. Usually you are quick and enthusiastic, with a charismatic personality. Your greatest assets are your strong instincts and the ability to learn quickly through combining theory and practice. On many occasions you manage to earn while learning new skills. Often you utilize your intuitive powers and are quick at recognizing opportunities when they arise. Having a number 15 birthday, you possess a talent for attracting money or receiving help and support from others. Although you are mentally adventurous, you nevertheless need to find a real base or a home that you can call your own. The subinfluence of the number 7 month indicates that you are rational and inquisitive, with a practical approach. You are able to quickly assess people and situations; however, often skeptical, you can also fluctuate between being confident and assertive and being self-doubting and unsure. Since you are highly intuitive, you may need to listen to your inner voice.

• *Positive:* willing, generous, responsible, kind, cooperative, appreciative, creative ideas

• *Negative:* restless, irresponsible, self-centered, loss of faith, worry, indecision, misusing power

Love & Relationships

Understanding and highly intuitive, you are emotionally honest and direct. Your strong character suggests you can be very protective of family members or people in your care. If you believe in someone, you will do anything to help and encourage them. Your inclination to take charge of situations, however, implies that you can become arrogant or domineering. It is often better to advise others and then step back and let them make up their own mind.

YOUR SPECIAL SOMEONE

If you are looking for an ideal partner, you may further enhance your luck by finding someone born on one of the following dates.

Love & friendship: Jan. 11, 13, 15, 17, 25, Feb. 9, 11, 13, 15, 23, Mar. 7, 9, 11, 13, 21, Apr. 5, 7, 9, 11, 19, May 3, 5, 7, 9, 17, 31, June 1, 3, 5, 7, 15, 29, July 1, 3, 5, 27, 29, 31, Aug. 1, 3, 11, 25, 27, 29, Sept. 1, 9, 23, 25, 27, Oct. 7, 21, 23, 25, Nov. 5, 19, 21, 23, Dec. 3, 17, 19, 21, 30

Beneficial: Jan. 1, 5, 20, Feb. 3, 18, Mar. 1, 16, Apr. 14, May 12, June 10, July 8, Aug. 6, Sept. 4, Oct. 2

Fatal attractions: Jan. 12, 13, 14, 15

Challenging: Jan. 6, 22, 24, Feb. 4, 20, 22, Mar. 2, 18, 20, Apr. 16, 18, May 16, 14, June 12, 14, July 10, 12, Aug. 8, 10, 31, Sept. 6, 8, 29, Oct. 4, 6, 27, Nov. 2, 4, 25, 30, Dec. 2, 23, 28

Soul mates: Jan. 6, 12, Feb. 4, 10, Mar. 2, 8, Apr. 6, May 4, June 2

July 16

♋ Receptive and intelligent, with common sense and intuitive abilities, you are often a self-assured Cancerian. Since you are able to learn new skills quickly, you are practical and decisive, able to combine your inner wisdom with good judgment. If you feel secure in your own knowledge, you can use your leadership abilities to rise to positions of authority or enjoy taking a leading stand, especially in family affairs.

The subinfluence of your decanate ruler, Pisces, implies that you have a strong sixth sense. Since you are receptive and sensitive to sound and vibration, you may find music to be a calming influence. Naturally gifted, you have many talents and can pick and choose the career you like.

Friendly and caring, you like to entertain or socialize. Although you have a warm heart, at times you will not accept interference from others, and your stubborn streak can cause you to act impatiently and appear intolerant.

A need for expansion and the ability to survey the whole suggests that you set high standards for yourself. Success can come through education and higher learning or through social, moral, or religious aspirations. All is possible if you can master self-discipline and overcome emotional insecurities.

After the age of six, when your progressed Sun moves into Leo, you become less shy or security-conscious. The Leo influence aids you to positively gain in confidence and performance capacity in your chosen field over the next thirty years. From the age of thirty-six onward, when your progressed Sun moves into Virgo, you probably will have a more practical and discriminating attitude, with service to others becoming a more important part of your life. At the age of sixty-six you experience another turning point as your progressed Sun moves into Libra, emphasizing harmony, relationships, and a need to expand your social circle.

FIXED STARS

Pollux, also known as the Boxing Twin or Hercules; Procyon

PRIMARY STAR

Star's name: Pollux, also known as the Boxing Twin or Hercules

Degree position: 22°15'–23°11' Cancer between the years 1930 and 2000

Magnitude: 1

Strength: ★★★★★★★★★

Orb: 2°30'

Constellation: Beta Gemini

Applicable days: July 13, 14, 15, 16, 17, 18

Star qualities: varied influences: Mars/Moon/Uranus

Description: a bright orange star located on the head of the southern Twin

PRIMARY STAR'S INFLUENCE

Pollux's influence suggests a subtle yet self-reliant, spirited, and brave nature. This star imparts a love of competitive sports. Pollux's negative influence is in hastiness and oversensitivity, which may create frustration and quarrels, resulting in unpleasant situations.

Linked to your Sun's degree, this star indicates love of adventure and a talent for sport. You are likely to go it alone or attempt to achieve success by your own effort. Pollux also imparts psychic abilities and the courage to pursue personal ideals and goals. Prominence in higher education and interests in philosophy are also indicated by the influence of this star.

Your Secret Self

Inside your sensitive heart are both a need for creativity and a strong drive for material success. Since at times you can be generous to a fault, your desire for money includes giving to others as well as protection for both yourself and your loved ones. You may have to be careful of losing energy to emotional worry or indecision, particularly involving close relationships.

With developed social skills and a desire to be of service to others, you may find your drive for material success is best channeled into areas that use your enormous potential. This includes creating positive opportunities to use the wealth of information that you possess. If you keep yourself mentally and creatively occupied, you will not have the time or the opportunity to dwell on events and worry unnecessarily.

Work & Vocation

As you possess strong leadership qualities, your greatest achievement is most likely to be at the forefront of your chosen profession. A caring or humanitarian side of your nature could provide you with the impetus to excel as a teacher, counselor, or social worker, or in a job that requires speaking up for others. This may include involvement in unions or politics. Other careers may include law or occupations of a philosophical or religious nature. However, the more practical side of your nature may also be attracted to business or banking. Alternatively, your creativity and quick way with words may lead you to writing, music, or drama.

Famous people who share your birthday include actress/dancer Ginger Rogers, Christian Science founder Mary Baker Eddy, actress Barbara Stanwyck, and writer Anita Brookner.

Numerology

A number 16 birthdate suggests that you are ambitious and emotional, caring and friendly. You often judge life according to how you feel, and you have a good insight into people. As a number 16 personality, you can experience inner tension when facing friction between a need for self-expression and responsibility to others. The creative ones among you have a talent for writing, with sudden flashes of inspiration. Although many of you come from a close family, you often choose to live alone or travel extensively. The subinfluence of the number 7 month indicates that you are rational and mentally quick. As you have strong instincts, you can anticipate what people may say or do and use it to your advantage. You enjoy learning new skills and like to be informed. You are blessed with a retentive memory and are bright and alert, though at times you may feel misunderstood or have difficulty expressing your feelings.

• *Positive:* higher education, responsibilities to home and family, integrity, intuitive, social, cooperative, insightful

• *Negative:* worry, never satisfied, irresponsible, opinionated, skeptical, selfish, irritable, fussy

YOUR SPECIAL SOMEONE

You are more likely to find people who will keep you curious and mentally active among those born on the following dates.

Love & friendship: Jan. 12, 16, 25, Feb. 10, 14, 23, 24, Mar. 8, 12, 22, 31, Apr. 6, 10, 20, 29, May 4, 8, 18, 27, June 2, 6, 16, 25, 30, July 4, 14, 23, 28, Aug. 2, 12, 21, 26, 30, Sept. 10, 19, 24, 28, Oct. 8, 17, 22, 26, Nov. 6, 15, 20, 24, 30, Dec. 4, 13, 18, 22, 28

Beneficial: Jan. 2, 13, 22, 24, Feb. 11, 17, 20, 22, Mar. 9, 15, 18, 20, 28, Apr. 7, 13, 16, 18, 26, May 5, 11, 16, 18, 26, June 3, 9, 12, 14, 22, July 1, 7, 10, 12, 20, Aug. 5, 8, 10, 18, Sept. 3, 6, 8, 16, Oct. 1, 4, 6, 14, Nov. 2, 4, 12, Dec. 2, 10

Fatal attractions: Jan. 13, 14, 15, 16, 25, Feb. 23, Mar. 21, Apr. 19, May 17, June 15, July 13, Aug. 11, Sept. 9, Oct. 7, Nov. 5, Dec. 3

Challenging: Jan. 7, 23, Feb. 5, 21, Mar. 3, 19, 29, Apr. 1, 17, 27, May 15, 25, June 13, 23, July 11, 21, 31, Aug. 9, 19, 29, Sept. 7, 17, 27, 30, Nov. 3, 13, 23, 26, Dec. 1, 11, 21, 24

Soul mates: Jan. 17, Feb. 15, Mar. 13, Apr. 11, May 9, June 7, July 5, Aug. 3, Sept. 1, Nov. 30, Dec. 28

Love & Relationships

Sensitive, highly intuitive, and intelligent, you seek the company of clever and interesting people who can offer you variety and fun. Your caring and sympathetic nature often suggests that others will come to you for advice and support in time of need. Often concerned with reforms and social issues, you can be an asset to your community and find yourself before the public. A tendency to become bored and restless implies that in personal relationships you need reassurance and affection, as well as a common interest.

July 17

Idealistic and enthusiastic, with an optimistic view, you are bright, with a keen mind and a thirst for knowledge. As a Cancerian, you are sensitive and shy, yet independent, with a strong need to succeed and accomplish. Your natural charm and spontaneous zeal imply that you possess grace and individuality as well as a youthful quality.

The subinfluence of your decanate ruler, Pisces, suggests that you are impressionable and imaginative, with strong intuition. Idealistic and receptive, you are able to put yourself in the position of others. Frequently well informed and multitalented, you can be very persuasive if you are positive and full of conviction.

Intelligent and confident, you are able to make quick decisions. At times you might be overly confident or headstrong and therefore act on impulse or appear irresponsible. Guard against a tendency to get emotionally excitable, as it shows more of your eccentricity than your individuality.

The urge to live an active life combined with your spirit of enterprise often suggests that your dreams can come true through perseverance and patience. The need to develop a more mature attitude often suggests that education is an essential component in your rise to success.

From the age of five through thirty-four, your progressed Sun moves through Leo, bringing a gradual increase in your confidence and social skills. There is a turning point in your life at age thirty-five as your progressed Sun enters Virgo, bringing more practical issues to prominence and making you more methodical and orderly. At the age of sixty-five, your progressed Sun enters Libra, placing an emphasis on social affairs, relationships, or developing an appreciation for art and beauty.

Fixed Stars

Pollux, also known as the Boxing Twin or Hercules; Procyon

Primary Star

Star's name: Pollux, also known as the Boxing Twin or Hercules

Degree position: 22°15'–23°11' Cancer between the years 1930 and 2000

Magnitude: 1

Strength: ★★★★★★★★★

Orb: 2°30'

Constellation: Beta Gemini

Applicable days: July 13, 14, 15, 16, 17, 18

Star qualities: varied influences: Mars/Moon/Uranus

Description: a bright orange star located on the head of the southern Twin

Primary Star's Influence

Pollux's influence suggests a subtle yet self-reliant, spirited, and brave nature. This star imparts a love of competitive sports. Pollux's negative influence is in hastiness and oversensitivity, which may create frustration and quarrels, resulting in unpleasant situations.

Linked to your Sun's degree, this star indicates love of adventure and a talent for sport. You are likely to go it alone or attempt to achieve success by your own effort. Pollux also imparts psychic abilities and the courage to pursue personal ideals and goals. Prominence in higher education and interests in philosophy are also indicated by the influence of this star.

Your Secret Self

As you are very intelligent and hold strong opinions, it is especially important for you to find opportunities to air your views. When these views are connected to an idealistic cause, then your fighting spirit is awakened by a sense of purpose. You possess a big heart with compassion for others, but you may have to balance this with your own need for self-expression and happiness.

Charismatic, you possess an attraction that draws people toward you. Having an androgynous quality, you can be very independent as well as sensitive. A material streak usually marks the importance of security in your life. Just be careful that you do not compromise your ideals for financial self-preservation.

Work & Vocation

As you are multitalented, you are able to get your ideas across in a creative and entertaining way. Your outstanding potential for acquiring knowledge may place you among the erudite or could serve you equally well in law or management. Your natural talents with the spoken and written word may be expressed through training, teaching, or writing. You may also show abilities for sales, lecturing, or promotion. With your strong principles and leadership skills, you can also be an excellent spokesperson, politician, or fighter for a cause. Alternatively, with your dramatic flair, you are likely to be able to earn your living through art, music, or drama. With your fine mind and potential for working hard for objectives, you have the capabilities to achieve in a major way.

Famous people who share your birthday include actors David Hasselhoff, Jimmy Cagney, and Donald Sutherland, and singers Diahann Carroll and Phoebe Snow.

Numerology

With a number 17 birthday, you are shrewd, with a reserved nature and good analytical abilities. Private, introspective, and independent, you rely on personal experience. With a strong interest in facts and figures, you frequently present a serious and thoughtful demeanor and like to take your time. Capable of long periods of concentration and endurance, you learn best through experience. Nevertheless, the less skeptical you are, the quicker you learn. The subinfluence of the number 7 month indicates that although you keep your opinions to yourself, you like to know what others are thinking. Since you can utilize your knowledge in a specific way, you develop your expertise and achieve success. By taking responsibility for your own actions, you can minimize worry and discontent. You may be more sensitive than you are willing to admit and at times find it difficult to express your feelings. Learn to differentiate between accepting advice and thinking that others are only interfering or criticizing.

• *Positive:* thoughtful, specialist, good planner, business sense, individual thinker, painstaking, accurate, skilled researcher, scientific

• *Negative:* stubborn, careless, moody, dogmatic, critical, worry, suspicious

Love & Relationships

Sensitive and thoughtful, you are usually an independent thinker who prefers to work out your problems without the help of others. You can be warm and intense on one hand, or aloof, on the other. You may need a very special link with your partner, as your ideal of love and devotion is so high. Although you are friendly and sociable, if you are insecure you may need to overcome a fear of being lonely or abandoned. When you find a long-term partner you can be loyal, caring, and very protective.

• *Positive:* competitive yet subtle and sensitive, the power of attainment
• *Negative:* crafty, rash nature, aggressive or selfish with a cruel streak, moodiness

See Appendix for additional fixed star readings.

YOUR SPECIAL SOMEONE

To find true happiness, you might look for a partner who is born on one of the following dates.

Love & friendship: Jan. 7, 10, 17, 27, Feb. 5, 8, 15, 25, Mar. 3, 6, 13, 23, Apr. 1, 4, 11, 21, May 2, 9, 19, June 7, 17, July 5, 15, 29, 31, Aug. 3, 13, 27, 29, 31, Sept. 1, 11, 25, 27, 29, Oct. 9, 23, 25, 27, Nov. 7, 21, 23, 25, Dec. 5, 19, 21, 23

Beneficial: Jan. 3, 5, 20, 25, 27, Feb. 1, 3, 18, 23, 25, Mar. 1, 16, 21, 23, Apr. 14, 19, 21, May 12, 17, 19, June 10, 15, 17, July 8, 13, 15, Aug. 6, 11, 13, Sept. 4, 9, 11, Oct. 2, 7, 9, Nov. 5, 7, Dec. 3, 5

Fatal attractions: Jan. 14, 15, 16, 17, Feb. 11, Mar. 9, Apr. 7, May 5, June 3, July 1

Challenging: Jan. 16, 24, Feb. 14, 22, Mar. 12, 20, Apr. 10, 18, May 8, 16, 31, June 6, 14, 29, July 4, 12, 27, Aug. 2, 10, 25, Sept. 8, 23, Oct. 6, 21, Nov. 4, 19, Dec. 2, 17

Soul mates: Jan. 16, Feb. 14, Mar. 12, Apr. 10, May 8, June 6, July 4, 31, Aug. 2, 29, Sept. 27, Oct 25, Nov. 23, Dec. 21

July 18

The power suggested by your birthday indicates that you are a seeker of knowledge who is thoughtful and intelligent. An ambitious individual with strong convictions, you possess a dynamic drive and persuasive manner. Assertive, magnetic, and highly intuitive, you have independent views and good reasoning powers.

The subinfluence of your decanate ruler, Pisces, suggests that you have a strong sense of vision and are ready to work to achieve your dreams. Imaginative and practical, you enjoy a mental challenge, but in your attempt to test your wits and intelligence, you can become argumentative, stubborn, or a daredevil.

With your quick mind and a wide range of interests, you can show versatility and enthusiasm. Your ability to see the big picture and your willingness to work hard suggest that you can establish yourself and successfully undertake large projects. In order to enhance your chances for success, education is a cornerstone for a solid foundation.

Although you are self-disciplined and educated, the true inspiration that you seek may lie in the realms of emotional satisfaction and fulfillment. By overpowering people with your mind, you do not actually gain an advantage, yet through the practice of being broad-minded, courteous, and compassionate, you gain their love and affection.

Your progressed Sun moves into Leo very early in your life, at the age of four. This increases your opportunities to develop more daring, as your power, creativity, and confidence increase. When your progressed Sun changes signs again and moves into Virgo at around the age of thirty-four, you become more discriminating, businesslike, and efficient. Another turning point occurs at the age of sixty-four, when your progressed Sun enters Libra, emphasizing issues around relationships, love, beauty, and harmony.

Your Secret Self

With naturally developed intuitive powers giving you something of a sixth sense about people, it pays for you to trust your first instincts regarding any situation. At times this can make you very cunning and ingenious, enabling you to turn situations to your advantage. Alternatively, you can show your generous and courteous nature by being a philanthropist or coming to the rescue of others.

You are likely to possess an almost inborn protection regarding money and usually enjoy good health. This good fortune can extend to opportunities for work that you find fulfilling, since you are unable to pretend enthusiasm when you do not feel it. Since your problems are rarely financial, your challenges may concern your spiritual quest.

Work & Vocation

Your natural leadership, keen intellect, and outstanding social skills enable you to be successful in almost any choice of career. You can excel in education, research, science, public relations, philosophy, and politics. Since you are never happy being told what to do, it is imperative not to find yourself in a servile position. If in business, your outstanding talent for organization and ability to think big make you an excellent problem solver. Your need for self-

FIXED STAR

Star's name: Procyon

Degree position: 24°48'–25°43' Cancer between the years 1930 and 2000

Magnitude: 1

Strength: ★★★★★★★★

Orb: 2°30'

Constellation: Alpha Canis Minor

Applicable days: July 16, 17, 18, 19, 20, 21

Star qualities: varied influences: Mercury/Mars or Jupiter/Uranus

Description: a yellow and white binary star located on the body of the Lesser Dog

PRIMARY STAR'S INFLUENCE

Procyon's influence bestows willpower, drive, and an ability to execute plans. This star also suggests much activity and unusual interests or occupations. Procyon imparts opportunities for wealth, success, and good fortune. This star frequently indicates a sudden turn of events that brings fame or notoriety as well as gains and losses. Therefore you may need to learn patience, and taking the time to plan will secure a more successful outcome. Ancient interpretations of this star also warn against bites from dogs.

Linked to your Sun's degree, this star grants courage, ingenuity, unusual talents, and a chivalrous nature. Procyon denotes that you will have many loyal friends who will come to your assistance and provide help when it is needed most. This star also foretells of sudden fortunes gained through gifts or legacies.

expression and a love for the dramatic may lure you to writing or the art and entertainment worlds. Whatever career you choose, you are likely to love diversity and be good at starting projects with excitement and willingness. A desire to aid the community in some way may increase later in life.

Famous people who share your birthday include politician Nelson Mandela, astronaut John Glenn, and tycoon Richard Branson.

Numerology

Determination and assertiveness are some of the attributes associated with the number 18 birthday. Often capable, hardworking, and responsible, you rise to a position of authority. Your strong business sense and organizational skills lead you to the world of commerce. As a number 18 personality, you may use your power to heal others, give sound advice, or solve other people's problems. However, you may have to learn how to distinguish between the use and misuse of power through learning to live with others. The subinfluence of the number 7 month indicates that you are intelligent and highly intuitive, with a discriminating mind. Often enthusiastic, with a charismatic personality, you are ambitious yet emotionally restless. Your greatest assets are your strong instincts and the ability to combine your practical skills with original thinking. Quick at recognizing possibilities and the potential of a situation, you possess a talent for utilizing opportunities.

• *Positive:* progressive, assertive, intuitive, courageous, resolute, healing ability, efficient, advisory skills

• *Negative:* uncontrolled emotions, lazy, lack of order, selfishness, failure to complete work, deceitful

YOUR SPECIAL SOMEONE

You might further help your chances of finding that special person by looking for someone born on one of the following dates.

Love & friendship: Jan. 1, 14, 28, 31, Feb. 12, 26, 29, Mar. 10, 24, 27, Apr. 8, 22, 25, May 6, 20, 23, June 4, 18, 21, July 2, 16, 19, 30, Aug. 14, 17, 28, 30, Sept. 12, 15, 26, 28, 30, Oct. 10, 13, 24, 26, 28, Nov. 8, 11, 22, 24, 26, Dec. 6, 9, 20, 22, 24

Beneficial: Jan. 26, Feb. 24, Mar. 22, Apr. 20, May 18, June 16, July 14, Aug. 12, Sept. 10, Oct. 8, Nov. 6, Dec. 4

Fatal attractions: Jan. 15, 16, 17, 18

Challenging: Jan. 3, 25, Feb. 1, 23, Mar. 21, Apr. 19, May 17, June 15, July 13, Aug. 11, Sept. 9, Oct. 7, Nov. 5, Dec. 3

Soul mates: Jan. 3, 10, Feb. 1, 8, Mar. 6, Apr. 4, May 2

Love & Relationships

Strong family links and an early influence from an older person often suggest that you may have a strong desire for independence. You may need to find a partner who is hardworking, is clever, and has a sense of the dramatic. Intuitive yet skeptical, you may become overly suspicious and need to learn about trust and respect. Otherwise you may find yourself bossing your partner, which ultimately is not what you want. Your natural charm draws others toward you and ensures your success socially.

July 19

FIXED STAR

Star's name: Procyon

Degree position: 24°48'–25°43' Cancer between the years 1930 and 2000

Magnitude: 1

Strength: ★★★★★★★★★

Orb: 2°30'

Constellation: Alpha Canis Minor

Applicable days: July 16, 17, 18, 19, 20, 21

Star qualities: varied influences: Mercury/Mars or Jupiter/Uranus

Description: a yellow and white binary star located on the body of the Lesser Dog

PRIMARY STAR'S INFLUENCE

Procyon's influence bestows willpower, drive, and an ability to execute plans. This star also suggests much activity and unusual interests or occupations. Procyon imparts opportunities for wealth, success, and good fortune. This star frequently indicates a sudden turn of events that brings fame or notoriety as well as gains and losses. Therefore you may need to learn patience, and taking the time to plan will secure a more successful outcome. Ancient interpretations of this star also warn against bites from dogs.

Linked to your Sun's degree, this star grants courage, ingenuity, unusual talents, and a chivalrous nature. Procyon denotes that you will have many loyal friends who will come to your assistance and provide help when it is needed most. This star also foretells of sudden fortunes gained through gifts or legacies.

Idealism and generosity are often associated with your birthday and endow you with compassionate understanding and a tender heart. As a Cancerian, you are sensitive and highly intuitive. Although you are often full of wonderful ideas, a tendency to worry may undermine your determination and self-esteem. This frequently suggests that positive thinking combined with imagination is your key to balance and inner peace.

The subinfluence of your decanate ruler, Pisces, implies that you are impressionable, with a strong sixth sense. Since you are receptive to color and sound, you may be artistically inclined or find music to be a calming influence.

By taking everything as a learning experience, you can overcome a tendency to become frustrated and impatient. Through being broad-minded and tolerant, you realize the infinite possibilities that are available to you.

Charming, friendly, and adventurous, with a need for close relationships, you often have an active social life. Since you need inspiration to explore your true mental potential, education or self-knowledge is advisable. This suggests that your abundance of feelings and mental creativity need to be channeled or find ways of self-expression.

Before the age of three, when your progressed Sun moves into Leo, you are inclined to be shy and sensitive. The strong Leo influence increases over the next thirty years, enabling you to grow in strength and confidence. After the age of thirty-three, when your progressed Sun moves into Virgo, you are likely to bring more patience and perfectionism to your talents and skills. At the age of sixty-three, when your progressed Sun moves into Libra, you experience a turning point that emphasizes the growing importance of your social and personal relationships, as well as increasing your appreciation of beauty and harmony.

Your Secret Self

You thrive on love and encouragement, as being appreciated makes you determined to try harder. Fair and responsible, you like to pay your debts; you come to learn that what you have sown you will reap. Through discipline of your mind and abilities, you are able to become more focused and make the most of your wonderful potential.

If you do not have outlets for your strong feelings, you may become despondent or depressed. By keeping a detached perspective, you learn to let go and welcome new opportunities into your life. Being a naturally good advisor, you may have to guard against becoming too caring, to the point of interfering, and may need to let others make their own mistakes. Nevertheless, since you are loyal and loving, you can be very protective of those you care about. Dramatic and creative, you can also inspire others with your idealism and enthusiastic approach.

Work & Vocation

Your enjoyment of dealing with people and your love of knowledge are likely to draw you toward occupations such as teacher, advisor, or social worker, or to the caring professions. A need to express your own ideas may also attract you to occupations such as design, writing, music, art, poetry, storytelling, or drama. Good with words, you stand up for your opinions and may feel at home in a career such as lawyer, reformer, or politician. With your organizational and managerial skills, you can also excel in business. Natural humanitarian and philosophical inclinations may attract you to religion or manifest as raising money for good causes.

Famous people who share your birthday include French painter Edgar Degas, gun inventor Samuel Colt, tennis star Ilie Nastase, and actor Anthony Edwards.

Numerology

Creative, sunny, and dynamic, yet humanitarian and sensitive, are some of the characteristics of the number 19 birthday. Decisive and resourceful, you possess depth of vision, but the dreamer side of your nature is compassionate, idealistic, and sensitive. The need to be someone may be the very thing that pushes you to be dramatic and claim center stage. Often there is a strong desire to establish an individual identity. However, to do so, you may first need to overcome the influence of peer-group pressure. Only through numerous experiences can you develop self-confidence or leadership abilities. To others you may appear confident, resilient, and resourceful, but inner tensions may cause emotional ups and downs. The subinfluence of the number 7 month indicates that you are analytical, thoughtful, and intuitive. Although you have a natural business sense, you can benefit greatly from developing your organizational and executive skills.

• *Positive:* dynamic, centered, creative, leader, lucky, progressive, optimistic, strong convictions, competitive, independent, gregarious

• *Negative:* self-centered, depressive, worried, fear of rejection, fluctuating moods, materialistic, egotistical, impatient

Love & Relationships

With a strong need for emotional security, you often seek a close relationship with a dependable person. Although relationships are very important to you, avoid a tendency to become too dependent on your partner or lover. Since you are sociable and popular, you enjoy other people's company and do not like being on your own. Caring and generous, you are often tempted to make sacrifices for those you love.

YOUR SPECIAL SOMEONE

You may find true love with those born on the following dates.

Love & friendship: Jan. 1, 15, 26, 29, 30, Feb. 13, 24, 27, 28, Mar. 11, 22, 25, 26, Apr. 9, 20, 23, 24, May 7, 18, 21, 22, June 5, 16, 19, 20, July 3, 14, 17, 18, 31, Aug. 1, 12, 15, 16, 29, 31, Sept. 10, 13, 14, 27, 29, Oct. 8, 11, 12, 25, 27, Nov. 6, 9, 10, 23, 25, Dec. 4, 7, 8, 21, 23, 29

Beneficial: Jan. 1, 2, 10, 27, Feb. 8, 25, Mar. 6, 23, Apr. 4, 21, May 2, 19, 30, June 17, 28, July 15, 26, Aug. 13, 24, Sept. 11, 22, Oct. 9, 20, Nov. 7, 18, Dec. 5, 16

Fatal attractions: Jan. 16, 17, 18, 19

Challenging: Jan. 17, 26, Feb. 15, 24, Mar. 13, 22, Apr. 11, 20, May 9, 18, June 7, 16, July 5, 14, Aug. 3, 12, 30, Sept. 1, 10, 28, Oct. 8, 26, 29, Nov. 6, 24, 27, Dec. 4, 22, 25

Soul mates: Jan. 21, Feb. 19, Mar. 17, Apr. 15, May 13, June 11, July 9, 29, Aug. 7, 27, Sept. 5, 25, Oct. 3, 23, Nov. 1, 21, Dec. 19

July 20

FIXED STAR

Star's name: Procyon

Degree position: 24°48'–25°43' Cancer between the years 1930 and 2000

Magnitude: 1

Strength: ★★★★★★★★★

Orb: 2°30'

Constellation: Alpha Canis Minor

Applicable days: July 16, 17, 18, 19, 20, 21

Star qualities: varied influences: Mercury/Mars or Jupiter/Uranus

Description: a yellow and white binary star located on the body of the Lesser Dog

PRIMARY STAR'S INFLUENCE

Procyon's influence bestows willpower, drive, and an ability to execute plans. This star also suggests much activity and unusual interests or occupations. Procyon imparts opportunities for wealth, success, and good fortune. This star frequently indicates a sudden turn of events that brings fame or notoriety as well as gains and losses. Therefore you may need to learn patience, and taking the time to plan will secure a more successful outcome. Ancient interpretations of this star also warn against bites from dogs.

Linked to your Sun's degree, this star grants courage, ingenuity, unusual talents, and a chivalrous nature. Procyon denotes that you will have many loyal friends who will come to your assistance and provide help when it is needed most. This star also foretells of sudden fortunes gained through gifts or legacies.

♋ The vitality and drive indicated by your birthday are often subdued by your friendly smile and charming personality. As a Cancerian, you are idealistic and intuitive, with strong determination and a powerful mind.

The subinfluence of your decanate ruler, Pisces, suggests that you are imaginative, with a sense of vision and the ambition to achieve your dreams. Inspired and practical, you enjoy a mental challenge, but in your attempt to test your wits and intelligence you can also become moody or stubborn.

Your potential for success depends on power and knowledge, and the more learned you become, the more focused you will be. There is a need to establish peace of mind and a firm foundation through a set of values and beliefs. Secure in your knowledge of what you believe and hold dear, you can accomplish and achieve. You are harmonious by nature, and your sensitivity implies that, being receptive to your immediate environment, you may need a positive atmosphere in order to flourish and thrive. Conversely, disharmony often brings out the worst in you, and when you find yourself in confrontational situations, you may succumb to power games or arguments. Nevertheless, you benefit from developing a diplomatic approach and, with your persuasive thinking and speech, can often convince others to change their minds.

From the age of two until thirty-two, while your progressed Sun is in the sign of Leo, you have many opportunities to use the sociable and dramatic side of your personality. Whether at work or socially, you learn to become more poised and self-assured. There is a change of emphasis after the age of thirty-two, when your progressed Sun moves into Virgo. After this period you will be inclined to be more orderly, practically motivated, and businesslike. At the age of sixty-two you experience another turning point as your progressed Sun moves into Libra, emphasizing your social life, relationships, and opportunities to develop any latent artistic or literary talents.

Your Secret Self

A deep desire to empower yourself and pass on your inspired knowledge may be challenged by the hard work needed to fulfill your enormous potential. Having leadership skills and seeing the opportunities within any situation, you have the ability to think in large terms. You have an optimistic view of life and a strong capacity for creative fantasy. By focusing your exceptional gifts on making your dreams come true, you can achieve something special.

You are attracted to people who possess a fine intellect, as they can stimulate and share your never-ending quest for knowledge. You may want to pursue higher education, or you may be drawn to more mystical subjects, as you are likely to possess an unconscious attraction to the process of enlightenment. This does not detract from a very earthy and mundane business sense that can commercialize your many talents.

Work & Vocation

Through the combination of your superb intellect and sensitivity, success in a people-related career is guaranteed. This could include professions such as counseling, education, law, or social reform. Your determination, ambition, and good organizational skills can also help you accomplish much in the world of business. You may have a special interest in working with children or dealing with food and items for the home. Alternatively, your vision and sense of structure may take you to careers such as photography or filmmaking. Equally, a need to express your more creative self may attract you to the world of art, music, drama, or entertainment. Being highly intuitive, you often possess natural healing ability that may attract you to the medical or alternative health professions.

Famous people who share your birthday include musician Carlos Santana, explorer Sir Edward Hillary, and actresses Diana Rigg and Natalie Wood.

Numerology

With a number 20 birthday, you are intuitive, sensitive, and adaptable, and you often see yourself as a part of a larger group. You enjoy cooperative activities, where you can interact, share experiences, or learn from others. Charming and gracious, you develop diplomatic and social skills, and can move in different social circles with ease. You may, however, need to develop your confidence or overcome a tendency to be easily hurt by the actions and criticism of others. In relationships and other associations, you must guard against an inclination to martyr yourself. The subinfluence of the number 7 month indicates that you are intelligent, perceptive, and reflective. Naturally versatile and imaginative, with strong instincts or psychic abilities, you can be creative and full of ideas. Often idealistic, you seek balance and harmony, and you can be inspired by ideas and people. At times you can be indecisive and need time alone away from others to think and reflect.

• *Positive:* good partnerships, gentle, tactful, receptive, intuitive, considerate, harmonious, agreeable, amicable, ambassador of goodwill

• *Negative:* suspicious, lack of confidence, timid, oversensitive, selfish, easily hurt, crafty

Love & Relationships

Often you believe that stability and a secure home are vital ingredients in a good love life. Usually you are attracted to those who share your ideas and principles. In your major relationships it may be advisable to find someone who is like-minded, with whom you can share the same level of understanding. Attracted to people who are clever and straightforward, you need mental stimulation and often learn a great deal from others.

YOUR SPECIAL SOMEONE

You may enjoy warm and tender relationships with those born on the following dates.

Love & friendship: Jan. 10, 13, 20, 30, Feb. 8, 11, 18, 28, Mar. 6, 9, 16, 26, Apr. 4, 7, 14, 24, May 2, 5, 12, 22, June 3, 10, 20, July 1, 8, 18, Aug. 6, 16, 30, Sept. 4, 14, 28, 30, Oct. 2, 12, 26, 28, 30, Nov. 10, 24, 26, 28, Dec. 8, 22, 24, 26

Beneficial: Jan. 12, 16, 17, 28, Feb. 10, 14, 15, 26, Mar. 8, 12, 13, 24, Apr. 6, 10, 11, 22, May 4, 8, 9, 20, 29, June 2, 6, 7, 18, 27, July 4, 5, 16, 25, Aug. 2, 3, 14, 23, Sept. 1, 12, 21, Oct. 10, 19, Nov. 8, 17, Dec. 6, 14

Fatal attractions: Jan. 17, 18, 19, 20, Mar. 31, Apr. 29, May 27, June 25, July 23, Aug. 21, Sept. 19, Oct. 17, Nov. 15, Dec. 17

Challenging: Jan. 6, 18, 22, 27, Feb. 4, 16, 20, 25, Mar. 2, 14, 18, 23, Apr. 12, 16, 21, May 10, 14, 19, June 8, 12, 17, July 6, 10, 15, Aug. 4, 8, 13, Sept. 2, 6, 11, Oct. 4, 9, Nov. 2, 7, Dec. 5

Soul mates: Mar. 28, Apr. 26, May 24, June 22, July 20, Aug. 18, Sept. 16, Oct. 14, Nov. 12, Dec. 10

July 21

FIXED STARS

Procyon; Altarf, also called the End

PRIMARY STAR

Star's name: Procyon

Degree position: 24°48'–25°43' Cancer between the years 1930 and 2000

Magnitude: 1

Strength: ★★★★★★★★

Orb: 2°30'

Constellation: Alpha Canis Minor

Applicable days: July 16, 17, 18, 19, 20, 21

Star qualities: varied influences: Mercury/Mars or Jupiter/Uranus

Description: a yellow and white binary star located on the body of the Lesser Dog

PRIMARY STAR'S INFLUENCE

Procyon's influence bestows willpower, drive, and an ability to execute plans. This star also suggests much activity and unusual interests or occupations. Procyon imparts opportunities for wealth, success, and good fortune. This star frequently indicates a sudden turn of events that brings fame or notoriety as well as gains and losses. Therefore you may need to learn patience, and taking the time to plan will secure a more successful outcome. Ancient interpretations of this star also warn against bites from dogs.

Linked to your Sun's degree, this star grants courage, ingenuity, unusual talents, and a chivalrous nature. Procyon denotes that you will have many loyal friends who will come to your as-

Receptive and intuitive, with an ambitious and resourceful character, you are revealed by your birthday to be a creative and astute personality. Your curiosity and understanding of what motivates others suggests that you are quick at assessing people and situations. As a Cancerian, you are sensitive, with a shrewd mind and good mental potential. Nevertheless, at times worry and skepticism imply that you may need to learn to trust your first instincts. Since you like to be mentally occupied and well informed, education or self-directed learning can help you develop your fine mind as well as your confidence.

The subinfluence of your decanate ruler, Pisces, empowers you with imagination and psychic abilities. Often autonomous, with a need to accomplish, you possess depth of thought and can develop your analytical skills. If inspired, you are usually adaptable and can cope with every situation. By developing a responsible attitude and remaining resolute, you never feel like a victim of destiny.

Your need to alternate between the conventional and the avant-garde implies that your individuality and creativity need some form of self-expression. Lack of mental stimulation, however, can cause a nervous disposition and bring on your tendency to be quarrelsome or stubborn.

Since your Sun progresses into Leo during the first year of your life, there are early opportunities in childhood to develop strength, creativity, and self-expression. Your increasing confidence is likely to continue until the age of thirty, when your focus will change to a more pragmatic and rational approach, with a growing desire for an orderly life. At the age of sixty there is another turning point as your progressed Sun enters Libra. This highlights the growing importance of relationships, your social circle, and an appreciation of beauty and harmony.

Your Secret Self

At times you have a high-spirited, childlike quality that delights in competition or creative challenges. You can enjoy friendly battles of wits and may take pleasure in asking subtly provocative questions. Although fun-loving, this part of you may want to avoid responsibilities, but if you believe in a project, you will become enthusiastic and work really hard to manifest your ideals. Although you are sociable, you may need time alone to recoup your energies and give you time to think.

Determination and a natural talent for understanding the value of things can help you attain wealth, but to achieve full satisfaction it may be necessary to balance these abilities with your deeper insight. By listening and trusting the quiet inner voice of your intuition rather than the rational mind, you are more likely to succeed. Fortunately, you possess a strong inner power that can always help you in times of difficulty.

Work & Vocation

Your imagination and keen intellect are likely to draw you toward occupations such as teaching, science, social work, or the caring professions. Your love of knowledge and a need to express your own unique individual ideas may also attract you particularly to writing or to occupations in design, music, art, or drama. You may possess either analytical or technical skills, which can help you in your career. Since you usually enjoy a good debate, your fighting and communication skills can aid you in politics, promotions, sales, and business. Your ability to raise funds for causes could mean that charity work would also be an excellent structure for your organizational and managerial skills.

Famous people who share your birthday include writer Ernest Hemingway, actor Robin Williams, violinist Isaac Stern, musician Cat Stevens, and writer/director Jonathan Miller.

sistance and provide help when it is needed most. This star also foretells of sudden fortunes gained through gifts or legacies.

- *Positive:* wealth and fortune, government positions, pride and dignity, prominence in religion
- *Negative:* snobbery, carelessness, clumsy, crafty, deceptive

See Appendix for additional fixed star readings.

Numerology

Dynamic drive and an outgoing personality are present in those with a number 21 birthday. Socially inclined, you have many interests and contacts and are generally fortunate. Showing others your friendly and gregarious personality, you are highly original and intuitive, with an independent spirit. With a number 21 birthday, you can be fun-loving, magnetic, and creative, with social charm. Alternatively, you can be shy and reserved, with a need to develop assertiveness, especially in close relationships. The subinfluence of the number 7 month indicates that you are intelligent and practical, with a strong sixth sense. At times, however, you may need to learn to trust others and overcome a tendency to be too skeptical or suspicious. Often outgoing, you need to interact with others and yet retain your originality and independence. Although you are sensitive, you can also be innovative and courageous, with plenty of energy.

- *Positive:* inspiration, creativity, love unions, long-lasting relationships, good with words
- *Negative:* dependency, nervous, loss of emotional control, lack of vision, disappointment, fear of change

YOUR SPECIAL SOMEONE

To keep you interested in a long-term relationship, you might want to look out for those born on the following dates.

Love & friendship: Jan. 21, 28, 31, Feb. 19, 26, 29, Mar. 17, 24, 27, Apr. 15, 22, 25, May 13, 20, 23, June 11, 18, 21, July 9, 16, 19, Aug. 7, 14, 17, 31, Sept. 5, 12, 15, 29, Oct. 3, 10, 13, 27, 29, 31, Nov. 1, 8, 11, 25, 27, 29, Dec. 6, 9, 23, 25, 27

Beneficial: Jan. 9, 12, 18, 24, 29, Feb. 7, 10, 16, 22, 27, Mar. 5, 8, 14, 20, 25, Apr. 3, 6, 12, 18, 23, May 1, 10, 16, 21, 31, June 2, 8, 14, 19, 29, July 6, 12, 17, 27, Aug. 4, 10, 15, 25, Sept. 2, 8, 13, 23, Oct. 6, 11, 21, Nov. 4, 9, 19, Dec. 2, 7, 17

Fatal attractions: Jan. 3, 18, 19, 20, 21, Feb. 1, Apr. 30, May 28, June 26, July 24, Aug. 22, Sept. 20, Oct. 18, Nov. 16, Dec. 14

Challenging: Jan. 7, 8, 19, 28, Feb. 5, 6, 17, 26, Mar. 3, 4, 15, 24, Apr. 1, 2, 13, 22, May 11, 20, June 9, 18, July 7, 16, Aug. 5, 14, Sept. 3, 12, Oct. 1, 10, Nov. 8, Dec. 6

Soul mates: Jan. 3, 19, Feb. 1, 17, Mar. 15, Apr. 13, May 11, June 9, July 7, Aug. 5, Sept. 3, Oct. 1

Love & Relationships

Friendly yet reserved, you are attracted to creative, independent, and hardworking individuals who know their own mind. In close relationships you need to establish your assertiveness from the beginning; however, you may also need to overcome a tendency to worry unnecessarily. Shrewd and self-reliant, you like to know what motivates others. When you open your heart and express your inner feelings, you can contribute a great deal to your relationships. Often it is women who will assist you or have a beneficial influence on your life.

July 22

As your birthday lies on the cusp of Cancer and Leo, you are sensitive yet assertive, with an ambitious nature. Usually sociable, your amiable personality is likely to exude a magnetic presence that can win you friends and influence others. Quietly forceful and direct, you are able to advance by the sheer power of your persistence.

Clever and considerate, you are a natural strategist and can combine your exceptionally perceptive mind with your practical abilities to make your dreams a reality. If you find a subject of interest that can capture your imagination, follow your heart and do not allow anxiety and worry to undermine your great potential.

Imaginative and competitive, you have ideas that can make you money, and since you are versatile, with many interests, you need to be organized in order to make full use of your abilities. Your desire for information often makes you very knowledgeable in your chosen field, while being verbally persuasive can give you a certain prestige. In the pursuit of your ambitions, guard against becoming overly serious, which often causes you unnecessary stress.

Up to the age of twenty-nine, your progressed Sun is in Leo. This emphasizes your creativity and sociability. After the age of thirty, when your progressed Sun moves into Virgo, you become more analytical, methodical, and orderly. This more practical perfectionism changes at the age of sixty, when your progressed Sun moves into Libra and you become more aware of your personal relationships and the need for harmony.

Fixed Star

Star's name: Altarf, also called the End

Degree position: 30° Cancer–1° Leo between the years 1930 and 2000

Magnitude: 3.5

Strength: ★★★★★

Orb: 1°40'

Constellation: Beta Cancer

Applicable days: July 21, 22

Star qualities: Mars

Description: an orange giant star located on the tip of the southern hind leg of the Crab

PRIMARY STAR'S INFLUENCE

Altarf's influence endows willpower, endurance, and advancement in life through one's own efforts. With stamina and a fighting spirit, you have an aptitude for overcoming difficulties and dangers. This star also warns against impulsiveness or overstraining.

Linked to your Sun's degree, Altarf bestows courage, determination, and the constant desire to be active and involved. This star bestows self-assurance and confidence as well as enthusiasm and a spirit of enterprise.

• *Positive:* active and productive, courage, self-assured

• *Negative:* waste of energy, impulsiveness, takes risks or gambles

Your Secret Self

Security comes from having a sense of purpose or a plan for the future. Thus, you may need to balance your ambition and desire to achieve with your tendency toward inertia. You have a good business sense, with the power to make money, and should avoid an unfounded fear of not having enough funds. Even though you are quite independent, you work well in cooperation with others and realize the value of partnerships or team efforts. Your lucky knack of making contacts and being able to commercialize your talents will always prove a source of financial protection for you.

Resolute and determined, you can regenerate yourself with your sheer willpower. This can be a healing force for good when used positively but emphasizes the need to always be fair and just in your dealings. You want recognition and you take pride in your efforts. Being a natural perfectionist, you are usually willing to work very hard to achieve your objectives.

Work & Vocation

With your gift of gab, you make an excellent salesperson, diplomat, politician, or agent. A love for knowledge indicates that you may become involved in education and work as a teacher or lecturer. Alternatively, your appreciation for the arts may inspire you to pursue a career in the theater, film, writing, fashion, interior design, or music. The culinary arts may also attract you to the kitchen, where you can combine your creativity with your love for food. On the other hand, your practical skills may lead you to become an engineer or technician. With your naturally caring and sympathetic nature, you may be drawn to occupations such as counselor, advisor, or childcare professional, or you may raise money for good causes.

Famous people who share your birthday are actors Terence Stamp and Danny Glover, Kennedy clan matriarch Rose Kennedy, politician Bob Dole, and designer Oscar de la Renta.

Numerology

With a number 22 birthdate, you are a proud, practical, disciplined, and highly intuitive individual. This is a master number and can vibrate both as number 22 and number 4. Honest and hardworking, with natural leadership abilities, you have a charismatic personality and a deep understanding of people. Although undemonstrative, you do show a caring, protective concern for the welfare of others. However, you never lose sight of your pragmatic or realistic stand. The subinfluence of the number 7 month indicates that you are sensitive and intelligent, with a love of knowledge and a strong sixth sense. Impressionable and receptive to your environment, you may need to explore ways to be creative and find emotional expression. Usually easygoing, you enjoy social activities and many interests, but will benefit from focusing on one particular objective. A blend of humility and confidence often challenges you to find a balance between ambition and willingness to work hard or taking the easy path and scattering your energies.

• *Positive:* universal, director, highly intuitive, pragmatic, practical, good with your hands, skillful, builder, good organizer, realist, problem-solver, achiever

• *Negative:* get-rich-quick schemes, nervous, bossy, materialistic, lack of vision, lazy, egotistical

Love & Relationships

Charm can be one of your greatest assets when socializing with friends and partners. With your fondness for the dramatic, your love life is not likely to be dull. Since emotional power is one of your strong points, your passions need expression. Still, it is better to avoid becoming too emotional or manipulative in order to secure long-term relationships. Once settled, you can be a loyal and caring friend and partner. You may, however, have to balance a conflict between your work and your relationships.

YOUR SPECIAL SOMEONE

While you can probably win many hearts, you may find relationships even more successful with people born on the following dates.

Love & friendship: Jan. 18, 22, Feb. 16, 20, Mar. 14, 18, 28, Apr. 12, 16, 26, May 10, 14, 24, June 8, 12, 22, July 6, 10, 20, 29, Aug. 4, 8, 18, 27, 30, Sept. 2, 6, 16, 25, 28, Oct. 4, 14, 23, 26, 30, Nov. 2, 12, 21, 24, 28, Dec. 10, 19, 22, 26, 28

Beneficial: Jan. 6, 10, 25, 30, Feb. 4, 8, 23, 28, Mar. 2, 6, 21, 26, Apr. 4, 19, 24, May 2, 17, 22, June 15, 20, 30, July 13, 18, 28, Aug. 11, 16, 26, Sept. 9, 14, 24, Oct. 7, 12, 22, Nov. 5, 10, 20, Dec. 3, 8, 18

Fatal attractions: Jan. 19, 20, 21, 22, May 29, June 27, July 25, Aug. 23, Sept. 21, Oct. 19, Nov. 17, Dec. 15

Challenging: Jan. 13, 29, 31, Feb. 11, 27, 29, Mar. 9, 25, 27, Apr. 7, 23, 25, May 5, 21, 23, June 3, 19, 21, July 1, 17, 19, Aug. 15, 17, Sept. 13, 15, Oct. 11, 13, Nov. 9, 11, Dec. 7, 9

Soul mates: Jan. 6, 25, Feb. 4, 23, Mar. 2, 21, Apr. 19, May 17, June 15, July 13, Aug. 11, Sept. 9, Nov. 7, Dec. 5

Leo

July 23–August 22

July 23

FIXED STARS

Although your Sun's degree is not linked to a fixed star, some of your other planets' degrees certainly will be. By having an astrological chart calculated, you can find the exact position of the planets on your date of birth. This will tell you which of the fixed stars listed in this book are relevant to you.

A spirit of enterprise, intelligence, sensitivity, and restlessness are some of the qualities associated with your birthdate. As you were born on the cusp of Leo and Cancer, you benefit from the influences of the Sun and Moon. The Sun in Leo, however, is predominant, and its influence suggests that dignity, pride, creativity, and a need for self-expression are vital parts of your character. Assertive from an early age, you are constantly seeking new interests and experiences. Your adventurous nature is eager to go anywhere, and often you like to take the lead.

Although your greatest asset is your quick and piercing mind, at times you can go a bit too fast. Your creative mental potential, however, is excellent for learning new skills and improving on existing systems. Whatever you do, your creative input and ingenuity can make a difference. With your strong instincts and unusual sense of humor, you can be witty and entertaining.

One of your greatest challenges may be impatience, and only by developing a more persevering attitude can you overcome your tendency to act too impulsively. When you find something worthwhile that interests you, your quick intelligence and versatility help you to successfully develop one particular line of work. If you improve your powers of concentration and mental endurance, you can become more pragmatic in your outlook and develop greater depth of thought.

To utilize the great potential indicated by your birthday, you may need to employ a scientific and logical approach. This will aid you to be more industrious and methodical, with particular reference to thoroughness and attention to detail. Among your many talents, you have the ability to come straight to the heart of a matter and solve problems swiftly and efficiently.

When you are age thirty, your progressed Sun moves into Virgo. Over the next thirty-year period you are likely to be influenced by this sign's qualities of practicality, discrimination, criticism, and perfectionism. At the age of sixty, when your progressed Sun enters Libra, there is a turning point for you that will highlight the growing importance of relationships, creativity, and harmony.

Your Secret Self

Idealistic and optimistic, with great enthusiasm for life, in your attempt to make it in a big way, you like to take a gamble. Although possessing an inner practical sense, you may have to learn that without patience, proper planning, and foresight, your dreams may turn out to be castles made of sand. Nevertheless, since you are often lucky, changing circumstances may bring you many blessings in disguise.

Since love and friendships are of prime importance, there may be lessons regarding loved ones. The restless side of your nature suggests that although you are very sensitive and emotional inside, you may at times be unsure of your feelings. This can lead you to become easily bored or to scatter your energies. A willingness to help others shows how compassionate you really are, although the pride associated with this birthdate suggests that you may be prone to flattery.

Work & Vocation

As you learn very quickly, you have the capability to achieve in many different occupations. Whatever career you choose, being ambitious and needing recognition often ensure that you rise to the top of your profession. A versatile side to your nature suggests that you may enjoy work that incorporates travel or variety. Being restless, you may experiment with many different kinds of experiences or occupations in your desire to find one that suits your adventurous nature. You may be particularly successful in business or any type of management position. With your love of freedom and spirit of enterprise, you may also wish to be independent and work for yourself.

Famous people who share your birthday include author Raymond Chandler, actor Michael Wilding, theosophist Max Heidel, and actor Woody Harrelson.

Numerology

Emotional sensitivity and creativity are some of the attributes of a number 23 birthday. Usually you are versatile and a quick thinker, with a professional attitude and a mind full of inventive ideas. With the number 23 influence, you can learn new subjects easily but may prefer practice to theory. Fond of travel, adventure, and meeting new people, the restlessness implied by the number 23 urges you to try many different kinds of experience, and you adapt to make the best of any situation. The subinfluence of the number 7 month indicates that although at times you encounter self-doubts, you prefer to make up your own mind. Usually multitalented and intelligent, you need to express yourself through mental pursuits. You can devote a great deal of time to work that demands detailed research or independent effort. Although you can appear thoughtful and cautious, you are imaginative and highly sensitive, with quick responses.

• *Positive:* loyal, responsible, travel, communicative, intuitive, creative, versatile, trustworthy, fame

• *Negative:* selfish, insecure, stubborn, uncompromising, fault-finding, withdrawn, prejudice

Love & Relationships

Gregarious and enthusiastic, you are attracted to imaginative people who can inspire and encourage you with their wisdom and knowledge. Your sensitivity and intuitive abilities suggest that you are a good judge of character and can be loving and supportive. Witty and proud, you like to play an important role in your social circle, yet a need for privacy also implies that you may be uneasy if someone intrudes on your personal life. Discontent may urge you to seek new and exciting experiences, which can include short-lived relationships or secret emotional involvements.

YOUR SPECIAL SOMEONE

To keep you interested in a long-term relationship, you might want to look out for those born on the following days.

Love & friendship: Jan. 13, 19, 23, Feb. 11, 17, 21, Mar. 9, 15, 19, 28, 29, 30, Apr. 7, 13, 17, 26, 27, May 5, 11, 15, 24, 25, 26, June 3, 9, 13, 22, 23, 24, July 1, 7, 11, 20, 21, 22, Aug. 5, 9, 18, 19, 20, Sept. 3, 7, 16, 17, 18, Oct. 1, 5, 14, 15, 16, 29, 31, Nov. 3, 12, 13, 14, 27, 29, Dec. 1, 10, 11, 12, 25, 27, 29

Beneficial: Jan. 7, 15, 20, 31, Feb. 5, 13, 18, 29, Mar. 3, 11, 16, 27, Apr. 1, 9, 14, 25, May 7, 12, 23, June 5, 10, 21, July 3, 8, 19, Aug. 1, 6, 17, 30, Sept. 4, 15, 28, Oct. 2, 13, 26, Nov. 11, 24, Dec. 9, 22

Fatal attractions: Jan. 19, 20, 21, 22

Challenging: Jan. 6, 14, 30, Feb. 4, 12, 28, Mar. 2, 10, 26, Apr. 8, 24, May 6, 22, June 4, 20, July 2, 18, Aug. 16, Sept. 14, Oct. 12, Nov. 10, Dec. 8

Soul mates: Apr. 30, May 28, June 26, July 24, Aug. 22, Sept. 20, Oct. 18, 30, Nov. 16, 28, Dec. 14, 26

July 24

♌ Ambitious, practical, and responsible, you are an idealistic Leo with a sympathetic and courageous heart. As a positive thinker with organizational and planning skills, you make good use of your wide knowledge. Being security-conscious, you like to set a solid foundation and build from there. Usually you are happier being active or working, rather than just wasting your energies in the pursuit of evanescent pleasure.

Since you are particularly drawn to people who are clever or interesting, you are liable to make contacts based on shared interests or the search for knowledge or wisdom. Education usually plays an important role in your advancement, whether early or later on in life. This may include self-directed study on a particular subject that inspires you. By using your refined common sense and cultivating your intuitive gifts, you often become an advisor to those around you.

Imaginative and full of money-making ideas, you have a good understanding of current trends and enjoy being creative while making money. In your eagerness to succeed, however, guard against being too critical, stubborn, or aggressive by learning to give and take, and by mastering the subtle art of negotiation.

When you are age twenty-nine, your progressed Sun moves into Virgo, commencing a thirty-year period of increasing emphasis on your work, practical efficiency, and productivity. You may start to draw more pleasure from being of service and doing your job well. Another turning point occurs at the age of fifty-nine, when your progressed Sun moves into Libra, stimulating you to be more diplomatic and placing more emphasis on relationships, balance, and harmonious surroundings.

Fixed Stars

Although your Sun's degree is not linked to a fixed star, some of your other planets' degrees certainly will be. By having an astrological chart calculated, you can find the exact position of the planets on your date of birth. This will tell you which of the fixed stars listed in this book are relevant to you.

Your Secret Self

As you are multitalented, you are interested in many subjects and like to keep yourself well informed by exploring new ideas. This prevents you from becoming bored or restless. Being idealistic, you need to strike a balance between fighting for what you believe in and accepting fate. When you establish a philosophy of life, you learn to accept your own limitations.

Although you always want to move on and progress, until you learn to be still and reflect or contemplate, you might find it hard to achieve inner peace. Introspection may prove a particularly useful tool in your quest for becoming whole. Your home may also be an important factor in finding security and protection for your emotional sensitivity. You are usually seeking some inner knowledge or wisdom that will give you inner love or serenity. This quest for wisdom will continue right through until the end of your life, and may be enhanced by the study of metaphysics or spirituality.

Work & Vocation

Pride and a strong sense of responsibility ensure that you want to do your job well. You make an excellent manager, executive, or leader and are likely to be resourceful. Being a good organizer and strategist, you can excel in commerce, particularly working in partnerships or in cooperative efforts. You could do equally well in promotion and advertising. Your fine mind may attract you to education, philosophy, religion, or psychology. With your strong sense of the dramatic, occupations such as actor, writer, or politician may provide a platform for your strong opinions.

Famous people who share your birthday include French author Alexandre Dumas, Zelda Fitzgerald (wife of author F. Scott Fitzgerald), and TV actress Linda Carter.

Numerology

With a number 24 birthday, you may dislike routine; however, you are hardworking, with practical abilities and sound judgment. The emotional sensitivity of the number 24 birthday suggests that you need to establish stability and order. Faithful and fair, though sometimes undemonstrative, you are inclined to believe that actions speak louder than words. With this pragmatic approach to life, you develop a good business sense and an ability to overcome obstacles and succeed. As a number 24 individual, you may have to overcome a tendency to be stubborn or fixed in your ideas. The subinfluence of the number 7 month indicates that you like to observe things carefully before you make up your mind. Since you are sensitive to structure and can easily create an efficient system, your creativity and practical skills prove beneficial.

• *Positive:* energy, idealist, practical skills, strong determination, honest, frank, fair, generous, love of home, active, energetic

• *Negative:* materialistic, too economical, instability, ruthless, dislikes routine, lazy, unfaithful, unstable, stubborn

Love & Relationships

Intuitive and shrewd, you are drawn to unusual relationships or to people who can inspire you to gain wider knowledge. Although for you home and family are important, an urge for freedom and independence suggests that an underlying restlessness and desire to accomplish may challenge your inclination to stay in one place for too long. You are usually attracted to those who know more than you do. Dramatic in your self-expression, you will always have a youthful and fun side to your personality.

YOUR SPECIAL SOMEONE

You might find just the right partner among those born on the following days.

Love & friendship: Jan. 3, 4, 14, 20, 24, Feb. 2, 12, 18, 22, Mar. 10, 16, 20, 29, 30, Apr. 8, 14, 18, 27, 28, May 6, 12, 16, 25, 26, 31, June 4, 10, 14, 23, 24, 29, July 2, 8, 12, 21, 22, 27, Aug. 6, 10, 19, 20, 25, Sept. 4, 8, 17, 18, 23, Oct. 2, 6, 15, 16, 21, 30, Nov. 4, 13, 14, 19, 28, 30, Dec. 2, 11, 12, 17, 26, 28, 30

Beneficial: Jan. 4, 8, 21, Feb. 2, 6, 19, Mar. 4, 17, 28, Apr. 2, 15, 16, May 13, 24, June 11, 22, July 9, 20, Aug. 7, 18, 31, Sept. 5, 16, 29, Oct. 3, 14, 27, Nov. 1, 12, 25, Dec. 10, 23

Fatal attractions: Jan. 3, 21, 22, 23, Feb. 1, May 31, June 29, July 27, Aug. 25, Sept. 23, Oct. 21, Nov. 19, Dec. 17

Challenging: Jan. 7, 10, 15, 31, Feb. 5, 8, 13, 29, Mar. 3, 6, 11, 27, Apr. 1, 4, 9, 25, May 2, 7, 23, June 5, 21, July 3, 19, Aug. 1, 17, Sept. 15, Oct. 13, Nov. 11, Dec. 9

Soul mates: Mar. 31, Apr. 29, May 27, June 25, July 23, Aug. 21, Sept. 19, Oct. 17, 29, Nov. 15, 27, Dec. 13, 25

July 25

♌ Creative, fun-loving, and entertaining with an ability to commercialize your talents, you are a sunny Leo full of charm, drive, and enthusiasm. The mental vitality and carefree attitude indicated by your birthdate, however, also carry a deeper and more introspective nature that may need to be developed.

The subinfluence of your ruling planet, the Sun, means that you are dignified and able to express the joys of life. Versatile and generous, with a curious mind, you usually have many interests or hobbies. Since you are sociable and gregarious, at times you may attempt too much and are in danger of scattering your energies. Nevertheless, you are skillful and artistic and have the potential for success through some type of creative pursuit. Athough intellectually bright, confusion as to what you really want to do may be a source of worry and indecision and may lead you to explore different options. If inspired, you are willing to develop the endurance and persistence needed to take on challenges and make impossible dreams come true.

Your pioneering, enterprising spirit and strong survival instincts make you a good strategist, and by developing a willingness to work for long-term results without instant rewards, you can show your dedication. Overcome a tendency to become emotionally insecure or jealous by learning to spontaneously trust your own instincts.

When you are age twenty-eight, your progressed Sun moves into Virgo. Over the next thirty-year period you are likely to develop your analytical skills and be influenced by this sign's qualities of practicality and efficiency. Another turning point occurs around the age of fifty-eight, when your progressed Sun moves into Libra, stimulating you to cooperate more with others, be diplomatic, and place more emphasis on your partnerships and harmony.

Your Secret Self

Through cultivating faith, you can learn to depend on your inner resources and diminish any doubts. Since you are clever and shrewd, you possess an ability to quickly appraise people and events. This psychological skill can be used purely to achieve material aims and objectives or to return some of your wisdom and experience to others. Although you need stimulating and challenging experiences that can push you forward, you may find yourself able to help others in unexpected ways.

Since you may be restless or impatient, you need to learn how to focus your energies by releasing them in a positive way through exercise, travel, or exciting explorations. Although you may find more business opportunities by being daring, be careful that your money does not go out as fast as it comes in.

Work & Vocation

Naturally dramatic and creative, you can utilize these gifts in any profession as well as in the world of entertainment. Although you seem confident, you may need to develop faith in your abilities and overcome self-doubt in any career you undertake. Being naturally charming and socially aware ensures your success in any people-related occupation as well as in politics or work in the community. Particularly good with words, you can excel as a writer, as a lecturer,

FIXED STARS

Although your Sun's degree is not linked to a fixed star, some of your other planets' degrees certainly will be. By having an astrological chart calculated, you can find the exact position of the planets on your date of birth. This will tell you which of the fixed stars listed in this book are relevant to you.

or in sales. Your need for a changing and varied career implies that you should avoid monotonous occupations. If in business, you are likely to take a creative approach and can work hard to support any cause that interests you. Similarly, your originality may find successful expression in art or music.

Famous people who share your birthday include artist Maxfield Parrish, painter Thomas Eakins, supermodel Iman, actress Estelle Getty, and actor Brad Renfro.

Numerology

Quick and energetic, though intuitive and thoughtful, as a number 25 individual, you need to express yourself through different experiences. These may include new and exciting ideas, people, or locations. A desire for perfection urges you to work hard and be productive. You may, however, need to be less impatient or critical if things do not happen according to plan. As a number 25, you possess strong mental energies that, when concentrated, aid you to look at all the facts and arrive at a conclusion faster than anyone else. Success and happiness come when you learn to trust your own instincts and develop perseverance and patience. The subinfluence of the number 7 month indicates that although at times you are secretive and fearful of showing your true feelings, you seek ways to express yourself. Usually you are instinctive and alert, and can gain skills and knowledge through both practical application and theory.

• *Positive:* highly intuitive, perfectionist, perceptive, creative mind, good at dealing with people

• *Negative:* impulsive, impatient, irresponsible, overly emotional, jealous, secretive, changing circumstances, critical, moody

Love & Relationships

Charming, dramatic, and creative, with a sensitive touch, you find it easy to make friends and influence people. Usually confident, with idealistic notions, you can be giving and loving. Although you are willing to make great sacrifices for those you love, you can sometimes appear selfish or withdrawn. You may have to be very discriminating about whom you choose for a love relationship, but once you have found the ideal mate you can be a loyal, caring, and devoted partner.

YOUR SPECIAL SOMEONE

If you are looking for someone special, you might find greater luck with those born on the following days.

Love & friendship: Jan. 21, 25, Feb. 19, 23, Mar. 17, 21, 30, Apr. 15, 19, 28, 29, May 13, 17, 26, 27, June 11, 15, 24, 25, 30, July 9, 13, 22, 23, 28, Aug. 7, 11, 20, 21, 26, 30, Sept. 5, 9, 18, 19, 24, 28, Oct. 3, 7, 16, 17, 22, 26, 29, Nov. 1, 5, 14, 15, 20, 24, 27, Dec. 3, 12, 13, 18, 22, 25, 27, 29

Beneficial: Jan. 5, 13, 16, 22, 28, Feb. 3, 11, 14, 20, 26, Mar. 1, 9, 12, 18, 24, 29, Apr. 7, 10, 16, 22, 27, May 5, 8, 14, 20, 25, June 3, 6, 12, 18, 23, July 1, 4, 10, 16, 21, Aug. 2, 8, 14, 19, Sept. 6, 12, 17, Oct. 4, 10, 15, Nov. 2, 8, 13, Dec. 6, 11

Fatal attractions: Jan. 21, 22, 23, 24, 25, June 30, July 28, Aug. 26, Sept. 24, Oct. 22, Nov. 20, Dec. 18

Challenging: Jan. 2, 23, 30, Feb. 21, 28, Mar. 19, 26, 28, Apr. 17, 24, 26, May 15, 22, 24, June 13, 20, 22, July 11, 18, 20, Aug. 16, 18, 19, Sept. 7, 14, 16, Oct. 5, 12, 14, Nov. 3, 10, 12, Dec. 1, 8, 10

Soul mates: Jan. 14, 22, Feb. 12, 20, Mar. 10, 18, Apr. 8, 16, May 6, 14, June 4, 12, July 2, 10, Aug. 8, Sept. 6, Oct. 4, Nov. 2

July 26

FIXED STARS

Although your Sun's degree is not linked to a fixed star, some of your other planets' degrees certainly will be. By having an astrological chart calculated, you can find the exact position of the planets on your date of birth. This will tell you which of the fixed stars listed in this book are relevant to you.

♌ Considerate and cheerful, with an ambitious personality, you can radiate confidence and be charming and generous. As a Leo, you are dignified and honorable, with a sharp intellect. This suggests that you are a good psychologist who understands people and what motivates them. With your personal touch, you have the talent for making people feel special and important.

The double influence of your ruling planet, the Sun, also suggests that you are proud, but you may have to learn to differentiate between being dignified and being arrogant. Since you like to be treated well and receive compliments, you may find it hard to accept criticism. By creating harmony and balance in relationships, you can communicate your thoughts and ideas more easily.

Although tenacious and persistent, with the power to pull through and endure, you may need to overcome a tendency to be too rigid in your outlook or be obstinate and impatient. With calmness, you can present new ideas to others in an entertaining and logical manner in order to persuade them to see things from your perspective. This helps you take the lead and use your ideas in a constructive way.

Incisive thinking and the ability to think fast indicate that you are an assertive communicator who likes to be direct and clear. Despite your mental precision, it may be wise to avoid an inclination for sarcasm when you need to release your frustrations.

Your natural vitality and desire to shine may draw you to sports, games, and social activities. From the age of twenty-seven, when your progressed Sun moves into Virgo, there is an increasing desire for practical order, analysis, and efficiency in your life. There is a turning point for you at the age of fifty-seven, when your progressed Sun enters Libra. From this time you may develop a desire to be more involved in your close personal relationships, and you may turn from more practical considerations to more aesthetic ones.

Your Secret Self

You are usually willing to work hard to achieve your objectives and want to be at the forefront of your activities. Headstrong, however, you can at times ignore your deep intuitive feelings in an attempt to get your own way. At times, you can display incredible moments of insight at lightning-fast speed. This can be reflected in a wonderful humorous outlook that carries a profound wisdom locked up behind a joker's facade.

You need to be constantly initiating new projects, preferably involving people. You are highly sociable and need the stimulation of lively debate to keep you on your toes. At times you can take a warm interest in the affairs of others, being kindly, considerate, and courteous. If you become too serious, however, you can turn stubborn and incite trouble.

Work & Vocation

Your natural confident front and enthusiasm, combined with your strong power to influence people, suggest that you can be an ideal leader. Your gift of gab plus your shrewd intellect make you an excellent candidate for a career such as promoter, negotiator, agent, or salesperson. Similarly, you can do well as a writer or lecturer. Being a naturally good psychologist, you may be drawn to professions such as counseling or public relations. If in the business world, your organizational and strategic skills often attract you to large projects. Alternatively, the entertainment or art world may appeal to you from the director's chair. Although independent, you may find many advantages to working cooperatively with others.

Famous people who share your birthday include Swiss psychologist and writer Carl Gustav Jung, playwright George Bernard Shaw, singer Mick Jagger, novelist Aldous Huxley, film directors Stanley Kubrick and Blake Edwards, and writer James Lovelock.

Numerology

With a number 26 birthday, you have a pragmatic approach to life, executive ability, and a good business sense. Usually responsible, with a natural aesthetic sense and a love of home, you need to build a solid foundation or find real stability. Often a tower of strength for others, you are willing to support friends, family members, and relatives who turn to you in time of need. You may nevertheless need to guard against materialistic tendencies and a desire to control situations or people. The subinfluence of the number 7 month indicates that you have to find a balance between your needs and your obligations to others. Being a perfectionist, you like to pay attention to small details and create beauty and harmony. The idealism and strength suggested by your birthday shows that you are a cautious character, with strong values and sound judgment.

- *Positive:* creative, practical, caring, responsible, proud of family, enthusiastic, courageous
- *Negative:* stubborn, rebellious, unstable relationships, unenthusiastic, lack of persistence

Love & Relationships

You are likely to possess a youthful and playful quality in your relationships that can be highly attractive but irresponsible. Being sociable and entertaining, you find it easy to make friends and are an excellent host. You enjoy sharing with those you love and can be warm and charming. Even though you may find playing the field attractive, you prefer establishing a more long-term commitment with someone who can understand your needs and desires.

YOUR SPECIAL SOMEONE

You might start to look for an exciting partner among those born on the following dates.

Love & friendship: Jan. 6, 16, 22, 26, Feb. 4, 14, 20, 24, Mar. 2, 12, 18, 22, Apr. 10, 16, 20, 30, May 8, 14, 18, 28, June 6, 12, 16, 26, July 4, 10, 14, 24, 31, Aug. 2, 8, 12, 22, 29, Sept. 6, 10, 20, 27, Oct. 4, 8, 18, 25, Nov. 2, 6, 16, 23, 30, Dec. 4, 14, 21, 28, 30

Beneficial: Jan. 6, 17, 23, 31, Feb. 4, 15, 21, 29, Mar. 2, 13, 19, 27, 30, Apr. 11, 17, 25, 28, May 9, 15, 23, 26, June 7, 13, 21, 24, July 5, 11, 19, 22, Aug. 3, 9, 17, 20, Sept. 1, 7, 15, 18, 30, Oct. 5, 13, 16, 28, Nov. 3, 11, 14, 26, Dec. 1, 9, 12, 24

Fatal attractions: Jan. 22, 23, 24, 25, 26

Challenging: Jan. 24, Feb. 22, Mar. 20, 29, Apr. 18, 27, 29, May 6, 16, 25, 27, 30, June 14, 22, 25, 28, July 12, 21, 23, 26, Aug. 10, 19, 21, 24, Sept. 8, 17, 19, 22, Oct. 6, 15, 17, 20, Nov. 4, 13, 15, 18, Dec. 2, 11, 13, 16

Soul mates: Jan. 13, Feb. 11, Mar. 9, Apr. 7, May 5, June 3, 30, July 1, 28, Aug. 26, Sept. 24, Oct. 22, Nov. 20, Dec. 18

July 27

♌ Friendly and understanding, with a sixth sense, you are a receptive Leo with strong character. Creative, with a thirst for knowledge and a strong need to explore, you are endowed with an imaginative and curious mind. You have a need to express yourself in thoughts and words or to initiate new ideas.

A determined and progressive thinker, you seek mental stimulation and recognize good ideas when you come across them. Quick on the uptake, you rarely miss an opportunity to keep up with the latest information and are usually a collector of books, magazines, or computer technology.

The subinfluence of your decanate ruler, Leo, indicates that you possess a lively personality, with charm and good looks. Being friendly, you enjoy intimate conversations and the personal touch. Nevertheless, you are often an extremist by nature and need to learn how to balance the generous side of your nature with a tendency to be overly sensitive, insecure, or stubborn.

Since you are social and gregarious, with forceful speech, you like to deal with the public at large and are good at diplomacy and public relations. When inspired, whatever you do, you usually start with great enthusiasm but not always enough preparation. This tendency can explain why you are inclined to get bored easily or lose heart, and suggests that having too many interests can distract your otherwise focused mind.

Being intuitive and practical, you are a productive idealist, and with your enthusiastic personality, erudition, and fertile imagination can produce impressive original thought. You may, however, need to learn how to turn your wonderful ideas into tangible concepts.

After the age of twenty-six, when your progressed Sun enters Virgo, you start to become less dominant as you center your attention on becoming more analytical, practical, and reflective. As your duties increase you will also find that you want to produce your work more perfectly and efficiently. From the age of fifty-six, when your progressed Sun moves into Libra, there is a change of emphasis in your life, and you become more easygoing, adaptable, and diplomatic.

Your Secret Self

Although personally ambitious, you may find your greatest pleasure comes from sharing with others. As you can be both independent and codependent, you may need to balance the emotional extremes of your nature in order to establish close and deep relationships. It may be necessary for you to pay special attention to ensure that all your associations are on an equal give-and-take basis.

You can be warm, loving, and highly idealistic. This may take you to high points of emotional inspiration, whether through art, music, or spirituality. The contrast between these heights and the mundane world and people's everyday personalities may sometimes cause inner tension. By spontaneously giving without expecting people to do things your way, you can avoid disappointment.

Work & Vocation

With your quick intelligence, exceptional memory, and leadership abilities, you can make a valuable contribution in almost any career. Given your attraction to people-related occupations and activities, you may excel as a salesperson, trainer, propagandist, or agent, or in public relations. Equally, you can excel as a writer, teacher, or administrator. If in business, you will probably want to direct the show, so you need to be self-employed or in a management position. Sharing your expertise can extend to being a lawyer or counselor, and you may find yourself working for a cause. Alternatively, you can also be attracted to careers that involve your appreciation of color, beauty and form, or music.

Famous people who share your birthday include country singer Bobbie Gentry, singer/actress Maureen McGovern, and poet Hilaire Belloc.

Numerology

The number 27 birthdate indicates that you are idealistic and sensitive. Intuitive and analytical, with a fertile and creative mind, you can impress others with your original thoughts. Although at times you appear secretive, overly rational, or detached, in fact you may be hiding inner tensions. In developing good communication skills, you can overcome a reluctance to express your deeper feelings. Education is essential for number 27 persons, and by developing depth of thought you become more patient and self-disciplined. The subinfluence of the number 7 month indicates that you are charismatic, with an imaginative mind and strong instincts. You are often forceful, determined, and observant and can pay a great deal of attention to details. By developing a positive attitude and learning to listen to others, you can overcome a tendency to be skeptical and suspicious. To gain a deeper understanding of life's wisdom, you may choose to ignore the advice of others and learn through personal experience.

• *Positive:* versatile, imaginative, creative, resolute, brave, good understanding, mentally capable, spiritual, inventive, mental strength

• *Negative:* disagreeable, quarrelsome, easily offended, argumentative, restless, nervous, mistrustful, overemotional

Love & Relationships

Although you are dynamic and forceful, you often think as a twosome. Friendly and sociable, you can attract others with your sunny personality, though you might prefer the intimacy of only a few close friends. Ambitious and self-motivated, you are usually attracted to hardworking individuals who are self-made. For happiness and long-lasting relationships, you may need to overcome a tendency to be too possessive or temperamental. However, in relationships you can be charming, loyal, and supportive.

YOUR SPECIAL SOMEONE

Your chances of finding a loving partner are increased with those born on the following dates.

Love & friendship: Jan. 1, 4, 27, 29, Feb. 2, 25, 27, Mar. 23, 25, Apr. 21, 23, May 19, 21, 29, June 17, 19, 27, July 15, 17, 25, Aug. 13, 15, 23, Sept. 11, 13, 21, Oct. 9, 11, 19, Nov. 7, 9, 17, Dec. 5, 7, 15

Beneficial: Jan. 3, 10, 15, 18, Feb. 1, 8, 13, 16, Mar. 6, 11, 14, 29, 31, Apr. 4, 9, 12, 27, 29, May 2, 7, 10, 25, 27, June 5, 8, 23, 25, July 3, 6, 21, 23, Aug. 1, 4, 19, 21, Sept. 2, 17, 19, Oct. 15, 17, Nov. 13, 15, Dec. 11, 13

Fatal attractions: Jan. 23, 24, 25, 26, 27, Apr. 30, May 28, June 26, July 24, Aug. 22, Sept. 20, Oct. 18, Nov. 16, Dec. 14

Challenging: Jan. 9, 14, 16, 25, Feb. 7, 12, 14, 23, Mar. 5, 10, 12, 21, 28, 30, Apr. 3, 8, 10, 19, 26, 28, May 1, 6, 8, 17, 24, 26, June 4, 6, 15, 22, 24, July 2, 4, 13, 20, 22, Aug. 2, 11, 18, 20, Sept. 9, 16, 18, Oct. 7, 14, 16, Nov. 5, 12, 14, Dec. 3, 10, 12

Soul mates: Dec. 29

July 28

♌ The emotional power suggested by your birthday endows you with a dynamic personality and shows you to be a charismatic, kind, and generous person with natural leadership ability. With your strong ambitions, courage, sensitivity, and quick responses, you have the potential for outstanding achievement.

The subinfluence of your decanate ruler, Leo, suggests that people are drawn to the confident and assured image you display. Although you are hardworking, a busy social life can also figure high on your list of priorities. Just ensure that it does not override the self-discipline required in order to make the most of your many wonderful talents.

Usually worldly and cultured, you like to be surrounded by quality and luxury and have an appreciation for beauty. If inspired, you may need to express yourself in a creative way and seek recognition through the worlds of theater, art, music, and entertainment. Gregarious and fun-loving, you can also be a diplomat when it is in your own interest.

Although usually a strong, proud, and dignified individual, you can at times be surprisingly modest. You may nevertheless need to overcome a tendency to be impatient or domineering that can stem from fixed and controlled emotions. As you like to think big or be excessive, guard against overdoing it either at work or at play, which could eventually put a strain on your health. Success can be achieved through your potential for hard work, strategy, and planning.

From childhood you are likely to be interested in social activities and developing your leadership abilities by being at the center of things. From the age of twenty-five onward, when your progressed Sun moves into Virgo, you will become more discriminating, practical, and thoughtful with your time and energy. You may look for ways to operate more efficiently, particularly in your working environment. When you reach the age of fifty-five your progressed Sun enters Libra for a thirty-year period. This is likely to emphasize your relationships as well as bring more harmony and balance into your life. This may also highlight a possible interest in writing, art, music, or healing.

Your Secret Self

Despite the fact that you ooze charm, wit, and creativity, and have the ability to entertain others, at times you may get overly serious or selfish, feeling that your efforts are not being appreciated. At these times you may be prone to becoming argumentative or self-indulgent. Channel these frustrations into being generous and detached in order to show your true humanitarian and compassionate nature. This ensures your popularity and gains you the recognition that you need.

Very intuitive, with a good sense of humor, you also need recognition from those you love. As you do not like to be alone, you may compromise for peace, home, and family. Watch that your love of sensuality and comfort does not deter you from the dynamic expression of your great potential.

Work & Vocation

With your natural dramatic sense and ability to lead, you can excel in the theater as an actor or director. Independent, with leadership ability, you will naturally rise to positions of power or may prefer to work for yourself. Multitalented, you also possess the ability to commercialize any of your talents, and you have the fortunate ability to make useful contacts. Possessing charm and advanced social skills, you are likely to succeed in any people-related activity. Your expertise with communication can be used in writing, lecturing, publishing, or sales. Combined with your confident front and competitive character, you can also be successful at business if you put in the necessary self-discipline. On the other hand, your humanitarian inclinations may direct you toward a career in social reform, health, and charity work. This birthdate can also indicate a gift for music.

Famous people born on your birthday are former First Lady Jacqueline Kennedy Onassis, children's writer Beatrix Potter, artist Marcel Duchamp, and musician Mike Bloomfield.

Numerology

Independent and idealistic, with determination and a pragmatic approach, you are often a law unto yourself. Like a number 1 individual, you are ambitious, direct, and enterprising. An inner conflict between wanting to be independent and wanting to be part of a team is also indicated. Always ready for action and new ventures, you courageously take on life's challenges, and with your enthusiasm you can easily inspire others, if not to join you, then at least to support you in your latest venture. As a number 28 birthday, you have leadership abilities and rely on your common sense, logic, and clear thinking. Often you take on responsibilities, but you can also be overly enthusiastic, impatient, or intolerant. The subinfluence of the number 7 month indicates that you may need to learn to trust your inner feelings in order to overcome issues concerning power and the material world. If doubtful and mistrusting, you may miss the opportunity to share your creative gifts with others.

• *Positive:* compassion, progressive, daring, artistic, creative, idealistic, ambitious, hardworking, stable home life, strong-willed

• *Negative:* daydreamer, unmotivated, lack of compassion, unrealistic, bossy, lack of judgment, aggressive, lack of confidence, too dependent on others, pride

Love & Relationships

Because of your romantic nature and generosity, people are easily drawn to your charismatic personality. Although nothing is too good for the ones you love, beware of becoming too domineering or overbearing. With your passionate temperament, you may experience strong attractions and even love at first sight. In order to achieve your desired goals, however, there must be a balance between your need for independence and the necessity for cooperation in love and work.

YOUR SPECIAL SOMEONE

You are more likely to have success in love and friendship with people born on the following dates.

Love & friendship: Jan. 2, 28, Feb. 26, Mar. 24, Apr. 22, May 20, 29, 30, June 18, 27, 28, July 16, 25, 26, Aug. 14, 23, 24, Sept. 12, 21, 22, Oct. 10, 19, 20, 29, 31, Nov. 8, 17, 18, 27, 29, Dec. 6, 15, 16, 25, 27

Beneficial: Jan. 2, 10, 13, 16, Feb. 8, 11, 14, Mar. 6, 9, 12, Apr. 4, 7, 10, May 2, 5, 8, June 3, 6, July 1, 4, 30, Aug. 2, 28, 30, Sept. 26, 28, Oct. 24, 26, Nov. 22, 24, Dec. 20, 22, 30

Fatal attractions: Jan. 24, 25, 26, 27, 28, Oct. 31, Nov. 29, Dec. 27

Challenging: Jan. 3, 9, 10, Feb. 1, 7, 8, Mar. 5, 6, 31, Apr. 3, 4, 29, May 1, 2, 27, June 25, July 23, Aug. 2, 21, 31, Sept. 19, 29, Oct 17, 27, Nov. 15, 25, Dec. 13, 23

Soul mates: Jan. 5, Feb. 3, Mar. 1, May 30, June 28, July 26, Aug. 24, Sept. 22, Oct. 20, Nov. 18, Dec. 16

July 29

FIXED STAR

Star's name: Praesepe, also called Praesaepe

Degree position: 6°16'–7°16' Leo, between the years 1930 and 2000

Magnitude: 5

Strength: ★★

Orb: 1°

Constellation: M44 Cancer

Applicable days: July 30, 31, August 1

Star qualities: Mars/Moon

Description: A star mass of more than forty stars located on the head of the Crab

PRIMARY STAR'S INFLUENCE

Praesepe imparts an adventurous yet industrious nature with good business acumen. This star also suggests good fortune and may indicate involvement in founding large businesses. Praesepe, however, also carries an influence that suggests impulsiveness and restlessness and warns against an inclination toward creating unnecessary trouble by being too insolent. This star also warns against involvement in lawsuits and risky dealings.

Linked to your Sun's degree, this star imparts energy and vitality, inner pride, and an ability to focus on goals with great determination. Once you make up your mind, you refuse to give up, but continue to strive toward your final objectives. This star's influence can attract friends, bring popularity, and lead to high-profile positions and even fame. Praesepe, however, warns against fluctuating moods, doubts, and fears, which could arise from misunderstandings

♌ An abundance of feeling, sensitivity, and imagination is usually associated with your birthday. Dramatic and talented, with a charming personality, you are a determined Leo who with inspiration and encouragement can reach great heights.

The subinfluence of your decanate ruler, Leo, suggests that, being proud and needing recognition, you display a confident and assured image. As you judge everything by the way you feel, you may need to find avenues for self-expression or an outlet for your artistic or creative talents. This suggests that your emotional range is tremendous, and with your thoughtfulness and warmth, you can win the admiration of others. If, on the other hand, you fail to get your own way, you can become dominating or melodramatic, with an inclination for emotional outbursts.

All your sensitivity does not detract from the fact that you also possess a tough business sense and an awareness of material considerations. This part of your personality can be resolute and inflexible, with a strong sense of duty. If especially interested in something, you can become really determined. Combined with your strong sense of vision and enthusiasm, you can inspire others; it might, however, be necessary to keep your feet on the ground by staying humble and well balanced.

After the age of twenty-four, when your progressed Sun enters Virgo, you begin to be less dominant, as your mental focus becomes more analytical, practical, and reflective. Your duties start to take up more of your time, and you may want to work more perfectly and efficiently. From the age of fifty-four, when your progressed Sun moves into Libra, there is a change of emphasis in your life and you become more relaxed, diplomatic, and creative, with your relationships playing a more important role in your life.

Your Secret Self

Always directed toward achievement, you need strong aims and objectives. With your large dreams, it is necessary to apply strong self-discipline and be very focused in order to accomplish them. One of your major challenges may come from negative thinking or expecting too much from others. This can cause frustration or disappointment that may lead to feelings of emotional dissatisfaction. With your potential to go from the depths of depression to the heights of inspired humanitarianism, it is vital to find positive outlets for your sensitive imagination and creative spirit. By harnessing all your dynamic emotions into work that has some sense of purpose, you are likely to find a deeper recognition of your inherent powerful role in society.

Work & Vocation

With your natural sense of authority, you do not like to be in a subservient position and may be at your best when working selflessly for a cause or an ideal. This could lead you to a career in politics, charity work, or social reform. Your excellent sense of the dramatic may fare well in acting or the world of entertainment, and you can share your knowledge with others through teaching or writing. Your sensitivity and sense of vision can help you become successful as a film director or photographer. Similarly, you have the ability to commercialize art or things of beauty and use your social skills to combine business and pleasure.

Famous people who share your birthday include statesman Dag Hammarskjöld, dictator Benito Mussolini, actress Clara Bow, and film director Bill Forsyth.

Numerology

As a number 29 individual, you have a powerful personality and extraordinary potential. You are highly intuitive, sensitive, and emotional. Inspiration is the key to your success story, and without it you may experience lack of purpose. Although you are a true dreamer, the extreme sides of your nature indicate that you may have to guard against alternating moods. If you trust your innermost feelings and open your heart to others, you can overcome your tendency to worry or use your mind as protective armor. Use your creative thoughts to achieve something special and unique that can motivate or be of service to others. The subinfluence of the number 7 month indicates that honesty and compassion are your true powers, and with them you can create love and harmony. While you are charismatic and forceful, if you wish to be in a position of authority, a responsible attitude, fairness, and integrity will gain you the respect and loyalty you want from others.

• *Positive:* inspirational, balance, inner peace, generous, successful, creative, intuitive, mystical, powerful dreams, worldly, faith

• *Negative:* unfocused, insecure, nervous, selfish, vain, moody, difficult, extremist, inconsiderate, overly sensitive

YOUR SPECIAL SOMEONE

Your opportunities to find that special person are greater with those born on the following dates.

Love & friendship: Jan. 3, 22, 25, 29, 30, Feb. 1, 20, 23, 27, 28, Mar. 18, 21, 25, 26, Apr. 16, 19, 23, 24, 28, May 14, 17, 21, 22, 26, 31, June 12, 15, 19, 20, 24, 29, July 10, 13, 18, 22, Aug. 8, 11, 15, 16, 20, 27, 29, 30, Sept. 6, 9, 13, 14, 18, 23, 27, 28, Oct. 4, 7, 11, 12, 16, 21, 25, 26, Nov. 2, 5, 9, 10, 14, 19, 23, 24, Dec. 3, 7, 8, 12, 17, 21, 22

Beneficial: Jan. 17, Feb. 15, Mar. 13, Apr. 11, May 9, 29, June 7, 27, July 5, 25, Aug. 3, 23, Sept. 1, 21, Oct. 19, 29, Nov. 17, 27, 30, Dec. 15, 25, 28

Fatal attractions: Jan. 25, 26, 27, 28, 29, May 31, June 29, July 27, Aug 25, 30, Sept. 23, 28, Oct. 21, 26, Nov. 19, 24, Dec 17, 22

Challenging: Jan. 20, 23, Feb. 18, 21, Mar. 16, 19, Apr. 14, 17, May 12, 15, June 10, 13, July 8, 11, Aug. 6, 9, Sept. 4, 7, Oct. 2, 5, Nov. 2, Dec. 1

Soul mates: Jan. 4, 31, Feb. 2, 29, Mar. 27, Apr. 25, May 23, June 21, July 19, Aug. 17, Sept. 15, Oct. 13, Nov. 11, Dec. 9

Love & Relationships

Drawn toward people of power and influence, you can be romantic and dramatic. However, on occasion your personal relationships may suffer from your contrasting moods. With your powerful emotions, you can be sensitive and caring, with a compassionate and expressive nature. Loyalty and devotion are very important to you, but avoid an inclination to be bossy and demanding. Through being responsible and giving, you often receive the respect and admiration of others.

July 30

♌ Your birthday suggests that you are creative and ambitious, possessing a dynamic emotional power and an attractive personality. Youthful and sociable, you prefer companionship to solitude. Although idealistic, you can be very aware of material considerations and usually have a good business sense.

With the added influence of your decanate ruler, Leo, you enjoy entertaining others and have a love of grandeur. Proud and dramatic, you project self-assurance and have a royal air about you. With the ability to shine in a crowd, you are warm-hearted and friendly. However, you may have to be careful that your strong ego does not lead you to become arrogant or temperamental.

A need for self-expression may lead you to creative outlets such as writing, drama, art, or music, and with your natural leadership you would enjoy being at the forefront of your crowd. Confident and courageous, you are usually willing to take risks and are capable of magnanimous gestures. In your desire for luxury, you may have to be careful of being overindulgent or extravagant. Nevertheless, confident and dignified, you can be highly entertaining and an excellent friend.

After the age of twenty-three, when your progressed Sun moves into Virgo for thirty years, there is an increasing need for practical order in your everyday existence. You will be more inclined to analyze things and look for ways to restructure your life so that it is generally healthier or more efficient. This continues until the age of fifty-three, when your progressed Sun enters Libra. As a turning point for you, this highlights the growing need for interaction with others and the importance of intimate relationships, creativity, and harmony.

Your Secret Self

With your enhanced sensitivity, you can be broad-minded and sympathetic to the problems of others. This may lead to your helping them through being a good listener or advisor. Creative and entertaining, you have the gift of uplifting people's spirits. An inner nobility bestows a natural grace and a freedom from limiting concepts.

With your heightened awareness, you may also be prone to go to extremes. On occasion, you can be overwhelmed or weighed down with an excess of feelings that can lead you to bury your sensitivities in feeling sorry for yourself or escaping. By concentrating on the needs of your own ego, you may become conceited or too self-involved and forget your high calling. When expressing your star quality, however, you bounce back from worry or misfortune to radiate love and warmth to your many admirers.

Work & Vocation

With your natural authority and ability to deal with people, you should ideally be in a leading position or in an occupation where you are given much freedom to do things your way. A natural diplomacy may lead you to vocations such as public relations or customer service, and your people skills can help you succeed in promotion or publishing. You can be especially good at businesses that involve socializing, such as clubs or restaurants, and as you enjoy en-

FIXED STARS

North Asellus; South Asellus; Praesepe, also called Praesaepe

PRIMARY STAR

Star's name: North Asellus
Degree position: 6°34'–7°35' Leo, between the years 1930 and 2000
Magnitude: 5
Strength: ★★
Orb: 1°
Constellation: Gamma Cancer
Applicable days: July 30, 31, August 1
Star qualities: Mars/Sun
Description: A pale yellow-white twin star located in the body of the Crab

PRIMARY STAR'S INFLUENCE

North Asellus bestows vitality and vigor, creative talent, love of the arts, and unexpected gains. Although both North and South Asellus impart a caring nature and therefore indicate responsibility, North Asellus is known as the beneficial star and endows powers of attainment plus a charitable and generous outlook. This star also suggests that intolerance and aggressive mannerisms do not achieve the desired results.

Linked to your Sun's degree, this star imparts a flair for dealing with the public, good social connections, and friends in influential positions. High preferment is indicated in education, especially philosophy and religion, or success in business and large corporations.

tertaining, you may be attracted to show business or the music industry. This birthdate can also involve an attraction for large-scale manufacturing.

Famous people who share your birthday include singer Kate Bush, auto manufacturer Henry Ford, actor Arnold Schwarzenegger, writer Emily Brontë, British athlete Daley Thompson, sculptor Henry Moore, director Peter Bogdanovich, and U.S. politician Patricia Schroeder.

Numerology

Creativity, friendliness, and sociability are just some of the attributes associated with the number 30 birthday. Ambitious, with creative potential, you can take ideas and expand them in your own dramatic style. With a number 30 birthday, you enjoy the good life and can be exceptionally charismatic and outgoing. Since you possess strong feelings, being in love or contented is a vital requirement. In your pursuit of happiness, avoid being lazy, overindulgent, impatient, or jealous, as these may cause you to experience emotional instability. Among those with number 30 birthdays, many will find recognition or fame, especially musicians, actors, and entertainers. The subinfluence of the number 7 month indicates that although you may appear confident, you can be shy or secretive and hide your opinions. Original and intuitive, you benefit from being multitalented. By avoiding worry and inner lack of trust, you can free your deeper feelings. If doubting or skeptical, you may miss the opportunity to develop your inner gifts.

- *Positive:* fun-loving, loyal, friendly, good synthesizer, talent with words, creative, lucky
- *Negative:* lazy, obstinate, erratic, impatient, insecure, indifferent, scatters energy

Love & Relationships

With your ability to be warm and entertaining, you are sure to have an active social life. A compelling need for love will probably draw you into all kinds of romantic relationships, some of which can prove to be more trouble than they are worth. Since you are so idealistic in affairs of the heart, you may need to work on being detached. By staying light-hearted you do not become overly serious or disappointed if your loved ones do not live up to your expectations. You can, however, be very universal in your love and extremely generous to those you hold dear.

YOUR SPECIAL SOMEONE

For your ideal partner, you might begin by looking for someone born on one of the following dates.

Love & friendship: Jan. 5, 10, 18, 19, 26, 30, Feb. 3, 8, 16, 17, 24, 28, Mar. 1, 6, 14, 15, 22, 26, Apr. 4, 12, 13, 20, 24, May 2, 10, 11, 18, 22, June 8, 9, 16, 20, 30, July 6, 7, 14, 18, 28, Aug. 4, 5, 12, 16, 26, 30, Sept. 2, 3, 10, 14, 28, Oct. 1, 8, 12, 22, 26, Nov. 6, 10, 20, 24, Dec. 4, 8, 18, 22, 30

Beneficial: Jan. 13, Feb. 11, Mar. 9, Apr. 7, May 5, June 3, 30, July 1, 28, Aug. 26, Sept. 24, Oct. 22, Nov. 20, Dec. 18

Fatal attractions: Jan. 26, 27, 28, 29

Challenging: Jan. 14, 24, Feb. 12, 22, Mar. 10, 20, Apr. 8, 18, May 6, 16, June 4, 14, July 2, 12, Aug. 10, Sept. 8, Oct. 6, Nov. 4, Dec. 2

Soul mates: July 30, Aug. 28, Sept. 26, Oct. 24, Nov. 22, Dec. 20

July 31

♌ The warm and friendly attributes of your birthday are enhanced by your charismatic and lively personality. Independent and ambitious, with the ability to plan on a large scale, you possess a keen intellect and are willing to work hard to attain your objectives. At times your sensitivity and sixth sense are heightened, and you become extremely intuitive. Generous and magnanimous, you may find that the money you earn keeps passing through your hands almost as quickly as it comes in. As you can be sociable and project the power of love, you are likely to be very popular.

With the added influence of your decanate ruler, Leo, you can influence others through your natural authoritive abilities. As a networker, you are particularly successful in people-related affairs or fronting social organizations. Luckily, as you are drawn toward riches and luxury, you possess the spirit of enterprise to make your grand dreams a reality. However, with your strong self-identity, you may need to be careful that you do not become opinionated or vain.

Although proud, dramatic, and idealistic, you can also be very practical. As a visionary, you usually enjoy pioneering a project or a belief that you find really interesting. At times, feeling oversensitive and vulnerable, you may have to guard against extremes. Fortunately, you are usually caring and understanding and possess a fighting spirit.

When you are age twenty-two, your progressed Sun moves into Virgo, commencing a thirty-year period of increasing emphasis on order, practical problem solving, and being more discriminating with your time and energy. Another turning point occurs at the age of fifty-two, when your progressed Sun moves into Libra, stimulating you to widen your social circle and placing more emphasis on relationships and the creative arts.

Fixed Stars

North Asellus; South Asellus; Praesepe, also called Praesaepe

Primary Star

Star's name: North Asellus
Degree position: 6°34'–7°35' Leo, between the years 1930 and 2000
Magnitude: 5
Strength: ★★
Orb: 1°
Constellation: Gamma Cancer
Applicable days: July 30, 31, August 1
Star qualities: Mars/Sun
Description: a pale yellow-white twin star located in the body of the Crab

Primary Star's Influence

North Asellus bestows vitality and vigor, creative talent, love of the arts, and unexpected gains. Although both North and South Asellus impart a caring nature and therefore indicate responsiblity, North Asellus is known as the beneficial star and endows powers of attainment plus a charitable and generous outlook. This star also suggests that intolerance and aggressive mannerisms do not achieve the desired results.

Linked to your Sun's degree, this star imparts a flair for dealing with the public, good social connections, and friends in influential positions. High preferment is indicated in education, especially philosophy and religion, or success in business and large corporations.

Your Secret Self

Inspired by intelligence, you respect those with knowledge and insight. Often a seeker yourself, you may go far and wide in your search for wisdom. This may involve travel that can be significant in expanding your horizons and social life. Generally honest and frank, you usually speak your mind but may prefer deeds to words. If you become restless or impatient, you may take hasty or impulsive action without thinking of the repercussions.

With your extreme sensitivity and need for love, you may find emotional fulfillment when working on your high ideals or projects of a humanitarian or universal nature. You possess a youthful quality that can at times give you a childlike innocence, but it may also suggest an inclination toward immaturity. Nevertheless, you take pleasure from entertaining and uplifting others with your talents.

Work & Vocation

Success with people is a foregone conclusion in any career that you choose. Ambitious, with organizational and leadership ability, you can succeed as a manager or administrator, or in any job that gives you as much freedom as possible. You are likely to do particularly well in law, education, or working with groups for the community. Your dramatic sense can help you excel as a performer or in politics. With your natural humanitarianism, you can also help other people, for example in the caring professions, as a physician, or in charity work. If in business, you may be drawn to work in large concerns. This birthdate is also excellent for writers, metaphysicians, or artists.

Famous people who share your birthday include actress Geraldine Chaplin, author and television presenter Jonathan Dimbleby, and actor Wesley Snipes.

Numerology

Strong willpower, determination, and an emphasis on self-expression are indicated by the number 31 birthday. You often combine your intuition and practical skill to make the right decisions. As a number 31 birthday, you have original ideas, a good sense of form, and the ability to succeed in business if you take your time and follow a practical plan of action. Good fortune and lucky opportunities are also suggested by this birthday, and you can be successful in turning your leisure-time pursuits into profitable ventures. As you are probably hardworking, time for love and having fun is crucial to you. The subinfluence of the number 7 month indicates that you are sensitive and thoughtful. Relationships are highly important to you, and you enjoy the company of others. Learning to stay balanced and overcoming a tendency toward fluctuating moods will prevent you from becoming overemotional or easily hurt.

• *Positive:* lucky, creative, original, builder, constructive, never gives up, practical, good conversationalist, responsible

• *Negative:* insecure, impatient, suspicious, easily discouraged, lack of ambition, selfish, stubborn

YOUR SPECIAL SOMEONE

Your chances of finding happiness and a loving partner are increased with those born on the following dates.

Love & friendship: Jan. 2, 3, 6, 9, 11, 21, 27, 31, Feb. 1, 4, 7, 9, 25, 29, Mar. 2, 5, 7, 17, 23, 27, Apr. 3, 5, 15, 21, 25, May 1, 3, 13, 19, 23, 30, June 1, 11, 17, 21, 28, July 9, 15, 19, 26, 29, Aug. 7, 13, 17, 24, 27, Sept. 5, 11, 15, 22, 25, Oct. 3, 9, 13, 20, 23, Nov. 1, 7, 11, 18, 21, 30, Dec. 5, 9, 16, 19, 28

Beneficial: Jan. 11, 16, 30, Feb. 9, 24, 28, Mar. 7, 22, 26, Apr. 5, 20, 24, May 3, 18, 22, 31, June 1, 16, 20, 29, July 14, 18, 27, Aug. 12, 16, 25, Sept. 10, 14, 23, Oct. 8, 12, 21, 29, Nov. 6, 10, 19, 27, Dec. 4, 8, 17, 25

Fatal attractions: Jan. 26, 27, 28, 29, 30

Challenging: Jan. 15, Feb. 13, Mar. 11, Apr. 9, May 7, 30, June 5, 28, July 3, 26, Aug. 1, 24, Sept. 22, Oct. 20, 30, Nov. 18, 28, Dec. 16, 26

Soul mates: Jan. 9, 29, Feb. 7, 27, Mar. 5, 25, Apr. 3, 23, May 1, 21, June 19, July 17, Aug. 15, Sept. 13, Oct. 11, Nov. 9, Dec. 7

Love & Relationships

With your charm and ability to radiate warmth, you can be attractive to others, whether in a crowd or on a one-to-one basis. Being very sociable, you make an excellent host or hostess and can be very compassionate about other people's problems. You are likely to be drawn to strong and determined people but may have to be careful of becoming involved in power plays with partners. Women of this birthdate especially are often willing to work hard to keep relationships harmonious, although both sexes can suffer from restlessness.

August 1

♌ Leadership, ambition, and a dramatic personality are indicated by your birthday. As a Leo, you are creative, with strong intuitive powers and a forceful demeanor. Although your adventurous nature seeks self-expression, a strong pragmatic view and concern for security suggest a materialistic overtone. This indicates that while idealism and vision play important roles in your life, worries about money or the lack of it keep your feet firmly on the ground. Nevertheless, you are a kind-hearted individual with strong emotions, humanitarian inclinations, and leadership abilities.

With the added influence of your decanate ruler, Leo, you are proud and dignified and can influence others through your natural executive abilities. Observant and perceptive, you have a good sense of values and are often resourceful. Quick to learn, you soon turn your interests and creative endeavors into successful commercial enterprises. By marketing your talents, you can impress others with your determination and organizational skills.

Generous, chivalrous, and assured, yet demanding and tense, is how others may describe you. This indicates that, due to emotional insecurity, you sometimes hide your true feelings. Loyal, diligent, and dependable, you take pride in your work. Although you can use your forceful speech to your advantage, a sharp tongue and an inclination to be overly dominant may undermine your great efforts.

When you are around the age of twenty-one, your progressed Sun moves into Virgo, commencing a thirty-year period of increased emphasis on order, efficiency, work, and health. You are also likely to gain an enhanced mental awareness of practical problem solving. Another turning point for you occurs around the age of fifty-one, when your progressed Sun moves into Libra, stimulating you to cooperate more with others, be diplomatic, and place more emphasis on creativity and partnerships.

Your Secret Self

Generous with your time and energy, you may have to watch out for a tendency to alternate between feelings of frustration and extravagant outbursts. This may lead to worry or indecision about material situations when it is not necessary. Possessing the ability to be detached and view your situation objectively, you are more than capable of handling any situation.

Courageous, independent, and inventive, with quick responses, you can make an excellent fighter for freedom, whether for yourself or others. With your fine mind, you can be direct and outspoken; your adventurous streak may spur you to seek out unusual and exciting experiences. A strong individualist, you have a wealth of creative ideas that can encourage you to become inspired and move into action.

Work & Vocation

Determined and strong-willed, you are liable to have an original approach to your career unless you settle for security below your outstanding potential. With your natural executive and leadership abilities, you should be in a managerial position or be given the freedom to work with some degree of independence. Possessing a fine mind and a flair for the technical or ana-

PRIMARY STAR

Star's name: North Asellus

Degree position: 6°34'–7°35' Leo between the years 1930 and 2000

Magnitude: 5

Strength: ★★

Orb: 1°

Constellation: Gamma Cancer

Applicable days: July 30, 31, August 1

Star qualities: Mars/Sun

Description: a pale yellow-white twin star located in the body of the Crab

PRIMARY STAR'S INFLUENCE

North Asellus bestows vitality and vigor, creative talent, love of the arts, and unexpected gains. Although both North and South Asellus impart a caring nature and therefore indicate responsiblity, North Asellus is known as the beneficial star and endows powers of attainment plus a charitable and generous outlook. This star also suggests that intolerance and aggressive mannerisms do not achieve the desired results.

Linked to your Sun's degree, this star imparts a flair for dealing with the public, good social connections, and friends in influential positions. High preferment is indicated in education, especially philosophy and religion, or success in business and large corporations.

lytical, you can excel in anything from science to writing and performing. Being very creative may inspire you to delve into the art or music world, where your shrewd ability to assess situations can help you commercialize your talents. Your ability to push through some kind of reform may attract you to work in organizations with a social conscience.

Famous people who share your birthday include musician Jerry Garcia, fashion designer Yves Saint-Laurent, actor Dom DeLuise, and author Herman Melville.

Numerology

The great desire to be first and independent is suggested by your birthdate. As a number 1, you are more inclined to be individual, innovative, and courageous, with plenty of energy. Often there is a need to establish a strong identity and develop assertiveness. The pioneering spirit indicated here encourages you to strike out alone. These self-starting forces can also stimulate you to develop executive or leadership abilities. Full of enthusiasm and original ideas, you can show others the way forward. Having a number 1 birthday, you may also need to learn that the world does not revolve around you; avoid an inclination to be self-centered or dictatorial. The subinfluence of the number 8 month indicates that you enjoy being in an influential position and have a strong desire for power and material success. You can gain the respect of others by being generous, fair, and just. To achieve your aims and objectives, develop your compassionate nature by using your sensitivity, integrity, and charismatic personality.

• *Positive:* leadership, creative, progressive, forceful, optimistic, strong convictions, competitive, independent, gregarious

• *Negative:* overbearing, jealous, egotistical, too proud, antagonistic, selfish, vacillating, impatient

Love & Relationships

Individual and dynamic, you enjoy meeting people from all walks of life. Being sociable, you enjoy the company of others, particularly those with creative ideas who stimulate you to express yourself. Although very loyal and willing to support those you love, you may still suffer from doubt or indecision in your relationships. To avoid disappointment, you may need to take your affairs of the heart fairly lightly and remember that you are meant to be happy.

YOUR SPECIAL SOMEONE

You may find emotional fulfillment and that special someone among those born on the following days.

Love & friendship: Jan. 4, 13, 14, 29, Feb. 11, 27, 29, Mar. 9, 15, 25, 27, Apr. 7, 23, 25, May 5, 21, 23, 29, June 3, 19, 21, 27, 30, July 1, 17, 19, 25, 28, Aug. 15, 17, 23, 26, Sept. 13, 15, 21, 24, Oct. 11, 13, 19, 22, 29, Nov. 9, 11, 17, 20, 27, Dec. 7, 9, 15, 18, 25

Beneficial: Jan. 11, Feb. 9, Mar. 7, 31, Apr. 5, 29, May 3, 27, 31, June 1, 25, 29, July 23, 27, 31, Aug. 21, 25, 29, 30, Sept. 19, 23, 27, 28, Oct. 17, 21, 25, 26, Nov. 15, 19, 23, 24, 30, Dec. 13, 17, 21, 22, 28

Fatal attractions: Jan. 12, 30, 31, Feb. 1, 10, Mar. 8, Apr. 6, May 4, June 2

Challenging: Jan. 10, Feb. 8, Mar. 6, 29, Apr. 4, 27, May 2, 25, June 23, July 21, Aug. 19, Sept. 17, Oct. 15, 31, Nov. 13, 29, 30, Dec. 11, 27, 28

Soul mates: Jan. 18, 24, Feb. 16, 22, Mar. 14, 20, Apr. 12, 18, May 10, 16, June 8, 14, July 6, 12, Aug. 4, 10, Sept. 2, 8, Oct. 6, Nov. 4, Dec. 2

August 2

♌ Your charismatic personality, charm, and love of pleasure and fun are usually eclipsed by a need to succeed or a strong desire for material gains. As a Leo, you are proud and outgoing, with a youthful or childlike quality and high spirits. Although you are determined and capable, a somewhat carefree attitude may be an obstacle to your attainment of success.

With the added influence of your decanate ruler, Leo, you enjoy entertaining others and have a love of grandeur. Dramatic, you project self-assurance and have a royal air about you. Sunny and spontaneous, you are often dignified and creative. Open to praise, you need to be appreciated and admired. Guard against fair-weather friends, who only tell you what you wish to hear. High-spirited and idealistic, yet ambitious and practical, you are an interesting combination of materialism and optimism.

Although you are spontaneous by nature, a love of freedom endows you with individuality. Joint efforts and collaboration with others usually produce profits and success, and a responsible attitude on your part will not go unnoticed. In the pursuit of your dream, your personal magnetism, versatility, and popularity will play important roles, and by being adaptable, witty, and entertaining, you win the hearts of many.

From the age of twenty, when your progressed Sun moves into Virgo, there is an increasing desire for practical order, analysis, and efficiency in your life. In the following thirty years, you will feel the need to become more health-conscious or introspective. There is another turning point for you at the begining of your fifties, when your progressed Sun enters Libra. From this time you may develop a desire to be more involved in your close personal relationships, and may turn from more practical considerations to more creative ones.

Fixed Stars

Although your Sun's degree is not linked to a fixed star, some of your other planets' degrees certainly will be. By having an astrological chart calculated, you can find the exact position of the planets on your date of birth. This will tell you which of the fixed stars listed in this book are relevant to you.

Your Secret Self

You are blessed with a strong personality, a good intellect, and an ability to learn quickly. Occasional moods of worry or confusion may leave you prone to temperamental behavior or escapism. These periods do not last for long, since your bright, personable, expressive qualities and many interests are likely to stimulate your need for creativity and new opportunities.

With your own unique approach to life, you like to be different and are usually ahead of your time. You can easily make friends with anyone and mix with people from all walks of life. Freedom and independence are liable to be high on your list of priorities, and you prefer to be honest with your feelings. You are aware of the image you project and can use this constructively to promote yourself. Receptive and influenced by your surroundings, you possess a friendly and warm personality, with good social skills and a diplomatic approach.

Work & Vocation

Having a naturally creative approach to life, you may find outlets for your emotional expression in the arts or the theater, especially as an actor or playwright. Your natural charm and charisma can prove particularly useful in promotion, sales, or negotiation. With excellent social and communication skills, you can prosper as a writer or in education, advertising, or publishing. All careers that use the personal touch, such as public relations, media, or counseling, can also be excellent outlets for your talents. With your strong independence, you need the freedom to work in your own way or may wish to become self-employed. Alternatively, you may do well in business, banking, or law.

Famous people who share your birthday include actor Peter O'Toole, writer James Baldwin, psychologist/journal keeper Ira Progoff, and actress Myrna Loy.

Numerology

Sensitivity and a strong need to be part of a group are suggested by a number 2 birthday. Adaptable and understanding, you enjoy cooperative activities where you can experience interaction with others. In your attempt to please those you like, you may run the risk of becoming overly dependent. Nevertheless, by developing confidence, you can overcome the tendency to get easily hurt by the action and criticism of others. The subinfluence of the number 8 month indicates that you are ambitious and determined, with practical and executive skills. Avoid becoming preoccupied with power and control by overcoming a tendency to be critical or demanding perfection. You may need to find a balance between being overly helpful and suddenly withdrawing. If insecure, you may find it hard to carry out your own personal plans. Conversely, if you find an original form of artistic or creative expression, you can make your dreams real.

- *Positive:* good partnerships, gentle, tactful, receptive, intuitive, considerate, harmonious, agreeable, ambassador of goodwill
- *Negative:* suspicious, lack of confidence, subservient, oversensitive, emotional, selfish, easily hurt, dishonest

Love & Relationships

Fun-loving and sociable, you can be a great friend and a good companion. Although loving and affectionate, you may have to be careful in choosing your relationships to ensure that they are long-lasting. You can be romantic with those you love and display honesty in your feelings, but in order to be happy, make sure you are also financially secure. With all your charm, you can be very attractive to the opposite sex and desire a relationship, but you may be pulled by an equally strong desire for freedom.

YOUR SPECIAL SOMEONE

To find long-lasting love and friendship, you may want to look among those born on the following dates.

Love & friendship: Jan. 6, 8, 10, 14, 23, 26, 28, Feb. 4, 10, 12, 21, 24, 26, Mar. 2, 10, 12, 19, 22, 24, Apr. 8, 14, 17, 20, 22, May 6, 15, 16, 18, 20, June 4, 13, 16, 18, July 2, 11, 14, 16, 20, Aug. 9, 12, 14, 22, Sept. 7, 10, 12, 24, Oct. 5, 8, 10, 26, Nov. 3, 6, 8, 28, Dec. 1, 4, 6, 30

Beneficial: Jan. 9, 12, Feb. 7, 10, Mar. 5, 8, Apr. 3, 6, May 1, 4, June 2, 30, July 28, Aug. 26, 30, 31, Sept. 24, 28, 29, Oct. 22, 26, 27, Nov. 20, 24, 25, Dec. 18, 22, 23, 29

Fatal attractions: Jan. 28, 29, 30, 31, Feb. 1, 2

Challenging: Jan. 11, 13, 29, Feb. 9, 11, Mar. 7, 9, 30, Apr. 5, 7, 28, May 3, 5, 26, 31, June 1, 3, 24, 29, July 1, 22, 27, Aug. 20, 25, Sept. 18, 23, 30, Oct. 16, 21, 28, Nov. 14, 19, 26, Dec. 12, 17, 24

Soul mates: Jan. 11, 12, 29, Feb. 9, 10, 27, Mar. 7, 8, 25, Apr. 5, 6, 23, May 3, 4, 21, June 1, 2, 19, July 17, Aug. 15, Sept. 13, Oct. 11, Nov. 9, Dec. 7

August 3

FIXED STARS

Although your Sun's degree is not linked to a fixed star, some of your other planets' degrees certainly will be. By having an astrological chart calculated, you can find the exact position of the planets on your date of birth. This will tell you which of the fixed stars listed in this book are relevant to you.

♌ Success-oriented, ambitious, and courageous, you are a lucky and optimistic individual with good business acumen and enormous schemes. Your birthday reveals you to be an adventurous and multitalented Leo with a need for achievement. Nevertheless, without inspiration, creative self-expression, and patience, many of your ideas and dreams will remain unfulfilled.

Although you possess excellent business sense and can be a shrewd investor or successful in speculating, the subinfluence of your decanate ruler, Sagittarius, suggests that you must also overcome an inclination to be overly optimistic or unrealistic. More often than not, you tend to believe that financial security can provide you with all the answers. But by seeing only material benefits, you can miss out on insight into what is truly worthwhile in life.

As a practical idealist, you have vision and leadership abilities and frequently manage to commercialize your abilities through self-promotion. Whatever you do in life, you are inclined to have grand dreams. This need to expand and extend may indicate that inner restlessness or dissatisfaction with your current situation encourages you to always go further in life.

In the pursuit of riches, it is frequently women who will assist you most on your road to success. Even if you are self-disciplined and hardworking, you have extravagant taste, as acquisitions are important to your sense of well-being.

After the age of nineteen, when your progressed Sun enters Virgo, you begin to be less dominant and become more analytical, practical, and reflective. Your duties start to take up more of your time, and you will find a need to work more perfectly and efficiently. From the age of forty-nine, when your progressed Sun moves into Libra, there is a change of emphasis in your life. From then on, you are apt to be more involved in your relationships as well as to widen your circle of friends. There is also a possibility that you will develop latent artistic or literary talents.

Your Secret Self

With your bright intellect and inventive thinking, you are often ahead of your time. Your original ideas and sense of nobility can point to an ability to shine when in a leading position. Being a shrewd judge of character, you can quickly assess people and circumstances. Since you also have excellent organizational potential, you are able to involve others in your plans and schemes. Your sudden flashes of insight and persuasive abilities can impress others and win them over to your point of view. Usually generous with your time and money, you work particularly well when helping others.

A rebellious streak can accent your desire for freedom. With your wit and intelligence, you can get by without much effort, but there is a danger of your choosing the easy way out. In order to realize your real abilities, you must rise to the challenges needed to stretch yourself to your true potential.

Work & Vocation

Your ambition and attractive personality can take you to the top in almost any career. Whether in banking or the arts, your dislike of taking orders can put you in a management or executive position. You should do particularly well in the theater as an actor, director, or scriptwriter. Alternatively, you may choose to use your people skills in business, where you can do well in sales, promotion, or negotiation. With your optimism and big plans, you like to initiate new projects where you have a leading role. Being good at delegating makes you an excellent administrator or may encourage you to work for yourself.

Famous people who share your birthday include actor Martin Sheen, singer Tony Bennett, British statesman Stanley Baldwin, film director John Landis, and fashion designer Anne Klein.

Numerology

Having a number 3 birthday, you are sensitive, with a need for creativity and emotional expression. Fun-loving and a good companion, you enjoy friendly social activities and many interests. Although you are versatile and expressive, with a need for different and exciting experiences, an inclination to get bored easily may cause you to become indecisive or spread yourself too thin. Although as a number 3, you are usually artistic and charming, with a good sense of humor, you may have to develop self-esteem and guard against tendencies to worry and emotional insecurities. The subinfluence of the number 8 month indicates that you use your creativity and imagination in a practical way. Although you are multitalented and a natural opportunist, you may be restless and tempted to do too many things at once. By becoming focused on a few projects, you can learn self-discipline and achieve success.

• *Positive:* humorous, happy, friendly, productive, creative, artistic, power to wish, freedom-loving, talent with words

• *Negative:* easily bored, vain, overimaginative, exaggerate, boastful, extravagant, self-indulgent, lazy, hypocritical, wasteful

Love & Relationships

Passionate and strong desires can make your love life an important area for you. A generous friend and lover, you are very popular, although at times you may become too dominating. Your charismatic appeal is likely to provide you with many social and romantic opportunities. Although you are usually loyal, it is possible that you may encounter a pull between your strong yearning for love and affection and your need for material security. Your need for freedom suggests that you may prefer to be in relationships that can give you enough space to feel independent.

YOUR SPECIAL SOMEONE

For love and friendship, you might just find the right person among those born on the following dates.

Love & friendship: Jan. 6, 10, 15, 29, 31, Feb. 4, 8, 13, 27, 29, Mar. 2, 11, 25, 27, Apr. 4, 9, 23, 25, May 7, 21, 23, June 5, 19, 21, July 3, 17, 19, 30, Aug. 1, 15, 17, 28, Sept. 13, 15, 26, Oct. 11, 13, 24, Nov. 9, 11, 22, Dec. 7, 9, 20

Beneficial: Jan. 13, 15, 19, Feb. 11, 13, 17, Mar. 9, 11, 15, Apr. 7, 9, 13, May 5, 7, 11, June 3, 5, 9, July 1, 3, 7, 29, Aug. 1, 5, 27, 31, Sept. 3, 25, 29, Oct. 1, 23, 27, Nov. 21, 25, Dec. 19, 23

Fatal attractions: Jan. 31, Feb. 1, 2, May 30, June 28, July 26, Aug. 24, Sept. 22, Oct. 20, Nov. 18, Dec. 16

Challenging: Jan. 12, Feb. 10, Mar. 8, Apr. 6, May 4, June 2, Aug. 31, Sept. 29, Oct. 27, 29, 30, Nov. 25, 27, 28, Dec. 23, 25, 26, 30

Soul mates: Jan. 2, 28, Feb. 26, Mar. 24, Apr. 22, May 20, June 18, July 16, Aug. 14, Sept. 12, Oct. 10, Nov. 8, Dec. 6

August 4

♌ Generous and broad-minded, you have a universal perspective, though a preoccupation with material concerns frequently limits your humanitarian inclinations. As a Leo, you are creative and magnanimous, with practical skills and powers of attainment. Friendly and cheerful, you attract people and can be popular. This also indicates strong leadership potential and suggests that you do not like to be in a subservient position.

The subinfluence of your decanate ruler, Sagittarius, encourages you to expand and, in combination with your optimistic outlook, inspires you to courageously take chances. When you fear the unknown, this influence can also work adversely and undermine your capability to perform record achievements. By trying to resist an inclination to be impatient and bossy, you can develop tolerance. Detachment and a balanced vocation attitude to life will enable you to avoid many frustrations and disappointments.

Adopting a responsible outlook may inspire you to explore your true potential and become a leading specialist in your chosen field. Although you prefer to deal with the larger picture, in your enthusiasm you may forget about the small but vital details. By learning to be thorough or methodical, you can enhance your prospects of success.

From childhood, you are likely to be interested in social activities and being at the center of things. From the age of eighteen onward, as your progressed Sun moves into Virgo for a thirty-year period, you gradually become more conscientious, thoughtful, reserved, and discriminating. You may be interested in becoming more efficient in your working environment. As your progressed Sun enters Libra, when you are age forty-eight, you reach a turning point. This brings a strong emphasis on your social relationships and partnerships. Your creative abilities are enhanced, and you may wish to develop any latent musical, artistic, or literary interests.

FIXED STAR

Star's name: Kochab

Degree position: 11°56'–12°45' Leo between the years 1930 and 2000

Magnitude: 2

Strength: ★★★★★★★

Orb: 2°10'

Constellation: Beta Ursa Minor

Applicable days: August 4, 5, 6, 7

Star qualities: Saturn/Mercury

Description: a giant orange star located in the Small Bear, also called the Little Dipper

PRIMARY STAR'S INFLUENCE

Kochab's influence bestows logic, concentration, and an ability to come straight to the point in discussion. Often you have a love of tidiness and good organizational skills. This star imparts stamina and opportunities to rise to a position of authority.

Linked to your Sun's degree, this star indicates that much can be achieved through determination. You have the ability to fight with energy and courage till the end, and you possess a never-give-up attitude. This star also warns against deceit and malicious or underhanded activities.

• *Positive:* determination, persistence, courage to overcome obstacles

• *Negative:* rashness, mischief, pessimism

Your Secret Self

You usually possess a youthful quality, and being happy and relaxed brings out your original sense of humor. Part of your clever, satirical wit may come from your natural psychological skills and ability to quickly evaluate people. A need for material security at all costs may cause a conflict between your ideals or desires and the limitations of your reality. By incorporating adventures, variety, and travel into your life, you can transform an inner restlessness into attainment of new goals.

By learning how to manage your assets and budget, you may avoid alternating periods of being well-off, generous, or extravagant with periods of being insecure due to a lack of funds. This will also help you overcome a fear of financial instability.

Work & Vocation

Since you are very independent and prefer to give orders rather than accept them, you are usually better in some position of authority or, if working within a group, where you have the freedom to operate in your own way. You are liable to succeed in teaching, lecturing, the theater, or running your own business. You are a good evaluator, and so the more pragmatic side of your nature may be drawn to real estate, banking, and the stock market. Alternatively, a humanitarian streak may find expression through the healing professions or in some form of social or community work.

Famous people who share your birthday include England's Queen Mother, poet Percy Bysshe Shelley, baseball player Roger Clemens, and Olympic athlete Mary Decker Slaney.

Numerology

The solid structure and orderly power suggested by the number 4 birthday indicate that you need stability and like to establish order. Endowed with energy, practical skills, and strong determination, you can achieve success through hard work. Security-conscious, you like to build a strong foundation for yourself and your family. A pragmatic approach to life confers a good business sense and an ability to achieve material success in life. As a number 4 individual, you are usually honest, frank, and fair. The challenges for a number 4 individual may include overcoming periods of instability or financial worry. The subinfluence of the number 8 month indicates that the way you manage your finances can make a great deal of difference to your life, and you may have to learn to be practical and economical. You like to think in a creative way and often lead and inspire others. Usually you have good reasoning powers and are a good planner or designer.

• *Positive:* well organized, self-discipline, steady, hardworking, organized, craftsmanship, good with your hands, pragmatism, trusting, exact

• *Negative:* uncommunicative, rigid, lazy, unfeeling, procrastination, bossy, hidden affections, resentful, strict

Love & Relationships

Although you are warm and loving, at times emotional inhibitions can make you seem cool and detached. Partnerships are very important in your life, even if you do not always express your feelings. Generally you are attracted to people who are mentally stimulating or with whom you share some type of intellectual activity. Although you are usually a good partner, if you have a stubborn streak, it may cause quarrels in relationships. Luckily, this does not last long, since, being understanding and caring, you are a good friend, host, and protective family member.

YOUR SPECIAL SOMEONE

Success in finding the right partner may be more easily achieved with those born on the following dates.

Love & friendship: Jan. 6, 7, 16, Feb. 4, 5, 14, Mar. 2, 12, 28, 30, Apr. 10, 26, 28, May 8, 24, 26, 30, June 6, 22, 24, 28, July 4, 20, 22, 26, 31, Aug. 2, 18, 20, 24, 29, Sept. 16, 18, 22, 27, Oct. 14, 16, 20, 25, Nov. 12, 14, 18, 23, Dec. 10, 12, 16, 21

Beneficial: Jan. 9, 14, 16, Feb. 7, 12, 14, Mar. 5, 10, 12, Apr. 3, 8, 10, May 1, 6, 8, June 4, 6, July 2, 4, Aug. 2, Sept. 30, Oct. 28, Nov. 26, 30, Dec. 24, 28, 29

Fatal attractions: Jan. 21, Feb. 19, Mar. 17, Apr. 15, May 13, June 11, July 9, Aug. 7, Sept. 5, Oct. 3, Nov 1

Challenging: Jan. 4, 13, 28, Feb. 2, 11, 26, Mar. 9, 24, Apr. 7, 22, May 5, 20, June 3, 18, July 1, 16, Aug. 14, Sept. 12, Oct. 10, 31, Nov. 8, 29, Dec. 6, 27

Soul mates: Jan. 15, 22, Feb. 13, 20, Mar. 11, 18, Apr. 9, 16, May 7, 14, June 5, 12, July 3, 10, Aug. 1, 8, Sept. 6, Oct. 4, Nov. 2

August 5

♌ Versatility, creativity, willpower, and determination are some of the qualities associated with your birthday. As a Leo, you are daring, ambitious, and dignified, but your strong sense of pride and materialistic inclinations suggest that financial security can be an important factor in your overall plans.

The subinfluence of your decanate ruler, Sagittarius, suggests that you enjoy being productive and usually have good moral values. You may, however, have to guard against tendencies to be too impatient or obstinate. Hardworking, you possess a practical business sense and good organizational abilities. With your forceful personality, you may have to be careful of being too headstrong or overpowering.

Although you have conservative views and an urge to climb up the ladder materially and socially, you nevertheless want to express your individuality. As someone who does not like to take orders from others, you frequently create your own ethics and code of conduct but must guard against being too opinionated. Women may prove to be especially beneficial to you, and learning to collaborate with others may bring rewarding experiences.

After the age of seventeen, when your progressed Sun moves into Virgo, there is an increased need for practical order in your daily existence. You will be more inclined to analyze things practically and look for ways to restructure your life so that it is generally better. This continues until the age of forty-seven, when your progressed Sun enters Libra. As a turning point, this highlights the growing importance of relationships, creativity, and harmony.

Fixed Stars

Kochab; Acubens, also called Sertan

Primary Star

Star's name: Kochab
Degree position: 11°56'–12°45' Leo between the years 1930 and 2000
Magnitude: 2
Strength: ★★★★★★★
Orb: 2°10'
Constellation: Beta Ursa Minor
Applicable days: August 4, 5, 6, 7
Star qualities: Saturn/Mercury
Description: a giant orange star located in the Small Bear, also called the Little Dipper

Primary Star's Influence

Kochab's influence bestows logic, concentration, and an ability to come straight to the point in discussion. Often you have a love of tidiness and good organizational skills. This star imparts stamina and opportunities to rise to a position of authority.

Linked to your Sun's degree, this star indicates that much can be achieved through determination. You have the ability to fight with energy and courage till the end, and you possess a never-give-up attitude. This star also warns against deceit and malicious or underhanded activities.

• Positive: determination, persistence, courage to overcome obstacles

Your Secret Self

Your practical determination, love of knowledge, and razor-sharp mind endow you with an ability to deal with any situation. A possible obstacle to your success is a tendency to become doubting or skeptical. In the event of your losing faith in either yourself or your abilities to achieve, there is a danger of coldness or isolation. By being daring and spontaneous, you can challenge yourself to be more dynamic and powerful.

Although at times you can be very concerned with material issues, it is through the use of your inner wisdom or spiritual insight that you can overcome life's difficulties. As you are likely to possess a strong personality and voice your opinions or make a stand, it is important to resist using power tactics to get your way. By trusting your intuition, you can build up your confidence and faith and achieve your inspired dreams.

Work & Vocation

Ambition, a good business sense, and the ability to take the lead are apt to help you in your climb to success. You enjoy power, structure, and effectiveness, yet you also possess an emotional perceptiveness and sensitivity. This combination could work effectively for you in all areas, from the handling of material assets to the creative world. Always aware of image, you may also possess a strong attraction for the theater or entertainment world. You may prefer to be in a position of power or self-employed, as you are not content to be subordinate. With your strength and determination, you usually excel in business, particularly sales; alternatively, you can become a good lawyer.

Famous people who share your birthday include basketball player Patrick Ewing, astronaut Neil Armstrong, film director John Huston, and actress Loni Anderson.

Numerology

Strong instincts, an adventurous nature, and a desire for freedom are all indicated by the number 5 birthday. The willingness to explore or try anything new, along with an enthusiastic approach, suggests that life will have a lot to offer you. Travel and many opportunities for change, some unexpected, may lead you to undergo a real transformation of views and beliefs. As a number 5 individual, you need to feel that life is exciting; however, you may also have to develop a responsible attitude and avoid tendencies such as unpredictability, excessiveness, and restlessness. You can achieve success by avoiding premature or speculative actions and through learning patience. The natural talent of a number 5 individual is knowing how to go with the flow and staying detached. The subinfluence of the number 8 month indicates that you are ambitious, with a sharp and active mind. Achievements and accomplishments are important for you, and since you are hardworking, with good managerial skills, you rise to positions of authority and influence.

• *Positive:* versatile, adaptable, progressive, strong instincts, magnetic, lucky, daring, freedom-loving, quick and witty, curious, mystical, sociable

• *Negative:* unreliable, changeable, procrastinator, inconsistent, overconfident, headstrong

Love & Relationships

You enjoy travel and meeting new people. Although very warm and sociable, you may be restless and indecisive about close relationships. This can be overcome by keeping yourself busy and creative, leaving you no time for doubt or worry. Music or the creative arts may prove especially uplifting for you. You have the ability to charm others with your optimism and generosity but may have to be careful of not becoming too bossy with those you love.

YOUR SPECIAL SOMEONE

For true love and happiness, you might be more successful with those born on the following dates.

Love & friendship: Jan. 1, 7, 17, 18, 20, Feb. 5, 15, 18, Mar. 3, 13, 16, 29, 31, Apr. 1, 11, 14, 27, 29, May 9, 12, 25, 27, June 7, 10, 23, 25, July 5, 8, 21, 23, Aug. 3, 6, 19, 21, Sept. 1, 4, 17, 19, Oct. 2, 15, 17, Nov. 13, 15, 30, Dec. 11, 13, 28

Beneficial: Jan. 15, 17, 28, Feb. 13, 15, 26, Mar. 11, 13, 24, Apr. 9, 11, 22, May 7, 9, 20, June 5, 7, 18, July 3, 5, 16, Aug. 1, 3, 14, Sept. 1, 12, Oct. 10, 29, Nov. 8, 27, Dec. 6, 25

Fatal attractions: Jan. 5, Feb. 1, 2, 3, 4, Mar. 1

Challenging: Jan. 4, 5, 14, Feb. 2, 3, 12, Mar. 1, 10, Apr. 8, 30, May 6, 28, June 4, 26, July 2, 24, Aug. 22, Sept. 20, Oct. 18, Nov. 16, Dec. 14

Soul mates: Jan. 2, Mar. 29, Apr. 27, May 25, June 23, July 21, Aug. 19, Sept. 17, Oct. 15, Nov. 13, Dec. 11

August 6

♌ Your birthday implies that under your sociable and idealistic demeanor may lie a practical nature seeking to commercialize on your talents. As a Leo, you are charming, romantic, and spontaneous, with creative gifts and an eye for color and style. The extreme sides of your nature show that, on one hand, you can be a tough disciplinarian, especially where money is concerned, and on the other hand, you can be a caring and compassionate humanitarian.

With the subinfluence of Jupiter, you are likely to be ambitious and full of vitality as well as direct and outspoken. Though a tendency to be critical implies that you may have to guard against having misgivings or being worried, inspiration is your key to motivation and success, and if stimulated, you are willing to put in the effort needed. Nevertheless, guard against becoming rigid and unspontaneous or doing things strictly out of duty. This may cause a sense of denial, lack of confidence, or feelings that you are unappreciated.

With your attractive personality, enthusiasm for life, and positive frame of mind, you can achieve great success. At times fortune will grant you a lucky break; however, guard against taking too much for granted and leaving all to chance.

When you are around the age of sixteen, your progressed Sun moves into Virgo, commencing a thirty-year period of increased emphasis on order, practical problem solving, and being more discriminating with your time and energy. Another turning point occurs at the age of forty-six, when your progressed Sun moves into Libra, stimulating you to widen your social circle, place more emphasis on your relationships, and develop any possible latent musical, artistic, or literary talents. From the age of seventy-six, when your progressed Sun enters Scorpio, you feel a need to get more in touch with your deeper emotions.

Your Secret Self

Although you may appear strong or tough on the outside, you possess an inner emotional sensitivity that can highlight the extremes of your character. When negative or too self-involved, your powerful emotions can be expressed as disappointment or loneliness, whereas when you are positive, you possess a universal love for all. Through your selflessness, you are willing to be of service to others without expecting much in return. It is important, though, to get the balance right between compromising yourself for the sake of harmony and being demanding. You may see this process working out in how you value yourself and how you allow people to treat you. With a strong desire to love and be loved, you are sensitive to the reactions of others. You possess a love of beauty and luxury and enjoy sharing.

Work & Vocation

With your charm and sense of values, you are excellent at combining business and pleasure. People respond to your sense of responsibility and ability to work hard. You are a networker, and one of your best assets is the ability to deal with people. You may excel in big business, merchandising, manufacturing, and banking, or may prefer to work for yourself. Talented, you are usually attracted to the theater or the world of entertainment. If utilizing the

---

PRIMARY STAR

Star's name: Kochab
Degree position: 11°56'–12°45' Leo between the years 1930 and 2000
Magnitude: 2
Strength: ★★★★★★★★
Orb: 2°10'
Constellation: Beta Ursa Minor
Applicable days: August 4, 5, 6, 7
Star qualities: Saturn/Mercury
Description: a giant orange star located in the Small Bear, also called the Little Dipper

PRIMARY STAR'S INFLUENCE

Kochab's influence bestows logic, concentration, and an ability to come straight to the point in discussion. Often you have a love of tidiness and good organizational skills. This star imparts stamina and opportunities to rise to a position of authority.

Linked to your Sun's degree, this star indicates that much can be achieved through determination. You have the ability to fight with energy and courage till the end, and you possess a never-give-up attitude. This star also warns against deceit and malicious or underhanded activities.

• *Positive:* determination, persistence, courage to overcome obstacles

more compassionate side of your nature, you may be drawn to child care, counseling, healing, or philanthropic work for the community. Alternatively, a strong appreciation of beauty, nature, and form may attract you to a creative career such as artist or designer.

Famous people who share your birthday include poet Lord Tennyson, actress Lucille Ball, actor Robert Mitchum, business tycoon Freddy Laker, painter Howard Hodgkin, and scientist Alexander Fleming.

Numerology

Compassion, idealism, and a caring nature are some of the attributes suggested by a number 6 birthday. This is the number of the perfectionist or the universal friend, and it indicates that you are frequently a humanitarian who can be responsible, loving, and supportive. With a number 6 birthday, you are frequently domestically inclined and a devoted parent. The more sensitive among you will need to find a form of creative expression and are drawn to the world of entertaining or art and design. You may need to develop more self-confidence and overcome tendencies such as interference, worry, and misplaced sympathy. The subinfluence of the number 8 month indicates that since you are quick to sense changes, you are cautious and a good judge of values. Although practical and economical, you are inclined to be idealistic and carefree. By trusting your intuition and learning about yourself, you can enjoy interaction with other people.

• *Positive:* worldly, universal brotherhood, friendly, compassionate, dependable, understanding, sympathetic, idealistic, domestically inclined, humanitarian, poised, artistic, balanced

• *Negative:* discontented, anxiety, shy, unreasonable, stubborn, disharmonious, domineering, selfish, suspicious, cynical, self-centered

Love & Relationships

Fun-loving and caring, you can be reliable and kind. At times you possess a childlike playfulness, and you are likely to always retain a certain youthfulness. Naturally charming and sociable, you are able to attract friends and admirers. In serious relationships you are romantic, idealistic, and loyal, but may have to resist either martyring yourself or being too possessive. You can be a devoted partner who is warm, caring, and loving.

YOUR SPECIAL SOMEONE

You might further improve your chances for building a long-lasting relationship by looking for someone born on one of the following dates.

Love & friendship: Jan. 4, 8, 9, 18, 19, 23, Feb. 2, 6, 7, 16, 17, 21, Mar. 4, 14, 15, 19, 28, 30, Apr. 2, 12, 13, 17, 26, 28, 30, May 10, 11, 15, 24, 26, 28, June 8, 9, 13, 22, 24, 26, July 6, 7, 11, 20, 22, 24, 30, Aug. 4, 5, 9, 18, 20, 22, 28, Sept. 2, 3, 7, 16, 18, 20, 26, Oct. 1, 5, 14, 16, 18, 24, Nov. 3, 12, 14, 16, 22, Dec. 1, 10, 12, 14, 20

Beneficial: Jan. 5, 16, 27, Feb. 3, 14, 25, Mar. 1, 12, 23, Apr. 10, 21, May 8, 19, June 6, 17, July 4, 15, Aug. 2, 13, Sept. 11, Oct. 9, 30, Nov. 7, 28, Dec. 5, 26, 30

Fatal attractions: Jan. 17, Feb. 2, 3, 4, 5, 15, Mar. 13, Apr. 11, May 9, June 7, July 5, Aug. 3, Sept. 1

Challenging: Jan. 1, 10, 15, Feb. 8, 13, Mar. 6, 11, Apr. 4, 9, May 2, 7, June 5, July 3, 29, Aug. 1, 27, Sept. 25, Oct. 23, Nov. 21, Dec. 19, 29

Soul mates: Aug. 30, Sept. 28, Oct. 26, Nov. 24, Dec. 22

August 7

♌ Idealistic, hardworking, and charming, you are charismatic, though reserved, with sound common sense. This birthday reveals you to be an artistic or creative Leo, with a kind heart and a strong sense of duty.

The subinfluence of your decanate ruler, Sagittarius, suggests that while you are usually frank and honest and a supporter of the less fortunate, there is a danger that in your dealings with others you may adopt a self-righteous or arrogant tone.

Your optimism and grand dreams are your motivating force and relate to your active and constructive mind. You may, however, need to develop a more realistic approach and overcome a tendency either to be overly optimistic or to harbor self-destructive thoughts. Among your many attributes is your ability to think in broad terms and be very persuasive.

Balancing between motivation and inertia, you desire success and prosperity, but without the right kind of support you may become easily discouraged or drift aimlessly until something or someone sparks your imagination. By practicing patience and persistence and keeping a positive mental attitude, you are guaranteed to achieve your objectives and well-earned success.

After the age of fifteen, when your progressed Sun moves into Virgo, there is an increased need for practical order in your day-to-day existence. You will be more inclined to analyze things and look for ways to restructure and improve your life. This continues until the age of forty-five, when your progressed Sun enters Libra. As a turning point for you, this highlights the growing importance of relationships, creativity, and harmony. When you are age seventy-five your progressed Sun enters Scorpio, emphasizing the importance of personal power and transformation.

Fixed Stars

Kochab; Acubens, also called Sertan; Dubhe

Primary Star

Star's name: Kochab
Degree position: 11°56'–12°45' Leo between the years 1930 and 2000
Magnitude: 2
Strength: ★★★★★★★
Orb: 2°10'
Constellation: Beta Ursa Minor
Applicable days: August 4, 5, 6, 7
Star qualities: Saturn/Mercury
Description: a giant orange star located in the Small Bear, also called the Little Dipper

Primary Star's Influence

Kochab's influence bestows logic, concentration, and an ability to come straight to the point in discussion. Often you have a love of tidiness and good organizational skills. This star imparts stamina and opportunities to rise to a position of authority.

Linked to your Sun's degree, this star indicates that much can be achieved through determination. You have the ability to fight with energy and courage till the end, and you possess a never-give-up attitude. This star also warns against deceit and malicious or underhanded activities.

• Positive: determination, persistence, courage to overcome obstacles

Your Secret Self

Because you are confident and compassionate, others often turn to you for support and encouragement. While you can give good advice, you may sometimes find it hard to practice what you preach. Creative and intuitive, you have a strong need for self-expression, which helps build your faith and confidence and is an outlet for any possible frustration or disappointment with yourself or others. Generous and warm-hearted, you genuinely care about people, and once you have set your mind on a goal, you can be very determined.

You may have to guard against lethargy or becoming too fixed. This may leave you resting in some comfortable and easy routine but not challenge you to achieve your full potential. An interesting combination of humanitarianism and a desire for the luxuries of life may stimulate you to make your grand dreams a reality.

Work & Vocation

Since you are friendly and charming and have the ability to speak out, you are able to excel in occupations that use people skills, such as in sales, agencies, or promotion. Your excellent mind and good organizational skills can attract you to business, where you are likely to become interested in large enterprises. The world of theater and entertainment can also be an area where you may prosper, making the best of your natural talent for performing. Alternatively, having a desire for truth and a philosophical approach to life may draw you to law, the clergy, or metaphysics. Since you can combine a flair for dealing with people and supporting the underdog, you may wish to fight for good causes.

Famous people who share your birthday include wartime spy Mata Hari, astrologer Alan Leo, flamenco guitarist Manitas De Plata, jazz musician Roland Kirk, film director Nicholas Ray, paleontologist Louis Leakey, and football Hall of Famer Alan Page.

Numerology

Analytical and thoughtful, number 7 individuals are frequently critical and self-absorbed. With a constant need for greater self-awareness, you enjoy gathering information and may be interested in reading, writing, or spirituality. Although shrewd, you may overrationalize or get lost in detail. A tendency to be enigmatic or secretive suggests that at times you feel misunderstood. The subinfluence of the number 8 month indicates that you are ambitious, with a good business sense. Although you usually do not like to get into debt, you need to learn how to manage your financial affairs. A desire to enjoy the good life suggests that you need something to motivate and inspire you; otherwise you can be in danger of drifting or becoming stuck in a rut. Willing to work hard for success, you often attract opportunities and can be lucky if traveling to foreign places.

• *Positive:* educated, trusting, meticulous, idealistic, honest, psychic, scientific, rational, reflective

• *Negative:* concealing, deceitful, unfriendly, secretive, skeptical, confused by details, nagging, detached, unfeeling, sensitive to criticism

Love & Relationships

Intuitive and reflective, with the ability to project love and a warm personality, you can be very popular. With your natural understanding, you can also attract people who may draw from your energy, so it is necessary to be discriminating in your choice of relationships. Since you usually have high ideals, you are willing to give much of yourself and may be disappointed if others are not as generous and giving as you.

YOUR SPECIAL SOMEONE

For love, devotion, and happiness, you might have better chances with those born on the following dates.

Love & friendship: Jan. 5, 9, 10, 18, 19, Feb. 3, 7, 8, 16, 17, Mar. 1, 5, 6, 14, 15, 31, Apr. 3, 12, 13, 29, May 1, 10, 11, 27, 29, June 8, 9, 25, 27, July 6, 7, 23, 25, 31, Aug. 4, 5, 21, 23, 29, Sept. 2, 3, 19, 21, 27, 30, Oct. 1, 17, 19, 25, 28, Dec. 13, 15, 21, 24

Beneficial: Jan. 1, 6, 17, Feb. 4, 15, Mar. 2, 13, Apr. 11, May 9, June 7, July 5, Aug. 3, Sept. 1, Oct. 31, Nov. 29, Dec. 27

Fatal attractions: Feb. 2, 3, 4, 5, 6

Challenging: Jan. 2, 16, Feb. 14, Mar. 12, Apr. 10, May 8, June 6, July 4, Aug. 2, Dec. 30

Soul mates: Jan. 11, 31, Feb. 9, 29, Mar. 7, 27, Apr. 5, 25, May 3, 23, June 1, 21, July 19, Aug. 17, Sept. 15, Oct. 13, Nov. 11, Dec. 9

August 8

♌ The dynamic power and restlessness indicated by your birthday suggest that life has a lot in store for you. As a Leo, you are both creative and ambitious, with a strong desire to achieve success and recognition.

The subinfluence of your decanate ruler, Sagittarius, implies that your optimism, enthusiasm, and persistent efforts can bring about great transformations in your circumstances and lifestyle. Hardworking and practical, you are a pragmatist who can think instinctively and quickly. Although productivity is often associated with your birthday, you may have to guard against being overly zealous or impatient.

Variety is the spice of life, and whatever you do, a routine and monotonous life is not for you. Meeting new people, traveling, and being versatile motivate you and urge you to take on life's challenges by having more adventures. Nevertheless, a strong need to feel settled and established develops later in life, and by learning to take responsibility and make long-term investments, you can feel more secure. A struggle between idealistic and materialistic tendencies nevertheless suggests that uncertainty and loss of focus may be your greatest challenge. An inclination to give up under stress or too quickly can be overcome by carefully planning your projects.

When you are age fourteen, your progressed Sun moves into Virgo, commencing a thirty-year period of increased emphasis on order, practical problem solving, and being more discriminating with your time and energy. Another turning point occurs at the age of forty-four, when your progressed Sun moves into Libra. This stimulates your need for balance and harmony and heightens your awareness of partnerships and relationships in general. When you are age seventy-four, your progressed Sun moves into Scorpio, highlighting your personal power and a need for more emotional depth in your life.

Fixed Stars

Dubhe; Acubens, also called Sertan

Primary Star

Star's name: Dubhe

Degree position: 14°9'–15°2' Leo between the years 1930 and 2000

Magnitude: 2

Strength: ★★★★★★★

Orb: 2°20'

Constellation: Alpha Ursa Major

Applicable days: August 6, 7, 8, 9, 10

Star qualities: varied interpretations: Mercury/Venus or Mars

Description: a yellow binary main star located on the back of the Greater Bear

Primary Star's Influence

Dubhe endows idealism, self-confidence, boldness, and pride. This star grants intelligence, articulate speech, and persuasive expression. Although you are probably adventurous, at times you may feel insecure and let suspicious and mistrustful thoughts cause you worry.

Linked to your Sun's degree, Dubhe bestows determination to succeed and to overcome obstacles. Love of learning and a desire to achieve may direct you toward higher studies, astrology, law, or the military. In turn, this may also reveal a flair for writing and philosophy. This star warns against becoming overly materialistic and suggests channeling your power positively lest it become destructive.

• *Positive:* higher learning, artistic talents, beautiful voice

Your Secret Self

Although at times you can make rapid and determined progress and advancement in life, this alternates with periods of inactivity. This may cause frustration and lack of self-esteem. To overcome the feeling of standing still, it may be necessary to develop detachment and not hold on to disappointment. By realizing that these periods are only temporary and will pass, you are able to take a long-term view and avoid becoming overly serious.

You have within you a wealth of creative ideas that can encourage you to be imaginative and ingenious and can stimulate you to use your initiative in bringing about something original. Finding this creative spark can assist you in enjoying life, having more fun, and resisting worry and indecision.

Work & Vocation

Although you are hardworking, with your love of change you are usually happier in activities or occupations that do not involve routine. You may be interested in the world of theater or entertainment but are not likely to persist if the financial rewards do not seem to be sufficient. Not liking to be in a subservient position, you may prefer working for yourself or being involved in management. Possessing imagination and a strong visual sense, you can be very successful in any career that involves image making. Work involving travel would also be ideal for your adventurous soul.

Famous people who share your birthday include actors Dustin Hoffman and Keith Carradine, singer Connie Stevens, artist Andy Warhol, actress Esther Williams, and Formula One race car driver Nigel Mansell.

Numerology

The power suggested by the number 8 birthday shows a character with strong values and sound judgment. The number 8 indicates that you aspire to great accomplishment and possess an ambitious nature. A desire for dominance, security, and material success is also indicated by this birthday. As a number 8 person, you have a natural business sense and will benefit greatly from developing organizational and executive skills. A strong need to feel secure or established urges you to make long-term plans and investments. The subinfluence of the number 8 month adds to your character. With your sharp and quick perception, you are usually good at assessing people and situations. Very efficient at your work, you are willing to work hard and take on responsibilities. Nevertheless, you may have to learn how to administer or delegate your authority in a fair and just way. Since pride comes before a fall, avoid becoming overconfident and vain.

• *Positive:* leadership, thoroughness, hardworking, authority, protection, power to heal, good judge of values

• *Negative:* impatient, wasteful, intolerant, overwork, domineering, easily discouraged, lack of planning

Love & Relationships

Attracted to strong personalities, you like those who have conviction and direction. Friendships are important to you, as you like to mix with people who can stimulate your mind as well as help you have a good time. There is a natural entertainer in you, which comes out in the company of those you love. You usually work for harmony in relationships, but if you become insecure, you may become quarrelsome. Learning to be patient with others helps smooth difficult situations.

YOUR SPECIAL SOMEONE

To stay youthful, happy, and in love, you might have more success with those born on the following dates.

Love & friendship: Jan. 6, 10, 20, 21, 29, Feb. 4, 8, 18, 19, 27, Mar. 2, 6, 16, 25, 28, 30, Apr. 4, 14, 23, 26, 28, 30, May 2, 12, 21, 24, 26, 28, 30, June 10, 19, 22, 24, 26, 28, July 8, 17, 20, 22, 24, 26, Aug. 6, 15, 18, 20, 22, 24, Sept. 4, 13, 16, 18, 20, 22, Oct. 2, 11, 14, 16, 18, 20, Nov. 9, 12, 14, 16, 18, Dec. 7, 10, 12, 14, 16

Beneficial: Jan. 7, 13, 18, 28, Feb. 5, 11, 16, 26, Mar. 3, 9, 14, 24, Apr. 1, 7, 12, 22, May 5, 10, 20, June 3, 8, 18, July 1, 6, 16, Aug. 4, 14, Sept. 2, 12, 30, Oct. 10, 28, Nov. 8, 26, 30, Dec. 6, 24, 28

Fatal attractions: Jan. 25, Feb. 4, 5, 6, 23, Mar. 21, Apr. 19, May 17, June 15, July 13, Aug. 11, Sept. 9, Oct. 7, Nov. 5, Dec. 3

Challenging: Jan. 3, 17, Feb. 1, 15, Mar. 13, Apr. 11, May 9, 30, June 7, 28, July 5, 26, 29, Aug. 3, 24, 27, Sept. 1, 22, 25, Oct. 20, 23, Nov. 18, 21, Dec. 16, 19

Soul mates: Jan. 18, Feb. 16, Mar. 14, Apr. 12, May 10, 29, June 8, 27, July 6, 25, Aug. 4, 23, Sept. 2, 21, Oct. 19, Nov. 17, Dec. 15

August 9

♌ Intuition, imagination, and pragmatism are some of the qualities associated with your birthday. As a Leo, you are usually confident, charming, and generous, though you also possess a sensitive nature.

The subinfluence of your decanate ruler, Sagittarius, suggests that by combining inspiration and enthusiasm with hard work, you are able to take advantage of opportunities that provide you with financial protection. This also indicates that money will never be your major problem, but in order to truly profit from this celestial benefactor, you have to put a strong emphasis on values and develop a responsible attitude.

Socially oriented, friendly, and gregarious, with a concern for the well-being of others, you have many acquaintances whom you support and encourage. The more inspired among you can be great humanitarians who devote their time and effort to good causes and charitable organizations.

Although you can concentrate with determination on the job at hand, you are often creative, with many interests. The pride you take in your work can also carry the sign of the perfectionist. Be careful that this sense of duty and self-control does not make you overly concerned with economy.

From childhood you are likely to be interested in social activities and developing your leadership abilities by being at the center of things. From the age of thirteen onward, as your progressed Sun moves into Virgo for a thirty-year period, you gradually become more conscientious and discriminating and react more efficiently to your working environment. At the age of forty-three you reach a turning point as your progressed Sun enters Libra. This brings a strong emphasis on your social relationships and partnerships. Your creative abilities are enhanced, and you may be drawn to develop your musical, artistic, or literary interests. When you are age seventy-three, your progressed Sun moves into Scorpio, highlighting issues concerning deep emotional change and transformation.

Fixed Star

Star's name: Dubhe

Degree position: 14°9'–15°2' Leo between the years 1930 and 2000

Magnitude: 2

Strength: ★★★★★★★

Orb: 2°20'

Constellation: Alpha Ursa Major

Applicable days: August 6, 7, 8, 9, 10

Star qualities: varied interpretations: Mercury/Venus or Mars

Description: a yellow binary main star located on the back of the Greater Bear

PRIMARY STAR'S INFLUENCE

Dubhe endows idealism, self-confidence, boldness, and pride. This star grants intelligence, articulate speech, and persuasive expression. Although you are probably adventurous, at times you may feel insecure and let suspicious and mistrustful thoughts cause you worry.

Linked to your Sun's degree, Dubhe bestows determination to succeed and to overcome obstacles. Love of learning and a desire to achieve may direct you toward higher studies, astrology, law, or the military. In turn, this may also reveal a flair for writing and philosophy. This star warns against becoming overly materialistic and suggests channeling your power positively lest it become destructive.

• Positive: higher learning, artistic talents, beautiful voice

• Negative: worry, insecurity, lack of imagination, inclination to materialism

Your Secret Self

If you trust your first instincts, you possess an emotional power that gives you the ability to intuitively understand other people's intentions. You also possess a sensitivity and subtle intuitive insight that can positively direct you if you listen to your own inner guidance.

Although you want material security, you may feel restless or impatient if your desire for excitement, action, or exploring new experiences is restricted. This discontent can lead you to some form of escapism, which may only compound the problem. You need to be continually searching and investigating in order to learn and inspire your spirit to break away from the rigid order of limitation. Your work is frequently an important key to feeling that you are fulfilling yourself and building something positive for the future.

Work & Vocation

Being ambitious, practical, and sociable can draw you toward good work opportunities. Whatever you do, you like to do it well, and you have a sense of organization, method, and order. With your negotiation skills, you are usually able to strike a good deal and get value for your money. In business you can do particularly well in merchandising, manufacturing, and anything in which you deal with the public. Alternatively, you may be drawn to the entertainment world, where your imagination and talents can help you become very successful. A latent humanitarian or religious streak may be developed to attract you to some form of work that is public-spirited.

Famous people who share your birthday include singer Whitney Houston, poet John Dryden, actress Melanie Griffith, singer-songwriter Joe Jackson, England's King Henry V, and child psychologist Jean Piaget.

Numerology

Benevolence, thoughtfulness, and sentimental sensitivity are all associated with the number 9 birthday. Tolerant and kind, you are often generous and liberal. Intuitive and psychic abilities point to a universal receptivity and, if channeled positively, may inspire you to seek a spiritual path. This birthday may suggest a need to overcome challenges and a tendency to be overly sensitive, with emotional ups and downs. You benefit greatly from world travel and interaction with people from all walks of life but may have to avoid unrealistic dreams or an inclination toward escapism. The subinfluence of the number 8 month indicates that you are strong-willed, with a desire for power and influence. Although you can be an idealist who is broad-minded, you are materially inclined. Driven by the need to achieve wealth and success, you often work hard and have many lucky opportunities.

• *Positive:* idealistic, humanitarian, creative, sensitive, generous, magnetic, poetic, charitable, giving, detached, lucky, popular

• *Negative:* frustrated, fragmented, unsure, selfish, impractical, worry

Love & Relationships

Your sociability, charismatic personality, and charm often attract many friends and admirers. Through the projection of your powerful feelings, you can express strong love and affection. If your emotions become repressed, however, there is a danger of being moody or becoming involved in power games. Nevertheless, you are usually willing to work at keeping the peace in your relationships and rarely give up easily.

YOUR SPECIAL SOMEONE

You might find emotional fulfillment and that special someone among those born on the following days.

Love & friendship: Jan. 7, 11, 21, 22, Feb. 5, 9, 19, 20, Mar. 3, 7, 18, 31, Apr. 1, 5, 16, 29, May 3, 14, 27, 29, June 1, 12, 25, 27, July 10, 23, 25, Aug. 8, 21, 23, 31, Sept. 6, 19, 21, 29, Oct. 4, 17, 19, 27, 30, Nov. 2, 15, 17, 25, 28, Dec. 13, 15, 23, 26

Beneficial: Jan. 8, 14, 19, Feb. 6, 12, 17, Mar. 4, 10, 15, Apr. 2, 8, 13, May 6, 11, June 4, 9, July 2, 7, Aug. 5, Sept. 3, Oct. 1, 29, Nov. 27, Dec. 25, 29

Fatal attractions: Feb. 5, 6, 7, 8

Challenging: Jan. 9, 18, 20, Feb. 7, 16, 18, Mar. 5, 14, 16, Apr. 3, 12, 14, May 1, 10, 12, June 8, 10, July 6, 8, 29, Aug. 4, 6, 27, Sept. 2, 4, 25, Oct. 2, 23, Nov. 21, Dec. 19

Soul mates: Jan. 9, Feb. 7, Mar. 5, Apr. 3, May 1, Oct. 30, Nov. 28, Dec. 26

August 10

♌ Your birthday reveals you to be intuitive, inventive, and original, an ambitious individual with great potential and leadership abilities. As a Leo, you are creative and talented, with an independent and unusual approach and a strong need for self-expression.

The subinfluence of your decanate ruler, Sagittarius, encourages you to travel and explore different experiences. Since you are versatile, with many interests, you may have to guard against dispersing your energies. By learning to focus and not wasting your time, you can obtain your heart's desire.

Your true showmanship indicates that you have the potential or mental capabilities for record achievements. Inspirational ideas and objective thinking will often assist you to overcome a tendency to be disappointed, indecisive, or worried. In your enthusiasm to take on life's challenges, however, guard against taking reckless chances by believing that new beginnings will solve all your past problems.

Although you rely on your common sense, an ability to see the numerous sides of every situation can at times bring about doubts and confusion. Nevertheless, you are a born strategist, with insight and strong instincts, and if faced with a problem, you can find a quick and inventive answer. Industrious and methodical, you have a pragmatic approach and openness that imply that you are frank and to the point.

When you are around the age of twelve, your progressed Sun moves into Virgo, commencing a thirty-year period of increasing emphasis on order, work, and efficiency as well as mental awareness of practical problem solving. Your progressed Sun moves into Libra when you are age forty-two. It marks a turning point, stimulating you to cooperate more with others, be diplomatic, and place more emphasis on your relationships. When you are age seventy-two, your progressed Sun moves into Scorpio, highlighting issues of personal power and transformation.

Fixed Stars

Dubhe, Merak

PRIMARY STAR

Star's name: Dubhe
Degree position: 14°9'–15°2' Leo between the years 1930 and 2000
Magnitude: 2
Strength: ★★★★★★★
Orb: 2°20'
Constellation: Alpha Ursa Major
Applicable days: August 6, 7, 8, 9, 10
Star qualities: varied interpretations: Mercury/Venus or Mars
Description: a yellow binary main star located on the back of the Greater Bear

PRIMARY STAR'S INFLUENCE

Dubhe endows idealism, self-confidence, boldness, and pride. This star grants intelligence, articulate speech, and persuasive expression. Although you are probably adventurous, at times you may feel insecure and let suspicious and mistrustful thoughts cause you worry.

Linked to your Sun's degree, Dubhe bestows determination to succeed and to overcome obstacles. Love of learning and a desire to achieve may direct you toward higher studies, astrology, law, or the military. In turn, this may also reveal a flair for writing and philosophy. This star warns against becoming overly materialistic and suggests channeling your power positively lest it become destructive.

Your Secret Self

When you substitute your creative spirit for material security, then you are achieving in the real sense of the word. At times, though, the fear of losing what you have already achieved may mean that you prefer to take the less interesting but safer option. This may deny you the opportunities to make dramatic changes, which involve taking some kind of risk. You can overcome this insecurity by recognizing that accomplishment is linked to doing what truly makes you happy.

You possess a strong inner desire for peace and harmony, which can be expressed through the arts or reflected in your love of home and family. You have a strong sense of responsibility and need to express yourself. Often idealistic, you can be very dedicated, especially if you support a cause that is near to your heart. Your capacity to love can be particularly expanded through the arts, drama, or music.

Work & Vocation

Creativity, sharp intelligence, and a capacity for hard work indicate that you have the potential to rise to the top of your chosen profession. You possess dramatic gifts that you can utilize in the theater, writing, or politics. However, with your natural business sense, you also possess a talent for merchandising and production. You may fare best in your own business, but whatever career you choose, you will always be looking to improve the way you work. Alternatively, a philosophical or humanitarian leaning may be satisfied through occupations such as the clergy, charity work, or philanthropy.

Famous people who share your birthday include U.S. president Herbert Hoover, singer Eddie Fisher, actress Norma Shearer, scientist Wolfgang Paul, actress Jane Wyatt, jazz singer Patti Austin, and actress Rosanna Arquette.

Numerology

Like those with a number 1 birthday, you usually strive to accomplish great endeavors. Nevertheless, you may have to overcome many obstacles before you achieve your goals. Energetic and original, you stand by your own beliefs even when they differ from others'. Your ability to be a self-starter with a pioneering spirit encourages you to travel far afield or strike out on your own. You may also learn that the world does not revolve around you, and should guard against selfishness and being dictatorial. Success and accomplishment are important to all individuals with number 10 birthdays, and frequently you find your way to the top of your profession. The subinfluence of the number 8 month indicates that you are a powerful character with strong convictions and an independent spirit. You are likely to be innovative, self-assured, and ambitious, though being multitalented suggests that you can try to accomplish too much, leading you to scatter your energies in too many directions.

• *Positive:* leadership, creative, progressive, forceful, optimistic, strong convictions, competitive, independent, gregarious

• *Negative:* overbearing, jealous, egotistical, too proud, antagonistic, lack of restraint, selfish, vacillating, impatient

Love & Relationships

You admire those who can accomplish much. You may be looking for such a high, idealistic love that it can sometimes be difficult for anyone to live up to your high hopes. As you may alternate between being loving, spontaneous, and affectionate and appearing cold or withdrawn, it is vital that you have space for yourself to balance your sensitivities. Your naturally friendly personality ensures that you have many friends, and being hospitable suggests that you are a good host or hostess.

YOUR SPECIAL SOMEONE

To improve on your chances of finding love and happiness, look out for those born on the following dates.

Love & friendship: Jan. 8, 22, 23, 26, Feb. 6, 20, 24, Mar. 4, 18, 22, Apr. 2, 16, 17, 20, 30, May 14, 18, 28, 30, June 12, 16, 26, 28, July 10, 14, 24, 26, Aug. 8, 12, 22, 24, Sept. 6, 10, 20, 22, 30, Oct. 4, 8, 18, 20, 28, Nov. 2, 6, 16, 18, 26, Dec. 4, 14, 16, 24

Beneficial: Jan. 9, 20, Feb. 7, 18, Mar. 5, 16, 29, Apr. 3, 14, 27, May 1, 12, 25, June 10, 23, July 8, 21, Aug. 6, 19, Sept. 4, 17, Oct. 2, 15, 30, Nov. 13, 28, Dec. 11, 26, 30

Fatal attractions: Jan. 27, Feb. 7, 8, 9, 25, Mar. 23, Apr. 21, May 19, June 17, July 15, Aug. 13, Sept. 11, Oct. 9, Nov. 7, Dec. 5

Challenging: Jan. 2, 10, 19, Feb. 8, 17, Mar. 6, 15, Apr. 4, 13, May 2, 11, June 9, July 7, 30, Aug. 5, 28, Sept. 3, 26, Oct. 1, 24, Nov. 22, Dec. 20, 30

Soul mates: Jan. 15, Feb. 13, Mar. 11, Apr. 9, May 7, June 5, July 3, Aug. 1, Oct. 29, Nov. 27, Dec. 25

August 11

♌ Action, inspiration, and creativity are some of the qualities associated with your birthday. With a pioneering spirit, you are an interesting mixture of idealism and a desire for money and status. As a Leo, you have charm and vitality, and with your friendly and gregarious personality, you are often described by others as an optimistic extrovert.

The subinfluence of your decanate ruler, Sagittarius, implies that because you are idealistic yet practical, you usually have the vision and ingenuity to turn your dreams into reality. This influence also indicates that your decisive attitude can be an important factor in your ability to overcome obstacles and periods of adversity. Jupiter's effect also points out that you have some exceedingly good ideas that can bring financial rewards.

The strong emphasis on relationships and partnerships linked to your birthday implies that although you can be mentally determined and single-minded, you may need to learn the art of compromise in order to benefit from what others have to offer. Friendly and enterprising, with a fondness for material comforts, you frequently seek associations that can bring you gain and further advancement. Lack of funds or a fear of not having enough money, however, can influence your otherwise good prospects, and you must avoid being materialistic or ruthless.

From the age of eleven, when your progressed Sun moves into Virgo for thirty years, there is an increasing need for a practical approach to life. You may gradually desire to become more efficient and discriminating with your time and energy. There is a turning point for you at the age of forty-one, when your progressed Sun enters Libra. At this time you may want to become more involved in your close personal relationships and may turn from practical considerations to more aesthetic ones. When you are age seventy-one, your progressed Sun enters Scorpio, and you may experience a new period of emotional change and transformation.

Your Secret Self

A strong need for recognition ensures that you want to be out front both materially and emotionally. Since you possess the power to achieve in a big way, it may be important to use this for emotional satisfaction as well as just material success. You may find your greatest fulfillment in satisfying your need to do something for the benefit of others.

With an inner sense of harmony, you desire life to be peaceful and contented, emphasizing the need for your home to be a safe and secure retreat from the world. This harmony can also stimulate musical, artistic, or creative skills that may be just waiting to be developed. Entertaining and sociable, you usually know how to relax and enjoy yourself. Just be careful that you do not compromise too much to keep the peace or allow anxiety to creep in and spoil your fun. Developing your inner sixth sense may be the key to using the tremendous latent abilities inherent in your birthday.

Work & Vocation

Friendly and generous, you have idealistic inclinations that may lead you to seek work that involves you with others. If you believe in a cause, you can be quite forceful or persuasive; as a

FIXED STAR

Star's name: Merak

Degree position: 18°29'–19°34' Leo between the years 1930 and 2000

Magnitude: 2

Strength: ★★★★★★★

Orb: 2°10'

Constellation: Alpha Ursa Major

Applicable days: August 10, 11, 12, 13, 14

Star qualities: Mars

Description: a white giant star located on the side of the Great Bear

PRIMARY STAR'S INFLUENCE

Merak imparts a love of command and leadership abilities, although it may also indicate an inclination to be overly dominant. Your determination means that you are likely to achieve much in life and succeed where others may fail.

Linked to your Sun's degree, this star bestows courage, assertiveness, and hot-blooded vitality. The power of attainment that is associated with this star ensures that your life will be full of activity. Merak's influence carries opportunities and possible fame and honors.

• *Positive:* love of life, active and creative, ambition, courage

• *Negative:* hastiness, stubbornness, overstrain

philanthropist, you have the power to do good in the community. In business, you have a flair for sales and promotion and can successfully negotiate contracts and business deals. Similarly, you can excel as an agent or business advisor. With your strong will and determination, you have much energy to direct toward accomplishment, and although you possess strong leadership skills, you may prefer to work in cooperation with others. You can also do well in the entertainment world, writing, or music.

Famous people who share your birthday include actress Arlene Dahl, wrestler Hulk Hogan, writers Enid Blyton and Alex Haley, and musician Phil Ochs.

Numerology

The special vibration of the master number 11 birthday suggests that idealism, inspiration, and innovation are highly important to you. A blend of humility and confidence challenges you to work toward self-mastery both materially and spiritually. Through experience you learn how to deal with both sides of your nature and develop a less extremist attitude by trusting your own feelings. Usually you are highly charged and enjoy vitality, but must avoid becoming overly anxious or impractical. The subinfluence of the number 8 month indicates that you can be determined and ambitious, with foresight and executive abilities. When you are creative and original you become optimistic, hardworking, and enthusiastic; however, you must learn to complete what you start and not leave a job half done. As fear often relates to being insecure about money and power, you may need to overcome a tendency to be arrogant or calculating. Learn to express your unique talent in order to unleash your true potential.

• *Positive:* focused, objective, enthusiastic, inspirational, spiritual, intuitive, intelligent, outgoing, inventive, artistic, service, healing ability, humanitarian, psychic

• *Negative:* superiority complex, aimless, overemotional, easily hurt, highly strung, selfish, lack of clarity

Love & Relationships

An ability to communicate your creative thoughts attracts you to artistic people. You are warm, friendly, and highly sociable. In your personal relationships you are especially drawn by powerful and intelligent individuals, although you may have to be careful not to become involved in arguments with loved ones. You are likely to be extremely generous with those you love and can be very loyal as a friend and lover. Usually willing to work hard to keep a relationship alive, you still need to keep some form of personal freedom.

YOUR SPECIAL SOMEONE

For security, mental stimulation, and love, you might want to begin looking for those born among the following dates.

Love & friendship: Jan. 3, 5, 23, Feb. 3, 11, 21, Mar. 9, 19, 28, 31, Apr. 7, 17, 26, 29, May 5, 15, 24, 27, 29, 31, June 3, 13, 22, 25, 27, 29, July 1, 11, 20, 23, 25, 27, 29, Aug. 9, 18, 21, 23, 25, 27, Sept. 7, 16, 19, 21, 23, 25, Oct. 5, 14, 17, 19, 21, 23, Nov. 3, 12, 15, 17, 19, 21, Dec. 1, 10, 13, 15, 17, 19

Beneficial: Jan. 3, 4, 10, 21, Feb. 1, 2, 8, 19, Mar. 6, 17, 30, Apr. 4, 15, 28, May 2, 13, 26, June 11, 24, July 9, 22, Aug. 7, 20, Sept. 5, 18, Oct. 3, 16, 31, Nov. 1, 14, 29, Dec. 12, 27

Fatal attractions: Jan. 22, 28, Feb. 8, 9, 10, 20, 26, Mar. 18, 24, Apr. 16, 22, May 14, 20, June 12, 18, July 10, 16, Aug. 8, 14, Sept. 6, 12, Oct. 4, 10, Nov. 2, 8, Dec. 6

Challenging: Jan. 11, 20, Feb. 9, 18, Mar. 7, 16, Apr. 5, 14, May 3, 12, 30, June 1, 10, 28, July 8, 26, 31, Aug. 6, 24, 29, Sept. 4, 22, 27, Oct. 2, 20, 25, Nov. 18, 23, Dec. 16, 21

Soul mates: Jan. 26, Feb. 24, Mar. 22, 30, Apr. 20, 28, May 18, 26, June 16, 24, July 14, 22, Aug. 12, 20, Sept. 10, 18, Oct. 8, 16, Nov. 6, 14, Dec. 4, 12

August 12

♌ Ambitious and creative, with strong intuitive powers and vitality, you have a birthday that reveals you to be an assertive individual with a positive perspective. As a Leo, you are forceful and determined, with a restless and assertive nature that normally assists you to get your own way. Your direct approach and alert responses suggest that you are able to quickly assess people and situations. By staying objective, you can also overcome a tendency to have fluctuating moods.

Your desire for success and security implies that you are keen to get the approval of others and therefore are usually friendly and gregarious. Your personal magnetism helps you to overcome early setbacks, and your intuitive powers frequently come to your assistance.

The influence of your decanate planet, Jupiter, suggests that you are daring and courageous, a dynamic person with a desire for recognition. As you are both sensitive and determined, with a strong desire for stability and advancement, you possess a duality that needs to be balanced. This implies that although you can be compassionate and understanding, you can also be authoritarian or domineering.

Since you are proud and dignified, you may be sensitive to other people's criticism. You may need to develop a more rational perspective, thus avoiding being hurt by others. With your no-nonsense approach and diplomatic skills, you enjoy work involving cooperation with others and are in your element when you can mix business and pleasure.

From childhood you are inclined to be sociable and friendly. When you are age ten, your progressed Sun enters Virgo for a thirty-year period. This indicates that you gradually become more practical and discriminating as well as increase your efficiency. As you reach the age of forty, your progressed Sun enters Libra, which can emphasize your relationships and a need to bring more beauty, harmony, and balance into your life. This can draw you to activities such as writing, art, music, or the healing arts. When you are age seventy, your progressed Sun moves into Scorpio, highlighting your emotional need for deep change and personal power.

Your Secret Self

As you are a person who can really make things happen, your focused willpower can be a formidable force to be reckoned with. For this reason you do not want fear to control your reactions, as you are likely to create exactly what you are concentrating on. When positively channeled, this power can be a tremendous energy to uplift others.

As you like to keep active and are excellent at wheeling and dealing, you often use your strategic skills, energy, and drive to overcome any obstacles in your path. You are liable to work best when inspired and listening to your intuition. As you have strong convictions, you normally take a determined stand on principles, even when you are wrong. This suggests that you may need to develop the art of negotiation and compromise in order to become more objective.

Work & Vocation

Ambitious and determined, you possess natural abilities for leadership and can also be very persuasive, especially when promoting ideas linked to financial gain. Magnanimous and kind,

---

FIXED STARS

Merak; Al Genubi, also called Asad Australis

PRIMARY STAR

Star's name: Merak
Degree position: 18°29'–19°34' Leo between the years 1930 and 2000
Magnitude: 2
Strength: ★★★★★★★
Orb: 2°10'
Constellation: Alpha Ursa Major
Applicable days: August 10, 11, 12, 13, 14
Star qualities: Mars
Description: a white giant star located on the side of the Great Bear

PRIMARY STAR'S INFLUENCE

Merak imparts a love of command and leadership abilities, although it may also indicate an inclination to be overly dominant. Your determination means that you are likely to achieve much in life and succeed where others may fail.

Linked to your Sun's degree, this star bestows courage, assertiveness, and hot-blooded vitality. The power of attainment that is associated with this star ensures that your life will be full of activity. Merak's influence carries opportunities and possible fame and honors.

• *Positive:* love of life, active and creative, ambition, courage

• *Negative:* hastiness, stubbornness, overstrain

See Appendix for additional fixed star readings.

you are excellent at dealing with people and can usually see opportunities. Whether in education, business, or the world of entertainment, you want the freedom to work in your own unique way. A dislike of taking orders may encourage you to seek executive positions or to work for yourself, but you are always able to negotiate a good deal or commercialize your talents.

Famous people who share your birthday include film director Cecil B. De Mille, guitarist Mark Knopfler, theosophist Madame Blavatsky, and actor George Hamilton.

Numerology

Usually you are intuitive, helpful, and friendly, with good reasoning power. Since you want to establish true individuality, you are often innovative. Naturally understanding and sensitive, you also know how to use tact and cooperative methods to achieve your aims and objectives. When you achieve a balance between your need for self-expression and your natural inclination to be supportive of others, you can find emotional satisfaction and personal fulfillment. You may nevertheless need to find the courage to stand on your own two feet and develop self-confidence or learn not to become easily discouraged by other people. The subinfluence of the number 8 month indicates that you are an ambitious and determined individual with strong intuitive powers. With your practical approach and executive abilities, you possess a dynamic drive and an outgoing personality. In life, you usually have many opportunities for advancement, and you often want to achieve prosperity or be in the spotlight.
- *Positive:* creative, attractive, initiative, disciplinarian, promote yourself or others
- *Negative:* reclusive, eccentric, uncooperative, overly sensitive, lack of self-esteem

Love & Relationships

You are likely to have an active social life, as you can be very entertaining and enjoy meeting new people. In your personal relationships your intense feelings can have you alternating between strong romantic idealism and very practical reality. Romantic at heart, you are interested in the chase, but once you have established a relationship you are prone to changing your feelings. Since you possess a strong need for independence, you will have to pick a partner who gives you the freedom you need. Proud of your family, you will move mountains to protect their interests.

YOUR SPECIAL SOMEONE

In order to find that special partner, you might begin by looking for those born on the following dates.

Love & friendship: Jan. 14, 15, 22, 24, 26, 31, Feb. 12, 22, 29, Mar. 10, 20, 27, Apr. 8, 18, 25, May 6, 16, 23, 30, June 4, 14, 21, 28, 30, July 2, 12, 19, 26, 28, 30, Aug. 10, 17, 24, 26, 28, Sept. 8, 15, 22, 24, 26, Oct. 6, 13, 20, 22, 24, 30, Nov. 4, 11, 18, 20, 22, 28, Dec. 2, 9, 16, 18, 20, 26, 29

Beneficial: Jan. 5, 22, 30, Feb. 3, 20, 28, Mar. 1, 18, 26, Apr. 16, 24, May 14, 22, June 12, 20, July 10, 18, 29, Aug. 8, 16, 27, 31, Sept. 6, 14, 25, 29, Oct. 4, 12, 23, 27, Nov. 2, 10, 21, 25, Dec. 9, 19, 23

Fatal attractions: Jan. 12, Feb. 9, 10, 11, Mar. 8, Apr. 6, May 4, June 2

Challenging: Jan. 16, 21, Feb. 14, 19, Mar. 12, 17, 30, Apr. 10, 15, 28, May 8, 13, 26, June 6, 11, 24, July 4, 9, 22, Aug. 2, 7, 20, Sept. 5, 18, Oct. 3, 16, Nov. 1, 14, Dec. 12

Soul mates: Jan. 25, Feb. 23, Mar. 21, Apr. 19, May 17, June 15, July 13, Aug. 11, Sept. 9, Oct. 7, Nov. 5, Dec. 3, 30

August 13

♌ Your birthday reveals you to be independent and creative, with an ability to lead and command—an intelligent individual with a shrewd practicality. As a Leo, you are dignified, courageous, and a force to be reckoned with. Through your abilities to think rationally, you learn to recognize the power of knowledge that is usually at your disposal.

Assertive, with practical common sense, you usually add self-discipline to the list of your attributes. You can achieve success through developing your mental powers and establishing yourself in your chosen field. Able to present a unique approach to a problem, you can give others practical advice and solutions. Women born on this day tend to think in an authoritative way and take charge of situations.

The subinfluence of your decanate ruler, Sagittarius, further emphasizes your commanding personality and a need for expansion. This can also imply that you can be stubborn and critical. Those who appear to know you well see you as a strange mixture of conservatism and dissidence, but never as boring or dull. Well informed, you enjoy arguments and debates, since you usually come out on top—though if you think you know it all, you can become domineering and may have to learn that being mentally aggressive or uncompromising does not always get you the results you desire.

When you are at the early age of nine, your progressed Sun moves into Virgo for a thirty-year period. This brings an increasing desire for practical order and security in your life. There is a turning point for you at the age of thirty-nine, when your progressed Sun enters Libra. From this time there is a greater emphasis on your personal relationships, and you may gradually become more amiable and collaborative. At the age of sixty-nine, when your progressed Sun enters Scorpio, you are likely to experience a deeper desire for emotional transformation.

FIXED STARS

Merak; Al Genubi, also called Asad Australis

PRIMARY STAR

Star's name: Merak

Degree position: 18°29'–19°34' Leo between the years 1930 and 2000

Magnitude: 2

Strength: ★★★★★★★

Orb: 2°10'

Constellation: Alpha Ursa Major

Applicable days: August 10, 11, 12, 13, 14

Star qualities: Mars

Description: a white giant star located on the side of the Great Bear

PRIMARY STAR'S INFLUENCE

Merak imparts a love of command and leadership abilities, although it may also indicate an inclination to be overly dominant. Your determination means that you can achieve much in life and succeed where others may fail.

Linked to your Sun's degree, this star bestows courage, assertiveness, and hot-blooded vitality. The power of attainment that is associated with this star ensures that your life will be full of activity. Merak's influence carries opportunities and possible fame and honors.

• *Positive:* love of life, active and creative, ambition, courage

• *Negative:* hastiness, stubbornness, overstrain

See Appendix for additional fixed star readings.

Your Secret Self

A need to work and accomplish often ensures that you take on a great deal of responsibility and do not like to waste your time. Although you are sensitive and vulnerable, you may not show this to people for fear of being controlled. Outwardly you may also appear proud or cynical, but in your heart you are altruistic and a campaigner for justice.

Your persistence and determination to accomplish is admirable, but you may have to overcome a tendency to be manipulative. Yet you do know the value of sharing and working cooperatively in order to achieve the best results. You are a good organizer, and if you are overloaded with work, you know how to delegate responsibilities to others. Although you are usually collaborative, a little amicable bantering with those closest to you shows your desire to be on top while keeping your sense of fun.

Work & Vocation

With your sharp intellect, perseverance, and ability to work hard, you inevitably rise to a position of authority in any career you choose. Your executive skills and natural communication abilities would be an asset to you in the business world. You are also particularly suited for intellectual professions, such as law, science, or teaching. A strong need to express yourself may find an outlet in writing or the entertainment business, and you may also be drawn to publishing or advertising. An inborn humanitarian streak may attract you to be a reformer, whether in society, religion, or politics.

Famous people who share your birthday include director Alfred Hitchcock, Wild West figure Annie Oakley, musician Dan Fogelberg, revolutionary dictator Fidel Castro, and hockey player Bobby Clarke.

Numerology

Emotional sensitivity, enthusiasm, and inspiration are often identified with the number 13 birthday. Numerologically, you are associated with ambition and hard work, and can accomplish much through creative self-expression. You may need to develop or cultivate a pragmatic outlook if you want to turn your creative talents into tangible products. Your original and innovative approach inspires new and exciting ideas that frequently result in work that impresses others. With a number 13 birthday, you are earnest, romantic, charming, and fun-loving, and with dedication you can achieve prosperity. The subinfluence of the number 8 month indicates that you are forceful and determined and like to be in control. By learning to focus on a particular goal and persevering, you often reach the top of your profession. Alternatively, since you have excellent practical and administrative skills, you can also rise to positions of authority. Learning about partnerships and cooperation will provide you with opportunities to share your great talents with others.

• *Positive:* ambitious, creative, freedom-loving, self-expressive, initiative
• *Negative:* impulsive, indecisive, bossy, unemotional, rebellious

Love & Relationships

Dynamic, with strong opinions, you are drawn to individuals who can match your fine mind. Being clever and magnetic, you have no trouble attracting friends and partners. You like to be open and direct in your dealings and need to know that you are building some sort of solid relationship with others. Do not let your rational approach spoil your normally positive outlook. You are likely to be very caring toward people in your circle and will do almost anything for those you love.

YOUR SPECIAL SOMEONE

You might be able to find true love and emotional security by looking for someone born on one of the following dates.

Love & friendship: Jan. 11, 13, 15, 17, 25, 26, Feb. 9, 11, 13, 15, 23, Mar. 7, 9, 11, 13, 21, Apr. 5, 7, 9, 11, 19, May 3, 5, 7, 9, 17, 31, June 1, 3, 5, 7, 15, 17, 29, July 1, 3, 5, 27, 29, 31, Aug. 1, 3, 11, 25, 27, 29, Sept. 1, 9, 23, 25, 27, Oct. 7, 21, 23, 25, Nov. 5, 19, 21, 23, Dec. 3, 17, 19, 21, 30

Beneficial: Jan. 1, 5, 20, Feb. 3, 18, Mar. 1, 16, Apr. 14, May 12, June 10, July 8, Aug. 6, Sept. 4, Oct. 2

Fatal attractions: Feb. 9, 10, 11, 12

Challenging: Jan. 6, 22, 24, Feb. 4, 20, 22, Mar. 2, 18, 20, Apr. 16, 18, May 14, 16, June 12, 14, July 10, 12, Aug. 8, 10, 31, Sept. 6, 8, 29, Oct. 4, 6, 27, Nov. 2, 4, 25, 30, Dec. 2, 23, 28

Soul mates: Jan. 6, 12, Feb. 4, 10, Mar. 2, 8, Apr. 6, May 4, June 2

August 14

♌ As you are pragmatic and hardworking, your birthday implies that your good judgment and creative mind will ensure your success and prosperity. As a Leo, you are naturally gifted and sociable, with a charming and attractive personality. Secure in your knowledge and highly intuitive, you are also receptive to your environment and happiest when active and productive.

The subinfluence of your decanate planet, Mars, adds to your vitality and enables you to achieve success. Nevertheless, you may need to overcome a tendency to be emotionally unsure or overly sensitive in order to realize your true potential.

Hardworking, honest, and direct is how others usually describe you. Although usually generous and sympathetic, you can be intolerant of ignorance or stupidity and display impatience. Since you are an independent thinker, you generally do not appreciate interference from others, which can bring out your stubborn streak.

The combination of your insight and logic is apt to lead you to positions of authority, and when it comes to communication, you can retaliate in just the right manner with your impressive speech. It is through developing trust in and receptivity to your inner voice that you gain the edge over others. With your power of resolution and determination, you like to put thought into action, while your natural curiosity inspires you to explore new territories.

When you are around the age of eight, your progressed Sun moves into Virgo, commencing a thirty-year period of increasing emphasis on practicality, order, and being more discriminating with your time and energy. Another turning point occurs at the age of thirty-eight, when your progressed Sun moves into Libra, stimulating you to develop any latent musical, artistic, or literary talents and to place more emphasis on your relationships. At the age of sixty-eight, when your progressed Sun enters Scorpio, there is another turning point that emphasizes the importance of emotional transformation and personal power.

Your Secret Self

You have high standards for yourself and want to succeed in a big way. Just remember that pure money or business success without a heart or creative element is not likely to bring you the happiness you seek. You respond to people and have a wonderful way of uplifting their spirits through your positive ideas and actions. Your strong dramatic side wants to inform as well as entertain, which makes an ideal combination for being a connector or link-up person for people from all different social groups.

You need success in order to prove your own faith in yourself. You may constantly be giving yourself challenges in order to show that you can overcome them and boost your confidence in the process. This can conquer a sense of doubt or distrust that can occasionally appear to threaten your peace of mind. Once things start moving for you, however, your strong sense of purpose ensures that nothing can stop you from achieving your tremendous potential.

Work & Vocation

Your natural dramatic gifts and sharp mind ensure that with self-discipline you can be at the forefront of your profession. You may have to be careful that an inner restlessness does not

---

FIXED STARS

Merak; Al Genubi, also called Asad Australis

PRIMARY STAR

Star's name: Merak

Degree position: 18°29'–19°34' Leo between the years 1930 and 2000

Magnitude: 2

Strength: ★★★★★★★

Orb: 2°10'

Constellation: Alpha Ursa Major

Applicable days: August 10, 11, 12, 13, 14

Star qualities: Mars

Description: a white giant star located on the side of the Great Bear

PRIMARY STAR'S INFLUENCE

Merak imparts a love of command and leadership abilities, although it may also indicate an inclination to be overly dominant. Your determination means that you are likely to achieve much in life and succeed where others may fail.

Linked to your Sun's degree, this star bestows courage, assertiveness, and hot-blooded vitality. The power of attainment that is associated with this star ensures that your life will be full of activity. Merak's influence carries opportunities and possible fame and honors.

• *Positive:* love of life, active and creative, ambition, courage

• *Negative:* hastiness, stubbornness, overstrain

See Appendix for additional fixed star readings.

stop you from fully developing your abilities. A need for variety usually points to your tendency to become bored if your work does not offer enough opportunity for change. With a natural business sense and organizational skills, you can succeed in commerce, banking, or law, or you may use your dramatic gifts in writing, music, or the theater. The caring or humanitarian side of your nature could provide you with the impetus to excel as a teacher, counselor, or social worker, or in a job that requires speaking up for others, such as union leader or politician. Alternatively, you may be drawn to the world of sport, where your ability to think big can take you to the top.

Famous people who share your birthday include actor Steve Martin, cartoonist Gary Larson, writer Danielle Steel, musician David Crosby, singer Sarah Brightman, and basketball player Magic Johnson.

Numerology

Intellectual potential, pragmatism, and determination are some of the qualities associated with the number 14 birthday. Indeed, as a number 14 individual, you frequently put your work first and judge yourself and others on the basis of career achievements. Although you need stability, the restlessness indicated by the number 14 urges you to forge ahead or take on new challenges in a constant attempt to improve your lot. This innate restlessness and constant lack of satisfaction may also inspire you to make a great many changes in your life, especially if you are not happy with your working conditions or financial status. With your perceptive mind, you respond quickly to problems and enjoy solving them. The subinfluence of the number 8 month indicates that you realize your own power and aspirations through hard work. Often practical, with a strong desire for prosperity, you have an original and innovative approach to problem solving, with new and exciting ideas that impress others.

- *Positive:* decisive actions, hardworking, lucky, creative, pragmatic, imaginative, industrious
- *Negative:* overly cautious or overly impulsive, thoughtless, stubborn

Love & Relationships

With your creativity and intelligence, you can mix business and pleasure. Friendly and sociable, you usually have many opportunities for love and romance. You may be particularly drawn to the company of those who are active and mentally stimulating. You need people who can appreciate your fast wit and sense of humor. Because of your ability to be sympathetic and understanding, others may come to you for support and advice.

YOUR SPECIAL SOMEONE

To find the partner or lover who will keep you interested and appreciate your sensitivity, you might start by looking for someone born on one of the following dates.

Love & friendship: Jan. 9, 12, 16, 25, Feb. 7, 10, 14, 23, 24, Mar. 8, 12, 22, 31, Apr. 3, 6, 10, 20, 21, 29, May 4, 8, 18, 27, June 2, 6, 16, 25, 30, July 4, 14, 23, 28, Aug. 2, 12, 21, 26, 30, Sept. 10, 19, 24, 28, Oct. 8, 17, 22, 26, Nov. 6, 15, 20, 24, 30, Dec. 4, 5, 13, 18, 22, 28

Beneficial: Jan. 2, 13, 22, 24, Feb. 11, 17, 20, 22, Mar. 9, 15, 18, 20, 28, Apr. 7, 13, 16, 18, 26, May 5, 11, 16, 18, 26, June 3, 9, 12, 14, 22, July 1, 7, 10, 12, 20, Aug. 5, 8, 10, 18, Sept. 3, 6, 8, 16, Oct. 1, 4, 6, 14, Nov. 2, 4, 12, Dec. 2, 10

Fatal attractions: Jan. 25, Feb. 11, 12, 13, 23, Mar. 21, Apr. 19, May 17, June 15, July 13, Aug. 11, Sept. 9, Oct. 7, Nov. 5, Dec. 3

Challenging: Jan. 7, 23, Feb. 5, 21, Mar. 3, 19, 29, Apr. 1, 17, 27, May 15, 25, June 13, 23, July 11, 21, 31, Aug. 9, 19, 29, Sept. 7, 17, 27, 30, Nov. 3, 13, 23, 26, Dec. 1, 11, 21, 24

Soul mates: Jan. 17. Feb. 15, Mar. 13, Apr. 11, May 9, June 7, July 5, Aug. 3, Sept. 1, Nov. 30, Dec. 28

August 15

♌ Since enthusiasm and intelligence are usually associated with your birthday, you are able to grasp information quickly. By accumulating knowledge, you can increase your assertiveness and self-confidence. As a Leo, you are easygoing and pleasant, with a youthful quality. Possessing a mind full of bright ideas, you need to channel your vitality and restless temperament through creative pursuits.

Idealistic and proud, with strong convictions, you have a natural flair for the spoken and written word. This contributes to your talent for writing or skill at teaching and lecturing. Although you rely on your own judgment, you prefer practice rather than theory, but your potential for accomplishment is enhanced if you combine both.

The subinfluence of your decanate ruler, Aries, suggests that you are ambitious and full of vigor and drive. By being responsible and taking a more reflective attitude, you are apt to be more successful. Once you have mastered your craft, you usually show others how talented and clever you really are. More often than not, you are inclined to be unconventional or progressive, with unusual interests and hobbies. If inspired, you may seek recognition through the theater, and with your personal magnetism and eagerness, you do not find it difficult to make the right impression. Although you are socially inclined and friendly, you also like to be carefree and different, and you rarely succumb to peer group pressure.

Your progressed Sun moves into Virgo for a thirty-year period as you reach the age of seven. During this period you will find it important to have practical order and efficiency in your daily life, particularly in your working environment. This continues until the age of thirty-seven, when your progressed Sun enters Libra. This turning point can stimulate you to develop any latent musical, artistic, or literary talents, and it highlights the importance of relationships. At the age of sixty-seven, you experience another turning point as your progressed Sun moves into Scorpio, emphasizing deep change, personal power, and transformation in your life.

Fixed Star

Star's name: Al Genubi, also called Asad Australis

Degree position: 19°44'–20°43' Leo between the years 1930 and 2000

Magnitude: 3

Strength: ★★★★★

Orb: 1°40'

Constellation: Epsilon Leo

Applicable days: August 12, 13, 14, 15

Star qualities: Saturn/Mars

Description: a yellow star located in the Lion's mouth

Primary Star's Influence

Al Genubi's influence imparts endurance, artistic talent, and the power of expression. This star also suggests that you possess a bold and daring personality.

Linked to your Sun's degree, Al Genubi endows determination, a need to be productive, and natural executive abilities. Your good organizational skills usually gain you positions of authority. Your need for self-expression and creativity may direct you toward the arts and more glamorous professions. This star warns that if you do not find ways to express yourself in a constructive manner, you may behave destructively.

• Positive: resilient, creative, artistic, vitality, personal magnetism

• Negative: domineering, proud, arrogant, cruel

Your Secret Self

A charismatic inner quality enables you to radiate love and positivity, emphasizing the importance of having an outlet for your self-expression. With your strong convictions and desire to be of service, you may enjoy leading some group or organization that is of use to others. Just be careful that you do not compromise too much of the idealistic side of your nature for the sake of material security. You are likely to triumph over any fears you may have about finances, which generally prove to be unfounded in the long term.

You combine in your temperament strong male and female elements, which can emphasize independence and determination as well as compassion and sensitivity. For your overall health it is vital to have these qualities in balance. With your willpower, determination, and sparkling individuality, you are a strong person who has outstanding potential for achieving good.

Work & Vocation

Your natural charm and business sense combine well to help you succeed, particularly in the world of sales, marketing, and promotion. A strong dramatic sense and love of knowledge can ensure that you excel either in the theater or in the lecture hall. You possess the ability to put your ideas across in an entertaining way, which can assist you in presentations, talks, or writing. An excellent fighter for a cause, you may be attracted to a career such as attorney or spokesperson, and if you are interested in reform, you may be drawn to a career in which you can speak up for others, such as union leader or politician. Similarly, your humanitarian instincts may lead you to counseling or social work. Whatever work you undertake, you would want the freedom to do it your own way and may prefer to be self-employed.

Famous people who share your birthday include Napoleon Bonaparte, Princess Anne, musician Oscar Peterson, cooking expert Julia Child, writer Sir Walter Scott, and mystic Sri Aurobindo.

Numerology

Versatility, enthusiasm, and restlessness are suggested by the number 15 birthday. Usually you are quick, with a charismatic personality. Your greatest assets are your strong instincts and the ability to learn quickly through combining theory and practice. On many occasions you manage to earn while learning new skills. Often you utilize your intuitive powers and are quick at recognizing opportunities when they arise. As a number 15 individual, you possess a talent for attracting money or receiving help and support from others. Carefree and resolute, you welcome the unexpected and like to take a gamble. Although you are naturally adventurous, you nevertheless need to find a real base or a home that you can call your own. The subinfluence of the number 8 month indicates that you are ambitious and determined, with a dynamic personality. With your foresight, organizational skills, and business acumen, you like to make long-lasting investments that help you to achieve prosperity and success.

• *Positive:* willing, generous, responsible, kind, cooperative, appreciative, creative ideas
• *Negative:* disruptive, irresponsible, self-centered, fear of change, loss of faith, indecision, materialistic

Love & Relationships

Sociable and warm, you can be very giving in relationships, although you also need personal freedom. You are capable of expressing a wide range of emotions, from sensitivity and caring to intense passion. A tendency to be idealistic also suggests that you may seek a partner that can inspire you and shares some of your interests. Responsibilities or burdens concerning others may also influence your relationships. Nevertheless, your charisma draws many friends and romantic opportunities and ensures your popularity.

YOUR SPECIAL SOMEONE

To find the right partner who will make you happy and keep you young at heart, you might look for someone born on one of the following dates.

Love & friendship: Jan. 2, 7, 10, 15, 17, 27, Feb. 5, 8, 15, 25, Mar. 3, 6, 13, 23, Apr. 1, 4, 11, 21, May 2, 9, 19, June 7, 17, July 5, 15, 29, 31, Aug. 3, 13, 27, 29, 31, Sept. 1, 11, 25, 27, 29, Oct. 9, 23, 25, 27, Nov. 7, 21, 23, 25, Dec. 5, 19, 21, 23

Beneficial: Jan. 3, 5, 20, 25, 27, Feb. 1, 3, 18, 23, 25, Mar. 1, 16, 21, 23, Apr. 14, 19, 21, May 12, 17, 19, June 10, 15, 17, July 8, 13, 15, Aug. 6, 11, 13, Sept. 4, 9, 11, 28, Oct. 2, 7, 9, 26, Nov. 5, 7, 24, Dec. 3, 5

Fatal attractions: Jan. 13, Feb. 11, 12, 13, Mar. 9, Apr. 7, May 5, June 3, July 1

Challenging: Jan. 16, 24, Feb. 14, 22, Mar. 12, 20, Apr. 10, 18, May 8, 16, 31, June 6, 14, 29, July 4, 12, 27, Aug. 2, 10, 25, Sept. 8, 23, Oct. 6, 21, Nov. 4, 19, Dec. 2, 17

Soul mates: Jan. 16, Feb. 14, Mar. 12, Apr. 10, May 8, June 6, July 4, 31, Aug. 2, 29, Sept. 27, Oct. 25, Nov. 23, Dec. 21

August 16

FIXED STARS

Although your Sun's degree is not linked to a fixed star, some of your other planets' degrees certainly will be. By having an astrological chart calculated, you can find the exact position of the planets on your date of birth. This will tell you which of the fixed stars listed in this book are relevant to you.

♌ Charming and friendly, with an intelligent and intuitive mind, you often conceal your discernment and astute perception. Although you can appear detached and thoughtful, you are sensitive and idealistic. As a Leo, you are self-assured and determined, with insight. This allows you to grasp ideas quickly and precisely. A pragmatic and direct approach usually contributes to your independent views and indicates that you possess persuasive speech.

The subinfluence of your decanate planet, Mars, grants vitality and adds to your mental potential. It encourages you to be more adventurous and daring and challenges the more introverted part of your nature. It may nevertheless also indicate a restless streak and hot-blooded temper. You may need to guard against worry or being too impulsive. Learn to finish what you start by practicing self-discipline to avoid becoming easily bored.

A need to receive the approval of others or the urge to shine suggests that you can enjoy being before the public. Although often serious, you can be enthusiastic and spontaneous when you find an interest that truly inspires you. Learn to trust your quick instincts and overcome a tendency to become too domineering or demanding.

From the early age of six, when your progressed Sun moves into Virgo, there commences a thirty-year period of increasing emphasis on being practical and building an orderly and efficient system for yourself, particularly in your work environment. At the age of thirty-six, when your progressed Sun moves into Libra, you experience a turning point and will start to place more importance on your relationships as well as develop any latent artistic, dramatic, or literary talent. When you are age sixty-six, your progressed Sun moves into Scorpio and highlights your personal power and a need for change or renewal. Your awareness strengthens with this trend.

Your Secret Self

You love to know what motivates others, and your ability to deal with people is a major part of your success. Much depends, therefore, on the harmony of your relationships, and you may need to strike a balance between great warmth and cool detachment. If you allow yourself to become too disappointed with others, you may be prone to despondency. However, when constructive, you can be very generous and hardworking, with a potential for extraordinary achievement.

With an innate practicality, you may find yourself as an advisor to others and are at your best when displaying modesty and compassion. As you can be financially fortunate, monetary problems can resolve themselves quickly. With a positive attitude and by tuning in to your powerful intuition you can move mountains.

Work & Vocation

Your people skills and fine intellect enable you to reach your potential in many different areas of life. Enthusiasm is a vital key to your success and is not something that you can fake. In business you will naturally be drawn to large enterprises or the media and are an excellent problem solver. Organizational and managerial abilities help you rise to positions of prominence. A flair for the dramatic, when combined with determination, can also ensure your success in show business. Whatever career you choose, you should avoid being in subservient positions, as you do not like being told what to do. Since you possess a fighting spirit, you may wish to work for worthwhile causes.

Famous people who share your birthday include singer/actress Madonna, fashion designer Katharine Hamnett, actor Timothy Hutton, T. E. Lawrence (Lawrence of Arabia), and Frank and Kathy Lee Gifford.

Numerology

The number 16 birthday suggests that you are thoughtful, sensitive, and friendly. Although analytical, you often judge life and people according to how you feel. As a number 16 personality, however, you can experience inner tensions when facing friction between a need for self-expression and responsibility to others. You may be interested in world affairs and may join international corporations or the media world. The creative ones among you have a talent for writing with sudden flashes of inspiration. With a number 16 birthday, you may need to learn how to balance between being overly confident and insecure. The subinfluence of the number 8 month indicates that although at times you are aloof or detached, you are usually practical, with a good sense of values. You like to be in a position of influence and power but need to exercise fair and just conduct. Worldly and proud, you can achieve a great deal with determination and faith.

- *Positive:* knowledgeable, responsibilities to home and family, integrity, intuitive, social, cooperative, insightful
- *Negative:* worry, never satisfied, self-promoting, opinionated, skeptical, fussy, irritable, unsympathetic

Love & Relationships

You may need to find a partner who is ambitious and naturally clever—someone you can rely on. An attraction to creative and successful people with acting skills suggests that you like glamour and socializing. Communicating your thoughts or ideas is also very important to you, as you respect knowledge and love sharing it. You may nevertheless have to guard against becoming bossy with your partners.

August 17

FIXED STARS

Although your Sun's degree is not linked to a fixed star, some of your other planets' degrees certainly will be. By having an astrological chart calculated, you can find the exact position of the planets on your date of birth. This will tell you which of the fixed stars listed in this book are relevant to you.

♌ Sociable and friendly, you are a creative Leo with a shrewd and intuitive mind. With your ability to grasp concepts very quickly, you can utilize situations to your advantage. A humanitarian with liberal and broad-minded views, you have a strong set of values. Since you can greatly benefit from self-discipline, it is important to acquire a good education or find something inspiring.

The need to express your wealth of ideas is perhaps due to the subinfluence of your decanate ruler, Aries, which suggests a necessity to be mentally active and productive. It may nevertheless indicate a restless streak and an inclination to fluctuate between being positive and creative and being worried and pessimistic. Avoid being critical and making heavy demands on yourself. You may need to guard against being too impulsive by learning to finish what you start or by practicing patience.

Although loyal and caring, you need to be less dogmatic or impetuous. In order to win the admiration you desire, you may need to show your loving nature rather than your discontent. Despite your generosity and spontaneity, emotional inhibitions can undermine your positive outlook. You need to be involved in exciting and emotionally fulfilling activities where you can express yourself dramatically.

Your progressed Sun moves into Virgo for a thirty-year period when you are age five. This emphasizes practical issues and a desire to gradually create for yourself an effective working environment. At the age of thirty-five, you reach a turning point as your progressed Sun enters Libra. This highlights your social relationships and partnerships. Your creative abilities are enhanced, and you may be drawn to develop your musical, artistic, or literary interests. After your mid-sixties, when your progressed Sun moves into Scorpio, you may wish to study the deeper meaning of life, gain greater emotional depth, and take on more challenges.

Your Secret Self

Your inner sensitivity may not be obvious from your proud exterior. Humanitarianism blends well with your sense of the dramatic, producing a need to express your ideas and creativity. Through your interest in people you can become a natural advisor to others, which can help you avoid personal dissatisfaction. You seek the security of home and family and have a strong awareness of your responsibilities. By developing your sense of values, you learn to keep a balance between being too extravagant and being too economical.

Keeping a detached viewpoint and having a positive belief system can manifest miracles in your life as well as help you overcome a possible tendency to depression or frustration. To avoid getting stuck in a comfortable rut, it may be necessary to persuade yourself to continually take on new challenges. Luckily, you respect knowledge and are usually looking for ways to improve yourself and your circumstances.

Work & Vocation

Your natural dramatic ability and ambition can help you climb up the ladder of success in the theater or entertainment world or may help you achieve in business or politics. Being a good psychologist, you enjoy working with people and can also succeed as a counselor or business advisor. Since you are a good organizer or manager, you are able to become a leader in your chosen field. Your communication skills and love of knowledge may draw you to writing, law, or education. Alternatively, your sensitivity and social conscience may attract you to healing or working for a cause.

Famous people who share your birthday include actors Robert De Niro and Sean Penn, singer Belinda Carlisle, actresses Mae West and Maureen O'Hara, race car driver Nelson Piquet, ice-skating star Robin Cousins, frontiersman Davy Crockett, and British poet laureate Ted Hughes.

Numerology

With a number 17 birthday, you are shrewd, with a reserved nature and good analytical abilities. An independent thinker, you benefit from being well educated or skillful. Usually you utilize your knowledge in a specific way in order to develop your expertise and can achieve material success or a prominent position as a specialist or researcher. Private, introspective, and detached, with a strong interest in facts and figures, you frequently present a serious and thoughtful demeanor and like to take your time. By developing your communication skills, you can discover much more about yourself from others. The subinfluence of the number 8 month indicates that although you are determined, with a good sense of values, at times your perfectionist, rigid views can undermine your progress. Avoid worry and suspicion. Since you wish to be influential and materially successful, you will need to work hard, develop sound judgment, and use your mental energies constructively.

• *Positive:* thoughtful, specialist, good planner, business sense, attracts money, individual thinker, painstaking, accurate, skilled researcher, scientific

• *Negative:* detached, lonely, stubborn, careless, moody, sensitive, narrow-minded, critical

Love & Relationships

Loving and caring, you can be a devoted partner. Being friendly and sociable, you usually have many friends and acquaintances. Your relationships play an important part in your life, and you can be very considerate of others' needs. Although very loyal and supportive of your partners, you may need to keep an emotional balance between being too dependent and being too dominant. Creative people have a positive influence on your life.

YOUR SPECIAL SOMEONE

In the search for that special someone who will bring out the best in you, look for those born on the following dates.

Love & friendship: Jan. 1, 9, 15, 26, 29, 30, Feb. 7, 13, 24, 27, 28, Mar. 11, 22, 25, 26, Apr. 3, 9, 20, 23, 24, May 7, 18, 21, 22, June 5, 16, 19, 20, July 3, 14, 17, 18, 31, Aug. 1, 12, 15, 16, 29, 31, Sept. 10, 13, 14, 27, 29, Oct. 8, 11, 12, 25, 27, Nov. 6, 9, 10, 23, 25, Dec. 4, 7, 8, 21, 23, 29

Beneficial: Jan. 1, 2, 10, 27, Feb. 8, 25, Mar. 6, 23, Apr. 4, 21, May 2, 19, 30, June 17, 28, July 15, 26, Aug. 13, 24, Sept. 11, 22, Oct. 9, 20, Nov. 7, 18, Dec. 5, 16

Fatal attractions: Feb. 11, 12, 13, 14, 15

Challenging: Jan. 17, 26, Feb. 15, 24, Mar. 13, 22, Apr. 11, 20, May 9, 18, June 7, 16, July 5, 14, Aug. 3, 12, 30, Sept. 1, 10, 28, Oct. 8, 26, 29, Nov. 6, 24, 27, Dec. 4, 22, 25

Soul mates: Jan. 21, Feb. 19, Mar. 17, Apr. 15, May 13, June 11, July 9, 29, Aug. 7, 27, Sept. 5, 25, Oct. 3, 23, Nov. 1, 21, Dec. 19

August 18

♌ Inspired and imaginative, with an active and inquisitive mind, you are a Leo with great potential. Although you are proud and dignified, with a desire to achieve success, you need to be motivated and determined to accomplish your objectives. Since you seek different experiences and can be adventurous, you are inclined to have a multitude of plans and ideas.

The subinfluence of your decanate ruler, Aries, adds courage to your personality. With your enterprising spirit, this influence also implies that you may be restless for action. Since you do not like to be in a subordinate position, you do not appreciate taking orders from others and like to make your own plans. Often you desire to take the lead or work independently, and with your good sense of structure, you also possess the ability to organize and execute projects.

Mentally quick and intelligent, you usually have an avid desire for knowledge and a need to express your thoughts and ideas. With your natural psychic gifts, you can detect others' motivations and sense hypocrisy. Since you are sensitive to your surroundings, you need to be in a positive environment, as you are aware of disharmonious and tense situations.

Your progressed Sun moves into Virgo when you are age four, commencing a thirty-year period of increasing emphasis on practical considerations and a need for order in your life. A turning point for you occurs at the age of thirty-four, when your progressed Sun moves into Libra, highlighting your awareness of relationships and stimulating you to develop any innate musical, literary, or artistic interests. After the age of sixty-four, when your progressed Sun enters Scorpio, you may seek more meaning in your life and bring on changes that can deepen your awareness.

FIXED STARS

Although your Sun's degree is not linked to a fixed star, some of your other planets' degrees certainly will be. By having an astrological chart calculated, you can find the exact position of the planets on your date of birth. This will tell you which of the fixed stars listed in this book are relevant to you.

Your Secret Self

By staying realistic and avoiding fantasy or escapism, you can rise to the challenge of disciplining your enormous mental potential. With your sensitivity and vivid imagination, occasionally it may be attractive to take the easy option. Knowledge and understanding may draw you toward spiritual or metaphysical ideas, and by nature you are friendly and communicative. With your love for debate, you have the skill to deal well with groups involved in reform or progressive movements.

You love power, particularly the power of knowledge, and respect those who have more information or wisdom than you do. You may, however, have to guard against mental power games or being manipulative when your ego becomes hooked into situations. Nevertheless, you have the ability to inspire others with your idealism, determination, and vision.

Work & Vocation

With your desire for the limelight, you could successfully pursue a theatrical career as an actor, dancer, or director. Similarly, your ambition could draw you to politics, law, or business, where you are likely to want a leading position. Not liking to take orders may incline you to become self-employed. A practical aptitude together with an organizational flair could suggest that you can achieve success in manufacturing, merchandising, or banking. An ability to relate to people indicates that you can excel in careers dealing with the public, especially education and social welfare. Alternatively, your sensitivity, special insight into psychology, and natural healing ability may draw you toward the medical or alternative health professions.

Famous people who share your birthday include actors Patrick Swayze, Robert Redford, and Martin Mull, director Roman Polanski, former U.S. secretary of defense Caspar Weinberger, and actress Shelley Winters.

Numerology

Determination, assertiveness, and ambition are some of the attributes associated with the number 18 birthday. Active, with a need for challenges, you like to keep busy and are frequently involved in some enterprise. Capable, hardworking, and responsible, you rise to positions of authority. Alternatively, your strong business sense and organizational skills lead you to the world of commerce. Since you may suffer from overwork, learn how to relax or slow down from time to time. As a number 18 personality, you may use your power to heal others, give sound advice, or solve other people's problems. The subinfluence of the number 8 month indicates that you are mentally quick and usually highly intuitive about people and situations. Although you can be restless and unsettled, you are efficient at your work and can execute plans with determination. You want recognition and are often in conflict between your idealistic beliefs and material inclinations.

• *Positive:* progressive, assertive, intuitive, courageous, resolute, healing ability, efficient, advisory skills

• *Negative:* uncontrolled emotions, lazy, lack of order, selfishness, callousness, difficulty completing work or projects, deceitful

Love & Relationships

Proud and dramatic, you have a charismatic personality that attracts others to you. In relationships it is very important for you to be honest and direct. With your sensitivity, you can be very affectionate and tender, but guard against escapism, whether through overindulgence or avoidance. With your warmth and sound advice, you have no problem attracting others. In your major relationships, it is important that you find someone who can offer you mental stimulation and with whom you can share your interests and values.

YOUR SPECIAL SOMEONE

You might find emotional fulfillment and that special someone among those born on the following days.

Love & friendship: Jan. 10, 13, 20, 25, 30, Feb. 8, 11, 18, 28, Mar. 6, 9, 16, 26, 30, Apr. 4, 7, 14, 24, 30, May 2, 5, 12, 22, June 3, 10, 20, July 1, 8, 18, Aug. 6, 16, 20, 30, Sept. 4, 14, 28, 30, Oct. 2, 12, 26, 28, 30, Nov. 10, 24, 26, 28, Dec. 8, 22, 24, 26

Beneficial: Jan. 12, 16, 17, 28, Feb. 10, 14, 15, 26, Mar. 8, 12, 13, 24, Apr. 6, 10, 11, 22, May 4, 8, 9, 20, 29, June 2, 6, 7, 18, 27, July 4, 5, 16, 25, Aug. 2, 3, 14, 23, Sept. 1, 12, 21, Oct. 10, 19, Nov. 8, 17, Dec. 6, 15

Fatal attractions: Feb. 14, 15, 16, Mar. 31, Apr. 29, May 27, June 25, July 23, Aug. 21, Sept. 19, Oct. 17, Nov. 15, Dec. 17

Challenging: Jan. 6, 18, 22, 27, Feb. 4, 16, 20, 25, Mar. 2, 14, 18, 23, Apr. 12, 16, 21, May 10, 14, 19, June 8, 12, 17, July 6, 10, 15, Aug. 4, 8, 13, Sept. 2, 6, 11, Oct. 4, 9, Nov. 2, 7, Dec. 5

Soul mates: Mar. 28, Apr. 26, May 24, June 22, July 20, Aug. 18, Sept. 16, Oct. 14, Nov. 12, Dec. 10

August 19

FIXED STARS

Alphard; Adhafera, also called Al-Serpha; Al Jabhah, also called the Forehead

PRIMARY STAR

Star's name: Alphard

Degree position: 26°17'–27°8' Leo, between the years 1930–2000

Magnitude: 2

Strength: ★★★★★★★

Orb: 2°10'

Constellation: Alpha Hydrae

Applicable days: August 19, 20, 21, 22

Star qualities: varied interpretations: Saturn/Venus and Sun/Jupiter

Description: a giant orange star located in the neck of the Hydra

PRIMARY STAR'S INFLUENCE

Alphard's influence bestows natural wisdom and a deep understanding of human nature. You appreciate the arts and have keen ambitions and a sensitive nature. Alphard warns against over-indulgence, intemperance, and lack of self-control. This star suggests turbulence and at times upheaval. Alphard also warns against all forms of poisoning and infections.

Linked to your Sun's degree, this star bestows executive abilities, positions of authority, and great opportunities for advancement. You tend to seek prominent positions and to be in the limelight. Nevertheless, you must always be fair and just, otherwise others will push you out. This applies also to work and relationships, where jealousy can creep in, although often you attempt to hide it.

♌ Dynamic and bright, with a gregarious personality, you need to shine and be noticed. As a Leo, you are also proud and self-confident, with a creative mind and a desire for self-expression.

The subinfluence of your decanate ruler, Aries, provides an added boost to your already energetic nature and suggests that you act with great assurance. Usually you seek a central role in situations and often take the lead. Mars's influence implies that you are enterprising and spontaneous, with an inclination to speculate, but should avoid get-rich-quick schemes. Since you like to have things your own way, you may need to develop a less dominant or egoistic character.

Although you are quick at assessing situations, you may need to overcome a tendency to overreact, become frustrated, or worry too much about money. Clever and shrewd, with a good mental potential, you like to keep yourself occupied and well informed. A mixture of cynicism and innocence indicates that you need to take responsibility for developing your fine mind and intuition. You are likely to possess a youthful quality, although work usually plays a prominent role in your life, especially as you get older. No matter what difficult situations you encounter in life, deep down you know that you possess the power to triumph over adversity.

When you are at the early age of three, your progressed Sun enters Virgo for a thirty-year period. This emphasizes the growing importance of creating a practical and orderly framework for yourself and accents the importance of service and paying attention to detail. When your progressed Sun moves into Libra, as you reach the age of thirty-three, there is a turning point in your life. At this time your relationships start to become more important and you may develop new diplomatic, social, or creative skills. At the age of sixty-three, when your progressed Sun moves into Scorpio, you may desire more emotional depth, intensity, and transformation.

Your Secret Self

Inspired by knowledge and wisdom, you need to stay positive and develop patience and tolerance. This helps you to keep your restless and active mind occupied and constructive. Quick and assertive, you have the ability to present new ideas to others and influence them with your thinking. Since you are a good evaluator, you are likely to work extremely hard in order to make a project you believe in a reality.

Strong willpower and determination help you accomplish in the material world, but to achieve total fulfillment, it is necessary to balance these forces with your intuitive insight. This indicates that you need to learn how to listen to the wisdom of your inner voice. When you combine your fine mind, courage, and originality, you can receive brilliant inspiration.

Work & Vocation

Highly ambitious, you can present a friendly and confident front. You possess a mental vitality that is good for debates and can win you arguments. This usually can help you prosper in law or politics. Similarly, you may prefer a career in sales or as an agent. As well as being analytical, you possibly possess technical skills that can aid you in your career. Your strong dramatic sense may attract you to the theater or entertainment world, but whatever you do, you will probably want to be in charge or direct the action. Alternatively, being so determined and businesslike, you may decide to work for yourself.

Famous people who share your birthday include President Bill Clinton, fashion designer Coco Chanel, philosopher P. D. Ouspensky, tycoon Malcolm Forbes, inventor Orville Wright, drummer Ginger Baker, and actress Jill St. John.

Numerology

Sunny, ambitious, and humanitarian are some of the ways people describe those with the number 19 birthday. Decisive and resourceful, you possess depth of vision, but the dreamer side of your nature is compassionate, idealistic, and creative. Although you are sensitive, the need to be someone may be the very thing that pushes you to be dramatic and claim center stage. Often there is a strong desire to establish an individual identity. To do so, you may first need to overcome the influence of peer group pressure. To others you may appear confident, resilient, and resourceful, but inner tensions may cause emotional ups and downs. Artistic and charismatic, you will find that the world is there for you to explore. The subinfluence of the number 8 month indicates that you possess stamina and vitality. Astute and determined, you rise to positions of authority and influence. Alternatively, your business and executive skills lead you to the world of commerce.

• *Positive:* dynamic, centered, creative, leader, lucky, progressive, optimistic, strong convictions, competitive, independent, gregarious

• *Negative:* self-centered, depressive, worry, fear of rejection, ups and downs, materialistic, egotistical, impatient

YOUR SPECIAL SOMEONE

You may be more likely to make a serious commitment with someone born on one of the following dates.

Love & friendship: Jan. 11, 21, 28, 31, Feb. 9, 19, 26, 29, Mar. 17, 24, 27, Apr. 5, 15, 22, 25, May 13, 20, 23, June 1, 11, 18, 21, July 9, 16, 19, Aug. 7, 14, 17, 31, Sept. 5, 12, 15, 29, Oct. 3, 10, 13, 27, 29, 31, Nov. 1, 8, 11, 25, 27, 29, Dec. 6, 9, 23, 25, 27

Beneficial: Jan. 9, 12, 18, 24, 29, Feb. 7, 10, 16, 22, 27, Mar. 5, 8, 14, 20, 25, Apr. 3, 6, 12, 18, 23, May 1, 10, 16, 21, 31, June 2, 8, 14, 19, 29, July 6, 12, 17, 27, Aug. 4, 10, 15, 25, Sept. 2, 8, 13, 23, Oct. 6, 11, 21, Nov. 4, 9, 19, Dec. 2, 7, 17

Fatal attractions: Jan. 3, Feb. 1, 15, 16, 17, Apr. 30, May 28, June 26, July 24, Aug. 22, Sep. 20, Oct. 18, Nov. 16, Dec. 14

Challenging: Jan. 7, 8, 19, 28, Feb. 5, 6, 17, 26, Mar. 4, 3, 15, 24, Apr. 1, 2, 13, 22, May 11, 20, June 9, 18, July 7, 16, Aug. 5, 14, Sept. 3, 12, Oct. 1, 10, Nov. 8, Dec. 6

Soul mates: Jan. 3, 19, Feb. 1, 17, Mar. 15, Apr. 13, May 11, June 9, July 7, Aug. 5, Sept. 3, Oct. 1

Love & Relationships

Assured and self-motivated, you can be understanding and considerate. Socially inclined, you have an ability to attract others that means you can always find friends and admirers. You are liable to be particularly interested in hardworking and intellectually stimulating people. Highly intuitive, you can sense what others are thinking or feeling; however, you need time to develop and build a trusting long-term relationship. Once committed, you can be a generous and kind partner.

August 20

FIXED STARS

Alphard; Adhafera, also called Al-Serpha; Al Jabhah, also called the Forehead

PRIMARY STAR

Star's name: Alphard

Degree position: 26°17'–27°8' Leo between the years 1930 and 2000

Magnitude: 2

Strength: ★★★★★★★

Orb: 2°10'

Constellation: Alpha Hydrae

Applicable days: August 19, 20, 21, 22

Star qualities: varied interpretations: Saturn/Venus and Sun/Jupiter

Description: a giant orange star located in the neck of the Hydra

PRIMARY STAR'S INFLUENCE

Alphard's influence bestows natural wisdom and a deep understanding of human nature. You appreciate the arts and have keen ambitions and a sensitive nature. Alphard warns against over-indulgence, intemperance, and a lack of self-control. This star suggests turbulence and at times upheaval. Alphard also warns against all forms of poisoning and infections.

Linked to your Sun's degree, this star bestows executive abilities, positions of authority, and great opportunities for advancement. You tend to seek prominent positions and to be in the limelight. Nevertheless, you must always be fair and just, otherwise others will push you out. This applies also to work and relationships, where jealousy can

♌ Friendly, charming, and ambitious, with a proud nature, you are a Leo who can create harmony and peace with your natural flair for people and social affairs. Intuitive and practical, you are able to blend your aspirations and exceptionally perceptive mind, but you need motivation, since you are prone to a love of ease and material comforts.

Luckily, the subinfluence of your decanate ruler, Aries, suggests that when you are goal-oriented, you possess energy and drive, especially in the pursuit of prestige and money. This also implies that you are willing to work hard in order to achieve positions of influence or success.

Although you are perceptive and responsible, at times you are inclined to worry about doing less than is expected of you, and you need recognition for your efforts. Nevertheless, you know how to mix business and pleasure and make others feel at ease. Since you know the value of things, you manage to overcome obstacles through determination and perseverance.

Your love for knowledge and the realization that it empowers you suggest that you like to share your ideas or information. With your natural sense for the dramatic, you can usually inspire others with your unique vision. At times a conflict between idealism and materialism suggests that you may need to develop a philosophy that can provide you with a clear path.

Until you reach the age of thirty-one, your progressed Sun is in Virgo, emphasizing the importance of practicality and order in your daily life. You may find yourself continually analyzing things in order to improve them. As your progressed Sun enters Libra when you are age thirty-two, there is a turning point for you that will highlight the growing importance of relationships, creativity, and balance. At the age of sixty-two, when your progressed Sun enters Scorpio, you are likely to direct your attention to the deeper and more transformative aspects of your psyche and achieve more personal power.

Your Secret Self

Your determination and a need to be in control suggest that you enjoy power. If used constructively, this can help you achieve in a dynamic way, but you may have to guard against a trace of ruthlessness or manipulation. Hardworking, with a natural business sense, you are able to commercialize your talents. Although independent, you realize the importance of working cooperatively with others.

At times you can be resolute, painstaking, and methodical, and at others you may feel a lack of purpose and stamina, so it may be important to keep a constructive balance between work and play in your life. Occasionally you may become anxious, and any fears you have regarding financial matters generally prove to be unfounded. Fortunately, you possess endurance and natural healing ability, so that even if things become very difficult, you have the capacity to rise above and triumph over adversity.

Work & Vocation

Clever and determined, you are most likely to succeed in careers that make the most of your mental potential. A flair for the dramatic and a need for self-expression may draw you to writing or the entertainment world. Similarly, your fine mind may be ideal in careers such as teaching, the media, and publishing. In business, a need to be in control suggests that you are highly independent and would do well working for yourself. Being a natural diplomat, you also may be attracted to politics or work involving public relations. This birthdate often indicates artistic or musical talent or philanthropic inclinations.

Famous people who share your birthday include former Indian prime minister Rajiv Gandhi, musician Isaac Hayes, singers Robert Plant and Jim Reeves, TV journalist Connie Chung, and former U.S. representative William Gray III.

Numerology

As a number 20 individual, you are intuitive, sensitive, adaptable, and understanding, and often see yourself as a part of a larger group. Usually you enjoy cooperative activities where you can interact, share experiences, or learn from others. Charming and gracious, you develop diplomatic and social skills and can move in different social circles with ease. You may, however, need to develop your confidence or overcome a tendency to be easily hurt by the actions and criticism of others or to be overly dependent. You are a master at creating a congenial and harmonious atmosphere. The subinfluence of the number 8 month suggests that you are pragmatic and determined, though an inner conflict between wanting to take the lead and wanting to be a part of a team is also indicated. Often you are ambitious, direct, and enterprising. Usually active and energetic, you courageously take on life's challenges. Among your many attributes are strong conviction, resourcefulness, and good judgment.

• *Positive:* good partnerships, gentle, tactful, receptive, intuitive, considerate, harmonious, agreeable, amicable, ambassador of goodwill

• *Negative:* suspicious, lack of confidence, subservient, timid, oversensitive, selfish, crafty

Love & Relationships

Intelligent and thoughtful, you can be understanding and stimulating company. Although very dramatic in your love life, you have a strong desire to keep the peace and create harmonious relationships. You may have to be aware of compromising yourself in the process and playing the martyr. Alternatively, you can also become too dominating, and therefore it may be important to establish a balance of power. Nevertheless, you are willing to give generously of your love and affection, and with your wonderful social skills, you can be charming and charismatic.

creep in, although often you attempt to hide it.

• *Positive:* confidence, can make a name for yourself, fame or notoriety

• *Negative:* legal entanglement and disputes, loss of self control, jealousy

See Appendix for additional fixed star readings.

YOUR SPECIAL SOMEONE

You might find a partner who will understand your sensitivity and need for love among those born on the following dates.

Love & friendship: Jan. 8, 12, 18, 22, Feb. 16, 20, Mar. 14, 18, 28, Apr. 6, 12, 16, 26, May 10, 14, 24, June 2, 8, 12, 22, July 6, 10, 20, 29, Aug. 4, 8, 18, 27, 30, Sept. 2, 6, 16, 25, 28, Oct. 4, 14, 23, 26, 30, Nov. 2, 12, 21, 24, 28, Dec. 10, 19, 22, 26, 28

Beneficial: Jan. 6, 10, 25, 30, Feb. 4, 8, 23, 28, Mar. 2, 6, 21, 26, Apr. 4, 19, 24, May 2, 17, 22, June 15, 20, 30, July 13, 18, 28, Aug. 11, 16, 26, Sept. 9, 14, 24, Oct. 7, 12, 22, Nov. 5, 10, 20, Dec. 3, 8, 18

Fatal attractions: Feb. 16, 17, 18, May 29, June 27, July 25, Aug. 23, Sept. 21, Oct. 19, Nov. 17, Dec. 15

Challenging: Jan. 13, 29, 31, Feb. 11, 27, 29, Mar. 9, 25, 27, Apr. 7, 23, 25, May 5, 21, 23, June 3, 19, 21, July 1, 17, 19, Aug. 15, 17, Sept. 13, 15, Oct. 11, 13, Nov. 9, 11, Dec. 7, 9

Soul mates: Jan. 6, 25, Feb. 4, 23, Mar. 2, 21, Apr. 19, May 17, June 15, July 13, Aug. 11, Sept. 9, Oct. 7, Nov. 5, Dec. 3

August 21

♌ Eager to achieve and action-oriented, you are a dynamic and versatile Leo with an ambitious nature and strong instincts. Usually proud and mentally quick, you are curious and determined to get your own way. Your optimistic outlook and spirit of enterprise urge you to live life to the fullest. This enthusiasm also suggests that you need to express your individuality in a creative way.

Although the subinfluence of your decanate ruler, Aries, adds vitality and drive to your personality, it also implies that you can act hastily or become bored easily. You may need to avoid being impulsive and initiating projects without planning in advance. The great potential indicated by your birthday also implies that you need to positively channel your energies to overcome your tendency to be dissatisfied.

You usually need constant mental stimulation and can entertain others with your quick wit and lively repartee. With your persuasive speech and sense of the dramatic, you can usually get your way by enchanting others. You do not suffer fools easily, however, and at times you can be too outspoken, selfish, or arrogant. Although you are multitalented and enjoy being active, you can gain from developing one particular skill and are likely to find great advantages through education and learning.

At the beginning of your life your progressed Sun moves into the sign of Virgo. Over the next thirty years you are apt to be influenced by this sign's qualities of practicality, criticism, and perfectionism. You may gradually become interested in being more efficient in your work environment. At the age of thirty-one you reach a turning point as your progressed Sun enters Libra. This brings a growing awareness of the importance of your relationships. Your creative abilities are enhanced, and you may be drawn to develop latent musical, artistic, or literary interests. When you reach the age of sixty-one, your progressed Sun enters Scorpio to highlight issues of personal power and transformation. This influence can also deepen your awareness and feelings.

Your Secret Self

Although your emotional sensitivity can make you very intuitive, it can also sometimes pull you in different directions. One part of you wants new and exciting things, and the other wants security and stability. If not constructively channeled, this can make you restless, unsettled, or prone to escapist tendencies. By continually having a positive plan for something new and uplifting, you avoid becoming cynical or rebellious. Pursuing your ideals and desire for truth stimulates you to be generous, compassionate, and humanitarian.

Frank and honest, you expect the same from others, but although you can be loving and caring, you may have to guard against a tendency to sarcasm. Travel and higher education can be excellent avenues for you to discover the more adventurous side of your nature. Since you are endowed with charm and spontaneity, you may also like to explore the hidden artistic or creative talents that are associated with your birthday.

Work & Vocation

As you assimilate knowledge very quickly on any subject that holds your interest, you may need variety to keep you continually challenged. Your lively intellect may draw you to a career

---

FIXED STARS

Regulus, also called the Lion's Heart; Alphard; Adhafera, also called Al-Serpha; Al Jabhah, also called the Forehead

PRIMARY STAR

Star's name: Regulus, also called the Lion's Heart

Degree position: 28°51'–29°48' Leo between the years 1930 and 2000

Magnitude: 1

Strength: ★★★★★★★★★

Orb: 2°30'

Constellation: Alpha Leonis

Applicable days: August 21, 22, 23, 24, 25, 26

Star qualities: Mars/Jupiter

Description: a brilliant white and blue triple star located on the body of the Lion

PRIMARY STAR'S INFLUENCE

Regulus is a royal star that takes a leading role among a nearly infinite cast of stars. Regulus imparts nobility, high honors, great charisma, and the power to project dignified personality. This star bestows a natural ability to make quick decisions and cope with demanding situations. It also imparts a desire for power and an ability to lead and command others. You have strong willpower and a love of enterprise, which often lead to a desire for freedom and independence. Regulus warns that these great benefits are not necessarily long-lasting.

in education, writing, or publishing. Ideally, you should be in an occupation that utilizes your excellent people skills, and if this involves foreign countries or change, then so much the better. Alternatively, your desire for self-expression can lead you to the art, music, or entertainment world, and sport can also be a positive outlet for your need for action.

Famous people who share your birthday include Princess Margaret, jazz pianist Count Basie, illustrator Aubrey Beardsley, singer Kenny Rogers, and basketball player Wilt Chamberlain.

Numerology

Dynamic drive and an outgoing personality are usually present in those with a number 21 birthday. Socially inclined, you have many interests and contacts and are generally fortunate. Usually you show others your friendly and gregarious personality. Intuitive, with an independent spirit, you are highly inventive and original. With a number 21 birthday, you can be fun-loving, magnetic, and creative, with social charm. Alternatively, you can be shy and reserved, with a need to develop assertiveness, especially in close relationships. In life you often have many opportunities and achieve success with other people. Although you can be inclined toward cooperative relationships or marriage, you always want to be acknowledged for your talents and abilities. The subinfluence of the number 8 month indicates that you are mentally restless, with strong instincts and willpower. Usually you are highly charged and enjoy vitality, but must avoid becoming overly anxious or impractical. Although you can learn quickly and adapt easily to new situations, you can also be inflexible and willful.

- *Positive:* inspiration, creativity, love unions, long-lasting relationships
- *Negative:* dependency, nervous, lack of vision, disappointment, worry

Love & Relationships

Witty and entertaining, you have a bright personality. Being friendly, you are a good mixer and inclined to have an active social life. You can be an excellent host and stimulating company. Drawn toward independent and successful people, when in a relationship you usually need to be free and self-reliant. One side of your love nature is very dramatic and loving, yet another may be secretive or suspicious, though you are liable to be very protective of your family or those in your care.

Linked to your Sun's degree, this star imparts ambition, power, and authority, and opportunities to rise to high positions in government and large corporations. If you do not have a position of prominence, you probably have influential friends. This star suggests that you should be kind to others on your way up, as you are likely to meet them on your way down.

- *Positive:* high-spirited, frankness, courage, honor and riches, rise to prominent positions, authority
- *Negative:* stubborn, unruly, domineering, greatness but also great failures (especially through dishonesty), fleeting success and fame

See Appendix for additional fixed star readings.

YOUR SPECIAL SOMEONE

You might find greater stability in love among people born on the following dates.

Love & friendship: Jan. 4, 13, 19, 23, Feb. 2, 11, 17, 21, Mar. 9, 15, 19, 28, 29, 30, Apr. 7, 13, 17, 26, 27, May 5, 11, 15, 24, 25, 26, June 3, 9, 13, 22, 23, 24, July 1, 7, 11, 20, 21, 22, Aug. 5, 9, 18, 19, 20, Sept. 3, 7, 16, 17, 18, Oct. 1, 5, 14, 15, 16, 29, 31, Nov. 3, 12, 13, 14, 27, 29, Dec. 1, 10, 11, 12, 25, 27, 29

Beneficial: Jan. 7, 15, 20, 31, Feb. 5, 13, 18, 29, Mar. 3, 11, 16, 27, Apr. 1, 9, 14, 25, May 7, 12, 23, June 5, 10, 21, July 3, 8, 19, Aug. 1, 6, 17, 30, Sept. 4, 15, 28, Oct. 2, 13, 26, Nov. 11, 24, Dec. 9, 22

Fatal attractions: Feb. 16, 17, 18, 19

Challenging: Jan. 6, 9, 14, 30, Feb. 4, 7, 12, 28, Mar. 2, 5, 10, 26, Apr. 3, 8, 24, May 1, 6, 22, June 4, 20, July 2, 18, Aug. 16, Sept. 14, Oct. 12, Nov. 10, Dec. 8

Soul mates: Apr. 30, May 28, June 26, July 24, Aug. 22, Sept. 20, Oct. 18, 30, Nov. 16, 28, Dec. 14, 26

August 22

♌ Being born on the cusp of Leo and Virgo, you are a creative thinker with a pragmatic approach. You often reveal a remarkable power of determination and a love of enterprise. Ambitious and proud, with a sense of honor, you know how to make good use of the knowledge at your disposal. Since you have the power to concentrate upon a particular project and act quickly and decisively, you are a capable organizer with a resolute mind.

The subinfluence of your decanate ruler, Aries, suggests that you enjoy living an active life. Daring and courageous, you have a dynamic personality and often appear forward and assertive. Your mind is full of ideas, and you are keen to realize your thoughts and plans. Although you are usually successful in your enterprises and appear conservative to others, you may need to overcome a tendency to be restless or impatient. You may have to avoid being stubborn by learning to balance your need for independence or freedom with a certain rebelliousness, especially in matters of authority.

Happier working than wasting your energy in the pursuit of pleasure, you need mental pursuits to keep you from being bored. Since you enjoy expanding your knowledge, education often proves beneficial, and you can achieve success through higher learning or self-study. Although you possess a strong materialistic streak, your idealistic inclinations suggest that you are a humanitarian who can campaign for a cause or an idea with great enthusiasm.

In the first year of your life your progressed Sun moves into the sign of Virgo. Over the next thirty years you are likely to be influenced by this sign's qualities of practical order and system. At the age of thirty you reach a turning point as your progressed Sun enters Libra. This brings a growing awareness of the importance of all your relationships. Your creative abilities are enhanced, and you may be drawn to develop latent musical, artistic, or literary interests as well as widen your social circle. There is another turning point when you are age sixty, as your progressed Sun moves into Scorpio, highlighting your increasing need for personal power and transformation. Your awareness usually increases due to this Sun progression.

Your Secret Self

Some of your challenges may involve sacrifice, selflessness, and humility. You have a strong awareness of your responsibilities, realizing that ultimately your peace of mind comes from working to create harmony in your environment. This may involve duties in the home or being a protector or advisor for others. With your strong views, this may also involve fighting for a cause.

Through your affection and forgiveness of others' faults, you can overcome many difficulties. You may, however, have to guard against being critical, domineering, or interfering. By learning to center yourself and stay calm or serene, you are able to handle possible restlessness. Alternatively, you may channel any dissatisfaction into seeking wisdom or travel. Although practical, you possess an inner emotional sensitivity, which may find fulfillment in the achievement of your high ideals.

Work & Vocation

You have the ability to lead and are a good planner and organizer. If in business, you may well be happier working for yourself; although independent, you may find that partnerships or

FIXED STARS

Regulus, also called the Lion's Heart; Alphard; Adhafera, also called Al-Serpha; Al Jabhah, also called the Forehead; Phecda, also called Phachd

PRIMARY STAR

Star's name: Regulus, also called the Lion's Heart

Degree position: 28°51'–29°48' Leo between the years 1930 and 2000

Magnitude: 1

Strength: ★★★★★★★★★

Orb: 2°30'

Constellation: Alpha Leonis

Applicable days: August 21, 22, 23, 24, 25, 26

Star qualities: Mars/Jupiter

Description: a brilliant white and blue triple star located on the body of the Lion

PRIMARY STAR'S INFLUENCE

Regulus is a royal star that takes a leading role among a nearly infinite cast of stars. Regulus imparts nobility, high honors, great charisma, and the power to project dignified personality. This star bestows a natural ability to make quick decisions and cope with demanding situations. It also imparts a desire for power and an ability to lead and command others. You have strong willpower and a love of enterprise, which often lead to a desire for freedom and independence. Regulus warns that these great benefits are not necessarily long-lasting.

team efforts could be very productive for you. Always full of ideas and with excellent people skills, you are highly likely to succeed in business, especially sales, promotion, or advertising. You may be drawn to professions that use your fine mind, such as education, writing, or law. Being gifted and dramatic, you can also become outstanding in the world of entertainment or music.

Famous people who share your birthday include composer Claude Debussy, musician John Lee Hooker, actress Valerie Harper, writers Ray Bradbury and Dorothy Parker, baseball player Carl Yastrzemski, football coach Bill Parcells, and U.S. general Norman Schwartzkopf.

Numerology

As a number 22 individual, you are a proud, practical, and highly intuitive person. This is a master number and can vibrate both as number 22 and as number 4. Often honest and hardworking, with natural leadership abilities, you have a charismatic personality and a deep understanding of people and what motivates them. Although undemonstrative, you often show a caring, protective concern for the welfare of others, yet you never lose sight of your pragmatic or realistic stand. Usually cultured and worldly, you have many friends and admirers. The more competitive among you achieve success and good fortune with help and encouragement from others. Many born on this date have strong links with brothers or sisters and can be protective and supportive of them. The subinfluence of the number 8 month indicates that you are reliable and efficient, with polished common sense. Since you are perceptive and imaginative, you enjoy solving problems and at times amaze others by producing simple solutions to difficult problems.

• *Positive:* universal, director, highly intuitive, pragmatic, practical, dexterous, skillful, builder, good organizer, realist, problem solver, achiever

• *Negative:* get-rich-quick schemes, nervous, bossy, materialistic, lack of vision, lazy, self-promoting

Love & Relationships

Your friendly and charismatic personality draws many people toward you and enhances your social life. In your close personal relationships you may sometimes find it difficult to express love, and you may be drawn to unusual individuals. Usually strong and independent, you can also be warm and protective of those you care for. You need someone intelligent who does not let you dominate him or her but at the same time keeps you feeling youthful and playful.

Linked to your Sun's degree, this star imparts ambition, power, authority, and opportunities to rise to a high position in government or large corporations. If you do not have a position of prominence, you probably have influential friends. This star suggests that you should be kind to others on your way up, as you are likely to meet them on your way down.

• *Positive:* high-spirited, frankness, courage, honor and riches, rise to prominent positions, authority

• *Negative:* stubborn, unruly, domineering, greatness but also great failures (especially through dishonesty), fleeting success and fame

See Appendix for additional fixed star readings.

YOUR SPECIAL SOMEONE

Your chances for happiness and love are better with someone born on one of the following dates.

Love & friendship: Jan. 3, 4, 14, 20, 24, 25, Feb. 2, 12, 14, 15, 16, 18, 22, Mar. 10, 16, 20, 29, 30, Apr. 8, 14, 18, 27, 28, May 6, 12, 16, 25, 26, 31, June 4, 10, 14, 23, 24, 29, July 2, 8, 12, 21, 22, 27, Aug. 6, 10, 19, 20, 25, Sept. 4, 8, 17, 18, 23, Oct. 2, 6, 15, 16, 21, 30, Nov. 4, 13, 14, 19, 28, 30, Dec. 2, 11, 12, 17, 26, 28, 30

Beneficial: Jan. 4, 8, 21, Feb. 2, 6, 19, Mar. 4, 17, 28, Apr. 2, 15, 16, May 13, 24, June 11, 22, July 9, 20, Aug. 7, 18, 31, Sept. 5, 16, 29, Oct. 3, 14, 27, Nov. 1, 12, 25, Dec. 10, 23

Fatal attractions: Jan. 3, Feb. 1, May 31, June 29, July 27, Aug. 25, Sept. 23, Oct. 21, Nov. 19, Dec. 17

Challenging: Jan. 7, 10, 15, 31, Feb. 5, 8, 13, 29, Mar. 3, 6, 11, 27, Apr. 1, 4, 9, 25, May 2, 7, 23, June 5, 21, July 3, 19, Aug. 1, 17, Sept. 15, Oct. 13, Nov. 11, Dec. 9

Soul mates: Mar. 31, Apr. 29, May 27, June 25, July 23, Aug. 21, Sept. 19, Oct. 17, 29, Nov. 15, 27, Dec. 13, 25

Virgo

August 23–September 22

August 23

♍ Being born on the cusp, you have the advantage of possessing both the friendly, warm, and sociable qualities of Leo and the intellectual sharpness of Virgo. Enterprising and hardworking, you can take on difficult and challenging projects, and once decided on a course of action you can be very determined. The combination of your astute observations and your need to express yourself can usually ensure your popularity. A tendency to impatience, indecision, and worry, however, may be one of the primary obstacles to your achievement.

With the added influence of your decanate ruler, Virgo, you can be shrewd and practical, with a desire for knowledge. Articulate and precise, you deliberate and analyze all the details before making a decision. Still, it may be necessary to avoid going over and over the same issues or becoming too critical of yourself and others. A talent for clear communication can be a particular asset in your climb to success.

In order to avoid frustration or irritability, it is important to discipline yourself and complete what you start, or an innate restlessness may cause you to diffuse your energies in too many directions. As you have a warm heart and a way with people, you find your relationships particularly important. Possessing the ability to be charming when necessary, you can draw others to you with your understanding and interesting personality.

After the age of thirty, when your progressed Sun moves into Libra, there is an increased emphasis on the needs of others and on relationships. Your sense of harmony and balance is likely to be enhanced, with the possibility of exploring artistic or creative outlets. This continues until the beginning of your sixties, when your progressed Sun enters Scorpio. As a turning point, this highlights the growing importance of touching deeper and more subtle aspects of your psyche and becoming more sensitive.

FIXED STARS

Regulus, also called the Lion's Heart; Phecda, also called Phachd

PRIMARY STAR

Star's name: Regulus, also called the Lion's Heart

Degree position: 28°51'–29°48' Leo between the years 1930 and 2000

Magnitude: 1

Strength: ★★★★★★★★

Orb: 2°30'

Constellation: Alpha Leonis (Leo)

Applicable days: August 21, 22, 23, 24, 25, 26

Star qualities: Mars/Jupiter

Description: a brilliant white and blue triple star located on the body of the Lion

PRIMARY STAR'S INFLUENCE

Regulus is a royal star that takes a leading role among a nearly infinite cast of stars. Regulus imparts nobility, high honors, great charisma, and the power to project a dignified personality. This star bestows a natural ability to make quick decisions and cope with demanding situations. It also imparts a desire for power and an ability to lead and command others. You have strong willpower and a love of enterprise, which often lead to a desire for freedom and independence. Regulus warns that these great benefits are not necessarily long-lasting.

Linked to your Sun's degree, this star imparts ambition, power, authority, and opportunities to rise to a high posi-

Your Secret Self

Possessing an inner nobility and pride, you do not like others to see you fail. As you may not persevere when bored, it is necessary for you to find things that are stimulating and challenging. It may be better to make your decisions carefully rather than act hastily and abandon projects later. Fortunately, with your ability to evaluate people quickly, you are a good psychologist who may rise to positions of authority because people respect your opinion.

Money may be a major factor in your uncertainty, which is not helped by a possible extravagant streak. Although at times you can be extremely successful, changeable circumstances in your finances suggest that you would be wise to save or plan. Travel or change are likely to play an important part in your life, so do not be afraid to branch out if promising prospects arise outside your usual routine. Although at times it may be necessary for you to have faith in yourself and build up your confidence, your natural business sense will always be a protection for you.

Work & Vocation

Your potential to be multitalented can ensure you success in many professions, but it is important to avoid monotonous occupations. With your communication skills and flair for dealing with people, you should excel in careers such as teaching, sales, writing, publishing, or the entertainment world. Alternatively, an ability for precision can lead you to engineering, science, or finely detailed artwork. Your practical sense can attract you to a career in banking, real estate, or working with other people's money. Whatever career you choose, you are likely to be a perfectionist and desire to do your job well.

Famous people who share your birthday include actors River Phoenix and Gene Kelly, musician Keith Moon, singer Bing Crosby, restaurateur Howard Johnson, actresses Shelley Long and Barbara Eden, journalist Henry Pringle, French king Louis XVI, and poet Edgar Lee Masters.

Numerology

Intuitive, emotionally sensitive, and creative are some of the ways others describe people with a number 23 birthday. Usually you are versatile, passionate, and a quick thinker, with a professional attitude and a mind full of creative ideas. With the number 23 influence, you can learn new subjects easily, but may prefer practice to theory. You are fond of travel, adventure, and meeting new people; the restlessness implied by the number 23 urges you to try many different kinds of experiences, and you are apt to make the most of any situation. Generally friendly and fun-loving, with courage and drive, you may need an active life in order to actualize your true potential. The subinfluence of the number 8 month indicates that you possess a strong character with an ambitious nature. If you are put in a position of trust, you may also have to learn how to be fair and just. Although you may be practical, a need for versatility often suggests that you can become easily bored if life becomes too uneventful.

• *Positive:* loyal, compassionate, responsible, loves travel, communicative, intuitive, creative, versatile, trustworthy

• *Negative:* selfish, insecure, stubborn, uncompromising, fault-finding, withdrawn, prejudiced

Love & Relationships

Often entertaining and versatile, you like to mix with different types of people. Restless and nervous, however, you can be indecisive about how you feel in relationships. When in love, you are often idealistic and willing to make sacrifices. At times, however, you can be overenthusiastic to start with and then become calculating or appear cold and uninterested. You may prefer a partner who is compassionate and who has faith in your capabilities.

tion in government or large corporations. If you do not have a position of prominence, you probably have influential friends. This star suggests that you should be kind to others on your way up, as you are likely to meet them on your way down.

• *Positive:* high-spirited, frankness, courage, honor and riches, rise to prominent positions, authority

Negative: stubborn, unruly, domineering, greatness but also great failures (especially through dishonesty), fleeting success and fame

See Appendix for additional fixed star readings.

YOUR SPECIAL SOMEONE

You might find a partner who is caring and loving among those born on the following dates.

Love & friendship: Jan. 11, 21, 25, Feb. 9, 19, 23, Mar. 17, 21, 30, Apr. 5, 15, 19, 28, 29, May 13, 17, 26, 27, June 11, 15, 24, 25, 30, July 9, 13, 22, 23, 28, Aug. 7, 11, 20, 21, 26, 30, Sept. 5, 9, 18, 19, 24, 28, Oct. 3, 7, 16, 17, 22, 26, 29, Nov. 1, 5, 14, 15, 20, 24, 27, Dec. 3, 12, 13, 18, 22, 25, 27, 29

Beneficial: Jan. 5, 13, 16, 22, 28, Feb. 3, 11, 14, 20, 26, Mar. 1, 9, 12, 18, 24, 29, Apr. 7, 10, 16, 22, 27, May 5, 8, 14, 20, 25, June 3, 6, 12, 18, 23, July 1, 4, 10, 16, 21, Aug. 2, 8, 14, 19, Sept. 6, 12, 17, Oct. 4, 10, 15, Nov. 2, 8, 13, Dec. 6, 11

Fatal attractions: Feb. 19, 20, 21, June 30, July 28, Aug. 26, Sept. 24, Oct. 22, Nov. 20, Dec. 18

Challenging: Jan. 2, 23, 30, Feb. 21, 28, Mar. 19, 26, 28, Apr. 17, 24, 26, May 15, 22, 24, June 13, 20, 22, July 11, 18, 20, Aug. 16, 18, 19, Sept. 7, 14, 16, Oct. 5, 12, 14, Nov. 3, 10, 12, Dec. 1, 8, 10

Soul mates: Jan. 14, 22, Feb. 12, 20, Mar. 10, 18, Apr. 8, 16, May 6, 14, June 4, 12, July 2, 10, Aug. 8, Sept. 6, Oct. 4, Nov. 2

August 24

You are mentally sharp, quiet, and self-assured, and there is more to you than meets the eye. Generally wanting things concise and direct, you can be persuasive by presenting new ideas in a logical manner. With the ability to be rational and hardworking, you often cope well with difficult situations. Your persistence and willpower are likely to show through and gain you respect and admiration from others.

The added influence of your decanate ruler, Virgo, suggests that you have quick, assertive communication and a penetrating intellect. This influence heightens your discrimination and diligence, enabling you to become an expert in your field. With your analytical approach to life, you are likely to pay attention to detail and prefer order or tidiness in your affairs. Nevertheless, guard against becoming overly fastidious or critical, or wasting your time in needless anxiety.

As you are inventive and original, new or stimulating experiences can enrich your life. Humanitarian inclinations may inspire you to promote freedom or progressive reforms. Being courageous and competitive, you may fight difficult but successful battles to overcome threatening situations. However, you may have to avoid occasionally becoming touchy, irritable, or provocative. Physical exercise may prove a positive antidote to counterbalance any excessive mental strain.

When you reach the age of twenty-nine, your progressed Sun moves into Libra, commencing a thirty-year period of increased emphasis on your partnerships, both personally and professionally. This is a time when you also have an increased sense of beauty and harmony in your relationships and may want to develop any creative potential you possess. Another turning point occurs at the age of fifty-nine, when your progressed Sun moves into Scorpio, stimulating you to seek deeper meaning to your life and placing more emphasis on making changes.

Fixed Stars

Regulus, also called the Lion's Heart; Phecda, also called Phachd

Primary Star

Star's name: Regulus, also called the Lion's Heart

Degree position: 28°51'–29°48' Leo between the years 1930 and 2000

Magnitude: 1

Strength: ★★★★★★★★

Orb: 2°30'

Constellation: Alpha Leonis (Leo)

Applicable days: August 21, 22, 23, 24, 25, 26

Star qualities: Mars/Jupiter

Description: a brilliant white and blue triple star located on the body of the Lion

Primary Star's Influence

Regulus is a royal star that takes a leading role among a nearly infinite cast of stars. Regulus imparts nobility, high honors, great charisma, and the power to project a dignified personality. This star bestows a natural ability to make quick decisions and cope with demanding situations. It also imparts a desire for power and an ability to lead and command others. You have strong willpower and a love of enterprise, which often lead to a desire for freedom and independence. Regulus warns that these great benefits are not necessarily long-lasting.

Linked to your Sun's degree, this star imparts ambition, power, authority, and opportunities to rise to a high posi-

Your Secret Self

Intense inner forces may cause you to alternate between extremes of uncertainty and a sense of being someone special. Cultivate positive thinking, trust your deeper intuitive understanding, and avoid periods of worry or doubt. Luckily, your wry sense of humor prevents you from taking yourself or others too seriously, easing any possible emotional tensions. With your high ideals, sense of the dramatic, and potential for leadership, you have the power to capitalize on your innate talents.

Because you are very sensitive, your relationships are likely to be especially important to you. It may be necessary to keep a balance between becoming overly dependent on others and staying independent. If you lose this balance, you may find that you may alternate between being optimistic and despondent. Consequently, it is important to keep open lines of communication with others.

Work & Vocation

A need to share your knowledge may be fulfilled in academic professions such as teaching or lecturing or through the world of promotion. Alternatively, your leadership abilities, organizational skills, and strategic planning ability may place you in the world of commerce. A love of detail and thoroughness often makes you an excellent researcher, scientist, financial analyst, or accountant. Being a hardworking and practical idealist may draw you to work in the community or in caring for the elderly. Attractions to professions such as counseling, health, and communications can also fulfill your humanitarian interests. Being a natural psychologist, you may be drawn toward occupations that involve personal contacts. You are likely to do particularly well with property or real estate.

Famous people who share your birthday include supermodel Claudia Schiffer, Chinese leader Deng Xiaoping, painter George Stubbs, writers Jorge Luis Borges and A. S. Byatt, and baseball player Cal Ripken Jr.

tion in government or large corporations. If you do not have a position of prominence, you probably have influential friends. This star suggests that you should be kind to others on your way up, as you are likely to meet them on your way down.

- *Positive:* high-spirited, frankness, courage, honor and riches, rise to prominent positions, authority
- *Negative:* stubborn, unruly, domineering, greatness but also great failures (especially through dishonesty), fleeting success and fame

See Appendix for additional fixed star readings.

Numerology

The emotional sensitivity of the number 24 birthday suggests that you seek balance and harmony. You are also receptive to form and structure and can easily create a complex yet efficient system. Faithful and fair, you are inclined to be undemonstrative, believing that actions speak louder than words. The main challenge for a number 24 birthday is to learn to associate with people from all walks of life, to overcome suspicious tendencies, and to build a secure home. The subinfluence of the number 8 month indicates that you are mentally active and conscientious, with a responsible attitude. You may need, however, to guard against destructive behavior, which can be interpreted by others as stubbornness. By learning to be light-hearted and expressive with your feelings, you often overcome a tendency to be overly serious. A pragmatic approach to life also gives you good business sense and an ability to achieve material success in life.

- *Positive:* energetic, idealistic, practical skills, strong determination, honest, frank, fair, generous, love of home, active
- *Negative:* materialistic, too economical, ruthlessness, dislikes routine, lazy, unfaithful, unstable, domineering, stubborn

YOUR SPECIAL SOMEONE

To find love and long-lasting relationships, you may wish to look out for someone born on one of the following dates.

Love & friendship: Jan. 6, 16, 22, 26, 27, Feb. 4, 14, 20, 24, Mar. 2, 12, 18, 22, 23, Apr. 10, 16, 20, 30, May 8, 14, 18, 28, June 6, 12, 16, 26, July 4, 10, 14, 24, 31, Aug. 2, 8, 12, 22, 29, Sept. 6, 10, 20, 27, Oct. 4, 8, 18, 25, Nov. 2, 6, 16, 23, 24, 30, Dec. 4, 14, 21, 22, 28, 30

Beneficial: Jan. 6, 17, 23, 31, Feb. 4, 15, 21, 29, Mar. 2, 13, 19, 27, 30, Apr. 11, 17, 25, 28, May 9, 15, 23, 26, June 7, 13, 21, 24, July 5, 11, 19, 22, Aug. 3, 9, 17, 20, Sept. 1, 7, 15, 18, 30, Oct. 5, 13, 16, 28, Nov. 3, 11, 14, 26, Dec. 1, 9, 12, 24

Fatal attractions: Feb. 18, 19, 20, 21

Challenging: Jan. 24, Feb. 22, Mar. 20, 29, Apr. 18, 27, 29, May 6, 16, 25, 27, 30, June 14, 22, 25, 28, July 12, 21, 23, 26, Aug. 10, 19, 21, 24, Sept. 8, 17, 19, 22, Oct. 6, 15, 17, 20, Nov. 4, 13, 15, 18, Dec. 2, 11, 13, 16

Soul mates: Jan. 13, Feb. 11, Mar. 9, Apr. 7, May 5, June 3, 30, July 1, 28, Aug. 26, Sept. 24, Oct. 22, Nov. 20, Dec. 18

Love & Relationships

You are likely to have a youthful side that will keep you constantly interested in new people and new places. Love and companionship are very important to you, but a tendency to mood swings may bring difficulties in relationships. Your need for fun makes you a good social mixer, and when relationships are based on mental affinity, they are usually successful. You may be drawn to those who can inspire your creativity or to a partner who can share your sense of humor.

August 25

FIXED STARS

Regulus, also called the Lion's Heart; Phecda, also called Phachd

PRIMARY STAR

Star's name: Regulus, also called the Lion's Heart

Degree position: 28°51'–29°48' Leo between the years 1930 and 2000

Magnitude: 1

Strength: ★★★★★★★★

Orb: 2°30'

Constellation: Alpha Leonis (Leo)

Applicable days: August 21, 22, 23, 24, 25, 26

Star qualities: Mars/Jupiter

Description: a brilliant white and blue triple star located on the body of the Lion

PRIMARY STAR'S INFLUENCE

Regulus is a royal star that takes a leading role among a nearly infinite cast of stars. Regulus imparts nobility, high honors, great charisma, and the power to project a dignified personality. This star bestows a natural ability to make quick decisions and cope with demanding situations. It also imparts a desire for power and an ability to lead and command others. You have strong willpower and a love of enterprise, which often lead to a desire for freedom and independence. Regulus warns that these great benefits are not necessarily long-lasting.

Linked to your Sun's degree, this star imparts ambition, power, authority, and opportunities to rise to a high

♍ The special influences of your birthday indicate that you possess a quick and creative mind that is constantly searching for new and exiting ideas to keep you intellectually stimulated. Strong-willed and pragmatic, yet imaginative and sensitive, you have the potential to make your ideals a reality.

With the influence of your decanate ruler, Virgo, you are likely to possess good general knowledge, to think progressively, and to love thoroughness and detail. Discriminating and methodical, you like to refine and improve on existing systems.

Mercury's effect is evident in the way you communicate your ideas: precisely and decisively. A love of words or language may endow you with a talent for writing or help you to become a specialist in your field. You may need, however, to avoid being overcritical or worrying about small or unimportant issues.

Although you possess nervous energy, when you do have a strong belief regarding a project, you will go all out until it is complete. This same natural enthusiasm often stimulates you to become a teacher, passing on your knowledge and experience. As you are ambitious, with strong desires, beware of being bossy by projecting your will onto others.

Possessing the ability to be charming and naturally diplomatic when it is needed, you are likely to be persuasive, with an interesting voice. Women of this birthday are often independent and enjoy initiating new projects. Both men and women of this birthdate like to keep themselves busy.

From childhood you are inclined to analyze situations practically in order to understand and improve them. Your progressed Sun moves into Libra when you reach the age of twenty-eight, and over the next thirty years you gradually become more aware of the importance of your social relationships and partnerships. Creative abilities are enhanced, and you may develop any latent musical, artistic, or literary interests. At the age of fifty-eight you reach another life turning point as your progressed Sun enters Scorpio. This brings an emphasis on change, a need for greater self-awareness, and personal power.

Your Secret Self

Although you are clever and intellectual, on an inner level you possess high ideals and intense emotional sensitivity. This can make you very vulnerable, particularly in the area of your relationships, so it is vital that you keep a balance between your need for independence and the needs of others. You make an excellent friend, warm and giving to those you love, though you feel incomplete without a mutually loving partner. Although young at heart, you may experience disappointment when others fail to live up to your high ideals. When despondent, you must guard against dealing with difficulties by becoming moody or an escapist. Your longing for love may find a creative outlet in service to others, art, music, literature, or spiritual experience. Particularly sensitive to discord, you need to surround yourself with a harmonious environment.

Work & Vocation

With your never-ending thirst for knowledge, you may be drawn to the academic world or a career as a trainer or teacher. Sharing all your expertise can extend to being a lawyer or counselor, and you may often find yourself working for a cause. Naturally thorough, you are likely to excel as a researcher, scientist, technician, or chemist. You may also fare well in mathematics or engineering or may be skilled with your hands. Being hardworking and interested in money issues, you may be drawn to business, where you prefer the freedom to work in your own way. At the other end of the scale, many of this birthday are often musical or artistic, and a love of language may attract you to writing. Possessing natural diplomatic skills, you may be attracted to a career as a promoter or agent.

Famous people who share your birthday include composer Leonard Bernstein, actors Sean Connery and Mel Ferrer, writers Martin Amis and Frederick Forsyth, and singer/songwriter Elvis Costello.

Numerology

Intuitive and thoughtful, yet quick and energetic, you need to express yourself through different experiences. With your number 25 birthday, a desire for perfection often urges you to work hard and be productive. Usually you are instinctive and alert, and you can gain more knowledge through practical application than mere theory. Good judgment and an eye for detail ensure successful accomplishment. You may have to develop a less skeptical attitude by overcoming a tendency to make erratic or impulsive decisions. As a number 25 individual, you possess strong mental energies that when concentrated aid you to look at all the facts and arrive at a conclusion faster than anyone else. The subinfluence of the number 8 month indicates that you are daring and innovative. Usually practical, you have natural business sense and will benefit greatly from developing your organizational and executive skills. A strong need to feel secure or established urges you to make long-term plans and investments.

• *Positive:* highly intuitive, perfectionist, perceptive, creative, good at dealing with people
• *Negative:* impulsive, impatient, irresponsible, overly emotional, jealous, secretive, critical, moody, nervous

YOUR SPECIAL SOMEONE

You might find a partner who will understand your sensitivity and need for love among those born on the following dates.

Love & friendship: Jan. 1, 4, 27, 28, 29, Feb. 2, 25, 27, Mar. 23, 25, Apr. 21, 23, May 19, 20, 21, 29, June 17, 19, 27, July 15, 17, 25, Aug. 13, 15, 23, Sept. 11, 13, 21, Oct. 9, 11, 19, Nov. 7, 9, 17, Dec. 5, 7, 15

Beneficial: Jan. 3, 10, 15, 18, Feb. 1, 8, 13, 16, Mar. 6, 11, 14, 29, 31, Apr. 4, 9, 12, 27, 29, May 2, 7, 10, 25, 27, June 5, 8, 23, 25, July 3, 6, 21, 23, Aug. 1, 4, 19, 21, Sept. 2, 17, 19, Oct. 15, 17, Nov. 13, 15, Dec. 11, 13

Fatal attractions: Feb. 20, 21, 22, 23, Apr. 30, May 28, June 26, July 24, Aug. 22, Sept. 20, Oct. 18, Nov. 16, Dec. 14

Challenging: Jan. 9, 14, 16, 25, Feb. 7, 12, 14, 23, Mar. 5, 10, 12, 21, 28, 30, Apr. 3, 8, 10, 19, 26, 28, May 1, 6, 8, 17, 24, 26, June 4, 6, 15, 22, 24, July 2, 4, 13, 20, 22, Aug. 2, 11, 18, 20, Sept. 9, 16, 18, Oct. 7, 14, 16, Nov. 5, 12, 14, Dec. 3, 10, 12

Soul mates: Dec. 29

Love & Relationships

Confident and realistic, you are charming and attractive. Often your easygoing nature and your ability to keep the peace ensure harmony in your relations with others. Since you are ambitious, you admire those who work hard. You prefer partnerships and can be loyal to the person you settle with. Although you are often devoted and giving, guard against becoming critical. Your natural charisma, however, can always magnetize people toward you.

August 26

♍ Natural leadership, a confident front, and generosity of spirit are qualities suggested by your birthday. Being warm, kind, and sociable, you will find that your friends are likely to play an important part in your life. Your sympathy, matched by your strong sense of justice, may cause you to defend the underdog or fight vigorously when principles are at stake. One of the few obstacles to your success may be an inability to discipline yourself when it is really necessary.

With the subinfluence of your decanate ruler, Virgo, you think very practically and are attracted by intelligent people. You like to make up your own mind about issues only after analyzing all the possible ramifications. Be careful to avoid continually going over the same issues and becoming anxious or overcritical. Being a good organizer, with a strong desire for order and cleanliness, you may feel happier when everything in life is running efficiently.

Projecting personal magnetism, you are interested in people and can be understanding and benevolent. Proud yet sensitive, you are likely to have a strong interest in home and family. With your open and amicable approach, you usually make friends easily with people of any age or background. As you possess a love of luxury and beautiful surroundings, it is fortunate that you also have a natural business ability to support your lifestyle.

In your early years you may be strongly influenced by a male figure such as a father or grandfather. When you reach the age of twenty-seven, your progressed Sun moves into Libra, commencing a thirty-year period during which there is an increasing emphasis on diplomacy, partnerships, and relationships. You are likely to gain an enhanced sense of balance and harmony that helps you to develop artistic or creative abilities. Another turning point for you occurs around the age of fifty-seven, when your progressed Sun moves into Scorpio, stimulating your sensitivity and causing you to seek more change and transformation in your life.

FIXED STAR

Star's name: Regulus, also called the Lion's Heart

Degree position: 28°51'–29°48' Leo between the years 1930 and 2000

Magnitude: 1

Strength: ★★★★★★★★

Orb: 2°30'

Constellation: Alpha Leonis (Leo)

Applicable days: August 21, 22, 23, 24, 25, 26

Star qualities: Mars/Jupiter

Description: a brilliant white and blue triple star located on the body of the Lion

PRIMARY STAR'S INFLUENCE

Regulus is a royal star that takes a leading role among a nearly infinite cast of stars. Regulus imparts nobility, high honors, great charisma, and the power to project a dignified personality. This star bestows a natural ability to make quick decisions and cope with demanding situations. It also imparts a desire for power and an ability to lead and command others. You have strong willpower and a love of enterprise, which often lead to a desire for freedom and independence. Regulus warns that these great benefits are not necessarily long-lasting.

Linked to your Sun's degree, this star imparts ambition, power, authority, and opportunities to rise to a high position in government or large corporations. If you do not have a position of prominence, you probably have influential friends. This star suggests that you should be kind to others on your way

Your Secret Self

Because you are proud and outwardly confident, people often do not see the more vulnerable and intuitive you. At times you may get overly serious, willful, or selfish, feeling that your hard efforts are not being appreciated. During these periods you may be prone to become frustrated or argumentative. Since you can also be very warm and magnanimous and may be willing to do almost anything for the people you love, you may need to learn emotional balance.

When you express your true humanitarian and compassionate nature, you can be very popular and gain the admiration that you need. You have a wonderful ability to utilize humor when giving others the benefit of your quick insight, and when you are really detached you can come out with sudden flashes of inspired wisdom.

Work & Vocation

Your organizational abilities and natural business acumen are likely to prove assets in any career, but may particularly draw you to the world of commerce or administration. Similarly, with your communication and social skills, you may excel in education, writing, or law. Your analytical ability and love of detail may draw you to the world of science, engineering, research, or industry. Alternatively, your love of people and way with words may attract you to sales or acting. A natural sympathy and humanitarian streak can find an outlet through counseling or fund-raising for charity. The combination of your intuition and rational mind may be particularly helpful in the healing professions.

Famous people who share your birthday include actor Macaulay Culkin, Queen Victoria's consort Prince Albert, writers Christopher Isherwood and Guillaume Apollinaire, musician Branford Marsalis, and vice-presidential candidate Geraldine Ferraro.

Numerology

The strength or power suggested by the number 26 birthday shows that you are a cautious character with strong values and sound judgment. A love of home and parental instincts may also suggest a need to build a solid foundation or find real stability. Often a tower of strength for others, you are willing to support friends, family members, and relatives who may turn to you in time of need. You may nevertheless need to guard against materialistic tendencies and a desire to control people or situations. The subinfluence of the number 8 month indicates that you aspire to great accomplishment and possess an ambitious nature. Although you are willing to work hard and take on responsibilities, try to avoid taking on more than your fair share of the workload. You have natural business sense and practical skills and can advise others about monetary matters. A strong need to feel secure or established urges you to make long-term plans and investments.

• *Positive:* creative, practical, caring, meticulous, idealistic, honest, responsible, proud of family, enthusiastic, courageous

• *Negative:* stubborn, rebellious, deceitful, unfriendly, unenthusiastic, lack of persistence, instability

Love & Relationships

With your giving nature and kindness, people are drawn to you. Although you can be idealistic with a strong need to be loved and appreciated, you may need to avoid a tendency to be domineering or overbearing. Being passionate, you may fall in love easily. However, in order to achieve your desired goals, there must be a balance between your need for independence and the necessity for cooperation in love and work.

up, as you are likely to meet them on your way down.

• *Positive:* high-spirited, frankness, courage, honor and riches, rise to prominent positions, authority

• *Negative:* stubborn, unruly, domineering, greatness but also great failures (especially through dishonesty), fleeting success and fame

YOUR SPECIAL SOMEONE

You are likely to have success in love and friendship with people born on the following dates.

Love & friendship: Jan. 2, 28, Feb. 26, Mar. 24, Apr. 22, May 20, 29, 30, June 18, 27, 28, July 16, 25, 26, Aug. 14, 23, 24, Sept. 12, 21, 22, Oct. 10, 19, 20, 29, 31, Nov. 8, 17, 18, 27, 29, Dec. 6, 15, 16, 25, 27

Beneficial: Jan. 2, 10, 13, 16, Feb. 8, 11, 14, Mar. 6, 9, 12, Apr. 4, 7, 10, May 2, 5, 8, June 3, 6, July 1, 4, 30, Aug. 2, 28, 30, Sept. 26, 28, Oct. 24, 26, Nov. 22, 24, Dec. 20, 22, 30

Fatal attractions: Feb. 23, 24, 25, 26, Oct. 31, Nov. 29, Dec. 27

Challenging: Jan. 3, 9, 10, Feb. 1, 7, 8, Mar. 5, 6, 31, Apr. 3, 4, 29, May 1, 2, 27, June 25, July 23, Aug. 2, 21, 31, Sept. 19, 29, Oct. 17, 27, Nov. 15, 25, Dec. 13, 23

Soul mates: Jan. 5, Feb. 3, Mar. 1, May 30, June 28, July 26, Aug. 24, Sept. 22, Oct. 20, Nov. 18, Dec. 16

August 27

♍ Charming and determined, with natural leadership ability, you have a birthday that suggests that you are a practical and shrewd visionary. With your capacity for discipline and hard work, once you have a definite goal you persevere until the end. You are capable of expressing a wide range of emotions. You can be compassionate and sensitive but also powerful and dominating.

With the subinfluence of your decanate ruler, Virgo, communication is particularly emphasized in your life. With your strong mental powers and sense of definition, you have a quick grasp of situations and can detect mistakes and understand complex issues. Having high standards and wanting method and order also imply that at times you may get carried away and become too critical.

When channeled constructively, your strong emotions can ensure your popularity, especially when you turn on your special charisma. You may have to avoid becoming impatient with others when they are too slow, and feeling a general dissatisfaction with your own lot.

Being intuitive as well as practical and mentally astute, you seek inspiration and work well in service to others. Idealistic and generous, you possess a strong sense of duty but can also be witty and entertaining. Many men of this birthday have developed the feminine side of their nature.

Until you reach the age of twenty-five, your progressed Sun is in Virgo, emphasizing the importance of being mentally focused and discriminating. At the age of twenty-six, when your progressed Sun moves into Libra, there is an increased need for partnership and relating to others. Your sense of balance, harmony, and beauty is likely to be enhanced, with the possibility of exploring literary, artistic, or creative outlets in some form. This continues until the age of fifty-six, when your progressed Sun enters Scorpio. This is a turning point for you, one that will highlight a growing need for emotional and spiritual regeneration as well as accenting joint finances.

FIXED STARS

Although your Sun's degree is not linked to a fixed star, some of your other planets' degrees certainly will be. By having an astrological chart calculated, you can find the exact position of the planets on your date of birth. This will tell you which of the fixed stars listed in this book are relevant to you.

Your Secret Self

Ambitious and hardworking, you are success-oriented and always seeking to better yourself. By releasing old worries or frustrations, you will find it easier to summon up the self-discipline needed to accomplish your great potential. By experiencing discontent and giving up too easily, you may get caught up in other people's dramas rather than focus on your own sense of purpose.

As you are often universal in your approach to life, you could find deeper fulfillment by finding an outlet for your latent humanitarianism, spirituality, or vivid imagination. Although you are willing to make sacrifices for others, it is necessary to do so from the goodness of your heart, with no hidden agendas. Your generosity and kindness are often repaid many times over.

Work & Vocation

You can be at your best when working selflessly for a cause or an ideal, which may lead you to a career in politics, charity work, or the healing professions. Since you enjoy sharing your knowledge with others, you can be an excellent teacher or writer. An appreciation of color and sound often indicates a flair for the arts or music. This also suggests that you can succeed as a dealer in the art world or in antiques, crafts, and design. A sense of structure can also help you in careers such as mathematics or architecture. Although you are efficient and thorough, if in business you may fare best when your sense of vision is creatively employed, such as in advertising or publishing. Alternatively, your gift of gab can take you into the world of sales or entertainment. When combined with your sympathetic understanding of people, you can nurture others in the world of health, counseling, or public service.

Famous people who share your birthday include missionary Mother Teresa, U.S. president Lyndon Johnson, Senator Bob Kerrey, philosopher G.F.W. Hegel, artist Man Ray, and politician Yasir Arafat.

Numerology

The number 27 birthday indicates that you are intuitive yet inquisitive, with a depth of thought that can be greatly enhanced by developing patience and self-control. You are often forceful, determined, and observant and can pay great attention to detail. Generally idealistic and sensitive, with a fertile and creative mind, you can impress others with your original thoughts and ideas. Developing good communication skills helps you to overcome a reluctance to express your deeper feelings. Education is especially beneficial for number 27 persons, and with the proper qualifications you can achieve success through writing, research, and work in large organizations. The subinfluence of the number 8 month indicates that you are mentally active and perceptive. As you need to express your powerful feelings, you often have a dynamic personality. By developing a more detached perspective, you may be able to listen to others and take on board their criticism or ideas.

• *Positive:* leadership, thoroughness, hardworking, traditional, authoritative, protective, the power to heal, good judge of values

• *Negative:* intolerant, restless, overworked, domineering, easily discouraged, lack of planning, controlling behavior

Love & Relationships

Dynamic and sensitive, with powerful emotions, you are usually drawn to creative individuals who know how to express themselves in words and ideas. Romantic and dramatic, you may need to beware of being drawn into unsuitable relationships. Socially inclined and a loyal friend, you can be generous and supportive. Since you often strive for powerful positions, you can be a faithful yet demanding partner who needs a strong expression of love for yourself and others.

YOUR SPECIAL SOMEONE

Your opportunities to find that special person are greater with those born on the following dates.

Love & friendship: Jan. 3, 16, 22, 25, 29, 30, Feb. 1, 14, 20, 23, 27, 28, Mar. 18, 21, 25, 26, Apr. 16, 19, 23, 24, 28, May 8, 14, 17, 21, 22, 26, 31, June 12, 15, 19, 20, 24, 29, July 10, 13, 18, 22, Aug. 8, 11, 15, 16, 20, 27, 29, 30, Sept. 6, 9, 13, 14, 18, 23, 27, 28, Oct. 4, 7, 11, 12, 16, 21, 25, 26, Nov. 2, 5, 9, 10, 14, 19, 23, 24, Dec. 3, 7, 8, 12, 17, 21, 22

Beneficial: Jan. 17, Feb. 15, Mar. 13, Apr. 11, May 9, 29, June 7, 27, July 5, 25, Aug. 3, 23, Sept. 1, 21, Oct. 19, 29, Nov. 17, 27, 30, Dec. 15, 25, 28

Fatal attractions: Feb. 23, 24, 25, May 31, June 29, July 27, Aug. 25, 30, Sept. 23, 28, Oct. 21, 26, Nov. 19, 24, Dec. 17, 22

Challenging: Jan. 20, 23, Feb. 18, 21, Mar. 16, 19, Apr. 14, 17, May 12, 15, June 10, 13, July 8, 11, Aug. 6, 9, Sept. 4, 7, Oct. 2, 5, Nov. 2, Dec. 1

Soul mates: Jan. 4, 31, Feb. 2, 29, Mar. 27, Apr. 25, May 23, June 21, July 19, Aug. 17, Sept. 15, Oct. 13, Nov. 11, Dec. 9

August 28

Sociable, warm, and friendly, you are revealed by your birthday to be young at heart. A strong sense of identity often puts you up front, where you are able to gain the approval you need. Capable of unselfish gestures toward those you love, you can also be understanding and a good listener. Be careful that immaturity or self-will does not spoil your attractive charm.

With the subinfluence of your decanate ruler, Virgo, you are clever, with a practical approach and natural business sense. Although you usually analyze situations very carefully, you may have to guard against becoming skeptical. Articulate and straightforward in speech, you value knowledge and expertise.

Playful and romantic, you possess a dynamic blend of idealism and pragmatism. Although you can procrastinate, once you set your mind on something you are willing to make great sacrifices to achieve your goals. As you enjoy a touch of glamour and can be attracted to the good life, you need an active social life and are known to be an entertaining companion. Cooperative and helpful, you can also provide emotional support for others. Although you will always have a youthful quality, it is through self-discipline that you are able to fully realize your potential.

When you reach the age of twenty-five, your progressed Sun moves into Libra, commencing a thirty-year period of increased emphasis on your partnerships, both personally and professionally. This is a time when you may also have an expanded sense of beauty and harmony and may want to develop any creative potential you possess. Another turning point occurs at the age of fifty-five, when your progressed Sun moves into Scorpio, stimulating you to seek deeper meaning to your life and placing more emphasis on transformation.

Fixed Stars

Although your Sun's degree is not linked to a fixed star, some of your other planets' degrees certainly will be. By having an astrological chart calculated, you can find the exact position of the planets on your date of birth. This will tell you which of the fixed stars listed in this book are relevant to you.

Your Secret Self

Warmhearted and loving, you seek harmonious relationships. Possessing an inner nobility and strong convictions, you may need to motivate yourself with constant challenges. This may be obstructed by a tendency to be impulsive and the desire for instant gratification. Since you enjoy having fun, you may choose to go for an easy option. Ultimately, this could cause you to lose your sense of purpose and direction.

As you are sensitive, with deep feelings, you may have to develop a detached view in order to avoid being easily hurt or feeling sorry for yourself. Learn to channel your excess emotion. By acting on your inner voice, you can begin to express yourself creatively and utilize your emotional powers. You are usually very generous and compassionate and enjoy being of service to others.

Work & Vocation

Your natural business sense can help you succeed in any undertaking, but you may be more drawn to careers that involve dealing with people. Your gift for communication may lead you to writing, education, or sales. As you enjoy entertaining others, you may also be drawn to show business or the music industry. A natural diplomacy may lead you to work in customer service or public relations, and your people skills can help you succeed in promotion or publishing. A natural aesthetic sense may draw you to occupations such as artist or designer and dealing with items and furnishings for the home.

Famous people who share your birthday include actors Charles Boyer, Ben Gazzara, and David Soul, and philosopher/writer Johann Wolfgang Goethe.

Numerology

Like a number 1 individual, you are ambitious, direct, and enterprising. Always ready for action and new ventures, you courageously take on life's challenges. With your enthusiasm you can easily inspire others, if not to join you, at least to support you in your latest venture. Although you are success-oriented and determined, family and home life are very important to you. Finding stability and taking care of your nearest and dearest may, at times, be a challenge for you. The subinfluence of the number 8 month indicates that you possess a highly intuitive and active mind. When taking on responsibilities, you like to be efficient but can also be impatient or intolerant. Emotionally dynamic, constantly on the go, you may need to learn how to relax. With your quick assessment of a situation you can easily solve problems. Avoid becoming overenthusiastic, initiating projects without a proper plan.

• *Positive:* progressive, daring, artistic, creative, compassionate, idealistic, ambitious, hardworking, stable home life, strong-willed

• *Negative:* daydreamer, unmotivated, lack of compassion, unrealistic, bossy, bad judgment, aggressive, lack of confidence, too dependent on others, pride

Love & Relationships

Although you often strive for autonomy and personal achievement, a powerful need for love is likely to draw you into all kinds of romantic affairs. You are often benevolent and caring, but a tendency to be idealistic and a perfectionist in relationships suggests that others may fail to live up to your expectations. Usually generous, with a charming personality and friendly nature, you can easily attract friends and partners, although some relationships may not prove to be worthwhile. Once you find your perfect mate, you can be very loving and supportive.

YOUR SPECIAL SOMEONE

For your ideal partner you might begin by looking for someone born on one of the following dates.

Love & friendship: Jan. 4, 5, 10, 18, 19, 26, 30, Feb. 2, 3, 8, 16, 17, 24, 28, Mar. 1, 6, 14, 15, 22, 26, Apr. 4, 12, 13, 20, 24, May 2, 10, 11, 18, 22, June 8, 9, 16, 20, 30, July 6, 7, 14, 18, 28, Aug. 4, 5, 12, 16, 26, 30, Sept. 2, 3, 10, 14, 28, Oct. 1, 8, 12, 22, 26, Nov. 6, 10, 20, 24, Dec. 4, 8, 18, 22, 30

Beneficial: Jan. 13, Feb. 11, Mar. 9, Apr. 7, May 5, June 3, 30, July 1, 28, Aug. 26, Sept. 24, Oct. 22, Nov. 20, Dec. 18

Fatal attractions: Feb. 23, 24, 25, 26

Challenging: Jan. 14, 24, Feb. 12, 22, Mar. 10, 20, Apr. 8, 18, May 6, 16, June 4, 14, July 2, 12, Aug. 10, Sept. 8, Oct. 6, Nov. 4, Dec. 2

Soul mates: July 30, Aug. 28, Sept. 26, Oct. 24, Nov. 22, Dec. 20

August 29

℔ Your birthday suggests that you are charismatic, warm, and ambitious, possessing a keen intellect and an enterprising spirit. Independent and success-oriented, you like to be active and think in grandiose terms. You may, however, have to avoid getting emotionally carried away or going to extremes.

With the subinfluence of Virgo, your decanate ruler, you possess a sharp, practical mind and are often a perfectionist. You are likely to pay attention to detail and want to refine your work. Nevertheless, you may need to refrain from continuously mulling over issues, since this can cause anxiety. Fortunately, your thirst for knowledge and a love of learning can keep you mentally occupied and stop you from becoming oversensitive.

Sociable and generous, you do well in people-related activities. Mind-broadening travel can be especially positive and bring you many new contacts. Possessing organizational skills and being adventurous, you also have the ability to make money. By applying the needed self-discipline, you can bring out your marvelous potential.

As dynamic and charming as you can be, sometimes you may become insecure, withdrawing to isolate yourself. By reconnecting to your intuition and idealistic vision, you soon return to being enthusiastic and creative.

From childhood you have been practical, analyzing situations in order to understand and improve them. After the age of twenty-four, as your progressed Sun moves into Libra for a thirty-year period, there is an increased need for partnership and relating. Your creative abilities are enhanced and you may develop any latent musical, artistic, or literary interests. Around the age of fifty-four you reach another life turning point as your progressed Sun enters Scorpio. This brings a strong emphasis on your emotional need for change, deeper awareness, and inner power.

Fixed Star

Star's Name: Alioth

Degree position: 7°52'–8°52' Virgo between the years 1930 and 2000

Magnitude: 2

Strength: ★★★★★★★

Orb: 2°10'

Constellation: Epsilon Ursa Major

Applicable days: August 29, 30, 31, September 1, 2, 3

Star qualities: Mars

Description: a blue-white star located in the tail of the Great Bear

PRIMARY STAR'S INFLUENCE

Alioth endows good judgment, a zest for life, and love of ease and comfort. Often you are broad-minded and inclined toward liberalism. This star imparts ambition to win, a competitive nature, and a constant need for activity. Alioth also imparts a talent for criticism and suggests that it should be used constructively.

Linked to your Sun's degree, Alioth's influence indicates an aptitude for business, sport, government posts, and dealing with the public. It can also stimulate thoroughness and the ability to exploit every situation, but warns against irritability and overconfidence.

• Positive: genuine, frank, endurance can overcome disappointment

• Negative: ruthlessness, egoism, destructiveness, obstinacy, overcritical

Your Secret Self

With your wealth of knowledge, you often possess a special gift for the written or spoken word and inspire and entertain others with your ideas. Although you are stimulated by intelligence, an inner restlessness may encourage you to explore many avenues in order to avoid becoming bored. Sensitive and imaginative, you possess a strong desire for freedom, but may have to beware of becoming a self-indulgent dreamer who fails to make your grand plans a reality.

Since you can become very passionate when really interested in a project, it is important to find an activity you love, then do it well. If too impatient, you may become distracted and take action without thinking or making the proper plans. At your best, you are optimistic, enthusiastic, and able to fulfill your high promise.

Work & Vocation

Ambitious, with leadership abilities, you may fare better in a position of management or working for yourself. At the least, you need as much freedom as possible within a job to operate in your own way. In order to avoid monotony, variety and change are necessary in any occupation you undertake. Your people skills aid you in any career you choose, and your emotional understanding and innate wisdom could take you into the caring professions or work that helps others. Your keen intellect could also lead you to education, law, science, writing, or politics. Alternatively, your practicality and enterprise may find an outlet in business or manufacturing. With your imagination and creativity, and with the right opportunities, you also could be very successful in the world of music and entertainment.

Famous people who share your birthday include singer Michael Jackson, actress Ingrid Bergman, actors Elliott Gould and Jason Priestley, singer Dinah Washington, jazz composer Charlie Parker, French painter Ingres, film director Richard Attenborough, news anchor Peter Jennings, and choreographer Mark Morris.

Numerology

As a number 29 individual, you are often highly intuitive, sensitive, and emotional. Your compassionate and understanding nature inspires humanitarianism and can encourage others to fulfill their hopes and aspirations. Although you are a true dreamer, the extreme sides of your nature indicate that you may have to guard against alternating moods. With a number 29 birthday, you need to be popular and may care what others think about you. The subinfluence of the number 8 month implies that you possess strong willpower and an ambitious nature. A need for self-expression suggests that you are imaginative and often seek emotional fulfillment. Although you usually appear ambitious and dynamic, you are often an idealist with a compassionate and sensitive nature. A need to be someone, however, may be the very thing that pushes you to be dramatic and claim center stage. Often there is a powerful desire to be original and establish an individual identity.

• *Positive:* inspirational, balanced, successful, mystical, creative, intuitive, powerful dreams, attention to detail, faith

• *Negative:* unfocused, moody, difficult, extremist, inconsiderate of others, isolated, overly sensitive

Love & Relationships

Charming and compelling, with a touch of the dramatic, you possess an enthusiastic personality. Often you are attracted to powerful people; however, you may need to avoid power challenges with partners. Women of this birthday are often willing to work hard to keep things comfortable and harmonious at home and in a relationship. Usually you are socially inclined and can make a good host or hostess. Often attracting more than one person and finding it hard to offend anyone, you can suffer difficulty in making relationship decisions.

YOUR SPECIAL SOMEONE

Your chances of finding happiness and a loving partner are increased with those born on the following dates.

Love & friendship: Jan. 2, 3, 6, 9, 10, 11, 21, 27, 31, Feb. 1, 4, 7, 8, 9, 25, 29, Mar. 2, 5, 6, 7, 17, 23, 27, Apr. 3, 4, 5, 15, 21, 25, May 1, 3, 13, 19, 23, 30, June 1, 11, 17, 21, 28, July 9, 15, 19, 26, 29, Aug. 7, 13, 17, 24, 27, Sept. 5, 11, 15, 22, 25, Oct. 3, 9, 13, 20, 23, Nov. 1, 7, 11, 18, 21, 30, Dec. 5, 9, 16, 19, 28 *Beneficial:* Jan. 11, 16, 30, Feb. 9, 24, 28, Mar. 7, 22, 26, Apr. 5, 20, 24, May 3, 18, 22, 31, June 1, 16, 20, 29, July 14, 18, 27, Aug. 12, 16, 25, Sept. 10, 14, 23, Oct. 8, 12, 21, 29, Nov. 6, 10, 19, 27, Dec. 4, 8, 17, 25

Fatal attractions: Feb. 24, 25, 26, 27

Challenging: Jan. 15, Feb. 13, Mar. 11, Apr. 9, May 7, 30, June 5, 28, July 3, 26, Aug. 1, 24, Sept. 22, Oct. 20, 30, Nov. 18, 28, Dec. 16, 26

Soul mates: Jan. 9, 29, Feb. 7, 27, Mar. 5, 25, Apr. 3, 23, May 1, 21, June 19, July 17, Aug. 15, Sept. 13, Oct. 11, Nov. 9, Dec. 7

August 30

♍ Expressive, hardworking, and caring, with an interest in people, you are a persuasive and original individual. With the ability to be both soft and loving, though tough and disciplined, you can express contrasting emotions.

With the subinfluence of your decanate ruler, Virgo, you have a sharp, analytical mind that picks up on every little detail. With a desire for knowledge and a need to improve yourself, you usually develop your ability to be articulate. Practical, with good concentration, you can be thorough and diligent in your work, but may have to avoid being overly critical of yourself or others in your search for perfection.

Sociable and charming, you like to make other people happy. Projecting a positive attitude or outlook toward life, you are at the same time realistic. Occasionally you may become overly serious or withdrawn, inhibiting your feelings or causing worry and negativity. You may also experience a conflict between your sense of duty and your heart's desire. By learning detachment and how to express the universal love and compassion inherent in your life path, you are able to experience more joyful emotional fulfillment.

From your early years, you are likely to be interested in analyzing situations practically in order to understand and improve them. When you reach the age of twenty-three, your progressed Sun moves into Libra, commencing a thirty-year period of increased emphasis on your partnerships, both personally and professionally. This is a time when you can have an increased sense of beauty and harmony and may want to develop any creative potential you possess. Another turning point occurs at the age of fifty-three, when your progressed Sun moves into Scorpio, placing more emphasis on the power of transformation and stimulating you to seek deeper emotional meaning in your life.

Your Secret Self

Often the demonstration of affection can be very important to you, as you may have experienced instances of controlled love in your life or in your home growing up. As you can be skeptical, you may need to learn faith and decide whom you can trust. By cultivating self-confidence, you are more able to take care of your needs. It may be particularly important how you value yourself and others and how you allow others to value you.

Money is important, but you are usually willing to work hard for it. You often work better when you allow your intuition to sense the right time for an idea or project and then act spontaneously rather than becoming restricted by too much structure. Being so sensitive, you need regular periods alone to reflect and connect to your deeper inspiration.

Work & Vocation

With your ability to be analytical or even technically minded, you may be drawn to work in research, science, or the health and medical world. Similarly, your sharp intellect and communication skills can aid you in education or writing. The more humanitarian side of your nature may be fulfilled in the caring professions or social reform, and your interest in people can make you an excellent counselor. With your thirst for knowledge and practical thinking, you

FIXED STAR

Star's name: Alioth

Degree position: 7°52'–8°52' Virgo between the years 1930 and 2000

Magnitude: 2

Strength: ★★★★★★★

Orb: 2°10'

Constellation: Epsilon Ursa Major

Applicable days: August 29, 30, 31, September 1, 2, 3

Star qualities: Mars

Description: a blue-white star located in the tail of the Great Bear

PRIMARY STAR'S INFLUENCE

Alioth endows good judgment, a zest for life, and love of ease and comfort. Often you are broad-minded and inclined toward liberalism. This star imparts ambition to win, a competitive nature, and a constant need for activity. Alioth also imparts a talent for criticism and suggests that it should be used constructively.

Linked to your Sun's degree, Alioth's influence indicates an aptitude for business, sport, government posts, and dealing with the public. It can also stimulate thoroughness and the ability to exploit every situation, but warns against irritability and overconfidence.

• Positive: genuine, frank, endurance can overcome disappointment

• Negative: ruthlessness, egoism, destructiveness, obstinacy, overcritical

may well become an expert in your chosen field or enter the world of business. Alternatively, your natural creativity and love of beauty may attract you to a career as a musician, actor, or entertainer. Similarly, with a feel for nature, you may also be drawn to a career such as landscape gardener.

Famous people who share your birthday include writer Mary Shelley, physicist Ernest Rutherford, actors Raymond Massey and Timothy Bottoms, baseball player Ted Williams, and investor Warren Buffet.

Numerology

Artistic and creative, friendly, and sociable are just some of the ways others describe people with the number 30 birthday. You enjoy the good life, love socializing, and can be exceptionally charismatic and loyal. Gregarious, with good taste and an eye for style and form, you can achieve success in all types of work concerning art, design, and music. Similarly, possessing a need for self-expression and a natural talent for words, you may excel at writing, speaking, or singing. You possess strong feelings, and being in love or contented is a vital requirement. In your pursuit of happiness, avoid being lazy or overindulgent. Among those with number 30 birthdays, many will find recognition or fame, especially musicians, actors, and entertainers. The subinfluence of the number 8 month indicates that you are hardworking and idealistic, with strong willpower and an ambitious nature. With sincere, spontaneous enthusiasm and an enterprising nature, you often take ideas and expand them in your own dramatic style.

- *Positive:* fun-loving, loyal, friendly, good conversationalist, creative, lucky
- *Negative:* lazy, obstinate, erratic, impatient, insecure, indifferent, scattered

Love & Relationships

Although you are an affectionate person, with a passionate and romantic nature, a need for variety and adventure implies that you may also become impatient and restless. You are often generous and giving, but at times you can become cold or withdrawn. In your relationships it is especially good for you to get away from routine by taking a short break or a quick pleasure trip. Sensitive to others, you may go through many changes in response to your partner's needs, so it is important to keep independent and enthusiastic.

YOUR SPECIAL SOMEONE

To find love and long-lasting relationships, look out for someone born on one of the following dates.

Love & friendship: Jan. 2, 9, 11, 12, 22, 25, Feb. 7, 10, 20, 23, 26, Mar. 5, 7, 8, 18, 21, Apr. 3, 5, 6, 16, 19, May 1, 4, 14, 17, 20, 24, 29, June 2, 12, 15, 27, July 10, 13, 16, 20, 25, 30, Aug. 9, 15, 24, 26, Sept. 7, 13, 22, 24, Oct. 4, 7, 10, 14, 19, 24, 28, 29, Nov. 2, 5, 8, 12, 17, 22, 26, 27, Dec. 3, 6, 10, 15, 20, 24, 25

Beneficial: Jan. 12, 23, 29, Feb. 10, 21, 27, Mar. 22, 26, Apr. 6, 17, 23, May 4, 15, 21, June 2, 13, 19, 28, 30, July 11, 17, 26, 28, Aug. 9, 15, 24, 26, Sept. 7, 13, 22, 24, Oct. 5, 11, 20, 22, Nov. 3, 9, 18, 20, 30, Dec. 1, 7, 16, 18, 28

Fatal attractions: Feb. 25, 26, 27, 28, July 29, Aug. 27, Sept. 25, Oct. 23, Nov. 21, Dec. 19

Challenging: Jan. 1, 4, 26, 30, Feb. 2, 24, 28, Mar. 22, 26, Apr. 20, 24, May 18, 22, 31, June 16, 20, 29, July 14, 18, 27, Aug. 12, 16, 25, 30, Sept. 10, 14, 23, 28, Oct. 8, 12, 21, 26, Nov. 6, 10, 19, 24, Dec. 4, 8, 17, 22

Soul mates: Jan. 20, Feb. 18, Mar. 16, Apr. 14, May 12, June 10, July 8, Aug. 6, Sept. 4, Oct. 2

August 31

♍ Your birthday shows you to be an industrious idealist with analytical skills, an active imagination, and powerful emotions. The unique combination of personal magnetism, communication skills, and determination gives you a creative flair for combining business and pleasure.

The double influence of Mercury implies clarity of vision and an ability to assimilate and analyze the smallest details. Usually articulate and discreet, you like to make up your own mind by methodical deduction. By refining and discriminating, you achieve excellence; just be careful that your pursuit for perfection does not turn into negative criticism and self-righteousness.

You have an appreciation of beauty and luxury and are likely to possess a good voice. It is through the use of your dynamic love, power, enthusiasm, and generosity that you can charm and impress others. At times you can be obstinate, withdrawn, or moody, challenging others to understand the many different facets of your personality.

Broad-minded, with a natural business sense, you communicate your values and show interest in money issues. Nevertheless, you possess an abundance of feelings and grand dreams.

A desire to transcend ordinary, mundane life may possibly manifest as an interest in metaphysical, mystical, or religious subjects. Since you can throw yourself wholeheartedly into a project if interested, you may have to be careful not to exhaust yourself by working too hard.

Your progressed Sun moves into Libra for a thirty-year period when you reach the age of twenty-two. From this time you gradually become more aware of the importance of your social relationships and partnerships. Your creative abilities and sense of harmony are enhanced and you may be drawn to develop any latent musical, artistic, or literary interests. At the age of fifty-two you reach another life turning point as your progressed Sun enters Scorpio. This brings a strong emphasis on a deeper need for emotional change, making you more self-reliant and in control.

FIXED STAR

Star's name: Alioth

Degree position: 7°52'–8°52' Virgo between the years 1930 and 2000

Magnitude: 2

Strength: ★★★★★★★

Orb: 2°10'

Constellation: Epsilon Ursa Major

Applicable days: August 29, 30, 31, September 1, 2, 3

Star qualities: Mars

Description: a blue-white star located in the tail of the Great Bear

PRIMARY STAR'S INFLUENCE

Alioth endows good judgment, a zest for life, and love of ease and comfort. Often you are broad-minded and inclined toward liberalism. This star imparts ambition to win, a competitive nature, and a constant need for activity. Alioth also imparts a talent for criticism and suggests that it should be used constructively.

Linked to your Sun's degree, Alioth's influence indicates an aptitude for business, sport, government posts, and dealing with the public. It can also stimulate thoroughness and the ability to exploit every situation, but warns against irritability and overconfidence.

• Positive: genuine, frank, endurance can overcome disappointment

• Negative: ruthlessness, egoism, destructiveness, obstinacy, overcritical

Your Secret Self

Your greatest potential may lie in an inner need to shine and inspire others, flowing from your natural honesty and high idealism. When developed, this asset will help you overcome everyday difficulties. If disturbed, you could become cold and lose faith, but once back on track you display a wonderful spontaneity and openness.

Since your birthday is identified with an emotional intensity, guard against using this in power tactics, especially when you are disappointed with others. There may be a conflict between your ideals and a very different reality. The key to your success lies in your compassionate understanding of people and situations. When this concern for others is combined with your enthusiasm and social skills, you can create harmony and happiness for yourself and those around you.

Work & Vocation

Your flair for people and a natural understanding of current trends can help you excel in promoting a vision in sales or media. The business world may also lure you to become an executive, entrepreneur, or philanthropist. While your analytical mind may be attracted to scientific research, editing, or education, your creative expression may prefer an outlet through writing, music, art, or the entertainment world. Many people of this birthdate are often dexterous. Being practical and exact can draw you to careers such as accountancy, working with property, or engineering. Alternatively, your idealism and sensitivity may lead you to charity work or the caring and medical professions.

Famous people who share your birthday include actors Richard Gere and James Coburn, educator Maria Montessori, singer/songwriter Van Morrison, violinist Itzhak Perlman, and composer Paul Winter.

Numerology

Strong willpower, determination, and an emphasis on self-expression are indicated by the number 31 birthday. Usually you are tireless and determined, with a desire to make material progress. You may have to learn, however, to accept the limitations of life and therefore need to build a solid foundation. Good fortune and lucky opportunities also suggest that you can be successful in turning your leisure-time pursuits into profitable ventures. Having fun is crucial to you, as you are very hardworking. You may have to guard against tendencies to be selfish or overly optimistic. The subinfluence of the number 8 month indicates that you are ambitious, practical, and intelligent, with executive skills and a need to accomplish. Since you are looking for emotional satisfaction, you may have to develop ways to assert yourself rather than succumb to overindulgence in material desires. You may also need to learn how to communicate your ideas or express your feelings more clearly and openly.

• *Positive:* lucky, creative, original, builder, constructive, persistent, practical, good conversationalist, responsible

• *Negative:* insecure, impatient, suspicious, easily discouraged, lack of ambition, selfish, stubborn

Love & Relationships

With your gregarious and charming personality, you can easily win people's hearts. Although you enjoy being social and outgoing, when you finally find your ideal partner you are loyal and make every effort to build a long-lasting relationship. Usually you marry for mental affinity and need a partner who can provide you with security and support. Encounters with people from foreign countries could bring special close friendships. By learning to overcome mental or nervous sensitivity, you can create greater balance and harmony.

YOUR SPECIAL SOMEONE

Finding your ideal partner may be easier with someone born on one of the following days.

Love & friendship: Jan. 8, 11, 23, 29, Feb. 6, 9, 27, Mar. 4, 7, 19, 25, 29, Apr. 2, 5, 23, 27, May 3, 21, 25, June 1, 19, 23, July 17, 21, Aug. 15, 19, 29, Sept. 13, 17, 27, Oct. 11, 15, 25, 29, 30, Nov. 9, 13, 23, 27, 28, Dec. 7, 11, 21, 25, 26

Beneficial: Jan. 13, 30, Feb. 11, 28, Mar. 9, 26, Apr. 7, 24, 30, May 5, 22, 28, June 3, 20, 26, July 1, 18, 24, 29, Aug. 16, 22, 25, Sept. 14, 20, 25, Oct. 12, 18, 23, Nov. 10, 16, 21, Dec. 8, 14, 19

Fatal attractions: Feb. 27, 28, 29, Oct. 30, Nov. 28, Dec. 26

Challenging: Jan. 5, 19, Feb. 3, 17, Mar. 1, 15, Apr. 13, May 11, June 9, 30, July 7, 28, 30, Aug. 5, 26, 28, Sept. 3, 24, 26, Oct. 1, 22, 24, Nov. 20, 22, Dec. 18, 20

Soul mates: Jan. 7, Feb. 5, Mar. 3, Apr. 4, Sept. 30, Oct. 28, Nov. 26, Dec. 24

September 1

♍ Independent, with a desire for prosperity, you have a birthday that suggests that you need to channel your innovative ideas into some form of accomplishment. Ambitious, you aim high and are naturally business-minded and good at commercializing your abilities. Quick at assessing people and situations, you can be creative, pioneering, and swift to see opportunities. Conscious of your appearance, you like to present a smart image that spells success.

The double impact of Virgo, which is both your planetary and decanate ruler, emphasizes your keen intellect and thirst for knowledge. This influence can also accent nervousness, so it may be necessary for you to ensure that you take regular breaks to keep calm. Communication, whether speaking or writing, is likely to be an area where you can excel, and with your precise mental approach you are likely to be articulate. With your high standards and thorough approach to work, be careful that you do not become too critical of yourself or others.

Since your potential for being financially successful is extremely high, you may only need to apply the necessary self-discipline and avoid procrastination to achieve results. Luckily, you are usually hardworking and a good planner or delegator. Although practical, you may like to take a risk when the odds are in your favor, and you want good returns for your work.

After the age of twenty-one, when your progressed Sun moves into Libra, there is an increased need for partnership and relating to others. Your sense of harmony, balance, and refinement is likely to be enhanced, with the possibility of your exploring literary, artistic, or creative interests. This continues on until the age of fifty-one, when your progressed Sun enters Scorpio. At this turning point you will probably realize the growing importance of touching deeper and more subtle aspects of your psyche as well as evaluating your own power.

Fixed Star

Star's name: Alioth

Degree position: 7°52'–8°52' Virgo between the years 1930 and 2000

Magnitude: 2

Strength: ★★★★★★★

Orb: 2°10'

Constellation: Epsilon Ursa Major

Applicable days: August 29, 30, 31, September 1, 2, 3

Star qualities: Mars

Description: a blue-white star located in the tail of the Great Bear

PRIMARY STAR'S INFLUENCE

Alioth endows good judgment, a zest for life, and a love of ease and comfort. Often you are broad-minded and inclined toward liberalism. This star imparts ambition to win, a competitive nature, and a constant need for activity. Alioth also imparts a talent for criticism and suggests that it should be used constructively.

Linked to your Sun's degree, Alioth's influence indicates an aptitude for business, sport, government posts, and dealing with the public. It can also stimulate thoroughness and the ability to exploit every situation, but warns against irritability and overconfidence.

• Positive: genuine, frank, endurance, can overcome disappointment

• Negative: ruthlessness, egoism, destructiveness, obstinacy, overcritical

Your Secret Self

An inner nobility suggests that you are proud and can be quietly dramatic. Being a practical idealist, you need to be of service to others and have a strong sense of purpose, or you may become restricted by materialism. At times you may be unexpectedly modest and at others confident and opinionated. As your ideas are original and ahead of their time, you need the freedom to express yourself. When you are positive and enthusiastic about a project, you have the ability to project this and excite others.

You are likely to be a natural networker who can link people from different groups. With your own philosophy of life, you are generally optimistic and good-humored. An urge to expand gives you a faculty to survey the whole; you are capable of leadership, foresight, and intuitive wisdom. The more you trust and apply this nonrational knowing to your everyday life, the more events will naturally fall into place.

Work & Vocation

With your organizing abilities, love of large enterprise, and ability to delegate, you would be excellent in business as an executive, a manager, or working for yourself. These same abilities would also aid you as an administrator, producer, or politician. Your skills in interacting with others could help you excel in education, writing, sales, or the communications world. Being competitive and thorough, and wanting to do a job well, you may become a specialist in your field or be drawn to research. Your desire to lead and pioneer could take you to careers as diverse as the military or the arts. Intuition and creativity are your natural talents, and by developing and refining these skills you are guaranteed success. It is important, however, in any career to stay as independent as possible.

Famous people who share your birthday include actress Lily Tomlin, boxer Rocky Marciano, singers Gloria Estefan and Barry Gibb, former Texas governor Ann Richards, and lawyer Alan Dershowitz.

Numerology

The great desire to be first and autonomous is suggested by your birthdate. As a number 1, you are inclined to be individual, innovative, and courageous, with plenty of energy. The pioneering spirit indicated here encourages you to make your own decisions or strike out alone. Full of enthusiasm and original ideas, you often show others the way forward. With a number 1 birthday, you may also need to learn that the world does not revolve around you. The subinfluence of the number 9 month indicates that you are highly intuitive and sensitive. Since you are influenced by your environment, you are also receptive to others. Often broadminded and a humanitarian, you seek fairness and justice. To others you may appear confident and resilient, but inner tensions may cause emotional ups and downs. Decisive and resourceful, you possess depth of vision, but the dreamer side of your nature is compassionate and idealistic.

• *Positive:* leadership, creative, progressive, forceful, optimistic, strong convictions, competitive, independent, gregarious

• *Negative:* overbearing, jealous, egotistical, antagonistic, lack of restraint, weak, unstable, impatient

Love & Relationships

Since you often have strong desires and feelings, you need to communicate on a personal level. You possess charm and a charismatic personality and can easily draw friends and admirers. You are attracted to optimistic people who can inspire you with new ideas and opportunities. Your love for freedom suggests that you may prefer to be in relationships that can give you enough space to feel independent. Since you may need to take your time where love is concerned, it is advisable not to make commitments too soon.

YOUR SPECIAL SOMEONE

To keep you interested in loving relationships, you might want to look out for those born on the following days.

Love & friendship: Jan. 6, 10, 15, 29, 31, Feb. 4, 13, 27, 29, Mar. 2, 11, 25, 27, Apr. 9, 25, 23, 30, May 7, 21, 23, 28, June 5, 19, 21, July 3, 17, 19, 30, Aug. 1, 15, 17, 28, Sept. 13, 15, 26, Oct. 11, 13, 24, Nov. 9, 11, 22, Dec. 7, 9, 20

Beneficial: Jan. 13, 15, 19, Feb. 11, 13, 17, Mar. 9, 11, 15, Apr. 7, 9, 13, May 5, 7, 11, June 3, 5, 9, July 1, 3, 7, 29, Aug. 1, 5, 27, 31, Sept. 3, 25, 29, Oct. 1, 23, 27, Nov. 21, 25, Dec. 19, 23

Fatal attractions: Feb. 28, 29, Mar. 1, May 30, June 28, July 26, Aug. 24, Sept. 22, Oct. 20, Nov. 18, Dec. 16

Challenging: Jan. 12, Feb. 10, Mar. 8, Apr. 6, May 4, June 2, Aug. 31, Sept. 29, Oct. 27, 29, 30, Nov. 25, 27, 28, Dec. 23, 25, 26, 30

Soul mates: Jan. 2, 28, Feb. 26, Mar. 24, Apr. 22, May 20, June 18, July 16, Aug. 14, Sept. 12, Oct. 10, Nov. 8, Dec. 6

September 2

♍ Your birthday suggests that you are practical yet sensitive, clever, friendly, and considerate. Enthusiastic and independent, you possess the ability to inspire others with your ideas and projects. Nevertheless, do not let frustration or disappointment spoil your big plans.

With the subinfluence of your decanate ruler, Virgo, you can be thorough, hardworking, methodical, and painstaking. As you possess a keen intellect, a desire for knowledge keeps you well informed. Although you carefully analyze situations, be wary of becoming too skeptical or constantly going over the same issues, causing worry and anxiety.

Naturally generous and a good psychologist, you can also be a person of extremes. At times you can be humanitarian and broad-minded and at others nervous and compulsive. Being a practical visionary, as well as resourceful, you prefer to be active rather than idle.

An inventive mind gives you quick responses and is particularly helpful when working in a team or partnership situation. Appearance is important, and you like to make a good impression. Enjoying the company of others, you can be warm and charming, with a sense of humor that can often get you out of a tight spot.

From childhood, you are likely to be constantly analyzing situations in order to improve them. However, when you reach the age of twenty, your progressed Sun moves into Libra, commencing a thirty-year period of increased emphasis on your partnerships and relating to others. This is a time when you may also have an increased sense of balance and harmony and may want to develop any creative potential you possess. Another turning point occurs at the age of fifty, when your progressed Sun moves into Scorpio, stimulating you to seek deeper meaning to your life and placing more emphasis on the power of transformation.

Your Secret Self

At times you are likely to experience a conflict between idealism and materialism. Being a good evaluator, with an instinct for money matters, you may find it more beneficial at times to take calculated risks. You also like some excitement. It can, however, still be a challenge to live well without becoming either too extravagant or too economical. Possible fluctuations in finances may necessitate a long-term plan to manage your assets.

The more you build up your confidence and self-esteem, the more life has to offer you. It will be easier if you develop detachment from your restrictions. Travel, new explorations, sports, and exercise are particularly advantageous. These help channel any possible restlessness and impatience you may have into more positive outlets and stimulate your adventurous spirit.

Work & Vocation

You may find you enjoy your work more if it involves broad variety. As you generally work well in partnerships or cooperatively with others, you may be drawn to careers in the media, counseling, social work, or public relations. The more practical side of your nature may find an outlet through banking, the stock market, or accountancy. As you may also possess analyti-

FIXED STARS

Alioth, Zosma

PRIMARY STAR

Star's name: Alioth

Degree position: 7°52'–8°52' Virgo between the years 1930 and 2000

Magnitude: 2

Strength: ★★★★★★★

Orb: 2°10'

Constellation: Epsilon Ursa Major

Applicable days: August 29, 30, 31, September 1, 2, 3

Star qualities: Mars

Description: a blue-white star located in the tail of the Great Bear

PRIMARY STAR'S INFLUENCE

Alioth endows good judgment, a zest for life, and a love of ease and comfort. Often you are broad-minded and inclined toward liberalism. This star imparts ambition to win, a competitive nature, and a constant need for activity. Alioth also imparts a talent for criticism and suggests that it should be used constructively.

Linked to your Sun's degree, Alioth's influence indicates an aptitude for business, sport, government posts, and dealing with the public. It can also stimulate thoroughness and the ability to exploit every situation, but warns against irritability and overconfidence.

• *Positive:* genuine, frank, endurance, can overcome disappointment

cal or technical skills, you may be attracted to a career in education, writing, or science. When your discrimination is combined with your compassion and desire to serve, you may be drawn to the healing professions or helping others. This birthdate can indicate possible success in show business, particularly music, as well as sport.

Famous people who share your birthday include tennis player Jimmy Connors, musician Russ Conway, actor Keanu Reeves, teacher/astronaut Christa McAuliffe, and football players Eric Dickerson and Terry Bradshaw.

Numerology

Sensitivity and a strong need to be part of a group is suggested by your number 2 birthday. Often you are adaptable and understanding, and you enjoy cooperative activities. A love of harmony and a desire to interact with others may inspire you to act as a mediator in family matters or become a peacemaker. In your attempt to please, you may run the risk of becoming overly dependent. The subinfluence of the number 9 month indicates that you are highly perceptive, imaginative, and sympathetic. Usually you are independent, broad-minded, and liberal, though at times you may have fixed ideas. As a humanitarian who seeks fairness and justice, with your foresight and progressive outlook, you can be spiritual yet practical. Avoid being hasty and overemotional, or reacting in an extreme manner. You may need to learn to communicate your thoughts and feelings in an open way.

• *Positive:* considerate, good partner, gentle, tactful, receptive, intuitive, harmonious, agreeable, ambassador of goodwill

• *Negative:* suspicious, lack of confidence, subservient, oversensitive, selfish, easily hurt, deceitful

Love & Relationships

A friendly communicator, you need a circle of friends who enjoy discussion or with whom you share some type of intellectual pursuits. Although you may sometimes seem too detached, you have a warm heart. At times, hidden insecurities may indicate that instead of being your usual diplomatic self, you can become argumentative, creating tension or unrest. Nevertheless, you are a loyal, loving, and supportive friend and partner.

YOUR SPECIAL SOMEONE

To find long-lasting happiness, security, and love, you might begin by looking for someone born on one of the following days.

Love & friendship: Jan. 2, 6, 16, 19, Feb. 4, 14, Mar. 2, 12, 28, 30, Apr. 10, 26, 28, May 8, 11, 24, 26, 30, June 6, 22, 24, 28, July 4, 20, 22, 26, 31, Aug. 2, 18, 20, 24, 29, Sept. 16, 18, 22, 27, Oct. 14, 16, 20, 25, Nov. 12, 14, 18, 23, Dec. 10, 12, 16, 21

Beneficial: Jan. 9, 14, 16, Feb. 7, 12, 14, Mar. 5, 10, 12, Apr. 3, 8, 10, May 1, 6, 8, June 4, 6, July 2, 4, Aug. 2, Sept. 30, Oct. 28, Nov. 26, 30, Dec. 24, 28, 29

Fatal attractions: Jan. 21, Feb. 19, 29, Mar. 1, 2, 17, Apr. 15, May 13, June 11, July 9, Aug. 7, Sept. 5, Oct. 3, Nov. 1

Challenging: Jan. 4, 13, 28, Feb. 2, 11, 26, Mar. 9, 24, Apr. 7, 22, May 5, 20, June 3, 18, July 1, 16, Aug. 14, Sept. 12, Oct. 10, 31, Nov. 8, 29, Dec. 6, 27

Soul mates: Jan. 15, 22, Feb. 13, 20, Mar. 11, 18, Apr. 9, 16, May 7, 14, June 5, 12, July 3, 10, Aug. 1, 8, Sept. 6, Oct. 4, Nov. 2

September 3

ℳ Your birthday suggests you are practical and friendly, a sharp and determined individual with strong willpower. An amiable companion, you are socially inclined and good company. As you possess the desire to constantly expand and improve yourself, you need only be clear about your goals to achieve success. This birthdate points to creative power as well as a capacity to overcome obstacles and perform record achievements.

With the subinfluence of your decanate ruler, Capricorn, you possess good concentration and a mind that assimilates and discriminates. Realistic and hardworking, you are methodical and a good organizer. Possessing a natural business sense, you have a no-nonsense approach and communicate in a clear and precise manner. Although reliable and thorough, you may have to avoid fault-finding or becoming stuck in a routine.

Ambitious, active, and productive, you are not apt to feel like a victim of destiny. Although you are persistent and enduring, avoid tasks that leave no room for new experiences. Being proud, you may have to refrain from being condescending to others; if tense, you may become irritable and frustrated. Luckily, you are also talented and quick-witted and can be the life and soul of the party. The more inspired among those born on this date often find self-expression through a love of art, music, or literature.

From childhood you are likely to be interested in analyzing situations in order to better understand and improve them. After the age of nineteen, as your progressed Sun moves into Libra for a thirty-year period, you gradually become more aware of the importance of your social relationships and partnerships. Your creative abilities are enhanced, and you may be drawn to develop any latent musical, artistic, or literary interests. At the age of forty-nine you reach another life turning point as your progressed Sun enters Scorpio. This brings a strong emphasis on a deeper need for change, transformation, and personal power.

FIXED STARS

Alioth, Zosma

PRIMARY STAR

Star's name: Alioth

Degree position: 7°52'–8°52' Virgo between the years 1930 and 2000

Magnitude: 2

Strength: ★★★★★★★

Orb: 2°10'

Constellation: Epsilon Ursa Major

Applicable days: August 29, 30, 31, September 1, 2, 3

Star qualities: Mars

Description: a blue-white star located in the tail of the Great Bear

PRIMARY STAR'S INFLUENCE

Alioth endows good judgment, a zest for life, and love of ease and comfort. Often you are broad-minded and inclined toward liberalism. This star imparts ambition to win, a competitive nature, and a constant need for activity. Alioth also imparts a talent for criticism and suggests that it should be used constructively.

Linked to your Sun's degree, Alioth's influence indicates an aptitude for business, sport, government posts, and dealing with the public. It can also stimulate thoroughness and the ability to exploit every situation, but warns against irritability and overconfidence.

• *Positive:* genuine, frank, endurance, can overcome disappointment

Your Secret Self

Your assertive and confident front often hides your sensitivity. Although at times you can be very concerned with material issues, it is through trusting your intuition that you can overcome a doubting or skeptical outlook. Although you need regular periods of rest or retreat, you may have to be careful not to isolate yourself. If you feel emotionally down, there is a danger you may become cold, obstinate, or domineering in your attempt to keep control of outside circumstances. When inspired, however, you are daring, fast, competitive, and spontaneous, truly able to express your sharp insight in a fun and creative way.

Your innate wisdom can manifest as natural authority, and your razor-sharp mind and love of knowledge endow you with an ability to deal with any situation. Possessing a strong personality and the potential for self-mastery, you have a power and strength that can uplift others and help you achieve your inspired dreams.

Work & Vocation

You enjoy power, structure, and efficiency, and you can excel particularly in business as an organizer, manager, or executive. Possessing a gift with words, you may also accomplish through law, writing, education, or politics. Communication in all forms, however, is likely to be part of your natural work experience. An amiable charm can also be of great assistance in your dealings with others and guarantees your success in people-related careers. Being very thorough and painstaking in your approach may attract you to research, science, or technical work. Since you are very independent and do not like taking orders, you may prefer being your own boss or delegating to others. A straightforward, matter-of-fact attitude may guarantee that you do not waste time but aim straight for your objectives.

Famous people who share your birthday include actor Charlie Sheen, blues musician Memphis Slim, actor Alan Ladd, physicist Carl Anderson, and writer Loren Eiseley.

Numerology

A need for love and creativity is indicated by the number 3 birthday. Often fun-loving and a good companion, you enjoy friendly social activities. You possess a strong need for self-expression and when positive can radiate the joy of life. An inclination to get bored easily, however, may cause you to become indecisive or spread yourself thin. Nevertheless, you are usually artistic and charming, with a good sense of humor. A talent with words may manifest through speaking, writing, or singing. Since you may need to develop self-esteem, guard against tendencies toward worry and other emotional insecurities. The subinfluence of the number 9 month indicates that you have good reasoning powers and are highly intuitive. Often you need to overcome restrictions and challenges before you find peace and harmony. With your insight you can often be a visionary but may have to learn to communicate your thoughts and feelings in an open way.

• *Positive:* humorous, happy, friendly, productive, creative, artistic, good conversationalist, power to wish, freedom-loving

• *Negative:* easily bored, vain, exaggerate, boastful, extravagant, self-indulgent, lazy, hypocritical

Love & Relationships

With your dynamic charm, you usually have many friends and acquaintances. Although you are hardworking, you enjoy having fun and socializing. You are often a tower of support for others, and your own need for love is not always obvious from your confident personality. Though you are usually attracted to powerful yet creative individuals, avoid martyring yourself. Since you are independent, at times you can be ambiguous about love, but once you settle down you can be faithful and caring.

YOUR SPECIAL SOMEONE

You might find a partner who will understand your sensitivity and need for love among those born on the following dates.

Love & friendship: Jan. 1, 7, 17, 20, 21, Feb. 5, 15, 18, Mar. 3, 13, 16, 29, 31, Apr. 1, 11, 14, 27, 29, May 9, 12, 13, 25, 27, June 7, 10, 23, 25, July 5, 8, 21, 23, Aug. 3, 6, 19, 21, Sept. 1, 4, 17, 19, Oct. 2, 15, 17, 23, Nov. 13, 15, 30, Dec. 11, 13, 19, 28

Beneficial: Jan. 15, 17, 28, Feb. 13, 15, 26, Mar. 11, 13, 24, Apr. 9, 11, 22, May 7, 9, 20, June 5, 7, 18, July 3, 5, 16, Aug. 1, 3, 14, Sept. 1, 12, Oct. 10, 29, Nov. 8, 27, Dec. 6, 25

Fatal attractions: Jan. 5, Feb. 3, Mar. 1, 2, 3

Challenging: Jan. 4, 5, 14, Feb. 2, 3, 12, Mar. 1, 10, Apr. 8, 30, May 6, 28, June 4, 26, July 2, 24, Aug. 22, Sept. 20, Oct. 18, Nov. 16, Dec. 14

Soul mates: Jan. 2, Mar. 29, Apr. 27, May 25, June 23, July 21, Aug. 19, Sept. 17, Oct. 15, Nov. 13, Dec. 11

September 4

♍ An interesting mixture of shrewd practicality and idealistic sensitivity, you are a hardworking and persuasive individual. A realist who is interested in people, you can be a loyal and faithful friend or companion. With the subinfluence of your decanate ruler, Capricorn, you possess the ability to work with meticulous precision. Your fine mind can analyze and research the details, but can also incline you to worry or become overcritical with yourself or others. Reliable and thorough, you can be most productive in your work but may have a conflict between duty and love.

Since you possess a desire for harmony, your appreciation of beauty and luxury, if developed, can lead to artistic or creative talent. You are likely to be a long-term planner, and although money is important, you are willing to work hard to acquire it. Protective of your family, you desire stability and need to be appreciated.

Although you can be charming and responsible, with a heightened awareness of relationships, you can also possess tightly controlled emotions. These extreme sides of your personality show, on one hand, a caring and humanitarian nature and, on the other, that you can sometimes be overly serious or rigid in your views.

After the age of eighteen, when your progressed Sun moves into Libra for a thirty-year period, there is an increased need for partnership and relating. Your sense of harmony and beauty are likely to be enhanced, with the possibility of exploring literary, artistic, or creative outlets in some form. This continues until the age of forty-eight, when your progressed Sun enters Scorpio. This is a turning point for you that will highlight a growing emphasis on emotional and spiritual regeneration as well as joint finances or corporate business activity. When you turn seventy-eight your progressed Sun moves into Sagittarius, accenting your personal philosophy and desire for truth.

Fixed Star

Star's name: Zosma

Degree position: 10°19'–11°14' Virgo between the years 1930 and 2000

Magnitude: 2.5

Strength: ★★★★★★

Orb: 2°10'

Constellation: Delta Leo

Applicable days: September 2, 3, 4, 5, 6

Star qualities: Saturn/Venus

Description: a white, pale yellow, and blue-violet triple star located on the Lion's back

PRIMARY STAR'S INFLUENCE

Zosma bestows a serious and responsible nature and an alert mind, but also warns against becoming overserious or selfish. You may experience changeable circumstances but should guard against unwarranted fears and anxieties. Positively, Zosma can impart a liberal attitude, charm, and a positive approach as well as unexpected success and advancement.

Linked to your Sun's degree, this star can help you gain power and convince others with your opinions. You can become influential and rise socially, as Zosma bestows friendliness and popularity. Although you can appear extroverted and gregarious, usually your nature is somewhat reserved. This star warns that only in time of need will you find out who are your true friends.

• Positive: loyal, dutiful, thoroughness

• Negative: shamelessness, egotistical, false friends, overseriousness

Your Secret Self

It may be important for you to learn to be emotionally detached without appearing cold or withdrawn. This allows you to be spontaneous without trying to be in control. Because you are so sensitive on an inner level, the demonstration of affection can be very important to you. Earlier in your life you may have experienced instances of controlled love, where you had to live up to other people's expectations, but as you learn to value yourself and your feelings you become more confident and less willing to compromise yourself for the approval of others. When negative, your powerful emotions can be expressed as disappointment, frustration, and an inability to let go of the past. When positive, you are generous and deeply loving. At these times your openness can expose you to a universal compassion or spiritual sensitivity that can heighten your desire to be of service to others.

Work & Vocation

Good at combining business and pleasure, you can be an excellent diplomat. An innate caring side to your nature may draw you to careers that involve service, such as counseling or teaching. Equally, the worlds of sales, commerce, and communications can be excellent outlets for your keen intellect and ability to deal with people. You possess a good business sense and are usually able to turn talents into financial assets. With possible technical as well as practical skills, you may be drawn to manufacturing, engineering, research, or even property speculation. Generally, you are likely to fare better in occupations that contain variety and change, as you do not like routine and may become bored. If in the healing world, you tend to take a very practical, down-to-earth approach.

Famous people who share your birthday include manufacturer Henry Ford II, writer Richard Wright, astrologer/writer Liz Greene, outlaw Jesse James, and architect Daniel Burnham.

Numerology

The solid structure and orderly power suggested by the number 4 birthday indicate that often you need stability and like to establish order. With a number 4 birthday, you are sensitive to form and composition. Security-conscious, you like to build a strong foundation for yourself and your family. Your pragmatic approach to life confers a good business sense and an ability to achieve material success in life. Faithful though undemonstrative, you are usually honest, frank, and fair. Nevertheless, you may have to learn how to express your feelings. The challenges for a number 4 individual may include overcoming periods of instability. The subinfluence of the number 9 month indicates that you are receptive, yet rational. Since you are also sensitive to your environment, you need time away from it all once in a while. Often reserved, yet broad-minded and humanitarian, you seek fairness and justice.

• *Positive:* well organized, self-disciplined, steady, hardworking, good with your hands, pragmatic, trusting, exact

• *Negative:* uncommunicative, repressed, rigid, lazy, unfeeling, procrastination, too economical, bossy, resentful, strict

Love & Relationships

Usually idealistic, sensitive, and charming, with the ability to captivate others, you can be romantic and loving. You take your personal relationships seriously and can be very committed. Avoid going too far on occasions and giving too much of yourself when it is not fully appreciated. Relationships can often be a mixed blessing for you if you lose your balance of power and independence, causing you to alternate between being warm and spontaneous, and tough and inflexible. You possess a strong need to express yourself, however, which, creatively used, can prove a source of delight and contentment. You can be very generous to the people you care for, and you take their needs seriously.

YOUR SPECIAL SOMEONE

You might find a partner who will understand your sensitivity and need for love among those born on the following dates.

Love & friendship: Jan. 4, 8, 9, 13, 18, 19, 23, Feb. 2, 6, 16, 17, 21, Mar. 4, 9, 14, 15, 19, 28, 30, Apr. 2, 12, 13, 17, 26, 28, 30, May 1, 5, 10, 11, 15, 24, 26, 28, June 8, 9, 13, 22, 24, 26, July 6, 7, 11, 20, 22, 24, 30, Aug. 4, 5, 9, 18, 20, 22, 28, Sept. 2, 3, 7, 16, 18, 20, 26, Oct. 1, 5, 14, 16, 18, 24, Nov. 3, 12, 14, 16, 22, Dec. 1, 10, 12, 14, 20

Beneficial: Jan. 5, 16, 27, Feb. 3, 14, 25, Mar. 1, 12, 23, Apr. 10, 21, May 8, 19, June 6, 17, July 4, 15, Aug. 2, 13, Sept. 11, Oct. 9, 30, Nov. 7, 28, Dec. 5, 26, 30

Fatal attractions: Jan. 17, Feb. 15, Mar. 1, 2, 3, 4, 13, Apr. 11, May 9, June 7, July 5, Aug. 3, Sept. 1

Challenging: Jan. 1, 10, 15, Feb. 8, 13, Mar. 6, 11, Apr. 4, 9, May 2, 7, June 5, July 3, 29, Aug. 1, 27, Sept. 25, Oct. 23, Nov. 21, Dec. 19, 29

Soul mates: Aug. 30, Sept. 28, Oct. 26, Nov. 24, Dec. 22

September 5

♍ Judicious, prudent, yet charming, you are a frank and open individual who possesses a kind heart and sound common sense. Although courteous and modest, you can still make big plans and are a good organizer. Friendly and agreeable in your approach, you have a need to be constantly learning and improving yourself. Be careful that dissatisfaction does not dampen your usual optimism.

With the subinfluence of your decanate ruler, Capricorn, you are realistic and hardworking, with keen perceptions. Independent and capable, you have an analytical approach and take pleasure in being productive. In your desire for perfection, guard against worrying over small issues and being too critical. This can induce a quick irritability that can spoil the harmony you seek.

This birthdate usually promises well-being, physical comfort, and economic security. You may be drawn toward freedom, change, or travel, but you equally need the stability of a strong home base. A restlessness can either spur you to achieve your grand plans or weaken your sense of purpose. If drifting, you may become too enmeshed in the problems of others. Your interest in a wide range of subjects can be a positive influence as long as you do not scatter your forces. You are usually able to succeed through perseverance and the tenacious pursuit of your plans.

From an early age you are likely to have been practical and analyzed situations in order to improve them. After the age of seventeen, when your progressed Sun moves into Libra, you grow more socially oriented, with a strong need to be popular and appreciated. Professional or personal partnerships start to play a more important part in your life. From the age of forty-seven, your power is enhanced when your progressed Sun moves into Scorpio, making you more self-reliant and in control. At the age of seventy-seven, you experience another turning point as your progressed Sun enters Sagittarius. This brings a new, more positive and expansive energy into your life.

Your Secret Self

It is important to build up your confidence, which may be strengthened by your ability to express yourself in all areas in your life. Although creative and intuitive, you may suffer from frustration and difficulty in making decisions about which way to go. This may not be helped by the fact that, being a good advisor, you attract people who want you to help them but are not always available for you. It may be necessary to let them learn through their own mistakes, rather than your always being there as a support.

When in a positive frame of mind, you have a broad-minded and universal approach to life, are sociable, and possess a very warm interest in people. At these times, you are able to make decisions that help you stay focused but detached. Education may be particularly helpful in your quest for self-awareness.

Work & Vocation

With a natural business sense, you are able to commercialize your talents. You need variety to prevent yourself from becoming bored, and so it is important that you not be stuck in a routine. The potential to be technical may draw you to science, engineering, or computers. A tal-

FIXED STAR

Star's name: Zosma

Degree position: 10°19'–11°14' Virgo between the years 1930 and 2000

Magnitude: 2.5

Strength: ★★★★★★★

Orb: 2°10'

Constellation: Delta Leo

Applicable days: September 2, 3, 4, 5, 6

Star qualities: Saturn/Venus

Description: a white, pale yellow, and blue-violet triple star located on the Lion's back

PRIMARY STAR'S INFLUENCE

Zosma bestows a serious and responsible nature and an alert mind, but also warns against becoming overserious or selfish. You may experience changeable circumstances but should guard against unwarranted fears and anxieties. Positively, Zosma can impart a liberal attitude, charm, and a positive approach as well as unexpected success and advancement.

Linked to your Sun's degree, this star can help you gain power and convince others with your opinions. You can become influential and rise socially, as Zosma bestows friendliness and popularity. Although you can appear extroverted and gregarious, usually your nature is somewhat reserved. This star warns that only in time of need will you find out who are your true friends.

• *Positive:* loyal, dutiful, thoroughness

• *Negative:* shamelessness, egotistical, false friends, overseriousness

ent for communication can help you in law or writing and make you an excellent critic. Similarly, success in dealing with people could draw you to promotion and sales. You are also likely to be successful in working with the earth, for instance in landscape gardening and building or in property speculation. A natural philosophical turn of mind may make professions in the clergy or education appealing to you. Alternatively, this birthdate can be an excellent influence for performers, composers, or songwriters.

Famous people who share your birthday include writer Arthur Koestler, composer John Cage, actress Raquel Welch, comedian Bob Newhart, singer Freddie Mercury, French king Louis XIV, director Werner Herzog, and cartoonist Cathy Guisewite.

Numerology

Strong instincts, an adventurous nature, and a desire for freedom are all indicated by the number 5 birthday. Travel and many opportunities for change, some unexpected, may lead you to undergo a real transformation of views and beliefs. Often the number 5 birthdate means that you have an active life and need to learn about patience and attention to detail; you can achieve success by avoiding premature or speculative actions. The natural talent of a number 5 individual is knowing how to go with the flow and staying detached. The subinfluence of the number 9 month indicates that you are rational, yet sensitive. As a humanitarian, you seek fairness and justice. With your foresight and progressive outlook, you can be spiritual, yet practical. Although you possess good business sense, you may need to work hard and put the effort in before you can gain success. Avoid being hasty or power-hungry.

• *Positive:* versatile, adaptable, progressive, magnetic, daring, freedom-loving, quick and witty, curious, mystical, sociable

• *Negative:* unreliable, changeable, procrastinator, inconsistent, undependable, overconfident, headstrong

Love & Relationships

Since you have a natural flair for dealing with people, you have the ability to make friends anywhere. With this capacity often comes the need to employ a certain amount of discretion. Generous and caring, you are likely to be popular with others. When positive, you can project a strong and powerful love that can bring you success romantically as well as socially. You can be very protective of your family, and you can be a loyal friend.

YOUR SPECIAL SOMEONE

You may find a longer-lasting relationship and stability with someone born on one of the following dates.

Love & friendship: Jan. 3, 5, 9, 10, 18, 19, Feb. 3, 7, 16, 17, Mar. 1, 5, 6, 14, 15, 31, Apr. 3, 12, 13, 29, May 1, 10, 11, 27, 29, June 8, 9, 25, 27, July 6, 7, 23, 25, 31, Aug. 4, 5, 21, 23, 29, Sept. 2, 3, 19, 21, 27, 30, Oct. 1, 17, 19, 25, 28, Dec. 13, 15, 21, 24

Beneficial: Jan. 1, 6, 17, Feb. 4, 15, Mar. 2, 13, Apr. 11, May 9, June 7, July 5, Aug. 3, Sept. 1, Oct. 31, Nov. 29, Dec. 27

Fatal attractions: Mar. 3, 4, 5, 6

Challenging: Jan. 2, 16, Feb. 14, Mar. 12, Apr. 10, May 8, June 6, July 4, Aug. 2, Dec. 30

Soul mates: Jan. 11, 31, Feb. 9, 29, Mar. 7, 27, Apr. 5, 25, May 3, 23, June 1, 21, July 19, Aug. 17, Sept. 15, Oct. 13, Nov. 11, Dec. 9

September 6

FIXED STARS

Although your Sun's degree is not linked to a fixed star, some of your other planets' degrees certainly will be. By having an astrological chart calculated, you can find the exact position of the planets on your date of birth. This will tell you which of the fixed stars listed in this book are relevant to you.

♍ The influence of this birthdate suggests that you are a practical idealist who needs stimulation and change to prevent you from becoming bored. Although you seek travel and adventure, you also need the security and comfort of your own home. Aware of image, you like to be popular and make a good impression.

The subinfluence of your decanate ruler, Capricorn, suggests that through hard work and perseverance you develop determination. With a mind that assimilates and discriminates, you possess keen perceptions and strong instincts. You may also be of service to your community as an advisor or specialist. Your work has a strong emphasis for you, but watch that restlessness or impatience does not cause you to become dissatisfied.

As you are likely to experience changeable financial situations in your life, it is advisable to save and consider long-term investments. These can work well for you and help you overcome any possible worry or anxiety about money. Versatile and adaptable, you can be highly focused when you have decided on a definite goal. Although you have a strong practical awareness, you also possess sensitive foresight, which can help you in the achievement of your grand visions.

After the age of sixteen, when your progressed Sun moves into Libra, there is an increased need for partnership and dealing with people on a one-to-one basis. Your sense of refinement and beauty is likely to be enhanced, with the possibility of your exploring literary, artistic, or creative interests. This continues until the age of forty-six, when your progressed Sun enters Scorpio. This turning point will highlight the growing importance of transformation as well as the evaluation of your own power. When you reach the age of seventy-six, your progressed Sun moves into Sagittarius, accenting your desire for more positivity and honesty.

Your Secret Self

If you channel your restlessness into something that really interests you, then you are able to become inspired enough to accept the responsibilities that bring you long-term satisfaction. At times you may suffer from self-doubt or insecurity, which come from not being certain you are making the right decisions. By being more detached, trusting that you will be taken care of in the larger plan, you are able to have a lighter and more creative approach to life.

An innate humanitarianism keeps you interested in people and enables you to maintain your sense of perspective. Sociable, with creative ideas, you may be happiest when expressing yourself. Your intuitive feelings are usually right and can often help you quickly judge others. You enjoy entertaining and can surprise people with your quick humor. A love of freedom may be linked with opportunities for travel and work in foreign countries.

Work & Vocation

Although you can be hardworking, you need a career that does not involve routine. Naturally analytical and able to carry out painstaking work, you could find fulfillment in research, science, or psychology. With a strong visual sense, you are also highly aware of image making and are suited for occupations such as advertising, media, graphics, or photography. If in business, you need variety and are not likely to stick with any work that does not reap financial rewards fairly quickly. Careers involving travel, sport, or leisure can also be excellent outlets for your energy and drive. People of this birthdate are often drawn to the health and medical world.

Famous people who share your birthday include scientist John Dalton, composer/ producer Billy Rose, social reformer Jane Addams, Kennedy patriarch Joseph Kennedy, and French general Marquis de Lafayette.

Numerology

Compassion, idealism, and a caring nature are some of the attributes suggested by a number 6 birthday. Frequently domestically inclined, you are a homemaker and a devoted parent. A desire for universal harmony and intense emotions often encourage you to work hard for what you believe in. The more sensitive among you will need to find a form of creative expression and are often drawn to the world of entertaining or art and design. The challenges for some number 6 individuals may include developing more self-confidence and compassion toward friends and neighbors as well as learning to be more responsible. The subinfluence of the number 9 month indicates that you are highly intuitive and sensitive. With your sympathy and understanding, you are often a visionary or a humanitarian who can be caring, loving, and supportive. With foresight and a progressive outlook, you can be spiritual, yet practical.

• *Positive:* worldly, universal brotherhood, friendly, compassionate, dependable, understanding, idealistic, poised, artistic, balanced

• *Negative:* discontented, anxious, shy, unreasonable, stubborn, outspoken, domineering, lack of responsibility, selfish, suspicious, self-centered

Love & Relationships

Friendly and outgoing, you are drawn to intelligent or entertaining individuals. Your desire for knowledge, which can lead to self-improvement and an inner youthful quality, is likely to stay with you throughout life and can help boost your social success. Although you can be very entertaining, you may have to work on issues of responsibility. You are nevertheless usually willing to work at keeping your relationships harmonious. Short breaks away with your partner usually work miracles at restoring your enthusiasm and adventurous spirit.

YOUR SPECIAL SOMEONE

For that someone special, you might want to look among those born on the following dates.

Love & friendship: Jan. 6, 10, 20, 21, 26, 29, Feb. 4, 8, 18, 27, Mar. 2, 6, 16, 25, 28, 30, Apr. 4, 14, 23, 26, 28, 30, May 2, 12, 13, 18, 21, 24, 26, 28, 30, June 10, 19, 22, 24, 26, 28, July 8, 17, 20, 22, 24, 26, Aug. 6, 15, 18, 20, 22, 24, Sept. 4, 13, 16, 18, 20, 22, Oct. 2, 11, 14, 16, 18, 20, Nov. 9, 12, 14, 16, 18, Dec. 7, 10, 12, 14, 16

Beneficial: Jan. 7, 13, 18, 28, Feb. 5, 11, 16, 26, Mar. 3, 9, 14, 24, Apr. 1, 7, 12, 22, May 5, 10, 20, June 3, 8, 18, July 1, 6, 16, Aug. 4, 14, Sept. 2, 12, 30, Oct. 10, 28, Nov. 8, 26, 30, Dec. 6, 24, 28

Fatal attractions: Jan. 25, Feb. 23, Mar. 3, 4, 5, 6, 21, Apr. 19, May 17, June 15, July 13, Aug. 11, Sept. 9, Oct. 7, Nov. 5, Dec. 3

Challenging: Jan. 3, 17, Feb. 1, 15, Mar. 13, Apr. 11, May 9, 30, June 7, 28, July 5, 26, 29, Aug. 3, 24, 27, Sept. 1, 22, 25, Oct. 20, 23, Nov. 18, 21, Dec. 16, 19

Soul mates: Jan. 18, Feb. 16, Mar. 14, Apr. 12, May 10, 29, June 8, 27, July 6, 25, Aug. 4, 23, Sept. 2, 21, Oct. 19, Nov. 17, Dec. 15

September 7

♍ The influence of your birthday suggests that you are a practical, clever, and sensitive individual with a need to build solid order in your life. There is a strong emphasis on your work that can prove especially fortunate in providing financial protection for you. With a fertile imagination and a good sense of values, you will find that through concentrated effort you can turn your visions into reality.

With the added influence of your decanate ruler, Capricorn, you are methodical and diligent, with innate common sense. The pride you take in your work can also carry the sign of the perfectionist. A sense of duty and control can make you responsible and skilled, but tightly controlled emotions can also lead to your becoming too serious, moody, or obstinate.

Idealistic and sensitive, you may wish to be of service to others. Since you can also be very businesslike, this powerful combination implies that you can be a compassionate realist. In order to avoid the mental stress that you can sometimes encounter, you need time for reflection, rest, or meditation. Practical skills, strong intuition, and an ability to concentrate with determination on the job in hand are just some of your many talents.

Around the time when you reach the age of fifteen, your progressed Sun moves into Libra, commencing a thirty-year period of growing emphasis on your social life and relationships, both personal and professional. This is a time when you may also have an increased sense of balance and harmony as well as a desire to develop any creative potential you possess. Another turning point occurs around the age of forty-five, when your progressed Sun moves into Scorpio, encouraging you to seek deeper meaning to your life and placing more emphasis on the power of transformation. When you reach the age of seventy-five, your progressed Sun moves into Sagittarius, stimulating a desire for expansion, truth, and positive ideals.

Your Secret Self

Although you are reliable and productive, an inner restlessness may spur you to explore new experiences and be more adventurous. If repressed, this can lead to dissatisfaction, and you may turn to escapism in order to compensate. Fortunately, a magnetic charm is there to save you from many difficult situations and draw people toward you.

Although one part of you wants life to be stable, secure, and predictable, another part does not want to be tied down and fears boredom. Be careful of falling into a rut if your situation becomes congenial and fairly smooth-running, as your opportunities are often away from your usual routine of home and work. You may need to develop patience and face the challenge of finding harmony within yourself.

Work & Vocation

Being practical and perceptive, you can succeed in just about any career, from scientific research and business to something more creative. As you like to create method and be thorough, having a practical plan for your big visions is vital. With your desire for order and keen intelligence, you are often drawn to commerce or industry, where you can use your organizational skills to excel. Employers are likely to appreciate your ability to work hard, your de-

FIXED STAR

Star's name: Mizar

Degree position: 14°36'–15°37' Virgo between the years 1930 and 2000

Magnitude: 2.5

Strength: ★★★★★★★

Orb: 2°10'

Constellation: Zeta Ursa Major

Applicable days: September 6, 7, 8, 9, 10, 11

Star qualities: Mars and Saturn/Venus

Description: a white and pale emerald star located on the tail of the Great Bear

PRIMARY STAR'S INFLUENCE

Mizar imparts ambition, a pragmatic nature, creativity, and artistic talents. This star, however, can also indicate disharmony and involvement in controversial issues.

Linked to your Sun's degree, this star indicates a prominence in writing and business and success in dealing with the general public. Mizar warns against being too critical and suggests using your mental powers in creative and positive ways.

• Positive: serious, responsible, creative

• Negative: rebellious, disharmonious, selfish

pendability, and your responsibility. With your communication and analytical skills, you may have an interest in teaching or writing. The more imaginative side of your nature may find an outlet through art, drama, or music.

Famous people who share your birthday include Queen Elizabeth I, singers Chrissie Hynde and Gloria Gaynor, musicians Sonny Rollins and Buddy Holly, film director Elia Kazan, actor Peter Lawford, artist Grandma Moses, banker J. P. Morgan, and French naturalist George Louis Count de Buffon.

Numerology

Analytical and thoughtful, number 7 individuals are often perfectionistic, critical, and self-absorbed. Preferring to make your own decisions, you frequently learn best through personal experience. This desire to learn can lead you into the academic world or to improving your skills. At other times, you can become overly sensitive to criticism by others and feel misunderstood. Your tendency to be enigmatic or secretive leads you to develop the art of asking subtle questions without letting anyone know what you really think. The subinfluence of the number 9 month indicates that you are perceptive and shrewd, with discriminative skills. Since you are influenced by your environment, you can easily sense changes in other people's moods. Often broad-minded and a humanitarian, you seek balance, fairness, and justice. With your insight, you can often be visionary; however, do not confuse fact with fantasy.

• *Positive:* educated, trusting, meticulous, idealistic, honest, psychic, scientific, rational, reflective

• *Negative:* concealing, deceitful, secretive, skeptical, confused, too detached, cold

Love & Relationships

Your practicality and matter-of-fact approach can often mask your emotional sensitivity. The ability you have to sense the feelings of others can help you in all your relationships. Nevertheless, if you withhold your own strong emotions you may be susceptible to moods or to isolating yourself. Build love relationships through knowledge of your loved one's needs and interests. Usually you are sociable, with a natural charm, often showing that you care through some practical act of service.

YOUR SPECIAL SOMEONE

Among those born on the following dates you may find someone with whom you can share your ideals more easily.

Love & friendship: Jan. 7, 11, 12, 22, Feb. 5, 9, 20, Mar. 3, 7, 8, 18, 31, Apr. 1, 5, 16, 29, May 3, 4, 14, 27, 29, June 1, 12, 25, 27, July 10, 23, 25, Aug. 8, 21, 23, 31, Sept. 6, 19, 21, 29, Oct. 4, 17, 19, 27, 30, Nov. 2, 15, 17, 25, 28, Dec. 13, 15, 23, 26

Beneficial: Jan. 8, 14, 19, Feb. 6, 12, 17, Mar. 4, 10, 15, Apr. 2, 8, 13, May 6, 11, June 4, 9, July 2, 7, Aug. 5, Sept. 3, Oct. 1, 29, Nov. 27, Dec. 25, 29

Fatal attractions: Mar. 5, 6, 7, 8

Challenging: Jan. 9, 18, 20, Feb. 7, 16, 18, Mar. 5, 14, 16, Apr. 3, 12, 14, May 1, 10, 12, June 8, 10, July 6, 8, 29, Aug. 4, 6, 27, Sept. 2, 4, 25, Oct. 2, 23, Nov. 21, Dec. 19

Soul mates: Jan. 9, Feb. 7, Mar. 5, Apr. 3, May 1, Oct. 30, Nov. 28, Dec. 26

September 8

♍ The influence of your birthday suggests that you are a creative and practical individual with an easygoing personality. Ambitious and enterprising, you possess natural business sense and an ability to present an unusual and original point of view. Although you usually appear bright and friendly, you also have a more serious side. Your strong need for self-expression may manifest itself socially or lead to writing or the arts. Your objective approach to life can be challenged by a tendency to worry or be indecisive, particularly about finances.

With the added influence of your decanate ruler, Capricorn, you have a meticulous approach to analyzing situations and can be hardworking and responsible. Since precision is important, you want to do a job well and have pride in your work. Although you possess a sharp mind that can be used for problem solving, you may need to avoid becoming too critical. With a good sense of values, you are likely to be quite economical or good at obtaining a bargain.

As you possess intuitive insight, you can be of great help in making decisions, though you may have to guard against becoming overly serious or moody. Alternatively, a desire to delve deeply into life may manifest as psychological skills, spiritual awareness, or a black-comedy sense of humor.

From childhood you are likely to be continually analyzing situations in order to understand and improve them. After the age of fourteen, however, as your progressed Sun moves into Libra for a thirty-year period, you gradually become more aware of the importance of your social relationships and partnerships. Your creative abilities are enhanced and you may be drawn to develop your musical, artistic, or literary interests. At the age of forty-four you reach another life turning point as your progressed Sun enters Scorpio. This brings a strong emphasis on your deeper need for power, intensity, and transformation. Your progressed Sun enters Sagittarius when you reach the age of seventy-four, stimulating a desire to expand your horizons, particularly through education, travel, or religion.

Your Secret Self

Clever and articulate, you can communicate your ideas with enthusiasm and sincerity. A good sense of values aids you in your search for unity. You may, however, encounter a conflict between your strong need for material security and your need for self-expression. Fortunately, as you are very intelligent and aware of your responsibilities, you are likely to be a powerful opponent and a good strategist.

As you are very sensitive to discord or unpleasantness, you may find that your sense of well-being is connected to the harmony of your surroundings. Ironically, if you lose your equilibrium, you may be tempted to become verbally cutting or interfering. Nevertheless, you possess a deep desire for love and harmony that can be channeled into art, music, or helping others.

Work & Vocation

Possessing a shrewd business sense, you are often successful in commerce or may use your sharp mind for research or science. You may be quite technical and apply this to any career

---

FIXED STAR

Star's name: Mizar

Degree position: 14°36'–15°37' Virgo between the years 1930 and 2000

Magnitude: 2.5

Strength: ★★★★★★

Orb: 2°10'

Constellation: Zeta Ursa Major

Applicable days: September 6, 7, 8, 9, 10, 11

Star qualities: Mars and Saturn/Venus

Description: a white and pale emerald star located on the tail of the Great Bear

PRIMARY STAR'S INFLUENCE

Mizar imparts ambition, a pragmatic nature, creativity, and artistic talents. This star, however, can also indicate disharmony and involvement in controversial issues.

Linked to your Sun's degree, this star indicates prominence in writing and business and success in dealing with the general public. Mizar warns against being too critical and suggests using your mental powers in creative and positive ways.

• *Positive:* serious, responsible, creative

• *Negative:* rebellious, disharmonious, selfish

you are interested in. With your original ideas and individual approach to life, you are attracted to writing or occupations involving communication. Intelligent and articulate, you may also find fulfillment in a career such as education. Similarly, a need for self-expression may draw you to the world of entertainment or politics. Seeking variety, you may change careers, or if you stay in the same occupation, you want to develop new ideas or improve the way you operate.

Famous people who share your birthday include comedians Peter Sellers and Sid Caesar, King Richard I (the Lionhearted), singer Patsy Cline, composer Antonin Dvorak, Senator Claude Pepper, and Eastern Orthodox Church patriarch Dimitrios I.

Numerology

The strength or power suggested by the number 8 birthday shows a character with strong values and sound judgment. The number 8 often indicates that you aspire to great accomplishment and possess an ambitious nature. A desire for dominance, security, and material success is also implied by this birthday. As a number 8 person, you have natural business sense and will benefit greatly from developing organizational and executive skills. You may have to learn how to administer or delegate your authority in a fair and just way. A strong need to feel secure or established urges you to make long-term plans and investments. The subinfluence of the number 9 month indicates that you are pragmatic and perceptive, with strong instincts. You like to utilize your knowledge in a creative and specific way and, with your imagination, can be original and productive.

• *Positive:* leadership, thoroughness, hardworking, authoritative, protective, power to heal, good judge of values

• *Negative:* impatient, wasteful, intolerant, miserly, restless, domineering, easily discouraged, lack of planning, controlling behavior

Love & Relationships

Being clever, original and sociable, you have no trouble attracting friends and admirers. Although spontaneous with your feelings, you can at times alternate between being loving and sensitive and being too detached. You may be looking for a special or spiritual link with your partner that may cause you to become critical if he or she does not live up to your high ideals. Practical issues of security may also influence your relationship decisions. Your friendly charm ensures your success in all social situations.

YOUR SPECIAL SOMEONE

You might find emotional fulfillment and that special someone among those born on the following days.

Love & friendship: Jan. 4, 8, 22, 23, 26, Feb. 6, 20, 24, Mar. 4, 18, 22, Apr. 2, 16, 20, 30, May 14, 15, 18, 28, 30, June 12, 16, 26, 28, July 10, 14, 24, 26, Aug. 8, 12, 22, 24, Sept. 6, 10, 20, 22, 30, Oct. 4, 8, 18, 20, 28, Nov. 2, 6, 16, 18, 26, Dec. 4, 14, 16, 24

Beneficial: Jan. 9, 20, Feb. 7, 18, Mar. 5, 16, 29, Apr. 3, 14, 27, May 1, 12, 25, June 10, 23, July 8, 21, Aug. 6, 19, Sept. 4, 17, Oct. 2, 15, 30, Nov. 13, 28, Dec. 11, 26, 30

Fatal attractions: Jan. 27, Feb. 25, Mar. 6, 7, 8, 9, 23, Apr. 21, May 19, June 17, July 15, Aug. 13, Sept. 11, Oct. 9, Nov. 7, Dec. 5

Challenging: Jan. 2, 10, 19, Feb. 8, 17, Mar. 6, 15, Apr. 4, 13, May 2, 11, June 9, July 7, 30, Aug. 5, 28, Sept. 3, 26, Oct. 1, 24, Nov. 22, Dec. 20, 30

Soul mates: Jan. 15, Feb. 13, Mar. 11, Apr. 9, May 7, June 5, July 3, Aug. 1, Oct. 29, Nov. 27, Dec. 25

September 9

♍ You are friendly and aware of yet practical and shrewd, and the influence of your birthday suggests that you are a constructive idealist. Energized by contact with people, you are a good strategist or planner who is capable of being single-minded and focused. Sociable and kind, you possess a love of humanity and a richness of feeling. Very determined, active, and hardworking, you have the potential to achieve your big plans.

With the subinfluence of your decanate ruler, Capricorn, you are realistic, precise, and articulate. You are also self-disciplined and have good communication skills. Eagerness for knowledge and an ability to analyze and be thorough can make you a good researcher or investigator.

It may, however, be necessary for you to balance the two sides of your nature. On one hand, you can be tough, obstinate, and demanding; on the other, you can be sensitive and extremely generous, especially with those you love.

You possess an active and intense imagination and in your idealistic quest for truth may be drawn to metaphysical or religious subjects. Although generally a practical optimist, you may at times have an ungrounded fear of not having enough money, even when you are doing quite well.

After you reach the age of thirteen, when your progressed Sun moves into Libra, there is an increased need for socializing, partnership, and relating. Your sense of harmony and balance is likely to be enhanced, with the possibility of exploring literary, artistic, or creative outlets in some form. This continues until the age of forty-three, when your progressed Sun enters Scorpio. This is a turning point for you that will highlight a growing emphasis on emotional and spiritual regeneration as well as joint finances or corporate business activity. At the age of seventy-three there is another turning point when your progressed Sun enters Sagittarius and you become more philosophical, with a need to expand your horizons, whether through travel or through mental pursuits.

Your Secret Self

A desire for material security, power, and prestige blends strangely with your high idealism. A strong motivator for you is a need for recognition, which can spur you to greater heights. You possess the energy and determination for substantial achievement but may find greater fulfillment satisfying your aspirations to help others. When driven by will, enthusiasm, and faith, you are able to achieve miracles.

You may encounter periods of weakness alternating with periods of remarkable progress and advancement. Getting in touch with your inner spiritual needs may help you develop a balance between your quest for pleasure and the more meaningful aspects of life. Fortunately, you will always keep a youthful or playful side, which can aid you in satisfying your lofty objectives.

Work & Vocation

Your natural diplomacy and expertise at making contacts can help you in all people-related careers. If you believe in a project, a person, or an idea, then your outstanding faith and en-

---

FIXED STAR

Star's name: Mizar
Degree position: 14°36'–15°37' Virgo between the years 1930 and 2000
Magnitude: 2.5
Strength: ★★★★★★★
Orb: 2°10'
Constellation: Zeta Ursa Major
Applicable days: September 6, 7, 8, 9, 10, 11
Star qualities: Mars and Saturn/Venus
Description: a white and pale emerald star located on the tail of the Great Bear

PRIMARY STAR'S INFLUENCE

Mizar imparts ambition, a pragmatic nature, creativity, and artistic talents. This star, however, can also indicate disharmony and involvement in controversial issues.

Linked to your Sun's degree, this star indicates prominence in writing and business and success in dealing with the general public. Mizar warns against being too critical and suggests using your mental powers in creative and positive ways.

• Positive: serious, responsible, creative

• Negative: rebellious, disharmonious, selfish

394

thusiasm can help you sell or promote your product. This is especially useful in the world of public relations, agencies, and negotiation. Possessing energy and drive, you may prefer working for yourself, but in cooperation with others. Your excellent analytical and communication skills may serve you well in research or writing, where you are likely to excel. Ideally, you should be in a position of authority and are a good advisor. Your active imagination may prove a great asset in the world of art, drama and music.

Famous people who share your birthday include singer Otis Redding, writers Leo Tolstoy and Cesare Pavese, actors Hugh Grant and Michael Keaton, skater John Curry, musician/ producer Dave Stewart, and illustrator Arthur Rackham.

Numerology

Benevolence, compassion, and sensitivity are all associated with the number 9 birthday. You are often considered intelligent and intuitive, with abilities that point to a universal receptivity. With a number 9 birthday, you usually feel that life is mapped out for you and does not leave you much room to maneuver. As well as learning to become impersonal, you may have to develop understanding, tolerance, and patience. You are likely to benefit greatly from world travel and interaction with people from all walks of life. Avoid unrealistic dreams or an inclination toward escapism. The subinfluence of the number 9 month strengthens your intuitive and receptive abilities. Since you are sensitive to your environment, you are often concerned with others' welfare. You may need to accept the limitations of life and understand that it is never fair or perfect. With your insight and sixth sense, you are often visionary, with psychic abilities.

• *Positive:* idealistic, humanitarian, creative, sensitive, generous, magnetic, poetic, charitable, giving, detached, lucky, popular

• *Negative:* frustrated, nervous, unsure, selfish, impractical, easily led, inferiority complex, fears, worry, isolated

Love & Relationships

As you need to communicate, you enjoy mixing with different social groups. Gregarious, yet assertive, you are attracted to intelligent people. You often have a wonderful gift for turning new friends into useful business contacts. Although you are drawn to mentally powerful individuals, avoid mind games with partners. Since you are very generous and supportive with the people you love, you often have loyal friends. Even though you make a caring partner, it is important to keep your independence.

YOUR SPECIAL SOMEONE

For security, mental stimulation, and love, you might want to begin looking for those born among the following dates.

Love & friendship: Jan. 3, 23, 24, Feb. 11, 21, Mar. 9, 19, 28, 31, Apr. 7, 17, 26, 29, May 5, 15, 16, 24, 27, 29, 31, June 3, 13, 22, 25, 27, 29, July 1, 11, 20, 23, 25, 27, 29, Aug. 9, 18, 21, 23, 25, 27, Sept. 7, 16, 19, 21, 23, 25, Oct. 5, 14, 17, 19, 21, 23, Nov. 3, 12, 15, 17, 19, 21, Dec. 1, 10, 13, 15, 17, 19

Beneficial: Jan. 3, 4, 10, 21, Feb. 1, 2, 8, 19, Mar. 6, 17, 30, Apr. 4, 15, 28, May 2, 13, 26, June 11, 24, July 9, 22, Aug. 7, 20, Sept. 5, 18, Oct. 3, 16, 31, Nov. 1, 14, 29, Dec. 12, 27

Fatal attractions: Jan. 22, 28, Feb. 20, 26, Mar. 6, 7, 8, 9, 18, 24, Apr. 16, 22, May 14, 20, June 12, 18, July 10, 16, Aug. 8, 14, Sept. 6, 12, Oct. 4, 10, Nov. 2, 8, Dec. 6

Challenging: Jan. 11, 20, Feb. 9, 18, Mar. 7, 16, Apr. 5, 14, May 3, 12, 30, June 1, 10, 28, July 8, 26, 31, Aug. 6, 24, 29, Sept. 4, 22, 27, Oct. 2, 20, 25, Nov. 18, 23, Dec. 16, 21

Soul mates: Jan. 26, Feb. 24, Mar. 22, 30, Apr. 20, 28, May 18, 26, June 16, 24, July 14, 22, Aug. 12, 20, Sept. 10, 18, Oct. 8, 16, Nov. 6, 14, Dec. 4, 12

September 10

♍ Determined and ambitious, you are a strong-willed individual with a no-nonsense approach. Intelligent, with natural diplomatic skills, you are quick to see opportunities. Your high idealism and friendly personality suggest that you can excel in almost anything.

With the subinfluence of your decanate ruler, Capricorn, you are realistic and hardworking. Meticulous, with keen perceptions, you have a serious and thorough approach to life. You can be a loyal and untiring worker when committed to a project or cause and are likely to give it your all.

Independent and productive, you possess a natural sense of authority and executive skills. Being practical, with an excellent understanding of values, you appreciate the good things in life. A desire for prestige and luxury is liable to motivate you into action, but you may have to guard against an extravagant streak. Capable of magnanimous gestures of generosity toward those you love, you can also be exacting about getting value for your money.

Although you have a strong sense of freedom, at times you may become impatient and dominate others. If opposed, you may display a more obstinate side to your nature. Ideally you should be in a position where your courage and ability to think on a grand scale put you in the forefront as an initiator. Your idealism and need for self-awareness may manifest as a strong humanitarian streak. This interest in people gives you a deeper understanding of others and helps you develop compassion.

After the age of twelve, when your progressed Sun moves into Libra, you grow more socially oriented, with a strong need to be popular and appreciated. You learn to become more diplomatic and enjoy harmonious and creative pursuits. From the age of forty-two your power is enhanced when your progressed Sun moves into Scorpio, making you more self-reliant and in control. When you reach the age of seventy-two your progressed Sun enters Sagittarius, accenting a desire to explore and expand your horizons, through travel, new interests, or education.

Your Secret Self

On an inner level you possess potent desires and emotions that may have placed you in situations you later questioned. These strong feelings can be channeled into a selfless love that is a powerful force for good in your life and the lives of others. You possess an innate understanding of people's needs and can usually bargain to get what you want. With your strong will and ability to make your wishes come true, it is important that you constantly check your motivation and be careful what you ask for.

You may possess a desire to create something of sizable proportions and are usually determined and highly motivated. Since you have a gift for dealing with people and making connections, you have the ability to improve the lives and circumstances of those you come in contact with if you stay positive.

Work & Vocation

Motivated by a strong combination of idealism and practicality, you possess natural abilities for leadership, particularly as a manager and entrepreneur. Possessing analytical skills, you

---

FIXED STAR

Star's name: Mizar

Degree position: 14°36'–15°37' Virgo between the years 1930 and 2000

Magnitude: 2.5

Strength: ★★★★★★

Orb: 2°10'

Constellation: Zeta Ursa Major

Applicable days: September 6, 7, 8, 9, 10, 11

Star qualities: Mars and Saturn/Venus

Description: a white and pale emerald star located on the tail of the Great Bear

PRIMARY STAR'S INFLUENCE

Mizar imparts ambition, a pragmatic nature, creativity, and artistic talents. This star, however, can also indicate disharmony and involvement in controversial issues.

Linked to your Sun's degree, this star indicates proficiency in writing and business and success dealing with the general public. Mizar warns against being too critical and suggests using your mental powers in creative and positive ways.

• *Positive:* serious, responsible, creative

• *Negative:* rebellious, disharmonious, selfish

may excel in research or make a good technician. Persuasive and enthusiastic, you may often promote ideas, products, or other people. Courageous and committed, you may pursue a career in commerce as a negotiator or financial advisor. Your communication skills or creativity would also enable you to consider a career in education, art, drama, or music. Sports could be an excellent outlet for your drive and enthusiasm.

Famous people who share your birthday include actress Amy Irving, fashion designer Karl Lagerfeld, golf champion Arnold Palmer, singer José Feliciano, paleontologist Stephen Jay Gould, poet H. D. (Hilda Doolittle), and baseball player Roger Maris.

Numerology

Like those with a number 1 birthday, you are ambitious and independent. Although you may have to overcome challenges before you reach your goals, with determination you often achieve your objectives. Your pioneering spirit frequently encourages you to travel far afield or strike out on your own. As a number 10 individual, you may also need to learn that the world does not revolve around you and that you should guard against being domineering. The subinfluence of the number 9 month indicates that you are creative, intuitive, and sensitive. As you are receptive, with foresight, you can be in tune with current trends. Although there is a strong need to establish a clear identity and accomplish things, you are likely to be proud, with an energetic personality and original ideas. To others you may appear confident, resilient, and resourceful, but inner tensions may cause emotional fluctuations.

• *Positive:* leadership, creative, progressive, forceful, optimistic, strong convictions, competitive, independent, gregarious

• *Negative:* overbearing, jealous, egotistical, too proud, antagonistic, lack of restraint, selfish, weak, unstable, impatient

Love & Relationships

An interesting mixture of idealism and practicality influences your relationships. Although you can be very loving, your strong emotions can sometimes make you prone to changing moods. Liking excitement and adventure, you need someone who keeps you constantly interested but who is also a hard worker. Even though you can be very supportive of your partners, in close relationships you need the freedom to be independent in your own right.

YOUR SPECIAL SOMEONE

For security, whether emotional or financial, you might want to begin looking for those born among the following dates.

Love & friendship: Jan. 3, 6, 14, 24, 31, Feb. 1, 12, 22, 29, Mar. 2, 10, 20, 27, Apr. 8, 18, 25, May 6, 16, 23, 30, June 4, 14, 21, 28, 30, July 2, 12, 19, 26, 28, 30, Aug. 10, 17, 24, 26, 28, Sept. 8, 15, 22, 24, 26, Oct. 6, 13, 20, 22, 24, 30, Nov. 4, 11, 18, 20, 22, 28, Dec. 2, 9, 16, 18, 20, 26, 29

Beneficial: Jan. 5, 22, 30, Feb. 3, 20, 28, Mar. 1, 18, 26, Apr. 16, 24, May 14, 22, June 12, 20, July 10, 18, 29, Aug. 8, 16, 27, 31, Sept. 6, 14, 25, 29, Oct. 4, 12, 23, 27, Nov. 2, 10, 21, 25, Dec. 9, 19, 23

Fatal attractions: Jan. 12, Feb. 10, Mar. 8, 9, 10, Apr. 6, May 4, June 2

Challenging: Jan. 16, 21, Feb. 14, 19, Mar. 12, 17, 30, Apr. 10, 15, 28, May 8, 13, 26, June 6, 11, 24, July 4, 9, 22, Aug. 2, 7, 20, Sept. 5, 18, Oct. 3, 16, Nov. 1, 14, Dec. 12

Soul mates: Jan. 25, Feb. 23, Mar. 21, Apr. 19, May 17, June 15, July 13, Aug. 11, Sept. 9, Oct. 7, Nov. 5, Dec. 3, 30

September 11

FIXED STARS

Although your Sun's degree is not linked to a fixed star, some of your other planets' degrees certainly will be. By having an astrological chart calculated, you can find the exact position of the planets on your date of birth. This will tell you which of the fixed stars listed in this book are relevant to you.

♍ Exceptional mental potential combined with sensitivity marks those with your birthday as something special. Articulate and hardworking, you like to be independent and in control. You recognize the power of knowledge and utilize it to your advantage. With all your talents, one of your possible problems may be underachievement. Careful and prudent, but also possessing an unconventional streak, you appear to others as confident and self-assured.

With the subinfluence of your decanate ruler, Capricorn, you possess depth of thought and can pay attention to detail. Your analytical skills endow you with good concentration and can make you a good psychologist or writer. Goal-oriented, you may sometimes be too critical or hard on yourself. Education, whether formal or self-directed, can be a vital key to bring out the best of your potential.

The leadership promised by your birthday is matched by your powers of perception. Both men and women of this day have to be careful of being too bossy or impatient. Frequently you can delegate work, as you have an insight into other people's rationales and understand their needs. Learning to trust your own intuition enables you to take on the challenges of developing an original creative talent or your business acumen.

After the age of eleven, when your progressed Sun moves into Libra, you grow more socially oriented, with a strong need to relate to people on a personal level. Your sense of refinement and beauty is likely to be strong, with the possibility of your exploring literary, artistic, or creative interests. From the age of forty-one your power is enhanced as your progressed Sun moves into Scorpio, making you more self-reliant and in control. At the age of seventy-one, when your progressed Sun moves into Sagittarius, you may desire to travel or expand your mental horizons.

Your Secret Self

When inspired, you are able to display amazing determination to accomplish your goals, but you also possess an innate understanding of the importance of teamwork. People may often underestimate your inner strength and tenacity and take you at face value. Little do they realize that you are a good actor and may also be hiding your sensitivity and fear of the unknown. By being diplomatic and assertive, you learn to trust your abilities and unlock the power of your potential.

Since you can use your knowledge in playful competitiveness, this can show you at your most witty and entertaining. Be careful that you do not go too far, becoming too serious or fixated on one issue. Keeping a balanced workload can certainly help you not to overtax your system. Often inspired, you have an inner idealist who fights injustice and is eager to help humanity.

Work & Vocation

As you usually do not like to take orders, you are better in a position of authority or self-employed. Your keen intelligence and organizational skills can make you an excellent administrator or lawyer. With your practical and analytical abilities, you can excel as an analyst, financial advisor, or statistician. Equally, you may prefer a career such as economist, researcher, scientist, or technician. This birthday is also excellent for teachers or writers. Since you take on responsibilities and work hard, others will appreciate your help and abilities. A humanitarian streak may attract you to a career as a reformer or therapist. Alternatively, your leadership abilities may lure you to the spotlight as a performer or politician.

Famous people who share your birthday include writers D. H. Lawrence, O. Henry, and Jessica Mitford, film director Brian DePalma, actress Hedy Lamarr, composer Arvo Pärt, and college football coach Paul "Bear" Bryant.

Numerology

The special vibration of the master number 11 birthday suggests that idealism, inspiration, and innovation are highly important to you. A blend of humility and confidence often challenges you to work toward self-mastery, both materially and spiritually. Although you possess intuitive powers, you may scatter your energies and often need to find a goal upon which you can focus. Usually you are highly charged and enjoy vitality but must avoid becoming overly anxious or impractical. The subinfluence of the number 9 month indicates that you are highly intuitive and sensitive. Since you are receptive, broad-minded, and a humanitarian, you can be concerned with people's welfare. By staying objective and using your diplomatic skills, you can establish strong links with others. Since you want to be supportive and helpful, you can assist others, but avoid being overly critical. With your insight, you are often visionary, with psychic abilities.

• *Positive:* balanced, focused, objective, enthusiastic, inspirational, spiritual, idealistic, intuitive, healing ability, humanitarian, psychic

• *Negative:* superiority complex, dishonest, aimless, overemotional, easily hurt, highly strung, selfish, lack of clarity, dominating, mean

Love & Relationships

Intelligent and observant, you are often a loyal and reliable partner or friend. Sincere and caring, you need a stable and honest relationship. Although you can refine and improve on situations, you may need to learn how to differentiate between being bossy and critical, and giving assistance to those around you. You usually get your own way through the art of negotiation.

YOUR SPECIAL SOMEONE

For that someone special you might want to look among those born on the following dates.

Love & friendship: Jan. 11, 13, 15, 17, 25, Feb. 9, 11, 13, 15, 23, Mar. 7, 9, 11, 13, 21, Apr. 5, 7, 9, 11, 19, May 3, 5, 7, 9, 17, 31, June 1, 3, 5, 7, 15, 29, July 1, 3, 5, 27, 29, 31, Aug. 1, 3, 11, 25, 27, 29, Sept. 1, 9, 23, 25, 27, Oct. 7, 21, 23, 25, Nov. 5, 19, 21, 23, Dec. 3, 17, 19, 21, 30

Beneficial: Jan. 1, 5, 20, Feb. 3, 18, Mar. 1, 16, Apr. 14, May 12, June 10, July 8, Aug. 6, Sept. 4, Oct. 2

Fatal attractions: Mar. 8, 9, 10, 11, 12

Challenging: Jan. 6, 22, 24, Feb. 4, 20, 22, Mar. 2, 18, 20, Apr. 16, 18, May 14, 16, June 12, 14, July 10, 12, Aug. 8, 10, 31, Sept. 6, 8, 29, Oct. 4, 6, 27, Nov. 2, 4, 25, 30, Dec. 2, 23, 28

Soul mates: Jan. 6, 12, Feb. 4, 10, Mar. 2, 8, Apr. 6, May 4, June 2

September 12

FIXED STAR

Star's name: Denebola

Degree position: 20°38'–21°31' Virgo between the years 1930 and 2000

Magnitude: 2

Strength: ★★★★★★★

Orb: 2°10'

Constellation: Beta Leo

Applicable days: September 12, 13, 14, 15, 16

Star qualities: varied influences: Saturn/Venus/Mercury and Mars

Description: a blue star located in the Lion's tail

PRIMARY STAR'S INFLUENCE

Denebola bestows good judgment, daring, courage, and a noble, generous nature. This star's influence can bring about exciting events and opportunities for advancement. You may have a natural talent for clear thinking and good values, accompanied by swift action. This star also indicates that you will be responsible and active on behalf of others. Denebola, however, also carries a reminder that benefits may not necessarily be long-lasting, and it warns against tendencies to get angry or anxious, which can spoil relationships.

Linked to your Sun's degree, this star imparts ingenuity and determination to acquire special skills. Rewards and honor through work are also indicated, and you may become a renowned specialist in your chosen field. Often gains and success come from work in the community and fulfilling public duties. Denebola may also impart

♍ Your birthdate indicates that you are an intelligent, friendly, sociable, and self-assured individual. As you have a quick mind, you are likely to enjoy wit, debate, or repartee and be a skilled commentator on others. Having the courage to speak your mind regardless of the repercussions, you prefer to be direct and honest. Naturally gifted, mentally receptive, generous, and optimistic, you need only apply self-discipline to live up to your outstanding potential.

With the added influence of your decanate ruler, Capricorn, you possess good concentration and like to be mentally thorough. Retaining your dignity and being able to work hard, you usually take your responsibilities seriously. This influence bestows a natural understanding of money and suggests that prestige and self-respect are important to you. Having practical common sense and being verbally skilled and incisive, you make an excellent critic. However, you may have to guard against nervous tension that may cause you to be a little too impatient or caustic.

With your ability to shine, you often take a leading position and have a way with people. You possess a philosophical inclination that can give you the ability to survey the whole or draw you toward things of a more humanitarian nature. When you are positive about your goals and vision, you are assured of success.

After the age of ten, when your progressed Sun moves into Libra, you have an increased need to be popular and appreciated as well as to learn more about yourself through close relationships with others. This continues until the beginning of your forties, when your progressed Sun enters Scorpio. This is a turning point for you that will highlight the growing importance of transformation as well as evaluating your own power and control. When you reach the age of seventy your progressed Sun moves into Sagittarius, highlighting a more expansive and philosophical approach to life.

Your Secret Self

Because you are a good actor, your outer assertive front may not show your inner sensitivity and need for creative expression. You are ambitious, with high standards for yourself and a strong drive for material success. Making the right choices is important, however, as you may need to guard against losing energy to emotional worry or indecision, particularly in your close relationships. Often interested in metaphysical or spiritual subjects, you have much to gain from developing your natural intuition or listening to your inner voice.

If your big plans occasionally fail, there is a chance that you may end up feeling sorry for yourself, though not for long, as you are determined to overcome obstacles and succeed. Your creative spirit ensures that you will always be looking for new and exciting ways to occupy your mind and expand your horizons.

Work & Vocation

With your excellent analytical skills, you are able to succeed in research, science, or psychology. Your quick intellect and talent with words indicate that you could also excel in

restlessness and warns against hasty decisions that you might later regret.
• *Positive:* self-control, generous, inventive, responsible, honorable
• *Negative:* rashness, lack of responsibility, impatience

writing, education, and the media. You may also succeed in law or publishing, but the practical side of your nature may attract you to the financial world, where you are likely to make an excellent banker, economist, or stockbroker. Similarly, you could prosper as a financial advisor, accountant, dealer, or negotiator. Alternatively, the caring or humanitarian side of your nature could provide you with the impetus to excel as a social worker or in a job that requires speaking up for others, such as union leader or politician. You may also be interested in careers of a philosophical or religious nature. If in the creative world, you can make an excellent designer or singer.

Famous people who share your birthday include athlete Jesse Owens, actress Linda Gray, actor Maurice Chevalier, singers Barry White and Maria Muldaur, explorer Henry Hudson, journalist H. L. Mencken, publisher Alfred A. Knopf, and painter Ben Shahn.

Numerology

Usually you are intuitive and friendly and possess good reasoning power. A desire to establish true individuality is often suggested by the number 12 birthday. Innovative and sensitive, you know how to use tact and cooperative methods to achieve your aims and objectives. To others you often appear confident, although self-doubts and suspicion can undermine your usual easygoing personality and positive outlook. When you achieve the balance between your need to define yourself and an inclination to be supportive of others, you can find emotional satisfaction and personal fulfillment. The subinfluence of the number 9 month indicates that you are witty, intuitive, and emotionally sensitive. Since you are likely to be intelligent and imaginative or creative, you need to find a way to express yourself freely. Avoid being hasty or scattering your energies in too many directions. Through communicating your thoughts and ideas, you can express your feelings and overcome a tendency to be misunderstood. With your foresight and progressive outlook, you can be spiritual, yet practical.
• *Positive:* creative, attractive, initiative, disciplinarian, assertive, confident
• *Negative:* reclusive, eccentric, uncooperative, overly sensitive, lack of self-esteem

YOUR SPECIAL SOMEONE

You might start to look for an exciting partner among those born on the following dates.

Love & friendship: Jan. 12, 16, 25, 29, Feb. 10, 14, 23, 24, Mar. 8, 12, 22, 25, 31, Apr. 6, 10, 20, 23, 29, May 4, 8, 18, 27, June 2, 6, 16, 25, 30, July 4, 14, 23, 28, Aug. 2, 12, 21, 26, 30, Sept. 10, 19, 24, 28, Oct. 8, 17, 22, 26, Nov. 6, 15, 20, 24, 30, Dec. 4, 13, 18, 22, 28

Beneficial: Jan. 2, 13, 22, 24, Feb. 11, 17, 20, 22, Mar. 9, 15, 18, 20, 28, Apr. 7, 13, 16, 18, 26, May 5, 11, 16, 18, 26, June 3, 9, 12, 14, 22, July 1, 7, 10, 12, 20, Aug. 5, 8, 10, 18, Sept. 3, 6, 8, 16, Oct. 1, 4, 6, 14, Nov. 2, 4, 12, Dec. 2, 10

Fatal attractions: Jan. 25, Feb. 23, Mar. 9, 10, 11, 12, 21, Apr. 19, May 17, June 15, July 13, Aug. 11, Sept. 9, Oct. 7, Nov. 5, Dec. 3

Challenging: Jan. 7, 23, Feb. 5, 21, Mar. 3, 19, 29, Apr. 1, 17, 27, May 15, 25, June 13, 23, July 11, 21, 31, Aug. 9, 19, 29, Sept. 7, 17, 27, 30, Nov. 3, 13, 23, 26, Dec. 1, 11, 21, 24

Soul mates: Jan. 17, Feb. 15, Mar. 13, Apr. 11, 22, May 9, June 7, July 5, Aug. 3, Nov. 30, Dec. 28

Love & Relationships

Friendly and intelligent, you often display a buoyant and witty personality. A certain discontent, however, indicates that you can get easily bored and look for those who offer you mental stimulation. In love you are loyal and supportive as long as you receive respect and are not taken for granted. Usually you like to be informed, and you take pleasure from trying out new activities or visiting new places. Similarly, you may enjoy taking courses of study where you can increase your knowledge or develop new skills and meet people who get you thinking. You will always have the ability to make friends and attract others.

September 13

♍ Independence, a quick intelligence, and practicality are qualities associated with your birthday. Sociable, with strong individuality, you enjoy and befriend people from all walks of life. Although sometimes nervous and excitable, you prefer to be direct and honest with your feelings. You possess a spirit of enterprise but may have to guard against stress caused by repressed emotions or taking on too much.

With the subinfluence of your decanate ruler, Taurus, you can be very charming and persuasive. A creative thinker, with a good sense of humor, you are likely to possess a pleasant voice and polite speech. An appreciation of beauty can bestow good taste and a love of luxury and comfort. Through education and the pursuit of knowledge you can easily develop your flair for the spoken and written word as well as improve your natural business sense.

Efficient and enthusiastic, you may have to guard against getting yourself worked up and becoming overly zealous or impatient. Although you are generally loyal and hardworking, it is important to learn self-discipline and develop your skills in order to bring out your wonderful potential. When interested in a project, you can become very eager, but in your desire to accomplish you may have to guard against being bossy. People of this birthday often possess a youthful or androgynous quality all of their life.

In early childhood you have a practical approach to whatever you do. After the age of nine, however, when your progressed Sun moves into Libra, there commences a thirty-year period of increased emphasis on personal relationships, your popularity, and partnerships in general. This is a time of increased awareness of balance and harmony, and you may want to develop any creative potential you possess. Another turning point occurs around the end of your thirties, when your progressed Sun moves into Scorpio, stimulating you to seek deeper meaning to your life and placing more emphasis on the power of transformation. When you reach sixty-nine your progressed Sun moves into Sagittarius, stimulating you to expand your horizons.

Your Secret Self

A charismatic warmth emanates from your caring heart. When directed outward this powerful projection of love can achieve miracles in helping others or in achieving some notable form of self-expression. When inspired, you possess a talent for getting your ideas across while keeping people entertained.

In your approach to life's challenges you are usually idealistic and optimistic, but sometimes can become skeptical. Although gifted and creative, you may have to be careful of financially playing it too safe, as material security can be a big issue for you. You need something solid and stable to rely upon or you may worry excessively about money, though any fears you have are usually groundless, given your excellent earning capacity.

Work & Vocation

Your persuasive powers and organizational abilities can certainly help you in careers such as sales, promotion, public relations, or politics. With your keen intellect and love of knowledge,

FIXED STAR

Star's name: Denebola

Degree position: 20°38'–21°31' Virgo between the years 1930 and 2000

Magnitude: 2

Strength: ★★★★★★★

Orb: 2°10'

Constellation: Beta Leo

Applicable days: September 12, 13, 14, 15, 16

Star qualities: varied influences: Saturn/Venus/Mercury and Mars

Description: a blue star located in the Lion's tail

PRIMARY STAR'S INFLUENCE

Denebola bestows good judgment, daring, courage, and a noble, generous nature. This star's influence can bring about exciting events and opportunities for advancement. You may have a natural talent for clear thinking and good values, accompanied by swift action. This star also indicates that you will be responsible and active on behalf of others. Denebola, however, also carries a reminder that benefits may not necessarily be long-lasting, and warns against tendencies to get angry or anxious, which can spoil relationships.

Linked to your Sun's degree, this star imparts ingenuity and determination to acquire special skills. Rewards and honor through work are also indicated, and you may become a renowned specialist in your chosen field. Often gains and success come from work in the community and fulfilling public duties. Denebola may also impart

restlessness and warns against hasty decisions that you might later regret.

• *Positive:* self-control, generous, inventive, responsible, honorable

• *Negative:* rashness, lack of responsibility, impatience

your aptitudes may lie in education, writing, or law. Your strong ideals and dynamism make you a fighter for a cause. Similarly, your natural business sense can help you succeed in commerce, real estate, accountancy, or the stock market. Not enjoying being in a subordinate position, you may fare well as a manager or administrator or being self-employed. Alternatively, sports are often an excellent outlet for your energy and drive, and your quest for self-expression may draw you to the theater or arts. In whatever career you choose you are usually willing to work hard to achieve your objectives.

Famous people who share your birthday include actresses Jacqueline Bisset and Claudette Colbert, singer Mel Tormé, writers Roald Dahl and J. B. Priestley, U.S. gymnastics coach Bela Karolyi, and biologist Walter Reed.

Numerology

Emotional sensitivity and inspiration are often identified with the number 13 birthday. Numerically, you are associated with hard work and can accomplish much through determination and being talented. You may, however, need to develop a pragmatic outlook if you want to turn your creative gifts into tangible products. With dedication you can achieve prosperity. Having a number 13 birthday, you can be charming and fun-loving, with a sociable personality. Like many individuals who share your birthdate, you may wish to travel or yearn to settle in a new environment to make a better life for yourself. The subinfluence of the number 9 month indicates that you are highly perceptive and sympathetic. Since you are influenced by your environment, you need to be decisive and take control of the direction in which your life is going. You may, however, need to overcome a tendency to be impatient, self-doubting, or restless. Often broad-minded and a humanitarian, with good reasoning powers, you seek fairness and practical solutions.

• *Positive:* ambitious, creative, freedom-loving, self-expressive, initiative
• *Negative:* impulsive, indecisive, bossy, unemotional, rebellious

YOUR SPECIAL SOMEONE

You might find a suitable relationship with someone who will understand your sensitivity and need for love among those born on the following dates.

Love & friendship: Jan. 2, 7, 10, 17, 27, Feb. 5, 8, 15, 25, Mar. 3, 6, 13, 23, Apr. 1, 4, 11, 21, May 2, 9, 19, June 7, 17, July 5, 15, 29, 31, Aug. 3, 13, 27, 29, 31, Sept. 1, 11, 25, 27, 29, Oct. 9, 23, 25, 27, 30, Nov. 7, 21, 23, 25, 28, Dec. 5, 19, 21, 23, 26

Beneficial: Jan. 3, 5, 20, 25, 27, Feb. 1, 3, 18, 23, 25, Mar. 1, 16, 21, 23, Apr. 14, 19, 21, May 12, 17, 19, June 10, 15, 17, July 8, 13, 15, Aug. 6, 11, 13, Sept. 4, 9, 11, Oct. 2, 7, 9, Nov. 5, 7, Dec. 3, 5

Fatal attractions: Jan. 13, Feb. 11, Mar. 9, 10, 11, 12, 13, Apr. 7, May 5, June 3, July 1

Challenging: Jan. 16, 24, Feb. 14, 22, Mar. 12, 20, Apr. 10, 18, May 8, 16, 31, June 6, 14, 29, July 4, 12, 27, Aug. 2, 10, 25, Sept. 8, 23, Oct. 6, 21, Nov. 4, 19, Dec. 2, 17

Soul mates: Jan. 16, Feb. 14, Mar. 12, Apr. 10, May 8, June 6, July 4, 31, Aug. 2, 29, Sept. 27, Oct. 25, Nov. 23, Dec. 21

Love & Relationships

Although you can be sociable and friendly, in personal relationships you can alternate between being observant and detached to being emotionally passionate. While you are often forthright, you can at times appear secretive and aloof. As you are often looking for an ideal love, if your expectations are too high, you may be prone to disappointments. Although there may be a danger of clandestine or unsuitable relationships, you can be a loving partner and a loyal friend. You usually particularly admire those who are clever and entertaining.

September 14

♍ The influence of your birthday indicates that you are an intelligent and ambitious individual with strong convictions. Independent and assertive, you are a seeker of knowledge and wisdom. When you find something you really believe in, you can project a remarkable enthusiasm that guarantees you success.

With the added influence of your decanate ruler, Taurus, you possess good communication skills and can be articulate and charming. You can deal with detail and be an excellent critic. Guard against becoming too impatient or bossy in your interaction with others. The influence of Venus also adds to your natural business sense and helps you appreciate the good things in life.

Usually independent, with a strong drive, you need to constantly challenge yourself to make the most of your talents and to avoid becoming bored. Although at times you can be arrogant or opinionated, on other occasions you may be strangely lacking in self-confidence. Fortunately, being friendly and sociable, you can quickly return to your usual optimistic self. Versatile and restless, you are likely to be driven to explore life through either travel or education. Since you can be highly persuasive, you have only to develop self-discipline in order to make the most of outstanding opportunities.

After the age of eight, when your progressed Sun moves into Libra, you begin to grow more socially oriented, with a strong need to be popular and appreciated. Over the next thirty years you learn to become more diplomatic and tactful through relating to others. From the age of thirty-eight your power is enhanced when your progressed Sun moves into Scorpio, making you more self-reliant and in control. When you reach the age of sixty-eight your progressed Sun enters Sagittarius, highlighting issues around truth, education, travel, or expanding your options.

FIXED STAR

Star's name: Denebola

Degree position: 20°38'–21°31' Virgo between the years 1930 and 2000

Magnitude: 2

Strength: ★★★★★★★

Orb: 2°10'

Constellation: Beta Leo

Applicable days: September 12, 13, 14, 15, 16

Star qualities: varied influences: Saturn/Venus/Mercury and Mars

Descripton: a blue star located in the Lion's tail

PRIMARY STAR'S INFLUENCE

Denebola bestows good judgment, daring, courage, and a noble, generous nature. This star's influence can bring about exciting events and opportunities for advancement. You may have a natural talent for clear thinking and good values, accompanied by swift action. This star also indicates that you will be responsible and active on behalf of others. Denebola, however, also carries a reminder that benefits may not necessarily be long-lasting, and warns against tendencies to get angry or anxious, which can spoil relationships.

Linked to your Sun's degree, this star imparts ingenuity and determination to acquire special skills. Rewards and honor through work are also indicated, and you may become a renowned specialist in your chosen field. Often gains and success come from work in the community and fulfilling public duties. Denebola may also impart

Your Secret Self

At times you can be extremely warm, generous, loving, and modest, and at others argumentative, manipulative, or stubborn. To balance these extremes within your nature, it is necessary to unite reason with intuition by listening for the silent voice of guidance inside yourself. This should not be too hard, as you already have a developed sixth sense about people and their motivations.

With a natural understanding of the value of knowledge and a good sense of structure, you respect those who have accomplished much or acquired wisdom. With your social skills and ability to organize, you are good at getting others to help you in your overall success. Luckily, a desire for honesty is a very strong part of your character. By using this to acknowledge your own failings, you are able to confront and work through difficult situations as well as heighten your sense of self-awareness.

Work & Vocation

You have good managerial abilities and a talent for solving problems. Writing is a skill that comes naturally to you and often can be used creatively or for business. You are not usually

restlessness and warns against hasty decisions that you might later regret.

- *Positive:* self-control, generous, inventive, responsible, honorable
- *Negative:* rashness, lack of responsibility, impatience

happy in subservient positions, so you fare better if you are in authority or working for yourself. Variety is important in any career; if your work includes travel, then so much the better. Your natural analytical skills may attract you to research, science, psychology, or education. If in business, you prosper when your work involves personal contacts. Whatever career you choose, you need to be genuinely enthusiastic, since you find it hard to fake interest.

Famous people who share your birthday include feminist Kate Millett, actress Zoe Caldwell, actor Jack Hawkins, and birth-control pioneer Margaret Sanger.

Numerology

Intellectual potential, a pragmatic outlook, and strong determination are some of the qualities associated with the number 14 birthday. Often you possess a strong desire to establish a firm foundation and achieve success through hard work. Like many individuals associated with this birthday, you can often reach the top of your profession. With your perceptive mind, you respond quickly to problems and enjoy solving them. With a number 14 birthdate, you like taking a risk or a gamble and may be lucky enough to gain a windfall. The subinfluence of the number 9 month indicates that you are discreet and sensitive. Learn to trust your own instincts or intuition and avoid being hasty or overly materialistic. Although you are usually hardworking, your adventurous nature and a desire for freedom indicate a willingness to explore and try anything new. With your enthusiastic approach, you will find that life will have a lot to offer. Travel and many opportunities for change, some unexpected, may lead you to undergo a real transformation of views and beliefs.

- *Positive:* decisive actions, hardworking, lucky, creative, pragmatic, imaginative, industrious
- *Negative:* overly cautious or overly impulsive, unstable, thoughtless, stubborn

Love & Relationships

You admire those with an unusual or original approach to life. You may also particularly want to find a partner who is disciplined and hardworking. With your charm and natural assertive demeanor, you often attract people who believe in you. In close relationships you need to be flexible and avoid becoming bossy or critical. A love of knowledge or wisdom may bring you nearer to your ideal partner. You require a certain amount of freedom in relationships, as you have a strong independent streak.

YOUR SPECIAL SOMEONE

With those born on the following dates your ideals might be realized more easily.

Love & friendship: Jan. 1, 13, 14, 28, 31, Feb. 12, 26, 29, Mar. 10, 24, 27, Apr. 8, 22, 25, May 5, 6, 20, 23, June 4, 18, 21, July 2, 16, 19, 30, Aug. 14, 17, 28, 30, Sept. 12, 15, 26, 28, 30, Oct. 10, 13, 24, 26, 28, Nov. 8, 11, 22, 24, 26, Dec. 6, 9, 20, 22, 24

Beneficial: Jan. 26, Feb. 24, Mar. 22, Apr. 20, May 18, June 16, July 14, Aug. 12, Sept. 10, Oct. 8, Nov. 6, Dec. 4

Fatal attractions: Mar. 12, 13, 14, 15

Challenging: Jan. 3, 25, Feb. 1, 23, Mar. 21, Apr. 19, May 17, June 15, July 13, Aug. 11, Sept. 9, Oct. 7, Nov. 5, Dec. 3

Soul mates: Jan. 3, 10, Feb. 1, 8, Mar. 6, Apr. 4, May 2

September 15

FIXED STAR

Star's name: Denebola

Degree position: 20°38'–21°31' Virgo between the years 1930 and 2000

Magnitude: 2

Strength: ★★★★★★★

Orb: 2°10'

Constellation: Beta Leo

Applicable days: September 12, 13, 14, 15, 16

Star qualities: varied influences: Saturn/Venus/Mercury and Mars

Description: a blue star located in the Lion's tail

PRIMARY STAR'S INFLUENCE

Denebola bestows good judgment, daring, courage, and a noble, generous nature. This star's influence can bring about exciting events and opportunities for advancement. You may have a natural talent for clear thinking and good values, accompanied by swift action. This star also indicates that you will be responsible and active on behalf of others. Denebola, however, also carries a reminder that benefits may not necessarily be long-lasting and warns against tendencies to get angry or anxious, which can spoil relationships.

Linked to your Sun's degree, this star imparts ingenuity and determination to acquire special skills. Rewards and honor through work are also indicated, and you may become a renowned specialist in your chosen field. Often gains and success come from work in the community and fulfilling public duties. Denebola may also impart

♍ Intelligent and friendly, you are revealed by your birthday to be a dependable individual with big plans. Loving knowledge, you are interested in many subjects but may be particularly drawn to world affairs. Since your image is usually important, in your desire to impress others you generally like the best. Direct and to the point, you can be kindhearted and generous, and although usually optimistic, you may have to overcome a tendency toward negative thinking.

With the added influence of your decanate ruler, Taurus, you are reliable and solid, with a strong need for love and affection. Since you have an appreciation of beauty and form, you can enjoy art, nature, and the good things in life. Articulate, with an ability to analyze detail, you possess creative communication skills, but you may have to guard against becoming critical or impatient. There is also a likelihood of your being quite thrifty or economical with money, yet you can be very generous with the people you love.

You are always ready to give your opinion, but sometimes your emotions can be blocked, producing frustration, shyness, or a stiff formality. Thinking too much can lead to worry, and in your desire to please you may often take on too much. When positive, however, your idealistic nature has inspired ideas and a desire to serve.

After the age of seven, when your progressed Sun moves into Libra, you have an increasing need for close personal relations and social acceptance. From this time your appreciation of beauty and harmony starts to become more enhanced, with the possibility of your exploring creative outlets. This continues until the age of thirty-seven, when your progressed Sun enters Scorpio. This is a turning point for you that will highlight a growing emphasis on emotional and spiritual regeneration as well as joint finances or corporate business activity. When you reach the age of sixty-seven, your progressed Sun enters Sagittarius, and you may start to become more interested in expanding your horizons.

Your Secret Self

Staying detached and developing a positive outlook and philosophy enable you to creatively channel your strong emotions and avoid dissatisfaction. An inner sensitivity highlights the importance of having a home or harmonious setting where you can feel safe and secure, as well as suggesting an inner need for peace and quiet.

You have a strong awareness of your responsibilities and are usually conscious of wanting to pay off your debts. However, it may be necessary to ensure that you constantly challenge yourself in new areas rather than sticking with the tried and true. A possible way to express yourself may be through ideas that emphasize the importance of associating with people who are mentally stimulating. Although you enjoy helping people and usually make a good advisor, you may have to be careful of interfering; sometimes it may be best to let others learn from their own mistakes.

Work & Vocation

Your keen intellect and analytical skills may lead you to a career in science, research, or medicine. Equally, you can excel in education, the legal profession, or politics. Your creative com-

restlessness and warns against hasty decisions that you might later regret.

• *Positive:* self-control, generous, inventive, responsible, honorable

• *Negative:* rashness, lack of responsibility, impatience

munication skills could also help you succeed in writing or in business. With a sense of order, proportion, and balance, you could fare well in careers such as architect, designer, artist, or mathematician. Being a natural advisor and analyst, you could work in the world of psychology or finance. Alternatively, a humanitarian streak may lead you to social reform or charity work.

Famous people who share your birthday include writers Agatha Christie and James Fenimore Cooper, film directors Oliver Stone and Jean Renoir, actor Tommy Lee Jones, President and Chief Justice William Howard Taft, and opera singer Jessye Norman.

Numerology

Usually you are quick and enthusiastic, with a charismatic personality. Your greatest assets are your strong instincts and the ability to learn through combining theory and practice. On many occasions you manage to earn while learning new skills. Often you utilize your intuitive powers and are able to recognize opportunities when they arise. With a number 15 birthday, you possess a talent for attracting money or receiving help and support from others. Successful conclusions to undertakings can become more frequent if you apply your practical skills to your original ideas and overcome your tendency to be restless or dissatisfied. The subinfluence of the number 9 month indicates that you are cautious and sensitive. By developing a realistic and sympathetic attitude, you can establish a more harmonious and congenial existence. With your foresight and progressive outlook, you can be conscientious and practical.

• *Positive:* willing, generous, responsible, kind, cooperative, appreciative, creative ideas

• *Negative:* disruptive, restless, irresponsible, self-centered, fear of change, loss of faith, worry, indecision

Love & Relationships

Having a close relationship is important to you, but avoid becoming too dependent on your partner. Usually you are idealistic, helpful, and creative, with social charm. Since you need a soul mate and dislike being alone, it is important to avoid substituting security for love and happiness. Although caring and generous, you need to stay detached and overcome a tendency to be critical. Learning to discuss and share your feelings with your partner can help you move forward in relationships.

YOUR SPECIAL SOMEONE

You might find a partner who will understand your sensitivity and need for love among those born on the following dates.

Love & friendship: Jan. 1, 5, 15, 26, 29, 30, Feb. 3, 13, 24, 27, 28, Mar. 11, 22, 25, 26, Apr. 9, 20, 23, 24, May 7, 18, 21, 22, June 5, 16, 19, 20, July 3, 14, 17, 18, 31, Aug. 1, 12, 15, 16, 29, 31, Sept. 10, 13, 14, 27, 29, Oct. 8, 11, 12, 25, 27, Nov. 6, 9, 10, 23, 25, Dec. 4, 7, 8, 21, 23, 29

Beneficial: Jan. 1, 2, 10, 27, Feb. 8, 25, Mar. 6, 23, Apr. 4, 21, May 2, 19, 30, June 17, 28, July 15, 26, Aug. 13, 24, Sept. 11, 22, Oct. 9, 20, Nov. 7, 18, Dec. 5, 16

Fatal attractions: Mar. 13, 14, 15, 16

Challenging: Jan. 17, 26, Feb. 15, 24, Mar. 13, 22, Apr. 11, 20, May 9, 18, June 7, 16, July 5, 14, Aug. 3, 12, 30, Sept. 1, 10, 28, Oct. 8, 26, 29, Nov. 6, 24, 27, Dec. 4, 22, 25

Soul mates: Jan. 21, Feb. 19, Mar. 17, Apr. 15, May 13, June 11, July 9, 29, Aug. 7, 27, Sept. 5, 25, Oct. 3, 23, Nov. 1, 21, Dec. 19

September 16

FIXED STARS

Denebola, Copula

PRIMARY STAR

Star's name: Denebola

Degree position: 20°38'–21°31' Virgo between the years 1930 and 2000

Magnitude: 2

Strength: ★★★★★★★★

Orb: 2°10'

Constellation: Beta Leo

Applicable days: September 12, 13, 14, 15, 16

Star qualities: varied influences: Saturn/Venus/Mercury and Mars

Descripton: a blue star located in the Lion's tail

PRIMARY STAR'S INFLUENCE

Denebola bestows good judgment, daring, courage, and a noble, generous nature. This star's influence can bring about exciting events and opportunities for advancement. You usually have a natural talent for clear thinking and good values, accompanied by swift action. This star also indicates that you will be responsible and active on behalf of others. Denebola, however, also carries a reminder that benefits may not necessarily be long-lasting, and warns against tendencies to get angry or anxious, which can spoil relationships.

Linked to your Sun's degree, this star imparts ingenuity and determination to acquire special skills. Rewards and honor through work are also indicated, and you may become a renowned specialist in your chosen field. Often

The influence of your birthday indicates that you can be smart and independent, yet friendly and sensitive. Intuitive and practically aware, you have an insight into people and situations. An ability to excel in all kinds of cerebral activities gives you the edge over others, but you still need the necessary self-discipline to fulfill your ambitious dreams.

With the added influence of your decanate ruler, Taurus, you possess charm and enjoy the good things in life. Love and affection are likely to be especially important to you. With creative communication skills, you are likely to have a pleasant voice and articulate speech. Venus's influence can also bestow a natural business sense that can lead you to good investments and attract money. Being able to handle all the details can help you both theoretically and practically.

You also possess a powerful desire for knowledge that will stay with you throughout life. This may inspire you to develop your wonderful intellectual potential through special training or education. You may, however, have to guard against becoming involved in mental power games with others.

Being a sensible visionary, you possess drive and imagination. These combine well when you are inspired and fighting for your ideals, and can endow you with the potential for tremendous success. A dislike of harshness implies that you need a positive environment, as you are very affected by disharmony around you. You can be a dreamer, so you need to channel your thoughts into creative outlets, but you may have to guard against believing the fantasy rather than the reality.

Your progressed Sun moves into Libra around the time you reach the age of six. Until the age of thirty-six, you may find that your relationships play an important part in your life, and you may want to be popular and appreciated. From the age of thirty-six onward your power is enhanced when the progressed Sun moves into Scorpio for thirty years, making you more self-reliant and in control. When your progressed Sun moves into Sagittarius as you reach the age of sixty-six, you become more optimistic and philosophical and may decide you want to expand your mind through travel or education.

Your Secret Self

Motivated by a deep and strong desire to empower yourself, you are always interested in self-improvement. It is necessary to build strength of character in order to avoid tendencies toward manipulation or escapism as the easy way out of difficult situations. Developing the highly sensitive and intuitive side to your nature can help you in your dealings with others and may even encourage an interest in mysticism or spirituality.

Attracted to intelligent and interesting people, you need positive role models to inspire you. With your capacity to excel in all kinds of intellectually challenging pursuits, you will work very hard when really interested in something. You may be happiest when passing on your inspiration or special insight to others.

Work & Vocation

A practical aptitude together with an organizational flair suggests that you can always achieve success in business. Alternatively, your keen analytical acumen may prefer an outlet through science, mathematics, or working with computers. Since you possess communication skills and social awareness, you may be drawn toward a career in education or law but are also likely to achieve in people-related occupations. Your special insight into psychology, diet, or natural healing ability may draw you toward the medical or alternative health professions. However, with your drive and ideas, you may wish to pass your knowledge on to others through more creative occupations such as acting or writing. You may also become involved with charitable organizations or work for worthwhile causes.

Famous people who share your birthday include blues musician B. B. King, actress Lauren Bacall, illusionist David Copperfield, comedienne Susan Ruttner, actor Peter Falk, biologist Albert Szent-Gyorgyi, yachtsman Dennis Connor, psychologist Karen Horney, and baseball player Orel Herschiser.

Numerology

A number 16 birthday suggests that you are ambitious, yet sensitive. Usually outgoing and sociable, you are friendly and thoughtful. You often judge life according to how you feel and have good insight and a caring nature. As a number 16 individual, you may be interested in world affairs and may join international corporations. The creative ones among you have a talent for writing with sudden flashes of inspiration. With a number 16 birthday, you may need to learn how to balance between being overconfident and doubtful and insecure. The subinfluence of the number 9 month indicates that you are observant and cautious. Since you are influenced by your feelings, you are likely to be receptive or impressionable, with strong instincts. The need to explore and grow through experience suggests that you may travel and be adventurous.

• *Positive:* responsible, integrity, intuitive, social, cooperative, insightful
• *Negative:* worry, never satisfied, irresponsible, self-promoting, opinionated, skeptical, fussy, irritable, selfish, unsympathetic

Love & Relationships

Often idealistic and caring, you can be a loyal friend and a responsible partner. Finding someone with whom you can share the same ideas and feelings is a prerequisite in your relationships. Your social and emotional relationships are likely to succeed with those who can inspire you and build up your confidence. Inquisitive, you like to find out what inspires or motivates others. When in love, you are warm, kind, and considerate.

gains and success come from work in the community and fulfilling public duties. Denebola may also impart restlessness and warns against hasty decisions that you might later regret.

• *Positive:* self-control, generous, inventive, responsible, honorable
• *Negative:* rashness, lack of responsibility, impatience

See Appendix for additional fixed star readings.

YOUR SPECIAL SOMEONE

To find long-lasting happiness, security, and a harmonious environment, you might begin by looking for someone born on one of the following days.

Love & friendship: Jan. 3, 10, 13, 20, 21, 30, Feb. 1, 8, 11, 18, 28, Mar. 6, 9, 16, 26, Apr. 4, 7, 14, 24, May 2, 5, 12, 22, June 3, 10, 20, July 1, 8, 18, Aug. 6, 16, 30, Sept. 4, 14, 28, 30, Oct. 2, 12, 26, 28, 30, Nov. 10, 24, 26, 28, Dec. 8, 22, 24, 26

Beneficial: Jan. 12, 16, 17, 28, Feb. 10, 14, 15, 26, Mar. 8, 12, 13, 24, Apr. 6, 10, 11, 22, May 4, 8, 9, 20, 29, June 2, 6, 7, 18, 27, July 4, 5, 16, 25, Aug. 2, 3, 14, 23, Sept. 1, 12, 21, Oct. 10, 19, Nov. 8, 17, Dec. 6, 15

Fatal attractions: Mar. 12, 13, 14, 15, 31, Apr. 29, May 27, June 25, July 23, Aug. 21, Sept. 19, Oct. 17, Nov. 15, Dec. 17

Challenging: Jan. 6, 18, 22, 27, Feb. 4, 16, 20, 25, Mar. 2, 14, 18, 23, Apr. 12, 16, 21, May 10, 14, 19, June 8, 12, 17, July 6, 10, 15, Aug. 4, 8, 13, Sept. 2, 6, 11, Oct. 4, 9, Nov. 2, 7, Dec. 5

Soul mates: Mar. 28, Apr. 26, May 24, June 22, July 20, Aug. 18, Sept. 16, Oct. 14, Nov. 12, Dec. 10

September 17

♍ The influence of your birthday indicates that you are a clever and perceptive individual with good communication skills. Independent and bright, you like to keep yourself informed. When inspired, you are able to act spontaneously and seize the opportunities of the moment. A tendency to doubt or lose faith, however, may cause you to become skeptical or worry.

The added influence of your decanate ruler, Taurus, suggests that you possess charm and a talent for words. Sociable and affectionate, you have an appreciation of beauty, color, and form. You may find the influence of women particularly helpful in achieving your goals. Practical and thorough, you are able to pay attention to detail and can become an expert in your field.

You are likely to find new and interesting developments stimulating, and you have the potential to be inventive, analytical, or technical. Although you possess quick responses, you also have the ability to work patiently at long and demanding tasks. You often crave excitement, and an innate restlessness may spur you to make many changes and to explore life through travel or education. These changes may bring uncertainty or unfounded fears regarding your finances and cause you to alternate between being economical and very generous. Learning to keep a creative balance between the old and new can help you avoid becoming dull by keeping you fresh and inspired.

When you reach the age of five, your progressed Sun moves into Libra, commencing a thirty-year period of increased emphasis on your social life and one-to-one relationships, both personal and professional. Another turning point occurs at the age of thirty-five, when your progressed Sun moves into Scorpio, stimulating you to seek deeper meaning to your life and placing more emphasis on the power of transformation. At the age of sixty-five your progressed Sun moves into Sagittarius and highlights a desire to explore new ideas or philosophies. You may wish to travel to different places and enjoy a different lifestyle.

Fixed Stars

Labrum, also called the Holy Grail; Copula

Primary Star

Star's name: Labrum, also called the Holy Grail

Degree position: 25°41'–26°21' Virgo between the years 1930 and 2000

Magnitude: 4

Strength: ★★★★

Orb: 1°30'

Constellation: Delta Crateris

Applicable days: September 17, 18, 19

Star qualities: Venus/Mercury

Description: a small yellow star located in the Cup

Primary Star's Influence

Labrum bestows intelligence and often imparts a creative and receptive nature with intuitive and psychic powers. This star also suggests that you have cosmopolitan views, a liberal outlook, and ecclesiastical inclinations. Frequently you will find an interest in history, philosophy, or religion and develop natural writing talents, which can lead to honor and wealth.

Linked to your Sun's degree, this star bestows determination and opportunities for success in dealing with the public. You may seek to express yourself through creative pursuits such as the performing arts, writing, presenting, communications, and the media. This star also points to a love of comfort

Your Secret Self

You possess an innate sense of the value of things and have the potential to be very successful financially. However, when you develop the wisdom of your intuition, you realize that money alone will never completely satisfy you. You are capable of profound flashes of deep insight but may need time and space for yourself to reflect and renew your energies. If you believe in a project, you will work really hard to manifest your ideals.

Since you need to feel productive and useful, as you get older your work is likely to play a prominent role in your life. It is therefore important that you believe your work is worthwhile. Since you can be mentally stubborn, you may have to remember to enjoy debating with others without becoming contentious.

Work & Vocation

With your attention to detail and thoroughness, you can excel in research or science. Practical and analytical, you may fare equally well as an economist, financial analyst, or accountant.

and pleasure and warns against over-indulgence and avoiding responsibility.

• *Positive:* creativity, education, artistic success, writing

• *Negative:* vanity and conceit, lack of drive, indulgence

See Appendix for additional fixed star readings.

Similarly, your ability for communication can help you succeed as a writer, critic, or lecturer or in the news and media world. You possess a mental vigor that is good for law, but you may prefer to work behind the scenes. The probability of your possessing technical skills may draw you toward working with computers or engineering. The medical and healing professions are also areas where you can enjoy sharing your knowledge with others.

Famous people who share your birthday include actress Anne Bancroft, singer Hank Williams, sailor Francis Chichester, writers Ken Kesey and William Carlos Williams, actor Roddy McDowall, racing driver Stirling Moss, Chief Justice Warren Burger, and Supreme Court Justice David Souter.

Numerology

As a number 17 individual, you are often shrewd, with a reserved nature and a well-reasoned approach in making decisions. Since you usually utilize your knowledge in a specific way, you can develop your expertise and achieve success or prominent positions as a specialist or researcher. Private, introspective, and detached, with a strong interest in facts and figures, you frequently present a serious and thoughtful demeanor and like to take your time. Capable of long periods of concentration and endurance, you can learn far more through experience. Nevertheless, the less skeptical you are, the quicker you learn. The subinfluence of the number 9 month indicates that you are practical and receptive. Well informed and a self-reliant thinker, you judge by your own personal experience and finally make up your own mind. With your foresight and progressive outlook, you can be spiritual, yet businesslike. Although financial security is important, avoid being materialistic.

• *Positive:* thoughtful, specialist, good planner, business sense, attracts money, painstaking, accurate, scientific

• *Negative:* detached, stubborn, carelessness, moody, sensitive, critical, worry, suspicious

Love & Relationships

Intuitive and intelligent, yet reserved, you do not like to reveal your thoughts or feelings. Since you are often highly aware, you can show a nervous side to your nature and need time to develop your relationships. You are likely to seek the company of ambitious and determined people who are hard-working. You need to build a loving relationship on trust and create harmony and peace.

YOUR SPECIAL SOMEONE

For security, mental stimulation, and love, you might want to begin looking for those born among the following dates.

Love & friendship: Jan. 21, 22, 28, 31, Feb. 19, 26, 29, Mar. 17, 24, 27, Apr. 15, 16, 22, 25, May 13, 20, 23, June 11, 18, 21, July 9, 16, 19, Aug. 7, 14, 17, 31, Sept. 5, 12, 15, 29, Oct. 3, 10, 13, 27, 29, 31, Nov. 1, 8, 11, 25, 27, 29, Dec. 6, 9, 23, 25, 27

Beneficial: Jan. 9, 12, 18, 24, 29, Feb. 7, 10, 16, 22, 27, Mar. 5, 8, 14, 20, 25, Apr. 3, 6, 12, 18, 23, May 1, 10, 16, 21, 31, June 2, 8, 14, 19, 29, July 6, 12, 17, 27, Aug. 4, 10, 15, 25, Sept. 2, 8, 13, 23, Oct. 6, 11, 21, Nov. 4, 9, 19, Dec. 2, 7, 17

Fatal attractions: Jan. 3, Feb. 1, Mar. 13, 14, 15, 16

Challenging: Jan. 7, 8, 19, 28, Feb. 5, 6, 17, 26, Mar. 3, 4, 15, 24, Apr. 1, 2, 13, 22, May 11, 20, June 9, 18, July 7, 16, Aug. 5, 14, Sept. 3, 12, Oct. 1, 10, Nov. 8, Dec. 6

Soul mates: Jan. 3, 19, Feb. 1, 17, Mar. 15, Apr. 13, May 11, June 9, July 7, Aug. 5, Sept. 3, Oct. 1

September 18

Ⅶ The influence of your birthday suggests that you are practical and perceptive, analytical and imaginative. Although you can be very determined, purposeful, and hardworking when you are interested in a project, at other times you can suffer from inertia and be quite happy to do nothing.

With the subinfluence of your decanate ruler, Taurus, love and affection are important to you. Since you desire peace, harmonious surroundings, and life's comforts, your home is likely to play a strong part in your life security. With the ability to pay attention to small details, you can be meticulous, but you may have to avoid continually going over the same issues until you become overcritical or anxious. You love knowledge and enjoy disseminating information to others.

Although you are sometimes nervous, your clear vision and practical approach can make you a good strategist. When you are able to combine this with your strong intuition, then you can achieve excellent results. It may be necessary for you to get a feel for a situation first before committing yourself to some form of structure, but once you give your word you are likely to take your responsibilities seriously.

When you reach the age of four your progressed Sun moves into Libra for a thirty-year period. This influence suggests that you are likely to be friendly and sociable from an early age. This highlights the importance of your relationships and diplomatic abilities. At the age of thirty-four you reach a life turning point as your progressed Sun enters Scorpio. This brings a strong emphasis on your deeper emotional need for change, intensity, and personal power. After the age of sixty-four, when your progressed Sun enters Sagittarius, you may become more adventurous, possibly exploring life through travel or higher education. You may meet people from foreign lands or go there yourself.

Your Secret Self

As a perfectionist, you may have to avoid being hard on yourself. You sometimes worry about doing less than is expected of you. Nevertheless, you possess an inner sense of power and determination that can overcome all obstacles and provide you with the recognition you need. When in powerful positions, you have to learn to be just and impartial and avoid being unfair or manipulative.

Although you work positively when you have a definite goal, you are well aware that you cannot do things without the cooperation of others. Fortunately, you have the skill of dealing with people on a personal level and an ability to make the right contacts, but you may have to overcome an unfounded fear of a lack of financial reserves. You may especially benefit from partnerships and shared projects.

Work & Vocation

Your meticulousness and perfectionism can help you succeed in careers such as researcher, statistician, economist, or accountant. Since cooperative efforts can aid your career advancement, you may decide to form a business partnership or work in a team. With your organiza-

FIXED STARS

Labrum, also called the Holy Grail; Copula; Zavijava, also called Al Araph; Al Kaid, also called Benetnash

PRIMARY STAR

Star's name: Labrum, also called the Holy Grail

Degree position: 25°41'–26°21' Virgo between the years 1930 and 2000

Magnitude: 4

Strength: ★★★★

Orb: 1°30'

Constellation: Delta Crateris

Applicable days: September 17, 18, 19

Star qualities: Venus/Mercury

Description: a small yellow star located in the Cup

PRIMARY STAR'S INFLUENCE

Labrum bestows intelligence and often imparts a creative and receptive nature, with intuitive and psychic powers. This star also suggests that you have cosmopolitan views, a liberal outlook, and ecclesiastical inclinations. Frequently you will find an interest in history, philosophy, or religion and develop natural writing talents, which can lead to honor and wealth.

Linked to your Sun's degree, this star bestows determination and opportunities for success in dealing with the public. You may seek to express yourself through creative pursuits such as the performing arts, writing, presenting, communications, and the media. This star also points to a love of comfort

• *Positive:* creativity, education, artistic success, writing

• *Negative:* vanity and conceit, lack of drive, indulgence

See Appendix for additional fixed star readings.

tional skills, you can also do well in authoritative positions such as manager, administrator, or executor, as well as in law and law enforcement. Occupations that may be excellent to keep your analytical skills sharpened include psychology, lecturing, and writing. You would do equally well in publishing, advertising, or the media. Alternatively, you could excel in the world of healing. You also possess the ability to raise money for good causes.

Famous people who share your birthday include actress Greta Garbo, writer Samuel Johnson, actor Jack Warden, singers Frankie Avalon and Jimmie Rodgers, astrologer Walter Koch, and physicist Edwin McMillan.

Numerology

Determination, assertiveness, and ambition are some of the attributes associated with the number 18 birthday. Dynamic and active, you frequently desire power and need constant challenge. At times you may be critical, hard to please, or inclined toward controversial issues. As a number 18 personality, you may use your power to help others, give sound advice, or solve other people's problems. Alternatively, your strong business sense and organizational skills lead you to the world of commerce. The subinfluence of the number 9 month indicates that you are a good strategist, with a need to be creative and independent. With your foresight and progressive outlook, you can be visionary, yet rational. Through benevolence, compassion, and sensitivity you learn and develop understanding, tolerance, and patience.

• *Positive:* progressive, assertive, intuitive, courageous, resolute, efficient, advisory skills

• *Negative:* uncontrolled emotions, lazy, lack of order, selfishness, failure to complete work on projects, misunderstood

YOUR SPECIAL SOMEONE

You might find emotional fulfillment and that special someone among those born on the following days.

Love & friendship: Jan. 8, 18, 22, Feb. 6, 16, 20, Mar. 14, 18, 28, Apr. 12, 16, 26, May 10, 14, 24, June 8, 12, 22, July 6, 10, 20, 29, Aug. 4, 8, 18, 27, 30, Sept. 2, 6, 16, 25, 28, Oct. 4, 14, 23, 26, 30, Nov. 2, 12, 21, 24, 28, Dec. 10, 19, 22, 26, 28

Beneficial: Jan. 6, 10, 25, 30, Feb. 4, 8, 23, 28, Mar. 2, 6, 21, 26, Apr. 4, 19, 24, May 2, 17, 22, June 15, 20, 30, July 13, 18, 28, Aug. 11, 16, 26, Sept. 9, 14, 24, Oct. 7, 12, 22, Nov. 5, 10, 20, Dec. 3, 8, 18

Fatal attractions: Mar. 13, 14, 15, 16, 17, May 29, June 27, July 25, Aug. 23, Sept. 21, Oct. 19, Nov. 17, Dec. 15

Challenging: Jan. 13, 29, 31, Feb. 11, 27, 29, Mar. 9, 25, 27, Apr. 7, 23, 25, May 5, 21, 23, June 3, 19, 21, July 1, 17, 19, Aug. 15, 17, Sept. 13, 15, Oct. 11, 13, Nov. 9, 11, Dec. 7, 9

Soul mates: Jan. 6, 25, Feb. 4, 23, Mar. 2, 21, Apr. 19, May 17, June 15, July 13, Aug. 11, Sept. 9, Nov. 7, Dec. 5

Love & Relationships

Charming and friendly, you usually enjoy socializing. Although you need love and affection, stability and security may be prerequisites in your relationships. You are attracted by intelligent people who inspire you, and you often want to share your need for self-expression with like-minded people. Although compassionate, romantic, and sensitive, you may need to guard against tendencies to be overemotional, insecure, or demanding when events do not meet with your approval.

September 19

FIXED STARS

Al Kaid, also called Benetnash; Labrum, also called the Holy Grail; Zavijava, also called Al Araph; Markeb

PRIMARY STAR

Star's name: Al Kaid, also called Benetnash

Degree position: 25°51'–26°50' Virgo between the years 1930 and 2000

Magnitude: 2

Strength: ★★★★★★★★

Orb: 2°10'

Constellation: Eta Ursa Major

Applicable days: September 18, 19, 20, 21, 22

Star qualities: Moon/Mercury

Description: a blue star located in the Great Bear

PRIMARY STAR'S INFLUENCE

Al Kaid imparts an active mind, a need for creative expression, intuitiveness, and an ability to adapt easily to new situations. You probably enjoy exchanging thoughts and ideas but may have a tendency to change your mind easily. This star indicates an aptitude for business and a fondness for power, and may grant opportunities for success, luck, and wealth.

Linked to your Sun's degree, Al Kaid's influence imparts a talent for business and points to success in dealing with the general public. You are inclined toward dealing with data, research, or exacting work that requires attention to detail. Al Kaid also tends to make you restless and ambitious and, at times,

♍ The influence of your birthday suggests that you are mentally sharp, fast, and instinctive, a practical and versatile individual. Since you are prone to become bored easily if things become too routine, you may seek out change and adventure or take on new challenges. Although you are mentally curious, restlessness or impatience may be a hurdle that you have to overcome in your rise to success.

With the subinfluence of your decanate ruler, Taurus, you possess charm and have a creative mentality. A natural business sense is combined with a love of the good life, as well as an appreciation of art and beauty. You have the ability to analyze any situation, and by developing methodical concentration and depth of thought, you achieve thoroughness and great skill at problem solving.

Your keen mentality comprehends information very quickly, and verbally you go straight to the heart of a matter. At other times you may become stubborn, cynical, or uncommunicative. Nevertheless, when your spirit of enterprise rekindles your optimism and sense of good fortune, you are good company and can be very entertaining.

From early childhood until you reach the age of thirty-two, your progressed Sun is in Libra, emphasizing your relationships and a need to be popular and appreciated. There is a turning point at the age of thirty-three, when your progressed Sun moves into Scorpio, suggesting that issues concerning your sense of personal power become more prominent and you become more self-reliant and in control. There may also be more of an accent on transformation or possibly joint finances. After sixty-three, when your progressed Sun moves forward into the sign of Sagittarius, you begin to look at life more philosophically. You seek more freedom and adventure in your life. This may also include education or travel abroad.

Your Secret Self

You may be more sensitive than you care to show. It may be necessary for you to find a form of expression for your strong emotions or else you could be prone to worry and indecision, particularly about material considerations. Although one part of you wants continual change, variety, or travel, another part wants life to be safe, secure, and financially solid. Integrating these opposites so that you are productively working on new and exciting projects may be an answer to this quandary.

Although creative and success-oriented, you may also be prone to escapist tendencies. These may be overcome by the development of your compassion and humanitarianism, as the idealistic you genuinely wishes to be of service to others.

Work & Vocation

In your choice of career you may have to guard against boredom, so it is important to select an occupation with constantly changing people or situations, such as working with the public or travel. Your quick intelligence and analytical skills enable you to assimilate information very quickly. This can help you in careers such as writing, law, teaching, and science as well as in business. Your restless nature and a desire to explore life could lead to changing your occupation or entering professions that entail a great deal of activity.

Famous people who share your birthday include actress/model Twiggy, author William Golding, Beatles manager Brian Epstein, actor Jeremy Irons, singer "Mama" Cass Elliot, designer Zandra Rhodes, and French cardinal Richelieu.

Numerology

Sunny, ambitious, and dynamic, yet idealistic and sensitive are some of the ways people would describe those with the number 19 birthday. Decisive and resourceful, you possess depth of vision, but the dreamer side of your nature is compassionate and impressionable. The need to be someone may be the very thing that pushes you to be dramatic and claim center stage. To others you may appear confident and resilient, but inner tensions may cause emotional ups and downs. Although proud, you may also need to learn that the world does not revolve around you. The subinfluence of the number 9 month indicates that you are highly perceptive. Since you are often a humanitarian, you may be concerned with the welfare of other people. If you set a high standard for yourself, you can be overly serious or critical of yourself and others. Although you are ambitious, self-doubt and insecurities may challenge your motivation.

• *Positive:* dynamic, centered, creative, leadership, progressive, optimistic, strong convictions, competitive, independent, gregarious

• *Negative:* self-centered, depressive, worry, fear of rejection, materialistic, egotistical, impatient

Love & Relationships

Although mentally quick, you are sensitive and receptive. A need for security and stability can be an important factor in your personal relationships. By taking your time and being patient, you learn whom to love and trust. This influence also suggests that rushing into relationships may cause you emotional tension, worry, or suspicion. A need to start again in new surroundings often plays an important role in shaping your personal life. With new opportunities come lessons in letting go of the past and having faith.

ruthless in your desire to reach the top. This star also gives a talent for criticism, which should be used in a positive way.

• *Positive:* active mind, good grasp or perception, sympathetic, kind, work with children

• *Negative:* criticism, gossip, worry, sensitive, nerves, propensity for lying, impatience, moody, overcritical

See Appendix for additional fixed star readings.

YOUR SPECIAL SOMEONE

To find security, trust, and love you might begin by looking for someone born on one of the following days.

Love & friendship: Jan. 4, 13, 19, 23, 24, Feb. 2, 11, 17, 21, 22, Mar. 9, 15, 19, 28, 29, 30, Apr. 7, 13, 17, 26, 27, May 5, 11, 15, 24, 25, 26, June 3, 9, 13, 22, 23, 24, July 1, 7, 11, 20, 21, 22, Aug. 5, 9, 18, 19, 20, Sept. 3, 7, 16, 17, 18, Oct. 1, 5, 14, 15, 16, 29, 31, Nov. 3, 12, 13, 14, 27, 29, Dec. 1, 10, 11, 12, 25, 27, 29

Beneficial: Jan. 7, 15, 20, 31, Feb. 5, 13, 18, 29, Mar. 3, 11, 16, 27, Apr. 1, 9, 14, 25, May 7, 12, 23, June 5, 10, 21, July 3, 8, 19, Aug. 1, 6, 17, 30, Sept. 4, 15, 28, Oct. 2, 13, 26, Nov. 11, 24, Dec. 9, 22

Fatal attractions: Mar. 15, 16, 17, 18

Challenging: Jan. 6, 14, 30, Feb. 4, 12, 28, Mar. 2, 10, 26, Apr. 8, 24, May 6, 22, June 4, 20, July 2, 18, Aug. 16, Sept. 14, Oct. 12, Nov. 10, Dec. 8

Soul mates: Apr. 30, May 28, June 26, July 24, Aug. 22, Sept. 20, Oct. 18, 30, Nov. 16, 28, Dec. 14, 26

September 20

♍ The influence of your birthday implies that you are a shrewd and practical individualist who is quick to see opportunities and enjoys learning. Clever and sensitive, you enjoy being actively productive and possess a spirit of enterprise. Usually optimistic, you like to be straightforward and honest, although you may need to develop patience and tolerance.

With the added influence of your decanate ruler, Taurus, you can be charming, be an intelligent conversationalist, and have an appreciation of beauty. Since you usually pay attention to detail, you are likely to be meticulous, with a good sense of form. Articulate and persuasive, you possess quick comprehension; writing or other forms of communication may play a strong part in your success. Although you have natural business sense and keen perceptions, you may have to guard against becoming overcritical.

Although very practical, you can also be idealistic and intuitive, with an ability to see the larger plan. Being naturally persuasive and enjoying some sharp wit, you are usually drawn to people who are clever or successful in their own right. These contacts can prove especially beneficial for you and your earning ability. Travel is also likely to play a part in inspiring you and stimulating you to be more daring.

From your early childhood until the age of thirty-one, your progressed Sun is in the sign of Libra, emphasizing a need to be popular and appreciated. Your relationships may prove especially important to you now. There is a turning point at the age of thirty-two, when your progressed Sun moves into Scorpio. Over the next thirty years your sense of personal power increases, making you more self-reliant and aware of emotional sensitivity. After sixty-two, when the progressed Sun moves forward into the sign of Sagittarius, you are likely to experience a desire to explore and expand your horizons. This could manifest physically through travel or mentally through study, and you are likely to develop a more philosophical outlook.

Fixed Stars

Al Kaid, also called Benetnash; Zavijava, also called Al Araph; Markeb

Primary Star

Star's name: Al Kaid, also called Benetnash

Degree position: 25°51'–26°50' Virgo between the years 1930 and 2000

Magnitude: 2

Strength: ★★★★★★★

Orb: 2°10'

Constellation: Eta Ursa Major

Applicable days: September 18, 19, 20, 21, 22

Star qualities: Moon/Mercury

Description: a blue star located in the Great Bear

Primary Star's Influence

Al Kaid imparts an active mind, a need for creative expression, intuitiveness, and an ability to adapt easily to new situations. You probably enjoy exchanging thoughts and ideas but may have a tendency to change your mind easily. This star indicates an aptitude for business and a fondness for power, and may grant opportunities for success, luck, and wealth.

Linked to your Sun's degree, Al Kaid's influence imparts a talent for business and points to success in dealing with the general public. You are inclined toward dealing with data, research, or exacting work that requires attention to detail. Al Kaid also tends to make you restless and ambitious and, at times, ruthless in your desire to reach the top.

Your Secret Self

Despite a desire for peace, you are likely to be constantly seeking mental stimulation. Learning to focus, reflect, or meditate will help keep you calm and deal with your inner restlessness. You are extremely sensitive and vulnerable, though on the surface you can appear confident and capable. This impressionable inner you may find it important to have a safe refuge from the world. Your home may therefore play an important part in your responsibilities and enable you to have a secure foundation from which to build. In your desire for harmony, however, guard against becoming stuck in a rut. Although aware of your responsibilities, you may have to learn the value of selflessness and how to make sacrifices. This can extend to fighting for a humanitarian cause or working to achieve peace in your environment.

Work & Vocation

You may be most likely to find fulfillment in careers that use your skills at dealing with people. Since you are full of ideas that can make money and are a good planner and organizer, you may succeed in sales, public relations, promotion, or advertising. Good at analyzing and collating information, you could also prosper in careers such as statistics, research, or education. Even though you have a sharp business sense, you may be more interested in occupations that use your creative side, such as writing, music, drama, or the arts. You are likely to fare especially well in working partnerships or team efforts. An idealistic streak could have you working in social reform, psychology, or public-spirited organizations.

Famous people who share your birthday include actress Sophia Loren, writer and social activist/writer Upton Sinclair, musician Jelly Roll Morton, basketball coach Red Auerbach, and psychologist Joyce Brothers.

This star also gives a talent for criticism, which should be used in a positive way.

• *Positive*: active mind, good grasp or perception, sympathetic, kind, work with children

• *Negative*: criticism, gossip, worry, sensitive, nerves, propensity for lying, impatience, moody, overcritical

See Appendix for additional fixed star readings.

Numerology

With a number 20 birthday, you are intuitive, adaptable, and understanding. Usually you enjoy cooperative activities where you can interact, share experiences, or learn from others. Often charming and gracious, you develop diplomatic skills and can move in different social circles with ease. You may, however, need to overcome a tendency to be hurt easily by the actions and criticism of others. In relationships you must guard against an inclination to martyr yourself, be mistrusting, or be overly dependent on others. The subinfluence of the number 9 month indicates that you are an idealistic visionary with a dynamic and forceful character. Often highly sensitive, you are influenced by your environment and are receptive to others. You are a master at creating a congenial and harmonious atmosphere. If you trust your innermost feelings, you can overcome your tendency to worry. Use your creative thoughts to achieve something special and unique that can inspire or be of service to others.

• *Positive*: good partnerships, gentle, tactful, receptive, intuitive, considerate, harmonious, agreeable, amicable, ambassador of goodwill

• *Negative*: suspicious, lack of confidence, subservient, oversensitive, emotional, selfish, easily hurt

Love & Relationships

Intelligent and thoughtful, with a rational approach, you usually have clear ideas about what you want from relationships. Nevertheless, you can become personally involved in unusual relationships or with unconventional individuals. Pragmatic by nature, you do not fall in love easily and often back out of unsuccessful relationships. Mentally quick, you need someone who can keep you interested and alert.

YOUR SPECIAL SOMEONE

For that special someone, you might want to look among those born on the following dates.

Love & friendship: Jan. 3, 4, 14, 20, 24, 25, Feb. 1, 2, 12, 18, 22, Mar. 10, 16, 20, 29, 30, Apr. 8, 14, 18, 27, 28, May 6, 12, 16, 25, 26, 31, June 4, 10, 14, 23, 24, 29, July 2, 8, 12, 21, 22, 27, Aug. 6, 10, 19, 20, 25, Sept. 4, 8, 17, 18, 23, Oct. 2, 6, 15, 16, 21, 30, Nov. 4, 13, 14, 19, 28, 30, Dec. 2, 11, 12, 17, 26, 28, 30

Beneficial: Jan. 4, 8, 21, Feb. 1, 2, 6, 19, Mar. 4, 17, 28, Apr. 2, 15, 16, May 13, 24, June 11, 22, July 9, 20, Aug. 7, 18, 31, Sept. 5, 16, 29, Oct. 3, 14, 27, Nov. 1, 12, 25, Dec. 10, 23

Fatal attractions: Jan. 3, Feb. 1, Mar. 16, 17, 18, 19, May 31, June 29, July 27, Aug. 25, Sept. 23, Oct. 21, Nov. 19, Dec. 11, 17

Challenging: Jan. 7, 10, 15, 31, Feb. 5, 8, 13, 29, Mar. 3, 6, 11, 27, Apr. 1, 4, 9, 25, May 2, 7, 23, June 5, 21, July 3, 19, Aug. 1, 17, Sept. 15, Oct. 13, Nov. 11, Dec. 9

Soul mates: Mar. 31, Apr. 29, May 27, June 25, July 23, Aug. 21, Sept. 19, Oct. 17, 29, Nov. 15, 27, Dec. 13, 25

September 21

M Your birthday indicates that you are independent and friendly, possessing great creative potential, and are socially inclined. With a need to express yourself, you are usually good with words, but you may have to guard against scattering your energy on too many interests or wasting it on worry and indecision.

With the added influence of your decanate ruler, Taurus, love and affection are important to you. Practical and articulate, you possess a thirst for knowledge and can be very charming. An appreciation of beauty and form bestows good taste and an ability to enjoy art, nature, and the good things in life. Although you have excellent communication skills and the ability to pay attention to detail, you may have to avoid continually going over the same small issues and thus becoming overcritical or anxious. Fortunately, this influence also bestows a natural business sense that can help you succeed in your rise to the top.

At times you can be extremely warm and optimistic, and at others you can become cold and irritable, especially if you do not have positive goals. Although naturally intuitive, you may have to overcome a skepticism toward spiritual matters. Your intellectual brightness, however, is likely to lead you to explore many avenues in your quest for wisdom.

Your progressed Sun moves into Libra during your early childhood, accenting a need to be appreciated. Your relationships are likely to play a particularly important role in your life up to the age of thirty-one, when there is a turning point as your progressed Sun moves into Scorpio. This influence increases your personal power, making you more determined and in control. After sixty-one, when the progressed Sun moves forward into the sign of Sagittarius, you become more philosophical, freedom-loving, and adventurous.

Fixed Stars

Al Kaid, also called Benetnash; Zavijava, also called Al Araph; Markeb

PRIMARY STAR

Star's name: Al Kaid, also called Benetnash
Degree position: 25°51'–26°50' Virgo between the years 1930 and 2000
Magnitude: 2
Strength: ★★★★★★★
Orb: 2°10'
Constellation: Eta Ursa Major
Applicable days: September 18, 19, 20, 21, 22
Star qualities: Moon/Mercury
Description: a blue star located in the Great Bear

Your Secret Self

Although you possess a good sense of values, you may need to overcome recurring doubts that undermine your confidence. By learning to use your intuitive powers, you can develop your faith and depend on your inner resources. You have an inner dignity and pride that cause you to dislike failure, but if afraid to take chances, you can reduce the likelihood of fulfilling your potential. As you can get bored easily, you need to find something that challenges and stimulates you. It is through perseverance and persistence that you can achieve your goals.

Usually versatile and successful, you can be impulsive, with an extravagant streak. If you take this into account, you will be able to control the fluctuations in your finances. A need for change and a desire to get away from restrictive circumstances can spur you to investigate many paths in your quest for satisfaction. This can include travel and work that can widen your horizons and provide you with new opportunities.

PRIMARY STAR'S INFLUENCE

Al Kaid imparts an active mind, a need for creative expression, intuitiveness, and an ability to adapt easily to new situations. You probably enjoy exchanging thoughts and ideas but may have a tendency to change your mind easily. This star indicates an aptitude for business and a fondness for power, and may grant opportunities for success, luck, and wealth.

Linked to your Sun's degree, Al Kaid's influence imparts a talent for business and points to success in dealing with the general public. You are inclined toward dealing with data, research, or exacting work that requires attention to detail. Al Kaid also tends to make you restless and ambitious and, at times, ruthless in your desire to reach the top.

Work & Vocation

Since a major part of your life centers on your work, it is important to make the most of your outstanding potential. Your consummate skill with words can help you excel as a writer or salesperson. Similarly, you can prosper as an agent, lawyer, actor, or politician, or in publishing. The creative abilities shown by your birthday can also find successful expression through music or singing. Alternatively, your natural business sense can help you in the world of commerce, where you are likely to take a creative approach to your work. You need to avoid monotonous occupations and may fare better when using your people skills. A desire to help others may manifest through counseling or teaching.

Famous people who share your birthday include authors Stephen King and H. G. Wells, singer/songwriter Leonard Cohen, writer/journalist Shirley Conran, actors Bill Murray and Larry Hagman, and composer Gustav Holst.

This star also gives a talent for criticism, which should be used in a positive way.
  • *Positive:* active mind, good grasp or perception, sympathetic, kind, work with children
  • *Negative:* criticism, gossip, worry, sensitive, nerves, propensity for lying, impatience, moody, overcritical

See Appendix for additional fixed star readings.

Numerology

Dynamic drive and an outgoing personality are often present in those with a number 21 birthday. Friendly and gregarious, you have many social contacts and a wide circle of friends. As a number 21 individual, you can be fun-loving, magnetic, and creative. Alternatively, you can be shy and reserved, with a need to develop assertiveness, especially in close relationships. Although you may be inclined toward cooperative associations or marriage, you always want to be acknowledged for your talents and abilities. The subinfluence of the number 9 month indicates that you are witty, discreet, and passionate, with a receptive sensitivity. As you are likely to be rational, yet imaginative, you need to find a way to express yourself freely. Avoid being indecisive or overly concerned with other people's opinions. Often broad-minded and a humanitarian, you seek fairness and justice. Avoid being hasty or scattering your energies in too many directions. With your insight, you can often be visionary.
  • *Positive:* inspiration, creativity, love unions, long-lasting relationships
  • *Negative:* dependency, nervous, temperamental, lack of vision, disappointment, fear of change

YOUR SPECIAL SOMEONE

You might find someone who is caring and loving among those born on the following dates.

Love & friendship: Jan. 11, 21, 25, Feb. 9, 19, 23, Mar. 17, 21, 30, Apr. 15, 19, 28, 29, May 3, 13, 17, 26, 27, June 11, 15, 24, 25, 30, July 9, 13, 22, 23, 28, Aug. 7, 11, 20, 21, 26, 30, Sept. 5, 9, 18, 19, 24, 28, Oct. 3, 7, 16, 17, 22, 26, 29, Nov. 1, 5, 14, 15, 20, 24, 27, Dec. 3, 12, 13, 18, 22, 25, 27, 29

Beneficial: Jan. 5, 13, 16, 22, 28, Feb. 3, 11, 14, 20, 26, Mar. 1, 9, 12, 18, 24, 29, Apr. 7, 10, 16, 22, 27, May 5, 8, 14, 20, 25, June 3, 6, 12, 18, 23, July 1, 4, 10, 16, 21, Aug. 2, 8, 14, 19, Sept. 6, 12, 17, Oct. 4, 10, 15, Nov. 2, 8, 13, Dec. 6, 11

Fatal attractions: Mar. 17, 18, 19, 20, June 30, July 28, Aug. 26, Sept. 24, Oct. 22, Nov. 20, Dec. 18

Challenging: Jan. 2, 23, 30, Feb. 21, 28, Mar. 19, 26, 28, Apr. 17, 24, 26, May 15, 22, 24, June 13, 20, 22, July 11, 18, 20, Aug. 16, 18, 19, Sept. 7, 14, 16, Oct. 5, 12, 14, Nov. 3, 10, 12, Dec. 1, 8, 10

Soul mates: Jan. 14, 22, Feb. 12, 20, Mar. 10, 18, Apr. 8, 16, May 6, 14, June 4, 12, July 2, 10, Aug. 8, Sept. 6, Oct. 4, Nov. 2

Love & Relationships

By nature, you are witty, entertaining, and fun to be with. Since you are usually amiable, generous, and gregarious, you find it easy to make friends and captivate people. Usually you are sensitive and idealistic, with a charming and romantic soul, but discontent and nervousness suggest that you can be critical or indecisive and change your mind about how you feel in relationships. Although you are able to make sacrifices in your love life, you can also run cold or become uncaring. You are often looking for a partner who is sensitive and understanding and who has faith in your abilities.

September 22

♍ Being on the cusp of Virgo and Libra indicates that you are fortunate enough to have the keen intellect of Virgo and the sociability of Libra. Basically practical, you can be persistent, meticulous, and precise, yet also have a competitive spirit. You are an original thinker who enjoys a good discussion or debate, but may have to guard against being too argumentative or sarcastic. Possessing the ability to be very diplomatic when necessary, however, you realize the advantages of working as part of a team.

With the added influence of your decanate ruler, Taurus, you can be articulate and shrewd, with a natural business sense. You are likely to have a pleasant voice, be charming, and have an appreciation for beauty and luxury. With your keen perceptions, you are very observant but may have to be careful of becoming overcritical. Your thirst for knowledge and sharp intellect may find you involved in many types of activities. When in the company of friends, you often enjoy friendly quips and have an unusual sense of humor.

Aware of your appearance, you like to make a good impression. For fulfillment, however, you may get the most satisfaction from manifesting your ideals or being of service to others. As you are highly intuitive, you must learn to trust your instincts.

Because your progressed Sun enters Libra in the first year of your life, you are likely to be bright and sociable as a child, with a need for harmonious surroundings. Until you reach the age of thirty, your relationships may play an important role in your life. After thirty, when your progressed Sun enters Scorpio, you experience a turning point when you start to become more emotionally self-reliant, in control, and less fearful. At the beginning of your sixties, when your progressed Sun moves into Sagittarius, you become more adventurous and philosophical, with an interest in travel, foreign people and places, or education.

Your Secret Self

You respond well to love and affection and can be warmhearted, generous, and good company. However, being proud and sometimes obstinate if challenged, you may become moody or irritable and suffer from nervous tension. You often protect your extreme sensitivity with your perceptive mind, but once you have really decided something, you can be very strong-willed and determined. This staying power can help you achieve outstanding success.

Your strong need to get to the depths of issues and discover what is lying beneath the surface can make you a good psychologist or stimulate you to investigate people's motives. As long as this does not make you suspicious, it can act as a tool for self-awareness. This insight can help you in your work and also encourages you to influence others.

Work & Vocation

With your analytical skills and critical expertise, you can make an excellent editor, writer, teacher, or scientist. Equally, with your flair for working with people, you can excel as an agent, salesperson or promoter, or in public relations. Alternatively, your leadership abilities, organizational skills, and strategic planning may place you in the world of commerce, where you can make an excellent negotiator or mentally challenge yourself by being involved with large proj-

FIXED STAR

Star's name: Al Kaid, also called Benetnash

Degree position: 25°51'–26°50' Virgo between the years 1930 and 2000

Magnitude: 2

Strength: ★★★★★★★

Orb: 2°10'

Constellation: Eta Ursa Major

Applicable days: September 18, 19, 20, 21, 22

Star qualities: Moon/Mercury

Description: a blue star located in the Great Bear

PRIMARY STAR'S INFLUENCE

Al Kaid imparts an active mind, a need for creative expression, intuitiveness, and an ability to adapt easily to new situations. You probably enjoy exchanging thoughts and ideas but may have a tendency to change your mind easily. This star indicates an aptitude for business and a fondness for power, and may grant opportunities for success, luck, and wealth.

Linked to your Sun's degree, Al Kaid's influence imparts a talent for business and points to success in dealing with the general public. You are inclined toward dealing with data, research, or exacting work that requires attention to detail. Al Kaid also tends to make you restless and ambitious and, at times, ruthless in your desire to reach the top. This star also gives a talent for criticism, which should be used in a positive way.

• *Positive:* active mind, good grasp or perception, sympathetic, kind, work with children

ects. Possessing a good sense of structure, you can also excel as an architect or draftsperson. With your humanitarian streak, you may be drawn to social reform or the healing world, where you can share your knowledge with others.

Famous people who share your birthday include author Fay Weldon, Olympic horseman Capt. Mark Phillips, musician Joan Jett, scientist Michael Faraday, and baseball coach Tommy Lasorda.

Numerology

With a number 22 birthdate, you are a practical, disciplined, and highly intuitive individual. This is a master number and can vibrate both as number 22 and number 4. Often honest and hardworking, with natural leadership abilities, you have a charismatic personality and a deep understanding of people. Although undemonstrative, you often show a caring, protective concern for the welfare of others. However, you never lose sight of your pragmatic or realistic stand. The subinfluence of the number 9 month indicates that you are ambitious, sensible, and cautious. Since you are also sensitive to others' feelings, you can be understanding and caring. Endowed with energy and enthusiasm, you can achieve success through hard work and determination. With your insight and strong instincts, you use your visionary abilities and can accomplish much through creative self-expression. You may, however, need to develop a pragmatic outlook and be economically minded.

• *Positive:* universal, director, highly intuitive, pragmatic, practical, good with your hands, skillful, builder, good organizer, realist, problem solver, achiever

• *Negative:* get-rich-quick schemes, nervous, bossy, materialistic, lack of vision, lazy, egotistical, grasping, self-promoting

Love & Relationships

Although you can have strong views and opinions, you are keen on partnerships. Since love and companionship are so important to you, often you give in or use your diplomatic skills to keep your relationships harmonious. Outgoing and proud, with a forceful poise, you are commanding yet alluring. Always looking for your ideal partner, you believe in lasting unions and can be loyal to the partner you settle with. On occasion, when you do not get the attention or affection you need, guard against becoming insecure or jealous.

YOUR SPECIAL SOMEONE

You might find a partner who will understand your sensitivity and need for love among those born on the following dates.

Love & friendship: Jan. 6, 16, 22, 26, Feb. 4, 14, 20, 24, Mar. 2, 12, 18, 22, Apr. 10, 16, 20, 30, May 8, 14, 18, 28, June 6, 12, 16, 26, July 4, 10, 14, 24, 31, Aug. 2, 8, 12, 22, 29, Sept. 6, 10, 20, 27, Oct. 4, 8, 18, 25, Nov. 2, 6, 16, 23, 30, Dec. 4, 14, 21, 28, 30

Beneficial: Jan. 6, 17, 23, 31, Feb. 4, 15, 21, 29, Mar. 2, 13, 19, 27, 30, Apr. 11, 17, 25, 28, May 9, 15, 23, 26, June 7, 13, 21, 24, July 5, 11, 19, 22, Aug. 3, 9, 17, 20, Sept. 1, 7, 15, 18, 30, Oct. 5, 13, 16, 28, Nov. 3, 11, 14, 26, Dec. 1, 9, 12, 24

Fatal attractions: Mar. 18, 19, 20, 21

Challenging: Jan. 24, Feb. 22, Mar. 20, 29, Apr. 18, 27, 29, May 6, 16, 25, 27, 30, June 14, 22, 25, 28, July 12, 21, 23, 26, Aug. 10, 19, 21, 24, Sept. 8, 17, 19, 22, Oct. 6, 15, 17, 20, Nov. 4, 13, 15, 18, Dec. 2, 11, 13, 16

Soul mates: Jan. 13, Feb. 11, Mar. 9, Apr. 7, May 5, June 3, 30, July 1, 28, Aug. 26, Sept. 24, Oct. 22, Nov. 20, Dec. 18

Libra

September 23–October 22

September 23

FIXED STARS

Although your Sun's degree is not linked to a fixed star, some of your other planets' degrees certainly will be. By having an astrological chart calculated, you can find the exact position of the planets on your date of birth. This will tell you which of the fixed stars listed in this book are relevant to you.

The influence of your birthday suggests that you are an intelligent yet sensitive individual, with a charming but straightforward style. Being born on the cusp of Virgo and Libra, you have the advantage of two sign rulers. One bestows a practical, keen intelligence and the other artistic talent. Unfortunately, this double influence can also make you a perfectionist who is inclined to self-indulgence. Nevertheless, the combination of your inquisitive mind, leadership skills, and sensitive emotions has the potential to take you to the top.

With the added influence of your decanate ruler, Libra, you can attract people with your agreeable manner and pleasant voice. Progressively minded, you have a desire for knowledge and enjoy initiating projects that keep you mentally stimulated. Although you appear easygoing, as an ambitious and willful individual, you have strong beliefs and will persist until you achieve your aims. With good social skills, you are a productive idealist who, with self-discipline and determination, is capable of making your desires a reality.

A creative thinker, with quick comprehension, you have a talent for communication. Although idealistic, you can also be quite money-conscious and enjoy beauty and luxury. You may, however, need to guard against extravagance or vanity. Using your fine intellect is an important part of your success, so you need work or other activities that keep you interested.

Before the age of twenty-nine, you are likely to be concerned with issues regarding money, creativity, and building harmony in your relationships. At the age of thirty, when your progressed Sun moves into Scorpio, there is a turning point that highlights a growing emphasis on deep emotional change and transformation. You may also become involved in joint finances or dealing with other people's money. Another turning point occurs at the age of sixty, when your progressed Sun moves into Sagittarius, indicating a need to become more adventurous and freedom-loving, possibly desiring to seek more education or travel.

Your Secret Self

Even though you appear self-reliant, you are very responsive to your partners or relationships. Affectionate and diplomatic, you can be friendly and stimulating company. If you lose emotional balance, however, you may become moody or cold, or lose interest. Even though you need people, it is vital that you stay independent within a personal relationship. This means that to stay happy, you require your partners to be fair and have an awareness of equal give-and-take.

Because you are sympathetic and capable, others are attracted to you for help and support. You are usually looking for your idealistic vision through a loving relationship or expression of art, music, or spirituality. If your inner sensitivity is restricted, you may become fearful and hostile. When positive, however, you are able to work very cooperatively with others, particularly in productive partnerships and group efforts.

Work & Vocation

Flexibility and natural communication skills suggest that you enjoy dealing with people and can be a good promoter or public-relations person. With charm and an ability to be persuasive, you often take a spokesperson role. Mindful of information, you may be drawn to a career in education or journalism and writing. Although you are adaptable, your pioneering thoughts imply that you can introduce fresh ideas or refine old concepts. If you believe in a person or cause, you can be a good agent or spokesperson. Alternatively, a love for music may draw you to the world of entertainment.

Famous people who share your birthday include musicians Bruce Springsteen, Ray Charles, and John Coltrane, singer Julio Iglesias, actor Mickey Rooney, and writer Walter Lippman.

Numerology

Intuitive, emotionally sensitive, and creative are some of the attributes of a person with a number 23 birthday. Usually you are versatile, passionate, and a quick thinker, with a professional attitude and a mind full of creative ideas. With the number 23 influence, you can learn new subjects easily but may prefer practice to theory. You are fond of travel, adventure, and meeting new people, and the restlessness implied by the number 23 urges you to try many different kinds of experiences. You are apt to make the most of any situation. Generally friendly and fun-loving, with courage and drive, you may need an active life in order to actualize your true potential. The subinfluence of the number 9 month indicates that you are intuitive and imaginative. Although you are multitalented and practical, you need to have order and develop patience. A tendency to get bored easily warns that you need to avoid changing course in midstream. You benefit from completing jobs before you move on to a new challenge.

• *Positive:* loyal, responsible, travel, communicative, intuitive, creative, versatile, trustworthy, fame

• *Negative:* selfish, insecure, stubborn, uncompromising, fault-finding, dull, withdrawn, prejudiced

Love & Relationships

With your ability to be charming, you can easily attract friends and partners. Although you may not commit yourself immediately, once you do, you are likely to go to great lengths to create harmony in your relationships. As you are a romantic and like emotional stability, you are generally loyal to your partner. Even if you become disillusioned, you are still likely to persevere in an attempt to keep your relationships congenial, especially if you are a woman. Men may not be as patient but are still idealistically attached to the idea of the perfect relationship.

YOUR SPECIAL SOMEONE

You might come close to finding that special person among those born on the following days.

Love & friendship: Jan. 1, 4, 27, 28, 29, Feb. 2, 25, 27, Mar. 23, 25, Apr. 21, 23, May 19, 21, 29, June 17, 19, 27, July 15, 17, 25, Aug. 13, 15, 23, Sept. 11, 13, 21, Oct. 9, 11, 19, Nov. 7, 9, 17, Dec. 5, 7, 15

Beneficial: Jan. 3, 10, 15, 18, Feb. 1, 8, 13, 16, Mar. 6, 11, 14, 29, 31, Apr. 4, 9, 12, 27, 29, May 2, 7, 10, 25, 27, June 5, 8, 23, 25, July 3, 6, 21, 23, Aug. 1, 4, 19, 21, Sept. 2, 17, 19, Oct. 15, 17, Nov. 13, 15, Dec. 11, 13

Fatal attractions: Mar. 19, 20, 21, 22, Apr. 30, May 28, June 26, July 24, Aug. 22, Sept. 20, Oct. 18, Nov. 16, Dec. 14

Challenging: Jan. 9, 14, 16, 25, Feb. 7, 12, 14, 23, Mar. 5, 10, 12, 21, 28, 30, Apr. 3, 8, 10, 19, 26, 28, May 1, 6, 8, 17, 24, 26, June 4, 6, 15, 22, 24, July 2, 4, 13, 20, 22, Aug. 2, 11, 18, 20, Sept. 9, 16, 18, Oct. 7, 14, 16, Nov. 5, 12, 14, Dec. 3, 10, 12

Soul mates: Dec. 29

September 24

FIXED STARS

Although your Sun's degree is not linked to a fixed star, some of your other planets' degrees certainly will be. By having an astrological chart calculated, you can find the exact position of the planets on your date of birth. This will tell you which of the fixed stars listed in this book are relevant to you.

♎ The influence of your birthday suggests that you are friendly, sympathetic, and kind, a social person with a strong sense of what is fair and right. You are likely to have a particular interest in home and family and be a diplomat in difficult situations. Generous and romantic, you possess a blend of charisma and leadership. Knowing how to use your influence socially, you are able to mix with people from all different walks of life.

With the added influence of your decanate ruler, Libra, you love luxury and beautiful surroundings. Your inspired ideas can help you develop your innate artistic or creative talents. You will, however, have to apply the necessary patience and self-discipline to bring out the best of your wonderful potential.

Life generally improves for you as you get older and become less dependent on others. You may need to stand up for your beliefs even when it creates confrontation. Being a good organizer and very sociable, however, you can make an excellent entertainer or host. With your love of pleasure and ease, it may be too easy to relax into a comfortable routine. In your mind, however, you have a rebellious humanitarian streak and a desire for action that can spur you to fight mediocrity.

Before the age of twenty-eight, you are likely to be interested in your social relationships and creating harmonious and luxurious surroundings for yourself. There is a change of emphasis in your life at twenty-nine, however, when your progressed Sun moves into Scorpio, highlighting issues concerning emotional change and causing a desire for deeper meaning in your life. Another turning point occurs at fifty-nine, when your progressed Sun moves into Sagittarius, stimulating you to become more adventurous and explore life mentally or physically, particularly through education or travel to foreign places. You may also meet people from different cultures who can widen your horizons.

Your Secret Self

When positive, you are able to be detached and look at life in a light, humorous, and entertaining way. When you are down, however, frustration or disappointment can be reflected in your relationships with others. You then can become controlling, or people may find it hard to reach you emotionally. If this occurs, you can stabilize your strong emotions by still being responsible but refusing to take yourself too seriously. Usually it is not long before your warmth, generosity, and kind nature return.

Possessing the potential for tremendous power, you can move others, particularly through being an artist, politician, entertainer, or spiritual leader. You respect people who can keep you on your toes mentally, and verbally respond as fast as you can. Being an excellent observer and shrewd judge of character can aid your understanding of human nature as well as help you make useful social contacts.

Work & Vocation

Creative and idealistic, you can work for a cause and inspire others to do well. You are generous, with practical abilities, and your charismatic and compelling personality implies that you can lead others, especially in organizing large events or social parties. Having diplomatic skills and charm enables you to win people over and be popular. As a networker with a humanitarian nature, you may become involved in fund-raising for charity. Willing to compromise, you can also be an excellent mediator. Responsible and hardworking, you may be interested in law and reforms. If you seek to express your powerful emotions you may succeed in writing, design, drama, music, or the arts.

Famous people who share your birthday include author F. Scott Fitzgerald, singer Anthony Newley, former Supreme Court Chief Justice John Marshall, Muppet creator Jim Henson, and photographer and musician Linda McCartney.

Numerology

As a number 24 individual, you may dislike routine; however, you are hardworking, with practical abilities and sound judgment. The emotional sensitivity of the number 24 birthday suggests that you need to establish stability and order. Faithful and fair, though sometimes undemonstrative, you are inclined to believe that actions speak louder than words. With this pragmatic approach to life, you develop good business sense and an ability to overcome obstacles and succeed. With a number 24 birthday, you may have to overcome a tendency to be stubborn or fixed in your ideas. The subinfluence of the number 9 month indicates that you are imaginative and generous, with depth of feeling. Idealistic and romantic, you can be a devoted friend and lover. Home and family play an important role in your life, and you are willing to make sacrifices for those you love. Creative self-expression is vital to your inner contentment; otherwise you may suffer from blocked emotions and frustration.

• *Positive:* idealist, practical skills, strong determination, honest, frank, fair, generous, love of home, energetic

• *Negative:* materialistic, instability, dislikes routine, lazy, unfaithful, domineering, stubborn

Love & Relationships

Charming and sociable, you have no problem attracting friends and partners. Love and a secure relationship are especially important for you, particularly as you have a strong need for a warm and secure home. In order to keep peace and harmony, you are usually willing to make sacrifices. Nevertheless, a stubborn streak suggests that if you believe in something, you can be inflexible. A loyal friend, with a warm and generous heart, you love entertaining others. Valuing companionship, you can also be a very supportive partner.

YOUR SPECIAL SOMEONE

For that special someone, look out for those born on the following days.

Love & friendship: Jan. 2, 5, 28, Feb. 3, 26, Mar. 1, 24, Apr. 22, May 20, 29, 30, June 18, 27, 28, July 16, 25, 26, Aug. 14, 23, 24, Sept. 12, 21, 22, Oct. 10, 19, 20, 29, 31, Nov. 8, 17, 18, 27, 29, Dec. 6, 15, 16, 25, 27

Beneficial: Jan. 2, 10, 13, 16, Feb. 8, 11, 14, Mar. 6, 9, 12, Apr. 4, 7, 10, May 2, 5, 8, June 3, 6, July 1, 4, 30, Aug. 2, 28, 30, Sept. 26, 28, Oct. 24, 26, Nov. 22, 24, Dec. 20, 22, 30

Fatal attractions: Mar. 21, 22, 23, Oct. 31, Nov. 29, Dec. 27

Challenging: Jan. 3, 9, 10, Feb. 1, 7, 8, Mar. 5, 6, 31, Apr. 3, 4, 29, May 1, 2, 27, June 25, July 23, Aug. 2, 21, 31, Sept. 19, 29, Oct. 17, 27, Nov. 15, 25, Dec. 13, 23

Soul mates: Jan. 5, Feb. 3, Mar. 1, May 30, June 28, July 26, Aug. 24, Sept. 22, Oct. 20, Nov. 18, Dec. 16

September 25

FIXED STARS

Although your Sun's degree is not linked to a fixed star, some of your other planets' degrees certainly will be. By having an astrological chart calculated, you can find the exact position of the planets on your date of birth. This will tell you which of the fixed stars listed in this book are relevant to you.

The influence of your birthday suggests that you are a charming, sensitive, and astute individual with a warm heart. Although idealistic and generous, with an active social life, you possess a strong sense of discipline or obligation. With a wide emotional range, you can go from being tough and detached to being caring and compassionate.

With the added influence of your decanate ruler, Libra, love and affection are especially important to you. Your social skills can ensure your success with people, especially when you turn on your special charisma. Being a good organizer, you enjoy putting people at their ease, and with your fast mind, you can be witty and entertaining. A need to express yourself and your creativity may find outlets through art, music, or drama, or at least you can become a fine appreciator. Financial matters are also likely to occupy your attention, and with your natural business sense you have the potential to commercialize your many talents.

Being an idealist, you will find it is important to have work or projects in your life that keep you constructively occupied. You generally like to keep busy. Being intuitive as well as mentally astute, you are likely to seek inspiration and work well in service to others. Being a sharp perfectionist, you may sometimes be too hard on yourself and others or become bossy and skeptical. When channeled constructively, however, your strong emotions can ensure remarkable success.

Before the age of twenty-seven, you are likely to be mainly concerned with developing your social skills, creative talents, and opportunities for financial success. At the age of twenty-eight, when your progressed Sun moves into Scorpio, there is a turning point that emphasizes a growing need for emotional change, power, and transformation. Another turning point occurs at the age of fifty-eight, when your progressed Sun moves into Sagittarius, indicating that you are likely to become more daring and forthright, with a need to expand your horizons and seek more inspiration and freedom.

Your Secret Self

By developing perseverance and a willingness to work, you are able to apply the self-discipline needed to fulfill the enormous potential of your birthdate. Always aware of success, you want to constantly improve your circumstances. With all your sensitivity and a love of pleasure, however, you may have to guard against any form of overindulgence or escapism.

Generally optimistic and friendly, you possess a wonderful imagination, dynamic emotions, and an ability to shine or stand out in a crowd. Nevertheless, a sense of soberness, frustration, or disappointment may emerge and cause you to become dissatisfied or even temperamental. By thinking universally, you are able to let go of difficulties or forgive. Your dealings with others improve and your confidence grows when you learn to trust your natural psychic abilities.

Work & Vocation

Imaginative and artistic, you enjoy expressing yourself and working in collaboration with others. Sociable, you like to mix with people of influence, be involved in politics, or work in the world of media, advertising, and publishing. With a flair for the arts, an eye for detail, and good taste, you usually recognize quality and craftsmanship. Creative and talented, you appreciate beauty and are usually interested in the arts, museums, antiques, or galleries. Alternatively, your powerful feelings may find expression in the healing professions, nursing, and caring for others. Intelligent and thoughtful, you enjoy sharing your knowledge with others and may aspire to be a teacher or lecturer, particularly in subjects such as literature, drama, art, or music.

Famous people who share your birthday include composer Dmitri Shostakovich, pianist Glenn Gould, actors Will Smith, Michael Douglas, Christopher Reeve, and Mark Hamilton, painter Mark Rothko, writer William Faulkner, and basketball player Scottie Pippin.

Numerology

Quick and energetic, though intuitive and thoughtful, with a number 25 birthday you need to express yourself through different experiences. These may include new and exciting ideas, people, or locations. A desire for perfection urges you to work hard and be productive. You may, however, need to be less impatient or critical if things do not happen according to plan. As a number 25 individual, you possess strong mental energies that when concentrated aid you to look at all the facts and arrive at a conclusion faster than anyone else. Success and happiness come when you learn to trust your own instincts and develop perseverance and patience. The subinfluence of the number 9 month indicates that you are sensitive and imaginative. Being a good judge of character, you need to learn to trust your inner feelings and intuition rather than be skeptical or full of self-doubt. Although you are charming and sociable, at times you can overreact or become overemotional and behave impulsively.

• *Positive:* highly intuitive, perfectionist, perceptive, creative mind, good at dealing with people

• *Negative:* impulsive, impatient, jealous, secretive, changing circumstances, critical, moody, nervous

Love & Relationships

With all your emotional power and charm, you are certainly in a position to attract others toward you. Although romantic and dramatic, you have a possible tendency for self-indulgence and indecision that may involve you in questionable relationships. Through exercising discrimination, however, you can be in an excellent position to achieve unions with those who can match you in mental agility, warmth, and loving. You may be particularly drawn to people who project power and determination. Once committed, however, you can be a loyal and faithful friend and partner.

YOUR SPECIAL SOMEONE

For that special person, you might look for someone born on one of the following dates.

Love & friendship: Jan. 3, 8, 22, 25, 29, 30, Feb. 1, 6, 20, 23, 27, 28, Mar. 18, 21, 25, 26, Apr. 2, 16, 19, 23, 24, 28, May 14, 17, 21, 22, 26, 31, June 12, 15, 19, 20, 24, 29, July 10, 13, 18, 22, Aug. 8, 11, 15, 16, 20, 27, 29, 30, Sept. 6, 9, 13, 14, 18, 23, 27, 28, Oct. 4, 7, 11, 12, 16, 21, 25, 26, Nov. 2, 5, 9, 10, 14, 19, 23, 24, Dec. 3, 7, 8, 12, 17, 21, 22

Beneficial: Jan. 17, Feb. 15, Mar. 13, Apr. 11, May 9, 29, June 7, 27, July 5, 25, Aug. 3, 23, Sept. 1, 21, Oct. 19, 29, Nov. 17, 27, 30, Dec. 15, 25, 28

Fatal attractions: Mar. 21, 22, 23, 24, May 31, June 29, July 27, Aug. 25, 30, Sept. 23, 28, Oct. 21, 26, Nov. 19, 24, Dec. 17, 22

Challenging: Jan. 20, 23, Feb. 18, 21, Mar. 16, 19, Apr. 14, 17, May 12, 15, June 10, 13, July 8, 11, Aug. 6, 9, Sept. 4, 7, Oct. 2, 5, Nov. 2, Dec. 1

Soul mates: Jan. 4, 31, Feb. 2, 29, Mar. 27, Apr. 25, May 23, June 21, July 19, Aug. 17, Sept. 15, Oct. 13, Nov. 11, Dec. 9

September 26

Ω You are charming and magnetic, projecting a warm and attractive personality. Being sociable and friendly, with a certain grace, you are also mentally astute and determined. As a sensitive romantic, your strong feelings can be a source of high inspiration. Unfortunately, they can also be a source for your frustration if others do not live up to your lofty ideals.

With the added influence of your decanate ruler, Libra, you have a good eye for color and feel happier when in beautiful surroundings. Being artistic and aware of image, as well as enjoying a touch of glamour, you are usually stylish and like to create a good impression. Gracious and refined, you possess natural diplomatic skills and an ability to make everyone feel at ease. Although you are a good socializer and can attract people with your agreeable manner, you may have to learn to be firm and decisive.

Playful and entertaining, you possess natural creative abilities that can be developed through patience and perseverance in writing, art, drama, or music. Just be careful that all this wonderful potential is not directed into self-indulgence or taking the easy option. Interested in people and emotionally supportive of others, you can be a positive influence on a personal level or in group efforts. One of the few obstacles to your success may be an inability to discipline yourself when it is really necessary.

Before the age of twenty-six, you are likely to be concerned with issues regarding money, creativity, and building harmony in your relationships. At the age of twenty-seven, when your progressed Sun moves into Scorpio, there is a turning point that indicates a period of transformation and highlights a growing need for intensity and emotional change. This can cause you to become more decisive and committed. Another turning point occurs at the age of fifty-seven, when your progressed Sun moves into Sagittarius. You may become more adventurous and freedom-loving, or you may find a new interest and start a new course of higher education. Alternatively, you may travel to foreign lands or meet people from different cultures.

Your Secret Self

Dramatic, proud, and noble, you do not always reveal your extreme sensitivity or vulnerability. This implies that when you develop your powerful intuition and learn to stay detached, you will be able to sense when situations do not feel right and avoid them, thus saving yourself from excesses of emotion. Being sympathetic and understanding, you may sometimes find yourself acting as an advisor. Remember to balance your generosity and compassion with detachment to escape taking on others' problems.

Warmhearted and in touch with the joy of life, you will always possess a youthful quality. Kind and magnanimous, you need people and usually seek companionship and harmonious relationships. When you find something you truly enjoy, you become dedicated and hardworking. You may find to your delight that bringing pleasure to others is highly rewarding.

Work & Vocation

Although you have a flair for business, your idealistic nature and desire for self-expression suggest that you are more suited to professions where you can be creative and collaborate with

---

FIXED STAR

Star's name: Zaniah

Degree position: 3°51'–4°43' Libra between the years 1930 and 2000

Magnitude: 4

Strength: ★★★★

Orb: 1°30'

Constellation: Eta Virgo

Applicable days: September 26, 27, 28, 29

Star qualities: Mercury/Venus

Description: a variable white star located on the southern wing of Virgo

PRIMARY STAR'S INFLUENCE

Zaniah's influence bestows refinement, congeniality, and a love of harmony and orderliness. Usually you possess a kind nature, with a charming personality, and probably have many friends. This star imparts popularity, honor, and success through social contacts.

Linked to your Sun's degree, Zaniah favors education, intellectual learning, and a natural talent for research and literature. With the help of this star, you may become a specialist in your subject of interest. You enjoy good working relationships with co-workers and make a good marriage partner. This star suggests that you have a very agreeable nature unless aroused.

• Positive: visionary, mentally keen, refiner, ability to handle detailed work

• Negative: vanity, conceit, lack of drive, squandering, looking for easy options

others. Sociable and friendly, you have a charm and easygoing personality that may draw you to public relations or working in customer service. If in sales, you need to believe in a product you are promoting; otherwise you may sound unconvincing. The ability to combine socializing with business suggests that you can enjoy working in restaurants, clubs, and bars. Alternatively, you may be drawn to teaching, especially films and drama, literature, and music. If blessed with a good voice, you may find yourself in the world of entertainment as an aspiring musician or singer.

Famous people who share your birthday include composer George Gershwin, writer T. S. Eliot, feminist Edith Abbott, singers Olivia Newton-John and Bryan Ferry, scientist Ivan Pavlov, tree planter "Johnny Appleseed" Chapman, and philosopher Martin Heidegger.

Numerology

With a number 26 birthday, you have a pragmatic approach to life, executive ability, and a good business sense. Usually responsible, with a natural aesthetic sense and a love of home, you need to build a solid foundation or find real stability. Often a tower of strength for others, you are willing to support friends and family members, who turn to you in times of need. You may nevertheless need to guard against materialistic tendencies and a desire to control situations or people. The subinfluence of the number 9 month indicates that you are imaginative and intuitive, with strong instincts. When motivated and ambitious, you like to utilize your knowledge in a creative and individual way. Although you prefer easy comfort and a carefree life, your idealism implies that when inspired, you can be dedicated and make great sacrifices. If you are self-disciplined and compassionate, your kindness to others is usually rewarded and your love restored.

• *Positive:* creative, practical, caring, responsible, proud of family, enthusiasm, courage

• *Negative:* stubborn, rebellious, unstable relationships, unenthusiastic, lack of persistence, instability

Love & Relationships

Friendly and charming, you can have an active social life and many friends and admirers. You respond well to group situations and can be the star of social gatherings. Although you are independent, idealism and a powerful need for love may draw you into unsuitable romantic relationships, so it may be necessary to exercise caution in all your personal affairs. A generous lover, you need to learn to stay detached and not give so much of yourself by becoming overserious. An altruistic and humanitarian attitude will enable you to put your love life into perspective.

YOUR SPECIAL SOMEONE

You might find a faithful and reliable lover or partner among those born on the following dates.

Love & friendship: Jan. 5, 9, 10, 18, 19, 26, 30, Feb. 3, 8, 16, 17, 24, 28, Mar. 1, 6, 14, 15, 22, 26, Apr. 4, 12, 13, 20, 24, May 1, 2, 10, 11, 18, 22, June 8, 9, 16, 20, 30, July 6, 7, 14, 18, 28, Aug. 4, 5, 12, 16, 26, 30, Sept. 2, 3, 10, 14, 28, Oct. 1, 8, 12, 22, 26, Nov. 6, 10, 20, 24, Dec. 4, 8, 18, 22, 30

Beneficial: Jan. 13, Feb. 11, Mar. 9, Apr. 7, May 5, June 3, 30, July 1, 28, Aug. 26, Sept. 24, Oct. 22, Nov. 20, Dec. 18

Fatal attractions: Mar. 22, 23, 24, 25

Challenging: Jan. 14, 24, Feb. 12, 22, Mar. 10, 20, Apr. 8, 18, May 6, 16, June 4, 14, July 2, 12, Aug. 10, Sept. 8, Oct. 6, Nov. 4, Dec. 2

Soul mates: July 30, Aug. 28, Sept. 26, Oct. 24, Nov. 22, Dec. 20

September 27

FIXED STAR

Star's name: Zaniah

Degree position: 3°51'–4°43' Libra between the years 1930 and 2000

Magnitude: 4

Strength: ★★★★

Orb: 1°30'

Constellation: Eta Virgo

Applicable days: September 26, 27, 28, 29

Star qualities: Mercury/Venus

Description: a variable white star located on the southern wing of Virgo

PRIMARY STAR'S INFLUENCE

Zaniah's influence bestows refinement, congeniality, and a love of harmony and orderliness. Usually you possess a kind nature with a charming personality and probably have many friends. This star imparts popularity, honor, and success through social contacts.

Linked to your Sun's degree, Zaniah favors education, intellectual learning, and a natural talent for research and literature. With the help of this star, you may become a specialist in your subject of interest. You enjoy good working relationships with co-workers and make a good marriage partner. This star suggests that you have a very agreeable nature unless aroused.

• *Positive:* visionary, mentally keen, refiner, ability to handle detailed work

• *Negative:* vanity, conceit, lack of drive, squandering, looking for easy options

♎ The power of your birthday implies that you are a warmhearted individual with charm and a spirit of enterprise. Honest and direct, you enjoy sharing with others and can be an excellent companion. Ambition often drives you to search for opportunities, and with your big plans, you need to keep yourself active. Due to your strong emotions, however, you may have to avoid going to extremes or acting too much on impulse.

With the added influence of your decanate ruler, Libra, you enjoy luxury and beauty and have a feel for color, form and sound. Liking to create a good image, you usually look attractive and are aware of your appearance. Courteous, friendly, and able to mix well, you possess natural diplomatic skills and an ability to make people relaxed. With your fine intellect, organizational skills, and adventurous nature, you also have the ability to make money. As you are idealistic or spiritually inclined, if this financial gain is also tied into a personal philosophy or social reform, then so much the better. A lack of self-discipline or indecision, however, may divert you from developing the wonderful potential inherent in your birthday.

Although you are usually optimistic, a tendency to be stubborn can, at times, alienate you from those you care for. Nevertheless, when you have positive outlets for your creativity and people skills, it brings out your enthusiasm and fighting spirit.

Before the age of twenty-five, you are likely to be mainly concerned with developing your social skills, creative talents, and opportunities for financial success. As you reach the age of twenty-six, when your progressed Sun moves into Scorpio, there is a turning point that emphasizes issues concerning emotional change and transformation. Another turning point occurs at the age of fifty-six, when your progressed Sun moves into Sagittarius. This indicates that you are likely to become more optimistic and expansive or seek inspiration, whether through personal contact, religion, education, or travel.

Your Secret Self

Possessing a youthful purity of heart, you enjoy entertaining others with your many talents. This childlike quality can sometimes reveal an immature streak, so you may need to look carefully at your responsibilities. A desire for movement and change often manifests as restlessness and impatience, but if you are inspired, it may stimulate you to explore and investigate new and exciting subjects or activities. Travel may also play a meaningful part in expanding your mental horizons or satisfying your desire for freedom.

As you admire intelligence, you have regard for those with wisdom or insight. Although you are sensitive and imaginative and respond well to idealism, you need persistence to make the most of your natural gifts. To avoid becoming bored, you may benefit from constantly updating your knowledge and skills or challenging yourself with bigger and better opportunities.

Work & Vocation

Determined and commanding, you are more comfortable in executive or management positions. As you need freedom to express yourself, you may prefer working independently or in a job that allows you to be a free agent. With your imagination and creativity, you could be very successful in the world of entertainment. Your keen intellect and persuasive manner suggest that as a humanitarian, you can succeed in bringing about reforms or work in education, law, science, writing, or politics. In order to avoid monotony, variety and change are necessary in any occupation you undertake. Compassionate and understanding, with the ability to uplift the spirit of others, you may be drawn to the caring professions or work that helps others.

Famous people who share your birthday include singer/songwriter Meat Loaf, King Louis XIII of France, mystic/saint Amritanandamayi, caricaturist George Cruikshank, actor William Conrad, American revolutionary Sam Adams, baseball player Mike Schmidt, and director Arthur Penn.

Numerology

The number 27 birthday indicates that you are idealistic and sensitive. As an intuitive and analytical individual with a fertile and creative mind, you can impress others with your original thoughts. Although at times you appear secretive or detached, in fact you may be hiding inner tensions. In developing good communication skills, you can overcome a reluctance to express your deeper feelings. Education is essential for number 27 persons, and by broadening your perspective, you become more patient and self-disciplined. The subinfluence of the number 9 month indicates that you are usually magnetic and charismatic, with a perceptive mind and a humanitarian nature. Although you can be generous and compassionate, you can become emotionally frustrated, suffering with fluctuating moods or indulging in escapism and self-pity. You benefit greatly from developing your understanding and tolerance as well as learning to become impersonal. Avoid being stubborn or argumentative when you feel emotionally insecure.

• *Positive:* versatile, imaginative, creative, resoluteness, bravery, good understanding, mentally capable, spiritual, inventive, mental strength

• *Negative:* disagreeable, easily offended, argumentative, restless, nervous, mistrusting, highly strung, tense

Love & Relationships

With your charismatic personality, you can really make a strong and lasting impression. Your warm and easy persona gives you the gift of putting others at their ease. A perfect host, you enjoy company and have many friends. Wearing your heart on your sleeve and needing large amounts of love and affection, you want a partner who can reciprocate your love and kindness. Drawn to powerful and determined individuals, you may have to be careful of becoming dependent on your partners. You have the fortunate ability to mix business and pleasure.

YOUR SPECIAL SOMEONE

For love and affection, you might want to look for that special someone among those born on the following dates.

Love & friendship: Jan. 2, 3, 6, 9, 10, 11, 21, 27, 31, Feb. 1, 4, 7, 8, 9, 25, 29, Mar. 2, 5, 7, 17, 23, 27, Apr. 3, 5, 15, 21, 25, May 1, 2, 3, 13, 19, 23, 30, June 1, 11, 17, 21, 28, July 9, 15, 19, 26, 29, Aug. 7, 13, 17, 24, 27, Sept. 5, 11, 15, 22, 25, Oct. 3, 9, 13, 20, 23, Nov. 1, 7, 11, 18, 21, 30, Dec. 5, 9, 16, 19, 28

Beneficial: Jan. 11, 16, 30, Feb. 9, 24, 28, Mar. 7, 22, 26, Apr. 5, 20, 24, May 3, 18, 22, 31, June 1, 16, 20, 29, July 14, 18, 27, Aug. 12, 16, 25, Sept. 10, 14, 23, Oct. 8, 12, 21, 29, Nov. 6, 10, 19, 27, Dec. 4, 8, 17, 25

Fatal attractions: Mar. 23, 24, 25, 26, 27

Challenging: Jan. 15, Feb. 13, Mar. 11, Apr. 9, May 7, 30, June 5, 28, July 3, 26, Aug. 1, 24, Sept. 22, Oct. 20, 30, Nov. 18, 28, Dec. 16, 26

Soul mates: Jan. 9, 29, Feb. 7, 27, Mar. 5, 25, Apr. 3, 23, May 1, 21, June 19, July 17, Aug. 15, Sept. 13, Oct. 11, Nov. 9, Dec. 7

September 28

♎ Charming, friendly, and intelligent, you tend to be a hardworking and perceptive individual. Compassionate and caring, you possess depth of feeling, yet you can also be shrewd, practical, and realistic. Persuasive, alert, and discerning, you have an interest in people that may manifest as a strong humanitarian streak or encourage you to fight for an idealistic cause.

With the added influence of your decanate ruler, Libra, the demonstration of love and affection is particularly important to you. Magnetism and refined social skills ensure that you enjoy putting others at ease and guarantee your success with people. A feel for beauty and the arts may find expression through music, painting, or drama as well as a desire to surround yourself with beauty, style, and luxury.

Financial matters are also likely to occupy much of your attention, and with your natural business sense and willingness to work hard, you have the potential to commercialize your many talents. Nevertheless, one of your challenges may be to obtain the right balance between work and play to ensure that life does not become overly serious or burdensome. You often work better when you allow your intuition to sense the right time for an idea or project and then act spontaneously rather than becoming restricted by too much structure.

Before the age of twenty-four, you are likely to be concerned with issues regarding money, creativity, and building harmony in your relationships. At the age of twenty-five, when your progressed Sun moves into Scorpio, you encounter a turning point that emphasizes a growing need for emotional change, personal power, and transformation in your life. This can cause you to become more decisive and committed. Another turning point occurs at the age of fifty-five, when your progressed Sun moves into Sagittarius. From this time you are likely to become more adventurous, freedom-loving, and philosophical, possibly desiring more inspiration through study or involvement with foreign people or places.

FIXED STAR

Star's name: Zaniah

Degree position: 3°51'–4°43' Libra between the years 1930 and 2000

Magnitude: 4

Strength: ★★★★

Orb: 1°30'

Constellation: Eta Virgo

Applicable days: September 26, 27, 28, 29

Star qualities: Mercury/Venus

Description: a variable white star located on the southern wing of Virgo

PRIMARY STAR'S INFLUENCE

Zaniah's influence bestows refinement, congeniality, and a love of harmony and orderliness. Usually you possess a kind nature, with a charming personality, and probably have many friends. This star imparts popularity, honor, and success through social contacts.

Linked to your Sun's degree, Zaniah favors education, intellectual learning, and a natural talent for research and literature. With the help of this star you may become a specialist in your subject of interest. You enjoy good working relationships with co-workers and make a good marriage partner. This star suggests that you have a very agreeable nature unless aroused.

• *Positive:* visionary, mentally keen, refiner, ability to handle detailed work

• *Negative:* vanity, conceit, lack of drive, squandering, looking for easy options

Your Secret Self

Emotionally generous with those you care for, you have the potential for powerful universal love and compassion. Being so sensitive, you need regular periods alone to reflect and connect to your deeper inspiration as well as short breaks away from your usual routine.

Occasionally you may take on other people's problems and make them your responsibility, or experience a conflict between your sense of duty and your heart's desire. This may cause you to become skeptical or withdrawn. By letting go and taking life as it comes, you learn to be more detached, trusting that life will spontaneously provide you with everything you need at the right time. Like everybody, you need love and approval, but these may have been previously withheld from you if you did not live up to other people's expectations. The more you value yourself and your feelings, the less you compromise yourself to get the affection you need, and thus you develop your self-confidence.

Work & Vocation

Ambitious and imaginative, you are likely to have grand plans and original ideas. Although you are sensitive and idealistic, you have a commanding and magnetic personality. As a humanitarian, you can be dedicated and hardworking. Seeking balance and harmony, you are fair and just, willing to fight for the underdog. Alternatively, your power of persuasion and bright ideas could motivate you to work in the world of advertising, the media, or publishing. If artistically inclined and full of passion, you may need to find ways to express your feelings through a creative outlet, especially music and drama.

Famous people who share your birthday include actress Brigitte Bardot, TV personality Ed Sullivan, actors Marcello Mastroianni and Peter Finch, Italian painter Michelangelo da Caravaggio, and director John Sayles.

Numerology

Independent and idealistic, with determination and a pragmatic approach, you are often a law unto yourself. Like a number 1 individual, you are ambitious, direct, and enterprising. An inner conflict between wanting to be independent and wanting to be part of a team is also indicated. Always ready for action and new ventures, you courageously take on life's challenges, and with your enthusiasm, you can easily inspire others, if not to join you, then at least to support you in your latest venture. With a number 28 birthday, you have leadership abilities; with common sense, you are able to think clearly. Although you can be responsible, avoid being overenthusiastic, impatient, or intolerant. The subinfluence of the number 9 month indicates that you are imaginative and intuitive, with strong premonitions. You benefit from developing your creativity or pursuing a career where you can be free to express yourself. Although you want affection and have a need to be part of a group, avoid martyring yourself.

• *Positive:* compassion, progressive, daring, artistic, idealistic, ambitious, hardworking, stable home life, strong-willed

• *Negative:* daydreamer, unmotivated, lack of compassion, unrealistic, bossy, lack of judgment, aggressive, lack of confidence, too dependent on others, pride

Love & Relationships

Your magnetic charm and natural friendliness can make you very attractive to others. Affectionate, caring, and tactile, you are very generous with those you love, though you may experience fluctuating moods that can cause you to act suddenly. Sensitive to others, you may go through many changes in response to your partner's needs, so it is important to stay independent. You need change and excitement in relationships to prevent you from becoming restless or stuck in a rut, so it is vital to schedule time for relaxation, travel, and fun. You fare better with a partner who shares your ideals.

YOUR SPECIAL SOMEONE

You might be lucky and find that special someone among those born on the following days.

Love & friendship: Jan. 2, 9, 11, 12, 22, 25, Feb. 7, 10, 20, 23, 26, Mar. 5, 8, 18, 21, Apr. 3, 6, 16, 19, May 1, 3, 4, 14, 17, 20, 24, 29, June 1, 2, 12, 15, 27, July 10, 13, 16, 20, 25, 30, Aug. 9, 15, 24, 26, Sept. 7, 13, 22, 24, Oct. 4, 7, 10, 14, 19, 24, 28, 29, Nov. 2, 5, 8, 12, 17, 22, 26, 27, Dec. 3, 6, 10, 15, 20, 24, 25

Beneficial: Jan. 12, 23, 29, Feb. 10, 21, 27, Mar. 22, 26, Apr. 6, 17, 23, May 4, 15, 21, June 2, 13, 19, 28, 30, July 11, 17, 26, 28, Aug. 9, 15, 24, 26, Sept. 7, 13, 22, 24, Oct. 5, 11, 20, 22, Nov. 3, 9, 18, 20, 30, Dec. 1, 7, 16, 18, 28

Fatal attractions: Mar. 24, 25, 26, 27, July 29, Aug. 27, Sept. 25, Oct. 23, Nov. 21, Dec. 19

Challenging: Jan. 1, 4, 26, 30, Feb. 2, 24, 28, Mar. 22, 26, Apr. 20, 24, May 18, 22, 31, June 16, 20, 29, July 14, 18, 27, Aug. 12, 16, 25, 30, Sept. 10, 14, 23, 28, Oct. 8, 12, 21, 26, Nov. 6, 10, 19, 24, Dec. 4, 8, 17, 22

Soul mates: Jan. 20, Feb. 18, Mar. 16, Apr. 14, May 12, June 10, July 8, Aug. 6, Sept. 4, Oct. 2

September 29

♎ The influence of your birthday shows you to be imaginative and romantic, yet possessing an emotional power that can make you a strong and determined individual. Through the use of your dynamic charm and natural business sense, you can display a talent for combining business and pleasure. Being very entertaining in the company of others, you are able to make an impression with your warmth and generosity.

With the added influence of your decanate ruler, Libra, you love luxury and harmonious surroundings. Appreciating beauty, color, and sound, you have innate artistic or creative talents that can be developed through singing, music, art, or drama. As you enjoy a touch of glamour, you usually look attractive and are aware of creating a good image. Gracious and friendly, you possess diplomatic skills and are an excellent negotiator. You have the ability to make money, but a lack of self-discipline or overindulgence may divert you from developing your wonderful potential.

The expression of love can be especially important to you, as you seek harmonious relationships. Nevertheless, as a Libra, your scales can tip, and although you possess a richness of feeling and are generally light-hearted, you may occasionally become moody or obstinate. This happens especially if you are disappointed that people or situations have not lived up to your high ideals or if your emotional intensity causes you to resort to power plays.

Before the age of twenty-three, you are likely to be mainly concerned with developing your social and financial skills, as well as putting emphasis on your relationships. At the age of twenty-four, when your progressed Sun moves into Scorpio, there is a turning point that highlights issues over the next thirty years concerning emotional change and transformation. Another turning point occurs at the age of fifty-four, when your progressed Sun moves into Sagittarius, suggesting that you may wish to be more adventurous, take greater risks, or expand your mind through further study and travel to foreign places.

Your Secret Self

Highly idealistic, you positively radiate when emotionally uplifting or inspiring others. It is important to have channels for your creativity and people skills in order to bring out your wonderful spontaneity, enthusiasm, and fighting spirit.

Although you are usually optimistic, a tendency toward emotional highs and lows can alienate you from those you care for. At these times, you may withdraw or go cold, so it is necessary to have faith that life will provide you with all you need or find positive outlets for your powerful emotions. Although you possess a dynamic vitality, your sensitivity may attract you to healing or more spiritual pursuits. Alternatively, you may use your compassion and understanding in helping those around you to achieve a better life.

Work & Vocation

Idealistic and dynamic, you possess a charismatic character and a forceful personality. Sociable and friendly, you have the ability to combine your business skills with pleasurable activities. A need to find emotional fulfillment suggests that you seek a vocation rather than menial

---

FIXED STAR

Star's name: Zaniah

Degree position: 3°51'–4°43' Libra between the years 1930 and 2000

Magnitude: 4

Strength: ★★★★

Orb: 1°30'

Constellation: Eta Virgo

Applicable days: September 26, 27, 28, 29

Star qualities: Mercury/Venus

Description: a variable white star located on the southern wing of Virgo

PRIMARY STAR'S INFLUENCE

Zaniah's influence bestows refinement, congeniality, and a love of harmony and orderliness. Usually you possess a kind nature with a charming personality, and you probably have many friends. This star imparts popularity, honor, and success through social contacts.

Linked to your Sun's degree, Zaniah favors education, intellectual learning, and a natural talent for research and literature. With the help of this star, you may become a specialist in your subject of interest. You enjoy good working relationships with co-workers and make a good marriage partner. This star suggests that you have a very agreeable nature unless aroused.

• *Positive:* visionary, mentally keen, refiner, ability to handle detailed work

• *Negative:* vanity, conceit, lack of drive, squandering, looking for easy options

work. You may be best suited to work for a cause or an ideal. Alternatively, you may be drawn to work in the public sector, politics, or social reform. If you want to explore your creativity, you can become successful in the film world. With a sense of the dramatic, you may succeed as an actor or prosper in the world of entertainment, where you can share your knowledge with others through teaching or writing.

Famous people who share your birthday include film directors Michelangelo Antonioni and Stanley Kramer, actress Anita Ekberg, painter Jacopo Tintoretto, singer Jerry Lee Lewis, British admiral Lord Nelson, and Polish politician Lech Walesa.

Numerology

As a number 29 individual, you have a powerful personality and extraordinary potential. You are highly intuitive, sensitive, and emotional. Inspiration is the key to your success story, and without it you may experience lack of purpose. Although you are a true dreamer, the extreme sides of your nature indicate that you may have to guard against alternating moods. If you trust your innermost feelings and open your heart to others, you can overcome your tendency to worry or employ your mind as protective armor. Use your creative thoughts to achieve something special and unique that can motivate or be of service to others. The subinfluence of the number 9 month indicates that you are concerned with others' welfare. Although you can be generous and kind, you set high standards for yourself and others. Your high expectations, however, can lead to disappointment and frustration. By learning to compromise and accept imperfection, you can learn to be contented with your lot.

• *Positive:* inspirational, balance, inner peace, generous, successful, creative, intuitive, mystical, powerful dreams, worldly, faith

• *Negative:* unfocused, insecure, nervous, moody, difficult, extremist, inconsiderate, isolated, overly sensitive

Love & Relationships

Friendly and warmhearted, you will find that social gatherings give you an opportunity to shine. Being passionate and romantic, you love flowers, hearts, and poems, but in a long-term relationship you need a partner who can provide you with stability and security. Since there is a possible danger of disillusionment in your relationships, you may have to be careful in your choice of partner and avoid being involved in power tactics or sulking. Nevertheless, your charismatic personality and charm often attract many admirers and friends, and with your powerful love and generosity, you have a lot to offer others.

YOUR SPECIAL SOMEONE

You might find greater emotional fulfillment and that special someone among those born on the following days.

Love & friendship: Jan. 8, 11, 12, 29, Feb. 6, 9, 27, Mar. 4, 7, 25, 29, Apr. 2, 5, 23, 27, May 3, 4, 21, 25, June 1, 2, 19, 23, July 17, 21, Aug. 15, 19, 29, Sept. 13, 17, 27, Oct. 11, 15, 25, 29, 30, Nov. 9, 13, 23, 27, 28, Dec. 7, 11, 21, 25, 26

Beneficial: Jan. 13, 30, Feb. 11, 28, Mar. 9, 26, Apr. 7, 24, 30, May 5, 22, 28, June 3, 20, 26, July 1, 18, 24, 29, Aug. 16, 22, 25, Sept. 14, 20, 25, Oct. 12, 18, 23, Nov. 10, 16, 21, Dec. 8, 14, 19

Fatal attractions: Mar. 25, 26, 27, 28, Oct. 30, Nov. 28, Dec. 26

Challenging: Jan. 5, 19, Feb. 3, 17, Mar. 1, 15, Apr. 13, May 11, June 9, 30, July 7, 28, 30, Aug. 5, 26, 28, Sept. 3, 24, 26, Oct. 1, 22, 24, Nov. 20, 22, Dec. 18, 20

Soul mates: Sept. 30, Oct. 28, Nov. 26, Dec. 24

September 30

♎ Imaginative yet analytical, you are a sensitive individual with a unique approach to life and are an interesting mixture of idealism and skepticism. Many of your major challenges may center around your emotional vulnerability and the failure of others to reach your high aspirations. You can, however, turn on the charm and be a highly creative thinker.

With the added influence of your decanate ruler, Libra, love and affection are especially important to you. A need to express yourself and your creativity may find outlets through art, writing, music, or drama, or at least you may become a fine appreciator. Refined and gracious, you are likely to have an agreeable manner and an attractive voice.

As a progressive thinker, you have a desire for knowledge and enjoy projects that keep you mentally stimulated. You possess critical and analytical abilities and often have technical skill. A tendency to be suspicious of others or to worry, however, may mar your usual light-hearted attitude.

The first half of your life may be more difficult than the second, due to your emotional sensitivity. Nevertheless, this can stimulate an intuitive or mystical side to your nature that will prove beneficial later in life.

Before the age of twenty-two, you are mainly concerned with creating harmony in your relationships, developing your creative and social skills, and finding opportunities for financial success. At the age of twenty-three, when your progressed Sun moves into Scorpio, you encounter a turning point that highlights issues concerning emotional intensity, change, and transformation over the next thirty years. Another turning point occurs at the age of fifty-three, when your progressed Sun moves into Sagittarius, indicating that you will want to expand your horizons and seek inspiration in life, whether through personal contact, religion, education, or travel.

Fixed Stars

Although your Sun's degree is not linked to a fixed star, some of your other planets' degrees certainly will be. By having an astrological chart calculated, you can find the exact position of the planets on your date of birth. This will tell you which of the fixed stars listed in this book are relevant to you.

Your Secret Self

Your powerful inner emotions need a positive channel for expression or else you may become moody. You possess, however, an enormous potential to realize the power of love and to channel it into the lives of others. At these times, you can become very charismatic and determined, inspiring or influencing people with your spontaneity, warm heart, and generosity. By organizing yourself and being persistent and businesslike, you are able to turn many of your heart's desires into a practical form.

A quest for a higher knowledge may move you toward projects or people that involve soul growth. You need to be constantly working and challenging yourself to achieve something that has some depth and purpose. This stops you from becoming overserious or too self-involved. Paradoxically, although you may have issues around being lonely or abandoned, you need periods alone for contemplation and self-analysis.

Work & Vocation

Gregarious and friendly, you fare better in occupations that involve creative thinking or dealing with the public. As an idealistic and loyal person, you enjoy working in partnerships or collaborating with others in a group effort. As a gifted and multitalented individual, you prefer working conditions that allow you time to play and have fun. If you want to succeed, you may have to work very hard to achieve stardom. With your natural diplomatic skills, you may prefer vocations such as public relations or customer service, and your people skills can help you succeed in promotion or publishing. As you enjoy entertaining, you can blend work and socializing in occupations involving clubs or restaurants, or you may be attracted to show business and the music industry.

Famous people who share your birthday include singer Johnny Mathis, actresses Angie Dickinson and Deborah Kerr, writers Truman Capote and W. S. Merwin, and actor Raymond Massey.

Numerology

Creativity, friendliness, and sociability are just some of the attributes associated with the number 30 birthday. Ambitious, with creative potential, you can take ideas and expand them in your own dramatic style. With a number 30 birthday, you enjoy the good life, and you can be exceptionally charismatic and outgoing. Since you possess strong feelings, being in love or contented is a vital requirement. In your pursuit of happiness, avoid being lazy or overindulgent and the tendency to be impatient or jealous, as these may cause you to experience emotional instability. Among those with number 30 birthdays, many will find recognition or fame, especially musicians, actors, and entertainers. The subinfluence of the number 9 month indicates that you are imaginative and intuitive. Being idealistic and dramatic, however, suggests that you can achieve your desires by becoming more realistic. If you are willing to persevere, work hard, and follow your beliefs and convictions with courage, you come to learn to enjoy your responsibilities. Avoid indulging in escapism; otherwise your aims or desires will remain unfulfilled dreams.

• *Positive:* fun-loving, loyal, friendly, good synthesizer, talent with words, creative, lucky
• *Negative:* lazy, obstinate, erratic, impatient, bad-tempered, insecure, indifferent, scatters energy

Love & Relationships

Although sensitive and idealistic, you also seek adventure to stop yourself from being bored or restless. Personal love may involve much change for you, so it is necessary to learn to adjust rather than become discouraged. As you sometimes take on other people's troubles, you may have to be extra discriminating in your choice of partners to avoid heartache. The demonstration of love and affection can be especially important to you, so it is necessary to be fair and open in all your dealings with others. You need some excitement in your love life to prevent you from becoming bored.

YOUR SPECIAL SOMEONE

You might start to look for an exciting partner among those born on the following dates.

Love & friendship: Jan. 9, 13, 30, Feb. 7, 11, 28, Mar. 5, 26, 30, Apr. 3, 24, 28, May 1, 22, 26, June 3, 20, 24, July 18, 22, 31, Aug. 16, 20, 29, 30, Sept. 14, 18, 27, 28, Oct. 12, 16, 25, 26, 31, Nov. 10, 14, 23, 24, 29, Dec. 8, 12, 21, 22, 27

Beneficial: Jan. 15, 22, 31, Feb. 13, 20, 29, Mar. 11, 18, 27, Apr. 9, 16, 25, May 7, 14, 23, 30, June 5, 12, 21, 28, July 3, 10, 19, 26, 30, Aug. 1, 8, 17, 24, 28, Sept. 6, 15, 22, 26, Oct. 4, 13, 20, 24, Nov. 2, 11, 18, 22, Dec. 9, 16, 20

Fatal attractions: Jan. 11, Feb. 9, Mar. 7, 26, 27, 28, 29, Apr. 5, May 3, June 1, Oct. 31, Nov. 29, Dec. 27

Challenging: Jan. 5, 8, 16, 21, Feb. 3, 6, 14, 19, Mar. 1, 4, 12, 17, Apr. 2, 10, 15, May 8, 13, June 6, 11, July 4, 9, 29, Aug. 2, 7, 27, Sept. 5, 25, Oct. 3, 23, Nov. 1, 21, Dec. 19

Soul mates: Jan. 13, Feb. 11, Mar. 9, Apr. 7, May 5, June 3, July 1, Aug. 31, Sept. 29, Oct. 27, Nov. 25, Dec. 23

October 1

Ω Independent and strong-willed, you are revealed by your birthday to be a dynamic yet charming and diplomatic Libra. Being ambitious, you want to constantly improve your situation. As you possess determination, business sense, and organizational skills behind a pleasant and amiable personality, with persistence and self-discipline you are bound to succeed.

The influence of your decanate ruler, Libra, suggests that demonstrating love and affection is particularly important to you. Magnetism and refined social skills ensure that you put others at ease and guarantee your success with people. A feel for the arts may find expression through music, painting, or drama as well as a desire to surround yourself with beauty, style, and luxury.

The motivating forces of your strong nature can be a need for security and power or a desire for material success and recognition. With the ability to think big, you need to be in a position of authority. A tendency to be proud, bossy, or self-oriented, however, suggests that you do not respond well to criticism and sometimes have to learn the hard way.

Talented and quick-witted, you are usually active and productive, with a sharp and keen intelligence. You may, however, have to guard against tendencies to be too impatient or obstinate. Nevertheless, if stimulated by a worthwhile project, you have the talent, vitality, and capacity to perform outstanding achievements.

Before the age of twenty-one, you are likely to be mainly concerned with your relationships and developing your social and financial skills. At the age of twenty-two, when your progressed Sun moves into Scorpio, you reach a turning point that over the next thirty years emphasizes issues concerning personal power, change, and transformation. Another turning point occurs at the age of fifty-two, when your progressed Sun moves into Sagittarius, suggesting that you may wish to take more risks in your life or expand your mind through study and travel. You may also have more connection with foreign people and places.

Fixed Star

Star's name: Vindemiatrix, also known as Vindemiator or the Grapes Gatherer

Degree position: 8°57'–9°57' Libra between the years 1930 and 2000

Magnitude: 3

Strength: ★★★★★

Orb: 1°40'

Constellation: Epsilon Virgo

Applicable days: October 1, 2, 3, 4

Star qualities: varied interpretations: Mercury/Saturn and Saturn/Venus/Mercury

Description: a bright yellow star located on the right wing of Virgo

PRIMARY STAR'S INFLUENCE

Vindemiatrix's influence indicates that although you possess a quick mind, at times you are impulsive or indiscreet. This star bestows concentration, logical thinking, and the ability to come straight to the point. You tend to approach problems methodically and persist until you resolve them. Vindemiatrix, however, also suggests that you can be obstinate or unyielding.

Linked to your Sun's degree, this star imparts leadership ability, pride, and a drive to accomplish and be recognized. You often conceal your cleverness and have a tendency to make insubstantial statements. This star also indicates that success comes mainly after effort, and it suggests a tendency to worry over money and failure even when there is no need to.

Your Secret Self

By trusting your quick and intuitive insight, you can often display a stoic wisdom gleaned from experience. As your natural leadership is revealed through self-mastery, you may not be living up to your true potential if you find yourself continually in menial positions. Dramatic and creative, your strength is in the dedication you show to a purpose or goal. It is therefore better for you to think big and aim for the top.

One of the possible hindrances to your achievement is a tendency to overtax your nervous system through being skeptical and worried. This can also isolate you from others, so you need to have faith in yourself and your abilities and make the most of your original and inventive ideas. Usually competitive and daring, you can be witty and spontaneous and thus inspire others with your talents. There is also a more hidden part of your nature that can manifest itself as a desire for solitude or self-analysis.

Work & Vocation

Intuitive and original, with a flair for socializing, you have a talent for mixing business and pleasure. Although you enjoy working with others, you prefer to take the lead rather than fol-

- *Positive:* reserved, clever, consistency, patience, methodical
- *Negative:* depression, worry, losses if not careful with monetary matters

low in others' footsteps. With diplomacy and executive skill, you usually occupy executive positions as a manager, organizer, or supervisor. Alternatively, you may decide to be self-employed. Having an understanding of people's needs suggests that you may choose to be of service to the public as a financial advisor or lawyer. An appreciation for beauty and the arts implies that you may run an agency or art gallery. If inspired by higher learning, you may take up theosophy, philosophy, or astrology.

Famous people who share your birthday include actress/singer Julie Andrews, U.S. president Jimmy Carter, actors Walter Matthau and Richard Harris, theosophist Annie Bessant, astrologer Marc Edmund Jones, and bank robber Bonnie Parker.

Numerology

As a number 1 person, you are more inclined to be individual, innovative, and courageous, with plenty of energy. Often there is a need to establish a strong identity and develop assertiveness. The pioneering spirit indicated here encourages you to strike out alone. These self-starting forces can also stimulate you to develop executive or leadership abilities. Full of enthusiasm and fresh ideas, you can show others the way forward. With a number 1 birthday, you may also need to learn that the world does not revolve around you, and you should avoid an inclination to be self-centered or dictatorial. The subinfluence of the number 10 month indicates that as a highly intuitive individual, you express yourself through inspired thoughts and original ideas. Although you are daring and decisive, at times you can find it hard to express your inner intimate feelings. As a dramatic and ambitious person, you can make a strong impression by yourself, but success often comes when you learn to collaborate with others.

- *Positive:* leadership, creative, progressive, forceful, optimistic, strong convictions, competitive, independent, gregarious
- *Negative:* overbearing, jealous, egotistical, too proud, antagonistic, lack of restraint, selfish, weak, vacillating, impatient

Love & Relationships

Friendly and charming, you have a desire to be popular with a wide circle of friends and acquaintances. Loyal and willing to make great sacrifices for those you love, you may nevertheless have to overcome a tendency to be manipulative or self-centered. Although love is very important to you, at times you may be indecisive and worry about your liaisons with others. A love of art and an appreciation for beauty and music suggest that you need an avenue for emotional self-expression and enjoy the company of creative people.

YOUR SPECIAL SOMEONE

You might find a partner who will understand your sensitivity and need for love among those born on the following dates.

Love & friendship: Jan. 1, 7, 17, 20, 30, Feb. 5, 15, 18, 28, Mar. 3, 13, 16, 29, 31, Apr. 1, 11, 14, 27, 29, May 9, 12, 22, 25, 27, June 7, 10, 23, 25, July 5, 8, 21, 23, Aug. 3, 6, 19, 21, Sept. 1, 4, 17, 19, Oct. 2, 15, 17, Nov. 13, 15, 30, Dec. 11, 13, 28

Beneficial: Jan. 15, 17, 28, Feb. 13, 15, 26, Mar. 11, 13, 24, Apr. 9, 11, 22, May 7, 9, 20, June 5, 7, 18, July 3, 5, 16, Aug. 1, 3, 14, Sept. 1, 12, Oct. 10, 29, Nov. 8, 27, Dec. 6, 25

Fatal attractions: Jan. 5, Feb. 3, Mar. 1, 27, 28, 29, 30

Challenging: Jan. 4, 5, 14, Feb. 2, 3, 12, Mar. 1, 10, Apr. 8, 30, May 6, 28, June 4, 26, July 2, 24, Aug. 22, Sept. 20, Oct. 18, Nov. 16, Dec. 14

Soul mates: Jan. 2, Mar. 29, Apr. 27, May 25, June 23, July 21, Aug. 19, Sept. 17, Oct. 15, Nov. 13, Dec. 11

October 2

FIXED STARS

Vindemiatrix, also called Vindemiator or the Grapes Gatherer; Caphir, also called Porrima

PRIMARY STAR

Star's name: Vindemiatrix, also known as Vindemiator or the Grapes Gatherer

Degree position: 8°57'–9°57' Libra between the years 1930 and 2000

Magnitude: 3

Strength: ★★★★★

Orb: 1°40'

Constellation: Epsilon Virgo

Applicable days: October 1, 2, 3, 4

Star qualities: varied interpretations: Mercury/Saturn and Saturn/Venus/Mercury

Description: a bright yellow star located on the right wing of Virgo

PRIMARY STAR'S INFLUENCE

Vindemiatrix's influence indicates that although you possess a quick mind, at times you are impulsive or indiscreet. This star bestows concentration, logical thinking, and the ability to come straight to the point. You tend to approach problems methodically and persist until you resolve them. Vindemiatrix, however, also suggests that you can be obstinate or unyielding.

Linked to your Sun's degree, this star imparts leadership ability, pride, and a drive to accomplish and be recognized. You often conceal your cleverness and have a tendency to make insubstantial statements. This star also

♎ Sociable, charming, and hardworking, you are a persuasive humanitarian who appreciates beauty and the arts. Although you are an idealist, you have a shrewd practical awareness that gives you the ability to turn your inspired dreams into tangible reality.

With the added influence of your decanate ruler, Libra, you possess natural diplomatic skills and an ability to make everyone feel at ease. People are attracted to your courteous and refined manner as well as to your skill in working cooperatively with others. You can be a loyal friend, an excellent parent, and very protective of your family members.

Appreciating beauty and possessing good taste, you are aware of your image and usually like to create a good impression. With a heightened awareness of color and sound, your innate artistic or creative talents can be developed to find expression in singing, music, art, or drama. Because you are sensitive to your environment, your home is liable to be warm and attractive.

Your idealism and romanticism may attract you to meaningful causes where you are likely to give generously of your time or money. Material security is also important to you, and generally you like to make long-term plans. Very determined when you have a goal in mind, you are usually willing to work hard for material achievement. A challenge, however, may be to keep the balance between your work and responsibility and your desire for love and pleasure.

Before the age of twenty, you are likely to be involved in social activity concerned with business or personal relations. At the age of twenty-one, when your progressed Sun moves into Scorpio, you reach a turning point that highlights a growing need for emotional change and intensity in your life. This may cause you to become more decisive and committed. Another turning point occurs at the age of fifty-one, when your progressed Sun moves into Sagittarius, indicating that you are likely to become daring or adventurous, possibly desiring to travel or seek more inspiration in your life through philosophical study.

Your Secret Self

Your inner sensitivity may not be immediately obvious from your outer personality. You are sympathetic, and with your strong feelings, you can identify with others' problems and reveal your potential for deep compassion and universal love. When you are able to view people and situations from this larger perspective, you can be very giving and detached, trusting that life will spontaneously fall into place in its own time. This awareness helps you avoid the need to control everything and becoming too serious, rigid, or frustrated.

Although friendly and caring, you can also be a person of extremes. When inspired, you are amusing, loving, and spontaneous, with a childlike sense of fun. You take life as it comes and have faith in the moment. If you allow yourself to become negative, however, you are in danger of becoming too self-sacrificing or sliding into self-pity and overindulgence. By finding a healthy balance between the material and the spiritual, you can find a wealth of inner love to help you overcome obstacles and make your wishes come true.

Work & Vocation

Creative and ambitious, you are highly intuitive, with a charming personality. You enjoy working with others and can succeed in occupations dealing with the public. You may be drawn to the world of media or public relations, or work as a social worker or negotiator. Intellectual and idealistic, you may be interested in a career as a teacher, psychologist, or counselor. Being artistic, with original ideas, you may be inspired to follow a career as an artist or a designer. If not artistically inclined, you may decide to use your charm and easygoing personality by joining the diplomatic corps and mix socializing, work, and travel. An ability to work with different people suggests that you can work in sales and promotion or fight for just causes as a mediator or arbitrator.

Famous people who share your birthday include Indian leader Mahatma Gandhi, comedians Groucho Marx and Bud Abbott, designer Donna Karan, writers Graham Greene and Wallace Stevens, and singer/songwriter Sting.

Numerology

Sensitivity and a strong need to be part of a group are suggested by a number 2 birthday. Adaptable and understanding, you enjoy cooperative activities where you can experience interaction with others. In your attempt to please those you like, however, you may run the risk of becoming overdependent. Nevertheless, by developing confidence, you can overcome the tendency to get easily hurt by the action and criticism of others. The subinfluence of the number 10 month indicates that you are idealistic and original, with strong convictions and a charismatic character. If you are inspired by an idea or a cause, you have the power to influence others to join your campaign. If insecure, however, you can become worried and indecisive about your personal needs and desires and lose your direction. Receptive and easily influenced by your environment, you need to express yourself through some creative pursuit and are often willing to work with others in order to achieve your goals.

• *Positive:* good partnerships, gentle, tactful, receptive, intuitive, agile, considerate, harmonious, agreeable, ambassador of goodwill

• *Negative:* suspicious, lack of confidence, subservient, oversensitive, emotional, selfish, easily hurt

Love & Relationships

Gregarious and friendly, you should find it easy to make friends and gain admirers. Because you are romantic, the expression of love, whether personal or universal, is likely to be very important to you. You are often willing to make great sacrifices for love; nevertheless, guard against doing things strictly out of duty, as this may cause you to feel unappreciated. As you may need the steadying influence of a stable partner, it is necessary to be very discriminating before you finally settle down in a long-term relationship. You are particularly drawn to intelligent and creative people.

indicates that success comes mainly after effort, and it implies a tendency to worry over money and failure even when there is no need to.

• *Positive:* reserved, clever, consistency, patience, methodical

• *Negative:* depression, worry, losses if not careful with monetary matters

See Appendix for additional fixed star readings.

YOUR SPECIAL SOMEONE

You might find a partner who will understand your sensitivity and need for love among those born on the following dates.

Love & friendship: Jan. 4, 8, 9, 17, 18, 19, 23, Feb. 2, 6, 16, 17, 21, Mar. 4, 14, 15, 19, 28, 30, Apr. 2, 12, 13, 17, 26, 28, 30, May 1, 10, 11, 15, 24, 26, 28, June 7, 8, 9, 13, 22, 24, 26, July 6, 7, 11, 20, 22, 24, 30, Aug. 4, 5, 9, 18, 20, 22, 28, Sept. 2, 3, 7, 16, 18, 20, 26, Oct. 1, 5, 14, 16, 18, 24, Nov. 3, 12, 14, 16, 22, Dec. 1, 10, 12, 14, 20

Beneficial: Jan. 5, 16, 27, Feb. 3, 14, 25, Mar. 1, 12, 23, Apr. 10, 21, May 8, 19, June 6, 17, July 4, 15, Aug. 2, 13, Sept. 11, Oct. 9, 30, Nov. 7, 28, Dec. 5, 26, 30

Fatal attractions: Jan. 17, Feb. 15, Mar. 13, 28, 29, 30, 31, Apr. 11, May 9, June 7, July 5, Aug. 3, Sept. 1

Challenging: Jan. 1, 10, 15, Feb. 8, 13, Mar. 6, 11, Apr. 4, 9, May 2, 7, June 5, July 3, 29, Aug. 1, 27, Sept. 25, Oct. 23, Nov. 21, Dec. 19, 29

Soul mates: Aug. 30, Sept. 28, Oct. 26, Nov. 24, Dec. 22

October 3

Ω Creative, kindhearted, and charismatic, you are an optimistic individual with a powerful imagination and an active mind. The combination of your organizational skills, ability to think on a grand scale, and strong need to express yourself can operate positively to help you achieve your heart's desires.

With the added influence of your decanate ruler, Libra, you love luxury and harmonious surroundings. Magnetism and refined social skills ensure your success with people. A good socializer, you are likely to be an excellent host. As you enjoy a touch of glamour, you usually look attractive and are aware of creating a good image. Appreciating beauty, color, and sound, you have innate artistic or creative talents that can be developed through singing, music, art, or drama. A possible danger to the realization of your wonderful potential may be a mixture of motivation and inertia, which could leave you stuck in a comfortable rut. Fortunately, a strong desire for the good things in life is likely to encourage you to make more of an effort.

Although not particularly aggressive for your own needs, you will fight hard to support the underdog or a meaningful cause. Inspired by many ideas, you can be determined and organized once you have set a definite goal and have a sense of purpose. Unfortunately, you may sometimes be subject to quick irritability or stubbornness, but at your best you are gracious and generous, with a good sense of humor.

Before the age of nineteen, you are likely to be mainly concerned with your relationships and developing your social and financial prospects. At the age of twenty, when your progressed Sun moves into Scorpio, you reach a turning point that starts to highlight issues concerning personal power, change, and transformation. Another turning point occurs at the age of fifty, when your progressed Sun moves into Sagittarius for a thirty-year period, suggesting that you may wish to take more risks in your life or expand your mind through study and travel. You may also have more connection with foreign people and places.

Your Secret Self

Although creative, imaginative, and highly intuitive, you need to strengthen your personal power through self-expression. At times worry, self-doubt, or indecision may keep you from the full demonstration of your many talents. Consequently, it is necessary for you to have a strong sense of your own aims and objectives in order to avoid losing yourself in other people or circumstances. By utilizing your broad-minded and universal approach to life, you are able to let go of situations that impede your progress.

Being sociable, with the sensitivity to put yourself in the place of others, you genuinely care about people. Unfortunately, other people around you may sometimes cause you to become disappointed or frustrated, so it is important to stay detached and cool. By keeping a positive mental attitude, you are able to combine your well-being with the physical comfort and economic security that are promised by your birthday.

Work & Vocation

Dynamic and versatile, you have a charming personality and an ability to promote your ideas. The harder you work, the better the result and the greater the rewards. In the world of com-

PRIMARY STAR

Star's name: Vindemiatrix, also known as Vindemiator or the Grapes Gatherer

Degree position: 8°57'–9°57' Libra between the years 1930 and 2000

Magnitude: 3

Strength: ★★★★★

Orb: 1°40'

Constellation: Epsilon Virgo

Applicable days: October 1, 2, 3, 4

Star qualities: varied interpretations: Mercury/Saturn and Saturn/Venus/Mercury

Description: a bright yellow star located on the right wing of Virgo

PRIMARY STAR'S INFLUENCE

Vindemiatrix's influence indicates that although you possess a quick mind, at times you are impulsive or indiscreet. This star bestows concentration, logical thinking, and the ability to come straight to the point. You tend to approach problems methodically and persist until you resolve them. Vindemiatrix, however, also suggests that you can be obstinate or unyielding.

Linked to your Sun's degree, this star imparts leadership ability, pride, and a drive to accomplish and be recognized. You often conceal your cleverness and have a tendency to make insubstantial statements. This star also indicates that success comes mainly after effort, and it implies a tendency to worry over money and failure even when there is no need to.

• *Positive:* reserved, clever, consistency, patience, methodical

• *Negative:* depression, worry, losses if not careful with monetary matters

See Appendix for additional fixed star readings.

merce, you can achieve success as a salesperson. Creative and gifted, you probably use your intuition to anticipate what the public wants. Fair and just, you may be drawn to practice law or politics to fight for or defend the underdog. If inspired by higher learning, you make an excellent teacher or preacher. Sociable and friendly, you may mix business and pleasure by working at a restaurant, a fashionable café, or a club. If interested in music and the arts, you may be drawn to performing arts, the theater, or the film and music industries.

Famous people who share your birthday include musician Lindsey Buckingham, etiquette expert Emily Post, occultist Paul Foster Case, actress Eleonora Duse, entertainer Chubby Checker, composer Steve Reich, and writers Gore Vidal and Thomas Wolfe.

Numerology

As a number 3 individual, you are sensitive, with a need for creativity and emotional expression. Fun-loving and a good companion, you enjoy friendly social activities and many interests. Although you are versatile and expressive, with a need for different and exciting experiences, an inclination to get bored easily may cause you to become indecisive or spread yourself too thinly. Although with a number 3 birthday you are usually artistic and charming, with a good sense of humor, you may have to develop self-esteem and guard against tendencies such as worry and emotional insecurities. The subinfluence of the number 10 month indicates that you are highly intuitive and independent. Although you are multitalented and original, a love of ease and a tendency to indulge in emotional insecurity suggests that you need to learn about self-control and discipline. Usually you express your humanitarian nature by helping or supporting others in times of trouble. Magnetic and charming, with inner wisdom, you need to trust your inner feelings and learn to be patient.

• *Positive:* humorous, happy, friendly, productive, creative, artistic, power to wish, freedom-loving, a talent with words

• *Negative:* easily bored, vain, overimaginative, exaggerate, unloving, boastful, extravagant, self-indulgent, lazy, hypocritical, wasteful

YOUR SPECIAL SOMEONE

For security, mental stimulation, and love, you might want to begin looking among those born on the following dates.

Love & friendship: Jan. 5, 9, 10, 18, 19, Feb. 3, 7, 8, 16, 17, Mar. 1, 5, 14, 15, 31, Apr. 3, 4, 12, 13, 29, May 1, 10, 11, 27, 29, June 8, 9, 25, 27, July 6, 7, 23, 25, 31, Aug. 4, 5, 21, 23, 29, Sept. 2, 3, 19, 21, 27, 30, Oct. 1, 17, 19, 25, 28, Dec. 13, 15, 21, 24

Beneficial: Jan. 1, 6, 17, Feb. 4, 15, Mar. 2, 13, Apr. 11, May 9, June 7, July 5, Aug. 3, Sept. 1, Oct. 31, Nov. 29, Dec. 27

Fatal attractions: Mar. 28, 30, 31, Apr. 1, 2

Challenging: Jan. 2, 16, Feb. 14, Mar. 12, Apr. 10, May 8, June 6, July 4, Aug. 2, Dec. 30

Soul mates: Jan. 11, 31, Feb. 9, 29, Mar. 7, 27, Apr. 5, 25, May 3, 23, June 1, 21, July 19, Aug. 17, Sept. 15, Oct. 13, Nov. 11, Dec. 9

Love & Relationships

Gregarious and friendly, you can be the life and soul of the party. With a strong sense of justice you usually take care of those you love and support your friends with encouraging words. You always remember those who have shown you kindness in the past. As you can be very loving and giving, do not allow others to become too dependent on you. You make a loyal and reliable friend and partner and, with your natural charm, are often popular with a large circle of acquaintances.

October 4

♎ Your birthday reveals you to be imaginative, sensitive, and creative, a Libra with an adventurous spirit. Honest and direct, you possess natural diplomatic skills and have a keen awareness of relationships. Being friendly and socially inclined, you have an attractive charm and are generally concerned with the image you present. With your versatile personality, you often seek out new and exciting experiences. You may, however, have to guard against tendencies to be too impatient or restless.

With the added influence of your decanate ruler, Aquarius, you are a creative and original thinker. Interested in the psychology of how people interrelate, you are open-minded and enjoy debate. Appreciating beauty and luxury, you have innate creative talents that can be developed to find expression in writing, music, art, or drama. Possessing the power to concentrate upon a particular aim and give it your full attention, you can be very determined once you have finally made up your mind.

Although travel often features prominently in your life, you also need the security and comfort of your own home. A struggle between idealistic and materialistic tendencies suggests that uncertainty, indecision, and loss of focus may be your greatest challenges.

At the age of nineteen, when your progressed Sun moves into Scorpio for thirty years, you reach a turning point in your life that highlights a growing need for emotional change, intensity, and transformation. Another turning point occurs at the age of forty-nine, when your progressed Sun moves into Sagittarius, indicating that you are likely to become more adventurous or philosophical. This may encourage you to study and broaden your horizons, or to have more of an interest in foreign people and places.

FIXED STARS

Vindemiatrix, also called Vindemiator or the Grapes Gatherer; Caphir, also called Porrima

PRIMARY STAR

Star's name: Vindemiatrix, also called Vindemiator or the Grapes Gatherer

Degree position: 8°57'–9°57' Libra between the years 1930 and 2000

Magnitude: 3

Strength: ★★★★★

Orb: 1°40'

Constellation: Epsilon Virgo

Applicable days: October 1, 2, 3, 4

Star qualities: varied interpretations: Mercury/Saturn and Saturn/Venus/Mercury

Description: a bright yellow star located on the right wing of Virgo

PRIMARY STAR'S INFLUENCE

Vindemiatrix's influence indicates that although you possess a quick mind, at times you are impulsive or indiscreet. This star bestows concentration, logical thinking, and the ability to come straight to the point. You tend to approach problems methodically and persist until you resolve them. Vindemiatrix, however, also suggests that you can be obstinate or unyielding.

Linked to your Sun's degree, this star imparts leadership ability, pride, and a drive to accomplish and be recognized. You often conceal your cleverness and have a tendency to make insubstantial statements. This star also

Your Secret Self

Sensitive, full of creative ideas, and possessing a strong sense of vision, you have the potential to manifest your original and inspired concepts. These can help you overcome possible worries about changing finances or insecurities around making the right decisions. Nevertheless, your need for self-expression and love of freedom ensure that, if despondent, you do not stay down for long.

Being clever, you learn quickly but need to develop detachment to avoid frustration or disappointment. The humanitarian side of your nature, however, is able to look past personal problems to a more universal perspective. Although you may have an extravagant streak, your knack for sensing when opportunities can offer a financial reward can help you rapidly advance in life.

Work & Vocation

Ambitious, capable, and versatile, you often have many interests and are likely to explore many avenues before you settle into a career. With your love of variety, it is vital to choose a career that can offer opportunities for progress and change and does not involve routine. Possessing a strong visual sense, you are highly aware of image making and are suitable for occupations in media, graphics, design, or photography. Generally hardworking, with people skills, you enjoy being creative and artistic and are likely to be successful in work connected with foreign places. With your capacity for deep thought, you may also become involved in careers that utilize your mental abilities, such as in research, philosophy, or education.

Famous people who share your birthday include actors Buster Keaton and Charlton Heston, actress Susan Sarandon, artist Jean Millet, designer Terence Conran, singer Patti LaBelle, writers Alvin Toffler and Jackie Collins, and Saint Francis of Assisi.

Numerology

The solid structure and orderly power suggested by the number 4 birthday indicate that you need stability and like to establish order. Endowed with energy, practical skills, and strong determination, you can achieve success through hard work. Security-conscious, you like to build a strong foundation for yourself and your family. A pragmatic approach to life confers a good business sense and an ability to achieve material success in life. As a number 4 person, you are usually honest, frank, and fair. The challenges for a number 4 individual may include overcoming periods of instability or financial worry. The subinfluence of the number 10 month indicates that you are ambitious and independent, with strong instincts and an inquisitive mind. Progressive and adaptable, you want to have the freedom to encounter different experiences. These may include travel for business and pleasure. Although you are witty and enthusiastic, willing to try anything new, on occasion you can be unpredictable or inconsistent and act in an irresponsible manner.

• *Positive:* organized, self-discipline, steady, hardworking, craftsmanship, good with your hands, pragmatism, trusting, exact

• *Negative:* uncommunicative, repressed, rigid, lazy, unfeeling, procrastination, too economical, bossy, hidden affections, resentful, strict

Love & Relationships

Charismatic and entertaining, you usually have many admirers. Since you are a Libra and socially inclined, love and friendships are especially important to you. With your quick and observant grasp of people and natural sense of humor, you can be an entertaining companion. Ideally, in relationships you need someone who is intelligent and with whom you can share your interests. At times, however, you may become reserved and not show your true feelings.

indicates that success comes mainly after effort, and it implies a tendency to worry over money and failure even when there is no need to.

• *Positive:* reserved, clever, consistency, patience, methodical

• *Negative:* depression, worry, losses if not careful with monetary matters

See Appendix for additional fixed star readings.

YOUR SPECIAL SOMEONE

You might find a partner who can help you express yourself and keep you mentally stimulated among those born on the following dates.

Love & friendship: Jan. 2, 6, 10, 20, 25, 29, Feb. 4, 8, 18, 27, Mar. 2, 6, 16, 25, 28, 30, Apr. 4, 14, 23, 26, 28, 30, May 2, 12, 21, 24, 26, 28, 30, June 10, 15, 19, 22, 24, 26, 28, July 8, 17, 20, 22, 24, 26, Aug. 6, 15, 18, 20, 22, 24, Sept. 4, 13, 16, 18, 20, 22, Oct. 2, 11, 14, 16, 18, 20, Nov. 9, 12, 14, 16, 18, Dec. 7, 10, 12, 14, 16

Beneficial: Jan. 7, 13, 18, 28, Feb. 5, 11, 16, 26, Mar. 3, 9, 14, 24, Apr. 1, 7, 12, 22, May 5, 10, 20, June 3, 8, 18, July 1, 6, 16, Aug. 4, 14, Sept. 2, 12, 30, Oct. 10, 28, Nov. 8, 26, 30, Dec. 6, 24, 28

Fatal attractions: Jan. 25, Feb. 23, Mar. 21, 30, 31, Apr. 1, 2, 19, May 17, June 15, July 13, Aug. 11, Sept. 9, Oct. 7, Nov. 5, Dec. 3

Challenging: Jan. 3, 17, Feb. 1, 15, Mar. 13, Apr. 11, May 9, 30, June 7, 28, July 5, 26, 29, Aug. 3, 24, 27, Sept. 1, 22, 25, Oct. 20, 23, Nov. 18, 21, Dec. 16, 19

Soul mates: Jan. 18, Feb. 16, Mar. 14, Apr. 12, May 10, 29, June 8, 27, July 6, 25, Aug. 4, 23, Sept. 2, 21, Oct. 19, Nov. 17, Dec. 15

October 5

♎ An interesting mixture of emotional vision and shrewd practicality is suggested by your birthdate. Charming, with a natural ability for dealing with the public, you are constantly seeking new experiences in your quest for self-discovery. A charismatic warmth endears you to others, but as important as relationships are in your life, you may not be satisfied unless you have an interesting or fulfilling occupation or activities.

With the added influence of your decanate ruler, Aquarius, you have inventive and productive ideas and may enjoy a good discussion. Broad-minded in your approach, you are interested in people and issues concerning freedom. You possess natural diplomatic skills as well as an ability to work cooperatively with others. An attraction toward the arts may find expression through music, painting, or drama as well as a desire to surround yourself with beauty, style, and luxury.

With a keen eye for opportunities, you possess good monetary potential and know how to negotiate a good deal. Being versatile, you also possess an ability to mix business and pleasure. When you perform a task, you like to do it well, as you have a sense of pride in your work. With all your talents, therefore, you need only to place an emphasis on hard work, values, and responsibility to succeed in a big way.

Up to the age of seventeen, you are mainly concerned with your relationships and developing your social awareness. At the age of eighteen, when your progressed Sun moves into Scorpio for thirty years, there is a turning point that emphasizes a growing need for emotional change and regeneration. Another turning point occurs at the age of forty-eight, when your progressed Sun moves into Sagittarius, suggesting that you may wish to take more risks in your life or expand your mind through study, inspiration, or travel. From the age of seventy-eight, when your progressed Sun enters Capricorn, you begin to place more emphasis on structure, stability, and security.

Your Secret Self

Although a pragmatist, you have an inner sensitivity that can draw you to an idealistic cause, with the possibility of your becoming a leading figure in humanitarian or religious movements. With your quick instincts, you often intuitively understand people or situations before you can engage processes of rational thought. Developing and trusting this intuitive ability helps advance your insight and solve problems.

As you usually become enthusiastic when you are involved in new projects or ideas, you may find yourself exploring physically or mentally in your quest to avoid boredom and routine. Travel can sometimes play a big part in enlarging your opportunities for success. If your need for excitement or new experience is restricted, you may feel restless or impatient and compensate by escaping or overindulging in the good things of life.

Work & Vocation

As an intelligent and creative individual who needs diversity, you are highly suited for occupations that can offer change and excitement. A flair for people and a dislike for routine suggests

FIXED STAR

Star's name: Algorab, also called Al Ghirab or the Crow
Degree position: 12°28'–13°22' Libra between the years 1930 and 2000
Magnitude: 3
Strength: ★★★★★
Orb: 1°30'
Constellation: Delta Corvi
Applicable days: October 5, 6, 7, 8
Star qualities: Mars/Saturn
Description: a pale yellow and purple binary star, located on the right wing of the Crow

PRIMARY STAR'S INFLUENCE

Algorab imparts a flair for business and enterprise and bestows determination and power to overcome challenges with charm and grace. This star indicates a reserved and studious nature, with ambition for recognition and success. Algorab also warns against destructiveness and deception from others.

Linked to your Sun's degree, this star imparts a talent for making a good impression and success in dealing with the public and in getting support or promotion from others. If in the public view, you can gain fame and popularity, although you must guard against scandals that can lose you your position.

• Positive: persistence, big enterprises, popularity, military honor
• Negative: unorthodox methods, working against the establishment

that you do better in occupations dealing with the public. If gifted and idealistic, you may want to pursue a career in the world of entertainment or music. If you become inspired by a moral cause or social injustice, you can become involved in social reforms or work for humanitarian groups. Although you can have periods of prosperity, you may indulge and experience the reverse. For security and stability, you may need to adopt a long-term savings policy.

Famous people who share your birthday include musicians Bob Geldof and Steve Miller, Czech president Vaclav Havel, astronaut Richard Gordon, pioneer filmmaker Louis Lumière, actress Glynis Johns, and auto racer Michael Andretti.

Numerology

Strong instincts, an adventurous nature, and a desire for freedom are all indicated by the number 5 birthday. The willingness to explore or try anything new and an enthusiastic approach suggest that life will have a lot to offer you. Travel and many opportunities for change, some unexpected, may lead you to undergo a real transformation of views and beliefs. With a number 5 birthday, you need to feel that life is exciting; however, you may also have to develop a responsible attitude and avoid tendencies such as unpredictability, excessiveness, and restlessness. The natural talent of a number 5 individual is knowing how to go with the flow and staying detached. The subinfluence of the number 10 month indicates that you are ambitious and determined when you set your mind on a plan or an ideal. Charismatic and gregarious, with an ability to attract opportunities, you like to have a wide circle of friends and make many contacts. Creative and multitalented, you usually manage to turn situations to your advantage, but avoid being critical or too demanding.

• *Positive:* versatile, adaptable, progressive, strong instincts, magnetic, lucky, daring, freedom-loving, quick and witty, curious, mystical, sociable

• *Negative:* unreliable, changeable, procrastinator, inconsistent, overconfident, headstrong

Love & Relationships

Others are drawn by your natural charm and magnetism. Being sociable and enjoying company, you should have no problem attracting friends and romantic partners. When you love, it is with power and deep feelings. As there is a possible danger of disillusionment in your relationships, you may have to be careful of becoming involved in emotional power games or sulking. Attracted to powerful people with big plans and strong ambitions, you can benefit from the assistance of influential people.

YOUR SPECIAL SOMEONE

You might come close to finding your true match with someone born on one of the following days.

Love & friendship: Jan. 7, 11, 12, 22, Feb. 5, 9, 10, 20, Mar. 3, 7, 18, 31, Apr. 1, 5, 16, 29, May 3, 14, 27, 29, June 1, 2, 12, 25, 27, July 10, 23, 25, Aug. 8, 21, 23, 31, Sept. 6, 19, 21, 29, Oct. 4, 17, 19, 27, 30, Nov. 2, 15, 17, 25, 28, Dec. 13, 15, 23, 26

Beneficial: Jan. 8, 14, 19, Feb. 6, 12, 17, Mar. 4, 10, 15, Apr. 2, 8, 13, May 6, 11, June 4, 9, July 2, 7, Aug. 5, Sept. 3, Oct. 1, 29, Nov. 27, Dec. 25, 29

Fatal attractions: Apr. 1, 2, 3, 4, 5

Challenging: Jan. 9, 18, 20, Feb. 7, 16, 18, Mar. 5, 14, 16, Apr. 3, 12, 14, May 1, 10, 12, June 8, 10, July 6, 8, 29, Aug. 4, 6, 27, Sept. 2, 4, 25, Oct. 2, 23, Nov. 21, Dec. 19

Soul mates: Jan. 9, Feb. 7, Mar. 5, Apr. 3, May 1, Oct. 30, Nov. 28, Dec. 26

October 6

Ω Your birthday shows you to be light, friendly, and congenial, a smart and creative Libra with original ideas. Diplomatic yet straight-speaking, you have an interest in people and are gracious and capable. Possessing natural shrewdness when it comes to financial affairs, you value security and appreciate the luxuries of life.

With the added influence of your decanate ruler, Aquarius, you have a strong mind and an interest in the avant-garde. Although you possess a touch of gentle charm and elegance, you can be very independent, with a need for freedom. Although sometimes critical, you are usually fairly easygoing, with a wonderful ability to make social contacts. A possible challenge to your stability may be an inclination to worry, particularly about monetary matters.

With a strong need for self-expression and having an appreciation of beauty, color, and sound, you may wish to develop your creative talents through writing, music, art, or drama. Whatever you do, you have good taste and an attraction to the unusual. Although sometimes indecisive, once set on a course of action you can be determined in achieving your objectives.

At the age of seventeen, when your progressed Sun moves into Scorpio, you reach a turning point in your life that emphasizes a growing need for emotional intensity, personal power, and transformation. Another turning point occurs at the age of forty-seven, when your progressed Sun moves into Sagittarius, influencing you to become more freedom-loving and to take more risks. From this time, you may also have more connection with foreign people and places or expand your mind through inspiration or study. From the age of seventy-seven, when your progressed Sun enters Capricorn, you begin to place more emphasis on security, discipline, and practical issues.

Your Secret Self

You are dependable and conscientious, and an awareness of your responsibilities can emphasize the importance of home and family in your life. As you learn very quickly and have the ability to solve problems, you often become an advisor to others. Just be careful that in your desire to help, you do not start to interfere or become anxious. You can make big sacrifices for those you love but are seldom swept off your feet by emotion. A desire for harmony and peace of mind may manifest as a need for regular periods of rest and recuperation.

Quick at assessing values, with an inner dramatic sense, you usually find yourself naturally taking a leadership position. Although you possess a good business sense, you may have to overcome a tendency to be too security-conscious or preoccupied with material concerns.

Work & Vocation

Creative and multitalented, with sharp intelligence, you possess excellent business acumen and the talent to merchandise your unique ideas. You may fare best as a self-employed person, running your own business. Whatever career you may choose, you will always be looking for ways to improve your working conditions. Intuitive and friendly, you are able to create a friendly and harmonious environment. An ability to write and an interest in public affairs and reforms suggest that you will be drawn to art, theater, writing, or music. With your natural

FIXED STAR

Star's name: Algorab, also called Al Ghirab or the Crow

Degree position: 12°28'–13°22' Libra between the years 1930 and 2000

Magnitude: 3

Strength: ★★★★★

Orb: 1°30'

Constellation: Delta Corvi

Applicable days: October 5, 6, 7, 8

Star qualities: Mars/Saturn

Description: a pale yellow and purple binary star located on the right wing of the Crow

PRIMARY STAR'S INFLUENCE

Algorab imparts a flair for business and enterprise and bestows determination and power to overcome challenges with charm and grace. This star indicates a reserved and studious nature with ambition for recognition and success. Algorab also warns against destructiveness and deception from others.

Linked to your Sun's degree, this star imparts a talent for making a good impression and success in dealing with the public and in getting support or promotion from others. If in the public view, you can gain fame and popularity, although you must guard against scandals that can lose you your position.

• *Positive:* persistence, big enterprises, popularity, military honor

• *Negative:* unorthodox methods, working against the establishment

business sense, you also possess a gift for promotion or production. Alternatively, a philosophical or humanitarian leaning may be satisfied through careers such as teaching and politics.

Famous people who share your birthday include actresses Britt Ekland and Carole Lombard, scientist/engineer George Westinghouse, explorer Thor Heyerdahl, singer Jenny Lind, and architect Le Corbusier.

Numerology

Compassion, idealism, and a caring nature are some of the attributes suggested by a number 6 birthday. This is the number of the perfectionist or the universal friend, and indicates that you are frequently a humanitarian who can be responsible, loving, and supportive. With a number 6 birthday, you are frequently domestically inclined and a devoted parent. The more sensitive among you will need to find a form of creative expression and are drawn to the world of entertaining or art and design. You may need to develop more self-confidence and overcome tendencies such as interfering, worry, and misplaced sympathy. The subinfluence of the number 10 month indicates that you are highly intuitive and original but also a perfectionist. Although you want peace and harmony, a tendency to be skeptical and undeceived suggests that self-doubt and worry can leave you wondering where your loyalty belongs. If you lack trust or faith in yourself and others, you may be constantly dissatisfied or discontented.

• *Positive:* worldly, universal brotherhood, friendly, compassionate, dependable, understanding, sympathetic, idealistic, domesticated, humanitarian, artistic

• *Negative:* discontented, anxiety, shy, unreasonable, disharmonious, domineering, lack of responsibility, selfish, suspicious, cynical, self-centered

Love & Relationships

Friendly and charming, you are able to fit into any social situation and can be a loving partner and supportive parent. Usually you are spontaneous, loyal, and giving, but if you are too concerned with your own agenda, you can occasionally appear cold or indifferent. If you set your goals too high, it may be difficult for anyone to live up to your expectations. Your gregarious and hospitable personality ensures that you have many friends and are a good host. Being creative and imaginative, you can be witty and entertaining.

YOUR SPECIAL SOMEONE

To find the ideal partner, you might start by looking for someone born on one of the following dates.

Love & friendship: Jan. 4, 8, 13, 22, 26, Feb. 2, 6, 20, 24, Mar. 4, 18, 22, Apr. 2, 16, 20, 30, May 14, 18, 28, 30, June 3, 12, 16, 26, 28, July 10, 14, 24, 26, Aug. 8, 12, 22, 24, Sept. 6, 10, 20, 22, 30, Oct. 4, 8, 18, 20, 28, Nov. 2, 6, 16, 18, 26, Dec. 4, 14, 16, 24

Beneficial: Jan. 9, 20, Feb. 7, 18, Mar. 5, 16, 29, Apr. 3, 14, 27, May 1, 12, 25, June 10, 23, July 8, 21, Aug. 6, 19, Sept. 4, 17, Oct. 2, 15, 30, Nov. 13, 28, Dec. 11, 26, 30

Fatal attractions: Jan. 27, Feb. 25, Mar. 23, Apr. 2, 3, 4, 5, 21, May 19, June 17, July 15, Aug. 13, Sept. 11, Oct. 9, Nov. 7, Dec. 5

Challenging: Jan. 2, 10, 19, Feb. 8, 17, Mar. 6, 15, Apr. 4, 13, May 2, 11, June 9, July 7, 30, Aug. 5, 28, Sept. 3, 26, Oct. 1, 24, Nov. 22, Dec. 20, 30

Soul mates: Jan. 15, Feb. 13, Mar. 11, Apr. 9, May 7, June 5, July 3, Aug. 1, Oct. 29, Nov. 27, Dec. 25

451

October 7

♎ The influence of your birthday reveals you to be a friendly, sharp, and honest Libra with excellent people skills. As you enjoy being active, you are usually planning some scheme or strategy. Once you set your heart on a goal, your determination and focus are admirable. Enterprising, with an attraction for material comforts, you have a knack for making contacts that can bring you gain and advancement.

With the added influence of your Sun in the decanate of Aquarius, you have original ideas and a shrewd understanding of humanity. Creative, with an interest and enjoyment in shaping things, you may be particularly interested in art, music, or metaphysical and religious subjects. Open-minded and liberal, you will stand up for your principles and for justice.

The strong emphasis on relationships and partnerships linked to your birthday reveals that you work better when in cooperation with others. At times you may have an unfounded fear of not having enough money, but you will always have the material protection of natural strategic skills and a talent for selling ideas. Once you have committed yourself to a concept or activity, you can project strong enthusiasm, toughness, and resolve. A humanitarian side to your nature is sensitive and idealistic and may find an outlet in helping your family, friends, or compassionate causes.

Up to the age of fifteen, you are mainly concerned with developing your social awareness. At the age of sixteen, when your progressed Sun moves into Scorpio, however, you experience a turning point that emphasizes, over the next thirty years, issues concerning emotional change, power, and regeneration. Another turning point occurs at the age of forty-six, when your progressed Sun moves into Sagittarius. This change suggests that you become more idealistic and optimistic, wishing to take more risks in your life or expand your self-expression through study and travel. From the age of seventy-six, when your progressed Sun enters Capricorn, you begin to place more emphasis on duties, practical goals, and a realistic outlook.

FIXED STAR

Star's name: Algorab, also called Al Ghirab or the Crow

Degree position: 12°28'–13°22' Libra between the years 1930 and 2000

Magnitude: 3

Strength: ★★★★★

Orb: 1°30'

Constellation: Delta Corvi

Applicable days: October 5, 6, 7, 8

Star qualities: Mars/Saturn

Description: a pale yellow and purple binary star located on the right wing of the Crow

PRIMARY STAR'S INFLUENCE

Algorab imparts a flair for business and enterprise and bestows determination and power to overcome challenges with charm and grace. This star indicates a reserved and studious nature, with ambition for recognition and success. Algorab also warns against destructiveness and deception from others.

Linked to your Sun's degree, this star imparts a talent for making a good impression and success in dealing with the public and in getting support or promotion from others. If in the public view, you can gain fame and popularity, although you must guard against scandals that can lose you your position.

• *Positive:* persistence, big enterprises, popularity, military honor

• *Negative:* unorthodox methods, working against the establishment

Your Secret Self

A strong need for recognition and status is often your motivating force. When this power is combined with your idealism, you can be driven to initiate new opportunities for success or be a force for good in the community. This helps you overcome a tendency to succumb to inertia or procrastination. Once you get moving, however, you are helped by your innate awareness that any efforts you put in now will ultimately be rewarded in the long term.

Although extremely generous to people you love and admire, your tendency to worry about money explains why you may occasionally appear materialistic. Nevertheless, you have the energy and determination for substantial achievement, but may find most satisfaction through helping others. By uniting your ambition and drive with your awareness of diplomacy and cooperative efforts, you can really achieve success.

Work & Vocation

Intuitive and idealistic, you enjoy collaborating with others, even though you like to make your own decisions. Alternatively, you may choose to be independent or be of service to others as an agent, salesperson, or promoter. An ability to put your thoughts and feelings down on paper suggests that you have a gift for writing. Education is a vocation that may prove especially meaningful for you. You may also be particularly good at selling or promoting an idea or product. Your business acumen and organizational skills can ensure your success in occupations such as financial advisor, counselor, and negotiator. Being sociable and an excellent networker indicates that you have the ability to make personal contacts and excel in careers involving people.

Famous people who share your birthday include psychiatrist R. D. Laing, singers Toni Braxton and John Mellencamp, TV commentator Clive James, South African archbishop Desmond Tutu, cellist Yo Yo Ma, and physicist Niels Bohr.

Numerology

Analytical and thoughtful, number 7 individuals are frequently discriminating and self-absorbed. With a constant need for greater self-awareness, you enjoy gathering information and may be interested in reading, writing, or spirituality. Although shrewd, you may overrationalize or get lost in detail. A tendency to be enigmatic or secretive suggests that at times you feel misunderstood. The subinfluence of the number 10 month indicates that you are ambitious and independent, with the ability to get things done. As a perfectionist with realistic expectations, you are able to combine your skills with delicate precision. Knowledgeable and entertaining, you have an ability to understand people that implies that you are intuitive and sensible. Although you need time alone, your flair for business and your friendly manner suggest that you prefer others' company rather than being alone. Always full of ideas, you need to be active and to put your practical skills to the test. If you feel a desire to fulfill some of your humanitarian ideals, you may use your healing powers to uplift others.

• *Positive:* educated, trusting, meticulous, idealistic, honest, psychic, scientific, rational, reflective

• *Negative:* concealing, uncommunicative, unfriendly, secretive, skeptical, confused, cold

Love & Relationships

Though you are attracted to powerful and clever people, intimacy and relationships can be very important to you. This may, however, not always be an easy area. Although you can be warm and generous with those you love, there are also times when you withdraw and become too self-oriented. Being very charming, you find it easy to attract others, but a love of mental challenge implies that you have to avoid becoming involved in battles of wills with others. Being smart, you usually enjoy the stimulation of like-minded individuals and can be a loyal friend and partner.

YOUR SPECIAL SOMEONE

For security, mental excitement, and love, you might want to begin looking among those born on the following dates.

Love & friendship: Jan. 3, 5, 23, Feb. 1, 11, 21, Mar. 9, 19, 28, 31, Apr. 7, 17, 26, 29, 30, May 5, 15, 24, 27, 28, 29, 31, June 3, 13, 22, 25, 27, 29, July 1, 11, 20, 23, 25, 27, 29, Aug. 9, 18, 21, 23, 25, 27, Sept. 7, 16, 19, 21, 23, 25, Oct. 5, 14, 17, 19, 21, 23, Nov. 3, 12, 15, 17, 19, 21, Dec. 1, 10, 13, 15, 17, 19

Beneficial: Jan. 3, 4, 10, 21, Feb. 1, 2, 8, 19, Mar. 6, 17, 30, Apr. 4, 15, 28, May 2, 13, 26, June 11, 24, July 9, 22, Aug. 7, 20, Sept. 5, 18, Oct. 3, 16, 31, Nov. 1, 14, 29, Dec. 12, 27

Fatal attractions: Jan. 22, 28, Feb. 20, 26, Mar. 18, 24, Apr. 2, 3, 4, 5, 6, 16, 22, May 14, 20, June 12, 18, July 10, 16, Aug. 8, 14, Sept. 6, 12, Oct. 4, 10, Nov. 2, 8, Dec. 6

Challenging: Jan. 11, 20, Feb. 9, 18, Mar. 7, 16, Apr. 5, 14, May 3, 12, 30, June 1, 10, 28, July 8, 26, 31, Aug. 6, 24, 29, Sept. 4, 22, 27, Oct. 2, 20, 25, Nov. 18, 23, Dec. 16, 21

Soul mates: Jan. 26, Feb. 24, Mar. 22, 30, Apr. 20, 28, May 18, 26, June 16, 24, July 14, 22, Aug. 12, 20, Sept. 10, 18, Oct. 8, 16, Nov. 6, 14, Dec. 4, 12

SUN: LIBRA

DECANATE: AQUARIUS/URANUS

DEGREE: 14°30'–15°30' LIBRA

MODE: CARDINAL

ELEMENT: AIR

FIXED STAR

Star's name: Algorab, also called Al Ghirab or the Crow

Degree position: 12°28'–13°22' Libra between the years 1930 and 2000

Magnitude: 3

Strength: ★★★★★

Orb: 1°30'

Constellation: Delta Corvi

Applicable days: October 5, 6, 7, 8

Star qualities: Mars/Saturn

Description: a pale yellow and purple binary star located on the right wing of the Crow

PRIMARY STAR'S INFLUENCE

Algorab imparts a flair for business and enterprise and bestows determination and power to overcome challenges with charm and grace. This star indicates a reserved and studious nature, with ambition for recognition and success. Algorab also warns against destructiveness and deception from others.

Linked to your Sun's degree, this star imparts a talent for making a good impression and success in dealing with the public and in getting support or promotion from others. If in the public view, you can gain fame and popularity, although you must guard against scandals that can lose you your position.

• *Positive:* persistence, big enterprises, popularity, military honor

• *Negative:* unorthodox methods, working against the establishment

Although you are charming and friendly, the urge for action and personal accomplishment revealed by your birthday suggests that you are a strong-willed and ambitious individual. Charismatic and determined, you possess intuitive leadership and the ability to mix business with pleasure. With a quick grasp of a situation, you prefer to be honest and straightforward. Enterprising and success-oriented, you have the ability to have fortunate ideas and to share them with others, and this is a major key to your success.

With the added influence of your decanate ruler, Aquarius, you can be inventive and productive and are often a good psychologist. Broad-minded in your approach, you have excellent skills for dealing with people, and you usually value freedom. Although independent, you enjoy exercising your natural diplomatic ability to work cooperatively with others as part of a team. There are times, however, when you are in danger of being too bossy or dictatorial, especially with people who fail to reach your high expectations.

Your active imagination and appreciation of the arts may possibly find expression through writing, music, painting, or drama as well as through a desire to surround yourself with beauty, style, and luxury. However, you may have to be careful that too great a love of the good life does not cause you to overindulge or place too much emphasis on material achievement.

At the age of fifteen, when your progressed Sun moves into Scorpio, you reach a turning point in your life that emphasizes issues regarding emotional change and personal transformation over the next thirty years. Another turning point occurs at the age of forty-five, when your progressed Sun moves into Sagittarius, indicating a growing need for freedom and a desire to expand your horizon and take more risks. From this time you may also have more connection with foreign people and places. From the age of seventy-five, when your progressed Sun enters Capricorn, you begin to take your duties and practical considerations more seriously.

Your Secret Self

Being a practical visionary, you are wise to trust your powerful instincts, and you work best when inspired. Needing constant adventure and change to keep yourself from becoming bored, you enjoy travel and being at the forefront of new trends and ideas. Although you possess a strong desire for money, power, and status, you can equally be an idealistic and sensitive humanitarian. This implies a necessity for balance between your natural compassion and a tendency to use power tactics or be self-seeking.

Magnanimous, kind, and generous, you become a dynamic force in helping others by uniting your intense will with your powerful emotions. Thinking on a grand scale, you make great plans, but you need to carry them out independently. Often this involves taking a risk or speculating, but a flair for spotting opportunities suggests that you usually get value for your money. With your active imagination, powers of persuasion, and excellent negotiation skills, you have the potential for outstanding achievement.

Work & Vocation

Dynamic and hardworking, you want to achieve much and are often an imaginative and enterprising entrepreneur. Although you can succeed in the commercial world, you may want to explore your creative talents by pursuing an artistic career. Having a captivating personality and powerful emotions implies that you can be passionate and idealistic about social reforms and find satisfaction working in the public sector or in politics. With your excellent negotiating skills, you may want to have a career in a big corporation as head of a department. Love of justice and honesty may lead you to politics or to work in the courts as a lawyer or an officer of the law. Alternatively, a love of beauty and art may compel you to work with museums and art galleries or as an antique dealer. If you believe in an idea or a person, you may work as an agent or a promoter.

Famous people who were born on your birthday include politician Jesse Jackson, actor Paul Hogan, actress Sigourney Weaver, actor/comic Chevy Chase, and Argentinian dictator Juan Perón.

Numerology

The power suggested by the number 8 birthday shows a character with strong values and sound judgment. The number 8 indicates that you aspire to great accomplishment and possess an ambitious nature. A desire for dominance, security, and material success is also indicated by this birthday. As a number 8 person, you have natural business sense and will benefit greatly from developing organizational and executive skills. A strong need to feel secure or established urges you to make long-term plans and investments. The subinfluence of the number 10 month indicates that you are highly intuitive, with a dynamic personality. Having faith in your abilities and trusting your inner wisdom enables you to combine your creativity with material success and make a forceful impression. Being motivated by high aspirations and a flair for people, you can turn your original ideas into profitable enterprises. Often you initiate new projects and work in the forefront of reforms or modernize existing systems.

• *Positive:* leadership, thoroughness, hardworking, tradition, authority, protection, power to heal, good judge of values

• *Negative:* impatient, wasteful, intolerant, miserly, restless, overwork, power-hungry, domineering, easily discouraged, lack of planning

Love & Relationships

Friendly, charming, and gregarious, yet assertive and outspoken, you usually have an active social life. Security-conscious, you may be tempted to marry for reasons other than love. Due to your ambition and determination, ideally you need a partner who is successful in his or her own right. As you may become restless in relationships and be prone to a change of heart, you may have to develop patience to stop you from becoming bored. This can be helped by putting time aside for travel or new and exciting experiences.

YOUR SPECIAL SOMEONE

You might find longer-lasting relationships and stability with someone born on one of the following dates.

Love & friendship: Jan. 6, 14, 24, 31, Feb. 4, 12, 22, 29, Mar. 2, 10, 20, 27, Apr. 8, 18, 25, May 6, 16, 23, 30, June 4, 14, 21, 28, 30, July 2, 12, 19, 26, 28, 30, Aug. 10, 17, 24, 26, 28, Sept. 8, 15, 22, 24, 26, Oct. 6, 13, 20, 22, 24, 30, Nov. 4, 11, 18, 20, 22, 28, Dec. 2, 9, 16, 18, 20, 26, 29

Beneficial: Jan. 5, 22, 30, Feb. 3, 20, 28, Mar. 1, 18, 26, Apr. 16, 24, May 14, 22, June 12, 20, July 10, 18, 29, Aug. 8, 16, 27, 31, Sept. 6, 14, 25, 29, Oct. 4, 12, 23, 27, Nov. 2, 10, 21, 25, Dec. 9, 19, 23

Fatal attractions: Jan. 12, Feb. 10, Mar. 8, Apr. 4, 5, 6, 7, May 4, June 2

Challenging: Jan. 16, 21, Feb. 14, 19, Mar. 12, 17, 30, Apr. 10, 15, 28, May 8, 13, 26, June 6, 11, 24, July 4, 9, 22, Aug. 2, 7, 20, Sept. 5, 18, Oct. 3, 16, Nov. 1, 14, Dec. 12

Soul mates: Jan. 25, Feb. 23, Mar. 21, Apr. 19, May 17, June 15, July 13, Aug. 11, Sept. 9, Oct. 7, Nov. 5, Dec. 3, 30

October 9

♎ Independent and clever, with a strong character, you are revealed by your birthday to be an honest and forthright Libra with natural confidence. The inherent leadership indicated by your birthday is matched by your excellent mental perception. Creative and observant, you recognize the power of knowledge, although you can also suffer from emotional tensions that cause discontent or undermine your usual confidence.

With the added influence of your Sun in the decanate of Aquarius, you have original ideas and a shrewd understanding of humanity. Women of this day often take charge of situations. A potential initiator of more progressive movements, you love the new and avant-garde. Open-minded and liberal, you will stand up for your principles, justice, and fair play. Ironically, you do not suffer fools gladly and at times can be bossy or domineering.

With your insight and desire for self-expression, you may be particularly interested in writing, art, music, or metaphysical and philosophical subjects. Although a pragmatist by nature, sometimes you can be radical or unconventional. It is wise to guard against a tendency to be contrary just for the sake of being difficult. By learning to be more compassionate and tolerant of other people's faults, you increase your chances for success in your dealings with others.

At the age of fourteen, when your progressed Sun moves into Scorpio, you reach a turning point in your life that emphasizes, over the next thirty years, issues concerning change and transformation of your personal motivation. Another turning point occurs at the age of forty-four, when your progressed Sun moves into Sagittarius, widening your perspective and indicating that you may wish to expand your mind and explore more possibilities through study, inspiration, and travel. From the age of seventy-four, when your progressed Sun enters Capricorn, you begin to place more emphasis on discipline and practical security.

Your Secret Self

With your quick responses and reactions, you are able to stand up for yourself and may even enjoy a little friendly rivalry or debate. Learning to trust your own intuition enables you to take on challenges such as developing an original artistic talent or your business acumen. Usually you enjoy being in control but can sometimes be erratic, have temper tantrums, or alternate between being overconfident and doubting yourself. Nevertheless, you possess an inner strength that can emerge and help you triumph over adversity.

Tenacious in the pursuit of your plans, you are usually willing to work hard. This can involve persevering and utilizing your uncompromising determination, especially for the attainment of long-term goals. Despite this, you may still need to develop self-discipline to bring out your outstanding potential. You are basically a humanitarian, and a combination of inner power and a skillful ability to deal with people can help you make your ideals a reality.

Work & Vocation

Intelligent, intuitive, and highly imaginative, you usually have many career opportunities. Interested in social reforms, you are particularly suited for intellectual professions such as law, education, scientific research, and writing. With your quick mind and ability to lead, you have

FIXED STAR

Star's name: Seginus

Degree position: 16°38'–17°20' Libra between the years 1930 and 2000

Magnitude: 3

Strength: ★★★★★

Orb: 1°40'

Constellation: Gamma Bootes

Applicable days: October 9, 10, 11, 12

Star qualities: Mercury/Saturn

Description: a small yellow and white star located on the left shoulder of Bootes

PRIMARY STAR'S INFLUENCE

Seginus's influence imparts a quick and keen mentality, many contacts, and popularity. This star indicates that you are versatile and a quick learner, but warns against an inclination to be inconsistent and make too many sudden changes.

Linked to your Sun's degree, Seginus bestows success in business, a natural aptitude for astrology and philosophy, or an inclination toward unusual interests. Sociable and friendly, you have many friends who will come to your aid when they are needed.

• Positive: cooperative, popularity, versatility

• Negative: losses through friendships and partnerships

strategic skills and administrative abilities that can be an asset to you in the business world. A desire for creativity and natural communication gifts imply that you need to express your individuality through pursuing a career in the world of fine arts and design or the theater and the performing arts, particularly music. As a humanitarian, you may be drawn to work in the health sector.

Famous people who share your birthday include singer/songwriters John Lennon, Sean Ono Lennon, and Jackson Browne, musician John Entwistle, director Jacques Tati, writer Miguel de Cervantes, and composer Camille Saint-Saëns.

Numerology

Benevolence, thoughtfulness, and sentimental sensitivity are all associated with the number 9 birthday. Tolerant and kind, you can be generous and liberal. Intuitive and psychic abilities point to a universal receptivity and, if channeled positively, may inspire you to seek a spiritual path. This birthday may suggest a need to overcome challenges and a tendency to be overly sensitive, with emotional ups and downs. You benefit greatly from world travel and interaction with people from all walks of life but may have to avoid unrealistic dreams or an inclination toward escapism. The subinfluence of the number 10 month indicates that, being both autonomous and humanitarian, you can inspire others with your positive outlook and determination. If blessed with the touch of genius, you may need to persevere in spite of obstacles in order to accomplish something unique or out of the ordinary. Avoid a tendency to be stubborn or domineering if you want others to turn to you for support and advice.

• *Positive*: idealistic, creative, sensitive, generous, magnetic, poetic, charitable, giving, detached, lucky, popular

• *Negative*: frustrated, nervous, fragmented, unsure, selfish, impractical, bitter, unethical, easily led, worried, isolated

Love & Relationships

Friends and admirers are usually drawn by your charisma and sharp intelligence. Frank and direct, you like to be truthful in all your dealings with others. Although sincere, romantic, and usually a loyal partner, at times you may alienate your loved ones by being bossy or too impatient. Nevertheless, you can also be very supportive, especially when giving practical help or advice. Ideally, you need a partner who can keep you mentally stimulated and can be as honest and straightforward as you are. You need a partner who will understand your vacillation between total confidence and self-doubt.

YOUR SPECIAL SOMEONE

To find long-lasting happiness and security, you might begin by looking for someone born on one of the following days.

Love & friendship: Jan. 7, 11, 13, 15, 16, 17, 25, Feb. 9, 11, 13, 14, 15, 23, Mar. 7, 9, 11, 12, 13, 21, Apr. 5, 7, 9, 11, 19, May 3, 5, 7, 9, 17, 31, June 1, 3, 5, 6, 7, 15, 29, July 1, 3, 5, 27, 29, 31, Aug. 1, 3, 11, 25, 27, 29, Sept. 1, 9, 23, 25, 27, Oct. 7, 21, 23, 25, Nov. 5, 19, 21, 23, Dec. 3, 17, 19, 21, 30

Beneficial: Jan. 1, 5, 20, Feb. 3, 18, Mar. 1, 16, Apr. 14, May 12, June 10, July 8, Aug. 6, Sept. 4, Oct. 2

Fatal attractions: Apr. 5, 6, 7, 8

Challenging: Jan. 6, 22, 24, Feb. 4, 20, 22, Mar. 2, 18, 20, Apr. 16, 18, May 16, 14, June 12, 14, July 10, 12, Aug. 8, 10, 31, Sept. 6, 8, 29, Oct. 4, 6, 27, Nov. 2, 4, 25, 30, Dec. 2, 23, 28

Soul mates: Jan. 6, 12, Feb. 4, 10, Mar. 2, 8, Apr. 6, May 4, June 2

October 10

♎ Your keen mind and sharp observations blend well with your idealism and ambition. As a Libra, you can also be very charming and gregarious, with an ability to deal with all types of people. Generous and kind, you enjoy giving to others but may have to beware of overindulgence in all its forms. Appreciating color, art, and beauty, you have a strong creative flair and enjoy luxury.

With the added influence of your decanate ruler, Aquarius, you usually desire to be in the forefront of new trends or ideas and possess strong individualism. Although you retain a touch of gentle charm and elegance, you can also be very willful and independent. Mentally competitive and sometimes critical, you are nevertheless usually easygoing. Your charismatic appeal is a great help in making social contacts. A possible challenge to your stability, however, may be an inclination to become stubborn and refuse to listen to advice from others.

Friendly and amusing, you like to entertain or socialize. Needing freedom and variety, you are likely to include travel as part of your agenda. A tendency to become impatient, however, can stop you from fully developing your innate talents. Fortunately, your optimistic view on life can help you recover quickly from any possible disappointments or setbacks.

From the age of thirteen onward, when your progressed Sun moves into Scorpio, you experience an emphasis on issues concerning emotional sensitivity, personal power, and transformation. Another turning point occurs at the age of forty-three, when your progressed Sun moves into Sagittarius, challenging you to expand your viewpoint and be more adventurous, whether mentally, physically, or spiritually. From the age of seventy-three, when your progressed Sun enters Capricorn, you begin to place a greater emphasis on structure, stability, and practical goals.

Your Secret Self

Desiring knowledge and thinking big, you have many ideas that can bring you financial returns. By overcoming an inclination to let materialistic matters dominate your life, however, you come to realize that there are many rewards that money cannot buy. It is through keeping faith in yourself and developing trust in your natural intuition that you can really succeed.

Being creative and sensitive, you may need to find some form of self-expression to give voice to your active mind and deepest feelings. This includes creating positive opportunities to use all the information that you possess. With a sense of the dramatic, you enjoy being entertaining. This can prove to be an excellent antidote to your experiences of doubt and indecision.

Work & Vocation

Capable and multitalented, you are both a humanitarian idealist and a high achiever. The ability to take charge and lead others suggests that you are more comfortable giving orders than taking them. With your organizational skills and desire to accomplish, you need a career that is challenging, where you can expand your knowledge. As an astute individual who is gifted with words and wit, you can excel in writing and literature or law and education. Alter-

FIXED STAR

Star's name: Seginus

Degree position: 16°38'–17°20' Libra between the years 1930 and 2000

Magnitude: 3

Strength: ★★★★★

Orb: 1°40'

Constellation: Gamma Bootes

Applicable days: October 9, 10, 11, 12

Star qualities: Mercury/Saturn

Description: a small yellow and white star located on the left shoulder of Bootes

PRIMARY STAR'S INFLUENCE

Seginus's influence imparts a quick and keen mentality, many contacts, and popularity. This star indicates that you are versatile and a quick learner, but warns against an inclination to be inconsistent and make too many sudden changes.

Linked to your Sun's degree, Seginus bestows success in business and a natural aptitude for astrology and philosophy or an inclination toward unusual interests. Sociable and friendly, you have many friends who will come to your aid when they are needed.

• *Positive:* cooperative, popularity, versatility

• *Negative:* losses through friendships and partnerships

natively, you can use your administrative skills in large corporations or succeed in the business world. Charming and sociable, you may be drawn to public work as a union leader or politician. As a benefactor, you can also initiate large projects that can help the community. Your need for artistic expression may lead you to the world of art and entertainment through the medium of music or drama.

Famous people who share your birthday include playwright Harold Pinter, musician/singer David Lee Roth, composer Giuseppe Verdi, pianist Thelonious Monk, painter Jean-Antoine Watteau, actress Dorothy Lamour, and actor Ben Vereen.

Numerology

Like someone with a number 1 birthday, you usually strive toward great endeavors to accomplish and achieve. Nevertheless, you may have to overcome some obstacles before you achieve your goals. Energetic and original, you stand by your own beliefs even when they differ from others'. Your ability to be a self-starter encourages you to travel far afield or strike out on your own. Success and accomplishment are important to all those with number 10 birthdays, and frequently you find the way to the top of your profession. The subinfluence of the number 10 month indicates that you are enterprising and hardworking. Although you rely on your intelligence and are quick at assessing situations and people, you have a strong intuitive sense that can dominate your thoughts and urges you to go by your feelings. Usually friendly, you can employ your persuasion and diplomatic skills to influence others to your way of thinking. You may also need to learn that the world does not revolve around you, and should guard against selfishness or being overemotional.

• *Positive:* leadership, creative, progressive, forceful, optimistic, strong convictions, competitive, independent, gregarious

• *Negative:* overbearing, jealous, egotistical, too proud, antagonistic, lack of restraint, selfish, vacillating, impatient

Love & Relationships

Being friendly, clever, and magnetic, you should have no trouble attracting friends and partners. Nevertheless, a certain underlying restlessness suggests that you can get bored easily or are unsure about how you truly feel in relationships. This may be avoided if you pick an intelligent and active partner who keeps you constantly stimulated mentally. You may find pleasure in trying out new activities, visiting new places, or taking courses of study where you can meet other clever people like yourself. As an excellent networker, you enjoy social occasions where you can mix with different types of people.

YOUR SPECIAL SOMEONE

For security, mental stimulation, and love, you might want to begin looking for those born among the following dates.

Love & friendship: Jan. 4, 9, 12, 16, 25, Feb. 2, 10, 14, 23, 24, Mar. 8, 12, 22, 31, Apr. 6, 10, 20, 29, May 4, 8, 18, 27, June 2, 6, 16, 25, 30, July 4, 14, 23, 28, Aug. 2, 12, 21, 26, 30, Sept. 10, 19, 24, 28, Oct. 8, 17, 22, 26, Nov. 6, 15, 20, 24, 30, Dec. 4, 13, 18, 22, 28

Beneficial: Jan. 2, 13, 22, 24, Feb. 11, 17, 20, 22, Mar. 9, 15, 18, 20, 28, Apr. 7, 13, 16, 18, 26, May 5, 11, 16, 18, 26, June 3, 9, 12, 14, 22, July 1, 7, 10, 12, 20, Aug. 5, 8, 10, 18, Sept. 3, 6, 8, 16, Oct. 1, 4, 6, 14, Nov. 2, 4, 12, Dec. 2, 10

Fatal attractions: Jan. 25, Feb. 23, Mar. 21, Apr. 5, 6, 7, 8, 9, 19, May 17, June 15, July 13, Aug. 11, Sept. 9, Oct. 7, Nov. 5, Dec. 3

Challenging: Jan. 7, 23, Feb. 5, 21, Mar. 3, 19, 29, Apr. 1, 17, 27, May 15, 25, June 13, 23, July 11, 21, 31, Aug. 9, 19, 29, Sept. 7, 17, 27, 30, Nov. 3, 13, 23, 26, Dec. 1, 11, 21, 24

Soul mates: Jan. 17, Feb. 15, Mar. 13, Apr. 11, May 9, June 7, July 5, Aug. 3, Sept. 1, Nov. 30, Dec. 28

October 11

♎ Very intelligent, with a gift for communicating ideas, you project enthusiasm, warmth, and personal magnetism. Although idealistic, you are usually willing to back your beliefs with actions. Naturally optimistic, with a youthful quality, you need only be responsible and apply the necessary self-discipline to bring out your wonderful potential.

With the added influence of your decanate ruler, Aquarius, you are an original and independent thinker. Combined with a spirit of enterprise and desire for freedom, you think big and are likely to campaign or fight for your convictions. Possessing charm and natural psychological skills, you have an ability to deal with people from all walks of life. Your persuasive powers and organizational ability can certainly help you in your climb to success.

With your strong Libra influence, you are a lover of beauty, nature, and the arts and have a strong need for self-expression. Many people of this birthday have an androgynous quality, being both independent and sensitive. A sense of refinement can bestow good taste and a love of luxury and comfort. When you add to your store of knowledge, your assertiveness and self-confidence increase. With your leadership potential and natural diplomatic skills, you have the ability to work cooperatively with others as part of a team. You may, however, need to avoid stress from taking on too much or being manipulative rather than dealing with people directly.

From the time you reach the age of twelve and onward, your progressed Sun moves into Scorpio. Usually you become more intense, with a growing emphasis on emotional change and a need for personal power. Another turning point occurs at the age of forty-two, when your progressed Sun moves into Sagittarius, stimulating you to widen your horizons, be more free, and seek inspiration, whether through study, personal contact, or travel. At the age of seventy-two, your progressed Sun moves into Capricorn, accenting a greater need for a practical and realistic approach to life.

Your Secret Self

You have the magnetism to captivate and enchant people through projecting the wealth of love and emotion within you. This ability suggests an inner grace, playfulness, and a desire for love and affection. When inspired to express yourself, you can be witty, buoyant, and full of enthusiasm to help your fellow human beings or an idealistic cause. In your drive to achieve, however, you may have to watch out for becoming bossy or extreme.

You are usually good with financial matters and have the ability to gain resources for yourself or others. In your overall life plan, material security may be a big issue, as you need something solid and stable to rely on. Nevertheless, avoid the temptation of always taking the safe route rather than really challenging yourself. Despite your fears to the contrary, as long as you develop patience and perseverance, your financial affairs usually turn out to be successful in the long term.

Work & Vocation

Intelligent and intuitive, you are multitalented and idealistic, with a wide choice of careers. You may be drawn to the world of commerce and use your persuasive charm in sales, promotion, or negotiation. With an ability to communicate ideas in an entertaining way, you may be drawn to occupations in education or training people in business. Equally, you can be attracted to writing, the law, public service, or politics. As an idealist with a spirit of enterprise, you may want to express yourself and develop your artistic talents. This can lead you to the world of art and design or advertising and media.

Famous people who share your birthday include actor Luke Perry, musicians Art Blakey and Daryl Hall, YMCA founder Sir George Williams, choreographer Jerome Robbins, and First Lady Eleanor Roosevelt.

Numerology

The special vibration of the master number 11 birthday suggests that idealism, inspiration, and innovation are highly important to you. A blend of humility and confidence challenges you to work toward self-mastery both materially and spiritually. Through experience you learn how to deal with both sides of your nature and develop a less extremist attitude by trusting your own feelings. Usually you are highly charged and enjoy vitality, but must avoid becoming overly anxious or impractical. The subinfluence of the number 10 month indicates that you are clever and versatile. Intelligent and friendly, you need to express your own individuality and be popular in your circle of friends. If you are unsure of a project's profitability, you may become impatient and try something new. Multitalented and idealistic, with many interests, you are rarely described as boring or dull. You need to stay focused on your aims and objectives, however, in order to achieve success. As you are often talented and freedom-loving, you benefit from exploring your creative abilities.

• *Positive:* balanced, focused, objective, enthusiastic, inspirational, idealistic, intelligent, outgoing, inventive, artistic, humanitarian, psychic

• *Negative:* superiority complex, aimless, overemotional, easily hurt, highly strung, selfish, lack of clarity, bossy

Love & Relationships

Romantic and idealistic, you seek relationships but also possess a strong need for freedom and independence. With all your charisma and intelligence, you should have no trouble attracting friends or admirers. Nevertheless, a tendency to alternate between being an intense and passionate lover and feeling a need to be independent and free may block some of your partnership opportunities. It is important to be discriminating to avoid becoming attached to unsuitable partners, but once you commit yourself, you are willing to work hard to make a relationship work.

YOUR SPECIAL SOMEONE

To find that special someone who will bring happiness to your life, you might look for someone born on one of the following days.

Love & friendship: Jan. 2, 7, 19, 17, 27, Feb. 5, 8, 15, 25, Mar. 3, 6, 13, 23, Apr. 1, 4, 11, 21, May 2, 9, 19, June 7, 17, July 5, 15, 29, 31, Aug. 3, 13, 27, 29, 31, Sept. 1, 11, 25, 27, 29, Oct. 9, 23, 25, 27, Nov. 7, 21, 23, 25, Dec. 5, 19, 21, 23

Beneficial: Jan. 3, 5, 20, 25, 27, Feb. 1, 3, 18, 23, 25, Mar. 1, 16, 21, 23, Apr. 14, 19, 21, May 12, 17, 19, June 10, 15, 17, July 8, 13, 15, Aug. 6, 11, 13, Sept. 4, 9, 11, Oct. 2, 7, 9, Nov. 5, 7, Dec. 3, 5

Fatal attractions: Jan. 13, Feb. 11, Mar. 9, Apr. 6, 7, 8, 9, May 5, June 3, July 1

Challenging: Jan. 16, 24, Feb. 14, 22, Mar. 12, 20, Apr. 10, 18, May 8, 16, 31, June 6, 14, 29, July 4, 12, 27, Aug. 2, 10, 25, Sept. 8, 23, Oct. 6, 21, Nov. 4, 19, Dec. 2, 17

Soul mates: Jan. 16, Feb. 14, Mar. 12, Apr. 10, May 8, June 6, July 4, 31, Aug. 2, 29, Sept. 27, Oct. 25, Nov. 23, Dec. 21

October 12

Ω A keen mind, friendliness, and sociability are just some of the attributes indicated by your date of birth. Enthusiastic and hardworking, when truly interested in a project or a cause you think creatively and have natural leadership abilities. An important part of your success is an ability to deal with people on a personal level. You love knowledge, but it is through learning self-mastery that you really achieve true satisfaction.

With the added influence of your decanate ruler, Aquarius, you have inventive and unique ideas that can be both productive and financially rewarding for you. You are quick to recognize new trends or concepts and usually enjoy expressing your ideas. Although independent, you possess natural diplomatic skills and an ability to work cooperatively with others as part of a team. Possessing a touch of gentle charm, you are generally easygoing. At times, however, you may become too dominant, critical, or stubborn.

Being very intelligent, valuing freedom, and having a warm heart, you have much to offer others. Your shrewd but restless mind gives you the ability to make quick decisions and often helps you to assess situations easily. Although self-assured, with strong convictions, on occasion you may worry or be strangely lacking in self-confidence. Fortunately, a determination to succeed regardless of difficulties will always help you come through.

From the age of eleven onward, when your progressed Sun moves into Scorpio, you experience an emphasis on issues concerning emotional change, power, and transformation. A turning point occurs at the age of forty-one, when your progressed Sun moves into Sagittarius, stimulating you to expand your perspective. You may have more contact with foreign people and places or take up a new interest. After the age of seventy-one, when your progressed Sun enters Capricorn, you will develop a more practical, concentrated, and goal-oriented approach.

FIXED STAR

Star's name: Seginus
Degree position: 16°38'–17°20' Libra
  between the years 1930 and
  2000
Magnitude: 3
Strength: ★★★★★
Orb: 1°40'
Constellation: Gamma Bootes
Applicable days: October 9, 10, 11, 12
Star qualities: Mercury/Saturn
Description: a small yellow and white
  star located on the left shoulder
  of Bootes

PRIMARY STAR'S INFLUENCE

Seginus's influence imparts a quick and keen mentality, many contacts, and popularity. This star indicates that you are versatile and a quick learner, but warns against an inclination to be inconsistent and make too many sudden changes.

Linked to your Sun's degree, Seginus bestows success in business, a natural aptitude for astrology and philosophy, or an inclination toward unusual interests. Sociable and friendly, you have many friends who will come to your aid when they are needed.

• *Positive:* cooperative, popularity, versatility

• *Negative:* losses through friendships and partnerships

Your Secret Self

One of your greatest assets can be your intuitive insight, but it may be necessary to listen to that quiet inner voice and learn about faith and trust. By applying wisdom, you are able to see the deeper philosophical or humorous approach to any situation. A strongly creative side to your nature guarantees that self-expression can be a vital part of your life plan and may stimulate a desire for music, art, or drama.

Much of your success is based on applying your ingenious ideas to practical situations and being prepared to put in the groundwork necessary to achieve your big plans. Generous with others, you know how to enjoy yourself but may have to be careful of overindulgence. An inner desire for honesty can override a manipulative streak and help you in your overall plans. When inspired, you can be extremely motivated and a source of encouragement for others.

Work & Vocation

Pragmatic and highly intuitive, you enjoy putting your creative thoughts to the test and showing others your unique capabilities. Among the many career choices you have, these can be highly suitable: psychologist, counselor, diplomat, lawyer. Your easy charm and organizational skills indicate that you can also succeed in people-related activities, whether in the business world or in the public sector. Articulate and sociable, you may be drawn to journalism and writing, academia, or the publishing world. Creative outlets are also likely to appeal to your imaginative mind. If talented as an actor, musician, or songwriter, you can reach the limelight when people recognize your gifts.

Famous people who share your birthday include opera singer Luciano Pavarotti, comedian Dick Gregory, occultist Alister Crowley, actress Susan Anton, and Scottish prime minister Ramsay MacDonald.

Numerology

People with the number 12 birthday are usually intuitive and friendly. Since you want to establish true individuality, you possess good reasoning and innovative power. Naturally understanding and sensitive, you also know how to use tact and cooperative methods to achieve your aims and objectives. When you achieve the balance between your need for self-expression and your natural inclination to be supportive of others, you can find emotional satisfaction and personal fulfillment. You may nevertheless need to find the courage to stand on your own two feet, develop self-confidence, or learn not to get easily discouraged by other people. The subinfluence of the number 10 month indicates that you are forceful and intelligent, with a need for stability and order. Determined and energetic, you enjoy working in collaboration with others as long as you can remain independent. Although you have a pragmatic approach to life and a good business sense, you may vacillate emotionally and at times overreact to situations or people. By expressing your feelings and using your diplomatic skills, however, you can smooth rough patches and overcome a tendency to be stubborn or tactless.

• *Positive:* creative, attractive, initiative, disciplinarian, promote yourself or others
• *Negative:* reserved, selfish, eccentric, uncooperative, oversensitive, lack of self-esteem, too shy

Love & Relationships

Being clever, you want a partner with whom you can be sociable and communicate your ideas. In close relationships you need to keep light and positive and avoid being irritable, bossy, or critical. Often finding yourself drawn to hardworking or powerful individuals, you may be pulled between a desire for independence and a desire for a close relationship. An urge for self-awareness suggests that you admire those with discipline and an original approach to life.

YOUR SPECIAL SOMEONE

Among those born on the following days you might just find that someone special who will inspire you with his or her unique personality.

Love & friendship: Jan. 1, 14, 28, 31, Feb. 12, 26, 29, Mar. 10, 24, 27, Apr. 8, 22, 25, May 6, 20, 23, June 4, 18, 21, July 2, 16, 19, 30, Aug. 14, 17, 28, 30, Sept. 12, 15, 26, 28, 30, Oct. 10, 13, 24, 26, 28, Nov. 8, 11, 22, 24, 26, Dec. 6, 9, 20, 22, 24

Beneficial: Jan. 26, Feb. 24, Mar. 22, Apr. 20, May 18, June 16, July 14, Aug. 12, Sept. 10, Oct. 8, Nov. 6, Dec. 4

Fatal attractions: Apr. 7, 8, 9, 10, 11

Challenging: Jan. 3, 25, Feb. 1, 23, Mar. 21, Apr. 19, May 17, June 15, July 13, Aug. 11, Sept. 9, Oct. 7, Nov. 5, Dec. 3

Soul mates: Jan. 3, 10, Feb. 1, 8, Mar. 6, Apr. 4, May 2

October 13

FIXED STARS

Although your Sun's degree is not linked to a fixed star, some of your other planets' degrees certainly will be. By having an astrological chart calculated, you can find the exact position of the planets on your date of birth. This will tell you which of the fixed stars listed in this book are relevant to you.

♎ Your birthday shows you to be practical, yet charming, a hardworking individual with a wealth of ideas. With your ability to grasp concepts very quickly, you can utilize situations to your advantage. Ambitious and resourceful, you enjoy debates and acquiring knowledge. Although you can be responsible, it still takes self-discipline to harness all the outstanding potential of your birthday.

With the added influence of your decanate ruler, Aquarius, you have a strong mind with independent views. With the ability to think big, you are usually interested in many subjects, and may be particularly drawn to world affairs. Possessing a spirit of enterprise and a desire for freedom, you are likely to campaign or fight for your beliefs.

Being a natural diplomat, you are skillful at relating to others and usually make a successful partner or team member. However, there are times when you may have to resist a tendency to become too domineering. With a strong set of values and organizational ability, you often have a gift for persuasive speech that can help you in your climb to success. Education and a positive philosophy can be vital keys to making the most of your possibilities. This helps you avoid impatience, frustration, or irritability and keeps you mentally active and productive.

From the age of ten, when your progressed Sun moves into Scorpio, you experience a growing emphasis over the next thirty years on issues concerning change, power, and transformation of your personal motivation. A turning point occurs at the age of forty, when your progressed Sun moves into Sagittarius, widening your perspective and indicating that you may become more optimistic and freedom-loving. This may include expanding your mind through study, travel, or new interests. After the age of seventy, when your progressed Sun enters Capricorn, you become more practical, cautious, and concentrated.

Your Secret Self

With your strong opinions and sense of the dramatic, you do not want to go unnoticed, and you prefer to be in a leading position. If you do not find any outlets to express your wonderful creativity or ideas, however, you may be prone to alternate between depression and arrogance. Nevertheless, your exterior can hide an inner sensitivity and imagination that when positively channeled can give you an exceptional sense of vision.

Although you can be thrifty and economical and enjoy negotiating a bargain, you can also be extremely generous with those you care for. Usually honest and direct with people, you prefer to pay your debts. Although you intend to be ambitious, your desire for harmony and the comforts of home can often prove a very attractive force. Learning to maintain a balance and developing inner peace can bring truly amazing results.

Work & Vocation

Creative and knowledgeable, you are usually mentally restless and witty, with a need to express yourself freely and without restrictions. If constantly told what to do, you can become antagonistic and argumentative. Being sociable and gregarious, you enjoy working in collaboration with others and may be drawn to a career in the public sector. Although you are interested in business, you are a humanitarian and may wish to pursue a career in the academic world or in teaching. If you want to develop your artistic gifts, you might choose to explore the world of show business or literature and writing, but you can also be a fine orator or lawyer. Caring and compassionate, you may decide to pursue a career as a social worker, counselor, or psychologist.

Famous people who share your birthday include former British prime minister Margaret Thatcher, singer/songwriter Paul Simon, comedian Lenny Bruce, musicians Pharaoh Sanders and Art Tatum, actor Yves Montand, and figure skater Nancy Kerrigan.

Numerology

Emotional sensitivity, enthusiasm, and inspiration are often identified with the number 13 birthday. Numerically, you are associated with ambition and hard work and can accomplish much through creative self-expression. You may need to develop or cultivate a pragmatic outlook if you want to turn your creative talents into tangible products. Your original and innovative approach inspires new and exciting ideas, frequently resulting in work that impresses others. With a number 13 birthday, you are earnest, romantic, charming, and fun-loving, and with dedication can achieve prosperity. The subinfluence of the number 10 month indicates that you are resilient, practical, and versatile. Being independent and self-reliant implies leadership skills and a need for freedom. Although to others you may appear certain and self-assured, emotional tensions and insecurities may cause you to vacillate and worry unnecessarily. By learning to be more patient and less restless, you can overcome a tendency to scatter your energies in too many directions.

- *Positive:* ambitious, creative, freedom-loving, self-expressive, initiative
- *Negative:* impulsive, indecisive, bossy, unemotional, rebellious

Love & Relationships

Relationships and companionship play a vital part in your life agenda. Nevertheless, it is essential to stay autonomous and never allow yourself to be in a dependent position. Although romantic, you may occasionally suffer inhibitions in expressing your true feelings. Your relationships are greatly improved, however, by the display of your affection. Once committed to a partner, you can be loyal and supportive.

YOUR SPECIAL SOMEONE

To find long-lasting happiness, security, and a harmonious environment, you might begin by looking for someone born on one of the following days.

Love & friendship: Jan. 1, 15, 26, 29, 30, Feb. 13, 24, 27, 28, Mar. 11, 22, 25, 26, Apr. 9, 20, 23, 24, May 7, 18, 21, 22, June 5, 16, 19, 20, July 3, 14, 17, 18, 31, Aug. 1, 12, 15, 16, 29, 31, Sept. 10, 13, 14, 27, 29, Oct. 8, 11, 12, 25, 27, Nov. 6, 9, 10, 23, 25, Dec. 4, 7, 8, 21, 23, 29

Beneficial: Jan. 1, 2, 10, 27, Feb. 8, 25, Mar. 6, 23, Apr. 4, 21, May 2, 19, 30, June 17, 28, July 15, 26, Aug. 13, 24, Sept. 11, 22, Oct. 9, 20, Nov. 7, 18, Dec. 5, 16

Fatal attractions: Apr. 9, 10, 11, 12

Challenging: Jan. 17, 26, Feb. 15, 24, Mar. 13, 22, Apr. 11, 20, May 9, 18, June 7, 16, July 5, 14, Aug. 3, 12, 30, Sept. 1, 10, 28, Oct. 8, 26, 29, Nov. 6, 24, 27, Dec. 4, 22, 25

Soul mates: Jan. 21, Feb. 19, Mar. 17, Apr. 15, May 13, June 11, July 9, 29, Aug. 7, 27, Sept. 5, 25, Oct. 3, 23, Nov. 1, 21, Dec. 19

October 14

FIXED STARS

Spica, also called Ishtar or Arista; Foramen

PRIMARY STAR

Star's name: Spica, also called Ishtar or Arista

Degree position: 22°51'–23°46' Libra between the years 1930 and 2000

Magnitude: 1

Strength: ★★★★★★★★★

Orb: 2°30'

Constellation: Alpha Virgo

Applicable days: October 14, 15, 16, 17, 18

Star qualities: varied: Venus/Mars or Venus/Jupiter/Mercury

Description: a brilliant white binary star located in the head of wheat in Virgo

PRIMARY STAR'S INFLUENCE

Spica is one of the predominant stars in the sky and it is of great importance. This star bestows good judgment and unexpected turns of good fortune. Spica also suggests refinement, interest in science, and love of culture and art. Honors and riches increase after your education is completed. Spica can also bring success in foreign lands, long voyages, and trading in imports and exports.

Linked to your Sun's degree, Spica offers eminent position, good social connections, success in business undertakings, and an ability to gain from new ideas and inventions. You have good concentration, are intuitive, and possess

♎ Charming and friendly, with a sensitive and powerful mind, you possess a strong desire for love and friendship. With your natural physical vitality, you probably attract much change and diversity into your life and enjoy being active. A dislike of discord or harshness implies that you are sensitive to your environment and need beautiful and harmonious surroundings.

With the added influence of your decanate ruler, Gemini, you are expressive and inquisitive, adaptable and versatile. Articulate, with a pleasant voice, you are a good conversationalist with a persuasive manner. Being a sweet-talker, however, you may occasionally find it tempting to take the easy way out of difficult situations and tell people what they want to hear. Nevertheless, you are sociable and easygoing, have an interest in human relationships, and are usually skillful at making contacts. With a love of luxury and the good life, you would be wise to guard against social excesses or overindulgence in any form.

Appreciating color and sound, you possess innate artistic talents that you may wish to develop through music, art, or drama. Alternatively, your natural business sense can be expanded and you may find yourself particularly lucky with investments. Your keen intellect is likely to keep you interested in constantly exploring new concepts and testing your wits and intelligence. Although you may suffer from indecision, when you have set your mind on something your power and determination can be formidable.

From the age of nine, when your progressed Sun moves into Scorpio, you experience a growing emphasis concerning your desire for personal power and transformation. A turning point occurs at the age of thirty-nine, when your progressed Sun moves into Sagittarius, widening your perspective and indicating that you may wish to expand your mind through new experiences, the study of philosophy and religion, or meeting foreign people and visiting foreign places. After the age of sixty-nine, when your progressed Sun enters Capricorn, you become more pragmatic, realistic, and structured.

Your Secret Self

With your extreme sensitivity and vivid imagination, you can either be a visionary or escape into fantasy. A highly intuitive side to your nature may encourage an interest in mysticism or spirituality and can prove to be a great asset in your dealings with others. However, you may have to guard against misusing your sensitivity through being deceptive or manipulative. Usually lucky, you can always get by, but by disciplining your mental potential, you can achieve outstanding results.

Having leadership skills and seeing the opportunities within any situation, you have the ability to think big and often like to take a risk. You may find most satisfaction, though, when passing on your knowledge, inspiration, or special insight to help others.

Work & Vocation

Receptive and charming, with a strong sense of vision, you are able to create new concepts that can assist you in careers such as style and image making or art and design. As an inquisitive individual with an interest in social issues, you make a good reporter, journalist, photographer, actor, or filmmaker. Your communication skills and social awareness can also inspire you to pursue a career in education. Intuitive and sensitive, you are spiritual, with insight into people's needs. These qualities may draw you to the clergy or the medical and alternative healing professions. A flair for mixing with others also suggests that you can succeed in public office or in people-related occupations.

Famous people who share your birthday include designer Ralph Lauren, poet e.e. cummings, Quaker leader William Penn, U.S. president Dwight Eisenhower, Irish prime minister Eamon de Valera, singer Cliff Richard, actor Roger Moore, and actress Lillian Gish.

Numerology

Intellectual potential, pragmatism, and determination are some of the qualities associated with the number 14 birthday. Indeed, as a number 14 individual, you frequently put your work first and judge yourself and others on the basis of career achievements. Although you need stability, the restlessness indicated by the number fourteen urges you to forge ahead or take on new challenges in a constant attempt to improve your lot. This innate restlessness and constant lack of satisfaction may also inspire you to make a great many changes in your life, especially if you are not happy with your working conditions or financial status. With your perceptive mind, you respond quickly to problems and enjoy solving them. The subinfluence of the number 10 month indicates that you are intuitive and idealistic, with a friendly manner. A willingness to compromise and adapt to situations enables you to create harmony and peace. Being stubborn, on the other hand, usually creates confrontations and emotional tension. If you are not career-oriented, you will invest your time and energy in home and family.

• *Positive:* decisive actions, hardworking, lucky, creative, pragmatic, imaginative, industrious
• *Negative:* overly cautious or overly impulsive, thoughtless, stubborn

Love & Relationships

Being friendly, you are able to mix with people from all social groups. Often attracted to people who are clever and straightforward, you need someone who can keep you mentally stimulated. Being sensitive and aware of subtle emotional changes, you can be very affectionate with your partners. There is a danger, however, that your restlessness may cause you to be bored or you may become involved in mental power games. Nevertheless, you can be very warm, tender, and loyal once you have finally settled down.

psychic abilities. Associations with intellectual activities and big organizations can bring success. You enjoy dealing with the public and can acquire immense wealth, especially from commercial enterprises.

• *Positive:* economical, pragmatic, focused goals

• *Negative:* too extravagant, constantly changing direction, unsettled mind

See Appendix for additional fixed star readings.

YOUR SPECIAL SOMEONE

For security, mental stimulation, and love, you might want to begin looking for those born on the following dates.

Love & friendship: Jan. 3, 10, 13, 20, 30, Feb. 1, 8, 11, 18, 28, Mar. 6, 9, 16, 26, Apr. 4, 7, 14, 24, May 2, 5, 12, 22, June 3, 10, 20, July 1, 8, 18, Aug. 6, 16, 30, Sept. 4, 14, 28, 30, Oct. 2, 12, 26, 28, 30, Nov. 10, 24, 26, 28, Dec. 8, 22, 24, 26

Beneficial: Jan. 12, 16, 17, 28, Feb. 10, 14, 15, 26, Mar. 8, 12, 13, 24, Apr. 6, 10, 11, 22, May 4, 8, 9, 20, 29, June 2, 6, 7, 18, 27, July 4, 5, 16, 25, Aug. 2, 3, 14, 23, Sept. 1, 12, 21, Oct. 10, 19, Nov. 8, 17, Dec. 6, 15

Fatal attractions: Mar. 31, Apr. 9, 10, 11, 12, 29, May 27, June 25, July 23, Aug. 21, Sept. 19, Oct. 17, Nov. 15, Dec. 17

Challenging: Jan. 6, 18, 22, 27, Feb. 4, 16, 20, 25, Mar. 2, 14, 18, 23, Apr. 12, 16, 21, May 10, 14, 19, June 8, 12, 17, July 6, 10, 15, Aug. 4, 8, 13, Sept. 2, 6, 11, Oct. 4, 9, Nov. 2, 7, Dec. 5

Soul mates: Mar. 28, Apr. 26, May 24, June 22, July 20, Aug. 18, Sept. 16, Oct. 14, Nov. 12, Dec. 10

October 15

Ω Charming, quick at assessing situations, and never lacking in inspiration, you are a sociable Libra with a flair for people and diplomacy. With an appreciation of beauty, color, and sound, you possess creative talents that you may wish to develop through artistic self-expression. Clever and shrewd, with good mental potential, you are likely to keep yourself active and be constantly upgrading your knowledge. Skeptical, yet with a certain childlike innocence, you gradually come to learn the benefits of listening to your intuition. This helps you to act spontaneously and seize the opportunities of the moment. Just be careful that in your quest for the best that life can offer, too great a love of luxury or social excesses do not deter you from your path.

With the added influence of your decanate ruler, Gemini, you are articulate and mentally curious. You are likely to have an interest in creative communication and education as well as a talent for writing. With a quick wit and pleasant voice, you have the potential for social entertaining and public speaking. Versatile and adaptable, you love to please and can talk to anyone about anything. It may be necessary, however, to keep yourself challenged intellectually and take responsibility for developing your fine mind to make the most of your wonderful cerebral potential.

Although generally easygoing and wishing to keep life harmonious, on occasion you may have to guard against becoming irritable, obstinate, or suffering from nervous tension. Yoga, martial arts, or sports can be a good release for your anxieties and help you balance your overactive mind.

From the age of eight, when your progressed Sun moves into Scorpio, there is a growing emphasis over the next thirty years on issues regarding emotional change and personal power. A turning point occurs as you reach the age of thirty-eight, when your progressed Sun moves into Sagittarius, expanding your mental perspective and indicating that you may wish to be more adventurous or take up new interests such as travel and visiting foreign places. After the age of sixty-eight, when your progressed Sun enters Capricorn, you become more pragmatic, cautious, and prudent.

Your Secret Self

With an ability to analyze people, you are a good psychologist and are usually skillful at making contacts. Your keen understanding of human nature, combined with your flashes of insight, can translate into a genuine desire to help others or a quest for wisdom. At times you are high-spirited and playful, with a love of entertaining. Alternatively, a more serious and introspective side to your personality occasionally needs solitude to reflect and relax. With all your many talents, you need only develop faith and discrimination to achieve outstanding success.

With an inner power and drive to accomplish, you can be very determined and, if inspired, will work really hard to manifest your plans and ideals. Understanding the value of things, you can be successful at acquiring wealth and status, though you need to have a strong sense of purpose to achieve satisfaction. By using your competitive spirit constructively, you can benefit from a most productive work influence.

Work & Vocation

Intelligent, with a friendly personality, you enjoy a challenge and are often mentally restless. Your enthusiasm and good communication skills grant success in occupations linked to pro-

FIXED STARS

Spica, also known as Ishtar or Arista; Foramen

PRIMARY STAR

Star's name: Spica, also known as Ishtar or Arista

Degree position: 22°51'–23°46' Libra between the years 1930 and 2000

Magnitude: 1

Strength: ★★★★★★★★★

Orb: 2°30'

Constellation: Alpha Virgo

Applicable days: October 14, 15, 16, 17, 18

Star qualities: varied: Venus/Mars or Venus/Jupiter/Mercury

Description: a brilliant white binary star located in the head of wheat in Virgo

PRIMARY STAR'S INFLUENCE

Spica is one of the predominant stars in the sky and it is of great importance. This star bestows good judgment and unexpected turns of good fortune. Spica also suggests refinement, interest in science, and love of culture and art. Honors and riches increase after your education is completed. Spica can also bring success in foreign lands, long voyages, and trading in imports and exports.

Linked to your Sun's degree, Spica offers eminent position, good social connections, success in business undertakings, and an ability to gain from new ideas and inventions. You have good concentration, are intuitive, and possess

motion, publishing, and education. A love of art suggests that you are creative and sensitive, with a talent for writing or music. Determined and persuasive, you can make the most of your communication skills as a lawyer, salesperson, or agent. Being analytical, you possibly possess technical skills that may find an outlet through working with computers and various types of engineering. By developing your fine mind, you may become involved in philosophy, metaphysics, or subjects of a more profound nature. A humanitarian streak may draw you to careers such as social work, psychology, or the healing professions.

Famous people who share your birthday include philosopher Friedrich Nietzsche, writers Oscar Wilde and P. G. Wodehouse, poet Virgil, Duchess of York Sarah Ferguson, businessman Lee Iaccoca, baseball player Jim Palmer, economist John Kenneth Galbraith, and actress/director Penny Marshall.

psychic abilities. Associations with intellectual activities and big organizations can bring success. You enjoy dealing with the public and can acquire immense wealth, especially from commercial enterprises.

• *Positive:* economical, pragmatic, focused goals

• *Negative:* too extravagant, constantly changing direction, unsettled mind

See Appendix for additional fixed star readings.

Numerology

Versatility, enthusiasm, and restlessness are suggested by the number 15 birthday. Your greatest assets are your strong instincts and the ability to learn quickly through combining theory and practice. Often you utilize your intuitive powers and are quick at recognizing opportunities when they arise. With a number 15 birthday, you possess a talent for attracting money or receiving help and support from others. Carefree and resolute, you welcome the unexpected and like to take a gamble. The subinfluence of the number 10 month indicates that you are highly intuitive and idealistic and need to trust your own feelings rather than overrationalize and have doubts. Usually stimulated by what you read or hear, you have a mind full of information and you benefit from directing your mental forces toward education, literature, and spirituality. Having faith in your inspired ideas and an eye for detail suggests that you can express yourself creatively through writing.

• *Positive:* willing, generous, responsible, kind, cooperative, appreciative, creative ideas

• *Negative:* disruptive, restless, irresponsible, unhelpful, self-centered, loss of faith, worry, indecision, misusing power

YOUR SPECIAL SOMEONE

For that someone special, you might want to look among those born on the following dates.

Love & friendship: Jan. 11, 21, 28, 31, Feb. 9, 19, 26, 29, Mar. 17, 24, 27, 31, Apr. 15, 22, 25, May 13, 20, 23, 27, June 1, 11, 18, 21, July 9, 16, 19, Aug. 7, 14, 17, 31, Sept. 5, 12, 15, 29, Oct. 3, 10, 13, 17, 27, 29, 31, Nov. 1, 8, 11, 25, 27, 29, Dec. 6, 9, 23, 25, 27

Beneficial: Jan. 9, 12, 18, 24, 29, Feb. 7, 10, 16, 22, 27, Mar. 5, 8, 14, 20, 25, Apr. 3, 6, 12, 18, 23, May 1, 10, 16, 21, 31, June 2, 8, 14, 19, 29, July 6, 12, 17, 27, Aug. 4, 10, 15, 25, Sept. 2, 8, 13, 23, Oct. 6, 11, 21, Nov. 4, 9, 19, Dec. 2, 7, 17

Fatal attractions: Jan. 3, Feb. 1, Apr. 10, 11, 12, 13, 30, May 28, June 26, July 24, Aug. 22, Sept. 20, Oct. 18, Nov. 16, Dec. 14

Challenging: Jan. 7, 8, 19, 28, Feb. 5, 6, 17, 26, Mar. 3, 4, 15, 24, Apr. 1, 2, 13, 22, May 11, 20, June 9, 18, July 7, 16, Aug. 5, 14, Sept. 3, 12, Oct. 1, 10, Nov. 8, Dec. 6

Soul mates: Jan. 3, 19, Feb. 1, 17, Mar. 15, Apr. 13, May 11, June 9, July 7, Aug. 5, Sept. 3, Oct. 1

Love & Relationships

Attracted to hardworking, ambitious, and self-made people, you need a partner who can keep up with your dynamic mental energy. With your natural charm, you should have no problem attracting admirers. Your skepticism, however, indicates that you probably take your time before committing yourself to a long-term relationship. Social contacts and group activities are important to you, as they help you develop your skills at analyzing people. Men of this birthday are particularly drawn to powerful and independent women, although women in general can prove particularly lucky for anybody born on this date. Once you do settle down, you can be very loyal and supportive.

October 16

Arcturus, also called the Bear Watcher, Alchameth, or Al Simak; Spica, also called Ishtar or Arista; Foramen

PRIMARY STAR

Star's name: Arcturus, also called the Bear Watcher, Alchameth, or Al Simak

Degree position: 23°15'–24°2' Libra between the years 1930 and 2000

Magnitude: 1

Strength: ★★★★★★★★★

Orb: 2°30'

Constellation: Alpha Bootes

Applicable days: October 16, 17, 18, 19, 20

Star qualities: Mars/Jupiter and Venus/Jupiter

Description: a golden orange and yellow star located on the left knee of Bootes

PRIMARY STAR'S INFLUENCE

Arcturus imparts artistic talent and success in the world of fine arts. This star can bestow riches, honors, and acclaim and bring prosperity. Arcturus may also bring success in foreign lands and through long journeys. This star warns against restlessness and anxious moments, which create instability in your life.

Linked to your Sun's degree, Arcturus imparts wealth and a good reputation. This star brings success after early setbacks and grants intuitive, psychic, or healing abilities. An inclination toward the legal profession or public

The influence of your birthday suggests that you are a charming, sensitive, and hardworking Libra who can also be very determined. Intuitive yet possessing business acumen, you are extremely purposeful when you are interested in a project or have set a definite goal. However, at other times you can suffer from indecision or inertia and procrastination, which can challenge your otherwise remarkable potential.

With the added influence of your decanate ruler, Gemini, you have an inquisitive and perceptive mind as well as good powers of speech. With an interest in relationships, you are usually skillful at diplomacy or making contacts. With a love of luxury and the good life, however, you would be wise to guard against social excesses or overindulgence in any form. Nevertheless, your creative mind is usually full of ideas and plans, and once set on a course of action, you have a tenacious approach to fulfilling your personal vision.

Although you project a sociable and amiable approach to life, you possess a strong sense of the dramatic and are very emotional. A powerful need for love and emotional satisfaction can be channeled into creative pursuits such as art, music, or drama, or may spur you to fight for an idealistic cause. Your farsightedness and natural practical approach make you a good strategist as well. There may nevertheless be times when you are prone to avoidance, guilt, or being too self-obsessed. By combining the two sides of your personality, you are able to establish harmony and equilibrium.

After you reach the age of seven, your progressed Sun moves into Scorpio, emphasizing issues concerning your emotional sensitivity and power. A turning point occurs at the age of thirty-seven, when your progressed Sun moves into Sagittarius, widening your perspective on life and indicating that you may wish to travel, study, or be adventurous. After the age of sixty-seven, when your progressed Sun enters Capricorn, you become more practical, mindful, and circumspect.

Your Secret Self

Cooperative efforts and partnerships are likely to play a major part in your life, as you possess natural diplomatic skills and an ability to deal with people on a personal level. Despite your special talent for making profitable contacts and commercializing your talents, sometimes you become anxious and worry unnecessarily about financial matters. Nevertheless, you may have to juggle the comfortable routine of home and family with being businesslike.

You enjoy a feeling of personal power, so you have to ensure that your motivation is always fair and just. Fortunately, you usually weigh situations carefully before coming to a final conclusion. Having a plan of action can stimulate your natural sense of structure and help you be more persistent and purposeful. This birthday indicates that you have the determination and resolve to triumph over obstacles or difficulties.

Work & Vocation

Idealistic and visionary, you are a peacemaker and a humanitarian who can inspire others to create harmony. Your willingness to compromise and work hard suggests that you are loyal and dedicated. An understanding of human nature and a love of knowledge may draw you to the academic world, where you would be an excellent teacher or lecturer. Your love of theater, music, and the arts suggests that you are creative and sensitive. You may want to pursue a career as a writer or work in the world of entertainment as a dramatist. If you are interested in the world of commerce, you may be drawn to advertising, TV, or publishing. Public-spirited and sociable, you may want to be involved in your community, raising money for good causes.

Famous people who share your birthday include dramatist Eugene O'Neill, Israeli prime minister David Ben Gurion, writer Gunther Grass, actresses Angela Lansbury and Suzanne Somers, lexicographer Noah Webster, and Supreme Court Justice William O. Douglas.

office may bring success. Alternatively, you may find an interest in writing on philosophical, spiritual, or religious subjects. This star suggests guarding against becoming too apprehensive and discontented by learning to accept calmly the ups and downs of life and staying detached.

• *Positive:* religious contacts, good judgment, long voyages, glamorous

• *Negative:* overindulgence, overly enthusiastic, laziness, negligence

See Appendix for additional fixed star readings.

Numerology

A number 16 birthday suggests that you are thoughtful, sensitive, and friendly. Although analytical, you often judge life and people according to how you feel. As a number 16 personality, however, you can experience inner tensions when facing friction between a need for self-expression and responsibility to others. You may be interested in world affairs and may join international corporations or the media world. The creative ones among you have a talent for writing with sudden flashes of inspiration. With a number 16 birthday, you may need to learn how to balance being overly confident with being doubtful and insecure. The subinfluence of the number 10 month indicates that you are ambitious, with leadership ability. Since you want security and stability, you are willing to make compromises in order to keep the status quo. Being emotional and creative suggests that you need to find ways to express your inspired ideas and establish your individuality. Faithful and caring, you are loyal to and supportive of those around you.

• *Positive:* wealth and fortune, government positions, pride and dignity, prominence in religion, love of knowledge, loyal

• *Negative:* snobbery, carelessness, crafty, deceptive

YOUR SPECIAL SOMEONE

In your quest for love, affection, and happiness, you might want to look among those born on the following dates.

Love & friendship: Jan. 8, 18, 22, Feb. 16, 20, Mar. 14, 18, 28, 31, Apr. 2, 12, 16, 26, May 10, 14, 24, June 8, 12, 22, July 6, 10, 20, 29, Aug. 4, 8, 18, 27, 30, Sept. 2, 6, 16, 25, 28, Oct. 4, 14, 23, 26, 30, Nov. 2, 12, 21, 24, 28, Dec. 10, 19, 22, 26, 28

Beneficial: Jan. 6, 10, 25, 30, Feb. 4, 8, 23, 28, Mar. 2, 6, 21, 26, Apr. 4, 19, 24, May 2, 17, 22, June 15, 20, 30, July 13, 18, 28, Aug. 11, 16, 26, Sept. 9, 14, 24, Oct. 7, 12, 22, Nov. 5, 10, 20, Dec. 3, 8, 18

Fatal attractions: Apr. 11, 12, 13, 14, May 29, June 27, July 25, Aug. 23, Sept. 21, Oct. 19, Nov. 17, Dec. 15

Challenging: Jan. 13, 29, 31, Feb. 11, 27, 29, Mar. 9, 25, 27, Apr. 7, 23, 25, May 5, 21, 23, June 3, 19, 21, July 1, 17, 19, Aug. 15, 17, Sept. 13, 15, Oct. 11, 13, Nov. 9, 11, Dec. 7, 9

Soul mates: Jan. 6, 25, Feb. 4, 23, Mar. 2, 21, Apr. 19, May 17, June 15, July 13, Aug. 11, Sept. 9, Oct. 7, Nov. 5, Dec. 3

Love & Relationships

Creative and dramatic, you possess a strong need for love and affection but are also willing to give much of yourself to those you love. With a wide emotional range, you can alternate between being sensitive and compassionate and being bossy and authoritarian. With all your charms, you may find yourself being drawn to other creative and dramatic people who can understand your passions and emotional needs. Alternatively, with your love of learning, you may look for people who have a greater awareness or intelligence than yourself.

October 17

♎ Versatile and sociable, you have an attraction for people and change that stimulates variety and excitement in your life. The influence of your birthday indicates that you are mentally quick and alert and are usually seeking new intellectual horizons to keep your inquisitive mind active. With a magnetic charm and fast wit, you can be very entertaining, although a tendency toward uncertainty or impatience can detract from your sense of purpose.

With the added influence of your decanate ruler, Gemini, you can be logical, articulate, and good at problem solving. The ability to be diplomatic yet go straight to the heart of a matter provides you with excellent communication skills. It would be wise, however, not to spoil your charms by being obstinate, calculating, or secretive. A feel for the arts may find expression through music, painting, or drama as well as a desire to surround yourself with beauty, style, and luxury.

Expressive and adaptable, you may need to develop your great mental potential through concentration and thoroughness. Being very instinctive and having a spirit of enterprise, you may work better when you think big and act upon your intuition rather than dwell in pessimism or indecision. Your desire for activity and good fortune can even extend to travel and opportunities to work abroad. With a love of luxury and the good life, you would be wise to guard against escapism or immoderation in any form.

After you reach the age of six, your progressed Sun moves into Scorpio, emphasizing over the next thirty years issues concerning your emotional power and transformation. A turning point occurs at the age of thirty-six, when your progressed Sun moves into Sagittarius, stimulating you to be more adventurous and freedom-loving or to widen your horizons. After the age of sixty-six, when your progressed Sun enters Capricorn, you become more practical, mindful, and prudent.

Your Secret Self

One side of your nature can be emotionally impulsive and restless, yet another side of you is cautious, with a desire to build for long-term security. With expensive tastes, you may need to keep yourself constructively occupied in order to fulfill your extravagant dreams. By staying positive and developing patience and tolerance, you are able to combine dynamic insight with the perseverance to achieve success.

Sensitive and intuitive, you respect those who possess knowledge or wisdom. A hidden desire for truth and integrity stimulates you to form your own philosophy in life. By being honest with yourself and avoiding hidden agendas, you gain the respect that you are seeking. An idealistic search for love and an inner need for self-expression may inspire you to write or constructively use your emotional energies for the benefit of others.

Work & Vocation

A need for variety and mental stimulation implies that you fare better in a job that offers change and advancement. Travel or working for export-import companies will enable you to

---

FIXED STARS

Arcturus, also called the Bear Watcher, Alchameth, or Al Simak; Spica, also called Ishtar or Arista; Foramen

PRIMARY STAR

Star's name: Arcturus, also called the Bear Watcher, Alchameth, or Al Simak

Degree position: 23°15'–24°2' Libra between the years 1930 and 2000

Magnitude: 1

Strength: ★★★★★★★★★

Orb: 2°30'

Constellation: Alpha Bootes

Applicable days: October 16, 17, 18, 19, 20

Star qualities: Mars/Jupiter and Venus/Jupiter

Description: a golden orange and yellow star located on the left knee of Bootes

PRIMARY STAR'S INFLUENCE

Arcturus imparts artistic talent and success in the world of fine arts. This star can bestow riches, honors, and acclaim, and bring prosperity. Arcturus may also bring success in foreign lands and through long journeys. This star warns against restlessness and anxious moments, which create instability in your life.

Linked to your Sun's degree, Arcturus imparts wealth and a good reputation. This star brings success after early setbacks and grants intuitive, psychic, or healing abilities. An inclination toward the legal profession or public

visit other continents. As an intelligent individual with strong views, you can do whatever you put your mind to, as long as you are interested and consistent. An ability to learn things quickly implies that you have to be careful not to become bored. An excellent communicator, you may enjoy working for the news media. Alternatively, you may be interested in research and academic studies or lecturing and training. Being sociable, you may become involved in public office or social services and work in the community. Having common sense and an ability to solve problems suggests that you may take up psychology or work as an advisor or counselor.

Famous people who share your birthday include actress Rita Hayworth, playwright Arthur Miller, daredevil Evel Knievel, journalist Jimmy Breslin, writer Nathanael West, and actor Montgomery Clift.

• *Positive:* religious contacts, good judgment, long voyages, glamorous

• *Negative:* overindulgence, overly enthusiastic, laziness, negligence

See Appendix for additional fixed star readings.

Numerology

With a number 17 birthday, you are shrewd, with a reserved nature and good analytical abilities. An independent thinker, you benefit from being well educated or skillful. Usually you utilize your knowledge in a specific way in order to develop your expertise, and you can achieve success or a prominent position as a specialist or researcher. Private, introspective, and detached, with a strong interest in facts and figures, you frequently present a serious and thoughtful demeanor and like to take your time. By developing your communication skills, you discover much more about yourself from others. The subinfluence of the number 10 month indicates that you are ambitious, with an idealistic and charismatic personality. Intelligent, with strong instincts and an eye for detail, you intuitively understand the problems you are facing. Although you possess common sense and are usually confident in your judgment, a tendency to be impatient or overenthusiastic suggests that you need to take your time and not act in haste.

• *Positive:* thoughtful, specialist, good planner, good business sense, attracts money, individual thinker, accurate, skilled researcher, scientific

• *Negative:* detached, stubborn, carelessness, moody, sensitive, narrow-minded, critical, worry

YOUR SPECIAL SOMEONE

To get both stability and excitement out of a relationship, you might like to look for those born on the following dates.

Love & friendship: Jan. 4, 13, 19, 23, 24, Feb. 11, 17, 21, Mar. 9, 15, 19, 28, 29, 30, Apr. 7, 13, 17, 26, 27, May 5, 11, 15, 24, 25, 26, 27, June 3, 9, 13, 22, 23, 24, July 1, 7, 11, 20, 21, 22, Aug. 5, 9, 18, 19, 20, Sept. 3, 7, 16, 17, 18, Oct. 1, 5, 14, 15, 16, 29, 31, Nov. 3, 12, 13, 14, 27, 29, Dec. 1, 10, 11, 12, 25, 27, 29

Beneficial: Jan. 7, 15, 20, 31, Feb. 5, 13, 18, 29, Mar. 3, 11, 16, 27, Apr. 1, 9, 14, 25, May 7, 12, 23, June 5, 10, 21, July 3, 8, 19, Aug. 1, 6, 17, 30, Sept. 4, 15, 28, Oct. 2, 13, 26, Nov. 11, 24, Dec. 9, 22

Fatal attractions: Apr. 13, 14, 15, 16

Challenging: Jan. 6, 14, 30, Feb. 4, 12, 28, Mar. 2, 10, 26, Apr. 8, 24, May 6, 22, June 4, 20, July 2, 18, Aug. 16, Sept. 14, Oct. 12, Nov. 10, Dec. 8

Soul mates: Apr. 30, May 28, June 26, July 24, Aug. 22, Sept. 20, Oct. 18, 30, Nov. 16, 28, Dec. 14, 26

Love & Relationships

Your need for variety and change is likely to spill over into your social life. Often drawn to strong people with initiative or insight, you are likely to have many opportunities for relationships. There is a danger of being secretive with your partners, so it is advisable to be as honest as possible to avoid repercussions later. Ruled by your feelings, you can, on one hand, look for stability and security, but on the other, you can also change mood and become restless, needing stimulating emotional experiences.

October 18

♎ Active and constructive, you are a creative individual with enterprising ideas. Willing to work hard when you are interested in a project, you need mental pursuits to stop you from becoming bored. A good planner with a pragmatic approach, you enjoy expanding your knowledge and putting it to good use.

With the added influence of your decanate ruler, Gemini, you are adaptable and versatile as well as verbally expressive. Although you like to be direct and honest with others, you are usually skillful at diplomacy and making contacts. A talent for problem solving and an instinct for people's needs can make you a good negotiator and advisor. The ability to communicate your ideas and philosophy of life can involve you in debates on subjects that interest you. Although idealistic, you may need to develop patience and tolerance, particularly when dealing with people less astute than yourself.

Innate artistic or creative talents may find expression through music, painting, writing, and drama. With your quick intelligence and intuition, you can be clever and amusing, with an inherent business sense. Being naturally persuasive yourself and enjoying some sharp wit, you are usually drawn to people who are clever or successful in their own right. Potentially a positive thinker, when enthusiastic and focused you have the ability to manifest your ideas into tangible reality. It would be wise, however, not to impair your wonderful potential by being too critical, rebellious, or obstinate.

From the time you reach the age of five onward, your progressed Sun moves into Scorpio and there is a growing emphasis on emotional change, power, and transformation. A turning point occurs at the age of thirty-five, when your progressed Sun moves into Sagittarius, stimulating you to be more adventurous and freedom-loving or to widen your horizons. Education may become a focal point, whether self-study or formal higher learning. After the age of sixty-five, when your progressed Sun enters Capricorn, you become more pragmatic, cautious, and mindful.

Your Secret Self

With an appreciation of color and sound, you may prefer to be surrounded with beauty, style, and luxury. You may, however, have to avoid overindulgence in any form of pleasure. By channeling the more restless side of your nature into being more focused, well informed, or positively adventurous, you manage to keep your enthusiasm very much alive. Possessing both an inner desire for peace of mind and a need to be constantly learning and exploring, you may be pulled in different directions until you learn to slow down. This involves simplifying your life and listening to your intuition.

Being very sensitive, you are aware of your responsibilities to others, particularly concerning family members and home. Kind and considerate, you can be an excellent advisor. Although at times you seem to know best, your good intentions may be understood by others as interference; by learning when not to take charge of situations, you can be supportive, yet detached.

Work & Vocation

Highly intuitive and imaginative, you are full of ideas that can make you money. With your organizational skills and determination, you are a good planner who thinks on a grand scale.

FIXED STARS

Arcturus, also called the Bear Watcher, Alchameth, or Al Simak; Spica, also called Ishtar or Arista

PRIMARY STAR

Star's name: Arcturus, also called the Bear Watcher, Alchameth, or Al Simak

Degree position: 23°15'–24°2' Libra between the years 1930 and 2000

Magnitude: 1

Strength: ★★★★★★★★★

Orb: 2°30'

Constellation: Alpha Bootes

Applicable days: October 16, 17, 18, 19, 20

Star qualities: Mars/Jupiter and Venus/Jupiter

Description: a golden orange and yellow star located on the left knee of Bootes

PRIMARY STAR'S INFLUENCE

Arcturus imparts artistic talent and success in the world of fine arts. This star can bestow riches, honors, and acclaim and bring prosperity. Arcturus may also bring success in foreign lands and through long journeys. This star warns against restlessness and anxious moments, which create instability in your life.

Linked to your Sun's degree, Arcturus imparts wealth and a good reputation. This star brings success after early setbacks, and grants intuitive, psychic, or healing abilities. An inclination toward the legal profession or public

Usually you want to take charge of situations and lead, or be your own boss. Friendly and sociable, you have a charismatic personality. If you believe in something, including yourself, you can be very persuasive and successful as an agent, salesperson, or promoter. Gifted and ambitious, you need to express yourself creatively and shine as an individual. As an intelligent person with common sense and practical abilities, you are often interested in social reforms and education.

Famous people who share your birthday include actor Jean-Claude van Damme, actress Melina Mercouri, tennis champion Martina Navratilova, singer/songwriter Chuck Berry, actor George C. Scott, singer/actress Lotte Lenya, philosopher Henri Bergson, and playwright Wendy Wasserstein.

Numerology

Determination, assertiveness, and ambition are some of the attributes associated with the number 18 birthday. Active, with a need for challenges, you like to keep busy and are frequently involved in some enterprise. Capable, hardworking, and responsible, you rise to positions of authority. Alternatively, your strong business sense and organizational skills lead you to the world of commerce. Since you may suffer from overwork, learn how to relax or slow down from time to time. As a number 18 personality, you can use your power to heal others, give sound advice, or solve other people's problems. The subinfluence of the number 10 month indicates that you want to accomplish and achieve. Although you are friendly and sociable, you have the courage to stand by your own beliefs even when they differ from others'. Being a forceful character with a keen intellect, you can influence others with your persuasive speech and charming manner, but you should guard against selfishness and being dictatorial.

• *Positive:* progressive, assertive, intuitive, courageous, resolute, healing ability, efficient, advisory skills

• *Negative:* uncontrolled emotions, lazy, lack of order, selfishness, callousness, failure to complete work or projects, deceitful

Love & Relationships

Relationships are very important to you even if you do not always demonstrate your feelings or affection. Nevertheless, you can be protective of those you care for. Often drawn to people who work hard, are unusual, or are from foreign lands, you need mental excitement or intellectual rapport. Charming and friendly, you usually enjoy socializing and can be witty and entertaining. Once you do decide to settle down, you can be a loyal and supportive partner.

office may bring success. Alternatively, you may find an interest in writing on philosophical, spiritual, or religious subjects. This star suggests guarding against becoming too apprehensive and discontented by learning to accept calmly the ups and downs of life and staying detached.

• *Positive:* religious contacts, good judgment, long voyages, glamorous

• *Negative:* overindulgence, overly enthusiastic, laziness, negligence

See Appendix for additional fixed star readings.

YOUR SPECIAL SOMEONE

For security and love, you might want to begin looking for those born on the following dates.

Love & friendship: Jan. 4, 14, 20, 24, 25, Feb. 2, 12, 15, 18, 22, 23, Mar. 10, 16, 20, 29, 30, Apr. 8, 14, 18, 27, 28, May 6, 12, 16, 25, 26, 31, June 4, 7, 10, 14, 23, 24, 29, July 2, 8, 12, 21, 22, 27, Aug. 6, 10, 19, 20, 25, Sept. 4, 8, 17, 18, 23, Oct. 2, 6, 15, 16, 21, 30, Nov. 4, 13, 14, 19, 28, 30, Dec. 2, 11, 12, 17, 26, 28, 30

Beneficial: Jan. 4, 8, 21, Feb. 2, 6, 19, Mar. 4, 17, 28, Apr. 2, 15, 16, May 13, 24, June 11, 22, July 9, 20, Aug. 7, 18, 31, Sept. 5, 16, 29, Oct. 3, 14, 27, Nov. 1, 12, 25, Dec. 10, 23

Fatal attractions: Jan. 3, Feb. 1, Apr. 13, 14, 15, 16, May 31, June 29, July 27, Aug. 25, Sept. 23, Oct. 21, Nov. 19, Dec. 17

Challenging: Jan. 7, 10, 15, 31, Feb. 5, 8, 13, 29, Mar. 3, 6, 11, 27, Apr. 1, 4, 9, 25, May 2, 7, 23, June 5, 21, July 3, 19, Aug. 1, 17, Sept. 15, Oct. 13, Nov. 11, Dec. 9

Soul mates: Mar. 31, Apr. 29, May 27, June 25, July 23, Aug. 21, Sept. 19, Oct. 17, 29, Nov. 15, 27, Dec. 13, 25

October 19

♎ The influence of your birthday indicates that you are a creative and optimistic Libra with a quick mind. Friendly, sociable, and imaginative, you can be charmingly assertive and have a need to be popular. You are adaptable and versatile; however, you may have to be careful that your many interests do not cause you to scatter your energies or be indecisive.

With the subinfluence of your decanate ruler, Gemini, you are expressive and a good conversationalist. The combination of your persuasive speech and dynamic charm ensures that you are usually skillful at making contacts and influencing others. Easygoing, you have an interest in human relationships and are good at dealing with people. The more doubting side of your nature, however, can cause you to worry or hide your feelings from others to protect your sensitivity.

Attracted to the creative arts and with a strong need to express yourself, you like to surround yourself with beauty or may even develop your innate artistic or literary talents. With a love of style, luxury, and the good life, you would be wise to guard against social excesses or overindulgence in any form. Fortunately, you are blessed with the grace of natural compassion that enables you to empathize with others. Developed, this gives you a humanitarian and altruistic desire to be of service. Nevertheless, with your warm heart and charisma, you may need to be careful that your social life does not take over your responsibilities.

From the age of four onward, when your progressed Sun moves into Scorpio, you experience a growing emphasis on emotional change, personal power, and regeneration. A turning point occurs at the age of thirty-four, when your progressed Sun moves into Sagittarius, indicating that you become more adventurous and freedom-loving, possibly desiring to travel or seek more education. After the age of sixty-four, when your progressed Sun enters Capricorn, you become more rational, sensible, and discerning, with a realistic point of view.

FIXED STAR

Star's name: Arcturus, also called the Bear Watcher, Alchameth, or Al Simak

Degree position: 23°15'–24°2' Libra between the years 1930 and 2000

Magnitude: 1

Strength: ★★★★★★★★

Orb: 2°30'

Constellation: Alpha Bootes

Applicable days: October 16, 17, 18, 19, 20

Star qualities: Mars/Jupiter and Venus/Jupiter

Description: a golden orange and yellow star located on the left knee of Bootes

PRIMARY STAR'S INFLUENCE

Arcturus imparts artistic talent and success in the world of fine arts. This star can bestow riches, honors, and acclaim, and bring prosperity. Arcturus may also bring success in foreign lands and through long journeys. This star warns against restlessness and anxious moments, which create instability in your life.

Linked to your Sun's degree, Arcturus imparts wealth and a good reputation. This star brings success after early setbacks and grants intuitive, psychic, or healing abilities. An inclination toward the legal profession or public office may bring success. Alternatively, you may find an interest in writing on philosophical, spiritual, or religious subjects. This star suggests guarding against becoming too apprehensive and discontented by learning to accept calmly

Your Secret Self

Proud, with a natural dramatic sense, you prefer to be in a leadership position. With a good sense of values, you are quick at assessing opportunities and evaluating people. This business sense, combined with a pioneering spirit, can help you achieve success. If you lose faith, however, you may be likely to become insecure or temperamental, which can cause you to place too much store in material power and status.

With your restlessness, you can become bored easily. This implies that you need to find activities that stimulate or challenge you, and persevere with them. Although at times you may suffer from a conflict between idealism and the mundane, usually variety and change can inspire you to become motivated and mobile. Travel can play an important role in your life, so if you feel restricted, do not be afraid to take chances and go further afield if promising prospects arise.

Work & Vocation

Versatile and multitalented, you need diversity and excitement. An ability to adapt to new circumstances suggests that you can learn quickly. Eloquent and charming, you can entertain others with your witty conversation or writing. This also suggests that you are a good salesperson

the ups and downs of life and staying detached.

• *Positive:* religious contacts, good judgment, long voyages, glamorous

• *Negative:* overindulgence, overly enthusiastic, laziness, negligence

or promoter. Sensitive and receptive to what the public wants, you can create styles and fashion or be involved in promotion, advertising, or politics. An ability to get along with others implies that you fare best in large organizations. Refined and meticulous, you can produce finely detailed artwork that needs precision, such as work in precious metals and stone. If you want to share your knowledge with others, you make a fine teacher, especially of art and drama, or you may choose to work as a counselor and uplift others with your kind words.

Famous people who share your birthday include singer/songwriter Peter Tosh, writer John le Carré, film pioneer Auguste Lumière, N.O.W. president Patricia Ireland, and actor John Lithgow.

Numerology

Ambition and humanitarianism are two of the characteristics of the number 19 birthday. Decisive and resourceful, you possess depth of vision, but the dreamer side of your nature is compassionate, idealistic, and creative. Although you are sensitive, the need to be someone may be the very thing that pushes you to be dramatic and claim center stage. Often there is a strong desire to establish an individual identity. To do so, you may first need to overcome the influence of peer group pressure. To others, you may appear confident, resilient, and resourceful, but inner tensions may cause emotional ups and downs. The subinfluence of the number 10 month indicates that you are self-reliant and original, with a charismatic personality. You have the ability to communicate your feelings with clarity and inspired thoughts. Although you often seek harmony and balance, you are prone to fluctuating moods, ranging from confidence to self-doubt. A need to be surrounded by people or be popular implies that you do not like to be isolated or alone.

• *Positive:* dynamic, centered, creative, leader, lucky, progressive, optimistic, strong convictions, competitive, independent, gregarious

• *Negative:* self-centered, depressive, worry, fear of rejection, ups and downs, materialistic, egotistical, impatient

YOUR SPECIAL SOMEONE

To find love, you might find a partner who is caring and loving among those born on the following dates.

Love & friendship: Jan. 21, 25, Feb. 19, 23, Mar. 17, 21, 30, Apr. 15, 19, 28, 29, May 13, 17, 26, 27, June 11, 15, 24, 25, 30, July 9, 13, 22, 23, 28, Aug. 7, 11, 20, 21, 26, 30, Sept. 5, 9, 18, 19, 24, 28, Oct. 3, 7, 16, 17, 22, 26, 29, Nov. 1, 5, 14, 15, 20, 24, 27, Dec. 3, 12, 13, 18, 22, 25, 27, 29

Beneficial: Jan. 5, 13, 16, 22, 28, Feb. 3, 11, 14, 20, 26, Mar. 1, 9, 12, 18, 24, 29, Apr. 7, 10, 16, 22, 27, May 5, 8, 14, 20, 25, June 3, 6, 12, 18, 23, July 1, 4, 10, 16, 21, Aug. 2, 8, 14, 19, Sept. 6, 12, 17, Oct. 4, 10, 15, Nov. 2, 8, 13, Dec. 6, 11

Fatal attractions: Apr. 14, 15, 16, 17, 18, June 30, July 28, Aug. 26, Sept. 24, Oct. 22, Nov. 20, Dec. 18

Challenging: Jan. 2, 23, 30, Feb. 21, 28, Mar. 19, 26, 28, Apr. 17, 24, 26, May 15, 22, 24, June 13, 20, 22, July 11, 18, 20, Aug. 16, 18, 19, Sept. 7, 14, 16, Oct. 5, 12, 14, Nov. 3, 10, 12, Dec. 1, 8, 10

Soul mates: Jan. 14, 22, Feb. 12, 20, Mar. 10, 18, Apr. 8, 16, May 6, 14, June 4, 12, July 2, 10, Aug. 8, Sept. 6, Oct. 4, Nov. 2

Love & Relationships

Friendly and popular, you find it easy to make friends and charm people. Usually attractive, you have admirers of the opposite sex. Nevertheless, there is a danger that if you allow yourself to run hot and cold, love can be a minefield, with your losses as many as your successes. You can be compassionate and caring and make sacrifices for those you love. Generous when socializing, you possess an alluring personal magnetism and are good with intimacy. You may, however, need to curb an extravagant or jealous streak.

October 20

FIXED STAR

Star's name: Arcturus, also called the Bear Watcher, Alchameth, or Al Simak

Degree position: 23°15'–24°2' Libra between the years 1930 and 2000

Magnitude: 1

Strength: ★★★★★★★★★

Orb: 2°30'

Constellation: Alpha Bootes

Applicable days: October 16, 17, 18, 19, 20

Star qualities: Mars/Jupiter and Venus/Jupiter

Description: a golden orange and yellow star located on the left knee of Bootes

PRIMARY STAR'S INFLUENCE

Arcturus imparts artistic talent and success in the world of fine arts. This star can bestow riches, honors, and acclaim, and bring prosperity. Arcturus may also bring success in foreign lands and through long journeys. This star warns against restlessness and anxious moments, which create instability in your life.

Linked to your Sun's degree, Arcturus imparts wealth and a good reputation. This star brings success after early setbacks and grants intuitive, psychic, or healing abilities. An inclination toward the legal profession or public office may bring success. Alternatively, you may find an interest in writing on philosophical, spiritual, or religious subjects. This star suggests guarding against becoming too apprehensive and discontented by learning to accept

♎ Mentally sharp and with the gift of persuasion, you are a Libra with charm and excellent people skills. With a need to be different, you are likely to project an attractive appearance and be drawn to original individuals. Being expressive and a shrewd observer of human behavior, you shine in social situations. Appreciating art, music, and creativity, you need to be surrounded by beauty, style, and luxury.

The subinfluence of your decanate ruler, Gemini, indicates that you are intellectually quick and able to impress people with words, either verbally or in writing. Being a good speaker and enjoying a debate comes from your ability to be decisively outspoken, yet diplomatic. You may have to be careful, however, that your humorous and cutting wit does not turn into sarcasm.

Having much to gain from cooperative efforts and partnerships, you particularly profit from personal contacts. Being provocative or manipulative, though, can lose you the many benefits of creating harmony and balance in relationships. Very determined when you have a goal in mind, you are capable of inventive and original achievements. However, you may need to protect your highly tuned nervous system to avoid becoming irritable or stressed.

From very early in your childhood, your progressed Sun moves into Scorpio, emphasizing your growing awareness of emotional change and personal power. A turning point occurs at the age of thirty-three when your progressed Sun moves into Sagittarius, indicating that you may wish to expand your horizons or travel. If education becomes a focal point, study of philosophy, psychology, and law can be beneficial. You are also likely to have more contact with foreign people and places. After the age of sixty-three, when your progressed Sun enters Capricorn, you become more practical, sensible, and prudent.

Your Secret Self

A tremendous inner power ensures that with dedication and hard work you can achieve almost anything. An active social life can be either a source of lively activity and entertainment or a distraction from achieving your outstanding potential—sometimes both. Whether socializing or working, you can project a warm and caring consideration for others that may even extend to humanitarian interests and activities.

Having a sixth sense about what motivates people, you can be highly intuitive. If you become too serious, however, you can be stubborn or moody. By staying independent and continually initiating new projects, you strengthen your sense of purpose and determination. Being dramatic and possessing a potential for leadership, you have the ability to effectively benefit from your outstanding potential.

Work & Vocation

Receptive and intuitive, you enjoy communicating with others and usually have a talent for words and writing. Shrewd and friendly, with a flair for people, you make an excellent mediator or negotiator. You can excel as an agent or salesperson as well, or in public relations or promotion. If you develop your creative gifts, you may choose a career in education as a teacher or lecturer or in publishing as a writer or journalist. Diplomatic and easygoing, with an ability to become involved on a personal level, you are a natural psychologist who can succeed in counseling, therapy, or the health professions. A need to express yourself and a love of the dramatic may lure you to the entertainment and art worlds. Alternatively, your leadership abilities, organizational skills, and strategic planning may place you in the world of commerce, where you can collaborate with others or be involved in large projects.

Famous people who share your birthday include actor Bela Lugosi, singer Tom Petty, French poet Arthur Rimbaud, architect Sir Christopher Wren, musician "Jelly Roll" Morton, and baseball players Micky Mantle and Keith Hernandez.

Numerology

With a number 20 birthday, you are intuitive, adaptable, and understanding, and often see yourself as a part of a larger group. Usually you enjoy cooperative activities where you can interact, share experiences, or learn from others. Charming and gracious, you develop diplomatic and social skills and can move in different social circles with ease. You may, however, need to develop your confidence or overcome a tendency to be easily hurt by the actions and criticism of others or to be overly dependent. You are a master at creating a congenial and harmonious atmosphere. The subinfluence of the number 10 month indicates that although you are self-assured and able to maintain an independent attitude, a need for love and intimacy suggests that you want to communicate your thoughts and ideas. While fun-loving and generous, you want approval and affection from those you love. If you remain decisive and positive in times of adversity, you can use your creativity and charismatic personality to influence others and make real advancement. A strong need for self-expression implies that you are gifted, usually with more than one interest.

• *Positive:* good partnerships, gentle, tactful, receptive, intuitive, considerate, harmonious, agreeable, amicable, ambassador of goodwill

• *Negative:* suspicious, lack of confidence, subservient, timid, oversensitive, selfish, easily hurt

Love & Relationships

Relationships can be very important to you, but it is vital not to find yourself in a dependent situation. Needing companionship, you usually dislike being alone for too long. Fortunately, your charm, diplomatic skills, and excellent powers of persuasion can help you find friends and lovers. However, at times your feelings can be extreme and difficult for others, even though you genuinely desire harmony. Being gracious, sociable, and entertaining, you make an excellent host.

YOUR SPECIAL SOMEONE

For prosperity and a long-lasting relationship, you might like to begin by looking for that special someone among those born on the following dates.

Love & friendship: Jan. 6, 16, 22, 26, Feb. 4, 14, 20, 24, Mar. 2, 12, 18, 22, Apr. 10, 16, 20, 30, May 8, 14, 18, 28, June 6, 12, 16, 26, July 4, 10, 14, 24, 31, Aug. 2, 8, 12, 22, 29, Sept. 6, 10, 20, 27, Oct. 4, 8, 18, 25, Nov. 2, 6, 16, 23, 30, Dec. 4, 14, 21, 28, 30

Beneficial: Jan. 6, 17, 23, 31, Feb. 4, 15, 21, 29, Mar. 2, 13, 19, 27, 30, Apr. 11, 17, 25, 28, May 9, 15, 23, 26, June 7, 13, 21, 24, July 5, 11, 19, 22, Aug. 3, 9, 17, 20, Sept. 1, 7, 15, 18, 30, Oct. 5, 13, 16, 28, Nov. 3, 11, 14, 26, Dec. 1, 9, 12, 24

Fatal attractions: Apr. 14, 15, 16, 17, 18, 19

Challenging: Jan. 24, Feb. 22, Mar. 20, 29, Apr. 18, 27, 29, May 6, 16, 25, 27, 30, June 14, 22, 25, 28, July 12, 21, 23, 26, Aug. 10, 19, 21, 24, Sept. 8, 17, 19, 22, Oct. 6, 15, 17, 20, Nov. 4, 13, 15, 18, Dec. 2, 11, 13, 16

Soul mates: Jan. 13, Feb. 11, Mar. 9, Apr. 7, May 5, June 3, 30, July 1, 28, Aug. 26, Sept. 24, Oct. 22, Nov. 20, Dec. 18

October 21

FIXED STARS

Although your Sun's degree is not linked to a fixed star, some of your other planets' degrees certainly will be. By having an astrological chart calculated, you can find the exact position of the planets on your date of birth. This will tell you which of the fixed stars listed in this book are relevant to you.

Ω A bright intellect and charming manner are revealed by the influence of your birthday. A progressive thinker with an inquisitive mind, you enjoy initiating projects that will keep you mentally enthusiastic. As a practical idealist, you see the value of intuition as well as pragmatism. You are sociable and magnetic, and a talent for dealing with people can be one of your major attributes.

With the subinfluence of your decanate ruler, Gemini, you are adaptable and versatile, with a flair for communication. Being highly strung and sensitive, however, indicates that you need to protect your delicate nervous system. Articulate, with good social skills, you are usually adept at diplomacy and making contacts. Always wanting the latest information and being able to enthuse others with your knowledge, you are often a natural teacher. In fact, education in any form is vital to make the most of your wonderful potential.

With a feel for the arts, you may find expression through music, painting, or drama as well as a desire to surround yourself with beauty, style, and luxury. Your refined nature is often displayed in a light-hearted personality, although you can experience times when you become very stubborn. Debates on subjects of interest and a talent for problem solving can keep your fine mind creatively occupied. When you lack mental stimulation, you are apt to scatter your energies on trivial or unimportant activities. Ambitious, with strong desires, you possess leadership skills but may have to beware of being bossy.

Your progressed Sun moves into Scorpio at the beginning of your life, emphasizing over the next thirty years issues concerning power and transformation. A turning point occurs at the age of thirty-two, when your progressed Sun moves into Sagittarius, stimulating you to be more adventurous and indicating that you may wish to study or travel. You are also likely to have more contact with foreign people and places. After the age of sixty-two, when your progressed Sun enters Capricorn, you become more pragmatic, cautious, and mindful.

Your Secret Self

Being outspoken yet instinctive about people's needs, you can be a good negotiator and advisor. Even though you appear independent, you are very responsive to your partners or associates. Sometimes afraid of being alone, you need to be careful of being overdependent or insecure in your relationships. By developing an awareness of balance and fair play, you can be generous with your love and attention and at the same time detached.

As a sensitive individual with exceptional imagination, you may choose to use these gifts through dedication to art and music, healing, spiritual experience, or an ideal. You can be a very good friend and a caring companion, but if your love is not reciprocated, you may be prone to escapism or becoming moody. Working cooperatively with others, either in partnerships or as part of a team, can prove to be especially important for your soul growth.

Work & Vocation

Ambitious and daring, with a love of knowledge, you can be an excellent trainer and teacher. Friendly and charming, with an easygoing personality, you enjoy working with people and can succeed in public relations and promotion. Multitalented, you may find that your problem is deciding exactly what you want to achieve. Often musical and artistic, with a flair for drama and speech, you can act in theater and film. You can also excel in writing, especially fiction, humor, and drama, where you can use your wit, imagination, and original ideas. If you believe in a cause, you make an excellent spokesperson. Loyal and dedicated, you usually work better in partnerships, but you want appreciation for your efforts.

Famous people who share your birthday include Nobel Prize founder Alfred Nobel, writers Samuel Coleridge and Ursula Le Guin, actress Carrie Fisher, Israeli prime minister Benjamin Netanyahu, musician Dizzy Gillespie, and baseball player Whitey Ford.

Numerology

Dynamic drive and an outgoing personality are usually present in those with a number 21 birthday. Socially inclined, you have many interests and contacts and are generally fortunate. Usually you show others your friendly and gregarious personality. Intuitive, with an independent spirit, you are highly inventive and original. With a number 21 birthday, you can be fun-loving and magnetic, with social charm. Alternatively, you can be shy and reserved, with a need to develop assertiveness, especially in close relationships. Although you can be inclined toward cooperative relationships or marriage, you always want to be acknowledged for your talents and abilities. The subinfluence of the number 10 month indicates that you are ambitious and direct. Inquisitive, multitalented, and intuitive, you need to work hard and develop self-discipline in order to commercialize your talents. With your practical skills and creative ideas, you are able to undertake large schemes and often enjoy initiating new projects.

• *Positive:* inspiration, creativity, love unions, long-lasting relationships

• *Negative:* dependency, nervous, temperamental, lack of vision, disappointment, fear of change

Love & Relationships

Charming and friendly, you have no trouble in attracting friends and admirers. In partnerships, you usually prefer hardworking and successful people. It is important to stay independent, yet be willing to give of yourself and play fair in all your relationships. It would be wise to avoid jealousy in your dealings with others, as it can spoil your caring and loving personality. Looking for that perfect partner, you believe in meaningful relationships and can be loyal to the person you settle down with.

YOUR SPECIAL SOMEONE

You might find a partner who will understand your sensitivity and need for love among those born on the following dates.

Love & friendship: Jan. 1, 4, 27, 29, Feb. 2, 25, 27, Mar. 23, 25, Apr. 21, 23, May 19, 21, 29, June 17, 19, 27, July 15, 17, 25, Aug. 13, 15, 23, Sept. 11, 13, 21, Oct. 9, 11, 19, Nov. 7, 9, 17, Dec. 5, 7, 15

Beneficial: Jan. 3, 10, 15, 18, Feb. 1, 8, 13, 16, Mar. 6, 11, 14, 29, 31, Apr. 4, 9, 12, 27, 29, May 2, 7, 10, 25, 27, June 5, 8, 23, 25, July 3, 6, 21, 23, Aug. 1, 4, 19, 21, Sept. 2, 17, 19, Oct. 15, 17, Nov. 13, 15, Dec. 11, 13

Fatal attractions: Apr. 16, 17, 18, 19, 20, 30, May 28, June 26, July 24, Aug. 22, Sept. 20, Oct. 18, Nov. 16, Dec. 14

Challenging: Jan. 9, 14, 16, 25, Feb. 7, 12, 14, 23, Mar. 5, 10, 12, 21, 28, 30, Apr. 3, 8, 10, 19, 26, 28, May 1, 6, 8, 17, 24, 26, June 4, 6, 15, 22, 24, July 2, 4, 13, 20, 22, Aug. 2, 11, 18, 20, Sept. 9, 16, 18, Oct. 7, 14, 16, Nov. 5, 12, 14, Dec. 3, 10, 12

Soul mates: Dec. 29

October 22

FIXED STARS

Magnetism, charm, and leadership are indicated by the special characteristics of your birthday. Diplomatic, with good social skills, you know how to court influence and use it to your advantage. With your strong sense of justice and sharp mental capabilities, you are more than able to hold your own in any situation. There is a danger, however, that indecision about any course of action or overindulgence in worldly pleasures can lure you away from your high ideals.

With the subinfluence of your decanate ruler, Gemini, you are very expressive and have a talent for communication. Naturally persuasive, with a shrewd understanding of human nature, you are sociable and easygoing. A dynamic charm ensures that you are amusing and friendly in social situations. You need only apply the necessary self-discipline to make the most of your outstanding potential.

With a strong interest in home and family and a love of comfort, you prefer to be surrounded by quality and luxury. With an interest in art and beauty and a need for self-expression, you may be drawn to writing, painting, or music. This does not take away from a natural business sense that helps you succeed in worldly terms. At times you are also able to act as an arbitrator or diplomat and bring peace and harmony to difficult situations. However, on other occasions you may be bossy or petty, which detracts from your usual easygoing style.

Your progressed Sun moves into Scorpio at the beginning of your life, emphasizing, over the next thirty years, issues concerning power and transformation. A turning point occurs at the age of thirty-one, when your progressed Sun moves into Sagittarius, stimulating you to be more optimistic and adventurous and indicating that you may wish to study or travel. You are likely to have more contact with foreign people and places. After the age of sixty-one, when your progressed Sun enters Capricorn, you become more pragmatic, mindful, and focused on your aims and objectives.

Your Secret Self

Generous and kind, you have a broad-minded detachment that allows you to feel an affinity with all of humankind. From time to time, though, you may be prone to hold in frustrations and disappointments, which are released through being overserious or argumentative. Although you can sometimes display selfish moods, you compensate by seeing the comedy of life and using your fast humor to deflate potentially difficult situations.

As you project a very confident front, your pride does not allow you to reveal your inner fears. You may have a need for something more meaningful in your life that can help you overcome trouble and be a source of wisdom. Your powerful feelings and sensitivity are linked to your intuition, so it pays to trust your instincts. When positive, you have an inner power that can manifest as healing or creative ability.

Work & Vocation

Elegant and dynamic, with practical skills, you are kind to people and have many contacts. Your charismatic personality and creativity suggest that you can excel in public relations, politics, humanitarian organizations, or international corporations. Multitalented and dramatic, you can choose any career you like, whether art, interior design, writing, music, or drama. Charming and generous, with advanced social skills, you can succeed as a negotiator or mediator and diplomat. Alternatively, because of your honesty and idealism, you may be drawn to the law as a lawyer, court officer, or judge. An ability to organize social events or raise money for charity and just causes indicates that you are persuasive and enterprising.

Famous people who share your birthday include psychologist/writer Timothy Leary, actresses Sarah Bernhardt and Catherine Deneuve, writer Doris Lessing, actors Jeff Goldblum and Derek Jacobi, and composer Franz Liszt.

Numerology

This is a master number and can vibrate both as number 22 and number 4. Often honest and hardworking, with natural leadership abilities, you have a charismatic personality and a deep understanding of people and what motivates them. Although undemonstrative, you often show a caring, protective concern for the welfare of others, yet you never lose sight of your pragmatic or realistic stand. Usually cultured and worldly, you have many friends and admirers. The more competitive among you achieve success and good fortune with help and encouragement from others. Many born on this date have strong links with brothers or sisters and can be protective and supportive of them. The subinfluence of the number 10 month indicates that you are ambitious and idealistic. Astute and highly intuitive, you need to learn to trust your own instincts. Your depth of feeling and need for self-expression imply that you are dynamic and motivated when inspired. An ability to endure and persevere suggests that you show your real character in times of stress and difficulties. Although you are generous and enthusiastic, at times you can be selfish or arrogant.

• *Positive:* universal, director, pragmatic, practical, good with your hands, skillful, builder, good organizer, realist, problem solver, achiever

• *Negative:* get-rich-quick schemes, nervous, bossy, materialistic, lack of vision, lazy, egotistical, grasping, self-promoting

Love & Relationships

You are romantic and magnanimous, and people are drawn to your friendly personality. With your strong emotions, you may experience powerful attractions, but as you do not like to be alone, you may compromise for peace, home, and family. Although idealistic, watch that your love of sensuality does not distract you from your utopian plans. Entertaining and warm, you make an excellent host.

YOUR SPECIAL SOMEONE

The ideal partner who will be lucky for you and make all your love wishes come true might be among those born on the following dates.

Love & friendship: Jan. 2, 28, Feb. 12, 26, Mar. 24, Apr. 22, May 20, 29, 30, June 4, 18, 27, 28, July 16, 25, 26, Aug. 14, 23, 24, Sept. 12, 21, 22, Oct. 10, 19, 20, 29, 31, Nov. 8, 17, 18, 27, 29, Dec. 6, 15, 16, 25, 27

Beneficial: Jan. 2, 10, 13, 16, Feb. 8, 11, 14, Mar. 6, 9, 12, Apr. 4, 7, 10, May 2, 5, 8, June 3, 6, July 1, 4, 30, Aug. 2, 28, 30, Sept. 26, 28, Oct. 24, 26, Nov. 22, 24, Dec. 20, 22, 30

Fatal attractions: Apr. 18, 19, 20, 21, Oct. 31, Nov. 29, Dec. 27

Challenging: Jan. 3, 9, 10, Feb. 1, 7, 8, Mar. 5, 6, 31, Apr. 3, 4, 29, May 1, 2, 27, June 25, July 23, Aug. 2, 21, 31, Sept. 19, 29, Oct. 17, 27, Nov. 15, 25, Dec. 13, 23

Soul mates: Jan. 5, Feb. 3, Mar. 1, May 30, June 28, July 26, Aug. 24, Sept. 22, Oct. 20, Nov. 18, Dec. 16

Scorpio

October 23–November 21

October 23

FIXED STARS

Although your Sun's degree is not linked to a fixed star, some of your other planets' degrees certainly will be. By having an astrological chart calculated, you can find the exact position of the planets on your date of birth. This will tell you which of the fixed stars listed in this book are relevant to you.

Born on the cusp of Libra and Scorpio, you are determined and receptive, with deep awareness. Impressionable and enterprising, you judge experiences by the way you feel and usually benefit from an extensive range of emotions. These go from being disciplined, with strong willpower, to being charming and charismatic. Hardworking and a networker, with a strong sixth sense, you constantly seek ways to interact with other people. Although you can be enthusiastic by nature, a pragmatic side to your character frequently suggests that you can rise above crises.

The subinfluence of your decanate ruler, Scorpio, implies that you possess great inner strength. Idealistic and understanding, you can be affectionate and perceptive. Your direct approach and sharp comments indicate that you are fearless and persistent. When challenged, you can show your opponent a daring and bold front. Your true tenacious spirit will usually rise if you feel threatened or insecure.

When you find an area of interest, you can become ambitious and determined to find out all you can about the subject. Although you can be impetuous or restless, you also possess a tender heart and can be kind and generous. You are usually well informed, and your quest for knowledge and a desire for self-expression indicate that you need to develop your fine mind.

Before the age of twenty-nine, you are likely to be concerned with issues regarding your emotional sensitivity and personal power. At the age of thirty, when your progressed Sun moves into Sagittarius, there is a turning point that highlights a growing need for freedom and expanding your horizons, whether through travel, education, or your philosophy of life. Another turning point occurs at the age of sixty, when your progressed Sun moves into Capricorn. This is likely to bring a more pragmatic, orderly, and security-conscious approach to life.

Your Secret Self

You possess a marvelous imagination and dynamic emotions but may sometimes experience frustration or disappointment that can cause you to become impatient or discontented. By exercising positive thinking, you will find it easier to let go of difficulties and summon up the self-discipline needed to live up to your great potential. Usually friendly, sensitive, and broadminded in your acceptance of others, by developing your universal approach to life you increase your generosity and compassion.

With a desire to always progress and advance in life, you can accrue special opportunities for success. Ambitious and competitive, with a quick intelligence, you are usually willing to work hard to accomplish your objectives. If you avoid the responsibility needed to fulfill your destiny, however, you may not be able to satisfy your strong need to build something of permanent value.

Work & Vocation

You possess the power to be very successful in people-related activities. If you fulfill your high calling and leadership potential, you are likely to be at the forefront of your career, particularly in the field of law, education, or business. Dramatic and expressive, you may enjoy occupations that allow you to be creative, such as in the world of art or entertainment. Alternatively, a strong sense of duty and a sensitive and caring nature suggest that you may be drawn to occupations that involve helping others, such as in public service, medicine, or the healing world generally. Having a strong imagination and sense of vision, you may wish to use this in careers in film or advertising.

Famous people who share your birthday include TV personality Johnny Carson, composer Albert Lortzing, Brazilian soccer player Pele, writers Robert Seymour Bridges and Michael Crichton, and football player Doug Flutie.

Numerology

Emotional sensitivity and creativity are two of the attributes of a number 23 birthday. Usually you are versatile and a quick thinker, with a professional attitude and a mind full of inventive ideas. With the number 23 influence, you can learn new subjects easily but may prefer practice to theory. You are fond of travel, adventure, and meeting new people; the restlessness implied by the number 23 urges you to try many different kinds of experience and helps you adapt to make the best of any situation. The subinfluence of the number 10 month indicates that you possess inner strength and great depth and are fiercely loyal. These qualities enable you to be brave and rise above difficulties. Self-reliant and purposeful, you prefer to be in control. Although you hide your feelings, your idealistic and truthful nature indicates that when you speak out, you can be brutally frank. Although at times you can be fearless, watch out that your sharp criticism does not offend others.

• *Positive:* loyal, responsible, travel, communicative, intuitive, fame, creative, versatile, trustworthy

• *Negative:* selfish, insecure, stubborn, fault-finding, dull, withdrawn, prejudiced

Love & Relationships

Sensitive and emotional, you can be an audacious and romantic idealist. Drawn toward forceful individuals, you make use of your powerful feelings by expressing your love dramatically. On occasion, however, your personal relationships may suffer from your contrasting moods or your excessive materialism. With your strong emotions, you can be caring, with a compassionate and demonstrative nature. Devotion and faithfulness are very important to you, but avoid an inclination to be commanding and forceful.

YOUR SPECIAL SOMEONE

You might find emotional fulfillment and that special someone among those born on the following days.

Love & friendship: Jan. 3, 19, 22, 25, 29, 30, Feb. 1, 17, 20, 23, 27, 28, Mar. 18, 21, 25, 26, Apr. 16, 19, 23, 24, 28, May 14, 17, 21, 22, 26, 31, June 9, 12, 15, 19, 20, 24, 29, July 10, 13, 18, 22, Aug. 8, 11, 15, 16, 20, 27, 29, 30, Sept. 6, 9, 13, 14, 18, 23, 27, 28, Oct. 4, 7, 11, 12, 16, 21, 25, 26, Nov. 2, 5, 9, 10, 14, 19, 23, 24, Dec. 3, 7, 8, 12, 17, 21, 22

Beneficial: Jan. 17, Feb. 15, Mar. 13, Apr. 11, May 9, 29, June 7, 27, July 5, 25, Aug. 3, 23, Sept. 1, 21, Oct. 19, 29, Nov. 17, 27, 30, Dec. 15, 25, 28

Fatal attractions: Apr. 19, 20, 21, 22, May 31, June 29, July 27, Aug. 25, 30, Sept. 23, 28, Oct. 21, 26, Nov. 19, 24, Dec. 17, 22

Challenging: Jan. 20, 23, Feb. 18, 21, Mar. 16, 19, Apr. 14, 17, May 12, 15, June 10, 13, July 8, 11, Aug. 6, 9, Sept. 4, 7, Oct. 2, 5, Nov. 2, Dec. 1

Soul mates: Jan. 4, 31, Feb. 2, 29, Mar. 27, Apr. 25, May 23, June 21, July 19, Aug. 17, Sept. 15, Oct. 13, Nov. 11, Dec. 9

October 24

♏ Youthful and creative, you are a Scorpio with inner nobility and a love for the good things in life. Although attracted by glamour, you are willing to work hard when you find an inspiring idea or a worthwhile cause.

The subinfluence of your decanate ruler, Scorpio, implies that you have a tenacious spirit and are daring and bold. Although at times your sharp and direct approach indicates that you are fearless and persistent, your ability to understand others implies that you can also be sympathetic and understanding. As a creative individual, you are emotionally warm, with a flair for social interactions. Usually attractive and graceful, with an ability to make yourself popular with other people, you often seek to express yourself artistically.

As you are emotionally perceptive, you can easily comprehend people's mood swings. Liable to make magnanimous gestures, you need to be appreciated and are a true friend and companion. Although you can be cooperative and helpful in group endeavors, when you become negative or perceive a lack of emotional support, you can feel resentful or sorry for yourself. By developing self-discipline, you realize that being responsible and patient has great benefits and rewards.

Up to the age of twenty-eight, you are concerned with issues regarding your emotional sensitivity and personal transformation. At the age of twenty-nine, when your progressed Sun moves into Sagittarius, there is a turning point that highlights a growing need for freedom and a more expansive outlook. This may involve taking more risks or expanding your mental perspective through a quest for truth, education, or travel. Another turning point occurs at the age of fifty-nine, when your progressed Sun moves into Capricorn, emphasizing a more serious, disciplined, and practical approach to life.

Your Secret Self

Being a natural actor as well as having excellent social skills, you are an expert at probing the motivation and hidden agendas of others without revealing anything of your own deeper self. This can protect your extreme sensitivity and enable you to feel in control. Generous and loving, you need people and harmonious relationships. Others appreciate your understanding, and you may sometimes find yourself advising those around you. It may be necessary, however, to develop detachment and a clear sense of boundaries to avoid being too generous and compassionate at your own expense.

Proud and intelligent, you need to constantly challenge yourself to get yourself moving. However, a desire for instant gratification or escapism through excess may slow you down in developing the self-discipline needed to achieve your outstanding potential. By trusting your powerful intuition, you are able to sense how far you can push situations or when to let go in order to avoid being hurt. A permanent youthful quality will always keep you in touch with the joy of life.

Work & Vocation

By combining your compelling charm, natural business sense, and people skills, you may be drawn to careers in public relations, sales, or publishing. You can be especially good at businesses that involve social interaction, such as promotion or being an agent for others. Alternatively, being creative and enjoying entertaining, you may be attracted to the arts, show business, or the music industry. With your natural understanding for the problems of others, you may find yourself a counselor or in the caring or healing professions. Your shrewd business sense helps you succeed in whatever career you may choose, but preferably you need the freedom to work in your own way.

Famous people who share your birthday include musician Bill Wyman, naturalist/microbiologist Anthony van Leeuwenhoek, actress Dame Sybil Thorndike, football player Y. A. Tittle, and actors F. Murray Abraham and Kevin Kline.

Numerology

With a number 24 birthday, you may dislike routine; however, you are hardworking, with practical abilities and sound judgment. The emotional sensitivity of the number 24 birthday suggests that you need to establish stability and order. Faithful and fair, though sometimes undemonstrative, you are inclined to believe that actions speak louder than words. With this pragmatic approach to life, you develop a good business sense and an ability to overcome obstacles and succeed. Having a number 24 birthday, you may have to get past a tendency to be stubborn or fixed in your ideas. The subinfluence of the number 10 month indicates that you are idealistic and independent, with great emotional power. Tenacious and fiercely loyal, you come to the aid of others in time of crisis. Self-reliant and courageous, you prefer to decide for yourself. Although winning is important, avoid a tendency to be self-centered or dictatorial. You can be evasive and secretive, but when you do speak your mind you can be critical and forthright.

• *Positive:* energy, idealist, practical skills, strong determination, honest, frank, fair, generous, love of home, active, energetic

• *Negative:* materialistic, too economical, instability, ruthless, dislikes routine, lazy, unfaithful, domineering and stubborn, vengeful, jealous

Love & Relationships

Highly sensitive, you have strong emotions and a compelling need for love, which are likely to draw you into all kinds of romantic liaisons. With your ability to be amiable and entertaining, you are sure to have an active social life. Although generous and idealistic, you can become captivated or overly serious about your relationships. In order to avoid unnecessary heartache, guard against letting your feelings dominate your mind. Through being responsible and adaptable, you often receive the respect and admiration of others.

YOUR SPECIAL SOMEONE

Sensual, loyal, and affectionate, you might find a partner who will understand your sensitivity and need for love among those born on the following dates.

Love & friendship: Jan. 5, 9, 10, 18, 19, 26, 30, 31, Feb. 3, 8, 16, 17, 24, 28, Mar. 1, 5, 6, 14, 15, 22, 26, Apr. 3, 4, 12, 13, 20, 24, May 2, 10, 11, 18, 22, June 8, 9, 16, 20, 30, July 6, 7, 14, 18, 28, Aug. 4, 5, 12, 16, 26, 30, Sept. 2, 3, 10, 14, 28, Oct. 1, 8, 12, 22, 26, Nov. 6, 10, 20, 24, Dec. 4, 8, 18, 22, 30

Beneficial: Jan. 13, Feb. 11, Mar. 9, Apr. 7, May 5, June 3, 30, July 1, 28, Aug. 26, Sept. 24, Oct. 22, Nov. 20, Dec. 18

Fatal attractions: April 20, 21, 22, 23

Challenging: Jan. 14, 24, Feb. 12, 22, Mar. 10, 20, Apr. 8, 18, May 6, 16, June 4, 14, July 2, 12, Aug. 10, Sept. 8, Oct. 6, Nov. 4, Dec. 2

Soul mates: July 30, Aug. 28, Sept. 26, Oct. 24, Nov. 22, Dec. 20

October 25

FIXED STARS

Although your Sun's degree is not linked to a fixed star, some of your other planets' degrees certainly will be. By having an astrological chart calculated, you can find the exact position of the planets on your date of birth. This will tell you which of the fixed stars listed in this book are relevant to you.

℧ Charismatic and dynamic, with powerful emotions, you are an ambitious and determined Scorpio who expects a great deal from life. Full of enthusiasm and a spirit of enterprise, you are imaginative and enjoy thinking on a grand scale. Highly intuitive, with analytical abilities, you have many interests and are usually involved in some venture or undertaking. A tendency to be impulsive, however, suggests that self-discipline and concentration are essential components in your formula for success.

The subinfluence of your decanate ruler, Scorpio, implies that your restless desire to accomplish compels you to find different modes of expression. Although sensual, you are fond of power, and you want to excel through the use of your cerebral capabilities. Your ability to overcome obstacles suggests that you can rejuvenate yourself and start all over again when necessary.

Although at times your discerning thoughts and reproach can overwhelm others, your ability to comprehend situations intuitively implies that you can also be sympathetic and understanding. As a sensitive individual, you often seek to express yourself artistically. Usually attractive and graceful, with an ability to make yourself popular, you have a flair for social interactions.

Before the age of twenty-seven, you are concerned with issues regarding your deep feelings and personal power. At the age of twenty-eight, when your progressed Sun moves into Sagittarius, there is a turning point that highlights optimism and a growing need for freedom and expanding your horizons, whether through your philosophy of life, education, or travel. Another turning point occurs at the age of fifty-eight, when your progressed Sun moves into Capricorn. This is likely to bring a more down-to-earth, sensible, and security-conscious approach to life.

Your Secret Self

With a strong sense of individuality and independence, as well as a spirit of enterprise, you can use your ambition to propel you into action and ensure that your big plans are successful. Being intelligent and possessing personal magnetism, you can be highly persuasive and have the gift of dealing easily with people from all walks of life. As a quick learner, you constantly seek new ideas and knowledge and are good at getting your own ideas across in an entertaining way.

An inner restlessness needs to be channeled into creative productivity, or it may cause you to become impatient and dissatisfied. By actively involving yourself in work or projects that keep your interest, you can avoid boredom and keep your ideals and spirit of adventure alive. Travel can often be a significant factor in expanding your horizons.

Work & Vocation

With your shrewd intelligence and the ability to think big, once you are really focused and determined you are capable of outstanding achievement in any field. With your charismatic personality and a natural flair for captivating people, you can do well in public-related occupations. Your sharp intellect can also help you succeed in science or education, but you may prefer to use your creative skills in art, drama, or music. Alternatively, being ambitious, with organizational skills and leadership ability, you can succeed in management, law, or business. Needing work that gives you as much freedom as possible, you may prefer to work for yourself.

Famous people who share your birthday include painter Pablo Picasso, violinist Midori, basketball coach Bobby Knight, composers Johann Strauss and Georges Bizet, and writer Harold Brodkey.

Numerology

You are quick and energetic, though intuitive and thoughtful. As a number 25 individual, you need to express yourself through different experiences. These may include new and exciting ideas, people, or locations. A desire for perfection urges you to work hard and be productive. You may, however, need to be less impatient or critical if things do not happen according to plan. As a number 25 person, you possess strong mental energies that when concentrated aid you to look at all the facts and arrive at a conclusion faster than anyone else. Success and happiness come when you learn to trust your own instincts and develop perseverance and patience. The subinfluence of the number 10 month indicates that although you are independent and charismatic, you need to enjoy your great inner power and be in control. Determined, with penetrating vision, you possess strong ambition and usually find ways to meet challenges or overcome obstacles. As a stubborn and tenacious individual with the power to heal others, you are fiercely loyal and never give up.

• *Positive:* highly intuitive, perfectionist, perceptive, creative mind, good at dealing with people

• *Negative:* impulsive, impatient, irresponsible, overly emotional, jealous, secretive, changing circumstances, critical, moody

Love & Relationships

Being active and dynamic yourself, in personal relationships you may favor strong, intelligent, and hardworking people who enjoy challenges or are in positions of authority. With your charm and sensitivity, you can make others feel secure and special. Sociable and hardworking, you like to entertain and often mix business and pleasure. When you feel in a generous mood, you can make magnanimous gestures of kindness and goodwill. Responsible and practical, you prefer order and planning for the future.

YOUR SPECIAL SOMEONE

If you are seeking stability and a special relationship, you might want to look among those born on the following dates.

Love & friendship: Jan. 2, 3, 6, 9, 10, 11, 17, 21, 27, 31, Feb. 1, 4, 7, 9, 25, 29, Mar. 2, 5, 7, 13, 17, 23, 27, Apr. 3, 5, 15, 21, 25, May 1, 3, 13, 19, 23, 30, June 1, 11, 17, 21, 28, July 5, 9, 15, 19, 26, 29, Aug. 7, 13, 17, 24, 27, Sept. 5, 11, 15, 22, 25, Oct. 3, 9, 13, 20, 23, Nov. 1, 7, 11, 18, 21, 30, Dec. 5, 9, 16, 19, 28

Beneficial: Jan. 11, 16, 30, Feb. 9, 24, 28, Mar. 7, 22, 26, Apr. 5, 20, 24, May 3, 18, 22, 31, June 1, 16, 20, 29, July 14, 18, 27, Aug. 12, 16, 25, Sept. 10, 14, 23, Oct. 8, 12, 21, 29, Nov. 6, 10, 19, 27, Dec. 4, 8, 17, 25

Fatal attractions: April 22, 23, 24, 25

Challenging: Jan. 15, Feb. 13, Mar. 11, Apr. 9, May 7, 30, June 5, 28, July 3, 26, Aug. 1, 24, Sept. 22, Oct. 20, 30, Nov. 18, 28, Dec. 16, 26

Soul mates: Jan. 9, 29, Feb. 7, 27, Mar. 5, 25, Apr. 3, 23, May 1, 21, June 19, July 17, Aug. 15, Sept. 13, Oct. 11, Nov. 9, Dec. 7

October 26

♏ Idealistic and ambitious, you are a sensitive Scorpio with intense feelings and strong desires. Charming and imaginative, you seek ways to express your powerful emotions or appetite for self-enjoyment. As a humanitarian, you can show great compassion and a willingness to support others. Although you can be impulsive and act upon your romantic notions, the practical side of your nature suggests that you can also be shrewd, calculating, and security-conscious.

The double influence of Pluto suggests that although you are sensitive, with immense charm, you can also be resolute and courageous, with a fighting spirit. This inner strength also points to a dynamic willpower, enabling you to rejuvenate yourself or overcome obstacles. Usually you are gregarious but reserved. Although you can have intense feelings, outwardly you remain calm and composed. Just guard against becoming inflexible, as it can work to your detriment.

Financial matters are also likely to occupy much of your attention, and with your natural business sense and willingness to work hard, you have the potential to commercialize your many talents. Nevertheless, one of your challenges may be to obtain the right balance between work and play to ensure that life does not become overly serious or burdensome. You often work better when you allow your intuition to sense the right time for an idea or project and then act spontaneously rather than becoming restricted by too much structure.

Before the age of twenty-six, you are concerned with issues regarding your acute emotional awareness and sense of personal power. At the age of twenty-seven, when your progressed Sun moves into Sagittarius, there is a turning point that highlights a growing need for adventure, more truth, inspiration, and freedom in your life. You become more optimistic and may desire to expand your mental outlook, perhaps through learning or contact with foreign people or places. Another turning point occurs at the age of fifty-seven, when your progressed Sun moves into Capricorn. This is likely to bring a more determined, disciplined, and pragmatic approach to achieving your goals.

Your Secret Self

With your magnanimous spirit and shrewd practicality, it is important to keep a balance between your high ideals and mundane reality. You usually enjoy luxury and have expensive tastes, but it is by using your potential for powerful, universal love and compassion that you are able to avoid much personal frustration or disappointment.

Although emotionally generous with those you care for, you can nevertheless be tough and dutiful. While discipline and self-mastery are very necessary to bring out the best of your talents, it is equally important not to be too hard on yourself. By learning to develop your faith and spontaneity, you can overcome a tendency to become too stubborn, withdrawn, or skeptical. With your sensitive power, you also need regular periods alone to reflect and connect to your natural intuitive insight.

Work & Vocation

Your keen intellect and good communication skills can help you succeed in any career, but you may be particularly attracted to large projects, law, or politics. With natural executive

FIXED STAR

Star's name: Princeps, also called Tsieh Kung

Degree position: 2°8'–2°50' Scorpio between the years 1930 and 2000

Magnitude: 3.5

Strength: ★★★★★

Orb: 1°30'

Constellation: Delta Bootes

Applicable days: October 26, 27, 28, 29

Star qualities: Mercury/Saturn

Description: a pale yellow giant star located in the spear shaft of Bootes

PRIMARY STAR'S INFLUENCE

Princeps suggests a keen mentality and a studious and profound mind, with a depth of understanding that favors research. This star bestows determination, resourcefulness, and a conservative outlook.

Linked to your Sun's degree, this star imparts prominence in education, science, or legal and government affairs. You have a competitive nature and a daring personality. Your subtle assertiveness and resourceful attitude help you to undertake and succeed with new or untried ideas. You have a reserved nature and will not commit yourself until you are sure where you stand. When you are convinced of the facts, you can be quite outspoken and are unafraid to be direct and stand your ground, as you prefer to be in control.

ability and a good business sense, you usually command respect from others through being hardworking and responsible. With your thirst for knowledge and practical thinking, you may well become an authority in your chosen field. An ability to be analytical or technical can draw you to work in science or the health and medical world. Alternatively, your natural creativity and love of beauty may attract you to a career as a musician, actor, or entertainer. The more humanitarian side of your nature may be fulfilled in the caring professions, philanthropic activities, or social reform.

Famous people who share your birthday include First Lady Hillary Rodham Clinton, actor Bob Hoskins, actress Jaclyn Smith, singer Mahalia Jackson, and French president François Mitterand.

Numerology

With a number 26 birthday, you have a pragmatic approach to life, executive ability, and a good business sense. Usually responsible, with a natural aesthetic sense and a love of home, you need to build a solid foundation or find real stability. Often a tower of strength for others, you are willing to support friends, family members, and relatives who turn to you in time of need. You may nevertheless need to guard against materialistic tendencies and a desire to control people or situations. The subinfluence of the number 10 month indicates that you are more inclined to be single-minded. You can also be courteous and courageous, with plenty of emotional power. If you are industrious and purposeful, winning is important, and initiating new ideas often leads to success. Generous and kind, you have the power to inspire others. As a perfectionist and an idealist, do not let your great sensitivity undermine your confidence or isolate you from others.

• *Positive:* creative, practical, caring, responsible, proud of family, enthusiastic, courageous

• *Negative:* stubborn, rebellious, unenthusiastic, lack of persistence

Love & Relationships

Although sensitive, with a compelling desire for love and affection, a need for variety and stimulating company suggests that you do not want your love life to become boring. Travel, or a break from routine with your friends or partner, is especially helpful to stop you from becoming overly serious or working too hard. However, new situations or unexpected events may sometimes cause unrest. If you become too keen in the beginning of a relationship, you can later become discouraged or lose interest. You benefit from developing a more patient approach and taking your time in forming relationships.

YOUR SPECIAL SOMEONE

To find love and a long-lasting companion, you may wish to look for someone born on one of the following dates.

Love & friendship: Jan. 2, 9, 12, 22, 25, Feb. 7, 10, 20, 23, 26, Mar. 5, 8, 18, 21, Apr. 3, 6, 16, 19, May 1, 4, 14, 17, 20, 24, 29, June 2, 12, 15, 27, July 10, 13, 16, 20, 25, 30, Aug. 9, 15, 24, 26, Sept. 7, 13, 22, 24, Oct. 4, 7, 10, 14, 19, 24, 28, 29, Nov. 2, 5, 8, 12, 17, 22, 26, 27, Dec. 3, 6, 10, 15, 20, 24, 25

Beneficial: Jan. 12, 23, 29, Feb. 10, 21, 27, Mar. 22, 26, Apr. 6, 17, 23, May 4, 15, 21, June 2, 13, 19, 28, 30, July 11, 17, 26, 28, Aug. 9, 15, 24, 26, Sept. 7, 13, 22, 24, Oct. 5, 11, 20, 22, Nov. 3, 9, 18, 20, 30, Dec. 1, 7, 16, 18, 28

Fatal attractions: Apr. 22, 23, 24, 25, July 29, Aug. 27, Sept. 25, Oct. 23, Nov. 21, Dec. 19

Challenging: Jan. 1, 4, 26, 30, Feb. 2, 24, 28, Mar. 22, 26, Apr. 20, 24, May 18, 22, 31, June 16, 20, 29, July 14, 18, 27, Aug. 12, 16, 25, 30, Sept. 10, 14, 23, 28, Oct. 8, 12, 21, 26, Nov. 6, 10, 19, 24, Dec. 4, 8, 17, 22

Soul mates: Jan. 20, Feb. 18, Mar. 16, Apr. 14, May 12, June 10, July 8, Aug. 6, Sept. 4, Oct. 2

October 27

℠ Your birthday shows you to be an imaginative and idealistic Scorpio with strong intuitive powers and powerful emotions. The unique combination of determination, personal magnetism, and penetrating insight makes you excellent at combining business and pleasure. Since at times your strong emotions may fluctuate, it is important that you recognize their power and learn to use them in a positive way. Finding creative outlets for self-expression can help you to avoid becoming too intense.

The double influence of Pluto suggests that you are magnetic and courageous, with a fighting spirit. This inner strength also points to a dynamic willpower that enables you to rejuvenate yourself or overcome obstacles. Usually you are friendly but reserved. Although you sometimes feel inner turbulence, outwardly you can remain calm and composed. Just guard against becoming inflexible, as it can work to your detriment.

Through the use of your dynamic appeal, energy, and generosity, you can charm and impress others. Alternating between being aloof or uncommunicative and being sympathetic and kind, you often remain a puzzle to others, as they fail to understand the many different aspects of your personality.

Before the age of twenty-five, you are largely concerned with the development of your sense of personal power and how to handle your deep emotions. After the age of twenty-six, when your progressed Sun moves into Sagittarius, you become more optimistic, with a growing need to be adventurous and seek opportunities. This may lead you to take chances, travel, or study. After the age of fifty-six, when your progressed Sun moves into Capricorn, you develop a more realistic and structured view and desire to be organized in order to actualize your potential.

Your Secret Self

Sociable and friendly, you become enthusiastic and light up when inspiring or entertaining others. Once your dynamic emotions are flowing, you are a positive force to be reckoned with. Ideally, you need direction for this spontaneous creativity. If your powerful emotions become blocked, however, you are liable to moods or can become withdrawn. By using your natural compassion and directing your powers of love toward concern for others, you can create harmony and happiness for yourself and those around you.

Naturally idealistic, you respond well to life's challenges when you have a cause to fight for. As your birthday is identified with dynamic force, however, guard against using this in power tactics, especially when you are disappointed with others. To empower yourself, you may have to learn to combine your intuition with faith. This enables you to achieve a sense of victory and successfully follow your dreams.

Work & Vocation

With your natural flair for people and an instinct for current trends, you can excel in promotion, sales, and media. Besides knowing what the public wants, you also have executive abilities and can succeed in the business world. Having a strong money sense suggests that you can

---

FIXED STAR

Star's name: Princeps, also called Tsieh Kung

Degree position: 2°8'–2°50' Scorpio between the years 1930 and 2000

Magnitude: 3.5

Strength: ★★★★★

Orb: 1°30'

Constellation: Delta Bootes

Applicable days: October 26, 27, 28, 29

Star qualities: Mercury/Saturn

Description: a pale yellow giant star located in the spear shaft of Bootes

---

PRIMARY STAR'S INFLUENCE

Princeps suggests a keen mentality and a studious and profound mind, with a depth of understanding that favors research. This star bestows determination, resourcefulness, and a conservative outlook.

Linked to your Sun's degree, this star imparts prominence in education, science, or legal and government affairs. You have a competitive nature and a daring personality. Your subtle assertiveness and resourceful attitude help you to undertake and succeed with new or untried ideas. You have a reserved nature and will not commit yourself until you are sure where you stand. When you are convinced of the facts, you can be quite outspoken and are unafraid to be direct and stand your ground, as you prefer to be in control.

become an entrepreneur or a philanthropist. Your strong creative expression may also find an outlet through music, the arts, or the world of entertainment. Alternatively, your natural ability to heal others may lead you to the caring or medical profession. This birthday often bestows writing gifts or an interest in education.

Famous people who share your birthday include singer Simon LeBon, violinist Nicolò Paganini, U.S. president Theodore Roosevelt, writers Dylan Thomas and Sylvia Plath, and comedian John Cleese.

Numerology

The number 27 birthdate indicates that you are idealistic and sensitive. Intuitive and analytical, with a fertile and creative mind, you can impress others with your original thoughts. Although at times you appear secretive, rational, or detached, in fact you may be hiding inner tensions. In developing good communication skills, you can overcome a reluctance to express your deeper feelings. Education is essential for number 27 persons, and by developing depth of thought you become more patient and self-disciplined. The subinfluence of the number 10 month indicates that you are original and dramatic. Your pride, determination, and strong morals suggest that you stand by your word. As a fiercely loyal individual, you have the ability to heal or help others rise above difficulties. A need for emotional fulfillment indicates that you can be productive and industrious when you believe in a cause.

• *Positive:* versatile, imaginative, creative, resolute, brave, good understanding, spiritual, inventive, mental strength

• *Negative:* disagreeable, quarrelsome, easily offended, restless, nervous, mistrusting, overemotional, tense

Love & Relationships

Although you are idealistic and faithful, in close relationships you can be possessive and jealous, especially when you feel insecure. As a responsible individual, you respect and admire hardworking people who are dedicated and loyal. Sensitive and a kind friend, you can be supportive and concerned for people's welfare, but avoid being overwhelmed by the problems of others. By learning to stay calm and detached, you can avoid unnecessary heartache.

YOUR SPECIAL SOMEONE

If you are looking for your ideal partner, you might start by looking for someone born on the following days.

Love & friendship: Jan. 8, 11, 12, 29, Feb. 6, 9, 27, Mar. 4, 7, 25, 29, Apr. 2, 5, 23, 27, May 3, 21, 25, 30, June 1, 19, 23, July 17, 21, Aug. 15, 19, 29, Sept. 13, 17, 27, Oct. 11, 15, 20, 25, 29, 30, Nov. 9, 13, 23, 27, 28, Dec. 7, 11, 21, 25, 26

Beneficial: Jan. 13, 30, Feb. 11, 28, Mar. 9, 26, Apr. 7, 24, 30, May 5, 22, 28, June 3, 20, 26, July 1, 18, 24, 29, Aug. 16, 22, 25, Sept. 14, 20, 25, Oct. 12, 18, 23, Nov. 10, 16, 21, Dec. 8, 14, 19

Fatal attractions: Apr. 23, 24, 25, 26, Oct. 30, Nov. 28, Dec. 26

Challenging: Jan. 5, 19, Feb. 3, 17, Mar. 1, 15, Apr. 13, May 11, June 9, 30, July 7, 28, 30, Aug. 5, 26, 28, Sept. 3, 24, 26, Oct. 1, 22, 24, Nov. 20, 22, Dec. 18, 20

Soul mates: Jan. 7, Feb. 5, Mar. 3, Apr. 1, Sept. 30, Oct. 28, Nov. 26, Dec. 24

October 28

A need to fulfill your noble ideals suggests that you are a powerful Scorpio with sensitive feelings. Autonomous and daring, you can achieve much if you develop faith in your abilities and do not lose heart. Being creative and imaginative, you possess an ability to communicate your vision, especially through wisdom and spirituality. With determination and perseverance, you can accomplish something unique and original.

The subinfluence of your decanate ruler, Scorpio, implies that you possess the power to overcome obstacles and reemerge unperturbed. Although you may at times appear vulnerable, your tenacity and dynamic power suggest that as long as you can keep your emotions in check, you can maintain a balanced perspective.

Although you can accomplish much by yourself, you benefit greatly from collaborating or interacting with others. As a humanitarian, you have strong personal morals or aspirations, but you need to avoid a tendency to impose your beliefs on others. Although you are willing to make sacrifices for those you love, you should avoid playing the martyr. You may need to learn how to compromise by remaining compassionate, yet detached.

Up to the age of twenty-four, you are occupied with your emotional sensitivity and need for personal transformation. At the age of twenty-five, when your progressed Sun moves into Sagittarius, there is a turning point that highlights a growing need for freedom and expanding your horizons, whether through travel, education, or your philosophy of life. Another turning point occurs at the age of fifty-five, when your progressed Sun moves into Capricorn. This is likely to bring you a more realistic and pragmatic approach to achieving your goals.

Your Secret Self

On an inner level you possess powerful and dynamic emotions that may not always be obvious from the outside. These may drive you to be constantly initiating new projects and, when channeled productively, can stop you from dwelling in moods or negative emotions. A desire to know what is beneath the surface of people or situations may cause you to delve into deeper and more profound levels of existence.

Highly intuitive, you gradually come to realize the power of love, which can prove to be a potent force in your relationships with others. The magnetic charm that you are able to project can be a great help in your overall success and enable you to inspire people with your charismatic enthusiasm. While you do have a strong interest in money issues, the expression of love and the fulfillment of your grand dreams can be especially important to you.

Work & Vocation

Being both analytical and intuitive in your thinking, you are drawn to careers that use creative thinking. This may include research in areas such as philosophy, science, psychology, or metaphysics. Alternatively, a possible technical aptitude may attract you to occupations such as working with computers or engineering. With your keen intellect and communication skills, you can also be successful as a writer, lecturer, or teacher. Although you possess leadership

FIXED STAR

Star's name: Princeps, also called Tsieh Kung

Degree position: 2°8'–2°50' Scorpio between the years 1930 and 2000

Magnitude: 3.5

Strength: ★★★★★

Orb: 1°30'

Constellation: Delta Bootes

Applicable days: October 26, 27, 28, 29

Star qualities: Mercury/Saturn

Description: a pale yellow giant star located in the spear shaft of Bootes

PRIMARY STAR'S INFLUENCE

Princeps suggests a keen mentality and a studious and profound mind, with a depth of understanding that favors research. This star bestows determination, resourcefulness, and a conservative outlook.

Linked to your Sun's degree, this star imparts prominence in education, science, or legal and government affairs. You have a competitive nature and a daring personality. Your subtle assertiveness and resourceful attitude help you to undertake and succeed with new or untried ideas. You have a reserved nature and will not commit yourself until you are sure where you stand. When you are convinced of the facts, you can be quite outspoken and are unafraid to be direct and stand your ground, as you prefer to be in control.

abilities, you may fare better through realizing the importance of teamwork or partnership. A humanitarian streak can also encourage you to work for the benefit of the community.

Famous people who share your birthday include actresses Julia Roberts and Jane Alexander, computer magnate Bill Gates, actress Joan Plowright, philosopher/writer Desiderius Erasmus, medical researcher Jonas Salk, explorer Captain James Cook, chef Auguste Escoffier, athlete Bruce Jenner, and painter Francis Bacon.

Numerology

Independent and determined, with a pragmatic approach, you are often a law unto yourself. Like a number 1 individual, you are ambitious, direct, and enterprising. An inner conflict between wanting to be independent and wanting to be part of a team is also indicated. Always ready for action and new ventures, you courageously take on life's challenges and, with your eagerness, you can easily inspire others, if not to join you, at least to support you in your latest venture. With a number 28 birthday, you have leadership abilities and can rely on your common sense, logic, and clear thinking. Often you take on responsibilities but can also be overly enthusiastic, impatient, or intolerant. The subinfluence of the number 10 month indicates that you are highly idealistic and sensitive, with strong premonitions or a sixth sense. Although strong-willed and determined, you benefit greatly from partnerships and collaborative efforts. Self-reliant and stubborn, you possess strong convictions, but by learning the art of diplomacy and compromise, you can achieve a great deal.

• *Positive:* compassion, progressive, daring, artistic, creative, idealistic, ambitious, hardworking, stable home life, strong-willed

• *Negative:* daydreamer, unmotivated, lack of compassion, unrealistic, bossy, lack of judgment, aggressive, lack of confidence, too dependent on others, pride

Love & Relationships

A need to be active and a love of variety suggest that you have diverse interests. Although you are an idealistic individual, with firm ideas about love, an unsettled and impatient spirit may sometimes create tension in close relationships. Nevertheless, being dutiful and devoted suggests that you are capable of making great sacrifices for those you love. If you are drawn into unusual relationships, circumstances can change rapidly and you have to adjust.

YOUR SPECIAL SOMEONE

To find long-lasting happiness, security, and a homey environment, you might begin by looking for someone born on one of the following days.

Love & friendship: Jan. 9, 20, 30, Feb. 7, 18, 28, Mar. 5, 16, 26, 30, Apr. 3, 24, 28, May 1, 22, 26, June 20, 24, July 8, 18, 22, 31, Aug. 16, 20, 29, 30, Sept. 14, 18, 27, 28, Oct. 12, 16, 25, 26, 31, Nov. 10, 14, 23, 24, 29, Dec. 8, 12, 21, 22, 27

Beneficial: Jan. 15, 22, 31, Feb. 13, 20, 29, Mar. 11, 18, 27, Apr. 9, 16, 25, May 7, 14, 23, 30, June 5, 12, 21, 28, July 3, 10, 19, 26, 30, Aug. 1, 8, 17, 24, 28, Sept. 6, 15, 22, 26, Oct. 4, 13, 20, 24, Nov. 2, 11, 18, 22, Dec. 9, 16, 20

Fatal attractions: Jan. 11, Feb. 9, Mar. 7, Apr. 5, 24, 25, 26, 27, May 3, June 1, Oct. 31, Nov. 29, Dec. 27

Challenging: Jan. 5, 8, 16, 21, Feb. 3, 6, 14, 19, Mar. 1, 4, 12, 17, Apr. 2, 10, 15, May 8, 13, June 6, 11, July 4, 9, 29, Aug. 2, 7, 27, Sept. 5, 25, Oct. 3, 23, Nov. 1, 21, Dec. 19

Soul mates: Jan. 13, Feb. 11, Mar. 9, Apr. 7, May 5, June 3, July 1, Aug. 31, Sept. 29, Oct. 27, Nov. 25, Dec. 23

October 29

♏ Idealistic and original, you are an inspired and warmhearted Scorpio with a strong sixth sense. With a generous nature and sociable inclinations, your easygoing manner can gain you many friends and make you popular. Multitalented and creative, you may also possess unique qualities that can impress others.

The subinfluence of your decanate ruler, Scorpio, implies that your insight and powerful perceptions can make you a natural investigator or lead you to explore the mysteries of life. Although alert and discriminating, you may sometimes be too intense with your crucial observations. Intuitive, with an inner strength, you have the ability to transform yourself through difficult situations. As a humanitarian, you are often kind and compassionate but may be prone to moods or mental restlessness.

When you recognize the power of compassion and love, you can create harmony and achieve inner peace or balance. Although you want love and comfort, by nature you are adventurous, with a restless streak. You like to broaden your horizons and be free, yet a need for emotional security suggests that you fare better when not isolated or alone. Although you are full of good intentions, a tendency to think that you know best implies that you may at times interfere in the affairs of others in an attempt to help. Nevertheless, you are loyal to and supportive of family members and are proud of your home.

Before the age of twenty-three, you are largely concerned with the development of your sense of personal power and how to handle your strong feelings. After the age of twenty-four, when your progressed Sun moves into Sagittarius, you become more optimistic and have a growing need to be adventurous; this may lead you to take more chances, travel, or study. After the age of fifty-four, when your progressed Sun moves into Capricorn, you become more realistic and organized in order to achieve your goals.

Your Secret Self

A desire for truth, knowledge, and power can enhance your abilities for creative thinking and problem solving as well as stimulating possible explorations into philosophical or metaphysical realms. Basically a positive thinker, you work better when you have a plan or strategy in place and are constructively busy. Shrewd and pragmatic, you have a natural flair for putting the knowledge you obtain to practical use, although you may need to avoid scattering your energies.

Along with an inventive mind that is capable of flashes of genius, you have a strong need for self-expression that may manifest socially or creatively. Unfortunately, you may also be prone to worry or indecision, particularly about material situations, so it is important to keep situations light. Your quick wit can make you attractive to others, but be sure to use your critical skills constructively.

Work & Vocation

Being a natural investigator, you are usually interested in delving beneath the surface, whether of people or of situations. This can suggest a possible interest in psychology, science, or meta-

FIXED STAR

Star's name: Princeps, also called Tsieh Kung

Degree position: 2°8'–2°50' Scorpio between the years 1930 and 2000

Magnitude: 3.5

Strength: ★★★★

Orb: 1°30'

Constellation: Delta Bootes

Applicable days: October 26, 27, 28, 29

Star qualities: Mercury/Saturn

Description: a pale yellow giant star located in the spear shaft of Bootes

PRIMARY STAR'S INFLUENCE

Princeps suggests a keen mentality and a studious and profound mind, with a depth of understanding that favors research. This star bestows determination, resourcefulness, and a conservative outlook.

Linked to your Sun's degree, this star imparts prominence in education, science, or legal and government affairs. You have a competitive nature and a daring personality. Your subtle assertiveness and resourceful attitude help you to undertake and succeed with new or untried ideas. You have a reserved nature and will not commit yourself until you are sure where you stand. When you are convinced of the facts, you can be quite outspoken and are unafraid to be direct and stand your ground, as you prefer to be in control.

physics. A desire for harmony may also attract you to music or healing. Although a part of you enjoys doing nothing, your strong sense of responsibility usually moves you into action. Working cooperatively with others in a team or partnership may prove particularly beneficial for you. Alternatively, if in business, you usually work better when using your people skills. A caring or humanitarian streak may draw you to charitable institutions or counseling.

Famous people who share your birthday include actresses Winona Ryder and Kate Jackson, actor Richard Dreyfuss, singers Melba Moore and Cleo Laine, writer James Boswell, and astronomer Edmund Halley.

Numerology

As a number 29 individual, you have a powerful personality and extraordinary potential. You are highly intuitive, sensitive, and emotional. Inspiration is the key to your success story, and without it you may experience lack of purpose. Although you are a true dreamer, the extreme sides of your nature indicate that you may have to guard against alternating moods. If you trust your innermost feelings and open your heart to others, you can overcome your tendency to worry or use your mind as protective armor. It would be best to utilize your creative thoughts to achieve something special and unique that can motivate or be of service to others. The subinfluence of the number 10 month indicates that although you have a desire to be first or independent, you benefit from working in collaboration with others. Usually you are ambitious, with remarkable ideas; however, you need to be decisive by remaining determined and realistic. When you are positive and full of enthusiasm, you are adaptable, innovative, and courageous, with plenty of energy.

• *Positive:* inspired, balanced, inner peace, generous, successful, creative, intuitive, mystical, powerful dreams, worldly, faith

• *Negative:* unfocused, insecure, nervous, selfish, vain, moody, difficult, extremist, isolated, overly sensitive

Love & Relationships

Although you are affectionate and self-sacrificing, at times you may become too involved in the lives of those you care for. Charming and idealistic, you are a kind and sentimental individual who is willing to help someone less fortunate than yourself. Although you are caring, you like to have financial security and be in the company of wealthy or influential people. By staying balanced and easygoing, you can create a harmonious atmosphere and allow others to feel secure and loved.

YOUR SPECIAL SOMEONE

You might find a partner who will understand your sensitivity and need for love among those born on the following dates.

Love & friendship: Jan. 10, 12, 15, 25, 28, Feb. 10, 13, 23, 26, Mar. 8, 10, 11, 21, 24, 31, Apr. 6, 9, 19, 22, 29, May 4, 7, 17, 20, 27, June 2, 5, 15, 18, 25, July 2, 3, 13, 16, 23, Aug. 1, 11, 14, 21, 31, Sept. 9, 12, 19, 29, Oct. 7, 10, 17, 27, Nov. 5, 8, 15, 25, Dec. 3, 6, 13, 23

Beneficial: Jan. 12, 23, 26, Feb. 10, 21, 24, Mar. 8, 19, 22, 28, Apr. 6, 17, 20, 26, May 4, 15, 18, 24, June 2, 13, 22, 16, July 11, 14, 20, 31, Aug. 9, 12, 18, 29, Sept. 7, 10, 16, 27, Oct. 5, 8, 14, 25, Nov. 3, 6, 12, 23, Dec. 1, 4, 10, 21

Fatal attractions: Apr. 25, 26, 27, 28, Nov. 30, Dec. 28

Challenging: Jan. 17, 18, 21, Feb. 15, 16, 19, Mar. 13, 14, 17, 29, Apr. 11, 12, 15, 27, May 9, 10, 13, 25, June 7, 8, 11, 23, July 5, 6, 9, 21, 30, Aug. 3, 4, 7, 19, 28, Sept. 1, 2, 5, 17, 26, Oct. 3, 15, 24, Nov. 1, 13, 22, Dec. 11, 20

Soul mates: Jan. 24, Feb. 22, Mar. 20, Apr. 18, 30, May 16, 28, June 14, 26, July 12, 24, Aug. 10, 22, Sept. 8, 20, Oct. 6, 18, Nov. 4, 16, Dec. 2, 14

October 30

♏ Charming and friendly, with a restless heart, you are a sensitive Scorpio who is versatile and adaptable. Since you have a desire for a full and varied life, you yearn for different experiences and new adventures. This need for personal freedom also suggests that it may be hard for you to find lasting satisfaction or that fluctuating moods can bring changing attitudes. Creative and colorful, you can usually communicate your ideas in a dramatic way.

The subinfluence of your decanate ruler, Scorpio, adds to your inner strength. Idealistic and sensitive, you can be affectionate, yet secretive. Your direct approach and sharp comments indicate that you can be a good satirist. Remember, however, that your criticism can be hurtful as well as amusing. When challenged, you can show your opponent a daring and bold front. Your true tenacious spirit usually comes to the fore if you feel threatened or insecure.

Although others see you as an exciting and stimulating companion, a quest for emotional fulfillment implies that you usually dislike restrictions and prefer to ignore limitations. Looking for ways to achieve emotional satisfaction, you often turn to travel and find that a change of atmosphere helps you to relax and feel optimistic. Even though work seems to interfere with your ideas of freedom, rewards usually come from being loyal, dutiful, and emotionally responsible.

Before the age of twenty-four, you are concerned with your emotional sensitivity and personal transformation. At the age of twenty-three, when your progressed Sun moves into Sagittarius, there is a turning point that emphasizes a growing need for more expansion and optimism in your life. This may come through mental development, education, or travel. Another turning point occurs at the age of fifty-three, when your progressed Sun moves into Capricorn; this begins to highlight practical issues of persistence, dedication, and realism.

Fixed Star

Star's name: Khambalia, also called Khamblia

Degree position: 5°53'–6°49' Scorpio between the years 1930 and 2000

Magnitude: 4

Strength: ★★★★

Orb: 1°30'

Constellation: Lambda Virgo

Applicable days: October 30, 31, November 1

Star qualities: Mercury/Mars

Description: a small white star located on the left foot of Virgo

PRIMARY STAR'S INFLUENCE

Khambalia imparts a quick mind and good debating skills. This star indicates changing circumstances, which might include unexpected gains. Khambalia's influence suggests that you have a pragmatic outlook and an inclination toward higher learning and education. Although friendly and sociable, often you may appear impersonal.

Linked to your Sun's degree, Khambalia offers success in business or politics and public office. You may become a specialist with unique abilities in your chosen profession. Occasionally this star can also bestow some unusual and outstanding talents that can bring changes in work and employment.

Your Secret Self

With your high ideals, you may feel that your sensitivity is not wasted when you are able to be of help to others. Since you can also be very businesslike, this powerful combination implies that you are a compassionate pragmatist. However, if you become disillusioned with others or too restless and impatient, you can be prone to channel your emotional sensitivities into escapism rather than confront your challenges directly or develop creative outlets for yourself.

Since you also possess a strong spirit of enterprise, you are usually enthusiastic, optimistic, and adventurous, and may possess a dynamic approach to satisfying your material needs. You may wish to channel your spiritual and creative forces into writing or turn your fine ideas into something tangible. Being very instinctive and capable of deep thought, you form instant opinions of people that are usually right. Often mentally quick and curious, with a unique sense of humor, you are good company and can be very entertaining.

Work & Vocation

Whatever career you undertake, it is necessary for you to have variety and change to prevent you from becoming bored. Although your home is important to you, if your work involves travel, then so much the better. Your magnetism and charm can certainly help you in activities dealing with the public. Usually, the bigger the enterprise you are involved with, the more you enjoy it. Possessing a talent with words and the ability to communicate ideas, you may particularly be attracted to writing, the media, or politics. Often this birthday suggests a talent for success in the theater or film.

Famous people who share your birthday include film director Louis Malle, body builder George Atlas, singer/songwriter Grace Slick, explorer Christopher Columbus, actor Henry Winkler, and writers Ezra Pound and Paul Valery.

Numerology

Creativity, friendliness, and sociability are just some of the attributes associated with the number 30 birthday. Ambitious, with creative potential, you can take ideas and expand them in your own dramatic style. You enjoy the good life and can be exceptionally charismatic and outgoing. Since you possess strong feelings, being in love or contented is a vital requirement. In your pursuit of happiness, avoid being lazy, overindulgent, impatient, or jealous, as these may cause you to experience emotional instability. Among those with number 30 birthdays, many will find recognition or fame, especially musicians, actors, and entertainers. The subinfluence of the number 10 month indicates that you need activity and excitement, but by being self-reliant and determined, you can achieve good results. Since you are likely to be autonomous by nature, you want to have the freedom to pursue your many interests. By remaining resolute and focused, you can turn your wild dreams into a reality.

• *Positive:* fun-loving, loyal, friendly, good synthesizer, talent with words, creative, lucky
• *Negative:* lazy, obstinate, erratic, impatient, insecure, indifferent, scatters energy

Love & Relationships

Although friendly, you can also be secretive and like to keep emotional control. You admire creative people who are focused and hardworking. Since you dislike monotony and can be indecisive about your feelings, you need to take your time to form long-term relationships. A need for personal freedom suggests that if a relationship gets into a rut or feels restrictive, you look out for a way to escape. Often changing circumstances bring a change of heart. Emotional restlessness implies that before you find your ideal partner you are likely to have many short-lived relationships. Your warm heart ensures your social success.

YOUR SPECIAL SOMEONE

You might start to look for an exciting partner who will keep you on your toes among those born on the following days.

Love & friendship: Jan. 6, 11, 14, 15, Feb. 4, 9, 12, Mar. 2, 7, 10, 11, 28, Apr. 5, 8, 26, 30, May 3, 6, 24, 28, June 1, 4, 22, 26, July 2, 3, 20, 24, Aug. 18, 22, Sept. 16, 20, 30, Oct. 14, 18, 28, Nov. 12, 16, 26, Dec. 10, 14, 24

Beneficial: Jan. 20, 24, Feb. 18, 22, Mar. 16, 20, 29, Apr. 14, 18, 27, May 12, 16, 25, June 10, 14, 23, 29, July 8, 12, 21, 27, Aug. 6, 10, 19, 25, 30, Sept. 4, 8, 17, 23, 28, Oct. 2, 6, 15, 21, 26, Nov. 4, 13, 19, 24, Dec. 2, 11, 17, 22

Fatal attractions: Apr. 26, 27, 28, 29, Aug. 31, Sept. 29, Oct. 27, Nov. 25, Dec. 23

Challenging: Jan. 22, 23, 27, Feb. 20, 21, 25, Mar. 18, 19, 23, Apr. 16, 17, 21, May 14, 15, 19, June 12, 13, 17, July 10, 11, 15, 31, Aug. 8, 9, 13, 29, Sept. 6, 7, 11, 27, Oct. 4, 5, 9, 25, Nov. 2, 3, 7, 23, Dec. 1, 5, 21

Soul mates: Jan. 23, Feb. 21, Mar. 19, Apr. 17, 29, May 15, 27, June 13, 25, July 11, 23, Aug. 9, 21, Sept. 7, 19, Oct. 5, 17, Nov. 3, 15, Dec. 1, 13

October 31

♏ Determined and productive, you are a pragmatic Scorpio with fixed views and a resolute nature. Although you possess strong feelings, by staying optimistic and putting on the charm you usually get your own way. Security-conscious and ambitious, you often take on responsibilities, but you may need to guard against overextending yourself.

The subinfluence of your decanate ruler, Scorpio, adds to your inner strength. Your direct approach and common sense indicate that you are a good strategist with an ability to communicate your ideas. As you are creative and idealistic, with a fine mind, self-expression is of prime importance. If you become preoccupied with self-fulfillment, however, you may let anxiety hamper your great potential and you may descend into inertia or laziness.

As someone who wants to build strong foundations, you are a real asset to others. Dedicated, you are willing to help people, especially if you feel inspired by a cause or an idea. Visionary and sensitive, you have a strong sense of justice, and your sincerity indicates that you are honest with your feelings. Your warm heart, however, can turn into stone if you feel threatened or cheated. When challenged, you can show your opponent a daring and bold front. Your true tenacious spirit usually comes to the fore if you feel intimidated or insecure.

Up to the age of twenty-one, you are concerned with emotional transformations in your life. After the age of twenty-two, when your progressed Sun moves into Sagittarius, you have a growing need for freedom and to expand your horizons, whether through education, your philosophy of life, or contact with foreign people or places. Another turning point occurs at the age of fifty-two, when your progressed Sun moves into Capricorn. This is likely to bring you a more serious, disciplined, and security-conscious approach to life.

FIXED STAR

Star's name: Khambalia, also called Khamblia

Degree position: 5°53'–6°49' Scorpio between the years 1930 and 2000

Magnitude: 4

Strength: ★★★★

Orb: 1°30'

Constellation: Lambda Virgo

Applicable days: October 30, 31, November 1

Star qualities: Mercury/Mars

Description: a small white star located on the left foot of Virgo

PRIMARY STAR'S INFLUENCE

Khambalia imparts a quick mind and good debating skills. This star indicates changing circumstances, which might include unexpected gains. Khambalia's influence suggests that you have a pragmatic outlook and an inclination toward higher learning and education. Although friendly and sociable, often you may appear impersonal.

Linked to your Sun's degree, Khambalia offers success in business, politics, or public office. You may become a specialist with unique abilities in your chosen profession. Occasionally this star can also bestow some unusual and outstanding talents that can bring changes in work and employment.

Your Secret Self

Beneath your easygoing exterior, you are ambitious and hardworking. When motivated or dedicated to a goal or purpose, you can be resolute in achieving your aims. Practical, you seek security and work better when you have a plan for what you want to achieve in the future. A sixth sense, particularly regarding material matters, bestows on you a shrewd sense of values and a rapid understanding of people. As well as being quick to see opportunities, you can also be a good organizer once determined. With your strong desires, however, you may have to be careful that excesses in any form do not dissipate your forces.

Frank and honest, you have a sharp and quick intelligence, good judgment, and the ability to overcome all obstacles if you apply self-discipline. Your birthday shows great potential for success in work, and usually your challenges are not financial. If you avoid the responsibility needed to fulfill your destiny, however, you may not be able to satisfy your strong need to build something of permanent value.

Work & Vocation

A capable and hard worker, you are suited for careers that can utilize your warm heart and practical approach. With a desire for social reform, you may fare particularly well in education, counseling, or philanthropic activities. With a desire to expand your mind, you are often attracted to psychology, philosophy, medicine, and the development of religious belief. Alternatively, your pragmatic nature and desire to build something of worth may attract you to the construction industry. A good parent and organizer, you enjoy being productive. A desire for self-expression may attract you to writing, literature, or performing. Whatever career you choose, your emotional honesty, fine mind, and organizational abilities can help you find success.

Famous people who share your birthday include painter Jan Vermeer, actor Michael Landon, TV newsperson Dan Rather, folksinger Tom Paxton, writer John Keats, TV newsperson Jane Pauley, and Republic of China president Chiang Kai-shek.

Numerology

Strong willpower, determination, and an emphasis on self-expression are indicated by the number 31 birthday. You often combine your intuition and practical skill to make the right decisions. With a number 31 birthday, you have original ideas, a good sense of form, and abilities to succeed in business if you take your time and follow a practical plan of action. As you are probably hardworking, time for love and having fun is crucial to you. The subinfluence of the number 10 month indicates that you are self-reliant and restless, with a need for variety and an active life. A tendency to think that the grass is greener on the other side of the fence can undermine your determination. Discover your objectives and stick to them. New opportunities or lucky breaks are also suggested by this birthday, and you can be successful in turning your leisure-time pursuits into profitable ventures.

• *Positive:* lucky, creative, original, builder, constructive, never give up, practical, good conversationalist, responsible

• *Negative:* insecure, impatient, suspicious, easily discouraged, lack of ambition, selfish, stubborn

Love & Relationships

Charming and friendly, you are group-oriented and enjoy being hospitable. A dislike of being alone suggests that you seek the company of others. If you overcome a fear of sharing your love and affection with someone else, you will probably find out how beneficial partnerships and collaborative ventures can be. Discriminating and intuitive, you often recognize other people's potential, although you guard against becoming overly dependent by learning to be happy with your lot.

YOUR SPECIAL SOMEONE

You might find a faithful and reliable lover or partner among those born on the following dates.

Love & friendship: Jan. 7, 12, 15, 16, 23, Feb. 5, 10, 13, Mar. 3, 8, 11, 12, 19, 29, Apr. 1, 6, 9, 27, May 4, 7, 25, 29, June 2, 5, 23, 27, July 3, 11, 21, 25, Aug. 1, 19, 23, Sept. 17, 21, Oct. 15, 19, 29, Nov. 13, 17, 27, Dec. 11, 15, 18, 25

Beneficial: Jan. 21, 25, Feb. 19, 23, Mar. 17, 21, 30, Apr. 15, 19, 28, May 13, 17, 26, June 11, 15, 24, 30, July 9, 13, 22, 28, Aug. 7, 11, 20, 26, 31, Sept. 5, 9, 18, 24, 29, Oct. 3, 7, 16, 22, 29, Nov. 1, 5, 14, 20, 25, Dec. 3, 12, 18, 23

Fatal attractions: Apr. 27, 28, 29, 30

Challenging: Jan. 5, 8, 28, Feb. 3, 6, 26, Mar. 1, 4, 24, Apr. 2, 22, May 20, June 18, July 16, Aug. 14, 30, Sept. 12, 28, 30, Oct. 10, 26, 28, Nov. 8, 24, 26, Dec. 6, 22, 24

Soul mates: Jan. 4, 10, Feb. 2, 8, Mar. 6, Apr. 4, May 2

November 1

♏ Independent and imaginative, you are a Scorpio who wants freedom. Charming, with a flair for people, you make friends easily and usually have an active life. Although gregarious, you tend to be a person with a sensitive soul and powerful emotions who needs to learn how to share or to be less self-centered.

With your insight, strong sense of justice, convictions, and sharp intellect, you like to speak your mind. Although you usually like to be in control, when fighting for others' rights you are idealistic and understanding, showing your true benevolent nature.

The subinfluence of your decanate ruler, Scorpio, implies that you possess stamina and determination. Inquisitive, you like to be honest and reveal the truth even though it may sometimes be unpleasant. When pressured or threatened, you can show your opponents a daring and bold front as well as your true tenacious spirit.

The desire for the good life usually motivates you to achieve, and if inspired by an ideal or a cause, you have the power to lead others. By not harboring resentment and learning to be responsible and considerate, you can win others' admiration and support. Although your direct approach and sharp comments show a side of you that is fearless and resilient, you can also be sympathetic and affectionate.

After the age of twenty-one, when your progressed Sun moves into Sagittarius, you become more optimistic and have a growing need for adventure or expansion. This may lead you to take more chances or explore life through travel or education. After the age of fifty-one, when your progressed Sun moves into Capricorn, you become more realistic, organized, and hardworking in order to achieve your goals.

Your Secret Self

With your charitable and altruistic approach to life, you are often in the position of supporting the underdog or helping and advising others. Frustration and disappointment may be a challenge, but by practicing patience and persistence and keeping a positive mental attitude, you are guaranteed well-earned success. Your agile mind allows you to grasp ideas very quickly, so education and acquiring knowledge can be a vital part of your self-confidence.

Creative and intuitive, you possess enhanced social or artistic skills and a need for self-expression. Your charisma, ability to be persuasive and charming, and intellectual brightness mark you out as an individual with something to say. You may be drawn to the study of philosophy, religion, or metaphysics, which can help you overcome a tendency to think negatively. Practical yet idealistic, you need to constantly challenge yourself in new areas to build up your sense of purpose, avoid inertia, and bring out the best of your remarkable potential.

Work & Vocation

An ability to promote an idea, plus your organizational skills, may lead you to excel in business, science, or law. Your strong desire to take the lead may, alternatively, take you to the world of sports. Your flair for business also suggests that you can achieve success in sales, promotion, banking, or real estate. Your need to explore and expand may urge you to travel or

FIXED STAR

Star's name: Khambalia, also called Khamblia

Degree position: 5°53'–6°49' Scorpio between the years 1930 and 2000

Magnitude: 4

Strength: ★★★★

Orb: 1°30'

Constellation: Lambda Virgo

Applicable days: October 30, 31, November 1

Star qualities: Mercury/Mars

Description: a small white star located on the left foot of Virgo

PRIMARY STAR'S INFLUENCE

Khambalia imparts a quick mind and good debating skills. This star indicates changing circumstances, which might include unexpected gains. Khambalia's influence suggests that you have a pragmatic outlook and an inclination toward higher learning and education. Although friendly and sociable, often you may appear impersonal.

Linked to your Sun's degree, Khambalia offers success in business, politics, or public office. You may become a specialist with unique abilities in your chosen profession. Occasionally this star can also bestow some unusual and outstanding talents that can bring changes in work and employment.

• *Positive:* dedication, higher learning, polished logic, power of thought

• *Negative:* argumentative, restlessness, unreliability

work abroad. Creative and imaginative, you may be drawn to careers such as writing, acting, or music and the arts. Equally, with a natural ability to deal with the public, you may be inspired to work for the benefit of others in psychology, education, or social work. Similarly, your special insight and compassion may draw you toward counseling or the healing world, in either the medical or alternative health professions.

Famous people who share your birthday include baseball player Fernando Valenzuela, writer Stephen Crane, chess champion Alexander Alekhine, golfer Gary Player, critic Edward Said, and musician Lyle Lovett.

Numerology

A great desire to be first and independent is suggested by your birthdate. As a number 1 individual, you are more inclined to be innovative and courageous, with plenty of energy. Often there is a need to establish a strong identity and develop assertiveness. The pioneering spirit indicated here encourages you to strike out alone. These self-starting forces can also stimulate you to develop executive or leadership abilities. Full of enthusiasm and original ideas, you can show others the way forward. With a number 1 birthday, you may also need to learn that the world does not revolve around you; avoid an inclination to be self-centered or dictatorial. The subinfluence of the number 11 month indicates that you are idealistic and full of ideas. Never described as boring, although sometimes opinionated, you are entertaining and interested in many diverse issues. For fulfillment, you need to be creative and innovative. Learn to focus on your goals and avoid scattering your energies.

• *Positive:* leadership, creative, progressive, forceful, optimistic, strong convictions, competitive, independent, gregarious

• *Negative:* overbearing, jealous, egotistical, too proud, antagonistic, lack of restraint, selfish, unstable, impatient

Love & Relationships

Magnetic and charismatic, you can make friends easily and have a way with people. Often attractive to the opposite sex and in demand, you may have difficulty in choosing a partner. As you have high expectations from relationships, you usually want someone who is protective of your interests, but you may need to avoid jealousy, possessiveness, and suspicious behavior. Nevertheless, being very sensitive, you usually do not like to hurt other people's feelings.

YOUR SPECIAL SOMEONE

For love and happiness, you may wish to choose a partner from among those born on the following dates.

Love & friendship: Jan. 3, 5, 9, 10, 18, 19, Feb. 1, 3, 7, 16, 17, Mar. 1, 5, 6, 14, 15, 31, Apr. 3, 12, 13, 29, May 1, 10, 11, 27, 29, June 8, 9, 25, 27, July 6, 7, 23, 25, 31, Aug. 4, 5, 21, 23, 29, Sept. 2, 3, 19, 21, 27, 30, Oct. 1, 17, 19, 25, 28, Dec. 13, 15, 21, 24

Beneficial: Jan. 1, 6, 17, Feb. 4, 15, Mar. 2, 13, Apr. 11, May 9, June 7, July 5, Aug. 3, Sept. 1, Oct. 31, Nov. 29, Dec. 27

Fatal attractions: Jan. 6, 7, 8, Apr. 29, 30, May 1

Challenging: Jan. 2, 16, Feb. 14, Mar. 12, Apr. 10, May 8, June 6, July 4, Aug. 2, Dec. 30

Soul mates: Jan. 11, 31, Feb. 9, 29, Mar. 7, 27, Apr. 5, 25, May 3, 23, June 1, 21, July 19, Aug. 17, Sept. 15, Oct. 13, Nov. 11, Dec. 9

November 2

♏ Sensitive and restless, you are a Scorpio with a dynamic personality and a need for variety. Usually life has a lot in store for you, and before settling down, you may experience numerous transformations. An innate restlessness implies that you can become easily bored in a monotonous atmosphere, while diversity can stimulate your mind.

If financial situations leave you dissatisfied, you are likely to search for better prospects. This urge to make a fresh start suggests that you may sometimes need to leave your past behind in order to move forward. For peace of mind and security, however, it would be advisable to consider long-term plans and investments.

Friendly and gregarious, you need to be involved in all sorts of social activities. The subinfluence of your decanate ruler, Scorpio, suggests that although you are tenacious, with power, determination, and drive, your gentle side shows your vulnerability. If these extremes become too excessive, your relationships may suffer.

You are an idealist, and at times your moods and sarcasm can clash with your good intentions and efforts. Receptive and clever, you learn quickly and have an instinctive understanding of others. By staying open-minded and optimistic, rather than becoming insecure, you come to learn that if you do not succeed the first time, you can always try again.

After the age of twenty, when your progressed Sun moves into Sagittarius, you feel a growing need for more expansion and optimism in your life. This may come through mental development, education, or travel, or you may have a desire to seek for truth or a philosophy in life. Another turning point occurs at the age of fifty, when your progressed Sun moves into Capricorn, highlighting the importance of order, structure, and realism in achieving your goals.

FIXED STAR

Star's name: Acrux

Degree position: 10°54'–11°50' Scorpio between the years 1930 and 2000

Magnitude: 1

Strength: ★★★★★★★★★

Orb: 2°30'

Constellation: Alpha Crux

Applicable days: November 2, 3, 4, 5, 6, 7

Star qualities: Jupiter

Description: a blue-white triple star, the brightest star in the Southern Cross

PRIMARY STAR'S INFLUENCE

Acrux bestows a love of knowledge, harmony, and justice. This star imparts an interest in philosophy, metaphysics, and astrology as well as granting psychic abilities. You have an inquisitive mind and probably an insatiable appetite for books or a desire to travel. Acrux may lead you toward research and education, the social sciences, philosophy, and religion.

Linked to your Sun's degree, Acrux suggests a sensitive and sentimental nature. This star imparts broadminded humanitarian beliefs, and you may be a seeker of justice. You may become a leader in your profession and can excel or gain a high position in affairs that concern humankind.

• Positive: justice, love toward your fellow man, compassion

• Negative: revenge, injustice, lack of feelings

Your Secret Self

Generous and broad-minded, you are intelligent and resourceful, and you like to keep busy. Although you may have an extravagant streak, money and security can often be a motivating factor to get you moving. However, a natural humanitarianism also gives you a strong interest in people and enables you to maintain your sense of perspective. By staying as detached as possible, you are able to avoid personal frustration or disappointment.

Sociable, with creative ideas, you may be happiest when expressing yourself. Your intuitive feelings are usually right and can often help you quickly judge others. At other times, you may suffer from an innate self-doubt that comes from not being certain you are making the right decisions. Nevertheless, you have a way with people and can be a fun companion, entertaining others with your wit and astute observations.

Work & Vocation

Although hardworking and ambitious, you have a love of variety that points to a career involving constant change. A fine intellect and shrewd business sense can help you succeed in finance, sales, or law. With your natural diplomacy, you may fare equally well in careers such as media, public relations, or arbitration. Alternatively, your sensitivity, imagination, and vision may find an outlet in music, drama, or photography. Being an idealist and a good psychologist, you may be equally drawn to therapy or fighting for a cause. Optionally, careers involving sport or leisure can be excellent outlets for your energy and drive.

Famous people who share your birthday include actor Burt Lancaster, writer Shere Hite, the Aga Khan III, pioneer Daniel Boone, actress Stephanie Powers, musician Keith Emerson, French queen Marie Antoinette, singer/songwriter k.d. lang, and commentator Patrick Buchanan.

Numerology

Sensitivity and a strong need to be part of a group are suggested by a number 2 birthday. Adaptable and understanding, you enjoy cooperative activities where you can experience interaction with others. In your attempt to please those you like, you may run the risk of becoming overly dependent. Nevertheless, by developing confidence, you can overcome the tendency to be easily hurt by the action and criticism of others. The subinfluence of the number 11 month indicates that you can express yourself and inspire others with your high ideals. Being innovative and having an interest in social reforms indicate that you need to be in the forefront of contemporary social groups. By persevering and being practical, you can attain your goals and objectives. Avoid taking on too many responsibilities or doing more than your fair share for other people.

• *Positive:* good partnerships, gentle, tactful, receptive, intuitive, considerate, harmonious, agreeable, ambassador of goodwill

• *Negative:* suspicious, lack of confidence, subservient, oversensitive, selfish, easily hurt, moody, deceitful

Love & Relationships

Imaginative and clever, you need to surround yourself with people who can inspire and motivate you. Secretive, you may sometimes be too reserved or shy to express your true feelings. Nevertheless, being sociable and entertaining, you have many friends and can be an interesting and amusing companion. Your close relationships are very important to you, so you are usually willing to work hard to make them a success.

YOUR SPECIAL SOMEONE

If you are looking for your ideal partner, you might find greater stability in love and friendships with someone born on one of the following dates.

Love & friendship: Jan. 2, 6, 10, 20, 26, 29, Feb. 4, 8, 18, 24, 27, Mar. 2, 6, 16, 25, 28, 30, Apr. 4, 14, 23, 26, 28, 30, May 2, 12, 21, 24, 26, 28, 30, June 10, 19, 22, 24, 26, 28, July 8, 14, 17, 20, 22, 24, 26, Aug. 6, 15, 18, 20, 22, 24, Sept. 4, 13, 16, 18, 20, 22, Oct. 2, 11, 14, 16, 18, 20, Nov. 9, 12, 14, 16, 18, Dec. 7, 10, 12, 14, 16

Beneficial: Jan. 7, 13, 18, 28, Feb. 5, 11, 16, 26, Mar. 3, 9, 14, 24, Apr. 1, 7, 12, 22, May 5, 10, 20, June 3, 8, 18, July 1, 6, 16, Aug. 4, 14, Sept. 2, 12, 30, Oct. 10, 28, Nov. 8, 26, 30, Dec. 6, 24, 28

Fatal attractions: Jan. 25, Feb. 23, Mar. 21, Apr. 19, 30, May 12, 17, June 15, July 13, Aug. 11, Sept. 9, Oct. 7, Nov. 5, Dec. 3

Challenging: Jan. 3, 17, Feb. 1, 15, Mar. 13, Apr. 11, May 9, 30, June 7, 28, July 5, 26, 29, Aug. 3, 24, 27, Sept. 1, 22, 25, Oct. 20, 23, Nov. 18, 21, Dec. 16, 19

Soul mates: Jan. 18, Feb. 16, Mar. 14, Apr. 12, May 10, 29, June 8, 27, July 6, 25, Aug. 4, 23, Sept. 2, 21, Oct. 19, Nov. 17, Dec. 15

November 3

℆ Although you often have a pragmatic approach to life, you are a sensitive and imaginative Scorpio. Usually determined, with a strong need for self-expression, you can combine practical skills with your creative talents. Friendly and sociable, you enjoy the company of others and can be very entertaining.

The subinfluence of your decanate ruler, Pisces, suggests that although you are sensible, learning to trust your instincts or first impressions can help you overcome your doubts and indecision. Neptune's influence grants you great inner vision, psychic abilities, and receptivity. Although you can be loyal and loving, you may have to guard against a tendency to be stubborn.

As a perfectionist who is talented and idealistic, you usually take pride in your work and add a touch of individualism to whatever you do. By avoiding the worry and emotional insecurity to which you are often prey, you will be able to execute your obligations to your satisfaction. Use charm and witty repartee rather than jealousy and sarcastic remarks when you want to put your views across.

You are often blessed with good economic circumstances, but if you do find yourself short of funds, your troubles are usually short-lived. Although your financial prospects are favorable, a strong emphasis on work implies that through perseverance and concentrated effort, you can take advantage of the many opportunities that come your way.

After the age of nineteen, when your progressed Sun moves into Sagittarius, you become more optimistic and have a growing need for a more expansive outlook; this may lead you to broaden your horizons, seek truth, travel, or study. After the age of forty-nine, when your progressed Sun moves into Capricorn, you become more practical, realistic, and organized in order to achieve our goals.

Your Secret Self

Although you project a strong image, an inner restlessness suggests that you need patience and must face the challenge of finding harmony within yourself. Although you have a pragmatic approach to life, a need for adventure and variety can lead you to explore new horizons, whether mentally or emotionally. If your powerful feelings become repressed, however, you may find yourself dissatisfied and escape through fantasy or self-indulgence as a form of compensation.

With your warm heart and sympathy, you can often sense the feelings of others. Your high ideals bring a desire for love and affection that may find creative outlets through the arts or spirituality. A need for personal freedom, however, can bring about changing attitudes or make you prone to fluctuating moods. Fortunately, your magnetic charm and acute perceptions can win you many favors and be keys to outstanding success.

Work & Vocation

Your birthday shows excellent opportunities for powerful enterprise and financial success if only you put in the necessary work. Ambitious, with negotiation skills, you are usually able to

FIXED STAR

Star's name: Acrux

Degree position: 10°54'–11°50' Scorpio between the years 1930 and 2000

Magnitude: 1

Strength: ★★★★★★★★★

Orb: 2°30'

Constellation: Alpha Crux

Applicable days: November 2, 3, 4, 5, 6, 7

Star qualities: Jupiter

Description: a blue-white triple star, the brightest star in the Southern Cross

PRIMARY STAR'S INFLUENCE

Acrux bestows a love of knowledge, harmony, and justice. This star imparts an interest in philosophy, metaphysics, and astrology as well as granting psychic abilities. You have an inquisitive mind and probably an insatiable appetite for books or a desire to travel. Acrux may lead you toward research and education, the social sciences, philosophy, and religion.

Linked to your Sun's degree, Acrux suggests a sensitive and sentimental nature. This star imparts broad-minded humanitarian beliefs, and you may be a seeker of justice. You may become a leader in your profession and can excel or gain a high position in affairs that concern humankind.

• *Positive:* justice, love toward your fellow man, compassion

• *Negative:* revenge, injustice, lack of feelings

strike a good deal and get value for your money, although you may have to avoid becoming stuck in a routine. With an innate practicality, you like to create method and order, so having a plan for your big visions is vital. Creative, with a natural talent with words, you are likely to also have latent writing skills that you may wish to cultivate. In business you are ideally suited for dealing with large projects and other people's money. Alternatively, you may use your sensitivity and creativity in some form of healing or self-expression.

Famous people who share your birthday include TV personality Roseanne, Israeli prime minister Yitzhak Shamir, Viscount Linley, actor Charles Bronson, boxer Larry Holmes, *Vogue* editor Anna Wintour, and writer André Malraux.

Numerology

With a number 3 birthday, you are sensitive, with a need for creativity and emotional expression. Fun-loving and a good companion, you enjoy friendly social activities and many interests. Although you are versatile and expressive, with a need for different and exciting experiences, an inclination to get bored easily may cause you to become indecisive or spread yourself too thinly. Although, as a number 3 individual, you are usually artistic and charming, with a good sense of humor, you may have to develop self-esteem and guard against tendencies such as worry and emotional insecurity. The subinfluence of the number 11 month indicates that you are enthusiastic and inspired. Supersensitive and imaginative, you have psychic abilities and receptivity. Although you are pragmatic, a tendency to fluctuate emotionally suggests that you need to stay single-minded and apply your inspirational ideas to some serviceable or creative use. If indecisive or insecure, you can succumb to a tendency toward self-indulgence or become scattered, with too many interests.

• *Positive:* humorous, happy, friendly, productive, creative, artistic, freedom-loving, a talent with words

• *Negative:* easily bored, vain, overimaginative, exaggerate, boastful, extravagant, self-indulgent, lazy, hypocritical, wasteful

Love & Relationships

Although you may seem quite down to earth, you are idealistic and romantic, with powerful yet sensitive feelings. You are usually willing to work hard to bring stability to your relationships and possess natural diplomatic skills when needed. If your strong emotions become blocked, however, you may experience changing moods or become dependent on your partner. You possess the ability to be both devotional and caring, yet tough and dutiful with those you love. You need people and are very sociable.

YOUR SPECIAL SOMEONE

Among those born on the following dates, you might find a partner who will understand your need for love and variety.

Love & friendship: Jan. 7, 11, 12, 22, Feb. 5, 9, 20, Mar. 3, 7, 8, 18, 31, Apr. 1, 5, 16, 29, May 3, 4, 14, 27, 29, June 1, 12, 25, 27, July 10, 23, 25, Aug. 8, 21, 23, 31, Sept. 6, 19, 21, 29, Oct. 4, 17, 19, 27, 30, Nov. 2, 15, 17, 25, 28, Dec. 13, 15, 23, 26

Beneficial: Jan. 8, 14, 19, Feb. 6, 12, 17, Mar. 4, 10, 15, Apr. 2, 8, 13, May 6, 11, June 4, 9, July 2, 7, Aug. 5, Sept. 3, Oct. 1, 29, Nov. 27, Dec. 25, 29

Fatal attractions: May 1, 2, 3, 4

Challenging: Jan. 9, 18, 20, Feb. 7, 16, 18, Mar. 5, 14, 16, Apr. 3, 12, 14, May 1, 10, 12, June 8, 10, July 6, 8, 29, Aug. 4, 6, 27, Sept. 2, 4, 25, Oct. 2, 23, Nov. 21, Dec. 19

Soul mates: Jan. 9, Feb. 7, Mar. 5, Apr. 3, May 1, Oct. 30, Nov. 28, Dec. 26

November 4

PRIMARY STAR

Star's name: Acrux
Degree position: 10°54'–11°50' Scorpio between the years 1930 and 2000
Magnitude: 1
Strength: ★★★★★★★★
Orb: 2°30'
Constellation: Alpha Crux
Applicable days: November 2, 3, 4, 5, 6, 7
Star qualities: Jupiter
Description: a blue-white triple star, the brightest star in the Southern Cross

PRIMARY STAR'S INFLUENCE

Acrux bestows a love of knowledge, harmony, and justice. This star imparts an interest in philosophy, metaphysics, and astrology as well as granting psychic abilities. You have an inquisitive mind and probably an insatiable appetite for books or a desire to travel. Acrux may lead you toward research and education, the social sciences, philosophy, and religion.

Linked to your Sun's degree, Acrux suggests a sensitive and sentimental nature. This star imparts broad-minded humanitarian beliefs, and you may be a seeker of justice. You may become a leader in your profession and can excel or gain a high position in affairs that concern humankind.

Inspired and idealistic, with a need to be creative and enterprising, you are a Scorpio who wants to be practical and down to earth. As a discerning individual with insight and determination, you are versatile, with natural business acumen. Often you intuitively know the answer to other people's problems. Astute and perceptive, with unique ideas, you can present a fresh and unusual point of view that has practical value and is elegant in its simplicity.

The subinfluence of your decanate ruler, Pisces, adds to your receptivity and implies that you can absorb the atmosphere around you. This influence also suggests that although you are imaginative, you can be prone to indecision and misunderstanding. A positive attitude, therefore, is essential to your well-being. By avoiding pessimism, you can focus your attention on matters at hand rather than scatter and diffuse your energies through nervous haste.

Although you have a flair for finances, worry and anxiety often revolve around money issues and can interfere with your ability to resolve problems or find easy solutions. Nevertheless, your inspirational ideas, bright outlook, and communication skills frequently give you the edge when the call is for originality. You are a perfectionist, and your thoroughness or concentration enables you to pick up on ideas and methods very quickly.

After the age of eighteen, when your progressed Sun moves into Sagittarius, you reach a turning point that emphasizes a growing need for freedom and optimism in your life. You may seek to expand your horizons through a quest for truth, mental development, education, or travel. Another turning point occurs at the age of forty-eight, when your progressed Sun moves into Capricorn and begins to highlight practical issues of persistence, dedication, and realism. From the age of seventy-eight, when your progressed Sun enters Aquarius, you begin to place more emphasis on independence, friendship, and group awareness.

Your Secret Self

Your inner sensitivity suggests a strong need for harmony, security, and affection. This implies that your home and family are particularly important to you. You run the risk, however, of caring so much that you become dominating and take charge of others' affairs to run them in your own way. By the power of your love and affection, however, you are able to practice forgiveness and overcome nearly all difficulties. Being a perfectionist, you can be very determined and devoted when committed to a cause or ideal.

Dramatic, with a strong awareness of values, you possess an ability to stand out from the crowd. An innate business sense enables you to turn any situation to your advantage as long as you do not become too materialistic or allow a desire for security to block you from taking risks. Charming and refined, you have only to apply the necessary self-discipline to your natural sense of leadership and intuitive perception to achieve remarkable results in life.

Work & Vocation

With your original ideas and individual approach to life, you may be attracted to writing or occupations involving communication. Possessing a shrewd business sense, you are often successful in commerce or may use your sharp mind for research, science, or medicine. Equally, your keen mental perceptions can draw you to philosophy, religion, or metaphysics. Given your intuitive understanding of people, any career that uses psychological skills is an excellent channel for your talents. Your natural dramatic sense can also attract you to politics or the entertainment world. Nevertheless, whatever career you choose, you will always have creative ideas and want to be constantly improving the way you work.

Famous people who share your birthday include actors Ralph Macchio and Art Carney, newsman Walter Cronkite, entertainer Will Rogers, photographer Robert Mapplethorpe, and actress Loretta Swit.

Numerology

The solid structure and orderly power suggested by the number 4 birthday indicate that you need stability and like to establish order. Endowed with energy, practical skills, and strong determination, you can achieve success through hard work. Security-conscious, you like to build a strong foundation for yourself and your family. A pragmatic approach to life confers a good business sense and an ability to achieve material success in life. As a number 4 individual, you are usually honest, frank, and fair. The challenges for a number 4 person may include overcoming periods of instability or financial worry. Loyal by nature, you gain from collaborating with others. The subinfluence of the number 11 month indicates that you are intuitive and creative, with a need for self-discipline. Idealistic and easygoing, you also desire harmony and balance. If you are discontented and unsettled, you may rebel and waste your wonderful ideas on impractical schemes. By taking your responsibilities seriously, you can achieve long-lasting stability.

• *Positive:* well organized, self-disciplined, steady, hardworking, organized, craftsmanship, good with your hands, pragmatic, trusting, exact

• *Negative:* unstable, destructive behavior, uncommunicative, repressed, rigid, lazy, unfeeling, procrastination, too economical, bossy, hidden affections, resentful, strict

YOUR SPECIAL SOMEONE

To find long-lasting happiness and security, you might begin by looking for someone born on one of the following days.

Love & friendship: Jan. 4, 8, 13, 22, 26, Feb. 6, 20, 24, Mar. 4, 13, 18, 22, Apr. 2, 16, 20, 30, May 14, 18, 28, 30, June 12, 16, 26, 28, July 5, 10, 14, 24, 26, Aug. 8, 12, 22, 24, Sept. 6, 10, 20, 22, 30, Oct. 4, 8, 18, 20, 28, Nov. 2, 6, 16, 18, 26, Dec. 4, 14, 16, 24

Beneficial: Jan. 9, 20, Feb. 7, 18, Mar. 5, 16, 29, Apr. 3, 14, 27, May 1, 12, 25, June 10, 23, July 8, 21, Aug. 6, 19, Sept. 4, 17, Oct. 2, 15, 30, Nov. 13, 28, Dec. 11, 26, 30

Fatal attractions: Jan. 27, Feb. 25, Mar. 23, Apr. 21, May 1, 2, 3, 4, 5, 19, June 17, July 15, Aug. 13, Sept. 11, Oct. 9, Nov. 7, Dec. 5

Challenging: Jan. 2, 10, 19, Feb. 8, 17, Mar. 6, 15, Apr. 4, 13, May 2, 11, June 9, July 7, 30, Aug. 5, 28, Sept. 3, 26, Oct. 1, 24, Nov. 22, Dec. 20, 30

Soul mates: Jan. 15, Feb. 13, Mar. 11, Apr. 9, May 7, June 5, July 3, Aug. 1, Oct. 29, Nov. 27, Dec. 25

Love & Relationships

As an idealistic and honest individual, you need to choose your partners cautiously, otherwise you may find them a disappointment. Being secretive suggests that you find it difficult to express your true feelings and so sometimes appear cold or indifferent. By staying sincere and confident, you can develop your emotional spontaneity to enhance loving relationships. Your creative approach to life ensures your success socially and enables you to mix with people from all walks of life.

November 5

♏ Intelligent and receptive, you are an astute Scorpio with deep feelings and strong inner powers. Inquisitive, with a discerning mind, you often attempt to gain strength through knowledge. Although outwardly calm, with a gentle composure, you can become intense, and your sharp criticism can at times be brutally frank. Determined and persistent, you also have strong convictions and a resolute attitude that can sometimes be interpreted as stubbornness.

The subinfluence of your decanate ruler, Pisces, adds power to your sensitivity and implies that you have the ability to instinctively comprehend issues. An ability to concentrate on one issue at a time indicates that you can specialize in one particular field of research or have original interests. Imaginative, with keen senses, you assimilate all that is around you. Although this influence suggests that you can be emotionally excessive or prone to fluctuating moods, you can achieve inner equilibrium by creating a balanced and harmonious atmosphere.

Your need for personal contacts means that, as a networker, you have a flair for people-related activities and usually thrive on new opportunities and contacts. Being mentally active, you enjoy a good intellectual challenge. An inclination to be argumentative, however, implies that when you do not get your own way you can become quarrelsome. Nevertheless, a desire to succeed or become involved in financial ventures indicates that you can benefit from associations or working for others.

After the age of seventeen, when your progressed Sun moves into Sagittarius, you start to become more optimistic. This may lead you to expand your mental outlook on life, take chances, or travel. Alternatively, you may desire more inner freedom and have a greater psychological interest in truth, philosophy, or the meaning of life. After the age of forty-seven, when your progressed Sun moves into Capricorn, you become more organized, industrious, and realistic, with a greater understanding of your goals and ambitions in life. From the age of seventy-seven, when your progressed Sun enters Aquarius, you begin to place more importance on companionship, freedom, and independence.

Your Secret Self

An interesting combination of high ideals and deep thought mixed with a practical desire for money, prestige, and luxury indicates that you may vacillate between these two extremes. Very strong-willed and determined when you have a goal in mind, you can impress others with your power and resolve. A good strategist, you possess the energy and determination for outstanding personal achievement, although you may find greater happiness using your focused willpower for the good of others.

Although you can often have an exceptionally perceptive mind, your tendency to alternate between ambition and inertia can challenge your otherwise great potential. Nevertheless, with your powers of concentration, need for recognition, and willingness to take on difficult and challenging work, you can be hardworking and dedicated. A strong need for harmony can be reflected in an appreciation or talent for art and music or by expression of a universal spirit.

Work & Vocation

Through your natural diplomatic skills and ability to make contacts, you are able to excel in careers that involve negotiation or arbitration, such as public relations, liaison and agency

PRIMARY STAR

Star's name: Acrux

Degree position: 10°54'–11°50' Scorpio between the years 1930 and 2000

Magnitude: 1

Strength: ★★★★★★★★★

Orb: 2°30'

Constellation: Alpha Crux

Applicable days: November 2, 3, 4, 5, 6, 7

Star qualities: Jupiter

Description: a blue-white triple star, the brightest star in the Southern Cross

PRIMARY STAR'S INFLUENCE

Acrux bestows a love of knowledge, harmony, and justice. This star imparts an interest in philosophy, metaphysics, and astrology as well as granting psychic abilities. You have an inquisitive mind and probably an insatiable appetite for books or a desire to travel. Acrux may lead you toward research and education, the social sciences, philosophy, and religion.

Linked to your Sun's degree, Acrux suggests a sensitive and sentimental nature. This star imparts broad-minded humanitarian beliefs, and you may be a seeker of justice. You may become a leader in your profession and can excel or gain a high position in affairs that concern humankind.

work, or business advising. You may also be particularly good at selling or promoting an idea or product. Totally determined once committed to a project, you have shrewd business sense and organizational skills that are likely to aid your success in whatever career you choose. Although you may prefer to work for yourself, you also realize the benefits of working cooperatively with others. Alternatively, a need for recognition may push you into the limelight in some capacity.

Famous people who share your birthday include singer Bryan Adams, playwright/actor Sam Shepard, actresses Vivien Leigh and Tatum O'Neal, singer/songwriter Art Garfunkel, and labor organizer Eugene Debs.

Numerology

Strong instincts, an adventurous nature, and a desire for freedom are all indicated by the number 5 birthday. The willingness to explore or try anything new and an enthusiastic approach suggest that life will have a lot to offer you. Travel and many opportunities for change, some unexpected, may lead you to undergo a real transformation of views and beliefs. With a number 5 birthday, you need to feel that life is exciting; however, you may also have to develop a responsible attitude and avoid tendencies such as unpredictability, excessiveness, and restlessness. You can achieve success by avoiding premature or speculative actions and through learning patience. The natural talent of a number 5 individual is knowing how to go with the flow and staying detached. The subinfluence of the number 11 month indicates that you are intuitive, with strong instincts. Intelligent and direct, you can communicate your ideas in a crystal-clear manner. Although you are receptive and sensitive to others, your humorous viewpoint can at times blend with your skepticism and produce a cynical wit.

• *Positive:* versatile, adaptable, progressive, strong instincts, magnetic, lucky, daring, freedom-loving, quick and witty, curious, mystical, sociable

• *Negative:* unreliable, changeable, procrastinator, inconsistent, undependable, overconfident, headstrong

Love & Relationships

Sensitive, with powerful emotions, you usually have a curious nature, with fixed beliefs and strong principles. As you admire powerful and independent people, you need a strong partner who can stand up to you and not be intimidated by your forceful personality. Although friendly and sociable, you may strike out on your own and try new challenges. Since you need to exercise your cerebral power, you prefer the company of intelligent individuals.

• *Positive:* justice, love toward your fellow man, compassion

• *Negative:* revenge, injustice, lack of feelings

See Appendix for additional fixed star readings.

YOUR SOMEONE SPECIAL

You might come close to finding your true match with someone born on one of the following dates.

Love and friendship: Jan. 2, 3, 23, Feb. 11, 21, Mar. 9, 19, 28, 31, Apr. 7, 17, 26, 29, May 5, 15, 24, 27, 28, 29, 31, June 3, 13, 22, 25, 26, 27, 29, July 1, 11, 20, 23, 25, 27, 29, Aug. 9, 18, 21, 23, 25, 27, Sept. 7, 16, 19, 21, 23, 25, Oct. 5, 14, 17, 19, 21, 23, Nov. 3, 12, 15, 17, 19, 21, Dec. 1, 10, 13, 15, 17, 19

Beneficial: Jan. 3, 4, 10, 21, Feb. 1, 2, 8, 19, Mar. 6, 17, 30, Apr. 4, 15, 28, May 2, 13, 26, June 11, 24, July 9, 22, Aug. 7, 20, Sept. 5, 18, Oct. 3, 16, 31, Nov. 1, 14, 29, Dec. 12, 27

Fatal attractions: Jan. 22, 28, Feb. 20, 26, Mar. 18, 24, Apr. 16, 22, May 3, 4, 5, 6, 14, 20, June 12, 18, July 10, 16, Aug. 8, 14, Sept. 6, 12, Oct. 4, 10, Nov. 2, 8, Dec. 6

Challenging: Jan. 11, 20, Feb. 9, 18, Mar. 7, 16, Apr. 5, 14, May 3, 12, 30, June 1, 10, 28, July 8, 26, 31, Aug. 6, 24, 29, Sept. 4, 22, 27, Oct. 2, 20, 25, Nov. 18, 23, Dec. 16, 21

Soul mates: Jan. 26, Feb. 24, Mar. 22, 30, Apr. 20, 28, May 18, 26, June 16, 24, July 14, 22, Aug. 12, 20, Sept. 10, 18, Oct. 8, 16, Nov. 6, 14, Dec. 4, 12

November 6

♏ Charming and gregarious, though motivated and ambitious, you are an enterprising Scorpio with vision and idealism. A need for personal fulfillment and a desire for action are often your motivating forces. Although you usually appear bright and amicable, occasionally circumstances can cause confusion and leave you feeling insecure or indecisive. Nevertheless, a lucky streak can get you out of many difficult situations, even when these are brought about by your own actions.

The subinfluence of your decanate ruler, Pisces, adds intuitive insight to your sensitivity and implies that you have the ability to instinctively comprehend or absorb the atmosphere around you. Imaginative, with keen senses, when inspired you enjoy being creative and fantasize or speculate to better your prospects. Inner equilibrium can be achieved by creating a balanced and harmonious atmosphere in your surroundings.

Happy when initiating new ideas, you like to be in the forefront of new trends. Creativity and practical skills are some of your many attributes, and the ability to present a new and unusual vision suggests that you have original thoughts. Usually a perfectionist, you are enabled, through inspirational ideas and positive perspective, to have the edge when the call is for ingenuity and drama.

After the age of sixteen, when your progressed Sun moves into Sagittarius, you start to become more positive and expansive in your outlook. This may lead you to higher education or travel, or stimulate you to be adventurous and take chances. You may wish to explore your psyche through philosophy, religion, or the quest for truth. From the age of forty-six, when your progressed Sun moves into Capricorn, you begin to take a more practical, realistic, and organized approach to life, with a strong need for order and structure. From the age of seventy-six, when your progressed Sun enters Aquarius, you begin to place more importance on friendship, independence, and humanitarian ideals.

Your Secret Self

Blessed with a talent for fortunate ideas, you often seek associations that can bring you gain and further advancement. A strong emphasis on relationships and partnerships implies that although you are a strong and forceful individual, you may have to learn the art of compromise in order to benefit from what others have to offer. With your intuitive farsightedness and quick grasp of situations, you are usually ready to make the most of opportunities presented to you, if not instigating them yourself.

You can be honest and extremely generous with those you love, but you also run the risk of spoiling your relationships through being domineering or self-destructive. Although you possess potent desires and emotions, by learning to be flexible and take criticism you can be more open to expressing the powerful, selfless love you possess at a deep level.

Work & Vocation

With your down-to-earth approach and natural diplomatic skills, you enjoy work involving cooperation with others and are in your element when you can mix business and pleasure or

PRIMARY STAR

Star's name: Acrux
Degree position: 10°54'–11°50' Scorpio between the years 1930 and 2000
Magnitude: 1
Strength: ★★★★★★★★★
Orb: 2°30'
Constellation: Alpha Crux
Applicable days: November 2, 3, 4, 5, 6, 7
Star qualities: Jupiter
Description: a blue-white triple star, the brightest star in the Southern Cross

PRIMARY STAR'S INFLUENCE

Acrux bestows a love of knowledge, harmony, and justice. This star imparts an interest in philosophy, metaphysics, and astrology as well as granting psychic abilities. You have an inquisitive mind and probably an insatiable appetite for books or a desire to travel. Acrux may lead you toward research and education, the social sciences, philosophy, and religion.

Linked to your Sun's degree, Acrux suggests a sensitive and sentimental nature. This star imparts broadminded humanitarian beliefs, and you may be a seeker of justice. You may become a leader in your profession and can excel or gain a high position in affairs that concern humankind.

when promoting ideas linked to financial gain. Being independent, with natural leadership skills, you do not like to take orders, and this may stimulate you to apply for management positions or work for yourself. With an urge for action and a talent for troubleshooting, you often thrive on new beginnings or challenges. Courageous yet persuasive, you can be very committed and enthusiastic once decided on an activity or career. Music or writing may also prove attractive to you, either professionally or as a creative release.

Famous people who share your birthday include director Mike Nichols, actress Sally Field, TV broadcaster/writer Melvyn Bragg, basketball inventor James Naismith, bandleader Ray Conniff, newsperson Maria Schriver, and composer John Philip Sousa.

Numerology

Compassion, idealism, and a caring nature are some of the attributes suggested by a number 6 birthday. This is the number of the perfectionist or the universal friend and indicates that you are frequently a humanitarian who can be responsible, loving, and supportive. With a number 6 birthday, you are often domestically inclined and a devoted parent. The more sensitive among you will need to find a form of creative expression and are drawn to the world of entertaining or art and design. You may need to develop more self-confidence and overcome tendencies such as interfering, worry, and misplaced sympathy. The subinfluence of the number 11 month indicates that you have powerful emotions and a strong character. Although you possess high ideals, you need to be determined, with patience and perseverance, in order to attain your goals. Innovative and imaginative, you like to plan for the future and feel materially secure. If discontented, you need to avoid being overcritical or domineering with others.

• *Positive:* worldly, universal brotherhood, friendly, compassionate, dependable, understanding, sympathetic, idealistic, domestically inclined, humanitarian, poised, artistic, balanced

• *Negative:* discontented, anxious, shy, unreasonable, stubborn, outspoken, disharmonious, perfectionist, domineering, lack of responsibility, selfish, suspicious, cynical, self-centered

Love & Relationships

Your strong personality combined with your ability to be warm and charming can be very attractive to others. Although you are an ambitious individual, you are also understanding and encouraging, willing to do anything for those you love. If you become impatient and move too fast in relationships, however, you may regret it later when you have time to think it through. Material considerations can also play a significant factor in your relationships, as security is important to you.

YOUR SPECIAL SOMEONE

To find long-lasting happiness and security, you might begin by looking for someone born on one of the following days.

Love & friendship: Jan. 14, 15, 24, 31, Feb. 12, 22, 29, Mar. 10, 11, 20, 27, Apr. 8, 18, 25, May 6, 16, 23, 30, June 4, 14, 21, 28, 30, July 2, 3, 12, 19, 26, 28, 30, Aug. 10, 17, 24, 26, 28, Sept. 8, 15, 22, 24, 26, Oct. 6, 13, 20, 22, 24, 30, Nov. 4, 11, 18, 20, 22, 28, Dec. 2, 9, 16, 18, 20, 26, 29

Beneficial: Jan. 5, 22, 30, Feb. 3, 20, 28, Mar. 1, 18, 26, Apr. 16, 24, May 14, 22, June 12, 20, July 10, 18, 29, Aug. 8, 16, 27, 31, Sept. 6, 14, 25, 29, Oct. 4, 12, 23, 27, Nov. 2, 10, 21, 25, Dec. 9, 19, 23

Fatal attractions: Jan. 12, Feb. 10, Mar. 8, Apr. 6, May 3, 4, 5, 6, June 2

Challenging: Jan. 16, 21, Feb. 14, 19, Mar. 12, 17, 30, Apr. 10, 15, 28, May 8, 13, 26, June 6, 11, 24, July 4, 9, 22, Aug. 2, 7, 20, Sept. 5, 18, Oct. 3, 16, Nov. 1, 14, Dec. 12

Soul mates: Jan. 25, Feb. 23, Mar. 21, Apr. 19, May 17, June 15, July 13, Aug. 11, Sept. 9, Oct. 7, Nov. 5, Dec. 3, 30

November 7

ℳ Independent and intelligent, you are a highly intuitive Scorpio with an ability to analyze and accumulate a great deal of information. Resourceful and smart, you recognize the power of knowledge or education. Perceptive and discerning, you welcome opportunities to exercise your mind through argument and debate. Usually you like to be in control, and you can appear to others as an authoritative individual with a commanding personality.

The subinfluence of your decanate ruler, Pisces, empowers you with imagination and an ability to delve deep into any particular area of interest. Imaginative, with psychic abilities, you enjoy being communicative and creative when inspired. With your vision and intuitive insight, you can easily evaluate the atmosphere around you.

A blend of caution and enthusiasm implies that you can alternate between being overconfident and self-doubting. Although a pragmatist by nature, at times you can also have unconventional ideas. This tendency to be an unorthodox thinker must not, however, become an excuse for being contrary just for the sake of being difficult. As others quickly recognize your strengths, you usually rise to a position of authority and power. Through patience and perseverance, you can endure great challenges and, with hard work, often achieve success.

After the age of fifteen, when your progressed Sun moves into Sagittarius, you start to become more optimistic, with a growing need for honesty and idealism in your life. It is a time for study, travel, and expanding your mental horizons. There is a turning point at the age of forty-five, when your progressed Sun moves into Capricorn. You are likely to become more practical, realistic, and organized in order to achieve your goals in life, and you have a strong need for order and structure. From the age of seventy-five, when your progressed Sun enters Aquarius, there is another change that emphasizes issues of friendship, independence, and humanitarian ideals.

FIXED STARS

Acrux; Alphecca; Al Genubi, also called South Scale or the South Claw

PRIMARY STAR

Star's name: Acrux

Degree position: 10°54'–11°50' Scorpio between the years of 1930 and 2000

Magnitude: 1

Strength: ★★★★★★★★★

Orb: 2°30'

Constellation: Alpha Crux

Applicable days: November 2, 3, 4, 5, 6, 7

Star qualities: Jupiter

Description: a blue-white triple star, the brightest star in the Southern Cross

PRIMARY STAR'S INFLUENCE

Acrux bestows a love of knowledge, harmony, and justice. This star imparts an interest in philosophy, metaphysics, and astrology as well as granting psychic abilities. You have an inquisitive mind and probably an insatiable appetite for books or a desire to travel. Acrux may lead you toward research and education, the social sciences, philosophy, and religion.

Linked to your Sun's degree, Acrux suggests a sensitive and sentimental nature. This star imparts broadminded humanitarian beliefs, and you may be a seeker of justice. You may become a leader in your profession and can excel or gain a high position in affairs that concern humankind.

Your Secret Self

Tough and determined, yet magnetic and charming, you are an interesting mixture of opposites. Along with a sharp wit and intelligence, you also possess a humanitarian streak that can give you quick insight into people. Responsible and hardworking, inside you you have an idealist who is keen to fight injustice. Nevertheless, a desire for power, money, or prestige can motivate you to climb the ladder of success.

Although independent, you know the value of sharing and working cooperatively in order to achieve the best results. To avoid dependent situations, it may be necessary to use your strong intuition to find just the right balance between standing up for your own ideas and being receptive to the opinions of others. A little competitive fun can help you keep your sense of humor.

Work & Vocation

With your keen intelligence and ability to lead, you usually have many different career opportunities and can succeed in any of them. Although you are independent, others appreciate your capacity for hard work and responsibility, so you often rise to a prominent position. With your quick mind, communication skills, and desire for knowledge, you may be drawn to a career as a writer or in education and research. Although you have an introspective or philosophical nature, you can also excel in theatrical or political endeavors. As you usually do not like to take orders, you prefer to be in charge or be self-employed.

Famous people who share your birthday include singer/songwriter Joni Mitchell, evangelist Billy Graham, scientist Marie Curie, singers Joan Sutherland and Johnny Rivers, ethologist Konrad Lorenz, and Russian general Leon Trotsky.

Numerology

Analytical and thoughtful, number 7 individuals are frequently critical and self-absorbed. With a constant need for greater self-awareness, you enjoy gathering information and may be interested in reading, writing, or spirituality. Although shrewd, you may overrationalize or get lost in detail. A tendency to be enigmatic or secretive suggests that at times you feel misunderstood. Mentally curious, you enjoy probing and investigating in an attempt to discover what lies beneath the surface. The subinfluence of the number 11 month indicates that you are highly intuitive, with powers of discrimination. Although you are intelligent, with penetrating thought, you can perform record achievements by letting your instincts and practical common sense guide you. Loyal, with strong convictions, you fare better in reforms and where you can inspire others with your humanitarian ideology.

To liberate your faith and great compassion, avoid using your power in a destructive way, and avoid rebelling against others.

• *Positive:* educated, trusting, meticulous, idealistic, honest, psychic, scientific, rational, reflective

• *Negative:* concealing, deceitful, unfriendly, secretive, skeptical, confused, nagging, detached, cold

YOUR SPECIAL SOMEONE

If you are looking for an ideal partner, you may enhance your luck by finding someone born on one of the following dates.

Love & friendship: Jan. 11, 13, 15, 17, 25, Feb. 9, 11, 13, 15, 23, Mar. 7, 9, 11, 13, 21, 29, Apr. 5, 7, 9, 11, 19, May 3, 5, 7, 9, 17, 31, June 1, 3, 5, 7, 15, 23, 29, July 1, 3, 5, 21, 27, 29, 31, Aug. 1, 3, 11, 25, 27, 29, Sept. 1, 9, 23, 25, 27, Oct. 7, 21, 23, 25, Nov. 5, 19, 21, 23, Dec. 3, 17, 19, 21, 30

Beneficial: Jan. 1, 5, 20, Feb. 3, 18, Mar. 1, 16, Apr. 14, May 12, June 10, July 8, Aug. 6, Sept. 4, Oct. 2

Fatal attractions: May 5, 6, 7, 8

Challenging: Jan. 6, 22, 24, Feb. 4, 20, 22, Mar. 2, 18, 20, Apr. 16, 18, May 14, 16, June 12, 14, July 10, 12, Aug. 8, 10, 31, Sept. 6, 8, 29, Oct. 4, 6, 27, Nov. 2, 4, 25, 30, Dec. 2, 23, 28

Soul mates: Jan. 6, 12, Feb. 4, 10, Mar. 2, 8, Apr. 6, May 4, June 2

Love & Relationships

You need a partner who will give you the freedom to be independent. Thoughtful and highly intuitive, you like to be honest with others. You are resourceful, too, and your character suggests that you can be forceful and compelling. When you love someone, you are supportive and reassuring. Although you are a caring person, your natural tendency to take control implies that at times you may become overbearing. When you commit yourself, however, you are responsible and love very deeply.

November 8

℠ Individual and intelligent, you are a sensitive Scorpio with a commanding personality. Although ambitious and forceful, with courage and commitment to your ideals, you can be kind and generous to the ones you love. Observant and highly intuitive, with a desire for knowledge, you quickly comprehend situations and as a result have interesting ideas. Farsighted, with executive skills, you can usually find yourself in the forefront of new trends and concepts.

The subinfluence of your decanate ruler, Pisces, implies that you are imaginative and talented, with a strong sixth sense. Naturally gifted, you seek ways to express yourself and are fortunate to be able to choose the career you like. Although you can be focused and determined, you may have to guard against a tendency to indulge in changeable moods, fantasy, or escapism.

A need for growth and the ability to review the whole suggests that you like to think on a grand scale. Self-assured and inquisitive, usually you do not welcome interference from others, and by showing a stubborn streak, you can appear restless or act impatient. Success can come through education, via higher learning, or through social, moral, or religious aspirations. All is possible if you develop patience, tolerance, and the self-discipline to overcome emotional insecurities.

From ages fourteen through thirty-three, when your progressed Sun is in Sagittarius, you seek freedom, positive ideals, and opportunities for expansion. Your urge to explore is at its strongest, and you may travel or develop an interest in religion, philosophy, or the meaning of life. At the age of forty-four, when your progressed Sun moves into Capricorn, there is a turning point as you start to become more practical, disciplined, and goal-oriented in the realization of your objectives. After the age of seventy-four, when your progressed Sun enters Aquarius, you begin to place more emphasis on friendship, independence, and group activities.

FIXED STAR

Star's name: Al Genubi, also called South Scale or the South Claw

Degree position: 14°6'–15°4' Scorpio between the years 1930 and 2000

Magnitude: 3

Strength: ★★★★★

Orb: 1°40'

Constellation: Alpha Libra

Applicable days: November 6, 7, 8, 9

Star qualities: varied interpretations: Jupiter/Mars/Saturn/Venus

Description: a pale yellow and white-gray binary star located in the southern scale of the Balance

PRIMARY STAR'S INFLUENCE

Al Genubi suggests that you may encounter changes and times of instability throughout life. This star also warns that you may need to follow orthodox ways or stay on the right side of the track. Success and accomplishment may be achieved through learning to overcome obstacles.

Linked to your Sun's degree, this star imparts the ability to focus on goals and objectives and thus overcome obstacles and disappointments. You may, however, need to avoid mental anxiety by learning that favors carry a price tag.

• *Positive:* learn to forgive, patience, perseverance

• *Negative:* unforgiving, dealing with unsavory characters, some legal problems

Your Secret Self

In order to fully utilize your quick wit, need for self-expression, and the sociable side of your nature, you may probably have to overcome an inclination toward uncertainty or indecision in your emotional relationships. Making choices and decisions may turn out to be one of the primary challenges to your otherwise well-structured mind. By using your gift with words and many creative talents, however, you are able to experience the joy of life.

Success-oriented, you usually have a plan or scheme in the pipeline. Being independent and a good networker or organizer, you may be put in charge of various projects. Very shrewd and quick at assessing people or environments, you usually like big projects and are constantly seeking opportunities. Your advancement in life is also helped by a kind generosity and optimism that endear you to others and increase your good fortune.

Work & Vocation

You prefer to be in some leading position; having excellent organizational skills can guarantee your success in business, particularly as a manager or administrator. Your probing mind may, alternatively, find interest and satisfaction in science or psychology. The more humanitarian side of your nature or your quick way with words could provide you with the impetus to excel as a teacher, counselor, or lawyer or in a job that requires speaking up for others. This may include involvement in social reform, unions, or politics. Optionally, your natural dramatic flair suggests that satisfaction could be found in the entertainment world. Other careers that may interest you include occupations of a philosophical, religious, or metaphysical nature.

Famous people who share your birthday include singers Bonnie Raitt and Ricki Lee Jones, actor Alain Delon, writer Margaret Mitchell, psychiatrist Herman Rorschach, heart surgeon Christiaan Barnard, and actress Katharine Hepburn.

Numerology

The power suggested by the number 8 birthday shows a character with strong values and sound judgment. The number 8 indicates that you aspire to great accomplishment and possess an ambitious nature. A desire for dominance, security, and material success is also indicated by this birthday. As a number 8 person, you have natural business sense and will benefit greatly from developing organizational and executive skills. A strong need to feel secure or established urges you to make long-term plans and investments. The subinfluence of the number 11 month indicates that you are intelligent, with the ability to turn your inspired ideas into tangible reality. Being productive and single-minded implies that you are willing to take on great responsibilities and work hard to achieve your objectives. Although you can rise to a position of influence, avoid being stubborn or domineering. In order to live up to your true potential, you need to be original and have faith in your abilities. It would be wise, however, not to succumb to becoming obsessive or overstraining your powers.

• *Positive:* leadership, thoroughness, hardworking, authority, protection, power to heal, good judge of values

• *Negative:* impatient, intolerant, overwork, domineering, easily discouraged, lack of planning, controlling behavior

Love & Relationships

Intelligent and highly intuitive, you prefer the company of clever or interesting people who can offer you mental stimulation. Your friendly and sympathetic nature suggests that others are drawn to you for guidance and support. Idealistic and ambitious, you can take responsibility for yourself and others. Although you appear strong and forceful, a sensitive side to your nature implies that at times you can be restless or emotionally insecure. With your excellent social skills, you usually have many friends and admirers.

YOUR SPECIAL SOMEONE

For security, reassurance, and affection, you might want to begin looking among those born on the following days.

Love & friendship: Jan. 4, 12, 16, 25, Feb. 10, 14, 23, 24, Mar. 8, 12, 22, 31, Apr. 6, 10, 20, 29, May 4, 8, 18, 27, June 2, 6, 16, 25, 29, 30, July 4, 14, 23, 28, Aug. 2, 12, 21, 26, 30, Sept. 10, 19, 24, 28, Oct. 8, 17, 22, 26, Nov. 6, 15, 20, 24, 30, Dec. 4, 13, 18, 22, 28

Beneficial: Jan. 2, 13, 22, 24, Feb. 11, 17, 20, 22, Mar. 9, 15, 18, 20, 28, Apr. 7, 13, 16, 18, 26, May 5, 11, 16, 18, 26, June 3, 9, 12, 14, 22, July 1, 7, 10, 12, 20, Aug. 5, 8, 10, 18, Sept. 3, 6, 8, 16, Oct. 1, 4, 6, 14, Nov. 2, 4, 12, Dec. 2, 10

Fatal attractions: Jan. 25, Feb. 23, Mar. 21, Apr. 19, May 5, 6, 7, 8, 17, June 15, July 13, Aug. 11, Sept. 9, Oct. 7, Nov. 5, Dec. 3

Challenging: Jan. 7, 23, Feb. 5, 21, Mar. 3, 19, 29, Apr. 1, 17, 27, May 15, 25, June 13, 23, July 11, 21, 31, Aug. 9, 19, 29, Sept. 7, 17, 27, 30, Nov. 3, 13, 23, 26, Dec. 1, 11, 21, 24

Soul mates: Jan. 17, Feb. 15, Mar. 13, Apr. 11, May 9, June 7, July 5, Aug. 3, Sept. 1, Nov. 30, Dec. 28

November 9

♏ As a sensitive, articulate, and spirited Scorpio, you demonstrate a fine intelligence and a love for knowledge. Enterprising and intuitive, with a youthful temperament, you prefer an active life and are usually spontaneous and expressive. Sometimes, however, you may need to guard against a tendency to immaturity, but by learning to concentrate on your responsibilities you can project a creative and disciplined image.

The subinfluence of your decanate ruler, Pisces, suggests that you are impressionable and imaginative, with strong premonitions. Idealistic and receptive, you can be very persuasive and possess strong convictions. Charming and sociable, you enjoy the company of others and can be an entertaining companion, especially in group gatherings. It would be wise, however, to guard against wasting your time on people of ambiguous character.

Strong willpower and an ability to be decisive suggest that you can plan and execute projects on a grand scale. Nevertheless, at times you may overreact by being too confident, headstrong, or impulsive. Becoming overexcitable only highlights eccentricity rather than individuality. For success, you benefit from being trusting and cooperative. By learning to discipline your restless mental energies, you can fulfill your dreams, turning your big ideas into tangible reality.

Between the ages of thirteen and forty-two, when your progressed Sun moves through Sagittarius, you feel a need to expand your horizons, take opportunities, and be more optimistic. This may also include exploring philosophical thought, education, or travel. At the age of forty-three, when your progressed Sun moves into Capricorn, there is a turning point as you start to become more industrious, pragmatic, and persevering, with a strong need for order and structure in your life. After the age of seventy-three, when your progressed Sun enters Aquarius, there is a change as you begin to place more emphasis on new ideas, companionship, and knowledge of human nature.

Fixed Star

Star's name: Al Genubi, also called South Scale or the South Claw
Degree position: 14°6'–15°4' Scorpio between the years 1930 and 2000
Magnitude: 3
Strength: ★★★★★
Orb: 1°40'
Constellation: Alpha Libra
Applicable days: November 6, 7, 8, 9
Star qualities: varied interpretations: Jupiter/Mars/Saturn/Venus
Description: a pale yellow and white-gray binary star located in the southern scale of the Balance

PRIMARY STAR'S INFLUENCE

Al Genubi suggests that you may encounter changes and times of instability throughout life. This star also warns that you may need to follow orthodox ways or stay on the right side of the track. Success and accomplishment may be achieved through learning to overcome obstacles.

Linked to your Sun's degree, this star imparts the ability to focus on goals and objectives and thus overcome obstacles and disappointments. You may, however, need to avoid mental anxiety by learning that favors carry a price tag.

• Positive: learn to forgive, patience, perseverance

• Negative: unforgiving, dealing with unsavory characters, some legal problems

Your Secret Self

You can be high-spirited, charming, and entertaining, with a warm heart, yet your desire for success springs from an interesting mixture of materialism and idealism. Although ambitious, you have a playful quality that is likely to stay with you throughout your life and show a side of you that is guaranteed to keep others fascinated. Friendly and enthusiastic, you will find that your people skills can certainly help you in your climb to the top.

Independent and success-oriented, you like to be active and think in grandiose terms. You may, however, have to avoid getting emotionally carried away or going to extremes. Being sensitive, you must avoid mind-altering substances of any description. As dynamic and charming as you can be, however, there may be times when you have secret fears or become too money-oriented. By reconnecting to your intuition and idealistic vision, you can return to your usual positive self.

Work & Vocation

As you possess strong leadership qualities, your greatest achievement is likely to be at the forefront of your chosen profession. Your outstanding potential for acquiring knowledge may place you among the scholarly or could serve you equally well in law, psychology, or medicine. Your natural talents with the spoken and written word can help you find fulfillment in teaching, lecturing, or writing. With your natural business sense, you may equally be drawn to the world of commerce and use your persuasive charm in sales, promotion, or negotiation. Optionally, with your strong principles you can be an excellent politician, spokesperson, or fighter for a cause. As a natural actor, you may be interested in the world of show business.

Famous people who share your birthday include writer Ivan Turgenev, writer/astronomer Carl Sagan, actresses Hedy Lamarr and Karen Dotrice, former U.S. vice president Spiro Agnew, golfer Tom Weiskopf, and baseball manager Whitey Herzog.

Numerology

Benevolence, thoughtfulness, and sentimental sensitivity are all associated with the number 9 birthday. Tolerant and kind, you are often generous and liberal. Intuitive and psychic abilities point to a universal receptivity and, if channeled positively, may inspire you to seek a spiritual path. This birthday may suggest a need to overcome challenges and a tendency to be overly sensitive, with emotional ups and downs. You benefit greatly from world travel and interaction with people from all walks of life, but may have to avoid unrealistic dreams or an inclination toward escapism. The subinfluence of the number 11 month indicates that you are intelligent and intuitive, with mediumistic abilities. As an imaginative and receptive person, you are aware of others' feelings. Although idealistic and generous, you can be secretive and sometimes conceal deep feelings that can turn to resentment. If you are too emotionally intense, you need to learn to be detached and optimistic. Use your diplomatic skill to smooth misunderstandings and avoid animosity.

• *Positive:* idealistic, humanitarian, creative, sensitive, generous, magnetic, poetic, charitable, giving, detached, lucky, popular

• *Negative:* frustrated, nervous, selfish, impractical, bitter, easily led, inferiority complex, fears, worry, isolated

Love & Relationships

Intelligent and sensitive, you are often an idealistic and thoughtful individual. When in the right mood, you can be spontaneous and passionate; however, when you are skeptical or mistrusting, you appear aloof and indifferent. You may need a special link with a partner you can trust, as your ideal of love is so high. Although you are friendly and sociable, you may need to overcome a fear of being lonely. Your natural understanding of human nature helps you through difficulties and makes you attractive to others.

YOUR SOMEONE SPECIAL

To find true happiness, you might just find the inspiring partner you are looking for among those born on the following dates.

Love & friendship: Jan. 7, 10, 17, 27, Feb. 5, 8, 15, 25, Mar. 3, 6, 13, 23, Apr. 1, 4, 11, 21, May 2, 9, 19, June 7, 17, July 5, 15, 29, 31, Aug. 3, 13, 27, 29, 31, Sept. 1, 11, 25, 27, 29, Oct. 9, 23, 25, 27, Nov. 7, 21, 23, 25, Dec. 5, 19, 21, 23

Beneficial: Jan. 3, 5, 20, 25, 27, Feb. 1, 3, 18, 23, 25, Mar. 1, 16, 21, 23, Apr. 14, 19, 21, May 12, 17, 19, June 10, 15, 17, July 8, 13, 15, Aug. 6, 11, 13, Sept. 4, 9, 11, Oct. 2, 7, 9, Nov. 5, 7, Dec. 3, 5

Fatal attractions: Jan. 13, Feb. 11, Mar. 9, Apr. 7, May 5, 6, 7, 8, 9, June 3, July 1

Challenging: Jan. 16, 24, Feb. 14, 22, Mar. 12, 20, Apr. 10, 18, May 8, 16, 31, June 6, 14, 29, July 4, 12, 27, Aug. 2, 10, 25, Sept. 8, 23, Oct. 6, 21, Nov. 4, 19, Dec. 2, 17

Soul mates: Jan. 16, Feb. 14, Mar. 12, Apr. 10, May 8, June 6, July 4, 31, Aug. 2, 29, Sept. 27, Oct. 25, Nov. 23, Dec. 21

November 10

Creative and intuitive, with a magnetic personality, you are an independent Scorpio who is assertive and persuasive. Although often you are freedom-loving, success comes from the constructive use of your willpower and ingenuity. As you are often courageous and have inspired ideas, you need to choose the path of hard work in order to fulfill your ambitious dreams.

The subinfluence of your decanate ruler, Pisces, suggests that you are imaginative and receptive, with strong convictions and a sense of vision. You enjoy a mental challenge, but in your attempt to test your wits and intelligence, try to guard against becoming too provocative or argumentative.

In order to enhance your chances for success, education is usually a cornerstone for the establishment of a solid foundation. With a quick mind and a wide range of interests, you show versatility and enthusiasm and can benefit extensively from travel and learning. As a seeker of knowledge who is thoughtful and intelligent, you usually develop independent views and good reasoning powers.

Although you are often self-disciplined, with a love of learning, the true inspiration for which you search may lie in the realm of emotional satisfaction and fulfillment. By controlling people through your willpower, you do not actually gain an advantage. It is through the art of being tolerant, amiable, and sympathetic that you gain the love and affection you seek.

Between the ages of twelve and forty-one, when your progressed Sun moves through Sagittarius, you become more open and honest, with a need for positive and optimistic ideals in life. A desire to expand your knowledge can manifest as a desire for adventure and freedom or travel and education. At the age of forty-two, when your progressed Sun moves into Capricorn, there is a turning point as you start to become more practical, disciplined, and goal-oriented. From the age of seventy-two, when your progressed Sun enters Aquarius, you begin to place more emphasis on friendship and knowledge of human nature.

Your Secret Self

Although you appear outwardly strong, your sensitivity and strong emotions imply that you may at times suffer from self-doubt. By learning to show your generosity and compassion, you can avoid being emotionally controlling or manipulative to compensate. The more you rely on your own intuitive power and insight, the more success you are likely to encounter in life. It is wise, nevertheless, to avoid worry and social excesses. When positive, however, you possess the dignity and modesty that come from a desire to give your best to your work.

Dynamic and creative, with sharp and quick mental responses, you have a positive vitality and the courage to fight adversity. With a desire to lead and exercise power, you can be ambitious and very determined. Charming, generous, and kind, with the ability to make yourself popular, you may also have to learn that being too direct or overbearing can push people away. Although you will always have a playful quality, it is through developing perseverance and a responsible attitude that you are able to make the most of your remarkable potential and achieve almost anything.

Work & Vocation

Your depth of knowledge, drive, and excellent social skills enable you to reach your potential in many different areas of life. Your probing mind may attract you to research, psychology, or

FIXED STARS

Although your Sun's degree is not linked to a fixed star, some of your other planets' degrees certainly will be. By having an astrological chart calculated, you can find the exact position of the planets on your date of birth. This will tell you which of the fixed stars listed in this book are relevant to you.

investigative work. Equally, you may excel in education or philosophy. In business, you will be naturally drawn to large enterprises and are an excellent problem solver. As you do not like to take orders, you need the freedom to work in your own way, and with the help of your organizational and managerial abilities you often rise to positions of prominence. Alternatively, a strong need for self-expression and a love for the dramatic may lure you to writing or the entertainment world. This birthday is also excellent for doctors and working with foreign people or places.

Famous people who share your birthday include actors Richard Burton, Claude Rains, and Roy Scheider, chef Robert Carrier, songwriter Tim Rice, English painter William Hogarth, sculptor Jacob Epstein, and writer Vachel Lindsay.

Numerology

Like someone with a number 1 birthday, you usually strive toward great endeavors. Nevertheless, you may have to overcome many obstacles before you arrive at your goals. Energetic and original, you stand by your own beliefs even when they differ from others'. Your ability to be a self-starter with a pioneering spirit encourages you to travel far afield or strike out on your own. You may also learn that the world does not revolve around you, and you should guard against selfishness and being dictatorial. Success and accomplishment are important to all number 10 individuals, and frequently you find the way to the top of your profession. The subinfluence of the number 11 month indicates that you are versatile, original, and multitalented. Strong convictions and a need to attain self-mastery imply that you can be spiritually aware. Although you possess an entertaining and witty personality, your carefree spirit needs direction and a purpose. At times, direct and opinionated, you say too much, but you are rarely accused of being dull or boring. As an ambitious individual, you must not overestimate your powers or become self-obsessed.

• *Positive:* leadership, creative, progressive, forceful, optimistic, strong convictions, competitive, independent, gregarious

• *Negative:* overbearing, jealous, egotistical, too proud, antagonistic, lack of restraint, selfish, weak, unstable, impatient

Love & Relationships

Strong and forceful, you respect those who are independent and knowledgeable. As an entertaining companion, you should have no trouble attracting friends and admirers. You usually look for a partner who is strong-willed and clever or who has qualities that you prize. Although you seem self-assured, on an intimate level you may have doubts about your own feelings and at times appear indecisive or skeptical. If suspicious, you may need to learn about trust and integrity. Although you can be creative and dramatic in your relationships, be careful of a tendency to become too demanding or stubborn.

YOUR SPECIAL SOMEONE

You might further help your chances of finding that special person by looking for someone born on one of the following dates.

Love & friendship: Jan. 1, 14, 19, 28, 31, Feb. 12, 26, 29, Mar. 10, 15, 24, 27, Apr. 8, 22, 25, May 6, 20, 23, June 4, 18, 21, July 2, 7, 16, 19, 30, Aug. 14, 17, 28, 30, Sept. 12, 15, 26, 28, 30, Oct. 10, 13, 24, 26, 28, Nov. 8, 11, 22, 24, 26, Dec. 6, 9, 20, 22, 24

Beneficial: Jan. 26, Feb. 24, Mar. 22, Apr. 20, May 18, June 16, July 14, Aug. 12, Sept. 10, Oct. 8, Nov. 6, Dec. 4

Fatal attractions: May 8, 9, 10, 11

Challenging: Jan. 3, 25, Feb. 1, 23, Mar. 21, Apr. 19, May 17, June 15, July 13, Aug. 11, Sept. 9, Oct. 7, Nov. 5, Dec. 3

Soul mates: Jan. 3, 10, Feb. 1, 8, Mar. 6, Apr. 4, May 2

November 11

♏ Sensitive and idealistic, you are an energetic Scorpio with tremendous mental potential if you are willing to discipline yourself through focusing on your objectives. Versatile and imaginative, you need to express your creative and emotional power. Composure and perseverance are often the keys to your success, and you are bound to make an impression by specializing in a particular area.

The subinfluence of your decanate ruler, Pisces, implies that you are receptive and highly intuitive, with psychic powers or a sixth sense. Although you constantly come up with remarkable ideas, a tendency to worry may undermine your convictions and self-esteem. This suggests that a pragmatic approach combined with poise and imagination are your balancing factors. Since you are receptive to vibration and rhythm, you may be creatively inclined or find music to be a positive influence.

Through being broad-minded and tolerant, you realize the infinite possibilities that are available to you. Although adventurous and keen on personal freedom, sharing and cooperative effort usually take you farther than traveling alone will. By seeing everything as a learning experience and listening to your inner voice, you come to value both your reason and intuition.

When you are aged eleven through forty, your progressed Sun is in Sagittarius, emphasizing a need for optimism and expansion through study, travel, or your personal quest for truth. At age forty-one, when your progressed Sun moves into Capricorn, there is a turning point as you start to take a more pragmatic, persistent, and realistic approach to life. At the age of seventy-one, when your progressed Sun enters Aquarius, you place more emphasis on new ideas, freedom, and companionship.

Your Secret Self

With an inner sense of the dramatic, you can project all emotions, from being tough, bossy, and determined to being sensitive, caring, and compassionate. Although generous and idealistic, with a warm heart, you also possess a strong sense of duty or obligation. Being intuitive as well as mentally astute, you are likely to seek inspiration and work well in service to others. A need to express yourself and your creativity may find outlets through art, music, or drama, or at least you can become a fine appreciator.

With a strong awareness of your responsibilities, you like to pay your debts but may sometimes be too hard on yourself or others. This may cause you to become depressed or frustrated. By having a positive philosophy in life or a meaningful cause or ideal, you are able to maintain a positive state of mind so your remarkable capabilities can shine through.

Work & Vocation

As you are able to put yourself in other people's positions, you are a good psychologist or advisor. A natural inclination for business combined with good organizational skills is likely to aid you in any career. With your love of knowledge and talent for communication, you could excel in teaching, science, or writing. By educating yourself, you are able to make the most of your

---

FIXED STAR

Star's name: Al Schemali, also called North Scale or the North Claw

Degree position: 18°23'–19°19' Scorpio between the years 1930 and 2000

Magnitude: 2.5

Strength: ★★★★★★

Orb: 1°30'

Constellation: Beta Libra

Applicable days: November 11, 12, 13

Star qualities: varied interpretations: Mercury/Jupiter and Jupiter/Mars

Description: a blue-white, sometimes pale emerald star located in the northern scale of the Balance

---

PRIMARY STAR'S INFLUENCE

Al Schemali offers opportunities for good fortune. You have a sound intellect and a flair for science or esoteric subjects, which highlights your intuitive and psychic abilities. This star may bestow honors, wealth, and riches and may also bring long-lasting happiness.

Linked to your Sun's degree, Al Schemali imparts a strong character, leadership abilities, and executive skills. With the help of this star's influence, you may enjoy promotion to a high position in your career and achieve success after initial difficulties. This star warns that you should avoid legal entanglements and questionable situations. On the other hand, trouble does not last long and good fortune returns if the correct choices are made.

potential. Occupations connected to the public or involving foreign lands could satisfy your love of variety and stop you from becoming bored. A need for service or being of use to your community can help you keep your feet on the ground and give you emotional satisfaction.

Famous people who share your birthday include actress Demi Moore, general George Patton, writers Kurt Vonnegut Jr. and Carlos Fuentes, comedian Jonathan Winters, and actor Leonardo DiCaprio.

Numerology

The special vibration of the master number 11 birthday suggests that idealism, inspiration, and innovation are highly important to you. A blend of humility and confidence challenges you to work toward self-mastery both materially and spiritually. Through experience you learn how to deal with both sides of your nature and develop a less extremist attitude by trusting your own feelings. Usually you are highly charged and enjoy vitality, but must avoid becoming overly anxious or impractical. The subinfluence of the number 11 month indicates that you are emotionally sensitive, with psychic abilities. Although you are receptive to positive influences around you, avoid any type of hostile environment, as it works negatively on your psyche. Staying balanced, determined, and focused enables you to receive a unique insight into people and ideas. Although you need freedom to operate independently, avoid being preoccupied with yourself and learn to work with others through collaborative endeavors. Combining your imaginative thought with your ingenuity and practical know-how can produce outstanding results.

• *Positive*: focused, objective, enthusiastic, inspirational, spiritual, intuitive, intelligent, outgoing, inventive, artistic, service, healing ability, humanitarian, psychic

• *Negative*: superiority complex, dishonest, aimless, overemotional, easily hurt, highly strung, selfish, lack of clarity, mean

YOUR SPECIAL SOMEONE

You might find long-lasting relationships and stability with someone born on one of the following days.

Love & friendship: Jan. 1, 5, 15, 26, 29, 30, Feb. 13, 24, 27, 28, Mar. 5, 11, 22, 25, 26, Apr. 9, 20, 23, 24, May 7, 18, 21, 22, June 5, 16, 19, 20, July 3, 14, 17, 18, 31, Aug. 1, 12, 15, 16, 29, 31, Sept. 10, 13, 14, 27, 29, Oct. 8, 11, 12, 25, 27, Nov. 6, 9, 10, 23, 25, Dec. 4, 7, 8, 21, 23, 29

Beneficial: Jan. 1, 2, 10, 27, Feb. 8, 25, Mar. 6, 23, Apr. 4, 21, May 2, 19, 30, June 17, 28, July 15, 26, Aug. 13, 24, Sept. 11, 22, Oct. 9, 20, Nov. 7, 18, Dec. 5, 16

Fatal attractions: May 9, 10, 11, 12

Challenging: Jan. 17, 26, Feb. 15, 24, Mar. 13, 22, Apr. 11, 20, May 9, 18, June 7, 16, July 5, 14, Aug. 3, 12, 30, Sept. 1, 10, 28, Oct. 8, 26, 29, Nov. 6, 24, 27, Dec. 4, 22, 25

Soul mates: Jan. 21, Feb. 19, Mar. 17, Apr. 15, May 13, June 11, July 9, 29, Aug. 7, 27, Sept. 5, 25, Oct. 3, 23, Nov. 1, 21, Dec. 19

Love & Relationships

You are idealistic, with a strong need for emotional security, so close relationships are an integral part of your happiness. Loyal and affectionate, you can be demonstrative with your feelings but need to guard against becoming overserious or insecure. Since you are sociable and popular, you enjoy other people's company and do not like being on your own. You are supportive of others, and you are often tempted to make sacrifices for those you love, but avoid becoming overly dependent on partners. Fortunately, you possess charm and wonderful people skills that can endear you to others and increase your social standing.

November 12

♏ Friendly and communicative, you are a multitalented Scorpio with a flair for dealing with people. Although at times you may appear unfeeling on the outside, you can be sensitive, with powerful emotions. Idealistic, you like to find out the truth and are often involved in exposing hidden issues. Your vitality and cerebral power are often subdued by your charming personality, but once you learn how to communicate your vision, you can inspire others with your originality and depth of feeling.

The subinfluence of your decanate ruler, Pisces, suggests that you are imaginative, with psychic ability as well as intense emotions. Since you enjoy a mental challenge and like to test your wits and intelligence, your easygoing manner can at times be misleading.

Confident in your knowledge, you can accomplish and achieve success, but the more learned you are, the more focused you become. Harmonious by nature, you have a need to establish peace of mind and create a congenial atmosphere through building a firm foundation and establishing a set of positive convictions. Alternatively, when you find yourself in confrontational situations, you may succumb to power games or become provocative and disagreeable. You benefit from enhancing your persuasive skills and diplomacy to convince others to change their mind.

When you are aged ten through thirty-nine, your progressed Sun is in Sagittarius, highlighting issues of adventure and freedom. You may wish to explore life by constantly expanding your mental outlook, whether through study, travel, or your personal quest for truth. At age forty, when your progressed Sun moves into Capricorn, there is a turning point as you start to take a more determined, disciplined, and realistic approach to life. This may involve manifesting more order and structure. At the age of seventy, when your progressed Sun enters Aquarius, you begin to place more emphasis on friendship, independence, and humanitarian ideals.

Your Secret Self

Highly intuitive, with a powerful sense of vision, you will find that self-discipline and concentration are essential to develop your amazing mental potential. Your ability to get by fairly easily without trying too hard may not do much to stimulate the hard work needed to fulfill your enormous potential. An understanding that knowledge is power ensures that you will always have a keen desire for new learning while keeping a certain childlike quality.

The subtlety and intelligence associated with your birthday suggests that you are likely to be interested in understanding the motives and secrets of others and are attracted to people who possess a fine intellect. Although you are aware of your innate wisdom, you may lack the patience to build on what you already know and must particularly avoid escapism through fantasy, alcohol, or drugs, due to your acute sensitivity.

Work & Vocation

With your ability to come across to others as really positive and charming, you can make your ideas known in an entertaining way. A good strategist, with people skills, you possess a natural

FIXED STAR

Star's name: Al Schemali, also called North Scale or the North Claw
Degree position: 18°23'–19°19' Scorpio between the years 1930 and 2000
Magnitude: 2.5
Strength: ★★★★★★
Orb: 1°30'
Constellation: Beta Libra
Applicable days: November 11, 12, 13
Star qualities: varied interpretations: Mercury/Jupiter and Jupiter/Mars
Description: a blue-white, sometimes pale emerald star located in the northern scale of the Balance

PRIMARY STAR'S INFLUENCE

Al Schemali offers opportunities for good fortune. You have a sound intellect and a flair for science or esoteric subjects, which highlights your intuitive and psychic abilities. This star may bestow honors, wealth, and riches and may also bring long-lasting happiness.

Linked to your Sun's degree, Al Schemali imparts a strong character, leadership abilities, and executive skills. With the help of this star's influence, you may enjoy promotion to a high position in your career and achieve success after initial difficulties. This star warns that you should avoid legal entanglements and questionable situations. On the other hand, trouble does not last long and good fortune returns if the correct choices are made.

aptitude for business, promotion, or sales. Not liking to take orders, however, suggests that you prefer management positions or may be inclined to become self-employed. Alternatively, with your desire for the limelight, you could successfully pursue a career as an actor, director, or politician. On the other hand, your keen intellect and communication skills could attract you to writing, law, education, or healing work.

Famous people who share your birthday include Princess Grace of Monaco, singer/songwriter Neil Young, composer Alexander Borodin, skater Tonya Harding, gymnast Nadia Comaneci, and Supreme Court Justice Harry Blackmun.

Numerology

With a number 12 birthday, usually you are intuitive, helpful, and friendly, with good reasoning powers. Since you want to establish true individuality, you are often innovative. Naturally understanding and sensitive, you also know how to use tact and cooperative methods to accomplish your aims and objectives. When you achieve a balance between your need for self-expression and your natural inclination to be supportive of others, you can find emotional satisfaction and personal fulfillment. You may nevertheless need to find the courage to stand on your own two feet and develop self-confidence or learn not to get easily discouraged by other people. The subinfluence of the number 11 month indicates that although you can express yourself, you are at times opinionated and outspoken. Being intuitive and versatile implies that you have many interests, but without perseverance and determination, you can waste your energy and spread yourself too thin. As a highly intuitive individual, you are a master at assessing people and finding out what lies beneath the surface.

• *Positive:* creative, attractive, initiative, disciplinarian, can promote yourself or others
• *Negative:* reclusive, eccentric, uncooperative, overly sensitive, lack of self-esteem

Love & Relationships

As you are likely to be powerful and assertive, you need to feel secure and in command of your life. Although idealistic and practical, you have a tendency to be stubborn, which implies that you become fixed in your basic beliefs and adhere to your own strict moral codes. In close relationships, learn to compromise rather than try to control your partner or make unreasonable demands. Sensitive, you need a peaceful and harmonious environment that can be mentally stimulating. Once committed to a relationship, you can be a very loyal and passionate yet tender partner.

YOUR SPECIAL SOMEONE

If you are looking for a stimulating relationship, you may want to seek those born on the following dates.

Love & friendship: Jan. 10, 13, 20, 21, 30, Feb. 8, 11, 18, 28, Mar. 6, 9, 16, 17, 26, Apr. 4, 7, 14, 24, May 2, 5, 12, 22, June 3, 10, 20, July 1, 8, 9, 18, Aug. 6, 16, 30, Sept. 4, 14, 28, 30, Oct. 2, 12, 26, 28, 30, Nov. 10, 24, 26, 28, Dec. 8, 22, 24, 26

Beneficial: Jan. 12, 16, 17, 28, Feb. 10, 14, 15, 26, Mar. 8, 12, 13, 24, Apr. 6, 10, 11, 22, May 4, 8, 9, 20, 29, June 2, 6, 7, 18, 27, July 4, 5, 16, 25, Aug. 2, 3, 14, 23, Sept. 1, 12, 21, Oct. 10, 19, Nov. 8, 17, Dec. 6, 15

Fatal attractions: Mar. 31, Apr. 29, May 9, 10, 11, 12, 27, June 25, July 23, Aug. 21, Sept. 19, Oct. 17, Nov. 15, Dec. 17

Challenging: Jan. 6, 18, 22, 27, Feb. 4, 16, 20, 25, Mar. 2, 14, 18, 23, Apr. 12, 16, 21, May 10, 14, 19, June 8, 12, 17, July 6, 10, 15, Aug. 4, 8, 13, Sept. 2, 6, 11, Oct. 4, 9, Nov. 2, 7, Dec. 5

Soul mates: Mar. 28, Apr. 26, May 24, June 22, July 20, Aug. 18, Sept. 16, Oct. 14, Nov. 12, Dec. 10

November 13

Creative and original, you are a practical and capable Scorpio with an astute mind and sharp intuition. Inspired and receptive, with curiosity and an observant eye, you like to find out what motivates others, and you are quick at assessing people and situations. Often independent, with a tenacious spirit, you possess depth of thought and can develop your intuitive and analytical skills.

The subinfluence of your decanate ruler, Cancer, empowers you with imagination and psychic abilities. If inspired, you are usually adaptable and can cope with every situation. Although you are shrewd and aware, at times skepticism or indecision can cause you to worry and be mistrustful; you may need to learn to have confidence in your first instincts. Since you like to be mentally occupied and well informed, education or self-directed learning can help you develop your fine mind as well as your confidence.

Your alternating between the conventional and the avant-garde implies that you need to express your individuality and creativity through finding mentally stimulating activities. Boredom and inactivity can cause a nervous disposition and bring on your tendency to be quarrelsome or provocative. Ambitious, you are willing to work hard and make a real effort in order to achieve your objectives; a positive perspective rather than cold cynicism makes your path to success a great deal smoother.

When you are aged nine through thirty-eight, your progressed Sun is in Sagittarius, highlighting issues of idealism, expansion, and opportunity. You may feel optimistic and able to take chances during this period. A desire for expansion may come through your work, education, or travel, or you may wish to explore your inner world through your personal quest for truth. At age thirty-nine, when your progressed Sun moves into Capricorn, you reach a turning point as you start to take a more disciplined, determined, and realistic approach to life. From the age of sixty-nine, when your progressed Sun enters Aquarius, you begin to place more emphasis on friendship and humanitarian ideals.

FIXED STAR

Star's name: Unukalhai

Degree position: 21°3'–21°54' Scorpio between the years 1930 and 2000

Magnitude: 2.5

Strength: ★★★★★

Orb: 1°40'

Constellation: Alpha Serpentis

Applicable days: November 13, 14, 15, 16

Star qualities: Saturn/Mars

Description: a pale orange-yellow star located on the neck of the Serpent

PRIMARY STAR'S INFLUENCE

Unukalhai imparts a bold and daring nature, determination, and endurance, which can help you overcome difficulties. This star also warns against keeping unsuitable company and suggests that although learning to do the right thing might be hard, it is also very rewarding.

Linked to your Sun's degree, Unukalhai imparts success in writing, politics, and affairs dealing with the public. This star bestows a good sense of structure and determination, although you may be obstinate. Unukalhai's influence also suggests that family matters need to be settled in a fair and just way and warns against involvement in feuds and legal battles.

• *Positive:* determination, endurance, power of resistance, overcoming challenges

• *Negative:* rebelliousness and quarrelsome, breaking the law, antiestablishment

Your Secret Self

Ambitious and determined, you have a desire for power and material success. With good financial know-how and strong survival instincts, you can accumulate wealth and utilize your surroundings to your advantage. You possess a direct and forthright approach to your goals that ensures that you do not waste time. Although you have a natural talent for making money, you may also need to develop your self-control and overcome a tendency to be manipulative, act ruthlessly, or carry materialism too far. Your strong motivation and capacity for hard work ensure that you are an achiever and have the potential to accomplish in a remarkable way.

Although you possess sharp, quick mental responses, you can also be very charming. You are an independent thinker who is particularly inventive when challenged but must guard against taking the easy option and not living up to your true potential. A youthful and playful quality is likely to stay with you all your life, but in your quest for achievement and mastery, you will need to be responsible and keep challenging yourself mentally. If you are feeling skeptical or cynical, you may need the faith to be more daring and spontaneous, as you usually work better when enjoying some friendly competition.

Work & Vocation

With your natural talent for understanding the value of things, you have a most productive work influence. This can help you in any career you choose, particularly business. If you believe in a project or are inspired, you will work really hard to manifest your objectives. This birthday often bestows a talent for writing or produces gifted teachers. You have a dynamic mental energy that is excellent for debating or law; or with your analytical mind, you may also be interested in psychology or research. The probability of your possessing technical skills may attract you to engineering or working with computers. The medical and healing professions are also areas where you can enjoy sharing your knowledge with others.

Famous people who share your birthday include writer Robert Louis Stevenson, astrologer/statistician Michel Gauqueli, actresses Linda Christian and Whoopi Goldberg, and U.S. Supreme Court Justice Louis Brandeis.

Numerology

Emotional sensitivity, enthusiasm, and inspiration are often identified with the number 13 birthday. Numerically, you are associated with ambition and hard work, and can accomplish much through creative self-expression. You may need to cultivate a pragmatic outlook if you want to turn your creative talents into tangible products. Your original and innovative approach inspires new and exciting ideas, which frequently result in work that impresses others. As a number 13 individual, you are earnest, romantic, charming, and fun-loving, and with dedication you can achieve prosperity. The subinfluence of the number 11 month indicates that you are astute and highly intuitive. Although you have many inspired thoughts, self-doubt can undermine your confidence and determination. Idealistic and thoughtful, you need a vision to steer you in the right direction. Being skeptical or doubting often gives rise to mistrust and emotional insecurity. By showing the humanitarian side of your nature, you can live up to your high ideals.

- *Positive:* ambitious, creative, freedom-loving, self-expressive, initiative
- *Negative:* impulsive, indecisive, bossy, unemotional, rebellious

Love & Relationships

Although you are devoted and affectionate to those you love, being secretive implies that you do not like to reveal your true feelings and may sometimes feel lonely. When in love, you need time to develop trust in your partner. Usually you are attracted to determined and hard-working or ambitious individuals. A tendency to worry or be suspicious indicates that you should guard against being resentful or vengeful. If you find an inspiring person whom you can trust, you can become a loyal and faithful partner.

YOUR SPECIAL SOMEONE

For security, mental stimulation, and love, you might want to begin looking for those born among the following dates.

Love & friendship: Jan. 21, 22, 28, 31, Feb. 19, 20, 26, 29, Mar. 17, 24, 27, Apr. 15, 22, 25, May 13, 20, 23, June 11, 18, 21, July 9, 10, 16, 19, Aug. 7, 14, 17, 31, Sept. 5, 12, 15, 29, Oct. 3, 10, 13, 27, 29, 31, Nov. 1, 8, 11, 25, 27, 29, Dec. 6, 9, 23, 25, 27

Beneficial: Jan. 9, 12, 18, 24, 29, Feb. 7, 10, 16, 22, 27, Mar. 5, 8, 14, 20, 25, Apr. 3, 6, 12, 18, 23, May 1, 10, 16, 21, 31, June 2, 8, 14, 19, 29, July 6, 12, 17, 27, Aug. 4, 10, 15, 25, Sept. 2, 8, 13, 23, Oct. 6, 11, 21, Nov. 4, 9, 19, Dec. 2, 7, 17

Fatal attractions: May 11, 12, 13, 14

Challenging: Jan. 7, 8, 19, 28, Feb. 5, 6, 17, 26, Mar. 4, 3, 15, 24, Apr. 1, 2, 13, 22, May 11, 20, June 9, 18, July 7, 16, Aug. 5, 14, Sept. 3, 12, Oct. 1, 10, Nov. 8, Dec. 6

Soul mates: Jan. 3, 19, Feb. 1, 17, Mar. 15, Apr. 13, May 11, June 9, July 7, Aug. 5, Sept. 3, Oct. 1

November 14

♏ As a Scorpio, you are quietly forceful and direct, with an ability to advance by the sheer power of your persistence. Usually composed and amiable, you have a sociable personality, which has a captivating presence that can win you friends and influence others.

The subinfluence of your decanate ruler, Cancer, suggests that you are receptive and discriminating, with psychic ability and deep, intense feelings. Your friendly style can at times hide the fact that you enjoy investigating and testing your inner strength with wit and intelligence. Although sensitive and considerate, you are a natural strategist with practical abilities, and you can combine your innovative ideas and determination to make your dreams a reality.

A blend of ambition and inertia implies that although you are clever and proficient, when you find a subject that captures your imagination you may need to develop self-discipline in order to remain focused on your goal. Since you can inspire others with your ideas and unique vision, do not allow your curiosity and many interests to distract you from your objectives or let anxiety and worry undermine your great potential. Your desire for information often makes you very knowledgeable in your chosen field, and since you are versatile and competitive, your ideas can make money for you. In the pursuit of your ambitions, guard against becoming overly serious, which often causes you unnecessary stress.

From age eight through thirty-seven, when your progressed Sun is in Sagittarius, you gradually become more optimistic, with a need for positivity, expansion, and idealism in your life. You may feel able to take more chances during this period; you may study or be involved with foreign people or places. At age thirty-eight, when your progressed Sun moves into Capricorn, you reach a turning point as you start to take a more realistic, persevering, and security-conscious approach to life, seeking more structure and order. At the age of sixty-eight, when your progressed Sun enters Aquarius, there is another change as you begin to place more importance on new ideas, humanitarianism, and companionship.

Your Secret Self

Dramatic, with an inner dignity, you can combine your sense of power and great determination to take you to the top. This emphasizes the importance of having clear goals or a sense of direction, as once you have made up your mind you can be resolute and persistent. You may have to be careful, however, that this does not become excessive and turn to just plain stubbornness. Nevertheless, with your natural business acumen, you maintain a strong protection around the area of your work as long as you are willing to put in the necessary discipline.

Although you have natural leadership abilities, you understand the advantages of teamwork and partnership. You have an innate skill for making contacts and being able to commercialize your talents. At times, however, you may get caught between work duties and relationships. It may be necessary to keep a balance so that you can be sensitive to the needs of others, but do not compromise too much of your personal power.

Work & Vocation

With your organizational skills, you can do well in business or in authoritative positions such as manager, administrator, or executor. Your keen mind and pleasure in mental pursuits could

PRIMARY STAR

Star's name: Agena
Degree position: 22°48'–23°45' Scorpio between the years 1930 and 2000
Magnitude: 1
Strength: ★★★★★★★★★
Orb: 2°30'
Constellation: Beta Centuris
Applicable days: November 14, 15, 16, 17, 18
Star qualities: varied influences: Venus/Jupiter or Mars/Mercury
Description: a small white star located on the right foreleg of the Centaur

PRIMARY STAR'S INFLUENCE

Agena bestows achievement and the rise to a high position. This star also imparts vitality and good health. Often you are refined and possess a high moral code, which may in turn bring friendship, success, and honors.

Linked to your Sun's degree, Agena bestows ambition and success. You are probably well connected or have prominent friends and associates. This star provides good social skills and the ability to attract wide popularity, which in turn brings opportunities. Agena encourages mental activity and quick, outspoken responses; however, it also suggests that speaking out of turn or being indiscreet can be costly.

equally lead you to a career in writing, teaching, research, or information technology. An ability to understand human nature indicates that occupations such as advisor, therapist, or psychologist could also be rewarding for you. Alternatively, your easy charm, natural flair for form and color, and sense of the dramatic could attract you to the theater, music, and the arts. In most instances cooperative efforts can greatly aid your career.

Famous people who share your birthday include Britain's Prince Charles, composer Aaron Copland, King Hussein of Jordan, former Indian prime minister Jawaharlal Nehru, heiress Barbara Hutton, painter Claude Monet, actress Louise Brooks, and former U.N. Secretary General Boutros Boutros-Ghali.

Numerology

Intellectual potential, pragmatism, and determination are some of the qualities of the number 14 birthday. Indeed, as a number 14 individual, you frequently put your work first and judge yourself and others on the basis of career achievements. Although you need stability, the restlessness indicated by the number 14 urges you to forge ahead or take on new challenges in a constant attempt to improve your lot. This innate restlessness and constant lack of satisfaction may also inspire you to make a great many changes in your life, especially if you are not happy with your working conditions or financial status. With your perceptive mind, you respond quickly to problems and enjoy solving them. The subinfluence of the number 11 month indicates that you are intelligent, idealistic, and highly intuitive. By combining your strong instincts with your practical skills and imaginative thoughts, you are able to produce original and creative ideas. Being less skeptical or stubborn and more trusting and flexible enables you to realize the benefits of staying liberal and open-minded.

• *Positive:* decisive actions, hardworking, lucky, creative, pragmatic, imaginative, industrious

• *Negative:* overly cautious or overly impulsive, unstable, thoughtless, stubborn

YOUR SPECIAL SOMEONE

You might find a partner who will understand your sensitivity and need for love among those born on the following days.

Love & friendship: Jan. 8, 12, 18, 22, Feb. 16, 20, Mar. 8, 14, 18, 28, Apr. 12, 16, 26, May 10, 14, 24, June 8, 12, 22, July 6, 10, 20, 29, Aug. 4, 8, 18, 27, 30, Sept. 2, 6, 16, 25, 28, Oct. 4, 14, 23, 26, 27, 30, Nov. 2, 12, 21, 24, 28, Dec. 10, 19, 22, 26, 28

Beneficial: Jan. 6, 10, 25, 30, Feb. 4, 8, 23, 28, Mar. 2, 6, 21, 26, Apr. 4, 19, 24, May 2, 17, 22, June 15, 20, 30, July 13, 18, 28, Aug. 11, 16, 26, Sept. 9, 14, 24, Oct. 7, 12, 22, 31, Nov. 5, 10, 20, Dec. 3, 8, 18

Fatal attractions: May 12, 13, 14, 15, 29, June 27, July 25, Aug. 23, Sept. 21, Oct. 19, Nov. 17, Dec. 15

Challenging: Jan. 13, 29, 31, Feb. 11, 27, 29, Mar. 9, 25, 27, Apr. 7, 23, 25, May 5, 21, 23, June 3, 19, 21, July 1, 17, 19, Aug. 15, 17, Sept. 13, 15, Oct. 11, 13, Nov. 9, 11, Dec. 7, 9

Soul mates: Jan. 6, 25, Feb. 4, 23, Mar. 2, 21, Apr. 19, May 17, June 15, July 13, Aug. 11, Sept. 9, Nov. 7, Dec. 5

Love & Relationships

As a sensitive and compassionate individual, you have a wide range of powerful emotions. Usually gregarious, you enjoy socializing and entertaining. Although you need love and affection, stability and security may be prerequisites in your relationships. You are attracted to dramatic and intelligent people who can inspire you to be creative and expressive. Once you are in a relationship, it is important to keep the balance between compromise and staying independent.

November 15

℠ Ambitious and intelligent, with an enterprising spirit, you are an active Scorpio with a restless nature. Your birthday implies that although your greatest asset is your quick and piercing mind, at times you can scatter your energies in too many directions and fail to find something that will keep you interested and satisfied. Your creative mental potential is, however, excellent for learning new skills and improving on existing knowledge. Whatever you do, your creative input and ingenuity can make a real difference.

The subinfluence of your decanate ruler, Cancer, suggests that you are versatile and imaginative, with strong instincts and intense feelings. With your unusual sense of humor, you can be witty and entertaining, but your friendly manner can sometimes be misleading, since you enjoy a mental challenge and like to test your intelligence against others.

Although you have the ability to come straight to the point of matters and solve problems swiftly and efficiently, guard against a tendency to be impatient. By developing a more persevering attitude, you can overcome your tendency to act impulsively. This will also aid you to be more industrious and methodical on issues that concern thoroughness and attention to detail.

While you are between the ages of seven and thirty-six, your progressed Sun is in Sagittarius, highlighting issues of expansion and opportunity. You may feel optimistic and able to take chances, and you desire to travel or study during this period. At age thirty-seven, when your progressed Sun moves into Capricorn, you reach a turning point as you start to take a more disciplined, determined, and realistic approach to life. You may have a stronger awareness of your goals and ambitions and have a greater need for order. From the age of sixty-seven, when your progressed Sun enters Aquarius, you start to place more emphasis on friendship, independence, and humanitarian ideals.

FIXED STARS

Agena, Unukalhai

PRIMARY STAR

Star's name: Agena

Degree position: 22°48'–23°45' Scorpio
between the years 1930 and 2000

Magnitude: 1

Strength: ★★★★★★★★

Orb: 2°30'

Constellation: Beta Centuris

Applicable days: November 14, 15, 16, 17, 18

Star qualities: varied influences: Venus/Jupiter or Mars/Mercury

Description: a small white star located on the right foreleg of the Centaur

PRIMARY STAR'S INFLUENCE

Agena bestows achievement and the rise to a high position. This star also imparts vitality and good health. Often you are refined and possess a high moral code, which may in turn bring friendship, success, and honors.

Linked to your Sun's degree, Agena bestows ambition and success. You are probably well connected or have prominent friends and associates. This star provides good social skills and the ability to attract wide popularity, which in turn brings opportunities. Agena encourages mental activity and quick, outspoken responses; however, it also suggests that speaking out of turn or being indiscreet can be costly.

Your Secret Self

You may mask your inner sensitivity to protect your vulnerability. At times you can be unsure of your feelings or experience a general dissatisfaction with life. To avoid becoming bored, you must keep your spirit of adventure alive. Travel, change, and a desire to be constantly exploring, whether mentally or physically, can help you find new and exciting experiences.

Your quick instincts can make you highly intuitive. Usually you work best on your first impression of a person or situation, which is invariably correct. You can develop this talent by having more faith in your perceptive abilities. Guiding your life by it, you gain deeper insight and wisdom and avoid escapism through overindulgence. Being willing to take a gamble for the sake of your grand plans, you are often lucky to be in the right place at the right time.

Work & Vocation

Whatever work you decide on, you learn very quickly, so you need activities that can keep you mentally challenged. Having an exceptional ability to talk to anybody from any walk of life as well as to make helpful contacts can certainly help you in all your endeavors. Needing variety, you may be drawn to careers that involve travel or constant change. You are ambitious and need recognition; this often ensures that you rise to the top of your profession. Careers that can use your quick intelligence may include business, law, or politics. Equally, you may use your dramatic gifts on the stage or through writing. With your love of freedom and restlessness, you may experiment with many different kinds of experiences or occupations in your desire to find one that suits your enterprising personality. Many people of this birthday often work for themselves.

Famous people who share your birthday include artist Georgia O'Keeffe, singer Petula Clark, astronomer William Herschel, conductor Daniel Barenboim, Nazi field marshal Erwin Rommel, industrialist Andrew Carnegie, writer J. G. Ballard, and Judge Joseph Wapner.

Numerology

Versatility, enthusiasm, and restlessness are suggested by the number 15 birthday. Usually you are quick, with a charismatic personality. Your greatest assets are your strong instincts and the ability to learn quickly through combining theory and practice. On many occasions you manage to earn while learning new skills. Often you utilize your intuitive powers and are quick at recognizing opportunities when they arise. As a number 15 birthday, you possess a talent for attracting money or receiving help and support from others. Although you are naturally adventurous, you nevertheless need to find a real base or a home that you can call your own. The subinfluence of the number 11 month indicates that although you have inner doubts, you have a strong character and are often determined and self-willed. By learning to utilize your natural common sense and sound judgment, you can overcome a fear of periods of instability. By being resolute yet flexible, you can welcome the unexpected and turn situations to your advantage.

• *Positive:* willing, generous, responsible, kind, cooperative, appreciative, creative ideas

• *Negative:* disruptive, irresponsible, self-centered, loss of faith, indecision, materialistic, misusing power

Love & Relationships

Although you are highly intuitive and sensitive, your skeptical attitude suggests that sometimes you can be doubting and noncommittal, preferring to keep your thoughts to yourself. You need mental stimulation and variety; otherwise you become bored easily. A need for security and stability can be an important factor in your personal relationships. By being patient and accepting or more discriminating, you learn whom to grow to love and trust. Do not let a self-destructive element or a desire to get even spoil your relationships. When positive, you can be generous and giving with those you love.

YOUR SPECIAL SOMEONE

To find long-lasting happiness and security, you might begin by looking for someone born on one of the following days.

Love & friendship: Jan. 13, 19, 23, 24, Feb. 22, 26, Mar. 9, 15, 19, 28, 29, 30, Apr. 7, 13, 17, 26, 27, May 5, 11, 15, 24, 25, 26, June 3, 9, 13, 22, 23, 24, July 1, 7, 11, 20, 21, 22, Aug. 5, 9, 18, 19, 20, Sept. 3, 7, 16, 17, 18, Oct. 1, 5, 14, 15, 16, 29, 31, Nov. 3, 12, 13, 14, 27, 29, Dec. 1, 10, 11, 12, 25, 27, 29

Beneficial: Jan. 7, 15, 20, 31, Feb. 5, 13, 18, 29, Mar. 3, 11, 16, 27, Apr. 1, 9, 14, 25, May 7, 12, 23, June 5, 10, 21, July 3, 8, 19, Aug. 1, 6, 17, 30, Sept. 4, 15, 28, Oct. 2, 13, 26, Nov. 11, 24, Dec. 9, 22

Fatal attractions: May 13, 14, 15, 16

Challenging: Jan. 6, 14, 30, Feb. 4, 12, 28, Mar. 2, 10, 26, Apr. 8, 24, May 6, 22, June 4, 20, July 2, 18, Aug. 16, Sept. 14, Oct. 12, Nov. 10, Dec. 8

Soul mates: Apr. 30, May 28, June 26, July 24, Aug. 22, Sept. 20, Oct. 18, 30, Nov. 16, 28, 30, Dec. 14, 26, 28

November 16

FIXED STARS

Agena, Unukalhai

PRIMARY STAR

Star's name: Agena

Degree position: 22°48'–23°45' Scorpio between the years 1930 and 2000

Magnitude: 1

Strength: ★★★★★★★★★

Orb: 2°30'

Constellation: Beta Centuris

Applicable days: November 14, 15, 16, 17, 18

Star qualities: varied influences: Venus/Jupiter or Mars/Mercury

Description: a small white star located on the right foreleg of the Centaur

PRIMARY STAR'S INFLUENCE

Agena bestows achievement and the rise to a high position. This star also imparts vitality and good health. Often you are refined and possess a high moral code, which may in turn bring friendship, success, and honors.

Linked to your Sun's degree, Agena bestows ambition and success. You are probably well connected or have prominent friends and associates. This star provides good social skills and the ability to attract wide popularity, which in turn brings opportunities. Agena encourages mental activity and quick, outspoken responses; however, it also suggests that speaking out of turn or being indiscreet can be costly.

• *Positive:* assertive, clever, stamina, popularity, good morals

♏ Intuitive and thoughtful, with a pragmatic approach, you are a Scorpio with good organizational and planning skills. As a rational thinker, you like to make good use of the wide knowledge you frequently acquire through your inquisitiveness and probing mind. As you are a perfectionist, this cerebral potential suggests that you like to solve problems and can succeed in research work and study.

The subinfluence of your decanate ruler, Cancer, empowers you with imagination and psychic abilities. This influence also suggests that you possess deep feelings and a capacity to express yourself dramatically through a dynamic unconscious. Idealistic, with a forceful personality, you have the ability to understand current trends and can enjoy being creative while making money if you do not succumb to being critical or fixed in your ideas.

Positive thinking and education, whether formal or self-directed, usually play an important role in your advancement. Although often skeptical, you may discover sometime in life a need to enhance your common sense by exploring a more philosophical or mystical perspective. You may even find yourself acting as an advisor to others. Since you are particularly drawn to people who are clever or interesting, you are liable to make contacts based on shared interests.

While you are between the ages of six and thirty-five, your progressed Sun is in Sagittarius, highlighting issues of adventure and expansion in life. You may feel optimistic or wish to extend your mental horizons through study or travel during this period. At age thirty-six, when your progressed Sun moves into Capricorn, you reach a turning point as you start to take a more practical, ordered, and realistic approach to life. From the age of sixty-six, when your progressed Sun enters Aquarius, you begin to increase your powers of observation and become more independent, humanitarian, and group-conscious.

Your Secret Self

Inside you are extremely sensitive and vulnerable, even though on the surface you appear confident, dramatic, and strong. You gradually come to realize that responsibility and hard work are the way to success, and you are willing to make sacrifices for your objectives or for others. A deep desire for harmony and simplicity may find expression through art and music; it may also emphasize the importance of your home and family.

Counterbalancing your desire for peace is a desire to move and be constantly exploring new mental horizons. The quest for knowledge and, ultimately, wisdom can take you into the world of education, travel, or new adventures. To avoid alternating between restlessness and getting stuck in a rut, it is important for you to lead a well-balanced life, reflect, and stay calm.

Work & Vocation

Practical and shrewd, you have an innate business sense. Employers respect your good organizational skills and the fact that you can be responsible. This can aid you in administration or managerial work. Being very independent, however, you like the freedom to work in your own way or may prefer to be self-employed. You are generally aware of the advantages of working cooperatively with others and may become involved in working partnerships. Your keen mind may attract you to research, education, law, or advisory positions. Some people of this birthday also have an interest in the study of philosophy, psychology, or metaphysics. Equally, you can be financially successful in sales, agencies, or promotion. You are a good long-term planner and usually enjoy fighting for a cause.

Famous people who share your birthday include actress Bo Derek, composer William Handy, boxer Frank Bruno, jockey Willie Carson, comedian Griff Rhys Jones, actor Burgess Meredith, scientist Werner Von Braun, and writer Chinua Achebe.

Numerology

A number 16 birthday suggests that you are thoughtful, sensitive, and friendly. Although analytical, you often judge life and people according to how you feel. As a number 16 personality, however, you can experience inner tensions when facing friction between a need for self-expression and responsibility to others. With this birthdate, you may be interested in world affairs and may join international corporations or the media world. If creative, you can have a talent for writing with sudden flashes of inspiration. You may need to learn how to balance between being overly confident and being doubtful and insecure. The subinfluence of the number 11 month indicates that although you are receptive and imaginative, with powerful emotions, you can be secretive and often hide your feelings by appearing collected or aloof. You may prefer to rationalize your feelings but are prone to strong emotional reactions or periods of emotional turbulence. These strong desires for self-fulfillment need to find expression through an ideal or a cause. Although your expectations of others are high, being unsympathetic or too critical can undermine your long-term plans.

• *Positive:* knowledgeable, responsibilities to home and family, integrity, intuitive, social, cooperative, insightful

• *Negative:* worry, never satisfied, irresponsible, self-promoting, opinionated, skeptical, fussy, irritable

Love & Relationships

Although you are a pragmatic and intelligent person, your idealistic and individual character suggests that often you are drawn to unconventional relationships or to people from foreign countries. You generally like someone who can positively stimulate your mind, and, once committed, you become loving, loyal, and supportive. Although you are a perfectionist, avoid imposing your ideals and beliefs on others, as they might resent your bossy approach. A touch of youthfulness and mischief will stay with you throughout your relationships to ensure that you do not take things too seriously.

YOUR SPECIAL SOMEONE

If you are looking for a partner, you might start by searching for someone born on one of the following days.

Love & friendship: Jan. 3, 4, 14, 17, 20, 24, 25, Feb. 1, 2, 12, 18, 22, Mar. 10, 13, 16, 20, 29, 30, 31, Apr. 8, 14, 18, 27, 28, May 6, 12, 16, 25, 26, 31, June 4, 10, 14, 23, 24, 29, July 2, 8, 12, 21, 22, 27, Aug. 6, 10, 19, 20, 25, Sept. 4, 8, 17, 18, 23, Oct. 2, 6, 15, 16, 21, 30, Nov. 4, 13, 14, 19, 28, 30, Dec. 2, 11, 12, 17, 26, 28, 30

Beneficial: Jan. 4, 8, 21, Feb. 1, 2, 6, 19, Mar. 4, 17, 28, Apr. 2, 15, 16, May 13, 24, June 11, 22, July 9, 20, Aug. 7, 18, 31, Sept. 5, 16, 29, Oct. 3, 14, 27, Nov. 1, 12, 25, Dec. 10, 23

Fatal attractions: Jan. 3, May 12, 13, 14, 15, 31, June 29, July 27, Aug. 25, Sept. 23, Oct. 21, Nov. 19, Dec. 11, 17

Challenging: Jan. 7, 10, 15, 31, Feb. 5, 8, 13, 29, Mar. 3, 6, 11, 27, Apr. 1, 4, 9, 25, May 2, 7, 23, June 5, 21, July 3, 19, Aug. 1, 17, Sept. 15, Oct. 13, Nov. 11, Dec. 9

Soul mates: Mar. 31, Apr. 29, May 27, June 25, July 23, Aug. 21, Sept. 19, Oct. 17, 29, Nov. 15, 27, Dec. 13, 25

November 17

♏ Your mental vitality and enthusiasm indicate that you are a sensitive but practical Scorpio who has an ability to commercialize your talents. Although usually witty and adaptable, you also have a deeper and more introspective nature that can at times make you appear modest or even secretive.

The subinfluence of your decanate ruler, Cancer, implies that you are imaginative and receptive, with an inquiring mind. Since you are intellectually bright, you may explore different options before you decide where your true talents lie. Although you can be versatile and mentally curious, do not allow your many interests or hobbies to confuse you or scatter your energies. Self-discipline and definite objectives often inspire you to develop the endurance and persistence needed to take on challenges and make impossible dreams come true. By developing a willingness to work for long-term results without instant rewards, you can show your talents and dedication.

Being an excellent judge of human nature indicates that you are a good strategist with an eye for detail. Often a perfectionist, you can be painstakingly accurate. Do not, however, allow this talent to turn to criticism. Pioneering, with an enterprising spirit, you also possess strong survival instincts. By learning to spontaneously trust your own instincts, you can overcome a tendency to be insecure or suspicious.

While you are between the ages of five and thirty-four, your progressed Sun is in Sagittarius, highlighting issues of expansion and opportunity. You may desire freedom, feel optimistic, and want to take chances during this period. At age thirty-five, when your progressed Sun moves into Capricorn, you reach a turning point as you start to take a more disciplined, determined, and serious approach to your goals and ambitions. At the age of sixty-five, when your progressed Sun enters Aquarius, you begin to place more emphasis on friendship, independence, humanitarian ideals, and group awareness.

FIXED STAR

Star's name: Agena

Degree position: 22°48'–23°45' Scorpio between the years 1930 and 2000

Magnitude: 1

Strength: ★★★★★★★★

Orb: 2°30'

Constellation: Beta Centuris

Applicable days: November 14, 15, 16, 17, 18

Star qualities: varied influences: Venus/Jupiter or Mars/Mercury

Description: a small white star located on the right foreleg of the Centaur

PRIMARY STAR'S INFLUENCE

Agena bestows achievement and the rise to a high position. This star also imparts vitality and good health. Often you are refined and possess a high moral code, which may in turn bring friendship, success, and honors.

Linked to your Sun's degree, Agena bestows ambition and success. You are probably well connected or have prominent friends and associates. This star provides good social skills and the ability to attract wide popularity, which in turn brings opportunities. Agena encourages mental activity and quick, outspoken responses; however, it also suggests that speaking out of turn or being indiscreet can be costly.

• Positive: assertive, clever, stamina, popularity, good morals

• Negative: rashness, indecision, lack of honor

Your Secret Self

Proud and dramatic, you have a natural business sense and a strong need for self-expression. Possessing an inventive mind and strong individuality, you may find that much satisfaction comes from fulfilling a need to do something different and original. Being an astute observer of people, with an innate understanding of values, enables you to advise or lead others. A possible hindrance to your success, however, is a tendency to worry, be indecisive, or become discouraged. Once set on a course of action, however, you can be determined and single-minded in achieving your objectives.

With a love of change and an innate restlessness, you need to find stimulating interests and persevere with them, as you can become bored easily. This implies that variety, adventure, or travel may play an important part in your life. Although ambitious, you may experience changing finances, so you should make allowances for this in your long-term plans. You may also have to watch out for a streak of extravagance or being too impulsive.

Work & Vocation

Your magnetic charm and social skills can help you achieve success in all people-related occupations. You are likely to take a creative approach to whatever you do and use your natural tal-

536

ent for conversation or words. This can help you in careers such as writing, lecturing, media, or sales. You are versatile, and your need for a changing and varied career implies that you should avoid monotonous occupations. Alternatively, the more theatrical side of your nature may find fulfillment through show business or politics, and you are likely to work hard to support a cause that interests you. A desire to find people's hidden motives may attract you to careers with a psychological edge, and your natural business sense can bring you good fortune financially.

Famous people who share your birthday include director Martin Scorsese, actors Danny De Vito and Rock Hudson, TV personality Jonathan Ross, Method actor/director Lee Strasberg, baseball player Tom Seaver, designer David Emanuel, Olympic athlete Bob Mathias, field marshal Viscount Montgomery, and actresses Lauren Hutton and Mary Elizabeth Mastrantonio.

Numerology

As a number 17 individual, you are shrewd, with a reserved nature and good analytical abilities. As an independent thinker, you benefit from being well educated or skillful. Usually you utilize your knowledge in a specific way in order to develop your expertise and can achieve material success or a prominent position as a specialist or researcher. Private, introspective, and detached, with a strong interest in facts and figures, you frequently present a thoughtful demeanor and like to take your time. By developing your communication skills, you can discover much more about yourself from others. The subinfluence of the number 11 month indicates that you are highly intuitive, with psychic abilities. Inquisitive, you like to uncover what is hidden beneath the surface. As you are multitalented and ambitious, you can be dramatic and magnetic. Although you are original and creative, with inspired thoughts, you need to stay resolute and focused in order to put your talents to good use.

• *Positive:* thoughtful, specialist, good planner, business sense, attracts money, individual thinker, painstaking, accurate, skilled researcher, scientific

• *Negative:* detached, stubborn, carelessness, moody, narrow-minded, critical, worry, suspicious

Love & Relationships

Although you are charming and romantic, with deep emotions, a tendency to be dissatisfied or uneasy suggests that at times you can be critical or indecisive about your feelings. Loyal and devoted, you are able to make sacrifices in your love life; however, you can also run cold or become overly serious. You are usually looking for a partner who has a big heart yet can be detached enough to give you the freedom you need.

YOUR SPECIAL SOMEONE

You might find emotional fulfillment and that special someone among those born on the following days.

Love & friendship: Jan. 11, 18, 21, 25, Feb. 19, 23, Mar. 7, 14, 17, 21, 30, Apr. 15, 19, 28, 29, May 13, 17, 26, 27, June 11, 15, 24, 25, 30, July 9, 13, 22, 23, 28, Aug. 7, 11, 20, 21, 26, 30, Sept. 5, 9, 18, 19, 24, 28, Oct. 3, 7, 16, 17, 22, 26, 29, Nov. 1, 5, 14, 15, 20, 24, 27, Dec. 3, 12, 13, 18, 22, 25, 27, 29

Beneficial: Jan. 5, 13, 16, 22, 28, Feb. 3, 11, 14, 20, 26, Mar. 1, 9, 12, 18, 24, 29, Apr. 7, 10, 16, 22, 27, May 5, 8, 14, 20, 25, June 3, 6, 12, 18, 23, July 1, 4, 10, 16, 21, Aug. 2, 8, 14, 19, Sept. 6, 12, 17, Oct. 4, 10, 15, Nov. 2, 8, 13, Dec. 6, 11

Fatal attractions: May 13, 14, 15, 16, June 30, July 28, Aug. 26, Sept. 24, Oct. 22, Nov. 20, Dec. 18

Challenging: Jan. 2, 23, 30, Feb. 21, 28, Mar. 19, 26, 28, Apr. 17, 24, 26, May 15, 22, 24, June 13, 20, 22, July 11, 18, 20, Aug., 16, 18, 19, Sept. 7, 14, 16, Oct. 5, 12, 14, Nov. 3, 10, 12, Dec. 1, 8, 10

Soul mates: Jan. 14, 22, Feb. 12, 20, Mar. 10, 18, Apr. 8, 16, May 6, 14, June 4, 12, July 2, 10, Aug. 8, Sept. 6, Oct. 4, Nov. 2

November 18

℞ Ambitious and forceful, you are a Scorpio who can radiate confidence and be charming and generous. Self-assured, you are not undermined by failure and rarely admit defeat. Your sharp intellect and social flair suggest that you are a good psychologist who understands people and what motivates them. As a networker with many contacts, you prefer the personal touch and have a talent for making people feel special and important.

The subinfluence of your decanate ruler, Cancer, suggests that you are intuitive and imaginative, with strong emotional instincts. An unusual sense of humor suggests that although you can be witty and entertaining, some of your remarks can also be sarcastic and cutting. Provocative, you enjoy a mental challenge and like to test your wits and intelligence against others'.

Often purposeful and determined, with the power to pull through and endure, you prefer to take the lead and use your ideas in a constructive way. Your strong convictions and a pragmatic approach enable you to think fast and be an assertive debater. When you are relaxed and free from stress, you can present your vision clearly and persuade others to see things from your perspective. When irritable, however, you may need to overcome a tendency to be cynical or fault-finding.

While you are between the ages of four and thirty-three, your progressed Sun is in Sagittarius, highlighting issues of freedom, adventure, and expansion in life. You may wish to extend your mental horizons during this period, whether through study, travel, or your personal quest for truth. At age thirty-four, when your progressed Sun moves into Capricorn, you reach a turning point as you start to take a more responsible, precise, and hardworking perspective on life, seeking structure and order. From the age of sixty-four, when your progressed Sun enters Aquarius, you begin to increase your powers of observation and become more independent, free, or humanitarian.

Your Secret Self

The extremes of your personality are reflected in your ability to be warm, friendly, and helpful, yet on other occasions you can be prone to dark moods. In order to avoid using your scorpionlike sting and causing trouble that you may later regret, it is necessary to use your sharp and probing mind to investigate your own power and motivation. When on a conscious quest for self-awareness, you are able to help many others along the way with your shrewd and insightful comments.

A more theatrical side to your nature needs people and enjoys an active social life. Pride can work for you positively to help you on to greater achievements. It can also, however, cause you to become arrogant or stubborn. To avoid this, you need to be constantly initiating new projects or activities where you can channel your tremendous inner power. This ensures that with dedication and hard work you can achieve almost anything.

Work & Vocation

You have determination, perseverance, and a willingness to work hard when committed to a project, and these qualities can help you achieve in any area of your career. With the ability

FIXED STAR

Star's name: Agena

Degree position: 22°48'–23°45' Scorpio between the years 1930 and 2000

Magnitude: 1

Strength: ★★★★★★★★

Orb: 2°30'

Constellation: Beta Centuris

Applicable days: November 14, 15, 16, 17, 18

Star qualities: varied influences: Venus/Jupiter or Mars/Mercury

Description: a small white star located on the right foreleg of the Centaur

PRIMARY STAR'S INFLUENCE

Agena bestows achievement and the rise to a high position. This star also imparts vitality and good health. Often you are refined and possess a high moral code, which may in turn bring friendship, success, and honors.

Linked to your Sun's degree, Agena bestows ambition and success. You are probably well connected or have prominent friends and associates. This star provides good social skills and the ability to attract wide popularity, which in turn brings opportunities. Agena encourages mental activity and quick, outspoken responses; however, it also suggests that speaking out of turn or being indiscreet can be costly.

• *Positive:* assertive, clever, stamina, popularity, good morals

• *Negative:* rashness, indecision, lack of honor

to turn on the charm when necessary and possessing a quick understanding of human nature, you can be particularly successful in any vocation that involves people . Your leadership qualities, organizational skills, and capacity for strategic planning are ideal for business, where you are likely to enjoy the challenge of large projects. Being very independent, you need to be allowed to work in your own way or may be self-employed. Alternatively, your sharp mind and keen intelligence may attract you to professions such as teaching, lecturing, or politics. Equally, your need for self-expression and a love for the dramatic may lure you into the art and entertainment worlds.

Famous people who share your birthday include astronaut Alan Shepard, singer Kim Wilde, actor David Hemmings, opera singer Amelita Galli-Curci, actor Marcello Mastroianni, poll analyst George Gallup, and actress Linda Evans.

Numerology

Determination, assertiveness, and ambition are some of the attributes associated with the number 18 birthday. Active, with a need for challenges, you like to keep busy and are frequently involved in some enterprise. Capable, hardworking, and responsible, you rise to positions of authority. Alternatively, your strong business sense and organizational skills may lead you to the world of commerce. Since you may suffer from overwork, learn how to relax or slow down from time to time. As a number 18 personality, you may use your powers positively by healing others. You can also give sound advice or solve other people's problems. The subinfluence of the number 11 month indicates that you are strong-willed and resolute. Often opinionated and sure of yourself, you can be charming and influence others. Nevertheless, as you are likely to demand your independence, guard against a tendency to be selfish or unruly. Multitalented and daring, you have inspired ideas and the courage to turn these into material success stories.

• *Positive:* progressive, assertive, intuitive, courageous, resolute, healing ability, efficient, advisory skills

• *Negative:* uncontrolled emotions, lazy, lack of order, selfishness, callousness, failure to complete work or projects

Love & Relationships

Young at heart, you like to have fun, are entertaining, and can be good company. You enjoy impressing others and can be generous but may sometimes need to avoid being irresponsible or selfish. Since love and companionship are so important to you, often you use your diplomatic skill to keep your relationships harmonious. Outgoing and proud, with a forceful personality, you are strong yet magnetically alluring. On occasion, guard against becoming temperamental.

YOUR SPECIAL SOMEONE

You might find a partner who will understand your sensitivity and need for love among those born on the following dates.

Love & friendship: Jan. 6, 16, 18, 22, 26, Feb. 4, 14, 20, 24, 25, Mar. 2, 12, 14, 18, 22, Apr. 10, 16, 20, 30, May 8, 14, 18, 28, June 6, 12, 16, 26, July 4, 10, 14, 24, 31, Aug. 2, 8, 12, 22, 29, Sept. 6, 10, 20, 27, Oct. 4, 8, 18, 25, Nov. 2, 6, 16, 23, 30, Dec. 4, 14, 21, 28, 30

Beneficial: Jan. 6, 17, 23, 31, Feb. 4, 15, 21, 29, Mar. 2, 13, 19, 27, 30, Apr. 11, 17, 25, 28, May 9, 15, 23, 26, June 7, 13, 21, 24, July 5, 11, 19, 22, Aug. 3, 9, 17, 20, Sept. 1, 7, 15, 18, 30, Oct. 5, 13, 16, 28, Nov. 3, 11, 14, 26, Dec. 1, 9, 12, 24

Fatal attractions: May 13, 14, 15, 16

Challenging: Jan. 24, Feb. 22, Mar. 20, 29, Apr. 18, 27, 29, May 6, 16, 25, 27, 30, June 14, 22, 25, 28, July 12, 21, 23, 26, Aug. 10, 19, 21, 24, Sept. 8, 17, 19, 22, Oct. 6, 15, 17, 20, Nov. 4, 13, 15, 18, Dec. 2, 11, 13, 16

Soul mates: Jan. 13, Feb. 11, Mar. 9, Apr. 7, May 5, June 3, 30, July 1, 28, Aug. 26, Sept. 24, Oct. 22, Nov. 20, Dec. 18

November 19

Creativity and emotional sensitivity are often part of your personal charm. Idealistic and forceful, with an inquisitive mind, you are a Scorpio with a love of knowledge that can urge you to be daring and original. As a progressive thinker with an innovative mind, you are often interested in social and educational reforms or are constantly seeking new and exciting ideas.

The subinfluence of your decanate ruler, Cancer, implies that you are imaginative, curious, and receptive. Since you are intellectually bright and versatile, you may explore different options before you decide where your true talents lie. The mental restlessness that is often associated with your birthday suggests that you can easily become bored when you lack mental stimulation and are, as a consequence, apt to scatter your energies on trivial pursuits.

With your artistic talents and desire for knowledge, you often gather information and develop good communication skills that can include a natural flair for writing. Your pragmatic approach and sharp intellect imply that you are confident and a good analyst of people and what motivates them. With your personal touch, you have the talent for making people feel special and important. Agreeable and diplomatic, you can be friendly and stimulating company, though when moody you may appear unfeeling or disinterested.

While you are between the ages of three and thirty-two, your progressed Sun is in Sagittarius, emphasizing issues of positive idealism, expansion, and opportunity. This period is good for study, travel, or an overall sense of freedom. At age thirty-three, when your progressed Sun moves into Capricorn, you reach a turning point as you start to take a more disciplined, structured, and realistic approach to life. From the age of sixty-three, when your progressed Sun enters Aquarius, you begin to place more emphasis on humanitarian ideals, independence, and friendship.

FIXED STARS

Although your Sun's degree is not linked to a fixed star, some of your other planets' degrees certainly will be. By having an astrological chart calculated, you can find the exact position of the planets on your date of birth. This will tell you which of the fixed stars listed in this book are relevant to you.

Your Secret Self

A hidden longing for love and peace may have you searching for a pure love or idealistic cause, but it is important that you are always aware of equality. Seemingly independent, you are wise enough to realize that you cannot go it alone. Partnerships, teamwork, or cooperative efforts can therefore play an especially important role in your life. Unless you ensure that you do not compromise too much of yourself in all your relationships, there is a danger of disappointment or emotional lows.

With your intense emotional sensitivity, you may need to balance the emotional extremes of your nature. Dynamic and dramatic, you are likely to find that people are naturally drawn to you because of your intelligence. As well as having a sharp mind, you can also be warm, loving, and understanding. This can lead to your becoming a leader, advisor, or protector of others.

Work & Vocation

With your leadership abilities, social skills, and keen intelligence, you can excel in almost any career. Being hardworking and interested in money issues, you may be drawn to business, where you prefer large projects and the freedom to work in your own way. Travel or variety may play a part in your work options. As you enjoy working for a cause, you can be drawn to social reform or may be a good promoter or spokesperson. Highly persuasive, you have verbal skills that may serve you well in media, politics, or law. Equally, you could succeed in sales, public relations, or advisory positions. Sharing all your knowledge and expertise can extend to being a lecturer or counselor.

Famous people who share your birthday include designer Calvin Klein, actresses Jodie Foster and Meg Ryan, TV host Dick Cavett, Indian prime minister Indira Gandhi, media tycoon Ted Turner, and astronaut Alan Shepard.

Numerology

Dynamic, ambitious, and humanitarian are some of the characteristics associated with the number 19 birthday. Decisive and resourceful, you possess depth of vision, but the dreamer side of your nature is compassionate, idealistic, and creative. Although you are sensitive, the need to be someone may be the very thing that pushes you to be dramatic and claim center stage. Often there is a strong desire to establish an individual identity. To do so, you may first need to overcome the influence of peer group pressure. To others, you may appear confident, resilient, and resourceful, but inner tensions may cause emotional ups and downs. Artistic and charismatic, you will find that the world is there for you to explore. The subinfluence of the number 11 month indicates that you are highly intuitive, with powerful emotions. With your insight, you can often be a visionary, but you may have to learn to communicate your thoughts and feelings in an open way. As a multitalented individual, you have good reasoning powers, but avoid being impatient or worried. Often you need to overcome restrictions and challenges before you find peace and harmony.

• *Positive:* dynamic, centered, creative, leader, lucky, progressive, optimistic, strong convictions, competitive, independent, gregarious

• *Negative:* self-centered, depressive, worry, fear of rejection, ups and downs, materialistic, egotistical, impatient

Love & Relationships

Practical and charismatic, you have an alluring and friendly personality. With your diplomatic skills, you are able to harmonize tense situations and relationships. You prefer active and aware people who have succeeded as a result of their own efforts. As you are emotionally intense, guard against coming on too strong and being possessive. You are often willing to work hard to achieve success in your relationships, and you make a loyal partner or friend.

YOUR SPECIAL SOMEONE

For security, mental stimulation, and love, you might want to begin looking among those born on the following days.

Love & friendship: Jan. 1, 4, 20, 27, 29, Feb. 2, 25, 27, Mar. 23, 25, Apr. 21, 23, May 19, 21, 29, June 17, 19, 27, July 15, 17, 25, Aug. 13, 15, 23, Sept. 11, 13, 21, Oct. 9, 11, 19, Nov. 7, 9, 17, Dec. 5, 7, 15

Beneficial: Jan. 3, 10, 15, 18, Feb. 1, 8, 13, 16, Mar. 6, 11, 14, 29, 31, Apr. 4, 9, 12, 27, 29, May 2, 7, 10, 25, 27, June 5, 8, 23, 25, July 3, 6, 21, 23, Aug. 1, 4, 19, 21, Sept. 2, 17, 19, Oct. 15, 17, Nov. 13, 15, Dec. 11, 13

Fatal attractions: Apr. 30, May 14, 15, 16, 17, 28, June 26, July 24, Aug. 22, Sept. 20, Oct. 18, Nov. 16, Dec. 14

Challenging: Jan. 9, 14, 16, 25, Feb. 7, 12, 14, 23, Mar. 5, 10, 12, 21, 28, 30, Apr. 3, 8, 10, 19, 26, 28, May 1, 6, 8, 17, 24, 26, June 4, 6, 15, 22, 24, July 2, 4, 13, 20, 22, Aug. 2, 11, 18, 20, Sept. 9, 16, 18, Oct. 7, 14, 16, Nov. 5, 12, 14, Dec. 3, 10, 12

Soul mates: Jan. 30, Feb. 28, July 18, Dec. 29

November 20

℠ Charismatic and intuitive, you are a friendly Scorpio with a winning smile and powerful emotions. Although usually a forceful character with a dynamic personality, you are kind and generous and, at times, surprisingly modest. You may need to overcome a tendency to be fixed and learn to let go of your controlled emotions. Ambitious and dramatic, with sensitivity and quick responses, you have the potential for outstanding creative achievement.

The subinfluence of your decanate ruler, Cancer, suggests that you are imaginative and like to be surrounded by quality and luxury. Gregarious and fun-loving, you can also be a diplomat when it is in your own interest. Although you are sensitive and guided by your feelings, a practical and hardworking nature suggests that only self-discipline is required in order to make the most of your many wonderful talents.

If inspired, you may need to express yourself in a creative way and seek recognition through the worlds of theater, art, music, and entertainment. Success can be achieved through determination and hard work. You may nevertheless need to overcome a tendency to be impatient, manipulative, or too domineering and develop your strategy and planning skills. Through collaboration and cooperative efforts you usually make your greatest contribution to your community or society.

Until you reach the age of thirty-one, your progressed Sun is in Sagittarius, encouraging you to move forward in life optimistically, searching for opportunities. You may feel adventurous and willing to take chances, have an interest in education, or feel drawn to foreign people or places. At age thirty-two, when your progressed Sun advances into Capricorn, you reach a turning point as you start to take a more practical, ambitious, and realistic approach to life, seeking order and structure. From the age of sixty-two, when your progressed Sun enters Aquarius, you begin to increase your powers of observation and become more experimental, independent, or group-conscious.

Fixed Star

Star's name: Bungula, also called Tolliman

Degree position: 28°36'–29°35' Scorpio between the years 1930 and 2000

Magnitude: 1

Strength: ★★★★★★★★★

Orb: 2°30'

Constellation: Alpha Centauri

Applicable days: November 20, 21, 22, 23, 24

Star qualities: Venus/Jupiter

Description: a brilliant white and yellow binary star located on the left foot of the Centaur

PRIMARY'S STAR'S INFLUENCE

Bungula bestows a passionate yet refined nature and beneficial social contacts. If you seek help, this star grants friends who will assist you when you need help most. It also imparts opportunities and positions of honor or power. Bungula nevertheless warns against extremist behavior and a fatalistic attitude.

Linked to your Sun's degree, this star indicates an ambitious nature, and the consistency and determination to achieve steady progress. It also warns of rivalry, envy, or self-centeredness.

• *Positive:* self-reliant, learn to share, generosity, popularity

• *Negative:* overly sensitive, falling out with other people, alienating yourself from others

Your Secret Self

Through self-analysis and humor you are able to balance the emotional extremes of your nature. Generous yet selfish, hardworking yet indulgent, tough yet sensitive, you can be an interesting mixture of opposites. Sociable and an expert at personal contact, your charm and your shrewd judgment of character can help you in all situations. Since you are often unhappy if alone, companionship is very important to you, and you will often compromise for peace. You may have to watch, however, that your love of sensuality and comfort does not deter you from the dynamic expression of your great potential.

Your strong intuition can be a great help in your own life and also in developing the more humanitarian and compassionate side of your nature. When operating positively, it enables you to be detached and self-assured and avoid falling into frustration or disappointment.

Work & Vocation

With the combination of your leadership abilities and emotional sensitivity, you will naturally rise to positions of power. Possessing charm and advanced social skills, you are likely to succeed in any people-related activity. Your communication skills may draw you toward occupations such as teacher, lecturer, writer, or salesperson. Your ability to make useful contacts can help you in business, especially combined with your ability to commercialize your talents. Alternatively, your natural dramatic sense can help you succeed in politics, the entertainment world, or the arts. On the other hand, your humanitarian inclinations may direct you toward a career in social reform or working for a cause.

Famous people who share your birthday include U.S. statesman Robert F. Kennedy, TV journalist Alistair Cooke, guitarist Duane Allman, comedian Dick Smothers, and writer Nadine Gordimer.

Numerology

With a number 20 birthday, you are intuitive, sensitive, adaptable, and understanding, and often see yourself as a part of a larger group. Usually you enjoy cooperative activities where you can interact, share experiences, or learn from others. Charming and gracious, you develop diplomatic and social skills and can move in different social circles with ease. You may, however, need to develop your confidence, overcome a tendency to be easily hurt by the actions and criticism of others, or avoid a tendency to become overly dependent. You are a master at creating a congenial and harmonious atmosphere. The subinfluence of the number 11 month indicates that you usually appear self-assured and practical, but inwardly you can possess deep feelings and are highly intuitive. Although you have a kind and gentle heart that can be generous and loyal, you can also be stubborn and suspicious. By learning to balance the extreme sides of your nature, you can create stability and order.

• *Positive:* good partnerships, gentle, tactful, receptive, intuitive, considerate, harmonious, agreeable, amicable, ambassador of goodwill

• *Negative:* suspicious, lack of confidence, oversensitive, emotional, selfish, easily hurt, dishonest

Love & Relationships

Social and generous, you can be kindhearted and have long-term friendships. When you become insecure, however, you can be possessive and selfish. Resilient and stubborn, with a strong sense of responsibility, in relationships you do not give up and are rarely the first one to leave. Although you possess deep and powerful emotions, you can also be secretive about the way you feel. Affectionate and passionate, you can be strong-willed or dramatic.

YOUR SPECIAL SOMEONE

For that special someone, you might find emotional fulfillment among those born on the following days.

Love & friendship: Jan. 2, 5, 14, 28, Feb. 26, Mar. 1, 10, 24, Apr. 22, May 20, 29, 30, June 18, 27, 28, July 16, 25, 26, Aug. 14, 23, 24, Sept. 12, 21, 22, Oct. 10, 19, 20, 29, 31, Nov. 8, 17, 18, 27, 29, Dec. 6, 15, 16, 25, 27

Beneficial: Jan. 2, 10, 13, 16, Feb. 8, 11, 14, Mar. 6, 9, 12, Apr. 4, 7, 10, May 2, 5, 8, June 3, 6, July 1, 4, 30, Aug. 2, 28, 30, Sept. 26, 28, Oct. 24, 26, Nov. 22, 24, Dec. 20, 22, 30

Fatal attractions: May 16, 17, 18, 19, Oct. 31, Nov. 29, Dec. 27

Challenging: Jan. 3, 9, 10, Feb. 1, 7, 8, Mar. 5, 6, 31, Apr. 3, 4, 29, May 1, 2, 27, June 25, July 23, Aug. 2, 21, 31, Sept. 19, 29, Oct. 17, 27, Nov. 15, 25, Dec. 13, 23

Soul mates: Jan. 5, Feb. 3, Mar. 1, May 30, June 28, July 26, Aug. 24, Sept. 22, Oct. 20, Nov. 18, Dec. 16

November 21

♏ Born on a cusp, you are influenced by both Scorpio and Sagittarius. Elegant and sociable, with an enterprising personality, you are a charming individual who can display a confident and assured image. With an abundance of feelings, sensitivity, and imagination, you are usually subtle and poised, yet a passionate side to your nature suggests that you are also determined and dramatic.

The subinfluence of your decanate ruler, Cancer, implies that you are intuitive and discerning, with strong premonitions. Usually you judge situations and experiences by the way you feel, and your emotional range can include great creativity, self-expression, or compassion and understanding. These usually win you the love and admiration you seek from others. If, on the other hand, you fail to get your own way, you can react too emotionally or become temperamental.

Ambitious, with enthusiasm and a strong sense of vision, you are dedicated and hardworking. Inspired by ideas, you seek ways to express yourself and find it easier to take the lead. This suggests that you fare better as someone who gives the orders rather than as a person in a subservient position. Idealistic and loyal, with a strong sense of duty, you usually let obligations take precedence over inclinations of the heart. Your sensitivity, however, does not detract from the fact that you possess good business sense and an awareness of material considerations. This part of your personality can be resolute and inflexible.

Until you reach the age of thirty, your Sun progresses through Sagittarius, highlighting issues of idealism, expansion, and opportunity. This period is good for study, travel, or your pursuit of truth and a positive philosophy. At age thirty-one there is a turning point when your progressed Sun moves into Capricorn. You start to take a more disciplined, determined, and realistic approach to life. From the age of sixty-one, when your progressed Sun enters Aquarius, you begin to place more of an emphasis on your personal freedom and the need to express your individuality. This can also accent issues of humanitarian ideals, friendship, and group awareness.

Your Secret Self

Competitive and success-oriented, you are always seeking to better yourself or improve your circumstances. By harnessing all your dynamic emotions into work that gives you a sense of purpose, you are likely to find a deeper awareness of your own inner power. In order to accomplish your grand dreams and fulfill your need to build something of long-lasting value, it is necessary to be very focused and self-disciplined.

By developing your natural humanitarianism, you are able to avoid personal dissatisfaction or disappointment with others. A great deal of your achievement depends on broadening your knowledge and expanding your universal understanding. By becoming mentally detached or objective, you are able to rise above difficult situations and solve problems with inspired thinking. Engaging and sociable, you can uplift others' spirits with your words of comfort and encouragement.

Work & Vocation

Hardworking and reliable, with a natural sense of authority, you invariably rise to positions of power. With your charm and warmth, you have a way with people but can also be a discipli-

FIXED STAR

Star's name: Bungula, also called Tolliman

Degree position: 28°36'–29°35' Scorpio between the years 1930 and 2000

Magnitude: 1

Strength: ★★★★★★★★

Orb: 2°30'

Constellation: Alpha Centauri

Applicable days: November 20, 21, 22, 23, 24

Star qualities: Venus/Jupiter

Description: a brilliant white and yellow binary star located on the left foot of the Centaur

PRIMARY STAR'S INFLUENCE

Bungula bestows a passionate yet refined nature and beneficial social contacts. If you seek help, this star grants friends who will assist you when you need it most. It also imparts opportunities and positions of honor or power. Bungula nevertheless warns against extremist behavior and a fatalistic attitude.

Linked to your Sun's degree, this star indicates an ambitious nature and the consistency and determination to achieve steady progress. It also warns of rivalry, envy, or self-centeredness.

• Positive: self-reliant, learn to share, generosity, popularity

• Negative: overly sensitive, falling out with other people, alienating yourself from others

narian. Although you are efficient and thorough, if in business you may fare best when your sense of vision is creatively employed, such as in advertising, publishing, or media. Idealistic, you can often be influential in social movements or work selflessly for a cause. This can lead you to a career in politics, charity work, or the healing professions. Since you have a way with words and enjoy sharing your knowledge with others, you can be an excellent teacher or writer. Alternatively, your sensitivity and imagination may find creative outlets through the arts.

Famous people who share your birthday include actresses Goldie Hawn and Juliet Mills, philosopher/writer Voltaire, writers Marilyn French and Beryl Bainbridge, painter René Magritte, baseball player Stan Musial, and *New Yorker* editor Tina Brown.

Numerology

Dynamic drive and an outgoing personality are usually present in those with a number 21 birthday. Socially inclined, you have many interests or contacts and are generally fortunate. Usually you show others your friendly and gregarious personality. Intuitive, with an independent spirit, you are highly inventive and original. As a number 21 individual, you can be fun-loving, magnetic, and creative, with social charm. Alternatively, you can be shy and reserved with a need to develop assertiveness, especially in close relationships. In life you often have many opportunities to show your multiple talents and leadership abilities. Although you can be inclined toward cooperative relationships, you always want to be acknowledged for your talents and abilities. The subinfluence of the number 11 month indicates that you can be inspired and receptive. Your ability to assess situations quickly implies that you have strong instincts and are mentally keen. Do not let doubt or suspicion undermine your confidence. If you learn to be patient, you can develop your creative flow and avoid impulsive actions.

- *Positive:* inspiration, creativity, love unions, long-lasting relationships
- *Negative:* dependency, nervous, loss of emotional control, lack of vision, fear of change

Love & Relationships

As an idealistic and intense individual, you have powerful emotions and strong desires. Dramatic and expressive, you can be very kind and supportive to those you love and are often a loyal and generous friend. Being security-conscious, you make sure everyone is well provided for. A tendency to attract unusual people suggests that you need to beware of questionable relationships. To establish harmony in partnerships, it is important to avoid negative thinking or a tendency to be bossy.

YOUR SPECIAL SOMEONE

You might find happiness and stability in relationships by looking for someone born on one of the following days.

Love & friendship: Jan. 3, 22, 25, 29, 30, Feb. 1, 20, 23, 27, 28, Mar. 18, 21, 25, 26, Apr. 16, 19, 23, 24, 28, May 14, 17, 21, 22, 24, 26, 31, June 12, 15, 19, 20, 24, 29, July 10, 13, 18, 22, Aug. 8, 11, 15, 16, 20, 27, 29, 30, Sept. 6, 9, 13, 14, 18, 23, 27, 28, Oct. 4, 7, 11, 12, 16, 21, 25, 26, Nov. 2, 5, 9, 10, 14, 19, 23, 24, Dec. 3, 7, 8, 12, 17, 21, 22

Beneficial: Jan. 17, Feb. 15, Mar. 13, Apr. 11, May 9, 29, June 7, 27, July 5, 25, Aug. 3, 23, Sept. 1, 21, Oct. 19, 29, Nov. 17, 27, 30, Dec. 15, 25, 28

Fatal attractions: May 18, 19, 20, 21, 31, June 29, July 27, Aug. 25, 30, Sept. 23, 28, Oct. 21, 26, Nov. 19, 24, Dec. 17, 22

Challenging: Jan. 20, 23, Feb. 18, 21, Mar. 16, 19, Apr. 14, 17, May 12, 15, June 10, 13, July 8, 11, Aug. 6, 9, Sept. 4, 7, Oct. 2, 5, Nov. 2, Dec. 1

Soul mates: Jan. 4, 31, Feb. 2, 29, Mar. 27, Apr. 25, May 23, June 21, July 19, Aug. 17, Sept. 15, Oct. 13, Nov. 11, Dec. 9

Sagittarius

November 22–December 21

SUN: SCORPIO/SAGITTARIUS CUSP

DECANATE: SAGITTARIUS/JUPITER

DEGREE: 29°30' SCORPIO–

0°30' SAGITTARIUS

MODE: MUTABLE

ELEMENT: FIRE

November 22

♐ Born on the cusp, you benefit from the influences of both Scorpio and Sagittarius. The Scorpio influence suggests that you are tenacious, sensitive, and highly intuitive. Your magnanimous gestures, enthusiasm, and joy for life show a playful and compassionate nature, implying that, under the influence of Sagittarius, you are idealistic and broad-minded.

The subinfluence of your decanate ruler, Sagittarius, suggests that you are inspired by travel, nature, and high aims, and often have an inclination toward philosophy and theology. Your optimism, strong instincts, and gregarious personality ensure that others are drawn to your friendly and easygoing manner. Your ability to make yourself popular indicates that you can entertain and enchant others with your innate charm. Although interested in new facts or ideas, you may have a very low boredom threshold. Friendly and cooperative, you can at times become overzealous. By becoming more reserved, you can moderate your eagerness.

Although generous both emotionally and materially, you may at times go to extremes by indulging in a life of luxury and glamour. If you allow yourself to become too much of an escapist who refuses to grow up, you will need to learn to take responsibility and have a more mature perspective. Nevertheless, when you do something you enjoy, you are capable of working very hard and with dedication and perseverance can accomplish and succeed.

Up to the age of twenty-nine, you will want to expand your horizons and seek opportunities, whether through enterprising ventures, study, or travel. At the age of thirty, when your progressed Sun moves into Capricorn, you start to become more practical, goal-oriented, and realistic in your approach to your achievements. Another turning point occurs at the age of sixty, when your progressed Sun moves into Aquarius. This highlights a growing need for freedom, new ideas, and expressing your individuality.

Your Secret Self

Although very self-willed, you possess sensitive emotions and seek inspiration. You may find your greatest pleasure, however, in being of service to others. Although caring, you may have to develop a detached perspective in order to avoid being easily hurt or feeling sorry for yourself. Your receptivity also bestows on you an exceptionally good sense of form and appreciation of art and music, which you may wish to develop or use as a healing force. Whatever you do in life, it is important to keep challenging yourself to bring out the best of your remarkable potential.

Creative, attractive, and a good listener, you need people and companionship, usually being unhappy on your own. Dramatic, with a sense of inner nobility and a warm heart, you enjoy an audience and will work hard to entertain and keep others happy. Although you are sociable, a tendency to self-indulgence or too much rich living may nevertheless be too tempting a distraction from realizing your high ideals.

Work & Vocation

Your advanced people skills, flair for business, and idealistic nature suggest that you are most suited to professions where you can collaborate with others. Your charm, talent for communication, and natural diplomacy may lead you to work in sales, promotion, agencies, or public

---

Star's name: Bungula, also called Tolliman

Degree position: 28°36'–29°35' Scorpio between the years 1930 and 2000

Magnitude: 1

Strength: ★★★★★★★★

Orb: 2°30'

Constellation: Alpha Centauri

Applicable days: November 20, 21, 22, 23, 24

Star qualities: Venus/Jupiter

Description: a brilliant white and yellow binary star located on the left foot of the Centaur

---

PRIMARY STAR'S INFLUENCE

Bungula bestows a passionate yet refined nature and beneficial social contacts. If you seek help, this star grants friends who will assist you when you need it most. It also imparts opportunities and positions of honor or power. Bungula nevertheless warns against extremist behaviors and a fatalistic attitude.

Linked to your Sun's degree, this star indicates an ambitious nature and the consistency and determination to achieve steady progress. It also warns of rivalry, envy, or self-centeredness.

• *Positive:* self-reliant, learn to share, generosity, popularity

• *Negative:* overly sensitive, falling out with other people, alienating yourself from others

548

relations. Equally, you can excel in the world of media, publishing, or politics. As you enjoy social interaction and entertaining others, you may be drawn to show business or the music industry. Alternatively, you may wish to share your ideas through the educational field. With your natural understanding for the problems of others, you may find yourself in the role of counselor or in the caring or healing professions. Optionally, the playful and competitive side of your nature may find a positive and financially lucrative outlet in the world of sports.

Famous people who share your birthday include actress Jamie Lee Curtis, writer George Eliot, tennis players Billie Jean King and Boris Becker, director Terry Gilliam, composer Benjamin Britten, songwriter Hoagy Carmichael, and former French president Charles de Gaulle.

Numerology

With a number 22 birthdate, you are a proud, practical, and highly intuitive individual. This is a master number and can vibrate both as number 22 and as number 4. Usually honest and hardworking, with natural leadership abilities, you have a charismatic personality and a deep understanding of people and what motivates them. Although undemonstrative, you often show a caring, protective concern for the welfare of others, yet you never lose sight of your pragmatic or realistic stand. Frequently cultured and worldly, you have many friends and admirers. The more competitive among you achieve success and good fortune with help and encouragement from others. Many born on this date have strong links with brothers or sisters and can be protective and supportive of them. The subinfluence of the number 11 month indicates that you are determined and intuitive, with deep feelings and high ideals. Usually you are sensitive, but by building a protective shield around yourself, you can appear insensitive and aloof. If you set your standards too high, you may suffer from discontent and become critical or unsympathetic.

• *Positive:* universal, director, highly intuitive, pragmatic, practical, dexterous, skillful, builder, good organizer, realist, problem solver, achiever

• *Negative:* get-rich-quick schemes, nervous, inferiority complex, bossy, materialistic, lack of vision, lazy, egotistical, self-promoting

Love & Relationships

Friendly and entertaining, yet sensitive and with strong emotions, you have a warm personality and a need for love and affection that can attract you to many different romantic relationships. These may sometimes prove to be unsuitable and not worth the effort. Youthful and idealistic, you can become strongly attached to partners, but to avoid unnecessary heartache, guard against becoming overly emotional. With your big heart, you can be both generous and compassionate with those you love.

YOUR SPECIAL SOMEONE

For your ideal partner, you might begin by looking for someone born on one of the following days.

Love & friendship: Jan. 5, 9, 10, 18, 19, 26, 30, Feb. 3, 8, 16, 17, 24, 28, Mar. 1, 6, 14, 15, 22, 26, 31, Apr. 4, 11, 12, 13, 20, 24, May 2, 10, 11, 18, 22, June 8, 9, 16, 20, 30, July 6, 7, 14, 18, 28, Aug. 3, 4, 5, 12, 16, 26, 30, Sept. 2, 3, 10, 14, 28, Oct. 1, 8, 12, 22, 26, Nov. 6, 10, 20, 24, Dec. 4, 8, 18, 22, 30

Beneficial: Jan. 13, Feb. 11, Mar. 9, Apr. 7, May 5, June 3, 30, July 1, 28, Aug. 26, Sept. 24, Oct. 22, Nov. 20, Dec. 18

Fatal attractions: May 20, 21, 22, 23

Challenging: Jan. 14, 24, Feb. 12, 22, Mar. 10, 20, Apr. 8, 18, May 6, 16, June 4, 14, July 2, 12, Aug. 10, Sept. 8, Oct. 6, Nov. 4, Dec. 2

Soul mates: Jan. 13, Feb. 11, Apr. 7, July 30, Aug. 28, Sept. 26, Oct. 24, Nov. 22, Dec. 20

November 23

♐ Gregarious and enthusiastic, you are an enterprising Sagittarian who is full of life. Charming and honest by nature, you have an ability to make friends and impress people. Since you have an adventurous nature and enjoy being active, you often have a full schedule and lead a busy life.

The subinfluence of your decanate ruler, Sagittarius, adds vitality to your restless nature and encourages you to take chances and broaden your horizons. Thoughtful and idealistic, you like to find out about new ideas and spread the word. Easily bored, however, you may need to develop a more diligent perspective by learning to be introspective and dependable. Avoid becoming scattered by getting carried away with too many aims. When inspired, you can act impulsively and take off in a new direction without prior planning. You may need to learn the discipline to back up your good intentions.

Creative and competitive, you have a fighting spirit, suggesting that you need to make things happen in a big way both emotionally and materially. With your executive skills and quick mind, you are versatile and talented. Spontaneous and outspoken, you can be direct and cutting, with others feeling that you show a lack of tenderness and tact. However, your compassion and warm heart usually compensate for verbal blunders.

Up to the age of twenty-eight, you are mainly concerned with issues of freedom and expanding your horizons, whether through travel, education, or your philosophy of life. A turning point occurs at the age of twenty-nine, when your progressed Sun moves into Capricorn. This is likely to bring a more pragmatic, orderly, and structured approach to life, with a stronger emphasis on achieving your major goals. There is another change of emphasis at fifty-nine, when your progressed Sun moves into Aquarius. This highlights a growing need for independence, progressive ideas, and expressing your own uniqueness.

Your Secret Self

Intelligent and enthusiastic, you love to learn and can comprehend information very quickly. You recognize the power of knowledge, and by gathering information, you build your wisdom, understanding, and confidence. Idealistic and proud, you have strong convictions and beliefs that you may wish to share through your natural flair for the written or spoken word. With your ardor and strong personal magnetism, you have the ability to inspire and impress others.

Your birthday promises a love of variety and a life of excitement and adventure. Any possible restlessness and impatience can be channeled into positive and constant self-improvement. Having the added advantage of being active as well as emotional and sensitive, you have a wide range to your personality and are therefore in a better position than most to achieve on a grand scale.

Work & Vocation

With your charismatic appeal and ability to deal with people, you may find yourself naturally gravitating to positions of leadership. Needing work that gives you as much freedom as possi-

---

FIXED STAR

Star's name: Bungula, also called Tolliman

Degree position: 28°36'–29°35' Scorpio between the years 1930 and 2000

Magnitude: 1

Strength: ★★★★★★★★

Orb: 2°30'

Constellation: Alpha Centauri

Applicable days: November 20, 21, 22, 23, 24

Star qualities: Venus/Jupiter

Description: a brilliant white and yellow binary star located on the left foot of the Centaur

PRIMARY STAR'S INFLUENCE

Bungula bestows a passionate yet refined nature and beneficial social contacts. If you seek help, this star grants friends who will assist you when you need it most. It also imparts opportunities and positions of honor or power. Bungula nevertheless warns against extremist behavior and a fatalistic attitude.

Linked to your Sun's degree, this star indicates an ambitious nature and the consistency and determination to achieve steady progress. It also warns of rivalry, envy, or self-centeredness.

• *Positive:* self-reliant, learn to share, generosity, popularity

• *Negative:* overly sensitive, falling out with other people, alienating yourself from others

ble, you may prefer to be in business for yourself. Ambitious and versatile, you need variety and change to keep your interest. Your keen intellect and persuasive manner suggest that as a humanitarian, you can succeed in bringing about reforms. Equally, you can succeed in education, law, science, writing, or politics. Emotionally sensitive, you have innate understanding that could take you into the caring professions or work that helps others. Alternatively, your spirit of enterprise may find an outlet in business. With your imagination, creativity, and natural flair for captivating people, you could equally be successful in the world of entertainment, particularly music.

Famous people who share your birthday include singer Bruce Hornsby, actors Boris Karloff, Harpo Marx, and Maxwell Caulfield, tennis player Lew Hoad, spiritual leader Sai Baba, and artist Erté.

Numerology

Emotional sensitivity and creativity are two of the attributes of a number 23 birthday. Usually you are versatile and a quick thinker, with a professional attitude and a mind full of inventive ideas. With the number 23 influence, you can learn new subjects easily but may prefer practice to theory. You are fond of travel, adventure, and meeting new people; the restlessness implied by the number 23 urges you to try many different kinds of experience, and you adapt to make the best of any situation. The subinfluence of the number 11 month indicates that you like to be methodical and rely on your own common sense. Although you are highly receptive to others, you generally make up your own mind. With faith and natural charm, you can communicate your powerful feelings and inspire those around you with a charitable viewpoint. A tendency to be highly charged when inspired suggests that you can be dramatic and creative.

• *Positive:* loyal, responsible, travel, communicative, intuitive, creative, versatile, trustworthy, fame

• *Negative:* selfish, insecure, stubborn, uncompromising, fault-finding, dull, withdrawn, prejudiced

Love & Relationships

With your charm and ability to radiate warmth, you can be attracted to people from different backgrounds. Wanting security and stability, you like to plan for the future. In your closer relationships you can be particularly drawn to strong-willed individuals who show a sense of purpose and determination. Being very sociable, you make an excellent host and can be very compassionate in regard to other people's problems.

YOUR SPECIAL SOMEONE

Your chances of finding happiness and a loving partner are increased with those born on the following dates.

Love & friendship: Jan. 2, 3, 6, 9, 10, 11, 21, 25, 27, 31, Feb. 1, 4, 7, 8, 9, 25, 29, Mar. 2, 5, 7, 17, 23, 27, Apr. 3, 4, 5, 15, 21, 25, May 1, 3, 13, 19, 23, 30, June 1, 11, 17, 21, 28, July 9, 15, 19, 26, 29, Aug. 7, 13, 17, 24, 27, Sept. 5, 11, 15, 22, 25, Oct. 3, 9, 13, 20, 23, Nov. 1, 7, 11, 18, 21, 30, Dec. 5, 9, 16, 19, 28

Beneficial: Jan. 11, 16, 30, Feb. 9, 24, 28, Mar. 7, 22, 26, Apr. 5, 20, 24, May 3, 18, 22, 31, June 1, 16, 20, 29, July 14, 18, 27, Aug. 12, 16, 25, Sept. 10, 14, 23, Oct. 8, 12, 21, 29, Nov. 6, 10, 19, 27, Dec. 4, 8, 17, 25

Fatal attractions: May 22, 23, 24, 25

Challenging: Jan. 15, Feb. 13, Mar. 11, Apr. 9, May 7, 30, June 5, 28, July 3, 26, Aug. 1, 24, Sept. 22, Oct. 20, 30, Nov. 18, 28, Dec. 16, 26

Soul mates: Jan. 9, 29, Feb. 7, 27, Mar. 5, 25, Apr. 3, 23, May 1, 21, June 19, July 17, Aug. 15, Sept. 13, Oct. 11, Nov. 9, Dec. 7

November 24

FIXED STARS

Bungula, also called Tolliman; Isidis, also called Dshubba; Graffia, also called Acrab or Frons Scorpi; Yed Prior

PRIMARY STAR

Star's name: Bungula, also called Tolliman

Degree position: 28°36'–29°35' Scorpio between the years 1930 and 2000

Magnitude: 1

Strength: ★★★★★★★★★

Orb: 2°30'

Constellation: Alpha Centauri

Applicable days: November 20, 21, 22, 23, 24

Star qualities: Venus/Jupiter

Description: a brilliant white and yellow binary star located on the left foot of the Centaur

PRIMARY STAR'S INFLUENCE

Bungula bestows a passionate yet refined nature and beneficial social contacts. If you seek help, this star grants friends who will assist you when you need it most. It also imparts opportunities and positions of honor or power. Bungula nevertheless warns against extremist behavior and a fatalistic attitude.

Linked to your Sun's degree, this star indicates an ambitious nature and the consistency and determination to achieve steady progress. It also warns of rivalry, envy, or self-centeredness.

• *Positive:* self-reliant, learn to share, generosity, popularity

♐ Expressive, with deep emotions, you are a romantic Sagittarian with a tender soul and great creative potential. Although you are intelligent and highly intuitive about people, your sensitive and impressionable nature suggests that you may need to be discriminating in your choice of friends. A serious side to your nature, however, implies that you are hardworking and practical, with a realistic view and a strong sense of duty. Loyal and faithful, at times to the point of self-denial, you can take things to heart and have conflicting desires.

The subinfluence of your decanate ruler, Sagittarius, indicates that you are optimistic and enthusiastic. At times shockingly direct, you speak before you think. When inspired, you have the potential to achieve intellectually and creatively. Constantly alert, you seek emotional fulfillment through travel and taking chances. A need for soul growth and moral aspirations suggest that you can find spirituality and philosophy rewarding and fulfilling. This will help you to develop foresight, and rather than seeing everything in terms of black or white, you will begin to understand concepts of wholeness that encompass the gray areas.

Usually you are honorable and sincere, with an interest in people. As an idealist, you can be quite persuasive, with the courage to fight for your cause. Although by being friendly and generous you can draw many people toward you, some of your emotional involvements can divert you from your path and thereby cause disappointment.

Up to the age of twenty-seven, you will want to be expanding your horizons and seeking opportunities, whether through enterprising ventures, study, or travel. At the age of twenty-eight, when your progressed Sun moves into Capricorn, you start to become more practical, goal-oriented, and realistic in your approach to your achievements. You will need more order and structure in your life. Another turning point occurs at the age of fifty-eight, when your progressed Sun moves into Aquarius. This highlights a growing need for freedom, new ideas, and expressing your individuality.

Your Secret Self

The extreme sides of your personality show, on one hand, a humanitarian nature that is compassionate and caring, and on the other hand that you can become tough and overserious. You may need to learn to balance a conflict between business and intimacy. By acting more spontaneously in life, without always trying to be in control, you will find your confidence increases as you have more faith and trust in your abilities.

The display of love and affection can be especially important for you. If you make too many concessions at your own expense to keep others happy, you may find yourself withdrawing and appearing cold. As you learn in life to give equal worth to your feelings as well as to those of others, you are able to stay caring yet still be emotionally detached.

Work & Vocation

Ambitious, hardworking, and imaginative, you can be a practical idealist with original notions and big plans. Your sharp intellect and good communication skills can certainly help you succeed in any line of work. Although sensitive, you have a strong and magnetic personality that can aid your success in any career. The more humanitarian side of your nature may be fulfilled in the caring professions or social reform, and your interest in people can make you an excellent counselor. Naturally philosophical, you may wish to express your ideas through teaching or writing. Alternatively, your natural creativity may attract you to a career as a musician, actor, or entertainer. You may travel for your work or even settle in a foreign place.

Famous people who share your birthday include artist Henri Toulouse-Lautrec, comedian Billy Connolly, cricketer Ian Botham, pianist Scott Joplin, actress Geraldine Fitzgerald, philosopher Spinoza, and authors William F. Buckley and Frances Hodgson Burnett.

Numerology

With a number 24 birthday, you may dislike routine; however, you are hardworking, with practical abilities and sound judgment. The emotional sensitivity of the number 24 birthday suggests that you need to establish stability and order. Faithful and fair, though sometimes undemonstrative, you are inclined to believe that actions speak louder than words. With this pragmatic approach to life, you develop a good business sense and an ability to overcome obstacles and succeed. Having a number 24 birthday, you may need to overcome a tendency to be stubborn or fixed in your ideas. The subinfluence of the number 11 month indicates that you are idealistic and optimistic. Your strong desire for self-expression can be productive emotionally and materially. Ambitious and security-conscious, you have a material streak and a taste for the good life. If you do not let your intense feelings get in the way of partnerships, you can benefit from the stability of domestic harmony.

• *Positive:* energy, idealist, practical skills, strong determination, honest, frank, fair, generous, love of home, active, energetic

• *Negative:* materialistic, instability, ruthless, lazy, unfaithful, domineering, stubborn, vengeful

Love & Relationships

As you are likely to be sensitive and restless, you need relationships that do not get stuck in a rut or become uneventful. It would be excellent for you to have adventures or take short breaks away with your partner. A tendency to change your feelings suggests that you need to take your time in forming relationships. Generous and idealistic, you often begin your personal associations with enthusiasm; later, however, you may lose interest. If discouraged by a lack of funds, this may interfere in your relationships and cause many changes.

YOUR SPECIAL SOMEONE

If you are looking for someone special, you might find stimulating company and a perfect partner among those born on the following dates.

Love & friendship: Jan. 2, 9, 11, 12, 22, 25, Feb. 7, 10, 20, 23, 26, Mar. 5, 8, 18, 21, Apr. 3, 5, 6, 16, 19, May 1, 4, 14, 17, 20, 24, 29, June 2, 12, 15, 27, July 10, 13, 16, 20, 23, 25, 30, Aug. 9, 15, 24, 26, Sept. 7, 13, 22, 24, Oct. 4, 7, 10, 14, 19, 24, 28, 29, Nov. 2, 5, 8, 12, 17, 22, 26, 27, Dec. 3, 6, 10, 11, 15, 20, 24, 25

Beneficial: Jan. 12, 23, 29, Feb. 10, 21, 27, Mar. 22, 26, Apr. 6, 17, 23, May 4, 15, 21, June 2, 13, 19, 28, 30, July 11, 17, 26, 28, Aug. 9, 15, 24, 26, Sept. 7, 13, 22, 24, Oct. 5, 11, 20, 22, Nov. 3, 9, 18, 20, 30, Dec. 1, 7, 16, 18, 28

Fatal attractions: May 21, 22, 23, 24, July 29, Aug. 27, Sept. 25, Oct. 23, Nov. 21, Dec. 19

Challenging: Jan. 1, 4, 26, 30, Feb. 2, 24, 28, Mar. 22, 26, Apr. 20, 24, May 18, 22, 31, June 16, 20, 29, July 14, 18, 27, Aug. 12, 16, 25, 30, Sept. 10, 14, 23, 28, Oct. 8, 12, 21, 26, Nov. 6, 10, 19, 24, Dec. 4, 8, 17, 22

Soul mates: Jan. 20, Feb. 18, Mar. 16, Apr. 14, May 12, June 10, July 8, Aug. 6, Sept. 4, Oct. 2

November 25

↗ Intuitive and idealistic, with a flair for the dramatic, you are a Sagittarian with powerful emotions, vitality, and drive. Although you are usually practical, a blend of optimism and skepticism implies that you need to find a balance between being overenthusiastic and being too critical.

The double influence of your ruling planet, Jupiter, implies that you seek to expand through travel and changes. Spirited and optimistic, you strive for honesty at all costs. At times you can be outspoken and direct. A need for emotional fulfillment indicates that you possess religious, spiritual, or moral aspirations. As you are likely to have strong desires and high ideals, you can be emotionally restless and ambitious. Sociable and generous, you thrive on affection and appreciation. When you turn on the charm, you can project charisma. Easily bored and prone to mood changes, however, you may show your emotional vulnerability, especially when others fail to match your high expectations.

As a progressive thinker, you have a desire for knowledge and enjoy projects that keep you mentally stimulated. Honorable and frank, you have critical and analytical abilities; as you like to speak your mind, at times you can be startlingly direct, especially when you voice your strong opinions. Nevertheless, you are kind and understanding, you have good advice to offer those you care for, and your loyalty knows no bounds.

Up to the age of twenty-six, you are mainly concerned with issues of freedom and expanding your opportunities, whether through taking chances, education, or travel. A turning point occurs at the age of twenty-seven, when your progressed Sun moves into Capricorn. This is likely to bring a more pragmatic, orderly, and structured approach to your life. There is another change of emphasis at age fifty-seven, when your progressed Sun moves into Aquarius. This highlights a growing need for independence, friendship, and original and progressive ideas. You may develop more of a desire for freedom and an interest in group affairs.

Fixed Stars

Isidis, also called Dshubba; Graffias, also called Acrab or Frons Scorpi; Yed Prior

PRIMARY STAR

Star's name: Isidis, also called Dshubba

Degree position: 1°33'–2°29' Sagittarius between the years 1930 and 2000

Magnitude: 2.5

Strength: ★★★★★★★

Orb: 1°40'

Constellation: Delta Scorpio

Applicable days: November 24, 25, 26

Star qualities: Mars/Saturn

Description: a bright star located near the right claw of the Scorpion

PRIMARY STAR'S INFLUENCE

Isidis imparts a liberal attitude, pride, and high aims. This star's influence grants ambition; you are competitive, with daring and unconventional views. Isidis warns against being impatient and also suggests guarding against keeping unreliable company.

Linked to your Sun's degree, this star encourages good education and an inclination toward higher learning in fields such as law, politics, philosophy, religion, metaphysics, and astrology. You are probably outgoing and enjoy popularity, many friends, and lasting partnerships. You may need to exercise discretion.

• *Positive:* outspoken and frank, educated, worldly

Your Secret Self

As you are sensitive and intuitive, when you act spontaneously you are able to shine and show others your warm emotional power. Although you can be enthusiastic and have a fighting spirit, one of your major challenges may be a tendency to be mistrustful, doubting yourself and others. You may find yourself becoming involved in power plays in your relationships. In order to avoid withdrawing and feeling isolated, you need to concentrate on positive thinking and having more confidence that you can make your high ideals a reality. Each step you take toward the fulfillment of your grand dreams will bring you satisfaction and rewards.

As you are a creative thinker and need to feel a sense of purpose in life, your work or activities can be especially important to you. Sometimes finding yourself in a position beneath your true talents may produce a conflict between your ideals and the very different reality of daily life. By applying perseverance and self-discipline to your wonderful sense of vision, you can eventually achieve the results you desire.

Work & Vocation

With your charismatic and dynamic personality, you can be a forceful influence in any career. Sociable and friendly, you have an ability to mix business and pleasure that can particularly

• *Negative:* indiscreet, opportunist, overly optimistic

See Appendix for additional fixed star readings.

help you in areas such as sales, promotion, or media. As well as having your finger on the pulse of public trends, you also have managerial abilities and can be very successful in the business world. Philanthropic and idealistic, you may be drawn to support a cause or work in the caring professions. While you may be mentally drawn to education, law, or large projects, a need for self-expression may attract you to find outlets through writing, music, art, or the entertainment world.

Famous people who share your birthday include singer Tina Turner, magazine publisher John F. Kennedy Jr., musician Bev Bevan, philanthropist Andrew Carnegie, baseball player Joe DiMaggio, composer/writer Virgil Thompson, and actor Ricardo Montalban.

Numerology

Quick and energetic, though intuitive and thoughtful, with a number 25 birthday you need to express yourself through different experiences. These may include new and exciting ideas, people, or locations. A desire for perfection urges you to work hard and be productive. You may, however, need to be less impatient or critical if things do not happen according to plan. As a number 25 individual, you possess strong mental energies that when concentrated aid you to look at all the facts and arrive at a conclusion faster than anyone else. Success and happiness come when you learn to trust your own instincts and develop perseverance and patience. The subinfluence of the number 11 month indicates that you are idealistic, with a need to broaden your outlook or be cosmopolitan. When you are inspired by a cause or an ideal, you can become a crusader with strong convictions. Charismatic and direct, you enjoy being part of a larger group or working with the public.

• *Positive:* highly intuitive, perfectionist, perceptive, creative mind, good at dealing with people

• *Negative:* impulsive, impatient, irresponsible, overly emotional, jealous, secretive, changing circumstances, critical, moody

Love & Relationships

Friendly and sociable, you can be devoted, but before you find your ideal love you are probably going to break a few hearts. A tendency for anxiety implies that you have a need for security. You respect and admire hardworking people who are dedicated and loyal. Responsible, you can work in harmony with your partner even though you are under pressure. You are an idealist, and if you believe in someone, you are loyal and supportive. Although you have strong family roots, you often want to travel far afield.

YOUR SPECIAL SOMEONE

You might find a long-lasting relationship and stability with someone born on one of the following dates.

Love & friendship: Jan. 8, 11, 12, 29, Feb. 6, 9, 27, Mar. 4, 7, 25, 29, Apr. 2, 5, 6, 23, 27, May 3, 21, 25, June 1, 19, 23, July 17, 21, Aug. 15, 19, 29, Sept. 13, 17, 27, Oct. 11, 15, 25, 29, 30, Nov. 9, 13, 23, 27, 28, Dec. 7, 11, 21, 25, 26

Beneficial: Jan. 13, 30, Feb. 11, 28, Mar. 9, 26, Apr. 7, 24, 30, May 5, 22, 28, June 3, 20, 26, July 1, 18, 24, 29, Aug. 16, 22, 25, Sept. 14, 20, 25, Oct. 12, 18, 23, Nov. 10, 16, 21, Dec. 8, 14, 19

Fatal attractions: May 23, 24, 25, 26, Oct. 30, Nov. 28, Dec. 26

Challenging: Jan. 5, 19, Feb. 3, 17, Mar. 1, 15, Apr. 13, May 11, June 9, 30, July 7, 28, 30, Aug. 5, 26, 28, Sept. 3, 24, 26, Oct. 1, 22, 24, Nov. 20, 22, Dec. 18, 20

Soul mates: Jan. 7, Feb. 5, Mar. 3, Apr. 1, Sept. 30, Oct. 28, Nov. 26, Dec. 24

November 26

Intuitive and sensitive, with powerful emotions, you are an idealistic Sagittarius with strong convictions. By living up to your high expectations and making your ideals a reality, you find joy and contentment.

The double influence of your ruling planet, Jupiter, implies that you are optimistic and honorable. Although you can be enthusiastic, one of your major challenges may be a tendency to be skeptical. This can also cause you to be suspicious, doubting yourself and others.

Being a person of extremes implies that because you are a perfectionist, you can be critical and outspoken; because you are a humanitarian, you are also often caring and kind, with a liberal attitude. When positive, you are idealistic and loyal, but when vulnerable, you can show the reverse side of your nature and be cold and unfeeling. Mentally restless, you can become easily bored unless you are inspired. You benefit greatly, therefore, from a quest for spiritual enlightenment that involves developing your religious and moral aspirations or expanding your intellectual horizons.

If you channel your enormous creative and emotional power, you can easily inspire others with your special artistic gifts. Imaginative yet analytical, you need a philosophy that can sustain you and help you establish a unique or independent approach to life.

Up to the age of twenty-five, you need the freedom to be adventurous and seek opportunities, whether through enterprising ventures, study, or travel. At the age of twenty-six, when your progressed Sun moves into Capricorn, you start to become more practical, goal-oriented, and realistic in your approach to your achievements. Another turning point occurs at the age of fifty-six, when your progressed Sun moves into Aquarius. This highlights a growing need for independence, group awareness, and expressing your individuality.

FIXED STARS

Isidis, also called Dshubba; Graffias, also called Acrab or Frons Scorpi; Yed Prior

PRIMARY STAR

Star's name: Isidis, also called Dshubba

Degree position: 1°33'–2°29' Sagittarius between the years 1930 and 2000

Magnitude: 2.5

Strength: ★★★★★★★

Orb: 1°40'

Constellation: Delta Scorpio

Applicable days: November 24, 25, 26

Star qualities: Mars/Saturn

Description: a bright star located near the right claw of the Scorpion

PRIMARY STAR'S INFLUENCE

Isidis imparts a liberal attitude, pride, and high aims. This star's influence grants ambition; you are competitive, with daring and unconventional views. Isidis warns against being impatient and also suggests guarding against keeping unreliable company.

Linked to your Sun's degree, this star encourages good education and an inclination toward higher learning in fields such as law, politics, philosophy, religion, metaphysics, and astrology. You are probably outgoing and enjoy popularity, many friends, and lasting partnerships. You may need to exercise discretion.

• *Positive:* outspoken and frank, educated, worldly

Your Secret Self

The magnetic charm that you are able to project can be a great help in your overall success and enables you to inspire and influence others. Possessing powerful inner emotions, you come to realize the importance of keeping a positive perspective. If you allow yourself to dwell in negativity, you can be prone to moodiness or feeling lonely. Alternatively, when ardent about a person or project you love, you can radiate enthusiasm and warmth. While you do have a strong interest in money issues, the expression of love and the fulfillment of your grand dreams can be especially important to you.

As you may particularly enjoy initiating new projects, it is vital to keep yourself actively working or creatively occupied. This helps you avoid times when you may become overly serious. Sensitive and highly intuitive, you have a desire to delve into deeper levels of awareness that may stimulate a need for self-analysis and personal realization.

Work & Vocation

With your fine analytical mind and your strong imagination, you are usually a creative thinker. You may wish to apply your problem-solving skills to business or employ them in areas such as education, philosophy, or writing. If technical, you may be drawn to occupations such as working with computers or engineering. If this involves creative thinking as well, such as in the world of computer games, so much the better. Being sensitive and having natural diplomatic skills, you may fare better in activities that involve you with other people. Being practical as well as intuitive, you have management potential, although your spirit of enterprise may stimulate you to work for yourself. A natural feel for color and form may, alternatively, attract you to the arts.

Famous people who share your birthday include musician John McVie, comedian Rich Little, English statesman William Pitt, actors Robert Goulet and Cyril Cusack, cartoonist Charles Schulz, and playwright Eugene Ionesco.

Numerology

Having a number 26 birthday, you possess a pragmatic approach to life, executive ability, and a good business sense. Usually responsible, with a natural aesthetic sense and a love of home, you need to create a harmonious environment for yourself or find real stability. Often a tower of strength for others, you are willing to support friends and family members who turn to you in time of need. You may nevertheless need to guard against materialistic tendencies and a desire to control situations or people. The subinfluence of the number 11 month indicates that you are optimistic and intuitive. Enterprising and ambitious, you have the opportunity to be responsible and original. When determined, you can be stubborn and follow only your inner voice. Being idealistic and adventurous, you can let your imagination sweep you off your feet and take you to faraway and inspiring places. The need to expand and explore suggests that you want to accomplish much. Staying focused and persevering implies that without a good incentive, you can lose heart and give up too easily.

• *Positive:* creative, practical, caring, responsible, proud of family, enthusiastic, courageous
• *Negative:* stubborn, rebellious, unstable relationships, unenthusiastic, lack of persistence

Love & Relationships

Sociable and friendly, you enjoy entertaining and being hospitable. Powerful inner emotions need a positive channel for expression, however, or you may become moody or bored. Being restless and eager suggests that there are many opportunities for change to satisfy your adventurous spirit. At times situations can change rapidly, unsettling you and your partner, especially if change is imposed on you both without notice. Although you can be stubborn, with fixed ideals, when in love you can be dutiful and devoted and make great sacrifices.

YOUR SPECIAL SOMEONE

For security, mental stimulation, and love, you might want to begin looking for those born among the following dates.

Love & friendship: Jan. 9, 13, 30, Feb. 7, 9, 28, Mar. 5, 26, 30, Apr. 3, 5, 24, 28, May 1, 22, 26, June 20, 24, July 18, 22, 31, Aug. 16, 20, 29, 30, Sept. 14, 18, 27, 28, Oct. 12, 16, 25, 26, 31, Nov. 10, 14, 23, 24, 29, Dec. 8, 12, 21, 22, 27

Beneficial: Jan. 15, 22, 31, Feb. 13, 20, 29, Mar. 11, 18, 27, Apr. 9, 16, 25, May 7, 14, 23, 30, June 5, 12, 21, 28, July 3, 10, 19, 26, 30, Aug. 1, 8, 17, 24, 28, Sept. 6, 15, 22, 26, Oct. 4, 13, 20, 24, Nov. 2, 11, 18, 22, Dec. 9, 16, 20

Fatal attractions: Jan. 11, Feb. 9, Mar. 7, Apr. 5, May 3, 24, 25, 26, 27, June 1, Oct. 31, Nov. 29, Dec. 27

Challenging: Jan. 5, 8, 16, 21, Feb. 3, 6, 14, 19, Mar. 1, 4, 12, 17, Apr. 2, 10, 15, May 8, 13, June 6, 11, July 4, 9, 29, Aug. 2, 7, 27, Sept. 5, 25, Oct. 3, 23, Nov. 1, 21, Dec. 19

Soul mates: Jan. 13, Feb. 11, Mar. 9, Apr. 7, May 5, June 3, July 1, Aug. 31, Sept. 29, Oct. 27, Nov. 25, Dec. 23

November 27

Idealistic and kindhearted, you are a creative Sagittarian with a charismatic personality and a winning smile. Sincere and truthful, yet shy and sensitive, you have many interests and are often multitalented. Although you judge life by your feelings, you are a good communicator, with imaginative thoughts. Being enthusiastic and optimistic, you usually attract many friends and like to include others in your plans and activities. Nevertheless, for soul growth and greater self-awareness, you need periods of solitude to develop your fine mind and philosophical perspective.

The double influence of your ruling planet, Jupiter, implies that you are striving for honesty in your spiritual and moral aspirations. Broad-minded, you seek to expand your horizons through travel and taking chances. As an original visionary, you need to find ways to express your wealth of emotions. Despite being charming, at times you can be shockingly direct and outspoken. It would be wise to guard against being too critical or unintentionally offensive.

Although you are blessed with common sense and practical skills, the dreamer side of your nature yearns for a utopian reality in idyllic locations. Mentally restless, you like adventure, yet a need for emotional security suggests that you fare better by not staying alone. Enthusiastic and optimistic, you like to see the broad plan. If you master your craft down to the finer details, you will encompass more and gain greater insight.

Up to the age of twenty-four you are optimistic, with a need to be adventurous and seek opportunities. This may lead you to take chances, travel, or study. At the age of twenty-five, when your progressed Sun moves into Capricorn, you start to become more pragmatic, orderly, and realistic in your approach to realizing your ambitions in life. Another turning point occurs at the age of fifty-five, when your progressed Sun moves into Aquarius. This highlights a growing need for more independence, group awareness, and progressive ideas.

Your Secret Self

Idealistic, with a fine mind, you are usually happiest when being productive and expanding your knowledge. Preferring to be frank and direct with others, you usually manage to combine being practical with being intuitive. Full of constructive ideas, you can be lucky in enterprising ventures, especially when you have a positive plan of what you intend to achieve. You may, however, need to develop patience and tolerance, particularly when dealing with people less aware than yourself.

Potentially highly creative, you have a strong need for self-expression that may manifest itself socially or through music, art, drama, or writing. With an objective and inventive mind that can alternate between flashes of genius and moments of rebelliousness, your ideas can often be ahead of their time. With your quick wit, you enjoy entertaining others but may have to be careful of a tendency to worry and be indecisive, particularly regarding money matters.

Work & Vocation

Although you possess a friendly and charming front, your fast mind is constantly coming up with new and original ideas that you can apply to your work. Your optimism and spirit of en-

FIXED STAR

Star's name: Graffias, also called Acrab or Frons Scorpi

Degree position: 2°12'–3°13' Sagittarius between the years 1930 and 2000

Magnitude: 3

Strength: ★★★★★

Orb: 1°40'

Constellation: Beta Scorpio

Applicable days: November 24, 25, 26, 27

Star qualities: Saturn/Mars

Description: a pale white and lilac triple star located on the head of the Scorpion

PRIMARY STAR'S INFLUENCE

Graffias bestows good business sense, wealth, and material power. Often this star grants an active mind and the desire to take risks. Graffias also indicates that success is achieved after many difficulties; therefore endurance and determination are the keys to achieving your goals. This star warns that benefits may not necessarily be long-lasting and suggests that too much activity may cause stress and bad health.

Linked to your Sun's degree, Graffias bestows success in politics and prominence in education, religion, and work linked to the public. This star suggests that high honors are often gained through hard work and service. You may possess the power to wish and get what you desire, but not always have the ability to enjoy fully the rewards of your hard-earned success.

terprise will have you making big plans in whatever career you choose. You may possess an interest in writing, metaphysics, or philosophy. Alternatively, a strong appreciation of harmony, color, and form may attract you to music or the arts. Although a part of you enjoys keeping things as they are for the sake of peace, your love of travel, desire for excitement, and strong sense of responsibility usually move you into action. Working cooperatively with others in a team or partnership may prove particularly beneficial for you.

Famous people you share your birthdate with are musician Jimi Hendrix, lawyer Caroline Kennedy Schlossberg, theater producer David Merrick, TV personality Buffalo Bob Smith, and actor/martial arts expert Bruce Lee.

Numerology

The number 27 birthdate indicates that you are idealistic and sensitive. Intuitive and analytical, with a fertile and creative mind, you can impress others with your original thoughts. Although at times you appear secretive, rational, or detached, in fact you may be hiding inner tensions. In developing good communication skills, you can overcome a reluctance to express your deeper feelings. Education is essential for number 27 persons, and by developing depth of thought you become more patient and self-disciplined. The subinfluence of the number 11 month indicates that you are highly intuitive, with psychic abilities and a flair for metaphysics. Idealistic and sensitive, with vision and imagination, you need to find ways to express yourself through writing and education. Although you are often a humanitarian with liberal views, you can experience doubts and emotional highs and lows if you lack faith or a philosophy to aspire to. Although you need time alone, avoid isolating yourself from others. You can achieve more peace by creating harmony around yourself.

• *Positive:* versatile, imaginative, creative, resolute, brave, good understanding, mentally capable, spiritual, inventive, mental strength

• *Negative:* disagreeable, quarrelsome, easily offended, argumentative, restless, nervous, mistrusting, overemotional, tense

Love & Relationships

Although you are an affectionate and idealistic individual, you rarely fall in love or get swept off your feet by your emotions. Liberal and easygoing, you make friends easily, but a need for financial security suggests that you may take financial considerations into account when choosing a partner. You like to associate with active, creative, and hardworking individuals and often receive support from your friends. As a good collaborator, you usually prefer to work in partnerships rather than alone or in seclusion.

YOUR SPECIAL SOMEONE

To keep you interested in a long-term relationship, you might want to look out for those born on the following days.

Love and friendship: Jan. 12, 14, 15, 25, 28, Feb. 10, 12, 13, 23, 26, Mar. 8, 11, 21, 24, 31, Apr. 6, 9, 19, 22, 29, May 4, 7, 17, 20, 27, 28, June 2, 4, 5, 15, 18, 25, July 3, 13, 16, 23, 24, Aug. 1, 11, 14, 21, 31, Sept. 9, 12, 19, 29, Oct. 7, 10, 17, 27, Nov. 5, 8, 15, 25, Dec. 3, 6, 13, 23

Beneficial: Jan. 12, 23, 26, Feb. 10, 21, 24, Mar. 8, 19, 22, 28, Apr. 6, 17, 20, 26, May 4, 15, 18, 24, June 2, 13, 22, 16, July 11, 14, 20, 31, Aug. 9, 12, 18, 29, Sept. 7, 10, 16, 27, Oct. 5, 8, 14, 25, Nov. 3, 6, 12, 23, Dec. 1, 4, 10, 21

Fatal attractions: May 25, 26, 27, 28, Nov. 30, Dec. 28

Challenging: Jan. 17, 18, 21, Feb. 15, 16, 19, Mar. 13, 14, 17, 29, Apr. 11, 12, 15, 27, May 9, 10, 13, 25, June 7, 8, 11, 23, July 5, 6, 9, 21, 30, Aug. 3, 4, 7, 19, 28, Sept. 1, 2, 5, 17, 26, Oct. 3, 15, 24, Nov. 1, 13, 22, Dec. 11, 20

Soul mates: Jan. 24, Feb. 22, Mar. 20, Apr. 18, 30, May 16, 28, June 14, 26, July 12, 24, Aug. 10, 22, Sept. 8, 20, Oct. 6, 18, Nov. 4, 16, Dec. 2, 14

November 28

FIXED STARS

Although your Sun's degree is not linked to a fixed star, some of your other planets' degrees certainly will be. By having an astrological chart calculated, you can find the exact position of the planets on your date of birth. This will tell you which of the fixed stars listed in this book are relevant to you.

A restless romantic, with many interests, you are an adventurous Sagittarian, full of hopes, ambition, and charm. As you are inspired by knowledge, if you are resolute and have a clear course of action, you can overcome a tendency to be dissatisfied with the mundane in life. Although your desire for change indicates an amount of uncertainty, it also suggests that you can have a varied and eventful life.

The double influence of your ruling planet, Jupiter, implies that you are witty, with a congenial nature. Usually full of enthusiasm and optimism, you are frank and outspoken. Idealistic and with strong convictions, you often strive for honesty at all costs. This influence can also inspire you to follow your heart in the pursuit of creative self-expression or religious and moral aspirations.

Interested in the idea of wholeness, you have foresight and a philosophical perspective. However, a tendency to neglect the small details suggests that you need to develop patience and avoid becoming bored or losing interest too quickly. Instead of moving swiftly from one subject to another, you may need to learn to focus on one particular objective in order to achieve your true potential.

Up to the age of twenty-three, you are mainly concerned with issues of freedom and expanding your horizons, whether through opportunities, your philosophy of life, education, or travel. A turning point occurs at the age of twenty-four, when your progressed Sun moves into Capricorn. This is likely to bring a more pragmatic, orderly, and structured approach to your life. You may have a greater awareness of your responsibilities and the work needed to achieve your goals. There is another change of emphasis at age fifty-four, when your progressed Sun moves into Aquarius. This highlights issues regarding friendship, group awareness, and independence.

Your Secret Self

Idealistic and imaginative, you may feel that your sensitivity is not wasted when you are able to use it creatively or to be of help to others. Since you also can be pragmatic and like order, this powerful combination implies that you can be a practical visionary. There may be a strong emphasis on work in your life, and through steady and consistent efforts you are able to establish for yourself a stable and financially beneficial situation.

You are likely to be constantly seeking new and exciting interests to keep your active mind stimulated. An inner restlessness, however, may sometimes cause you discontent or make you prone to escapism. It is important, therefore, to keep yourself constructively focused on positive goals. A fascination for people and change can prompt you to go exploring through education or travel in your quest for variety and a mental challenge.

Work & Vocation

Although you will always be exploring new areas in your desire for variety, you gradually overcome a tendency to believe that the grass is always greener on the other side of the fence. Find-

560

ing productive work that is not restrictive to your free spirit helps you to be satisfied with your lot. Ambitious, you aim high and have leadership potential. Although you are independent, you also gain from teamwork or partnerships. If you can incorporate your desire for travel into your work, then so much the better. You may alternatively wish to develop your innate literary or musical talents. Whatever career you choose, you will be happiest when using your warm charm and people skills in some form of dynamic action.

Famous people who share your birthday include songwriter Randy Newman, poet/artist William Blake, U.S. senator Gary Hart, writers Nancy Mitford, Friedrich Engels, and Rita Mae Brown, and band leader Paul Shaffer.

Numerology

Independent and idealistic, with determination and a pragmatic approach, you are often a law unto yourself. Like a number 1 individual, you are ambitious, direct, and enterprising. An inner conflict between wanting to be independent and wanting to be part of a team is also indicated. Always ready for action and new ventures, you courageously take on life's challenges, and with your enthusiasm you can easily inspire others, if not to join you, at least to support you in your latest venture. With a number 28 birthday, you have leadership abilities and rely on your common sense, logic, and clear thinking. Often you take on responsibilities, but you can also be overly enthusiastic, impatient, or intolerant. The subinfluence of the number 11 month indicates that you are inspired and restless, seeking emotional fulfillment. Although you want success and stability, being adventurous and zealous suggests that at times you are willing to take chances in order to obtain more out of life.

• *Positive:* compassion, progressive, daring, artistic, creative, idealistic, ambitious, hardworking, stable home life, strong-willed

• *Negative:* daydreamer, unmotivated, lack of compassion, unrealistic, bossy, lack of judgment, aggressive, lack of confidence, too dependent on others, pride

Love & Relationships

A love for variety and action suggests that you are a restless individual with an appreciation for beauty and an eye for style. At times, however, you may become impersonal or indecisive about your feelings. You are adventurous and optimistic, though changing circumstances imply that you may find it hard to commit yourself to a long-lasting relationship. As you dislike monotony, you may have many short-lived relationships until you find your ideal partner. You admire creative people who are hardworking and decisive about where they are going.

YOUR SPECIAL SOMEONE

If you are looking for someone special, you might find stimulating company and a perfect partner among those born on the following dates.

Love & friendship: Jan. 6, 7, 10, 11, 14, Feb. 4, 9, 12, Mar. 2, 7, 10, 28, Apr. 1, 4, 5, 8, 26, 30, May 3, 6, 24, 28, June 1, 4, 22, 26, July 2, 20, 24, Aug. 18, 22, Sept. 16, 20, 30, Oct. 14, 18, 28, Nov. 12, 16, 26, Dec. 10, 14, 24

Beneficial: Jan. 20, 24, Feb. 18, 22, Mar. 16, 20, 29, Apr. 14, 18, 27, May 12, 16, 25, June 10, 14, 23, 29, July 8, 12, 21, 27, Aug. 6, 10, 19, 25, 30, Sept. 4, 8, 17, 23, 28, Oct. 2, 6, 15, 21, 26, Nov. 4, 13, 19, 24, Dec. 2, 11, 17, 22

Fatal attractions: May 25, 26, 27, 28, Aug. 31, Sept. 29, Oct. 27, Nov. 25, Dec. 23

Challenging: Jan. 22, 23, 27, Feb. 20, 21, 25, Mar. 18, 19, 23, Apr. 16, 17, 21, May 14, 15, 19, June 12, 13, 17, July 10, 11, 15, 31, Aug. 8, 9, 13, 29, Sept. 6, 7, 11, 27, Oct. 4, 5, 9, 25, Nov. 2, 3, 7, 23, Dec. 1, 5, 21

Soul mates: Jan. 23, Feb. 21, Mar. 19, Apr. 17, 29, May 15, 27, June 13, 25, July 11, 23, Aug. 9, 21, Sept. 7, 19, Oct. 5, 17, Nov. 3, 15, Dec. 1, 13

November 29

FIXED STARS

Although your Sun's degree is not linked to a fixed star, some of your other planets' degrees certainly will be. By having an astrological chart calculated, you can find the exact position of the planets on your date of birth. This will tell you which of the fixed stars listed in this book are relevant to you.

♐ Receptive and resourceful, with vitality and drive, you are a compassionate Sagittarian who wants emotional stability. As a highly intuitive individual, you are able to understand people and their motives, but your desire for emotional security suggests that you need to know where you stand with people. Although you are idealistic by nature, your ambition and a strong practical sense imply that you can be forceful and effective if you keep your feet firmly on the ground.

The double influence of your ruling planet, Jupiter, implies that you are an honorable and idealistic individual who is striving for honesty at all costs. Enthusiastic and optimistic, with possible religious or moral aspirations, you have foresight and may be interested in philosophy. A need to expand and explore indicates that you are likely to travel far afield in search of truth and enlightenment. But in your attempt to put the world to rights, avoid being too rigid or inflexible.

As a sincere and frank person with strong convictions and opinions, you prefer to be outspoken and direct. You are usually loyal and honorable, and when you make a promise you like to keep your word. An ability to work hard and be dedicated implies that others rely on you to fulfill your obligations. Though you are spontaneous and generous, try to balance your need for fairness with your philanthropic gestures. Self-satisfaction and fulfillment can be achieved through linking your emotional and practical necessities.

Up to the age of twenty-two, you are optimistic and will want to expand your opportunities, whether through enterprising ventures, study, or travel. At the age of twenty-three, when your progressed Sun moves into Capricorn, you start to become more practical, goal-oriented, and realistic in your approach to your achievements. This can involve a greater need for order and structure in your life. Another turning point occurs at the age of fifty-three, when your progressed Sun moves into Aquarius. This highlights a growing need for freedom, new ideas, and expressing your individuality.

Your Secret Self

As well as being practical and determined, you can also be creative, witty, and entertaining. Being able to appreciate beauty and the good things in life, you are likely to have good taste and enjoy luxury. Although you are usually very friendly and helpful, there is a danger that you may sometimes adopt a self-righteous or arrogant tone that will cause you to antagonize others. Your problems are rarely financial, however, as you possess a special ability for sensing opportunities as well as a shrewd pragmatism.

Always seeking higher and bigger objectives, you are success-oriented and have good work prospects. With a sharp and quick intelligence, you can be highly motivated when really interested in achieving an objective. Although you prefer large projects, try not to overlook the details, as they are part of the whole. At best you can be an inspired thinker, with a gift to offer others through your work or creative expression.

Work & Vocation

With a strong desire for truth and justice and a humanitarian side to your nature, you may find yourself working for a cause or be drawn to law, politics, and social reform. You may wish to combine these talents with your imagination and emotional sensitivity and become a writer or enter the caring professions. Alternatively, being a good planner and organizer, you enjoy being productive and may use these talents in business or administration. Naturally philanthropic and a good parent, you may wish to help others through charity work or fund-raising for your local community.

Famous people who share your birthday include writers Louisa May Alcott and C. S. Lewis, jazz musician Chuck Mangione, film director Busby Berkeley, civil rights leader Adam Clayton Powell Jr., Green party leader Petra Kelly, and former French prime minister Jacques Chirac.

Numerology

As a number 29 individual, you have a powerful personality and extraordinary potential. You are highly intuitive, sensitive, and emotional. Inspiration is the key to your success story, and without it you may experience lack of purpose. Although you are a true dreamer, the extreme sides of your nature indicate that you may have to guard against alternating moods. If you trust your innermost feelings and open your heart to others, you can overcome your tendency to worry or use your mind as protective armor. Use your creative thoughts to achieve something special and unique that can motivate or be of service to others. The subinfluence of the number 11 month indicates that, being a humanitarian and idealistic, you seek emotional fulfillment or contentment. Keen to explore or discover new ideas, you enjoy being inquisitive and adventurous. Although you are optimistic, with firm convictions, you need to remain practical and use your common sense when embarking on new ventures. Having faith and broadening your horizons through education and study usually bring enlightenment and spiritual awareness.

• *Positive:* inspirational, balance, inner peace, generous, successful, creative, intuitive, mystical, powerful dreams, worldly, faith

• *Negative:* unfocused, insecure, nervous, selfish, vain, moody, difficult, extremist, inconsiderate, isolated, overly sensitive

Love & Relationships

Hospitable and charming, you enjoy being gregarious and sociable. As you need to be with people, you are always involved in some collaborative effort. Being group-oriented suggests that you do not like to be alone; be careful, however, of becoming manipulative or overdependent on partners or friends. Home and family are particularly important to you, and you like to make your house a warm, friendly, and inviting place.

YOUR SPECIAL SOMEONE

If you are looking for love or your soul mate, you might find happiness with someone born on one of the following days.

Love & friendship: Jan. 1, 7, 12, 15, 19, Feb. 5, 10, 13, Mar. 3, 8, 11, 29, Apr. 1, 6, 9, 27, May 4, 7, 25, 29, June 2, 5, 23, 27, July 3, 21, 25, Aug. 1, 5, 19, 23, Sept. 17, 21, Oct. 15, 19, 29, Nov. 13, 17, 27, Dec. 11, 15, 18, 25

Beneficial: Jan. 21, 25, Feb. 19, 23, Mar. 17, 21, 30, Apr. 15, 19, 28, May 13, 17, 26, June 11, 15, 24, 30, July 9, 13, 22, 28, Aug. 7, 11, 20, 26, 31, Sept. 5, 9, 18, 24, 29, Oct. 3, 7, 16, 22, 29, Nov. 1, 5, 14, 20, 25, Dec. 3, 12, 18, 23

Fatal attractions: May 28, 29, 30, 31

Challenging: Jan. 5, 8, 28, Feb. 3, 6, 26, Mar. 1, 4, 24, Apr. 2, 22, May 20, June 18, July 16, Aug. 14, 30, Sept. 12, 28, 30, Oct. 10, 26, 28, Nov. 8, 24, 26, Dec. 6, 22, 24

Soul mates: Jan. 4, 10, Feb. 2, 8, Mar. 6, Apr. 4, 7, May 2

November 30

♐ Creative and versatile, with excellent communication skills, you are a gifted Sagittarian with imagination and a lively personality. As an adaptable and multi-faceted individual, you are enthusiastic and inquisitive. Finding certainty in personal relationships helps you to be consistent with your feelings. Your ability to express yourself indicates that you are articulate, with quick responses. Although you are usually charming, eloquent, and amusing, occasionally you can be argumentative or outspoken and use your sharp tongue to express your feelings. Adventurous and romantic, with a love of the dramatic, you can sometimes get emotionally carried away or be prone to overindulge.

The double influence of your ruling planet, Jupiter, implies that you are usually optimistic and idealistic, with a humanitarian nature. A certain restlessness and a tendency to become easily bored imply that you enjoy challenges and need excitement or different experiences. Creative, with a flair for literature and writing, you benefit from finding ways to express yourself intellectually and emotionally.

Although you can be enterprising and adventurous or eager for travel and change, on occasion you may experience doubts and feel insecure, if you are honest about your feelings. Highly intuitive, you prefer to trust your own instincts, but by learning to be patient you realize that acting impulsively can be unwise.

Up to the age of twenty-one, you are mainly concerned with issues of freedom and expanding your horizons, whether through travel, education, or your philosophy of life. A turning point occurs when you reach the age of twenty-two, as your progressed Sun moves into Capricorn. This is likely to bring a more pragmatic, orderly, and structured approach to your life. You experience another change of emphasis at age fifty-two, when your progressed Sun moves into Aquarius. This highlights issues regarding friendship, group awareness, and independence.

Your Secret Self

Although you possess deep feelings, your strong need for love and self-expression may not always be obvious from the outside. Your sensitivity can be very useful in artistic pursuits or helping others, but you may have to avoid becoming overemotional or too self-involved. On the other hand, it may be better to trust your heart and powerful intuition rather than be too rational. Nevertheless, with your strong willpower, sense of the dramatic, and persuasive speech, you have the potential to achieve remarkable success.

Strong intuition, good judgment, and superior mental abilities are indicated by your birthday. This combination of wisdom and logic is likely to lead you to positions of authority. Sociable and dramatic, with keen intelligence and a desire to see the big picture, you often enjoy networking and sharing information. Good at instructing other people, you may, however, have to avoid sometimes becoming stubborn when dealing with interference from others.

Work & Vocation

Ambitious and sociable, with a quick mind, you have excellent communication skills that can be your greatest assets. You may decide to use these as a writer or in the world of sales, politics,

FIXED STAR

Star's name: Antares, also called Anti Aries or the Rival of Mars

Degree position: 8°48'–9°49' Sagittarius between the years 1930 and 2000

Magnitude: 1

Strength: ★★★★★★★★★

Orb: 2°30'

Constellation: Alpha Scorpio

Applicable days: November 30, December 1, 2, 3, 4, 5

Star qualities: Mars/Jupiter, also Jupiter/Venus

Description: a binary star, fiery red and emerald green, located in the body of the Scorpion

PRIMARY STAR'S INFLUENCE

Antares is one of the four royal stars and therefore is of great importance. This star imparts an adventurous nature, keen mentality, broad-minded outlook, and liberal attitude. It also indicates unexpected events, lucky breaks, and numerous opportunities for travel to foreign lands. Antares bestows courage, strong convictions, and a daring character. However, it also warns against rashness, destructive behavior, obstinacy, and vengeful acts.

Linked to your Sun's degree, Antares imparts an interest in education, politics, or business dealing with the public. You are probably idealistic, optimistic, and willing to fight for just

or entertainment. Once you overcome any possible indecisiveness as to your vocation, you are in a position to apply your natural creative approach to any career you choose. With a desire for action, you usually thrive on variety and travel. Education, whether formal or self-directed, is likely to play an important part in your climb to success. Dynamic yet friendly, you have a gift with words that can help you advance in your career and enhance your overall popularity.

Famous people who share your birthday include singers Billy Idol and June Pointer, British prime minister Winston Churchill, political activist Abbie Hoffman, and writers Jonathan Swift, Mark Twain, and David Mamet.

Numerology

Creativity, friendliness, and sociability are just some of the attributes associated with the number 30 birthday. Ambitious, with creative potential, you can take ideas and expand them in your own dramatic style. Having a number 30 birthday, you enjoy the good life and are usually charismatic and outgoing. Since you possess strong feelings, being in love or contented is a vital requirement. In your pursuit of happiness, stay loyal and avoid being lazy or overindulgent. If you become impatient or jealous, you can experience emotional instability. Among those with number 30 birthdays, many will find recognition or fame, especially musicians, actors, and entertainers. The subinfluence of the number 11 month indicates that you are highly sensitive, with high hopes and expectations. Although you have the power to obtain your heart's desire, when you achieve your objectives you may realize that in fact you want something entirely different. A tendency to be restless or become bored may also undermine your staying power and determination. Although you are usually gifted, restlessness and indecision may cause you to doubt your capabilities. If inspired, however, you can rise to the heights of creativity and demonstrate how gifted and dedicated you really are.

• *Positive:* fun-loving, loyal, friendly, good synthesizer, talent with words, creative, lucky
• *Negative:* lazy, obstinate, erratic, impatient, insecure, indifferent, scatters energy

YOUR SPECIAL SOMEONE

For love and mental stimulation, you might want to begin looking for those born among the following days.

Love & friendship: Jan. 2, 8, 19, 28, Feb. 6, 26, Mar. 4, 24, 30, Apr. 2, 22, 28, May 20, 26, 30, June 18, 24, 28, July 16, 22, 26, Aug. 5, 14, 20, 24, Sept. 12, 18, 22, Oct. 1, 10, 16, 20, 30, Nov. 8, 14, 18, 28, Dec. 6, 12, 16, 26

Beneficial: Jan. 18, 21, 22, Feb. 16, 19, 20, Mar. 14, 17, 18, 31, Apr. 12, 15, 16, 29, May 10, 13, 14, 27, June 8, 11, 12, 25, July 6, 9, 10, 23, Aug. 4, 7, 8, 21, 30, Sept. 2, 5, 6, 19, 28, 30, Oct. 3, 4, 17, 26, 28, Nov. 1, 2, 15, 24, 26, Dec. 13, 22, 24

Fatal attractions: May 27, 28, 29, 30, Oct. 29, Nov. 27, Dec. 25

Challenging: Jan. 29, Feb. 27, Mar. 25, Apr. 23, May 21, June 19, July 17, Aug. 15, 30, Sept. 13, 28, Oct. 11, 26, Nov. 9, 24, Dec. 7, 22

Soul mates: Jan. 24, 27, 28, Feb. 22, 25, 26, Mar. 20, 23, 24, Apr. 18, 21, 22, May 16, 19, 20, June 14, 17, 18, 30, July 12, 15, 16, 28, Aug. 10, 13, 14, 26, Sept. 8, 11, 12, 24, Oct. 6, 9, 10, 22, Nov. 4, 7, 8, 20, Dec. 2, 5, 6, 18, 30

Love & Relationships

Optimistic, you enjoy mixing socially and being popular. Although you are charismatic, a tendency to think too much and maybe daydream, or a need for variety and mental stimulation, implies that you can become unsettled or indecisive about long-term commitments. If in doubt, avoid being a martyr or wasting your time and energy on the wrong person. Usually you are attracted to individuals who are friendly or knowledgeable and educated. Often both sexes find that women can be particularly valuable to or supportive of them.

December 1

FIXED STARS

Antares, also called Anti Aries or the Rival of Mars; Han

PRIMARY STAR

Star's name: Antares, also called Anti Aries or the Rival of Mars

Degree position: 8°48'–9°49' Sagittarius between the years 1930 and 2000

Magnitude: 1

Strength: ★★★★★★★★★

Orb: 2°30'

Constellation: Alpha Scorpio

Applicable days: November 30, December 1, 2, 3, 4, 5

Star qualities: Mars/Jupiter, also Jupiter/Venus

Description: a binary star, fiery red and emerald green, located in the body of the Scorpion

PRIMARY STAR'S INFLUENCE

Antares is one of the four royal stars and therefore is of great importance. This star imparts an adventurous nature, keen mentality, broad-minded outlook, and liberal attitude. It also indicates unexpected events, lucky breaks, and numerous opportunities for travel to foreign lands. Antares bestows courage, strong convictions, and a daring character. However, it also warns against rashness, destructive behavior, obstinacy, and vengeful acts.

Linked to your Sun's degree, Antares imparts an interest in education, politics, or business dealing with the public. You are probably idealistic, optimistic, and willing to fight for just

Independent and ambitious, you are a determined Sagittarian with idealistic aspirations. Although you need the freedom to express yourself and pursue your aims and interests, you are also a sociable and charming individual. Enthusiastic and optimistic, you like to leave your options open for opportunities or adventure, and you do well by staying focused.

The double influence of your ruling planet, Jupiter, implies that you prefer to see the broad plan rather than the fine detail, and you are a good organizer. Although you may be occupied with mundane issues, your need for spiritual insight implies that you seek a practical philosophy to help you feel confident and secure. The dynamic power and the restlessness indicated by your birthday suggest that life has a lot in store for you. Although productivity is associated with your birthday, you may have to guard against being overly zealous or impatient.

A struggle between idealistic and materialistic tendencies suggests that a scattering of your energies or lack of self-motivation may be your greatest challenges. An inclination to give up under stress or become easily bored can be overcome by carefully planning your projects and persevering in what you aim for. If you are hardworking and practical, you can use natural common sense and intuition to think instinctively and quickly. At times direct and outspoken, with strong opinions, you take a gamble and strive for honesty at all costs.

Up to the age of twenty, you are optimistic and adventurous, with a strong desire to expand your opportunities. This may be through taking chances, education, or travel. A turning point occurs as you reach the age of twenty-one, when your progressed Sun moves into Capricorn. This brings a more pragmatic, orderly, and structured approach to your life. You acquire a greater sense of how to realistically achieve your goals. There is another change of emphasis at age fifty-one, when your progressed Sun moves into Aquarius. This highlights issues regarding friendship, group awareness, and independence. You may decide to share some of your more progressive ideas with others.

Your Secret Self

With your dynamic emotions and sensitive power, you can quickly judge situations by the way you feel. As you are very instinctive, your first reactions about people are usually right. With a wide emotional range, you can go from being warm, gentle, and compassionate to being strong and resolute. Although you may suffer at times from restlessness and impatience, once you set your mind on a job, you like to do it well and can be relentlessly persistent.

You are an interesting mixture of charm, practical organization, and fertile imagination, and your work can be an important outlet for your energy and talents. Diligent and concentrated effort must be applied in order to take advantage of your remarkable potential, but fortunately your hard work will give you financial protection. With a good sense of vision and a strong emphasis on values, you are in a position to positively influence others.

Work & Vocation

Independent and strong-willed, you have natural leadership abilities that can ensure your success at the forefront of your field if you are only willing to exercise the necessary self-discipline. You are practical, with an honest and direct approach, and others appreciate knowing where they stand with you. Your organizational skills show a talent for administration, but this may not provide enough stimulation to keep you happy unless it also involves people and variety. With your original ideas, you often enjoy initiating your own projects or do much to improve existing systems.

Famous people who share your birthday include comedian/director Woody Allen, comedian Richard Pryor, musician Jaco Pastorius, ballerina Alicia Markova, singer/actress Bette Midler, and golfer Lee Trevino.

causes. Antares also bestows a talent for writing and a religious outlook that seeks knowledge and wisdom. Although Antares bestows honor and riches, these are not necessarily long-lasting. With Antares's influence, unforeseen circumstances can change situations suddenly for good or bad.

• *Positive:* courageous, worldly, travel to foreign lands, higher education

• *Negative:* hot temper, outspoken, rebellious, destructive behavior

See Appendix for additional fixed star readings.

Numerology

The great desire to be first and independent is suggested by your birthdate. As a number 1 individual, you are inclined to be innovative and courageous, with plenty of energy. Often there is a need to establish a strong identity and develop assertiveness. The pioneering spirit indicated here encourages you to strike out alone. These self-starting forces can also stimulate you to develop executive or leadership abilities. Full of enthusiasm and original ideas, you can show others the way forward. With a number 1 birthday, you may also need to learn that the world does not revolve around you; avoid an inclination to be self-centered or dictatorial. The subinfluence of the number 12 month indicates that you are friendly, with a generous personality. Although you are idealistic, with a daring and optimistic attitude, you want to keep your feet firmly on the ground and use your good common sense. Although you usually have no trouble convincing or attracting others, you may need to learn when to take the lead and when to accept change and compromise.

• *Positive:* leadership, creative, progressive, forceful, optimistic, strong convictions, competitive, independent, gregarious

• *Negative:* overbearing, jealous, egotistical, too proud, antagonistic, lack of restraint, selfish, unstable, impatient

YOUR SPECIAL SOMEONE

To find long-lasting happiness and security, you might begin by looking for someone born on one of the following days.

Love & friendship: Jan. 1, 7, 11, 12, 22, 27, Feb. 5, 9, 20, Mar. 3, 7, 18, 26, 31, Apr. 1, 5, 16, 29, May 3, 14, 27, 29, June 1, 12, 25, 27, July 10, 23, 25, Aug. 8, 16, 21, 23, 31, Sept. 6, 19, 21, 29, Oct. 4, 17, 19, 27, 30, Nov. 2, 15, 17, 25, 28, Dec. 13, 15, 23, 26

Beneficial: Jan. 8, 14, 19, Feb. 6, 12, 17, Mar. 4, 10, 15, Apr. 2, 8, 13, May 6, 11, June 4, 9, July 2, 7, Aug. 5, Sept. 3, Oct. 1, 29, Nov. 27, Dec. 25, 29

Fatal attractions: May 30, 31, June 1, 2

Challenging: Jan. 9, 18, 20, Feb. 7, 16, 18, Mar. 5, 14, 16, Apr. 3, 12, 14, May 1, 10, 12, June 8, 10, July 6, 8, 29, Aug. 4, 6, 27, Sept. 2, 4, 25, Oct. 2, 23, Nov. 21, Dec. 19

Soul mates: Jan. 9, Feb. 7, Mar. 5, Apr. 3, May 1, Oct. 30, Nov. 28, Dec. 26

Love & Relationships

Idealistic and sociable, you seek emotional stability and security. As a charismatic personality, you often attract many friends and admirers. Usually harmonious and kind, you are willing to work at keeping the peace in your relationships and rarely give up on a partner you love. Although you can express feelings of love and affection, you can become inconsiderate or willful if your emotions become repressed.

December 2

♐ Versatile and sociable, you are an intuitive Sagittarian with an enterprising spirit. Idealistic and sensitive, you have a restless nature that seeks variety. As a resourceful and courageous individual, you enjoy an element of risk that can bring you excitement and opportunities. Full of enthusiasm and bright ideas, you can be creative and inspirational.

The influence of your decanate ruler, Sagittarius, implies that you prefer to see the broad plan rather than the finer details. Usually optimistic and humanitarian, you have foresight that suggests that you are interested in ideas that encompass the whole. Your assertiveness urges you to be competitive and adventurous; even so, cooperative ventures often bring added benefits. With a natural flair for literature and writing, you benefit from finding ways to express yourself intellectually and emotionally. In your enthusiasm to take on life's challenges, however, guard against taking reckless chances by believing that new beginnings will solve all your past problems.

Since you have original thoughts and excellent executive ability, you are a natural strategist who is able to find practical solutions to problems and get things moving quickly. Although you rely on your common sense, an independent and unusual approach endows you with an ability to see the various sides of every situation. By being patient, however, you manage to avoid scattering your energies on worries and doubts. Industrious and methodical, you have an open and pragmatic approach, implying that you are frank and direct and usually go straight to the heart of the matter.

Up to the age of nineteen, you will want to expand your horizons and seek opportunities, whether through enterprising ventures, study, or travel. At the age of twenty, when your progressed Sun moves into Capricorn, you start to become more practical, goal-oriented, and realistic in your approach to your achievements. This can involve a greater need for order and structure in your life. Another turning point occurs at the age of fifty, when your progressed Sun moves into Aquarius. This highlights a growing need for more freedom and independence. As well as having a desire to express your individuality, you can become more humanitarian and group-conscious in your approach and experimental in your lifestyle.

FIXED STARS

Antares, also called Anti Aries or the Rival of Mars; Han

PRIMARY STAR

Star's name: Antares, also called Anti Aries or the Rival of Mars

Degree position: 8°48'–9°49' Sagittarius between the years 1930 and 2000

Magnitude: 1

Strength: ★★★★★★★★★

Orb: 2°30'

Constellation: Alpha Scorpio

Applicable days: November 30, December 1, 2, 3, 4, 5

Star qualities: Mars/Jupiter, also Jupiter/Venus

Description: a binary star, fiery red and emerald green, located in the body of the Scorpion

PRIMARY STAR'S INFLUENCE

Antares is one of the four royal stars and therefore of great importance. This star imparts an adventurous nature, keen mentality, broad-minded outlook, and liberal attitude. It also indicates unexpected events, lucky breaks, and numerous opportunities for travel to foreign lands. Antares bestows courage, strong convictions, and a daring character. However, it also warns against rashness, destructive behavior, obstinacy, and vengeful acts.

Linked to your Sun's degree, Antares imparts an interest in education, politics, or business dealing with the public. You are probably idealistic, optimistic, and willing to fight for just

Your Secret Self

Your inner sensitivity may not always be obvious from your confident front. Being a problem-solver who is looking for deeper meaning in life, you often intuitively know the answer to other people's dilemmas. Responsible, with a strong need for love and affection, you are willing to go to great lengths to create harmony, even to the point of making sacrifices for others. You run the risk of caring so much, however, that even with the best of intentions you may become domineering or interfering. By using the power of love, you are able to overcome obstacles and forgive others to create the peace you so strongly seek.

Dramatic, proud, and strong-willed, you do not like to be in subservient positions. A good awareness of values and an innate business sense enable you to turn any situation to your advantage as long as you do not become too preoccupied with material concerns. Although charming, at times you may have to guard against being too outspoken or verbally cutting. Nevertheless, with your inner strength and charismatic personality, you only have to apply the necessary self-discipline to achieve outstanding success in life.

Work & Vocation

Your keen intelligence and excellent communication skills point to a remarkable capacity for achievement. You may have to guard against taking on too much, or overcome a tendency to doubt yourself. As a rebel with a cause, you may become a pioneer in social or educational reforms. Constantly updating your ideas, you may decide to change your career or at least improve the way you work. Being naturally sociable as well as having shrewd business acumen point you toward careers that may incorporate both of these characteristics, such as sales, publishing, or media. Alternatively, you may want to use your highly creative approach to life through writing or the the arts. A philosophical or humanitarian leaning may be satisfied through occupations such as charity work, religion, or becoming a philanthropist. You may particularly reap benefits from travel or working in partnerships.

Famous people who share your birthday include tennis player Monica Seles, impressionist painter Georges Seurat, opera star Maria Callas, designer Gianni Versace, and writer Nicos Kazantzakis.

Numerology

Sensitivity and a strong need to be part of a group are suggested by the number 2 birthday. You enjoy cooperative activities where you can experience interaction with others. In your attempt to please those you like, you may run the risk of becoming overly dependent. Nevertheless, by developing confidence, you can overcome the tendency to get easily hurt by the actions and criticism of others. The subinfluence of the number 12 month indicates that you are creative and multitalented, with strong instincts. Being highly intuitive, with a keen mind, you are friendly and adaptable. A need for mental stimulation and a restless nature imply that you benefit from self-discipline and staying consistent. You also need to develop your diplomatic skills and be less blunt or outspoken. By becoming more self-disciplined and patient, you learn to trust your own instincts.

• *Positive:* good partnerships, gentle, tactful, receptive, intuitive, considerate, harmonious, agreeable, ambassador of goodwill

• *Negative:* suspicious, lack of confidence, subservient, oversensitive, deceitful, selfish, moodiness, easily hurt

Love & Relationships

Idealistic and honest, you need to choose your partners carefully; otherwise it may be difficult for anyone to live up to your high expectations. Although your naturally friendly personality ensures that you have many friends, having two sides to your nature implies that you may alternate between being optimistic, spontaneous, and affectionate and appearing indifferent or withdrawn. These changing moods can leave others wondering or bewildered. Often looking for an almost spiritual bond, you can go to great lengths to help those you love.

causes. Antares also bestows a talent for writing and a religious outlook that seeks knowledge and wisdom. Although Antares confers honor and riches, these are not necessarily long-lasting. With Antares's influence, unforeseen circumstances can change situations suddenly for good or bad.

• *Positive:* courageous, worldly, travel to foreign lands, higher education

• *Negative:* hot temper, outspoken, rebellious, destructive behavior

See Appendix for additional fixed star readings.

YOUR SPECIAL SOMEONE

If you are looking for friendship or love, you might find an inspiring partner among those born on the following days.

Love & friendship: Jan. 4, 8, 13, 22, 26, Feb. 6, 20, 24, Mar. 4, 18, 22, Apr. 2, 7, 16, 20, 30, May 14, 18, 28, 30, June 12, 16, 26, 28, July 10, 14, 23, 24, 26, Aug. 8, 12, 22, 24, Sept. 6, 10, 20, 22, 30, Oct. 4, 8, 18, 20, 28, Nov. 2, 6, 16, 18, 26, Dec. 4, 14, 16, 24

Beneficial: Jan. 9, 20, Feb. 7, 18, Mar. 5, 16, 29, Apr. 3, 14, 27, May 1, 12, 25, June 10, 23, July 8, 21, Aug. 6, 19, Sept. 4, 17, Oct. 2, 15, 30, Nov. 13, 28, Dec. 11, 26, 30

Fatal attractions: Jan. 27, Feb. 25, Mar. 23, Apr. 21, May 19, 30, 31, June 1, 2, 17, July 15, Aug. 13, Sept. 11, Oct. 9, Nov. 7, Dec. 5

Challenging: Jan. 2, 10, 19, Feb. 8, 17, Mar. 6, 15, Apr. 4, 13, May 2, 11, June 9, July 7, 30, Aug. 5, 28, Sept. 3, 26, Oct. 1, 24, Nov. 22, Dec. 20, 30

Soul mates: Jan. 15, Feb. 13, Mar. 11, Apr. 9, May 7, June 5, July 3, Aug. 1, Oct. 29, Nov. 27, Dec. 25

December 3

FIXED STARS

Antares, also called Anti Aries or the Rival of Mars; Rastaban; Han

PRIMARY STAR

Star's name: Antares, also called Anti Aries or the Rival of Mars

Degree position: 8°48'–9°49' Sagittarius between the years of 1930 and 2000

Magnitude: 1

Strength: ★★★★★★★★★

Orb: 2°30'

Constellation: Alpha Scorpio

Applicable days: November 30, December 1, 2, 3, 4, 5

Star qualities: Mars/Jupiter, also Jupiter/Venus

Description: a binary star, fiery red and emerald green, located in the body of the Scorpion

PRIMARY STAR'S INFLUENCE

Antares is one of the four royal stars and therefore of great importance. This star imparts an adventurous nature, keen mentality, broad-minded outlook, and liberal attitude. It also indicates unexpected events, lucky breaks, and numerous opportunities for travel to foreign lands. Antares bestows courage, strong convictions, and a daring character. However, it also warns against rashness, destructive behavior, obstinacy, and vengeful acts.

Linked to your Sun's degree, Antares imparts an interest in education and politics or business dealing with the public. You are probably idealistic, optimistic, and willing to fight for a

Creative and versatile, with a flair for people, you are a charming and friendly Sagittarian with a pragmatic approach. A willingness to compromise and cooperate with others usually leads you to successful joint ventures that can be of immense benefit to you and your co-workers. Although often fortunate, you may need to overcome a tendency to scatter your energies by learning to focus your enterprising spirit on the most important issues.

The subinfluence of your decanate ruler, Aries, adds vitality to your bright outlook and optimistic nature. Energetic and determined, you have the ability to overcome obstacles. This assertiveness also urges you to be adventurous and expand your horizons. Being alert, with excellent executive ability, you enjoy an element of risk that can bring you good fortune and excitement. Your fighting spirit and creative thinking suggest that you need freedom of expression and like to get things moving quickly.

Cerebral and intuitive, you are a humanitarian who enjoys intellectual activities. These can fire your imagination and inspire your idealistic beliefs or spur your interest in metaphysical and religious subjects. Although you have many wonderful money-making ideas, a conflict between your ideals and reality suggests that you need to have realistic goals. If not, you may experience a concern about not having enough money, or periods of weakness may alternate with periods of determined progress and advancement in life.

Up to the age of eighteen, you are optimistic and adventurous, with a strong desire to expand your opportunities. This may be through taking chances, education, or travel. A turning point occurs as you reach the age of nineteen, when your progressed Sun moves into Capricorn. This brings a more pragmatic, orderly, and structured approach to your life. You have a more realistic sense of how to achieve your goals. There is another change of emphasis at age forty-nine, when your progressed Sun moves into Aquarius. This highlights issues regarding friendship, group awareness, and independence.

Your Secret Self

Although publicly very active, with a strong need for recognition, you also possess an inner desire for peace and tranquility. This may lead you to develop artistic and creative pursuits or emphasize the importance of your home as a retreat from the world. By learning to balance your dynamic, worldly ambitions with your desire for a simple life, you can avoid going to extremes or becoming too self-absorbed. You can use your excellent intuitive sense in your practical affairs by getting a feel for a situation before committing yourself to some form of structure.

A strong desire to be materially successful implies that you usually enjoy initiating projects you feel can really succeed. As you can be very determined, you can be a powerful force when directed toward a goal. A strong inner need for material success, power, and prestige blends peculiarly with a high idealism, and you are liable to work best when inspired and listening to your intuition. When positively channeled, your power can be a tremendous energy for the uplifting of others.

Work & Vocation

Although independent, with leadership skills, you also realize the importance of acting cooperatively with others. This may encourage you to become involved in working partnerships or projects involving teamwork. With your positive enthusiasm and vitality, you can be especially good at selling or promoting an idea or product. Your relationship skills and ability to make contacts ensure that people-related careers such as public relations specialist, advisor, go-between, and agent, are ideal. Clever and creative, you may well choose a career in music, literature, art, or drama. Idealistic as well as practical, you may find particular enjoyment in work that helps others.

Famous people who share your birthday include film director Jean-Luc Godard, writer Joseph Conrad, singer Ozzy Osbourne, psychologist Anna Freud, singer Andy Williams, and figure skater Katarina Witt.

Numerology

With a number 3 birthday, you are sensitive, with a need for creativity and emotional expression. Fun-loving and a good companion, you enjoy friendly social activities and many interests. Although you are versatile and expressive, with a need for different and exciting experiences, an inclination to get bored easily may cause you to become indecisive or spread yourself too thinly. Although, as a number 3 individual, you are usually artistic and charming, with a good sense of humor, you may have to develop self-esteem and guard against tendencies such as worry and emotional insecurities. The subinfluence of the number 12 month indicates that you are freedom-loving, idealistic, and direct, with a trusting and optimistic outlook. Usually you have many contacts and enjoy being popular. A need to be active and enterprising suggests that you enjoy being part of a social group or a large family. A need to be active and adventurous also implies that you need variety; otherwise you may become bored and restless.

• *Positive:* humorous, happy, friendly, productive, creative, artistic, the power to wish, freedom-loving, a talent with words

• *Negative:* easily bored, vain, overimaginative, exaggerate, boastful, extravagant, self-indulgent, lazy, hypocritical

Love & Relationships

Friendly and idealistic, you are attracted to intelligent and powerful people who have strong convictions. Warm and affectionate, you are highly sociable, with a wide circle of friends. Although you can be optimistic and generous with those you love, you also have strong personal desires and ambitions that can sometimes cause you to seem calculating. Although you are usually willing to make sacrifices to keep your relationships alive, you need to maintain a certain amount of your personal freedom. Friends can sometimes prove to be helpful in business situations.

just cause. Antares also bestows a talent for writing and a religious outlook that seeks knowledge and wisdom. Although Antares confers honor and riches, these are not necessarily long-lasting. With Antares's influence, unforeseen circumstances can change situations suddenly for good or bad.

• *Positive:* courageous, worldly, travel to foreign lands, higher education

• *Negative:* hot temper, outspoken, rebellious, destructive behavior

See Appendix for additional fixed star readings.

YOUR SPECIAL SOMEONE

You might find a partner who will understand your sensitivity and need for love among those born on the following days.

Love & friendship: Jan. 3, 6, 23, Feb. 11, 21, Mar. 9, 19, 28, 31, Apr. 7, 11, 17, 26, 29, May 5, 15, 24, 27, 29, 31, June 3, 13, 22, 25, 27, 29, July 1, 11, 20, 23, 25, 27, 29, Aug. 3, 9, 18, 21, 23, 25, 27, Sept. 7, 16, 19, 21, 23, 25, Oct. 5, 14, 17, 19, 21, 23, Nov. 3, 12, 15, 17, 19, 21, Dec. 1, 10, 13, 15, 17, 19

Beneficial: Jan. 3, 4, 10, 21, Feb. 1, 2, 8, 19, Mar. 6, 17, 30, Apr. 4, 15, 28, May 2, 13, 26, June 11, 24, July 9, 22, Aug. 7, 20, Sept. 5, 18, Oct. 3, 16, 31, Nov. 1, 14, 29, Dec. 12, 27

Fatal attractions: Jan. 22, 28, Feb. 20, 26, Mar. 18, 24, Apr. 16, 22, May 14, 20, 30, June 1, 2, 3, 12, 18, July 10, 16, Aug. 8, 14, Sept. 6, 12, Oct. 4, 10, Nov. 2, 8, Dec. 6

Challenging: Jan. 11, 20, Feb. 9, 18, Mar. 7, 16, Apr. 5, 14, May 3, 12, 30, June 1, 10, 28, July 8, 26, 31, Aug. 6, 24, 29, Sept. 4, 22, 27, Oct. 2, 20, 25, Nov. 18, 23, Dec. 16, 21

Soul mates: Jan. 26, Feb. 24, Mar. 22, 30, Apr. 20, 28, May 18, 26, June 16, 24, July 14, 22, Aug. 12, 20, Sept. 10, 18, Oct. 8, 16, Nov. 6, 14, Dec. 4, 12

December 4

Optimistic and ambitious, you are a spirited Sagittarian with a pragmatic approach and a determined nature. Your strong desires and bold drive for money and prestige imply that, with courage and commitment, you often achieve your objectives and ideals. Forceful and highly individualistic, with a need for freedom, you thrive on new beginnings and opportunities to expand your horizons.

The subinfluence of your decanate ruler, Aries, adds to your assertiveness and urges you to be adventurous and independent. Competitive, with a spirit of enterprise, you like to be active, alert, and daring. With your excellent executive abilities, you enjoy an element of risk that accompanies challenges, and usually you manage to make things move along quickly.

Idealistic, with a good business sense, you have fortunate ideas and the ability to realize them. Your farsightedness and comprehension imply that you are often able to spot new trends and situations. You enjoy initiating projects or being in the forefront of modern concepts and projects. Although you are resourceful and courageous, a tendency to adhere to your principles out of stubbornness rather than real conviction suggests that you need to learn to compromise rather than be domineering.

Up to the age of seventeen, you are mainly concerned with issues of freedom, adventure, and opportunity. At the age of eighteen, when your progressed Sun moves into Capricorn, you start to become more practical, goal-oriented, and realistic in your approach to your achievements. This may involve more order and structure in your life. Another turning point occurs at the age of forty-eight, when your progressed Sun moves into Aquarius. This highlights a growing need for freedom, new ideas, and expressing your individuality. You are likely to place more emphasis on group endeavors or the importance of friendship.

Your Secret Self

Although independent, you have a gift for dealing with people and making connections. Your relationships can be especially important, and you realize the advantages of working as part of a team or in a partnership. Being idealistic, with a shrewd business sense, you can be a practical visionary who excels at promoting an idea or a cause. Although you may sometimes experience groundless fears around money issues, your powers of persuasion and excellent negotiation skills mean that you have the potential for remarkable success.

Strong-willed and magnanimous, you have a powerful desire for love and self-expression. This desire combines with a natural humanitarian streak, so that when you are positively focused you can become a dynamic force helping others. Enthusiastic, you make great plans but often need to do things your way. By finding a middle path between idealism and ambition, love and money, compassion and power, you can be capable of inspired leadership.

Work & Vocation

Enterprising, ambitious, and hardworking, you have strong willpower and ability to see opportunities that can help you in your rise to success. The combination of your relationship skills and determination enables you to cooperate with others in a dynamic and positive way.

FIXED STARS

Antares, also called Anti Aries or the Rival of Mars; Rastaban

PRIMARY STAR

Star's name: Antares, also called Anti Aries or the Rival of Mars

Degree position: 8°48'–9°49' Sagittarius between the years 1930 and 2000

Magnitude: 1

Strength: ★★★★★★★★

Orb: 2°30'

Constellation: Alpha Scorpio

Applicable days: November 30, December 1, 2, 3, 4, 5

Star qualities: Mars/Jupiter, also Jupiter/Venus

Description: a binary star, fiery red and emerald green, located in the body of the Scorpion

PRIMARY STAR'S INFLUENCE

Antares is one of the four royal stars and therefore of great importance. This star imparts an adventurous nature, keen mentality, broad-minded outlook, and liberal attitude. It also indicates unexpected events, lucky breaks, and numerous opportunities for travel to foreign lands. Antares bestows courage, strong convictions, and a daring character. However, it also warns against rashness, destructive behavior, obstinacy, and vengeful acts.

Linked to your Sun's degree, Antares imparts an interest in education, politics, or business dealing with the public. You are probably idealistic, optimistic, and willing to fight for just

As you think on a large scale and have excellent negotiating skills, you may want to be an entrepreneur or have a career in big corporations or management. With your art of persuasion, you may also wish to pursue a career in commerce, such as arbitrator, agent, or financial advisor. Although your enthusiasm may lead you to commercially promote ideas, products, or other people, your equally strong idealism may lead you to promote a cause. You may want to explore your creative talents by pursuing an artistic career.

Famous people who share your birthday include artist Wassily Kandinsky, TV personality Wink Martindale, poet Rainer Maria Rilke, actor Jeff Bridges, and biologist R. R. Mann.

causes. Antares also bestows a talent for writing and a religious outlook that seeks knowledge and wisdom. Although Antares confers honor and riches, these are not necessarily long-lasting. With Antares's influence, unforeseen circumstances can change situations suddenly for good or bad.

• *Positive:* courageous, worldly, travel to foreign lands, higher education

• *Negative:* hot temper, outspoken, rebellious, destructive behavior

See Appendix for additional fixed star readings.

Numerology

The solid structure and orderly power suggested by the number 4 birthday indicate that you need stability and like to establish order. Endowed with energy, practical skills, and strong determination, you can achieve success through hard work. Security-conscious, you like to build a strong foundation for yourself and your family. A pragmatic approach to life confers a good business sense and an ability to achieve material success in life. As a number 4 individual, you are usually honest, frank, and fair. The challenges for a number 4 individual may include overcoming periods of instability or financial worry. The subinfluence of the number 12 month indicates that although you are friendly and sociable, you can be direct and outspoken. Inquisitive and doubting, you enjoy testing your competence and intelligence against the odds. As a free thinker, you can be quite stubborn and single-minded once you have decided on a course of action. Although you are full of dynamic drive, you need stability and patience in order to channel your energies into something useful or a meaningful purpose.

• *Positive:* well organized, self-disciplined, steady, hardworking, organized, craftsmanship, good with your hands, pragmatism, trusting, exact

• *Negative:* unstable, destructive behavior, uncommunicative, repressed, rigid, lazy, unfeeling, procrastination, too economical, bossy, hidden affections, resentful, strict

YOUR SPECIAL SOMEONE

In order to find someone who can meet your ideals, you might like to begin by looking for those born on the following dates.

Love & friendship: Jan. 6, 14, 21, 24, 31, Feb. 4, 12, 19, 22, 29, Mar. 10, 20, 27, Apr. 8, 18, 25, May 6, 16, 23, 30, June 4, 14, 21, 28, 30, July 2, 12, 19, 26, 28, 30, Aug. 10, 17, 24, 26, 28, Sept. 8, 15, 22, 24, 26, Oct. 6, 13, 20, 22, 24, 30, Nov. 4, 11, 18, 20, 22, 28, Dec. 2, 9, 16, 18, 20, 26, 29

Beneficial: Jan. 5, 22, 30, Feb. 3, 20, 28, Mar. 1, 18, 26, Apr. 16, 24, May 14, 22, June 12, 20, July 10, 18, 29, Aug. 8, 16, 27, 31, Sept. 6, 14, 25, 29, Oct. 4, 12, 23, 27, Nov. 2, 10, 21, 25, Dec. 9, 19, 23

Fatal attractions: Jan. 12, Feb. 10, Mar. 8, Apr. 6, May 4, June 1, 2, 3, 4, 5

Challenging: Jan. 16, 21, Feb. 14, 19, Mar. 12, 17, 30, Apr. 10, 15, 28, May 8, 13, 26, June 6, 11, 24, July 4, 9, 22, Aug. 2, 7, 20, Sept. 5, 18, Oct. 3, 16, Nov. 1, 14, Dec. 12

Soul mates: Jan. 25, Feb. 23, Mar. 21, Apr. 19, May 17, June 15, July 13, Aug. 11, Sept. 9, Oct. 7, Nov. 5, Dec. 3, 30

Love & Relationships

Dynamic and thoughtful, you want personal freedom and an active social life. A tendency to change your feelings implies that even at the last minute doubts can creep in before you commit yourself to long-term relationships. In your intimate partnerships your intense feelings can have you fluctuating between idyllic optimism and very practical reality. Since you desire to be autonomous, you will have to pick a partner who can provide you with the freedom you need to be happy.

December 5

↗ Intelligent and determined, you are a versatile and restless Sagittarian who is destined to succeed through knowledge, maturity, and polished skills of discrimination. Your optimism and desire to lead an active life suggest that you need the freedom to express yourself emotionally and mentally.

The subinfluence of your decanate ruler, Aries, adds to your assertiveness and urges you to be adventurous and independent. Although you have the ability to display a confident front and show others your excellent executive ability, your own doubt and insecurities may undermine your sense of purpose and confuse you as to what your objectives truly are.

By the tenacious pursuit of your plans, you develop the patience and perseverance required to attain your long-term goals. Outspoken and straightforward, you have suggestions for reforms and an original outlook that indicate that you are knowledgeable and authoritative. Women of this day tend to think in a decisive way and take charge of situations.

Shrewd, with a blend of conservatism and rebelliousness, you may be direct and outspoken, but never boring or dull. Through your ability to think rationally, you learn to recognize the power of knowledge that is usually at your disposal. But if you enthusiastically pursue a rebellious cause, you may be in danger of scattering your energies, or you may become too willful or stubborn and regret it later.

Up to the age of sixteen, you are optimistic and adventurous, with a strong desire to expand your opportunities. This may be through taking chances, education, or travel. A turning point occurs as you reach the age of seventeen, when your progressed Sun moves into Capricorn. This brings a more pragmatic, orderly, and structured approach to your life. You develop a more realistic sense of how to achieve your goals and are more aware of security. There is another change of emphasis at age forty-seven, when your progressed Sun moves into Aquarius. This highlights issues regarding independence and expressing progressive or original ideas. You may have a greater desire for freedom as well as a better understanding of group awareness or humanitarian ideals.

Your Secret Self

With your strong character, you are often goal-oriented and ambitious, possessing an overriding sense of duty and a tenacious personality. Responsible and enjoying power, you usually prefer to be in control. With your quick mental responses, you are usually well able to stand up for yourself and may even enjoy a little friendly rivalry or debate. Hardworking and persistent in the pursuit of your objectives, you can exhibit uncompromising determination.

Although very independent and a natural leader, you are aware of the importance of teamwork or cooperative efforts. While your relationships or working partnerships may play an important part in your life, it is important to get the balance right between your needs and the needs of others. To avoid emotional tensions or arrogance, you may fare best when using your innate diplomatic skills. Nevertheless, because you are proud, your outer appearance may often be a false front to hide your sensitivity, idealism, and inner strength.

Work & Vocation

With your ability to work hard and a capacity to take responsibility, you may find yourself naturally gravitating to positions of authority. Your keen intelligence and original ideas may

FIXED STARS

Antares, also called Anti Aries or the Rival of Mars; Rastaban

PRIMARY STAR

Star's name: Antares, also called Anti Aries or the Rival of Mars

Degree position: 8°48'–9°49' Sagittarius between the years 1930 and 2000

Magnitude: 1

Strength: ★★★★★★★★

Orb: 2°30'

Constellation: Alpha Scorpio

Applicable days: November 30, December 1, 2, 3, 4, 5

Star qualities: Mars/Jupiter, also Jupiter/Venus

Description: a binary star, fiery red and emerald green, located in the body of the Scorpion

PRIMARY STAR'S INFLUENCE

Antares is one of the four royal stars and therefore of great importance. This star imparts an adventurous nature, keen mentality, broad-minded outlook, and liberal attitude. It also indicates unexpected events, lucky breaks, and numerous opportunities for travel to foreign lands. Antares bestows courage, strong convictions, and a daring character. However, it also warns against rashness, destructive behavior, obstinacy, and vengeful acts.

Linked to your Sun's degree, Antares imparts an interest in education, politics, or business dealing with the public. You are probably idealistic, optimistic, and willing to fight for a just

particularly draw you to careers such as education, philosophy, or scientific research. Magnanimous and kind, you are excellent at dealing with people and can usually see opportunities. A dislike of taking orders may encourage you to seek management positions or to work for yourself, as you prefer the freedom to work in your own unique way. Humanitarianism and possible spiritual aspirations can steer you toward social reform or religion. Alternatively, a natural sense of the dramatic may attract you to some aspect of the entertainment world.

Famous people who share your birthday include opera singer José Carreras, U.S. president Martin Van Buren, film directors Fritz Lang and Otto Preminger, singer/songwriters J. J. Cale and Little Richard, astrologer Robert Hand, poet Christina Rossetti, animator Walt Disney, and writer Joan Didion.

Numerology

Strong instincts, an adventurous nature, and a desire for freedom are all indicated by the number 5 birthday. The willingness to try anything new and an enthusiastic approach suggest that life will have a lot to offer you. Travel and many opportunities for change, some unexpected, may lead you to undergo a real transformation of views and beliefs. With a number 5 birthday, you need to feel that life is exciting; however, you may also have to develop a responsible attitude and avoid tendencies such as unpredictability, excessiveness, and restlessness. You can achieve success by avoiding premature or speculative actions and through learning patience. The natural talent of a number 5 individual is knowing how to go with the flow and staying detached. The subinfluence of the number 12 month indicates that you are highly intuitive and creative, with practical abilities and a persuasive manner. Although intelligent and broad-minded, you are sometimes impatient and tense, especially if things do not move quickly enough. You want personal freedom and are often a fighter against injustice.

• *Positive:* versatile, adaptable, progressive, strong instincts, magnetic, lucky, daring, freedom-loving, quick and witty, curious, mystical, sociable

• *Negative:* unreliable, changeable, procrastinator, inconsistent, undependable, overconfident, headstrong

Love & Relationships

Intelligent and knowledgeable, you have an authoritative poise that attracts many admirers. Being responsible and thoughtful, you are honest and direct. If you believe in someone, you will be very supportive and reassuring. Although you are caring, your inclination to take charge of situations implies that at times you may become self-imposing or domineering. It is therefore better to merely suggest to others a course of action or let them make up their own mind. You admire emotionally balanced people who are contented and happy. Your need for a secure foundation in life often adds emphasis to the importance of your marriage, or, if you are single, of a strong home base.

cause. Antares also bestows a talent for writing and a religious outlook that seeks knowledge and wisdom. Although Antares confers honor and riches, these are not necessarily long-lasting. With Antares's influence, unforeseen circumstances can change situations suddenly for good or bad.

• *Positive:* courageous, worldly, travel to foreign lands, higher education

• *Negative:* hot temper, outspoken, rebellious, destructive behavior

See Appendix for additional fixed star readings.

YOUR SPECIAL SOMEONE

If you are looking for an ideal partner, you may further enhance your luck by finding someone born on one of the following dates.

Love & friendship: Jan. 7, 11, 13, 15, 17, 25, Feb. 5, 9, 11, 13, 15, 23, Mar. 7, 9, 11, 13, 21, Apr. 1, 5, 7, 9, 11, 19, May 3, 5, 7, 9, 17, 31, June 1, 3, 5, 7, 15, 29, July 1, 3, 5, 27, 29, 31, Aug. 1, 3, 11, 25, 27, 29, Sept. 1, 9, 23, 25, 27, Oct. 7, 21, 23, 25, Nov. 5, 19, 21, 23, Dec. 3, 17, 19, 21, 30

Beneficial: Jan. 1, 5, 20, Feb. 3, 18, Mar. 1, 16, Apr. 14, May 12, June 10, July 8, Aug. 6, Sept. 4, Oct. 2

Fatal attractions: June 2, 3, 4, 5

Challenging: Jan. 6, 22, 24, Feb. 4, 20, 22, Mar. 2, 18, 20, Apr. 16, 18, May 16, 14, June 12, 14, July 10, 12, Aug. 8, 10, 31, Sept. 6, 8, 29, Oct. 4, 6, 27, Nov. 2, 4, 25, 30, Dec. 2, 23, 28

Soul mates: Jan. 6, 12, Feb. 4, 10, Mar. 2, 8, Apr. 6, May 4, June 2

December 6

With intelligence and good judgment at your disposal, you are a perceptive Sagittarian with powerful feelings and high ideals. By developing your instincts and intuitive powers, you learn to utilize the power of positive thinking to eliminate your worries and emotional insecurities.

The subinfluence of your decanate ruler, Aries, adds to your vitality and urges you to be adventurous and independent. But in order to achieve your objectives, in the big world, you need to stay resolute and optimistic. Multitalented and enthusiastic, with a need to express your originality and individuality, you may need to pay attention to detail and focus on what you want to achieve.

Since you are an independent thinker, you do not value intervention from others and can sometimes show an inflexible streak. Nevertheless, whatever you wish to achieve in life, it can be advantageous to search for truth and wisdom or to embark on a spiritual quest. As a perfectionist with excellent executive abilities, you can undertake large projects and be dedicated and hardworking. Friendly and sociable, with compassion and a humanitarian streak, you have a wide circle of friends and an outgoing personality. Although usually charming, generous, and sympathetic, you can also be intolerant of ignorance. At such times you display impatience and do not suffer fools gladly.

Between the ages of sixteen and forty-five, as your progressed Sun moves through Capricorn, you emphasize practical issues and a need for order and structure in your life. A turning point occurs at the age of forty-six, when your progressed Sun moves into Aquarius. This highlights a growing desire for more independence, group awareness, and progressive ideas. You may also feel more experimental. Another turning point occurs at age seventy-six, when your progressed Sun moves into Pisces. This is likely to place more emphasis on your emotional receptivity, imagination, or psychic awareness.

Your Secret Self

The ability to express yourself can prove valuable in releasing your emotional uncertainties and preventing you from becoming overly sensitive. This self-expression can also stimulate your joy of life and encourage you to be happy and creative. Being inventive, quick-witted, and imaginative, you may find that inspiration can be a strong factor in your success, whether through your social life or through developing talents in art, music, drama, or writing. Worry or indecision, particularly regarding emotional affairs, may turn out to be one of the main challenges to your otherwise well-structured mind.

Success-oriented, ambitious, and courageous, you are a lucky and optimistic individual with good business acumen and large schemes. Often, however, you may be inclined to believe that financial security can provide you with all the answers. But by seeing only the material benefits, you can miss out on insight into what is truly worthwhile in life. Fortunately, you are connected to an intuitive source of higher knowledge that can bring you much personal happiness and fulfillment, particularly through being of service to others.

Work & Vocation

With your keen intelligence and enterprising spirit, you usually enjoy a challenge and are constantly updating your knowledge. As you prefer large projects and do not like to be subordi-

---

FIXED STAR

Star's name: Rastaban

Degree position: 10°49'–11°42'
    Sagittarius between the years
    1930 and 2000

Magnitude: 2.5

Strength: ★★★★★★★

Orb: 1°40'

Constellation: Beta Draconis

Applicable days: December 3, 4, 5, 6

Star qualities: Saturn/Mars

Description: an irregular, variable, giant
    red and blue-yellow binary star,
    located in the head of the
    Dragon

PRIMARY STAR'S INFLUENCE

Rastaban imparts strong convictions, determination, and success in dealing with the general public. This star may also indicate opportunities for unusual discoveries and inventions as well as changes and unexpected turns of fortune. Rastaban bestows great courage, daring, and an ambitious nature. Often, through the help of others, you may gain power and fame.

Linked to your Sun's degree, Rastaban imparts executive abilities, an ambitious nature, and persistence. This may eventually lead to high positions in careers such as education, religion, science, and innovative research.

Horses are also associated with this star, and working with them may be a desired career.

• *Positive:* endurance, patience, pragmatic outlook

• *Negative:* rebellious and antiestablishment, lack of drive

nate to others, you ideally need a career where you can retain some control or authority. Your quest for truth and idealism may attract you to law, counseling, or social reform, especially when you are in a position to speak up for the rights of others. Your intuitive intellect may equally find fulfillment through the educational world, scientific research, metaphysics, or philosophy. The more practical side of your nature, however, may be attracted to business, where your organizational skills, convincing speech, and many talents can help you achieve in a big way. Alternatively, a deep need for harmony may draw you to music or the arts.

Famous people who share your birthday include songwriter Ira Gershwin, actress Agnes Moorehead, jazz composer Dave Brubeck, swimmer Eleanor Holm, boxing promoter Don King, and photojournalist Alfred Eisenstadt.

Numerology

Idealism, creativity, and a compassionate nature are some of the attributes suggested by a number 6 birthday. This is the number of the perfectionist or the universal friend and indicates that you are frequently a humanitarian who can be responsible, loving, and supportive. With a number 6 birthday, you are frequently domestically inclined and a devoted parent. The more sensitive among you will need to find a form of creative expression and are drawn to the world of entertaining or art and design. You may need to develop more self-confidence and overcome tendencies such as interference, worry, and misplaced sympathy. The subinfluence of the number 12 month indicates that you are imaginative and charitable. Although you are a visionary with an optimistic outlook and intelligence, you need to learn to trust your intuition and develop your psychic abilities. Broad-minded and original, you often seek a path to higher learning and can benefit greatly from studying metaphysics or philosophy. By taking others' needs into consideration and accepting your responsibilities, you usually find peace of mind and overcome anxiety.

• *Positive:* worldly, universal brotherhood, compassionate, dependable, understanding, sympathetic, idealistic, domesticated, humanitarian, poised, artistic

• *Negative:* discontented, anxious, shy, unreasonable, stubborn, outspoken, perfectionist, domineering, lack of responsibility, suspicious, self-centered

Love & Relationships

Friendly and perceptive, you prefer the company of intelligent and forceful people who can offer you interesting conversation and mental stimulation. Having an amicable and sympathetic nature suggests that others are drawn to you in time of need for guidance and support. Idealistic and ambitious, you can take responsibility for yourself and others. Although in relationships you appear strong and forceful, a sensitive side to your nature implies that at times you can become restless or bored. Although often interested in foreign people or places, you still need the security of home.

YOUR SPECIAL SOMEONE

For affection, security, and reassurance, you might want to begin looking for those born among the following days.

Love & friendship: Jan. 4, 9, 12, 16, 25, 30, Feb. 10, 14, 23, 24, Mar. 8, 12, 22, 31, Apr. 3, 6, 10, 20, 29, May 4, 8, 18, 27, June 2, 6, 16, 25, 30, July 4, 14, 23, 28, Aug. 2, 12, 16, 21, 26, 30, Sept. 10, 19, 24, 28, Oct. 8, 17, 22, 26, Nov. 6, 15, 20, 24, 30, Dec. 4, 13, 18, 22, 28

Beneficial: Jan. 2, 13, 22, 24, Feb. 11, 17, 20, 22, Mar. 9, 15, 18, 20, 28, Apr. 7, 13, 16, 18, 26, May 5, 11, 16, 18, 26, June 3, 9, 12, 14, 22, July 1, 7, 10, 12, 20, Aug. 5, 8, 10, 18, Sept. 3, 6, 8, 16, Oct. 1, 4, 6, 14, Nov. 2, 4, 12, Dec. 2, 10

Fatal attractions: Jan. 25, Feb. 23, Mar. 21, Apr. 19, May 17, June 2, 3, 4 5, 6, 15, July 13, Aug. 11, Sept. 9, Oct. 7, Nov. 5, Dec. 3

Challenging: Jan. 7, 23, Feb. 5, 21, Mar. 3, 19, 29, Apr. 1, 17, 27, May 15, 25, June 13, 23, July 11, 21, 31, Aug. 9, 19, 29, Sept. 7, 17, 27, 30, Nov. 3, 13, 23, 26, Dec. 1, 11, 21, 24

Soul mates: Jan. 17, Feb. 15, Mar. 13, Apr. 11, May 9, June 7, July 5, Aug. 3, Sept. 1, Nov. 30, Dec. 28

December 7

FIXED STARS

Although your Sun's degree is not linked to a fixed star, some of your other planets' degrees certainly will be. By having an astrological chart calculated, you can find the exact position of the planets on your date of birth. This will tell you which of the fixed stars listed in this book are relevant to you.

Determined and intuitive, with cerebral powers, you are a Sagittarian on a quest for enlightenment or greater self-awareness. Usually intelligent and enthusiastic, with the ability to comprehend information quickly, you possess ingenious ideas that need to be channeled through mental and creative pursuits.

The subinfluence of your decanate ruler, Aries, suggests that you are ambitious and full of vitality, with a restless temperament. Inquisitive and adventurous, you enjoy an element of risk that can bring excitement and new opportunities. As a creative thinker, you like to gather information, and by amassing knowledge, you often assert your self-confidence. Talented and clever, with a flair for the spoken and written word, you possess a youthful quality, personal magnetism, and spontaneity. With the ability to communicate your thoughts, you usually do not find it difficult to make the right impression.

Although you are socially inclined, your individual philosophical perspective and self-reliant attitude indicate that you prefer to think independently and rarely succumb to peer group pressure. This also contributes to your individuality, skeptical outlook, and need for creative self-expression. Idealistic, you are willing to fight against injustice. If, however, your progressive notions are unconventional, you may appear impulsive and rebellious.

Between the ages of fifteen and forty-four, as your progressed Sun moves through Capricorn, you feel a need for a practical and realistic approach to achieving your goals in life. A turning point occurs at the age of forty-five, when your progressed Sun moves into Aquarius. This highlights a desire for more independence and expressing your individuality. You may become involved with issues of freedom, group awareness, or humanitarian ideals. Another change of emphasis occurs at age seventy-five, when your progressed Sun moves into Pisces. This is likely to highlight your emotional receptivity, imagination, or spiritual inner world.

Your Secret Self

Charismatic and ambitious, you have charm and a warm heart. As you are sociable and generous, you do particularly well in people-related activities. Independent and success-oriented, you like to be active and think in grandiose terms. With your powerful convictions and desire to be of service, you may enjoy supporting an ideal or leading a movement that is of practical use to others. Although you can show deep compassion, your strong emotions may mean you need to avoid going to extremes or acting too much on impulse.

Honest and direct, you enjoy sharing with others and can be an excellent companion. In contrast to the more idealistic side of your nature, a materialistic streak points to the importance of security in your life. Just be careful that you do not compromise too much of your spirit for the sake of financial protection. Nevertheless, with your youthful enthusiasm, strong individuality, and quick intelligence, you are in the fortunate position of inspiring and entertaining others with your wealth of information.

Work & Vocation

With your sharp intelligence and excellent analytical and communication skills, you can particularly excel as a writer, as a spokesperson, or in education. Equally, with your ability to get your ideas across, you may be attracted to law, academia, and politics. Possessing a positive attitude, big plans, and charismatic personality, you can also succeed in large corporations and gain promotion to positions of responsibility. Alternatively, you may be drawn to the world of commerce and use your persuasive charm in sales, promotion, or negotiation. Your need for self-expression indicates that your creative talents can equally lead you to the world of music, art, or drama.

Famous people who share your birthday include linguist Noam Chomsky, singer/songwriters Harry Chapin and Tom Waits, basketball player Larry Bird, actress Ellen Burstyn, writer Willa Cather, and baseball player Johnny Bench.

Numerology

Analytical and thoughtful, number 7 individuals are frequently critical and self-absorbed. With a constant need for greater self-awareness, you enjoy gathering information and may be interested in reading, writing, or spirituality. Although shrewd, you may overrationalize or get lost in detail. A tendency to be enigmatic or secretive suggests that at times you feel misunderstood. As a seeker of knowledge, you benefit greatly from education and especially the study of metaphysics, philosophy, and law. The subinfluence of the number 12 month indicates that you are highly intuitive and imaginative. Independent and capable, you have grand plans and original ideas. Optimistic and carefree, you like to make your own decisions. At times you can be unintentionally insensitive to others, saying whatever is on your mind without a second thought. Nevertheless, thanks to your innocent charm, your frank manner and childish impoliteness are often forgiven. By learning to collaborate and develop your diplomatic skills, you can overcome a tendency to be opinionated or to appear skeptical and provocative.

• *Positive:* educated, trusting, meticulous, idealistic, honest, psychic, scientific, rational, reflective

• *Negative:* concealing, deceitful, unfriendly, secretive, skeptical, malicious, cold, unfeeling

Love & Relationships

Idealistic and mystical, you seek relationships that are truly meaningful. Having two sides to your nature suggests that while you can be spontaneous and passionate, your more thoughtful side needs space and time to be alone, making you sometimes appear aloof and indifferent. If you feel disheartened or let down, you can usually mend bridges by being honest and open about your feelings. Otherwise, skepticism and issues concerning mistrust can spoil friendships and intimate relationships. Avoid being drawn to secret affairs or becoming attached to unsuitable partners who can become a burden later. You need an intelligent partner who can keep up with your quick mind and ever-expanding quest for knowledge.

YOUR SPECIAL SOMEONE

To find true happiness, you might just find the inspiring partner you are looking for among those born on the following dates.

Love & friendship: Jan. 2, 7, 10, 17, 27, 31, Feb. 5, 8, 15, 25, Mar. 3, 6, 13, 23, Apr. 1, 4, 11, 21, 27, May 2, 9, 19, June 7, 17, July 5, 15, 29, 31, Aug. 3, 13, 27, 29, 31, Sept. 1, 11, 25, 27, 29, Oct. 9, 23, 25, 27, Nov. 7, 21, 23, 25, Dec. 5, 19, 21, 23

Beneficial: Jan. 3, 5, 20, 25, 27, Feb. 1, 3, 18, 23, 25, Mar. 1, 16, 21, 23, Apr. 14, 19, 21, May 12, 17, 19, June 10, 15, 17, July 8, 13, 15, Aug. 6, 11, 13, Sept. 4, 9, 11, Oct. 2, 7, 9, Nov. 5, 7, Dec. 3, 5

Fatal attractions: Jan. 13, Feb. 11, Mar. 9, Apr. 7, May 5, June 3, 4, 5, 6, 7, July 1

Challenging: Jan. 16, 24, Feb. 14, 22, Mar. 12, 20, Apr. 10, 18, May 8, 16, 31, June 6, 14, 29, July 4, 12, 27, Aug. 2, 10, 25, Sept. 8, 23, Oct. 6, 21, Nov. 4, 19, Dec. 2, 17

Soul mates: Jan. 16, Feb. 14, Mar. 12, Apr. 10, May 8, June 6, July 4, 31, Aug. 2, 29, Sept. 27, Oct. 25, Nov. 23, Dec. 21

December 8

Intelligent and inspired, your dynamic personality suggests that you are a Sagittarian with a forceful mind and an ambitious nature. Although you appear resourceful and courageous, your sensitivity and strong emotions imply that you may at times have self-doubts or insecure feelings. By learning to show your generosity and compassion, you can avoid being emotionally controlling or manipulative.

The subinfluence of your decanate ruler, Aries, adds to your vitality, determination, and assertiveness, making you think independently. Although you are usually cautious, an adventurous streak suggests that you like an element of risk, which can bring changes and excitement. Since you have excellent executive ability, you like to take charge of situations. Your spirit of enterprise and need to freely express yourself indicate that you do not like to be confined.

Your intelligence and intuitive instinct usually make a powerful combination that urges you to be creative and materially successful. Idealistic and opinionated, at times you can be restless or bored, and since you do not take orders well, you may also become argumentative and uncompromising. With self-discipline, optimism, enthusiasm, and your love of knowledge, you are often inspired to bring about reforms or be inventive, pioneering new ideas.

While you are between the ages of fourteen and forty-three, your progressed Sun moves through Capricorn, emphasizing practical issues and a need for order and structure in your life. A turning point occurs at the age of forty-four, when your progressed Sun moves into Aquarius. This highlights a growing desire for more independence, group awareness, and progressive ideas. You may want freedom or feel more experimental. Another turning point occurs at age seventy-four, when your progressed Sun moves into Pisces. This is likely to make you more emotionally sensitive, sympathetic, and imaginative. This is a time when artistic, creative, or spiritual talents are accentuated.

FIXED STAR

Star's name: Sabik

Degree position: 16°58'–17°59'
Sagittarius between the years
1930 and 2000

Magnitude: 2.5

Strength: ★★★★★★

Orb: 1°40'

Constellation: Eta Ophiuchi

Applicable days: December 8, 9, 10, 11

Star qualities: varied influences:
Saturn/Venus and Jupiter/Venus

Description: a pale yellow star located
on the left knee of Ophiuchus

PRIMARY STAR'S INFLUENCE

Sabik's influence suggests honesty and moral courage. This star also urges you to remain true to your nature and to avoid dishonesty and wastefulness. It suggests that it may be necessary to exercise judgment and avoid underhanded dealings, no matter how lucrative they may seem.

Linked to your Sun's degree, Sabik bestows sincerity, honorable conduct, and a love of justice. You may seek spiritual wisdom and have inclinations toward philosophical studies as well as unconventional or controversial subjects. This star grants changes for the better, and undesirable situations often end up being blessings in disguise. It also indicates that no matter what the circumstances, good morals and convictions will see you through difficult times.

• *Positive:* morals and courage, overcoming obstacles

• *Negative:* wastefulness, dishonesty, deception, lack of morals

Your Secret Self

Although you have a youthful quality, you are also an independent thinker with a quick and shrewd understanding of the motivation of others. Highly intuitive, you have almost a sixth sense about situations; this can help you if you trust your own inner guidance. Although you can be very inventive when challenged, guard against a tendency to take the easy option, as it is through developing perseverance and a responsible attitude that you can achieve remarkable results.

With your innate practicality and natural business sense, financial problems are usually resolved quickly. Your good fortune can extend to opportunities for work that you find fulfilling. Success comes especially from genuine enthusiasm, which is not something that you can fake. The combination of your desire to be direct and honest, your dynamic drive, and your positive determination can help you achieve extraordinary results in life.

Work & Vocation

You have a talent for solving problems and good organizational and managerial abilities, so in business you may be naturally drawn to large enterprises. Since you are never happy being told what to do, it is better for you to be in a position of authority or working for yourself. A strong dramatic sense, when combined with your need for self-expression, can ensure your success in music, writing, art, and the entertainment business. Many people of this birthday are drawn to metaphysics or positive mind training. Your fighting spirit can help you overcome any obstacles you may encounter in your work.

Famous people who share your birthday include singers Sinead O'Connor and Jim Morrison, actress Kim Basinger, artist Diego Rivera, composer Jean Sibelius, actors David Carradine and Maximilian Schell, and entertainer Sammy Davis Jr.

Numerology

The power suggested by the number 8 birthday shows a character with strong values and sound judgment. The number 8 indicates that you aspire to great accomplishment and possess an ambitious nature. A desire for dominance, security, and material success is also indicated by this birthday. As a number 8 person, you have natural business sense and will benefit greatly from developing organizational and executive skills. A strong need to feel secure or established urges you to make long-term plans and investments. The subinfluence of the number 12 month indicates that you are optimistic and charismatic. Usually you are forceful, full of vitality and willpower, and so it is important for you to have your opinions respected. When inspired, you can express yourself clearly and be very persuasive. Although you possess a strong materialistic streak, you are inclined toward philosophy and intellectual pursuits. A need to be popular suggests that when determined and positive, you are capable of achieving harmony and unity in your environment.

• *Positive:* leadership, thoroughness, hardworking, authority, protection, power to heal, good judge of values
• *Negative:* impatient, wasteful, intolerant, overwork, domineering, easily discouraged, lack of planning, controlling behavior

Love & Relationships

Attracted to people who can inspire you intellectually, you often seek individuals who are unique and independent. Usually you admire those who have good practical knowledge and wisdom and who are kind and helpful, with plenty of good advice. Although you portray a confident front, a tendency to vacillate between optimism and pessimism suggests that you may have doubts about your feelings. When insecure, you may attempt to dominate others. If you are hardworking and career-oriented, make sure you allow time for partners, loved ones, and socializing.

YOUR SPECIAL SOMEONE

You are more likely to find that special individual by looking for someone born on one of the following dates.

Love & friendship: Jan. 1, 13, 14, 22, 28, 29, 31, Feb. 12, 26, 29, Mar. 10, 24, 27, Apr. 8, 16, 22, 25, May 6, 20, 23, June 4, 18, 21, July 2, 16, 19, 30, Aug. 14, 17, 28, 30, Sept. 12, 15, 26, 28, 30, Oct. 10, 13, 24, 26, 28, Nov. 8, 11, 22, 24, 26, Dec. 6, 9, 20, 22, 24

Beneficial: Jan. 26, Feb. 24, Mar. 22, Apr. 20, May 18, June 16, July 14, Aug. 12, Sept. 10, Oct. 8, Nov. 6, Dec. 4

Fatal attractions: June 5, 6, 7, 8

Challenging: Jan. 3, 25, Feb. 1, 23, Mar. 21, Apr. 19, May 17, June 15, July 13, Aug. 11, Sept. 9, Oct. 7, Nov. 5, Dec. 3

Soul mates: Jan. 3, 10, Feb. 1, 8, Mar. 6, Apr. 4, May 2, Aug. 31

December 9

Mental creativity, sensitivity, and a positive frame of mind are the keys to your achievements and success. Sociable and friendly, you are an optimistic Sagittarian who is full of life. A blend of fortunate opportunities and challenges, however, implies that you need to find a balance between enthusiasm and frustration. By taking life in your stride, you learn that through perseverance, patience, and determination you can overcome difficulties.

The subinfluence of your decanate ruler, Aries, adds to your assertiveness and urges you to be creative and adventurous. Astute and intuitive, with an ability to comprehend ideas instantly, you can turn difficult circumstances to your advantage. As a humanitarian with progressive and liberal views, you have a strong set of beliefs.

Since you possess an active and productive mind, you have a wealth of imaginative ideas. You may need to be involved in exciting and emotionally fulfilling activities where you can express yourself mentally and emotionally. Nevertheless, you may also have a restless streak and an inclination to fluctuate between being positive and creative and being worried and pessimistic. You may need to guard against being too impulsive by learning to finish what you start or being calmer. Although you have excellent executive ability, your tendency to be critical means you can make burdensome demands on yourself or others. Rather than show discontent, you may be wiser to show your usual generous and loving nature.

Between the ages of thirteen and forty-two, as your progressed Sun moves through Capricorn, you feel a need for a practical and realistic approach to achieving your goals in life. A turning point occurs at the age of forty-three, when your progressed Sun moves into Aquarius. This highlights a desire for more independence and expressing your individuality. You may become involved with issues of freedom, group awareness, or humanitarian ideals. Another change occurs at age seventy-three, when your progressed Sun moves into Pisces. This is likely to highlight your emotional receptivity, imagination, or compassion.

Your Secret Self

An inner sensitivity underlies your confident front. Your strong emotions and sense of the dramatic, when channeled constructively, can ensure your popularity, especially when you turn on your special charm. Imaginative and with strong opinions, you need to express your creativity and ideas. If this need is not fulfilled, you can become deeply frustrated or disappointed, especially if others do not live up to your expectations. Disciplining your mind and continually educating yourself, however, give you confidence and encourage you to make the most of your potential.

A sense of duty implies that you want to be responsible and not have any outstanding liabilities. With a need for security and congenial surroundings, you make your home particularly important in your overall life plan. Alternatively, your need for harmony can be reflected through an appreciation or talent for art, drama, writing, or music.

Work & Vocation

Your love of knowledge and need to express your ideas may attract you to careers such as writing, science, or education. Equally, as you usually enjoy a good debate, your fighting and com-

FIXED STAR

Star's name: Sabik

Degree position: 16°58'–17°59'
    Sagittarius between the years
    1930 and 2000

Magnitude: 2.5

Strength: ★★★★★★★

Orb: 1°40'

Constellation: Eta Ophiuchi

Applicable days: December 8, 9, 10, 11

Star qualities: varied influences:
    Saturn/Venus and Jupiter/Venus

Description: a pale yellow star located
    on the left knee of Ophiuchus

PRIMARY STAR'S INFLUENCE

Sabik's influence shows honesty and moral courage. This star urges you to remain true to your nature and to avoid dishonesty and wastefulness. It suggests a need to exercise judgment and avoid underhanded dealings, no matter how lucrative they may seem.

Linked to your Sun's degree, Sabik bestows sincerity, honorable conduct, and a love of justice. You may seek spiritual wisdom and have inclinations toward philosophical studies as well as unconventional or controversial subjects. This star grants changes for the better, and undesirable situations often end up being blessings in disguise. It also indicates that no matter what the circumstances, good morals and convictions will see you through difficult times.

• *Positive:* morals and courage, overcoming obstacles

• *Negative:* wastefulness, dishonesty, deception, lack of morals

munication skills could be combined in an occupation such as lawyer, reformer, or politician. As you are a good organizer or manager and possess a keen money sense, you can also excel in business or become a leader in your chosen field. An innate humanitarianism may alternatively draw you toward the caring professions or worthwhile causes. With an inner sense of the dramatic, you may prefer to express yourself through the world of entertainment.

Famous people who share your birthdate are actors Kirk Douglas and Beau Bridges, actress Dame Judi Dench, actor/directors John Malkovich and John Cassavetes, and singer Joan Armatrading.

Numerology

Benevolence, thoughtfulness, and sentimental sensitivity are all associated with the number 9 birthday. Tolerant and kind, you are often generous and liberal. Intuitive and psychic abilities point to a universal receptivity and, if channeled positively, may inspire you to seek a spiritual path. This birthday may suggest a need to overcome challenges and a tendency to be overly sensitive, with emotional ups and downs. You benefit greatly from world travel and interaction with people from all walks of life but may have to avoid unrealistic dreams or an inclination toward escapism. The subinfluence of the number 12 month indicates that you are a humanitarian with idealistic and optimistic views. A need for variety and being gifted suggests that you want the freedom to explore and enjoy different experience. You may therefore need to cultivate an independent perspective and find expression for your many talents. Although you are creative and charming, you can possess a tendency toward irritability. Being mentally active, you benefit greatly from broadening your mind through learning and developing patience and perseverance.

• *Positive:* idealistic, humanitarian, creative, sensitive, generous, magnetic, poetic, charitable, giving, detached, lucky, popular

• *Negative:* frustrated, nervous, fragmented, unsure, selfish, impractical, unethical, easily led, inferiority complex, worry, isolated

Love & Relationships

Sociable and considerate, you enjoy other people's company and do not like being on your own. Sensitive and idealistic, with a strong need for emotional security, you seek a close relationship with a partner who is devoted and affectionate. Although you can be loyal, loving, and generous yourself, you also want the freedom to travel and explore different experiences. Since you do not like to be restricted, you may need to find a partner who will not tie you down with heavy responsibilities. As a kind and charitable individual, you are often tempted to make sacrifices for those you love, but avoid becoming overdependent on others.

YOUR SPECIAL SOMEONE

You might find your loving partner among those born on the following days.

Love & friendship: Jan. 1, 5, 9, 15, 26, 29, 30, Feb. 13, 24, 27, 28, Mar. 11, 22, 25, 26, Apr. 3, 9, 19, 20, 23, 24, May 7, 18, 21, 22, June 5, 16, 19, 20, July 3, 14, 17, 18, 31, Aug. 1, 12, 15, 16, 29, 31, Sept. 10, 13, 14, 27, 29, Oct. 8, 11, 12, 25, 27, Nov. 6, 9, 10, 23, 25, Dec. 4, 7, 8, 21, 23, 29

Beneficial: Jan. 1, 2, 10, 12, 27, Feb. 8, 10, 25, Mar. 6, 23, Apr. 4, 8, 21, May 2, 6, 19, 30, June 4, 17, 28, July 2, 15, 26, Aug. 13, 24, Sept. 11, 22, Oct. 9, 20, Nov. 7, 18, Dec. 5, 16

Fatal attractions: June 8, 9, 10, 11

Challenging: Jan. 17, 26, Feb. 15, 24, Mar. 13, 22, Apr. 11, 20, May 9, 18, June 7, 16, July 5, 14, Aug. 3, 12, 30, Sept. 1, 10, 28, Oct. 8, 26, 29, Nov. 6, 24, 27, Dec. 4, 22, 25

Soul mates: Jan. 21, Feb. 19, Mar. 17, Apr. 15, May 13, June 11, July 9, 29, Aug. 7, 27, Sept. 5, 25, Oct. 3, 23, Nov. 1, 21, Dec. 19

December 10

♐ Ambitious and independent, you are an intelligent Sagittarian with imaginative and inspired thoughts. Your active and enquiring mind urges you to find success through being original and innovative. Although daring and adventurous, you have a piercing clarity and pragmatic approach that suggest you seek freedom and self-mastery over your mental and emotional forces. A good business sense indicates that, with motivation, you can also initiate successful financial ventures.

The subinfluence of your decanate ruler, Aries, adds fortitude and defiance to your enterprising spirit. Since you seek different experiences and can be adventurous, you are inclined to have a multitude of plans and ideas. This influence also implies that you are competitive and restless for action and often enjoy an element of risk. As you prefer to take the lead, you do not like to be in a subordinate position or take orders from others. Independent and possessing executive abilities, you like to organize and execute grand projects.

Mentally sharp, you usually have an avid desire for learning and a need to gather information or knowledge. You are also likely to have an interest in the study of philosophy, psychology, or religious thought. Highly intuitive and with psychic gifts, you are quick to understand others and sense hypocrisy. Despite your strength, you need to be in pleasant environments where you can relax and enjoy a harmonious atmosphere.

Between the ages of twelve and forty-one, as your progressed Sun moves through Capricorn, you emphasize practical issues and a need for order and structure in your life. A turning point occurs at the age of forty-two, when your progressed Sun moves into Aquarius. This highlights a growing desire for more independence, group awareness, and progressive ideas. You may want freedom or feel more experimental. Another turning point occurs at age seventy-two, when your progressed Sun moves into Pisces. This is likely to make you more emotionally sensitive, sympathetic, and imaginative.

FIXED STAR

Star's name: Sabik

Degree position: 16°58′–17°59′
Sagittarius between the years 1930 and 2000

Magnitude: 2.5

Strength: ★★★★★★★

Orb: 1°40′

Constellation: Eta Ophiuchi

Applicable days: December 8, 9, 10, 11

Star qualities: varied influences:
Saturn/Venus and Jupiter/Venus

Description: a pale yellow star located on the left knee of Ophiuchus

PRIMARY STAR'S INFLUENCE

Sabik's influence shows honesty and moral courage. This star urges you to remain true to your nature and avoid dishonesty and wastefulness. It suggests that there is a need to exercise judgment and avoid underhanded dealings, no matter how lucrative they may seem.

Linked to your Sun's degree, Sabik bestows sincerity, honorable conduct, and love of justice. You may seek spiritual wisdom and have inclinations toward philosophical studies as well as unconventional or controversial subjects. This star grants changes for the better, and undesirable situations often end up being blessings in disguise. It also indicates that no matter what the circumstances, good morals and convictions will see you through difficult times.

• Positive: morals and courage, overcoming obstacles

• Negative: wastefulness, dishonesty, deception, lack of morals

Your Secret Self

Intuitive and highly strung, you have an extreme sensitivity that makes you receptive to the feelings and motivations of others. Your outstanding visionary sense and individuality suggest that you may wish to develop your innate spiritual, artistic, or creative talents. Although mental power is your greatest gift, avoid wasting it through being manipulative or in mind games with others.

As you are very clever and like to take chances, you may often rely on your natural luck. This may tempt you to take the easy way out rather than find the self-discipline and responsibility needed to live up to your exceptional potential. While being popular ensures that you have an active social life, do not allow escapist tendencies to become a further hindrance to your achievements. Understanding the power of knowledge, you seek inspiration for yourself and others and fare better when your remarkable talents are dedicated to an ideal.

Work & Vocation

Positive and charming, with a shrewd business sense, you have a natural flair for people that ensures your success in careers dealing with the public. Your sharp mind and talent with words make you an excellent candidate for a career such as writer, teacher, lawyer, promoter, or salesperson. Sensitive and a natural psychologist, you may find that occupations involving personal contacts, such as therapy or alternative healthcare, could also be rewarding. Not liking to take orders, however, suggests that you prefer management positions or may be inclined to become self-employed. With your outstanding imagination, you may alternatively wish to use your visionary talents in art, film, drama, or architecture.

Famous people who share your birthday include actor Kenneth Branagh, actresses Dorothy Lamour and Susan Dey, TV journalist Chet Huntley, writer Emily Dickinson, and experimental filmmaker Michael Snow.

Numerology

Like someone with a number 1 birthday, you usually strive toward great accomplishments. Nevertheless, you may have to overcome many obstacles before you achieve your goals. Energetic and original, you stand by your own beliefs even when they differ from others'. Your ability to be a self-starter with a pioneering spirit encourages you to travel far afield or strike out on your own. You may also learn that the world does not revolve around you; guard against selfishness and being dictatorial. Success and accomplishment are important to all those with a number 10 birthday, and frequently you find the way to the top of your profession. The subinfluence of the number 12 month indicates that you are optimistic, enterprising, and multitalented. Although you are friendly, idealistic, and humanitarian, you do not like your authority or opinions questioned or opposed. Creative and inventive, you can use your vision and resourcefulness to oversee large projects.

• *Positive:* leadership, creative, progressive, forceful, optimistic, strong convictions, competitive, independent, gregarious

• *Negative:* overbearing, jealous, egotistical, too proud, antagonistic, selfish, weak, vacillating, impatient

Love & Relationships

Charming, friendly, and sociable, you usually find it easy to attract friends and admirers. Being kind, you can be a sensitive and caring lover but in the long term need a partner who can keep you mentally stimulated or inspired. As you are probably idealistic, with fixed moral codes, you can sometimes appear stubborn. With your direct approach, you prefer to be honest with your loved ones but may sometimes have to be careful to be tactful.

YOUR SPECIAL SOMEONE

If you are looking for a relationship, you may find your ideal partner among those born on the following dates.

Love & friendship: Jan. 8, 10, 13, 20, 30, Feb. 1, 8, 11, 18, 28, Mar. 6, 9, 16, 26, Apr. 4, 7, 14, 24, May 2, 5, 12, 22, June 3, 10, 20, July 1, 8, 18, Aug. 6, 16, 30, Sept. 4, 14, 28, 30, Oct. 2, 12, 26, 28, 30, Nov. 10, 24, 26, 28, Dec. 8, 22, 24, 26

Beneficial: Jan. 12, 16, 17, 28, Feb. 10, 14, 15, 26, Mar. 8, 12, 13, 24, Apr. 6, 10, 11, 22, May 4, 8, 9, 20, 29, June 2, 6, 7, 18, 27, July 4, 5, 16, 25, Aug. 2, 3, 14, 23, Sept. 1, 12, 21, Oct. 10, 19, Nov. 8, 17, Dec. 6, 15

Fatal attractions: Mar. 31, Apr. 29, May 27, June 7, 8, 9, 10, 11, 25, July 23, Aug. 21, Sept. 19, Oct. 17, Nov. 15, Dec. 17

Challenging: Jan. 6, 18, 22, 27, Feb. 4, 16, 20, 25, Mar. 2, 14, 18, 23, 28, Apr. 12, 16, 21, May 6, 10, 14, 19, June 4, 8, 12, 17, July 6, 10, 15, Aug. 4, 8, 13, Sept. 2, 6, 11, Oct. 4, 9, Nov. 2, 7, Dec. 5

Soul mates: Mar. 28, Apr. 26, May 24, June 22, July 20, Aug. 18, Sept. 16, Oct. 14, Nov. 12, Dec. 10

December 11

Enthusiastic and adventurous, with an easygoing personality, you are a shrewd Sagittarian with an optimistic outlook. Dynamic and bright, you have a gregarious personality; if you avoid an inclination to indulge in worry or self-doubt, the cards are usually stacked in your favor. Highly intuitive and aware, you need to combine your cerebral power with your premonitions and learn to trust your own feelings.

The subinfluence of your decanate ruler, Aries, provides an added boost to your already energetic nature and suggests that you are spontaneous and enterprising. No matter what difficult situations you encounter in life, inwardly you know that you possess the power to triumph over adversity. Mars's influence also implies that since you enjoy speculations with an element of risk, you learn to quickly assess situations but should avoid get-rich-quick schemes.

Although you are idealistic and sensitive, a belief in material comfort urges you to work hard and seek opportunities to make your fortune. Although you are quick to respond, you may need to overcome a tendency to overreact, become frustrated, or worry too much about money. A mixture of cynicism and innocence indicates that you need to take responsibility for developing your fine mind and inner faith.

Between the ages of eleven and forty, as your progressed Sun moves through Capricorn, you feel a need for a practical and realistic approach to achieving your goals in life. A turning point occurs at the age of forty-one, when your progressed Sun moves into Aquarius. This highlights a desire for more independence and expressing your individuality. You may become involved with issues of freedom, group awareness, or humanitarian ideals. Another turning point occurs at age seventy-one, when your progressed Sun moves into Pisces. This is likely to highlight your emotional inner world, imagination, receptivity, and sensitivity.

Your Secret Self

A major motivating force of your dynamic nature is the need for security and power or a desire for material success and recognition. Although you possess a natural talent for understanding the value of things, as well as a most productive work influence, you may have to develop your self-control and overcome a tendency to be manipulative or ruthless, or to carry materialism to extremes. If you really believe in a project or are inspired, however, you will work hard to manifest your objectives and have the capacity to perform outstanding achievements.

Although you possess a youthful and high-spirited quality, accomplishment through work gradually plays a more prominent role in your life. When inspired, you are prepared to drive yourself hard to convert your ideals into a tangible reality. By giving yourself regular periods alone to reflect and restore your energy, you can connect to your natural intuitive insight and avoid becoming skeptical or withdrawn.

Work & Vocation

Your dynamic mental energy, enthusiasm, and ability to think on a large scale can make you ideally suited for careers in business, debating, law, or research. If you believe in a project or are inspired, you will work really hard to manifest your objectives. With your fine mind, you could also be a gifted teacher, or you may wish to use your communication talents through writing. If technically inclined, you may be drawn toward working with computers or engineering. Alternatively, you may sharpen your mental skills and find satisfaction in the world of science. Whichever career you choose, your natural executive skills may place you in a position of management or power. With your talent for understanding the value of things and a desire to share your knowledge, you have a most productive work influence.

Famous people who share your birthday include writer Aleksandr Solzhenitsyn, heiress Christina Onassis, singer Jermaine Jackson, composer Hector Berlioz, film producer Carlo Ponti, film director Susan Seidelman, former New York mayor Fiorello LaGuardia, and writer Naguib Mahfouz.

Numerology

The special vibration of the master number 11 birthday suggests that idealism, inspiration, and innovation are highly important to you. A blend of humility and confidence challenges you to work toward self-mastery, both materially and spiritually. Through experience you learn how to deal with both sides of your nature and develop a less extremist attitude by trusting your own feelings. Usually you are highly charged and enjoy vitality but must avoid becoming overly anxious or impractical. The subinfluence of the number 12 month indicates that you are energetic, highly intuitive, and enterprising, with a freedom-loving spirit. Although you are friendly and easygoing, with a charming personality, you are ambitious and determined with an inclination to take charge. If insecure, you can become suspicious or restless and nervous. Enthusiastic and daring, you are eager to free yourself from restrictions and are often willing to take a chance to improve your circumstances.

• *Positive:* focused, objective, enthusiastic, inspirational, spiritual, intuitive, intelligent, outgoing, inventive, artistic, service, healing ability, humanitarian, psychic

• *Negative:* superiority complex, worry, aimless, overemotional, easily hurt, highly strung, selfish, confused, mean

Love & Relationships

As you are both highly intuitive and sensitive as well as sociable and easygoing, you can be secretive and not let anyone know what is on your mind. When in love, you need time to adjust to and accept your partner. A tendency to worry or be skeptical suggests that you can suffer from stress or anxiety. Usually you admire ambitious and hardworking individuals who are practical, independent, and confident enough to live by their own convictions.

YOUR SPECIAL SOMEONE

Loyal, devoted, and affectionate to those you love, you might find longer-lasting relationships and stability with someone born on one of the following dates.

Love & friendship: Jan. 11, 21, 25, 28, 31, Feb. 9, 19, 26, 29, Mar. 17, 21, 24, 27, Apr. 5, 15, 22, 25, May 13, 20, 23, June 11, 18, 21, July 9, 16, 19, Aug. 7, 11, 14, 17, 31, Sept. 5, 12, 15, 29, Oct. 3, 10, 13, 27, 29, 31, Nov. 1, 8, 11, 25, 27, 29, Dec. 6, 9, 23, 25, 27

Beneficial: Jan. 9, 12, 18, 24, 29, Feb. 7, 10, 16, 22, 27, Mar. 5, 8, 14, 20, 25, Apr. 3, 6, 12, 18, 23, May 1, 10, 16, 21, 31, June 2, 8, 14, 19, 29, July 6, 12, 17, 27, Aug. 4, 10, 15, 25, Sept. 2, 8, 13, 23, Oct. 6, 11, 21, Nov. 4, 9, 19, Dec. 2, 7, 17

Fatal attractions: May 28, June 6, 7, 8, 9, 10, 11, 12, 26, July 24, Sept. 20

Challenging: Jan. 7, 8, 19, 28, Feb. 5, 6, 17, 26, Mar. 3, 4, 15, 24, Apr. 1, 2, 13, 22, May 11, 20, June 9, 18, July 7, 16, Aug. 5, 14, Sept. 3, 12, Oct. 1, 10, Nov. 8, Dec. 6

Soul mates: Jan. 3, 19, Feb. 1, 17, Mar. 15, Apr. 13, May 11, June 9, July 7, Aug. 5, Sept. 3, Oct. 1

December 12

FIXED STARS

Although your Sun's degree is not linked to a fixed star, some of your other planets' degrees certainly will be. By having an astrological chart calculated, you can find the exact position of the planets on your date of birth. This will tell you which of the fixed stars listed in this book are relevant to you.

Sociable and friendly, you are an idealistic Sagittarian with a love of knowledge and a strong sixth sense. As a practical visionary with a responsible nature, you have an excellent business sense and good timing, often seeing ahead. Although you are usually ambitious, an inclination to indulge in worry may undermine your otherwise optimistic outlook. This blend of enterprise and inertia suggests that you need to find an inspiring, unique vision that you can share with others.

The subinfluence of your decanate ruler, Aries, shows you to be courageous, with vitality and drive. As a humanitarian, you may develop a conflict between idealism and materialism, and so you will probably need to develop a philosophy that can provide you with clear insight. It also implies that when you are inspired by a cause, you are willing to work hard in order to contribute your talents and skills.

As you know how to mix business and pleasure and make others feel at ease, you can achieve material success and a position of influence. Creative and intelligent, you need to express your aspirations and exceptionally perceptive mind through intellectual pursuits rather than indulge in a love of ease and material comforts.

Between the ages of ten and thirty-nine, as your progressed Sun moves through Capricorn, you emphasize practical issues and a need for order and structure in your life. A turning point occurs at the age of forty, when your progressed Sun moves into Aquarius. This highlights a growing desire for more independence, group awareness, and progressive ideas. You may want freedom or feel more experimental. Another change of emphasis occurs at age seventy, when your progressed Sun moves into Pisces. This is likely to make you more emotionally sensitive, sympathetic, and imaginative. This is often a time when artistic, creative, or spiritual talents are accentuated.

Your Secret Self

As you possess an inner sense of power and great determination, once you have made up your mind you can be relentless in the pursuit of your objectives. Since you are ambitious and need to feel productive, your work can play an especially significant role in your life story. It is important, however, for you to have a clear goal and a plan of action in order to fully commercialize your talents and abilities.

Although you have people skills and an ability to make the right contacts, it is important in your relations with others not to find yourself in a dependent position. If you do, you may overcompensate by becoming too dominant. By keeping a balance between needing others and being independent, you are able to make the best of your many talents. Although you may experience fears around issues of money, these are generally unfounded. You may be particularly fortunate through partnerships or cooperative efforts.

Work & Vocation

You are likely to succeed in careers that make the most of your mental potential, such as teaching, writing, or politics. With your powers of persuasion and bright ideas, you could also succeed in the world of advertising, media, or publishing. Being ambitious, you aim high and can be totally determined in the pursuit of your goals. Alternatively, a natural creativity and dramatic sense can draw you to the theater or the arts. Having a natural understanding of people, you may also be attracted to occupations that involve personal contact or being an advisor to others.

Famous people who share your birthday include Frank Sinatra, fashion designer Jasper Conran, playwright John Osborne, singer Dionne Warwick, writer Gustave Flaubert, musician Grover Washington Jr., actor Edward G. Robinson, and painter Helen Frankenthaler.

Numerology

Usually you are intuitive, helpful, and friendly and possess good reasoning power. Since you want to establish true individuality, you are often innovative. Naturally understanding and sensitive, you also know how to use tact and cooperative methods to achieve your aims and objectives. When you achieve the balance between your need for self-expression and the natural inclination to be supportive of others, you can find emotional satisfaction and personal fulfillment. You may nevertheless need to find the courage to stand on your own two feet and learn not to get easily discouraged by other people. The subinfluence of the number 12 month indicates that you are idealistic and ambitious. Usually you can express yourself clearly and, with your high receptivity, assess people and situations accurately. If competitive, you need to believe in your goal in order to succeed. Your ability to make fair and just decisions can create harmony and help others feel united and secure. If in doubt and suspicious, however, you can become bored or anxious, creating tension and disharmony.

- *Positive:* creative, attractive, initiative, disciplinarian, promote yourself or others
- *Negative:* reclusive, eccentric, uncooperative, overly sensitive, lack of self-esteem

Love & Relationships

Sociable and generous, you have a love for the dramatic. Usually you are drawn to creative or theatrical individuals with drive and enthusiasm. Being emotionally sensitive also suggests that you have a passionate nature with strong desires. Although you are loyal and dynamic, guard against being too intense or bossy. Since you can be light-hearted and entertaining, avoid taking emotional issues too seriously, especially if things do not work the way you planned them.

December 13

♐ Enthusiastic and creative, you are a multitalented Sagittarian with an astute mind and an optimistic personality. Your plans may include adventures and extensive travel abroad. Inspired and ambitious, you can achieve your aims by focusing on your objectives and persevering until they come to pass. Although you can be fun-loving and free, with a restless nature, a desire for stability suggests that you also need to develop a practical and realistic perspective.

The subinfluence of your decanate ruler, Leo, adds to your self-confidence; with a spirit of enterprise and hope, you can enjoy many fortunate opportunities. If you indulge in self-righteousness, you can become opinionated and self-centered. Alternatively, as an idealistic humanitarian, you have noble and lofty ideas that can extend your horizons. Mentally quick and alert, you have intelligence and strong instincts that help you grow through developing a broader, philosophical view of life.

Capable of deep thought and mental endurance, you have a scientific approach and rationality that suggest you are an excellent problem solver. A thirst for variety implies that you need activity, mental stimulation, and constant movement; otherwise you can become bored or dissatisfied. Although your unusual sense of humor implies that you can be entertaining and witty, you do not suffer fools gladly, and can at times be outspoken or brutally frank.

Between the ages of nine and thirty-eight, as your progressed Sun moves through Capricorn, you feel a need for a practical and realistic approach to achieving your goals. A turning point occurs at the age of thirty-nine, when your progressed Sun moves into Aquarius. This highlights a desire to be more independent and express your individuality. You may become involved with issues of freedom, group awareness, or humanitarian ideals. Another change of emphasis occurs at age sixty-nine, when your progressed Sun moves into Pisces. This is likely to highlight your emotional sensitivity, psychic awareness, and imagination.

Your Secret Self

Your strong feelings can sometimes be buffeted by conflicting ideals. On one hand, you want constant change; on the other, you want practicality and security. By realizing that you have to build a foundation to whatever you want to achieve, by persevering and not giving up too easily if you become bored or impatient, you can achieve excellent results. It is usually better for you to specialize and learn one or two areas of interest in depth rather than chase too many aims and objectives.

As well as sensitivity, you possess good organizational skills and a creative intellect. With your intuition and warmth, you have a natural gift for dealing with people. Although you can be charming, sometimes restlessness may stop you from expressing the dynamic love that is a strong part of your personality. By enthusiastically working toward your ideals, you keep positively focused, thus inspiring others and making things happen in a big way.

Work & Vocation

Whatever career you choose will require variety and mental challenge, as you pick up information very quickly. Occupations that involve travel can be particularly beneficial for you, as can any work that keeps you mentally stimulated. Having an ability to talk to people from all

FIXED STAR

Star's name: Rasalhague, also called the Serpent Charmer

Degree position: 21°28′–22°26′ Sagittarius between the years 1930 and 2000

Magnitude: 2

Strength: ★★★★★★★★

Orb: 2°10′

Constellation: Alpha Ophiuchi

Applicable days: December 13, 14, 15, 16

Star qualities: Saturn/Venus

Description: a bright white and blue sapphire star located on the head of Ophiuchus

PRIMARY STAR'S INFLUENCE

Rasalhague imparts a desire for knowledge and education, humanitarianism, and a broad-minded or liberal perspective. You may also be interested in philosophy and religion and have a gift for visualization.

Linked to your Sun's degree, Rasalhague suggests a reserved yet thoughtful nature. This star may indicate success in business through the ability to concentrate on large projects or think in worldly terms. Often this star suggests great individual achievement or that you will be ahead of your time. Rasalhague can also make you suspicious, and it implies that learning to trust others may bring popularity and widen your circle of friends.

• *Positive:* connected with large enterprises, involvement in sports, good income

• *Negative:* suspicious, scattered energies, overly serious

walks of life as well as an ability to make helpful contacts can certainly assist you in all your endeavors. Although ambitious, with your restlessness and love of freedom, you may experiment with many different kinds of experiences or occupations in your desire to find one that suits your enterprising personality.

Famous people who share your birthday include actors Robert Lindsay, Dick Van Dyke, and Christopher Plummer, comedian Jim Davidson, guitarist Carlos Montoya, writer Lauren van der Post, and former U.S. First Lady Mary Todd Lincoln.

Numerology

Emotional sensitivity, enthusiasm, and inspiration are often identified with the number 13 birthday. Numerically, you are associated with ambition and hard work, and you can accomplish much through creative self-expression. You may need to cultivate a pragmatic outlook if you want to turn your creative talents into tangible products. Your original and innovative approach inspires new and exciting ideas, which frequently result in work that impresses others. With a number 13 birthday, you are earnest, romantic, charming, and fun-loving, and with dedication and patience you can achieve prosperity. The subinfluence of the number 12 month indicates that you can have difficulty deciding what you want. Worried that you may miss out on something, you may try to do too much and thus scatter your energies. Although you are friendly, optimistic, and keen on partnerships, you think independently and want to stay autonomous and free. Intelligent and restless, you benefit greatly from developing a solid philosophy or using your common sense to pursue comprehensive education or higher learning.

• *Positive:* ambitious, creative, freedom-loving, self-expressive, initiative
• *Negative:* impulsive, indecisive, bossy, unemotional, rebellious

Love & Relationships

As you like new beginnings and opportunities, you need to be in the company of mentally stimulating people who are adventurous, idealistic, and enterprising; otherwise you may become bored and restless. A secretive side to your nature implies that you prefer to keep your thoughts to yourself and rarely speak openly about your true feelings. By being patient and discriminating, you develop loving relationships. Usually you need to be careful about mixing personal relationships with business. If you are mistrustful or skeptical, relationships may suffer from your unwillingness to become fully committed. If inspired by other individuals, you need to be careful not to get carried away with their plans and ideas and get sidetracked.

YOUR SPECIAL SOMEONE

You may be more successful finding your ideal partner among those born on the following dates.

Love & friendship: Jan. 13, 19, 23, 28, Feb. 11, 17, 21, Mar. 9, 15, 19, 24, 28, 29, 30, Apr. 7, 13, 17, 26, 27, May 5, 11, 15, 24, 25, 26, June 3, 9, 13, 22, 23, 24, July 1, 7, 11, 20, 21, 22, Aug. 5, 9, 14, 18, 19, 20, Sept. 3, 7, 16, 17, 18, Oct. 1, 5, 14, 15, 16, 29, 31, Nov. 3, 12, 13, 14, 27, 29, Dec. 1, 10, 11, 12, 25, 27, 29

Beneficial: Jan. 7, 15, 20, 31, Feb. 5, 13, 18, 29, Mar. 3, 11, 16, 27, Apr. 1, 9, 14, 25, May 7, 12, 23, June 5, 10, 21, July 3, 8, 19, Aug. 1, 6, 17, 30, Sept. 4, 15, 28, Oct. 2, 13, 26, Nov. 11, 24, Dec. 9, 22

Fatal attractions: June 10, 11, 12, 13

Challenging: Jan. 6, 14, 30, Feb. 4, 12, 28, Mar. 2, 10, 26, Apr. 8, 24, May 6, 22, June 4, 20, July 2, 18, Aug. 16, Sept. 14, Oct. 12, Nov. 10, Dec. 8

Soul mates: Apr. 30, May 28, June 26, July 24, Aug. 22, Sept. 20, Oct. 18, 30, Nov. 16, 28, Dec. 14, 26

December 14

♐ Although you are a restless and idealistic Sagittarian who yearns for adventure, travel, and excitement, your common sense and need for stability and security imply that you are also shrewd and observant. Nevertheless, your desire for variety and change suggests that you are not likely to rest on your laurels and settle for less than the best.

The subinfluence of your decanate ruler, Leo, adds to your self-confidence, and with an optimistic spirit and enthusiasm, you can have many noble or lofty ideas. Outspoken, you usually have strong convictions and opinions that need to be expressed. Active, with good organizational skills, you are happier working or planning rather than wasting your energy on trivial pursuits. As you like to set a solid foundation and build from there, you can also benefit from working on ideals or long-term projects that you believe in.

Intelligent and intuitive, you know how to make use of any information at your disposal. Inspired by wisdom and desiring knowledge, you often take up education to prevent yourself from becoming bored. This suggests that you can benefit from exploring philosophy and spirituality. Whether your study is self-directed or conventional, you enjoy all kinds of mental pursuits that allow you to expand your horizons.

While you are between ages eight and thirty-seven, your progressed Sun moves through Capricorn. This brings a growing need for practical order and structure into your life, gradually making you more goal-oriented and responsible. There is a turning point at age thirty-eight when your progressed Sun moves into Aquarius, highlighting a desire for independence, progressive ideas, and expressing your individuality. Another change of emphasis occurs at age sixty-eight, when your progressed Sun moves into Pisces, accenting issues of emotional sensitivity, imagination, and psychic awareness.

FIXED STAR

Star's name: Rasalhague, also called the Serpent Charmer

Degree position: 21°28'–22°26' Sagittarius between the years 1930 and 2000

Magnitude: 2

Strength: ★★★★★★★★

Orb: 2°10'

Constellation: Alpha Ophiuchi

Applicable days: December 13, 14, 15, 16

Star qualities: Saturn/Venus

Description: a bright white and blue sapphire star located on the head of Ophiuchus

PRIMARY STAR'S INFLUENCE

Rasalhague imparts a desire for knowledge and education, humanitarianism, and a broad-minded or liberal perspective. You may also be interested in philosophy and religion and have a gift for visualization.

Linked to your Sun's degree, Rasalhague suggests a reserved yet thoughtful nature. This star may indicate success in business through the ability to concentrate on large projects or think in worldly terms. Often this star suggests great individual achievement or that you will be ahead of your time. Rasalhague can also make you suspicious and implies that learning to trust others may bring popularity and widen your circle of friends.

• *Positive:* connected with large enterprises, involvement in sports, good income

• *Negative:* suspicious, scattered energies, overly serious

Your Secret Self

Although you appear confident, an inner dichotomy reveals both a need to seek new and exciting experiences and a desire for peace of mind. Although your restlessness drives you to succeed, it can also cause a dissatisfaction that can lead to escapism or overindulgence. It is important, therefore, to establish a well-balanced life. By learning to be introspective and calm, you can develop patience and inner serenity.

Your quick instincts and sensitivity can make you highly intuitive. By developing these qualities, you can utilize your insight and gain wisdom that can influence and inspire others. In your desire to help, however, you may have to be careful of becoming too critical or dominating. Being idealistic and wanting to improve the world, you often feel happiest when you are selflessly supporting a cause or helping others.

Work & Vocation

With your spirit of enterprise and good organizational skills, you usually think big. Your quick and shrewd mind is likely to be full of money-making ideas that can help you succeed in business, particularly in sales, agency work, or promotion. Being very independent, you need the freedom to work in your own way but are still keenly aware of the advantages of working cooperatively with others. This may lead you to partnerships or team efforts that could be very productive for you. With your polished common sense and personal philosophy, you may become an advisor to others or be particularly interested in the study of psychology or spiritual thought. An ability to articulate your ideas and your love of knowledge or wisdom may, alternatively, draw you to the world of writing, advertising, or publishing. Many people of this birthday are attracted to the world of sports.

Famous people who share your birthday include actresses Jane Birkin, Patty Duke, and Lee Remick, bandleader Spike Jones, tennis player Stan Smith, writer Shirley Jackson, and U.S. senator Margaret Chase Smith.

Numerology

Intellectual potential, pragmatism, and determination are some of the qualities of the number 14 birthday. Indeed, with this birthdate you frequently put your work first and judge yourself and others on the basis of career achievements. Although you need stability, the restlessness indicated by the number 14 urges you to forge ahead or take on new challenges in a constant attempt to improve your lot. This innate restlessness and constant lack of satisfaction may also inspire you to make a great many changes in your life, especially if you are not happy with your working conditions or financial status. With your perceptive mind, you respond quickly to problems and enjoy solving them. The subinfluence of the number 12 month indicates that you are idealistic and ambitious, with an adventurous nature. Even though you have a practical approach and common sense, you want excitement and often test your wits by taking risks. However, avoid taking financial chances that can get you into serious debt. If you realize that knowledge is power, you can grow and expand beyond your wildest dreams.

• *Positive:* decisive actions, hardworking, lucky, creative, pragmatic, imaginative, industrious

• *Negative:* overly cautious or overly impulsive, unstable, thoughtless, stubborn

Love & Relationships

Inquisitive and mentally quick, you like to mix with people who are positive and enterprising and who can inspire and motivate you. Although you can be idealistic and romantic, you are not always good at expressing your more intimate feelings. When you decide to commit yourself to a partner, however, you can be loyal and loving. Money and financial security may be important factors in your relationships, as you usually want security and comfort. Often you are attracted to intelligent individuals who are unusual but sure of themselves. Although you are caring, it would be wise to avoid being too bossy with your loved ones.

YOUR SPECIAL SOMEONE

If you are seeking an inspiring partner, you might start by looking for someone born on one of the following days.

Love & friendship: Jan. 3, 4, 14, 17, 20, 24, Feb. 1, 2, 12, 18, 22, Mar. 10, 16, 20, 29, 30, Apr. 8, 11, 14, 18, 27, 28, May 6, 12, 16, 25, 26, 31, June 4, 10, 14, 23, 24, 29, July 2, 8, 12, 21, 22, 27, Aug. 3, 6, 10, 19, 20, 25, Sept. 4, 8, 17, 18, 23, Oct. 2, 6, 15, 16, 21, 30, Nov. 4, 13, 14, 19, 28, 30, Dec. 2, 11, 12, 17, 26, 28, 30

Beneficial: Jan. 4, 8, 21, Feb. 1, 2, 6, 19, Mar. 4, 17, 28, Apr. 2, 15, 16, May 13, 24, June 11, 22, July 9, 20, Aug. 7, 18, 31, Sept. 5, 16, 29, Oct. 3, 14, 27, Nov. 1, 12, 25, Dec. 10, 23

Fatal attractions: May 31, June 11, 12, 13, 14, 15, 29, July 27, Aug. 25, Sept. 23, Oct. 21, Nov. 19, Dec. 11, 17

Challenging: Jan. 7, 10, 15, 31, Feb. 5, 8, 13, 29, Mar. 3, 6, 11, 27, Apr. 1, 4, 9, 25, May 2, 7, 23, June 5, 21, July 3, 19, Aug. 1, 17, Sept. 15, Oct. 13, Nov. 11, Dec. 9

Soul mates: Mar. 31, Apr. 29, May 27, June 25, July 23, Aug. 21, Sept. 19, Oct. 17, 29, Nov. 15, 27, Dec. 13, 25

December 15

♐ Creative and imaginative, you are a multitalented Sagittarian with a dynamic personality and many interests. Bright and sociable, you usually lead an active life and, with your optimistic outlook, are charming and friendly. As you possess many talents, being decisive and pragmatic can enhance your chances for success.

The subinfluence of your decanate ruler, Leo, adds to your optimism and self-confidence and indicates that you are proud and enterprising. Your need for security implies that you are constantly searching for an ideal situation that can provide you with mental stimulation and variety. Your intellectual brightness may lead you to explore many subjects, though this may also be a source of confusion if you have too many objectives. This also indicates that dissatisfaction is likely to be a major challenge, and if monetary issues such as lack of funds are a problem, you may become cynical or worried. Although sometimes indecisive, once set on a course of action you can be determined and single-minded in achieving your objectives.

Mentally quick and witty, with an insight into people, you are curious about everything and everyone. Although you enjoy collaborating with others, you can at times be unpredictable and act impulsively, causing unease and misunderstanding. Fortunately, you are usually sensitive and intuitive enough to sense tension and act tactfully when necessary.

From age seven to thirty-six, as your progressed Sun moves through Capricorn, you have a growing awareness of your goals and ambitions in life and emphasize a practical and realistic approach. There is a turning point at age thirty-seven, when your progressed Sun moves into Aquarius, highlighting a growing need for independence, progressive ideas, and expressing your own individuality. At sixty-seven, your progressed Sun moves into Pisces, accenting your emotional sensitivity, imagination, and intuition.

FIXED STARS

Rasalhague, also called the Serpent Charmer; Lesuth, also called the Sting

PRIMARY STAR

Star's name: Rasalhague, also called the Serpent Charmer

Degree position: 21°28'–22°26' Sagittarius between the years 1930 and 2000

Magnitude: 2

Strength: ★★★★★★★

Orb: 2°10'

Constellation: Alpha Ophiuchi

Applicable days: December 13, 14, 15, 16

Star qualities: Saturn/Venus

Description: a bright white and blue sapphire star located on the head of Ophiuchus

PRIMARY STAR'S INFLUENCE

Rasalhague imparts a desire for knowledge and education, humanitarianism, and a broad-minded or liberal perspective. You may also be interested in philosophy and religion and have a gift for visualization.

Linked to your Sun's degree, Rasalhague suggests a reserved yet thoughtful nature. This star may indicate success in business through the ability to concentrate on large projects or think in worldly terms. Often this star suggests great individual achievement or that you will be ahead of your time. Rasalhague can also make you suspicious and implies that learning to trust others may bring popularity and widen your circle of friends.

Your Secret Self

As a clever conversationalist with polished social skills, you are aware of human nature and are able to mix with people from all walks of life. A natural business sense and an innate understanding of values bestow leadership skills and the ability to quickly judge the motives of others. Possessing an inventive mind and strong individuality, you may find that your greatest satisfaction in life comes from developing your natural humanitarianism or expressing your strong originality.

The quick and instinctive qualities suggested by your birthdate blend well with your visionary and versatile personality. Being proud, you find it important to present a good image, and you are likely to be drawn to the company of intelligent people. Seeking variety and action to curb an inner restlessness, you need to focus and develop determination and self-awareness to overcome limitations. As money can be a major factor in your uncertainty, try to avoid being too extravagant by making allowances for the likelihood of fluctuating finances.

Work & Vocation

As you can pick up on situations extremely quickly, you can become bored easily and dislike routine. This suggests that you need a career with variety and are likely to be constantly on the move. Do not be afraid to take chances and go further afield if promising job prospects arise, as this usually turns out well for you. With your charm and exceptional social skills, you need an occupation that deals with people. Your persuasive manner and easy way with words can enable you to be a writer or teacher or to excel in sales. In business, you are likely to take a creative approach and prefer large projects. Alternatively, the more dramatic side of your nature may find fulfillment through performing or music, where you can express your original ideas and approach.

Famous people who share your birthday include actor Don Johnson, actresses Liv Ullman and Stephanie Lawrence, tycoon J. Paul Getty, writer Edna O'Brien, and engineer Alexander Eiffel.

Numerology

Versatility, enthusiasm, and restlessness are suggested by the number 15 birthday. Usually you are quick, with a charismatic personality. Your greatest assets are your strong instincts and the ability to learn quickly through combining theory and practice. On many occasions you manage to earn while learning new skills. Often you utilize your intuitive powers and are quick at recognizing opportunities when they arise. Carefree and resolute, you welcome the unexpected and like to take a risk. Although you are naturally adventurous, you nevertheless need to find a real base or home that you can call your own. The subinfluence of the number 12 month indicates that you are idealistic and optimistic, with psychic abilities. If inspired by a concept or a person, you become eager and passionate, but you can quickly lose interest and become bored. Multitalented, with many interests, you want to expand and grow intellectually through study and travel. Although you may experience fluctuations in your financial circumstances, usually you possess a talent for attracting money or receiving help and support from others.

• *Positive:* willing, generous, responsible, kind, cooperative, appreciative, creative ideas
• *Negative:* disruptive, irresponsible, self-centered, fear of change, worry, indecision, materialistic

Love & Relationships

Gregarious and charming, you find it easy to make friends and communicate with people. Generous when socializing, you are also able to make others feel at ease in your company. Worry and insecurity often center on lack of money and can cause stress to stable relationships; therefore you must learn to think positively and have faith. As you are usually attractive, you have no difficulty finding partners. When in love, you can be compassionate and caring and make allowances, putting others' needs before your own. Nevertheless, a tendency toward fluctuating moods implies that although you are usually warm and tender, when you feel insecure you can switch your feelings off and be cold and uncaring.

YOUR SPECIAL SOMEONE

You might find a partner who will inspire you among those born on the following dates.

Love & friendship: Jan. 11, 21, 25, Feb. 19, 23, Mar. 17, 21, 30, Apr. 5, 15, 19, 28, 29, May 13, 17, 26, 27, June 11, 15, 24, 25, 30, July 9, 13, 22, 23, 28, Aug. 7, 11, 20, 21, 26, 30, Sept. 5, 9, 18, 19, 24, 28, Oct. 3, 7, 16, 17, 22, 26, 29, Nov. 1, 5, 14, 15, 20, 24, 27, Dec. 3, 12, 13, 18, 22, 25, 27, 29

Beneficial: Jan. 5, 13, 16, 22, 28, Feb. 3, 11, 14, 20, 26, Mar. 1, 9, 12, 18, 24, 29, Apr. 7, 10, 16, 22, 27, May 5, 8, 14, 20, 25, June 3, 6, 12, 18, 23, July 1, 4, 10, 16, 21, Aug. 2, 8, 14, 19, Sept. 6, 12, 17, Oct. 4, 10, 15, Nov. 2, 8, 13, Dec. 6, 11

Fatal attractions: June 13, 14, 15, 16, 30, July 28, Aug. 26, Sept. 24, Oct. 22, Nov. 20, Dec. 18

Challenging: Jan. 2, 23, 30, Feb. 21, 28, Mar. 19, 26, 28, Apr. 17, 24, 26, May 15, 22, 24, June 13, 20, 22, July 11, 18, 20, Aug. 16, 18, 19, Sept. 7, 14, 16, Oct. 5, 12, 14, Nov. 3, 10, 12, Dec. 1, 8, 10

Soul mates: Jan. 14, 22, Feb. 12, 20, Mar. 10, 18, Apr. 8, 16, May 6, 14, June 4, 12, July 2, 10, Aug. 8, Sept. 6, Oct. 4, Nov. 2

December 16

♐ As a sociable networker with idealistic notions, you are an ambitious and cosmopolitan Sagittarian who enjoys social encounters. Proud and charismatic, you can win approval with your charm and friendly personality. As a humanitarian, you can show love and affection as a way to express your powerful emotions, but if you are self-seeking, you can be boastful.

The subinfluence of your decanate ruler, Leo, adds to your self-confidence; with the spirit of hope and optimism, you often have noble and lofty ideas. Although you can show great generosity and kindness, emotional conflict between duty and your desire for freedom implies that you can sometimes be unsure of where your loyalties lie. When emotionally dissatisfied, you can be extravagant in an attempt to impress others. Nevertheless, your sensitivity shows that you have a compassionate heart. By developing a more philosophical view, you can balance these extremes of your nature.

Intelligent and with a penetrating intellect, you have excellent communication skills and enjoy learning, debating, and discussions. Since you are also witty, with a sense of humor, you have a way with people and can be engaging and amusing. When overly confident or moody, however, avoid being cynical or using your sharp tongue to create tension and disputes.

Between the ages of six and thirty-five, as your progressed Sun moves through Capricorn, you feel a need for a practical and realistic approach to achieving your goals in life. A turning point occurs at the age of thirty-six, when your progressed Sun moves into Aquarius. This highlights a desire to be more free from responsibilities, more independent, and to express your individuality. You may become involved with issues of universal spirituality, group awareness, or humanitarian ideals. Another turning point occurs at age sixty-six, when your progressed Sun moves into Pisces. This is likely to highlight your emotional inner world, sensitivity, and imagination.

Your Secret Self

Strong-willed, gregarious, and fun-loving, you can also be a diplomat when it is in your own interests. When these traits are coupled with your natural sense of the dramatic, people are drawn to the confident and assured image you display. Your emotional power endows you with a strong personality and shows you to be a charismatic and generous individual with natural leadership ability. If inspired, you may need to express yourself in a creative way and seek recognition through the worlds of theater, art, music, or writing. Although you are hardworking, a busy social life can also figure high on your list of priorities. Just ensure that it does not override the need for self-discipline required to make the most of your many marvelous talents.

With your sharp mind and ability to go straight to the heart of a matter, you are excellent at problem solving or may particularly enjoy initiating new projects. By developing your sensitivity, you can come to understand yourself and life at a deeper level and so avoid possible periods of frustration or depression. An ability to see the paradoxes and ridiculousness of life can help keep you humorous and mentally balanced. It is important to keep yourself busy working or creatively occupied in order to utilize your potential for outstanding achievement.

FIXED STARS

Rasalhague, also called the Serpent Charmer; Lesuth, also called the Sting

PRIMARY STAR

Star's name: Rasalhague, also called the Serpent Charmer
Degree position: 21°28'–22°26'
    Sagittarius between the years
    1930 and 2000
Magnitude: 2
Strength: ★★★★★★★
Orb: 2°10'
Constellation: Alpha Ophiuchi
Applicable days: December 13, 14, 15, 16
Star qualities: Saturn/Venus
Description: a bright white and blue sapphire star located on the head of Ophiuchus

PRIMARY STAR'S INFLUENCE

Rasalhague imparts a desire for knowledge and education, humanitarianism, and a broad-minded or liberal perspective. You may also be interested in philosophy and religion and have a gift for visualization.

Linked to your Sun's degree, Rasalhague suggests a reserved yet thoughtful nature. This star may indicate success in business through the ability to concentrate on large projects or think in worldly terms. Often this star suggests great individual achievement or that you will be ahead of your time. Rasalhague can also make you suspicious and implies that learning to trust others may bring popularity and widen your circle of friends.

Work & Vocation

Your sharp and quick mentality can be your most valuable asset and can prove especially helpful in a career as a writer, lecturer, or politician. You have a spirit of enterprise, determination, and a willingness to work hard when committed to a project, and these can help you achieve in any area of your career. Your leadership qualities, organizational skills, and capacity for strategic planning are ideal for business, where you are likely to enjoy the challenge of large projects. Enjoying freedom, you need to be allowed to work in your own way or may decide to work for yourself. Alternatively, your need for self-expression and a love for the dramatic may draw you to music, art, or acting. As a natural psychologist, you may also enjoy a career that utilizes an understanding of human nature.

Famous people who share your birthday include writer Jane Austen, anthropologist Margaret Mead, composer Ludwig van Beethoven, playwright/composer Noel Coward, and writers Arthur C. Clarke and Philip K. Dick.

Numerology

A number 16 birthday suggests that you are thoughtful, sensitive, and friendly. Although analytical, you often judge life and people according to how you feel. As a number 16 personality, however, you can experience inner tensions when facing friction between a need for self-expression and responsibility to others. You may be interested in world affairs and may join international corporations or the media world. The creative ones among you have a talent for writing with sudden flashes of inspiration. With a number 16 birthday, you may need to learn how to balance between being overly confident and being insecure. The subinfluence of the number 12 month indicates that you are optimistic and daring, with a need to expand and grow. Intuitive and analytical, you are a shrewd psychologist, with good insight into people and what motivates them. Able to offer the right incentives, you can mix business and pleasure, and you enjoy putting on a show. Although you are kind and friendly, beware of being arrogant, selfish, or self-promoting.

• *Positive:* knowledgeable, responsibilities to home and family, integrity, intuitive, social, cooperative, insightful

• *Negative:* worry, never satisfied, irresponsible, opinionated, skeptical, fussy, irritable, unsympathetic

Love & Relationships

Knowing people from different backgrounds implies that you like mixing in various circles. Friendly and easygoing, with a good sense of humor, you enjoy being sociable and having fun. Young at heart and passionate, you want to experience different types of relationships and need to avoid settling down too early in life. Usually you are attracted to those who are artistically talented or creative in business. Self-conscious, you like to present a smart image and impress others, often making spontaneous and magnanimous gestures of kindness. You are hospitable, enjoy having friends over, and can be very entertaining.

YOUR SPECIAL SOMEONE

For security, mental stimulation, and love, you might want to begin looking for those born on the following dates.

Love & friendship: Jan. 6, 16, 18, 22, 26, Feb. 4, 14, 20, 24, Mar. 2, 12, 18, 22, Apr. 10, 12, 16, 20, 30, May 8, 14, 18, 28, June 6, 12, 16, 26, July 4, 10, 14, 24, 26, 31, Aug. 2, 4, 8, 12, 22, 29, Sept. 6, 10, 20, 27, Oct. 4, 8, 18, 25, Nov. 2, 6, 16, 23, 30, Dec. 4, 14, 21, 28, 30

Beneficial: Jan. 6, 17, 23, 31, Feb. 4, 15, 21, 29, Mar. 2, 13, 19, 27, 30, Apr. 11, 17, 25, 28, May 9, 15, 23, 26, June 7, 13, 21, 24, July 5, 11, 19, 22, Aug. 3, 9, 17, 20, Sept. 1, 7, 15, 18, 30, Oct. 5, 13, 16, 28, Nov. 3, 11, 14, 26, Dec. 1, 9, 12, 24

Fatal attractions: June 14, 15, 16, 17

Challenging: Jan. 24, Feb. 22, Mar. 20, 29, Apr. 18, 27, 29, May 6, 16, 25, 27, 30, June 14, 22, 25, 28, July 12, 21, 23, 26, Aug. 10, 19, 21, 24, Sept. 8, 17, 19, 22, Oct. 6, 15, 17, 20, Nov. 4, 13, 15, 18, Dec. 2, 11, 13, 16

Soul mates: Jan. 13, Feb. 11, Mar. 9, Apr. 7, May 5, June 3, 30, July 1, 28, Aug. 26, Sept. 24, Oct. 22, Nov. 20, Dec. 18

December 17

↗ Inquisitive and ambitious, you are a Sagittarian with a dynamic personality and a compelling desire for knowledge. Optimistic and creative, you possess a wonderful imagination and are willing to take chances and be innovative. Though you are ambitious, with strong desires, beware of being bossy and projecting your will onto others. Your quick comprehension and creative mind imply that to keep yourself intellectually stimulated, you need to constantly search for new and exciting ideas.

The subinfluence of your decanate ruler, Leo, adds vitality and self-confidence to your independent outlook. Strong-willed and enterprising, with excellent practical skills, you can turn your lofty ideas into tangible products. Whether in the forefront or behind the scenes, your contribution can make a great deal of difference.

Although you are discriminating and methodical, your ability to see the whole and to think progressively suggests that you like to refine and improve on existing systems. You may need, however, to avoid being too critical or worrying about small or insignificant issues. An interest in higher learning may lead you to philosophy and spirituality, and since you can communicate your ideas in a precise and decisive way, you may be drawn to academic investigation. A love of words or language may also endow you with a talent for writing.

Between the ages of five and thirty-four, as your progressed Sun moves through Capricorn, you focus on practical issues and a need for order and structure in your life. A turning point occurs at the age of thirty-five, when your progressed Sun moves into Aquarius. This highlights a growing desire for more independence, group awareness, and progressive ideas. You may want freedom or feel more experimental. Another turning point occurs at age sixty-five, when your progressed Sun moves into Pisces. This is likely to make you more receptive, emotionally sensitive, sympathetic, and imaginative. This is a time when artistic, creative, or spiritual talents are accentuated.

FIXED STARS

Lesuth, also called the Sting; Aculeus

PRIMARY STAR

Star's name: Lesuth, also called the Sting

Degree position: 23°2'–24°0' Sagittarius between the years 1930 and 2000

Magnitude: 3

Strength: ★★★★★

Orb: 1°40'

Constellation: Nu Scorpio

Applicable days: December 15, 16, 17, 18

Star qualities: Mercury/Mars

Description: a small quadruple-star system surrounded by a nebula, located on the stinger of the Scorpion

PRIMARY STAR'S INFLUENCE

Lesuth imparts a quick and keen mind, assertiveness, and self-motivation. You are probably ambitious, with sound judgment and a sociable nature. This star bestows creativity, inventiveness, and opportunities to work on new discoveries or enjoy unexpected benefits and good fortune.

Linked to your Sun's degree, Lesuth indicates success in public affairs, a flair for writing, or an inclination toward education and higher learning. You are probably inventive and inquisitive and contribute to society through your discoveries. You make a good detective or investigator because of your quick and active mind. You are outspoken, hardworking, and full of vitality, with swift actions. Nevertheless, you must learn to channel all your energy

Your Secret Self

Being charming, you can be friendly and stimulating company and possess a natural gift for dealing with people. Your good communication skills, agreeable manner, and social grace allow you to play the refined diplomat. Aware of image, you can make yourself attractive to others, but you may have to be careful of a streak of vanity or conceit.

Even though you are affectionate and caring and need people, it is vital that you stay independent in your personal relationships with others. By keeping a healthy balance, you avoid hidden fears or becoming moody. With your high ideals and active imagination, you are a creative thinker and a practical visionary. You may use these abilities to advance in a material sense; alternatively, you may be drawn to the development of your innate creative and spiritual talents. Although you have a shrewd awareness regarding money, you are also able to promote an idea or cause and are usually willing to work hard to achieve your objectives.

Work & Vocation

With your quick mental perception, ability to take the lead, and love of knowledge, you may be drawn to teaching, whether in the classroom or as a trainer in management. Equally, you can succeed in writing, science, or research, where you can utilize your keen mentality. Having excellent people skills also ensures your success in business, sales, public relations, or promotion. Although independent, you may see particularly beneficial results from working in partnerships or as part of a team. If using the more artistic side of your personality, you may achieve fulfillment through musical and creative pursuits.

Famous people who share your birthday include writer Erskine Caldwell, physician/ alchemist Philippus Paracelsus, scientist Humphry Davy, physicist Joseph Henry, poet John Greenleaf Whittier, journalist William Safire, and writer Ford Madox Ford.

Numerology

With a number 17 birthday, you are shrewd, with a reserved nature and good analytical abilities. As an independent thinker, you benefit from being well educated or skillful. Usually you utilize your knowledge in a specific way in order to develop your expertise and can achieve material success or a prominent position as a specialist or researcher. Private, introspective, and detached, with a strong interest in facts and figures, you frequently present a serious and thoughtful demeanor and like to take your time. By developing your communication skills, you can discover much more about yourself from others. The subinfluence of the number 12 month indicates that you are intuitive and multitalented. When inspired, you are motivated and dynamic, with a need to express yourself. Usually you are direct and outspoken, with strong opinions, but prone to impatience and restlessness. If indecisive or worried, you can vacillate emotionally and financially. By developing perseverance and learning to be diplomatic and trusting in your dealings with others, you can benefit from collaborations and partnerships.

• *Positive:* thoughtful, specialist, good planner, business sense, attracts money, individual thinker, painstaking, accurate, skilled researcher, scientific

• *Negative:* detached, stubborn, moody, sensitive, narrow-minded, critical, worry, suspicion

Love & Relationships

Inquisitive and mentally restless, you like to be in the company of intelligent people who are creative and enterprising and who succeed as a result of their ingenuity and hard work. As you often think of yourself as part of a group and have an attractive personality, you have no difficulty finding friends and partners. Although mentally independent, at times you can become emotionally insecure, especially if you do not receive reassurance from your partner. Usually you believe in long-term relationships and seek someone reliable whom you can trust and settle down with.

into worthwhile projects and avoid activities that could bring danger or legal entanglements.

• *Positive:* shrewd, creative, determination, common sense

• *Negative:* tendency to exaggeration, turbulence

See Appendix for additional fixed star readings.

YOUR SPECIAL SOMEONE

You are likely to be more fortunate with someone born on one of the following dates.

Love & friendship: Jan. 1, 4, 20, 27, 29, Feb. 2, 25, 27, Mar. 23, 25, Apr. 4, 21, 23, May 19, 21, 29, June 17, 19, 27, July 15, 17, 25, Aug. 6, 13, 15, 23, Sept. 11, 13, 21, Oct. 9, 11, 19, Nov. 7, 9, 17, Dec. 5, 7, 15

Beneficial: Jan. 3, 10, 15, 18, Feb. 1, 8, 13, 16, Mar. 6, 11, 14, 29, 31, Apr. 4, 9, 12, 27, 29, May 2, 7, 10, 25, 27, June 5, 8, 23, 25, July 3, 6, 21, 23, Aug. 1, 4, 19, 21, Sept. 2, 17, 19, Oct. 15, 17, Nov. 13, 15, Dec. 11, 13

Fatal attractions: Apr. 30, May 28, June 15, 16, 17, 18, 26, July 24, Aug. 22, Sept. 20, Oct. 18, Nov. 16, Dec. 14

Challenging: Jan. 9, 14, 16, 25, Feb. 7, 12, 14, 23, Mar. 5, 10, 12, 21, 28, 30, Apr. 3, 8, 10, 19, 26, 28, May 1, 6, 8, 17, 24, 26, June 4, 6, 15, 22, 24, July 2, 4, 13, 20, 22, Aug. 2, 11, 18, 20, Sept. 9, 16, 18, Oct. 7, 14, 16, Nov. 5, 12, 14, Dec. 3, 10, 12

Soul mates: Dec. 29

December 18

FIXED STARS

Lesuth, also called the Sting; Aculeus

PRIMARY STAR

Star's name: Lesuth, also called the Sting

Degree position: 23°2'–24°0' Sagittarius between the years 1930 and 2000

Magnitude: 3

Strength: ★★★★★

Orb: 1°40'

Constellation: Nu Scorpio

Applicable days: December 15, 16, 17, 18

Star qualities: Mercury/Mars

Description: a small quadruple-star system surrounded by a nebula, located on the stinger of the Scorpion

PRIMARY STAR'S INFLUENCE

Lesuth imparts a quick and keen mind, assertiveness, and self-motivation. You are probably ambitious, with sound judgment and a sociable nature. This star bestows creativity, inventiveness, and opportunities to work on new discoveries or enjoy unexpected benefits and good fortune.

Linked to your Sun's degree, Lesuth indicates success in public affairs, a flair for writing, or an inclination toward education and higher learning. You are probably inventive and inquisitive and contribute to society through your discoveries. You make a good detective or investigator because of your quick and active mind. You are outspoken, hardworking, and full of vitality, with swift actions. Nevertheless, you must learn to channel all your energy into

Charming and ambitious, with powerful feelings, you are a sensitive Sagittarian with a chivalrous heart and a determined nature. Cosmopolitan and friendly, you seek recognition and emotional fulfillment. By finding a proper channel to express your dramatic nature, you can achieve success and emotional stability. If you utilize your diplomatic skills and learn to collaborate, you may find that partnerships and group efforts can yield great rewards.

The subinfluence of your decanate ruler, Leo, imbues your self-confidence with the spirit of hope and creativity. Optimistic, you can extend your horizons through travel and new opportunities. Stubborn and proud, you have your own strong sense of justice and morals but, being capable of magnanimous gestures of goodwill, you can also be generous and warmhearted.

Although you are self-possessed and understanding, if you insist on having things your own way, you can also be demanding or critical. As you like to be surrounded by quality and luxury, your desire for an extravagant lifestyle suggests that you are willing to work hard in order to maintain a high standard of living. You may have to watch, however, that your love of sensuality or overindulgence does not deter you from the self-discipline needed to fulfill your great potential.

Between the ages of four and thirty-three, as your progressed Sun moves through Capricorn, you feel a need for a practical and realistic approach to achieving your goals in life. A turning point occurs at the age of thirty-four, when your progressed Sun moves into Aquarius. This highlights a desire for more independence and expressing your individuality. You may become involved with issues of freedom, group awareness, or humanitarian ideals. Another turning point occurs at age sixty-four, when your progressed Sun moves into Pisces. This is likely to highlight your emotional receptivity, imagination, or psychic awareness.

Your Secret Self

Charismatic, sociable, and an expert at personal contact, you have charm and are a shrewd judge of people's motivation; these qualities can help you in all situations. The combination of your sharp intellect and psychological skills suggests that your humor can be both insightful and cutting as well as very entertaining. Sometimes provocative, you also enjoy a mental challenge and like to test your wits and intelligence against others'. Nevertheless, companionship is very important to you, and you will often compromise for peace.

When you have a goal or sense of purpose, you can be extremely dedicated and hardworking. When faced with setbacks, you can develop tremendous endurance to carry on and are capable of great sacrifice. It may be necessary to learn to balance the extremes of your nature, however, as you are capable of going from the heights to the depths, being either humanitarian, compassionate, and detached or frustrated, depressed, and overserious. Through self-analysis and trusting your deeper insight, you can make the most of your exceptional talents.

Work & Vocation

Ambitious, charismatic, and independent, you will naturally rise to positions of power where you can use your natural leadership ability. Possessing charm and advanced social skills, you are likely to succeed in most people-related activities. If you work hard, your enterprising spirit, confident front, and competitive character can help you be successful in business, especially as you have a knack for making useful contacts. Your gift for communication can also be used in writing, sales, publishing, or teaching. With your sense of the dramatic, you can excel in the entertainment world or in politics. Alternatively, you may use the more humanitarian side of your nature through charity work, social reform, or fund-raising.

Famous people who share your birthday include actor Brad Pitt, film director Steven Spielberg, political activist Steve Biko, musician Keith Richards, artist Paul Klee, and actress Betty Grable.

Numerology

Determination, assertiveness, and ambition are some of the attributes associated with the number 18 birthday. Active, with a need for challenges, you like to keep busy and are frequently involved in some enterprise. Capable, hardworking, and responsible, you rise to positions of authority. Your strong business sense and organizational skills may lead you to the world of commerce. Since you may suffer from overwork, learn how to relax or slow down from time to time. As a number 18 personality, you may use your power to heal others, give sound advice, or solve other people's problems. The subinfluence of the number 12 month indicates that you are honest and idealistic, with powerful feelings; you need to grow and expand to find emotional fulfillment. You are multitalented and versatile, but if you are without an outlet to express yourself, you may become restless and unsettled. Although you are generous and friendly, you can also appear proud and arrogant. It would be wise to learn to be less demanding and avoid imposing your will on others.

• *Positive:* progressive, assertive, intuitive, courageous, resolute, healing ability, efficient, advisory skills

• *Negative:* overly sensitive, controlled emotions, lazy, lack of order, selfishness

Love & Relationships

Dynamic and ruled by your emotions, you are drawn to powerful people. Generous and compassionate, you are confident and like to make a good impression. Although you are loyal and caring, at times you can become disillusioned or emotionally blocked and find it hard to express how you truly feel. While you often seek peace and harmony in relationships, you may resent change and become too bossy or stubborn. Often willing to be patient and make sacrifices in order to keep your relationships, you also need to learn when to let go if things are not working out.

worthwhile projects and avoid activities that could bring danger or legal entanglements.

• *Positive:* shrewd, creative, determination, common sense

• *Negative:* tendency to exaggeration, turbulence

See Appendix for additional fixed star readings.

YOUR SPECIAL SOMEONE

If you are looking for an inspiring relationship, you might find your loving partner among those born on the following days.

Love & friendship: Jan. 2, 28, Feb. 26, Mar. 24, Apr. 22, May 20, 29, 30, June 18, 27, 28, July 16, 25, 26, Aug. 14, 23, 24, Sept. 12, 21, 22, Oct. 10, 19, 20, 29, 31, Nov. 8, 17, 18, 27, 29, Dec. 6, 15, 16, 25, 27

Beneficial: Jan. 2, 10, 13, 16, Feb. 8, 11, 14, Mar. 6, 9, 12, Apr. 4, 7, 10, May 2, 5, 8, June 3, 6, July 1, 4, 30, Aug. 2, 28, 30, Sept. 26, 28, Oct. 24, 26, Nov. 22, 24, Dec. 20, 22, 30

Fatal attractions: Oct. 31, Nov. 29, Dec. 27

Challenging: Jan. 3, 9, 10, Feb. 1, 7, 8, Mar. 5, 6, 31, Apr. 3, 4, 29, May 1, 2, 27, June 25, July 23, Aug. 2, 21, 31, Sept. 19, 29, Oct. 17, 27, Nov. 15, 25, Dec, 13, 23

Soul mates: Jan. 5, Feb. 3, Mar. 1, May 30, June 28, July 26, Aug. 24, Sept. 22, Oct. 20, Nov. 18, Dec. 16

December 19

FIXED STARS

Etamin, Aculeus

PRIMARY STAR

Star's name: Etamin

Degree position: 26°55'–27°57'
Sagittarius between the years
1930 and 2000

Magnitude: 2.5–3

Strength: ★★★★★

Orb: 1°40'

Constellation: Gamma Draconis

Applicable days: December 19, 20, 21

Star qualities: Mars/Moon

Description: a red giant binary star
located in the Dragon's eye

PRIMARY STAR'S INFLUENCE

Etamin bestows a keen mentality, enthusiasm, individuality, and a pioneering spirit. Often you are self-assured but at times overconfident, which results in hasty actions that lead to loss of position.

Linked to your Sun's degree, this star encourages you to pursue a career in higher education, writing, publishing, or the legal profession. Usually Etamin imparts an assertive and determined nature with an interest in unusual subjects, ideas, and issues.

• *Positive:* willpower, fighting spirit, ambition, sincerity

• *Negative:* impulsive actions, quarrels, irritability, moodiness

See Appendix for additional fixed star readings.

Sociable and versatile, you are a sensitive Sagittarian with powerful feelings and creative talents. Although multitalented, with dramatic self-expression, intellectually you are apt to be practical and have an exceptional sense of structure. When your dynamic emotions are channeled productively, you can ensure a successful outcome, but you may have to overcome a tendency to be dissatisfied or impatient when events happen too slowly or not according to plan. Since you want to achieve much, you may need to learn that only through hard work and perseverance can you really accomplish and succeed in life.

The subinfluence of your decanate ruler, Leo, adds to your self-confidence. With the spirit of hope and optimism, you can expand your horizons. As a proud person with a resolute and determined nature, you prefer to lead rather than be in subordinate positions.

Although rational and intelligent, you have a broad emotional range, suggesting that you base your judgment on how you feel. When interested in something or someone, you involve yourself wholeheartedly; otherwise you can become bored and lose interest. Your strong sense of duty implies that, being loyal and faithful, you are willing to work hard, be dedicated, or make real sacrifices. At times this sense of duty dominates the inclinations of your heart, and you may then become frustrated or temperamental or succumb to emotional restlessness.

Between the ages of three and thirty-two, as your progressed Sun moves through Capricorn, you focus on practical issues and a need for order and structure in your life. A turning point occurs at the age of thirty-three, when your progressed Sun moves into Aquarius. This highlights a growing desire for more personal freedom, group awareness, and progressive humanitarian ideas. You may want independence or feel more experimental. Another turning point occurs at age sixty-six, when your progressed Sun moves into Pisces. This is likely to make you more receptive, emotionally sensitive, sympathetic, and imaginative. This is a time when artistic, creative, or spiritual talents are accentuated.

Your Secret Self

Friendly and intelligent, you like to communicate your ideas and share your knowledge. With the ability to think universally, you can be humanitarian, broad-minded, and detached, preferring to be direct and honest in your approach. Kindhearted and generous to the ones you love, you may nevertheless have to overcome a tendency to think negatively or guard against being critical or opinionated. Through working with positive thinking, you can develop the mental discipline needed to overcome obstacles and achieve success.

Aligned to success, you can be ambitious and hardworking. Being directed toward achievement, you need strong aims and objectives, and you work better when driven by an inner vision of what you want to accomplish. This keeps your wonderful imagination clearly focused and helps you avoid emotional discontent.

Work & Vocation

The combination of your optimistic attitude and sensitive leadership can ensure your success in people-related activities. Intelligent and thoughtful, you may wish to share your knowledge with others through teaching or writing. Being creative and talented, you can excel in music and artistic pursuits; you also have the ability to mix business and pleasure and commercialize art. Equally, your excellent sense of the dramatic may serve you well in acting or the world of entertainment. Preferring to be in control, you do not usually like to be in deferential positions and may be at your best when working selflessly for a cause or an ideal. Your sense of vision may also draw you to the media world, advertising, or publishing. Alternatively, the compassionate side of your nature may find expression in the healing professions, caring for others, or public service.

Famous people who share your birthday include singer Edith Piaf, actor Ralph Richardson, actress Cicely Tyson, producer David Susskind, singer/musician Maurice White, writer Jean Genet, and anthropologist Richard Leakey.

Numerology

Ambitious and humanitarian are some of the ways others would describe people with the number 19 birthday. Decisive and resourceful, you possess depth of vision, but the dreamer side of your nature is compassionate, idealistic, and creative. Although you are sensitive, the need to be someone may be the very thing that pushes you to be dramatic and claim center stage. Often there is a strong desire to establish an individual identity. To do so, you may first need to overcome the influence of peer group pressure. To others, you may appear confident, resilient, and resourceful, but inner tensions may cause emotional ups and downs. Artistic and charismatic, you will find that the world is there for you to explore. The subinfluence of the number 12 month indicates that you are visionary and honorable, with powerful emotions. Your practical skills and commanding personality imply that usually you like to take charge of situations and need the freedom to express yourself without restrictions. By learning to stay positive or adopting a philosophical perspective, you can overcome challenges or a tendency to become frustrated when facing delays or obstacles.

• *Positive:* dynamic, focused, creative, leader, lucky, progressive, optimistic, strong convictions, competitive, independent, gregarious

• *Negative:* self-centered, worry, fear of rejection, ups and downs, materialistic

Love & Relationships

Your powerful love expression usually draws you toward strong or dramatic personalities. Although you are romantic and sensitive, a need for stability and security implies that you should be careful about your choice of partners. Since emotional satisfaction can be realized if you develop your great potential, avoid indulging in worry, negative thinking, suspicion, or jealousy. Supportive and protective, you can be a devoted friend and partner. By learning to be patient and tolerant, you can overcome a tendency to become mentally frustrated when things don't go according to plan.

YOUR SPECIAL SOMEONE

You might find longer-lasting relationships and stability with someone born on one of the following dates.

Love & friendship: Jan. 3, 8, 22, 25, 29, 30, Feb. 1, 6, 20, 23, 27, 28, Mar. 18, 21, 25, 26, 30, Apr. 16, 19, 23, 24, 28, May 14, 17, 21, 22, 26, 31, June 12, 15, 19, 20, 24, 29, July 10, 13, 18, 22, Aug. 8, 11, 15, 16, 20, 27, 29, 30, Sept. 6, 9, 13, 14, 18, 23, 27, 28, Oct. 4, 7, 11, 12, 16, 21, 25, 26, Nov. 2, 5, 9, 10, 14, 19, 23, 24, Dec. 3, 7, 8, 12, 17, 21, 22

Beneficial: Jan. 17, Feb. 15, Mar. 13, Apr. 11, May 9, 29, June 7, 27, July 5, 25, Aug. 3, 23, Sept. 1, 21, Oct. 19, 29, Nov. 17, 27, 30, Dec. 15, 25, 28

Fatal attractions: May 31, June 17, 18, 19, 20, 29, July 27, Aug. 25, 30, Sept. 23, 28, Oct. 21, 26, Nov. 19, 24, Dec. 17, 22

Challenging: Jan. 20, 23, Feb. 18, 21, Mar. 16, 19, Apr. 14, 17, May 12, 15, June 10, 13, July 8, 11, Aug. 6, 9, Sept. 4, 7, Oct. 2, 5, Nov. 2, Dec. 1

Soul mates: Jan. 4, 31, Feb. 2, 29, Mar. 27, Apr. 25, May 23, June 21, July 19, Aug. 17, Sept. 15, Oct. 13, Nov. 11, Dec. 9

December 20

♐ Receptive and charming, you are a gracious and enchanting Sagittarian with an engaging personality. Cooperative and helpful in group endeavors, you offer emotional support and encouragement to those you befriend. As an idealist with strong humanitarian inclinations, you may be drawn to devote yourself to a cause or a vocation. Although you are imaginative, with noble and lofty ideas, you can also be proud and inclined toward extravagance and overindulgence.

The subinfluence of your decanate ruler, Leo, adds to your self-confidence; with a spirit of hope and optimism, you can extend your horizons. You are mentally astute and very determined, and when positive you develop patience and a philosophical view that strengthen your character mentally and spiritually.

As an impressionable romantic, you can have deep feelings that may be a source of inspiration. They can also unfortunately be a cause of frustration, especially if you are unable to fulfill your high expectations. An inclination to do what is nice and easy rather than what is part of your duty or responsibility implies that you need to develop self-discipline rather than indulge in instant gratification or impulsive behavior.

Compassionate and charitable, you enjoy mixing with different people, as you seek harmonious relationships. When you discover something inspiring that you can really enjoy, you are willing to dedicate yourself and work extremely hard.

Until you reach the age of thirty-one, your progressed Sun moves through Capricorn, emphasizing a need for a practical and realistic approach to achieving your goals in life. A turning point occurs at the age of thirty-two, when your progressed Sun moves into Aquarius. This highlights a desire to be more independent and express your individuality. You may become involved with issues of freedom, group awareness, or humanitarian ideals. Another turning point occurs at age sixty-two, when your progressed Sun moves into Pisces. This is likely to highlight your emotional receptivity and imagination or spiritual inner world.

FIXED STARS

Etamin, Acumen

PRIMARY STAR

Star's name: Etamin

Degree position: 26°55'–27°57'
Sagittarius between the years
1930 and 2000

Magnitude: 2.5–3

Strength: ★★★★★

Orb: 1°40'

Constellation: Gamma Draconis

Applicable days: December 19, 20, 21

Star qualities: Mars/Moon

Description: a red giant binary star located in the Dragon's eye

PRIMARY STAR'S INFLUENCE

Etamin bestows a keen mentality, enthusiasm, individuality, and a pioneering spirit. You are often self-assured but can at times be overconfident, which results in hasty actions that may lead to loss of position.

Linked to your Sun's degree, this star encourages you to pursue a career in higher education, writing, publishing, or the legal profession. Usually Etamin imparts an assertive and determined nature with an interest in unusual subjects, ideas, and issues.

• *Positive:* willpower, fighting spirit, ambition, sincerity

• *Negative:* impulsive actions, quarrels, irritability, moodiness

See Appendix for additional fixed star readings.

Your Secret Self

Highly sociable, you need people and can be generous, kind, and magnanimous. Seeking compatible and sympathetic relationships with others, you can be an excellent friend or companion. Being proud and dramatic, you do not always reveal your extreme sensitivity, as you like to be in control; if you become hurt, you may have to avoid playing the martyr or feeling sorry for yourself. This same sensitivity, however, can also make you highly intuitive, and if it is developed, it can give you access to higher or more profound levels of existence.

A permanent youthful quality combines well with your sense of loving to keep you in touch with your joyful inner child. This playful quality may be expressed through art, music, writing, and drama, or it may enable you to delight and entertain others. With your wonderful imagination, dynamic emotions, and natural compassion, you have the ability to lift people's spirits and really enjoy life.

Work & Vocation

Your warm personality and overriding charm guarantee you success in occupations that deal with people. You can be especially good at businesses that involve social interaction, such as public relations, promotion, sales, or being an agent for others. A natural empathy can also draw you to counseling, healing, or helping others. Your shrewd business sense helps you succeed in whatever career you may choose, but preferably you need the freedom to work in your own way. Alternatively, being creative, you may be attracted to writing, music, the arts, or the entertainment business. Your natural playfulness may also find expression in the sports world.

Famous people who share your birthday include psychic Uri Geller, philosophers Sidney Hook and Susanne Langer, actor Kiefer Sutherland, baseball team owner Branch Rickey, writer Max Lerner, and racing driver Paddy McNally.

Numerology

With a number 20 birthday, you are intuitive, sensitive, adaptable, and understanding, and often see yourself as a part of a larger group. Usually you enjoy cooperative activities where you can interact, share experiences, or learn from others. Charming and gracious, you develop good diplomatic and social skills and can move in different social circles with ease. You may, however, need to develop your confidence or overcome a tendency to be easily hurt by the actions and criticism of others or be overly dependent. You are a master at creating a congenial and harmonious atmosphere. The subinfluence of the number 12 month indicates that you are astute and receptive, with a restless nature. You benefit from trusting your strong instincts, since you are often very perceptive in your assessment of people and their motives. Although you are ambitious and determined, your idealistic vision may cause you to vacillate between wanting personal advancement and sacrificing your personal wishes for the sake of the common good.

• *Positive:* good partnerships, gentle, tactful, receptive, intuitive, considerate, harmonious, agreeable, amicable, ambassador of goodwill

• *Negative:* suspicious, lack of confidence, oversensitive, selfish

Love & Relationships

Your need for emotional stimulation shows your powerful feelings. Restless and highly sensitive, you have idealistic inclinations that are probably going to entice you to try many different relationships. Since you are willing to make sacrifices for those you love and cherish, you need to take your time to find a suitable partner. Youthful and enthusiastic, you like to be spontaneous, but by becoming strongly attached to partners you run the risk of getting overly serious. This may sometimes prove to be a costly and unnecessary heartache.

YOUR SPECIAL SOMEONE

You might find a partner who will understand your sensitivity and need for love among those born on the following dates.

Love & friendship: Jan. 5, 10, 18, 19, 20, 26, 30, Feb. 3, 8, 16, 17, 24, 28, Mar. 1, 6, 14, 15, 22, 26, Apr. 4, 12, 13, 20, 24, 30, May 2, 10, 11, 12, 18, 22, June 8, 9, 16, 20, 30, July 6, 7, 14, 18, 28, Aug. 4, 5, 12, 16, 26, 30, Sept. 2, 3, 10, 14, 28, Oct. 1, 8, 12, 22, 26, Nov. 6, 10, 20, 24, Dec. 4, 8, 18, 22, 30

Beneficial: Jan. 13, Feb. 11, Mar. 9, Apr. 7, May 5, June 3, 30, July 1, 28, Aug. 26, Sept. 24, Oct. 22, Nov. 20, Dec. 18

Fatal attractions: June 16, 17, 18, 19, 20

Challenging: Jan. 14, 24, Feb. 12, 22, Mar. 10, 20, Apr. 8, 18, May 6, 16, June 4, 14, July 2, 12, Aug. 10, Sept. 8, Oct. 6, Nov. 4, Dec. 2

Soul mates: July 30, Aug. 28, Sept. 26, Oct. 24, Nov. 22, 23, Dec. 20, 21

SUN: SAGITTARIUS/CAPRICORN
CUSP
DECANATE: LEO/SUN
DEGREE: 28°30'–29°30' SAGITTARIUS
MODE: MUTABLE
ELEMENT: FIRE

December 21

♐ Born on the cusp of Sagittarius and Capricorn, you benefit from Jupiter's optimism and Saturn's realism. Charismatic and versatile, you have a dynamic personality and a desire to achieve on a grand scale. Your powerful emotions are your motivating force, and you want to realize your creative potential by turning your dreams into tangible reality. Although you are active and full of drive, having strong desires also implies that if you become excitable and rush into new projects without prior planning, you may miss some of your best opportunities. By restraining your inclination to be impatient and learning to focus on fewer goals, you become more responsible and reap the rewards.

The subinfluence of your decanate rulers, Leo and Saturn, adds to your self-confidence and strengthens your determination. Usually you are creative, idealistic, and full of noble ideas. Amiable and kindhearted, you have a lively expression of feeling and, with your direct approach, are also honest and friendly. When full of vitality, you can inspire others with your enthusiasm and spirit of enterprise.

Gracious, amicable, and able to mix with people from all walks of life, you possess natural diplomatic skills and an ability to make others feel at ease. Benevolence and an urge to grow and expand suggest that you can achieve much by yourself. Nonetheless, the tremendous potential indicated by your birthday is truly realized if you are engaged in collaborative ventures that can benefit not only yourself but others as well.

Up to the age of thirty, as your progressed Sun moves through Capricorn, you focus on practical issues and a need for order and structure in your life. A turning point occurs at the age of thirty-one, when your progressed Sun moves into Aquarius. This highlights a growing desire for more independence and original, progressive ideas. You may want freedom or feel a need to find your place within groups. Another turning point occurs at age sixty-one, when your progressed Sun moves into Pisces. This is likely to make you more emotionally sensitive, sympathetic, and imaginative. This is a time when artistic, creative, or spiritual talents are accentuated.

Fixed Stars

Etamin, Acumen, Sinistra, Spiculum

PRIMARY STAR

Star's name: Etamin
Degree position: 26°55'–27°57'
 Sagittarius between the years
 1930 and 2000
Magnitude: 2.5–3
Strength: ★★★★★
Orb: 1°40'
Constellation: Gamma Draconis
Applicable days: December 19, 20, 21
Star qualities: Mars/Moon
Description: a red giant binary star
 located in the Dragon's eye

PRIMARY STAR'S INFLUENCE

Etamin bestows a keen mentality, enthusiasm, individuality, and a pioneering spirit. You are often self-assured but at times overconfident, which results in hasty actions that may lead to loss of position.

 Linked to your Sun's degree, this star encourages you to pursue a career in higher education, writing, publishing, or the legal profession. Usually Etamin imparts an assertive and determined nature with an interest in unusual subjects, ideas, and issues.

 • *Positive:* willpower, fighting spirit, ambition, sincerity

 • *Negative:* impulsive actions, quarrels, irritability, moodiness

See Appendix for additional fixed star readings.

Your Secret Self

With a never-ending quest for knowledge, you will enjoy learning until the end of life. Your natural charm and spontaneous zeal imply that, as well as a youthful quality, you possess grace and individuality. Frequently well-informed and multitalented, you can be very persuasive if you are positively confident. Enthusiastic and intelligent, you are able to grasp ideas and information very quickly and apply them to your life. Be careful, however, of a tendency toward pride or emotional inflation that can take you very high, then leave you disappointed later.

With your love of variety and strong personal magnetism, you have the ability to influence and motivate others. Your desire for movement and change occasionally manifests as restlessness or impatience, but if you are inspired, it may stimulate you to explore and investigate new and exciting subjects or activities.

Work & Vocation

With your ambition, shrewd intelligence, and ability to think big, once you are really focused and determined you are capable of outstanding achievement in any field. With natural leadership abilities, you need the freedom to operate in your own way, so you usually fare better in a position of management or working for yourself. With your charismatic personality and a natural flair for captivating people, you can do especially well in public-related occupations, the entertainment world, or politics. Alternatively, your organizational skills, practicality, and enterprise may find positive outlets in business. You may experience a conflict, however, between your own personal ambitions and a desire for humanitarian ideals. Your sharp intellect can also help you succeed in science or education, but you may prefer to use your creative skills in art, drama, or music.

Famous people who share your birthday include musician Frank Zappa, dictator Joseph Stalin, prime minister Benjamin Disraeli, actress Jane Fonda, tennis player Chris Evert, athlete Florence Griffith Joyner, and TV host Phil Donahue.

Numerology

Dynamic drive and an outgoing personality are usually present in those with a number 21 birthday. Socially inclined, you have many interests and contacts and are generally fortunate. Usually you show others your friendly and gregarious personality. Intuitive and with an independent spirit, you are highly inventive and original. With a number 21 birthday, you can be fun-loving, magnetic, and creative, with social charm. In life you often have many opportunities to work in collaboration with other people and achieve success. Although you can be inclined toward cooperative relationships or marriage, you always want to be acknowledged for your talents and abilities. The subinfluence of the number 12 month indicates that you are optimistic and creative, with imagination and high ideals. Usually a perfectionist, you need to stay realistic in order to avoid disappointments. An ability to create harmony and a congenial atmosphere suggests that you have the power to make others feel at ease. Persuasive and charismatic, you are also able to influence others.

• *Positive:* inspiration, creativity, love unions, long-lasting relationships
• *Negative:* dependency, nervous, termperamental, lack of vision, disappointment, fear of change

Love & Relationships

An ability to relate to different people allows you to accept universal concepts of love and compassion. Charismatic and dynamic, with a responsible attitude, you prefer order and like to plan. Usually you are drawn to relationships that can offer long-term security and stability. You may favor hardworking and ambitious people in positions of power and authority who enjoy challenges. Although you can be understanding and humanitarian, you want to find true emotional satisfaction and not settle for second best.

YOUR SPECIAL SOMEONE

You might find stability, stimulating company, and the perfect partner among those born on the following dates.

Love & friendship: Jan. 2, 3, 6, 9, 10, 11, 21, 27, 29, 31, Feb. 1, 4, 7, 9, 25, 29, Mar. 2, 5, 7, 17, 23, 25, 27, Apr. 3, 4, 5, 15, 21, 25, May 1, 3, 13, 19, 23, 30, June 1, 11, 17, 21, 28, July 9, 15, 19, 26, 29, Aug. 7, 13, 17, 24, 27, Sept. 5, 11, 15, 22, 25, Oct. 3, 9, 13, 20, 23, Nov. 1, 7, 11, 18, 21, 30, Dec. 5, 9, 16, 19, 28

Beneficial: Jan. 11, 16, 30, Feb. 9, 24, 28, Mar. 7, 22, 26, Apr. 5, 20, 24, May 3, 18, 22, 31, June 1, 16, 20, 29, July 14, 18, 27, Aug. 12, 16, 25, Sept. 10, 14, 23, Oct. 8, 12, 21, 29, Nov. 6, 10, 19, 27, Dec. 4, 8, 17, 25

Fatal attractions: June 19, 20, 21, 22
Challenging: Jan. 15, Feb. 13, Mar. 11, Apr. 9, May 7, 30, June 5, 28, July 3, 26, Aug. 1, 24, Sept. 22, Oct. 20, 30, Nov. 18, 28, Dec. 16, 26

Soul mates: Jan. 9, 29, Feb. 7, 27, Mar. 5, 25, Apr. 3, 23, May 1, 21, June 19, July 17, Aug. 15, Sept. 13, Oct. 11, Nov. 9, Dec. 7

Capricorn

December 22–January 20

SUN: CAPRICORN/SAGITTARIUS
CUSP
DECANATE: CAPRICORN/SATURN
DEGREE: 29°30'–0°30' CAPRICORN
MODE: CARDINAL
ELEMENT: EARTH

December 22

♑ Magnetic and charming, yet hardworking, you possess outstanding potential for achievement if you only apply the necessary self-discipline. Being born on a cusp, you have the advantage of both the realistic and pragmatic perspective of Capricorn and the Sagittarian ability to see positive opportunities. Together these qualities can help you achieve positions of leadership, where you are able to use your refined social skills and emotional sensitivity in your adept dealings with people.

With the subinfluence of your decanate ruler, Capricorn, you are ambitious and have a strong sense of duty. A touch of perfectionism implies that if you undertake a job, you want to do it properly. Your good sense of structure gives you natural business abilities and helps you organize your goals. Financial matters are likely to occupy much of your attention, and you have the capability to commercialize your many talents. You may have to be careful, however, that your preoccupation with materialism or prestige does not distract you from your high ideals. In fact, one of your challenges may be to obtain the right balance between work and play and thus ensure that life does not become arduous.

Caring and kind, you possess deep feelings and enjoy putting others at their ease. Your interest in people may manifest as a strong humanitarian streak that may encourage you to fight for an idealistic cause. Friendly and naturally persuasive, you have refined conversational skills and are expert at the personal touch. A feel for beauty and the arts may find expression through music, art, or drama as well as a desire to surround yourself with style and luxury.

Up to the age of twenty-nine, you are likely to be goal-oriented and have a practical approach to your achievements. At the age of thirty, when your progressed Sun moves into Aquarius, you reach a turning point that highlights a growing need for freedom, new ideas, and expressing your individuality. Another turning point occurs at the age of sixty, when your progressed Sun moves into Pisces. This is likely to bring more emphasis on your emotional receptivity, imagination, or psychic awareness.

Your Secret Self

Although you can be very generous, warm, and spontaneous, you also possess an ability to be tough and dutiful. This may sometimes cause a conflict between your affections and your work. With your extreme sensitivity and strong emotions, you can suffer deeply from disappointment or frustration if you focus on negativity and are unable to let go of the past. By thinking positively and taking life as it comes, you learn to be more detached and less cynical, trusting that life will spontaneously provide you with everything you need at the right time.

While growing up, you may have experienced instances of controlled love and had to live up to others' expectations. By building faith and confidence in your abilities, you are in a position to give compassionate care to others by intuiting in the moment what feels right for you.

Work & Vocation

Although sensitive and creative, you are practical by nature. You may be attracted to the financial world, where you are likely to make an excellent economist, analyst, or stockbroker. Alter-

FIXED STAR

Star's name: Sinistra
Degree position: 28°46'–29°44'
  Sagittarius between the years
  1930 and 2000
Magnitude: 3
Strength: ★★★★★
Orb: 1°40'
Constellation: Nu Ophiuchi
Applicable days: December 21, 22, 23
Star qualities: Venus/Saturn
Description: a dwarf orange star located
  in the left hand of Ophiuchus

PRIMARY STAR'S INFLUENCE

Sinistra bestows success in business enterprises, good executive abilities, leadership potential, and an independent or original personality. This star, however, also imparts restlessness and a constant need for change, which may result in fluctuating circumstances. Often you seek powerful and influential positions.

Linked to your Sun's degree, Sinistra bestows high aspirations and a daring and original yet contentious nature. Achievements in business, the legal profession, government, or dealing with the public are all indicated by the influence of this star. Alternatively, you may have aspirations for higher learning, religion, and philosophy. There are also opportunities to make a name for yourself and achieve fame or notoriety.

• *Positive:* high position in public life
• *Negative:* domineering, unfeeling, overserious

natively, you can become an advisor or a business accountant. A flair for dealing with people may encourage you to work as a negotiator or dealer. Ambitious, you prefer to be in a leading position. As you possess excellent organizational skills, you can achieve success as a politician, manager, or administrator. You may also be attracted to research and science or work for the community. Conversely, as you are creative and multitalented, you may be drawn toward design, drama, or music.

Famous people who share your birthday include singers Maurice and Robin Gibb, baseball player Steve Carlton, former First Lady Claudia "Lady Bird" Johnson, TV personality Noel Edmonds, opera composer Puccini, and actress Peggy Ashcroft.

Numerology

With a number 22 birthdate, you are a practical, disciplined, and highly intuitive individual. This is a master number and can vibrate both as number 22 and as number 4. Often honest and hardworking, with natural leadership abilities, you have a charismatic personality and a deep understanding of people. Although undemonstrative, you often show a caring and protective concern for the welfare of others. You never lose sight, however, of your pragmatic or realistic stand. The subinfluence of the number 12 month indicates that you are ambitious and idealistic. Being both optimistic and skeptical implies that much depends on your frame of mind. When you are positive, your ideas can turn out to be highly profitable, but you must guard against depression and emotional anxiety. Highly receptive, you have strong premonitions, but if you doubt yourself, these turn to worry. A need to create harmony and a calm environment can enhance your chances of achieving inner peace and tranquility.

• *Positive:* universal, original, highly intuitive, pragmatic, practical, good with your hands, skillful, builder, good organizer, realist, problem solver, achiever

• *Negative:* get-rich-quick schemes, inferiority complex, bossy, materialistic, lazy, egotistical

Love & Relationships

With your intuition and understanding, you can easily relate to others. Friendly and affectionate, you need people and relationships. Although you are usually generous and caring, there can be times when you become oversensitive and withdrawn. At these times you may appear cold, so it is necessary for you to rebalance yourself. Change, travel, or physical exercise can all help you recover your usual good spirits. Romantic and sensitive with humanitarian and universal concepts, you enjoy sharing experiences and can be a loyal and supportive partner or friend.

YOUR SPECIAL SOMEONE

To find love and long-lasting relationships, you may want to look out for someone born on one of the following dates.

Love & friendship: Jan. 2, 7, 9, 11, 12, 22, 25, Feb. 7, 10, 20, 23, 26, Mar. 5, 8, 18, 21, Apr. 3, 6, 16, 19, May 1, 3, 4, 14, 17, 20, 24, 29, June 2, 12, 15, 27, July 10, 13, 16, 20, 25, 30, Aug. 9, 15, 24, 26, Sept. 7, 13, 22, 24, Oct. 4, 7, 10, 14, 19, 24, 28, 29, 30, Nov. 2, 5, 8, 12, 17, 22, 26, 27, 28, Dec. 3, 6, 10, 15, 20, 24, 25

Beneficial: Jan. 12, 23, 29, Feb. 10, 21, 27, Mar. 22, 26, Apr. 6, 17, 23, May 4, 15, 21, June 2, 13, 19, 28, 30, July 11, 17, 26, 28, Aug. 9, 15, 24, 26, Sept. 7, 13, 22, 24, Oct. 5, 11, 20, 22, Nov. 3, 9, 18, 20, 30, Dec. 1, 7, 16, 18, 28

Fatal attractions: June 20, 21, 22, 23, July 29, Aug. 27, Sept. 25, Oct. 23, Nov. 21, Dec. 19

Challenging: Jan. 1, 4, 26, 30, Feb. 2, 24, 28, Mar. 22, 26, Apr. 20, 24, May 18, 22, 31, June 16, 20, 29, July 14, 18, 27, Aug. 12, 16, 25, 30, Sept. 10, 14, 23, 28, Oct. 8, 12, 21, 26, Nov. 6, 10, 19, 24, Dec. 4, 8, 17, 22

Soul mates: Jan. 20, Feb. 18, Mar. 16, Apr. 14, May 12, June 10, July 8, Aug. 6, Sept. 4, Oct. 2

December 23

♑ The influences of your birthday suggest that you are practical yet imaginative, a strong individual with a desire for action. Although you have the drive and determination to achieve prosperity in life, it is through your emotional power to influence people that you can really obtain satisfaction.

With the subinfluence of your decanate ruler, Capricorn, you can be ambitious and hardworking. Being persistent, you have the energy to achieve the goals you have undertaken. Although you are usually courteous and friendly, a tendency to repress your strong emotions may sometimes leave you appearing cold and undemonstrative. Nevertheless, through the use of your dynamic charm and ability to entertain others, you can also make an impression with your warmth and generosity.

With a talent for combining business and pleasure, you have a drive for material gain and status. Usually you possess a wealth of feelings and great dreams. As long as you are willing to put in the necessary effort, your intuitive intellect and outstanding imagination can be valuable assets in your climb to the top. Although versatile, you may need to channel any possible restlessness into a focused desire for positive change.

Before the age of twenty-eight, you are likely to be concerned with practical issues regarding your career or responsibilities. At the age of twenty-nine, when your progressed Sun moves into Aquarius, there is a turning point that highlights a growing need to be more independent and able to express your own unique vision. Another turning point occurs at the age of fifty-nine, when your progressed Sun moves into Pisces. This is likely to bring more emphasis on enhanced emotional sensitivity, and you are likely to be more receptive to your creative urges.

Fixed Star

Star's name: Polis

Degree position: 2°15'–3°14' Capricorn between the years 1930 and 2000

Magnitude: 4

Strength: ★★★★

Orb: 1°30'

Constellation: Mu Sagittarius

Applicable days: December 23, 24, 25, 26

Star qualities: Jupiter/Mars

Description: a blue and white triple star located in the upper part of the bow of the Archer

PRIMARY STAR'S INFLUENCE

Polis bestows keen perception and the power to focus upon a particular goal. This star encourages you to search for success and good fortune and grants the determination to rise to high positions. The ability to make quick and fortunate decisions imparts leadership abilities. This star also warns against a tendency to be rebellious and domineering.

Linked to your Sun's degree, Polis imparts a pioneering and courageous nature, many opportunities, endurance, and high ambitions. You are proud and seek to make a name for yourself, whether it results in fame or notoriety. This star can also impart success in higher education, with special interests in spirituality. Polis also warns against a tendency to dominate situations and take the lead unless you are the initiator of the enterprise.

Your Secret Self

Proud and independent, you need positive outlets for your enormous emotional power. Although practical and down to earth, you also have the ability to inspire others with your ideals and spontaneity. Mentally very shrewd about people, with an altruistic or humanitarian side to your nature, you can excel in activities that require dealing with people.

The differing sides of your personality may sometimes confuse those around you. Usually you are very sociable and strong, yet a tendency to isolate yourself can sometimes leave you feeling lonely. If you withdraw, you can also show a stubborn streak that affects your relationships with others. A desire to transcend the mundane can help you overcome these tendencies and inspire you to share your generosity, vision, and innate compassion with others.

Work & Vocation

As a resourceful individual with a strong personality, you possess a natural business sense and can succeed in all kinds of people-related occupations. Usually versatile and responsible, you are hardworking and dedicated. Since you have excellent executive abilities, working in large corporations often enables you to secure an executive position as a manager or administrator. Your charm, persuasive manner, and communication skills also point to success in the worlds of sales, promotion, and negotiation. Creative, you may be inspired by occupations connected with photography, writing, art, music, and drama. You can commercialize your talents through whatever career you choose as long as you are willing to work hard to achieve your objectives.

Famous people who share your birthday include Japanese emperor Akihito, Queen Silvia of Sweden, Mormon founder Joseph Smith, writer Robert Bly, musician Chet Baker, and U.S. Supreme Court Justice John Jay.

Numerology

Intuition, emotional sensitivity, and creativity are some of the attributes of a number 23 birthday. Usually you are versatile, passionate, and a quick thinker, with a professional attitude and a mind full of creative ideas. With the number 23 influence, you can learn new subjects easily but may prefer practice to theory. You are fond of travel, adventure, and meeting new people; the restlessness implied by the number 23 urges you to try many different kinds of experiences, and you are apt to make the most of any situation. Generally friendly and fun-loving, with courage and drive, you may need an active life in order to actualize your true potential. The subinfluence of the number 12 month indicates that you need to express your feelings clearly and persevere in spite of initial difficulties. To avoid emotional upset, you may need to discipline yourself and refrain from outbursts when you don't get your own way. By developing the art of give and take, you also learn to stay impersonal.

• *Positive:* loyal, compassionate, responsible, loves travel, communicative, intuitive, creative, versatile, trustworthy

• *Negative:* selfish, insecure, stubborn, uncompromising, fault-finding

YOUR SPECIAL SOMEONE

For that special someone, you may wish to look among those born on the following dates.

Love & friendship: Jan. 8, 11, 12, 29, Feb. 6, 9, 27, Mar. 4, 7, 25, 29, Apr. 2, 5, 23, 27, May 3, 4, 21, 25, June 1, 19, 23, July 17, 21, Aug. 15, 19, 29, Sept. 13, 17, 27, Oct. 11, 15, 25, 29, 30, Nov. 9, 13, 23, 27, 28, Dec. 7, 11, 21, 25, 26

Beneficial: Jan. 13, 30, Feb. 11, 28, Mar. 9, 26, Apr. 7, 24, 30, May 5, 22, 28, June 3, 20, 26, July 1, 18, 24, 29, Aug. 16, 22, 25, Sept. 14, 20, 25, Oct. 12, 18, 23, Nov. 10, 16, 21, Dec. 8, 14, 19

Fatal attractions: June 21, 22, 23, Oct. 30, Nov. 28, Dec. 26

Challenging: Jan. 5, 19, Feb. 3, 17, Mar. 1, 15, Apr. 13, May 11, June 9, 30, July 7, 28, 30, Aug. 5, 26, 28, Sept. 3, 24, 26, Oct. 1, 22, 24, Nov. 20, 22, Dec. 18, 20

Soul mates: Jan. 7, Feb. 5, Mar. 3, Apr. 1, Sept. 30, Oct. 28, Nov. 26, Dec. 24

Love & Relationships

Although you are active and restless, you desire emotional tranquillity. Desiring harmony, you will often seek or make efforts to keep the peace, so partnerships and home play a strong part in your life agenda. Your strong emotions, however, also point to a need to express yourself positively; otherwise you may hold in emotions that can cause problems later. With your dynamic charm, nevertheless, you can easily win people's hearts and attract admirers. Although you have powerful love to offer others, in a long-term relationship you need a partner who can provide you with material stability and security.

December 24

♑ With your practical nature and strong emotional ideals, you are a refined and pragmatic individual with a sensitive intellect. Highly intuitive, yet rational, you can use your critical abilities professionally or for self-analysis. Just be careful that a tendency to be skeptical does not close your mind to the various possibilities and opportunities open to you.

With the subinfluence of your decanate ruler, Capricorn, you are ambitious and have a strong awareness of your responsibilities. Persevering, you have the power to slowly advance toward your goals and overcome difficulties. Preferring to work with a structured system, you can be reliable and take your tasks seriously. Be careful, however, that your self-restraint does not turn into melancholy or make you seem stubborn or cold.

Usually you have a realistic approach to life and can be charming and talented. A gift for creative thinking may manifest through writing, speaking, or other forms of communication. With your diplomacy, attractive voice, and amiable personality, you are able to win friends and sway others. When insecure, you may possess a fear of being alone or abandoned. You do need, however, regular periods of peace and privacy for introspection.

Up to the age of twenty-seven you have a desire for order and structure in your life, and practical considerations are important. At the age of twenty-eight, when your progressed Sun moves into Aquarius, there is a turning point that highlights a growing need for independence and autonomy. You become more sociable and group-conscious as well as desiring to express your own individuality. Another turning point occurs at the age of fifty-eight, when your progressed Sun moves into Pisces. This is likely to bring more emphasis to your emotional receptivity, imagination, or psychic and spiritual awareness.

FIXED STAR

Star's name: Polis

Degree position: 2°15'–3°14' Capricorn between the years 1930 and 2000

Magnitude: 4

Strength: ★★★★

Orb: 1°30'

Constellation: Mu Sagittarius

Applicable days: December 23, 24, 25, 26

Star qualities: Jupiter/Mars

Description: a blue and white triple star located in the upper part of the bow of the Archer

PRIMARY STAR'S INFLUENCE

Polis bestows keen perception and the power to focus upon a particular goal. This star encourages you to search for success and good fortune and grants the determination to rise to high positions. The ability to make quick and fortunate decisions imparts leadership abilities. This star also warns against a tendency to be rebellious and domineering.

Linked to your Sun's degree, Polis imparts a pioneering and courageous nature, many opportunities, endurance, and high ambitions. You are proud and seek to make a name for yourself, whether it results in fame or notoriety. This star can impart success in higher education, with special interests in spirituality. Polis also warns against a tendency to dominate situations and take the lead unless you are the initiator of the enterprise.

Your Secret Self

With a strong inner emotional power, you have the ability to charm, uplift, or inspire others. Your powerful imagination and keen practicality can combine to make you a realistic visionary. It would be wise, however, to guard against using your sense of fantasy in daydreaming or escape. When positively focused, you possess the ability to project powerful love and determination in a combination that is guaranteed to bring you success.

Although an engaging charm and leadership abilities can help you in your climb to the top, at times you may be such a perfectionist that people cannot reach your high ideals. This can bring possible misunderstandings or difficulty in communicating your ideas. With your sharp mind, it is important to keep yourself busy in order to make the most of your many gifts. Through developing your deeper intuitive sensitivity, you can come to understand yourself better and thus avoid becoming too serious or depressed. By keeping your sense of humor and enjoying the pleasure of initiating new activities, you are able to keep yourself creatively occupied.

Work & Vocation

Determined and self-reliant, you are often intuitive and intelligent, with ambition and drive. Your fine intellect suggests that you like to use your business acumen and be enterprising. You also have a talent for solving problems, as well as excellent organizational and managerial abilities. If inspired, you may choose to develop your natural writing skills. Alternatively, you can use your talents to administer art in national institutions. Attracted to public life, you can become involved in education, politics, acting, or the entertainment world. Despite being very practical, you may be attracted to philosophy, metaphysics, or mysticism. A love of variety and a need to be active and independent may inspire you to be self-employed.

Famous people who share your birthday include astronomer Tycho Brahe, blues singer Leadbelly, choreographer Robert Joffrey, billionaire Howard Hughes, seer Nostradamus, and actress Ava Gardner.

Numerology

The emotional sensitivity of the number 24 birthday suggests that you seek balance and harmony. You are also receptive to form and structure and can easily create a complex yet efficient system. Although idealistic, faithful, and fair, you are inclined to be undemonstrative, believing that actions speak louder than words. The main challenge for a number 24 individual is to learn to associate with people from all walks of life, to overcome suspicious tendencies, and to build a secure home. The subinfluence of the number 12 month indicates that you are highly perceptive, with strong ambitions. You are friendly and sociable, but a tendency to be easily annoyed or hurt suggests that at times you take issues too much to heart. An inclination to alternate between being confident and independent and being vulnerable and self-doubting also implies that you need to seek balance and harmony in all your relationships. By staying open-minded and liberal, you are able to see the broader picture. Nevertheless, you are serious, efficient, hardworking, and trustworthy.

• *Positive:* energetic, idealistic, practical skills, strong determination, tolerant, frank, fair, generous, love of home, active
• *Negative:* materialistic, jealous, ruthlessness, dislike routine, lazy, unfaithful, stubborn

YOUR SPECIAL SOMEONE

You might start to look for an interesting companion among those born on the following dates.

Love & friendship: Jan. 9, 13, 30, Feb. 7, 28, Mar. 5, 26, 30, Apr. 3, 24, 28, May 1, 5, 22, 26, June 3, 20, 24, July 18, 22, 31, Aug. 16, 20, 29, 30, Sept. 14, 18, 27, 28, Oct. 12, 16, 25, 26, 31, Nov. 10, 14, 23, 24, 29, Dec. 8, 12, 21, 22, 27

Beneficial: Jan. 15, 22, 31, Feb. 13, 20, 29, Mar. 11, 18, 27, Apr. 9, 16, 25, May 7, 14, 23, 30, June 5, 12, 21, 28, July 3, 10, 19, 26, 30, Aug. 1, 8, 17, 24, 28, Sept. 6, 15, 22, 26, Oct. 4, 13, 20, 24, Nov. 2, 11, 18, 22, Dec. 9, 16, 20

Fatal attractions: Jan. 11, Feb. 9, Mar. 7, Apr. 5, May 3, June 1, 22, 23, 24, 25, Oct. 31, Nov. 29, Dec. 27

Challenging: Jan. 5, 8, 16, 21, Feb. 3, 6, 14, 19, Mar. 1, 4, 12, 17, Apr. 2, 10, 15, May 8, 13, June 6, 11, July 4, 9, 29, Aug. 2, 7, 27, Sept. 5, 25, Oct. 3, 23, Nov. 1, 21, Dec. 19

Soul mates: Jan. 13, Feb. 11, Mar. 9, Apr. 7, May 5, June 3, July 1, Aug. 31, Sept. 29, Oct. 27, Nov. 25, Dec. 23

Love & Relationships

With your love for truth and beauty, you can be honest and direct. Idealistic in love, you seek exciting and stimulating friends and partners. Having a natural charm can endear you to others and help your popularity. As you are likely to experience many emotional changes in your relationships, it is better to be versatile and adapt rather than be inflexible. As you are sensitive, the demonstration of love and affection can be especially important to you and help you overcome an emotional restlessness. Your need for a strong home base and security may be the thing that finally helps you settle down.

December 25

♑ The influences of your birthday show you to be a practical and affectionate individual with a strong desire for harmony. As charm is likely to be one of your major assets, your ability to deal with people can greatly aid your success. A congenial and smart communicator, you possess original and inventive ideas and are often ahead of your time. Although shrewd and independent, you possess a genuine care and concern for others that can extend to your supporting an idealistic cause.

With the subinfluence of your decanate ruler, Capricorn, you are dependable and have a strong awareness of your responsibilities. Establishing a secure home is important to you, and you are willing to work hard to keep your loved ones protected. If you undertake a job, you want to do it well and are willing to make sacrifices to achieve your objectives. A good sense of structure helps you organize your goals and gives you natural business abilities.

You like to live well, but this does not detract from an innate humanitarian or philanthropic side to your personality. With your desire to help, you can often advise or help manage the affairs of others. If this is carried too far, however, there is a danger you may take over and become too critical, dominating, or interfering. Nevertheless, you usually want to keep the peace and are broad-minded and trustworthy.

Before the age of twenty-six you are likely to have a pragmatic, realistic, and goal-oriented approach to your achievements. At the age of twenty-seven, when your progressed Sun moves into Aquarius, you reach a turning point that highlights a growing need to express more freedom and independence. You may want to experiment with different concepts, make new friends, or become involved with group activities. Another turning point occurs at the age of fifty-seven, when your progressed Sun moves into Pisces. This is likely to bring more emphasis on your enhanced sensitivity and feelings. You may become more sympathetic and compassionate toward others or become involved in artistic or mystical pursuits.

Your Secret Self

With your keen intellect, idealism, and natural philosophical perspective, you are usually happiest when constructively busy and expanding your knowledge. Education, whether formal or self-directed, can be a vital key to your success and advancement. Generally honest and direct, you can also be highly intuitive about situations as well as about other people's motivation. With good strategic skills and an ability to see the larger plan, you often have surges of optimism and inspiration that can help you move forward in a bold and enterprising way.

With the ability to learn quickly, you have a creative approach to life and a desire for self-expression. You need to be with people, and an inner restlessness may cause you to explore many socially related activities. As you are interested in many different areas, staying focused is important to stop you from becoming scattered, indecisive, or worried. By staying humble and sensitive to the needs of others, you can develop great tolerance and emotional satisfaction in life.

Work & Vocation

Enterprising and idealistic, you are a humanitarian with philanthropic inclinations. As a charming and receptive individual, you are good at dealing with people. A career in public life can suit your personality and you can succeed admirably in politics, the healing professions, or public organizations. A love of knowledge and an interest in metaphysics may inspire you to study and teach history, philosophy, or astrology. Alternatively, being technically inclined and having an interest in mathematics may inspire you to study science, astronomy, chemistry, or biology. Creative, with a need for self-expression, you may take up writing or develop your artistic talents.

Famous people who share your birthday include actress Sissy Spacek, former Egyptian president Anwar Sadat, musician Noel Redding, singer Annie Lennox, actor Humphrey Bogart, cosmetics tycoon Helena Rubinstein, writer Carlos Castaneda, and Civil War nurse Clara Barton.

Numerology

Intuitive and thoughtful, yet quick and energetic, with a number 25 birthday you need to express yourself through different experiences. A desire for perfection often urges you to work hard and be productive. Usually you are instinctive and alert, and can gain more knowledge through practical application than mere theory. Good judgment and an eye for detail ensure successful accomplishment. You may have to develop a less skeptical attitude by overcoming a tendency to make erratic or impulsive decisions. As a number 25 personality, you possess strong mental energies that when concentrated can aid you to look at all the facts and arrive at a conclusion faster than anyone else. The subinfluence of the number 12 month indicates that you are helpful and friendly, with an attractive personality. Your strong convictions and an inclination to think independently suggest that you are intelligent and practical. Although you are usually faithful and dependable, a tendency to be critical or interfering advises that you need to remain broad-minded and humble.

• *Positive:* highly intuitive, perfectionist, perceptive, creative, good at dealing with people

• *Negative:* impulsive, impatient, irresponsible, overemotional, jealous, secretive, moody, nervous

Love & Relationships

A strong need for love and affection may cause you to seek an idealistic romance. Being friendly, you are often drawn to people-related activities, but with your sensitivity it would be wise to guard against social excesses. Although your charm can attract admirers, it is important to pick your partners carefully to avoid unfortunate emotional involvements. By ensuring an equal balance in your partnerships, you do not become dependent. As you have a strong need for harmony and inner peace, a secure home base may play an important part in your decisions.

YOUR SPECIAL SOMEONE

For love and a stable relationship, you may want to look out for someone born on one of the following days.

Love & friendship: Jan. 9, 14, 15, 25, 28, Feb. 10, 13, 23, 26, Mar. 8, 11, 21, 24, 31, Apr. 6, 9, 19, 22, 29, May 4, 6, 7, 17, 20, 27, June 2, 5, 15, 18, 25, July 3, 13, 16, 23, Aug. 1, 11, 14, 21, 31, Sept. 9, 12, 19, 29, Oct. 7, 10, 17, 27, Nov. 5, 8, 15, 25, Dec. 3, 6, 13, 23

Beneficial: Jan. 12, 23, 26, Feb. 10, 21, 24, Mar. 8, 19, 22, 28, Apr. 6, 17, 20, 26, May 4, 15, 18, 24, June 2, 13, 16, 22, July 11, 14, 20, 31, Aug. 9, 12, 18, 29, Sept. 7, 10, 16, 27, Oct. 5, 8, 14, 25, Nov. 3, 6, 12, 23, Dec. 1, 4, 10, 21

Fatal attractions: June 23, 24, 25, 26, Nov. 30, Dec. 28

Challenging: Jan. 17, 18, 21, Feb. 15, 16, 19, Mar. 13, 14, 17, 29, Apr. 11, 12, 15, 27, May 9, 10, 13, 25, June 7, 8, 11, 23, July 5, 6, 9, 21, 30, Aug. 3, 4, 7, 19, 28, Sept. 1, 2, 5, 17, 26, Oct. 3, 15, 24, Nov. 1, 13, 22, Dec. 11, 20

Soul mates: Jan. 24, Feb. 22, Mar. 20, Apr. 18, 30, May 16, 28, June 14, 26, July 12, 24, Aug. 10, 22, Sept. 8, 20, Oct. 6, 18, Nov. 4, 16, Dec. 2, 14

December 26

♑ With your dynamic emotions, intuition, and warmth, you have a natural gift for dealing with people. Your Capricorn birthday suggests that your innate practicality enables you to work enthusiastically toward your ideals. As well as charm, you possess good organizational skills and a creative intellect. Be careful, however, that an inner restlessness does not deter you from realizing your unique potential.

With the subinfluence of your decanate ruler, Capricorn, you are reliable and have a strong sense of duty. Faithful and loyal, you can be ardent in your desire to help others. Although capable of good concentration when interested in a project, you may still need to develop patience if you tend to become bored too quickly.

Full of big plans and a desire for action, freedom, and adventure, you can have a varied and eventful life. Financial problems, however, may sometimes interfere with the expression of your heart's desires, or it may seem that satisfaction is always around the corner. Through self-analysis, being responsible, and learning to let go of the past, you can avoid emotional instability.

Up to the age of twenty-five you feel a need for order and structure in your life, and practical considerations are important. At the age of twenty-six, when your progressed Sun moves into Aquarius, you reach a turning point that highlights a growing need for independence and liberation from the mundane. You become more sociable and group conscious as well as desiring to express your own individuality. Another turning point occurs at the age of fifty-six, when your progressed Sun moves into Pisces. This is likely to bring increased emphasis to your emotional receptivity, imagination, or psychic and spiritual awareness.

FIXED STAR

Star's name: Polis

Degree position: 2°15'–3°14' Capricorn between the years 1930 and 2000

Magnitude: 4

Strength: ★★★★

Orb: 1°30'

Constellation: Mu Sagittarius

Applicable days: December 23, 24, 25, 26

Star qualities: Jupiter/Mars

Description: a blue and white triple star located in the upper part of the bow of the Archer

PRIMARY STAR'S INFLUENCE

Polis bestows keen perception and the power to focus upon a particular goal. This star encourages you to search for success and good fortune and grants the determination to rise to high positions. The ability to make quick and fortunate decisions imparts leadership abilities. This star also warns against a tendency to be rebellious and domineering.

Linked to your Sun's degree, Polis imparts a pioneering and courageous nature, many opportunities, endurance, and high ambitions. You are proud and seek to make a name for yourself, whether it results in fame or notoriety. This star can impart success in higher education, with special interests in spirituality. Polis also warns against a tendency to dominate situations and take the lead unless you are the initiator of the enterprise.

Your Secret Self

Although practical, inwardly you are extremely sensitive and intuitive. With your high ideals and longing for love, you may become involved in humanitarian causes, artistic self-expression, or searching for truth in spiritual experience. Along with an equally strong need to build a solid order in your life, there is an emphasis on your work that can prove especially fortunate in providing you with financial protection. With a fertile imagination and a good sense of values, you will find that through persistent and concentrated efforts you can turn your visions into reality.

Your spirit of enterprise suggests that you have a need for action and adventure. If this is repressed, you may experience a lack of consistency and go from being restless and impatient at one extreme to inertia at the other. To avoid a tendency toward escapism or daydreaming, it is vital for you to stay focused on creative and exciting projects and activities. When optimistic and enthusiastic, you are able to inspire others and make things happen on a grand scale.

Work & Vocation

Intelligent and purposeful, with determination and drive, you prefer a large business and a great deal of activity. Self-reliant, you enjoy succeeding through your own efforts and hard work. Although you enjoy business and material success, you may want to pursue a career in publishing or advertising and promotion. A talent with words and the ability to communicate ideas indicate that you can accomplish much as a writer or work in the media, the theater, or the film world. Practical and with good organizational skills, you can be efficient and authoritative. Whatever career you assume, to avoid boredom you need challenges and diversity.

Famous people who share your birthday include Communist leader Mao Zedong, Indian mystic Mother Meera, record producer Phil Spector, writer Henry Miller, actor Richard Widmark, and entertainer Steve Allen.

Numerology

The strength or power suggested by the number 26 birthday shows that you are a cautious character with strong values and sound judgment. Parental instincts and a love of home may also suggest a need to build a solid foundation or find real stability. Often a tower of strength for others, you are willing to support friends and family members who may turn to you in time of need. You may nevertheless need to guard against materialistic tendencies and a desire to control people or situations. The subinfluence of the number 12 month indicates that you are gregarious and amiable, with an enterprising spirit. Intuitive and intelligent, with executive skills, you have inspired ideas and an ability to turn them to tangible products and achieve financial success. Usually you know how to take advantage of new situations. Inner dissatisfaction with your circumstances, however, may bring unrest. This constant search for peace implies that you need to establish balance and harmony.

• *Positive:* creative, practical, caring, meticulous, idealistic, honest, responsible, proud of family, enthusiastic, courageous
• *Negative:* stubborn, rebellious, unfriendly, lack of persistence, instability

Love & Relationships

Capable of turning on the charm, you can easily attract others. Very sociable, you may find yourself drawn to creative and hardworking people who stimulate these qualities in yourself. With your powerful need for love, however, choices regarding your love partners may prove difficult until you learn to stay detached. Creative but bored by routine, you may have many short-lived relationships until you find your ideal partner. Once you find your true love, you are capable of being loyal and loving.

YOUR SPECIAL SOMEONE

You may find someone who understands your sensitivity and needs more easily among those born on the dates listed below.

Love & friendship: Jan. 6, 11, 14, 26, Feb. 4, 9, 12, Mar. 2, 7, 10, 28, Apr. 5, 8, 20, 26, 30, May 3, 6, 24, 28, June 1, 4, 22, 26, July 2, 20, 24, Aug. 18, 22, Sept. 10, 16, 20, 30, Oct. 14, 18, 28, Nov. 12, 16, 26, Dec. 10, 14, 24

Beneficial: Jan. 20, 24, Feb. 18, 22, Mar. 16, 20, 29, Apr. 14, 18, 27, May 12, 16, 25, June 10, 14, 23, 29, July 8, 12, 21, 27, Aug. 6, 10, 19, 25, 30, Sept. 4, 8, 17, 23, 28, Oct. 2, 6, 15, 21, 26, Nov. 4, 13, 19, 24, Dec. 2, 11, 17, 22

Fatal attractions: June 24, 25, 26, 27, Aug. 31, Sept. 29, Oct. 27, Nov. 25, Dec. 23

Challenging: Jan. 22, 23, 27, Feb. 20, 21, 25, Mar. 18, 19, 23, Apr. 16, 17, 21, May 14, 15, 19, June 12, 13, 17, July 10, 11, 15, 31, Aug. 8, 9, 13, 29, Sept. 6, 7, 11, 27, Oct. 4, 5, 9, 25, Nov. 2, 3, 7, 23, Dec. 1, 5, 21

Soul mates: Jan. 23, Feb. 21, Mar. 19, Apr. 17, 29, May 15, 27, June 13, 25, July 11, 23, Aug. 9, 21, Sept. 7, 19, Oct. 5, 17, Nov. 3, 15, Dec. 1, 13

December 27

FIXED STAR

Star's name: Kaus Borealis

Degree position: 5°20'–6°19' Capricorn between the years 1930 and 2000

Magnitude: 3

Strength: ★★★★★★

Orb: 1°40'

Constellation: Lambda Sagittarius

Applicable days: December 27, 28, 29

Star qualities: Mercury/Mars

Description: a giant orange star located in the northern part of the bow of the Archer

PRIMARY STAR'S INFLUENCE

Kaus Borealis imparts intelligence, a keen mentality, energetic and impressive speech, and good communication skills. A love of discussion and debate is also indicated by this star; however, at times you appear aggressive or argumentative. Frequently this star bestows ability at repartee, humanitarian tendencies, and an idealistic nature with a keen sense of justice. This star may also force changes on you and challenge your obstinacy.

Linked to your Sun's degree, Kaus Borealis imparts resoluteness and an inner driving force to achieve positions of influence. Your leadership ability and ingenuity are often recognized by others and lead to accomplishment or promotion. Nevertheless, an inner restlessness and a continual need to forge ahead may suggest discontent.

• *Positive:* versatile, determined, knowledgeable, outspoken

• *Negative:* lack of satisfaction, extremist, opinionated

♑ With your strong feelings and innate practicality, you like to know where you stand, whether with people or in the world. Your Capricorn birthday suggests a need for a strong foundation in life that blends well with your sense of honesty and directness. Although you are idealistic by nature, your ambition suggests that you can be enterprising and hardworking. People are very important to you, and your ability to play the charming diplomat can help you succeed in all activities having to do with the public.

With the subinfluence of your decanate ruler, Capricorn, you can be persevering and goal-oriented. A shrewd intellect and sense of discrimination endow you with good judgment and common sense. As a good strategist and planner, you enjoy being constructive but may have to watch a tendency to become overconfident or preoccupied with self-fulfillment.

Being sensitive and intuitive, you benefit from trusting your own feelings, which are usually right. You enjoy entertaining, and usually know how to mix your work and social life. Be careful, however, of a self-indulgent streak that can incline you to indulge in emotional excesses.

Before the age of twenty-four, you are likely to have a realistic approach to your achievements and a strong sense of what you want from life. At the age of twenty-five, when your progressed Sun moves into Aquarius, you reach a turning point that highlights a growing need to express freedom and independence. You may want to experiment with different concepts, make new friends, or become involved with humanitarian or group activities. Another turning point occurs at the age of fifty-five, when your progressed Sun moves into Pisces. This probably emphasizes your enhanced sensitivity and feelings. You may become more receptive toward others or sympathetic and compassionate. By allowing your imagination to flow, you can become engaged in artistic or mystical pursuits.

Your Secret Self

Although you have an easygoing exterior, you can be motivated and success-oriented, particularly if you have a plan of action. Broad-minded, you may be drawn to travel or to the study of philosophical or spiritual subjects. This does not detract from your shrewd practicality, which allows you to see opportunities and get value for your money.

With your quick mind and sharp comments, you possess a flair for being witty and entertaining. Confident in your opinions, you may have to watch a tendency to get carried away and become arrogant. A sixth sense, particularly regarding material matters, endows you with financial protection and a quick understanding of people. When you add your dedication to a goal or purpose, you have only to make the effort to build a solid foundation to your achievements in order to perform miracles and achieve long-lasting success.

Work & Vocation

Ambitious and hardworking, with a flair for dealing with the public, you have natural healing ability. You are suited to occupations that can utilize your easygoing personality and practical competence. Usually composed and understanding, with an ability to listen, you can counsel people or be an advisor. With a desire for social reform, you may fare particularly well in education and research. As you are a good organizer and have a desire to build something worthwhile, you may become involved in philanthropic activities. Alternatively, a desire for self-expression may attract you to writing, literature, or the performing arts. Interest in metaphysics and technical ability suggest that you may wish to explore astronomy and astrology.

Famous people who share your birthday include actress Marlene Dietrich, astronomer/astrologer Johannes Kepler, chemist Louis Pasteur, and actor Gerard Depardieu.

Numerology

You are intuitive yet inquisitive, and the number 27 birthday indicates that your depth of thought can be greatly enhanced by developing patience and self-control. You are often forceful, determined, and observant and can pay great attention to detail. Generally idealistic and sensitive, with a fertile and creative mind, you can impress others with your original thought and ideas. Developing good communication skills helps you to overcome a reluctance to express your deeper feelings. Education is beneficial for number 27 persons and, with the proper qualifications, you can achieve success through writing, research, and work in large organizations. The subinfluence of the number 12 month indicates that you are talented and ambitious. Security-conscious, you like to think realistically but on a grand scale. When you learn to trust your intuition, you become even-tempered, with polished common sense, and can solve problems by looking at the broader picture. Then you also feel relaxed and project a confident front in public.

- *Positive:* leadership, thoroughness, hardworking, traditional, authoritative, protective, the power to heal, good judge of values
- *Negative:* intolerant, miserly, restless, overworked, domineering, easily discouraged, lack of planning

Love & Relationships

Your need for people suggests that love and relationships are particularly important to you. With your warm personality, you are likely to have many friends and work well in group efforts or partnerships. With a strong love of home and family, you feel that having roots and a solid foundation in life can be a significant part of your life plan. As you generally do not like to be alone, be careful not to become dependent in your romantic affairs. With your intense emotions, you can be devoted, loyal, and caring but may also have to watch out for occasional domineering behavior.

YOUR SPECIAL SOMEONE

You might find emotional fulfillment and that special someone among those born on the following days.

Love & friendship: Jan. 7, 12, 15, 27, Feb. 5, 10, 13, Mar. 3, 8, 11, 29, Apr. 1, 6, 9, 19, 27, May 4, 7, 25, 29, June 2, 5, 23, 27, July 3, 21, 25, Aug. 1, 19, 23, Sept. 11, 17, 21, Oct. 15, 19, 29, Nov. 13, 17, 27, Dec. 11, 15, 18, 25

Beneficial: Jan. 21, 25, Feb. 19, 23, Mar. 17, 21, 30, Apr. 15, 19, 28, May 13, 17, 26, June 11, 15, 24, 30, July 9, 13, 22, 28, Aug. 7, 11, 20, 26, 31, Sept. 5, 9, 18, 24, 29, Oct. 3, 7, 16, 22, 29, Nov. 1, 5, 14, 20, 25, Dec. 3, 12, 18, 23

Fatal attractions: June 26, 27, 28

Challenging: Jan. 5, 8, 28, Feb. 3, 6, 26, Mar. 1, 4, 24, Apr. 2, 22, May 20, June 18, July 16, Aug. 14, 30, Sept. 12, 28, 30, Oct. 10, 26, 28, Nov. 8, 24, 26, Dec. 6, 22, 24

Soul mates: Jan. 4, 10, Feb. 2, 8, Mar. 6, Apr. 4, May 2

December 28

♑ The influence of your birthday suggests that you are a charming and intelligent Capricorn who is sensitive and personable, yet hardworking. As you are well informed on many subjects and enthusiastic when involved in new projects, education can prove to be a significant factor in your life. Although you are quick, witty, and sociable, indecision or worry may turn out to be the primary challenge to your otherwise well-structured mind.

The subinfluence of your decanate ruler, Capricorn, suggests that in order to fulfill your need for self-expression, you probably have to overcome an inclination to be serious or shy. As an idealist, you have leadership and executive abilities. These talents particularly apply to establishing better conditions for others. By realizing the importance of organization or a good system, you can use your common sense and idealism as a source of inspiration and bring people together, especially if there is a mutual interest.

Since you possess a fast mind and hate to be bored, you are likely to restlessly search for new and original pursuits to keep you engrossed. Just be careful that this does not lead to nervousness, uncertainty, or emotional discontent. Ambitious, persistent, and practical, you can put up with difficult circumstances, but once you have had enough, you can become adamant. Since this birthday usually gives intuitive or psychic gifts, with age there is often a growing recognition of a higher wisdom.

After the age of twenty-four, when your progressed Sun goes into Aquarius, you become less influenced by appearances, more independent, and more trusting of your individuality. You may be more interested in unusual subjects, group affairs, or humanitarian issues. Another turning point occurs at the age of fifty-four, when your progressed Sun enters Pisces. From this time, there is more of an emphasis on your emotional needs and ideals, with an enhancement of your sensitivity and imagination.

Fixed Star

Star's name: Kaus Borealis

Degree position: 5°20'–6°19' Capricorn between the years 1930 and 2000

Magnitude: 3

Strength: ★★★★★

Orb: 1°40'

Constellation: Lambda Sagittarius

Applicable days: December 27, 28, 29

Star qualities: Mercury/Mars

Description: a giant orange star located in the northern part of the bow of the Archer

PRIMARY STAR'S INFLUENCE

Kaus Borealis imparts intelligence, a keen mentality, energetic and impressive speech, and good communication skills. A love of discussion and debate is also indicated by this star; however, at times you appear aggressive or argumentative. Frequently this star bestows ability at repartee, humanitarian tendencies, and an idealistic nature with a keen sense of justice. This star may also force changes on you and challenge your obstinacy.

Linked to your Sun's degree, Kaus Borealis imparts resoluteness and a drive to achieve positions of influence. Your leadership ability and ingenuity are often recognized by others and lead to accomplishment or promotion. Nevertheless, an inner restlessness and continual need to forge ahead may suggest discontent.

Your Secret Self

Deeply emotional and sensitive, you have an inner quest for love and affection that may not be noticed by others. You should always trust your heart rather than your head, which may at times be too rational or calculating. You are quietly dramatic, so guard against melancholy or selfishness by developing some form of creative pursuit, particularly music, that will enable you to express your powerful feelings of love.

Being highly intelligent, with personal magnetism, you have a strong sense of individuality. A spirit of enterprise can push your ambition into action and ensure that your big plans are successful. You may, however, have to guard against a rebellious or stubborn streak, which can undermine the self-discipline needed to make the most of your potential. Fortunately, you are connected to an intuitive source of higher knowledge that can bring you personal happiness and fulfillment through being of service to others.

Work & Vocation

Persuasive and charming, with organizational skills, you are ambitious and multitalented. Your interest in knowledge and your communication skills can lead you to a career in education, publishing, market research, media, or writing. Alternatively, you can demonstrate your administrative skills in the business world, politics, charitable organizations, and large enterprises such as the civil service. Enterprising, you will probably change your vocation at least once, as you need people and variety in your work environment. With an ability to think on a grand scale and a strong sense of independence, you may prefer the option of working as a freelancer or becoming self-employed.

Famous people born on your birthday are U.S. president Woodrow Wilson, actress Maggie Smith, actor Denzel Washington, and violinist Nigel Kennedy.

Numerology

Like a number 1 individual, you are ambitious, direct, and enterprising. Always ready for action and new ventures, you courageously take on life's challenges. With your enthusiasm, you can easily inspire others, if not to join you, at least to support you in your latest adventure. Although you are success-oriented and determined, family and home life are very important to you. Finding stability and taking care of your nearest and dearest may at times be a challenge for you. The subinfluence of the number 12 month indicates that you are idealistic and multi-talented, with a strong need to express yourself. When you believe in something, you are firm and inflexible. Although you dislike change, you like to plan ahead and safeguard the future. Emotionally sensitive and highly intuitive, you prefer to put your creative talents to some practical use. An ability to think on a large scale suggests that when you let your imagination flow, you can be resourceful and original.

• *Positive:* progressive, daring, artistic, creative, compassionate, idealistic, ambitious, hardworking, stable home life, strong-willed

• *Negative:* daydreamer, unmotivated, lack of compassion, unrealistic, bossy, bad judgment, lack of confidence, too dependent on others, pride

YOUR SPECIAL SOMEONE

You might find a long-lasting relationship with someone born on one of the following dates.

Love & friendship: Jan. 1, 2, 8, 19, 28, Feb. 6, 26, Mar. 4, 24, 30, Apr. 2, 22, 28, May 11, 20, 26, 30, June 18, 24, 28, July 16, 22, 26, Aug. 14, 20, 24, Sept. 3, 12, 18, 22, Oct. 10, 16, 20, 30, Nov. 8, 14, 18, 28, Dec. 6, 12, 16, 26

Beneficial: Jan. 18, 21, 22, Feb. 16, 19, 20, Mar. 14, 17, 18, 31, Apr. 12, 15, 16, 29, May 10, 13, 14, 27, June 8, 11, 12, 25, July 6, 9, 10, 23, Aug. 4, 7, 8, 21, 30, Sept. 2, 5, 6, 19, 28, 30, Oct. 3, 4, 17, 26, 28, Nov. 1, 2, 15, 24, 26, Dec. 13, 22, 24

Fatal attractions: June 26, 27, 28, 29, Oct. 29, Nov. 27, Dec. 25

Challenging: Jan. 29, Feb. 27, Mar. 25, Apr. 23, May 21, June 19, July 17, Aug. 15, 30, Sept. 13, 28, Oct. 11, 26, Nov. 9, 24, Dec. 7, 22

Soul mates: Jan. 24, 27, 28, Feb. 22, 25, 26, Mar. 20, 23, 24, Apr. 18, 21, 22, May 16, 19, 20, June 14, 17, 18, 30, July 12, 15, 16, 28, Aug. 10, 13, 14, 26, Sept. 8, 11, 12, 24, Oct. 6, 9, 10, 22, Nov. 4, 7, 8, 20, Dec. 2, 5, 6, 18, 30

Love & Relationships

Your natural charm and amiable personality guarantee friendships, and once you have overcome your shyness and ultrasensitivity, you become a witty and highly entertaining companion. In your personal relationships you are drawn to creative or intelligent people with strong personalities with whom you can have a mental rapport. An element of doubt or uncertainty may cause indecisiveness and affect your relationships. By keeping yourself positive and creatively occupied, you are able to stay light-hearted and avoid worry.

December 29

Sensitive, with a natural gift for dealing with people, you are a charming and creative Capricorn. Your good communication skills, agreeable manner, and social grace allow you to play the courteous diplomat. Although you have high ideals, you can also be practical, and usually you are willing to work hard in order to achieve your objectives.

With the subinfluence of your decanate ruler, Capricorn, you can be dedicated and conscientious when you believe in a cause or a project. As a pragmatist and good planner, you enjoy being constructive and have a shrewd understanding of how to sell or promote an idea or product. An ungrounded fear of not having enough money may sometimes emerge to cause you concern, but your excellent people skills and commitment will always ensure that you have ample funds at your disposal.

Highly imaginative, you are a creative thinker and hardworking visionary. You may use these abilities to advance in business; alternatively, you may be inspired by your innate artistic and spiritual talents. Having a pleasant voice and being aware of your image, you can appear attractive to others. Combined with your love of luxury, you may have to be careful of a streak of vanity or extravagance.

After the age of twenty-three, when your progressed Sun goes into Aquarius, you become less influenced by rules and tradition. By letting go of the past, you become more independent and trusting of your own unique perspective. You may become interested in group affairs, humanitarian issues, or expressing your individuality. Another turning point occurs at the age of fifty-three, when your progressed Sun enters Pisces. From this time, there is more of an emphasis on your emotional inner life, reflected through your visions, dreams, and intuitive understanding of your relationships with others.

Fixed Star

Star's name: Kaus Borealis

Degree position: 5°20'–6°19' Capricorn between the years 1930 and 2000

Magnitude: 3

Strength: ★★★★★★

Orb: 1°40'

Constellation: Lambda Sagittarius

Applicable days: December 27, 28, 29

Star qualities: Mercury/Mars

Description: a giant orange star located in the northern part of the bow of the Archer

Primary Star's Influence

Kaus Borealis imparts intelligence, a keen mentality, energetic and impressive speech, and good communication skills. A love of discussion and debate is also indicated by this star; however, at times you appear aggressive or argumentative. Frequently this star bestows ability at repartee, humanitarian tendencies, and an idealistic nature with a keen sense of justice. This star may also force changes on you and challenge your obstinacy.

Linked to your Sun's degree, Kaus Borealis imparts resoluteness and a drive to achieve positions of influence. Your leadership ability and ingenuity are often recognized by others and lead to accomplishment or promotion. Nevertheless, an inner restlessness and continual need to forge ahead may suggest discontent.

• Positive: versatile, determined, knowledgeable, outspoken

• Negative: lack of satisfaction, extremist, opinionated

Your Secret Self

Although love is especially important to you, the quest for knowledge and the development of your deeper understanding are also vital to your emotional fulfillment. Education, whether self-directed or through more formal channels, can be a key to stimulating your desire for information and wisdom.

A need to constantly initiate new projects that keep you mentally challenged suggests that you may find satisfaction in greater self-awareness and the opportunity to share your findings with others. When your self-mastery and knowledge are combined, you may find yourself as an advisor to others or that you have natural leadership qualities. By connecting your natural idealism and compassion to a larger framework, you can also avoid pessimism or negative thinking.

Work & Vocation

Charming and charismatic, you are engaging and thoughtful. An ability to work with the public suggests that you can accomplish much in sales and promotion. Interested in knowledge, you may be drawn to a career in education as a teacher or lecturer. Since you also have technical abilities, you may be interested in information and communication technology. An ability to assimilate information and utilize it may inspire you to learn many languages and work in international organizations as an interpreter. Alternatively, you may wish to pursue a career in politics or public service. An interest in the arts and a talent for writing may inspire you to compose music, write poetry, or play a musical instrument.

Famous people who share your birthday include actors Jon Voight and Ted Danson, cellist Pablo Casals, actress Mary Tyler Moore, and singer Marianne Faithfull.

Numerology

As a number 29 individual, you are often highly intuitive, sensitive, and emotional. Your compassionate and understanding nature inspires humanitarianism and can encourage others to fulfill their hopes and aspirations. Although you are a true dreamer, often the extreme sides of your personality indicate that you have to guard against alternating moods. With a number 29 birthday, you need to be popular and may care what others think about you. The subinfluence of the number 12 month implies that you are sociable and friendly, although you may appear shy and reserved. A pragmatic outlook and a willingness to work hard for material prosperity imply that although you are security-conscious, you may need to overcome a tendency to worry about money. You like the freedom of being independent, but learning to share and trust may benefit you greatly in close relationships, partnerships, or collaborating with others in a group effort.

• *Positive:* inspirational, balanced, successful, mystical, creative, intuitive, powerful dreams, attention to detail, faith

• *Negative:* unfocused, moody, difficult, extremist, inconsiderate of others, overly sensitive

Love & Relationships

A strong need for companionship emphasizes the importance of your personal relationships. Although always looking for an ideal love, you are stimulated by successful and creative people and prefer to associate with those of wealth, status, or artistic ability. Once committed to a relationship, you will work hard to keep peace and harmony, even to the point of making sacrifices. You can find friends and enjoyment through sharing your mutual creative and intellectual interests.

YOUR SPECIAL SOMEONE

For your ideal partner, you might begin by looking for someone born on one of the following days.

Love & friendship: Jan. 5, 6, 14, 16, 31, Feb. 12, 14, Mar. 1, 2, 10, 12, 31, Apr. 8, 10, 25, 29, May 6, 8, 27, June 4, 6, 25, July 2, 4, 23, 29, Aug. 2, 21, 27, Sept. 15, 19, 25, Oct. 17, 23, 31, Nov. 15, 21, 29, Dec. 13, 19, 27

Beneficial: Jan. 19, 22, 30, Feb. 17, 20, 28, Mar. 15, 18, 26, Apr. 13, 16, 24, 30, May 11, 14, 22, 28, June 9, 12, 20, 26, July 7, 10, 18, 24, Aug. 5, 8, 16, 22, Sept. 3, 6, 14, 20, Oct. 1, 4, 12, 18, 29, Nov. 2, 10, 16, 27, Dec. 8, 14, 25

Fatal attractions: June 27, 28, 29, 30

Challenging: Jan. 11, 25, 26, Feb. 9, 23, 24, Mar. 7, 21, 22, Apr. 5, 19, 20, May 3, 17, 18, 29, June 1, 15, 16, 27, July 13, 14, 25, Aug. 11, 12, 23, Sept. 9, 10, 21, 30, Oct. 7, 8, 19, 28, Nov. 5, 6, 17, 26, Dec. 3, 4, 15, 24

Soul mates: May 31, June 29, July 27, Aug. 25, Sept. 23, Oct. 21, Nov. 19, Dec. 17

December 30

VS With good communication skills and a unique perspective on life, you tend to be a practical, sharp, and amusing Capricorn. A creative approach to life suggests that you are friendly and sociable, with a strong desire for love and self-expression. Just be careful that a tendency to worry or be indecisive does not spoil your remarkable potential.

With the subinfluence of your decanate ruler, Capricorn, you are always aware that you do not get anything in life without effort. Having strong willpower, you are usually dedicated and hardworking when you are involved in exciting activities. Your many interests and a desire for variety suggest that you can enjoy different experiences; you may have to beware, however, of scattering your forces in too many directions.

Being smart and responsive, you have a strong need to be with people and often act as a messenger of ideas. Although your sensitivity can be useful in artistic pursuits or helping others, you may have to avoid overreacting emotionally or becoming too self-absorbed. Impressionable when it comes to your environment, you need to be in harmonious surroundings. This can help you develop your innate universal understanding and emotional detachment, thus avoiding disappointment with others.

Before the age of twenty-one, you are likely to be cautious and realistic in your approach to life. After the age of twenty-two, however, when your progressed Sun moves into Aquarius, you become less influenced by the opinions of others, more independent, and desirous of expressing your individuality. Friends, group affairs, or humanitarian issues may start to play a stronger role in your life. Another turning point occurs at the age of fifty-two, when your progressed Sun enters Pisces. From this time there is an emphasis on your enhanced sensitivity and feeling. You will be more receptive and imaginative, or you may experience an urge to develop or appreciate creative talents.

FIXED STAR

Star's name: Facies

Degree position: 7°12'–8°24' Capricorn between the years 1930 and 2000

Magnitude: 5

Strength: ★★

Orb: 1°

Constellation: M22 Sagittarius

Applicable days: December 29, 30, 31

Star qualities: Sun/Mars

Description: a bright open star cluster and nebula located in the bow of the Archer

PRIMARY STAR'S INFLUENCE

Facies imparts assertiveness, a fighting spirit, and a fearless natures. You are full of vitality and vigor, and usually you wish to exercise power and have the necessary leadership qualities. Facies grants the ability to make decisions quickly, and you are a good strategist who can enjoy competitive activities and win.

Linked to your Sun's degree, this star bestows success in business and dealing with the public as well as strong willpower, inner drive, and a competitive spirit. This star also warns that the constant need to be number one may involve some risks, and suggests avoiding underhanded dealings and dangerous situations.

• *Positive:* will to live, active life, power of attainment, decisiveness

• *Negative:* overstrain, obstinacy, inclination to quarrel

Your Secret Self

As loving and affectionate as you are, a strong inner desire for material success can motivate you into action. Your need for money and status can at times clash with your sensitive ideals. This indicates that you may vacillate between the two extremes or be at your best when receiving financial rewards for supporting a cause or belief. While you possess inherent leadership skills, it would be wise to avoid becoming too demanding.

When positively inspired, you are able to spread happiness to all. Intelligent and well informed, you dislike boredom and are likely to search restlessly for new and original pursuits to keep your mind engrossed. A basic uncertainty about emotional concerns or discontent with your situation may drain you of your positivity. It is therefore important to continually find creative outlets for your many talents. With age you gradually come to realize the importance of a higher wisdom that can help you utilize your innate intuitive gifts.

Work & Vocation

Creative and dynamic, you have an engaging personality and a down-to-earth approach. With your natural diplomatic skills, you enjoy work involving cooperation with others and are in your element when you can mix business and pleasure. If you believe in an idea or a project, you show commitment and enthusiasm. Being independent, with natural leadership skills, you prefer to delegate tasks rather than take orders. This may stimulate you to apply for management positions or work for yourself. With an urge for action and a talent for inspiring others, you often thrive on new beginnings or exciting challenges. Art, music, or writing may also prove attractive to you, either professionally or as a recreational activity.

Famous people who share your birthday include writer Rudyard Kipling, blues guitarist Bo Diddley, singer Patti Smith, comedienne Tracey Ullman, and baseball player Sandy Koufax.

Numerology

Artistic, friendly, and sociable are just some of the ways others would describe people born on this day. You enjoy the good life, love socializing, and can be exceptionally charismatic, loyal, and friendly. Gregarious, with good taste and an eye for style and form, you can achieve success in all types of work concerning art, design, and music. Similarly, a need for self-expression and a natural talent for words may inspire you to explore writing, speaking, or singing. You possess strong feelings, and being in love or contented is a vital requirement. In your pursuit of happiness, avoid being lazy or overindulgent. Among those with number 30 birthdays, many will find recognition or fame, especially musicians, actors, and entertainers. The subinfluence of the number 12 month indicates that you are idealistic, with the ability to captivate others. Aesthetic and particular, you like to pay attention to details, but a tendency to be fastidious suggests that you should refrain from criticizing. An ability to synthesize concepts and expand them often allows you to initiate new projects or revive old ideas by injecting them with new life.

- *Positive:* fun-loving, loyal, friendly, good conversationalist, creative, lucky
- *Negative:* lazy, obstinate, erratic, impatient, temperamental, jealous, insecure, indifferent

Love & Relationships

Witty and dynamic, you have a charming and charismatic personality. Friendly and sociable, you can attract the love and affection you need from others. Women can play an especially fortunate part in assisting you in life. You may particularly enjoy the company of dramatic and creative people, who can encourage you to become more gregarious and dramatic. At times, however, doubt or indecision may affect your close relationships, and you can then become influenced by issues of security.

YOUR SPECIAL SOMEONE

Your chances of finding happiness and a loving partner are increased with those born on the following dates.

Love & friendship: Jan. 5, 6, 7, 15, 17, Feb. 3, 5, 13, 15, Mar. 1, 2, 3, 11, 13, Apr. 1, 9, 11, 27, 30, May 7, 9, 28, June 5, 7, 26, July 3, 5, 24, 30, Aug. 1, 3, 22, 28, Sept. 1, 17, 20, 26, Oct. 18, 24, Nov. 16, 22, 30, Dec. 14, 20, 28

Beneficial: Jan. 8, 20, 31, Feb. 6, 18, 29, Mar. 4, 16, 27, Apr. 2, 14, 25, May 12, 23, 29, June 10, 21, 27, July 8, 19, 25, Aug. 6, 17, 23, Sept. 4, 15, 21, Oct. 2, 3, 13, 19, 30, Nov. 11, 17, 28, Dec. 9, 15, 26

Fatal attractions: June 28, 29, 30, July 1

Challenging: Jan. 11, 12, 27, Feb. 9, 10, 25, Mar. 7, 8, 23, Apr. 5, 6, 21, May 3, 4, 19, 30, June 1, 2, 17, 28, July 15, 26, Aug. 13, 24, Sept. 11, 22, Oct. 9, 20, 29, Nov. 7, 18, 27, Dec. 5, 16, 25

Soul mates: Jan. 26, Feb. 24, Mar. 22, Apr. 20, May 18, June 16, July 14, Aug. 12, Sept. 10, Oct. 8, Nov. 6, 30, Dec. 4, 28

December 31

V♑ Serious yet charismatic, you have a strong sense of presence and individuality that marks you out as someone special. With your audacious charm, you like to be the center of attention and are extremely persistent in obtaining your objectives. Sometimes melancholy or pessimistic, but always self-aware, you organize your life along practical lines to get the maximum returns from any situation. Through self-discipline you are able to make the most of your many talents and remarkable potential.

The subinfluence of your decanate ruler, Capricorn, indicates that you are keen on timing and structure. Consequently, you may experience considerable anxiety during periods of change and instability. A desire to be impeccably reliable also suggests that you like to take charge or be in control. Your pragmatism and strong awareness of material considerations, however, can sometimes cause you to vacillate between being mercenary and being capable of profound insight.

Striving to be independent, you are aware of image and first impressions. Being hard-working and organized, once committed to a project or cause you are capable of remarkable output. Usually dramatic, with powerful projection and strong opinions, you need to find some form of self-expression through which you can obtain the respect you desire. Often you are blessed with strong intuitive gifts and an ability to fight difficult situations and be self-regenerating.

Before the age of twenty, you are inclined to have a need for practical order and structure in your life. After the age of twenty-one, when your progressed Sun moves into Aquarius, you become less influenced by tradition and more independent. New opportunities to present your own unique perspective may encourage you to take an interest in group affairs or humanitarian issues. Another turning point occurs at the age of fifty-one, when your progressed Sun enters Pisces. From this time, there is more of an emphasis on developing sensitivity, imagination, and a strong inner life. This can be reflected through your visions, dreams, and emotional ideals.

Your Secret Self

A wonderful childlike innocence will stay with you throughout your life. Not only can this give you a youthful quality, but it also enables you to be imaginative and creative. Although you are usually positive and optimistic, there are times when you may succumb to anxieties or imaginary fears.

At your best you can be amazingly strong and possess an almost transcendent humility. You are willing to make sacrifices and share your deep compassion in helping or being of service to others. Obstacles to realizing your profound potential are a selfish and dramatic streak or an oversensitivity that can cause you to exaggerate every failure into a tragedy. Although some of the lessons in your youth may have been uncomfortable, as you get older and wiser you benefit from these experiences. An increase in self-discipline is often needed in order to achieve fulfillment and happiness.

Work & Vocation

Usually enterprising and multitalented, you have a wide choice of options at your disposal. Ambitious and goal-oriented, with excellent business skills, you are willing to work hard, es-

FIXED STAR

Star's name: Facies

Degree position: 7°12'–8°24' Capricorn between the years 1930 and 2000

Magnitude: 5

Strength: ★★

Orb: 1°

Constellation: M22 Sagittarius

Applicable days: December 29, 30, 31

Star qualities: Sun/Mars

Description: a bright open star cluster and nebula located in the bow of the Archer

PRIMARY STAR'S INFLUENCE

Facies imparts assertiveness, a fighting spirit, and a fearless nature; you are full of vitality and vigor. Usually you wish to exercise power and have the necessary leadership qualities. Facies grants the ability to make decisions quickly, and you are a good strategist who can enjoy competitive activities and win.

Linked to your Sun's degree, this star bestows success in business and dealing with the public. Facies bestows strong willpower, inner drive, and a competitive spirit. This star also warns that the constant need to be number one may involve some risks, and suggests avoiding underhanded dealings and dangerous situations.

• Positive: will to live, active life, power of attainment, decisiveness

• Negative: overstrain, obstinacy, inclination to quarrel

pecially when inspired by a project or interested in a special subject. Since you want to excel at what you do, having a vocation, rather than just a career, is likely to take you to the top of your profession. Independent, with a pragmatic approach and executive skills, you enjoy organizing big events. Dramatic, sensitive, and creative, you are highly suitable for the theater or the opera. A talent for words and writing can inspire you to put pen to paper. With an engaging voice and a knack for conversation, you are an excellent orator, teacher, or lecturer.

Famous people who share your birthday include artist Henri Matisse, beauty entrepreneur Elizabeth Arden, astrologer Noel Tyl, singers John Denver, Donna Summer, and Odetta, and actors Ben Kingsley and Anthony Hopkins.

Numerology

Strong willpower, determination, and an emphasis on self-expression are indicated by the number 31 birthday. Usually you are tireless and determined, with a desire to make material progress. You may have to learn, however, to accept the limitations of life and build a solid foundation. Good fortune and lucky opportunities also suggest that you can be successful in turning your leisure-time pursuits into profitable ventures. Having fun is crucial to you, as you are very hardworking. You may have to guard against tendencies to be selfish or overly optimistic. The subinfluence of the number 12 month indicates that you are creative and multitalented. Although you are sociable and friendly, you are an independent thinker and therefore a law unto yourself. Adventurous and enterprising, you seek fulfillment through personal expression. Your inner growth occurs through overcoming obstacles and challenges. If you want to gain true wisdom, you should turn away from the material world or from occupations that provide only financial benefits.

• *Positive:* lucky, creative, original, builder, constructive, persistent, practical, good conversationalist, responsible

• *Negative:* insecure, impatient, suspicious, easily discouraged, lack of ambition, selfish, stubborn

Love & Relationships

With your charm, charisma, and natural dramatic sense, you can easily attract friends and admirers. Although very protective of those you love or those in your care, you can also at times be quite demanding. Hospitable and attentive, you can be an excellent host and show a genuine concern for others. While you may occasionally suffer from down moods, you can be a warm, responsible, and affectionate lover and a loyal companion.

January 1

♑ The influence of your birthday suggests that you are an ambitious and down-to-earth Capricorn who prefers to be in positions of power. Self-mastery and a strong sense of purpose are vital keys to your success and happiness; without these, you may be prone to restlessness and discontent. You possess a tremendous potential for inspired leadership if you do not shy away from your responsibilities.

With the subinfluence of your decanate ruler, Taurus, once you decide on a course of action you have the power to attain your goal, even if it takes a long time. Practical, with the ability to endure, you can be very hardworking when interested in a project or an activity. Loyal and dedicated, you are capable of making great sacrifices for what you want. You possess an appreciation or talent for music or drama, which you can develop for pleasure and relaxation. You may, however, need to avoid being bossy or selfish, which can spoil your otherwise good fortune.

Your versatility and desire for change can bring you an interest in many different subjects. Being clever and desiring knowledge, you are drawn to people of intelligence. In your early years you develop an independent attitude, which you rely on throughout your life. Not renowned for taking advice from others, you can be stubborn or obstinate on occasion. One of your challenges is to rise above petty emotional considerations and express ideal love through service.

Before the age of nineteen you are likely to take your approach to life quite seriously. After the age of twenty, however, when your progressed Sun moves into Aquarius, you become less influenced by the opinions of others, more independent, and keen to express your individuality. Friends, group affairs, or humanitarian issues may start to play a stronger role in your life. By middle age, you should have your goals clearly defined in order to avoid frustration and impatience. Another turning point occurs at the age of fifty, when your progressed Sun enters Pisces. From this time, there is an emphasis on your enhanced sensitivity and feeling. You will be more receptive and imaginative or may experience an urge to develop your creative talents. By learning to trust your intuition, you develop self-assurance and have a clearer vision.

Your Secret Self

Although you possess an inner knowing, nobility, and pride, there can also be a deeper feeling that you are not good enough, and this often drives you to accomplish. If you feel uncertain yourself, you may set about trying to control other people or situations. You may need to acknowledge that you desire popularity or acceptance from others, even though this may cause you some embarrassment. Each individual battle you fight, however, gradually builds up your self-confidence. Strength comes from a realistic appraisal of your talents and limitations and an understanding of the power of your potential.

While you may have all your defenses well fortified in early life, as you get older you are likely to become less serious and more light-hearted. Having learned many of your lessons the hard way, you become your own finest authority figure, very self-reliant and determined.

Work & Vocation

Authoritative and independent, with administrative skills and executive abilities, you like to take charge or be in a leading position. Intuitive and shrewd, you can comprehend what moti-

---

FIXED STAR

Star's name: Pelagus, also called Nunki

Degree position: 11°15'–12°21'
Capricorn between the years
1930 and 2000

Magnitude: 2

Strength: ★★★★★★★

Orb: 2°10'

Constellation: Sigma Sagittarius

Applicable days: January 1, 2, 3, 4, 5

Star qualities: Mercury/Jupiter

Description: a star located on the vane of the arrow at the Archer's hand

PRIMARY STAR'S INFLUENCE

Pelagus's influence bestows a love of truthfulness, a strong character, and a direct and assertive manner. This star imparts determination to achieve success and sound common sense. Pelagus urges the individual toward education and higher learning, especially in science, philosophy, history, and spirituality. This star also indicates an outspoken personality and strong convictions.

Linked to your Sun's degree, Pelagus bestows creativity and a wealth of ideas, a rise to influential public position, and favorable conditions at home and with family matters. You can make a name for yourself, and even though you sometimes become involved in complex situations, you usually come out unscathed.

• *Positive:* higher learning, sound common sense, love of truth

• *Negative:* controversial, failure through dishonesty

vates other people. With your business skills and enterprising approach, you are usually self-employed, or you may work as an originator, politician, or producer. If employed by others, you are usually an executive, manager, or foreman. With the potential to excel in all kinds of creative endeavors and business enterprise, you especially like to work for big corporations and government establishments, where you can display your leadership abilities. Usually you prefer to specialize in a particular field and have a formal profession rather than being involved in pure business. Hardworking and dedicated, you need to learn to take other people's needs into consideration.

Famous people who share your birthday include FBI chief J. Edgar Hoover, writer J. D. Salinger, American revolutionary Paul Revere, and U.S. politician Barry Goldwater.

Numerology

The great desire to be first and autonomous is suggested by your birthdate. With a number 1 birthday, you are inclined to be individualistic, innovative, and courageous, with plenty of energy. The pioneering spirit indicated here encourages you to make your own decisions or strike out alone. Full of enthusiasm and original ideas, you often show others the way forward. With a number 1 birthday, you may also need to learn that the world does not revolve around you. The subinfluence of the number 1 month indicates that you are creative and highly intuitive, with a perceptive and idealistic nature. Inspired and resolute, you have a forceful character. Usually, you like to dictate to others and are better at giving orders than receiving them. If you find it hard to express your feelings, you may appear cold or uncaring. Learn to trust your powerful intuition and do not entertain negative thoughts. You may need to learn the art of compromise by avoiding a tendency to be inflexible or adamant.

• *Positive:* leadership, creative, progressive, forceful, optimistic, strong convictions, competitive, independent, gregarious

• *Negative:* jealous, egotistical, antagonistic, lack of restraint, impatient

Love & Relationships

Intelligent and with quick understanding, you get bored easily and need variety and adventure in your social life. Attracted to resourceful people, you can be a loyal friend or partner. With your strong personality, you do not usually suffer fools gladly but can be very charming when necessary. With your need for knowledge, order, and security, you can be a good parent but may have to watch being overbearing with those you love. As much as you need love yourself, it does not override practical considerations. Nevertheless, the more affection you show to others, the better.

YOUR SPECIAL SOMEONE

You might find stimulating company and happiness among those born on the following dates.

Love & friendship: Jan. 9, 30, Feb. 7, 28, Mar. 5, 26, Apr. 3, 24, May 1, 22, 30, 31, June 20, 28, 29, July 18, 26, 27, Aug. 16, 24, 25, Sept. 14, 22, 23, Oct. 12, 20, 21, Nov. 10, 18, 19, Dec. 8, 16, 17, 29

Beneficial: Jan. 4, 6, 8, 21, Feb. 2, 4, 19, Mar. 2, 17, Apr. 15, May 13, June 11, July 9, Aug. 7, Sept. 5, Oct. 3, Nov. 1

Fatal attractions: July 1, 2, 3, 4, 5

Challenging: Jan. 25, Feb. 23, Mar. 21, 31, Apr. 19, 29, May 17, 27, June 15, 25, July 13, 23, Aug. 11, 21, Sept. 9, 19, Oct. 7, 17, Nov. 5, 15, Dec. 3, 13

Soul mates: Jan. 2, 13, Feb. 11, Mar. 9, Apr. 17, May 5, Nov. 21

January 2

♑ The influence of your birthday shows you to be ambitious and persistent, a serious and hardworking Capricorn. As a practical and down-to-earth individual with sharp mental abilities, you show an excellent capacity for learning. Education is particularly helpful for bringing out the best of your potential. One of your major lessons, however, is mastering a positive attitude toward money and relationships.

With the subinfluence of your decanate ruler, Taurus, there is a strong need for love and affection and harmonious working relationships. A lover of beauty and the arts, you can be creative but like to put your talents to a useful purpose. You have an innate understanding of the value of things and are practical enough to get the best out of situations. Due to your love of quality and luxury, however, you may not stop to consider whether you are spending more than you can afford.

Your original ideas and ability to be a shrewd judge of human nature suggest that you have excellent opportunities for success. Your date of birth does imply, however, a need for a certain amount of hard work and self-discipline in order to achieve your goals. Fortunately, you are born with the endurance to accomplish your ambitions, as long as you avoid tension in your relationships. One of your major challenges is to acknowledge and believe in your abilities. If you cannot manage this, you will find that you are taking positions well beneath your capabilities.

Before the age of eighteen you are likely to have a strong need for practical order and structure in your life. After the age of nineteen, when your progressed Sun moves into Aquarius, you desire more independence and freedom, with friendship becoming more important in your life. You may have an interest in more unusual subjects or want to express your own unique ideas. Another turning point occurs at the age of forty-nine, when your progressed Sun enters Pisces. From this time there is more of an emphasis on developing your sensitivity and a strong inner life. This can be reflected through your visions, dreams, and emotional ideals.

FIXED STAR

Star's name: Pelagus, also called Nunki

Degree position: 11°15'–12°21'
    Capricorn between the years
    1930 and 2000

Magnitude: 2

Strength: ★★★★★★★

Orb: 2°10'

Constellation: Sigma Sagittarius

Applicable days: January 1, 2, 3, 4, 5

Star qualities: Mercury/Jupiter

Description: a star located on the vane of the arrow at the Archer's hand

PRIMARY STAR'S INFLUENCE

Pelagus's influence bestows a love of truthfulness, strong character, and a direct and assertive manner. This star imparts determination to achieve success and sound common sense. Pelagus urges you toward education and higher learning, especially science, philosophy, history, and spirituality. This star also indicates an outspoken personality and strong convictions.

Linked to your Sun's degree, Pelagus bestows creativity and a wealth of ideas, a rise to influential public position, and favorable conditions at home and with family matters. You can make a name for yourself, and even though you sometimes become involved in complex situations, you usually come out unscathed.

• *Positive:* higher learning, sound common sense, love of truth

• *Negative:* controversial, failure through dishonesty

Your Secret Self

An innate ability to turn anything into a business must not be confused with the success that comes from doing something you believe is of real value. Although you possess an excellent capacity for earning wealth, pursuing activities for mere financial gain is liable to leave you outwardly successful but not always inwardly content. It is therefore important to learn to translate your money skills into worthy projects that in turn leave you feeling happier.

Being determined, you always aim for the top. You enjoy power and find strength in dedicating yourself to a specific goal or purpose. Without this control, you may become insecure and stubborn or you may even experience extremes of mood, from passion to indifference. Nevertheless, being sensitive provides the protection of intuitive insight that in turn can help solve many of life's dilemmas for yourself or others.

Work & Vocation

Ambitious and creative, with success in mind, you often collaborate with others in business. Usually you are highly intuitive and have a strong intellectual potential. When these are combined with your sensitivity, you do well in healing, teaching, or scientific research. Authoritative and hardworking, you often act as a media and public relations person, arbitrator, or manager for other people. A good psychologist, you have a natural disposition for writing that may be developed later on in life. Alternatively, you may choose to explore your creativity through art, photography, music, or the theater. Since you need to express yourself and gain wisdom, pure business is not satisfactory in the long run. The best field may be education or service to the community as a social worker and educator.

Famous people who share your birthday include writer Isaac Asimov, opera singer Renata Tebaldi, dancer Vera Zorina, French saint Thérèse de Lisieux, and photographer David Bailey.

Numerology

Sensitivity and a strong need to be part of a group are suggested by your number 2 birthday. Often you are adaptable and understanding, and you enjoy cooperative activities. A love of harmony and a desire to interact with others may inspire you to act as a mediator or become a peacemaker. In your attempt to please, you may run the risk of becoming overdependent. The subinfluence of the number 1 month indicates that you are highly intuitive and imaginative. The initiatory spirit indicated here encourages you to make your own decisions or strike out alone. You are inclined to be independent, innovative, and courageous, with plenty of energy. Usually you are broad-minded and liberal, though at times you may have fixed ideas. As a humanitarian who is sympathetic, you seek wisdom and justice. A need to explore the mysteries of life may inspire you to study and teach metaphysics and philosophy. Avoid being hasty and overemotional, reacting in an extreme manner to situations. You may find that you are happiest when serving the public and bringing about reforms or enlightment.

• *Positive:* considerate, good partner, gentle, tactful, receptive, intuitive, harmonious, agreeable, ambassador of goodwill

• *Negative:* suspicious, lack of confidence, timid, oversensitive, selfish, easily hurt, deceitful

Love & Relationships

Sensual and with strong attractions, you desire love and affection. With your need for companionship, it is important to have friendship in your love relationships. You must avoid getting petty or frustrated in your daily affairs, as this can be a source of discontent in relationships. Usually you are loyal to and supportive of your partner. You can be generous with the people you love, although there may be conflict in relationships or marriage around issues of money. You may possibly find that later in life others will turn to you for advice and guidance.

YOUR SPECIAL SOMEONE

For that special person you might try someone born on one of the following dates.

Love & friendship: Jan. 4, 18, 21, 31, Feb. 2, 16, 19, 29, Mar. 14, 17, 27, Apr. 12, 15, 25, 27, May 10, 13, 23, 25, June 8, 11, 21, July 6, 9, 19, 31, Aug. 4, 7, 17, 29, Sept. 2, 15, 17, 27, 30, Oct. 3, 13, 25, 28, Nov. 1, 11, 13, 23, Dec. 9, 21, 24, 30

Beneficial: Jan. 6, Feb. 4, Mar. 2, May 30, June 28, July 26, Aug. 24, Sept. 22, 30, Oct. 20, 28, Nov. 18, 26, Dec. 16, 24

Fatal attractions: June 30, July 3, 4, 5, 6, 28, Aug. 26, Sept. 24, Oct. 22, Nov. 20, Dec. 18

Challenging: Jan. 27, Feb. 25, Mar. 23, Apr. 21, May 19, June 17, July 15, Aug. 13, Sept. 11, Oct. 9, Nov. 7, Dec. 5

Soul mates: Jan. 17, 19, Feb. 15, 17, Mar. 13, 15, Apr. 11, 13, May 9, 11, June 7, 9, July 5, 7, Aug. 3, 5, Sept. 1, 3, Oct. 1

SUN: CAPRICORN
DECANATE: TAURUS/VENUS
DEGREE: 11°–13° CAPRICORN
MODE: CARDINAL
ELEMENT: EARTH

January 3

♑ You are a dynamic and creative Capricorn, with sharp, quick mental responses. If you are interested in a project or idea, the influence of your birthday makes you ambitious and hardworking. Usually you are an independent thinker who is particularly inventive when challenged, but you must guard against taking the easy option and not living up to your true potential. Although you will always have a youthful quality, it is through developing perseverance and a responsible attitude that you are able to achieve almost anything.

With the subinfluence of your decanate ruler, Taurus, you can be extremely charming, especially when it is in your own interests. Appearance is important to you, and you have a keen eye for style and beauty. This date of birth often bestows musical or dramatic appreciation or talent that you may wish to develop. With good financial know-how and strong survival instincts, you can accumulate wealth and utilize your surroundings to your advantage. Essential to your success and accomplishment are education, planning, and a dedicated, methodical approach.

You have the choice between using the discipline of your birthday or being manipulative to attain your desires. It is wise to avoid negative thinking and a worrisome attitude. When positive, you possess a certain dignity that comes from an awareness of your high calling, yet you still remain modest and maintain a desire to give your best to your work. Although you have a tendency to be skeptical, you come to develop an independent and free-thinking philosophy.

Before the age of seventeen you are likely to be watchful in your approach to life. After the age of eighteen, however, when your progressed Sun moves into Aquarius, you become more independent and less influenced by tradition or the opinions of others. You have a strong desire to express your individuality; friends, group affairs, or humanitarian issues may also start to play a stronger role in your life. By your middle years you come to realize that nothing is free and in order to succeed you must invest time and effort. Another turning point occurs at the age of forty-eight, when your progressed Sun enters Pisces. From this time, there is an emphasis on your enhanced sensitivity and feelings. You will be more receptive, imaginative, and compassionate or be drawn to spiritual interests.

FIXED STAR

Star's name: Pelagus, also called Nunki
Degree position: 11°15'–12°21'
    Capricorn between the years
    1930 and 2000
Magnitude: 2
Strength: ★★★★★★★
Orb: 2°10'
Constellation: Sigma Sagittarius
Applicable days: January 1, 2, 3, 4, 5
Star qualities: Mercury/Jupiter
Description: a star located on the vane
    of the arrow at the Archer's hand

PRIMARY STAR'S INFLUENCE

Pelagus's influence bestows a love of truthfulness, strong character, and a direct and assertive manner. This star imparts sound common sense and determination to achieve success. Pelagus urges the individual toward education and higher learning, especially science, philosophy, history, and spirituality. This star also indicates an outspoken personality and strong convictions.

Linked to your Sun's degree, Pelagus bestows creativity and a wealth of ideas, a rise to influential public position, and favorable conditions at home and with family matters. You can make a name for yourself, and even though you sometimes become involved in complex situations, you usually come out unscathed.

• Positive: higher learning, sound common sense, love of truth

• Negative: controversial, failure through dishonesty

Your Secret Self

Success comes when you experience real enthusiasm; it is not something you can fake. By feeling spirited, you are able to give your all. This imbues you with a firm inner conviction that you are going to win and achieve extraordinary results. In your quest for achievement and mastery, you need to keep mentally challenging yourself. When in doubt, you may respond with skepticism or cynicism. By having faith instead, you can be more daring and spontaneous, and if you include friendly competition, you usually enjoy your work better.

As you like current and exciting concepts or activities, you enjoy initiating new ventures and getting others moving in an adventurous way. Good at fighting for humanitarian issues or pushing forward some type of reform, you can inspire others to take action. With your natural awareness that knowledge is power, you harbor an excellent ability to mentally structure your achievements and hence possess the potential for outstanding success. In later years you experience some powerful realizations as you come to understand the value of love.

Work & Vocation

Enterprising and idealistic, with executive abilities, you are an initiator or a good trouble-shooter. Intuition and an ability to think quickly imply that you need to be active and like things to be well defined. An ability to mix business and pleasure indicates that you are friendly and helpful. If in business, you need to have faith and a vision in order to succeed. As a maverick, you are enterprising and original, but need to use orthodox methods. Your courage and idealism may inspire you to fight against social injustice. With your leadership and organizational skill, you usually take charge of situations. Your friendly approach can also be good for sales and promotion. As a humanitarian or social reformer, you make an excellent teacher, and a talent for writing suggests that you can put pen to paper.

Famous people born on your birthday include actor Mel Gibson, musician Stephen Stills, actress Victoria Principal, writer J. R. R. Tolkien, record producer George Martin, and film director Sergio Leone.

Numerology

A need for creativity is indicated by the number 3 birthday. Often fun-loving and a good companion, you enjoy friendly social activities. You possess a strong need for self-expression, and when positive you can radiate the joy of life. An inclination to get bored easily, however, may cause you to become indecisive or spread yourself thin. Nevertheless, you are usually artistic and engaging, with a good sense of humor. A talent with words may manifest through speaking, writing, or singing. The subinfluence of the number 1 month indicates that you are autonomous and independent. Full of enthusiasm and original ideas, you often show others the way forward. As a serious and hardworking individual, you like to put your imaginative thoughts to practical use. Innovative and courageous, you do not worry about speaking your mind but usually do it in a charming way. The enterprising spirit indicated here encourages you to experiment with different concepts and make your own decisions or strike out alone.

• *Positive:* humorous, happy, friendly, productive, creative, artistic, good conversationalist, power to wish, freedom-loving

• *Negative:* easily bored, vain, boastful, extravagant, self-indulgent, lazy, doubtful

Love & Relationships

With an inclination for independence, you still need a strong and stable home base. Women of this birthday are often attracted to men who are daring risk takers and pioneers. While you have a youthful and playful streak, once you settle down and become responsible you can be a very loyal and faithful friend or partner. Occasionally, however, you may experience a certain emotional remoteness in relationships. Nevertheless, being quite sociable and charming, you draw people toward you and can be very entertaining.

January 4

♑ Success-oriented, you are a frank and honest Capricorn who is willing to work hard to achieve your objectives. Ambitious and competitive, you have a sharp and quick intellect, good judgment, and the ability to overcome all obstacles if you apply self-discipline. However, if you avoid the responsibility needed to fulfill your high destiny, you may not be able to satisfy your strong urge to build something of long-lasting value.

With the supporting influence of your decanate ruler, Taurus, you can express artistic and creative abilities either in your career or as a pastime. The influence of Venus can bestow charm and a flair for being witty, entertaining, and sociable. With an expansive viewpoint and a love of variety, you may be drawn to travel or the study of philosophical or spiritual subjects. This does not detract from a shrewd practicality that allows you to gain value for money and make the most of any situation.

Although you are confident of your opinions and quick with your responses, there is a danger that in your dealings with others you may become arrogant or impatient. While you can have a very pragmatic approach to life and show a real power for accumulating wealth, you may find greater satisfaction in concerns of a more profound nature.

From the age of seventeen, when your progressed Sun enters Aquarius, you become more group-oriented, less conservative, and more freedom-loving. In your middle years you will reap the benefits of your labor as long as you have applied yourself to hard work and dedication. If you seek a new direction, you must approach it cautiously in order to avoid sudden changes and unwise speculations that may arise from boredom. After the age of forty-seven, when your progressed Sun moves into Pisces, your emotional sensitivity is enhanced and you develop a stronger inner life. This can be reflected in your visions, dreams, and ideals. In later years you are likely to retain a youthful outlook.

Your Secret Self

Your strong and assured front often hides your powerful emotions and sensitivity. With your strong imagination and receptive nature, you can be a practical visionary who is able to connect to the mass collective. Through compassion, you realize that you have a gift to offer others. You can be dramatic and proud, and the translation of these qualities into your work or creative expression can be a vital key to your success. Alternatively, if you do not channel your sensitivity into positive outlets or recognize the importance of work in your life, you may be prone to escapism, lack of clarity, or mood swings.

Usually genial in your approach, you are interested in a wide range of subjects, particularly education, philosophy, law, religion, travel, or politics. At your best you can be an inspired thinker or uplifting conversationalist, talking about your pet subject with great enthusiasm.

Work & Vocation

Sociable and friendly, you possess good communication skills and have a flair for dealing with the public. As this birthday implies a need for transformation and variety in your occupation,

FIXED STAR

Star's name: Wega, also called Vulture
Degree position: 14°20'–15°19'
    Capricorn between the years
    1930 and 2000
Magnitude: 1
Strength: ★★★★★★★★★
Orb: 2°30'
Constellation: Alpha Lyra
Applicable days: January 4, 5, 6, 7, 8
Star qualities: varied interpretations:
    Venus/Mercury, also Jupiter/Saturn
Description: a bright white and blue
    sapphire star located in the lower
    part of the Lyre

PRIMARY STAR'S INFLUENCE

Wega bestows leadership ability and a sociable and outgoing personality. Usually you possess an idealistic and optimistic outlook and have creative abilities and a talent for writing. This star, however, also implies that changeable circumstances can bring about fluctuating periods of success and suggests that only with determination can you ensure stability.

Linked to your Sun's degree, Wega imparts success and opportunities to rise to high positions. This star may bring you into contact with influential people, and this might lead to honor and popularity. Wega's influence also suggests that changeable circumstances may cause success to be short-lived. You probably enjoy work in a governmental position or dealing with the general public. This star also warns against being too critical or abrupt.

you need plenty of activity to avoid procrastination. Success often lies along commercial lines, making you a good manager or planner. Employment may also come through government agencies such as the civil service, police work, and local authorities. A love of knowledge implies that you can be an excellent teacher or trainer. With your imagination, wit, and natural talent for entertainment, you can mix work with social activities or enter the world of showbiz.

Famous people who share your birthday include actress Dyan Cannon, scientist Sir Isaac Newton, boxer Floyd Patterson, fairy tale writer Jacob Grimm, shorthand inventor Isaac Pitman, and inventor of writing system for the blind Louis Braille.

Numerology

The solid structure and orderly power suggested by the number 4 birthday indicate that often you need stability and like to establish order. As a number 4 individual, you are sensitive to form and composition. Security-conscious, you like to build a strong foundation for yourself and your family. Your pragmatic approach to life confers a good business sense and an ability to achieve material success. Faithful though undemonstrative, you are usually honest, frank, and fair. Nevertheless, you may have to learn how to express your feelings. The challenges for a number 4 individual may include overcoming periods of instability. The subinfluence of the number 1 month indicates that you are ambitious and enterprising, with an independent outlook. Innovative and inquisitive, with plenty of energy, you are usually hardworking and serious, with a desire to achieve a great deal. Mentally sharp and intuitive, you are inclined to make your own decisions or strike out alone. Being authoritative implies that you prefer to give out orders, rather than be in a subordinate position. When inspired with original ideas, you often show others the way forward.

• *Positive:* well organized, self-disciplined, steady, hardworking, good with your hands, pragmatic, trusting, exact

• *Negative:* uncommunicative, repressed, lazy, procrastination, too economical, bossy, resentful

Love & Relationships

Dynamic and witty, you can be very charming. When you are gregarious and kind, you have many friends and an active social life. As you enjoy lightness and creativity, you may be happiest when sharing these with partners and others. You may, however, be indecisive when it comes to definite commitment and may have to beware of money matters affecting your relationships. Romantically, although you can appear indifferent at times, underneath lies a sensitive and compassionate soul.

YOUR SPECIAL SOMEONE

You could delay settling down, but may be more likely to reveal your loving nature to people born on the following dates.

Love & friendship: Jan. 3, 14, 24, 28, Feb. 1, 12, 22, 26, Mar. 10, 20, Apr. 8, 18, May 6, 16, 20, 31, June 4, 14, 29, July 2, 12, 27, Aug. 10, 25, 31, Sept. 8, 12, 23, 29, Oct. 6, 21, 27, Nov. 4, 19, 25, Dec. 2, 17, 23

Beneficial: Jan. 1, 11, Feb. 9, Mar. 7, 28, Apr. 5, 26, 30, May 3, 24, 28, June 1, 22, 26, July 20, 24, Aug. 18, 22, Sept. 16, 20, 30, Oct. 14, 18, 28, Nov. 12, 16, 26, Dec. 10, 14, 24

Fatal attractions: July 4, 5, 6, 7

Challenging: Jan. 17, 20, Feb. 15, 18, Mar. 13, 16, Apr. 11, 14, May 9, 12, June 7, 10, July 5, 8, Aug. 3, 6, Sept. 1, 4, Oct. 2

Soul mates:, July 29, Aug. 27, Sept. 25, Oct. 23, 31, Nov. 21, 29, Dec. 19, 27

January 5

♑ Your Capricorn birthday shows you to be a charismatic, loyal, and hardworking individual who, with a worthwhile goal or sense of purpose, can be extremely dedicated. Practical and down to earth, when faced with setbacks you develop tremendous endurance to carry on and are capable of great sacrifice. This birthday bestows extraordinary potential but also suggests the influence of extremes; very universal and detached, or depressed and overserious.

The supporting influence of your decanate ruler, Taurus, gives you charm and creative abilities. Your prominent social skills ensure an ease at interrelating with those around you. Enjoying the good things of life, you prefer to be in harmonious or even luxurious surroundings. Unconventional and aware of image, you like to be well groomed and often have an original way of dressing.

Possessing good organizational skills, you work better when you think positively and have a plan of action. You benefit from investing effort in projects that are long-lasting, and should avoid dubious get-rich-quick schemes. You have a strong inclination for adventure and travel and may even settle away from your native home.

After the age of sixteen, when your progressed Sun moves into Aquarius, you become less traditional and more independent, with a growing desire to express your individuality. Friendship, group affairs, or humanitarian issues may start to play a stronger role in your life. Another turning point occurs at the age of forty-six, when your progressed Sun enters Pisces. From this time, there is an increased emphasis on your enhanced sensitivity and feelings. At the highest level you will be seeking a mystical or spiritual connection, but on a mundane level this may result in confusion or daydreaming. You will become more receptive and imaginative and may experience an urge to develop or appreciate creative gifts.

Your Secret Self

If you can harness your potential for enormous emotional power and combine this with a strong sense of direction, you can be a leader in the arts, entertainment, politics, or spiritual affairs. When your strong self-will is positively focused, you can accomplish miracles and be extremely compassionate. If you indulge in negative thoughts, however, you can become dictatorial and ruthless or be prone to frustration and disappointment. When you learn the lesson of being truly detached without being cold, which may not be until later in life, you gain enormous inner freedom and a desire for knowledge of a deeper or more profound nature.

A love of harmony can inspire you to seek peace. With your subtle sensitivity and desire to transcend the mundane, you possess heightened perceptions of light, color, form, and sound, which you can channel into artistic, musical, or spiritual pursuits. With a strong sense of responsibility toward others, you often seek true wisdom or an ideal world.

Work & Vocation

Friendly and generous, yet ambitious and hardworking, you need harmonious working relations and a congenial environment. Your ability to make contacts and deal with people sug-

---

FIXED STAR

Star's name: Wega, also called Vulture

Degree position: 14°20'–15°19'
Capricorn between the years 1930 and 2000

Magnitude: 1

Strength: ★★★★★★★★

Orb: 2°30'

Constellation: Alpha Lyra

Applicable days: January 4, 5, 6, 7, 8

Star qualities: varied interpretations:
Venus/Mercury, also Jupiter/Saturn

Description: a bright white and blue sapphire star located in the lower part of the Lyre

---

PRIMARY STAR'S INFLUENCE

Wega bestows leadership ability and a sociable and outgoing personality. Usually you possess an idealistic and optimistic outlook and have creative abilities and a talent for writing. This star, however, also implies that changeable circumstances can bring about fluctuating periods of success and suggests that only with determination can you ensure stability.

Linked to your Sun's degree, Wega imparts success and opportunities to rise to high positions. This star may bring you into contact with influential people, and this might lead to honor and popularity. Wega's influence also suggests that changeable circumstances may cause success to be short-lived. You probably enjoy work in a governmental position or dealing with the general public. This star also warns against being too critical or abrupt.

gests that you can excel as a mediator, manager, or agent. Usually you have a sense of what the public wants, due to an understanding of the collective dream. Although you often want to succeed in the business world, your true talent lies in pursuing a vocation that involves service to others through education and spirituality. A talent for writing, drama, and music suggests that you have powerful feelings that need expressing.

Famous people who share your birthday include spiritual master Paramahansa Yogananda, actress Diane Keaton, German politician Konrad Adenauer, guitarist Jimmy Page, actor Robert Duvall, and choreographer Alvin Ailey.

Numerology

Strong instincts, an adventurous nature, and a desire for freedom are all indicated by the number 5 birthday. Travel and many opportunities for change, some unexpected, may lead you to undergo a real transformation of views and beliefs. Often having a number 5 birthdate means that you have an active life and need to learn about patience and attention to detail. Usually you can achieve success by avoiding premature or speculative actions. The natural talent of a number 5 individual is knowing how to go with the flow and staying detached. The subinfluence of the number 1 month indicates that you are proud, ambitious, and independent. As a sensitive and intuitive person, you are compassionate, with a sympathetic nature and generous heart. Your determined spirit indicates that you need to make your own decisions or strike out alone. Although at times you may be full of enthusiasm, a need to learn to persevere may cause you to feel frustrated. This suggests that at times you may act in haste or show a tendency to be impatient.

• *Positive:* versatile, adaptable, progressive, magnetic, daring, freedom-loving, quick and witty, curious, mystical, sociable

• *Negative:* unreliable, procrastinator, inconsistent, overconfident, resistance to change

Love & Relationships

People are drawn to you by your personal magnetism, and therefore you usually find it easy to make friends. When you express love, it is often powerful and intense. Desiring freedom, and sometimes involved in unusual types of partnerships, you value friendship and a wider, more humanitarian approach to relationships. Men of this birthday may be attracted toward rather strong and forceful women. Companionship is important to you, but avoid becoming too dependent on partners or others. Besides having a need for a loving relationship, you are also attracted to people of intelligence. Once you find your perfect love, you can be loyal and faithful.

YOUR SPECIAL SOMEONE

For warm and tender relationships, you may wish to look for those born on the following dates.

Love & friendship: Jan. 5, 17, 19, Feb. 3, 15, 17, Mar. 13, 15, Apr. 11, 13, May 9, 11, June 7, 9, 30, July 5, 7, 28, 30, Aug. 3, 5, 26, 28, Sept. 1, 3, 24, 26, Oct. 1, 22, 24, Nov. 20, 22, Dec. 18, 20, 30

Beneficial: Jan. 20, 29, Feb. 18, 27, Mar. 16, 25, Apr. 14, 23, May 12, 21, June 10, 19, July 8, 17, Aug. 6, 15, Sept. 4, 13, Oct. 2, 11, 29, Nov. 9, 27, Dec. 7, 25

Fatal attractions: Mar. 29, Apr. 27, May 25, June 23, July 5, 6, 7, 8, 21, Aug. 19, Sept. 17, Oct. 15, Nov. 13, Dec. 11

Challenging: Jan. 14, 27, Feb. 12, 25, Mar. 10, 23, Apr. 8, 21, May 6, 19, June 4, 17, July 2, 15, Aug. 13, Sept. 11, Oct. 9, Nov. 7, Dec. 5

Soul mates:, June 30, July 28, Aug. 26, Sept. 24, Oct. 22, 29, Nov. 20, 27, Dec. 18, 25

January 6

ᚷ Tough and determined, yet magnetic and charming, you are an interesting mixture of opposites. Your birthday suggests that you are a practical visionary who is willing to work hard to achieve your ideals; you have the advantage of possessing a tremendous energy that enables you to achieve in life. A desire for power, money, and prestige can motivate you to climb the ladder of success. Along with a sharp wit and intelligence, you also have a humanitarian streak that can give you quick insight into people and inspire you to greater heights.

With the subinfluence of your decanate ruler, Taurus, you retain a love for art or beauty as well as a gift for accumulating riches. Highly creative, you prefer to put your talents to some practical use and are often willing to make sacrifices to achieve your objectives. It would be wise nonetheless to avoid taking life too seriously, as it can leave you emotionally frustrated or disappointed. At other times, however, you can be extremely compassionate, detached, and full of universal love.

As a strong individual, you are often goal-conscious, ambitious, and tenacious, with an overriding sense of duty. Philosophical in your thinking, you can positively accept the experience gained as the result of previous difficulties in life.

After the age of fifteen, when your progressed Sun moves into Aquarius, you become less influenced by tradition, more independent, and trusting of your own unique perspective. You may also start to be more interested in group affairs or humanitarian issues. Another turning point occurs at the age of forty-five, when your progressed Sun enters Pisces. From this time, there is more of an emphasis on developing your sensitivity and a vivid inner life. This can be reflected through your visions, dreams, and emotional ideals. In later years you may find that your emotional fulfillment will depend upon the personal expression of love that you display toward others as well as the realization that money or power is not the answer to everything.

Your Secret Self

The quest for knowledge is a vital key to your success and achievement. Education of some description will ensure the development of your enormous potential. An inner pride stops you from displaying your doubts or indecision and often places you in positions of leadership rather than in situations where you are subordinate to others. Desiring originality in your life, you have something to say that is a bit different. Having a willful temperament, you may sometimes be restless, but it is through your more persevering and strategic characteristics that you can achieve long-term results. Beware of becoming involved in power games, as these can deplete your positive energies.

With a strong need for recognition, you find it especially hard to be taken for granted. You have a strong sense of responsibility, and you may have to maintain a balance between your duties and your ideals. Highly intuitive, you usually operate best when you get a feel for a situation first before making commitments.

Work & Vocation

Forceful and determined, you have a bold facade that hides your doubts and insecurities but assists you in all matters dealing with the public. Ideally suited for the healing professions, you

FIXED STAR

Star's name: Wega, also called Vulture

Degree position: 14°20'–15°19' Capricorn between the years 1930 and 2000

Magnitude: 1

Strength: ★★★★★★★★

Orb: 2°30'

Constellation: Alpha Lyra

Applicable days: January 4, 5, 6, 7, 8

Star qualities: varied interpretations: Venus/Mercury, also Jupiter/Saturn

Description: a bright white and blue sapphire star located in the lower part of the Lyre

PRIMARY STAR'S INFLUENCE

Wega bestows leadership ability and a sociable and outgoing personality. Usually you possess an idealistic and optimistic outlook and have creative abilities and a talent for writing. This star, however, also implies that changeable circumstances can bring about fluctuating periods of success and suggests that only with determination can you ensure stability.

Linked to your Sun's degree, Wega imparts success and opportunities to rise to high positions. This star may bring you into contact with influential people, and this might lead to honor and popularity. Wega's influence also suggests that changeable circumstances may cause success to be short-lived. You probably enjoy work in a governmental position or dealing with the general public. This star also warns against being too critical or abrupt.

make an excellent physician or alternative health care practitioner. With your business skills and natural gift for helping others, you can also be an accomplished counselor, psychologist, advisor, negotiator, or dealer. Inspired and intelligent, you may be drawn toward religion and spirituality. As a visionary, you may enter the film industry or work for companies that sell an image or a vision. Although personal fulfillment comes through work and productive activities, you may need to avoid a possible danger of becoming a workaholic.

Famous people who share your birthday include poets Kahlil Gibran and Carl Sandburg, U.S. statesman Benjamin Franklin, golfer Nancy Lopez, writers Alan Watts and E. L. Doctorow, composer Alexander Scriabin, and painter Gustave Dore.

Numerology

Compassion, idealism, and a caring nature are some of the attributes suggested by a number 6 birthday. Frequently domestically inclined, you are a homemaker and a devoted parent. Intense emotions and a desire for universal harmony often encourage you to work hard for what you believe in. The more sensitive among you will need to find a form of creative expression and are often drawn to the world of entertaining or art and design. The challenges for some people with number 6 birthdates may include developing more humility and showing compassion toward friends and neighbors as well as learning to be more responsible. The subinfluence of the number 1 month indicates that you are ambitious and proud, with a strong character. Although you have an excellent business sense and executive abilities, avoid becoming materialistic. Usually autonomous, proud, and practical, you are highly intuitive, with strong values and sharp instincts. By staying broad-minded and liberal, you can overcome a tendency to be critical or too authoritative.

• *Positive:* worldly, universal brotherhood, friendly, compassionate, dependable, understanding, idealistic, poised, artistic, balanced

• *Negative:* shy, unreasonable, stubborn, outspoken, domineering, lack of responsibility, selfish, cynical, self-centered

Love & Relationships

Dyanmic, practical, and protective, you tend to work hard for people you love but at times may have to be careful not to take over or be too bossy. Your friendships and romantic aspirations may well be connected with your career and ambitions, and you are likely to be drawn toward powerful individuals with strong positions or social connections. Though you are loyal and responsible, beware that possible indecision or moodiness does not dampen your happiness.

YOUR SPECIAL SOMEONE

Your chances of success in relationships are better with people born on the following dates.

Love & friendship: Jan. 9, 16, 18, 26, 31, Feb. 7, 14, 16, 24, 29, Mar. 5, 12, 14, 22, 27, Apr. 3, 10, 12, 20, 25, May 1, 8, 10, 18, 23, June 6, 8, 16, 21, July 4, 6, 14, 19, 31, Aug. 2, 4, 12, 17, 29, Sept. 2, 10, 15, 27, Oct. 8, 13, 25, Nov. 6, 11, 23, Dec. 4, 9, 21, 30

Beneficial: Jan. 1, 21, Feb. 19, Mar. 17, Apr. 15, May 13, June 11, July 9, Aug. 7, Sept. 5, Oct. 3, 30, Nov. 1, 28, Dec. 26

Fatal attractions: July 6, 7, 8, 9, 10

Challenging: Mar. 29, Apr. 27, May 25, June 23, July 21, Aug. 19, Sept. 17, Oct. 15, Nov. 13, Dec. 11

Soul mates: Jan. 27, Feb. 25, Mar. 23, 30, Apr. 21, 28, May 19, 26, June 17, 24, July 15, 22, Aug. 13, 20, Sept. 11, 18, Oct. 9, 16, Nov. 7, 14, Dec. 5, 12

January 7

♑ You are a clever, intuitive, and hardworking individual, and the influence of your birthday implies that your sensitive intellect can be the vital ingredient in your success. Although practical and down to earth, you also have the ability to inspire others with your ideals and spontaneity. Mentally very shrewd about people, you have an altruistic or humanitarian side to your nature, and you can excel in activities that require good people skills.

With the supporting influence of your decanate ruler, Taurus, and your strong sense of dedication, success in art, music, and literary or other creative endeavors is particularly emphasized. With the ability to combine business with socializing, you like to think big and aim for the top. You may, however, need to guard against a stubborn or contrary streak in your nature that refuses to conform for the sake of being difficult.

Although you can be sociable, the occasional tendency to isolate yourself implies that sometimes you may feel lonely. You may need to keep a balance between the differing aspects of your personality, particularly those of material ambition, your ideals, and your spiritual awareness. Nevertheless, you are also liable to experience sudden realizations and unexpected changes of good fortune and gains, particularly from cooperative activities or travel.

From the ages of fourteen to forty-three, when your progressed Sun moves through Aquarius, you tend to be group-oriented, less traditional or serious, and more freedom-loving. You may be attracted by unusual interests or have a strong desire to express your individuality. After the age of forty-four, when your progressed Sun moves into Pisces, your emotional sensitivity grows and you develop a more meaningful inner life. This can be reflected in your visions, dreams, and ideals. At the age of seventy-four there is another turning point as your progressed Sun enters Aries, emphasizing a need to take the initiative and be brave and direct in your relationships with others.

Your Secret Self

One of your major challenges is to recognize your inner power and learn to refuse offers of positions beneath your capabilities. At times you may find yourself working for people who do not have your level of awareness, and so it is important to have faith in your outstanding potential and talents. Receptive to new ideas and interested in freedom and reforms, you can be inventive and progressive and hence harbor a need to express your original opinions. Your independent thinking can also make you confrontational, but if you direct your argumentative inclinations into developing debating skills and communication, you can really excel. While you may not push yourself to the forefront, you are naturally suited for leadership of some description.

Sensitive, you may be prone to moods at times, leading you to withdraw or appear cold. Nevertheless, this awareness can also enhance your intuition and give you a sixth sense about people or circumstances. When you totally trust your inspired thoughts and perceptive insight, you link to your source of spontaneity and wisdom. This helps you radiate warmth and a powerful love that can magnetize or enchant others.

Work & Vocation

Even though you have a sharp business sense, you may be more interested in something that combines your executive and leadership ability with your exceptional imagination and cre-

FIXED STAR

Star's name: Wega, also called Vulture

Degree position: 14°20'–15°19'
    Capricorn between the years
    1930 and 2000

Magnitude: 1

Strength: ★★★★★★★★★

Orb: 2°30'

Constellation: Alpha Lyra

Applicable days: January 4, 5, 6, 7, 8

Star qualities: varied interpretations:
    Venus/Mercury, also Jupiter/Saturn

Description: a bright white and blue
    sapphire star located in the lower
    part of the Lyre

PRIMARY STAR'S INFLUENCE

Wega bestows leadership ability and a sociable and outgoing personality. Usually you possess an idealistic and optimistic outlook and have creative abilities and a talent for writing. This star, however, also implies that changeable circumstances can bring about fluctuating periods of success and suggests that only with determination can you ensure stability.

Linked to your Sun's degree, Wega imparts success and opportunities to rise to high positions. This star may bring you in contact with influential people, and this might lead to honor and popularity. Wega's influence also suggests that changeable circumstances may cause success to be short-lived. You probably enjoy work in a governmental position or dealing with the general public. This star also warns against being too critical or abrupt.

ative talents. This could manifest in writing, drama, or the arts. Good organizing ability, idealism, and a humanitarian streak could have you working in large or public organizations. Careerwise, the accent is on your mental and creative abilities. You may wish to pursue a career as a teacher, advisor, or social worker. If in business, you may work as an agent or negotiator, or as a mediator who handles the financial affairs of others. Often willing to work behind the scenes, you can be a producer or promoter. You are advised not to settle for less than your high potential indicates. Humanitarian, you may wish to devote your life to social reforms.

Famous people who share your birthday include actor Nicholas Cage, singer/songwriter Kenny Loggins, flutist Jean-Pierre Rampal, and St. Bernadette of Lourdes.

Numerology

Analytical and thoughtful, number 7 individuals are often perfectionistic, critical, and self-absorbed. Preferring to make your own decisions, you frequently learn best through personal experience. This desire to learn can lead you into the academic world or to improving your skills. At times, you can become oversensitive to criticism from others and feel misunderstood. Your tendency to be inquisitive and enigmatic leads you to develop the art of asking subtle questions without letting anyone know what you really think. The subinfluence of the number 1 month indicates that you are perceptive and shrewd, with discriminative abilities. The great desire to be first and autonomous is also suggested by your birthday. A tendency to be skeptical suggests that although you are intuitive, you are likely to doubt your own decisions and worry. Practical, you want to commercialize your ideas and are often a specialist in one particular area. Meticulous and hardworking, you usually decide on an academic career and can excel in research, writing, or administration.

• *Positive:* educated, trusting, meticulous, idealistic, honest, psychic, scientific, rational, reflective

• *Negative:* concealing, skeptical, confused, nagging, malicious, detached

Love & Relationships

Romantically, your charm can easily win you friends and admirers. Attracted to people with intelligence, you may be better off with a partner who possesses as broad a vision as you do. It may be wise, however, to avoid being too bossy in close associations. With the ability to endure, you can also be very loyal once in a committed relationship. Your keen mental prowess and unusual interests suggest that friendship and companionship may be linked to work or mentally stimulating social activities.

YOUR SPECIAL SOMEONE

You may enjoy a very rewarding relationship with people born on the following dates.

Love & friendship: Jan. 21, 28, 31, Feb. 19, 26, 29, Mar. 17, 24, 27, Apr. 15, 22, 25, May 13, 20, 23, June 11, 18, 21, July 9, 16, 19, Aug. 7, 14, 17, 31, Sept. 5, 12, 15, 29, Oct. 3, 10, 13, 27, 29, 31, Nov. 1, 8, 11, 25, 27, 29, Dec. 6, 9, 23, 25, 27

Beneficial: Jan. 9, 12, 18, 24, 29, Feb. 7, 10, 16, 22, 27, Mar. 5, 8, 14, 20, 25, Apr. 3, 6, 12, 18, 23, May 1, 4, 10, 16, 21, 31, June 2, 8, 14, 19, 29, July 6, 12, 17, 27, Aug. 4, 10, 15, 25, Sept. 2, 8, 13, 23, Oct. 6, 11, 21, Nov. 4, 9, 19, Dec. 2, 7, 17

Fatal attractions: Jan. 3, Feb. 1, July 7, 8, 9, 10, 11

Challenging: Jan. 7, 8, 19, 28, Feb. 5, 6, 17, 26, Mar. 3, 4, 15, 24, Apr. 1, 2, 13, 22, May 11, 20, June 9, 18, July 7, 16, Aug. 5, 14, Sept. 3, 12, Oct. 1, 10, Nov. 8, Dec. 6

Soul mates: Jan. 3, 19, Feb. 1, 17, Mar. 15, Apr. 13, May 11, June 9, July 7, Aug. 5, Sept. 3, Oct. 1

January 8

FIXED STAR

Star's name: Wega, also called Vulture

Degree position: 14°20'–15°19'
 Capricorn between the years
 1930 and 2000

Magnitude: I

Strength: ★★★★★★★★

Orb: 2°30'

Constellation: Alpha Lyra

Applicable days: January 4, 5, 6, 7, 8

Star qualities: varied interpretations:
 Venus/Mercury, also Jupiter/Saturn

Description: a bright white and blue
 sapphire star located in the lower
 part of the Lyre

PRIMARY STAR'S INFLUENCE

Wega bestows leadership ability and a sociable and outgoing personality. Usually you possess an idealistic and optimistic outlook and have creative abilities and a talent for writing. This star, however, also implies that changeable circumstances can bring about fluctuating periods of success and suggests that only with determination can you ensure stability.

Linked to your Sun's degree, Wega imparts success and opportunities to rise to high positions. This star may bring you into contact with influential people, and this might lead to honor and popularity. Wega's influence also suggests that changeable circumstances may cause success to be short-lived. You probably enjoy work in a governmental position or dealing with the general public. This star also warns against being too critical or abrupt.

VS Your Capricorn birthday points to a personality that is strong, dedicated, and ambitious, yet subtle, unassuming, and refined. Although determined, competitive, and hardworking, you also possess imagination, sensitivity, and charismatic charm. With all your practicality and worldly sense, it is important that you not lose sight of the intuitive insight or sense of vision implied by your birthday.

With the subinfluence of your decanate ruler, Taurus, your flair for music, the arts, and dealing with money can often bring you success and fulfillment. When interacting with others, you profit from your excellent people skills and talents. With an appreciation of beauty, glamour, and the good life, you prefer to be in harmonious or even luxurious environments. Although you possess the ability to enchant others, they may not see that behind your bold facade you may occasionally suffer from inner confusion or doubt.

While you suffer from a touch of inertia as far as your grand dreams and ideals are concerned, the thought of material success usually moves you into action. Strong-willed and bright, you have the ability to assimilate knowledge quickly if you are interested. Your enthusiasm for projects you love can be most impressive. This can help you overcome a sensitive nervousness or discontent that could attract you to destructive pastimes such as drugs or drink. However, your strong sense of style, coupled with a flair for the dramatic, ensures that you can stand out in a crowd.

In your youth a powerful woman may make an impact on you. From the age of thirteen to forty-two, when your progressed Sun moves through Aquarius, you tend to be less traditional or cautious, more freedom-loving, and group-oriented. You may develop unconventional interests or have a strong desire to express your individuality. After the age of forty-three, when your progressed Sun moves into Pisces, your emotional sensitivity and intuition increase. You may place more importance on your dreams, ideals, or spiritual or psychic awareness. At the age of seventy-three, there is another turning point as your progressed Sun enters Aries. This accents a need to take direct action on issues that affect you, rather than being too passive.

Your Secret Self

Through your inspired awareness and development of self-discipline, you are able to realize your enormous potential. Many of your lessons in life regard your work. Fortunately, you are able to see the advantages of working cooperatively with others in a team, and partnerships can be beneficial for you. It is important, however, not to become dependent on anything or anyone, as you can become fearful and too serious.

It is necessary to learn detachment at a very deep level, and this may not be fully understood until somewhat later in life. When you recognize this need you empower yourself with inner freedom and a desire for things of a more humanitarian or profound nature. Highly intuitive, you have an urge to transcend the mundane that can stimulate you to produce original work or bring you into contact with foreign countries.

Work & Vocation

Ambitious and practical, with social skills, you need to be in contact with other people or to work in collaboration with other individuals. An ability to work hard and pay attention to detail implies that you can excel as a scientist, religious worker, or lecturer and educator. If in business, you can succeed in serving the public or work for reforms. Charismatic and individual, with a charming voice and a need for self-expression, you may be drawn to the realms of business and entertainment. You can also communicate, teach, and inspire others in areas such as politics, spirituality, and philosophy. Alternatively, your sensitivity and sense of harmony may draw you toward the arts and music.

Famous people who share your birthday include singers Elvis Presley, David Bowie, and Shirley Bassey, comedian Soupy Sales, and scientist Stephen Hawking.

Numerology

The strength or power suggested by the number 8 birthday shows a character with strong values and sound judgment. The number 8 often indicates that you aspire to great accomplishment and possess an ambitious nature. A desire for dominance, security, and material success is also implied by this birthday. As a number 8 person, you have natural business sense and will benefit greatly from developing organizational and executive skills. You may have to learn how to administer or delegate your authority in a fair and just way. A strong need to feel secure or established urges you to make long-term plans and investments. The subinfluence of the number 1 month indicates that you are enterprising, discerning, and efficient. The creative vitality indicated here encourages you to express yourself and make your own judgments or strike out alone. Imaginative and original, with practical ideas, you like to be methodical and utilize your knowledge in a productive way. Although you are determined and full of eagerness, you may need to develop tolerance and be less domineering.

• *Positive:* leadership, thoroughness, hardworking, authoritative, protective, power to heal, good judge of values

• *Negative:* impatient, wasteful, intolerant, domineering, easily discouraged, lack of planning

YOUR SPECIAL SOMEONE

You might find a faithful and reliable lover or partner among those born on the following dates.

Love & friendship: Jan. 6, 20, 22, 24, 30, Feb. 4, 18, 20, 22, 28, Mar. 2, 16, 18, 20, 26, 29, Apr. 14, 16, 18, 24, 27, May 12, 14, 16, 22, 25, June 10, 12, 14, 20, 23, July 8, 10, 12, 18, 21, Aug. 6, 8, 10, 16, 19, Sept. 4, 6, 8, 14, 17, Oct. 2, 4, 6, 12, 15, Nov. 2, 4, 10, 13, Dec. 2, 8, 11

Beneficial: Jan. 1, 3, 4, 14, Feb. 1, 2, 12, Mar. 10, 28, Apr. 8, 26, 30, May 6, 24, 28, June 4, 22, 26, July 2, 20, 24, Aug. 18, 22, Sept. 16, 20, Oct. 14, 18, Nov. 12, 16, Dec. 10, 14

Fatal attractions: Jan. 11, Feb. 9, Mar. 7, Apr. 5, May 3, June 1, July 8, 9, 10, 11, 12

Challenging: Jan. 3, 5, Feb. 1, 3, Mar. 1, July 31, Aug. 29, Sept. 27, 30, Oct. 25, 28, Nov. 23, 26, 30, Dec. 21, 24, 28

Soul mates: Jan. 5, 12, Feb. 3, 10, Mar. 1, 8, Apr. 6, May 4, June 2

Love & Relationships

Your personal charisma ensures that you shine socially, although many of your main lessons in life concern close personal relationships. You are drawn toward successful and mentally stimulating people, and when enthusiastic about a relationship you give it everything. You can be a passionate and warm lover, though you may be prone to moods. Your home is likely to be especially important to you as a refuge from the world.

January 9

♑ The influence of your birthday suggests that you are a practical and hardworking Capricorn with the ability to endure. Security-conscious, you like to build on the basis of long-lasting results, and once you are committed to a person or project, you can be loyal, dutiful, and responsible. A universal quality to your thinking can manifest as a humanitarian interest in others. It would be wise, however, to avoid negative thinking, which is likely to bring on feelings of frustration and impatience and thereby make it difficult to realize your ideals and wishes.

With the supporting influence of your decanate ruler, Taurus, you possess natural creative talents. You may wish to develop these through the arts in order to give expression to your imagination and sensitive emotions, or you may use your talents and charm in your dealings with people. A longing for love and affection points to a need for approval and emphasizes the importance of relationships in your life.

A love of beauty and the good life suggests that you prefer to be surrounded by harmony and luxury, but a dislike of discord may cause you to hide your head in the sand and avoid necessary confrontation. Although at times you will have to face obstacles and disappointment, avoid letting pessimism or materialism get the better of you. Detachment rather than inflexibility is often the key to solving many of your problems. Fortunately, you possess the perseverance and intelligence to win through sheer determination.

From the age of twelve to forty-one, when your progressed Sun moves through Aquarius, you gradually become more independent, although you value friendship. You may be attracted by unusual interests or humanitarian issues, or you may have a strong desire to express your individuality. After the age of forty-two, when your progressed Sun moves into Pisces, your emotional sensitivity becomes enhanced and you develop a more meaningful inner life. This can be reflected in your visions, dreams, and ideals. In your middle years, after numerous changes, you are likely to find gains through partnership and cooperative relationships. At the age of seventy-two, there is another turning point as your progressed Sun enters Aries, emphasizing a need to take the initiative and be brave and direct in your relationships with others. New beginnings are also indicated with this progression.

Your Secret Self

Your dynamic emotions need positive channels of expression, or you may become caught up in other people's dramas. A natural ability to help others will enable you to feel more fulfilled and aid you in gaining friends. When feeling self-assured, you are able to project the power of love and magnetize others with your charismatic appeal.

Practical yet imaginative, you like order and have a good sense of vision. You need a plan and a strong sense of purpose, or your restlessness may cause you to overindulge as a form of escapism. With a desire for self-improvement and a strong emphasis on work in your life, you must apply diligence and concentrated effort so as to take advantage of your true potential. You will find, however, that if you work hard, financial protection will always appear when you really need it.

Work & Vocation

Enterprising and imaginative, you may want to have the freedom to do as you wish and be independent. A need for variety and change suggests that you are likely to combine travel and work. Your desire for activity and progress may lead you to experiment with many occupations. Whatever you do, avoid routine and mundane jobs that do not promise advancement or excitement. Idealistic and creative, with a poetic heart, you may be drawn to the worlds of art and music. If you are interested in business and social reforms, marketing, economics, promotion, and politics are just a few of the careers that you may find interesting. An ability to think quickly and a charming personality suggest that you may want to combine traveling with business and work as a tour operator, travel agent, long-distance commuter, or salesperson.

Famous people who share your birthday include former U.S. president Richard Nixon, singers Joan Baez and Crystal Gale, writer Simone de Beauvoir, and entertainer Gypsy Rose Lee.

Numerology

Benevolence, compassion, and sensitivity are all associated with the number 9 birthday. You are often considered intelligent and intuitive, with psychic abilities that point to a universal receptivity. With a number 9 birthday, you usually feel that life is mapped out for you and does not leave you much room to maneuver. As well as learning to become impersonal, you may have to develop understanding, tolerance, and patience. You are likely to benefit greatly from world travel and interaction with people from all walks of life. Avoid unrealistic dreams or an inclination toward escapism. The subinfluence of the number 1 month strengthens your intuitive powers and receptivity. Ambitious and determined, you can be resolute and commanding. With your insight and sixth sense, you are often visionary. Imaginative and idealistic, you need to learn to trust your own instincts. A great desire to be first and autonomous implies that you may need to accept the limitations of life and understand that it is never fair or perfect. At times you may be asked to abandon your personal plans, and you will learn that the world does not revolve around you.

• *Positive:* idealistic, humanitarian, creative, sensitive, generous, magnetic, poetic, charitable, giving, detached, lucky, popular

• *Negative:* frustrated, nervous, fragmented, selfish, impractical, easily led, worry

Love & Relationships

Idealistic about the perfect partner, you may even opt for platonic relationships if you fail to find anyone who can measure up to your high ideals. To avoid disappointment and frustration, you may have more luck with a partner who has a humanitarian nature. Some people of this birthday choose partners that they either put on a pedestal or attempt to rescue, so it is important to be discriminating in your choice of relationships. Once committed, however, you are a loyal and faithful partner.

YOUR SPECIAL SOMEONE

You may be lucky in love with persons born on the following dates.

Love & friendship: Jan. 1, 7, 21, 23, 31, Feb. 5, 19, 21, 29, Mar. 3, 17, 19, 27, Apr. 1, 15, 17, 25, May 13, 15, 23, June 11, 13, 21, July 9, 11, 19, Aug. 7, 9, 17, Sept. 5, 7, 15, Oct. 3, 5, 13, Nov. 1, 3, 11, Dec. 1, 9

Beneficial: Jan. 5, 16, 18, Feb. 3, 14, 16, Mar. 1, 12, 14, 29, Apr. 10, 12, 27, May 8, 10, 25, 29, June 6, 8, 23, 27, July 4, 6, 21, 25, Aug. 2, 4, 19, 23, Sept. 2, 17, 21, Oct. 15, 19, Nov. 13, 17, Dec. 11, 15, 29

Fatal attractions: Jan. 6, 30, Feb. 4, 28, Mar. 2, 26, Apr. 24, May 22, June 20, July 9, 10, 11, 12, 13, 18, Aug. 16, Sept. 14, Oct. 12, Nov. 10, Dec. 8

Challenging: Jan. 4, Feb. 2, May 29, 31, June 27, 29, 30, July 25, 27, 28, Aug. 23, 25, 26, 30, Sept. 21, 23, 24, 28, Oct. 19, 21, 22, 26, Nov. 17, 19, 20, 24, Dec. 15, 17, 28, 22

Soul mates: Jan. 23, Feb. 21, Mar. 19, Apr. 17, May 15, June 13, July 11, 31, Aug. 9, 29, Sept. 7, 27, Oct. 5, 25, Nov. 3, 23, Dec. 1, 21

January 10

VS Your Capricorn birthday indicates that you are practical, friendly, and determined, a strong-willed individual with a direct approach. A sixth sense, particularly regarding material matters, endows you with a shrewd sense of values and a quick understanding of people. When your instincts are combined with your dedication to a goal or purpose, you can be resolute in achieving your aims. Ambitious, with a need to lead the action, you need only apply the necessary self-discipline to achieve remarkable success.

With the supporting influence of your decanate ruler, Taurus, an ability to turn on the charm can enhance your sociability and success. You may wish to surround yourself with beauty, style and luxury. Although material security, status, and prestige can be important, you will strive to achieve results when you find something of interest. Liking the good life, however, and knowing how to enjoy yourself, you may have to beware of overindulgence or becoming too materialistic.

Your warmth and magnetic appeal ensure that you are fortunate in people-related activities. As you seek harmonious relationships with others, you are sensitive to your environment. Usually you desire security and like to build a good foundation for whatever you want to do in life. With hard work and a positive attitude, you have the drive to move mountains and can impress others with your knowledge and achievements.

From the age of eleven to forty, when your progressed Sun moves through Aquarius, you have a growing desire to be independent as well as a heightened interest in friendship or group awareness. You may need to express your own unique ideas or be experimental. After the age of forty-one, when your progressed Sun moves into Pisces, your emotional sensitivity becomes refined and you develop a stronger sense of vision. This may encourage you to seek idealistic or spiritual goals. At the age of seventy-one there is a turning point as your progressed Sun enters Aries, emphasizing a desire for active self-orientation in your affairs.

FIXED STAR

Star's name: Deneb, also called Al Danab

Degree position: 18°49'–19°55' Capricorn between the years 1930 and 2000

Magnitude: 3

Strength: ★★★★★

Orb: 1°40'

Constellation: Zeta Aquila

Applicable days: January 9, 10, 11, 12

Star qualities: Mars/Jupiter

Description: a green star located in the eye of the Eagle

PRIMARY STAR'S INFLUENCE

Deneb imparts leadership abilities and bestows a liberal attitude and a broad-minded nature. Optimistic, enterprising, and daring, you are enthusiastic and ambitious, with sound common sense and an ability to act assertively.

Linked to your Sun's degree, this star bestows success in dealing with the public and an inclination toward business and the legal profession. You probably possess leadership and executive skills, a strong will, and the ability to instruct others. This star imparts an independent and dynamic personality or true individuality, which gives you opportunities for advancement through courage and enthusiasm.

• *Positive:* enterprising spirit, competitive, ambitious

• *Negative:* hastiness, impatience, dishonesty, negligence

Your Secret Self

Success-oriented and an independent thinker, you recognize the power of knowledge and expertise. Being mentally keen as well as practical, you are excellent at problem solving. Your sensitive and intuitive intellect is capable of inspired thinking that may attract you to writing, art, philosophy, religion, or metaphysics. Another aspect of your personality is an ability to influence others with your spirited enthusiasm. This can place you naturally in positions of leadership, although you may have to guard against becoming too stubborn or willful.

Generous and kind, you can be very caring at times. Your problems are rarely financial but are more likely to be emotional, particularly issues of being disappointed with others. Fortunately, your ability to see opportunities can often give you a lucky break and help you change situations for the better.

Work & Vocation

Hardworking and ambitious, with a pragmatic approach, you like to think independently and are often an entrepreneur, producer, or promoter. Skill with your hands and a desire to build something solid may draw you to the business world. You may be drawn to construction and engineering or work as a builder or troubleshooter. If attracted to the arts, you want to see financial rewards and are likely to succeed in advertising and promotion or manufacturing and management. Although you have excellent business skills, you may be interested in philosophy, religion, or metaphysics. As a curious and inventive individual, you want to explore the unknown and sometimes have a maverick quality.

Famous people who share your birthday include singer Rod Stewart, painter James McNeill Whistler, singer Pat Benatar, actor Sal Mineo, religious reformer John Calvin, musician Max Roach, dancer Ray Bolger, and boxer George Foreman.

Numerology

Like those with a number 1 birthday, you are enterprising and independent. Although you may have to overcome challenges before you achieve your goals, with determination you often achieve your objectives. Your pioneering spirit frequently encourages you to travel far afield or strike out on your own. As a number 10 individual, you may also learn that although with perseverance you can achieve a great deal, you should guard against being self-centered or domineering. The subinfluence of the number 1 month indicates that you are full of drive and high aspiration. Usually creative and innovative, you have a commanding presence and executive abilities. Intelligent, you prefer to lead rather than take orders from others. A need for a challenge suggests that you want to test your intelligence and wits. At times you may have to stand on your own two feet in order to build your confidence. When self-assured, you are hardworking and ambitious. Although usually you seek a well-balanced outlook and stability, at times you can become emotionally frustrated and unable to show your feelings. As a person who wants to achieve success, you may need to develop your diplomatic skills or learn to compromise.

• *Positive:* leadership, creative, progressive, forceful, optimistic, strong convictions, competitive, independent, gregarious

• *Negative:* overbearing, jealous, egotistical, antagonistic, selfish, vacillating, impatient

Love & Relationships

With your elegant taste and sense of style, you are likely to have an attractive home in which to entertain friends and acquaintances. Ambitious and preferring to be associated with people of intelligence or success, you are not likely to spend much time with life's underachievers. While often passionate, you still do not lose your practical perspective. Usually magnanimous and generous with those you love, you can become surprisingly thrifty on occasion. Proud and with magnetic charm, you should find it easy to attract partners, but be careful that material considerations do not become too important a factor in your close relationships.

YOUR SPECIAL SOMEONE

For that special someone, you might want to look among those born on the following dates.

Love & friendship: Jan. 8, 12, 17, 20, 22, 24, Feb. 6, 15, 18, 20, 22, Mar. 4, 13, 16, 18, 20, 28, Apr. 2, 11, 14, 16, 18, 26, May 9, 12, 14, 16, June 7, 10, 12, 14, July 5, 8, 10, 12, 30, Aug. 3, 6, 8, 10, 28, Sept. 1, 4, 6, 8, 16, 26, Oct. 2, 4, 6, 24, Nov. 2, 4, 22, Dec. 2, 20

Beneficial: Jan. 6, 23, Feb. 4, 21, Mar. 2, 19, 30, Apr. 17, 28, May 15, 26, 30, June 13, 24, 28, July 11, 22, 26, Aug. 9, 20, 24, Sept. 7, 18, 22, Oct. 5, 16, 20, Nov. 3, 14, 18, Dec. 1, 12, 16, 30

Fatal attractions: Jan. 7, Feb. 5, Mar. 3, Apr. 1, July 10, 11, 12, 13, 14

Challenging: Jan. 5, 26, 29, Feb. 3, 24, 27, Mar. 1, 22, 25, Apr. 20, 23, May 18, 21, June 16, 19, 30, July 14, 17, 28, Aug. 12, 15, 26, 31, Sept. 10, 13, 24, 29, Oct. 8, 11, 22, 27, Nov. 6, 9, 20, 25, Dec. 4, 7, 18, 23

Soul mates: Jan. 30, Feb. 28, Mar. 26, Apr. 24, May 22, June 20, July 18, Aug. 16, Sept. 14, Oct. 12, 31, Nov. 10, 29, Dec. 8, 27

January 11

♑ Your birthday indicates that you are a hard worker with a strong idealistic and creative spirit. Although a serious and ambitious Capricorn, you can also be extremely charming and warm, with a natural talent for dealing with people. Individual and aware of appearances, you like to be well groomed and often have an original way of dressing. Although strong-willed and determined, you may vacillate at times between faith and doubt, which can cause you worry or indecision.

The subinfluence of your decanate ruler, Virgo, makes you mentally keen and alert, with a good ability to concentrate. Shrewd and purposeful, you are excellent at problem solving and like to see things through to their final conclusion. Being pragmatic and a good strategist, you prefer to put your many talents to some practical use; once you decide on a course of action, you have the power to attain your goal if you apply the necessary effort. Nevertheless, it would be better to avoid taking life too seriously, which could leave you feeling emotionally frustrated or disappointed. These same powerful emotions can also be used constructively through compassion and a universal attitude.

With your many diverse interests and need for action, you should enjoy travel and adventure. With an appreciation of beauty and a desire for glamour and the good life, luckily you possess the financial potential to accumulate wealth. Women may prove to be of particularly beneficial influence in your life in general.

From the age of ten to thirty-nine, when your progressed Sun moves through Aquarius, you have a growing need for freedom and independence. You can develop a heightened interest in friendship or group awareness and may need to express your individuality. After the age of forty, when your progressed Sun moves into Pisces, your emotional sensitivity becomes emphasized and you develop a stronger sense of vision. This may encourage you to seek idealistic or spiritual goals. By your middle years, your work is likely to involve travel and change, which will have a positive effect on your life. At the age of seventy, there is a turning point as your progressed Sun enters Aries, accenting a need to be direct and active in your affairs and in your relationships with others.

Your Secret Self

With the right attitude, you have the potential to inspire others with your ideals and imagination, so avoid investing your emotional energies in small or unimportant events, which can divert you from your positive and worldly goals. By concentrating on your creative energies, you are able to achieve productive results. Take time to regenerate yourself by paying attention to your diet and health and learn to relax now and then.

Although you possess the ability to enchant others, they may not see that behind your bold front you occasionally suffer from inner confusion. In later years wisdom will come through the culmination of your spiritual development, universal understanding, and natural mystical potential. Guard against being impulsive, acting extravagant, or falling for get-rich-quick schemes by investing in long-term plans.

Work & Vocation

Self-expression, freedom, and mental stimulation should be the foundation of your career. As you do not like to take orders from others, you may prefer to be self-employed. Usually a law

FIXED STAR

Star's name: Deneb, also called Al Danab

Degree position: 18°49'–19°55' Capricorn between the years 1930 and 2000

Magnitude: 3

Strength: ★★★★★

Orb: 1°40'

Constellation: Zeta Aquila

Applicable days: January 9, 10, 11, 12

Star qualities: Mars/Jupiter

Description: a green star located in the eye of the Eagle

PRIMARY STAR'S INFLUENCE

Deneb imparts leadership abilities and bestows a liberal attitude and a broad-minded nature. Optimistic, enterprising, and daring, you are enthusiastic and ambitious, with sound common sense and an ability to act assertively.

Linked to your Sun's degree, this star bestows success in dealing with the public and an inclination toward business and the legal profession. You probably possess leadership and executive skills, a strong will, and the ability to instruct others. This star imparts an independent and dynamic personality or true individuality, which gives you opportunities for advancement through courage and enthusiasm.

• *Positive:* an enterprising spirit, competitive, ambitious

• *Negative:* hastiness, impatience, dishonesty, negligence

unto yourself, you are dynamic and enterprising. With your universal compassion and independent thinking, you can pursue a career in teaching, counseling, or psychology. An interest in religion, philosophy, and metaphysics implies a talent for astrology. Usually women play an active part in your career advancement. A knack for words, imagination, and communication skills suggest a flair for writing, music, or the arts. Idealistic, you may want to work for reforms and fight injustice by pursuing a career as a person in the clergy, politician, or civil servant.

Famous people who share your birthday include U.S. statesman Alexander Hamilton, musician Clarence Clemons, singer Naomi Judd, and psychologist William James.

Numerology

The special vibration of the master number 11 birthday suggests that idealism, inspiration, and innovation are highly important to you. A blend of humility and confidence often challenges you to work toward self-mastery, both materially and spiritually. Usually you are highly charged and enjoy vitality but must avoid becoming overly anxious or impractical. The subinfluence of the number 1 month indicates that you are independent and enterprising, with a need to express yourself creatively. Although friendly and outgoing, you dislike restrictions and prefer to act freely and be autonomous. Developing your diplomatic skills and learning to compromise, however, can help you to find a middle ground and be less self-seeking. Innovative and with plenty of energy, you are multitalented, with many interests. At times you may be outspoken, but you are an entertaining person and are never boring. Although you possess intuitive powers and are determined, you need a goal upon which you can focus rather than scatter your energies in many directions.

• *Positive:* balanced, focused, objective, enthusiastic, inspirational, spiritual, idealistic, intuitive, healing ability, humanitarian, psychic

• *Negative:* superiority complex, aimless, overemotional, easily hurt, selfish, lack of clarity, dominating

Love & Relationships

Being charming and magnetic, you can draw people toward you. Usually you are more interested in those who stimulate your mind or inspire you creatively. It can be very advantageous if you also share a joint interest or purpose. Since you are sensitive, with strong emotions, it might be helpful to regularly spend time alone, collecting your thoughts and feelings. This allows you to intuitively sense what is right for you in your relationships and helps you keep the balance between being independent and needing others. You usually work better when you have faith in yourself and keep your partners on their toes with a little friendly rivalry.

YOUR SPECIAL SOMEONE

You are likely to have luck with someone born on one of the following dates.

Love & friendship: Jan. 9, 13, 23, 25, 27, Feb. 7, 21, 23, 25, Mar. 5, 19, 21, 23, 29, Apr. 3, 17, 19, 21, 27, 30, May 1, 5, 15, 17, 19, 25, 28, June 13, 15, 17, 23, 26, July 11, 13, 15, 21, 24, Aug. 9, 11, 13, 19, 22, Sept. 7, 9, 11, 17, 20, Oct. 5, 7, 9, 15, 18, Nov. 3, 5, 7, 13, 16, Dec. 1, 3, 5, 11, 14

Beneficial: Jan. 2, 4, 7, Feb. 2, 5, Mar. 3, Apr. 1, May 31, June 29, July 27, 31, Aug. 25, 29, Sept. 23, 27, Oct. 21, 25, Nov. 19, 23, Dec. 17, 21

Fatal attractions: Jan. 8, 14, Feb. 6, 12, Mar. 4, 10, Apr. 2, 8, May 6, June 4, July 2, 11, 12, 13, 14, 15

Challenging: Jan. 6, 19, 29, Feb. 4, 17, 27, Mar. 2, 15, 25, Apr. 13, 23, May 11, 21, June 9, 19, July 7, 17, Aug. 5, 15, Sept. 3, 13, 30, Oct. 1, 11, 28, Nov. 9, 26. Dec. 7, 24, 29

Soul mates: Jan. 16, 21, Feb. 14, 19, Mar. 12, 17, Apr. 10, 15, May 8, 13, June 6, 11, July 4, 9, Aug. 2, 7, Sept. 5, Oct. 3, Nov. 1

January 12

♑ Your birthday shows you to be friendly and hardworking, a practical Capricorn with compelling personal charm. Although you are independent, your natural diplomatic skills suggest that you can work well in cooperative or teamwork situations. Down to earth in your approach, you can also be highly imaginative, with a strong sense of vision.

The subinfluence of your decanate ruler, Virgo, indicates that you are responsible, with clear goals and keen perceptions. Being methodical, you take pride in your work; once decided on a course of action, you have the power to attain your objective, regardless of the time involved. This birthday suggests that your work has an especially strong emphasis for you. You may, however, have to avoid a tendency to become so absorbed in your interests that you neglect your immediate surroundings.

With both practical business sense and sensitive emotions, you will find that it is important to develop a sense of balance in your life. This helps you avoid unknown fears or hidden tensions that may lead you to escapism or instability. Although you possess a strong understanding of the material world, an inclination toward humanitarian or mystical subjects may draw you to spiritual or metaphysical studies. The combination of your sensitivity, inventive mind, and quick insight can also give you a shrewd understanding of human nature. Preferring to keep active, you may be of service to your community as an advisor or specialist.

From the age of nine to thirty-eight, when your progressed Sun moves through Aquarius, you become less influenced by traditional views and more independent. You learn to trust your own individual perspective. You may develop an interest in groups or humanitarian issues and have a strong need for friendship. Another turning point occurs at the age of thirty-nine, when your progressed Sun enters Pisces. From this time, there is more of an emphasis on your emotional inner life, reflected through your visions, dreams, and emotional ideals. This may encourage you to seek idealistic or spiritual goals. At the age of sixty-nine, there is another turning point as your progressed Sun enters Aries, accenting a desire for an active and direct approach to the people and situations in your life.

Your Secret Self

One of your major challenges is to put those inspired ideas and grand dreams into action. Helped by your quick intelligence and an inner nobility, you can also find yourself in leadership positions. Although clever and gifted, you may still experience periods of self-doubt or feelings of inferiority. By recognizing the power of your knowledge and developing your natural intuitive sense, you can confidently take the initiative and convert your ideals into a reality.

Although part of you would be quite happy just to relax at home in a comfortable routine, your natural sense of responsibility prods you into action. An inner desire for harmony can translate into a love of music, art, or peaceful surroundings. Even though you can sometimes become anxious, at your best you can enchant others with your qualities of compassion and inner strength.

Work & Vocation

Friendly and diplomatic, you enjoy all kinds of activities that involve partnerships or collaborating with others. A way with words implies that you also have excellent writing skills, and if

FIXED STAR

Star's name: Deneb, also called Al Danab

Degree position: 18°49'–19°55' Capricorn between the years 1930 and 2000

Magnitude: 3

Strength: ★★★★★

Orb: 1°40'

Constellation: Zeta Aquila

Applicable days: January 9, 10, 11, 12

Star qualities: Mars/Jupiter

Description: a green star located in the eye of the Eagle

PRIMARY STAR'S INFLUENCE

Deneb imparts leadership abilities and bestows a liberal attitude and a broad-minded nature. Optimistic, enterprising, and daring, you are enthusiastic and ambitious, with sound common sense and an ability to act assertively.

Linked to your Sun's degree, this star bestows success in dealing with the public and an inclination toward business and the legal profession. You probably possess leadership and executive skills, a strong will, and the ability to instruct others. This star imparts an independent and dynamic personality or true individuality, which gives you opportunities for advancement through courage and enthusiasm.

• *Positive:* enterprising spirit, competitive, ambitious

• *Negative:* hastiness, impatience, dishonesty, negligence

you have an ear for music, you can compose and play; you may also wish to paint and draw. Competitive and ambitious, you may choose drama and sporting activities. If self-employed, you can excel as a buyer and trader or agent and negotiator. Alternatively, you may choose a career in public relations or counseling. If working in the civil service, you are ideally suited to being a diplomat and commercial attaché. An interest in the visual arts, such as photography and design, may inspire your inventive temperament. Unafraid of new inventions, you may be drawn to information technology and related industries.

Famous people who share your birthday include artist John Singer Sargent, U.S. statesman John Hancock, spiritual teacher Swami Vivekananda, writer Jack London, and actress Kirstie Alley.

Numerology

Usually you are intuitive and friendly, possessing good reasoning power. A desire to establish true individuality is often suggested by the number 12 birthday. Innovative and sensitive, you know how to use tact and cooperative methods to achieve your aims and objectives. To others you often appear confident, although self-doubt and suspicion can undermine your usual easygoing personality and positive outlook. When you achieve a balance between your need to define yourself and an inclination to be supportive of others, you can find emotional satisfaction and personal fulfillment. The subinfluence of the number 1 month indicates that you are ambitious and hardworking, with practical abilities. Intelligent and courageous, as an autonomous individual, you are inclined to be innovative, with executive skills. Although you have a desire to be first and strike out alone, you benefit greatly from partnerships and collaborating with others. Nevertheless, as you are enthusiastic and original, you prefer to be a leader rather than a follower.

- *Positive:* creative, attractive, initiative, disciplinarian, assertive, confident
- *Negative:* reclusive, eccentric, uncooperative, overly sensitive, lack of self-esteem

Love & Relationships

Although you are outwardly sociable, at heart you may be quietly reserved. Marriage or a settled relationship can be particularly important to you, especially with your love of home. You are usually loyal and willing to make sacrifices to keep your relationships harmonious. You may have to be careful, however, of falling into a rut or through lack of communication becoming detached and hence appearing cold or indifferent. Although relationships are very important to you, remember to keep a balance between staying independent and being actively involved in relationships.

January 13

FIXED STARS

Although your Sun's degree is not linked to a fixed star, some of your other planets' degrees certainly will be. By having an astrological chart calculated, you can find the exact position of the planets on your date of birth. This will tell you which of the fixed stars listed in this book are relevant to you.

Strong willpower and a sharp mind are some of the qualities implied by your date of birth. As a determined Capricorn, you must keep yourself busy working or creatively occupied in order to make the most of your many talents. By developing your heightened intuitive sensitivity, you can come to understand yourself and life at a deeper level and so avoid possible periods of frustration. A winning charm and leadership abilities can help you in your climb to the top.

The subinfluence of your decanate ruler, Virgo, makes you mentally keen and alert, with good concentration. With the ability to go straight to the heart of a matter, you are a practical and direct thinker with sound common sense. You may particularly enjoy initiating new projects or problem solving. Preferring precision and accuracy, you will work steadily and with disciplined effort once you have decided on your goal. By taking time out to relax or by assessing whether you have lost your sense of humor, you can judge whether you have gone a little too far and become too serious.

Although you are a pragmatist, your sensitivity, fertile imagination, and inspired thinking mean that you can also be an idealist. This may lead you to feel happiest when working hard on a project or cause about which you feel deeply. Being stubborn, uncompromising, or willful, however, may prove to be the major block to the use of the tremendous power contained in your birthday.

From the age of eight to thirty-seven, when your progressed Sun moves through Aquarius, you have a growing need for freedom and independence. You can develop a heightened interest in friendship or group awareness and may need to express your individuality. After the age of thirty-eight, when your progressed Sun moves into Pisces, your emotional sensitivity becomes emphasized and you develop a stronger sense of vision. This may encourage you to seek idealistic or spiritual goals. At the age of sixty-eight there is a turning point as your progressed Sun enters Aries, accenting a need to be direct and active in your affairs and in your relationships. You can also take the lead and inspire others.

Your Secret Self

With an acute sensitivity, you possess strong intuition and the potential for wisdom. By trusting your instinctive reactions to people or situations, you come to learn about your inner strength and spontaneous awareness. These can also help you realize that your high ideals may not necessarily be found in other people. The price for your high ideals may be that you sometimes have to stand alone. Artistic and refined, you have an ability for visionary and creative thinking that can lead you to writing or mystical pursuits. As a perfectionist with analytical or critical talents, you can demonstrate humility and dedication to your work.

Your sharp intellect and natural psychological skills keep you interested in people's motivation and bestow an innate gift for self-analysis. You usually prefer the personal touch and have a talent for making people feel special. With your unusual humor, you also enjoy a mental challenge and like to test your wits and intelligence against others.

Work & Vocation

Hardworking and dedicated, you are a creative individual with leadership ability. If you are working for others, your employers or superiors will appreciate your responsible attitude and broad-minded approach to original ideas. Self-disciplined, you can stay calm in times of crisis. Intuitive, you also have the ability to solve problems and work as an advisor or a specialist in your field. An interest in history, philosophy, and spirituality often leads you to explore metaphysics. An interest in education suggests that you can be an accomplished teacher or writer. Alternatively, you may choose to work as a counselor or administrator.

Famous people who share your birthday include singer Sophie Tucker, philosopher George Gurdjieff, astrologer Geoffrey Cornelius, and actor Robert Stack.

Numerology

Emotional sensitivity and inspiration are often identified with the number 13 birthday. Numerically, you are associated with hard work, and you can accomplish much through determination and creative self-expression. You may, however, need to develop a pragmatic outlook if you want to turn your talents and artistic gifts into tangible products. With dedication you can achieve prosperity or recognition. With a number 13 birthday, you can be charming and fun-loving, with a sociable personality. Like many individuals who share your birthdate, you may find traveling a rewarding experience, or you may yearn to settle in a new environment to make a better life for yourself. The subinfluence of the number 1 month indicates that you are intelligent, with strong instincts, spontaneity, and inspired thoughts. Enchanted by wisdom or knowledge, you may turn your back on the material world to seek enlightenment in spirituality. Usually autonomous and innovative, you have courage and plenty of energy. The pioneering spirit indicated here encourages you to explore new objectives, territories, or concepts. Usually you make your own decisions or strike out alone. Full of enthusiasm and original ideas, you often show others the way forward.

• *Positive:* ambitious, original, creative, freedom-loving, self-expressive, initiative
• *Negative:* impulsive, indecisive, bossy, unemotional, rebellious

Love & Relationships

In your finer moments, you project charm and openness and have no problem attracting friends and admirers. You need love, but sometimes feeling inhibited or shy may block your communication with others. This may not be helped by possible conflicts between love and duty or work. You can, however, be extremely loyal once committed to a partner, and you have a strong need for security. The more universal you become, the less likely you are to take your personal life too seriously, and thus you can avoid disappointment. Ideally, it would be better to find a partner who shares your interests, hopes, and aspirations.

YOUR SPECIAL SOMEONE

You may have luck with a partner born on one of the following dates.

Love & friendship: Jan. 11, 20, 24, 25, 27, 29, Feb. 9, 18, 23, 25, 27, Mar. 7, 16, 21, 23, 25, Apr. 5, 14, 19, 21, 23, May 3, 12, 16, 17, 19, 21, June 1, 10, 15, 17, 19, July 8, 13, 15, 17, Aug. 6, 11, 13, 15, Sept. 4, 8, 9, 11, 13, Oct. 2, 7, 9, 11, Nov. 5, 7, 9, Dec. 3, 5, 7

Beneficial: Jan. 9, 26, Feb. 7, 24, Mar. 5, 22, Apr. 3, 20, May 1, 18, 29, June 16, 27, July 14, 25, 29, 30, Aug. 12, 23, 27, 28, 31, Sept. 10, 21, 25, 26, 29, Oct. 8, 19, 23, 24, 27, Nov. 6, 17, 21, 22, 25, Dec. 4, 15, 19, 20, 23

Fatal attractions: Jan. 16, Feb. 14, Mar. 12, Apr. 10, May 8, June 6, July 4, 13, 14, 15, 16, 17, Aug. 2

Challenging: Jan. 8, 29, 31, Feb. 6, 27, 29, Mar. 4, 25, 27, 28, Apr. 2, 23, 25, 26, May 21, 23, 24, June 19, 21, 22, July 17, 19, 20, Aug. 15, 17, 18, Sept. 13, 15, 16, Oct. 11, 13, 14, 30, Nov. 9, 11, 12, 28, Dec. 7, 9, 10, 26

Soul mates: May 30, June 28, July 26, Aug. 24, Sept. 22, 30, Oct. 20, 28, Nov. 18, 26, Dec. 16, 24

January 14

FIXED STARS

Although your Sun's degree is not linked to a fixed star, some of your other planets' degrees certainly will be. By having an astrological chart calculated, you can find the exact position of the planets on your date of birth. This will tell you which of the fixed stars listed in this book are relevant to you.

♑ Friendly, practical, and hardworking, you are an intuitive and imaginative individual with sound common sense. Your birthday shows that your magnetic charm is likely to help you in your dealings with others and combines well with your natural sense of leadership. A logical thinker with a creative flair, you respect people with knowledge and like to be informed. Clever, ambitious, and independent, you have talents that can bring you much success in life, particularly when you avoid negative thinking.

With the subinfluence of your decanate ruler, Virgo, you are a methodical and careful worker who pays attention to detail. Although you retain a basic shyness or reserve, you have good communication skills and can go straight to the heart of a matter. You have a touch of the perfectionist, so you can make precise and accurate observations, though you may have to avoid being overcautious or serious.

Receptive to new ideas, you are inventive and progressive and have a need to convey your originality. Although you are interested in freedom and reform, at times your dislike of restriction can turn into a stubborn or contrary streak. Preferring to be active, you have a quick intelligence that suggests that you need variety and new experiences to stop you from becoming bored, but it is wise not to let an inner restlessness cause you to move too quickly or impulsively.

From age seven to thirty-six, when your progressed Sun moves through Aquarius, you have a growing desire to be independent as well as a heightened interest in friendship or group awareness. You may need to express your own unique ideas or be experimental. After the age of thirty-seven, when your progressed Sun moves into Pisces, your sensitivity is enhanced and you develop a stronger awareness of your emotional needs. Your sense of vision may encourage you to seek idealistic or spiritual goals. At the age of sixty-seven there is a turning point as your progressed Sun enters Aries, emphasizing a desire for active self-promotion and taking the initiative in life.

Your Secret Self

Although you appear confident, you can be prone to worry or indecision and be inwardly more complex than you seem. A need to express yourself may manifest through creative talents in music, art, or drama, and if you can discipline yourself to develop your ideas, you can succeed in a big way. A need to be popular suggests that you also need the approval of others, and you may mask your impatience if it is in your own interests. Yet, inspired by example, you can be a true visionary and humanitarian, fighting for causes and your ideals.

Interested in everything and everyone, you often try to do too much. Spending periods alone in reflection, contemplation, or meditation is particularly good for developing your inner calm. You succeed best in an activity that you love, as this is when you are able to feel your most powerful. By building a strong sense of purpose and having faith in yourself and what life can provide, you can achieve miracles.

Work & Vocation

Creative and pragmatic, you are often a shrewd judge of people and values. Versatile and multitalented, you can achieve a great deal if you invest time and effort. Usually ambitious and competitive, you can master your craft, whether you draw or cook. Good administrative skills suggest that you want leadership or management positions. Friendly and with excellent communication skills, you may be interested in teaching or work in the media, or public relations, advertising, and promotion. If you decide you want to pursue a career in business, you may be attracted to banking and the stock exchange. Persuasive and commanding, you can succeed in anything that involves people by using your common sense and compassion.

Famous people who share your birthday include actress Faye Dunaway, singer LL Cool J, humanitarian Albert Schweitzer, photographer Cecil Beaton, and writers Yukio Mishima and John Dos Passos.

Numerology

Intellectual potential, a pragmatic outlook, and strong determination are some of the qualities associated with the number 14 birthday. Often you possess a strong desire to establish a firm foundation and achieve success through hard work. Like many individuals associated with this birthday, you can often reach the top of your profession. With your perceptive mind you respond quickly to problems and enjoy solving them. With a 14 birthdate, you like taking a risk or a gamble or may be lucky to gain a windfall. The subinfluence of the number 1 month indicates that you are original and idealistic but often inquisitive and stubborn or set in your ways. The great desire to be first and autonomous usually suggests that by developing your creative gifts, you can rise to a position of prominence in your profession. The experimental essence indicated here encourages you to make your own judgment or strike out alone. When innovative and full of enthusiasm, you often show others the way forward by introducing reforms or original ideas.

- *Positive:* decisive actions, hardworking, lucky, creative, pragmatic, imaginative, industrious
- *Negative:* overcautious, impulsive, unstable, thoughtless, stubborn

Love & Relationships

Generous and friendly when socializing, you are a good mixer and enjoy the company of others. Interested in self-improvement, you are often drawn to clever people who are busy advancing themselves. Your love of knowledge also suggests that you enjoy groups where you can learn new information or skills. Although honest and direct with your thoughts, in relationships you may sometimes have difficulty expressing your feelings or alternately may become too controlling. You work particularly well in partnerships where you have similar interests or are actively working on joint projects

YOUR SPECIAL SOMEONE

You may try many experiments in your quest for love, but for that special someone you might want to begin looking for those born among the following dates.

Love & friendship: Jan. 4, 10, 11, 12, 26, 28, 30, 31, Feb. 2, 9, 10, 24, 26, 28, Mar. 7, 8, 22, 24, 26, Apr. 5, 6, 20, 22, 24, 30, May 3, 4, 18, 20, 22, 28, 31, June 1, 2, 16, 18, 20, 26, 29, July 14, 16, 18, 24, 27, Aug. 12, 14, 16, 22, 25, Sept. 10, 12, 14, 20, 23, Oct. 8, 10, 12, 18, 21, Nov. 6, 8, 10, 16, 19, Dec. 4, 6, 8, 14, 17

Beneficial: Jan. 3, 10, 29, Feb. 1, 8, 27, Mar. 6, 25, Apr. 4, 23, 25, May 2, 21, 23, June 19, July 17, 30, Aug. 15, 28, Sept. 13, 15, 26, Oct. 11, 24, Nov. 9, 22, Dec. 7, 20

Fatal attractions: Jan. 11, Feb. 9, Mar. 7, Apr. 5, May 3, June 1, July 14, 15, 16, 17, 18

Challenging: Jan. 9, Feb. 7, Mar. 5, 28, Apr. 3, 26, May 1, 24, June 22, July 20, Aug. 18, Sept. 16, Oct. 14, 30, 31, Nov. 12, 28, 29, Dec. 10, 26, 27

Soul mates: Jan. 7, Feb. 5, Mar. 3, Apr. 1, May 29, June 27, July 25, Aug. 23, Sept. 21, Oct. 19, Nov. 17, Dec. 15

657

January 15

FIXED STAR

Star's name: Terebellum

Degree position: 24°52'–25°55'
Capricorn between the years
1930 and 2000

Magnitude: 5

Strength: ★★

Orb: 1°

Constellation: Omega Sagittarius

Applicable days: January 15, 16, 17

Star qualities: Venus/Saturn

Description: an orange-red star in the four-sided figure in the tail of the Archer

PRIMARY STAR'S INFLUENCE

Terebellum imparts a clear and pragmatic outlook, with an ambitious and determined personality. Often you succeed after overcoming difficulties. This star indicates that you are responsible and dutiful and can endure hardship and struggle. This star may also suggest that you can experience doubts and inner conflicts between personal desires and duties to others.

Linked to your Sun's degree, this star bestows cleverness and ambition to rise to prominent positions. Terebellum, however, warns that you may nevertheless be crafty and suggests guarding against mischief and wrongdoing. This star indicates that good fortune and success can be achieved, but often at considerable expense or sacrifice.

• *Positive:* ambitious, devotion, sentimental, clever

• *Negative:* mercenary, ruthlessness, crafty, self-seeking

Your birthday shows you to be an ambitious and determined Capricorn who is a good judge of values. Quietly dramatic, with inherent leadership skills, you have a persistence and dedication to your goals that can help you reach high positions. Realistic and pragmatic, you are a straight-talking individual, although a natural flair for people ensures your success in social situations. A tendency to allow yourself to get overconcerned by materialism may be one of the few stumbling blocks to the realization of your remarkable promise.

With the subinfluence of your decanate ruler, Virgo, you have excellent communication skills and an ability to pay attention to detail. Logical and mentally thorough, you show good concentration and are capable of deep thought. You may have to be careful, however, that with your natural critical abilities you do not appear too pointed in your observations. A preference to have everything clearly defined and explained can aid you to solve problems easily or enhance your natural business sense.

With your strong character, you are able to combine your creativity with a spirit of enterprise. Since you possess good judgment and an ability to evaluate people and situations, you may find yourself speaking on others' behalf or fighting for human rights. Independent, self-willed, and dynamic, you possess good organizational skills and an ability to inspire others.

From the age of six to thirty-five, when your progressed Sun moves through Aquarius, you become group-oriented, less serious, and more freedom-loving. You may be attracted by unusual interests or have a strong desire to express your individuality. After the age of thirty-six, when your progressed Sun moves into Pisces, your emotional sensitivity becomes enhanced and you develop a stronger inner life. This can be reflected in your visions, dreams, and ideals. At the age of sixty-six, there is a turning point when your progressed Sun enters Aries, emphasizing a need to take the initiative and be brave and direct in your relationships with others.

Your Secret Self

A humanitarian and detached side to your personality can encourage you to be generous with your time or money. With an ability to inject energy into a cause or a project you support, you can stimulate and inspire others to action. Allowing yourself to dwell on the past can cause frustration or disappointment, and a tendency to vacillate between being too security-conscious and being too extravagant suggests that you need to develop your economic acumen.

An inner creativity can inspire you to great heights or encourage some tangible form of self-expression. At these times, you can be very light-hearted, sociable, and able to express the joys of life. If you spread out into many areas, however, you may encounter worry and indecision about your choices. Often ahead of your time, you have unusual and inventive ideas, a quick, dry wit, and an ability to be very entertaining.

Work & Vocation

Idealistic and resolute, with a Midas touch, you could achieve success in education, research, and science. A good sense of structure may inspire you to build or work on some large business project. Whether an architect, a manager, or in government service, you are likely to be magnanimous and dramatic. When successful, you may enjoy being a philanthropist or an initiator. Creative and technical, with a flair for the avant-garde, you may work as an art dealer, curator, or art administrator. Eloquent and entertaining, you may be drawn to the theater, opera, or music. Alternatively, you may be attracted to groups and organizations as a trade-union leader or civil rights campaigner willing to fight for humanitarian causes.

Famous people who share your birthday include civil rights leader Martin Luther King Jr., playwright Molière, drummer Gene Krupa, tycoon Aristotle Onassis, physicist Edward Teller, and Cardinal John O'Connor.

Numerology

Usually you are quick and enthusiastic, with a charismatic personality. Your greatest assets are your strong instincts and the ability to learn through combining theory and practice. On many occasions you manage to earn while learning new skills. Often you utilize your intuitive powers and are able to recognize opportunities when they arise. With a number 15 birthday, you possess a talent for attracting money or receiving help and support from others. Successful conclusions to undertakings can become more frequent if you apply your practical skills to your original ideas and overcome your tendency to be restless or dissatisfied. The subinfluence of the number 1 month indicates that you are individual and innovative, with endurance and plenty of energy. The initiative and vitality indicated here encourage you to take chances, especially if you are inspired by an idea or a business opportunity. Astute and autonomous, you like to take the initiative or show others the way forward.
- *Positive:* willing, generous, responsible, kind, cooperative, appreciative, creative ideas
- *Negative:* disruptive, restless, irresponsible, self-centered, loss of faith, worry

Love & Relationships

Being friendly, with a strong desire to express yourself, ensures that you have an active social life. Many women of this birthdate are drawn to men who prefer to live an exciting, fast-paced, or daring kind of life. As an inventive and original person, you can also be attracted to clever people who stimulate your mind. Uncertainty or indecisiveness concerning close relationships, however, can become a source of worry or disappointment unless you learn to keep a responsible yet light-hearted attitude.

YOUR SPECIAL SOMEONE

To find long-lasting happiness, security, and love, you might begin by looking for someone born on one of the following days.

Love & friendship: Jan. 13, 26, 29, Feb. 11, 27, 29, Mar. 9, 25, 27, Apr. 7, 23, 25, May 5, 18, 21, 23, 29, June 3, 19, 21, 27, 30, July 1, 17, 19, 25, 28, Aug. 15, 17, 23, 26, Sept. 10, 13, 15, 21, 24, Oct. 11, 13, 19, 22, 29, Nov. 9, 11, 17, 20, 27, Dec. 4, 7, 9, 15, 18, 25

Beneficial: Jan. 11, Feb. 9, Mar. 7, 31, Apr. 5, 29, May 3, 27, 31, June 1, 25, 29, July 23, 27, 31, Aug. 21, 25, 29, 30, Sept. 19, 23, 27, 28, Oct. 17, 21, 25, 26, Nov. 15, 19, 23, 24, 30, Dec. 13, 17, 21, 22, 28

Fatal attractions: Jan. 12, Feb. 10, Mar. 8, Apr. 6, May 4, June 2, July 15, 16, 17, 18, 19

Challenging: Jan. 10, Feb. 8, Mar. 6, 29, Apr. 4, 27, May 2, 25, June 23, July 21, Aug. 19, Sept. 17, Oct. 15, 31, Nov. 13, 29, 30, Dec. 11, 27, 28

Soul mates: Jan. 18, 24, Feb. 16, 22, Mar. 14, 20, Apr. 12, 18, May 10, 16, June 8, 14, July 6, 12, Aug. 4, 10, Sept. 2, 8, Oct. 6, Nov. 4, Dec. 2

January 16

♑ Your birthday suggests that you are a sociable, charming, practical Capricorn with a strong sense of values. Your personal magnetism and ability to quickly assess people and situations can help you advance in life. With a strong sense of your own individuality, you are very aware of image and like to look presentable. Security-conscious, you prefer to plan ahead and are persistent in achieving your chosen objectives.

With the subinfluence of your decanate ruler, Virgo, you like to adhere to a structured system, work with a schedule, or write lists. Mentally sharp and verbally precise, you are a good critic and prefer to be honest and direct. Although retaining a certain shyness or reserve, you are sociable, with good communication skills. Needing recognition, you are usually ambitious and determined, but occasionally you may have doubts and are reluctant to move forward. With a natural business sense, however, you are loyal and responsible once committed to a project.

An ability to befriend people from all walks of life can manifest as a humanitarian interest in others. Although you are tough and practical, your eagerness and idealism imply that you are an interesting combination of materialism and enthusiasm. A love of beauty and the good life suggests that you prefer to be surrounded by harmony and luxury and enjoy a touch of glamour.

While you are between the ages of five and thirty-four, your progressed Sun is in Aquarius, highlighting your individuality, desire for freedom, and group awareness. At age thirty-five, as your progressed Sun moves into Pisces, there is a turning point that emphasizes the importance of needing to feel more in touch with your emotions and heightens your sense of vision. Another change at age sixty-five, when your progressed Sun moves into Aries, accents a desire for self-assertion, more action, and new beginnings.

Your Secret Self

Dignified and creative, you have expressive qualities that ensure many interests and opportunities. Personal magnetism and a need for variety will continually bring new experiences into your life, with a possibility of contacts abroad. This can create difficulties in decision making. It would be wise, therefore, to avoid worry or negative thinking, which makes it difficult to realize your ideals. By developing faith you will find it easier to access your outstanding potential.

With a shrewd intellect and an ability to learn quickly, you value knowledge. Original yourself, you are a good judge of public trends and are usually ahead of your time. Although you can be serious, you will always have an inner playful quality that can be enchanting. Be careful, however, of a self-centered streak that can sometimes emerge to spoil your relationships. Nevertheless, your adeptness at putting your ideas across in an informative and entertaining way can captivate and inspire others.

Work & Vocation

Your personality and communication skills suggest that you can be a positive force in sales, teaching, entertainment, or politics. You are practical, ambitious, and hardworking, and in

FIXED STAR

Star's name: Terebellum

Degree position: 24°52'–25°55'
Capricorn between the years
1930 and 2000

Magnitude: 5

Strength: ★★

Orb: 1°

Constellation: Omega Sagittarius

Applicable days: January 15, 16, 17

Star qualities: Venus/Saturn

Description: an orange red star in the
four-sided figure in the tail of the
Archer

PRIMARY STAR'S INFLUENCE

Terebellum imparts a clear and pragmatic outlook with an ambitious and determined personality. Often you succeed after overcoming difficulties. This star indicates that you are responsible and dutiful and can endure hardship and struggle. This star may also suggest that you can experience doubts and inner conflicts between personal desires and duties to others.

Linked to your Sun's degree, this star bestows cleverness and an ambition to rise to prominent positions. Terebellum, however, warns that you may nevertheless be sharp and suggests guarding against mischief and wrongdoing. This star indicates that good fortune and success can be achieved, but often at a considerable expense or sacrifice.

• *Positive:* ambitious, devotion, sentimental, clever

• *Negative:* mercenary, ruthlessness, crafty, self-seeking

business your charm is likely to be a valuable asset in promoting yourself, a product, or a cause. Equally, your personal touch can help you succeed in publishing or advertising. Since you possess strong values as well as good organizational abilities, this can be advantageous to you in occupations such as administration or law. Alternatively, having a naturally creative approach to life, you may find outlets for your emotional expression through music, writing, or the arts. Whatever career you choose, you can enjoy success in dealing with the public.

Famous people born on your birthday include singer Sade, choreographer Merce Cunningham, actress/singer Ethel Merman, baseball player Dizzy Dean, writer Susan Sontag, model Kate Moss, and naturalist Dian Fossey.

Numerology

The number 16 birthday suggests that you are ambitious, yet sensitive. Usually outgoing and sociable, you are friendly and thoughtful. Although you are analytical, you often judge life according to how you feel. Intuitive, you have good insight and a caring nature. As a number 16 individual, you may be interested in world affairs and may join international corporations. The gifted ones among you have a talent for writing with sudden flashes of inspiration. You may need to learn how to balance between being overconfident and being doubtful or insecure. The subinfluence of the number 1 month indicates that you are self-reliant and resourceful. Enterprising, you enjoy taking the lead and initiating new projects. As a perceptive and creative individual, you can formulate new concepts and provide an unusual and original perspective. A need for security implies that you are efficient and realistic, and usually a long-term planner.

• *Positive:* higher education, responsibilities to home and family, integrity, intuitive, social, cooperative, insightful

• *Negative:* worry, dissatisfaction, irresponsible, opinionated, skeptical, selfish, unsympathetic

Love & Relationships

Being sociable, you have an ability to make friends easily. Valuing friendship, you are loyal to those you care for. As you want financial security, practical considerations often play a strong part in your romantic partnerships. A longing for love and affection emphasizes the importance of relationships in your life, although you may sometimes appear aloof and give others the wrong impression. It may be necessary to balance your need for intimacy and your need for freedom.

YOUR SPECIAL SOMEONE

You may have good luck with someone born on one of the following dates.

Love & friendship: Jan. 2, 6, 8, 14, 23, 26, 27, 28, Feb. 4, 10, 12, 21, 24, 26, Mar. 2, 10, 12, 19, 22, 24, Apr. 8, 14, 17, 20, 22, May 6, 15, 16, 18, 19, 20, 30, June 4, 13, 16, 18, July 2, 11, 14, 16, 20, Aug. 9, 12, 14, 22, Sept. 7, 10, 11, 12, 24, Oct. 5, 8, 10, 26, Nov. 3, 6, 8, 28, Dec. 1, 4, 6, 30

Beneficial: Jan. 9, 12, 18, Feb. 7, 10, Mar. 5, 8, Apr. 3, 6, May 1, 4, 10, June 2, 30, July 28, Aug. 26, 30, 31, Sept. 24, 28, 29, Oct. 22, 26, 27, Nov. 20, 24, 25, Dec. 18, 22, 23, 29

Fatal attractions: July 16, 17, 18, 19

Challenging: Jan. 11, 13, 29, Feb. 9, 11, Mar. 7, 9, 30, Apr. 5, 7, 28, May 3, 5, 26, 31, June 1, 3, 24, 29, July 1, 22, 27, Aug. 20, 25, Sept. 18, 23, 30, Oct. 16, 21, 28, Nov. 14, 19, 26, Dec. 12, 17, 24

Soul mates: Jan. 12, 29, Feb. 10, 27, Mar. 8, 25, Apr. 6, 23, May 4, 21, June 2, 19, July 17, Aug. 15, Sept. 13, Oct. 11, Nov. 9, Dec. 7

January 17

♑ Determined and pragmatic, you are a dynamic Capricorn with a straightforward style. Independent and success-oriented, you need change and adventure to keep your interest and to stop you from becoming restless or impatient. Confident, you usually work best when you think optimistically about large projects. These can motivate you into action, and once focused on a goal you will work hard to achieve your grand plans.

With the subinfluence of your decanate ruler, Virgo, you possess a fast mind, quick responses, and an ability to evaluate situations rapidly. Good concentration and common sense suggest that you can be thorough and capable of deep thought. With your high standards and competent approach to work, be careful that you do not become too demanding of yourself or others.

Naturally business-minded, you are good at commercializing your abilities and seeing opportunities when they arise. Ambitious, you aim high and enjoy power and influence. With an ability to project positive enthusiasm or excite other people, you make a good organizer or natural leader.

Your generosity and assurance attract others and increase your general good fortune. Sometimes emotional moods may cause you to suffer from nervous tension, so it is necessary to lead a well-balanced life and stay healthy.

From the age of four to thirty-three, when your progressed Sun moves through Aquarius, you become aware of your freedom and independence. You may be group-oriented, feel attracted by unusual interests, or have a strong desire to express your individuality. After the age of thirty-four, when your progressed Sun moves into Pisces, your emotional sensitivity becomes enhanced and you develop a stronger inner life. This can be shown through your dreams and ideals. At the age of sixty-four there is a turning point as your progressed Sun enters Aries, emphasizing a need to take the initiative and be brave and direct in your relationships with others.

Your Secret Self

Proud and dramatic, you are socially inclined but prefer to take the lead. With your natural curiosity and inventive thinking, you are often ahead of your time. You may even be interested in reforms and changing attitudes in society. If disciplined and hardworking, you also possess the ability to accumulate wealth but may find more satisfaction from being at the center of altruistic activities. It is often through developing your natural sixth sense that you gain many advantages and rewards.

A desire for self-mastery and an inquisitive nature will always inspire you to investigate new areas. If you do not believe in your own talents, however, you may find yourself taking positions well beneath your capabilities. Luckily, you are born with the endurance to accomplish your ambitions. It would be wise, however, to listen to what others have to say and avoid an inclination to be stubborn. With your intuition, communication skills, and need for self-expression, however, you possess excellent opportunities for success.

Work & Vocation

Dynamic and intuitive, you are ambitious and determined to achieve success by your own merit. Intelligent and practical, you like to plan on a large scale. Since you possess executive

---

FIXED STAR

Star's name: Terebellum

Degree position: 24°52'–25°55'
    Capricorn between the years
    1930 and 2000

Magnitude: 5

Strength: ★★

Orb: 1°

Constellation: Omega Sagittarius

Applicable days: January 15, 16, 17

Star qualities: Venus/Saturn

Description: an orange-red star in the
    four-sided figure in the tail of the
    Archer

PRIMARY STAR'S INFLUENCE

Terebellum imparts a clear and pragmatic outlook with an ambitious and determined personality. Often you succeed after overcoming difficulties. This star indicates that you are responsible and dutiful and can endure hardship and struggle. This star may also suggest that you can experience doubts and inner conflicts between personal desires and duties to others.

Linked to your Sun's degree, this star bestows cleverness and ambition to rise to prominent positions. Terebellum, however, warns that you may nevertheless be crafty and suggests guarding against mischief and wrongdoing. This star indicates that good fortune and success can be achieved but often at a considerable expense or sacrifice.

• *Positive:* ambitious, devotion, sentimental, clever

• *Negative:* mercenary, ruthlessness, crafty, self-seeking

skills, you can succeed at delegating and supervising others. Often you are drawn to a career in law, politics, or the civil service. If you are interested in monetary affairs, you may work in banking or for a large insurance company. An interest in food and the service industries suggests that you may be in the restaurant and hotel business. Well educated and with a talent for writing, you may be inspired to become a teacher, writer, or counselor. When wealthy, you may become a patron and a philanthropist who supports just causes. If you desire only money and material power, you may resort to fortune-hunting or get-rich-quick schemes.

Famous people who share your birthday include actor Jim Carrey, David Lloyd George, boxer Joe Frazier, gangster Al Capone, hair stylist Vidal Sassoon, playwright Anton Chekhov, and boxer Muhammad Ali.

Numerology

As a number 17 individual, you are often shrewd, with good reasoning ability. Since you usually utilize your knowledge in a specific way, you can develop your expertise and achieve success or a prominent position as a specialist or researcher. Private, introspective, and detached, with a strong interest in facts and figures, you frequently present a serious and thoughtful demeanor and like to take your time. Capable of long periods of concentration and endurance, you can learn best through experience. Nevertheless, the less skeptical you are, the quicker you learn. The subinfluence of the number 1 month indicates that you are highly intuitive and ambitious. Inclined to be individual and innovative, you are analytical, a good planner, and independent. Courageous and with plenty of energy, your adventurous spirit encourages you to think on a grand scale or strike out alone. Full of enthusiasm and original ideas, you often prefer to lead or show others the way forward.

• *Positive:* thoughtful, specialist, good planner, business sense, attracts money, painstaking, accurate, scientific

• *Negative:* detached, stubborn, carelessness, moody, narrow-minded, critical, worry, suspicious

Love & Relationships

Usually you are loyal and generous to those you love. Friendly and sociable, it is important for you to be respected by others. With your strong feelings, you can sometimes reveal a dramatic and passionate nature, although you do not lose sight of practical issues. While you have a need for love and affection, your desire for freedom suggests that you may prefer to be in relationships that can offer you enough space to feel independent. You are attracted to powerful, optimistic, or influential people who can inspire you with new ideas and opportunities.

YOUR SPECIAL SOMEONE

For love and friendship, you might just find the right person among those born on the following days.

Love & friendship: Jan. 5, 6, 10, 11, 15, 29, 31, Feb. 4, 13, 27, 29, Mar. 2, 6, 11, 25, 27, Apr. 9, 23, 25, May 2, 3, 7, 21, 23, June 5, 19, 21, July 3, 17, 19, 30, Aug. 1, 15, 17, 28, Sept. 13, 15, 26, Oct. 11, 13, 24, Nov. 9, 11, 22, Dec. 7, 9, 20

Beneficial: Jan. 13, 15, 19, Feb. 11, 13, 17, Mar. 9, 11, 15, Apr. 7, 9, 13, 24, May 5, 7, 11, June 3, 5, 9, July 1, 3, 7, 29, Aug. 1, 5, 27, 31, Sept. 3, 16, 25, 29, Oct. 1, 23, 27, Nov. 21, 25, Dec. 19, 23

Fatal attractions: May 30, June 28, July 17, 18, 19, 20, 26, Aug. 24, Sept. 22, Oct. 20, Nov. 18, Dec. 16

Challenging: Jan. 12, Feb. 10, Mar. 8, Apr. 6, May 4, June 2, Aug. 31, Sept. 29, Oct. 27, 29, 30, Nov. 25, 27, 28, Dec. 23, 25, 26, 30

Soul mates: Jan. 2, 28, Feb. 26, Mar. 24, Apr. 22, May 20, June 18, July 16, Aug. 14, Sept. 12, Oct. 10, Nov. 8, Dec. 6

January 18

♑ With your smart and shrewd approach to life and a charming personality, you have a head start over others in your ability to succeed in life. Ambitious and broad-minded, with strong leadership potential, you prefer to give the orders, but may have to resist going too far and becoming bossy. Fortunately, a humanitarian side to your personality suggests that you are a good judge of character and enjoy helping others.

With the subinfluence of your decanate ruler, Virgo, you have a keen intellect and good communication skills. Your excellent sense of structure indicates that you possess natural business sense and a willingness to work hard for success. Practical and perceptive, you can make astute observations, but you may have to avoid a tendency to be critical. Common sense and good concentration imply that you are capable of deep thought and productive results.

Sociable and friendly, when relaxed you can also display an original sense of humor or satire. A tendency to disappointment or frustration, however, may sometimes drain you of your positivity. It is important to stay detached and see the larger picture. By being broad-minded, you can afford to be generous with others and show them a side to your nature that is warm, giving, and magnanimous. Inventive and with original ideas, you have the potential to inspire others with your enthusiasm and grand plans.

While you are between the ages of three and thirty-two your progressed Sun is in Aquarius, highlighting your individuality, friendship, desire for freedom, and group awareness. At age thirty-three, as your progressed Sun moves into Pisces, there is a turning point that emphasizes the importance of your sensitivity, imagination, and need to feel more in touch with your emotions. Another change at age sixty-three, when your progressed Sun moves into Aries, accents a desire for self-assertion, more action, and new beginnings.

Fixed Stars

Although your Sun's degree is not linked to a fixed star, some of your other planets' degrees certainly will be. By having an astrological chart calculated, you can find the exact position of the planets on your date of birth. This will tell you which of the fixed stars listed in this book are relevant to you.

Your Secret Self

Business acumen and an instinct for money matters help you to become a good evaluator. This can extend to being a good judge of people and situations that combines well with your liberal outlook. Possessing natural authority, you may feel a responsibility to pass this knowledge on to others and can therefore be an excellent fighter for just causes or ideals. Be careful, however, that a touch of materialism does not distract you from your high aims.

Seeking adventure and change, you need variety in your life to prevent you from becoming bored. If too confined by structure or responsibilities, you may become restless and impatient. By striking a balance, you can avoid going to extremes and indulging yourself in material extravagances to make up for emotional dissatisfaction. By finding ways of expressing your dynamic sensitivity, you can use your subtle ability to enchant others. That ability, together with your fast responses enables you to keep others entertained and uplifted.

Work & Vocation

Capable and creative, you are often interested in combining your talents with your practical abilities. An excellent image maker, you may become involved in the world of advertising, fashion, or media. Idealistic and progressive, you may be interested in teaching, training, or charity work. If in business, intuition and a strong sixth sense may help you to succeed in the world of banking, investment, and the stock exchange. Alternatively, you can use your compassionate nature by joining the healing professions or work in science and technology as a researcher. The dramatic side of your personality may inspire you to write or join the world of film and theater as an actor, promoter, or producer.

Famous people who share your birthday include actors Kevin Costner, Cary Grant, and Danny Kaye, conservationist David Bellamy, writer A. A. Milne, and film director John Boorman.

Numerology

Determination, assertiveness, and ambition are some of the attributes associated with the number 18 birthday. Dynamic and active, you frequently desire power and need constant challenge. At times you may be critical or hard to please or inclined toward controversial issues. As a number 18 personality, you may use your power to help others, give sound advice, or solve other people's problems. Alternatively, your strong business sense and organizational skills can lead you to the world of commerce. The subinfluence of the number 1 month indicates that you are original and multitalented. Imaginative and full of ideas, you need to find ways to express yourself creatively and autonomously. As a good strategist, you can turn your wonderful ideas into tangible products. The great desire to be first and innovative encourages you to make your own decisions or strike out alone. You are confident and have plenty of energy, and your charm and enthusiasm can inspire others to support your latest plans. Although lucky, you may need to learn that sometimes the world does not revolve around you.

• *Positive:* progressive, assertive, intuitive, courageous, resolute, efficient, advisory skills
• *Negative:* uncontrolled emotions, lazy, lack of order, selfishness, failure to complete work or projects, misunderstood

Love & Relationships

It is important in your relationships to keep a sense of balance. At times you may appear cool or detached and at other times you can be warm and caring. A vital part of your agenda is to have friends and partners who can keep challenging you mentally; otherwise you may become somewhat compulsive or argumentative. Working too hard and not giving your partners enough of your time can also present possible problems. It is better, therefore, to have companions who are also fairly independent in their own right. Nevertheless, you are loyal, loving, and a supportive friend and partner.

YOUR SPECIAL SOMEONE

You might come close to finding that special person among those born on the following days.

Love & friendship: Jan. 2, 6, 7, 11, 16, Feb. 4, 14, Mar. 2, 12, 28, 30, Apr. 10, 26, 28, May 3, 8, 24, 26, 30, June 6, 22, 24, 28, July 4, 20, 22, 26, 31, Aug. 2, 18, 20, 24, 29, Sept. 16, 18, 22, 27, Oct. 14, 16, 20, 25, Nov. 12, 14, 18, 23, Dec. 10, 12, 16, 21

Beneficial: Jan. 9, 14, 16, Feb. 7, 12, 14, Mar. 5, 10, 12, Apr. 3, 8, 10, May 1, 6, 8, June 4, 6, July 2, 4, Aug. 2, Sept. 30, Oct. 28, Nov. 26, 30, Dec. 24, 28, 29

Fatal attractions: Jan. 21, Feb. 19, Mar. 17, Apr. 15, May 13, June 11, July 9, 18, 19, 20, 21, 22, Aug. 7, Sept. 5, Oct. 3, Nov. 1

Challenging: Jan. 4, 13, 28, Feb. 2, 11, 26, Mar. 9, 24, Apr. 7, 22, May 5, 20, June 3, 18, July 1, 16, Aug. 14, Sept. 12, Oct. 10, 31, Nov. 8, 29, Dec. 6, 27

Soul mates: Jan. 15, 22, Feb. 13, 20, Mar. 11, 18, Apr. 9, 16, May 7, 14, June 5, 12, July 3, 10, Aug. 1, 8, Sept. 6, Oct. 4, Nov. 2

January 19

V♑ Strong will and determination are just some of the characteristics related to your Capricorn birthday. With your sharp intelligence, practicality, and desire for recognition, you do not like to be taken for granted. With natural business sense and the potential for leadership, you are active and productive, and you prefer to be ruling your own affairs. If you are willing to work hard, your birthday shows distinct indications of remarkable success.

With the subinfluence of your decanate ruler, Virgo, you can be structured and efficient, with good communication skills. You may have a gift for writing or speaking and use this as part of your work. As you usually think big and enjoy power, a strong need for security and material success can motivate you to achieve and accomplish. A tendency to be arrogant, bossy, or self-oriented, however, suggests that you may not always respond well to criticism, and this can affect your relationships with others. By developing your diplomatic skills and by learning to collaborate, you improve your powers of influence.

Quick-witted and talented, you possess good organizational abilities. You may, however, have to guard against tendencies to be too impatient or headstrong. Luckily, this same dogged determination is what helps you overcome difficulties and gives you the strength to perform outstanding achievements.

From the age of two to thirty-one, when your progressed Sun moves through Aquarius, you have a growing desire to be independent as well as a heightened interest in friendship or group awareness. You may need to express your own unique ideas or be experimental. After the age of thirty-two, when your progressed Sun moves into Pisces, your emotional sensitivity becomes refined and you develop a stronger sense of vision. This may encourage you to seek idealistic or spiritual goals. At the age of sixty-two there is a turning point as your progressed Sun enters Aries, emphasizing a desire for new beginnings or active self-assertiveness.

FIXED STARS

Although your Sun's degree is not linked to a fixed star, some of your other planets' degrees certainly will be. By having an astrological chart calculated, you can find the exact position of the planets on your date of birth. This will tell you which of the fixed stars listed in this book are relevant to you.

Your Secret Self

Proud and alert, you value the wisdom learned from practical experience and hard work rather than just theory. The secret power here is self-mastery, which can provide deeper satisfaction than mere material gain. By trusting your intuitive insight and developing your willpower, you can become an authority in your field of experience.

One of the possible hindrances to your achievement is a tendency to be too cynical, cold, or doubting. Inner faith, therefore, is an important part of your confidence, as it encourages you to be more daring and spontaneous. Your competitive spirit and enthusiasm, when channeled positively, can inspire you to accumulate wealth and gain knowledge.

Work & Vocation

Ambitious and competitive, you want to be in a position of power, where you can use your influence. In business, you usually want to take on responsibilities and work hard in order to rise to the executive and managerial level. An excellent organizer or supervisor, you are efficient and able to pay attention to detail. As you often do not like to be told what to do, you may choose to be self-employed, working as an expert, consultant, or advisor. You may be interested in law, public service, or large organizations. Individual and original, you may wish to explore your creative powers through writing, painting, music, or drama. A need to be active suggests that you can enjoy sports and be a successful athlete.

Famous people who share your birthday include writer Edgar Allan Poe, artist Paul Cézanne, singers Janis Joplin, Dolly Parton, and Phil Everly, actor Michael Crawford, tennis player Stefan Edberg, and photographer Cindy Sherman.

Numerology

With a number 19 birthday, you are sunny, ambitious, and dynamic, yet idealistic and sensitive. Decisive and resourceful, you possess depth of vision, but the dreamer side of your nature is compassionate and impressionable. The need to be someone may be the very thing that pushes you to be dramatic and claim center stage. To others you may appear confident and resilient, but inner tensions may cause emotional ups and downs. Although proud, you may also need to learn that the world does not revolve around you. The subinfluence of the number 1 month indicates that you are highly perceptive, with an ambitious personality. Although you may start a project with great enthusiasm, learn to finish what you started. Issues concerning balance and fairness imply that you need to be constantly even-handed and just. Avoid overreacting to situations by staying impersonal. Autonomous and idealistic, you are inclined to be individual, innovative, and courageous, with plenty of energy. The initiatory force indicated here encourages you to make your own judgment or strike out alone. As a leader, you can often show others the way forward.

• *Positive:* dynamic, centered, creative, leadership, progressive, optimistic, strong convictions, competitive, independent, gregarious

• *Negative:* self-centered, worry, fear of rejection, materialistic, egotistical, impatient

Love & Relationships

Sociable, with a strong need for emotional expression, you enjoy the company of others. Although you can be loyal, at times you can suffer from worry or indecision regarding your affairs of the heart and may have many choices in your quest for the ideal love. You may have to balance your deeper and more serious side with a lighter and more romantic part of your personality. Nevertheless, charm can be an asset in entertaining others and can help you become an excellent host.

YOUR SPECIAL SOMEONE

You might find a partner who will understand your sensitivity and need for love among those born on the following dates.

Love & friendship: Jan. 1, 7, 12, 17, 20, 21, Feb. 5, 15, 18, Mar. 3, 13, 16, 29, 31, Apr. 1, 11, 14, 27, 29, May 9, 12, 13, 25, 27, June 7, 10, 23, 25, July 5, 8, 21, 23, Aug. 3, 6, 19, 21, Sept. 1, 4, 5, 17, 19, Oct. 2, 15, 17, Nov. 13, 15, 30, Dec. 11, 13, 28

Beneficial: Jan. 15, 17, 28, Feb. 13, 15, 26, Mar. 11, 13, 24, Apr. 9, 11, 22, 28, May 7, 9, 20, June 5, 7, 18, July 3, 5, 16, Aug. 1, 3, 14, Sept. 1, 12, 18, Oct. 10, 29, Nov. 8, 27, Dec. 6, 25

Fatal attractions: Jan. 5, Feb. 3, Mar. 1, July 19, 20, 21, 22, 23

Challenging: Jan. 4, 5, 14, Feb. 2, 3, 12, Mar. 1, 10, Apr. 8, 30, May 6, 28, June 4, 26, July 2, 24, Aug. 22, Sept. 20, Oct. 18, Nov. 16, Dec. 14

Soul mates: Jan. 2, Mar. 29, Apr. 27, May 25, June 23, July 21, Aug. 19, Sept. 17, Oct. 15, Nov. 13, Dec. 11

SUN: CAPRICORN/AQUARIUS CUSP

DECANATE: VIRGO/MERCURY

DEGREE: 28° CAPRICORN–

0° AQUARIUS

MODE: CARDINAL

ELEMENT: EARTH

January 20

Your birthday shows you to be a persuasive and charming individual, practical and hardworking, yet sensitive. Born on the cusp, you also possess an Aquarian interest in people and show a keen understanding of relationships. Skill in working cooperatively with others can help you in your overall success. Your pragmatic approach to life suggests that you possess a strong sense of loyalty and are capable of endurance. The challenge you may be facing, however, is to keep the balance between your desire to fulfill your obligations and your need for freedom, spontaneity, and pleasure.

With the subinfluence of your decanate ruler, Virgo, you are a methodical and careful worker who pays attention to detail. Although you retain a certain shyness or reserve, you have good communication skills and can go straight to the heart of a matter. With a touch of the perfectionist and critical skills, you want to do a job properly and can make precise and accurate observations. A sense of duty and control can make you dependable and skilled, but tightly controlled emotions can also lead to your becoming too serious, rigid, or stubborn.

With a love of beauty and a good sense of form, you may wish to develop your creative gifts through art, music, or writing. Your home is liable to be warm and attractive, as you possess good taste and enjoy luxury. Although money is important, you are willing to work hard to acquire it and need the security of long-term plans.

Until you reach the age of thirty your progressed Sun is in Aquarius, highlighting your individuality, desire for freedom, and group awareness. It may be necessary for you to express your independence, and friends may be especially important to you. At age thirty-one, as your progressed Sun moves into Pisces, there is a turning point that heightens your sense of vision and emphasizes the importance of needing to feel more in touch with your emotions. Another change at age sixty-one, when your progressed Sun moves into Aries, accents a desire for self-assertion, more action, and new beginnings. This may inspire you to take more leadership roles.

Fixed Star

Star's name: Altair, also called Al Tair or the Eagle

Degree position: Aquarius 0°47'–1°43' between the years 1930 and 2000

Magnitude: 1

Strength: ★★★★★★★★

Orb: 2°30'

Constellation: Alpha Aquila

Applicable days: January 20, 21, 22, 23, 24

Star qualities: Mars/Jupiter, Uranus, Mercury

Description: a white and yellow star in the neck of the Eagle

PRIMARY STAR'S INFLUENCE

Altair bestows strong desires, confidence, ambition, and a liberal attitude, yet an unyielding nature as well. This star indicates that although you can be radical and rebellious or sometimes cause trouble by throwing a monkey wrench in the works, your originality, eccentricity, and ingenious ideas often compensate for your misbehavior. Altair also bestows sudden bursts of wealth or success through new inventions but warns that fluctuating circumstances can frequently endanger positions of authority.

Linked to your Sun's degree, this star imparts originality, popularity, and adventurous tendencies. Altair also urges you to seek knowledge and reveals a talent for writing and education. Often ambitious and daring, you seek a change of fortune and may enjoy unexpected gains or other benefits. Group-

Your Secret Self

Your tough front often conceals your extreme inner sensitivity. Love and relationships are especially important to you, and you often have a desire to make other people happy. This can be expressed as a humanitarian caring or compassion for the feelings of others. At times, however, you may feel frustration and disappointment because you cannot relax and let go. You may have experienced instances of conditional love earlier in your life, where you have had to meet another's expectations before you received the love and affection you needed. It is important, therefore, that in your desire to love and be loved you do not compromise too much of your true self or overcompensate by withdrawing and becoming cold or melancholic as a protection mechanism.

In your desire for peace and harmony, you are usually willing to work hard to deal with the obstacles in your path. Through this you come to realize the significance of valuing yourself and trusting your feelings.

Work & Vocation

Sociable and good at combining business and pleasure, you often accomplish more by working with other people. Usually you use your communication and diplomatic skill to persuade

• *Positive:* original, inventive, individual, humanitarian, creative

• *Negative:* rebellious, antagonistic, unpredictable

others to your way of thinking. Imaginative, entertaining, and original, you like to use your humor and charm when doing business with others. Often astute and caring, you can accomplish in the medical world and the healing professions. A firm approach to health and good business sense imply that you can also work as a teacher, counselor, and advisor. Alternatively, as a multitalented individual with a need to be creative, you can put pen to paper and write or paint as well as compose music or make films.

Famous people who share your birthday include film directors David Lynch and Federico Fellini, actress Patricia Neal, and actor George Burns.

Numerology

Having a number 20 birthday, you are intuitive, adaptable, and understanding. Usually you benefit from cooperative activities where you can interact, share experiences, or learn from others. Often charming and gracious, you develop diplomatic skills and can move in different social circles with ease. You may, however, need to overcome a tendency to be hurt easily by the actions and criticism of others. Avoid an inclination to martyr yourself or to be mistrusting or self-seeking. The subinfluence of the number 1 month indicates that you are ambitious and determined, with a forceful character. Individual, innovative, and creative, you are courageous and have plenty of energy when you are inspired. Although friendly and charming, you may also need to learn that the world does not revolve around you. In relationships, you may need to balance your own wishes with the needs and desires of others. Nevertheless, when you learn to trust your inner feelings and have faith in your abilities, you can succeed by commercializing your artistic talents.

• *Positive:* good partnerships, gentle, tactful, receptive, intuitive, considerate, harmonious, agreeable, amiable, ambassador of goodwill

• *Negative:* suspicious, lack of confidence, timid, oversensitive, selfish, crafty

Love & Relationships

Your natural charm and sociability indicate that you have a large circle of friends with whom you are generous and giving. Idealistic and romantic, you have a strong need for love, which suggests that the demonstration of affection can be very important to you. With your stoic strength, you can be a loyal and faithful friend and very protective of your family members. This means you are often willing to make sacrifices for those you love, but you may need to be careful not to play the martyr. Some people of this birthdate find close relationships with those of a different age group.

YOUR SPECIAL SOMEONE

You might find stability in relationships by looking for someone born on the following dates.

Love & friendship: Jan. 4, 8, 9, 13, 18, 19, 23, Feb. 2, 6, 16, 17, 21, Mar. 4, 14, 15, 19, 28, 30, Apr. 2, 12, 13, 17, 26, 28, 30, May 1, 5, 10, 11, 15, 24, 26, 28, June 8, 9, 13, 22, 24, 26, July 6, 7, 11, 20, 22, 24, 30, Aug. 4, 5, 9, 18, 20, 22, 28, Sept. 2, 3, 7, 16, 18, 20, 26, Oct. 1, 5, 14, 16, 18, 24, Nov. 3, 12, 14, 16, 22, Dec. 1, 10, 12, 14, 20

Beneficial: Jan. 5, 16, 27, Feb. 3, 14, 25, Mar. 1, 12, 23, Apr. 10, 21, 29, May 8, 19, June 6, 17, July 4, 15, Aug. 2, 13, Sept. 11, 19, Oct. 9, 30, Nov. 7, 28, Dec. 5, 26, 30

Fatal attractions: Jan. 17, Feb. 15, Mar. 13, Apr. 11, May 9, June 7, July 5, 20, 21, 22, 23, 24, Aug. 3, Sept. 1

Challenging: Jan. 1, 10, 15, Feb. 8, 13, Mar. 6, 11, Apr. 4, 9, May 2, 7, June 5, July 3, 29, Aug. 1, 27, Sept. 25, Oct. 23, Nov. 21, Dec. 19, 29

Soul mates: Aug. 30, Sept. 28, Oct. 26, Nov. 24, Dec. 22

Aquarius

January 21–February 19

SUN: AQUARIUS/CAPRICORN CUSP
DECANATE: AQUARIUS/URANUS
DEGREE: 29°30' CAPRICORN–
1°30' AQUARIUS
MODE: FIXED
ELEMENT: AIR

January 21

 Born on the cusp of Aquarius and Capricorn, you have the advantage of being both friendly and charismatic, yet shrewd and practical. Frank and honest, with strong convictions and sharp intellect, you like to be direct and speak your mind. Original in your approach, you enjoy learning and can be prudent and discerning. Although you possess an easygoing style, you may also have to overcome a tendency to be irritable, as it might estrange you from others.

With the added influence of your Sun in the decanates of Aquarius and Virgo, you can be an inspired thinker with an ability to make accurate observations, particularly about people. Capable of good concentration, you usually take your work seriously. You can be a skillful problem solver. With a touch of the perfectionist, however, you may have to avoid becoming overly critical. Broad-minded and humanitarian, you are a free thinker who is willing to fight injustice and for the rights of others. Often original and ahead of your time with your ideas, you can be highly inventive, but may have to guard against becoming too abrupt or frank, causing upset to others.

Although part of you just wants peace and quiet, a desire for the good life usually motivates you to achieve. If inspired by an ideal or a cause, you will work twice as hard. Being confident and caring, you may find that others often turn to you for support or advice.

Up until you reach the age of twenty-nine, your progressed Sun moves through Aquarius, highlighting issues of freedom, independence, and the need to express your individuality. After the age of thirty, when your progressed Sun moves into Pisces, you become more sensitive and aware of emotional issues. You may develop a greater sense of vision or have more access to your inner world. At the age of sixty, you reach another turning point, as your progressed Sun enters Aries, accenting a greater self-orientation; you also start to feel more confident and assertive. This influence may inspire you to begin new projects.

Fixed Stars

Altair, also called Al Tair or the Eagle; Albireo

PRIMARY STAR

Star's name: Altair, also called Al Tair or the Eagle

Degree position: Aquarius 0°47'–1°43' between the years 1930 and 2000

Magnitude: 1

Strength: ★★★★★★★★★

Orb: 2°30'

Constellation: Alpha Aquila

Applicable days: January 20, 21, 22, 23, 24

Star qualities: Mars/Jupiter, Uranus, Mercury

Description: a white and yellow star in the neck of the Eagle

PRIMARY STAR'S INFLUENCE

Altair bestows strong desires, confidence, ambition, and a liberal attitude, yet an unyielding nature as well. This star indicates that although you can be radical and rebellious or sometimes cause trouble by throwing a monkey wrench in the works, your originality, eccentricity, and ingenious ideas often compensate for your misbehavior. Altair also bestows sudden bursts of wealth or success through new inventions but warns that fluctuating circumstances can frequently endanger positions of authority.

Linked to your Sun's degree, this star imparts originality, popularity, and

Your Secret Self

With your creative approach, you have many inspired ideas. You may wish to develop these and build up your confidence through some form of self-expression, whether art, music, writing, or drama. Alternatively, you may use your gentle charm and social skills to great success in your dealings with others. In order to avoid scattering your energies or being indecisive, you need to develop persistence and a strong sense of purpose.

Although you generally possess a detached and universal mentality, at times you may suffer from frustration. If disappointed with others, you may become resentful or rebellious. By letting go of the past and concentrating all your mental energies on your positive goals, you can avoid wasted energy. Having the added advantage of natural intuition can be a tremendous benefit if you trust your sixth sense about people and the final outcome of situations.

Work & Vocation

Being born on the cusp, you have the practical business sense of Capricorn that desires prestige as well as the insight into human nature that comes with Aquarius. This enables you to mix business with your social life. Dynamic and versatile, you have a charming personality and an ability to promote your ideas. This can help you particularly in the world of sales, promotion, and public relations. You can also succeed in commerce or banking, where you are likely to use your people skills. Alternatively, with your strong sense of justice, you may be drawn to defend the underdog through the law or politics. Similarly, your desire to expand your knowledge can attract you to work in education, philosophy, or science. Creative and gifted, you could equally be inspired to work in careers such as design, art, acting, or music.

Famous people who share your birthday include designer Christian Dior, actors Paul Scofield, Telly Savalas, and Geena Davis, composer Jerome Kern, and opera singer Placido Domingo.

adventurous tendencies. Altair also urges you to seek knowledge and reveals a talent for writing and education. Often ambitious and daring, you seek a change of fortune and may enjoy unexpected gains or other benefits. Group-oriented, you can make friends and influence people.

• *Positive:* original, inventive, individual, humanitarian, creative

• *Negative:* rebellious, antagonistic, unpredictable

See Appendix for additional fixed star readings.

Numerology

Dynamic drive and an outgoing personality are usually present in those with a number 21 birthday. Socially inclined, you have many contacts and interests. Usually you show others your friendly and gregarious personality. Intuitive, with an independent spirit, you are highly inventive and original. Having a number 21 birthday, you can be fun-loving and magnetic, with grace and charm. Alternatively, you can be shy and reserved, with a need to develop assertiveness, especially in close relationships. Although you can be inclined toward cooperative relationships or marriage, you always want to be acknowledged for your talents and abilities. The subinfluence of the number 1 month indicates that you are enterprising, with an independent outlook. Observant and innovative, with an inquisitive mind and plenty of energy, you need to work hard in order to achieve recognition and success, although you are usually ambitious. At times you may be stubborn and make your own decisions or strike out alone. When inspired, you have original ideas and a unique perspective.

• *Positive:* inspiration, creativity, love unions, long-lasting relationships
• *Negative:* dependency, nervous, lack of vision, fear of change

YOUR SPECIAL SOMEONE

Success in finding the right partner may be more easily achieved with those born on the following dates.

Love & friendship: Jan. 5, 9, 18, 19, 23, Feb. 3, 7, 16, 17, Mar. 1, 5, 14, 15, 31, Apr. 3, 12, 13, 29, May 1, 10, 11, 15, 27, 29, June 8, 9, 25, 27, July 6, 7, 23, 25, 31, Aug. 4, 5, 21, 23, 29, Sept. 2, 3, 7, 19, 21, 27, 30, Oct. 1, 17, 19, 25, 28, Dec. 13, 15, 21, 24

Beneficial: Jan. 1, 6, 17, Feb. 4, 15, Mar. 2, 13, Apr. 11, 30, May 9, 28, June 7, July 5, Aug. 3, 22, Sept. 1, Oct. 31, Nov. 29, Dec. 27

Fatal attractions: July 22, 23, 24, 25

Challenging: Jan. 2, 16, Feb. 14, Mar. 12, Apr. 10, May 8, June 6, July 4, Aug. 2, Dec. 30

Soul mates: Jan. 11, 31, Feb. 9, 29, Mar. 7, 27, Apr. 5, 25, May 3, 23, June 1, 21, July 19, Aug. 17, Sept. 15, Oct. 13, Nov. 11, Dec. 9

Love & Relationships

Charismatic and idealistic, you have high expectations of relationships. A flair for dealing with people indicates that you can mix well with others. Although you can at times overreact, you are a humanitarian who is very protective of those you love. Avoid letting others take advantage of your good nature if you do not want to be distracted from your own goals. Your strong personality combined with your warmth and charm can be very attractive to others.

January 22

≋ Clever and instinctive, you are an Aquarian who is active but sensitive, with a desire for change. As you dislike routine, variety or travel is likely to play a strong part in your life story, with the possibility of your working or living in a foreign country. Honest and direct, you have a shrewd business sense and visionary ability. Aware of impressions, you find it important to present a good image to others. To curb an inner restlessness, however, you need to focus and develop patience and perseverance.

With the added influence of your Sun in the decanate of Aquarius, you are friendly, outgoing, and people-oriented. You may also have a more unusual or eccentric side to your nature. With an objective and inventive mind, you can have flashes of genius and are able to quickly judge character in others. Your individual perspective can place you ahead of your time, although if carried too far, you can become contrary, rebellious, or stubborn.

As a practical idealist, you have the ability and self-discipline to work hard in order to make your dreams a reality. Sometimes you may be tempted to take the path of instant rewards rather than build for the future. To overcome any possible anxiety about changeable financial situations in your life, it is advisable to save and consider long-term investments.

Until you reach the age of twenty-eight, your progressed Sun is in Aquarius, highlighting issues of personal freedom and friendship and expressing your individuality. At the age of twenty-nine, when your progressed Sun moves into Pisces, you start to become more emotionally aware, developing a greater sense of vision and more access to your inner world. At the age of fifty-nine there is a turning point as your progressed Sun enters Aries. This influence can make you more confident, assertive, and ambitious, possibly initiating new ventures or activities.

FIXED STARS

Altair, also called Al Tair or the Eagle; Albireo

PRIMARY STAR

Star's name: Altair, also called Al Tair or the Eagle

Degree position: Aquarius 0°47'–1°43' between the years 1930 and 2000

Magnitude: 1

Strength: ★★★★★★★★★

Orb: 2°30'

Constellation: Alpha Aquila

Applicable days: January 20, 21, 22, 23, 24

Star qualities: Mars/Jupiter, Uranus, Mercury

Description: a white and yellow star in the neck of the Eagle

Your Secret Self

A quick learner, you need outlets for your inner creativity. Through self-expression and standing by your decisions, you can learn to eliminate worry or self-doubt from your life. Versatile and adaptable, you can be highly focused when you have decided on a definite goal. Although you have a strong practical awareness, you also possess a sensitive foresight that can help you in the achievement of your grand visions.

Generous and broad-minded, you have a universal perspective. Being friendly, you attract people and can be popular. This adds to your leadership capabilities and suggests that you do not like to be in subservient positions. Although you have natural business sense, be careful that becoming overly preoccupied with material concerns does not limit your wonderful humanitarian potential.

PRIMARY STAR'S INFLUENCE

Altair bestows strong desires, confidence, ambition, and a liberal attitude, yet an unyielding nature as well. This star indicates that although you can be radical and rebellious or sometimes cause trouble by throwing a monkey wrench in the works, your originality, eccentricity, and ingenious ideas often compensate for your misbehavior. Altair also bestows sudden bursts of wealth or success through new inventions but warns that fluctuating circumstances can frequently endanger positions of authority.

Linked to your Sun's degree, this star imparts originality, popularity, and adventurous tendencies. Altair also urges you to seek knowledge and re-

Work & Vocation

Although hardworking and ambitious, you have a love of variety that points to a career that involves fast changes and does not entail a predictable routine. Occupations that involve travel may particularly suit your adventurous spirit. You need work that can be practical yet satisfy your idealism. If in business, you can use your visionary ability to project into the future or sell your ideas to others. Whatever career you choose, you will have a need for action. Alternatively, you may use your imagination and sensitivity in the arts as an actor or musician or in the healing world.

Famous people who share your birthday include poet Lord Byron, singers Michael Hutchence and Sam Cooke, philosopher Sir Francis Bacon, actor John Hurt, and film director D. W. Griffith.

See Appendix for additional fixed star readings.

veals a talent for writing and education. Often ambitious and daring, you seek a change of fortune and may enjoy unexpected gains or other benefits. Group-oriented, you can make friends and influence people.

• *Positive:* original, inventive, individual, humanitarian, creative

• *Negative:* rebellious, antagonistic, unpredictable

Numerology

This is a master number and can vibrate both as number 22 and as number 4. Often honest and hardworking, with natural leadership abilities, you have a charismatic personality and a deep understanding of people and what motivates them. Although undemonstrative, you often show a caring, protective concern for the welfare of others, yet you never lose sight of your pragmatic or realistic stand. Usually cultured and worldly, you have many friends and admirers. The more competitive among you achieve success and good fortune with help and encouragement from others. The subinfluence of the number 1 month indicates that you are ambitious and enterprising, with an independent outlook. Although you are determined to establish stability and security, a restless streak implies that you need the freedom to know that you can enjoy a whole range of opportunities without being restricted. Mentally sharp and intuitive, you are inclined to make your own decisions or strike out alone. As a humanitarian with a realistic approach, you can be a tower of strength for others in times of trouble.

• *Positive:* universal, director, highly intuitive, pragmatic, practical, good with your hands, skillful, builder, good organizer, problem solver, achiever

• *Negative:* nervous, inferiority complex, bossy, materialistic, lack of vision, lazy, egotistical

YOUR SPECIAL SOMEONE

For true love and happiness, you might be more successful with those born on the following dates.

Love & friendship: Jan. 6, 10, 20, 24, 29, Feb. 4, 8, 18, 27, Mar. 2, 6, 16, 25, 28, 30, Apr. 4, 14, 23, 26, 27, 28, 30, May 2, 12, 21, 24, 26, 28, 30, June 10, 19, 22, 24, 26, 28, July 8, 17, 20, 22, 24, 26, Aug. 6, 15, 18, 20, 22, 24, 30, Sept. 4, 13, 16, 17, 18, 20, 22, Oct. 2, 11, 14, 16, 18, 20, Nov. 9, 12, 14, 16, 18, Dec. 7, 10, 12, 14, 16

Beneficial: Jan. 7, 13, 18, 28, Feb. 5, 11, 16, 26, Mar. 3, 9, 14, 24, Apr. 1, 7, 12, 22, May 5, 10, 20, June 3, 8, 18, July 1, 6, 16, Aug. 4, 14, Sept. 2, 12, 30, Oct. 10, 28, Nov. 8, 26, 30, Dec. 6, 24, 28

Fatal attractions: Jan. 25, Feb. 23, Mar. 21, Apr. 19, May 17, June 15, July 13, 22, 23, 24, 25, 26, Aug. 11, Sept. 9, Oct. 7, Nov. 5, Dec. 3

Challenging: Jan. 3, 17, Feb. 1, 15, Mar. 13, Apr. 11, May 9, 30, June 7, 28, July 5, 26, 29, Aug. 3, 24, 27, Sept. 1, 22, 25, Oct. 20, 23, Nov. 18, 21, Dec. 16, 19

Soul mates: Jan. 18, Feb. 16, Mar. 14, Apr. 12, May 10, 29, June 8, 27, July 6, 25, Aug. 4, 23, Sept. 2, 21, Oct. 19, Nov. 17, Dec. 15

Love & Relationships

With your advanced social skills, you usually have many friends and admirers. Receptive and friendly, with a need for mental stimulation, you are likely to seek the company of intelligent people. In order to achieve peace and harmony, you are often willing to make concessions or sacrifices. Friendships are important to you, as you like to mix with people who can inspire you to be adventurous and help you have a good time. You come into your own when entertaining the people you love.

January 23

PRIMARY STAR

Star's name: Altair, also called Al Tair or the Eagle

Degree position: Aquarius 0°47'–1°43' between the years 1930 and 2000

Magnitude: 1

Strength: ★★★★★★★★★

Orb: 2°30'

Constellation: Alpha Aquila

Applicable days: January 20, 21, 22, 23, 24

Star qualities: Mars/Jupiter, Uranus, Mercury

Description: a white and yellow star in the neck of the Eagle

PRIMARY STAR'S INFLUENCE

Altair bestows strong desires, confidence, ambition, and a liberal attitude, yet an unyielding nature as well. This star indicates that although you can be radical and rebellious or sometimes cause trouble by throwing a monkey wrench in the works, your originality, eccentricity, and ingenious ideas often compensate for your misbehavior. Altair also bestows sudden bursts of wealth or success through new inventions but warns that fluctuating circumstances can frequently endanger positions of authority.

Linked to your Sun's degree, this star imparts originality, popularity, and adventurous tendencies. Altair also urges you to seek knowledge and re-

 Intuitive yet practical, you are a hardworking Aquarian with a strong insight into people. Preferring to be methodical and organized, you like to build a solid foundation to whatever you want to achieve in life. Although pragmatic, you can also be sensitive with a fertile imagination.

With the added influence of your Sun in the decanate of Aquarius, you have an inventive mind, especially when it comes to problem solving. Sociable and friendly, you need people and like to present a good image. Instinctively, you have an astute understanding of character and motivation that can bestow strong humanitarian tendencies. With your great mental potential you can experience moments of high inspiration or intuition but may also have to overcome a tendency to be stubborn or obstinate.

Honest and direct, you possess a magnetic charm that can save you from many difficult situations and draw people toward you. Although you are sociable, a certain reserve suggests that you are prone to occasionally suppressing or inhibiting your emotions. Usually thrifty and economical, you put a great emphasis on work. As a practical idealist, you need only to apply diligent and concentrated effort in order to take advantage of your special potential.

Until you reach the age of twenty-seven your progressed Sun is in Aquarius, highlighting issues of personal freedom, friendship, and expressing your individuality. At the age of twenty-eight, when your progressed Sun moves into Pisces, you become more emotionally sensitive and receptive, with your psychic impressions of others becoming stronger. At the age of fifty-eight there is another turning point as your progressed Sun enters Aries. This influence accents a greater self-orientation and a need for new activities as you start to feel more confident and assertive.

Your Secret Self

Although you can work hard and be responsible, you also need variety and change in your life; otherwise, you may become impatient or restless. Desiring order and security, you also want freedom and dislike being tied down. These contrasting sides to your personality suggest that you need to periodically break away from your routine and be a bit more adventurous. This may also inspire you to be more dynamically productive.

With your high ideals, dreams, and emotional power, you possess a strong inner need for love, affection, and self-expression. If obstructed, you may be prone to alternating moods or escapism. With patience, you can enjoy the challenge of actively finding harmony within yourself. As a strong visionary, you have much to offer others with your foresight and sensitive depth of understanding.

Work & Vocation

Your inventive mind needs to be constantly stimulated, and with your people skills you may be happy in careers dealing with the public. Your more practical side may be drawn to business, while your humanitarian inclinations may attract you to counseling or social reform. Your practical and responsible approach ensures that employers notice and respect your talents. Although organized and methodical, you do not like to be in a job that is boring. As you are likely to be good with your hands, you may use your dexterity in some practical application. If you develop your innate creativity, you will invariably want to express yourself in an original or unique way.

Famous people who share your birthday include painter Edouard Manet, actor Humphrey Bogart, Princess Caroline of Monaco, French actress Jeanne Moreau, singer Anita Pointer, entertainer Chita Rivera, and Russian film director Sergei Eisenstein.

• *Positive:* original, inventive, individual, humanitarian, creative

• *Negative:* rebellious, antagonistic, unpredictable

See Appendix for additional fixed star readings.

Numerology

Intuition, emotional sensitivity, and creativity are some of the attributes of a number 23 birthday. Usually you are versatile, passionate, and a quick thinker, with a professional attitude and a mind full of creative ideas. With the number 23 influence, you can learn new subjects easily but may prefer practice to theory. You are fond of travel, adventure, and meeting new people; the restlessness implied by the number 23 urges you to try many different kinds of experiences, and you are apt to make the most of any situation. Generally friendly and fun-loving, with courage and drive, you may need an active life in order to actualize your true potential. The subinfluence of the number 1 month indicates that you are autonomous, enthusiastic, and original. Although you have an independent and progressive outlook, you can benefit greatly from collaborating with others. By creating a harmonious atmosphere, you are able to relax and achieve inner peace. You may, however, have to overcome a tendency to be stubborn or inflexible about emotional issues.

• *Positive:* loyal, responsible, travel, communicative, intuitive, creative, versatile, trustworthy, fame

• *Negative:* selfish, insecure, stubborn, fault-finding, withdrawn, prejudiced

YOUR SPECIAL SOMEONE

For love, devotion, and happiness, you might have more chances with those born on the following dates.

Love & friendship: Jan. 7, 11, 12, 22, 25, Feb. 5, 9, 20, Mar. 3, 7, 18, 31, Apr. 1, 5, 16, 29, May 3, 4, 14, 17, 27, 29, June 1, 12, 25, 27, July 10, 23, 25, Aug. 8, 21, 23, 31, Sept. 6, 9, 19, 21, 29, Oct. 4, 17, 19, 27, 30, Nov. 2, 15, 17, 25, 28, Dec. 13, 15, 23, 26

Beneficial: Jan. 8, 14, 19, 30, Feb. 6, 12, 17, Mar. 4, 10, 15, Apr. 2, 8, 13, 24, May 6, 11, June 4, 9, July 2, 7, Aug. 5, Sept. 3, Oct. 1, 29, Nov. 27, Dec. 25, 29

Fatal attractions: July 24, 25, 26, 27

Challenging: Jan. 9, 18, 20, Feb. 7, 16, 18, Mar. 5, 14, 16, Apr. 3, 12, 14, May 1, 10, 12, June 8, 10, July 6, 8, 29, Aug. 4, 6, 27, Sept. 2, 4, 25, Oct. 2, 23, Nov. 21, Dec. 19

Soul mates: Jan. 9, Feb. 7, Mar. 5, Apr. 3, May 1, Oct. 30, Nov. 28, Dec. 26

Love & Relationships

Friendly and receptive, you are a humanitarian with a good understanding of people. A need for variety and a tendency to become restless imply that you benefit from the company of mentally stimulating people who can keep you interested in new and progressive ideas. Since you have plenty of love to give, you benefit from finding the right kind of person who can appreciate your sensitivity. A need to find a channel for expression can help you be creative and avoid fluctuating moods, which cause you to sulk or be difficult. Even though you are usually loyal in relationships, you still need the freedom to be yourself.

January 24

You are a friendly and creative Aquarian with an easygoing personality and an original approach to life. Ambitious and resourceful, you possess natural business sense and a desire for harmony. You have an interest in people and a natural humanitarian quality that together suggest you can mix easily in any social circle. Your many interests may sometimes bring quandaries regarding decision making. Your inspirational ideas and objective thinking, however, can help overcome a tendency to become worried, particularly about finances. Your excellent mental potential and desire for self-expression suggest that you are capable of outstanding achievements.

With the added influence of your Sun in the decanate of Aquarius, you are amiable, outgoing, and people-oriented. Although you usually appear light and congenial, you also have a more discerning and serious side that may attract you to philosophy or can be used for problem solving. With your original ideas, you are often ahead of your time and can be witty and entertaining. As you are independent, freedom is important to you, but avoid becoming too self-willed or contrary.

Usually hardworking, you can be judicious and practical. You also enjoy obtaining a bargain. Straight-speaking, you have the ability to go directly to the heart of a matter and can use your excellent communication skills in your climb to success.

Until you reach the age of twenty-six your progressed Sun moves through Aquarius, highlighting issues of freedom, friendship, and independence. After the age of twenty-seven, when your progressed Sun moves into Pisces, you become more sensitive and aware of emotional issues. You may develop a greater sense of vision or have more access to your inner world. At the age of fifty-seven there is another turning point as your progressed Sun enters Aries. This accents new beginnings in your life as you start to feel more confident, assertive, and daring.

Fixed Stars

Altair, also called Al Tair or the Eagle; Dabih; Giedi, also called Al Jady; Oculus

PRIMARY STAR

Star's name: Altair, also called Al Tair or the Eagle

Degree position: 0°47'–1°43' Aquarius between the years 1930 and 2000

Magnitude: 1

Strength: ★★★★★★★★★

Orb: 2°30'

Constellation: Alpha Aquila

Applicable days: January 20, 21, 22, 23, 24

Star qualities: Mars/Jupiter, Uranus, Mercury

Description: a white and yellow star in the neck of the Eagle

PRIMARY STAR'S INFLUENCE

Altair bestows strong desires, confidence, ambition, and a liberal attitude, yet an unyielding nature as well. This star indicates that although you can be radical and rebellious or sometimes cause trouble by throwing a monkey wrench in the works, your originality, eccentricity, and ingenious ideas often compensate for your misbehavior. Altair also bestows sudden bursts of wealth or success through new inventions but warns that fluctuating circumstances can frequently endanger positions of authority.

Linked to your Sun's degree, this star imparts originality, popularity, and adventurous tendencies. Altair also urges you to seek knowledge and re-

Your Secret Self

An inner desire for love, affection, and harmony can manifest in your life through creative pursuits or a strong love of home and family. You may take a rather protective attitude toward people around you, which can result in your becoming critical or taking on their troubles as your own. Even though you may have good intentions, you benefit from learning not to take over people's lives but to let them solve their own problems. When you combine your compassion with your natural humanitarianism, you may decide to look for a deeper meaning to life and help others or support an idealistic cause.

Multitalented, you have unique qualities and a spark of genius at times that can impress others. Although you seek self-expression, your concerns regarding money and security suggest a materialistic overtone that may stop you from taking chances in life. Possessing natural leadership skills and a fighting spirit suggests that you are not likely to stay in an unsatisfactory position for long.

Work & Vocation

With your original ideas, keen intelligence, and individual approach to life, you are likely to succeed in any career, particularly one involving communication. Within your work you want to be constantly improving the way you operate. You are often shrewd and successful in business. You may also use your sharp mind for research or solving problems. A strong desire for self-expression can bring you success in writing, music, and the entertainment world. Although you are attracted to careers that deal with the public, you are also capable of deep thought and may have an interest in philosophy, religion, or law. With your desire to expand and share your knowledge, you may become interested in social or educational reforms.

Famous people who share your birthday include singer Neil Diamond, actress Nastassja Kinski, writer Edith Wharton, and actor John Belushi.

Numerology

As a number 24 individual, you may dislike routine; however, you are hardworking, with practical abilities and sound judgment. The emotional sensitivity of the number 24 birthday suggests that you need to establish stability and order. Faithful and fair, though sometimes undemonstrative, you are inclined to believe that actions speak louder than words. With this pragmatic approach to life, you develop good business sense and an ability to surmount obstacles and succeed. With a number 24 birthday, you may have to overcome a tendency to be stubborn or fixed in your ideas. The subinfluence of the number 1 month indicates that you are independent and idealistic. As a serious individual, you like to put your imaginative thoughts to practical use. Being a progressive thinker, you may be interested in humanitarian issues and drawn toward public life or reforms, especially in education and politics. Innovative and courageous, you speak your mind, but usually do it in a charming way. The enterprising spirit indicated here encourages you to experiment with different concepts and make up your own mind or strike out alone.

• *Positive:* energy, idealist, practical skills, strong determination, honest, frank, fair, generous, love of home, active, energetic

• *Negative:* materialism, too economical, dislikes routine, lazy, unfaithful, domineering, stubborn

Love & Relationships

Individual and sensitive, you need time and space for yourself. As an idealist, you can have such high expectations that sometimes it is difficult for anyone to live up to them. Although you can be loving and spontaneous, you are also capable of showing others a cold shoulder and appearing too detached. As you can be generous and giving, watch out that you do not make too many sacrifices you might later regret. Being friendly, you attract others and can fare particularly well in group situations.

veals a talent for writing and education. Often ambitious and daring, you seek a change of fortune and may enjoy unexpected gains or other benefits. Group-oriented, you can make friends and influence people.

• *Positive:* original, inventive, individual, humanitarian, creative

• *Negative:* rebellious, antagonistic, unpredictable

See Appendix for additional fixed star readings.

YOUR SPECIAL SOMEONE

You might find emotional fulfillment and that special someone among those born on the following days.

Love & friendship: Jan. 4, 8, 13, 22, 26, Feb. 2, 6, 20, 24, Mar. 4, 18, 22, Apr. 2, 16, 20, 30, May 5, 14, 18, 28, 30, June 3, 12, 16, 26, 28, July 10, 14, 24, 26, Aug. 8, 12, 22, 24, Sept. 6, 10, 20, 22, 30, Oct. 4, 8, 18, 20, 28, Nov. 2, 6, 16, 18, 26, Dec. 4, 14, 16, 24

Beneficial: Jan. 9, 20, Feb. 7, 18, Mar. 5, 16, 29, Apr. 3, 14, 27, May 1, 12, 25, 31, June 10, 23, July 8, 21, Aug. 6, 19, 25, Sept. 4, 17, 23, Oct. 2, 15, 30, Nov. 13, 28, Dec. 11, 26, 30

Fatal attractions: Jan. 27, Feb. 25, Mar. 23, Apr. 21, May 19, June 17, July 15, 24, 25, 26, 27, 28, Aug. 13, Sept. 11, Oct. 9, Nov. 7, Dec. 5

Challenging: Jan. 2, 10, 19, Feb. 8, 17, Mar. 6, 15, Apr. 4, 13, May 2, 11, June 9, July 7, 30, Aug. 5, 28, Sept. 3, 26, Oct. 1, 24, Nov. 22, Dec. 20, 30

Soul mates: Jan. 15, Feb. 13, Mar. 11, Apr. 9, May 7, June 5, July 3, Aug. 1, Oct. 29, Nov. 27, Dec. 25

January 25

FIXED STARS

Dabih; Giedi, also called Al Jady; Oculus; Bos

PRIMARY STAR

Star's name: Dabih

Degree position: 3°4'–4°3' Aquarius between the years 1930 and 2000

Magnitude: 3

Strength: ★★★★★

Orb: 1°40'

Constellation: Beta Capricorn

Applicable days: January 23, 24, 25, 26

Star qualities: Saturn/Venus and Saturn/Uranus

Description: a binary orange-yellow and blue star located in the left eye of the Goat

PRIMARY STAR'S INFLUENCE

Dabih imparts positions of trust and authority, and bestows a responsible nature that may gain you public recognition. Dabih also suggests that you may have a reserved nature and a tendency to be mistrustful. It warns against unsavory associations or losses through friends.

Linked to your Sun's degree, this star imparts determination and success through steady progress and hard work. Dabih also suggests that you should proceed cautiously and use conventional methods to gain opportunities for promotion.

• *Positive:* hard work, dedication, perseverance

≈ Friendly and generous, you are an active and intelligent Aquarian with a spirit of success. Sharp and aware, you can be hardworking and disciplined. As a determined individual with good strategies, you can concentrate your energy and drive on achieving your goals. Your innate business sense can assist you to commercialize your talents, but your natural idealism may also involve you in activities or projects that help others.

With the added influence of your Sun in the decanate of Aquarius, you are a shrewd judge of character, with strong insight into people's motivation. Broad-minded and humanitarian, you are a free thinker with inventive and original ideas. Friendship is especially important to you and, being amiable and sociable, you have a gift for making new contacts. With your quick reactions and strong sense of individuality, you are rarely boring, but you may have to watch a tendency toward nervous haste.

With two extremes in your nature, you can be either ruthlessly determined, businesslike, and assertive, or compassionate, sensitive, and visionary. By learning to stay well balanced, you are able to creatively combine these qualities to manifest your dreams and ideals. Sometimes others may interpret your detachment as coldness or indifference, but it is your skill in working cooperatively with others that can be one of your greatest assets.

Until you reach the age of twenty-five your progressed Sun is in Aquarius, highlighting issues of personal freedom, friendship, and expressing your individuality. At the age of twenty-six, when your progressed Sun moves into Pisces, emotional concerns take on more importance in your life as you become more sensitive and impressionable. You may have more contact with your dreams or inner world. At the age of fifty-six there is a turning point as your progressed Sun enters Aries. This dynamic influence accents leadership and greater self-orientation as you start to feel more assertive and confident. This may inspire you to begin new projects.

Your Secret Self

The urge for action and personal accomplishment revealed by your birthday suggests that you are a strong-willed and ambitious individual. With your endurance and strong survival instincts, you can be persistent, but you may have to avoid becoming obstinate or impatient. Although you may sometimes get too caught up in the material world and worry unnecessarily about money, the ability to have fortunate ideas and share them with others is a major part of your success.

Your idealism and active imagination can be expressed through an interest in the arts, music, religion, or spirituality. With your grand dreams, drive, and determination, it is surprising that you can also be prone to inertia. You can keep your life in harmony by utilizing your universal perspective. This connects you to your innate compassion and often inspires you to altruistic endeavors.

Work & Vocation

Being inventive and a sharp judge of character can be especially helpful to you in any career, but particularly writing and counseling. Friendly and able to work well with others, you have a natural ease in making contacts that can prove to be helpful in your life plan. Intuitive and idealistic, you enjoy collaborating with others even though you are independent and like to make your own decisions. You may be particularly good at selling or promoting an idea or product. Equally, your business acumen, organizational skills, and ability to deal with people on a one-to-one level can ensure your success in occupations such as financial advisor or negotiator. Being sensitive and a perfectionist, you may wish to develop your creative skills to a high professional level in music, writing, or the arts.

Famous people who share your birthday include writers Somerset Maugham and Virginia Woolf, cellist Jacqueline Du Pre, poet Robert Burns, conductor Wilhelm Furtwangler, singer Etta James, and Philippine president Corazon Aquino.

Numerology

Quick and energetic, as well as intuitive and thoughtful, you need to express yourself through different experiences. These may include pursuing new and exciting ideas, meeting new people, or going to new locations. Having a number 25 birthday, you are likely to feel a desire for perfection urging you to work hard and be productive. You may, however, need to be less impatient or critical if things do not happen according to plan. With this birthdate, you possess strong mental energies that aid you in looking at all the facts and arriving at a conclusion faster than anyone else. Success and happiness come when you learn to trust your own instincts and develop perseverance and patience. The subinfluence of the number 1 month indicates that you are usually intuitive and ambitious. When self-assured, you show a great deal of enthusiasm and willingness to collaborate with others. If in doubt, however, you may be mistrustful and uncooperative. Innovative and courageous, you speak your mind but usually do it in a charming way. Since you are concerned with security, you need stability to keep you balanced and relaxed.

• *Positive:* highly intuitive, perfectionist, perceptive, creative mind, good at dealing with people

• *Negative:* impatient, irresponsible, overly emotional, jealous, secretive, changing circumstances, critical, moody

Love & Relationships

Gregarious and group-oriented, you are a networker who enjoys making contacts and meeting people. Usually you have an active social life, and you can mix business with pleasure. All your relationships are very important to you, and you will make an effort to keep in touch with all your friends and acquaintances. You tend to like the company of intelligent and powerful people. You may have to be careful, however, not to become manipulative with partners. Although at times you may have concerns with money issues, you can be very generous with the people you love.

YOUR SPECIAL SOMEONE

To improve on your chances of finding love and happiness, look out for those born on the following dates.

Love & friendship: Jan. 3, 6, 23, 28, Feb. 11, 21, Mar. 9, 19, 28, 31, Apr. 7, 17, 26, 29, May 5, 15, 24, 27, 29, 31, June 3, 13, 18, 22, 25, 27, 29, July 1, 11, 20, 23, 25, 27, 29, Aug. 9, 18, 21, 23, 25, 27, Sept. 7, 16, 19, 21, 23, 25, Oct. 5, 10, 14, 17, 19, 21, 23, Nov. 3, 12, 15, 17, 19, 21, Dec. 1, 10, 13, 15, 17, 19

Beneficial: Jan. 3, 4, 10, 21, Feb. 1, 2, 8, 19, Mar. 6, 17, 30, Apr. 4, 15, 28, May 2, 13, 26, June 11, 24, July 9, 22, Aug. 7, 20, Sept. 5, 18, 22, Oct. 3, 16, 31, Nov. 1, 14, 29, Dec. 12, 27

Fatal attractions: Jan. 22, 28, Feb. 20, 26, Mar. 18, 24, Apr. 16, 22, May 14, 20, June 12, 18, July 10, 16, 26, 27, 28, 29, Aug. 8, 14, Sept. 6, 12, Oct. 4, 10, Nov. 2, 8, Dec. 6

Challenging: Jan. 11, 20, Feb. 9, 18, Mar. 7, 16, Apr. 5, 14, May 3, 12, 30, June 1, 10, 28, July 8, 26, 31, Aug. 6, 24, 29, Sept. 4, 22, 27, Oct. 2, 20, 25, Nov. 18, 23, Dec. 16, 21

Soul mates: Jan. 26, Feb. 24, Mar. 22, 30, Apr. 20, 28, May 18, 26, June 16, 24, July 14, 22, Aug. 12, 20, Sept. 10, 18, Oct. 8, 16, Nov. 6, 14, Dec. 4, 12

January 26

The influence of your Aquarius birthday implies that you are a strong-willed individualist who likes to be in the forefront of new trends and ideas. Charismatic and determined, you possess intuitive leadership and the ability to mix business and pleasure. The urge for action and personal accomplishment revealed by your birthday suggests that you are ambitious and success-oriented. With your quick grasp of situations, you prefer to be honest and straightforward in your approach. Possessing strong drive and an enterprising spirit, you have the potential to manifest your grand dreams as tangible reality.

With the added influence of your Sun in the Aquarius decanate, you are a broad-minded humanitarian with a rebellious streak. Constructively harnessed, this could help you become a pioneer of new ventures. Paradoxically, although you do not like your personal freedom restricted, you may run the risk of being bossy in your attempt to do things your own way. Naturally direct, with a good sense of values, you usually present an assertive yet friendly personality.

While you have excellent skills for dealing with people, patience may not be one of your strongest attributes. This can cause you to alternate between restlessness, on one hand, and making magnanimous gestures, on the other. One of your primary assets, however, is the ability to understand what motivates others. By combining this with your very fortunate ideas, idealism, and down-to-earth approach, you can achieve success and prosperity.

Until you reach the age of twenty-four your progressed Sun moves through Aquarius, highlighting issues of freedom and independence. You develop a heightened interest in friendship or group awareness and need to express your individuality. After the age of twenty-five, when your progressed Sun moves into Pisces, you become more sensitive and have to deal with more emotional issues. You may develop a greater sense of vision or have more access to your inner world. At the age of fifty-five there is another turning point as your progressed Sun enters Aries. This accents a need to take the initiative and be direct and active in your relationships with others. You will start to feel more confident and daring and may initiate new plans and activities.

FIXED STARS

Dabih, Oculus, Bos

PRIMARY STAR

Star's name: Dabih

Degree position: 3°4'–4°3' Aquarius between the years 1930 and 2000

Magnitude: 3

Strength: ★★★★★

Orb: 1°40'

Constellation: Beta Capricorn

Applicable days: January 23, 24, 25, 26

Star qualities: Saturn/Venus and Saturn/Uranus

Description: a binary orange-yellow and blue star located in the left eye of the Goat

PRIMARY STAR'S INFLUENCE

Dabih imparts positions of trust and authority, and bestows a responsible nature that may gain you public recognition. Dabih also suggests that you may have a reserved nature and a tendency to be mistrustful. It warns against unsavory associations or losses through friends.

Linked to your Sun's degree, this star imparts determination and success through steady progress and hard work. Dabih also suggests that you should proceed cautiously and use conventional methods to gain opportunities for promotion.

• *Positive:* hard work, dedication, perseverance

• *Negative:* overly suspicious, mistrustful

See Appendix for additional fixed star information.

Your Secret Self

Given your power to manifest what you want in life, it is vital that you be clear about what you wish for. To others you may sometimes appear detached, yet you possess powerful inner feelings and desires. These strong emotions need to be acknowledged and channeled through positive outlets. When directed into selfless love and helping others, your personality and high ideals can prove to be a remarkable force for good.

You possess a natural talent for business along with a flair for making contacts. Constantly evaluating your own self-worth and the advantages to be gained from situations, you love to bargain or make things happen. Even when you are doing well, you may entertain the fear of not having enough money. By staying connected to your strong spirit, however, you will always have more than enough.

Work & Vocation

Motivated by the strong combination of idealism and practicality, you possess natural abilities for leadership. In business you have a healthy perspective on money, but guard against power struggles and being critical of others. You thrive on new beginnings or challenges, and you have the wonderful ability to spot opportunities. With your enthusiasm and persuasive speech, you can often sell ideas or promote products and other people. As a person with courage, commitment, and executive abilities, you may pursue a career in commerce as a negotiator, agent, or financial advisor. Alternatively, your individual and unique approach to life may find expression in the creative world.

Famous people who share your birthday include actor Paul Newman, military leader Douglas MacArthur, singers Eartha Kitt, Eddie Van Halen, and Anita Baker, political activist Angela Davis, violinist Stephane Grappelli, film director Roger Vadim, and hockey player Wayne Gretsky.

Numerology

With a number 26 birthday, you have a pragmatic approach to life, executive ability, and a good business sense. Usually responsible, with a natural aesthetic sense and a love of home, you need to build a solid foundation or find real stability. Often a tower of strength for others, you are willing to support friends and family members who turn to you in time of need. You may nevertheless need to guard against materialistic tendencies and a desire to control situations or people. The subinfluence of the number 1 month indicates that you are intuitive and independent, with an enterprising spirit. A need for freedom suggests that you require room to maneuver or take advantage of opportunities when they occur. Broad-minded yet practical, you can anticipate trends. Full of enthusiasm and original ideas, you often show others the way forward. As a serious and hardworking individual, you are able to make real progress, and usually you put your imaginative thoughts to practical use. Although you can achieve a great deal through your own efforts, you need the cooperation of others in order to achieve real success.

• *Positive:* creative, practical, caring, responsible, proud of family, enthusiasm, courage
• *Negative:* stubborn, rebellious, unstable relationships, unenthusiastic, lack of persistence

Love & Relationships

A tendency to change your feelings about affairs of the heart suggests, among other things, that you need variety and movement. You need to develop patience to see how things turn out rather than acting too much on impulse and regretting it later. Usually you enjoy an active life, meeting new people, and experiencing different situations. Your ideal partner would be someone who is able to keep you interested and on your toes as well as being loving and understanding. Being independent, even within a loving relationship you need the freedom to operate in your own way.

YOUR SPECIAL SOMEONE

For security, mental stimulation, and love, you might want to begin looking for those born among the following dates.

Love & friendship: Jan. 6, 14, 22, 24, 31, Feb. 4, 12, 22, 29, Mar. 10, 20, 27, Apr. 8, 18, 25, May 6, 16, 23, 25, 30, June 4, 14, 21, 28, 30, July 2, 12, 19, 26, 28, 30, Aug. 10, 17, 24, 26, 28, Sept. 8, 15, 22, 24, 26, Oct. 4, 6, 13, 15, 20, 22, 24, 30, Nov. 4, 11, 18, 20, 22, 28, Dec. 2, 9, 16, 18, 20, 26, 29

Beneficial: Jan. 5, 22, 30, Feb. 3, 20, 28, Mar. 1, 18, 26, Apr. 16, 24, May 14, 22, June 12, 20, July 10, 18, 29, Aug. 8, 16, 27, 31, Sept. 6, 14, 25, 27, 29, Oct. 4, 12, 23, 27, Nov. 2, 10, 21, 23, 25, Dec. 9, 19, 23

Fatal attractions: Jan. 12, Feb. 10, Mar. 8, Apr. 6, May 4, June 2, July 28, 29, 30, 31

Challenging: Jan. 16, 21, Feb. 14, 19, Mar. 12, 17, 30, Apr. 10, 15, 28, May 8, 13, 26, June 6, 11, 24, July 4, 9, 22, Aug. 2, 7, 20, Sept. 5, 18, Oct. 3, 16, Nov. 1, 14, Dec. 12

Soul mates: Jan. 25, Feb. 23, Mar. 21, Apr. 19, May 17, June 15, July 13, Aug. 11, Sept. 9, Oct. 7, Nov. 5, Dec. 3, 30

January 27

≈≈ Clever, intuitive, and a strong individualist, you are knowledgeable with quick perceptions. Your Aquarius birthday implies that you are independent, with an ability to lead, and that you would rather take charge than answer to superiors. Assertive, with common sense, you are usually willing to work hard to achieve your objectives. With your outstanding intellect and intuition, you have only to develop the necessary self-discipline to fulfill your remarkable potential.

With the added influence of your Sun in the decanate of Aquarius, you are friendly, outgoing, and people-oriented. Able to present a unique approach to a problem, you can give others practical advice and solutions. You may also have a more unusual or eccentric side to your nature. Your individualistic thinking can place you ahead of your time, although there is also a danger of becoming stubborn or rebellious.

By a tenacious pursuit of your plans, you develop the patience and perseverance required to attain your long-term goals. With an objective and inventive mind, you can have flashes of genius and your instincts about other people are usually right. As a good judge of character, you are straightforward and outspoken. Your original perspective can inspire you to instigate reform and renew outdated systems. Women of this day tend to think in a decisive way and often take command of situations rather than be passive observers.

Until you reach the age of twenty-three your progressed Sun is in Aquarius, highlighting issues of personal freedom, friendship, and expressing your individuality. At the age of twenty-four, when your progressed Sun moves through Pisces, you become more emotionally sensitive, develop a greater sense of vision, or have more access to your inner world. At the age of fifty-four there is a turning point as your progressed Sun enters Aries. This influence can start to make you more confident, assertive, and ambitious, possibly initiating or leading new activities.

Fixed Stars

Although your Sun's degree is not linked to a fixed star, some of your other planets' degrees certainly will be. By having an astrological chart calculated, you can find the exact position of the planets on your date of birth. This will tell you which of the fixed stars listed in this book are relevant to you.

Your Secret Self

When you have set yourself a definite goal, you can be determined and uncompromising in achieving your objectives. This same resolve can help you overcome obstacles in your life and make you capable of great accomplishments. Enjoying power, you like to be in control but should avoid becoming involved in tactics or psychological games. Your strong sense of duty and desire for material success suggest that you take your work or responsibilities seriously.

Although independent, you usually work well in group situations or partnerships. As a good team member, you understand the dynamics of compromise in a working relationship. Although you do not suffer fools gladly, you usually achieve more when you use your inherent diplomatic skills rather than take a dogmatic approach. When dealing with people on a one-to-one basis, you have the skill to make others feel special.

Work & Vocation

Your keen intelligence is likely to be the strongest influence on the career you choose. Needing work that keeps you mentally stimulated, you can be clever, responsible, and hardworking.

Given the opportunity, you usually rise to positions of authority. Your natural humanitarianism can attract you to social or educational reform, but you could equally excel in politics or progressive movements for human rights. Your organizational skills and natural communicative abilities would be an asset if you are in business or practicing law. Being very independent, however, you may wish to freelance and work for yourself. Your understanding of human nature can be helpful in careers such as counseling or medicine. A desire to express your creativity and individuality could lead you to the arts, the theater, and particularly music.

Famous people who share your birthday include composer Wolfgang Amadeus Mozart, actress Bridget Fonda, pianist John Ogden, writer Lewis Carroll (aka Charles Dodgson), and publisher William Randolph Hearst Jr.

Numerology

The number 27 birthdate indicates that you are idealistic and sensitive. Intuitive and analytical, with a fertile and creative mind, you can impress others with your original thoughts. Although at times you appear secretive, rational, or detached, in fact, you may be hiding inner tensions. In developing good communication skills, you can overcome a reluctance to express your deeper feelings. Education is essential for number 27 persons, and by developing depth of thought you become more patient and self-disciplined. The subinfluence of the number 1 month indicates that you are gifted and imaginative, with strong instincts or psychic abilities. As an independent thinker, you are autonomous and assertive, with a broad-minded perspective. Full of enthusiasm and original ideas, you have a progressive outlook, suggesting that you often show others the way forward. Although idealistic, you are a serious and hardworking individual and like to put your thoughts to practical use. Innovative and courageous, you do not hesitate to speak your mind on issues close to your heart or to experiment with different concepts. Usually you make up your own mind.

• *Positive:* versatile, imaginative, creative, brave, good understanding, mentally capable, spiritual, inventive, mental strength

• *Negative:* easily offended, argumentative, restless, mistrustful, overly emotional, tense

Love & Relationships

Humanitarian and progressive, you have a need for people, suggesting that love and relationships are especially important to you. You are emotionally honest and intelligent, and others admire your abilities and rational outlook. With a need for stability and emotional security, you may feel that having a family and a strong foundation in life is a significant part of your overall plan. With your strong emotions, you can be devoted, loyal, and caring, but may also have to watch out for occasionally becoming domineering.

YOUR SPECIAL SOMEONE

In order to find that special partner, you might wish to look for those born on the following dates.

Love & friendship: Jan. 7, 8, 11, 13, 15, 17, 25, Feb. 5, 7, 9, 11, 13, 15, 23, Mar. 7, 9, 11, 13, 21, Apr. 2, 5, 7, 9, 11, 19, May 3, 5, 7, 9, 17, 31, June 1, 3, 5, 7, 15, 29, July 1, 3, 5, 27, 29, 31, Aug. 1, 3, 11, 25, 27, 29, Sept. 1, 9, 23, 25, 27, Oct. 7, 21, 23, 25, Nov. 5, 19, 21, 23, Dec. 3, 17, 19, 21, 30

Beneficial: Jan. 1, 5, 20, 29, Feb. 3, 18, Mar. 1, 16, Apr. 14, May 12, June 10, 17, July 8, Aug. 6, Sept. 4, Oct. 2, 9

Fatal attractions: July 28, 29, 30, 31

Challenging: Jan. 6, 22, 24, Feb. 4, 20, 22, Mar. 2, 18, 20, Apr. 16, 18, May 14, 16, June 12, 14, July 10, 12, Aug. 8, 10, 31, Sept. 6, 8, 29, Oct. 4, 6, 27, Nov. 2, 4, 25, 30, Dec. 2, 23, 28

Soul mates: Jan. 6, 12, Feb. 4, 10, Mar. 2, 8, Apr. 6, May 4, June 2

January 28

FIXED STARS

Although your Sun's degree is not linked to a fixed star, some of your other planets' degrees certainly will be. By having an astrological chart calculated, you can find the exact position of the planets on your date of birth. This will tell you which of the fixed stars listed in this book are relevant to you.

Ambitious and smart, you are an Aquarian with a fast mind and natural intuition. Charming and attractive, you can project a self-assured image to others.

Being generous and friendly, with good social skills, suggests that you are invariably popular. Talented and possessing good judgment, you feel secure in your knowledge and prefer to think independently. With your quick reactions and strong sense of individuality, you are rarely boring, but you may have to watch a tendency to be impatient.

With the added influence of your Sun in the Aquarius decanate, you are an original and broad-minded humanitarian with a rebellious streak. Productively channeled, this could help you become a pioneer of new and progressive ideas and endeavors. As a good psychologist, you possess a shrewd insight into people's character and motivation that can help you in your climb to the top.

Friendship can be an integral part of your emotional development. Being warm and sociable, you are a good networker, with a gift for making new contacts. Ironically, although you do not like interference from others or having your personal freedom restricted, you may sometimes run the risk of becoming stubborn or bossy yourself. Original and inventive, you have a fast, assertive, and concise mind that loves wit, satire, or quick repartee. If threatened, you can be competitive and have the power to verbally retaliate in just the right manner. Although a good critic, you must be careful not to take this too far and use words as a weapon to be hurtful.

Until you reach the age of twenty-two your progressed Sun is in Aquarius, highlighting issues of personal freedom, friendship, and expressing your individuality. At the age of twenty-three, when your progressed Sun moves into Pisces, you become more emotionally aware and receptive, with an emphasis on your dreams and natural intuition. At the age of fifty-three there is a turning point as your progressed Sun enters Aries. This influence accents greater self-orientation as you start to feel more confident and daring.

Your Secret Self

Dramatic, sensitive, and creative, you have a strong need for self-expression. Although you are usually optimistic, discontent or indecision about emotional concerns can sometimes prove to be a challenge. Your idealism can be a source of inspiration, however; as you dislike being bored, you are likely to be constantly searching for new and original pursuits to keep your mind engrossed and uplifted. With your innate intuitive or psychic gifts, you may discover a growing recognition of a higher wisdom.

Success-oriented, with an ability to see the large picture, you have big plans and can be very enterprising. Ambitious and courageous, you are naturally lucky, with good business acumen. Be careful, however, of a tendency to think that financial security can provide you with all the answers. This emphasizes the need to adhere to choices that can enhance your sense of values, identity, and self-esteem.

Work & Vocation

As an astute, charming, and witty individual who is gifted with words, you fare well in any career that involves communication, particularly writing, media, or speaking up for others. With a desire to expand your knowledge, you may be equally drawn to education, science, literature, or law. Capable and multitalented, you are both a humanitarian idealist and a high achiever. This side of your nature may feel more at home counseling, doing community work, or fighting for a social or political cause. With natural leadership and the ability to think big, you can use your administrative skills in large corporations or succeed in the business world. Alternatively, your need for artistic expression can attract you to the world of art and entertainment, particularly through the media of music and drama.

Famous people who share your birthday include pianist Arthur Rubinstein, novelist Colette, ballet dancer Mikhail Baryshnikov, actor Alan Alda, and painter Jackson Pollock.

Numerology

Independent and idealistic, with determination and a pragmatic approach, you are often a law unto yourself. Like a number 1 individual, you are ambitious, direct, and enterprising. An inner conflict between wanting to be independent and wanting to be part of a team is also indicated. Always ready for action and new ventures, you courageously take on life's challenges, and with your enthusiasm you can easily inspire others, if not to join you, then at least to support you in your latest venture. As a number 28 individual, you have leadership abilities and rely on your common sense, logic, and clear thinking. Although you can be responsible, avoid being overly enthusiastic, impatient, or intolerant. The subinfluence of the number 1 month indicates that you are full of enthusiasm and original ideas. Shrewd and instinctive, you have a need for activity and mental challenge that implies that you can achieve a great deal and are apt to do so from an early age. Although you are practical, your values may change through experience and you will express yourself in a different way. To find inner peace, you may need to create a harmonious atmosphere and a loving and caring environment.

• *Positive:* compassion, progressive, daring, artistic, creative, idealistic, ambitious, hardworking, stable home life, strong-willed

• *Negative:* daydreamer, unmotivated, lack of compassion, unrealistic, bossy, lack of judgment

Love & Relationships

Intelligent and determined, you enjoy the company of clever individuals who are mentally stimulating or adventurous. A tendency to become bored easily implies that you also prefer active people who are doers. Since you may have doubts about intimate relationships, you may feel more comfortable in a platonic relationship where you both share the same interests. When you give your heart to someone, you are loyal, loving, and supportive.

January 29

FIXED STARS

Although your Sun's degree is not linked to a fixed star, some of your other planets' degrees certainly will be. By having an astrological chart calculated, you can find the exact position of the planets on your date of birth. This will tell you which of the fixed stars listed in this book are relevant to you.

 Strong-willed and intelligent, you are an Aquarian with excellent communication skills. You may decide to use your natural rebellious streak to support the rights of others, and with your wealth of knowledge, you often act as a mediator. Your personal magnetism and creative talents can draw others toward you; you are likely to be popular and mix easily with people from all walks of life. Often sparkling and with strong characteristics, you manage to keep people entertained while still getting your message across.

With the added influence of your Sun in the Aquarius decanate, your inventive ideas can often be ahead of their time. Independent and freedom-loving, you have a need to do things your way. Very sociable, you value friendship and frequently have a wide, humanitarian approach to relationships. Honest in your feelings, you can be enthusiastic and eager in your approach when you find a person or project you really enjoy. Being high-strung and excitable, however, means that you should avoid stress from taking on too much or being unpredictable.

Idealistic and with strong convictions, you have a natural flair for the spoken and written word. This contributes to a possible talent for writing or a skill at teaching and lecturing. Although you are practical and have organizing ability, you can sometimes be carried away with optimism and the spirit of enterprise. Outspoken and full of life, you love action and want to make things happen in a big way. Although you are talented and determined, be careful that pride does not cause you to be obstinate or stubborn.

Until you reach the age of twenty-one your progressed Sun moves through Aquarius, highlighting issues of freedom, independence, and the need to express your individuality. After the age of twenty-two, when your progressed Sun moves into Pisces, you become more sensitive and aware of emotional issues. You may develop a greater sense of vision or have more access to your inner world. At the age of fifty-two there is another turning point when your progressed Sun enters Aries, accenting a greater self-orientation as you start to feel more confident and assertive, with a greater need to pioneer new areas of interest.

Your Secret Self

Very persuasive, you are an interesting mixture of materialism and idealism. Although you may worry excessively about money matters or material security, your birthdate indicates a natural financial protection, ensuring that whatever you give can be replaced. An appreciation for beauty and the good life suggests that you love luxury with a touch of glamour. Original in any form of artistic or creative expression, you enjoy the interesting and the unusual.

Charming and warmhearted, you possess strong emotions. A charismatic inner quality enables you to radiate love and positivity, emphasizing the importance of having an outlet for your self-expression. Due to your strong feelings, however, you may have to avoid going to extremes or acting too much on impulse. Your temperament combines strong male and female elements that can emphasize both independence and determination as well as compassion and sensitivity.

Work & Vocation

With your sharp intelligence, you have many career choices. An ability to communicate your ideas can attract you to lecturing, teaching, or writing. With your positive attitude and easygoing personality, you can succeed in people-related careers and gain promotion to positions of responsibility. You may be drawn to the world of commerce and use your persuasive charm in sales, promotion, or negotiation. You are equally likely to be attracted to law, academia, or politics. Alternatively, your need for self-expression can lead you to the media or entertainment business.

Famous people who share your birthday include TV host Oprah Winfrey, feminist Germaine Greer, actors Tom Selleck and W. C. Fields, political revolutionary Thomas Paine, and playwright Anton Chekhov.

Numerology

As a number 29 individual, you have a powerful personality and extraordinary potential. You are highly intuitive, sensitive, and emotional. Inspiration is the key to your success story, and without it you may experience lack of purpose. Although you are a true dreamer, the extreme sides of your nature indicate that you may have to guard against alternating moods. If you trust your innermost feelings and open your heart to others, you can overcome a tendency to worry or use your mind as protective armor. Use your creative thoughts to achieve something special and unique that can motivate or be of service to others. The subinfluence of the number 1 month indicates that you are intuitive and receptive, with a humanitarian nature. Creative and intelligent, you can excel in all types of activities that require individuality and an astute mind. The enterprising spirit indicated here encourages you to experiment with different concepts and make up your own mind or strike out alone. Liberal and full of enthusiasm, you like to explore new ideas and are often interested in technical information or applying new discoveries. Although you are imaginative and inventive, you like to put your ideas to practical use.

• *Positive:* inspirational, balance, inner peace, generous, successful, creative, intuitive, mystical, powerful dreams, worldly, faith

• *Negative:* unfocused, insecure, moody, difficult, extremist, inconsiderate, overly sensitive

Love & Relationships

Usually honest and direct, you enjoy sharing your many interests with others and can be an excellent companion. Spontaneous and idealistic, you need an inspiring bond with your partner. A fear of being deserted or lonely, however, may sometimes cause you to appear aloof or uncaring, or cause you to become attached to unsuitable partners. You may have to be careful not to appear so detached and independent that your partner assumes that you do not need him or her. Clever and intuitive yourself, you enjoy the company of creative people and make a generous and loyal friend.

YOUR SPECIAL SOMEONE

You may be more likely to make a serious commitment with someone born on one of the following dates.

Love & friendship: Jan. 2, 7, 10, 17, 22, 27, 31, Feb. 5, 8, 15, 25, Mar. 3, 6, 13, 23, Apr. 1, 4, 11, 16, 21, May 2, 9, 19, 23, June 7, 12, 17, 23, July 5, 15, 29, 31, Aug. 3, 13, 27, 29, 31, Sept. 1, 11, 25, 27, 29, Oct. 4, 9, 13, 23, 25, 27, Nov. 7, 21, 23, 25, Dec. 5, 19, 21, 23

Beneficial: Jan. 3, 5, 20, 25, 27, Feb. 1, 3, 18, 23, 25, Mar. 1, 16, 21, 23, Apr. 14, 19, 21, May 12, 17, 19, June 10, 15, 17, July 8, 13, 15, Aug. 6, 11, 13, Sept. 4, 9, 11, 28, Oct. 2, 7, 9, Nov. 5, 7, 24, Dec. 3, 5

Fatal attractions: Jan. 13, Feb. 11, Mar. 9, Apr. 7, May 5, June 3, July 1, 31, August 1, 2

Challenging: Jan. 16, 24, Feb. 14, 22, Mar. 12, 20, Apr. 10, 18, May 8, 16, 31, June 6, 14, 29, July 4, 12, 27, Aug. 2, 10, 25, Sept. 8, 23, Oct. 6, 21, Nov. 4, 19, Dec. 2, 17

Soul mates: Jan. 16, Feb. 14, Mar. 12, Apr. 10, May 8, June 6, July 4, 31, Aug. 2, 29, Sept. 27, Oct. 25, Nov. 23, Dec. 21

January 30

FIXED STARS

Although your Sun's degree is not linked to a fixed star, some of your other planets' degrees certainly will be. By having an astrological chart calculated, you can find the exact position of the planets on your date of birth. This will tell you which of the fixed stars listed in this book are relevant to you.

≈≈ Your birthday indicates that you are friendly, enthusiastic, and success-oriented, a freedom-loving Aquarian with big ideas. Assertive and dynamic, you have a warm way with people and an ease in social situations. With your keen intellect and rational approach, you love knowledge, but it is through gaining wisdom that you reach contentment.

With the added influence of your Sun in the Aquarius decanate, you are a broad-minded humanitarian with a rebellious streak. As an objective thinker with an inventive mind, you can have inspired and unique ideas that can reward you financially. With your shrewd insight, you are usually able to quickly judge others' character. Your insight and forward thinking can place you ahead of your time, although there is also the danger that you may go too far and become stubborn or critical.

You are quick to recognize new trends or concepts, and usually you enjoy expressing your ideas. Although self-assured, with strong convictions, at times you may be prone to worry and to act impulsively. A need to receive the approval of others or the urge to shine suggests that you can enjoy being before the public. You can become spirited and excited when you find an interest that truly inspires you and convey this to others through your persuasive speech.

Until you reach the age of twenty, your progressed Sun is in Aquarius, highlighting issues of personal freedom, friendship, and expressing your individuality. At the age of twenty-one, when your progressed Sun moves through Pisces, you become more emotionally sensitive, develop a greater sense of working toward your dreams, or have more access to your inner world. At the age of fifty-one there is a turning point as your progressed Sun enters Aries. This influence can start to make you more confident, assertive, and dynamic as you really start to come into your own.

Your Secret Self

Highly intuitive, you need to listen for and trust your inner guidance. This can help you find a balance between your vision and reality. Once you have developed a plan to achieve your goals, it is necessary to stick to it regardless of difficulties. A genuine desire to give your best to your work can help you stay modest and honorable. Your determination to succeed will always help you win.

Ambitious, you do not usually like to take orders from others and are therefore better suited for positions of authority. Quick to spot opportunities, you possess a strong practicality and organizational skills. Although friendly, with an astute mentality, you may show your impatience by failing to be a good listener or becoming bored easily. Capable of outstanding success, however, you can move mountains with your positive attitude.

Work & Vocation

Your shrewd understanding of human nature, charm, and organizational skills indicate that you have the potential to prosper in many people-related activities, whether in the business world, education, or government. Independent, confident, and friendly, you will find that your natural leadership skills can place you in executive positions, management, or working for yourself. Willing to put in much effort when you find an area of interest, you want to constantly improve yourself. With your creative and inventive ideas, you can be a good communicator, writer, or negotiator as well as succeed in the entertainment world.

Famous people who share your birthday include actress Vanessa Redgrave, steam engine inventor James Watt, U.S. president Franklin Roosevelt, actor Gene Hackman, and singer Jody Watley.

Numerology

Artistic, friendly, and sociable are just some of the ways others would describe people with the number 30 birthday. You enjoy the good life and socializing, and you can be exceptionally charismatic, loyal, and friendly. Gregarious, with good taste and an eye for style and form, you can achieve success in all types of work concerning art, design, and music. Similarly, a need for self-expression and a natural talent for words may inspire you to explore writing, speaking, or singing. You possess strong feelings, and being in love or contented is a vital requirement. In your pursuit of happiness, avoid being lazy or overindulgent. Among those with number 30 birthdays, many will find recognition or fame, especially musicians, actors, and entertainers. The subinfluence of the number 1 month indicates that you are ambitious and idealistic, with creative thoughts. The ability to revive old ideas by injecting them with a new life suggests that you can synthesize concepts and expand on them. Although you are friendly and receptive, you may need to learn to compromise and avoid being stubborn or bossy if you want people to enjoy your witty and sociable nature.

- *Positive:* fun-loving, loyal, friendly, good conversationalist, creative, lucky
- *Negative:* lazy, obstinate, impatient, temperamental, jealous, indifferent, scattered

YOUR SPECIAL SOMEONE

You can find your ideal partner and greater stability in love with someone born on one of the following dates.

Love & friendship: Jan. 1, 8, 14, 23, 28, 31, Feb. 12, 26, 29, Mar. 10, 24, 27, Apr. 2, 8, 22, 25, May 6, 20, 23, June 4, 13, 18, 21, July 2, 16, 19, 30, Aug. 14, 17, 28, 30, Sept. 12, 15, 26, 28, 30, Oct. 10, 13, 24, 26, 28, Nov. 8, 11, 22, 24, 26, Dec. 6, 9, 20, 22, 24

Beneficial: Jan. 26, Feb. 24, Mar. 22, Apr. 20, May 18, June 16, July 14, Aug. 12, Sept. 10, 29, Oct. 8, Nov. 6, Dec. 4, 22

Fatal attractions: Aug. 1, 2, 3, 4

Challenging: Jan. 3, 25, Feb. 1, 23, Mar. 21, Apr. 19, May 17, June 15, July 13, Aug. 11, Sept. 9, Oct. 7, Nov. 5, Dec. 3

Soul mates: Jan. 3, 10, Feb. 1, 8, Mar. 6, Apr. 4, May 2

Love & Relationships

Individual and independent, you are likely to have many interests and be involved in many activities. Usually you want to form relationships with powerful people who are established and autonomous. Sometimes partnerships can be difficult due to an uncertainty about how you truly feel. You need a hardworking partner that you can look up to or depend on. Alternatively, you may find your career more interesting and devote yourself to accomplishment and hard work. You may particularly enjoy socializing with clever and creative people who can stimulate your intellect.

January 31

≈≈ Quick and inventive, you are revealed by your Aquarius birthday to be a generous and creative individual with a friendly manner. Freedom-loving and independent, you can display open-minded and humanitarian qualities as well as be progressive in your views. Being very intelligent, you have an expansive and universal approach that may take you traveling or studying in your never-ending quest for knowledge.

With the added influence of your Sun in the decanate of Gemini, you can be a skillful and engaging communicator, whether speaking or writing. Being mentally active and curious by nature suggests that you possess a gift for objective thinking and can synthesize information from many sources, presenting it in an original way. Although you are often ahead of your time, avoid letting your rebellious streak turn you into an obstinate or stubborn individual.

An exceptional thinker, with a touch of the mad genius, you can be mentally inspired and become quite excitable. A flair for observing people can help you make astute and insightful comments on others. A tendency to be impatient, however, may cause you to become bored easily and distract you from persevering and developing your unique potential.

Until you reach the age of nineteen your progressed Sun moves through Aquarius, highlighting issues of freedom, independence, and the need to express your individuality. After the age of twenty, when your progressed Sun moves into Pisces, you become more receptive, sensitive to your feelings, and aware of image. You may develop a greater sense of vision or have more access to your subconscious world. At the age of fifty there is another turning point as your progressed Sun enters Aries, emphasizing your fighting spirit and leadership. You may need to break away from the past as you become more assertive and ambitious, possibly initiating new ventures.

Fixed Stars

Your Secret Self

You have great imagination and creative powers. These energies should be accessed in order to allow you the freedom to flow with your original ideas. By relying on your own inspiration and inner guidance, you can make decisions that alter your life. Be careful not to settle for less just because you are worried you might upset your security. Dramatic, you have a strong need to express your feelings and share your ideas. If these needs are left unfulfilled, you may experience frustration or melancholy. Interested in a wide range of subjects, particularly philosophy, religion, travel, and politics, you can be an inspired thinker or uplifting conversationalist.

You benefit greatly from disciplining your mind through learning new skills and education. Whether you are unorthodox or conventional, knowledge can be a vital key to your success. By learning patience and tolerance and having something to believe in, you are able to keep positive and achieve remarkable results despite any outer difficulties.

Work & Vocation

A natural inclination for business combined with good organizational and managerial skills is likely to aid you in any career. With your love of gathering information and a talent for communication, you could excel in teaching, science, or writing. Equally, you could make a good orator or lawyer. With your humanitarian tendencies, you have a natural understanding of people and may be drawn to counseling or social reform. Occupations connected to the public or foreign lands could satisfy your love of variety and prevent you from becoming bored. Creative as well as knowledgeable, you may decide to develop your artistic and musical gifts or enter the world of show business.

Famous people who share your birthday include singer/musician Phil Collins, composers Franz Schubert and Philip Glass, writer Norman Mailer, comedienne Carol Channing, singers John Lydon and Mario Lanza, and baseball pitcher Nolan Ryan.

Numerology

Strong willpower, determination, and an emphasis on self-expression are indicated by the number 31 birthday. Usually you are tireless and determined, with a desire to make material progress. You may have to learn, however, to accept the limitations of life and therefore need to build a solid foundation. Good fortune and lucky opportunities also suggest that you can be successful in turning your leisure-time pursuits into profitable ventures. Having fun is crucial to you, as you are very hardworking. You may have to guard against a tendency to be selfish or overly optimistic. The subinfluence of the number 1 month indicates that you are intuitive, multitalented, and enterprising. Although you are shrewd, with a creative mind and a strong desire for security, you are likely to be restless or impatient. By staying positive and optimistic and knowing how to go with the flow, you learn about patience and paying attention to detail. Innovative, with an inquisitive mind, you are usually ambitious and willing to work hard in order to achieve recognition and success. When inspired, you have original ideas and a unique perspective.

• *Positive:* lucky, creative, original, builder, constructive, persistent, practical, good conversationalist, responsible

• *Negative:* insecure, impatient, suspicious, easily discouraged, lack of ambition, selfish, stubborn

Love & Relationships

Friendly and outgoing, you are spontaneous and sociable, with an ability to attract others. But if you are insecure, be careful not to become too dominating. Creative, with a sense of the dramatic, you enjoy mentally stimulating and original people who like to express themselves. Although you can be devoted and loving, a dislike of being alone implies that you should avoid becoming overdependent on your partners. Being clever, with definite opinions, you tend to particularly enjoy social occasions that include a lively debate.

YOUR SPECIAL SOMEONE

Your chances for happiness and love are better with someone born on one of the following dates.

Love & friendship: Jan. 1, 5, 9, 15, 26, 29, 30, Feb. 13, 24, 27, 28, Mar. 11, 22, 25, 26, Apr. 9, 20, 23, 24, May 7, 18, 21, 22, June 5, 16, 19, 20, July 3, 14, 17, 18, 31, Aug. 1, 12, 15, 16, 29, 31, Sept. 10, 13, 14, 27, 29, Oct. 8, 11, 12, 25, 27, Nov. 6, 9, 10, 23, 25, Dec. 4, 7, 8, 21, 23, 29

Beneficial: Jan. 1, 2, 10, 14, 27, Feb. 8, 12, 25, Mar. 6, 10, 23, Apr. 4, 8, 21, May 2, 6, 19, 30, June 4, 17, 28, July 2, 15, 26, Aug. 13, 24, Sept. 11, 22, 30, Oct. 9, 20, Nov. 7, 18, Dec. 5, 16

Fatal attractions: Aug. 2, 3, 4, 5

Challenging: Jan. 17, 26, Feb. 15, 24, Mar. 13, 22, Apr. 11, 20, May 9, 18, June 7, 16, July 5, 14, Aug. 3, 12, 30, Sept. 1, 10, 28, Oct. 8, 26, 29, Nov. 6, 24, 27, Dec. 4, 22, 25

Soul mates: Jan. 21, Feb. 19, Mar. 17, Apr. 15, May 13, June 11, July 9, 29, Aug. 7, 27, Sept. 5, 25, Oct. 3, 23, Nov. 1, 21, Dec. 19

February 1

≈≈ Your Aquarius birthday suggests that individuality and a creative intellect are your strongest personality traits. With your sharp mind and quick responses, you enjoy a mental challenge. You can achieve power through your work, which enables you to build good structures and develop determination and discipline. The combination of your intuitive skills and practical talents indicates that you need only apply a little effort to reap immediate positive rewards.

With the added influence of your Sun in the decanate of Gemini, flashes of inspiration come to you naturally and add to your superior mental abilities. Curious, you are constantly accumulating and updating your knowledge so that you can present your ideas in stimulating and convincing ways. When used negatively, however, these same energies can make you erratic or easily excitable.

Quietly dramatic, you need to be active and accomplish things, preferably leading the action and being at the forefront of ideas. Proud of your achievement, you like to get people going in an exciting and adventurous way, inspiring them to take positive action. Ambitious and competitive, you may fight for humanitarian issues or push forward some type of reform. Beware of taking the route of expediency to achieve your goals rather than doing what you know is right.

Until you reach the age of eighteen your progressed Sun is in Aquarius, highlighting issues of personal freedom, friendship, and expressing your individuality. At the age of nineteen, when your progressed Sun moves through Pisces, your dreams and visions become more prominent and you develop your emotional receptivity. At the age of forty-nine there is a turning point as your progressed Sun enters Aries. This influence accents greater self-awareness as you start to feel more confident and assertive, which may inspire you to initiate new activities.

FIXED STAR

Star's name: Armus

Degree position: 11°45'–12°45'
Aquarius between the years 1930 and 2000

Magnitude: 5

Strength: ★★

Orb: 1°

Constellation: Eta Capricorn

Applicable days: February 1, 2, 3

Star qualities: Mars/Mercury

Description: a small orange and red star located in the heart of the Goat

PRIMARY STAR'S INFLUENCE

Armus imparts originality, inventiveness, and a contentious nature, along with a quick mind and the ability to impress others. Armus bestows a special talent for speech and quick repartee. This star also warns against being argumentative or disagreeable, and against an inner restlessness that can cause instability.

Linked to your Sun's degree, this star imparts independence, quick action, and an alert mind. You are probably socially inclined and achieve success through dealing with the general public.

• Positive: common sense, ability to judge, skill, impressive speech

• Negative: irritability, mental tension, nervousness, quarrelsome

Your Secret Self

You are fascinated by the new and unusual and refuse to conform to traditional and narrow ways of thinking. Although sometimes stubborn, you are particularly inventive when challenged. With your special understanding of human behavior, you benefit from mixing with people more knowledgeable than yourself, and in turn you are willing to inspire others.

With your mental dynamism, you can take quick and decisive action and are good at getting yourself out of difficult situations. As you dislike constraint of any kind, you may have to learn to overcome sudden flashes of anger or obstinacy that can cause trouble. When in touch with your powerful inner vitality, you are daring and spontaneous, full of the conviction that you are going to win or achieve extraordinary results. As this natural enthusiasm is not something you can fake, you should concentrate on what positively moves your spirit.

Work & Vocation

With your charismatic abilities, you have a flair for working with people. In business you like activities that are defined, and you usually rise to management or executive positions.

Friendly, with persuasive powers, you can be particularly successful in sales and promotion. You prefer careers that need action and quick thinking; your courage could help you fight battles for others or stand against social injustice. With your constant need for variety, you would do well to avoid a routine job. Your inventive ideas can often involve you in progressive research and new innovations that allow you to express your individuality.

Famous people who share your birthday include actor Clark Gable, Russian president Boris Yeltsin, director John Ford, physicist Fritjof Capra, actress Sherilyn Fenn, and singers Rick James and Don Everly.

Numerology

As a number 1 personality, you are more inclined to be individual, innovative, and courageous, with plenty of energy. Often there is a need to establish a strong identity and develop assertiveness. The pioneering spirit indicated here encourages you to strike out alone. These self-starting forces can also stimulate you to develop executive or leadership abilities. Full of enthusiasm and original ideas, you can show others the way forward. With a number 1 birthday, you may also need to learn that the world does not revolve around you and avoid an inclination to be self-centered or dictatorial. The subinfluence of the number 2 month indicates that you are highly receptive and intuitive. Although you can be friendly and sociable, you are an individual with a strong character. This suggests that with age you realize your unique qualities and become more assertive and self-reliant. As a humanitarian, you are universal and progressive, willing to work for social reforms and just causes. Without faith or insight into your higher self, you may feel insecure and indecisive. With vision and ingenuity, however, you can inspire others, especially if you use your creativity and develop your unique perspective.

• *Positive:* leadership, creative, progressive, forceful, optimistic, strong convictions, competitive, independent, gregarious

• *Negative:* jealous, egotistical, antagonistic, lack of restraint, selfish, unstable, impatient

Love & Relationships

Although you are progressive and independent, you still want a secure base and a stable home. Usually you are attracted to strong individuals who think for themselves. As long as you have the freedom to do as you please, you can be a very loyal and faithful friend or partner. Being sociable and charming, you draw people toward you and can be very entertaining.

YOUR SPECIAL SOMEONE

To keep you interested in a long-term relationship, you might want to look for those born on the following days.

Love & friendship: Jan. 1, 4, 5, 11, 21, 24, Feb. 2, 3, 9, 19, 22, Mar. 1, 7, 17, 20, Apr. 5, 15, 18, 30, May 1, 13, 16, 28, June 11, 14, 26, July 9, 12, 24, Aug. 7, 10, 22, Sept. 5, 8, 20, Oct. 3, 6, 18, Nov. 1, 4, 16, Dec. 2, 14

Beneficial: Jan. 14, 23, 27, Feb. 12, 21, 25, Mar. 19, 23, Apr. 17, 21, May 15, 19, June 13, 17, July 11, 15, 31, Aug. 9, 13, 29, Sept. 7, 11, 27, Oct. 9, 25, Nov. 3, 7, 23, Dec. 1, 5, 21

Fatal attractions: Aug. 4, 5, 6, 7

Challenging: Jan. 17, Feb. 15, Mar. 13, Apr. 11, May 9, June 7, July 5, Aug. 3, Sept. 1

Soul mates: Jan. 30, Feb. 28, Mar. 26, 29, Apr. 24, 27, May 22, 25, June 20, 23, July 18, 21, Aug. 16, 19, Sept. 14, 17, Oct. 12, 15, Nov. 10, 13, Dec. 8, 11

February 2

Independent and success-oriented, you are an Aquarian with strong individual traits. The influence of your birthday suggests that with your expansive viewpoint and powerful imagination, you are an independent thinker who has inspired ideas. Friendly and sociable, with a shrewd understanding of human nature, you can be a sensitive humanitarian. Intellectually creative, you have a fast mind that stimulates you to seek variety or be continually acquiring knowledge. You may therefore have to avoid a tendency to become impatient or get bored easily.

With the added influence of your Sun in the Gemini decanate, you are interested in the latest ideas and innovations and tend to show your free spirit in a nonconformist way. Witty and amusing, you can be a clever conversationalist and have a gift with the written or spoken word. Although independent and self-willed, you are also aware of the advantages of working cooperatively with others and can make a good team member when you believe in an undertaking. Objective in your views, you like to be frank and honest in your dealings with others. You may have to be careful of being so detached that at times you appear to others as indifferent.

Ambitious and with an enterprising outlook, you are usually willing to work hard to achieve your objectives. Being successful in your work is important to you, and often your life revolves around career activities, special projects, and the need for constant improvement. Persistence and discipline will bring you the success you so strongly desire.

Until you reach the age of seventeen your progressed Sun moves through Aquarius, highlighting issues of freedom, independence, and the need to express your individuality. After the age of eighteen, when your progressed Sun moves into Pisces, you become more sensitive, receptive, and aware of emotional issues. At the age of forty-eight there is another turning point as your progressed Sun enters Aries, emphasizing a need to break away from the past and become more bold and assertive. When your progressed Sun enters Taurus, at age seventy-eight, you have a stronger need for stability and practical security.

Your Secret Self

Although outwardly you appear assertive or even aloof, inside you are extremely sensitive. Nevertheless, you can be dramatic and proud, and when you discover that you possess something special, you realize that you have a gift to offer others. As a visionary who is impressionable, you can appreciate color and sound and enchant others through creative pursuits such as music, art, or writing. Alternatively, with your refined ideals and compassion, you may develop your natural inclination toward philosophy or mysticism. If you do not find productive channels for your sensitivity, there is a danger that you may be prone to moods or escapism.

A strong desire for honesty can underlie all your activities. You genuinely want to build a better future for yourself, your loved ones, and the world. This may involve making sure your foundations are strong before you rush off to the next step.

Work & Vocation

Your charm and magnetism can help you succeed in most people-related careers. Your curiosity about people may lead you to explore subjects such as psychology, sociology, or politics.

FIXED STARS

Dorsum, Armus

PRIMARY STAR

Star's name: Dorsum

Degree position: 12°51'–13°50'
Aquarius between the years 1930 and 2000

Magnitude: 4

Strength: ★★★★

Orb: 1°30'

Constellation: Theta Capricorn

Applicable days: February 2, 3, 4

Star qualities: Jupiter/Saturn

Description: a small white-blue star located on the back of the Goat

PRIMARY STAR'S INFLUENCE

Dorsum bestows an ability to attain far-reaching objectives through perseverance and patience. Often industrious, you can achieve success in dealing with public affairs.

Linked to your Sun's degree, this star imparts slow but steady advancement, and progress is usually linked to responsibility. Dorsum encourages you to explore and develop your writing skills.

• *Positive:* sense of duty, diplomatic, willingness to serve

• *Negative:* tension, discontent, lack of patience

See Appendix for additional fixed star readings.

Independent, you may prefer to be your own boss and have much freedom within the confines of your work. Your quick mind and communication skills may lead you to writing or education through teaching and lecturing. Alternatively, your sensitivity may draw you toward music, the arts, or healing. As you may get bored easily, it would be better that you have a job with much variety or travel.

Famous people who share your birthday include writers James Joyce and Ayn Rand, psychologist Havelock Ellis, violinist Jascha Heifetz, singer Graham Nash, and actresses Farrah Fawcett and Holly Hunter.

Numerology

Sensitivity and a strong need to be part of a group are suggested by a number 2 birthday. Adaptable and understanding, you enjoy cooperative activities where you can experience interaction with others. In your attempt to please those you like, you may run the risk of becoming overly dependent. Nevertheless, by developing confidence, you can overcome the tendency to get easily hurt by the actions and criticism of others. The subinfluence of the number 2 month indicates that you are receptive and intuitive. As a humanitarian, you are liberal and progressive, with an interest in people, reforms, and just causes. Cooperative and supportive, you need stability and like to establish order. Security-conscious, you can plan ahead and persevere with long-term projects. Although you are an idealist, your pragmatic approach to life confers a good business sense and an ability to achieve material success. Since you are blessed with a sixth sense, your perception about people is usually right, so it is best to learn to trust your own feelings.

• *Positive:* good partnerships, gentle, tactful, receptive, intuitive, agile, considerate, harmonious, agreeable, ambassador of goodwill

• *Negative:* suspicious, lack of confidence, oversensitive, selfish, deceitful

Love & Relationships

Sociable and friendly, you enjoy group activities and meeting new people. Ambitious and hardworking, you have a need for security that implies you are loyal and protective. Indecision and worry, however, may cause you to doubt your intimate feelings and your choice of whom to settle down with. If you have concerns about financial issues, they may hinder or put stress on your relationship. Although you are sensitive, romantically you sometimes appear a bit aloof or too practical.

YOUR SPECIAL SOMEONE

If you are looking for someone special, you might find greater luck with those born on the following days.

Love & friendship: Jan. 3, 14, 24, 28, Feb. 1, 12, 22, Mar. 10, 20, Apr. 8, 18, May 6, 16, 31, June 4, 14, 18, 29, July 2, 12, 27, Aug. 10, 25, 31, Sept. 8, 23, 29, Oct. 6, 10, 21, 27, Nov. 4, 19, 25, Dec. 2, 17, 23

Beneficial: Jan. 1, 11, Feb. 9, Mar. 7, 28, Apr. 5, 26, 30, May 3, 24, 28, June 1, 22, 26, July 20, 24, Aug. 18, 22, Sept. 16, 20, 30, Oct. 14, 18, 28, Nov. 12, 16, 26, Dec. 10, 14, 24

Fatal attractions: Aug. 4, 5, 6, 7

Challenging: Jan. 17, 20, Feb. 15, 18, Mar. 13, 16, Apr. 11, 14, May 9, 12, June 7, 10, July 5, 8, Aug. 3, 6, Sept. 1, 4, Oct. 2

Soul mates: July 29, Aug. 27, Sept. 25, Oct. 23, 31, Nov. 21, 29, Dec. 19, 27

February 3

Your birthday implies that you are an independent Aquarian with good social skills. Original and friendly, you have a natural understanding of human nature.

Your fascination for people encourages you to mix with different social groups in your quest for creative stimulation and self-realization. Impressionable, you are aware of image and enjoy a touch of glamour. Although you are normally bright, with the gift to enchant others, you may need to learn to let go and avoid holding on to frustrations or disappointments. This can cause you to suffer or make you overserious.

With the added influence of your Sun in the decanate of Gemini, you can have flashes of inspiration that add to your superior mental abilities. Excellent communication skills indicate persuasive speech and a special talent with words. Mentally sharp and receptive to new ideas, you are often ahead of your time. Objective in your views, you have a desire to be continually learning.

With personal magnetism, you often radiate individuality. Companionship and friendship are especially important areas in your life, and you often have an unusual or more humanitarian approach to relationships. With your subtle sensitivity and desire to transcend the mundane, you possess heightened perceptions of light, color, form, and sound, which you may wish to channel into artistic, musical, or spiritual pursuits.

In youth, your father figure may have been rather too restrictive an influence on you. Between the ages of seventeen and forty-six, when your progressed Sun moves through Pisces, you become more sensitive and imaginative. You develop a greater sense of imagination and vision or have more access to your inner world. At the age of forty-seven there is a turning point as your progressed Sun enters Aries, making you more confident, assertive, and ambitious, possibly initiating new ventures or activities. When your progressed Sun enters Taurus, at age seventy-seven, you have a stronger need for practical security and stability.

Fixed Stars

Dorsum, Armus

PRIMARY STAR

Star's name: Dorsum

Degree position: 12°51'–13°50'
Aquarius between the years 1930 and 2000

Magnitude: 4

Strength: ★★★★

Orb: 1°30'

Constellation: Theta Capricorn

Applicable days: February 2, 3, 4

Star qualities: Jupiter/Saturn

Description: a small white-blue star located on the back of the Goat

PRIMARY STAR'S INFLUENCE

Dorsum bestows an ability to attain far-reaching objectives through perseverance and patience. Often industrious, you can achieve success in dealing with public affairs.

Linked to your Sun's degree, this star imparts slow but steady advancement, and progress is usually linked to responsibility. Dorsum also encourages you to explore and develop your writing skills.

• Positive: sense of duty, diplomatic, willingness to serve

• Negative: tension, discontent, lack of patience

See Appendix for additional fixed star readings.

Your Secret Self

When your strong self-will is positively focused, you can cut through difficulties to achieve in a remarkable way. With the ability to take the lead, you can channel your strong inner emotional power to attain positions of influence and authority. Being sensitive to those around you suggests a need for a strong home base and peaceful and harmonious surroundings.

When positive, you are hardworking, diligent, and responsible, with the ability to be thorough. Capable of being very universal and detached, you may be drawn toward fulfilling your ideals or being of service to others. This can help you overcome possible periods of instability or confusion. Although you can sometimes appear aloof in order to protect yourself from being hurt, you can show your warmth, deep feelings, and compassion when you really care.

Work & Vocation

It is usually through the expression of your original ideas and unique perspective that you can achieve the greatest success. Being friendly, you need good working relationships with those around you and have an ability to make contacts. This can help you in the world of sales or public relations, especially as you have an intuitive understanding of what the public wants. With your natural gift for words, you could be a good writer or lecturer and may be particularly drawn to creative pursuits. Whether scientific, creative, or in business, you are likely to succeed, particularly when working on something you believe in. Alternatively, with your understanding of human nature, you can also be drawn to working with children, counseling, or social work.

Famous people who share your birthday include writers Gertrude Stein and James Michener, actress Morgan Fairchild, artist Norman Rockwell, football player Fran Tarkenton, and musician Dave Davies.

Numerology

As a number 3 individual, you are sensitive, with a need for creativity and emotional expression. Fun-loving and a good companion, you enjoy friendly social activities and many interests. You are versatile and expressive, with a need for different and exciting experiences, but an inclination to get bored easily may cause you to become indecisive or spread yourself too thin. Although with a number 3 birthday you are usually artistic and charming, with a good sense of humor, you may have to develop self-esteem and guard against tendencies such as worry and emotional insecurities. The subinfluence of the number 2 month indicates that you are receptive and idealistic, with a flair for dealing with people. Ambitious yet charming, you know how to use your diplomatic skills and friendly personality. A need to express your talents suggests that you can be dramatic and dynamic when you have a goal or a purpose. Although usually generous and kind, at times you can become frustrated or impatient; this may lead you to overreact or act on impulse, resulting in extravagance and self-indulgence.

• *Positive:* humorous, happy, friendly, productive, creative, artistic, freedom-loving, a talent with words

• *Negative:* easily bored, exaggerate, extravagant, self-indulgent, lazy, hypocritical

Love & Relationships

Although you have powerful emotions and a great desire for love, you need independence and freedom to express yourself. Romantically, you have charm and charisma, which provide you with an easy manner. Aware of your image, you like to present yourself well and make the right impression. Since you like to be spontaneous, you may at times act on the spur of the moment. People are drawn to your sparkling personality and magnetism. Men of this day may be particularly attracted by independent and forceful women.

YOUR SPECIAL SOMEONE

You may find it easier to build happy relationships with people born on the following days.

Love & friendship: Jan. 8, 17, 19, Feb. 15, 17, Mar. 13, 15, Apr. 11, 13, May 9, 11, June 7, 9, 30, July 5, 7, 28, 30, Aug. 3, 5, 26, 28, Sept. 1, 3, 24, 26, Oct. 1, 22, 24, Nov. 20, 22, Dec. 18, 20, 30

Beneficial: Jan. 20, 29, Feb. 18, 27, Mar. 16, 25, Apr. 14, 23, May. 12, 21, June 10, 19, July 8, 17, Aug. 6, 15, Sept. 4, 13, Oct. 2, 11, 29, Nov. 9, 27, Dec. 7, 25

Fatal attractions: Mar. 29, Apr. 27, May 25, June 23, July 21, Aug. 5, 6, 7, 8, 19, Sept. 17, Oct. 15, Nov. 13, Dec. 11

Challenging: Jan. 14, 20, 27, Feb. 12, 25, Mar. 10, 23, Apr. 8, 21, May 6, 19, June 4, 10, 17, July 2, 15, Aug. 13, Sept. 11, Oct. 2, 9, Nov. 7, Dec. 5

Soul mates: June 30, July 28, Aug. 26, Sept. 24, Oct. 22, 29, Nov. 20, 27, Dec. 18, 25

February 4

≈≈ Your birthday indicates that you are friendly but determined, an ambitious Aquarian with original ideas. Strong-willed, with the capacity for hard work, you may encounter a possible conflict between materialism and your ideals. A strong emotional driving force together with a natural business sense nevertheless provides you with the opportunity to successfully combine both sides of your nature to be a practical idealist.

The added influence of your Sun in the Gemini decanate enables you to communicate your ideas in a realistic, dynamic, and convincing way. Clever and inventive, you grasp information very quickly and have a sharp wit, good judgment, and reasoning powers. Being very independent, you do not like your personal freedom restricted, but you may run the risk of being domineering in your attempt to do things your own way.

Determined and enterprising, with organizational abilities, you have the power to undertake almost any project. It would be wise, however, to guard against a tendency to take on more than you can handle. Naturally direct, with your own brand of values, you are an interesting mixture of opposites and usually present a tough yet charming personality. A desire for power, money, and prestige is usually balanced by a strong humanitarian streak that can give you quick insight into individuals and society as a whole.

Between the ages of sixteen and forty-five, when your progressed Sun moves through Pisces, you become more sensitive, receptive, and aware of emotional issues. Your imagination and sense of vision are enhanced. At the age of forty-six there is a turning point as your progressed Sun enters Aries, emphasizing a need to break away from the past and become bolder and more assertive. In your middle years your ability to tackle large projects successfully is highlighted by strong and decisive actions. When your progressed Sun enters Taurus, at age seventy-six, you have a greater need for practical security and stability.

Your Secret Self

Your self-confident front often hides your insecurities and your need for love. By expressing your natural creativity, whether through your approach to life, artistic pursuits, or with friends, you can avoid indecision and worry. Naturally dramatic, you have a need to lead or be where the action is. Intelligent, you do not suffer fools easily. Pride can give you a natural sense of nobility or can work against you if you become too stubborn or self-willed.

Knowledge has a strong influence in your life and is vital to your inner quest. With endurance, a need for recognition, and a strong sense of duty, you have a tenacious approach to fulfilling your own vision. If you use your excellent intuitive sense in your practical affairs, you are able to establish a concrete foundation upon which you can build your aspirations. Honest and direct, with a clear intention, patience, and perseverance, you are able to bring about long-term success.

Work & Vocation

Your determination and awareness of power and structure can give you a natural business sense. With your inventive and original ideas, you can be successful in many different areas

FIXED STAR

Star's name: Dorsum

Degree position: 12°51'–13°50'
Aquarius between the years 1930 and 2000

Magnitude: 4

Strength: ★★★★

Orb: 1°30'

Constellation: Theta Capricorn

Applicable days: February 2, 3, 4

Star qualities: Jupiter/Saturn

Description: a small white-blue star located on the back of the Goat

PRIMARY STAR'S INFLUENCE

Dorsum bestows an ability to attain far-reaching objectives through perseverance and patience. Often industrious, you can achieve success in dealing with public affairs.

Linked to your Sun's degree, this star imparts slow but steady advancement, and progress is usually linked to responsibility. Dorsum also encourages you to explore and develop your writing skills.

• *Positive:* sense of duty, diplomatic, willingness to serve

• *Negative:* tension, discontent, lack of patience

in life. With your good communication skills, you may be drawn to writing, education, publishing, or the media. There may also be an attraction to the stage or politics. Being a natural psychologist can help you in all careers, including business, or you may specialize as a therapist or counselor. As a humanitarian, you may be interested in new social movements, and occupations involving people can play a major role in your life.

Famous people who share your birthday include U.S. vice president Dan Quayle, rock star Alice Cooper, civil rights pioneer Rosa Parks, Argentine president Isabel Perón, aviator Charles Lindbergh, feminist Betty Friedan, and actress Ida Lupino.

Numerology

The solid structure and orderly power suggested by the number 4 birthday indicate that you need stability and like to establish order. Endowed with energy, practical skills, and strong determination, you can achieve success through hard work. Security-conscious, you like to build a strong foundation for yourself and your family. A pragmatic approach to life confers good business sense and an ability to achieve material success in life. As a number 4 personality, you are usually honest, frank, and fair. The challenges for a number 4 individual may include overcoming periods of instability or financial worry. The subinfluence of the number 2 month indicates that you are receptive and idealistic. Usually your home and family are important to you. You may even benefit from real estate and property. Although you are hardworking, you enjoy the good life and can be self-indulgent. At times your generosity and caring nature go too far and can be interpreted by others as interference. Nevertheless, you can be a loyal and supportive partner or parent.

• *Positive:* well organized, self-disciplined, steady, hardworking, craftsmanship, good with your hands, pragmatism, trusting, exact

• *Negative:* unstable, destructive behavior, uncommunicative, repressed, lazy, unfeeling, procrastination, too economical, bossy, resentful

Love & Relationships

Although you appear easygoing and amiable, you have to be careful not to be bossy or domineering. Your friendship and romantic aspirations may well be connected with your career ambitions. Usually you are attracted to leaders or powerful people with social connections. Loyal and responsible, you can be a tower of strength to those around you.

YOUR SPECIAL SOMEONE

Your chances of romantic success are better with people born on the following dates.

Love & friendship: Jan. 4, 8, 9, 16, 18, 26, 31, Feb. 2, 7, 14, 16, 24, 29, Mar. 4, 5, 12, 14, 22, 27, Apr. 3, 10, 12, 20, 25, May 1, 8, 10, 18, 23, June 6, 8, 16, 21, July 4, 6, 14, 19, 31, Aug. 2, 4, 12, 17, 29, Sept. 2, 10, 15, 27, Oct. 8, 13, 25, Nov. 6, 11, 23, Dec. 4, 9, 21, 30

Beneficial: Jan. 1, 21, Feb. 19, Mar. 17, Apr. 15, May. 13, June 10, 11, July 9, Aug. 7, Sept. 5, Oct. 2, 3, 30, Nov. 1, 28, Dec. 26

Fatal attractions: Aug. 7, 8, 9, 10

Challenging: Mar. 29, Apr. 27, May 25, June 23, July 21, Aug. 19, Sept. 17, Oct. 15, Nov. 13, Dec. 11

Soul mates: Jan. 27, Feb. 25, Mar. 23, 30, Apr. 21, 28, May 19, 26, June 17, 24, July 15, 22, Aug. 13, 20, Sept. 11, 18, Oct. 9, 16, Nov. 7, 14, Dec. 5, 12

February 5

Your birthday reveals you to be an objective, intuitive, strong individual with an original personality. You are clever, with flashes of inspiration; your constant curiosity about life and people is coupled with the need for change and variety. This usually helps you to develop your unique ideas. It would be wise, however, not to let restlessness or a tendency to vacillate emotionally spoil your remarkable potential.

With the subinfluence of your decanate ruler, Gemini, you have quick mental responses and an ability to make split-second decisions. Receptive to new ideas, you are often progressive and ahead of your time. With a desire to continually learn, you also have good communication skills or a gift for writing. Although objective in your views, you may have to avoid being so detached that others can perceive you as cold. Nevertheless, as a humanitarian with an independent view, you are also aware of the advantages of working cooperatively with others and can make a good team member when you believe in a project.

With an advanced view of life, you value knowledge and freedom and are often concerned with social reform. Your autonomous thinking can sometimes make you confrontational, but if you direct your argumentative inclinations into developing debating skills, you can really excel. Although you may be inclined toward religion and spirituality, you are more likely to have your own belief system. With a touch of the mad genius, you may also have to be wary of being impatient, stubborn, or temperamental. Physical activity can have a healing effect on your nervous system and make you more relaxed and agreeable.

In youth, you are quick to learn and react. While you are between the ages of fifteen and forty-four, when your progressed Sun moves through Pisces, your emotional sensitivity becomes emphasized and you develop your imagination. This may encourage you to seek idealistic, creative, or spiritual goals. After the age of forty-five, when your progressed Sun moves into Aries, you have a need to be more assertive, active, and directive in your daily affairs, possibly pioneering new ventures. At the age of seventy-five there is another turning point as your progressed Sun enters Taurus, accenting a need for more stability and security.

Your Secret Self

Multitalented, you have a unique perspective on many different areas of life. Although sometimes you may find yourself at odds with people who do not have your level of awareness, you need to be patient. It may also be necessary to discipline yourself and have faith in your own abilities in order to make the most of your talents and earning potential. An innate understanding of values enables you to advise others through being an excellent commentator on their situation, whether on a psychological or a material level.

Being sensitive, with a highly tuned nervous system, you need to find quiet times alone for introspection and regenerating your forces. These periods can especially inspire you in the areas of art, music, drama, or more mystical interests. By avoiding worry over money or frustration from wanting to live beyond your means, you are able to enjoy the power of your dynamic emotions, and with your energy and generosity you can charm and impress others.

Work & Vocation

Having good organizing abilities, you have the potential to rise to high positions. With the accent on your mental and communicative skills, you could be an excellent teacher, counselor,

FIXED STARS

Although your Sun's degree is not linked to a fixed star, some of your other planets' degrees certainly will be. By having an astrological chart calculated, you can find the exact position of the planets on your date of birth. This will tell you which of the fixed stars listed in this book are relevant to you.

psychologist, or social reformer. Even though you have a sharp business sense and can be successful handling the financial affairs of others, you may be more interested in a career that demands creativity and imagination, such as writing, drama, or the arts. On the other hand, your love for freedom and the need to test your own mental ability may prompt you to run your own business or be self-employed. Alternatively, with your humanitarian streak, you may find yourself working for public-spirited organizations.

Famous people who share your birthday include actresses Charlotte Rampling and Barbara Hershey, baseball player Hank Aaron, British politician Sir Robert Peel, entertainer Bobby Brown, U.S. statesman Adlai Stevenson, and writer William Burroughs.

Numerology

Strong instincts, an adventurous nature, and a desire for freedom are all indicated by the number 5 birthday. The willingness to try anything new and an enthusiastic approach suggest that life will have a lot to offer you. Travel and many opportunities for change, some unexpected, may lead you to undergo a real transformation of views and beliefs. With a number 5 birthday, you need to feel that life is exciting; however, you may also have to develop a responsible attitude and avoid tendencies such as unpredictability, excessiveness, and restlessness. The natural talent of a number 5 individual is knowing how to go with the flow or learning to let go. The subinfluence of the number 2 month indicates that you are diplomatic, with a friendly and sociable nature. Although you have a flair for dealing with people, you can at times be reserved and mistrustful. You nevertheless enjoy collaborating with others, especially when you can mix work with pleasure. Intuitive and adaptable, you are usually courteous and sensitive to other people's feelings. You thrive on encouragement and need to keep yourself mentally occupied.

• *Positive:* versatile, adaptable, progressive, strong instincts, magnetic, lucky, daring, freedom-loving, quick and witty, curious, mystical, sociable

• *Negative:* unreliable, procrastinator, inconsistent, overconfident

Love & Relationships

With your charm, wit, and ability to uplift and inspire others, you usually have many friends and a successful social life. Romantically, you are attracted to clever people with strong personalities. As you seek mental stimulation as well as romance, companionship may be linked to work or intellectually oriented social activities. Although drawn to powerful and intelligent people, you would be wise to avoid being too bossy with your partners yourself.

YOUR SPECIAL SOMEONE

You may find it easier to find love and companionship with someone born on one of the following dates.

Love & friendship: Jan. 21, 28, 29, 31, Feb. 19, 26, 29, Mar. 17, 24, 27, Apr. 3, 15, 22, 25, May 13, 20, 23, June 11, 18, 19, 21, July 9, 16, 19, Aug. 7, 14, 17, 31, Sept. 5, 12, 15, 29, Oct. 3, 10, 11, 13, 27, 29, 31, Nov. 1, 8, 11, 25, 27, 29, Dec. 6, 9, 23, 25, 27

Beneficial: Jan. 9, 12, 18, 24, 29, Feb. 7, 10, 16, 22, 27, Mar. 5, 8, 14, 20, 25, Apr. 3, 6, 12, 18, 23, May 1, 4, 10, 16, 21, 31, June 1, 2, 8, 14, 19, 29, July 6, 12, 17, 27, Aug. 4, 10, 15, 25, Sept. 2, 8, 13, 23, Oct. 6, 11, 21, Nov. 4, 9, 19, Dec. 2, 7, 17

Fatal attractions: Jan. 3, Feb. 1, Aug. 7, 8, 9, 10

Challenging: Jan. 7, 8, 19, 28, Feb. 5, 6, 17, 26, Mar. 3, 4, 15, 24, Apr. 1, 2, 13, 22, May 11, 20, June 9, 18, July 7, 16, Aug. 5, 14, Sept. 3, 12, Oct. 1, 10, Nov. 8, Dec. 6

Soul mates: Jan. 3, 19, Feb. 1, 17, Mar. 15, Apr. 13, May 11, June 9, July 7, Aug. 5, Sept. 3, Oct. 1

February 6

With your Aquarius birthday, you are a charismatic individual who is friendly, idealistic, and a natural diplomat. Although socially inclined and outwardly charming, you can also be reserved and responsible, with a serious attitude. While you possess a strong worldly sense, it is important not to lose sight of your intuitive insight or vision. A desire to explore knowledge implies that you are constantly educating yourself. Through this study you can often find the self-discipline needed to unlock your outstanding potential.

With the subinfluence of your decanate ruler, Gemini, you are clever and possess good communication skills. Independent and objective in your views, at times you can be quite outspoken. Original and inventive, you have good judgment and reasoning powers. The combination of your ability to be persuasive and your practical skills can also help you in your climb to success.

Since you are usually responsible and hardworking, you are often asked to take charge of projects or assist others. An equally strong desire for peace and harmony can sometimes leave you wanting to keep things as they are. You may find that if you are reluctant to change, you can get stuck in a rut. Fortunately, the thought of material success usually motivates you into action.

While you are between the ages of fourteen and forty-three, when your progressed Sun moves through Pisces, your emotional sensitivity is enhanced, making you more imaginative, receptive, and aware of your social life. You may become more visionary or mediumistic, interested in developing your creative talents. There is a turning point at age forty-four, when your progressed Sun enters Aries. Your ambition and determination become more apparent and you start to show a more assertive character. You may be involved in starting new projects or pioneering original ideas. Another change of emphasis occurs at age seventy-four, when your progressed Sun enters Taurus, highlighting a greater need for stability, security, and emotional steadiness.

Your Secret Self

Interested in social reform, you possess a humanitarian awareness that inspires collaboration with others. You see the advantages of working for progressive group ideals. But you can also be self-willed, and there may be times when you need to learn to differentiate between stubbornness and perseverance. By staying positively detached and broad-minded, you can avoid seeming cold or indifferent. You may need to learn to bide your time in order to avoid periods of frustration and disappointment. Nevertheless, you are responsible, with an ability to inspire and enchant others, and you often seek an ideal world or true wisdom.

Many of your life lessons revolve around your work. Partnerships are likely to play a vital part in your life, and sharing is a key to your success. You are usually good at relating to others on a one-to-one basis. In order to avoid becoming fearful or too serious, however, it is important to keep the balance between working cooperatively with others and keeping your own independence.

Work & Vocation

A strong sense of justice inspires you to seek equal rights and good working conditions for yourself or others; this may draw you to the world of politics or social and community affairs.

Whatever career you choose, you need to exercise your advanced people skills. With an ability to communicate, teach, or inspire others, you may be interested in education, research, or social reform. If you are not using the more humanitarian or political side of your nature, your ability to captivate an audience may draw you toward the entertainment world.

Famous people who share your birthday include U.S. president Ronald Reagan, actress Zsa Zsa Gabor, singers Axl Rose, Bob Marley, and Natalie Cole, baseball player Babe Ruth, actor Rip Torn, and film director François Truffaut.

Numerology

Compassion, idealism, and a caring nature are some of the attributes suggested by a number 6 birthday. This is the number of the perfectionist or the universal friend, and indicates that you are frequently a humanitarian who can be responsible, loving, and supportive. With a number 6 birthday, you are frequently domestically inclined and a devoted parent. The more sensitive among you will need to find a form of creative expression and are drawn to the world of entertaining or art and design. You may need to develop more self-confidence and overcome tendencies such as interference, worry, and misplaced sympathy. The subinfluence of the number 2 month indicates that you are intuitive, courteous, and idealistic. As a receptive and adaptable individual, you are caring and often liberal. Usually keen on new concepts and reforms, you are a humanitarian at heart. When you collaborate with others, you are hardworking and practical, and often willing to share your good fortune and valuable insight.

• *Positive:* worldly, universal brotherhood, friendly, compassionate, dependable, understanding, sympathetic, idealistic, domestically inclined, humanitarian, poised, artistic, balanced

• *Negative:* discontented, shy, unreasonable, stubborn, outspoken, disharmonious, perfectionist, domineering, lack of responsibility, suspicious, cynical, self-centered, interfering

Love & Relationships

You are usually attracted to people who can keep up with your stream of ideas and enthusiasm or those who are inventive and successful in their own right. When you find someone to love, you can be full of eagerness and willingness to contribute to the relationship. Drawn toward intelligent people, you need a clever and informed partner. Your charismatic personality ensures that you will have many friends and social contacts. Marriage and stability are often important elements in your view of life.

YOUR SPECIAL SOMEONE

You may find happiness and companionship with people born on the following dates.

Love & friendship: Jan. 6, 20, 22, 24, 28, 30, Feb. 4, 18, 20, 22, 28, Mar. 2, 16, 18, 20, 26, 29, Apr. 14, 16, 18, 24, 27, May 12, 14, 16, 22, 25, June 10, 12, 14, 18, 20, 23, July 8, 10, 12, 18, 21, Aug. 6, 8, 10, 16, 19, Sept. 4, 6, 8, 14, 17, 29, Oct. 2, 4, 6, 12, 15, Nov. 2, 4, 10, 13, 25, Dec. 2, 8, 11

Beneficial: Jan. 1, 3, 4, 14, 23, Feb. 1, 2, 12, Mar. 10, 28, Apr. 8, 17, 26, 30, May 6, 24, 28, June 4, 22, 26, July 2, 20, 24, Aug. 18, 22, Sept. 16, 20, Oct. 14, 18, Nov. 12, 16, Dec. 10, 14

Fatal attractions: Jan. 11, Feb. 9, Mar. 7, Apr. 5, May 3, June 1, July 8, 9, 10, 11

Challenging: Jan. 3, 5, Feb. 1, 3, Mar. 1, July 31, Aug. 29, Sept. 27, 30, Oct. 25, 28, Nov. 23, 26, 30, Dec. 21, 24, 28

Soul mates: Jan. 5, 12, Feb. 3, 10, Mar. 1, 8, Apr. 6, May 4, June 2

February 7

≈ Your Aquarius birthday shows you to be an original and progressive individual with keen mental abilities. Enthusiastic, inventive, and humanitarian, you love freedom and benefit from exploring many avenues in your search for variety or interesting subjects. Be careful, however, that this does not turn into a nervous restlessness that prevents you from developing your fine talents.

With the subinfluence of your decanate ruler, Gemini, you are curious by nature and have a gift for objective thinking or scientific research. A skillful and engaging communicator, you possess a flair for making astute observations about people. Your expansive and universal sense may inspire you to travel or study in your never-ending quest for knowledge. This natural curiosity may also lead you to present your explorations in such a convincing way that you decide to become a storyteller or a writer. A tendency to get bored easily, however, may make it more difficult to persevere and achieve your unique potential.

Detachment and your universal quality are keys to solving many of your problems. Be careful, however, to avoid inflexibility and feelings of frustration and impatience, since they can undermine your determination to realize your goals and ambitions. To achieve your objectives, you benefit more from combining your strong imagination and idealism with your sharp intellect.

While you are between the ages of thirteen and forty-two, when your progressed Sun moves through Pisces, your emotional sensitivity becomes enhanced and you develop a stronger inner life. This can be reflected in your visions, dreams, and ideals as well as in your social life. At the age of forty-three there is a turning point as your progressed Sun enters Aries, emphasizing a need to take the initiative and be brave and direct in your relationships with others. Alternatively, you may develop your relationship skills. Another change of emphasis occurs at age seventy-three, when your progressed Sun enters Taurus, highlighting a greater need for a practical approach to life as well as financial security.

Your Secret Self

Your strong emotions and warm heart suggest that you are an individual who enjoys sharing experiences with others. Courteous and friendly, you possess natural diplomatic skills and an ability to make people feel relaxed. A charismatic inner quality enables you to radiate love and positivity, emphasizing the importance of having an outlet for your self-expression. Due to your strong feelings, however, you may have to create a balance and refrain from going to extremes by overreacting. Nevertheless, you possess charm, and with your power of love, you need only to find fulfilling activities or relationships to bring out the best in you.

Honest and direct, you can be an excellent companion, with a natural ability to help others. As well as charm, you also have ambition and a spirit of enterprise. Although these qualities often drive you to search for opportunities and keep you active, you also possess a need for security and strong foundations. To achieve harmony, you may be required to plan your actions and use your organizational skills.

Work & Vocation

With your desire for change and excitement, it would be best for you to avoid monotonous work. Careers that involve variety or travel would be ideal for your spirit of adventure. You may be a good salesperson with an ability to promote ideas, people, or products. With your strong imagination and need for self-expression, you can discipline your inner restlessness through writing, drama, or the arts. Alternatively, you may combine your receptivity and analytical ability in the world of science or research. With your strong humanitarian leanings, you may be attracted to careers that involve social reform, such as politics or education. A natural compassion may draw you to the world of health care or healing.

Famous people born on your birthday include psychologist Alfred Adler, writers Laura Ingalls Wilder, Charles Dickens, and Sinclair Lewis, and actress Juliette Greco.

Numerology

Analytical and thoughtful, number 7 individuals are frequently critical and self-absorbed. With a constant need for greater self-awareness, you enjoy gathering information and may be interested in reading, writing, or spirituality. Although shrewd, you may overrationalize or get lost in detail. A tendency to be enigmatic or secretive suggests that at times you feel misunderstood. As an independent thinker, you like to have the freedom to make your own decisions and mistakes. The subinfluence of the number 2 month indicates that you are highly intuitive and sensitive. A dislike for monotony implies that at times you can become impatient or highly strung. An emotional restlessness suggests that you enjoy excitement and need plenty of activity. Progressive and liberal, you are interested in people and are usually involved in cooperative efforts. Since you thrive on encouragement, you need supportive people around you who can inspire you to persevere or assist you when you need help. Beware of those who undermine your abilities, but listen to what others have to say before you make up your mind.

• *Positive:* educated, trusting, meticulous, idealistic, honest, psychic, scientific, rational, reflective

• *Negative:* deceitful, unfriendly, secretive, skeptical, confused, detached

Love & Relationships

Very sensitive in matters of the heart, you would be wise to enter relationships carefully rather than be too impulsive. When you fall in love your feelings run very deep, and you can remain loyal even through periods of difficulty or sacrifice. In relationships, your high expectations may sometimes lead to disappointment if others cannot live up to your ideals. By learning to be detached, you can avoid possible frustration. You are attracted by clever people, but it may be better to pick a partner who can be as humanitarian and broad-minded as you.

YOUR SPECIAL SOMEONE

You may be lucky in love with a person born on one of the following dates.

Love & friendship: Jan. 1, 7, 11, 21, 23, 31, Feb. 5, 19, 21, 29, Mar. 3, 17, 19, 27, Apr. 1, 15, 17, 25, May 13, 15, 23, June 11, 13, 21, July 9, 11, 19, Aug. 7, 9, 17, Sept. 5, 7, 15, Oct. 3, 5, 13, Nov. 1, 3, 11, 27, Dec. 1, 9, 24

Beneficial: Jan. 5, 16, 18, Feb. 3, 14, 16, Mar. 1, 12, 14, 29, Apr. 10, 12, 27, May 8, 10, 25, 29, June 6, 8, 23, 27, July 4, 6, 21, 25, Aug. 2, 4, 19, 23, Sept. 2, 17, 21, Oct. 15, 19, Nov. 13, 17, Dec. 11, 15, 29

Fatal attractions: Jan. 6, 30, Feb. 4, 28, Mar. 2, 26, Apr. 24, May 22, June 20, July 18, Aug. 9, 10, 11, 12, 16, Sept. 14, Oct. 12, Nov. 10, Dec. 8

Challenging: Jan. 4, Feb. 2, May 29, 31, June 27, 29, 30, July 25, 27, 28, Aug. 23, 25, 26, 30, Sept. 21, 23, 24, 28, Oct. 19, 21, 22, 26, Nov. 17, 19, 20, 24, Dec. 15, 17, 18, 22

Soul mates: Jan. 23, Feb. 21, Mar. 19, Apr. 17, May 15, June 13, July 11, 31, Aug. 9, 29, Sept. 7, 27, Oct. 5, 25, Nov. 3, 23, Dec. 1, 21

February 8

♒ Sociable and friendly, you have a strong-willed individuality that marks you out as an Aquarian with charismatic charm and strong views. Generous and direct, you need people and enjoy the good life. Quick to spot opportunities, you have a practical outlook and organizational skills. These, coupled with drive and determination, inspire you to think on a grand scale and to project success.

With the subinfluence of your decanate ruler, Gemini, you love to communicate, whether through speaking or writing. An exceptional thinker, you have the ability to acquire information and knowledge from many sources and to present your ideas in an original and interesting way. With a touch of the mad genius, you can be mentally inspired and become quite excitable. Often ahead of your time, you have inventive and progressive ideas. A rebellious streak can be reflected in your appearance or lifestyle, but sometimes it can become a problem, especially if you become too eccentric or stubborn.

Being confident and friendly ensures that you are lucky in people-related activities. With your astute mentality, you can learn skills quickly, but a tendency to become easily bored suggests that misunderstandings with others can occur if you do not take the time to listen. Nevertheless, because you seek harmonious relationships with others, you are intuitive about people and your environment.

While you are between the ages of twelve and forty-one, when your progressed Sun moves through Pisces, your emotional sensitivity becomes emphasized and you develop a stronger sense of vision. This may encourage you to seek idealistic, artistic, or spiritual goals. After the age of forty-two, when your progressed Sun moves into Aries, you have a need to be more assertive, active, and directive in your daily affairs, possibly pioneering new ventures. At the age of seventy-two there is another turning point as your progressed Sun enters Taurus, accenting a need for more financial stability and security.

Fixed Star

Star's name: Castra

Degree position: 19°30'–20°12'
Aquarius between the years 1930 and 2000

Magnitude: 4

Strength: ★★★★

Orb: 1°30'

Constellation: Epsilon Capricorn

Applicable days: February 8, 9, 10

Star qualities: Jupiter/Saturn

Description: a small yellow-orange star located in the belly of the Goat

PRIMARY STAR'S INFLUENCE

Castra imparts leadership ability, assertiveness, and prominence in public office. This star also suggests that patience and hard work lead to success but that destructive behavior may result in failure.

Linked to your Sun's degree, Castra can bestow honors in writing and achievement in higher education. You may well have an interest in philosophy or astrology. This star may also grant you intuitive and psychic abilities.

• *Positive:* perseverance, ambition, philosophical thinking

• *Negative:* lack of self-confidence, pessimism

Your Secret Self

You thrive on acquiring knowledge that you feel will enhance your personal power. Smart, with executive abilities, you are ambitious and enthusiastic when you find a subject or project that really interests you. Capable of accomplishment and success, you can move mountains with a positive attitude, although you may need to develop humility to avoid becoming arrogant or overbearing. As a creative person, you have natural talents that may lead you to activities such as music, art, writing, or drama, where you are likely to excel.

Warm and generous, with common sense, you are capable of giving others practical and useful help and support. You want to build strong foundations to your achievements and are usually willing to work hard to actualize your goals. However, you may have to be careful of a tendency to overindulge in the good life that may distract from your lofty aims and ideals.

Work & Vocation

With your spirit of enterprise, drive, and people skills, you have no trouble creating a career for yourself. Being independent, however, you usually do not like to take orders and may prefer to work for yourself or in a career where you are given much freedom. Practical and a good organizer, you like to build a solid foundation to your achievements, which can serve you well as an entrepreneur or a manager or in the construction business. Good communication skills can help you in sales, advertising, and media. Alternatively, your sense of the dramatic could attract you to the entertainment world, where you could be successful as an actor, director, or writer.

Famous people who share your birthday include actress Lana Turner, actors James Dean, Jack Lemmon, and Nick Nolte, astrologer Evangeline Adams, writer Jules Verne, philosopher Emmanuel Swedenborg, film director King Vidor, composer John Williams, and philosopher Martin Buber.

Numerology

The power suggested by this birthday shows a character with strong values and sound judgment. The number 8 indicates that you aspire to great accomplishments and possess an ambitious nature. A desire for dominance, security, and material success is also indicated by this birthday. As a number 8 person, you have natural business sense and will benefit greatly from developing your organizational and executive skills. A strong need to feel secure or established urges you to make long-term plans and investments. The subinfluence of the number 2 month indicates that you are receptive and highly intuitive. Although you are friendly and sociable, with a flair for people, you are usually self-reliant and have a strong independent streak. Nevertheless, you are considerate and sensitive to other people's feelings and are often courteous, with a romantic nature. Highly intuitive and original, you are ambitious and creative, with a strong need to express your emotional sensitivity. Although on many occasions your common sense tells you that you are right, avoid being arrogant or too critical.

• *Positive:* leadership, thoroughness, hardworking, tradition, authority, protection, power to heal, good judge of values

• *Negative:* impatient, wasteful, intolerant, miserly, restless, overwork, easily discouraged, lack of planning, controlling

Love & Relationships

Practical, with common sense and a love for the good things in life, you know how to enjoy yourself or entertain other people. Usually you like to be associated with ambitious and hardworking people who are success-oriented. As you are proud and security-conscious, prestige and money may be important factors in relationships. With excellent taste and a love of beauty, you can appreciate quality. You enjoy making magnanimous gestures of generosity to those in your favor and make a very valuable friend.

YOUR SPECIAL SOMEONE

For a long-term relationship, you may be lucky in love with persons born on the following dates.

Love & friendship: Jan. 8, 14, 17, 20, 22, 24, Feb. 6, 15, 18, 20, 22, Mar. 4, 13, 16, 18, 20, Apr. 2, 8, 11, 14, 16, 18, May 9, 12, 14, 16, June 4, 7, 10, 12, 13, 14, July 5, 8, 10, 12, 30, Aug. 3, 6, 8, 10, 28, Sept. 1, 4, 6, 8, 26, Oct. 2, 4, 6, 24, Nov. 2, 4, 22, Dec. 2, 20

Beneficial: Jan. 6, 23, Feb. 4, 21, Mar. 2, 19, 30, Apr. 17, 28, May 15, 26, 30, June 13, 24, 28, July 11, 22, 26, Aug. 9, 20, 24, Sept. 7, 18, 22, Oct. 5, 16, 20, Nov. 3, 14, 18, Dec. 1, 12, 16, 30

Fatal attractions: Jan. 7, Feb. 5, Mar. 3, Apr. 1, Aug. 10, 11, 12, 13

Challenging: Jan. 5, 26, 29, Feb. 3, 24, 27, Mar. 1, 22, 25, Apr. 20, 23, May 18, 21, June 16, 19, 30, July 14, 17, 28, Aug. 12, 15, 26, 31, Sept. 10, 13, 24, 29, Oct. 8, 11, 22, 27, Nov. 6, 9, 20, 25, Dec. 4, 7, 18, 23

Soul mates: Jan. 30, Feb. 28, Mar. 26, Apr. 24, May 22, June 20, July 18, Aug. 16, Sept. 14, Oct. 12, 31, Nov. 10, 29, Dec. 8, 27

February 9

Creative and original, you are a friendly Aquarian with an independent personality. Mentally quick and receptive, you can be persuasive and charismatic. Your intuitive and humanitarian nature provides you with a unique perspective on life and suggests that you are sociable and a good observer of human behavior. Multitalented and with many choices, you would be wise to avoid worry and indecision, as these may undermine your confidence and sap your vital energy.

With the subinfluence of your decanate ruler, Gemini, you possess an inventive approach to problem solving. Broad-minded and unconventional in some of your ideas, you may experience flashes of inspiration. Needing freedom, you can sometimes appear very detached, and others may interpret your manner as being cold or uninterested.

Since you enjoy bringing innovations to outdated ideas, you may find that your progressive ideas are ahead of their time. Although inspiration can take you to great heights, mental discipline is essential in order to avoid plummeting to equally great lows. The combination of your universal understanding and natural mystical potential, however, can be developed to bring much wisdom into your life and the lives of others.

Personal magnetism and the need for constant variety suggest that you will make many contacts and experience different circumstances in your life, with a possibility of involvements abroad. Although with your many interests there is a danger of becoming scattered, you can be very focused and hardworking when committed to a project or activity.

While you are between the ages of eleven and forty, when your progressed Sun moves through Pisces, your emotional sensitivity and imagination are accentuated. This makes you more impressionable or aware of your social life, dreams, and creative or spiritual gifts. At the age of forty-one there is a turning point as your progressed Sun enters Aries, emphasizing a need to actively take the initiative in all your affairs, possibly starting new ventures or pioneering progressive ideas. Another change of emphasis occurs at age seventy-one when your progressed Sun enters Taurus, highlighting a greater need for stability and a practical approach to life.

Your Secret Self

A strong inner desire for harmony can be reflected in a love of home and family. You may sometimes take a protective attitude toward those around you in an attempt to solve their difficulties. Even though you may have the best intentions, you may need to learn not to take over people's lives but to let them learn through dealing with their own problems. Advancement comes from decisive action, so it is important to define your sense of purpose and accept the responsibility of your more difficult challenges in order to fulfill your true potential.

A youthful or playful quality will remain with you throughout life. Being aware of image and wanting to express your own unique style imply that you can explore your creativity through artistic pursuits. Although you crave harmony and a utopian ideal, it is through facing your responsibilities that you can achieve long-lasting rewards.

Work & Vocation

As a compassionate and independent thinker, you may want to pursue a career in teaching, writing, counseling, psychology, or social reform. Multitalented, you are likely to receive more

FIXED STAR

Star's name: Castra

Degree position: 19°30'–20°12'
Aquarius between the years 1930 and 2000

Magnitude: 4

Strength: ★★★★

Orb: 1°30'

Constellation: Epsilon Capricorn

Applicable days: February 8, 9, 10

Star qualities: Jupiter/Saturn

Description: a small yellow-orange star located in the belly of the Goat

PRIMARY STAR'S INFLUENCE

Castra imparts leadership ability, assertiveness, and prominence in public office. This star also suggests that patience and hard work lead to success and that destructive behavior may result in failure.

Linked to your Sun's degree, Castra can bestow honors in writing and achievement in higher education. You may well have an interest in philosophy or astrology. This star may also grant you intuitive and psychic abilities.

• *Positive:* perseverance, ambition, philosophical thinking

• *Negative:* lack of self-confidence, pessimism

satisfaction from a fulfilling vocation than from just financial rewards. Travel and change are likely to play an important part in your work and lifestyle. If you decide to pursue a career in public service, you may be drawn to administration or law and politics or work as a government official. Since you possess a latent talent to access the collective dreams and yearnings of a generation, you may wish to explore your creativity through the arts and the theater or design and technology.

Famous people who share your birthday include writers Alice Walker and Brendan Behan, singer Carole King, actress Mia Farrow, actor Joe Pesci, and biologist Jacques Monod.

Numerology

Benevolence, thoughtfulness, and sentimental sensitivity are all associated with the number 9 birthday. Tolerant and kind, you are often generous and liberal. Intuitive and psychic abilities point to a universal receptivity and, if channeled positively, may inspire you to seek a spiritual path. This birthday may suggest a need to overcome challenges and a tendency to be oversensitive, with emotional ups and downs. You benefit greatly from world travel and interaction with people from all walks of life but may have to avoid unrealistic dreams or an inclination toward escapism. The subinfluence of the number 2 month indicates that you are sensitive and receptive, but a tendency to vacillate suggests that you need to maintain a balanced outlook. In order to achieve and succeed, you need to find something that can truly inspire you to develop your talents. Being versatile, you enjoy a variety of interests, and your independent nature implies that you need the freedom to be spontaneous and mentally creative.

• *Positive:* idealistic, humanitarian, creative, sensitive, generous, magnetic, poetic, charitable, giving, detached, lucky, popular

• *Negative:* frustrated, fragmented, selfish, impractical, easily led, inferiority complex, worry

Love & Relationships

Being friendly and sociable, you have an ability to attract many types of people. Since you can alternate between being very generous and expressive and appearing unfeeling, you need to establish balance and harmony in your relationships. As you are attracted to intelligent people, it would be beneficial to share some sort of intellectual activity or joint interest with your mate. A modern-thinking individual, you may choose a more unusual or alternative approach to relationships.

YOUR SPECIAL SOMEONE

You are likely to have more fun and luck with someone born on one of the following dates.

Love and friendship: Jan. 7, 9, 23, 25, 27, Feb. 5, 7, 21, 23, 25, Mar. 5, 19, 21, 23, 29, Apr. 3, 17, 19, 21, 27, 30, May 1, 15, 17, 19, 25, 28, June 3, 13, 15, 17, 23, 26, July 11, 13, 15, 21, 24, Aug. 9, 11, 13, 19, 22, Sept. 7, 9, 11, 17, 20, Oct. 5, 7, 9, 15, 18, Nov. 3, 5, 7, 13, 16, 28, Dec. 1, 3, 5, 11, 14

Beneficial: Jan. 2, 4, 7, 26, Feb. 2, 5, Mar. 3, Apr. 1, May 31, June 16, 29, July 27, 31, Aug. 25, 29, Sept. 23, 27, Oct. 21, 25, Nov. 19, 23, Dec. 17, 21

Fatal attractions: Jan. 8, 14, Feb. 6, 12, Mar. 4, 10, Apr. 2, 8, May 6, June 4, July 2, Aug. 11, 12, 13, 14

Challenging: Jan. 6, 19, 29, Feb. 4, 17, 27, Mar. 2, 15, 25, Apr. 13, 23, May 11, 21, June 9, 19, July 7, 17, Aug. 5, 15, Sept. 3, 13, 30, Oct. 1, 11, 28, Nov. 9, 26, Dec. 7, 24, 29

Soul mates: Jan. 16, 21, Feb. 14, 19, Mar. 12, 17, Apr. 10, 15, May 8, 13, June 6, 11, July 4, 9, Aug. 2, 7, Sept. 5, Oct. 3, Nov. 1

February 10

≈≈ Kindhearted and hardworking, you are a strong-willed Aquarian with sound common sense. Your charisma and ability to deal with people on an individual level suggest that you possess natural diplomatic skills and can work well in cooperative or teamwork situations. Although practical, preferring to keep busy, you are also sensitive, with a vivid imagination.

With the subinfluence of your decanate ruler, Libra, you have charm and a strong intuition about people. As an observer of human nature, you have an awareness that deepens with age. Although independent, you need to be in touch with people and can obtain satisfaction from being of service to others. With your autonomous perspective, you need freedom and do not like to be restrained. Inventive, you have good powers of perception and are an excellent problem solver.

Although at times you may become irritable or display stubbornness, at other times you can enchant others with your sensitivity, caring, and compassion. Active and down to earth in your approach, you also have high ideals and a strong sense of vision. A clear picture of what you want to achieve usually motivates you into action. In order to stay on top of situations, you would be wise to regularly review your life plans. By leading a balanced life, you can avoid becoming involved in restrictive situations or overindulgence as a form of escapism.

While you are between the ages of ten and thirty-nine, when your progressed Sun moves through Pisces, your emotional sensitivity becomes emphasized and you develop a way to deal with your feelings. You may be encouraged to go after some of your dreams. After the age of forty, when your progressed Sun moves into Aries, you have a need to be more assertive, active, and directive in your daily affairs, possibly pioneering new ventures. At the age of seventy there is another turning point as your progressed Sun enters Taurus, accenting a need for more financial stability and security and a greater attraction to nature.

Your Secret Self

Although you are amiable and diplomatic, you also possess power and determination. Responsible and a good organizer, with an inner nobility and pride, you are often put in important positions or in charge of others. With your sharp and shrewd intellect, you have an honest and straightforward style that people interpret as natural confidence. Being highly intuitive, you usually work best when you trust your first impressions of people or situations.

Your responsibilities can extend to your home and family, which play an especially important part in your life. A strong inner desire for peace and harmony may sometimes cause you to repress your anger or become stuck in a rut. If so, this can cause emotional tensions, moods, or fear of the unknown. By learning to confront your feelings and anxieties, you can stretch yourself into new areas and keep yourself fresh. Through expanding your horizons, you are able to balance your need to help others with your skills and expertise and enjoy new and interesting or relaxing pursuits.

Work & Vocation

Independent and clever, you want to have the freedom to do as you wish. You may resent being told what to do or what is best, so you may work better as a manager. As an intuitive person, you are a good judge of character, and with your excellent business sense you have an ability to spot a bargain. Good at buying and selling, you may be drawn to business as a negotiator or an agent. A flair for people implies that you can succeed as a politician or work for the public as a civil servant or administrator. With your desire to help others, you may be drawn to charities, to work in the religious or spiritual field, or to assist those who are disadvantaged. Creative, you may choose to explore drama and sports or music, art, and photography. Your inventive nature may inspire you to work in research or new technology.

Famous people who share your birthday include actors Jimmy Durante and Robert Wagner, writers Boris Pasternak and Berthold Brecht, British prime minister Harold Macmillan, Olympic swimmer Mark Spitz, and singers Roberta Flack and Leontyne Price.

Numerology

Like those with a number 1 birthday, you usually strive toward great endeavors. Nevertheless, you may have to overcome some obstacles before you achieve your goals. Energetic and original, you stand by your own beliefs even when they differ from others'. Your pioneering spirit and ability to be a self-starter also encourage you to travel far afield or strike out on your own. You may also need to learn that the world does not revolve around you, and you should guard against selfishness and being dictatorial. Success and accomplishment are important to all number 10 birthdays, and frequently you find the way to the top of your profession. The subinfluence of the number 2 month indicates that you are intuitive and adaptable, with a friendly personality. At times, however, you may have too many choices and feel confused as to what you should be doing. Usually you are diplomatic and sociable, with a flair for people, and can benefit greatly from collaborating with others. Although you are ambitious, a tendency to rely on others may undermine your decisiveness. As a considerate and sensitive person, you can be receptive to other people's feelings.

• *Positive:* leadership, creative, progressive, forceful, optimistic, strong convictions, competitive, independent, gregarious

• *Negative:* overbearing, jealous, egotistical, antagonistic, lack of restraint, selfish, vacillating, impatient

Love & Relationships

Being friendly, you enjoy socializing and collaborating with others, especially if you feel you can contribute something of worth. Since you can benefit from partnerships, it is important to master the arts of diplomacy and negotiation. As you enjoy comfort, you may be inclined to settle for security; your need for inspiration, however, often encourages you to seek relationships that involve some kind of intellectual challenge. If you become oversensitive, you may be prone to fluctuating moods or misunderstandings with others through lack of communication. Usually you are a loyal partner that others can count on for love and support.

YOUR SPECIAL SOMEONE

To find emotional fulfillment and that special someone, you may want to look among those born on the following days.

Love & friendship: Jan. 10, 14, 26, 28, Feb. 8. 24, 26, Mar. 6, 22, 24, 30, Apr. 4, 8, 20, 22, 28, May 2, 18, 20, 26, 29, June 4, 16, 18, 24, 27, July 14, 16, 22, 25, Aug. 12, 14, 20, 23, 30, Sept. 10, 12, 18, 21, 28, Oct. 8, 10, 16, 19, 26, Nov. 6, 8, 14, 17, 24, Dec. 4, 6, 12, 15, 22

Beneficial: Jan. 8, Feb. 6, Mar. 4, 28, Apr. 2, 26, May 24, June 22, 30, July 20, 28, 29, Aug. 18, 26, 27, 30, Sept. 16, 24, 25, 28, Oct. 14, 22, 23, 26, 29, Nov. 12, 20, 21, 24, 27, Dec. 10, 18, 19, 22, 25

Fatal attractions: Jan. 15, Feb. 13, Mar. 11, Apr. 9, May 7, June 5, July 3, Aug. 1, 12, 13, 14, 15

Challenging: Jan. 7, 9, 30, Feb. 5, 7, 28, Mar. 3, 5, 26, Apr. 1, 3, 24, May 1, 22, June 20, July 18, Aug. 16, Sept. 14, Oct. 12, 29, Nov. 10, 27, Dec. 8, 25, 30

Soul mates: Jan. 8, 27, Feb. 6, 25, Mar. 4, 23, Apr. 2, 21, May 19, June 17, July 15, Aug. 13, Sept. 11, Oct. 9, Nov. 7, Dec. 5

February 11

Strong-willed and original, you are a determined Aquarian with an inventive mind and a sharp insight into human nature. With imagination and a desire to be at the forefront of progressive trends, you seek new and exciting ventures to keep your active mind occupied. With your physical stamina and drive, you have the perseverance to overcome obstacles or frustrations as long as you keep your mind positively focused.

With the subinfluence of your decanate ruler, Libra, you are friendly and affectionate, with a strong need for social interaction. You may possess creative talents and have an original approach to your relationships. An ability to mix with all types of people indicates that there is a prominent humanitarian side to your nature. A natural rebel with advanced ideas, you are capable of bringing reforms to outdated systems. It would be wise, however, to avoid being stubborn or self-willed, as this may ultimately work against you.

With your sensitivity and strong emotions, you are often an idealist and are likely to be happiest when working hard on a project or cause about which you feel deeply. Astute and receptive, you are clever enough to pick up on situations immediately. By keeping yourself creatively occupied or active, you can avoid becoming bored and fulfill your great potential.

While you are between the ages of nine and thirty-eight, when your progressed Sun moves through Pisces, your emotional sensitivity becomes enhanced and you develop your imagination. This can be reflected in your dreams and ideals as well as in your social life. At the age of thirty-nine there is a turning point as your progressed Sun enters Aries, emphasizing a need to actively take the initiative and be brave and direct in your relationships with others. This may involve pioneering new activities in your life. Another change of emphasis occurs at age sixty-nine, when your progressed Sun enters Taurus, highlighting a greater need for a practical approach to life and financial security.

FIXED STARS

Sad Al Suud; Deneb Algedi; Nashira, also called the Bringer of Good Tidings

PRIMARY STAR

Star's name: Sad Al Suud

Degree position: 22°24'–23°20'
Aquarius between the years 1930 and 2000

Magnitude: 3

Strength: ★★★★★

Orb: 1°30'

Constellation: Beta Aquarius

Applicable days: February 11, 12, 13, 14

Star qualities: varied influences:
Mercury/Saturn and Sun/Uranus

Description: a pale yellow star located on the left shoulder of Aquarius

PRIMARY STAR'S INFLUENCE

Sad Al Suud's influence suggests creativity, imagination, intuition, and psychic abilities. You may find interest in astrology and metaphysical studies. Usually you are domestically inclined and love your home. This star also bestows a happy family life and gains through marriage.

Linked to your Sun's degree, this star indicates originality, success dealing with the public, and interest in astrology, philosophy, or spirituality. You are probably competitive, original, and inventive. This star also suggests the occurrence of some strange or unexpected events.

• *Positive:* originality, creativity, lucky changes, new opportunities

Your Secret Self

Highly intuitive, with innate spiritual potential, you can benefit greatly from developing this side of your nature. Through self-analysis and periods of introspection, you can stay in touch with your inner sensitivity and spontaneity, allowing life to unfold in its own time. This helps you to relax and avoid possible periods of suspicion or isolation. If you set your expectations too high, people may find it hard to reach your high ideals of perfection.

Biting repartee and a sense of satire can help you see life's irony in a lighter way and keep you mentally balanced. You can be provocative, and although you enjoy entertaining others, you love a mental challenge in which you can test your wits and intelligence against others'. Although you are very independent, as a networker with many contacts you prefer the personal touch and work well in partnerships or as a member of a team. Your determination and leadership ability work to your benefit and qualify you for advancement in all areas of life.

Work & Vocation

With your sharp insight and powerful instincts, you are dynamic and receptive, with executive ability. Your humanitarian inclinations may draw you to work with people as a psychologist or counselor. Inventive and progressive, with an interest in research and information technology, you enjoy being in the forefront of new industries. You are hardworking and dedicated, and your employers or superiors will appreciate your discipline and broad-minded approach to new and original ideas. As you are able to stay calm in a crisis, you enjoy solving problems and making discoveries. Usually you can work well as an advisor or a specialist, or working for yourself. An interest in education suggests that you can be an accomplished teacher or writer. Alternatively, you may choose to study philosophy and spirituality or explore metaphysics.

Famous people who share your birthday include inventor Thomas Edison, designer Mary Quant, actresses Jennifer Aniston and Tina Louise, writer Fyodor Dostoyevsky, and actor Burt Reynolds.

Numerology

The special vibration of the master number 11 birthday suggests that idealism, inspiration, and innovation are highly important to you. A blend of humility and confidence challenges you to work toward self-mastery both materially and spiritually. Through experience you learn how to deal with both sides of your nature and develop a less extremist attitude by trusting your own feelings. Usually you are highly charged and enjoy vitality, but must avoid becoming overanxious or impractical. The subinfluence of the number 2 month indicates that you are intuitive and receptive. As a sensitive individual, you are diplomatic and sociable, with a humanitarian perspective. You benefit greatly from association and partnership, especially if those around you are encouraging and supportive. Although adaptable, you can at times become discouraged too easily due to fears or a mistrust of people. You are inventive and talented, and if you have a special quest or interest, follow your heart and do not let others undermine your confidence, especially if you are breaking new ground and experimenting with original concepts.

• *Positive:* balanced, focused, objective, enthusiastic, inspirational, spiritual, idealistic, intuitive, intelligent, outgoing, inventive, artistic, service, healing ability, humanitarian, has faith, psychic

• *Negative:* superiority complex, aimless, overemotional, easily hurt, selfish, lack of clarity, dominating

Love & Relationships

Idealistic and unconventional, you are keen on progressive concepts and usually enjoy the company of unorthodox individuals who are willing to embrace new ideas. At times you can alternate between being sensitive, unpretentious, and caring and being stubborn or selfish. You may also have an inner conflict between your high ideals and practical considerations. Although you need deep intimacy, at times you may feel inhibited and unable to express your powerful emotions. Generally, however, you are a wonderful friend and ally who is willing to use your strong will to help and support those you love.

YOUR SPECIAL SOMEONE

You might find someone who shares your high ideals and aspirations among those born on the following dates.

Love & friendship: Jan. 11, 15, 20, 25, 27, 28, 29, Feb. 9, 18, 23, 25, 27, Mar. 7, 16, 21, 23, 25, Apr. 5, 9, 14, 19, 21, 23, May 3, 12, 17, 19, 21, June 1, 5, 10, 15, 17, 18, 19, July 8, 13, 15, 17, Aug. 6, 11, 13, 15, Sept. 4, 9, 11, 13, Oct. 2, 7, 9, 11, Nov. 5, 7, 9, Dec. 3, 5, 7

Beneficial: Jan. 9, 26, Feb. 7, 24, Mar. 5, 22, Apr. 3, 20, May 1, 18, 29, June 7, 16, 27, July 14, 25, 29, 30, Aug. 12, 23, 27, 28, 31, Sept. 10, 21, 25, 26, 29, Oct. 8, 19, 23, 24, 27, Nov. 6, 17, 21, 22, 25, Dec. 4, 15, 19, 20, 23

Fatal attractions: Jan. 16, Feb. 14, Mar. 12, Apr. 10, May 8, June 6, July 4, Aug. 2, 13, 14, 15, 16

Challenging: Jan. 8, 29, 31, Feb. 6, 27, 29, Mar. 4, 25, 27, 28, Apr. 2, 23, 25, 26, May 21, 23, 24, June 19, 21, 22, July 17, 19, 20, Aug. 15, 17, 18, Sept. 13, 15, 16, Oct. 11, 13, 14, 30, Nov. 9, 11, 12, 28, Dec. 7, 9, 10, 26

Soul mates: May 30, June 28, July 26, Aug. 24, Sept. 22, 30, Oct. 20, 28, Nov. 18, 26, Dec. 16, 24

February 12

FIXED STARS

Sad Al Suud; Deneb Algedi; Nashira, also called the Bringer of Good Tidings

PRIMARY STAR

Star's name: Sad Al Suud

Degree position: 22°24'–23°20'
Aquarius between the years 1930 and 2000

Magnitude: 3

Strength: ★★★★★

Orb: 1°30'

Constellation: Beta Aquarius

Applicable days: February 11, 12, 13, 14

Star qualities: varied influences:
Mercury/Saturn and Sun/Uranus

Description: a pale yellow star located on the left shoulder of Aquarius

PRIMARY STAR'S INFLUENCE

Sad Al Suud's influence suggests creativity, imagination, intuition, and psychic abilities. You may find interest in astrology and metaphysical studies. Usually you are domestically inclined and love your home. This star also bestows a happy family life and gains through marriage.

Linked to your Sun's degree, this star indicates originality, success dealing with the public, and interest in astrology, philosophy, or spirituality. You are probably competitive, original, and inventive. This star also suggests the occurrence of some strange or unexpected events.

• *Positive:* originality, creativity, lucky changes, new opportunities

~~~ You are an original, intelligent, and creative Aquarian with an easy charm and good social skills. You possess leadership potential and a fine, objective mind that can quickly assess people, situations, and new ideas. Ambitious and clever, you like to think big; just be careful that with your multiple talents and abilities you do not dissipate your energies in too many directions.

With the subinfluence of your decanate ruler, Libra, you can be charming, sociable, and able to mix with people from all walks of life. Although you can sometimes appear offhand or detached, you crave affection and a warm circle of friends. An interesting blend of contrasts, you possess a humanitarian spirit, yet you love obtaining a good deal or bargain. Your natural diplomacy and ease in making contacts combined with an ability to sell your ideas can do much to enhance your success.

Beneath your cool and detached exterior you are often more complex than you seem. By channeling your inner restlessness into self-discipline, you can make those wonderfully creative and imaginative ideas a reality. Having an innate sense of values, you quickly rise to the top of any situation; watch out, however, that your natural leadership does not degenerate into bossiness or stubbornness. At your best you are independent, highly enthusiastic, dynamic, and inventive, with your own unique style.

While you are between the ages of eight and thirty-seven, when your progressed Sun moves through Pisces, your emotional sensitivity is enhanced, making you more imaginative, receptive, and aware of your social life. You may become more visionary or interested in developing creative or spiritual talents. There is a turning point at age thirty-eight, when your progressed Sun enters Aries. Your ambition and determination become more apparent, and you start to really come into your own. You may be involved in starting new projects or pioneering new ideas. Another change of emphasis occurs at age sixty-eight, when your progressed Sun enters Taurus, highlighting a greater need for stability, security, and emotional steadiness.

Your Secret Self

Your subtle artistic talents and quick intelligence suggest you have many hidden facets to your personality. Quick wit and a strong need for self-expression may partly satisfy your adventurous nature. It would be wise, however, to guard against wasting your precious energy in self-doubt, indecision, or worry. By developing your inner faith and self-discipline and by learning to trust your innate intuitive powers, you can achieve tremendous success. This may involve refusing to take positions beneath your talents and capabilities.

Being highly creative, you can possess a driving force that spurs you on to fresh achievements. Sensitive and highly strung, however, you may find that spending periods alone in reflection, contemplation, or meditation are particularly good for developing your inner calm.

Work & Vocation

Your good business sense implies that with your communication skills and executive ability, you are able to negotiate well with people. You may be drawn toward careers in the public sector. Interested in education and learning, you may choose to be a teacher or lecturer. An interest in public affairs suggests that you may enter politics or work as a counselor or advisor. Authoritative and capable, you may want to enter the world of business and become involved in manufacturing, accountancy, publishing, or advertising. Alternatively, your independent and creative spirit may lead you to writing, acting, or the arts in general. With your objective and unorthodox mind, you may be inspired to become a scientist or inventor. As a natural humanitarian and philanthropist, you can make a valuable contribution to your chosen cause. You are inquisitive, and if you are interested in other cultures, you may become an archeologist or anthropologist.

Famous people who share your birthday include U.S. president Abraham Lincoln, biologist Charles Darwin, musician Ray Manzarek, TV personality Arsenio Hall, and director Franco Zeffirelli.

Numerology

People with a number 12 birthday are usually intuitive and friendly. Since you want to establish true individuality, you possess good reasoning power and are usually innovative. Naturally understanding and sensitive, you also know how to use tact and cooperative methods to achieve your aims and objectives. When you achieve a balance between your need for self-expression and your natural inclination to be supportive of others, you can find emotional satisfaction and personal fulfillment. You may nevertheless need to find the courage to stand on your own two feet and develop self-confidence or learn not to get easily discouraged by other people. The subinfluence of the number 2 month indicates that you are receptive, with diplomatic skills and a flair for people. As a humanitarian, you are considerate and sensitive to other people's feelings. You may have to learn, however, to counteract your busy social life with your work and commitments. Although you can be intuitive and adaptable, your restless nature implies that at times you can display impatience or domineering tendencies. With an interest in learning and reforms, you are keen on progressive concepts and social issues, especially education and politics.

- *Positive:* creative, attractive, initiative, disciplinarian, promote yourself or others
- *Negative:* reclusive, eccentric, uncooperative, overly sensitive, lack of self-esteem

Love & Relationships

Friendly, sociable, and fun-loving, you find it easy to communicate with all types of people. Usually you like those who are mentally stimulating or groups where you can share your interests and learn. Up on current trends, you are self-aware and prefer like-minded people who are interested in self-improvement. In personal relationships, however, you may need to avoid a tendency to be bossy. Progressive, you may choose to experiment in your quest for love. Your sensitivity suggests that your detached exterior sometimes masks a difficulty in demonstrating your deep emotions.

YOUR SPECIAL SOMEONE

You may have luck in your relationships with persons born on the following dates.

Love & friendship: Jan. 4, 11, 12, 26, 28, 30, Feb. 2, 9, 10, 24, 26, 28, Mar. 7, 8, 22, 24, 26, Apr. 5, 6, 10, 20, 22, 24, 30, May 3, 4, 18, 20, 22, 28, 31, June 1, 2, 6, 16, 18, 20, 26, 29, July 14, 16, 18, 24, 27, Aug. 12, 14, 16, 22, 25, Sept. 10, 12, 14, 20, 23, Oct. 8, 10, 12, 13, 18, 21, Nov. 6, 8, 10, 16, 19, Dec. 4, 6, 8, 14, 17

Beneficial: Jan. 3, 10, 29, 31, Feb. 1, 8, 27, Mar. 6, 25, Apr. 4, 23, May 2, 21, 23, June 19, July 17, 30, Aug. 15, 28, Sept. 13, 26, Oct. 11, 24, Nov. 9, 22, Dec. 7, 20

Fatal attractions: Jan. 11, Feb. 9, Mar. 7, Apr. 5, May 3, June 1, Aug. 14, 15, 16, 17

Challenging: Jan. 9, Feb. 7, Mar. 5, 28, Apr. 3, 26, May 1, 24, June 22, July 20, Aug. 18, Sept. 16, Oct. 14, 30, 31, Nov. 12, 28, 29, Dec. 10, 26, 27

Soul mates: Jan. 7, Feb. 5, Mar. 3, Apr. 1, May 29, June 27, July 25, Aug. 23, Sept. 21, Oct. 19, Nov. 17, Dec. 15

February 13

≈ With good communication skills and inventive ideas, you are an original and talented Aquarian with a sense of the dramatic. Your strong character indicates that you take pride in your work but dislike being in subservient positions. Diligent and dependable, with a creative approach, you enjoy being part of associations or groups where you can play a leading role.

With the subinfluence of your decanate ruler, Libra, you are sociable, charming, and able to interrelate with people from all social circles. A natural diplomacy and good sense of values can also help you in your overall success, since it gives you excellent bargaining or negotiating skills. With your original approach, awareness of image, and love of beauty, you may wish to express your individuality through literary or artistic pursuits. Possessing a strong need for love and affection, you feel that relationships are very important.

Astute and with a keen eye, you have a capacity for precise thinking that implies you are capable of analyzing issues in depth. A natural rebel and also a humanitarian, you are willing to fight for the rights of others and give your support to an idealistic cause. Although you prefer to deal with people in a direct and forthright way, you may have to guard against being bossy or too verbally sharp.

While you are between the ages of seven and thirty-six, when your progressed Sun moves through Pisces, your emotional sensitivity becomes emphasized and you develop a stronger sense of vision. Your feelings may encourage you to seek idealistic, creative, or spiritual goals. After the age of thirty-seven, when your progressed Sun moves into Aries, you have a need to be more assertive, active, and directive in your daily affairs, possibly pioneering new ventures. At the age of sixty-seven there is another turning point as your progressed Sun enters Taurus, accenting a need for more financial stability and security and a love of nature.

Your Secret Self

Although you are ambitious and have shrewd business sense, at times worry or indecision about money and material situations can prevent you from fully enjoying your outstanding creative potential. Keeping a lighter perspective through a positive mental approach and cutting down on extravagances help you keep life simpler and easier. Courageous, with a free spirit, you are capable of inspired ideas. By combining these ideas with self-discipline, you are capable of achieving outstanding success.

Generous and broad-minded, you have a universal perspective that can help you lead others. Enjoying excitement, you can excel at motivating other people or pushing for changes and reforms. Although you are sometimes obstinate, detachment and a balanced attitude to life will enable you to avoid many frustrations and disappointments. Being sensitive, you need regular periods of rest and play to recharge your nervous energies.

Work & Vocation

With your intelligence and practical skills, you are inventive and original. Creative and versatile, you need variety and different ways to express yourself. Although you enjoy large projects

---

FIXED STARS

Sad Al Suud; Deneb Algedi; Nashira, also called the Bringer of Good Tidings

---

PRIMARY STAR

Star's name: Sad Al Suud

Degree position: 22°24'–23°20'
Aquarius between the years 1930 and 2000

Magnitude: 3

Strength: ★★★★★

Orb: 1°30'

Constellation: Beta Aquarius

Applicable days: February 11, 12, 13, 14

Star qualities: varied influences:
Mercury/Saturn and Sun/Uranus

Description: a pale yellow star located on the left shoulder of Aquarius

---

PRIMARY STAR'S INFLUENCE

Sad Al Suud's influence suggests creativity, imagination, intuition, and psychic abilities. You may find interest in astrology and metaphysical studies. Usually you are domestically inclined and love your home. This star also bestows a happy family life and gains through marriage.

Linked to your Sun's degree, this star indicates originality, success dealing with the public, and interest in astrology, philosophy, or spirituality. You are probably competitive, original, and inventive. This star also suggests the occurrence of some strange or unexpected events.

• *Positive:* originality, creativity, lucky changes, new opportunities

and collaborating with others, you may feel restricted if in a subservient position. Ideally, you need a career where you can be self-employed or retain some control or authority. Your intuitive intellect may draw you to scientific research, education, metaphysics, or philosophy. Alternatively, your caring nature may find a place in the world of counseling, social work, or fighting for the rights of others. Being multitalented and having a fine appreciation of art, music, and drama may also lead you to a career in the arts, media, or entertainment world. Your ability to push through some kind of reform may attract you to humanitarian causes or public service.

Famous people who share your birthday include singers Peter Gabriel and Tennessee Ernie Ford, actresses Kim Novak and Stockard Channing, and actors Oliver Reed and George Segal.

Numerology

Emotional sensitivity, enthusiasm, and inspiration are often identified with the number 13 birthday. Numerically, you are associated with ambition and hard work, and can accomplish much through creative self-expression. You may need to cultivate a pragmatic outlook if you want to turn your creative talents into tangible products. Your original and innovative approach inspires new and exciting ideas, which frequently result in work that impresses others. With a number 13 birthday, you are earnest, romantic, charming, and fun-loving, and with dedication you can achieve prosperity. The subinfluence of the number 2 month indicates that you are receptive and idealistic, with a flair for dealing with people. Ambitious yet charming, you know how to use your diplomatic skills and friendly personality to achieve success socially and financially. A need to express your talents suggests that you can be dramatic and dynamic when you have a goal or a purpose. Although usually generous and kind, at times you can overreact or be extravagant or self-indulgent. You usually benefit from cooperative effort but prefer to be in a leading position or take charge.

• *Positive:* ambitious, creative, freedom-loving, self-expressive, initiative
• *Negative:* impulsive, indecisive, bossy, unemotional, rebellious, egotistical

Love & Relationships

Sociable and friendly, with a witty and entertaining personality, you have many friends and acquaintances. Usually you are interested in intelligent and creative people who can inspire you to express yourself. Although you need love and affection, indecision or uncertainty may cause confusion about long-term relationships. By learning to stay detached and keeping yourself creative, you can avoid dwelling on or worrying about your personal life. Having a humanitarian side to your personality emphasizes the importance of friendship in your life.

YOUR SPECIAL SOMEONE

Your opportunities to find that special person are greater with those born on the following dates.

Love & friendship: Jan. 13, 17, 29, Feb. 11, 27, 29, Mar. 9, 25, 27, Apr. 7, 11, 23, 25, May 5, 21, 23, 29, June 3, 7, 19, 21, 27, 30, July 1, 17, 19, 25, 28, Aug. 15, 17, 23, 26, Sept. 13, 15, 21, 24, Oct. 11, 13, 19, 22, 29, Nov. 9, 11, 17, 20, 27, Dec. 7, 9, 15, 18, 25

Beneficial: Jan. 11, Feb. 9, Mar. 7, 31, Apr. 5, 29, May 3, 27, 31, June 1, 9, 25, 29, July 23, 27, 31, Aug. 21, 25, 29, 30, Sept. 19, 23, 27, 28, Oct. 1, 17, 21, 25, 26, Nov. 15, 19, 23, 24, 30, Dec. 13, 17, 21, 22, 28

Fatal attractions: Jan. 12, Feb. 10, Mar. 8, Apr. 6, May 4, June 2, Aug. 15, 16, 17, 18

Challenging: Jan. 10, Feb. 8, Mar. 6, 29, Apr. 4, 27, May 2, 25, June 23, July 21, Aug. 19, Sept. 17, Oct. 15, 31, Nov. 13, 29, 30, Dec. 11, 27, 28

Soul mates: Jan. 18, 24, Feb. 16, 22, Mar. 14, 20, Apr. 12, 18, May 10, 16, June 8, 14, July 6, 12, Aug. 4, 10, Sept. 2, 8, Oct. 6, Nov. 4, Dec. 2

February 14

 Your birthday shows you to be friendly and charming, an intelligent Aquarian with a warm heart. With grace added to your individuality, you possess refined social skills that can aid you in your overall success. Your strong imagination and awareness of image give you an ability to be creative or to make a good impression on others.

With the added influence of your Sun in the decanate of Libra, you are amiable and easygoing, with a need for affection and harmonious relationships. A lover of beauty, art, and music, you possess innate creative talents. You may wish to employ self-discipline to develop these into a powerful form of self-expression. Enjoying luxury and style, you can be attracted to the best that life can offer.

Direct and honest in your communications with others, you prefer life to be simple. With a natural insight into people's motivation, you are a good psychologist and natural humanitarian. Sometimes aloof, you protect yourself from being hurt by appearing detached. You may have to be careful, however, that others do not interpret these signals wrongly and think that they are not wanted. A youthful quality is likely to stay with you throughout your life and show a side of you that is guaranteed to keep others enchanted or entertained.

When you are between the ages of six and thirty-five, your progressed Sun moves through Pisces, and your emotional sensitivity and imagination are emphasized. This can be reflected in your visions, dreams, and ideals as well as in your social life. At the age of thirty-six there is a turning point as your progressed Sun enters Aries, emphasizing a need to actively take more initiative and be assertive, become involved in leadership and pioneering ideas, or be direct in your relationships with others. Another change of emphasis occurs at age sixty-six, when your progressed Sun enters Taurus, highlighting a greater need for a practical approach to life and financial security.

FIXED STARS

Sad Al Suud, Deneb Algedi

PRIMARY STAR

Star's name: Sad Al Suud

Degree position: 22°24'–23°20'
     Aquarius between the years 1930
     and 2000

Magnitude: 3

Strength: ★★★★★★

Orb: 1°30'

Constellation: Beta Aquarius

Applicable days: February 11, 12, 13, 14

Star qualities: varied influences:
     Mercury/Saturn and Sun/Uranus

Description: a pale yellow star located
     on the left shoulder of Aquarius

PRIMARY STAR'S INFLUENCE

Sad Al Suud's influence suggests creativity, imagination, intuition, and psychic abilities. You may find interest in astrology and metaphysical studies. Usually you are domestically inclined and love your home. This star also bestows a happy family life and gains through marriage.

Linked to your Sun's degree, this star indicates originality and success dealing with the public. You are probably competitive, original, and inventive. This star also suggests the occurrence of some strange or unexpected events.

• *Positive:* originality, creativity, lucky changes, new opportunities

• *Negative:* scandals, hasty action that can backfire

See Appendix for additional fixed star readings.

Your Secret Self

With your wide range of interests and desires, you may sometimes encounter indecision about your life choices or have a conflict between your ideals and mundane reality. Your bright personality and expressive qualities, however, can help you keep life in perspective. Try not to let a need for material security stop you from taking creative chances.

Although practical, you also possess psychic or intuitive gifts that if developed could greatly aid your self-awareness and desire to help others. Although you possess an inner playfulness, learning to take responsibility can help bring stability into your life and enhance your chances for success. Dramatic, with a mind full of bright ideas, you need to channel your vitality and restless temperament through creative pursuits. A constant desire for knowledge will stay with you throughout your life and help keep you enthusiastic and youthful.

Work & Vocation

Individual and determined, you have charm and vitality. In business, you use your personality to promote yourself and like to take opportunities to advance. Usually hardworking, with practical skills and executive ability, you can succeed in business and sales or promoting merchandise by creating an image. A flair for dealing with people also suggests that you can work as a public servant or a networker in large corporations. Alternatively, you may run an agency or work in media and publishing. Banking, insurance, and the stock exchange may appeal to you. You may also choose to go it alone and start your own business. If you want an exciting and varied life, you may choose a career in show business.

Famous people who share your birthday include director Alan Parker, trade unionist James Hoffa, comedian Jack Benny, abolitionist Frederick Douglass, and choreographer Gregory Hines.

Numerology

Intellectual potential, pragmatism, and determination are some of the qualities associated with the number 14 birthday. Indeed, with this birthdate you frequently put your work first and judge yourself and others on the basis of career achievements. Although you need stability, the restlessness indicated by the number 14 urges you to forge ahead or take on new challenges in a constant attempt to improve your lot. This innate restlessness and constant lack of satisfaction may also inspire you to make a great many changes in your life, especially if you are not happy with your working conditions or financial status. With your perceptive mind, you respond quickly to problems and enjoy solving them. The subinfluence of the number 2 month indicates that you are intuitive and discriminating. A tendency to be critical and self-absorbed suggests that you are often a perfectionist but can indulge in skeptical rationalization. Although you are receptive and intuitive, you may be prone to restlessness and lack of faith. Since you prefer to make your own decisions, frequently you learn best through personal experience.

• *Positive:* decisive action, hardworking, lucky, creative, pragmatic, imaginative, industrious
• *Negative:* overly cautious or overly impulsive, unstable, thoughtless, stubborn

Love & Relationships

Charming and individual, you like to be free to take advantage of the opportunities that are available to you. Since you make friends easily, you have many social opportunities and acquaintances. Many of your opportunities come through people you know. Although you are practical and possess good common sense, you need to take your time in choosing your relationships carefully; otherwise you feel restricted or may lose interest. Honest and direct yourself, you may be particularly interested in a partner who can be practical yet imaginative or sensitive. Although you value relationships, you also need freedom within a partnership.

YOUR SPECIAL SOMEONE

Your chances of finding a loving partner for a long-term relationship are increased with those born on the following dates.

Love & friendship: Jan. 6, 8, 14, 18, 23, 26, 28, Feb. 4, 10, 12, 21, 24, 26, Mar. 2, 10, 12, 19, 22, 24, Apr. 8, 12, 14, 17, 20, 22, May 6, 15, 16, 18, 20, 22, June 4, 13, 16, 18, 20, July 2, 11, 14, 16, 20, Aug. 4, 9, 12, 14, 22, Sept. 7, 10, 12, 24, Oct. 5, 8, 10, 12, 26, Nov. 3, 6, 8, 28, Dec. 1, 4, 6, 30

Beneficial: Jan. 9, 12, 17, Feb. 7, 10, Mar. 5, 8, Apr. 3, 6, May 1, 4, June 2, 7, 30, July 28, Aug. 26, 30, 31, Sept. 24, 28, 29, Oct. 22, 26, 27, Nov. 20, 24, 25, Dec. 18, 22, 23, 29

Fatal attractions: Aug. 16, 17, 18, 19

Challenging: Jan. 11, 13, 29, Feb. 9, 11, Mar. 7, 9, 30, Apr. 5, 7, 28, May 3, 5, 26, 31, June 1, 3, 24, 29, July 1, 22, 27, Aug. 20, 25, Sept. 18, 23, 30, Oct. 16, 21, 28, Nov. 14, 19, 26, Dec. 12, 17, 24

Soul mates: Jan. 12, 29, Feb. 10, 27, Mar. 8, 25, Apr. 6, 23, May 4, 21, June 2, 19, July 17, Aug. 15, Sept. 13, Oct. 11, Nov. 9, Dec. 7

February 15

≈ An original thinker with a quick mind, you are a generous and kind Aquarian with a strong awareness of values. Friendly and enthusiastic, your ability to learn fast can help you acquire many talents in life. A charismatic communicator with an innate business sense, you are frequently able to see opportunities and commercialize your gifts.

With the added influence of your Sun in the decanate of Libra, you can mix with all types of people and have the power to influence them with your inventive ideas. Charming and affectionate, with a strong need for social interaction, you also possess a humanitarian side to your nature. A natural diplomacy and ease in making contacts combined with an ability to sell your ideas can do much to enhance your success. With an appreciation of beauty, style, and luxury, you can often have expensive tastes.

With your sense of vision or ability to see the bigger plan, you can often see ahead and be an excellent organizer. Not liking to be small or petty, you usually work better with a positive goal in mind. Although your rebellious side can work well in bringing positive change, it would be wise to avoid going too far and becoming contrary or stubborn. Talented and quick at evaluating situations, you have a fortunate ability to materialize your dreams. Just be careful that in the pursuit of your desires you do not preoccupy yourself with material concerns.

Between the ages of five and thirty-four, when your progressed Sun moves through Pisces, you develop a stronger sense of subtlety and your emotional sensitivity becomes emphasized. You may be encouraged to seek idealistic or creative goals. After the age of thirty-five, when your progressed Sun moves into Aries, you have a need to be more assertive, active, and directive in your daily affairs, possibly pioneering new ventures. At the age of sixty-five there is another turning point as your progressed Sun enters Taurus, accenting a need for more financial stability and security and a pragmatic approach to life.

Fixed Stars

Although your Sun's degree is not linked to a fixed star, some of your other planets' degrees certainly will be. By having an astrological chart calculated, you can find the exact position of the planets on your date of birth. This will tell you which of the fixed stars listed in this book are relevant to you.

Your Secret Self

Dramatic and proud, you appear confident and often rise to positions of authority. A good networker, you can often link people from different groups and find satisfaction in helping others. A natural sense of refinement or artistic appreciation may stimulate you to develop your creative talents, if not for a career, then as a relaxing pastime. Although you have the ability to manage financially without too much effort, it is through developing your inner ideals and natural wisdom that you can find your biggest rewards.

Fortunately, you possess a sense of endurance that can help you accomplish your aims and objectives. If you find yourself in positions well beneath your capabilities, you may not be recognizing your tremendous potential. By being willing to put in the work and the necessary self-discipline, you have excellent opportunities for success.

Work & Vocation

Being good at delegating and having an interest in public affairs suggest that you can work as an official or civil servant. You have excellent business sense, and with your communication skills and executive ability, you are able to negotiate well with people or work as a counselor or advisor. An interest in education and learning may draw you toward teaching or writing. Interested in new technological discoveries, you may be working with computers or in engineering. If in the business world, you could be drawn to banking and the service industries. Creative, you may be inspired to produce original works of art. As a natural humanitarian, you can also make a valuable contribution to your chosen cause. Wealthy individuals with this birthday are often philanthropists and art patrons.

Famous people who share your birthday include actresses Jane Seymour, Claire Bloom, and Marisa Berenson, astronomer Galileo Galilei, singer Melissa Manchester, actor John Barrymore, and jeweler Charles Tiffany.

Numerology

Versatility, enthusiasm, and restlessness are suggested by the number 15 birthday. Your greatest assets are your strong instincts and the ability to learn quickly through combining theory and practice. Often you utilize your intuitive powers and are quick at recognizing opportunities when they arise. As a number 15 individual, you possess a talent for attracting money or receiving help and support from others. Carefree and resolute, you welcome the unexpected and like to take a gamble. The subinfluence of the number 2 month indicates that you are receptive and highly intuitive. Although you are enterprising and hardworking, you enjoy socializing, but you need to learn how to be confrontational without being domineering or aggressive. Restless and mentally active, you have drive and ambition, but avoid overwork or resorting to greed or wasteful indulgence. Quick and alert, you need to express your dramatic dynamism through responsible and creative planning. When enthusiastic and optimistic, you benefit from collaborating with others, as long as you finish what you start.

• *Positive:* willing, generous, responsible, kind, cooperative, appreciative, creative ideas, enterprising

• *Negative:* restless, irresponsible, self-centered, fear of change, loss of faith, worry, indecision, materialistic

Love & Relationships

Popular and outgoing, you are likely to have many acquaintances and friends. As a loyal partner, you can give generously to your friends and those you love. Your charm can attract many social and romantic opportunities. Intelligent and dynamic, you enjoy the company of forceful people with charismatic personalities. Although you have powerful feelings and desires for love and affection, you may sometimes have difficulty deciding who is the right partner for you. Your friendliness and charisma, however, always ensure your social success.

YOUR SPECIAL SOMEONE

If you are looking for someone special, you might find greater luck with those born on the following days.

Love & friendship: Jan. 6, 15, 18, 29, 31, Feb. 4, 13, 27, 29, Mar. 2, 11, 25, 27, Apr. 9, 12, 23, 25, May 7, 21, 23, June 1, 5, 19, 21, July 3, 17, 19, 30, Aug. 1, 15, 17, 28, Sept. 13, 15, 26, Oct. 1, 11, 13, 24, Nov. 9, 11, 22, Dec. 7, 9, 20

Beneficial: Jan. 13, 15, 19, Feb. 11, 13, 17, 19, Mar. 9, 11, 15, Apr. 7, 9, 13, May 5, 7, 11, June 3, 5, 9, 11, July 1, 3, 7, 29, Aug. 1, 5, 27, 31, Sept. 3, 25, 29, Oct. 1, 3, 23, 27, Nov. 21, 25, Dec. 19, 23

Fatal attractions: May 30, June 28, July 26, Aug. 17, 18, 19, 20, 24, Sept. 22, Oct. 20, Nov. 18, Dec. 16

Challenging: Jan. 12, Feb. 10, Mar. 8, Apr. 6, May 4, June 2, Aug. 31, Sept. 29, Oct. 27, 29, 30, Nov. 25, 27, 28, Dec. 23, 25, 26, 30

Soul mates: Jan. 2, 28, Feb. 26, Mar. 24, Apr. 22, May 20, June 18, July 16, Aug. 14, Sept. 12, Oct. 10, Nov. 8, Dec. 6

February 16

 Intelligent and with a universal perspective, you are a friendly and independent Aquarian. Your birthday indicates that although you are usually generous, kind, and open, you also have a side to your nature that can be introspective or critical. Your strong instincts for leadership suggest that you do not like to be in subservient positions and that you are often a good judge of values.

With the added influence of your Sun in the decanate of Libra, you possess good social and communication skills. Needing people, love, and affection, you find that relationships are very important to you. Witty and cultured, you have quick reactions and a humanitarian viewpoint. Although you are independent, your easy ability to deal with others helps you work well as part of a team. An eccentric instability, however, implies that you may get bored easily and find it hard to listen or communicate without rhetoric.

Preferring to keep active, you can be productive and resourceful. With a touch of the mad genius, you can have inspired and unique ideas. An exceptional thinker and good synthesizer of information, you enjoy learning and sharing your knowledge with others. When you are preoccupied with your own thoughts, however, your mental focus can be elsewhere, and you may appear absent-minded. Although you can usually be quite detached, sometimes a tendency to hold on to disappointments or frustration may undermine your positive plans and goals. Releasing the past enables you to live more happily in the present.

While you are between the ages of four and thirty-three, when your progressed Sun moves through Pisces, your emotional sensitivity increases, making you more imaginative, receptive, and emotionally aware of your social life. You may also become visionary or interested in developing creative talents. There is a turning point at age thirty-four, when your progressed Sun enters Aries. Your ambition and determination become apparent and you start to really come into your own. Another change of emphasis occurs at age sixty-four, when your progressed Sun enters Taurus, influencing you to be more practical, with a need for stability, security, and emotional steadiness.

FIXED STARS

Although your Sun's degree is not linked to a fixed star, some of your other planets' degrees certainly will be. By having an astrological chart calculated, you can find the exact position of the planets on your date of birth. This will tell you which of the fixed stars listed in this book are relevant to you.

Your Secret Self

With an innate practical sense, you can quickly assess the worth of an idea or project. This combines well with your natural psychological skills, and so you are also able to evaluate people's character or motivation, which often places you in a leading role. A need for material security can play an important role in decision making; just be careful that it does not undermine your soul growth. Fortunately, your zany sense of humor can help you keep it all in a balanced perspective.

By incorporating variety into your life, an inner restlessness or impatience can be channeled into dynamic change, adventure, travel, or physical exercise. You may have to make allowances for varying financial circumstances, which can leave you alternating between extravagance and thriftiness. Perseverance and long-term plans can help you avoid dissatisfaction with material limitations.

Work & Vocation

Independent and progressive, you can express yourself in writing or speech. With this gift, you may choose a career in education as a teacher or lecturer. Idealistic and outspoken, you are observant and articulate, with an eye for detail. This suggests that you may decide to use your analytical skills to review and correct others' work or have a job in the media as a journalist or reporter. Alternatively, your executive skills and business sense may draw you to the world of commerce or banking and the stock market. If, on the other hand, you want to explore your creativity, you may be inspired to participate in the world of sports, art, or show business. Humanitarian and dynamic, you can use your practical skills through charity work or causes that are concerned with political affairs and social reforms.

Famous people who share your birthday include tennis star John McEnroe, director John Schlesinger, singer/politician Sonny Bono, actor Levar Burton, and political scientist George Kennan.

Numerology

The number 16 birthday suggests that you are thoughtful, sensitive, and friendly. Although analytical, you often judge life and people according to how you feel. As a number 16 personality, however, you can experience inner tensions when facing friction between a need for self-expression and your responsibility to others. With this birthdate, you may be interested in world affairs and may join international corporations or the media world. The creative ones among you have a talent for writing with sudden flashes of inspiration. You may need to learn how to balance between being overly confident and being doubtful and insecure. The subinfluence of the number 2 month indicates that you seek inner harmony and are often intuitive and highly idealistic. As a humanitarian you can be caring and kind, willing to do your utmost for whatever cause you believe in. Although you can be sensitive to others, a tendency to be suspicious or moody suggests that sometimes you can shift back and forth from being generous and enthusiastic to being insecure and indecisive. You may need to overcome a tendency to be restless or impatient.

• *Positive:* higher education, responsibilities to home and family, integrity, intuitive, social, cooperative, insightful

• *Negative:* worry, never satisfied, irresponsible, self-promoting, opinionated, skeptical

Love & Relationships

You may be most fulfilled when enjoying the company of others. This may include socializing with mentally stimulating people or those with whom you share some joint interest. By avoiding a tendency to become overly serious or argumentative, you are able to stay detached and keep a balanced perspective. Intelligent and shrewd, you can create harmony and long-term satisfaction by bringing your natural psychological skills to your relationships.

YOUR SPECIAL SOMEONE

To keep you interested in a long-term relationship, you might want to look for those born on the following days.

Love & friendship: Jan. 6, 11, 16, Feb. 4, 14, Mar. 2, 12, 28, 30, Apr. 10, 26, 28, May 8, 24, 26, 30, June 1, 6, 22, 24, 28, July 4, 20, 22, 26, 31, Aug. 2, 18, 20, 24, 29, Sept. 16, 18, 22, 27, 28, Oct. 14, 16, 20, 25, Nov. 12, 14, 18, 23, Dec. 10, 12, 16, 21

Beneficial: Jan. 9, 14, 16, Feb. 7, 12, 14, Mar. 5, 10, 12, Apr. 3, 8, 10, May 1, 6, 8, June 4, 6, 12, July 2, 4, Aug. 2, Sept. 30, Oct. 4, 28, Nov. 26, 30, Dec. 24, 28, 29

Fatal attractions: Jan. 21, Feb. 19, Mar. 17, Apr. 15, May 13, June 11, July 9, Aug. 7, 19, 20, 21, 22, 23, Sept. 5, Oct. 3, Nov. 1

Challenging: Jan. 4, 13, 28, Feb. 2, 11, 26, Mar. 9, 24, Apr. 7, 22, May 5, 20, June 3, 18, July 1, 16, Aug. 14, Sept. 12, Oct. 10, 31, Nov. 8, 29, Dec. 6, 27

Soul mates: Jan. 15, 22, Feb. 13, 20, Mar. 11, 18, Apr. 9, 16, May 7, 14, June 5, 12, July 3, 10, Aug. 1, 8, Sept. 6, Oct. 4, Nov. 2

February 17

FIXED STARS

Although your Sun's degree is not linked to a fixed star, some of your other planets' degrees certainly will be. By having an astrological chart calculated, you can find the exact position of the planets on your date of birth. This will tell you which of the fixed stars listed in this book are relevant to you.

 Your Aquarius birthday shows you to be strong-willed and determined, a practical individualist with an active mind. Ambitious and persistent, you have a strong presence and good organizational skills that point to a desire for continual improvement, both materially and socially. Active and productive, you enjoy power, so you may need to continually challenge yourself. Although you possess a natural ability to take the lead, you may benefit from developing your patience in order to avoid being too domineering. Fortunately, you possess the capacity to overcome obstacles and perform outstanding achievements.

With the added influence of your Sun in the decanate of Libra, you can be sociable and amusing, with a sense of artistic or creative appreciation. You are particularly likely to gain from female acquaintances and have a warm circle of friends. With the ability to be charming in your dealings with others when necessary, you can mix business with pleasure.

With your inventive or analytical mind, you can often create original or financially lucrative concepts. A setback to your possible achievements, however, may be an obstinate or rebellious attitude. If left unchecked, this may cause self-destructive behavior.

Up to the age of thirty-two, when your progressed Sun moves through Pisces, you develop a stronger inner life and your emotional sensitivity becomes enhanced. This can be reflected in your visions, dreams, and ideals as well as in your social life. At the age of thirty-three, there is a turning point as your progressed Sun enters Aries, emphasizing a need to actively take the initiative, pioneer ideas, or be brave and direct in your relationships with others. Another change of emphasis occurs at age sixty-three, when your progressed Sun enters Taurus, highlighting a greater need for stability and a practical approach to life.

Your Secret Self

Hardworking, you have endurance, stamina, and courage. Being proud and dramatic, you may have to refrain from occasionally being patronizing or, if tense, becoming irritable. Through developing self-mastery, you gain a deep sense of satisfaction and are able to help others with your direct, down-to-earth common sense and through lessons learned from personal experience.

Enjoying mental competition, you can be as quick as lightning with your comments. When you establish your inner faith, you can be daring enough to be spontaneous and follow your spirit. This can help you overcome a tendency to be skeptical or doubting. When your love of knowledge and quick insight are combined with your natural business acumen, you have the power to achieve remarkable results in life.

Work & Vocation

Hardworking, creative, and independent, you have unique talents and executive skills. Possessing good reasoning powers, you like to investigate issues and get to the bottom of things. You can be drawn to a career as a detective or work as a lawyer. Practical, you may use your organizational ability to administer large businesses. Alternatively, with your talent for putting your thoughts on paper and your imaginative mind, you can turn to writing and education or training people in technical skills. Since you value your independence, and do not like to take orders, you usually prefer to be in positions of authority; you can be an excellent manager or supervisor.

Famous people who share your birthday include basketball player Michael Jordan, black rights activist Huey Newton, authors Ruth Rendell and Isabelle Eberhardt, female impersonator Barry Humphries, and actor Alan Bates.

Numerology

With a number 17 birthday, you are shrewd, with a reserved nature, good analytical abilities, and writing skills. Inquisitive and original, you are an independent thinker who benefits from being well educated or skillful. Usually you utilize your knowledge in a specific way in order to develop your expertise and can achieve material success or a prominent position as a specialist or researcher. Private, introspective, and detached, with a strong interest in facts and figures, you frequently present a serious and thoughtful demeanor and like to take your time. By developing your communication skills, you can discover much about yourself from others. The subinfluence of the number 2 month indicates that you are receptive and intuitive. Although you can be friendly and sociable, your independent nature suggests that you have original thoughts and a unique perspective. If you lack faith or insight into your higher self, you may feel doubtful or indecisive. As a humanitarian, you are universal and progressive, willing to work for social reforms and just causes.

• *Positive:* thoughtful, specialist, good planner, good business sense, attracts money, individual thinker, painstaking, accurate, skilled researcher, scientific

• *Negative:* detached, stubborn, carelessness, moody, narrow-minded, critical, worry, suspicion

Love & Relationships

Sociable and bright, you enjoy the company of interesting or unusual people and can easily mix with different groups of people. At times, however, you can be indecisive or uncertain about your love and long-term commitments. Often attracted to powerful yet creative individuals, your need for love, intimacy, and understanding is contrary to your strong and self-assured image. When in love, you may need to avoid martyring yourself or being temperamental. You like to have your own way, but you can be loyal and caring.

YOUR SPECIAL SOMEONE

You might find a partner who will understand your sensitivity and need for love among those born on the following dates.

Love & friendship: Jan. 7, 17, 20, 21, Feb. 5, 15, 18, Mar. 3, 13, 16, 29, 31, Apr. 1, 11, 14, 15, 27, 29, May 9, 12, 25, 27, June 7, 10, 11, 23, 25, July 5, 8, 21, 23, Aug. 3, 6, 19, 21, Sept. 1, 4, 17, 19, Oct. 2, 3, 15, 17, Nov. 13, 15, 30, Dec. 11, 13, 28

Beneficial: Jan. 15, 17, 24, 28, Feb. 13, 15, 22, 26, Mar. 11, 13, 24, Apr. 9, 11, 22, May 7, 9, 20, June 5, 7, 14, 18, July 3, 5, 16, Aug. 1, 3, 14, Sept. 1, 12, Oct. 6, 10, 29, Nov. 8, 27, Dec. 6, 25

Fatal attractions: Jan. 5, Feb. 3, Mar. 1, Aug. 21, 22, 23

Challenging: Jan. 4, 5, 14, Feb. 2, 3, 12, Mar. 1, 10, Apr. 8, 30, May 6, 28, June 4, 26, July 2, 24, Aug. 22, Sept. 20, Oct. 18, Nov. 16, Dec. 14

Soul mates: Jan. 2, Mar. 29, Apr. 27, May 25, June 23, July 21, Aug. 19, Sept. 17, Oct. 15, Nov. 13, Dec. 11

February 18

FIXED STARS

Although your Sun's degree is not linked to a fixed star, some of your other planets' degrees certainly will be. By having an astrological chart calculated, you can find the exact position of the planets on your date of birth. This will tell you which of the fixed stars listed in this book are relevant to you.

 Dynamic, persuasive, and a strong individualist, you are an interesting mixture of material drive and humanitarian ideals. Sociable and charming, yet reserved, you enjoy power and initiating new projects. One of your main challenges may be to keep a balance between your work and your intimate relationships.

With the added influence of your Sun in the Libra decanate, you have a feel for beauty and the arts and an appreciation of aesthetics. Being naturally dramatic, you have unique ideas that may find expression through music, writing, or drama. Although independent, you place a high worth on your relationships, and you recognize the advantages of working in partnerships or in a team. Interested in people, you like to take a leading role but may have to avoid being too critical or controlling.

You can be vulnerable yet tough, and others may find your blend of love and discipline hard to understand. Financial matters are likely to occupy much of your attention, but with your shrewd business sense and determination, you have the potential to market your talents. Resolute and dedicated when you have a goal, you like to create something original. When you have faith, you usually find that everything just flows spontaneously into place. When you doubt, however, you may hold on to the past and lose your sense of timing. You often have the fortunate ability to see self-discipline as a positive investment rather than as a denial.

Up to the age of thirty-one, when your progressed Sun moves through Pisces, you develop a stronger sense of vision and your emotional sensitivity becomes emphasized. This may encourage you to seek idealistic, artistic, or spiritual goals. After the age of thirty-two, when your progressed Sun moves into Aries, you have a need to be more assertive, active, and directive in your daily affairs, possibly pioneering new ventures. At the age of sixty-two there is another turning point as your progressed Sun enters Taurus, accenting a need for more practical stability and security.

Your Secret Self

On an inner level, you are extremely sensitive, especially to the expression of love and feelings. You may have encountered difficulties growing up concerning the display of emotion. At times this may have caused you to become skeptical or withdrawn. When you trust others enough to open your heart wide, you can be extremely generous and compassionate. This universal feeling may even stimulate an interest in mystical or spiritual experience. By learning to let go and take life as it comes, you become more detached, seeing life with the aid of a dry sense of humor.

As you have deep feelings and a humanitarian spirit, this may encourage you to fight strongly for an ideal or a cause. Highly intuitive, you often work best when you trust your own instincts and go by first impressions.

Work & Vocation

Hardworking and dutiful, you are willing to make sacrifices, but you need to keep a healthy balance between duty and time for relaxation and recreational pursuits. Being independent, you want to have enough freedom to express your original thoughts. You blossom with encouragement and positive feedback from those you work with. Usually idealistic and charming, you enjoy working with the public and are highly supportive of social reforms. Intuitive and intelligent, with a talent for business, you are also suited for a career in administration, where you can use your critical and analytical skills to advise others. Friendly and diplomatic, you have a flair for combining business and pleasure. You may need to make sure, however, that you do not take others too seriously by taking offense.

Famous people who share your birthday include artist Yoko Ono, actors John Travolta and Matt Dillon, actress Cybill Shepherd, violinist Niccolò Paganini, guitarist Andrés Segovia, mystic Ramakrishna, magazine publisher Helen Gurley Brown, and writer Toni Morrison.

Numerology

Determination, assertiveness, and ambition are some of the attributes associated with the number 18 birthday. Active, with a need for challenges, you like to keep busy and are frequently involved in some enterprise. Capable, hardworking, and responsible, you rise to positions of authority. Alternatively, your strong business sense and organizational skills lead you to the world of commerce. Since you may suffer from overwork, learn how to relax or slow down from time to time. As a number 18 personality, you may use your power to heal others, give sound advice, or solve other people's problems. The subinfluence of the number 2 month indicates that you are intuitive and creative, with inspirational and original thoughts. Although you are receptive and friendly, a dislike for restriction and responsibilities implies that you do not want to be tied down by a routine. Although you are idealistic, with good practical skills and original ideas, you need to learn to stay balanced in order to achieve inner peace and tranquility.

• *Positive:* progressive, assertive, intuitive, courageous, resolute, healing ability, efficient, advisory skills

• *Negative:* uncontrolled emotions, lazy, lack of order, selfishness, failure to complete work or projects

Love & Relationships

Intuitive and sensitive, you need the freedom to express your deep feelings. Friendly and clever, you enjoy the company of creative people who know how to enjoy themselves. Usually you want meaningful or serious relationships and are loyal and loving. When in a spontaneous mood, you like to follow your heart and do things with your partners or friends on the spur of the moment. In relationships, however, your willingness to make sacrifices for those you love implies a need to exercise some discrimination. Friendship is an important element of your partnerships.

SUN: AQUARIUS/PISCES CUSP

DECANATE: LIBRA/VENUS

DEGREE: 29°30' AQUARIUS–

0°30' PISCES

MODE: FIXED/MUTABLE

ELEMENT: AIR/WATER

FIXED STARS

Fom Al Haut, Sad Al Melik

PRIMARY STAR

Star's name: Fom Al Haut

Degree position: 2°51'–3°51' Pisces between the years 1930 and 2000

Magnitude: 1

Strength: ★★★★★★★★★

Orb: 2°30'

Constellation: Alpha Piscis Australis

Applicable days: February 19, 20, 21, 22, 23, 24, 25

Star qualities: Venus/Mercury

Description: a reddish white star located in the mouth of the southern Fish

---

PRIMARY STAR'S INFLUENCE

Fom Al Haut is one of the four royal stars and marks the winter solstice. Fom Al Haut is an especially powerful star and thus bestows good fortune, success, and a keen mentality. This star may also indicate a need to change from a material view to a more spiritual one.

Linked to your Sun's degree, this star imparts good rhythm, receptivity, and a tendency to go with the current. Easily influenced by your environment, you are self-seeking and may need to find creative self-expression. This star also suggests that legacies and inheritance can be expected, but warns against squandering or spending them quickly.

 Being born on the cusp of Aquarius and Pisces, you have the advantage of being mentally inventive, sensitive, and idealistic. Direct and frank in your communication, you prefer to be honest in your relationships with others. Friendly, warm, and outgoing, you have a gift for dealing with people. You may have to overcome a tendency to be irritable or stubborn, however, that can spoil your charismatic appeal and separate you from others.

With the added influence of your Sun between the Libra and Pisces decanates, you can be romantic, creative, and visionary, with an intuitive intellect. Gregarious, you need people and are likely to have an active social life. Image and status can be important to you, so you usually present yourself to others in a dignified way. Nevertheless, you also have a more unusual or eccentric side to your nature that can be reflected in your original and unique ideas, which are often ahead of their time.

With an innate business sense, you can be fortunate to see opportunities. A tendency to become discouraged or get stuck in a rut may sometimes deter you from putting in the hard work, perseverance, and determination needed to achieve your objectives. When positive and optimistic, however, you are capable of inspired thinking and determination. With your sense of justice and compassion, you have strong convictions and will often stand up for your ideals or fight for others.

Until you reach the age of thirty, when your progressed Sun moves through Pisces, your emotional sensitivity is enhanced, making you imaginative, receptive, and aware of your social peer group. You may become visionary or interested in developing creative or spiritual talents. There is a turning point at age thirty-one, when your progressed Sun enters Aries. Your ambition and determination become more apparent and you begin to really come into your own. You may be involved in starting new projects or pioneering new ideas. Another change of emphasis occurs at age sixty-one, when your progressed Sun enters Taurus, highlighting a greater need for financial stability, security, and emotional steadiness.

Your Secret Self

With an inner desire for self-expression, you may become attracted to writing, art, music, or drama, whether professionally or for relaxation. Taking a light and creative approach to problem solving helps you avoid worry and indecision. Advantages and opportunities can come from unexpected sources and may appear fairly minor, but they should not be ignored, as they may often turn out to be significant to you later.

Broad-minded and humanitarian, you can view life with a universal perspective. At times, however, you may experience an unconscious discontent that comes from disappointment with your situation or with others. When you feel this frustration, avoid the temptation to give up too quickly or take the easy way out. By developing mental detachment and perseverance, you can gain confidence and achieve outstanding success.

Work & Vocation

Your charismatic personality and flair for people suggest that you enjoy working with the public. Persuasive and conscious of your image, you can work in sales and promotion or advertising. Alternatively, you may want to express yourself through design and fashion or acting, dancing, or singing. Witty, with a good sense of humor, you can be entertaining and might run a club successfully. Since you like to meet as many people as possible, you can fare better in large organizations, where you can hope to advance and rise to the top of your profession. In order to achieve, however, you need to work hard, finish what you have started, and not leave everything to the eleventh hour.

Famous people who share your birthday include astronomer Nicholas Copernicus, singer Smokey Robinson, writer Amy Tan, actress Merle Oberon, actor Lee Marvin, British royal family member Prince Andrew, and supermodel Cindy Crawford.

Numerology

Sunny, ambitious, and humanitarian are some of the ways others would describe people with the number 19 birthday. Decisive and resourceful, you possess depth of vision, but the dreamer side of your nature is compassionate, idealistic, and creative. Although you are sensitive, the need to be someone may be the very thing that pushes you to be dramatic and claim center stage. Often there is a strong desire to establish an individual identity. To do so, you may first need to overcome the influence of peer group pressure. To others, you may appear confident, resilient, and resourceful, but inner tensions may cause emotional ups and downs. The subinfluence of the number 2 month indicates that you are receptive and intuitive, with a dramatic personality. You thrive on encouragement and are susceptible to your environment. As a courteous and romantic individual, you are considerate and sensitive to other people's feelings. Although you are friendly and sociable, with a flair for people, at times your moody and restless nature exposes your vulnerability. Although you can be adaptable, do not let others influence your decision making.

• *Positive:* dynamic, centered, creative, leader, lucky, progressive, optimistic, strong convictions, competitive, independent, gregarious, disciplined

• *Negative:* self-centered, worry, fear of rejection, ups and downs, materialistic, egotistical, impatient

Love & Relationships

Fun-loving and gregarious, you are often popular and have no problem attracting admirers. It may be necessary to develop strong discrimination, however, to avoid giving your heart to those who are undeserving of your warmth and devotion. Caring, sympathetic, and appearing confident, you may find that people turn to you for advice or support, but as it is not always reciprocal, you may need to learn whom to let into your close circle of friends. Generous and giving to those you love, you have an open and winning charm that can prove to be a valuable asset in your relationships.

YOUR SPECIAL SOMEONE

Success in love and friendship is more likely with those born on the following dates.

Love & friendship: Jan. 5, 9, 18, 19, 23, Feb. 3, 7, 16, 17, 21, Mar. 1, 5, 14, 15, 31, Apr. 3, 12, 13, 29, May 1, 10, 11, 27, 29, June 4, 8, 9, 25, 27, July 6, 7, 23, 25, 31, Aug. 4, 5, 21, 23, 29, Sept. 2, 3, 19, 21, 27, 30, Oct. 1, 17, 19, 25, 28, Dec. 13, 15, 21, 24

Beneficial: Jan. 1, 6, 17, Feb. 4, 15, Mar. 2, 13, Apr. 11, May 9, June 7, July 5, Aug. 3, Sept. 1, Oct. 31, Nov. 29, Dec. 27

Fatal attractions: Aug. 22, 23, 24, 25

Challenging: Jan. 2, 16, Feb. 14, Mar. 12, Apr. 10, May 8, June 6, July 4, Aug. 2, Dec. 30

Soul mates: Jan. 11, 31, Feb. 9, 29, Mar. 7, 27, Apr. 5, 25, May 3, 23, June 1, 21, July 19, Aug. 17, Sept. 15, Oct. 13, Nov. 11, Dec. 9

Pisces

February 20–March 20

February 20

H Charming and socially inclined, you are a receptive Piscean with a friendly personality. As an easygoing person with a sensitive nature, you have a flair for dealing with people from all walks of life. Although creative and versatile, you may have difficulty deciding exactly what your aims are. Quietly ambitious and determined, however, you are willing to make the necessary changes and are likely to travel far in order to find your true identity.

The added influence of your Sun in the decanate of Pisces brings intuition to your visionary and imaginative mind as well as depth to your idealistic nature. By learning to trust your premonitions, you come to know your strengths and failings as well as those of others. Your youthful and positive outlook is your true asset, and with determination and hard work you can overcome the obstacles in your path. Although you are adaptable and can fit easily into new circumstances, a dislike of routine and a restless spirit imply that you can too easily become dissatisfied with your current situation.

By realizing that periods of progress and advancement in your life are often followed by periods of recession, you can keep financial circumstances steady through long-term investment rather than immediate compensation. As success and rewards usually come through perseverance and sticking firmly to your principles, you may need to learn that impatience often has the reverse effect, causing you worry or insecurity.

Aware of image and with a strong sense of vision, you often have many creative ideas. Inspired by example, you are often stimulated to search for idealistic situations that can provide you with mental stimulation and variety.

Until you reach the age of twenty-nine, your progressed Sun moves through Pisces, accenting your sensitivity and feelings. You may find yourself searching for an ideal situation or relationship or just something more magical in your life. From the age of thirty, when your progressed Sun moves into Aries, you start to become more confident, assertive, and ambitious. You are likely to start new ventures or take the initiative in your dealings with others. At the age of sixty there is another turning point as your Sun enters Taurus. After this time, you slow down and have a practical need for more stability and financial security in your life.

Your Secret Self

Mentally quick and bright, you usually possess many talents, so you need to be decisive and practical to avoid confusion and achieve your objectives. Once set on a course of action, however, you can be very determined and single-minded.

Being a natural psychologist, you possess a quick insight into people and a desire to learn. Sociable and smart, you usually enjoy an active life and can be friendly, witty, and charming. At times, however, you may be prone to frustration with your financial situation, and this can cause you to have outbursts of extravagance. By developing a universal and humanitarian perspective, you become more detached and relaxed about your material circumstances. With your natural foresight, you often work better when you intuitively get a feel for a situation before making things happen. By keeping focused and developing your self-awareness, you have more realistic goals and can overcome restraints to realize your remarkable potential.

Work & Vocation

Although you are hardworking, your ambition suggests you need a career that can offer prospects for progress. With your quick intellect, you usually want an active life that includes

---

FIXED STARS

Fom Al Haut; Sad Al Melik

PRIMARY STAR

Star's name: Fom Al Haut

Degree position: 2°51'–3°51' Pisces between the years 1930 and 2000

Magnitude: 1

Strength: ★★★★★★★★

Orb: 2°30'

Constellation: Alpha Piscis Australis

Applicable days: February 19, 20, 21, 22, 23, 24, 25

Star qualities: Venus/Mercury

Description: a reddish white star located in the mouth of the southern Fish

PRIMARY STAR'S INFLUENCE

Fom Al Haut is one of the four royal stars and marks the winter solstice. Fom Al Haut is an especially powerful star and thus bestows good fortune, success, and a keen mentality. This star may also indicate a need to change from a material view to a more spiritual one.

Linked to your Sun's degree, this star imparts good rhythm, receptivity, and a tendency to go with the current. Easily influenced by your environment, you are self-seeking and may need to find creative self-expression. This star also suggests that legacies and inheritance can be expected but warns against squandering or spending them quickly.

• *Positive:* learn to budget, idealistic, imaginative, creative

change and travel. As you are a sensitive person, a congenial atmosphere at work is a must. If you do not get along with your boss or fellow employees, you are likely to abandon the job and look elsewhere. Being versatile, you can quickly learn new skills and adapt to situations. An eye for form and color indicates an interest in art and design. Equally, your sense of rhythm or sensitivity can attract you to music and dancing or health and healing work. Sociable, with an easygoing personality, you can also succeed in all kinds of public relations occupations. Alternatively, a career in sports may inspire you to compete or teach. Usually you need a job that does not involve mundane routine and challenges your imagination.

Famous people who share your birthday include actors Kelsey Grammer and Sidney Poitier, society figure Ivana Trump, singers Kurt Cobain and Buffy Sainte-Marie, photographer Ansel Adams, and director Robert Altman.

Numerology

With a number 20 birthday, you are intuitive, sensitive, and understanding, and often see yourself as a part of a larger group. Usually you enjoy cooperative activities where you can interact, share experiences, or learn from others. Charming and gracious, you develop diplomatic and people skills and can move in different social circles with ease. You may, however, need to develop your confidence to overcome a tendency to be easily hurt by the actions and criticism of others or be overdependent. You are a master at creating a congenial and harmonious atmosphere. The subinfluence of the number 2 month indicates that you are adaptable and practical. A need for stability is emphasized if you lack a methodology. Sensitivity to your environment and a love of harmony may inspire you to act as a mediator or a peacemaker. By developing patience and learning to trust your instincts, you overcome self-doubts and build a more assertive personality.

• *Positive:* considerate, good partner, gentle, tactful, receptive, intuitive, harmonious, agreeable, ambassador of goodwill

• *Negative:* suspicious, lack of confidence, oversensitive, emotional, selfish, easily hurt

Love & Relationships

Friendly and sociable, you often work for peace and harmony in relationships. Friendships are important to you, and you usually mix with people who can stimulate your mind as well as help you have a good time. Frequently a natural entertainer, you can be witty and make others laugh, especially when in the company of those you love. Although you may settle down with one person, a need for change and variety may inspire you to travel or extend your social group.

YOUR SPECIAL SOMEONE

For security, mental stimulation, and love, you might want to begin looking among those born on the following dates.

Love & friendship: Jan. 6, 10, 20, 24, 29, Feb. 4, 8, 18, 27, Mar. 2, 6, 16, 25, 28, 30, Apr. 4, 14, 23, 26, 28, 30, May 2, 12, 21, 24, 26, 28, 30, June 10, 19, 22, 24, 26, 28, July 8, 12, 17, 20, 22, 24, 26, Aug. 6, 15, 18, 20, 22, 24, Sept. 4, 13, 16, 18, 20, 22, Oct. 2, 11, 14, 16, 18, 20, Nov. 4, 9, 12, 14, 16, 18, Dec. 7, 10, 12, 14, 16

Beneficial: Jan. 7, 13, 18, 28, Feb. 5, 11, 16, 26, Mar. 3, 9, 14, 24, Apr. 1, 7, 12, 22, May 5, 10, 20, June 3, 8, 18, July 1, 6, 16, Aug. 4, 14, Sept. 2, 12, 30, Oct. 10, 28, Nov. 8, 26, 30, Dec. 6, 24, 28

Fatal attractions: Jan. 25, Feb. 23, Mar. 21, Apr. 19, May 17, June 15, July 13, Aug. 11, 23, 24, 25, 26, Sept. 9, Oct. 7, Nov. 5, Dec. 3

Challenging: Jan. 3, 17, Feb. 1, 15, Mar. 13, Apr. 11, May 9, 30, June 7, 28, July 5, 26, 29, Aug. 3, 24, 27, Sept. 1, 22, 25, Oct. 20, 23, Nov. 18, 21, Dec. 16, 19

Soul mates: Jan. 18, Feb. 16, Mar. 14, Apr. 12, May 10, 29, June 8, 27, July 6, 25, Aug. 4, 23, Sept. 2, 21, Oct. 19, Nov. 17, Dec. 15

SUN: PISCES

DECANATE: PISCES/NEPTUNE

DEGREE: 1°30'–2°30' PISCES

MODE: MUTABLE

ELEMENT: WATER

FIXED STARS

Fom Al Haut; Sad Al Melik

PRIMARY STAR

Star's name: Fom Al Haut

Degree position: 2°51'–3°51' Pisces
   between the years 1930 and
   2000

Magnitude: 1

Strength: ★★★★★★★★

Orb: 2°30'

Constellation: Alpha Piscis Australis

Applicable days: February 19, 20, 21, 22,
   23, 24, 25

Star qualities: Venus/Mercury

Description: a reddish white star located
   in the mouth of the southern Fish

PRIMARY STAR'S INFLUENCE

Fom Al Haut is one of the four royal stars and marks the winter solstice. Fom Al Haut is an especially powerful star and thus bestows good fortune, success, and a keen mentality. This star may also indicate a need to change from a material view to a more spiritual expression.

Linked to your Sun's degree, this star imparts good rhythm, receptivity, and a tendency to go with the current. Easily influenced by your environment, you are self-seeking and may need to find creative self-expression. This star also suggests that legacies and inheritance can be expected but warns against squandering or spending them quickly.

• *Positive:* learn to budget, idealistic, imaginative, creative

February 21

Practical yet imaginative, you are a sensitive Piscean with a strong need for self-expression. As a versatile and creative individual, you are impressionable and enthusiastic when captivated by a person or an idea. Having a sensible outlook, you are often concerned with building a secure foundation for yourself. Restrictions or a tedious routine can, however, unsettle your mutable nature. Although you do not like to be pinned down, when necessary you can exhibit how adaptable and methodical you really are.

The added influence of your Sun in the decanate of Pisces adds intuition to your receptivity, and with your mediumistic powers, you easily pick up on currents and trends. Rhythmic, you have an ear for music and a possible talent for dancing. If you lack direction, you can be influenced by peer group pressure; rather than stand alone, you will go with the flow or choose escapism as an easy way out.

Although you are often lucky financially, a strong emphasis on work implies that through diligent and concerted efforts you often establish a safeguarded and prosperous position. Generally loyal and businesslike, you tend to take your responsibilities seriously. When you carry out your duties, you like to do them well and have a sense of pride in your work.

Until you reach the age of twenty-eight your progressed Sun moves through Pisces, placing the emphasis on your emotional development, dreams for the future, and sensitivity. While you are between the ages of twenty-nine and fifty-eight your progressed Sun moves through Aries. This influence suggests that you develop your assertiveness and enjoy being active and adventurous. After the age of fifty-nine, when your progressed Sun moves into Taurus, you may become calmer and more steady, with a possible stronger interest in nature. There is also an increased need to be established and feel secure.

Your Secret Self

Although you can be pragmatic, with a desire for stability and security, you may need to apply concentrated efforts to overcome an inner impatience. If this restlessness gets out of hand, you may become prone to escapism or vacillating moods. However, when your fertile imagination is channeled creatively into practical activities, you can be most productive.

Possessing an inner charm, you can project a warm heart. A desire for action, freedom, and adventure suggests that you can have a varied and eventful life. It is important to enjoy and live in the present, as you may have a tendency to believe that satisfaction is always just around the corner. With your high ideals and visionary sense, you may express your dreams and longing for love through creative pursuits or helping others. Alternatively, having a sense of duty and being a perfectionist, you may prefer to direct attention to taking pride in your work.

Work & Vocation

Although you have a pragmatic approach and good common sense, you do not like to be limited or restricted by routine and monotony. Sensitive and imaginative, you are both inspirational and practical. Although you want order, you may have difficulties finding out exactly what you want to achieve, and so you may try out various alternatives. If you are in business, your organizational skills can help you to achieve good results. Fortunately, you have fine opportunities as long as you are willing to work hard for your success. Sociable and outgoing, you can excel in all kinds of public relations careers, particularly in the music industry, fashion, and the art and design world. A good sense of rhythm suggests that you can also succeed in music or dance. Dexterous, you may be interested in making or building things with your hands.

Famous people who share your birthday include singer Nina Simone, fashion designer Hubert de Givenchy, Russian statesman Alexei Kosygin, writer Anaïs Nin, poet W. H. Auden, and director Sam Peckinpah.

Numerology

Dynamic drive and an outgoing personality are usually present in those with a number 21 birthday. Socially inclined, you have many interests and contacts and are generally fortunate. Usually you show others your friendly and gregarious personality. Intuitive, with an independent spirit, you are highly inventive and original. As a number 21 individual, you can be fun-loving and magnetic, with social charm. Alternatively, you can be shy and reserved, with a need to develop assertiveness, especially in close relationships. Although you can be inclined toward cooperative relationships or marriage, you always want to be acknowledged for your talents and abilities. The subinfluence of the number 2 month indicates that although strong-willed or stubborn, you are receptive and influenced by your environment or peer group. If self-doubting, you may scatter your energies in different directions, making you unable to take full advantage of the great opportunities that are in store for you. A need for activity suggests that you have to find ways to express yourself. Finding a stabilizing yet exciting occupation may inspire you spiritually and emotionally.

• *Positive:* inspiration, creativity, love unions, long-lasting relationships
• *Negative:* dependency, loss of emotional control, lack of vision, disappointment, fear of change

Love & Relationships

Sociable and friendly, you thrive on sociable activities and friendly gatherings. Powerful emotions and a sensitive heart suggest that you have a great deal of love to give. If your strong feelings are not channeled, however, you may be subject to moods or liable to sulk. You may have to learn to take your time in order to make sure you know exactly whom you want to be with. Beware of either becoming involved in a rescuer role by taking on someone you feel needs help, or falling into a victim role yourself. To find happiness you may need someone who is exciting and generous. but can provide you with the stability you need.

YOUR SPECIAL SOMEONE

You might start to look for a fun-loving partner who can understand the power of your love among those born on the following dates.

Love & friendship: Jan. 7, 11, 16, 22, Feb. 5, 9, 20, Mar. 3, 7, 18, 31, Apr. 1, 5, 16, 29, May 3, 14, 16, 27, 29, June 1, 6, 12, 25, 27, July 4, 10, 13, 23, 25, Aug. 8, 21, 23, 31, Sept. 6, 19, 21, 29, Oct. 4, 17, 19, 27, 30, Nov. 2, 5, 15, 17, 25, 28, Dec. 13, 15, 23, 26

Beneficial: Jan. 8, 14, 19, Feb. 6, 12, 17, Mar. 4, 10, 15, Apr. 2, 8, 13, May 6, 11, June 4, 9, 28, July 2, 7, Aug. 5, Sept. 3, Oct. 1, 29, Nov. 18, 27, Dec. 25, 29

Fatal attractions: Aug. 24, 25, 26, 27

Challenging: Jan. 9, 18, 20, Feb. 7, 16, 18, Mar. 5, 14, 16, Apr. 3, 12, 14, May 1, 10, 12, June 8, 10, July 6, 8, 29, Aug. 4, 6, 27, Sept. 2, 4, 25, Oct. 2, 23, Nov. 21, Dec. 19

Soul mates: Jan. 9, Feb. 7, Mar. 5, Apr. 3, May 1, Oct. 30, Nov. 28, Dec. 26

February 22

H Your birthday reveals you to be a highly intuitive, adaptable Piscean with a unique perspective on life. Imaginative and receptive, you display a creative approach to problem solving that suggests you are a pragmatist who can experience inspirational moments of pure genius.

The added influence of your Sun in the decanate of Pisces strengthens your sensitivity and psychic awareness, indicating that you pick up on the different moods around you as well as social currents and trends. Although you are contemplative, your ideas can be ahead of their time and sometimes at odds with others'. If you lack direction, you can be influenced by peer group pressures and rather than stand alone, you go with the flow or choose escapism as an easy way out.

Although you may sometimes appear evasive or unpredictable, your quick wit and creative talents make you very attractive to others. As a versatile individual, you have many interests and some unusual hobbies. If you are unable to express yourself, you may succumb to worry or, if indecisive, may scatter your energies. Although you are able to maintain a cheerful and friendly perspective, a more serious side to your personality usually appears when financial issues are discussed.

Until you reach the age of twenty-seven your progressed Sun moves through Pisces, placing emphasis on your sensitivity and emotional interactions with others. While you are between the ages of twenty-eight to fifty-seven your progressed Sun moves through Aries. This influence suggests that you will enter a new phase by becoming more determined and spirited, and this may result in a strong desire for new ventures. After the age of fifty-eight, when your progressed Sun moves into Taurus, your need to be established and feel secure will increase, coupled with a wish for more calm and emotional steadiness.

Your Secret Self

Responsible and home-loving, you need to find peace within yourself. Often willing to make sacrifices to help those close to you, you have deep love and affection but are seldom swept off your feet by emotion. If you become overly responsible and take on problems that are not yours, it may cause you to be prone to anxiety. Your high ideals and desire for harmony may inspire you to express yourself, whether socially, in creative pursuits, or by fighting for a cause.

With a natural business sense and the ability to lead, you are seldom in a lowly position. Observant and perceptive, you have a good sense of values and are often resourceful. Although you can impress others with your bargaining and evaluation skills, be careful not to compromise your ideals just for security. Proud and dramatic, you are quick to learn, and can soon turn your interests and creative endeavors into successful commercial enterprises.

Work & Vocation

Creative and intelligent, you possess a good mind, strong imagination, and good organizational skills. Friendly and naturally diplomatic, you can win favor in people-related occupations. Your good communication skills suggest success through writing or a career that

---

FIXED STARS

Fom Al Haut; Sad Al Melik; Deneb Adige, also called Al Dhanab

PRIMARY STAR

Star's name: Fom Al Haut

Degree position: 2°51'–3°51' Pisces between the years 1930 and 2000

Magnitude: 1

Strength: ★★★★★★★★

Orb: 2°30'

Constellation: Alpha Piscis Australis

Applicable days: February 19, 20, 21, 22, 23, 24, 25

Star qualities: Venus/Mercury

Description: a reddish white star located in the mouth of the southern Fish

PRIMARY STAR'S INFLUENCE

Fom Al Haut is one of the four royal stars and marks the winter solstice. Fom Al Haut is an especially powerful star and thus bestows good fortune, success, and a keen mentality. This star may also indicate a need to change from a material view to a more spiritual one.

Linked to your Sun's degree, this star imparts good rhythm, receptivity, and a tendency to go with the current. Easily influenced by your environment, you are self-seeking and may need to find creative self-expression. This star also suggests that legacies and inheritance can be expected but warns against squandering or spending them quickly.

• Positive: learn to budget, idealistic, imaginative, creative

involves public relations. Although very sensitive, you also possess a natural business sense that can help you succeed in commerce. As you usually work best when inspired, you may need to constantly reevaluate your work to keep your interest alive. A side to your nature that is interested in philosophy or helping others may attract you to the clergy, social reform, politics, or the world of health. Alternatively, being rhythmic suggests that you may have an ear for music or a talent for dancing. A strong desire for self-expression can bring you success in music and the theater.

Famous people who share your birthday include actress Drew Barrymore, racing driver Niki Lauda, film director Luis Buñuel, actor Kyle MacLachlan, Boy Scouts founder Robert Baden-Powell, composer Frederic Chopin, U.S. senator Edward Kennedy, U.S. president George Washington, and basketball player Julius Erving.

Numerology

As a number 22 individual, you are a proud, practical, and highly intuitive person. Since this is a master number, it can vibrate both as number 22 and as number 4. Often honest and hardworking, with natural leadership abilities, you have a charismatic personality and a deep understanding of people. Although undemonstrative, you can show a caring and protective concern for the welfare of others. The subinfluence of the number 2 month indicates that although you are a perfectionist and a humanitarian, you need to have realistic aims and objectives. Do not martyr yourself to those who are not worthy of your kindness. The subinfluence of the number 2 month indicates that you build a protective wall around yourself if you feel indecisive or vulnerable. Avoid overreacting or being critical if you want to get along better with those you love. A love of harmony and desire for inner peace suggest that you are by nature compassionate and idealistic.

• *Positive:* universal, director, highly intuitive, pragmatic, practical, good with your hands, skillful, builder, good organizer, realist, problem solver, achiever

• *Negative:* get-rich-quick schemes, nervous, bossy, materialistic, lack of vision, lazy, egotistical

Love & Relationships

If too idealistic, you may hold on to high notions about love, so it can be difficult for loved ones to live up to your expectations. Sympathetic and kind, you will make sacrifices for those you love. Although you can be spontaneous and giving, there is a danger that, if too preoccupied with your own needs, you may on occasion come across as cold or detached. It is therefore important to stay balanced and appear positive rather than overreact. Creative and versatile, you enjoy socializing and have a talent for mixing work with pleasure. You can be loyal and supportive to your friends and partners.

YOUR SPECIAL SOMEONE

You might just find the inspiring partner you are looking for among those born on the following dates.

Love & friendship: Jan. 4, 8, 22, 26, Feb. 6, 20, 24, Mar. 4, 18, 22, Apr. 2, 16, 20, 30, May 14, 18, 28, 30, June 12, 16, 26, 28, 29, July 10, 14, 24, 26, Aug. 8, 12, 22, 24, Sept. 6, 10, 20, 22, 30, Oct. 4, 8, 18, 20, 21, 28, Nov. 2, 6, 16, 18, 26, Dec. 4, 14, 16, 24

Beneficial: Jan. 9, 20, Feb. 7, 18, Mar. 5, 16, 29, Apr. 3, 14, 27, May 1, 12, 25, June 10, 23, July 8, 21, Aug. 6, 19, Sept. 4, 17, Oct. 2, 15, 30, Nov. 13, 28, Dec. 11, 26, 30

Fatal attractions: Jan. 27, Feb. 25, Mar. 23, Apr. 21, May 19, June 17, July 15, Aug. 13, 25, 26, 27, Sept. 11, Oct. 9, Nov. 7, Dec. 5

Challenging: Jan. 2, 10, 19, Feb. 8, 17, Mar. 6, 15, Apr. 4, 13, May 2, 11, June 9, July 7, 30, Aug. 5, 28, Sept. 3, 26, Oct. 1, 24, Nov. 22, Dec. 20, 30

Soul mates: Jan. 15, Feb. 13, Mar. 11, Apr. 9, May 7, June 5, July 3, Aug. 1, Oct. 29, Nov. 27, Dec. 25

February 23

PRIMARY STAR

Star's name: Fom Al Haut

Degree position: 2°51'–3°51' Pisces between the years 1930 and 2000

Magnitude: 1

Strength: ★★★★★★★★★

Orb: 2°30'

Constellation: Alpha Piscis Australis

Applicable days: February 19, 20, 21, 22, 23, 24, 25

Star qualities: Venus/Mercury

Description: a reddish white star located in the mouth of the southern Fish

PRIMARY STAR'S INFLUENCE

Fom Al Haut is one of the four royal stars and marks the winter solstice. Fom Al Haut is an especially powerful star and thus bestows good fortune, success, and a keen mentality. This star may also indicate a need to change from a material view to a more spiritual one.

Linked to your Sun's degree, this star imparts good rhythm, receptivity, and a tendency to go with the current. Easily influenced by your environment, you are self-seeking and may need to find creative self-expression. This star also suggests that legacies and inheritance can be expected but warns against squandering or spending them quickly.

H Your birthday reveals you to be a receptive, dynamic, friendly, and active Piscean who can achieve success through partnerships and cooperative endeavors. Although you are restless by nature, your life is oriented toward social interaction and develops through people-related experiences.

The added influence of your Sun in the decanate of Pisces strengthens your receptivity, and with your sixth sense, you pick up on the moods of people around you. Although sensitive and imaginative, you have business acumen and ideas that can bring financial rewards. Being rhythmic, you often have an ear for music or a natural talent for dancing. If you lack direction, you can be influenced by peer group pressure; rather than stand alone, you go with the flow or choose escapism as an easy way out.

Ambitious and versatile, you have an ability to mix business with pleasure that suggests you are a good networker, and can learn to mix with people from all walks of life. As you can be very determined, you are a powerful force when inspired by an aim or an idea. Although you have a strong desire to achieve success, a sensitive, imaginative, and idealistic side to your nature implies that you need to find balance in your life and overcome unfounded fears about lack of funds.

Until you reach the age of twenty-six your progressed Sun moves through Pisces, accenting your sensitivity and feelings. You may find yourself searching for an ideal situation or relationship or just something more magical in your life. From the age of twenty-seven, when your progressed Sun moves into Aries, you start to become more confident, assertive, and ambitious. You are likely to start new ventures or take the initiative in your dealings with others. At the age of fifty-seven there is another turning point as your Sun enters Taurus. After this time, you slow down and have a need for more stability and financial security in your life.

Your Secret Self

Visionary and idealistic, yet with a desire for money, power, and prestige, you are ambitious and motivated. Although you are capable of hard work and a methodical execution of your plans, a tendency to become bored easily suggests that if there is no financial incentive or quick returns, you are apt to abandon your plans and look for better prospects elsewhere. With your intuitive awareness of the law of cause and effect, you innately understand that without making the necessary effort, you cannot have your just rewards.

Having leadership abilities and a need for recognition implies that you think on a universal scale. Conceptual, with a desire for harmony, you enjoy new beginnings but need to avoid becoming anxious or restless. As a generous and versatile individual, you are tolerant and resourceful, with a need for realistic goals. An extravagant streak implies that at times you may overspend, but a need for money and security usually motivates you to be enterprising and take new opportunities.

Work & Vocation

Imaginative yet determined, you possess a friendly personality that can ensure your success in people-related careers. A need for recognition may push you into the forefront of your area of expertise. With a special skill for selling an idea or cause you believe in, you can particularly succeed in promotional work or negotiating deals. You may do well in occupations that involve foreign countries, such as import-export or travel. Although you may prefer to work for yourself, you are also a good team member. While you have a natural business sense, a sensitivity to color, sound, and form may draw you to artistic, dramatic, or musical forms of expression. Totally determined once committed to a project, you have shrewd business sense and organizational skills that are likely to aid your success in whatever career you choose.

Famous people who share your birthday include actor Peter Fonda, chef Anton Mosimann, actress Julie Walters, banker M. A. Rothschild, writer Samuel Pepys, guitarist Johnny Winter, and NAACP founder W. E. B. Du Bois.

Numerology

Intuitive, emotionally sensitive, and creative, you are usually versatile, passionate, and a quick thinker, with a professional attitude. With a number 23 birthday, you have a mind full of creative ideas and are usually multi-talented. You are fond of travel, adventure, and meeting new people; the restlessness implied by the number 23 urges you to try many different kinds of experience, as you adapt to situations easily. Friendly and fun-loving, with courage and drive, you may need an active life in order to actualize your true potential. The subinfluence of the number 2 month indicates that although you enjoy cooperative activities, you like to stay independent and make up your own mind. You benefit greatly from broadening your horizons through exploring different subjects and developing faith in your abilities. A love of harmony and a need for peace and quiet may inspire you to express your original thoughts and unique talents.

• *Positive:* loyal, responsible, travel, communicative, intuitive, creative, versatile, trustworthy, fame

• *Negative:* selfish, insecure, stubborn, uncompromising, fault-finding, prejudiced

Love & Relationships

Usually you have an active social life and many friends. Since your relationships are important, you are willing to make the effort to keep them alive. With your strong principles, you need a partner who can stand up to you and not be intimidated by your forceful personality. Although on the whole you are friendly and easygoing, you enjoy a mental challenge and debates. Although you are interested in mental power or strong individuals, avoid mentally dominating others or falling victim to others dominating you. Nonetheless, kind and understanding, you are very generous with the people you care for and will go to great lengths for those you love.

YOUR SPECIAL SOMEONE

For security, mental stimulation, and love, you might begin by looking among those born on the following dates.

Love & friendship: Jan. 3, 23, Feb. 11, 21, 25, Mar. 9, 19, 28, 31, Apr. 7, 17, 26, 29, May 5, 15, 24, 27, 29, 31, June 3, 13, 22, 25, 27, 29, July 1, 11, 15, 20, 23, 25, 27, 29, Aug. 9, 18, 21, 23, 25, 27, Sept. 7, 16, 19, 21, 23, 25, Oct. 5, 14, 17, 19, 21, 23, Nov. 3, 7, 12, 15 17, 19, 21, Dec. 1, 10, 13, 15 17, 19

Beneficial: Jan. 3, 4, 10, 21, Feb. 1, 2, 8, 19, Mar. 6, 17, 30, Apr. 4, 15, 28, May 2, 13, 26, June 11, 24, July 9, 22, Aug. 7, 20, Sept. 5, 18, 24, Oct. 3, 16, 22, 31, Nov. 1, 14, 29, Dec. 12, 27

Fatal attractions: Jan. 22, 28, Feb. 20, 26, Mar. 18, 24, Apr. 16, 22, May 14, 20, June 12, 18, July 10, 16, Aug. 8, 14, 26, 27, 28, 29, Sept. 6, 12, Oct. 4, 10, Nov. 2, 8, Dec. 6

Challenging: Jan. 11, 20, Feb. 9, 18, Mar. 7, 16, Apr. 5, 14, May 3, 12, 30, June 1, 10, 28, July 8, 26, 31, Aug. 6, 24, 29, Sept. 4, 22, 27, Oct. 2, 20, 25, Nov. 18, 23, Dec. 16, 21

Soul mates: Jan. 26, Feb. 24, Mar. 22, 30, Apr. 20, 28, May 18, 26, June 16, 24, July 14, 22, Aug. 12, 20, Sept. 10, 18, Oct. 8, 16, Nov. 6, 14, Dec. 4, 12

February 24

♓ Your Pisces birthday reveals you to be self-motivated and imaginative, as well as a receptive and independent individual. Idealistic, with powerful feelings and a willingness to work hard, you can be very generous and protective of those you love. Although you are amiable and gracious, with a pragmatic approach, a blend of high ideals and a practical desire for money and luxury indicate that you may vacillate between extremes. By finding a just cause that can both inspire you and provide a financial incentive, you can overcome a tendency to be ruled by your forceful emotions.

The added influence of your Sun in the Pisces decanate strengthens your intuitive powers, though occasionally it may also result in fluctuating moods and restlessness. Mentally sharp and receptive to new trends and ideas, you are able to welcome social reform. Although you are usually imaginative and contemplative, your unsettled nature can sometimes cause you to be at odds with others. If you lack direction, you can be influenced by peer group pressure; rather than stand alone, you might go with the flow or choose escapism as an easy way out.

Since you enjoy new beginnings, ideally you should be an initiator. This also suggests that you should avoid getting stuck in a rut and becoming impatient. As long as you keep faith in yourself, your no-nonsense approach, original ideas, and intuition guarantee you success.

Until you reach the age of twenty-five, your progressed Sun moves through Pisces, placing the emphasis on your emotional development and intuition as well as your dreams for the future. While you are between the ages of twenty-six and fifty-five, your progressed Sun moves through Aries. This influence suggests that you develop your assertiveness and enjoy being active and adventurous. This is a good time to initiate projects, be involved in leadership, or learn to be more straightforward in your relationships. After the age of fifty-six, when your progressed Sun moves into Taurus, you become calmer and steadier, with a possible greater interest in nature. There is also an increased need to be established and feel secure.

Fixed Stars

Fom Al Haut; Deneb Adige, also called Al Dhanab

PRIMARY STAR

Star's name: Fom Al Haut

Degree position: 2°51'–3°51' Pisces between the years 1930 and 2000

Magnitude: 1

Strength: ★★★★★★★★★

Orb: 2°30'

Constellation: Alpha Piscis Australis

Applicable days: February 19, 20, 21, 22, 23, 24, 25

Star qualities: Venus/Mercury

Description: a reddish white star located in the mouth of the southern Fish

PRIMARY STAR'S INFLUENCE

Fom Al Haut is one of the four royal stars and marks the winter solstice. Fom Al Haut is an especially powerful star and thus bestows good fortune, success, and a keen mentality. This star may also indicate a need to change from a material view to a more spiritual one.

Linked to your Sun's degree, this star imparts good rhythm, receptivity, and a tendency to go with the current. Easily influenced by your environment, you are self-seeking and may need to find creative self-expression. This star also suggests that legacies and inheritance can be expected but warns against squandering or spending them quickly.

• Positive: learn to budget, idealistic, imaginative, creative

Your Secret Self

Charming and cooperative, you enjoy socializing and often have a charismatic personality. As a networker, you are capable of making the right contacts and mixing business with pleasure. Imaginative and original, you are usually a good strategist, with executive abilities. When you are enthusiastic about new projects or ideas, your dynamic nature reveals a great deal of energy and determination. Your intuitive skills and business acumen enable you to see financial opportunities before the rest, and you usually have many inspired ideas to make money.

Although at times you can be quite bossy, an ability to work with others suggests that you know how to use diplomacy and negotiate a compromise. Your personal relationships are extremely important, both as a mirror of your own self-awareness and because they provide you with an avenue for expressing your powerful love and emotions.

Work & Vocation

Strong desires and motivation suggest that you are idealistic, with material inclinations. Intuitive and receptive, you have an excellent talent for dealing with people and can act as a financial advisor, mediator, or negotiator. You thrive on new beginnings or challenges, and in business you have a special ability to spot opportunities or talented people. Imaginative and sensitive to color and form, you can express yourself through interior design or styling. Alternatively, you may choose to follow your adventurous spirit in search of fortune. This may include travel to faraway places in order to experience different ways of life. Another option for your many talents and individuality may be to find a career in the creative world as a writer, actor, or painter.

Famous people who share your birthday include painter Winslow Homer, fairy-tale writer Wilhelm Grimm, French racing driver Alain Prost, musician Nicky Hopkins, and actors James Farentino, Edward James Olmos, and Abe Vigoda.

Numerology

The emotional sensitivity of the number 24 birthday suggests that you may need to establish harmony and order. Usually honest, dependable, and security-conscious, you need the love and support of a partner and enjoy building a strong foundation for yourself and your family. A pragmatic approach to life also gives you a good business sense and an ability to achieve material success. As a number 24 individual, you may have to overcome periods of instability and a tendency to be stubborn or fixed in your ideas. The subinfluence of the number 2 month indicates that as a networker with a desire to interact with others, you may collaborate in group efforts or act as a mediator. Efficient, you have determination and good organizational skills. All you need for outstanding success, therefore, is self-discipline and the desire to make something of yourself. Discerning in your assessment of others, you need to learn to trust your intuition. If you lack motivation, you can become restless and scatter your energies.

• *Positive:* energy, idealist, practical skills, strong determination, honest, frank, fair, generous, love of home active, energetic

• *Negative:* materialism, too economical, instability, dislikes routine, lazy, unfaithful, domineering, stubborn, vengeful

YOUR SPECIAL SOMEONE

For mental stimulation, love, and friendship, you might want to begin looking among those born on the following dates.

Love & friendship: Jan. 14, 24, 31, Feb. 12, 22, 29, Mar. 10, 20, 27, Apr. 8, 18, 25, May 6, 16, 23, 30, June 4, 14, 18, 21, 28, 30, July 2, 12, 16, 19, 26, 28, 30, Aug. 10, 17, 24, 26, 28, Sept. 8, 15, 22, 24, 26, Oct. 6, 13, 20, 22, 24, 30, Nov. 4, 8, 11, 18, 20, 22, 28, Dec. 2, 9, 16, 18, 20, 26, 29

Beneficial: Jan. 5, 22, 30, Feb. 3, 20, 28, Mar. 1, 18, 26, Apr. 16, 24, May 14, 22, June 12, 20, July 10, 18, 29, Aug. 8, 16, 27, 31, Sept. 6, 14, 25, 29, Oct. 4, 12, 23, 27, Nov. 2, 10, 21, 25, Dec. 9, 19, 23

Fatal attractions: Jan. 12, Feb. 10, Mar. 8, Apr. 6, May 4, June 2, Aug. 27, 28, 29, 30

Challenging: Jan. 16, 21, Feb. 14, 19, Mar. 12, 17, 30, Apr. 10, 15, 28, May 8, 13, 26, June 6, 11, 24, July 4, 9, 22, Aug. 2, 7, 20, Sept. 5, 18, Oct. 3, 16, Nov. 1, 14, Dec. 12

Soul mates: Jan. 25, Feb. 23, Mar. 21, Apr. 19, May 17, June 15, July 13, Aug. 11, Sept. 9, Oct. 7, Nov. 5, Dec. 3, 30

Love & Relationships

Charming and friendly, you usually enjoy an active life and meeting new people. A tendency to be easily bored, however, indicates that you may need someone who can keep you on your toes and constantly interested. You ideally need a strong partner who will be as hardworking as yourself. Your strong desire for love and affection can eventually cause you to settle down and commit yourself. If you take your time in choosing the right friends or partners, you are likely to be less impetuous about love and relationships.

February 25

FIXED STARS

Fom Al Haut; Deneb Adige, also called Al Dhanab

PRIMARY STAR

Star's name: Fom Al Haut

Degree position: 2°51'–3°51' Pisces between the years 1930 and 2000

Magnitude: 1

Strength: ★★★★★★★★

Orb: 2°30'

Constellation: Alpha Piscis Australis

Applicable days: February 19, 20, 21, 22, 23, 24, 25

Star qualities: Venus/Mercury

Description: a reddish white star located in the mouth of the southern Fish

PRIMARY STAR'S INFLUENCE

Fom Al Haut is one of the four royal stars and marks the winter solstice. Fom Al Haut is an especially powerful star and thus bestows good fortune, success, and a keen mentality. This star may also indicate a need to change from a material view to a more spiritual one.

Linked to your Sun's degree, this star imparts good rhythm, receptivity, and a tendency to go with the current. Easily influenced by your environment, you are self-seeking and may need to find creative self-expression. This star also suggests that legacies and inheritance can be expected but warns against squandering or spending them quickly.

• Positive: learn to budget, idealistic, imaginative, creative

♓ Your sensitivity and mental power combine to mark your Pisces birthday as something special. Inspired and imaginative, you are an articulate and hardworking individual who likes to be independent and in control. As you are both intuitive and rational, by recognizing the power of knowledge and utilizing your natural discrimination you make the most of your intelligence. With all your talents, one of your possible problems may be underachievement. Careful and prudent, but also possessing an unconventional streak, you appear to others as confident and self-assured.

With the added influence of your Sun in the decanate of Pisces, you possess mediumistic powers and depth of thought. These enhance your analytical skills and endow you with an ability to pick up on the different moods around you as well as social currents and trends. Although this influence can give you a unique insight into people and situations, it may also cause you to experience periods of confusion and self-doubt.

If you lack direction, you can be influenced by peer group pressure; rather than stand alone, you may go with the flow or choose escapism as an easy way out. As a goal-oriented person, you may sometimes be too critical or hard on yourself. Learning to trust your own intuition enables you to take on the challenges of developing an original view. Education, whether formal or self-directed, can be a vital key to bring out the best of your potential.

Until you reach the age of twenty-four your progressed Sun moves through Pisces, placing the emphasis on your sensitivity and emotional interactions with others. While you are between the ages of twenty-five and fifty-four your progressed Sun moves through Aries. This influence suggests that you will enter a new phase by becoming more assertive, determined, and spirited, which may result in a strong desire for new ventures. After the age of fifty-five, when your progressed Sun moves into Taurus, your need to be established and feel materially secure will increase, coupled with a wish for more calm and steadiness in your life.

Your Secret Self

Strong and determined, yet alluring and engaging, you are an interesting blend of opposites. Intelligent and observant, with a quick wit and a sharp tongue, you also possess a perceptive insight into other people's psychology. Idealistic and hardworking, you are a self-reliant individual who is willing to fight injustice. Nonetheless, a desire for power, money, or prestige can also motivate you to achieve.

Although usually independent, you know the value of sharing and working cooperatively with others in order to achieve the best results. Sometimes you can persevere in situations with an amazing determination. It would be wise, however, to avoid subservient positions, as you are likely to react strongly to power games from authority figures. As you are usually conscientious and eager to help others, you may have to ensure that you do not cause yourself stress by taking on too much.

Work & Vocation

Intelligent and receptive, you possess a strong personality and leadership abilities. As employers appreciate your ability to take responsibility and work hard, you can rise to high positions. If in business, you can commercialize your knowledge. Alternatively, you may wish to pursue a career in education through teaching or lecturing. If you want to explore your creative abilities, you can develop your writing skills or be involved in large projects, preferably directing the action. An ability to organize and refine systems may inspire you to take an administrative job where you can organize others with your talent for efficiency. As a humanitarian, you are interested in reforms and better conditions in the workplace. If you are spiritually inclined, you may explore philosophy or have religious aspirations.

Famous people who share your birthday include musician George Harrison, composer G. F. Handel, mystic Meher Baba, French painter Pierre-Auguste Renoir, English film director David Puttnam, nutrition expert Adelle Davis, comedian/actor Zeppo Marx, and actor Tom Courtenay.

Numerology

As a number 25 individual, you are quick and energetic as well as intuitive and thoughtful, and you need to express yourself through different experiences. These may include new and exciting ideas, people, or locations. A desire for perfection urges you to work hard and be productive. You may, however, need to be less impatient or critical if things do not happen according to plan. With a number 25 birthday, you possess strong mental energies that when concentrated aid you to look at all the facts and arrive at a conclusion faster than anyone else. Success and happiness come when you learn to trust your own instincts and develop perseverance and patience. The subinfluence of the number 2 month indicates that you are sensitive and intelligent. Relationships are usually an area where you can learn and develop. By staying positive and not allowing inner fears to undermine your creative flow, you can refine your intuitive and psychic skills. A practical humanitarian, you can contribute a great deal to groups or organizations with which you are involved.

• *Positive:* highly intuitive, perfectionist, perceptive, creative mind, good at dealing with people

• *Negative:* impulsive, impatient, irresponsible, jealous, secretive, changing circumstances, critical, moody, nervous

Love & Relationships

Although you are emotionally sensitive, your ability to be direct also implies that you can be outspoken. You admire those who are positive, emotionally honest, and straightforward. Although you are responsible and idealistic, your pride suggests that in partnerships you prefer to keep the upper hand. When negative, you may have to avoid being domineering or projecting your own feelings of frustration and dissatisfaction onto other family members. Loyal and security-conscious, however, you can be devoted and very protective of those you love. Your home is your castle, where you can retreat from the stresses of work and outside pressure. Usually you are a warm and caring host and enjoy entertaining others.

YOUR SPECIAL SOMEONE

You may find love and happiness with someone born on one of the following dates.

Love & friendship: Jan. 11,13,15,17, 25, Feb. 9,11,13,15,23, Mar. 7,9,11,13, 21, Apr. 5, 7. 9,11,19, May 3,5,7,9,17, 31, June 1, 3, 5, 7, 15, 29, July 1, 3, 5, 17, 27, 29, 31, Aug. 1, 3,11, 25, 27, 29, Sept. 1, 9, 23, 25, 27, Oct. 7, 21, 23, 25, Nov. 5, 9,19, 21, 23, Dec. 3,17,19, 21, 30

Beneficial: Jan. 1, 5, 20, Feb. 3, 18, Mar. 1,16, Apr. 14, May 12, June 10, July 8, Aug. 6, Sept. 4, Oct. 2

Fatal attractions: Aug. 28, 29, 30, 31

Challenging: Jan. 6, 22, 24, Feb. 4, 20, 22, Mar. 2,18, 20, Apr. 16,18, May 14, 16, June 12,14, July 10,12, Aug. 8,10, 31, Sept. 6, 8, 29, Oct. 4, 6, 27, Nov. 2, 4, 25, 30, Dec. 2, 23, 28

Soul mates: Jan. 6, 12, Feb. 4, 10, Mar. 2, 8, Apr. 6, May 4, June 2

February 26

FIXED STARS

Deneb Adige, also called Al Dhanab; Skat

PRIMARY STAR

Star's name: Deneb Adige, also called Al Dhanab

Degree position: 4°19'–4°55' Pisces between the years 1930 and 2000

Magnitude: 1

Strength: ★★★★★★★★★

Orb: 2°30'

Constellation: Alpha Cygnus

Applicable days: February 22, 23, 24, 25, 26, 27

Star qualities: Venus/Mercury

Description: a brilliant white star located in the tail of the Swan

PRIMARY STAR'S INFLUENCE

Deneb Adige's influence bestows intelligence and the capability to grasp information quickly. This star imparts versatility and idealism as well as psychic abilities. Friendly and likable, you may need to be careful in your choice of friends.

Linked to your Sun's degree, this star imparts a talent for writing, a love of literature, and a possible interest in astrology. Deneb Adige can bring popularity and success in dealing with the public. This star can also indicate some difficulties in childhood that leave a strong impression.

• *Positive:* articulate, imaginative, astute mind, good intellect

Sociable and intuitive, you are an idealistic Piscean with practical skills and exceptional mental receptivity. Naturally talented and versatile, with the opportunity to lead a busy and eventful life, you seek to fulfill yourself through expressing your own individuality. Although mentally restless, you achieve emotional security and peace of mind by working hard and building a solid foundation for yourself and those you love. Taking the lead may appeal to you more than obeying orders does. If you attempt to do too much, however, you are in danger of taking on more than you can master and may end up accomplishing very little.

The added influence of your Sun in the Pisces decanate enhances your good judgment with imagination and psychic abilities, allowing you to blend inner wisdom with logic. By training yourself to trust your own instincts, you come to feel secure in your knowledge and display a confident and decisive character.

As a perfectionist, you usually take your responsibilities seriously. You may, however, have to guard against nervous tension, which can cause you to be impatient or critical. Mentally sharp and discerning, you possess the competence to speak your mind in a direct and honest way. This suggests that you have the skills to communicate your ideas and opinions either directly or through witty repartee.

Until you reach the age of twenty-three your progressed Sun moves through Pisces, accenting your sensitivity and feelings. You may find yourself searching for an ideal situation or relationship or just something more magical in your life. From the age of twenty-four, when your progressed Sun moves into Aries, you start to become more confident, assertive, and ambitious. You are likely to start new ventures or be in leading positions. At the age of fifty-four there is another turning point as your Sun enters Taurus. After this time you slow down and have a need for more stability and financial security in your life.

Your Secret Self

Although highly intelligent, you are also very sensitive and intuitive, with a strong need for self-expression. While being witty and friendly, you may have to overcome an inclination to be uncertain about your deeper personal feelings, especially in your intimate relationships. Making choices and decisions may be one of the challenges to your otherwise rational mind. Often interested in metaphysical or spiritual subjects, you have much to gain from developing your natural intuition or listening to your inner voice.

Your strong practical sense suggests that you are ambitious and shrewd, with an ability to quickly assess people or situations. Be careful, however, of a tendency to think that financial security can provide you with all the answers. Nonetheless, your strong sense of purpose and a need to accomplish imply that you have high standards and are usually success-oriented. This need for activity indicates that you usually have a plan or scheme in the pipeline. An ability to think independently reveals that you can undertake large projects and oversee large enterprises. Usually you respond to limitations and criticism by proving the doubting person wrong.

Work & Vocation

Imaginative and practical, you usually seek a career where you can expand your knowledge and skills. Preferring work that is creative and mentally stimulating, you have a strong sense of vision and natural foresight. Your talent for words indicates that you can succeed in the world of communications, particularly writing and literature, education, or the media. If scientifically minded, you may choose a career in chemistry or engineering. Alternatively, you may prefer banking or law. Well organized and authoritative, you can excel in whatever you do. If you are interested in reform, you may be drawn to areas where you can speak up for others, such as union work or politics. Similarly, your humanitarian instincts may lead you to fight for a cause or help others through counseling or social work. Your need for artistic expression could be best satisfied through the media of art and design, music, or drama.

Famous people who share your birthday include writer Victor Hugo, musicians Fats Domino and Johnny Cash, industrialist Sir James Goldsmith, showman Buffalo Bill Cody, and comedian/actor Jackie Gleason.

Numerology

With a number 26 birthday, you have a pragmatic approach to life, executive ability, and a good business sense. Usually responsible, with a natural aesthetic sense and a love of home, you need to build a solid foundation or find real stability. Often a tower of strength for others, you are willing to support friends and family members who turn to you in time of need. You may nevertheless need to guard against materialistic tendencies and a desire to control people or situations. The subinfluence of the number 2 month indicates that you are intuitive, with a strong sixth sense as well as practical abilities. In your attempt to please, you may run the risk of becoming overly dependent. A desire to accomplish inspires you to be innovative and think on a grand scale. Although you are receptive to the opinions of others, you resent interference from those around you. When resolute, you like to be in control of your own decision making.

• *Positive:* creative, practical, caring, responsible, proud of family, enthusiasm, courage
• *Negative:* stubborn, rebellious, unstable relationships, unenthusiastic, lack of persistence

Love & Relationships

Highly intuitive and mentally restless, you like intelligent people who want to accomplish and achieve. Although you are sensitive and sympathetic, relationships are subject to changes, and at times you may feel unsettled. New opportunities or meeting exciting people may influence your plans, as you like variety and mental stimulation. You need a partner who possesses a good intellect and with whom you can share your love for knowledge.

YOUR SPECIAL SOMEONE

For that special partner or friend, you might want to begin looking for those born among the following dates.

Love & friendship: Jan. 12, 16, 25, Feb. 10, 14, 23, 24, Mar. 8, 12, 22, 31, Apr. 6, 10, 20, 29, May 4, 8, 18, 27, June 2, 6, 16, 25, 30, July 4, 14, 18, 23, 28, Aug. 2, 12, 21, 26, 30, Sept. 10, 19, 24, 28, Oct. 8, 17, 22, 26, Nov. 6, 10, 15, 20, 24, 30, Dec. 4, 13, 18, 22, 28

Beneficial: Jan. 2, 13, 22, 24, Feb. 11, 17, 20, 22, Mar. 9, 15, 18, 20, 28, Apr. 7, 13, 16, 18, 26, May 5, 11, 16, 18, 26, June 3, 9, 12, 14, 22, July 1, 7, 10, 12, 20, Aug. 5, 8, 10, 18, Sept. 3, 6, 8, 16, Oct. 1, 4, 6, 14, Nov. 2, 4, 12, Dec. 2, 10

Fatal attractions: Jan. 25, Feb. 23, Mar. 21, Apr. 19, May 17, June 15, July 13, Aug. 11, 30, 31, Sept. 1, 9, Oct. 7, Nov. 5, Dec. 3

Challenging: Jan. 7, 23, Feb. 5, 21, Mar. 3, 19, 29, Apr. 1, 17, 27, May 15, 25, June 13, 23, July 11, 21, 31, Aug. 9, 19, 29, Sept. 7, 17, 27, 30, Nov. 3, 13, 23, 26, Dec. 1, 11, 21, 24

Soul mates: Jan. 17, Feb. 15, Mar. 13, Apr. 11, May 9, June 7, July 5, Aug. 3, Sept. 1, Nov. 30, Dec. 28

February 27

FIXED STARS

Deneb Adige, also called Al Dhanab; Skat

PRIMARY STAR

Star's name: Deneb Adige, also called Al Dhanab

Degree position: 4°19'–4°55' Pisces between the years 1930 and 2000

Magnitude: 1

Strength: ★★★★★★★★★

Orb: 2°30'

Constellation: Alpha Cygnus

Applicable days: February 22, 23, 24, 25, 26, 27

Star qualities: Venus/Mercury

Description: a brilliant white star located in the tail of the Swan

PRIMARY STAR'S INFLUENCE

Deneb Adige's influence bestows intelligence and the capability to grasp information quickly. This star imparts versatility and idealism as well as psychic abilities. Friendly and likable, you may need to be careful in your choice of friends.

Linked to your Sun's degree, this star imparts a talent for writing, a love of literature, and a possible interest in astrology. Deneb Adige can bring popularity and success in dealing with the public. This star can also indicate some difficulties in childhood that leave a strong impression.

• *Positive:* articulate, imaginative, astute mind, good intellect

♓ Intelligent and receptive, with an idealistic nature, you are a sensitive Piscean with high aspirations. As a visionary, you possess a youthful or androgynous quality that implies a fresh look on life but also mental restlessness. Thus your potential is often enhanced by a responsible and mature attitude. Although sometimes evasive, you prefer to be direct and honest with your feelings. You possess a spirit of enterprise but may have to guard against stress caused by repressed emotions or being overly enthusiastic.

The added influence of your Sun in the Pisces decanate suggests that you are intuitive, imaginative, and multitalented, with a wealth of ideas. Although you can be sympathetic and charming, with an alluring demeanor, you can be enigmatic and uncommunicative when the mood takes you.

Although sociable, you have an independent view of life. When inspired by a cause or an idea you can become very eager, but in your desire to accomplish you may have to guard against being bossy. As a creative thinker with a love of knowledge, you enjoy many interests. Through education and the pursuit of knowledge you can easily develop your flair for the spoken and written word as well as improve your natural business sense. An appreciation of art and beauty can bestow good taste and a love of luxury and comfort.

Until you reach the age of twenty-two your progressed Sun moves through Pisces, placing the emphasis on your emotional development and intuition. While you are between the ages of twenty-three and fifty-two your progressed Sun moves through Aries. This influence suggests that you develop your assertiveness and enjoy being active and adventurous. After the age of fifty-three, when your progressed Sun moves into Taurus, you may become more creative and interested in nature, luxury, or the good life. There is also an increased need to be established and feel secure.

Your Secret Self

Charming and entertaining, you can be high-spirited and young at heart. Your desire for success reveals an interesting blend of materialism and idealism. Although you are ambitious, a carefree quality is likely to keep you optimistic and enthusiastic throughout your life and show a side of you that is guaranteed to keep others fascinated. You are friendly and outgoing, and your people skills can certainly help you in your climb to the top.

Although your image and material security are important, there may be times when you have secret fears or become too money-oriented. Nevertheless, you are usually focused on success, with an active mind and imaginative ideas. You will always have a youthful quality that, combined with your powerful emotions and compassion, enables you to uplift people with your enthusiasm and playful spirit.

Work & Vocation

Intelligent and astute, you have a persuasive manner and are an excellent promoter. If in business, you can work in advertising or sales. Since you have a charming and positive personality, you are suited for any career dealing with the public. Interested in modern ideas and keen to

748

learn, you may turn to education. With your enthusiasm, you can be an excellent and inspiring teacher or lecturer. As a humanitarian, you could also be a good attorney, politician, or spokesperson who fights for just causes. Your executive skills and enterprising spirit suggest that you can start your own business or work as a director or head of a department or company. As long as you take your responsibilities seriously, you can achieve a great deal with your vitality and determination. Since you grasp situations very quickly, education can particularly help you advance in life. By continually learning new skills, you stay young and in high spirits.

Famous people who share your birthday include actresses Elizabeth Taylor and Joanne Woodward, consumer advocate Ralph Nader, poet H. W. Longfellow, philosopher Rudolf Steiner, singer Michael Bolton, and writer John Steinbeck.

Numerology

Intuitive yet analytical, you have a depth of thought that can be greatly enhanced by developing patience and self-control. The number 27 birthdate indicates that you are determined and observant and can pay great attention to detail. Although at times you appear secretive, rational, or detached, in fact you may be hiding inner tensions. In developing good communication skills, you can overcome a reluctance to express your deeper feelings. The subinfluence of the number 2 month indicates that, sensitive and with a strong need to be part of a group, you are adaptable and understanding, and enjoy cooperative activities. Since you are receptive and inquisitive, you need to learn to trust your intuition in order to channel your thoughts effectively and gain greater awareness. By learning to stay balanced and detached, you can interact with others and yet remain independent. Avoid becoming anxious or nervous when you face opposition. Develop your humanitarian traits by showing others your compassionate nature. If overconfident, you may let success go to your head.

• *Positive:* versatile, imaginative, creative, resoluteness, bravery, good understanding, mentally capable, spiritual, inventive, mental strength

• *Negative:* quarrelsome, restless, nervous, mistrusting, overly emotional

Love & Relationships

Charming, intelligent, and young at heart, you are likely to be sociable and popular. Intense and sensitive, you can go from being spontaneous and kind to being cold and aloof. You often seek an ideal love with a strong link. At times responsibilities to others can delay your plans or affect your relationships. Attractive, you should have no difficulty finding friends or partners. Ironically, you may sometimes have a fear of being lonely or abandoned and have to learn to compromise and adjust to others. When you do find your ideal love, however, you can be a loyal friend and a loving partner.

YOUR SPECIAL SOMEONE

For that special someone, you might want to look among those born on the following dates.

Love & friendship: Jan. 7, 10, 17, 27, Feb. 5, 8, 15, 25, Mar. 3, 6, 13, 23, Apr. 1, 4, 11, 21, May 2, 9, 19, June 7, 17, July 5, 15, 19, 29, 31, Aug. 3, 13, 27, 29, 31, Sept. 1, 11, 25, 27, 29, Oct. 9, 23, 25, 27, Nov. 7, 11, 21, 23, 25, Dec. 5, 19, 21, 23

Beneficial: Jan. 3, 5, 20, 25, 27, Feb. 1, 3, 18, 23, 25, Mar. 1, 16, 21, 23, Apr. 14, 19, 21, May 12, 17, 19, June 10, 15, 17, 23, July 8, 13, 15, Aug. 6, 11, 13, Sept. 4, 9, 11, Oct. 2, 7, 9, 26, Nov. 5, 7, 13, Dec. 3, 5

Fatal attractions: Jan. 13, Feb. 11, Mar. 9, Apr. 7, May 5, June 3, July 1, Aug. 31, Sept. 1, 2

Challenging: Jan. 16, 24, Feb. 14, 22, Mar. 12, 20, Apr. 10, 18, May 8, 16, 31, June 6, 14, 29, July 4, 12, 27, Aug. 2, 10, 25, Sept. 8, 23, Oct. 6, 21, Nov. 4, 19, Dec. 2, 17

Soul mates: Jan. 16, Feb. 14, Mar. 12, Apr. 10, May 8, June 6, July 4, 31, Aug. 2, 29, Sept. 27, Oct. 25, Nov. 23, Dec. 21

February 28

Although you are friendly and witty, with a congenial personality, the qualities associated with your Pisces birthday suggest that you are competitive, hardworking, and intelligent. As sensitivity and intuition are among your prime assets, you have high hopes and grand dreams. Although you are multitalented, your wonderful potential may not be realized without self-discipline, perseverance, and determination. With a flair for people, you often achieve success through collaborative efforts.

The influence of your Sun in the decanate of Pisces implies that you can add vision and imagination to your receptivity and creativity. Although often artistic and impressionable, with humanitarian inspirations, underneath it all you have a shrewd mind and good business sense.

As a thoughtful and intelligent seeker of knowledge, you possess a dynamic drive and persuasive manner. In order to enhance your chances for success, education is a cornerstone for the establishment of a solid foundation. Inspiring and practical, you enjoy a mental challenge, but in your attempt to test your wits and aptitude, you can become controversial, obstinate, or evasive. An enterprising individual with strong convictions, you have independent views and good reasoning powers.

Until you reach the age of twenty-one your progressed Sun moves through Pisces, placing emphasis on your sensitivity and emotional interactions with others. Your early life may have been particularly influenced by a strong male figure. While you are between the ages of twenty-two and fifty-one your progressed Sun moves through Aries. This influence suggests that you will enter a new phase by becoming more determined, assertive, and spirited, which may result in a strong desire for new ventures. After the age of fifty-two, when your progressed Sun moves into Taurus, your need to be materially established and feel secure will increase, coupled with a wish for more calm and emotional steadiness.

Your Secret Self

As a persuasive individual, with insight and deep awareness, you have the choice between attaining your desires by learning to listen to your inner wisdom and high principles or getting what you want by being manipulative. The more responsible and righteous your actions, the higher you are likely to rise in life. Since you possess a distinct dignity that comes from an awareness of your morals and idealistic nature, it is advisable to avoid being too selfish or indulgent.

Although you know things instinctively, you possess excellent common sense and quick mental responses. These usually keep you alert and inspire you to fight adversity. Charming, generous, and kind, with the ability to make yourself popular, you may also have to learn that being too arrogant can push people away. Although you will always have a playful quality, it is through developing perseverance and being reliable that you are able to make the most of your outstanding potential.

Work & Vocation

The combination of your sharp mind and advanced social skills enables you to be successful in many different areas of life. Your desire to mentally explore everything that interests you

---

Star's name: Skat

Degree position: 7°51'–8°40' Pisces between the years 1930 and 2000

Magnitude: 3.5–4

Strength: ★★★★

Orb: 1°30'

Constellation: Delta Aquarius

Applicable days: February 26, 27, 28, 29

Star qualities: varied interpretations: Saturn/Jupiter or Uranus/Venus/Mercury

Description: a small star located on the right leg of Aquarius

PRIMARY STAR'S INFLUENCE

Skat's influence bestows idealism, artistic flair, and a receptive mind. This star indicates that you often have a romantic nature, good fortune, success, and lasting happiness.

Linked to your Sun's degree, this star imparts sensitivity, idealism, and psychic ability, and offers success in dealing with the general public. You probably enjoy popularity and gain help from friends in times of need. This star, however, warns against being overemotional and suggests that you may need to overcome a tendency to overreact to criticism.

• *Positive:* creativity, rhythm, sensitivity, patience

• *Negative:* inconstancy, moodiness, nervousness

may attract you to education, science, research, or philosophy. Equally, your fine mind can make you an excellent problem solver. Although you love travel, a natural restlessness may block some of your work opportunities. Preferring to take the lead, you are better in a management position or working for yourself. If in business, you are aided by your superior organizational skills and enterprising spirit. Much success comes through natural enthusiasm for your work, which is not something that you can feign. A desire to help others usually becomes stronger with age. Your need for self-expression and a love for the dramatic may, alternatively, lure you to writing or the art and entertainment worlds.

Famous people who share your birthday include racing driver Mario Andretti, dancer Vaslav Nijinsky, chemist Linus Pauling, actress Bernadette Peters, musician Brian Jones, and architect Frank Gehry.

Numerology

Independent and idealistic, with determination and a pragmatic approach, you are often a law unto yourself. Like a number 1 individual, you are ambitious, direct, and enterprising. An inner conflict between wanting to be independent and wanting to be part of a team is also indicated. Always ready for action and new ventures, you courageously take on life's challenges; with your enthusiasm, you can easily inspire others, if not to join you, at least to support you in your latest venture. Having a number 28 birthday, you possess leadership abilities and rely on your common sense, logic, and clear thinking. Although you can be responsible, avoid being overenthusiastic, impatient, or intolerant. The subinfluence of the number 2 month indicates that you are receptive, with an ability to intuitively understand what drives other people. You benefit from different kinds of personal interactions. Although critical of others, you may sometimes need to take a closer look at your own failings. A need to create balance implies that you benefit from learning the art of give-and-take.

• *Positive:* compassion, progressive, daring, artistic, creative, idealistic, ambitious, hardworking, stable home life, strong-willed

• *Negative:* daydreamer, unmotivated, lack of compassion, unrealistic, bossy, lack of judgment, aggressive, lack of confidence, too dependent on others, pride

Love & Relationships

Your numerous activities and strong desire for independence may sometimes interfere with your relationships. You usually admire those who have good practical knowledge and wisdom or who are kind and helpful, with plenty of good advice. Although you are mentally powerful, you need a partner who can understand your vulnerability. When you show your sensitive side, you can create warmer and closer relationships.

YOUR SPECIAL SOMEONE

If you are looking for that special person with whom to form a longer-lasting relationship, keep an eye out for people born on the following dates.

Love & friendship: Jan. 1, 8, 14, 28, 31, Feb. 12, 26, 29, Mar. 10, 24, 27, Apr. 8, 22, 25, May 6, 20, 23, June 4, 18, 21, July 2, 16, 19, 20, 30, Aug. 14, 17, 28, 30, Sept. 12, 15, 26, 28, 30, Oct. 10, 13, 24, 26, 28, Nov. 8, 11, 12, 22, 24, 26, Dec. 6, 9, 20, 22, 24

Beneficial: Jan. 26, Feb. 24, Mar. 22, Apr. 20, May 18, June 16, 24, July 14, Aug. 12, Sept. 10, Oct. 8, Nov. 6, 14, Dec. 4, 29

Fatal attractions: Aug. 31, Sept. 1, 2, 3

Challenging: Jan. 3, 25, Feb. 1, 23, Mar. 21, Apr. 19, May 17, June 15, July 13, Aug. 11, Sept. 9, Oct. 7, Nov. 5, Dec. 3

Soul mates: Jan. 3, 10, Feb. 1, 8, Mar. 6, Apr. 4, May 2

February 29

Determination, imagination, and creative self-expression are all qualities revealed by your Pisces birthday. As an idealistic and compassionate person, you have intuitive understanding and a warm heart. Although you have a wealth of remarkable ideas, a tendency to become anxious may weaken your resolve and self-confidence.

The added influence of your Sun in the decanate of Pisces implies that you are impressionable, with a strong sixth sense. Charming, you can enchant others with your inspired visions and idealism. Although the combination of imagination and positive thinking is often your key to success and happiness, you also need to be realistic and occupy yourself with mundane matters. Since you are receptive to sound, you have good timing and rhythm and may find music to be a relaxing influence.

As you need motivation to explore your true mental potential, education or self-knowledge is advisable. By taking everything as a learning experience, you can overcome a tendency to become frustrated and impatient. A flair for people suggests that through being broad-minded and tolerant, you realize the infinite possibilities available to you.

Until you reach the age of twenty your progressed Sun moves through Pisces, accenting your sensitivity and feelings. You may find yourself searching for an ideal situation or relationship, or you may have a strong inner life. From the age of twenty-one, when your progressed Sun moves into Aries, you start to become more confident, assertive, and ambitious. You are likely to start new ventures or be more straightforward in your relationships with others. At the age of fifty-one there is another turning point as your Sun enters Taurus. After this time you slow down and have a need for more stability and financial security in your life.

Your Secret Self

Your wide range of emotions suggests that you are dramatic and creative, with a strong need to express yourself. If you are unable to reveal your feelings and ideas, you may become depressed or disappointed with others. In order to achieve the great potential of your birthday, you may need to develop a positive philosophy about life that includes patience and perseverance. Often gifted, you may find outlets for your creativity through art, music, or drama, or at least you can become a fine appreciator.

With a strong awareness of your responsibilities, you like to pay your debts but may sometimes be too hard on yourself or others. Although usually generous and idealistic, with a warm heart, you also possess a strong sense of duty, obligation, and loyalty. Since education, whether conventional or unorthodox, is a vital key to your success, you need to constantly update your knowledge and keep yourself mentally occupied.

Work & Vocation

With your love of knowledge and talent for communication, you can excel in careers such as education or science. A natural inclination for business combined with good organizational or managerial skills is likely to aid you in any occupation you undertake. A flair with color and sound can possibly attract you to the world of art and design, poetry, music, or dance. Equally,

---

FIXED STAR

Star's name: Skat

Degree position: 7°51'–8°40' Pisces between the years 1930 and 2000

Magnitude: 3.5–4

Strength: ★★★★

Orb: 1°30'

Constellation: Delta Aquarius

Applicable days: February 26, 27, 28, 29

Star qualities: varied interpretations: Saturn/Jupiter or Uranus/Venus/Mercury

Description: a small star located on the right leg of Aquarius

---

PRIMARY STAR'S INFLUENCE

Skat's influence bestows idealism, artistic flair, and a receptive mind. This star indicates that you often have a romantic nature, good fortune, success, and lasting happiness.

Linked to your Sun's degree, this star imparts sensitivity, idealism, and psychic ability, and offers success in dealing with the general public. You probably enjoy popularity and gain help from friends in times of need. This star, however, warns against being overemotional and suggests that you may need to overcome a tendency to overreact to criticism.

• *Positive:* creativity, rhythm, sensitivity, patience

• *Negative:* inconstancy, moodiness, nervousness

you may be interested in literature or writing imaginative stories. Natural sympathy and a philosophical streak may draw you to religion or supporting the underdog. Alternatively, your sense of the dramatic may help you succeed in show business.

Famous people who share your birthday include composer Gioacchino Rossini, bandleader Jimmy Dorsey, actor James Mitchell, Shaker founder Anne Lee, and singer/actress Dinah Shore.

Numerology

Idealistic visionaries with a dynamic and forceful character, number 29 individuals have powerful personalities and extraordinary potential. Inspiration is the key to your success story, and without it you may experience a lack of purpose. Although you are a true dreamer, the extreme sides of your nature indicate that you may have to guard against alternating moods, going from being very friendly and warm to being cold and uncaring, or from optimistic to pessimistic. Quite observant, you still may have to learn how to be less critical or doubting and more considerate of those around you. The subinfluence of the number 2 month indicates that you are observant and sensitive, with powerful emotions. A desire to communicate or express yourself suggests that you need to interact with others. Multitalented, you benefit from putting your ideas to practical use. In your attempts to please others, you may find that not all of your good intentions are welcome.

• *Positive:* inspirational, balanced, inner peace, generous, creative, intuitive, mystical, powerful dreams, faith, worldly, successful

• *Negative:* unfocused, moody, difficult, extremist, inconsiderate, overly sensitive

Love & Relationships

Although relationships are very important to you, beware of becoming dependent on your partners. You may need to cultivate an independent perspective and find outlets for expression of your many talents. As a faithful individual, you seek a loyal and affectionate spouse who will always be there for you. Being demonstrative with your feelings, you like to establish a long-lasting relationship with one person. With your warm personality, you like to socialize and have friends around, and you can be very entertaining.

YOUR SPECIAL SOMEONE

For security, strong emotional bonds, and love, you may be more lucky with those born on the following days.

Love & friendship: Jan. 1, 15, 26, 29, 30, Feb. 13, 24, 27, 28, Mar. 11, 22, 25, 26, Apr. 9, 20, 23, 24, May 7, 18, 21, 22, June 5, 16, 19, 20, 23, July 3, 14, 17, 18, 31, Aug. 1, 12, 15, 16, 29, 31, Sept. 10, 13, 14, 27, 29, Oct. 8, 11, 12, 25, 27, Nov. 6, 9, 10, 13, 23, 25, Dec. 4, 7, 8, 21, 23, 29

Beneficial: Jan. 1, 2, 10, 14, 27, Feb. 8, 25, Mar. 6, 23, Apr. 4, 21, May 2, 6, 19, 30, June 4, 17, 28, July 2, 15, 26, Aug. 13, 24, Sept. 11, 22, Oct. 9, 20, Nov. 7, 18, Dec. 5, 16

Fatal attractions: Aug. 31, Sept. 1, 2, 3, 4

Challenging: Jan. 17, 26, Feb. 15, 24, Mar. 13, 22, Apr. 11, 20, May 9, 18, June 7, 16, July 5, 14, Aug. 3, 12, 30, Sept. 1, 10, 28, Oct. 8, 26, 29, Nov. 6, 24, 27, Dec. 4, 22, 25

Soul mates: Jan. 21, Feb. 19, Mar. 17, Apr. 15, May 13, June 11, July 9, 29, Aug. 7, 27, Sept. 5, 25, Oct. 3, 23, Nov. 1, 21, Dec. 19

March 1

FIXED STARS

Although your Sun's degree is not linked to a fixed star, some of your other planets' degrees certainly will be. By having an astrological chart calculated, you can find the exact position of the planets on your date of birth. This will tell you which of the fixed stars listed in this book are relevant to you.

H Your Pisces birthday shows you to be an idealistic and hardworking individual who, with a sense of purpose or a clear objective, can be determined and dedicated. By combining your creativity and practical abilities, you can show your true originality. You may benefit, however, from staying detached and learning to let go rather than taking life too seriously. Although you may at times face adversity and frustration, your endurance and charismatic enthusiasm help you attract assistance from others.

The added influence of your Sun in the decanate of Pisces indicates that you are sensitive and impressionable, with a strong sense of vision. Being a sympathetic individual, you are receptive to the feelings of others but need to beware of fluctuating or nervous moods. These emotional extremes imply that you benefit from thinking positively and being in harmonious surroundings. An ability to access the collective unconscious suggests that you are naturally psychic; when this is combined with your advanced social skills, you have a gift for dealing with people. If unhappy, however, avoid indulging in escapism or self-pity.

Ambitious, you possess excellent executive skills and the potential for leadership. Being a good organizer, you work better when you have a plan for the future. As you usually benefit most from long-term investments, you should avoid ambiguous get-rich-quick schemes.

Until you reach the age of nineteen your progressed Sun moves through Pisces, placing the emphasis on your sensitivity, receptivity to your surroundings, and emotional needs. While you are between the ages of twenty and forty-nine your progressed Sun moves through Aries. This influence suggests that you will enter a new phase by becoming more assertive, daring, and spirited, which can result in a desire for new ventures. After the age of fifty, when your progressed Sun moves into Taurus, your need to be established and feel financially secure will increase, coupled with a desire for a calmer life.

Your Secret Self

Having emotional power suggests that you have a magnetic personality and the potential for being compassionate and generous. When your strong self-will is positively focused, you can accomplish miracles through your determination and strong convictions. If you indulge in negative thoughts, you can become extremely stubborn. This can also cause you heartache or depression. When you begin to express your true feelings, you can achieve inner freedom by being detached without appearing ruthless or cold.

A desire for knowledge of a more profound nature suggests that you have a love for harmony and peace. With your subtle sensitivity, you possess enhanced perceptions of color, light, and sound that you may wish to channel into artistic, musical, or spiritual pursuits. Through selflessness and a universal approach to life, you achieve true happiness and satisfaction.

Work & Vocation

Naturally friendly yet ambitious, you have an ability to initiate projects and make contacts. Your ease at dealing with people can help you in any career, but your sensitivity suggests that you need harmonious working relations to be happy. Although you have administrative and managerial skills and can succeed in business, you may be more emotionally satisfied using your imagination and sense of originality. If in the sales world, you have an ability to make friends with your clients and also have a psychic awareness of what the public wants. By being of service to others or taking a spiritual approach to your work, you can find deeper fulfillment. You may wish to express your emotions through an innate talent for writing, drama, or music. Being independent, you may do better working for yourself.

Famous people who share your birthday include actor David Niven, painter Sandro Botticelli, singer/actor Harry Belafonte, former Israeli prime minister Yitzhak Rabin, bandleader Glenn Miller, and singer Roger Daltrey.

Numerology

As a number 1 individual, you are inclined to be individual, innovative, and courageous, with plenty of energy. Often there is a need to establish a strong identity and develop assertiveness. The pioneering spirit indicated here encourages you to strike out alone. These self-starting forces can also stimulate you to develop executive or leadership abilities. Full of enthusiasm and original ideas, you can show others the way forward. With a number 1 birthday, you may also need to learn that the world does not revolve around you and avoid an inclination to be self-centered or dictatorial. The subinfluence of the number 3 month indicates that you need to express your feelings. Relationships, companionship, and friendships are very important to your emotional growth. By learning to focus on one particular goal, you can avoid losing sight of your purpose. Nevertheless, a need to expand and explore implies that you are likely to travel and may even settle in a foreign land.

• *Positive:* leadership, creative, progressive, forceful, optimistic, strong convictions, competitive, independent, gregarious

• *Negative:* overbearing, jealous, egotistical, proud, antagonistic, lack of restraint, selfish, unstable, impatient

Love & Relationships

Charming and charismatic, you are often easygoing and friendly. Usually you are drawn toward strong and forceful individuals. A need to express your feelings implies that you can sparkle in social events. Generous and kind, you are willing to do your utmost for those you love. You usually admire those who are mentally sharp and decisive. When at ease, you can be entertaining and witty. Often involved in unusual types of relationships, you need a great deal of freedom and space.

YOUR SPECIAL SOMEONE

You might find a partner who will understand your sensitivity, strong passions, and need for love among those born on the following dates.

Love & friendship: Jan. 7, 8, 17, 19, Feb. 15, 17, Mar. 3, 13, 15, Apr. 11, 13, May 9, 11, June 7, 9, 30, July 5, 7, 28, 30, Aug. 3, 5, 26, 28, Sept. 1, 3, 24, 26, Oct. 1, 22, 24, Nov. 20, 22, Dec. 18, 20, 30

Beneficial: Jan. 20, 29, Feb. 18, 27, Mar. 16, 25, Apr. 14, 23, May. 12, 21, June 10, 19, July 8, 17, Aug. 6, 15, Sept. 4, 13, Oct. 2, 11, 29, Nov. 9, 27, Dec. 7, 25

Fatal attractions: Mar. 29, Apr. 27, May 25, June 23, July 21, Aug. 19, Sept. 1, 2, 3, 4, 17, Oct. 15, Nov. 13, Dec. 11

Challenging: Jan. 14, 27, Feb. 12, 25, Mar. 10, 23, Apr. 8, 21, May 6, 19, June 4, 17, July 2, 15, Aug. 13, Sept. 11, Oct. 9, Nov. 7, Dec. 5

Soul mates: June 30, July 28, Aug. 26, Sept. 24, Oct. 22, 29, Nov. 20, 27, Dec. 18, 25

March 2

FIXED STARS

Although your Sun's degree is not linked to a fixed star, some of your other planets' degrees certainly will be. By having an astrological chart calculated, you can find the exact position of the planets on your date of birth. This will tell you which of the fixed stars listed in this book are relevant to you.

Idealistic yet practical, you are shown by your Pisces birthday to be an impressionable yet intelligent and determined individual. Although you are charming and easygoing, you possess a strong character and are often objective and enterprising. You usually benefit from partnerships, but avoid becoming domineering or involved in power struggles with partners, especially when they refuse to take notice of your practical advice or authoritative position.

The added influence of your Sun in the decanate of Cancer indicates that you are highly imaginative, intuitive, and receptive. As a humanitarian, you are usually sensitive and caring, with a universal sense of family. This also suggests that you can use your knowledge to help people. Sympathetic, you are receptive to the needs of others and may benefit from staying detached and refraining from fluctuating moods. If unhappy, avoid indulging in risk taking as a means of escapism.

Magnetic and charming, yet tough and resolute, you are often a blend of caution and eagerness. Witty and logical, you can quickly assess people and their motives. A desire for money and prestige helps you get moving and implies that, as a hardworking visionary, you have extensive energy with which to achieve in life.

Until you reach the age of eighteen your progressed Sun moves through Pisces, placing the emphasis on your sensitivity, emotional development, and dreams for the future. While you are between the ages of nineteen and forty-eight, your progressed Sun moves through Aries. This influence suggests that you gradually develop your self-confidence and assertiveness, and you enjoy being active and adventurous. This is a good time to take the initiative and learn to be more straightforward. After the age of forty-nine, when your progressed Sun moves into Taurus, you may become more emotionally steady and practical. There is also an increased need to be established and financially secure as well as to be nourished by beauty and nature.

Your Secret Self

Although you seem amiable, your dynamic personality reveals an inner nobility, intelligence, and strong determination. A love for learning and a need to be informed emphasize how important knowledge is to your inner quest. Education often ensures the development of your enormous potential. Philosophical in your thinking, you can see the experience gained from previous difficulties in life. Usually you are progressive, and deep inside there is a strong sense that you have something worthwhile to say.

While you are prone to worry, your pride stops you from displaying your doubts or indecision; it also often places you in positions of leadership rather than subordinate to others. Having a strong sense of duty and responsibility, you may have to maintain a balance between your duties and your ideals. As a perfectionist, you may need to overcome a tendency to criticize or be too demanding by focusing your attention on being of service to others. With a strong need for recognition, you find it especially hard to be taken for granted. Beware of becoming involved in power games, as these can deplete your positive energies.

Work & Vocation

Determined and progressive, you enjoy putting new ideas and methods into practice. Intelligent as well as sensitive, you may find that occupations relating to people are most interesting.

There may be an attraction to the stage or politics; you are likely to succeed before the public in some way. With your original and inventive ideas, you may be interested in education, writing, or social reform. Having power and innate business acumen suggests that you can achieve much in life, although you may be happier if your plans include your natural sense of vision. Although personal fulfillment comes through work and productive activities, you may need to avoid taking on too much. The medical and healing professions can also be good outlets for your talents. You usually work well cooperatively as part of a team or partnership.

Famous people who share your birthday include Russian statesman Mikhail Gorbachev, singers Lou Reed, Karen Carpenter, and Jon Bon Jovi, composer Kurt Weill, actress Jennifer Jones, and entertainer Desi Arnaz.

Numerology

Sensitivity and a strong need to be part of a group are suggested by a number 2 birthday. Adaptable and understanding, you enjoy cooperative activities in which you can experience interaction with others. In your attempt to please those you like, you may run the risk of becoming overly dependent. Nevertheless, by developing confidence you can overcome the tendency to get easily hurt by the action and criticism of others. The subinfluence of the number 3 month indicates that, capable and intuitive and with a sharp intellect, you need to find a purpose or an exciting project to occupy yourself with. Your birthday implies that you are likely to have many changes in your social contacts as well as opportunities for travel. When you are insecure, your restlessness and ever-changing moods may at times cause difficulties with others, but with love and understanding you can make relationships work through your subtle power of persuasion. Avoid relationships that involve power games and manipulative strategies.

• *Positive:* good partnerships, gentle, tactful, receptive, intuitive, agile, considerate, harmonious, agreeable, ambassador of goodwill

• *Negative:* suspicious, lack of confidence, oversensitive, selfish, easily hurt

Love & Relationships

Friends and admirers are attracted by your strength and charisma. Although you are protective and loving, you may have to overcome an inclination to be controlling or bossy. Your friendships and romantic aspirations may be connected with your career and ambitions. You are likely to be drawn toward powerful people with social connections. A willingness to work hard for those you love indicates that you are loyal and responsible. Romantically, your quest for love may be influenced by practical considerations and a need for security.

YOUR SPECIAL SOMEONE

Your chances of success are more likely to occur with people born on the following dates.

Love & friendship: Jan. 9, 16, 18, 26, 31, Feb. 7, 14, 16, 24, 29, Mar. 5, 12, 14, 22, 27, Apr. 3, 10, 12, 20, 25, May 1, 8, 10, 12, 18, 23, June 6, 8, 16, 21, July 4, 6, 8, 14, 19, 31, Aug. 2, 4, 12, 17, 29, Sept. 2, 10, 15, 27, Oct. 8, 13, 25, Nov. 6, 11, 23, Dec. 4, 9, 21, 30

Beneficial: Jan. 1, 21, Feb. 19, Mar. 17, Apr. 15, May 13, June 11, July 9, Aug. 7, Sept. 5, Oct. 3, 30, Nov. 1, 28, Dec. 26

Fatal attractions: Sept. 2, 3, 4, 5

Challenging: Mar. 29, Apr. 27, May 25, June 23, July 21, Aug. 19, Sept. 17, Oct. 15, Nov. 13, Dec. 11

Soul mates: Jan. 27, Feb. 25, Mar. 23, 30, Apr. 21, 28, May 19, 26, June 17, 24, July 15, 22, Aug. 13, 20, Sept. 11, 18, Oct. 9, 16, Nov. 7, 14, Dec. 5, 12

March 3

Your Pisces birthday shows that you are a versatile, imaginative, and sensitive individual with subtle perceptions. Your powerful feelings and need for freedom suggest that, as a creative person, you benefit from finding ways to express yourself. An inner nobility and pride imply that you have grand dreams, but you may need to avoid indulging in unrealistic fantasies. Idealistic and romantic, you can be sympathetic and compassionate.

The added influence of your Sun in the decanate of Cancer indicates that you are impressionable and receptive. You usually have a sixth sense and strong premonitions. As you possess a wealth of feelings, you are protective and caring. Having faith in what you do is highly important; if you lose hope, you can go from optimism and brightness to being cold or withdrawn. Purposeful and determined, however, you usually come out of these moods quickly and easily.

An ability to combine business and pleasure suggests that, being sociable and friendly, you benefit from group activities and partnerships. As a clever and witty person, you can also be spontaneous and highly entertaining. Although you are very shrewd about people, avoid becoming sarcastic or involved in arguments and acts of jealousy with loved ones.

While you are between the ages of eighteen and forty-seven your progressed Sun moves through Aries. This influence suggests that you develop your assertiveness and enjoy being active and courageous. After the age of forty-eight, when your progressed Sun moves into Taurus, you feel an increased need for practicality, stability, and financial security. You may become more calm, emotionally steady, and attracted by nature. At the age of seventy-eight there is a turning point when your progressed Sun enters Gemini. This suggests that your curiosity grows and you start to transform your way of thinking. This highlights your interest in communication and learning new subjects.

Your Secret Self

Proud and sensitive, with a good understanding of values, you will find that one of your challenges is to recognize your inner power and not settle for less than you deserve. If you let money become too important an issue or you lack self-esteem and confidence in your abilities, you may find yourself in work beneath your high calling. A sharp understanding of people makes you an excellent observer of human behavior as well as an individualist who values freedom.

Inventive and progressive, you need to express your original ideas and talents. Although your sensitivity can sometimes cause changing moods, if you are inspired, you entertain and uplift others. Idealistic and sensitive, you may be particularly inspired in the areas of art, music, drama, or more mystical interests. When positive, you can project dynamic charm, enthusiasm, and generosity.

Work & Vocation

Your keen business sense in combination with your intuitive and imaginative abilities can inspire you to become an innovator or reformer. Your gift with words and exceptional imagination could manifest creatively in writing, drama, or the arts. Alternatively, with executive and leadership ability and good organizational skills, you can handle the affairs of others. Your love for freedom and the need to test your mental abilities, however, may prompt you to be self-employed. Being idealistic, with a humanitarian streak, could have you working in altruistic organizations, and often you are willing to act behind the scenes. This birthday can also produce wise counselors and teachers.

Famous people who share your birthday include inventor Alexander Graham Bell, actress Jean Harlow, Olympic athlete Jackie Joyner-Kersee, illustrator/cartoonist Ronald Searle, jet-setter Lee Radziwill, Romanian president Ion Iliescu, and singer Lou Reed.

Numerology

A need for love, creativity, and sensitivity are all indicated by the number 3 birthday. Easygoing and a good companion, you enjoy friendly social activities and many interests. Versatility and a need for self-expression lead you to seek numerous experiences. An inclination to get bored easily, however, may cause you to become indecisive or spread yourself too thin. Although you can be enthusiastic and charming, with a good sense of humor, you may have to develop self-esteem to guard against worry. Personal relationships and a loving atmosphere are of prime importance to you, as they endow you with hope and inspiration. The subinfluence of the number 3 month indicates that you need to turn your imaginative and creative ideas into tangible reality; otherwise they may remain unfulfilled dreams. Proud and idealistic, you need to develop faith in your abilities by refraining from feeling imperfect or unprepared. When you are optimistic, your personality shines with love, generosity, and creativity. When negative, however, you may be prone to excessive emotional intensity.
- *Positive:* humorous, happy, friendly, productive, creative, artistic, loving, freedom-loving, talent with words
- *Negative:* easily bored, jealous, vain, exaggerate, extravagant, self-indulgent, lazy, possessive, spoiled

Love & Relationships

Romantically, your charm and fun-loving personality can easily win you friends and admirers. Usually you admire intelligent individuals who achieve success through their own efforts. Friendship and companionship may be linked to work or intellectually oriented social activities. Gregarious and spontaneous, you can be the life and soul of the party when you are in the right kind of mood. Attracted to people with cerebral power, you like to debate and communicate your ideas. Avoid being too bossy or possessive, however, as it shows your insecurities and anxiety.

YOUR SPECIAL SOMEONE

You may find love, mental excitement, and consideration with someone born on one of the following dates.

Love & friendship: Jan. 21, 28, 31, Feb. 19, 26, 27, 29, Mar. 17, 24, 27, Apr. 15, 22, 23, 25, May 13, 20, 23, June 11, 18, 21, July 9, 16, 17, 19, Aug. 7, 14, 17, 31, Sept. 5, 12, 15, 29, Oct. 3, 10, 13, 27, 29, 31, Nov. 1, 8, 9. 11, 25, 27, 29, Dec. 6, 9, 23, 25, 27

Beneficial: Jan. 9, 12, 18, 24, 29, Feb. 7, 10, 16, 22, 27, Mar. 5, 8, 14, 20, 25, Apr. 3, 6, 12, 18, 23, May 1, 4, 10, 16, 21, 31, June 2, 8, 14, 19, 29, July 6, 12, 17, 27, Aug. 4, 10, 15, 25, Sept. 2, 8, 13, 23, Oct. 6, 11, 21, Nov. 4, 9, 19, Dec. 2, 7, 17

Fatal attractions: Jan. 3, Feb. 1, Sept. 3, 4, 5, 6

Challenging: Jan. 7, 8, 19, 28, Feb. 5, 6, 17, 26, Mar. 3, 4, 15, 24, Apr. 1, 2, 13, 22, May 11, 20, June 9, 18, July 7, 16, Aug. 5, 14, Sept. 3, 12, Oct. 1, 10, Nov. 8, Dec. 6

Soul mates: Jan. 3, 19, Feb. 1, 17, Mar. 15, Apr. 13, May 11, June 9, July 7, Aug. 5, Sept. 3, Oct. 1

SUN: PISCES

DECANATE: CANCER/MOON

DEGREE: 12°30'–14° PISCES

MODE: MUTABLE

ELEMENT: WATER

FIXED STAR

Star's name: Achernar

Degree position: 14°17'–15°11' Pisces between the years 1930 and 2000

Magnitude: 1

Strength: ★★★★★★★★

Orb: 2°30'

Constellation: Alpha Eridanus

Applicable days: March 3, 4, 5, 6, 7, 8

Star qualities: Jupiter

Description: a blue-white star located at the mouth of the river Eridani

---

PRIMARY STAR'S INFLUENCE

Achernar's influence stimulates expanded vision and the ability to see the whole. You are likely to have an optimistic outlook, a love of justice, and high aspirations. This star bestows success and a flair for dealing with the general public. Achernar may also direct you toward philosophy and religion.

Linked to your Sun's degree, this star bestows a generous, patient, and optimistic nature. This star gives prominence in higher education and a talent for writing. Rewards for outstanding work may be indicated. Achernar suggests that you can achieve success in business and dealing with the general public. If you gain fame, it is often long-lasting.

• *Positive:* justice, social sense, aspirations

• *Negative:* impressionability, escapism, speculation, misunderstandings

---

Your Pisces birthday points to a practical and dedicated personality who is both ambitious and determined, yet subtle and genteel. Although hardworking and competitive, you are also a creature of fantasy, sensitivity, and charisma. Despite all your worldly, sophisticated charm, you possess powerful intuitive insight.

The added influence of your Sun in the decanate of Cancer indicates that you are impressionable and receptive. Although you have high aims and objectives, a touch of lethargy suggests that you need material incentives to motivate you to accomplish. As a sympathetic individual, you are receptive to others' feelings but need to beware of fluctuating moods or worry. An ability to sense the deeper emotions of other people suggests that you are naturally psychic. If unhappy, avoid indulging in escapism or self-pity.

Strong-willed and bright, you have the ability to assimilate knowledge quickly if you are inspired or interested. Although you need stability and security, avoid boring and tedious activities, as these may ultimately lead to anxiety. A need for security and emotional satisfaction suggests that partnerships and friendships are especially important to you. Although you are naturally cooperative, by taking responsibility and developing self-discipline you can increase your initiative and self-confidence.

Until you reach the age of sixteen your progressed Sun moves through Pisces, placing the emphasis on your sensitivity, receptivity to your surroundings, and emotional needs. While you are between the ages of seventeen and forty-six your progressed Sun moves through Aries. This influence suggests that you will enter a new phase by becoming more assertive, daring, and spirited; this may result in a desire for new ventures. After the age of forty-seven, when your progressed Sun moves into Taurus, your need to be established and feel financially secure will increase, coupled with a wish for more emotional stability. At the age of seventy-seven, when your progressed Sun moves into Gemini, you start to become more curious and interested in different forms of communication, possibly taking up a new interest.

Your Secret Self

Friendly and outgoing, you enjoy working cooperatively with others in a team and usually see the advantages of operating in partnerships. If you have a tendency to worry or dwell on the past, then you need to learn about detachment. This implies that it is important not to become dependent on anything or anyone, as this can result in your becoming overly serious. By learning to let go, you develop a strong sense of personal freedom and are able to connect to a deeper universal level.

A natural diplomacy can give you an ease with people in social situations. Although many of your lessons in life regard your work, relationships are particularly important to your well-being. Although you are willing to make sacrifices for those you love, be careful not to martyr yourself. By ensuring that you always keep the balance of power equal in all your relationships and developing self-discipline, you can unlock your amazing potential.

Work & Vocation

Your social skills indicate that you usually work well in people-related careers. Highly intuitive and imaginative, you may decide to exercise your talents through creative pursuits such as art, hairdressing, dancing, music, or acting. You may also be attracted to writing in any form. Equally, your sensitive and sympathetic nature can lead you to careers involving counseling, teaching, or service in the community. Hardworking, with an instinctive business sense, you are also likely to be motivated by a desire for the good things in life. In your desire for harmonious surroundings, however, try to avoid getting stuck in too much of a routine.

Famous people who share your birthday include composer Antonio Vivaldi, writer Alan Sillitoe, racing driver Jim Clark, actress Paula Prentiss, psychologist Hans Eysenck, and actor John Garfield.

Numerology

Endowed with energy, practical skills, and strong determination, you can achieve success through hard work. With a number 4 birthday, you are sensitive to form and composition and are able to create practical systems. Security-conscious, you like to build a strong foundation for yourself and your family. A pragmatic approach to life confers a good business sense and an ability to move forward and achieve material success in life. You are usually honest, frank, and fair; nevertheless, you may have to learn to be more diplomatic and avoid a tendency to be stubborn or tactless. The subinfluence of the number 3 month indicates that, being versatile and creative, you must put your ideas to practical use. In order to combat your tendency for procrastination, you need structure and constant mental stimulation. As you enjoy a variety of social activities and interests, you may need to learn to focus on fewer aims. Usually you are a charming and entertaining companion, but emotional insecurities imply that at times you appear reserved. You possess good analytical skills, and by asserting yourself you can make others take more notice of your opinions.

• *Positive:* well organized, self-disciplined, steady, hardworking, craftsmanship, good with your hands, pragmatism, trusting, exact

• *Negative:* unstable, uncommunicative, repressed, lazy, procrastination, too economical, bossy, hidden affections, resentful

Love & Relationships

Your charismatic personality ensures that you have many friends and good social contacts. Although there may be some hidden uncertainty about close personal relationships, you usually associate with intelligent people who are assertive and mentally stimulating. You admire hardworking individuals who are determined in their approach to life challenges. A love of knowledge and admiration for those who possess inner wisdom suggest that you enjoy educational courses and collaborating with others. When you are enthusiastic about a relationship, you are willing to invest your time and money.

YOUR SPECIAL SOMEONE

You may find love and happiness with someone born on one of the following dates.

Love & friendship: Jan. 6, 20, 22, 24, 27, 30, Feb. 4, 18, 20, 22, 28, Mar. 2, 16, 18, 20, 26, 29, Apr. 14, 16, 18, 24, 27, May 2, 12, 14, 16, 22, 25, June 10, 12, 14, 20, 23, July 8, 10, 12, 15, 16, 18, 21, Aug. 6, 8, 10, 16, 19, Sept. 4, 6, 8, 14, 17, Oct. 2, 4, 6, 12, 15, Nov. 2, 4, 10, 13, 17, Dec. 2, 8, 11

Beneficial: Jan. 1, 3, 4, 12, 14, Feb. 1, 2, 12, Mar. 10, 28, Apr. 8, 26, 30, May 6, 24, 28, June 4, 22, 26, July 2, 11, 20, 24, Aug. 18, 22, Sept. 16, 20, Oct. 14, 18, Nov. 3, 12, 16, Dec. 10, 14

Fatal attractions: Jan. 11, Feb. 9, Mar. 7, Apr. 5, May 3, June 1, Sept. 4, 5, 6, 7, 8

Challenging: Jan. 3, 5, Feb. 1, 3, Mar. 1, July 31, Aug. 29, Sept. 27, 30, Oct. 25, 28, Nov. 23, 26, 30, Dec. 21, 24, 28

Soul mates: Jan. 5, 12, Feb. 3, 10, Mar. 1, 8, Apr. 6, May 4, June 2

March 5

Ⅱ Dynamic and idealistic, you are an ambitious and restless Piscean dreamer. Sensitive and highly intuitive, you can harness your powerful imagination through creative and productive endeavors. A need for variety implies that you constantly search for different and exciting ways to express your feelings. With an impulsive streak, you can sometimes act spontaneously in a moment of enthusiasm.

The added influence of your Sun in the decanate of Cancer indicates that you have a strong sixth sense and a need for the support of family or friends. Impressionable and receptive, you can easily access the feelings of others and are naturally psychic. As a sympathetic and caring individual, you may have to be careful not to take on other people's problems as your own. Although you are hardworking and practical, at times your powerful emotions can cause you to be tense and dramatic.

Compassionate by nature, you usually expect a great deal from others and are often willing to make sacrifices for the ones you love. If you are facing obstacles and disappointment, try to avoid letting pessimism or materialism get the better of you. When unhappy, however, avoid hiding your head in the sand or indulging in escapism and self-pity. By learning to trust your strong instincts, you can take advantage of the unexpected turns in life. A natural business sense and a love of travel and change may inspire you to experiment with different activities and occupations.

Until you reach the age of fifteen your progressed Sun is in Pisces, indicating that you are idealistic, loving, and versatile but that a tendency to be overemotional may cause you to become bored easily. While you are between the ages of sixteen and forty-five your progressed Sun moves through Aries, suggesting that you gradually become more confident, assertive, and ambitious. You may decide to start new ventures and find probable gains through cooperative ventures. At the age of forty-six there is another turning point as your Sun enters Taurus. After this time you slow down and have a need for more stability and financial security in your life. From the age of seventy-six, when your progressed Sun enters Gemini, you develop a heightened interest in communication and the exchange of ideas.

Your Secret Self

Your powerful emotions and sensitive nature suggest that you can achieve success through the power of love. If your strong feelings are not channeled or put to practical use, they can sometimes work to your disadvantage and you can become overemotional. When those feelings are positively used, however, you are dramatic and dynamic with creative talents, especially acting and performing.

Sociable and idealistic, with inspired thoughts, you can be both practical and imaginative. To utilize your great possibilities, you need a clear vision of what you want to achieve and methodical planning. Fortunately, you possess a good practical sense of values and a financial protection that comes from hard work. This strong emphasis on your work implies that through diligent and concentrated efforts you are able to make your lofty dreams a reality.

Work & Vocation

Sensitive and imaginative, with a desire for change and excitement, you may be most attracted to careers that involve variety or travel. Your natural dynamics can help you succeed in the

FIXED STAR

Star's name: Achernar
Degree position: 14°17'–15°11' Pisces between the years 1930 and 2000
Magnitude: 1
Strength: ★★★★★★★★★
Orb: 2°30'
Constellation: Alpha Eridanus
Applicable days: March 3, 4, 5, 6, 7, 8
Star qualities: Jupiter
Description: a blue-white star located at the mouth of the river Eridani

PRIMARY STAR'S INFLUENCE

Achernar's influence stimulates expanded vision and the ability to see the whole. You are likely to have an optimistic outlook, a love of justice, and high aspirations. This star bestows success and a flair for dealing with the general public. Achernar may also direct you toward philosophy and religion.

Linked to your Sun's degree, this star bestows a generous, patient, and optimistic nature. This star gives prominence in higher education and a talent for writing. Rewards for outstanding work may be indicated. Achernar suggests that you can achieve success in business and dealing with the general public. If you gain fame, it is often long-lasting.

• Positive: justice, social sense, aspirations

• Negative: impressionability, escapism, speculation, misunderstandings

business world. Your caring nature suggests a possible interest in social reform or working in the world of healing and health or child care. Many people of this birthday use their visionary skills in the art, design, film, and fashion worlds. Alternatively, you may wish to explore the more theatrical side of your personality, either in the entertainment world or through politics. Whatever career you choose, it is vital to avoid monotonous work. With the ability to see business opportunities, you could be involved in sales, promotion, or dealings with foreign countries.

Famous people who share your birthday include Chinese premier Chou En-lai, British musical star Elaine Paige, actors Dean Stockwell and Rex Harrison, actress Samantha Eggar, and film director Pier Paolo Pasolini.

Numerology

Your enthusiastic approach and willingness to try anything new suggest that life will have a lot to offer you. Travel and opportunities for change, some unexpected, may lead you to undergo a real transformation of views and beliefs. With a number 5 birthday, you need to feel that life is exciting. Nevertheless, you may need to develop a responsible attitude and avoid tendencies such as unpredictability and restlessness. The natural talent of a number 5 individual is knowing how to go with the flow and staying detached. The subinfluence of the number 3 month indicates that you are sociable and outgoing. Although you want security and stability, a tendency to become bored easily implies that you need variety, though it would be wise to develop patience and tolerance. You possess a strong need for self-expression and when positive can radiate the joy of life. A talent with words may indicate that you need to learn how to utilize the abundance of your creative power. Learning to endure in spite of challenges and delays allows you to take control.

• *Positive:* versatile, adaptable, progressive, strong instincts, magnetic, lucky, daring, freedom-loving, quick and witty, curious, mystical, sociable

• *Negative:* unreliable, procrastinator, inconsistent, overconfident

Love & Relationships

Romantic and idealistic about relationships, you may sometimes choose platonic relationships, as it is hard to find a partner who measures up to your high ideals. You admire individuals who are creative or humanitarian and idealistic. When you fall in love, you love deeply and usually remain loyal through periods of difficulty. Although you are caring and supportive, avoid overreacting to others or martyring yourself by staying realistic and detached.

YOUR SPECIAL SOMEONE

You may be luckier in forming lasting relationships and finding love with someone born on one of the following dates.

Love & friendship: Jan. 1, 7, 21, 23, 31, Feb. 5, 19, 21, 29, Mar. 3, 7, 17, 19, 27, Apr. 1, 15, 17, 25, May 3, 13, 15, 23, June 11, 13, 21, July 9, 11, 18, 19, Aug. 7, 9, 17, Sept. 5, 7, 15, Oct. 3, 5, 13, Nov. 1, 3, 10, 11, Dec. 1, 9

Beneficial: Jan. 5, 16, 18, Feb. 3, 14, 16, Mar. 1, 12, 14, 29, Apr. 10, 12, 27, May 8, 10, 25, 29, June 6, 8, 23, 27, July 4, 6, 21, 25, Aug. 2, 4, 19, 23, Sept. 2, 17, 21, Oct. 15, 19, Nov. 13, 17, Dec. 11, 15, 29

Fatal attractions: Jan. 6, 30, Feb. 4, 28, Mar. 2, 26, Apr. 24, May 22, June 20, July 18, Aug. 16, Sept. 5, 6, 7, 8, 9, 14, Oct. 12, Nov. 10, Dec. 8

Challenging: Jan. 4, Feb. 2, May 29, 31, June 27, 29, 30, July 25, 27, 28, Aug. 23, 25, 26, 30, Sept. 21, 23, 24, 28, Oct. 19, 21, 22, 26, Nov. 17, 19, 20, 24, Dec. 15, 17, 18, 22

Soul mates: Jan. 23, Feb. 21, Mar. 19, Apr. 17, May 15, June 13, July 11, 31, Aug. 9, 29, Sept. 7, 27, Oct. 5, 25, Nov. 3, 23, Dec. 1, 21

March 6

H Your Pisces birthday reveals you to be an idealistic individual with a good sense of values and practical skills. Friendly, kind, and often blessed with vitality and drive, you are a strong-willed person with a direct and frank approach. Highly intuitive, especially in matters concerning financial affairs, you are able to take advantage of excellent job opportunities. When you set your heart on an ideal or a cause, you can be both dedicated and determined.

The added influence of your Sun in the decanate of Cancer indicates that usually your sixth sense about people is correct. With an ability to recognize a good bargain when you see one, you do not miss many opportunities. As a sympathetic individual, you are receptive to the feelings of others but need to beware of fluctuating moods. With a natural ability to lead, you usually fare better giving orders than receiving them. In order to achieve success, you need only apply the necessary self-discipline.

Blessed with excellent health and knowing how to enjoy yourself, you relish the good life. You may have to beware, however, of overindulgence or becoming too materialistic. Avoid coming across as bossy or arrogant by showing your humble and gentle side. If you lack discipline, you may be uncertain of your values and beliefs, but with the right attitude you can move mountains and impress others with your knowledge and capabilities.

Until you reach the age of fourteen your progressed Sun moves through Pisces, placing the emphasis on your emotional development. While you are between the ages of fifteen and forty-four, your progressed Sun moves through Aries. This influence suggests that you gradually develop your assertiveness and enjoy being active and adventurous. This is a good time to take the initiative and learn to be more straightforward. After the age of forty-five, when your progressed Sun moves into Taurus, you may become more emotionally steady and practical. You also have an increased need to be established and financially secure as well as to be nourished by beauty and nature. At the age of seventy-five your progressed Sun moves into Gemini, emphasizing communication and the desire to study or talk.

FIXED STAR

Star's name: Achernar

Degree position: 14°17'–15°11' Pisces between the years 1930 and 2000

Magnitude: 1

Strength: ★★★★★★★★★

Orb: 2°30'

Constellation: Alpha Eridanus

Applicable days: March 3, 4, 5, 6, 7, 8

Star qualities: Jupiter

Description: a blue-white star located at the mouth of the river Eridani

PRIMARY STAR'S INFLUENCE

Achernar's influence stimulates expanded vision and the ability to see the whole. You are likely to have an optimistic outlook, a love of justice, and high aspirations. This star bestows success and a flair for dealing with the general public. Achernar may also direct you toward philosophy and religion.

Linked to your Sun's degree, this star bestows a generous, patient, and optimistic nature. This star gives prominence in higher education and a talent for writing. Rewards for outstanding work may be indicated. Achernar suggests that you can achieve success in business and dealing with the general public. If you gain fame, it is often long-lasting.

• *Positive:* justice, social sense, aspirations

• *Negative:* impressionability, escapism, speculation, misunderstandings

Your Secret Self

With your love for knowledge, you usually feel happier when well informed or when you have the skills to work out your problems. Your strong mental willpower, when used positively, encourages you to think independently and constructively. Usually very smart and determined, with an eye for detail, you are inquisitive and inventive. A tendency to become bored, however, implies that you thrive on variety and have an enthusiasm for new interests.

Capable of being very hardworking when interested, you learn quickly. Warm and creative, you possess a social grace and feel at ease in your interactions with others. An inclination to be self-indulgent, however, may create tension in love relationships. When you turn on the charm, though, you can be highly magnetic, with the ability to make yourself popular with others.

Work & Vocation

With your strong visionary sense and practical spirit of enterprise, you are often willing to organize or direct large undertakings. A good organizer, you have an excellent sense of form and are usually willing to work hard. With a need for harmony and self-expression, you can be strongly attracted by artistic or creative pursuits such as dance, music, drama, or writing. Possessing good social skills also enables you to work successfully in careers that deal with the public. You can combine your shrewd business understanding with your natural creativity and social skills to help you reach the top in the world of finance. Alternatively, a desire to help others may attract you to the caring, healing, or medical professions.

Famous people who share your birthday include painter and sculptor Michelangelo, poet Elizabeth Barrett Browning, comedian Lou Costello, singers Kiri Te Kanawa and Mary Wilson, Olympic athlete Dick Fosbury, writer Gabriel García Márquez, and actor Tom Arnold.

Numerology

Compassion, idealism, and a caring nature are some of the attributes suggested by a number 6 birthday. Often a visionary or a humanitarian, you can be responsible, loving, and supportive. Although you are usually worldly and career-oriented, with a number 6 birthday you can be a homemaker and a devoted parent. The more sensitive among you will need to find a form of creative expression and are often drawn to the world of entertainment or art and design. The challenges for some number 6 individuals may include developing self-confidence or being more commanding. The subinfluence of the number 3 month indicates that you are sensitive, with a strong sixth sense. Fun-loving and a good companion, you enjoy friendly social activities and many interests. Since you are versatile, with a need for different and exciting experiences, an inclination to get bored easily may cause you to become indecisive or spread yourself too thin. Curiosity and a need to discover a meaning to the broader picture of life suggest a necessity for spiritual development.

• *Positive:* worldly, friendly, compassionate, dependable, sympathetic, idealistic, domestically inclined, humanitarian, poised, artistic, balanced

• *Negative:* discontented, anxious, shy, unreasonable, stubborn, outspoken, domineering, irresponsible, cynical, self-centered

Love & Relationships

Charming and good-natured, you like to be associated with success and prestige. A taste for the good life implies that you are drawn toward luxury and appreciate quality. Money and good prospects are also important factors in relationships. Usually you know how to enjoy yourself or entertain people and like to associate with those who have potential. Magnanimous and kind, you like generous people but need to avoid overindulgence.

YOUR SPECIAL SOMEONE

If you are looking for security, harmony, wealth, and happiness, you might be luckier with someone born on one of the following dates.

Love and friendship: Jan. 7, 8, 17, 20, 22, 24, Feb. 6, 15, 18, 20, 22, Mar. 4, 13, 16, 18, 20, Apr. 1, 2, 11, 14, 16, 18, 26, May 9, 12, 14, 16, June 7, 10, 12, 14, July 5, 8, 10, 12, 20, 30, Aug. 3, 6, 8, 10, 28, Sept. 1, 4, 6, 8, 26, Oct. 2, 4, 6, 24, Nov. 2, 4, 12, 22, Dec. 2, 20

Beneficial: Jan. 6, 23, Feb. 4, 21, Mar. 2, 19, 30, Apr. 17, 28, May 15, 26, 30, June 13, 24, 28, July 11, 22, 26, Aug. 9, 20, 24, Sept. 7, 18, 22, Oct. 5, 16, 20, Nov. 3, 14, 18, Dec. 1, 12, 16, 30

Fatal attractions: Jan. 7, Feb. 5, Mar. 3, Apr. 1, Sept. 6, 7, 8, 9

Challenging: Jan. 5, 26, 29, Feb. 3, 24, 27, Mar. 1, 22, 25, Apr. 20, 23, May 18, 21, June 16, 19, 30, July 14, 17, 28, Aug. 12, 15, 26, 31, Sept. 10, 13, 24, 29, Oct. 8, 11, 22, 27, Nov. 6, 9, 20, 25, Dec. 4, 7, 18, 23

Soul mates: Jan. 30, Feb. 28, Mar. 26, Apr. 24, May 22, June 20, July 18, Aug. 16, Sept. 14, Oct. 12, 31, Nov. 10, 29, Dec. 8, 27

March 7

H Imaginative, idealistic, and thoughtful, you are a creative and discriminating Piscean who is full of ideas. Although blessed with a vivid inner life, in order to achieve success and prosperity you need to find a practical purpose for your wonderful thoughts and dreams.

The added influence of your Sun in the decanate of Cancer implies that you are intuitive, with an ability to access the collective unconscious. As you usually have a wealth of feelings, you are a sensitive and kind person. When you are optimistic and positive, your caring and sympathetic nature can bring light and hope to any situation. Although you are receptive to others' feelings, you may need to beware of fluctuating moods. If unhappy, avoid indulging in worry or fantasy. Develop your intuitive side by trusting your strong sixth sense.

Though you present a bright and confident front to the world, you conceal a more serious and deep side to your nature. Being versatile and multitalented indicates that making the right choices can be difficult. Advancement usually comes from decisive action rather than worry and indecision. It is better to invest in long-term plans and firm foundations rather than immediate returns. Although you possess great ideas, you must learn to be patient as well as listen to the advice of others. By learning to stay detached and let go of the past, you can avoid periods of being frustrated or disappointed.

While you are between the ages of fourteen and forty-three your progressed Sun moves through Aries. This influence suggests that you gradually develop your confidence and enjoy being active and assertive. After the age of forty-four, when your progressed Sun moves into Taurus, you feel an increased need for stability and financial security. You may become more emotionally stable, with a possible stronger interest in nature. At the age of seventy-four there is a turning point when your progressed Sun enters Gemini. This suggests that your curiosity grows and you start to transform your way of thinking. This also highlights your interest in communication and learning new subjects.

Your Secret Self

Although you are idealistic and highly intuitive, you may vacillate between faith and self-doubt. By being afraid to take risks, especially where your security is concerned, you may experience frustration or dissatisfaction with yourself and others. It is through facing your doubts and fears that you can truly find faith in yourself and discover what life has to offer you. With a positive perspective, you have the potential to inspire others with your ideals and imagination. You may need to learn to concentrate on your true goals by avoiding scattering your energies on unimportant issues or events.

Although you want to surround yourself with harmony and beauty, at a deep level many of your personal challenges may concern your attitude toward money and material considerations. You may find it difficult to accept the responsibility of your more difficult challenges. By focusing on your creative energies, you are able to achieve original and productive results. Take time to regenerate yourself by paying attention to your diet and health as well as learning to relax.

Work & Vocation

Sensitive yet analytical, you have a strong need for self-expression. When this is combined with your imagination and visionary sense, you may wish to pursue a career in photography,

FIXED STAR

Star's name: Achernar

Degree position: 14°17'–15°11' Pisces between the years 1930 and 2000

Magnitude: 1

Strength: ★★★★★★★★★

Orb: 2°30'

Constellation: Alpha Eridanus

Applicable days: March 3, 4, 5, 6, 7, 8

Star qualities: Jupiter

Description: a blue-white star located at the mouth of the river Eridani

PRIMARY STAR'S INFLUENCE

Achernar's influence stimulates expanded vision and the ability to see the whole. You are likely to have an optimistic outlook, a love of justice, and high aspirations. This star bestows success and a flair for dealing with the general public. Achernar may also direct you toward philosophy and religion.

Linked to your Sun's degree, this star bestows a generous, patient, and optimistic nature. This star gives prominence in higher education and a talent for writing. Rewards for outstanding work may be indicated. Achernar suggests that you can achieve success in business and dealing with the general public. If you gain fame, it is often long-lasting.

• Positive: justice, social sense, aspirations

• Negative: impressionability, escapism, speculation, misunderstandings

art, or film, or use your emotional impressionability in music or dance. Alternatively, you may be drawn to the caring professions, such as the medical world, teaching, social work, or charity and voluntary work. The influence of this birthday also suggests that there may be interests or work involving foreign countries. If in the business world, you can use your people skills to help you achieve success. Fluctuating circumstances in your working environment can point to changes in your career. Whatever work you choose, your keen intelligence and intuitive sense can help you to learn quickly.

Famous people who share your birthday include composer Maurice Ravel, Dutch painter Piet Mondrian, horticulturist Luther Burbank, tennis player Ivan Lendl, photographer Lord Snowden, and actress Anna Magnani.

Numerology

Analytical and thoughtful, number 7 individuals are frequently critical and self-absorbed. With a constant need for greater self-awareness, you enjoy gathering information and may be interested in reading, writing, or spirituality. Although shrewd, you may overrationalize or get lost in detail. A tendency to be enigmatic or secretive suggests that at times you feel misunderstood. The subinfluence of the number 3 month indicates that although you are sensitive and idealistic, with a need for close personal relationships, you prefer at times to be on your own. Analytical and inquisitive, you like to ask subtle questions without letting anyone know what you really think. A tendency to be skeptical or too proud also suggests that you need to develop your communication skills in order to avoid misunderstandings. Happiest when you are extending your knowledge and broadening your horizons, you benefit from all kinds of intellectual pursuits. A seeker of wisdom, you can find inspiration in studying metaphysics, philosophy, or the healing arts.

• *Positive:* educated, trusting, meticulous, idealistic, honest, psychic, scientific, rational, reflective

• *Negative:* concealing, unfriendly, secretive, skeptical, confused, detached

Love & Relationships

As you are likely to attract all types of people, you need to be discriminating in your choice of friends. Achieving emotional balance can prevent you from alternating between being emotionally expressive and appearing cold or withdrawn. It is particularly important that you are honest with your partners. Usually you are attracted to intelligent people with whom you can share some sort of intellectual activity. Charming and friendly, you have no problem making friends or finding lovers. With your gentle mannerisms and creative approach to life, you can enchant others.

YOUR SPECIAL SOMEONE

You are likely to have more luck with someone born on one of the following dates.

Love & friendship: Jan. 9, 23, 25, 27, Feb. 7, 21, 23, 25, Mar. 5, 19, 21, 23, 29, Apr. 3, 17, 19, 21, 27, 30, May 1, 15, 17, 19, 25, 28, June 13, 15, 17, 23, 26, 27, July 11, 13, 15, 21, 24, Aug. 9, 11, 13, 19, 22, Sept. 7, 9, 11, 17, 20, Oct. 5, 7, 9, 15, 18, 30, Nov. 3, 5, 7, 13, 16, 17, Dec. 1, 3, 5, 11, 14, 26

Beneficial: Jan. 2, 4, 7, 26, Feb. 2, 5, Mar. 3, Apr. 1, May 31, June 29, July 14, 27, 31, Aug. 25, 29, Sept. 23, 27, Oct. 21, 25, Nov. 6, 19, 23, Dec. 17, 21

Fatal attractions: Jan. 8, 14, Feb. 6, 12, Mar. 4, 10, Apr. 2, 8, May 6, June 4, July 2, Sept. 7, 8, 9, 10

Challenging: Jan. 6, 19, 29, Feb. 4, 17, 27, Mar. 2, 15, 25, Apr. 13, 23, May 11, 21, June 9, 19, July 7, 17, Aug. 5, 15, Sept. 3, 13, 30, Oct. 1, 11, 28, Nov. 9, 26, Dec. 7, 24, 29

Soul mates: Jan. 16, 21, Feb. 14, 19, Mar. 12, 17, Apr. 10, 15, May 8, 13, June 6, 11, July 4, 9, Aug. 2, 7, Sept. 5, Oct. 3, Nov. 1

March 8

♓ Your birthday shows you to be a hardworking and pragmatic Piscean with a friendly and charming personality. Although you are direct and prompt in your approach, you are inspired and highly imaginative. Often self-reliant and with a strong sense of purpose, you have natural diplomatic skills that imply that you prefer to work in collaboration with others as a leading member of a team. Avoid becoming involved in power games or manipulative tactics, however.

The added influence of your Sun in the decanate of Cancer indicates that you are receptive and sensitive. As you usually have powerful thoughts and an ability to sense the subconscious of others, you are naturally psychic about what motivates them. As a caring individual, you are sympathetic to others' feelings but need to beware of fluctuating moods. If insecure, avoid resorting to arguments just for the sake of being difficult; escapism or self-pity will not serve you well, either.

Although you are ambitious and have good business sense, your birthday suggests that, due to your mental dynamism, you need to constantly reestablish a balance in your life. By creating harmony, you are able to overcome inner tensions and unexplained anxieties. An inclination for metaphysical subjects may draw you to spirituality or philosophy. When inspired by a cause or an idea, you are able to learn your subject thoroughly and even contribute your own original thoughts.

While you are between the ages of thirteen and forty-two your progressed Sun moves through Aries, suggesting that you gradually become more confident, assertive, and ambitious. You may prefer a leading role or start new ventures. At the age of forty-three there is a turning point as your Sun enters Taurus. After this time, you slow down and have a need for more stability and financial security in your life. From the age of seventy-three, when your progressed Sun enters Gemini, you develop a heightened interest in communication and the exchange of ideas.

Your Secret Self

Intelligent and imaginative, you learn to value wisdom and understanding. Your desire for knowledge and your enterprising spirit can be your motivating forces. Although part of you would be quite happy just to relax at home and get stuck in a comfortable routine, your challenge is often concerned with the drive and determination that it takes to put your wonderful ideas into practice or turn your dreams into action. Your natural sense of leadership and pride suggests that unless you are mentally stimulated, you may not be tapping into your true potential.

Highly intuitive and imaginative, you need something to inspire you to act independently. Usually you have original and progressive beliefs but need a creative outlet to express yourself. Leading a well-balanced life can be a key to your happiness. To avoid anxiety, especially worries connected to your work, you may need to break away from your day-to-day routine through other interests, hobbies, or travel.

Work & Vocation

Friendly and cooperative, you work well in activities that involve partnerships or collaborating with others. With natural business sense, you can succeed in commerce, banking, or financial

---

FIXED STAR

Star's name: Achernar

Degree position: 14°17'–15°11' Pisces between the years 1930 and 2000

Magnitude: 1

Strength: ★★★★★★★★★

Orb: 2°30'

Constellation: Alpha Eridanus

Applicable days: March 3, 4, 5, 6, 7, 8

Star qualities: Jupiter

Description: a blue-white star located at the mouth of the river Eridani

PRIMARY STAR'S INFLUENCE

Achernar's influence stimulates expanded vision and an ability to see the whole. You are likely to have an optimistic outlook, a love of justice, and high aspirations. This star bestows success and a flair for dealing with the general public. Achernar may also direct you toward philosophy and religion.

Linked to your Sun's degree, this star bestows a generous, patient, and optimistic nature. This star gives prominence in higher education and a talent for writing. Rewards for outstanding work may be indicated. Achernar suggests that you can achieve success in business and dealing with the general public. If you gain fame, it is often long-lasting.

• Positive: justice, social sense, aspirations

• Negative: impressionability, escapism, speculation, misunderstandings

ventures, but ideally you need to combine this with your people skills or creativity. Administrative work of any type can be aided by your superior organizational skills. Being diplomatic can help you in many different areas, such as public relations work and negotiations. Equally, your intuitive powers can always provide you with a sixth sense about your work opportunities. An interest in the arts and visual concepts such as photography and design may inspire your inventive temperament, or you may be drawn to writing, music, drama, or dance. Sensitive and with a need for creativity, you have the potential to put your ideas to practical use.

Famous people who share your birthday include actress Lynn Redgrave, writer Kenneth Grahame, painter Anselm Kiefer, ballet dancer Lynn Seymour, singer/actor Mickey Dolenz, singer Carole Bayer Sager, actor Aidan Quinn, and U.S. Supreme Court Justice Oliver Wendell Holmes.

Numerology

The power suggested by the number 8 birthday shows a character with strong values and sound judgment. The number 8 indicates that you aspire to great accomplishment and possess an ambitious nature. A desire for dominance, security, and material success is also indicated by this birthday. As a number 8 person, you have natural business sense and will benefit greatly from developing organizational and executive skills. A strong need to feel secure or established urges you to make long-term plans and investments. The subinfluence of the number 3 month indicates that you are multitalented and imaginative. At times your intuitive powers can provide you with flashes of inspiration. Sensitive and with a need for creativity, you use your ideas in a practical way. But as a natural opportunist, beware of attempting to do too many things at once. By becoming focused on a few projects, you can learn self-discipline and patience, which can lead to successful achievements. In order to achieve your aims, use your powers of persuasion to support and encourage rather than to manipulate partners and loved ones.

• *Positive:* leadership, thoroughness, hardworking, authority, protection, power to heal, good judge of values

• *Negative:* impatient, intolerant, restless, overwork, domineering, easily discouraged, lack of planning

Love & Relationships

Although stability and home life are important, you have to find ways to express yourself and not allow your love life to become boring or monotonous. Finding a balance between duties and leisure time can help things flow. Although harmony and security or a settled relationship seem particularly important to you, you may become moody with your loved ones if you feel discontented or become too dependent on partners. Fortunately, when you focus your friendly charm and sensitive understanding on others, you have the ability to make them feel really special. Using your natural diplomatic skills can bring peace and harmony to your relationships with others.

YOUR SPECIAL SOMEONE

You might find friendship or a faithful lover or partner among those born on the following dates.

Love & friendship: Jan. 10, 26, 28, Feb. 8, 21, 24, 26, Mar. 6, 22, 24, 30, Apr. 4, 20, 22, 28, May 2, 18, 20, 26, 29, June 16, 18, 24, 27, July 11, 14, 16, 22, 25, Aug. 12, 14, 20, 23, 30, Sept. 10, 12, 18, 21, 28, Oct. 8, 10, 16, 19, 26, Nov. 3, 6, 8, 14, 17, 24, Dec. 4, 6, 12, 15, 22

Beneficial: Jan. 8, Feb. 6, Mar. 4, 28, Apr. 2, 26, May 24, June 22, 30, July 20, 28, 29, Aug. 18, 26, 27, 30, Sept. 16, 24, 25, 28, Oct. 14, 22, 23, 26, 29, Nov. 12, 20, 21, 24, 27, Dec. 10, 18, 19, 22, 25

Fatal attractions: Jan. 15, Feb. 13, Mar. 11, Apr. 9, May 7, June 5, July 3, Aug. 1, Sept. 8, 9, 10, 11

Challenging: Jan. 7, 9, 30, Feb. 5, 7, 28, Mar. 3, 5, 26, Apr. 1, 3, 24, May 1, 22, June 20, July 18, Aug. 16, Sept. 14, Oct. 12, 29, Nov. 10, 27, Dec. 8, 25, 30

Soul mates: Jan. 8, 27, Feb. 6, 25, Mar. 4, 23, Apr. 2, 21, May 19, June 17, July 15, Aug. 13, Sept. 11, Oct. 9, Nov. 7, Dec. 5

March 9

H Highly intuitive and sensitive, you are a reserved but observant Piscean with hidden powers and determination. Mentally sharp, you like to initiate new ventures and be in a leading position. Idealistic and with deep feelings, you need challenges to bring about the transformation that you seek in order to let your true character rise to the surface.

The added influence of your Sun in the decanate of Cancer indicates that you have a fertile imagination. As you usually have a wealth of feelings, you are also sensitive and caring. When sympathetic and receptive to the feelings of others you can be very supportive and loyal, but avoid taking on other people's problems. An ability to access the collective unconscious suggests that you are aware of current moods but need to beware of your own fluctuating emotions. If dissatisfied, avoid indulging in escapism, worry, or self-pity.

Since you are multitalented, it is important that you keep yourself occupied with work and express yourself creatively. Being stubborn or self-willed, however, may prove to be an obstacle to the great potential indicated by this birthday. By developing your heightened receptivity, you can begin to comprehend yourself and life at a deeper level. Inspired by new beginnings, you feel confident and hopeful when you are working hard on a project you have faith in.

Until you reach the age of eleven your progressed Sun moves through Pisces, placing an emphasis on your sensitivity, impressionability to your surroundings, and emotional needs. While you are between the ages of twelve and forty-one your progressed Sun moves through Aries. This influence suggests that you gradually become more assertive, daring, and spirited, which may result in a strong desire for new ventures. After the age of forty-two, when your progressed Sun moves into Taurus, your need to be established and feel financially secure will increase, coupled with a wish for more calm and emotional steadiness. At the age of seventy-two, when your progressed Sun moves into Gemini, you start to become more curious and interested in different forms of communication, possibly taking up a new interest.

Your Secret Self

Although you can develop excellent communication skills, you may at times be highly idealistic and have difficulty expressing your true feelings. Nevertheless, a need for personal or intimate relationships is a vital key to your happiness. Learning to stay detached, expecting less of others, or standing on your own two feet gives you the confidence you desire. It may also help you to overcome suspicion or the fear of being alone. Meticulous and tidy, you like to pay attention to detail and may want to develop your critical and analytical skills.

Your leadership ability, determination, and capacity for hard work point out that once you have made up your mind, you can advance in any field of endeavor. As a perfectionist with highly idealistic and romantic notions, you have a strong need to express your creative talents. By having a meaningful cause to support, you are able to successfully channel your high ideals, quick insight, and compassion to help others.

Work & Vocation

Broad-minded and hardworking, you can be very dedicated to a project when interested. Your ability to quickly grasp concepts and be responsible is appreciated by your employers. With

FIXED STARS

Although your Sun's degree is not linked to a fixed star, some of your other planets' degrees certainly will be. By having an astrological chart calculated, you can find the exact position of the planets on your date of birth. This will tell you which of the fixed stars listed in this book are relevant to you.

your innate leadership skills, you are able to influence others and stay calm in times of crisis. Intuitive and imaginative, you possess a good sense of vision that you can use for problem solving, for foresight, or in the visual arts. You could also be interested in music or dance. Alternatively, you may choose to work as a counselor or administrator. An interest in education suggests that you can be an accomplished teacher or writer. Some people of this birthday have a strong interest in religion or spirituality and are drawn to help others through the caring professions or altruistic endeavors.

Famous people who share your birthday include chess player Bobby Fischer, cosmonaut Yuri Gagarin, jazz musician Ornette Coleman, singer Jackie Wilson, guitarist Robin Trower, and author Mickey Spillane.

Numerology

Benevolence, thoughtfulness, and sentimental sensitivity are all associated with the number 9 birthday. Tolerant and kind, you are often generous and liberal. Intuitive and psychic abilities point to a universal receptivity and, if channeled positively, may inspire you to seek a spiritual path. This birthday may suggest a need to overcome challenges, a tendency to be overly sensitive, and emotional ups and downs. You benefit greatly from world travel and interaction with people from all walks of life, but may have to avoid unrealistic dreams or an inclination toward escapism. The subinfluence of the number 3 month indicates that you are idealistic, creative, and imaginative. Usually you are perceptive, accommodating, and friendly. Naturally understanding and sympathetic, you also know how to use tact and cooperative methods to achieve your aims and objectives. Intelligent, you also possess good reasoning power. Since you want to establish true individuality, you are often innovative. In order to overcome challenges, you need to develop self-discipline and determination.

• *Positive:* idealistic, humanitarian, creative, sensitive, generous, magnetic, poetic, detached, lucky, popular

• *Negative:* frustrated, nervous, selfish, impractical, easily led, inferiority complex, worry

Love & Relationships

Sensitive and receptive, you need to find a partner whom you can trust and who will share your deep feelings of intimacy. You may need to guard against becoming preoccupied with self-interests that can separate you from others or to avoid an inclination to be suspicious by learning to overcome your shyness. You are more suited to someone who shares your high ideals and aspirations. Your dynamic drive and power to initiate new projects can always gain you the admiration of others.

YOUR SPECIAL SOMEONE

Your ideals may be realized more easily with those born on the following dates.

Love & friendship: Jan. 11, 20, 25, 27, 29, Feb. 9, 18, 23, 25, 27, Mar. 7, 16, 21, 23, 25, Apr. 5, 14, 19, 21, 23, 29, May 3, 12, 17, 19, 21, June 1, 10, 15, 17, 19, 25, July 8, 13, 15, 17, Aug. 6, 11, 13, 15, Sept. 4, 9, 11, 13, Oct. 2, 7, 9, 11, Nov. 5, 7, 9, 15, Dec. 3, 5, 7

Beneficial: Jan. 9, 26, Feb. 7, 24, Mar. 5, 22, Apr. 3, 20, May 1, 18, 29, June 16, 27, July 14, 25, 29, 30, Aug. 12, 23, 27, 28, 31, Sept. 10, 21, 25, 26, 29, Oct. 8, 19, 23, 24, 27, Nov. 6, 17, 21, 22, 25, Dec. 4, 15, 19, 20, 23

Fatal attractions: Jan. 16, Feb. 14, Mar. 12, Apr. 10, May 8, June 6, July 4, Aug. 2, Sept. 8, 9, 10, 11, 12

Challenging: Jan. 8, 29, 31, Feb. 6, 27, 29, Mar. 4, 25, 27, 28, Apr. 2, 23, 25, 26, May 21, 23, 24, June 19, 21, 22, July 17, 19, 20, Aug. 15, 17, 18, Sept. 13, 15, 16, Oct. 11, 13, 14, 30, Nov. 9, 11, 12, 28, Dec. 7, 9, 10, 26

Soul mates: May 30, June 28, July 26, Aug. 24, Sept. 22, 30, Oct. 20, 28, Nov. 18, 26, Dec. 16, 24

March 10

The mixture of ambition and idealism suggested by your birthday indicates that you are a perceptive Piscean with a pragmatic approach. You are a gifted and versatile individual, and when you become inspired you often take the leading role, showing others your originality and administrative skills.

The added influence of your Sun in the decanate of Cancer brings imagination to your natural intuitive abilities. Although independent, you have a strong desire for security, so your home and family are especially important parts of your life. Endowed with psychic or mediumistic talents, you need to trust your inner feelings. When you have premonitions, events usually come about just as you knew they would. Although your warmth and sympathetic nature imply that you can be tolerant and compassionate, your pride and sensitivity indicate that you can get easily hurt and are prone to moodiness.

Although you are capable of hard work and blessed with good business sense, you need to express yourself by doing something unconventional and creative. Receptive to new ideas and experiences, you desire room to maneuver freely; although you are materially aware, you dislike a mundane routine. You desire freedom, but your easy charm and warm and friendly manner can make you popular with others. Subtle and with the gift of diplomacy, you can be direct without being offensive. An attraction for beauty suggests that you can be stylish and have a love of the creative arts.

Until you reach the age of ten your progressed Sun moves through Pisces, highlighting issues regarding your emotional sensitivity and dreams for the future. While you are between the ages of eleven and forty your progressed Sun moves through Aries. This influence suggests that you gradually develop your confidence and assertiveness, with a desire to be more active and adventurous. This is a good time to take the initiative and learn to be more straightforward. After the age of forty-one, when your progressed Sun moves into Taurus, you enter a new phase. This emphasizes an increased need to be solidly established and financially secure as well as to be nourished by beauty and nature. At the age of seventy-one your progressed Sun moves into Gemini, emphasizing communication and desire for new interests.

Your Secret Self

Naturally dramatic and sociable, you usually appear self-assured. If on an inner level you lack the self-confidence to strike out on your own, however, you may end up in situations that do not utilize your full capabilities and talents. Although you usually have a wide range of interests, by focusing on one particular idea or project you are more able to fully express your strong creativity.

Bright and adaptable, you have a quick understanding of people. This insight helps you to achieve in life and ensures your success in social situations. Generous and understanding, you often attempt to keep the peace by using your diplomacy and natural charm. Although friendly, you do not reveal all of yourself to others and often need periods of being alone to reflect and find your center of stillness. Developing your strong intuition allows you to have faith in your own abilities and avoid worry and indecision.

Work & Vocation

People-related occupations are likely to bring you the most satisfaction. Your natural psychological skills could also prove helpful in sales, advertising, or counseling work. Although you

FIXED STARS

Although your Sun's degree is not linked to a fixed star, some of your other planets' degrees certainly will be. By having an astrological chart calculated, you can find the exact position of the planets on your date of birth. This will tell you which of the fixed stars listed in this book are relevant to you.

can collaborate and work well in a team situation, you usually do not like to take orders from others. This suggests that you are better in a leadership position or working for yourself. Your natural dramatic sense and strong imagination may find release through music, art, dance, or drama. Writing can prove to be an equally positive outlet for the creative side of your nature. Sympathetic and intuitive, you could be attracted to the caring professions. As you usually love travel, you may also become involved in businesses that deal with foreign countries. Others will appreciate your ability to bring new and original ideas to your work.

Famous people who share your birthday include actress Sharon Stone, jazz composer Bix Beiderbecke, actor Chuck Norris, U.S. abolitionist Harriet Tubman, and British royal family member Prince Edward.

Numerology

Like those with a number 1 birthday, you are ambitious and independent. Although you may have to overcome challenges before you achieve your goals, with determination you often accomplish your objectives. Your pioneering spirit frequently encourages you to travel far afield or strike out on your own. With a number 10 birthday, you may also need to learn that the world does not revolve around you and that you should guard against being domineering. The subinfluence of the number 3 month indicates that you need to find ways to express yourself. Amiable and friendly, you enjoy social activities and usually have many interests. Versatile, with a restless streak, you run the risk of becoming bored too easily or spreading yourself too thin, unless you are self-disciplined. Although you can be enthusiastic, with a good sense of humor, you may have to develop self-esteem in order to guard against worry. Avoid being bossy or too critical in personal relationships. A loving atmosphere is of prime importance to you, as it fills you with hope and inspiration.

• *Positive:* leadership, creative, progressive, forceful, optimistic, strong convictions, competitive, independent, gregarious

• *Negative:* overbearing, jealous, egotistical, pride, selfish, impatient

Love & Relationships

As you have a wonderful friendly charm that can attract friends and admirers, you are sure to have an active social life and enjoy entertaining. You usually enjoy the company of intelligent people who can introduce you to new ideas, or you may like to join groups where you can gain information and learn practical skills. Your need for balance and harmony implies that you achieve more by using diplomatic methods and interpersonal skills with your partner or associates rather than being dogmatic.

YOUR SPECIAL SOMEONE

For security, mental stimulation, and love, you might want to begin looking for those born among the following dates.

Love & friendship: Jan. 4, 11, 12, 16, 26, 28, 30, Feb. 2, 9, 10, 24, 26, 28, Mar. 7, 8, 22, 24, 26, Apr. 5, 6, 20, 22, 24, 30, May 3, 4, 8, 18, 20, 22, 28, 31, June 1, 2, 16, 18, 20, 26, 29, July 4, 14, 16, 18, 24, 27, Aug. 12, 14, 16, 22, 25, Sept. 10, 12, 14, 20, 23, Oct. 8, 10, 12, 18, 21, Nov. 6, 8, 10, 16, 19, Dec. 4, 6, 8, 14, 17

Beneficial: Jan. 3, 10, 29, 31, Feb. 1, 8, 27, 29, Mar. 6, 25, 27, Apr. 4, 23, 25, May 2, 21, 23, June 19, 21, July 17, 19, 30, Aug. 15, 17, 28, Sept. 13, 15, 26, Oct. 11, 13, 24, Nov. 9, 11, 22, Dec. 7, 9, 20

Fatal attractions: Jan. 11, Feb. 9, Mar. 7, Apr. 5, May 3, June 1, Sept. 10, 11, 12, 13

Challenging: Jan. 9, Feb. 7, Mar. 5, 28, Apr. 3, 26, May 1, 24, June 22, July 20, Aug. 18, Sept. 16, Oct. 14, 30, 31, Nov. 12, 28, 29, Dec. 10, 26, 27

Soul mates: Jan. 7, Feb. 5, Mar. 3, Apr. 1, May 29, June 27, July 25, Aug. 23, Sept. 21, Oct. 19, Nov. 17, Dec. 15

March 11

H Inspired and idealistic, you are a dynamic and enthusiastic Piscean with strong material values. Endowed with inner strength and powers of perception, you like to take the lead or be in the forefront of new and innovative projects. A preoccupation with material concerns and a need for financial security imply that you like to combine your imaginative and creative talents with commercial enterprises. With your desire for the good life, however, you may have to avoid overindulgence or being extravagant.

The added influence of your Sun in the decanate of Cancer suggests that you possess powerful intuition or a strong sixth sense. With your fertile imagination, you can have vision and foresight. Although practical skills and good judgment override other factors, an ability to access the collective unconscious makes you aware of public trends.

As a humanitarian with determination and strong convictions, you possess idealistic notions. As you also have the capacity to be persistent and diligent, success is yours if you do not allow yourself to get overly concerned by materialism. Although you can respond quickly and intuitively, by learning to stay calm and avoiding compulsive or erratic activities you become more patient and less domineering.

While you are between the ages of ten and thirty-nine your progressed Sun moves through Aries. This influence suggests that you gradually develop your assertiveness and self-confidence as well as enjoy being active and courageous. After the age of forty, when your progressed Sun moves into Taurus, you have an increased need for stability and financial security. You become more relaxed and determined, but a reluctance to change can reveal signs of stubbornness. At the age of seventy there is a turning point when your progressed Sun enters Gemini. This suggests that your curiosity grows and you start to transform your way of thinking. This also highlights your interest in communication and learning new subjects.

Fixed Stars

Although your Sun's degree is not linked to a fixed star, some of your other planets' degrees certainly will be. By having an astrological chart calculated, you can find the exact position of the planets on your date of birth. This will tell you which of the fixed stars listed in this book are relevant to you.

Your Secret Self

At times indecision or worry, particularly regarding financial issues, can undermine your wonderful creativity. When inspired, you have an original approach and are capable of deep thought. Having courage and an independent spirit stimulates you to seek personal freedom and enables you to react quickly to situations. Although you can be expressive, avoid scattering your energies among too many interests. Self-discipline brings out the best of your extraordinary potential.

Generous when positive but frustrated when down, you will see that the greater your detachment, the more you are able to avoid disappointment. Your keen mind and visionary ability help you see on a large scale. By utilizing your organizing abilities and fighting spirit, you are able to apply your worldly knowledge to achieve, either in personal terms or in supporting a meaningful cause.

Work & Vocation

You can be an excellent manager or administrator and usually do better in life when in positions of authority. An innate understanding of money and values may draw you to business, where you can do particularly well, especially when combining your practical, imaginative, and creative skills. Your ability to push through some kind of reform may attract you to leadership in such organizations as trade unions or encourage you to fight for the rights of others. An excellent spokesperson, you may become involved in politics to get your message across. If not a freedom fighter, you may be interested in education or some other form of public service. A need to express your individuality and creativity may draw you to the world of art, music, dance, or entertainment.

Famous people who share your birthday include media tycoon Rupert Murdoch, British prime minister Harold Wilson, science fiction writer Douglas Adams, silent-film actress Dorothy Gish, and singer Bobby McFerrin.

Numerology

The special vibration of the master number 11 birthday suggests that idealism, inspiration, and innovation are highly important to you. A blend of humility and confidence challenges you to work toward self-mastery both materially and spiritually. Through experience you learn how to deal with the different sides of your nature and develop a less extremist attitude by trusting your own feelings. Usually you are highly charged and enjoy vitality, but must avoid becoming overly anxious or impractical. The subinfluence of the number 3 month indicates that you are sensitive and imaginative, with mental dynamism and quick responses. Usually enthusiastic and enterprising, you are willing to take a chance and make a fresh start. If independent, you are not the type to sit around, as you need variety and activity. You not only know what you want but are resourceful enough to know the fastest way of obtaining it. Usually you are dexterous, with a flair for technical work that demands skill and precision. Sociable and proud, you care about your image and appearance.

• *Positive:* balanced, focused, objective, enthusiastic, inspirational, spiritual, idealistic, intuitive, intelligent, outgoing, inventive, artistic, healing ability, humanitarian, faith

• *Negative:* superiority complex, dishonest, aimless, overemotional, easily hurt, selfish, dominating

Love & Relationships

Outgoing and sociable, you enjoy interacting with others and like to make a good impression. Usually you desire the company of optimistic and pragmatic people who can give sound advice or solve problems. As a dynamic and dramatic individual, you must be careful of being too bossy with your spouse or associates. You can benefit greatly from mixing with people who are mentally stimulating or participating in groups where you can be creatively expressive.

March 12

H Congenial and charming, with youthful charisma, you are a friendly Piscean with an enthusiastic approach. As you are likely to be high-spirited and idealistic, you may find that you grow old more slowly than other people. The peculiar mixture of materialism and idealism suggested by your birthday implies that although you possess a determined and ambitious nature and a good head for business, you enjoy excitement and are conscious of your image. This suggests that you are keen to find the funds that can provide you with the good life. As a quick learner, you may find that the road to success often involves developing new skills and applying them creatively.

The added influence of your Sun in the decanate of Scorpio suggests that you possess second sight or natural psychic abilities. An inclination toward investigating parapsychology, telepathy, or clairvoyance can lead you to mystical realizations. With your powerful perceptions and depth of feeling, your inquisitive mind enjoys getting to the bottom of things. If you find true inspiration, you are often willing to work hard and can achieve prosperity and fame.

Kindhearted, adaptable, and sociable, you are usually witty and entertaining, with a desire to be accepted and popular. Aware of your image, you need to feel good and look well groomed, often spending your money on clothes and luxury goods. Although you like to be independent, joint efforts and collaboration with others can yield profits and success. With a responsible attitude, you often make excellent contributions to your team.

Between the ages of nine and thirty-eight, as your progressed Sun moves through Aries, you gradually become more assertive and ambitious. As your confidence grows, you may decide to take the initiative and pioneer new ventures or be stronger in your relationships with others. At the age of thirty-nine there is another turning point as your Sun enters Taurus. After this time you slow down and have a greater need for more stability and financial security in your life. From the age of sixty-nine, when your progressed Sun enters Gemini, you develop a heightened interest in communication and the exchange of ideas.

Your Secret Self

Although you may be gifted and skillful, without effort and determination your talents may not be fully realized. Your bright personality and youthful expression suggest that you are idealistic and full of life. Since you often have many diverse interests and activities, you are advised to have clear goals and learn to stay focused.

Intelligent and ambitious, you may sometimes be caught between what inspires you and what is financially lucrative. One side of you may be drawn toward an easy, luxurious lifestyle, whereas a desire for inspiration can spur you to work hard to fulfill your ideals. Learning to make the right decisions and stand by them is therefore important to your well-being. A wonderful ability to entertain and enchant others stays with you throughout your life.

Work & Vocation

With your personal charm and social skills, any line of activity that involves people can give you the greatest fulfillment. Your charisma, leadership qualities, and organizational skills indi-

---

FIXED STAR

Star's name: Markab

Degree position: 22°29'–23°22' Pisces between the years 1930 and 2000

Magnitude: 2.5–3

Strength: ★★★★★★★

Orb: 1°40'

Constellation: Alpha Pegasus

Applicable days: March 12, 13, 14, 15, 16

Star qualities: Mars/Mercury

Description: a bright white star located on the wing of Pegasus

---

PRIMARY STAR'S INFLUENCE

Markab's influence bestows a spirit of enterprise, powers of resolution, and a determined mind. This star imparts a love of discussion or argument, good judgment, practical skills and dexterity, and quickness at repartee. You probably have the ability to retaliate in the right manner with impressive speech and can utilize situations to your advantage.

Linked to your Sun's degree, Markab bestows love of travel, creative and artistic talents, and success in dealing with the public. This star brings an aptitude for business and material gain, which may be achieved through the ability to think and act quickly and intuitively. You may feel stimulated to pursue an interest in higher education, spirituality, philosophy, or writing. Markab also warns against complacency and a lack of enthusiasm, which you may need to overcome.

cate a potential to reach the top in your chosen field. In business you can use your ease with people particularly well in sales, promotion, publishing, or the media. With a gift for words, you may also excel as a writer or lecturer. Your need for self-expression and love for the dramatic can lure you into the art, music, and entertainment worlds. Original and talented, with a strong awareness of values, you can combine your business sense with your quick insight into others to create material success.

Famous people who share your birthday include entertainer Liza Minnelli, writer Jack Kerouac, musician/songwriters James Taylor and Paul Kantner, jazz singer Al Jarreau, and playwright Edward Albee.

Numerology

Usually you are intuitive, helpful, and friendly, possessing good reasoning power. Since you want to establish true individuality, you are often innovative. Naturally understanding and sensitive, you also know how to use tact and cooperative methods to achieve your aims and objectives. When you achieve a balance between your need for self-expression and your natural inclination to be supportive of others, you can find emotional satisfaction and personal fulfillment. You may nevertheless need to find the courage to stand on your own two feet and develop self-confidence or learn not to get easily discouraged by other people. The subinfluence of the number 3 month indicates that you are multitalented and sensitive. Friendly, you enjoy social activities and many interests. A need for self-expression often leads you to seek many different experiences. Idealistic and a perfectionist, you need to create a harmonious ambiance and avoid a tendency to worry or criticize. As well as a loving atmosphere, personal relationships are of prime importance to you, as they endow you with hope and inspiration.

• *Positive:* creative, attractive, initiative, discipline, self-promotion

• *Negative:* reclusive, eccentric, uncooperative, overly sensitive, low self-esteem

Love & Relationships

An ability to make friends easily suggests that you are easygoing and sociable. Usually you have many interests and enjoy mixing business with pleasure. You admire people who are successful whether creatively or financially, and with your social skills you can benefit through friends and acquaintances. It may be wise to take your time in choosing your partners carefully, however, to ensure long-lasting relationships. With your warm and creative outlook, you can uplift others, but you may also have to learn to express your own needs.

YOUR SPECIAL SOMEONE

For long-term relationships and love, you might start to look for an exciting partner among those born on the following dates.

Love & friendship: Jan. 6, 8, 14, 23, 26, 28, Feb. 4, 10, 12, 21, 24, 26, Mar. 2, 10, 12, 19, 22, 24, Apr. 8, 14, 17, 20, 22, May 6, 15, 16, 18, 20, June 4, 13, 16, 18, 28, July 2, 11, 14, 16, 20, Aug. 9, 12, 14, 22, Sept. 7, 10, 12, 24, Oct. 5, 8, 10, 23, 26, Nov. 3, 6, 8, 15, 28, Dec. 1, 4, 6, 30

Beneficial: Jan. 9, 12, Feb. 7, 10, Mar. 5, 8, Apr. 3, 6, May 1, 4, June 2, 30, July 28, Aug. 26, 30, 31, Sept. 24, 28, 29, Oct. 22, 26, 27, Nov. 20, 24, 25, Dec. 18, 22, 23, 29

Fatal attractions: Sept. 12, 13, 14, 15, 16

Challenging: Jan. 11, 13, 29, Feb. 9, 11, Mar. 7, 9, 30, Apr. 5, 7, 28, May 3, 5, 26, 31, June 1, 3, 24, 29, July 1, 22, 27, Aug. 20, 25, Sept. 18, 23, 30, Oct. 16, 21, 28, Nov. 14, 19, 26, Dec. 12, 17, 24

Soul mates: Jan. 12, 29, Feb. 10, 27, Mar. 8, 25, Apr. 6, 23, May 4, 21, June 2, 19, July 17, Aug. 15, Sept. 13, Oct. 11, Nov. 9, Dec. 7

March 13

H Your birthday reveals you to be a multitalented, perceptive, and optimistic Piscean with a strong desire to achieve success. Although you have a need to express yourself creatively and practically, without determination and perseverance you will not be able to manifest your many creative ideas.

The added influence of your Sun in the decanate of Scorpio adds depth to your dynamic emotions, sensitivity, and intuitive feelings. As a practical idealist with leadership ability, you are a good planner and delegator. As a visionary with foresight and emotional power, you have the power to transform your life expression. If inspired, you can concentrate with great intensity on your objectives. An interest in metaphysical subjects suggests that you are capable of developing your telepathic and psychic abilities.

Possessing excellent business sense, you can be a shrewd competitor in commercial enterprises or become involved in large projects and speculations. If materially inclined, you often have extravagant tastes, with possessions being important to your sense of self-worth. If making money becomes too much of a preoccupation, however, you have to be aware of what you are compromising in your quest for success. Generous and optimistic, you do not like to be small or petty, preferring to think in terms of large rewards.

Until you reach the age of seven your progressed Sun moves through Pisces, placing an emphasis on your sensitivity, receptivity to your surroundings, and emotional needs. While you are between the ages of eight and thirty-seven your progressed Sun moves through Aries. This influence suggests that you will gradually become more assertive, daring, and spirited. This may spur you to start projects and become more confident. After the age of thirty-eight, when your progressed Sun moves into Taurus, your need to be established and feel secure will increase, coupled with a wish for more calm and emotional steadiness. At the age of sixty-eight, when your progressed Sun moves into Gemini, you start to become more curious about different forms of communication, possibly taking up a new interest.

Your Secret Self

Highly intuitive and ambitious, you are sensitive and intelligent, with an ability to quickly evaluate people as well as your situation. With good organizational abilities and the skills to oversee large projects, you enjoy keeping yourself busy. An inner sense of dignity or pride suggests that you do not enjoy restrictive tasks or work that lacks mental challenge. Energetic and inquisitive, you come to learn the value of knowledge. As your ideas are original and often ahead of their time, you need the freedom to express yourself.

Generous and kind and very persuasive, you usually work better in a leadership position. You are a natural networker who may know people from different groups. Often hardworking, imaginative, and inventive, you can recognize opportunities for expansion. You also possess the ability to accumulate wealth but may find more satisfaction from being able to help others or from philanthropic projects. When you are positive and enthusiastic about an undertaking, you have the ability to project this and excite others. Benefits will come from connections with women, especially in education and work.

Work & Vocation

Imaginative, with a keen mind and an inborn business sense, you have the gift of being able to commercialize your many talents. Your ease in dealing with the public and good communica-

---

FIXED STAR

Star's name: Markab

Degree position: 22°29'–23°22' Pisces between the years 1930 and 2000

Magnitude: 2.5–3

Strength: ★★★★★★★

Orb: 1°40'

Constellation: Alpha Pegasus

Applicable days: March 12, 13, 14, 15, 16

Star qualities: Mars/Mercury

Description: a bright white star located on the wing of Pegasus

PRIMARY STAR'S INFLUENCE

Markab's influence bestows a spirit of enterprise, powers of resolution, and a determined mind. This star imparts a love of discussion or argument, good judgment, practical skills and dexterity, and quickness at repartee. You probably have the ability to retaliate in the right manner with impressive speech and can utilize situations to your advantage.

Linked to your Sun's degree, Markab bestows love of travel, creative and artistic talents, and success in dealing with the public. This star brings an aptitude for business and material gain, which may be achieved through the ability to think and act quickly and intuitively. You may feel stimulated to pursue an interest in higher education, spirituality, philosophy, or writing. Markab also warns against complacency and a lack of enthusiasm, which you may need to overcome.

tion skills can be a big advantage in sales and marketing or publishing. Alternatively, some people of this birthdate become involved in science or research. Although you have a natural talent for business, you can display planning or organizational skills in whatever occupation you choose. Enjoying travel, you may also find yourself becoming involved in work having to do with overseas destinations. Career choices such as teaching, lecturing, or writing may provide you with the freedom to operate in your own way.

Famous people who share your birthday include astronomer Percival Lowell, singer Neil Sedaka, entertainer Tessie O'Shea, Scientology founder L. Ron Hubbard, musician Dick Katz, and publisher Walter Annenberg.

Numerology

Emotional sensitivity, enthusiasm, and inspiration are often identified with the number 13 birthday. Numerically, you are associated with ambition and hard work, and can accomplish much through creative self-expression. You may need to cultivate a pragmatic outlook if you want to turn your creative talents into tangible products. Your original and innovative approach inspires new and exciting ideas, which frequently result in work that impresses others. With a number 13 birthday, you are earnest, romantic, charming, and fun-loving, and with dedication you can achieve prosperity. The subinfluence of the number 3 month indicates that you are creative and imaginative. Intelligent and sensitive, you are full of wonderful ideas and grand plans. Usually easygoing and a good companion, you enjoy friendly social activities. Versatility and a need for self-expression lead you to seek numerous experiences. An inclination to get bored easily, however, may cause you to become indecisive or spread yourself too thin. Your tendency to be skeptical may cause you to feel emotionally insecure, so you benefit from having faith and trusting your intuition.

• *Positive:* ambitious, creative, freedom-loving, self-expressive, initiative
• *Negative:* impulsive, indecisive, bossy, unemotional, rebellious, egotistical

Love & Relationships

Sociable and friendly, you need to be popular and often enjoy new emotional experiences. A tendency to become bored implies that you need to find a person who will be stimulating and encouraging. Usually you possess dynamic emotions and admire people who are charismatic, with powerful personalities. Dramatic, you can make magnanimous gestures and be very helpful to others in time of need. With your strong feelings and desire for affection, you are a considerate and loyal friend.

YOUR SPECIAL SOMEONE

Your charm is likely to attract many social and romantic opportunities, but for that someone special you might want to look among those born on the following dates.

Love & friendship: Jan. 6, 10, 15, 29, 31, Feb. 4, 13, 27, 29, Mar. 2, 11, 25, 27, Apr. 9, 23, 25, May 2, 7, 21, 23, June 5, 19, 21, July 3, 7, 17, 19, 30, Aug. 1, 15, 17, 28, Sept. 13, 15, 26, Oct. 1, 11, 13, 24, Nov. 9, 11, 22, Dec. 7, 9, 20

Beneficial: Jan. 13, 15, 19, Feb. 11, 13, 17, Mar. 9, 11, 15, Apr. 7, 9, 13, May 5, 7, 11, June 3, 5, 9, July 1, 3, 7, 29, Aug. 1, 5, 27, 31, Sept. 3, 25, 29, Oct. 1, 23, 27, Nov. 21, 25, Dec. 19, 23

Fatal attractions: May 30, June 28, July 26, Aug. 24, Sept. 13, 14, 15, 16, 22, Oct. 20, Nov. 18, Dec. 16

Challenging: Jan. 12, Feb. 10, Mar. 8, Apr. 6, May 4, June 2, Aug. 31, Sept. 29, Oct. 27, 29, 30, Nov. 25, 27, 28, Dec. 23, 25, 26, 30

Soul mates: Jan. 2, 28, Feb. 26, Mar. 24, Apr. 22, May 20, June 18, July 16, Aug. 14, Sept. 12, Oct. 10, Nov. 8, Dec. 6

March 14

FIXED STAR

Star's name: Markab

Degree position: 22°29'–23°22' Pisces between the years 1930 and 2000

Magnitude: 2.5–3

Strength: ★★★★★★★

Orb: 1°40'

Constellation: Alpha Pegasus

Applicable days: March 12, 13, 14, 15, 16

Star qualities: Mars/Mercury

Description: a bright white star located on the wing of Pegasus

PRIMARY STAR'S INFLUENCE

Markab's influence bestows a spirit of enterprise, powers of resolution, and a determined mind. This star imparts a love of discussion or argument, good judgment, practical skills and dexterity, and quickness at repartee. You probably have the ability to retaliate in the right manner with impressive speech and can utilize situations to your advantage.

Linked to your Sun's degree, Markab bestows love of travel, creative and artistic talents, and success in dealing with the public. This star brings an aptitude for business and material gain, which may be achieved through the ability to think and act quickly and intuitively. You may feel stimulated to pursue an interest in higher education, spirituality, philosophy, or writing. Markab also warns against complacency and a lack of enthusiasm, which you may need to overcome.

H Although you are a receptive and sensitive Piscean, your dynamic and restless nature urges you to explore the many possibilities available to you in this lifetime. Your potential for success lies in your intelligence, versatility, and self-reliant spirit. Generous and liberal, you are attractive to others and usually popular. Your universal outlook encourages a humanitarian approach to life and stimulates your natural sense of humor.

The added influence of your Sun in the decanate of Scorpio indicates that you are a person of extremes. Idealistic and imaginative, yet pragmatic and with a strong material sense, you are an interesting mixture of opposites. Usually you are magnetic and discerning, with strong premonitions, penetrating thoughts, and psychic abilities. Although you often appear calm, frustration or disappointment can push you to express inner tensions, especially via sarcastic remarks. Being multitalented, ambitious, and a good evaluator, however, means that you have the potential for achieving your grand objectives.

Usually independent, you may resent taking orders from others. This suggests that you do not like to be in subservient positions and you fare better when using your leadership potential. How you manage your assets may at times be a cause for concern, especially if you are prone to bouts of extravagance. Decisions made in haste or on the spur of the moment can leave you financially on the spot. With calculated risks, however, your timing can be excellent, making you luckier than most people.

While you are between the ages of seven and thirty-six your progressed Sun moves through Aries. This influence suggests that you gradually become more confident and assertive, which may result in your having a strong self-orientation or a pioneering spirit. After you reach the age of thirty-seven, when your progressed Sun moves into Taurus, your need to be established and financially secure will increase, coupled with a wish for more practicality in your life. At the age of sixty-seven, when your progressed Sun moves into Gemini, you start to become more involved with communication, highlighting a need for mental stimulation or new interests.

Your Secret Self

A natural authority springs from your inner pride and sense of drama. This can take you to positions of responsibility, where you are able to use your many talents. An inherent impatience or restlessness suggests that you seek to dissolve any restrictions or limitations put on you. If your circumstances do not provide you with new opportunities or chances for advancement, you may wish to travel and explore new prospects elsewhere.

As well as possessing a good sense of values and an instinct for financial matters, you can also make an excellent fighter for a cause or ideal. Changing finances, however, may sometimes curb your aspirations, so it may be necessary to budget or plan for the future rather than go for immediate rewards. By staying as detached as possible, you avoid being too security-conscious and are able to use your universal outlook to achieve remarkable results.

Work & Vocation

Careers that use your sharp intellect or communication skills, such as scientist, lawyer, teacher, or writer, are likely to bring you success. With your high ideals and humanitarianism, you usually want to help in the cause of progress. With your imagination and fine mind, you enjoy exploring new ideas and knowledge that can make you more productive. Alternatively, you may be creatively inspired and express your sensitivity through art, music, or the entertainment world. A compassionate side to your nature may find expression through the healing professions or social work.

Famous people who share your birthday include physicist Albert Einstein, composers Georg Telemann and Quincy Jones, actors Michael Caine and Billy Crystal, immunologist Paul Ehrlich, and actress Rita Tushingham.

Numerology

Intellectual potential, pragmatism, and determination are some of the qualities of the number 14 birthday. Indeed, with this birthday you frequently put your work first and judge yourself and others on the basis of career achievements. Although you need stability, the restlessness indicated by the number 14 urges you to forge ahead or take on new challenges in a constant attempt to improve your lot. This innate restlessness and constant lack of satisfaction may also inspire you to make a great many changes in your life, especially if you are not happy with your working conditions or financial status. With your perceptive mind, you respond quickly to problems and enjoy solving them. The subinfluence of the number 3 month indicates that you are sensitive, with powerful emotions. Although you are idealistic and creative, your ambition is to be productive; with extraordinary surges of energy, you are capable of achieving a great deal. An inclination to get bored easily, however, may cause you to become indecisive or spread yourself too thin. A positive environment is essential for you, as you thrive on inspiration and excitement.

• *Positive:* decisive actions, hardworking, lucky, creative, pragmatic, imaginative, industrious

• *Negative:* overly cautious or overly impulsive, unstable, thoughtless, stubborn

Love & Relationships

Your warm heart may not be immediately obvious from your casual personality. You may be happiest when socializing with people who get you thinking or with whom you share some type of intellectual or creative activity. Although you are a good communicator, at times you may need to stay detached and avoid becoming overserious due to hidden insecurities. Fortunately, intuitive and amusing, you can ease tense situations with your unusual sense of humor or satire.

YOUR SPECIAL SOMEONE

For security, mental stimulation, and love, you might want to begin looking among those born on the following dates.

Love & friendship: Jan. 6, 11, 16, Feb. 4, 14, Mar. 2, 12, 28, 30, Apr. 10, 26, 28, May 3, 8, 24, 26, 30, June 1, 6, 22, 24, 28, July 4, 20, 22, 26, 31, Aug. 2, 18, 20, 24, 29, Sept. 16, 18, 22, 27, Oct. 14, 16, 20, 25, Nov. 12, 14, 18, 23, Dec. 10, 12, 16, 21

Beneficial: Jan. 9, 14, 16, Feb. 7, 12, 14, Mar. 5, 10, 12, Apr. 3, 8, 10, May 1, 6, 8, June 4, 6, July 2, 4, Aug. 2, Sept. 30, Oct. 28, Nov. 26, 30, Dec. 24, 28, 29

Fatal attractions: Jan. 21, Feb. 19, Mar. 17, Apr. 15, May 13, June 11, July 9, Aug. 7, Sept. 5, 14, 15, 16, 17, Oct. 3, Nov. 1

Challenging: Jan. 4, 13, 28, Feb. 2, 11, 26, Mar. 9, 24, Apr. 7, 22, May 5, 20, June 3, 18, July 1, 16, Aug. 14, Sept. 12, Oct. 10, 31, Nov. 8, 29, Dec. 6, 27

Soul mates: Jan. 15, 22, Feb. 13, 20, Mar. 11, 18, Apr. 9, 16, May 7, 14, June 5, 12, July 3, 10, Aug. 1, 8, Sept. 6, Oct. 4, Nov. 2

SUN: PISCES
DECANATE: SCORPIO/PLUTO
DEGREE: 23°30'–24°30' PISCES
MODE: MUTABLE
ELEMENT: WATER

March 15

$\mathcal{H}$ Imaginative and intuitive, you are a Piscean who seeks security and harmony. Amiable and modest, you can attract admirers with your friendly and charming personality. Usually you have many opportunities to succeed materially and socially, and your strong sense of values suggests that financial security may play an important part in your life plan. Although you have the dynamic drive to gain a certain degree of power or achieve prestige or recognition, a tendency to scatter your energies on too many interests may undermine your determination.

The added influence of your Sun in the decanate of Scorpio implies that you are inquisitive, with a probing mind. Interested in the unknown, you enjoy exploring new concepts or unearthing the truth. Your growth and strength come from the capacity to overcome difficulties. When you are inspired by a cause or an idea, you usually find within you the inspiration and creative power to perform record achievements.

As you often alternate between feelings of distrust and hope, sometimes you can appear restless or self-doubting and at other times you come across as self-reliant, assured, and even domineering. This can easily cause unrest in your environment through quarrels or conflict with your superiors. By learning to relax and avoiding feeling irritable or aggressive, you can restore the peace.

While you are between the ages of six and thirty-five your progressed Sun moves through Aries. This influence suggests that you gradually develop your confidence and assertiveness. After the age of thirty-six, when your progressed Sun moves into Taurus, you feel an increased need for stability and financial security. You become more relaxed and determined, but a reluctance to change can be a sign of obstinacy. At the age of sixty-six there is a turning point when your progressed Sun enters Gemini. This suggests that your curiosity grows and starts to transform your way of thinking, possibly encouraging an interest in learning new subjects.

Your Secret Self

Being proud and dramatic and disliking failure, you feel that it is important to do things right and keep your sense of self-respect. You possess an innate wisdom, which you may keep hidden from others. This may manifest as a desire for solitude or a deeper insight into life's mysteries. Occasionally, however, you may become too impatient, stubborn, or confused and need to develop tolerance or to listen to the advice of others. With a discerning inner strength, however, you have the power to rise above any difficulties and uplift others with your strong spirit.

In order to achieve your true potential, you may need to recognize that knowledge is your path to success. In the event of your losing faith in either yourself or your abilities to achieve, there is a danger of isolation or secrecy. This may cause you to become mistrustful or doubting. Highly intuitive, however, you are a perceptive observer who is quick on the uptake. When you trust your spontaneous first impressions and act on them, you are able to live in the present moment rather than the past or the future.

Work & Vocation

Sensitive yet determined, you have an ability to work hard that can help you reach the top in your chosen field. You enjoy power and efficiency, so you may succeed in business or govern-

FIXED STAR

Star's name: Markab
Degree position: 22°29'–23°22' Pisces between the years 1930 and 2000
Magnitude: 2.5–3
Strength: ★★★★★★★
Orb: 1°40'
Constellation: Alpha Pegasus
Applicable days: March 12, 13, 14, 15, 16
Star qualities: Mars/Mercury
Description: a bright white star located on the wing of Pegasus

PRIMARY STAR'S INFLUENCE

Markab's influence bestows a spirit of enterprise, powers of resolution, and a determined mind. This star imparts a love of discussion or argument, good judgment, practical skills and dexterity, and quickness at repartee. You probably have the ability to retaliate in the right manner with impressive speech and can utilize situations to your advantage.

Linked to your Sun's degree, Markab bestows love of travel, creative and artistic talents, and success in dealing with the public. This star brings an aptitude for business and material gain, which may be achieved through the ability to think and act quickly and intuitively. You may feel stimulated to pursue an interest in higher education, spirituality, philosophy, or writing. Markab also warns against complacency and a lack of enthusiasm, which you may need to overcome.

ment, particularly as an administrator, supervisor, or manager. You can also excel in advertising, law, science, or banking. Achievement is likely in sales, negotiation, or careers that involve investigation. Alternatively, an idealistic side to your nature may prefer public service or the caring professions. As you do not like taking orders and are very independent, you may enjoy being your own boss. If you are using the more creative side of your nature, you can be particularly good at music.

Famous people who share your birthday include singers Terence Trent D'Arby and Michael Love, musician Phil Lesh, scientist Alexander Popov, singer/songwriters Sly Stone, Lightnin' Hopkins, and Ry Cooder, and U.S. president Andrew Jackson.

Numerology

Versatility, enthusiasm, and restlessness are suggested by the number 15 birthday. Your greatest assets are your strong instincts and the ability to learn quickly through combining theory and practice. Often you utilize your intuitive powers and are quick at recognizing opportunities when they arise. With a number 15 birthday, you possess a talent for attracting money or receiving help and support from others. Carefree and resolute, you welcome the unexpected and like to take a gamble. The subinfluence of the number 3 month indicates that you are receptive and versatile. Charming and friendly, you enjoy social activities and many interests. Multitalented and ambitious, you need to find self-expression through different experiences and much activity. An inclination to get bored easily, however, may cause you to become restless or spread yourself too thin. Although you are enthusiastic and entertaining, with a good sense of humor, you may have to develop self-esteem to guard against worry and other emotional insecurities. Personal relationships and a loving atmosphere are of prime importance to you, as they endow you with hope and inspiration.

• *Positive:* willing, generous, responsible, kind, cooperative, appreciative, perceptive, enthusiasm, creative ideas

• *Negative:* restless, irresponsible, self-centered, fear of change, worry, indecisive, materialistic, misusing power

Love & Relationships

Sociable and friendly, you are sensitive and idealistic, with a need to communicate your feelings. When in love, you can be devoted and thoughtful. If you are doubtful or indecisive, uncertainties about love can cause anxieties and confusion. Once you have made up your mind, however, you are loyal and fully committed. Usually you enjoy relationships in which you can share your creative ideas or activities.

YOUR SPECIAL SOMEONE

You might find a partner who will understand your sensitivity and need for love among those born on the following dates.

Love & friendship: Jan. 7, 13, 17, 20, Feb. 5, 15, 18, Mar. 3, 13, 16, 29, 31, Apr. 1, 11, 14, 27, 29, May 5, 9, 12, 25, 27, June 7, 10, 23, 25, July 1, 5, 8, 21, 23, Aug. 3, 6, 19, 21, Sept. 1, 4, 17, 19, Oct. 2, 15, 17, Nov. 13, 15, 30, Dec. 11, 13, 28

Beneficial: Jan. 15, 17, 28, Feb. 13, 15, 26, Mar. 11, 13, 24, Apr. 9, 11, 22, May 7, 9, 20, June 5, 7, 18, July 3, 5, 11, 16, Aug. 1, 3, 14, Sept. 1, 12, Oct. 10, 29, Nov. 3, 8, 27, Dec. 6, 25

Fatal attractions: Jan. 5, Feb. 3, Mar. 1, Sept. 15, 16, 17, 18

Challenging: Jan. 4, 5, 14, Feb. 2, 3, 12, Mar. 1, 10, Apr. 8, 30, May 6, 28, June 4, 26, July 2, 24, Aug. 22, Sept. 20, Oct. 18, Nov. 16, Dec. 14

Soul mates: Jan. 2, Mar. 29, Apr. 27, May 25, June 23, July 21, Aug. 19, Sept. 17, Oct. 15, Nov. 13, Dec. 11

March 16

♓ Friendly and sociable, you often come across as an idealistic Piscean with an easy-going personality and charming nature. Although you may appear calm, you are a complex mixture of spirituality and materialism. On one hand, you have the vision and the practical skills to enter into the world of commerce and make your mark as a persuasive and successful entrepreneur or businessperson. On the other hand, your mystical and philanthropic inclinations may inspire you to be spontaneous and pursue a humanitarian cause, displaying your more compassionate nature.

The added influence of your Sun in the decanate of Scorpio implies that you are perceptive and intelligent. Although you seek to increase your understanding, you are often an introvert. With the power to heal, you are capable of transforming yourself and starting all over again. Although you have a penetrating mind and are a good investigator, you are not always keen on divulging information about yourself.

To express yourself, you may choose to unleash your imaginative thoughts through writing or other creative pursuits. Since you are often sensitive to your environment, the key to your happiness is through establishing inner harmony and peace. Your confidence increases if you replace your doubts with commitment and faith in your abilities.

Between the ages of five and thirty-four, as your progressed Sun moves through Aries, you gradually become more confident, assertive, and ambitious. You may decide to pioneer new endeavors or learn to be straightforward in your dealings with others. At the age of thirty-five there is another turning point as your Sun enters Taurus. After this time you slow down and have a need for more permanence and financial protection in your life. From the age of sixty-five, when your progressed Sun enters Gemini, you develop a heightened interest in communication and the exchange of ideas.

Fixed Stars

Markab; Scheat

Primary Star

Star's name: Markab

Degree position: 22°29'–23°22' Pisces between the years 1930 and 2000

Magnitude: 2.5–3

Strength: ★★★★★★★★

Orb: 1°40'

Constellation: Alpha Pegasus

Applicable days: March 12, 13, 14, 15, 16

Star qualities: Mars/Mercury

Description: a bright white star located on the wing of Pegasus

Primary Star's Influence

Markab's influence bestows a spirit of enterprise, powers of resolution, and a determined mind. This star imparts a love of discussion or argument, good judgment, practical skills and dexterity, and quickness at repartee. You probably have the ability to retaliate in the right manner with impressive speech and can utilize situations to your advantage.

Linked to your Sun's degree, Markab bestows love of travel, creative and artistic talents, and success in dealing with the public. This star brings an aptitude for business and material gain, which may be achieved through the ability to think and act quickly and intuitively. You may feel stimulated to pursue an interest in higher education, spirituality, philosophy, or writing. Mar-

Your Secret Self

Love and relationships are especially important to you, and you often have a desire to make other people happy. This can be expressed as humanitarian caring or warmhearted generosity. Sensitive and receptive to your surroundings, however, you may find it hard to be spontaneous or demonstrate your affection in an open way if you feel restricted. As financial security and self-worth are also important to your well-being, you may sometimes be caught between duty and your personal desires. Through your experiences, you come to value the power of love.

Being idealistic, you may be tested as to how far you will compromise to get the rewards that you need and deserve. It is important to establish a balance between standing up for your rights and being caring and sensitive.

Work & Vocation

Charming and imaginative, with a sensitive eye for color and style, you can succeed as a designer and image maker. Although you are sociable and gregarious, you take financial considerations seriously and are good at combining business and pleasure. A need to express yourself implies that if you are not creative yourself, you like to work with beautiful objects and are often drawn to dealing in art or antiques. Alternatively, your imaginative and original thoughts may draw you to writing and journalism or the media and publishing world. A networker who is interested in people, you can be an excellent diplomat or mediator. As a humanitarian and spiritual person, you also have unique powers to heal and comfort those less fortunate than yourself.

Famous people who share your birthday include comedian Jerry Lewis, actress Isabelle Huppert, director Bernardo Bertolucci, actor Hardy Kruger, and songwriter Nancy Wilson.

Numerology

A number 16 birthday suggests that you are thoughtful, sensitive, and friendly. Although analytical, you often judge life and people according to how you feel. As a number 16 personality, however, you can experience inner tensions when facing friction between a need for self-expression and responsibility to others. With a number 16 birthday, you may be interested in world affairs and may join international corporations or the media world. The creative ones among you have a talent for writing with sudden flashes of inspiration. You may need to learn how to balance between being overly confident and being doubtful and insecure. The subinfluence of the number 3 month indicates that you are idealistic, creative, and full of original thoughts. Although you are easygoing and friendly, you like to make up your own mind and are usually autonomous. Intuitive and sensitive, you may need to develop faith in your abilities and guard against business worries. Although you may think that money can solve all your problems, your emotional insecurities usually have very little to do with financial matters. When inspired, you are dynamic and motivated and able to use your power to encourage others rather than dictate your own wishes.

• *Positive:* higher education, responsibilities to home and family, integrity, intuitive, social, cooperative, insightful

• *Negative:* worry, irresponsible, self-promoting, opinionated, skeptical, fussy, irritable, selfish

Love & Relationships

Idealistic and young at heart, for love and a happy relationship you are often willing to make some kind of sacrifice. Romantic by nature, you often believe that love and devotion can conquer all. Just be careful not to martyr yourself to someone unworthy of you. On occasion you may end up with someone from a different age group or background. Generous and loving, you can be a caring and protective partner. Although you can be gentle, in relationships you prefer to be honest and have a strong sense of responsibility.

kab also warns against complacency and a lack of enthusiasm, which you may need to overcome.

• *Positive:* energetic, creative, enterprising

• *Negative:* fault-finding, willfulness, irritability, rashness and premature actions

See Appendix for additional fixed star readings.

YOUR SPECIAL SOMEONE

If you are looking for your ideal friend or relationship, you may have better luck with someone born on one of the following dates.

Love & friendship: Jan. 4, 8, 9, 18, 19, 23, Feb. 2, 6, 16, 17, 21, Mar. 4, 14, 15, 19, 28, 30, Apr. 2, 12, 13, 17, 26, 28, 30, May 1, 10, 11, 15, 24, 26, 28, June 8, 9, 13, 22, 24, 26, July 6, 7, 11, 20, 22, 24, 30, Aug. 4, 5, 9, 18, 20, 22, 28, Sept. 2, 3, 7, 16, 18, 20, 26, Oct. 1, 5, 14, 16, 18, 24, Nov. 3, 12, 14, 16, 22, Dec. 1, 10, 12, 14, 20

Beneficial: Jan. 5, 16, 27, Feb. 3, 14, 25, Mar. 1, 12, 23, Apr. 10, 21, May 8, 19, June 6, 17, July 4, 15, Aug. 2, 13, Sept. 11, Oct. 9, 30, Nov. 7, 28, Dec. 5, 26, 30

Fatal attractions: Jan. 17, Feb. 15, Mar. 13, Apr. 11, May 9, June 7, July 5, Aug. 3, Sept. 1, 16, 17, 18, 19

Challenging: Jan. 1, 10, 15, Feb. 8, 13, Mar. 6, 11, Apr. 4, 9, May 2, 7, June 5, July 3, 29, Aug. 1, 27, Sept. 25, Oct. 23, Nov. 21, Dec. 19, 29

Soul mates: Aug. 30, Sept. 28, Oct. 26, Nov. 24, Dec. 22

March 17

Intuitive and analytical, you are a sensitive Piscean with a pragmatic approach. Although you have high aspirations and ideals, you are also likely to be preoccupied with material interests. Often charismatic and with creative talents, you are imaginative and receptive; your difficulty, however, may be in creating harmony through self-expression. When you feel suppressed, you are inclined to indulge in worry, doubts, or pessimistic thoughts. Success usually comes as a result of hard work and dedication. To reap your rewards, therefore, you must first complete your tasks and obligations.

The added influence of your Sun in the decanate of Scorpio suggests that you possess second sight and are usually highly intuitive. With your powerful perceptions and depth of feeling, your inquisitive mind enjoys getting to the bottom of things.

Because you are compassionate, frank, and honest, others turn to you in times of need, and usually you find yourself supporting the underdog. As an individual with common sense and good organizational abilities, you like to think on a grand scale. When you feel optimistic, you can be an inspired thinker or uplifting conversationalist. Although you are generally constructive in outlook, sometimes dissatisfaction with yourself and others may make you overly critical. Travel is particularly beneficial for you, as it fits well with your desire to improve yourself through expanding your knowledge.

While you are between the ages of four and thirty-three your progressed Sun moves through Aries. This influence suggests that you gradually become more assertive, daring, and spirited, resulting in a strong desire for new ventures. After you reach the age of thirty-four, when your progressed Sun moves into Taurus, your need to be established and feel secure will increase, coupled with a wish for more calm and emotional steadiness. At the age of sixty-four, when your progressed Sun moves into Gemini, you start to become more curious about different forms of communication, possibly taking up a new interest.

FIXED STAR

Star's name: Scheat

Degree position: 28°14'–29°6' Pisces between the years 1930 and 2000

Magnitude: 2

Strength: ★★★★★★★

Orb: 2°10'

Constellation: Beta Pegasus

Applicable days: March 16, 17, 18, 19, 20, 21

Star qualities: Mars/Mercury or Saturn/Mercury

Description: a giant deep orange-yellow star located on the left leg of Pegasus

PRIMARY STAR'S INFLUENCE

Scheat's influence imparts determination but also stubbornness. This star suggests that you are a dreamer and an idealist, with an enterprising nature. You probably have many friends and enjoy a good social life in which you have a sense of belonging.

Linked to your Sun's degree, Scheat bestows success in dealing with the general public, as well as a talent for metaphysics, astrology, and esoteric subjects. You probably possess psychic or intuitive ability and a strong imagination. This star also indicates that success is not necessarily long-lasting and suggests a need to exercise caution in your choice of friends, acquaintances, or business colleagues.

• Positive: resolution, common sense, discussion, enterprise, determination

• Negative: danger by water, rashness, obstinate

Your Secret Self

Receptive and charitable, you usually prefer unpretentious and straightforward individuals. Blessed with a caring nature, you are often in a position to help or advise others. Although you can appear confident and purposeful, frustration and disappointment may be a challenge. By practicing patience and persistence, however, you can keep a positive mental attitude and achieve well-earned success. An ability to grasp ideas very quickly implies that education and acquiring knowledge can be a vital part of your self-confidence.

Charismatic and charming, with intellectual brightness, you are an individual with creative thoughts and a strong need for self-expression. You may also be drawn to the study of philosophy, religion, or metaphysics, which can help you overcome a tendency to think negatively. In your desire for harmony your home can play an especially important role, satisfying your need for peace and security.

Work & Vocation

Although you have excellent business sense and an optimistic outlook, you may need to learn that there's no such thing as a free lunch. Talented and dynamic, with an interest in a wide range of subjects, you need to persevere and be diligent. A tendency to do things at the last minute or leave work unfinished may cause you frustration and anxiety. If you work hard, however, and pay attention to detail, you can attain prominent positions. You can usually excel in sales and promotion. Often you can produce art for the masses and turn your talents into commercial success. Good outcomes can also be achieved through education, travel, public service, or politics. Good at dealing with people, you may also be drawn to law, philosophy, or religion. Being creative, you can also choose to express your strong emotions through dance, art, music, or drama.

Famous people who share your birthday include ballet dancer Rudolf Nureyev, actors Rob Lowe, Patrick Duffy, and Kurt Russell, children's book illustrator Kate Greenaway, golfer Bobby Jones, and singers John Sebastian and Nat King Cole.

Numerology

As a number 17 individual, you are shrewd, with a reserved nature and good analytical abilities. As an independent thinker, you benefit from being well educated or skillful. Usually you utilize your knowledge in a specific way in order to develop your expertise and can achieve material success or a prominent position as a specialist or researcher. Private, introspective, and detached, with a strong interest in facts and figures, you frequently present a serious and thoughtful demeanor and like to take your time. By developing your communication skills, you can discover much about yourself from others. The subinfluence of the number 3 month indicates that you are receptive, with a strong sixth sense and powerful premonitions. When inspired, you have wonderful ideas and imaginative thoughts that are worth writing down. Kind and idealistic, you are a magnet to those who need encouragement and reassurance. Easygoing and a good companion, you enjoy friendly social activities and many interests. Versatility and a need for self-expression lead you to all kinds of creative experiences. Personal relationships and a loving atmosphere are of prime importance to you, as they endow you with hope and inspiration.

• *Positive:* thoughtful, specialist, good planner, good business sense, attracts money, individual thinker, painstaking, accurate, skilled researcher, scientific

• *Negative:* stubborn, carelessness, moody, sensitive, fixed ideas, critical, worry, suspicion

Love & Relationships

Dynamic and loving, you often attract many admirers. Usually fortunate, you enjoy mixing with different types of people. With the power to captivate others comes the necessity to distinguish between true and fair-weather friends. Otherwise you can draw toward you individuals who demand too much of your time or distract you from your purpose. Although you have a great deal of love to give, avoid overreacting when you show your true feelings. Generous and compassionate, you can be caring and supportive of your partners and friends.

YOUR SPECIAL SOMEONE

You might find a partner who will understand your sensitivity, strong passions, and need for love among those born on the following dates.

Love & friendship: Jan. 3, 5, 9, 18, 19, Feb. 1, 3, 7, 16, 17, Mar. 1, 5, 14, 15, 31, Apr. 3, 12, 13, 29, May 1, 10, 11, 27, 29, June 8, 9, 25, 27, July 6, 7, 11, 23, 25, 31, Aug. 4, 5, 21, 23, 29, Sept. 2, 3, 19, 21, 27, 30, Oct. 1, 17, 19, 25, 28, Nov. 3, Dec. 13, 15, 21, 24

Beneficial: Jan. 1, 6, 17, Feb. 4, 15, Mar. 2, 13, Apr. 11, May 9, June 7, July 5, Aug. 3, Sept. 1, Oct. 31, Nov. 29, Dec. 27

Fatal attractions: Sept. 17, 18, 19, 20, 21

Challenging: Jan. 2, 16, Feb. 14, Mar. 12, Apr. 10, May 8, June 6, July 4, Aug. 2, Dec. 30

Soul mates: Jan. 11, 31, Feb. 9, 29, Mar. 7, 27, Apr. 5, 25, May 3, 23, June 1, 21, July 19, Aug. 17, Sept. 15, Oct. 13, Nov. 11, Dec. 9

SUN: PISCES

DECANATE: SCORPIO/PLUTO

DEGREE: 26°30'–27°30' PISCES

MODE: MUTABLE

ELEMENT: WATER

FIXED STAR

Star's name: Scheat

Degree position: 28°14'–29°6' Pisces between the years 1930 and 2000

Magnitude: 2

Strength: ★★★★★★★

Orb: 2°10'

Constellation: Beta Pegasus

Applicable days: March 16, 17, 18, 19, 20, 21

Star qualities: Mars/Mercury or Saturn/Mercury

Description: a giant deep orange-yellow star located on the left leg of Pegasus

PRIMARY STAR'S INFLUENCE

Scheat's influence imparts determination but also stubbornness. This star suggests that you are a dreamer and an idealist, with an enterprising nature. You probably have many friends and enjoy a good social life in which you have a sense of belonging.

Linked to your Sun's degree, Scheat bestows success in dealing with the general public, as well as a talent for metaphysics, astrology, and esoteric subjects. You probably possess psychic or intuitive ability and a strong imagination. This star also indicates that success is not necessarily long-lasting and suggests a need to exercise caution in your choice of friends, acquaintances, or business colleagues.

• *Positive:* resolution, common sense, discussion, enterprise, determination

• *Negative:* danger by water, rashness, obstinate

Sensitive and restless, you are a Piscean who wants to exceed the boundaries of existence through travel and transformation. Intuitive and spontaneous, you are imaginative and young at heart. As a visionary and multitalented individual, you need to find some kind of creative self-expression. The only obstacle that stands in your way may be a lack of perseverance or a desire to see immediate financial rewards for your efforts.

The subinfluence of your decanate ruler, Scorpio, increases your determination to initiate changes in order to transform and better yourself. Often it is through periods of difficulty that you realize your true strength. Although naturally modest and receptive, you have insight and profound understanding, suggesting that you can empower yourself by being able to understand the many sides to any issue and the correct timing of future events.

Fluctuations in circumstances and an extravagant side to your nature suggest that you often desire an expensive lifestyle. This, however, also implies that you need to develop patience and self-restraint, working within a disciplined structure or a budget. By learning that opportunities for long-lasting success can be utilized more effectively with poise and preparation, you can maintain the kind of life you want.

While you are between the ages of three and thirty-two your progressed Sun moves through Aries. This influence suggests that you gradually become more confident and assertive, which may result in your initiating projects or having a sense of self-orientation. After the age of thirty-three, when your progressed Sun moves into Taurus, you have an increasing need to be established and feel secure coupled with a wish for more practicality in your life. At the age of sixty-three, when your progressed Sun moves into Gemini, you start to become more involved with communication and need more mental stimulation.

Your Secret Self

Generous and broad-minded, you are intelligent and resourceful, and you like to keep busy. At a deep level you may at times allow self-doubt or insecurity to undermine your creativity, causing you to be uncertain about making the right decisions in life. Your humanitarian nature, however, is able to put everything in perspective and help you overcome a tendency to worry. By learning to relax, you can let your natural talent express itself, and enjoy life.

Witty and entertaining, you have a way with people and enjoy friendly social gatherings. Although you may have an extravagant streak, money and security can often be a motivating factor for you. A strong interest in people and the ability to make astute observations imply that your intuitive feelings are usually right and can often help you quickly judge others. By staying as detached as possible, you are able to avoid personal frustration or disappointment.

Work & Vocation

Although you are hardworking, you need to avoid mundane occupations that do not offer variety and new incentive for progress. Working in a constantly changing or exciting atmosphere can keep you interested and mentally stimulated. Careers that involve travel and working with the public will suit your restless temperament. A need for adventure implies that you want to have as many experiences in your early life as you can before you settle down to a more permanent situation. With your imagination, sense of vision, and structure, you may be interested in a career as a designer, artist, architect, or filmmaker. Equally, a good sense of rhythm may attract you to music or dance. As a humanitarian, you may be inspired to help, teach, or instruct others. Alternatively, your strong business sense and organizational skills may lead you to the world of commerce.

Famous people who share your birthday include clairvoyant Edgar Cayce, country singer Charlie Pride, British prime minister Neville Chamberlain, soul singer Wilson Pickett, composer Nicolai Rimsky-Korsakov, writers John Updike and George Plimpton, and U.S. president Grover Cleveland.

Numerology

Determination, assertiveness, and ambition are some of the attributes associated with the number 18 birthday. Active, with a need for challenges, you like to keep busy and are frequently involved in some enterprise. Capable, hardworking, and responsible, you rise to positions of authority. Since you may suffer from overwork, learn how to relax or slow down from time to time. As a number 18 personality, you may use your power to heal others, give sound advice, or solve other people's problems. The subinfluence of the number 3 month indicates that you are idealistic and sensitive. Easygoing and a good companion, you enjoy friendly social activities and many interests. Versatility and a need for self-expression imply that you benefit by being active and productive. A humanitarian streak implies that if you join large institutions, you usually concentrate on improvement and reforms. An inclination to get bored easily may inspire you to travel, but avoid spreading yourself too thin. Usually enthusiastic and charming, with a good sense of humor, you may have to develop self-esteem and learn to stay detached.

- *Positive:* progressive, assertive, intuitive, courageous, resolute, healing ability, efficient, advisory skills
- *Negative:* uncontrolled emotions, lazy, lack of order, selfishness, callousness

Love & Relationships

Although you are receptive and sensitive, you can be independent-minded. Friendly and sociable, you are often attracted to people who can stimulate your mind and imagination. You are intelligent and restless, and usually relationships are important to you, as you enjoy mixing with different types of people. With your natural sense of humor, you can be entertaining in the company of those you love. You usually fare better with an intelligent partner or one who shares your interests.

YOUR SPECIAL SOMEONE

If you are searching for that special person, you might start to look for an exciting and fun-loving partner among those born on the following dates.

Love & friendship: Jan. 6, 10, 20, 29, Feb. 4, 8, 18, 27, Mar. 2, 6, 16, 20, 25, 28, 30, Apr. 4, 14, 23, 26, 28, 30, May 2, 12, 16, 21, 24, 26, 28, 30, June 10, 19, 22, 24, 26, 28, July 8, 12, 17, 20, 22, 24, 26, Aug. 6, 15, 18, 20, 22, 24, Sept. 4, 13, 16, 18, 20, 22, Oct. 2, 11, 14, 16, 18, 20, Nov. 4, 9, 12, 14, 16, 18, Dec. 7, 10, 12, 14, 16

Beneficial: Jan. 7, 13, 18, 28, Feb. 5, 11, 16, 26, Mar. 3, 9, 14, 24, Apr. 1, 7, 12, 22, May 5, 10, 20, June 3, 8, 18, July 1, 6, 16, Aug. 4, 14, Sept. 2, 12, 30, Oct. 10, 28, Nov. 8, 26, 30, Dec. 6, 24, 28

Fatal attractions: Jan. 25, Feb. 23, Mar. 21, Apr. 19, May 17, June 15, July 13, Aug. 11, Sept. 9, 19, 20, 21, Oct. 7, Nov. 5, Dec. 3

Challenging: Jan. 3, 17, Feb. 1, 15, Mar. 13, Apr. 11, May 9, 30, June 7, 28, July 5, 26, 29, Aug. 3, 24, 27, Sept. 1, 22, 25, Oct. 20, 23, Nov. 18, 21, Dec. 16, 19

Soul mates: Jan. 18, Feb. 16, Mar. 14, Apr. 12, May 10, 29, June 8, 27, July 6, 25, Aug. 4, 23, Sept. 2, 21, Oct. 19, Nov. 17, Dec. 15

SUN: PISCES

DECANATE: SCORPIO/PLUTO

DEGREE: 27°30'–28°30' PISCES

MODE: MUTABLE

ELEMENT: WATER

FIXED STAR

Star's name: Scheat

Degree position: 28°14'–29°6' Pisces between the years 1930 and 2000

Magnitude: 2

Strength: ★★★★★★★

Orb: 2°10'

Constellation: Beta Pegasus

Applicable days: March 16, 17, 18, 19, 20, 21

Star qualities: Mars/Mercury or Saturn/Mercury

Description: a giant deep orange-yellow star located on the left leg of Pegasus

---

PRIMARY STAR'S INFLUENCE

Scheat's influence imparts determination but also stubbornness. This star suggests that you are a dreamer and an idealist with an enterprising nature. You probably have many friends and enjoy a good social life in which you have a sense of belonging.

Linked to your Sun's degree, Scheat bestows success in dealing with the general public, as well as a talent for metaphysics, astrology, and esoteric subjects. You probably possess psychic or intuitive ability and strong imagination. This star also indicates that success is not necessarily long-lasting and suggests a need to exercise caution in your choice of friends, acquaintances, or business colleagues.

• Positive: resolution, common sense, discussion, enterprise, determination

• Negative: danger by water, rashness, obstinate

ℋ Determined and intuitive, you are a receptive Piscean with motivation and dynamic drive. As a pragmatic and imaginative individual, you want stability and security, yet you thrive on variety and activity. Your career usually plays a significant role in your life, and through dedication and hard work you can establish an enduring and successful position.

The added influence of your Sun in the Scorpio decanate implies that you are observant and discriminating. Although you have a penetrating mind and are a good investigator, you are not always keen on revealing yourself. Seeking to increase your understanding through self-mastery, you find your creative expression by taking the lead and being enterprising. With the power to heal, you are capable of transforming yourself and starting all over again. By combining your organizational skills and strong instincts, you can turn situations to your advantage or create tangible products from your inspired ideas.

Idealistic, you take pride in your work and are often willing to dedicate yourself to a cause or a project. Although you are usually protected financially, it is through perseverance and commitment to your objectives that you can succeed. As a loyal individual, you tend to take your responsibilities seriously, but a need to unwind enables you to relax and take a more friendly approach.

Until you reach the age of thirty-one your progressed Sun moves through Aries. This influence suggests that you develop your assertiveness and enjoy being active and courageous. After the age of thirty-two, when your progressed Sun moves into Taurus, you feel an increased need for stability and financial security. You become more relaxed and determined, but a reluctance to change can reveal signs of stubbornness. At the age of sixty-two there is a turning point when your progressed Sun enters Gemini. This suggests that your curiosity grows and you start to transform your way of thinking. This also highlights your interest in communication and learning new subjects.

Your Secret Self

As you usually have vitality and strong instincts, you need emotional and mental stimulation. A desire for action and excitement suggests that you enjoy exploring new ideas or initiating original projects. A lack of activity or change may contribute to feelings of unease, and you can become restless and impatient without knowing why. In order to compensate, avoid indulging in escapism.

Since half of you wants variety and adventure and the other half seeks stability and security, you may need to create a balanced environment where you can have both opportunities for advancement and predictability. Interested in change and reform, you can stimulate others into action. Although charming and sociable, you have a need for emotional contentment and require inner tranquility and peace. Rather than aim in different directions, listen to your strong inner perceptions and your life will flow more smoothly.

Work & Vocation

Blessed with excellent career opportunities, you may have difficulty deciding what you want to achieve. A practical approach and good organizational skills mean that you can take on an executive role or a position of authority. Although you can succeed in the business world, a need to be creative suggests that you are too idealistic to be content with financial benefits alone. Unless you can also find some emotional satisfaction, you may lose interest and seek new opportunities or challenges. You usually fare better in large organizations where there are opportunities for advancement. Alternatively, you may want to be your own boss and be independent. A love of travel and variety suggests that you are interested in different experiences and keen on working in new locations.

Famous people who share your birthday include actresses Glenn Close and Ursula Andress, writers Philip Roth and Irving Wallace, actor Bruce Willis, and U.S. Supreme Court Justice Earl Warren.

Numerology

Ambitious and dynamic, yet creative, idealistic, and sensitive, you are a true number 19 individual. Decisive and resourceful, you possess depth of vision, but the dreamer side of your nature is compassionate and impressionable. The need to be someone may be the very thing that pushes you to be dramatic and claim center stage. To others you may appear confident and resilient, but inner tensions or doubts may cause emotional ups and downs. If you set standards that are too high, you can be overserious or too critical of yourself and others. The subinfluence of the number 3 month indicates that you are highly perceptive. As an assertive and multitalented individual, your opportunities for success are enhanced by your ability to establish a stable environment in which you can channel your energies constructively. When committed, you can use your versatility and ingenuity to introduce new attitudes or improve working conditions. Although material success is important to you, your desire for self-mastery and transformation implies that your highest reward is the integration of wisdom and emotional expression.

• *Positive:* dynamic, centered, creative, leadership, progressive, optimistic, strong convictions, competitive, independent, gregarious

• *Negative:* self-centered, worry, fear of rejection, materialistic, egotistical, impatient, escapism

Love & Relationships

Charismatic and friendly, you like to mix with a wide variety of people. When you love, it is with power and deep feelings. Although you usually establish long-lasting friendships and have strong bonds with others, you do not like to be restricted by too much routine or responsibilities. A need for stability and security suggests that you seek a partner who can be exciting yet reliable and trustworthy. Changing circumstances in your life imply that you may need to take your time before you commit yourself to long-term relationships.

YOUR SPECIAL SOMEONE

You might find a faithful and trustworthy lover or partner who will appreciate your special talents among those born on the following dates.

Love & friendship: Jan. 7, 11, 22, 25, Feb. 5, 9, 20, Mar. 3, 7, 18, 31, Apr. 1, 5, 16, 29, May 3, 14, 17, 27, 29, June 1, 12, 25, 27, July 10, 13, 23, 25, Aug. 8, 21, 23, 31, Sept. 6, 19, 21, 29, Oct. 4, 17, 19, 27, 30, Nov. 2, 5, 15, 17, 25, 28, Dec. 13, 15, 23, 26

Beneficial: Jan. 8, 14, 19, Feb. 6, 12, 17, Mar. 4, 10, 15, Apr. 2, 8, 13, May 6, 11, June 4, 9, July 2, 7, Aug. 5, Sept. 3, Oct. 1, 29, Nov. 27, Dec. 25, 29

Fatal attractions: Sept. 20, 21, 22, 23, 24

Challenging: Jan. 9, 18, 20, Feb. 7, 16, 18, Mar. 5, 14, 16, Apr. 3, 12, 14, May 1, 10, 12, June 8, 10, July 6, 8, 29, Aug. 4, 6, 27, Sept. 2, 4, 25, Oct. 2, 23, Nov. 21, Dec. 19

Soul mates: Jan. 9, Feb. 7, Mar. 5, Apr. 3, May 1, Oct. 30, Nov. 28, Dec. 26

SUN: PISCES/ARIES CUSP

DECANATE: SCORPIO/PLUTO,
ARIES/MARS

DEGREE: 28°30'–29°30' PISCES

MODE: MUTABLE

ELEMENT: WATER

March 20

ℋ Born on the cusp of Pisces and Aries, you benefit from the influence of both signs. Idealistic and purposeful, you are able to turn your imaginative ideas to practical use. Although you are sensitive, ambitious, and multitalented, you aim to achieve a great deal. Astute and receptive, you have the ability to come straight to the point of a matter. Your strong urge for self-expression, however, may be challenged by your doubts and worries. In order to achieve your dreams, you need to trust your own decisions regardless of financial obstacles.

The added influence of your Sun in the decanates of Scorpio and Aries points to your intuitive ability to pick up on hidden agendas very quickly and your desire to get to the bottom of things. When you feel positive, you can be self-assured, daring, and bold, with original and inspired ideas. Although you often appear light and congenial, a closer look reveals a more serious side that may be interested in the study of more unusual, philosophical, or spiritual subjects.

Although you are able to achieve much through your unique qualities, learning to use your charm and diplomatic skills will enhance your chances for success. Your interest in people shows your natural humanitarian qualities. Partnerships or working as part of a team can often play an important role in your advancement.

Until you reach the age of thirty your progressed Sun moves through Aries, suggesting that you gradually develop your ambitious plans along with your confidence. You may wish to pioneer or experiment with new pursuits. At the age of thirty-one you encounter another turning point as your Sun enters Taurus. After this time you become more practical and security-conscious, with a greater desire for luxuries and beauty. From the age of sixty-one, when your progressed Sun enters Gemini, you develop a heightened interest in communication and the exchange of ideas.

Your Secret Self

Idealistic and practical, you can enjoy being enterprising and working for a worthwhile cause. Although you have a strong need for material security, you are not willing to compromise on issues that are close to your heart. Nonetheless, you are more than willing to assist others or give valuable advice. You thrive on encouragement, and your love of harmony and peace implies that you will do your utmost to restore the balance to tense situations.

If you do believe in a cause, you will give it your full support and use your persuasive ways to convince others. Always willing to share your knowledge, you can make great contributions to partnerships or groups. Romantic and idealistic, you want true love and affection, but in reality you are practical, security-conscious, and seldom swept off your feet by emotion. You may also come to learn the difference between interfering in others' lives and offering advice when it is needed.

Work & Vocation

Having a competitive streak, you want to succeed and be creative. You may be attracted to the world of sports, music, or the theater. Persuasive, you can promote your ideas. You often excel in sales and careers that deal with the public. As a capable and methodical individual, you may

FIXED STAR

Star's name: Scheat

Degree position: 28°14'–29°6' Pisces between the years 1930 and 2000

Magnitude: 2

Strength: ★★★★★★★

Orb: 2°10'

Constellation: Beta Pegasus

Applicable days: March 16, 17, 18, 19, 20, 21

Star qualities: Mars/Mercury or Saturn/Mercury

Description: a giant deep orange-yellow star located on the left leg of Pegasus

PRIMARY STAR'S INFLUENCE

Scheat's influence imparts determination but also stubbornness. This star suggests that you are a dreamer and an idealist with an enterprising nature. You probably have many friends and enjoy a good social life in which you have a sense of belonging.

Linked to your Sun's degree, Scheat bestows success in dealing with the general public as well as a talent for metaphysics, astrology, and esoteric subjects. You probably possess psychic or intuitive ability and a strong imagination. This star also indicates that success is not necessarily long-lasting and suggests a need to exercise caution in your choice of friends, acquaintances, or business colleagues.

be interested in large projects where you can exhibit your administrative skills. Original and versatile in whatever career you choose, you like to make changes and bring improvements or reforms to the workplace. Intelligent and articulate, you can accomplish through teaching and writing or communication. Possessing a shrewd business sense, you are often successful in commerce, or you may use your sharp mind for research and problem solving.

Famous people who share your birthday are actors William Hurt and Sir Michael Redgrave, playwright Henrik Ibsen, former Canadian prime minister Brian Mulroney, pianist Sviatoslav Richter, director Spike Lee, actress Holly Hunter, hockey player Bobby Orr, and public television personality Fred (Mr.) Rogers.

Numerology

As a number 20 individual, you are intuitive, sensitive, adaptable, and understanding, and often see yourself as a part of a larger group. Usually you enjoy cooperative activities where you can interact, share experiences, or learn from others. Charming and gracious, you develop diplomatic and people skills and can move in different social circles with ease. You may, however, need to develop your confidence in order to overcome a tendency to be overly dependent or too easily hurt by the actions and criticism of others. You are a master at creating a congenial and harmonious atmosphere. The subinfluence of the number 3 month indicates that you are creative and sensitive. Easygoing and a good companion, you enjoy friendly social activities and many interests. Versatility and a need for self-expression lead you to seek numerous experiences. An inclination to get bored easily, however, may cause you to become indecisive or spread yourself too thin. Although you can be enthusiastic and charming, with a good sense of humor, you may have to develop self-esteem to guard against worry and other emotional insecurities. You work better with hope and inspiration.

• *Positive:* good partnerships, gentle, tactful, receptive, intuitive, considerate, harmonious, agreeable, amicable, ambassador of goodwill

• *Negative:* suspicious, lack of confidence, oversensitive, selfish, easily hurt, crafty

Love & Relationships

Sensitive and receptive, usually you are intuitive and spontaneous. Although you are prepared to do a great deal for the ones you love, another side to your nature indicates that sometimes you can appear indifferent or restless. As you are more sensitive than you seem, it is vital that you create a harmonious environment for yourself where you can relax and unwind. If you are looking for an ideal love, it might be difficult for anyone to live up to your high expectations. Thoughtful and kind, however, you seek stability and will remain loyal to your chosen partner.

YOUR SPECIAL SOMEONE

If you are looking for a dynamic yet sensitive partner, you might find a longer-lasting relationship with someone born on one of the following dates.

Love & friendship: Jan. 4, 8, 13, 22, 26, Feb. 6, 20, 24, Mar. 4, 18, 22, Apr. 2, 16, 20, 30, May 14, 18, 28, 30, June 12, 16, 26, 28, July 1, 10, 14, 24, 26, Aug. 8, 12, 22, 24, Sept. 6, 10, 20, 22, 30, Oct. 4, 8, 18, 20, 28, Nov. 2, 6, 16, 18, 26, Dec. 4, 14, 16, 24

Beneficial: Jan. 9, 20, Feb. 7, 18, Mar. 5, 16, 29, Apr. 3, 14, 27, May 1, 12, 25, June 10, 23, July 8, 21, Aug. 6, 19, Sept. 4, 17, 22, 23, 24, Oct. 2, 15, 30, Nov. 13, 28, Dec. 11, 26, 30

Fatal attractions: Jan. 27, Feb. 25, Mar. 23, Apr. 21, May 19, June 17, July 15, Aug. 13, Sept. 11, Oct. 9, Nov. 7, Dec. 5

Challenging: Jan. 2, 10, 19, Feb. 8, 17, Mar. 6, 15, Apr. 4, 13, May 2, 11, June 9, July 7, 30, Aug. 5, 28, Sept. 3, 26, Oct. 1, 24, Nov. 22, Dec. 20, 30

Soul mates: Jan. 15, Feb. 13, Mar. 11, Apr. 9, May 7, June 5, July 3, Aug. 1, Oct. 29, Nov. 27, Dec. 25

Appendix of
Fixed Stars

For those whose birthdays are influenced by more than one fixed star, here is a complete listing of fixed stars and their attributes. You may also use this appendix in conjunction with a professionally cast astrological chart to learn more about the significance of these celestial bodies.

Aries

DENEB KAITOS

Star's name: Deneb Kaitos, also called Dipda
Degree position: 1°32'–2°27' Aries between the years 1930 and 2000
Magnitude: 2
Strength: ★★★★★★★
Orb: 2°10'
Constellation: Beta Ceti
Applicable days: March 21, 22, 23, 24, 25, 26
Star qualities: Saturn
Description: a yellow-orange star located at the tail of the Whale

Deneb Kaitos indicates a restrained nature and an ability to move ahead with determination. It also imparts an inherent restlessness, which can lead to spurts of activity followed by periods of recuperation. This star warns against misuse of force and suggests that these individuals should learn how to relax their minds by thinking positively; they may also need to spend time alone.

Linked to your Sun's degree, this star bestows organizational skills and emphasizes duties and responsibilities. With discipline and control it is possible to achieve much. This star may also warn against a tendency to becoming frustrated.

• *Positive:* perseverance, determination
• *Negative:* repression or frustration, doing things on impulse, changing direction without thinking

ALGENIB

Star's name: Algenib, also called the Carrier or the Wing
Degree position: 8°10'–9°4' Aries between the years 1930 and 2000
Magnitude: 3
Strength: ★★★★★★
Orb: 2°
Constellation: Alpha Pegasi
Applicable days: March 29, 30, 31, April 1, 2
Star qualities: Mars/Mercury
Description: a small white star located in the wing on the side of Pegasus

Algenib imparts powers of thought, a positive and active mind that is capable of great accomplishment through ideas and actions. This star conveys resolution, determination, and enthusiasm, with competitive tendencies. It also enhances the speed of one's mental processes and gives the confidence to retaliate in just the right manner with impressive speech. This star also warns against being quick-tempered and reckless.

Linked to your Sun's degree, this star imparts good business skills, a love of learning, an interest in religious affairs, and a talent for writing. Algenib may also suggest a need for privacy and time alone. It indicates success in dealing with the public.

• *Positive:* decisiveness, spirit of enterprise, strong will, a fighting spirit, verbal repartee
• *Negative:* criticism, sarcasm, headstrong behavior, depressions, argumentative

SIRRAH

Star's name: Sirrah, also called Alpheratz and Caput Andromeda
Degree position: 13°11'–14°13' Aries between the years 1930 and 2000
Magnitude: 2
Strength: ★★★★★★★
Orb: 2°10'
Constellation: Alpha Andromedae
Applicable days: April 2, 3, 4, 5, 6, 7
Star qualities: Jupiter/Venus
Description: a blue, white, and purple binary star located in the Head of Andromeda

Sirrah signifies good relationships with others and popularity. It bestows a harmonious nature and benefits from good social connections. This star can also grant honor and wealth, cheerfulness, optimism, versatility, and sound judgment. It warns, however, against being too outspoken or taking popularity for granted.

Linked to your Sun's degree, this star indicates that usually you can achieve your heart's desire as long as you are clear about your objectives. Sometimes after you obtain what you want, you are at a loss as to what to do next. However, since one of your natural attributes is knowing the right people and being at the right place at the right time, this state does not tend to last long.

• *Positive:* warm heart, joy, popularity, attractive personality
• *Negative:* self-conceit, excess

BATEN KAITOS

Star's name: Baten Kaitos, also called Cetus or Zeta Ceti
Degree position: 20°57'–21°49' Aries between the years 1930 and 2000
Magnitude: 3.5–4
Strength: ★★★★
Orb: 1°30'
Constellation: Zeta Ceti
Applicable days: April 10, 11, 12, 13
Star qualities: Saturn
Description: a topaz-yellow star located in the body of the Whale

Baten Kaitos imparts cautiousness, a serious outlook, and sincerity. It also implies responsibility, a straightforward approach, and an ability to overcome great challenges. Often it indicates a preference for working in solitude and a tendency to be impatient if restricted.

Linked to your Sun's degree, this star indicates that you may need to learn how to adjust to changed circumstances, as there is a likelihood of alteration in fortunes and lifestyle. Just when you think that the dust has settled, upheaval occurs. There are, however, also good opportunities for travel or changes of residence due to work.

• *Positive:* thoughtfulness, modesty, dedication, diligence, endurance
• *Negative:* melancholy, selfishness, instability

AL PERG

Star's name: Al Perg, also called Kullat Nuti or Piscium
Degree position: 25°50'–26°46' Aries between the years 1930 and 2000
Magnitude: 3.5–4
Strength: ★★★★★
Orb: 1°30'
Constellation: Eta Piscium
Applicable days: April 15, 16, 17, 18
Star qualities: Saturn and Jupiter
Description: a binary star located in the cord near the tail of the Northern Fish

Al Perg bestows determination to realize one's objectives. Success comes with patience and steadfastness, but not without struggle. Accomplishment and recognition can be achieved through perseverance and dedication. This star also implies that dissatisfaction with oneself as well as with others may cause irritability.

Linked to your Sun's degree, this star denotes achievement, with a slow and steady rise to greater power, and a preference for work in government and political affairs.

• *Positive:* happiness in solitude, sense of duty, straightforwardness, honesty
• *Negative:* inconstancy, discontent, moodiness, emotional tensions, changing objectives

VERTEX

Star's name: Vertex, also called Great Nebulae
Degree position: 26°51'–27°47' Aries between the years 1930 and 2000
Magnitude: 3.5–4
Strength: ★★★★★
Orb: 1°
Constellation: M31 Andromedae
Applicable days: April 16, 17, 18, 19
Star qualities: Mars/Moon
Description: a great nebula located on the north side of the head of Andromeda

Vertex endows an ambitious nature and a drive to excel. By nature you need to be first; you possess a fighting spirit. This star also imparts strong inner tensions, which can bring about impulsive or premature actions.

Linked to your Sun's degree, this star indicates high preferment in dealing with the public. Leadership qualities, idealism, and a desire to fight for just causes are some of the qualities of Vertex. Turbulence, however, is also possible.

• *Positive:* competitiveness, passion, vigor and enthusiasm, forceful expression
• *Negative:* restlessness, changeable moods, irritability

MIRACH

Star's name: Mirach, also called Andromeda's Girdle
Degree position: 29°17' Aries to 0°24' Taurus between the years 1930 and 2000
Magnitude: 2
Strength: ★★★★★★★
Orb: 2°10'
Constellation: Beta Andromedae
Applicable days: April 18, 19, 20, 21, 22, 23
Star qualities: Neptune and Venus
Description: a reddish yellow star located in the side of the girdle of Andromeda

Mirach bestows sensitivity, a dreamy and idealistic nature, and a refined sense of beauty. Frequently you have a gregarious and cheerful outlook, personal charm, a desire for happiness, and a love of company. The positive influence that this star carries endows you with imaginative power, inspiration, and ideas based on artistic creation. Often you possess mediumistic tendencies and a love of daydreaming. Although adventurous, you can also be devoted and visionary. You have a stimulating influence on others and can make friends easily. Often you are helped in life by others.

Linked to your Sun's degree, this star bestows a talent for composing or playing music. Your goal may be to create the real out of the ideal. This star also implies that eccentricity might be linked to a lack of self-confidence.

• *Positive:* altruism, brilliant mind, inclination to mysticism, idealism, good taste, artistic talents, wide range of interests

• *Negative:* secret bad habits, romantic preoccupation, excessive idealism

Taurus

MIRA

Star's name: Mira or Stella Mira
Degree position: 0°33'–1°32' Taurus between the years 1930 and 2000
Magnitude: 2–10
Strength: ★★★★★
Orb: 1°30'
Constellation: Omicron Ceti
Applicable days: April 20, 21, 22, 23
Star qualities: Saturn/Jupiter
Description: an orange-red star located in the tail of the Whale

Mira endows perseverance, consciousness of objectives, a sense of duty, and an ability to overcome obstacles through endurance. This star, however, also warns against an inclination toward materialism. Dissatisfaction with yourself as well as others often leads to confusion or frustration and an unsettled existence. Cultivating patience is therefore essential. Mira, however, also bestows a scientific and resourceful mind, which can develop original ideas.

Linked to your Sun's degree, this star imparts determination and preferment in legal affairs, government, and dealing with the public.

• *Positive:* diligence, sense of duty, straightforwardness, sincerity

• *Negative:* instability, irritability, frustration

EL SCHERATAIN

Star's name: El Scheratain, also called Sharatan
Degree position: 2°58'–3°58' Taurus between the years 1930 and 2000
Magnitude: 2.5–3
Strength: ★★★★★★★
Orb: 2°
Constellation: Beta Arietis
Applicable days: April 22, 23, 24, 25
Star qualities: Mars/Saturn
Description: a pearl-white star located in the north horn of the Ram

El Scheratain imparts endurance, the power to overcome by resistance, and energy. Through determination, this star sug-

gests that you can develop leadership abilities and achieve honors and good fortune. The influence of this star also indicates that irritating occurrences need to be addressed with patience. Individuals influenced by this star need to avoid frustration or indecision, as it may deplete their powers.

Linked to your Sun's degree, this star bestows a preference for work requiring endurance and good physical strength. You may achieve distinction in your field. El Scheratain, however, also carries a negative influence, suggesting a tendency to dominate or control situations, thus creating problems.

• *Positive:* persistence, indefatigable strength

• *Negative:* destructive force, stubbornness, lack of energy, lack of vitality

HAMAL

Star's name: Hamal, also called Al Hamal or the Sheep
Degree position: 6°43'–7°38' Taurus between the years 1930 and 2000
Magnitude: 2
Strength: ★★★★★★★★
Orb: 2°10'
Constellation: Alpha Arietis
Applicable days: April 25, 26, 27, 28, 29, 30
Star qualities: combined influences of Mars and Saturn
Description: an orange-yellow star located in the forehead of the Ram

Hamal endows restlessness and a drive to excel, together with an influence of rebelliousness. This star suggests that competitiveness and drive for success may at times challenge you to use unorthodox methods in order to achieve your goals.

Linked to your Sun's degree, this star bestows the power to overcome obstacles with concentration and persistence but warns against being inconsiderate to others or using force to get your own way. Only through patience can you develop your skills, talents, and abilities. Hamal may also suggest a danger of putting money at the top of your priorities.

• *Positive:* patience, discipline, hard work, concentrated energy, leadership

• *Negative:* use of force, unscrupulousness, keeping unsuitable company

SCHEDIR

Star's name: Schedir, also called Sader
Degree position: 6°51'–7°57' Taurus between the years 1930 and 2000
Magnitude: 2.5
Strength: ★★★★★★★
Orb: 2°
Constellation: Alpha Cassiopeia
Applicable days: April 26, 27, 28, 29, 30
Star qualities: Saturn

Description: a multiple and slightly variable main blue star located at Alpha Cassiopeia

Schedir's influence assists receipt of help from people in influential positions. Often Schedir bestows mystical inclinations, and although outwardly these individuals appear serious, they can enjoy or desire the good life.

Linked to your Sun's degree, this star frequently grants a talent for writing, and success in matters dealing with the general public.

- *Positive:* support from others, determination, consistency
- *Negative:* inclination toward materialism, overly serious

ALAMAK

Star's name: Alamak, also called Almach
Degree position: 13°15'–14°20' Taurus between the years 1930 and 2000
Magnitude: 2
Strength: ★★★★★★★
Orb: 2°10'
Constellation: Gamma Andromedae
Applicable days: May 2, 3, 4, 5, 6, 7
Star qualities: Venus
Description: a binary star, orange, emerald, and blue, located on the left foot of Andromeda

Alamak bestows artistic and musical talent, a good voice, and social popularity. This star also imparts good fortune and success, and you can achieve honors or receive unexpected gains. If you are industrious and patient, success can be attained, as can love, romance, and happiness in domestic affairs.

Linked to your Sun's degree, this star grants honors through writing and creative pursuits, success in dealing with the public at large, and achievements in public affairs, particularly in affairs connected to the law and legal profession. Alamak also indicates that you can often gain fame and prestige.

- *Positive:* creative talents, loving nature, ability to attract material success
- *Negative:* selfishness, indulgence, extravagance

MENKAR

Star's name: Menkar
Degree position: 13°20'–14°14' Taurus between the years 1930 and 2000
Magnitude: 2.5
Strength: ★★★★★★
Orb: 1°40'
Constellation: Alpha Ceti
Applicable days: May 3, 4, 5, 6
Star qualities: Saturn
Description: a bright orange-red star located in the jaw of the Whale

Menkar foretells of many challenges and a need to persevere. Often you are devoted and sympathetic and have an ability to display compassion. Even though, at times, there may be difficult family situations, you can carry your share of the responsibility with pride and determination.

Linked to your Sun's degree, this star suggests that through patience and a responsible attitude, you can achieve success. It carries a warning, however, that legacies and inheritance might be bound up in family disagreements. Menkar also denotes a good voice but warns of some trouble with the throat.

- *Positive:* devoted, considerate, compassionate
- *Negative:* give up too quickly, resentful, irresponsible, wallowing in self pity

ZANRAK

Star's name: Zanrak
Degree position: 22°33'–23°32' Taurus between the years 1930 and 2000
Magnitude: 3
Strength: ★★★★★★
Orb: 1°40'
Constellation: Gamma Eridani
Applicable days: May 13, 14, 15, 16
Star qualities: Saturn
Description: a red star located in the river Eridanus

Zanrak imparts seriousness and a pragmatic outlook, together with a tendency to take life too seriously. This star's influence also suggests oversensitivity to other people's opinions and a pessimistic outlook.

Linked to your Sun's degree, this star can impart a preference for writing, business, and dealing with the public. Zanrak also warns that you can become isolated or encounter obstacles. There are also indications that you are strongly influenced by your immediate environment and need support from other family members.

- *Positive:* pragmatism, seriousness, responsibility, sensitivity
- *Negative:* overly serious or somber demeanor

CAPULUS

Star's name: Capulus, also called Gyrus
Degree position: 23°15'–24°27' Taurus between the years 1930 and 2000
Magnitude: 4
Strength: ★★★★
Orb: 1°30'
Constellation: M34 Perseus
Applicable days: May 13, 14, 15
Star qualities: Mars/Mercury
Description: a binary cluster located in the sword hand of Perseus

Capulus imparts power of thought, a quick mind, and realization of ideas and plans. There are also indications that you are ambitious or competitive, which at times can cause rashness, indecision, and changeable views. A love of conversation and debate is also indicated by this star and endows you with impressive speaking abilities and quick repartee. Capulus warns against using talents in a destructive manner, sarcasm, and becoming involved in controversies.

Linked to your Sun's degree, this star bestows persistence, endurance, determination, and an ability to focus your energy. Capulus's influence enables you to achieve a prominent position in your field and may also encourage you to study philosophy, astrology, or metaphysics. Alternatively, this star may indicate success in dealing with the public at large.

- *Positive:* ambitious, good sense of humor
- *Negative:* sarcastic, critical, too competitive, destructive

ALGOL

Star's name: Algol, also called Caput Medusae
Degree position: 25°13'–26°21' Taurus between the years 1930 and 2000
Magnitude: 2.5
Strength: ★★★★★★★
Orb: 2°
Constellation: Beta Perseus
Applicable days: May 15, 16, 17, 18, 19
Star qualities: Saturn/Jupiter
Description: a white binary and variable star located in the Medusa's head held in the hand of Perseus

This star carries a double meaning: on one hand, it endows high spiritual values, and on the other, it suggests misfortune and lack of satisfaction or spirituality. When positive, you have the potential to become a leader through achievement and outstanding character, or to be of benefit to the community. This star suggests that bereavement may have a strong impact on a person's life and is often prominent for individuals who counsel the bereaved.

Linked to your Sun's degree, Algol bestows victory after struggle or victory over others in conflict and dispute. Yet it also carries a warning about scattering your energy and becoming confused. This star suggests the importance of maintaining correct conduct, thus avoiding legal entanglements and unsuitable company, which may lead to involvement in vendettas, family feuds, or physical conflicts.

- *Positive:* high spiritual values, correct conduct
- *Negative:* misfortune, impatience, misconduct, keeping bad company

ALCYONE

Star's name: Alcyone
Degree position: 29° Taurus–0°6' Gemini between the years 1930 and 2000
Magnitude: 3
Strength: ★★★★★★
Orb: 1°40'
Constellation: Eta Taurus
Applicable days: May 19, 20, 21, 22
Star qualities: Moon/Mars
Description: a green and yellow principal star in the Pleiades cluster, located on the shoulder of the Bull (it is the brightest star of the Pleiades)

Alcyone imparts openness and frankness, honesty, and sincerity. Restlessness and impulsive actions can also be associated with this star. By nature, you are forceful and purposeful, yet when feelings intensify you are inclined to act on impulse. This may cause turbulence and bring about changed circumstances. This star also warns against fevers and problems with eyesight.

Linked to your Sun's degree, Alcyone bestows love, eminence, and a talent for leadership. This star often indicates that you can enjoy success in legal and public matters or use your creative mind to develop your writing skills.

- *Positive:* creative mind, honesty, enthusiasm
- *Negative:* cantankerousness, moodiness, temperamental behavior

Gemini

PRIMA HYADUM

Star's name: Prima Hyadum
Degree position: 4°41'–5°46' Gemini between the years 1930 and 2000
Magnitude: 4
Strength: ★★★★
Orb: 1°30'
Constellation: Gamma Taurus
Applicable days: May 24, 25, 26, 27, 28
Star qualities: varied interpretations: Saturn/Mercury or Mars/Neptune
Description: an orange star, the chief star of the Hyades, which consists of 132 stars, located at the northern eye and marking the forehead of the Bull

Prima Hyadum grants energy, ambition, and a desire for prestige, leading to achievement or great success. This star suggests a need for study and education in order to develop clear thinking. Prima Hyadum, however, also carries an influence that implies contradictions in fortunes or times of turbulence.

Linked to your Sun's degree, this star imparts a talent for writing, business, sport, astrology, and success through working with the public. There is also a chance of fame and fortune and opportunities for popularity or notoriety. Prima Hyadum warns against tendencies toward greed and exploitation of others, and suggests refraining from hasty decisions, which may cause upheaval.

- *Positive:* writing, education, communication
- *Negative:* restlessness, lack of knowledge, greed

AIN

Star's name: Ain
Degree position: 7°30'–8°26' Gemini between the years 1930 and 2000
Magnitude: 4
Strength: ★★★★
Orb: 1°30'
Constellation: Epsilon Taurus
Applicable days: May 27, 28, 29
Star qualities: Mercury/Mars
Description: an orange star located in the northern eye of the Bull

Ain imparts a keen mind, love of discussion, ability to judge, and swift repartee. You are often energetic and assertive, and you possess the ability to retaliate in the right manner with articulate speech. This star, however, also warns against dishonesty and legal problems.

Linked to your Sun's degree, this star highlights preferment in study, writing, and higher learning, which may include the occult and astrology. The influence of this star bestows energy and determination to get what you want from life. You can succeed in your chosen career and make a lasting contribution. Ain also carries an influence suggesting that a rise is sometimes followed by a fall, and warns against getting entangled in illegal matters, which could prove disastrous.

- *Positive:* power of thought, quickness at repartee, ability to judge
- *Negative:* restlessness, irritability, lack of knowledge, quarrel

ALDEBARAN

Star's name: Aldebaran, also called Al Dabbaran, the Follower
Degree position: 8°48'–9°45' Gemini between the years 1930 and 2000
Magnitude: 1
Strength: ★★★★★★★★★
Orb: 2°30'
Constellation: Alpha Taurus
Applicable days: May 28, 29, 30, 31, June 1, 2
Star qualities: Mars/Mercury/Jupiter
Description: a giant rose-red star, located in the left eye of the Bull

Aldebaran is one of the four Royal Stars or Watchers of the Heavens and therefore is considered of prime importance. It bestows high aims, honor, intelligence, eloquence, and integrity. You are often courageous and can achieve positions of responsibility and good fortune. In many cases, however, success can be short-lived. This star imparts sharp, impressive speech and the ability to discuss and debate. It also bestows a tendency toward argumentativeness and self-destruction. Other warnings from this star concern jealousy from others, or making enemies, and damage to the eyes.

Linked to your Sun's degree, this star bestows extraordinary mental energy, providing the ability to get on with life and achieve through considerable determination and persistence. Aldebaran also indicates success, especially in dealing with the public. This star grants the ability to think big and undertake or concentrate on large projects. One important warning about Aldebaran is that fame or success may have a price or sacrifice attached to it. The most beneficial influence of this star is a strong preference for study, writing, and educational reform.

- *Positive:* theological aptitude, love of hermeneutics, expressiveness, popularity
- *Negative:* notoriety, lack of focus, anxiety

RIGEL

Star's name: Rigel
Degree position: 15°50'–16°40' Gemini between the years 1930 and 2000
Magnitude: 1
Strength: ★★★★★★★★★★
Orb: 2°30'
Constellation: Beta Orionis
Applicable days: June 3, 4, 5, 6, 7, 8, 9
Star qualities: varied influences: Mars/Jupiter or Saturn/Jupiter
Description: a brilliant blue-white double star located on the left foot of Orion

Rigel confers the ability to rise quickly in life, imparts strong willpower and an ambitious nature, and stimulates the mind to acquire wider general knowledge. A love of action and lucky breaks often stimulate you to be competitive. The ability to develop a scientific mind and even be inventive is linked to this star. Rigel can bestow honor, material riches, and lasting success.

Linked to your Sun's degree, this star suggests that you have a courageous and bold personality, with a broad or liberal outlook. You can also be hardworking, with good business sense and a flair for politics and public affairs. A strong preference for astrology, study, and higher education is also indicated by Rigel. This star indicates that great success can be achieved through assertiveness and a forthright approach, but warns against being too outspoken.

- *Positive:* founder of large enterprises, liberal, education, common sense
- *Negative:* short temper, insolent or unruly, demanding, restless

BELLATRIX

Star's name: Bellatrix, also called the Female Warrior
Degree position: 19°58'–20°54' Gemini between the years 1930 and 2000
Magnitude: 1.5
Strength: ★★★★★★★★
Orb: 2°10'
Constellation: Gamma Orionis
Applicable days: June 9, 10, 11, 12, 13
Star qualities: Mars/Mercury
Description: a large pale white-yellow star located on the left shoulder of Orion

Bellatrix's influence imparts power of thought, common sense, and an ability to assess situations quickly. This star also indicates wealth and good social contacts. Bellatrix bestows an articulate, intelligent, quick mind. You are probably eloquent, with a forceful, strong vocal expression and fondness of power. For women, this star frequently imparts a masculine mental approach. Bellatrix bestows authoritativeness, ambition, energy, and desire for civil or political honor.

Linked to your Sun's degree, this star denotes changeable circumstances; riches and honor may not be long-lasting. There is also an inclination toward research, mechanical abilities, and a scientific approach.
- *Positive:* common sense, intelligent, good contacts, communicative
- *Negative:* vacillation, rash, headstrong, indecisive in business, must learn to listen to others, sudden turns of events and turbulence

CAPELLA

Star's name: Capella, also called Little She-Goat and Amalthea
Degree position: 20°52'–21°48' Gemini between the years 1930 and 2000
Magnitude: 1
Strength: ★★★★★★★★★★
Orb: 2°30'
Constellation: Alpha Aurigae
Applicable days: June 9, 10, 11, 12, 13, 14
Star qualities: Mercury/Mars
Description: a large bright white star located on the body of the Goat in the arms of Auriga

Capella grants an energetic nature, inquisitiveness, and a love of learning. This star encourages an interest in research and new inventions. It imparts honor and prominent positions of trust. You may also acquire wealth and success.

Linked to your Sun's degree, this star indicates a tendency to be verbose and suggests that you avoid being too talkative. Capella advises learning to listen to others in order to avoid misunderstandings.
- *Positive:* trustworthy, loyalty, inquisitive mind, comprehensive knowledge
- *Negative:* argumentative, indecision, worry, lack of interest, wasted mental energy

PHACT

Star's name: Phact
Degree position: 21°08'–21°46' Gemini between the years 1930 and 2000
Magnitude: 2.5–3
Strength: ★★★★★★
Orb: 1°40'
Constellation: Alpha Columbae
Applicable days: June 11, 12, 13, 14
Star qualities: Mercury/Venus with Uranus influence
Description: a small bright binary star located at the base of the right wing of the Dove

Phact bestows artistic talent and intelligence, as well as a sense of rhythm. It reveals a flair for creative thinking and an interest in mathematics, music, or education. You are friendly and lovable, with good fortune.

Linked to your Sun's degree, this star grants popularity and social contacts, especially with young people. Phact's influence points to opportunities and success in careers associated with the arts. With this star you can become a good communicator or mediator and work with the public. Phact also grants a touch of ingenuity and mediumistic abilities.
- *Positive:* hopefulness, charm, creative talents
- *Negative:* too talkative, doubts, insecurities

MINTAKA

Star's name: Mintaka, also called Cingula Orionis
Degree position: 21°30'–22°16' Gemini between the years 1930 and 2000
Magnitude: 2.5–3
Strength: ★★★★★★
Orb: 1°40'
Constellation: Delta Orion
Applicable days: June 12, 13, 14, 15
Star qualities: Mercury/Saturn/Jupiter

Description: A brilliant white and pale violet variable binary star located in the belt of Orion alongside the star Alnilam

This star imparts good fortune, luck, and dignity. Thinking positively, you can make the best of any situation. Mintaka bestows courage, an industrious nature, and good timing. Executive and managerial capabilities and lasting happiness are also indicated by this star.

Linked to your Sun's degree, this star offers a piercing and sharp mind, good judgment, and memory. You are probably discreet, with a cautious nature, and with patience can bring changes for the better. You have a good sense of timing and a natural talent for turning situations to your advantage. This star gives a strong preference for education.

• *Positive:* see opportunities, good judgment, managerial capabilities

• *Negative:* changeable, frustration, inconsistency, lack of endurance

EL NATH

Star's name: El Nath
Degree position: 21°36'–22°41' Gemini between the years 1930 and 2000
Magnitude: 2
Strength: ★★★★★★★★
Orb: 2°10'
Constellation: Beta Taurus
Applicable days: June 11, 12, 13, 14, 15, 16
Star qualities: Mars/Mercury
Description: a giant brilliant white and pale gray binary star located at the tip of the northern horn of the Bull

El Nath imparts ambition, determination, and achievement through enterprise. This star also bestows good luck and acclaim. The influence of El Nath endows you with intelligence and a quick grasp of situations. Honors can be attained through research and scientific work or study of philosophy, theology, or history.

Linked to your Sun's degree, this star imparts a good mind, assertive manner, and comprehensive knowledge. El Nath also empowers you through the ability to speak persuasively, and encourages success through work in the legal system and government positions.

• *Positive:* high education, impressive speech, realization of thoughts and plans, outstanding achievements

• *Negative:* headstrong, critical and fault-finding, controversial, stubborn

ENSIS

Star's name: Ensis
Degree position: 22°2'–22°57' Gemini between the years 1930 and 2000
Magnitude: 4.5
Strength: ★★★
Orb: 1°
Constellation: M42 Orinis
Applicable days: June 13, 14, 15
Star qualities: Mars/Moon
Description: the Great Nebula located in the sheath of Orion

Ensis endows you with a defiant nature, driving ambition, and a constant desire to forge ahead. This star also warns against restlessness and hastiness, which can cause unnecessary upheaval.

Linked to your Sun's degree, this star can endow tremendous energy, drive, and willpower. Ensis suggests that you have intense emotions and are daring, with an ability to initiate projects with great vigor. The negative influence of this star is in the bestowal of a restless and impatient spirit, which may result in mood swings or emotional outbursts.

• *Positive:* ambitious, daring, leadership, energy, vigor, drive

• *Negative:* impatience, restlessness, anger, moodiness, quarrelsome

ALNILAM

Star's name: Alnilam, also called Al Nitham or the String of Pearls
Degree position: 22°29'–23°22' Gemini between the years 1930 and 2000
Magnitude: 2
Strength: ★★★★★★★★
Orb: 2°10'
Constellation: Epsilon Orion
Applicable days: June 12, 13, 14, 15, 16, 17
Star qualities: varied influences: Jupiter/Saturn and Mercury/Saturn
Description: a bright white star located in the center of the belt of Orion

Alnilam bestows fleeting fame and wealth or public honors. The influence of this star is therefore likely to be of short duration. This star grants a keen and daring personality, but it warns against being headstrong or rash, or changing direction without a suitable strategy.

Linked to your Sun's degree, this star denotes a strong character, full of energy and determination. Alnilam encourages you to undertake large projects or to be enterprising, although it also suggests that you must think before making any statements. Often by avoiding stubbornness and frustration you can use your enormous vitality on something positive and worthwhile.

• *Positive:* daring, energetic, ambitious, gains and victory

• *Negative:* rashness, instability, making sudden changes when convenient to yourself

AL HECKA

Star's name: Al Hecka
Degree position: 23°48'–24°25' Gemini between the years
1930 and 2000
Magnitude: 2
Strength: ★★★★★★★
Orb: 1°40'
Constellation: Zeta Taurus
Applicable days: June 14, 15, 16, 17
Star qualities: Mars or Saturn/Mercury
Description: a bluish star located on the Bull's south,
or following, Horn

Al Hecka bestows a proud, assertive nature, and fondness of power. You probably have leadership abilities and the determination to achieve wealth and fame. This star also denotes a mischievous nature and warns against associating with dubious characters.

Linked to your Sun's degree, this star imparts a reserved but enterprising spirit. Your talent for organization is coupled with a studious or hard-working nature. Al Hecka endows an inquisitive and pragmatic outlook as well as executive abilities, which can be beneficial when dealing with the public. This star also warns against suspicious circumstances and danger from others through deceit.

• *Positive:* practical, hard working, determination
• *Negative:* one who questions everything

POLARIS

Star's name: Polaris, also known as Al Rukkabah or the Pole Star
Degree position: 27°35'–28°33' Gemini between the years
1930 and 2000
Magnitude: 2
Strength: ★★★★★★★
Orb: 2°10'
Constellation: Alpha Ursa Minor
Applicable days: June 17, 18, 19, 20, 21, 22
Star qualities: Saturn/Venus
Description: a yellow and pale white binary star located in the tail of
the Lesser Bear

Polaris bestows spiritual powers, discretion, and clear aims and objectives. You can gain respect from others, as well as encouragement to pursue and achieve your goals. This star implies that recognition often comes after delays and obstacles. Through continual striving and a get-up-and-go attitude, you can earn rewards. Legacies and inheritance, however, are frequently accompanied by misunderstandings and disputes.

Linked to your Sun's degree, this star indicates an inclination for spirituality, religion, and philosophy. Polaris may also

bestow a flair for dealing with the public. This star frequently suggests that you are subject to changes in fortune through unforeseen events.

• *Positive:* dutiful, good instincts, clear aims and objectives, good boundaries
• *Negative:* unfeeling, overly serious, inhibited emotional expression

BETELGEUZE

Star's name: Betelgeuze
Degree position: 27°46'–28°42' Gemini between the years
1930 and 2000
Magnitude: 1
Strength: ★★★★★★★★★
Orb: 2°30'
Constellation: Alpha Orionis
Applicable days: June 18, 19, 20, 21, 22, 23
Star qualities: Mars/Mercury
Description: a variable orange-red star located on the right
shoulder of Orion

Betelgeuze imparts an ability to judge, an optimistic outlook, a quick mind, and a competitive nature. This star also bestows luck and success through resolution and determination. You may receive honor for outstanding achievement and may also gain material wealth.

Linked to your Sun's degree, this star shows a talent for philosophy and an aptitude for metaphysical studies. Belelgeuze imparts success in sport and legal affairs as well as generally carrying a good influence in all matters dealing with others. Although honor and wealth can be achieved, they are not necessarily long-lasting, for there is an ever-present danger of sudden loss.

• *Positive:* good judgment, problem solving, harmony of action and thought
• *Negative:* obstinate, argumentative, antagonist

MENKALINAN

Star's name: Menkalinan, also known as Shoulder of the Rein-Holder
Degree position: 28°56'–29°54' Gemini between the years
1930 and 2000
Magnitude: 2
Strength: ★★★★★★★
Orb: 2°10'
Constellation: Beta Aurigae
Applicable days: June 19, 20, 21, 22, 23
Star qualities: Jupiter with influences of Mars/Mercury/Venus
Description: a bright yellow star located on the right
shoulder of Auriga

Menkalinan bestows an energetic, assertive, and competitive nature as well as a sharp, active mind. This star also imparts quick actions and restlessness. Menkalinan promises success, honors, and popularity but also warns against sudden changes, hasty actions, or destructiveness.

Linked to your Sun's degree, Menkalinan assures achievement and success if you proceed steadily and avoid creating unnecessary turbulence. This star suggests that it will be in your interest to develop a think-before-you-act mentality, warning against hasty action.

• *Positive:* power of resolution, quick thinking, assertive mind, love of debate, the power to retaliate, impressive speaking

• *Negative:* nervousness, rashness, love of quarreling, headstrong, obstinate, critical

Cancer

TEJAT

Star's name: Tejat, also called Tejat Prior
Degree position: 2°27'–3°26' Cancer between the years 1930 and 2000
Magnitude: 3
Strength: ★★★★★★
Orb: 1°40'
Constellation: Eta Gemini
Applicable days: June 23, 24, 25, 26
Star qualities: Mercury/Venus
Description: an orange-red binary, variable star located on the left foot of the northern Twin

Tejat imparts confidence, pride, dignity, and a refined nature. The influence of this star denotes a wealth of feelings, a sense and appreciation of beauty, and artistic and literary abilities. Tejat also grants cheerfulness, a sense of humor, and the knowledge that two heads are better than one. Many benefits can come from cooperation, associative thinking, and developing a diplomatic yet persuasive manner. Tejat, however, warns that this talent can be used negatively to be cunning, overly confident, or inconsistent. It also warns against possible legal difficulties.

Linked to your Sun's degree, this star bestows appreciation for beauty, artistic talent, literary skills, and unusual interests. Tejat bestows a light-hearted nature, yet it also warns against a lack of drive and a tendency to be inconsistent. With this star you may experience some instability or change.

• *Positive:* thoughts of love, artistic sense, love union, writing skills

• *Negative:* inclination to squander, light-hearted living, vanity, conceit

DIRAH

Star's name: Dirah, also called Nuhaiti
Degree position: 4°19'–5°17' Cancer between the years 1930 and 2000
Magnitude: 3
Strength: ★★★★★★
Orb: 1°40'
Constellation: Mu Gemini
Applicable days: June 25, 26, 27, 28
Star qualities: Mercury/Venus
Description: a yellow and blue binary star located in the left foot of the northern Twin

Dirah imparts a sound mind and creative ideas. This star bestows forceful speech accompanied by a witty, sociable, and friendly personality. Often a good communicator, you enjoy discussion, debate, and group popularity. There are also indications that you like music and orderliness and have a flair for making things look elegant and refined. Dirah bestows a talent for writing that, if developed, can bring honor and riches.

Linked to your Sun's degree, this star bestows the ability to make a favorable impression upon those you come into contact with and to gain wide popularity. Dirah's influence suggests prominence in public affairs, academic study, and writing, as well as success in education, literature, and publishing or politics. You may excel in sport, or enjoy studying astrology and esoteric subjects.

• *Positive:* creativity, wit, communication skills, love of art and beauty

• *Negative:* vanity, conceit, squandering, immature

ALHENA

Star's name: Alhena or Al-Hena, also called the Bright Foot of Gemini
Degree position: 8°7'–9°7' Cancer between the years 1930 and 2000
Magnitude: 2
Strength: ★★★★★★★★
Orb: 2°10'
Constellation: Gamma Gemini
Applicable days: June 28, 29, 30, July 1, 2
Star qualities: Mercury/Venus or Moon/Venus with Jupiter
Description: a brilliant white star in the left foot of the southern Twin

Alhena's influence can bestow prominence in the art world and denotes a refined, lovable, and affable nature. You may be interested in spirituality or art and science. This star also indicates that you take pride in achievement, whether great or small. A love of ease and luxury is also suggested.

Linked to your Sun's degree, this star denotes artistic inclinations, interest in the sciences, and prominence in the study of astrology or metaphysics. You have a charismatic personality and can prosper through social affairs and all dealings with the public. You are motivated by desire for pleasure and luxury. This star is also associated with Achilles' heel and therefore warns against foot injuries.

• *Positive:* tactful, the joy of living, sociability, stylish with film-star mannerisms

• *Negative:* lazy, overindulgent, wasteful, conceited, proud

SIRIUS

Star's name: Sirius
Degree position: 13°6'–14°2' Cancer between the years 1930 and 2000
Magnitude: 1
Strength: ★★★★★★★★★
Orb: 2°30'
Constellation: Alpha Canis Major
Applicable days: July 3, 4, 5, 6, 7, 8
Star qualities: varied interpretations: Moon/Jupiter/Mars
Description: a brilliant white and yellow binary star, located in the mouth of the Great Dog; linked to the Egyptian god Osiris

Sirius bestows an optimistic, broad outlook and the ability to make loyal friends in high places. With this star's influence, you can enjoy prosperity and success and can act as guardian or have a custodial position. Often, and without much effort, you can receive favors from superiors. Sirius may indicate honor, wealth, and fame as well as an opportunity to exercise power and leadership qualities. Sirius may also encourage rebellious or daredevil behavior, and it thus warns against the danger of pushing ahead prematurely.

Linked to your Sun's degree, this star suggests success in business, domestic happiness, and an inclination toward the arts, astrology, philosophy, or higher learning. If honor comes too early, you might be unprepared and unable to cope with success. Frequently you present a royal demeanor, and you are successful in dealing with the public. This star also indicates that you are trustworthy and can act as custodian of other people's property.

• *Positive:* faithfulness, important responsibilities, joy of living, love of enterprise, successful, creative activities

• *Negative:* the urge for freedom at any cost, misuse of power and positions of trust

CANOPUS

Star's name: Canopus
Degree position: 13°58'–15° Cancer between the years 1930 and 2000
Magnitude: 1
Strength: ★★★★★★★★★
Orb: 2°30'
Constellation: Alpha Carinae
Applicable days: July 4, 5, 6, 7, 8, 9, 10
Star qualities: Saturn/Jupiter and Moon/Mars

Description: a yellow-white star located in one of the oars of the ship Argo

The Egyptian god Canopus, patron of ships and voyages, is linked to this star, which bestows travel and suggests long voyages. This star imparts a kind nature, conservatism, astuteness, and success through education and academic achievements. You have the ability to acquire comprehensive knowledge as well as work for the community. This star also warns about family and relations, domestic afflictions, and troubles with a parent.

Linked to your Sun's degree, this star bestows success in public affairs and attainment of far-reaching objectives through industrious effort. Fame can also be achieved but is not always long-lasting. There may be some minor problems on the domestic front or with friends and relatives, although help is there when it is needed most.

• *Positive:* earnestness, commitment, love of travel, perseverance, success in law

• *Negative:* frustration, discontent, most problems are of your own doing, involvement in lawsuits

AL WASAT

Star's name: Al Wasat
Degree position: 17°32'–18°34' Cancer between the years 1930 and 2000
Magnitude: 4
Strength: ★★★★
Orb: 1°30'
Constellation: Delta Gemini
Applicable days: July 9, 10, 11, 12, 13
Star qualities: Saturn
Description: a yellow and blue binary star located in the waist area of the Twins

Al Wasat imparts intelligence, persistence, and a pragmatic outlook. This star conveys an ability to speak clearly and to the point and bestows prominence in public affairs or management as a result. This star warns against trying too hard and depleting your energies. Al Wasat also suggests that you must avoid acting in a destructive manner, causing unnecessary stress, and creating uneasy situations, which you might later regret.

Linked to your Sun's degree, Al Wasat imparts endurance, common sense, and an inherent drive to forge ahead with determination. This star also suggests that you should avoid being too pushy and learn to channel your energies into a worthwhile cause.

• *Positive:* rewards depend on past efforts, determination

• *Negative:* hustler, aggressive, pessimistic, destructive behavior

PROPUS

Star's name: Propus
Degree position: 17°59'–19°3' Cancer between the years 1930 and 2000
Magnitude: 4
Strength: ★★★★
Orb: 1°30'
Constellation: Iota Gemini
Applicable days: July 10, 11, 12, 13
Star qualities: Mercury/Venus
Description: a small binary star located between the shoulders of the Twins

Propus endows a keen mentality and articulate self-expression. Gregarious, affable, and witty, you may enjoy eminence and success through artistic pursuits or dealing with the public. You are probably sensitive, with strong feelings and a love of ease and luxury.

Linked to your Sun's degree, Propus's influence can direct you toward artistic pursuits. There is a natural talent for astrology, writing, and public speaking. This star will also assist in developing a forceful approach in order to get your ideas across, or to undertake creative work.

• *Positive:* good voice, impressive speech, love of music, creative talents
• *Negative:* hypersensitivity, sweet talker, arrogance, lack of drive to reach goals or objectives

CASTOR

Star's name: Castor
Degree position: 19°16'–20°13' Cancer between the years 1930 and 2000
Magnitude: 2
Strength: ★★★★★★★
Orb: 2°10'
Constellation: Alpha Gemini
Applicable days: July 10, 11, 12, 13, 14, 15
Star qualities: varied influences of Mercury, Venus, Mars, and Jupiter
Description: a binary star, bright white and pale white, located on the head of the northern Twin

Castor's influence bestows a quick mind and keen intellect. This star indicates fluctuating circumstances of gains alternating with losses, and sudden rises in fortune that may be followed by a fall.

Linked to your Sun's degree, Castor bestows energetic characteristics and a talent for wit and satire, but also a tendency to cynicism. This star imparts a flair for writing and good communication skills. You are probably interested in public affairs and may choose a career in the media. This star also imparts opportunities in foreign affairs, as well as good intuition and talent for metaphysical studies.

• *Positive:* can bring sudden rises in status and turns in fortune, keen intelligence, creative ability
• *Negative:* fame but sometimes at a high price, self-sacrificing

POLLUX

Star's name: Pollux, also known as the Boxing Twin or Hercules
Degree position: 22°15'–23°11' Cancer between the years 1930 and 2000
Magnitude: 1
Strength: ★★★★★★★★★
Orb: 2°30'
Constellation: Beta Gemini
Applicable days: July 13, 14, 15, 16, 17, 18
Star qualities: varied influences: Mars/Moon/Uranus
Description: a bright orange star located on the head of the southern Twin

Pollux's influence suggests a subtle yet self-reliant, spirited, and brave nature. This star imparts a love of competitive sports. Pollux's negative influence is in hastiness and oversensitivity, which may create frustration and quarrels, resulting in unpleasant situations.

Linked to your Sun's degree, this star indicates love of adventure and a talent for sport. You are likely to go it alone or attempt to achieve success by your own effort. Pollux also imparts psychic abilities and the courage to pursue personal ideals and goals. Prominence in higher education and interests in philosophy are also indicated by the influence of this star.

• *Positive:* competitive yet subtle and sensitive, the power of attainment
• *Negative:* crafty, rash nature, aggressive or selfish with a cruel streak, moodiness

PROCYON

Star's name: Procyon
Degree position: 24°48'–25°43' Cancer between the years 1930 and 2000
Magnitude: 1
Strength: ★★★★★★★★★
Orb: 2°30'
Constellation: Alpha Canis Minor
Applicable days: July 16, 17, 18, 19, 20, 21
Star qualities: varied influences: Mercury/Mars or Jupiter/Uranus
Description: a yellow and white binary star located on the body of the Lesser Dog

Procyon's influence bestows willpower, drive, and an ability to execute plans. This star also suggests much activity and unusual interests or occupations. Procyon imparts opportunities for wealth, success, and good fortune. This star frequently indicates a sudden turn of events that brings fame or notoriety as well as gains and losses. Therefore you may need to learn patience, and taking the time to plan will secure a more successful outcome. Ancient interpretations of this star also warn against bites from dogs.

Linked to your Sun's degree, this star grants courage, ingenuity, unusual talents, and a chivalrous nature. Procyon denotes that you will have many loyal friends who will come to your assistance and provide help when it is needed most. This star also foretells of sudden fortunes gained through gifts or legacies.

• *Positive:* wealth and fortune, government positions, pride and dignity, prominence in religion
• *Negative:* snobbery, carelessness, clumsy, crafty, deceptive

ALTARF

Star's name: Altarf, also called the End
Degree position: 30° Cancer–1° Leo between the years 1930 and 2000
Magnitude: 3.5
Strength: ★★★★★
Orb: 1°40'
Constellation: Beta Cancer
Applicable days: July 21, 22
Star qualities: Mars
Description: an orange giant star located on the tip of the southern hind leg of the Crab

Altarf's influence endows willpower, endurance, and advancement in life through one's own efforts. With stamina and a fighting spirit, you have an aptitude for overcoming difficulties and dangers. This star also warns against impulsiveness or overstraining.

Linked to your Sun's degree, Altarf bestows courage, determination, and the constant desire to be active and involved. This star bestows self-assurance and confidence as well as enthusiasm and a spirit of enterprise.

• *Positive:* active and productive, courage, self-assured
• *Negative:* waste of energy, impulsiveness, takes risks or gambles

Leo

PRAESEPE

Star's name: Praesepe, also called Praesaepe
Degree position: 6°16'–7°16' Leo between the years 1930 and 2000
Magnitude: 5
Strength: ★★
Orb: 1°
Constellation: M44 Cancer

Applicable days: July 30, 31, August 1
Star qualities: Mars/Moon
Description: a star mass of more than forty stars located on the head of the Crab

Praesepe imparts an adventurous yet industrious nature with good business acumen. This star also suggests good fortune and may indicate involvement in founding large businesses. Praesepe, however, also carries an influence that suggests impulsiveness and restlessness and warns against an inclination toward creating unnecessary trouble by being too insolent. This star also warns against involvement in lawsuits and risky dealings.

Linked to your Sun's degree, this star imparts energy and vitality, inner pride, and an ability to focus on goals with great determination. Once you make up your mind, you refuse to give up, but continue to strive toward your final objectives. This star's influence can attract friends, bring popularity, and lead to high-profile positions and even fame. Praesepe, however, warns against fluctuating moods, doubts, and fears, which could arise from misunderstandings with others, and may result in self-destructive behavior.

• *Positive:* enthusiasm, spirit of enterprise, strong will, openness, frankness
• *Negative:* aimlessness, defiance, incompatible, misunderstood personality, reclusive

NORTH ASELLUS

Star's name: North Asellus
Degree position: 6°34'–7°35' Leo, between the years 1930 and 2000
Magnitude: 5
Strength: ★★
Orb: 1°
Constellation: Gamma Cancer
Applicable days: July 30, 31, August 1
Star qualities: Mars/Sun
Description: a pale yellow-white twin star located in the body of the Crab

North Asellus bestows vitality and vigor, creative talent, love of the arts, and unexpected gains. Although both North and South Asellus impart a caring nature and therefore indicate responsibility, North Asellus is known as the beneficial star and endows powers of attainment plus a charitable and generous outlook. This star also suggests that intolerance and aggressive mannerisms do not achieve desired results.

Linked to your Sun's degree, this star imparts a flair for dealing with the public, good social connections, and friends in influential positions. High preferment is indicated in education, especially philosophy and religion, or success in business and large corporations.

- *Positive:* fearless, competitive nature, very patient until a course of action is determined
- *Negative:* hastiness, stubbornness, restlessness

SOUTH ASELLUS

Star's name: South Asellus

Degree position: 7°44'–8°44' Leo between the years 1930 and 2000

Magnitude: 4

Strength: ★★★★

Orb: 1°30'

Constellation: Delta Cancer

Applicable days: July 30, 31, August 1, 2, 3

Star qualities: Mars/Sun

Description: a pale yellow twin star located in the body of the Crab

South Asellus suggests that you must take great care to be a responsible individual, especially when in authoritative positions. The warning that this star carries indicates that you may have to guard against being a daredevil and putting your life at risk. South Asellus also warns against making slanderous statements, which can backfire and cause loss of reputation or domestic problems.

Linked to your Sun's degree, this star in a favorable configuration with other planets imparts a charitable and generous outlook with preferment for business. South Asellus also imparts energy and determination but less flair for dealing with the public than its twin star, North Asellus. This star suggests that exercising caution may help with social connections and friends in influential positions. Nevertheless, some mistakes may result in misunderstandings and cause loss of credibility or trouble in business.

- *Positive:* thoughtful and caring, caution
- *Negative:* outspoken and careless, offensive

KOCHAB

Star's name: Kochab

Degree position: 11°56'–12°45' Leo between the years 1930 and 2000

Magnitude: 2

Strength: ★★★★★★★★

Orb: 2°10'

Constellation: Beta Ursa Minor

Applicable days: August 4, 5, 6, 7

Star qualities: Saturn/Mercury

Description: a giant orange star located in the Small Bear, also called the Little Dipper

Kochab's influence bestows logic, concentration, and an ability to come straight to the point in discussion. Often you have a love of tidiness and good organizational skills. This star imparts stamina and opportunities to rise to a position of authority.

Linked to your Sun's degree, this star indicates that much can be achieved through determination. You have the ability to fight with energy and courage till the end, and you possess a never-give-up attitude. This star also warns against deceit and malicious or underhanded activities.

- *Positive:* determination, persistence, courage to overcome obstacles
- *Negative:* rashness, mischief, pessimism

ACUBENS

Star's name: Acubens, also called Sertan

Degree position: 12°40'–13°36' Leo between the years 1930 and 2000

Magnitude: 4

Strength: ★★★★

Orb: 1°30'

Constellation: Alpha Cancer

Applicable days: August 5, 6, 7, 8

Star qualities: Mercury/Saturn

Description: a double star with white and red constituents, located in the southern claw of the Crab

Acubens imparts a logical and rational mind, perseverance, and high ideals. You can appear forceful and may be quite outspoken. This star bestows depth of thought and a talent for organization but may also reveal domineering tendencies.

Linked to your Sun's degree, Acubens endows good structure and executive abilities. There is an inborn potential for making outstanding contributions to your field of expertise. Preferment for education, including the study of astrology and science, are also indicated and may reveal a talent for writing. This star was originally associated with hiding places and refuge for outlaws and thus warns of working against the establishment.

- *Positive:* pragmatic nature, patience and determination
- *Negative:* speculator, rebel, restlessness, misuse of knowledge

DUBHE

Star's name: Dubhe

Degree position: 14°9'–15°2' Leo between the years 1930 and 2000

Magnitude: 2

Strength: ★★★★★★★★

Orb: 2°20'

Constellation: Alpha Ursa Major

Applicable days: August 6, 7, 8, 9, 10

Star qualities: varied interpretations: Mercury/Venus or Mars

Description: a yellow binary main star located on the back of the Greater Bear

Dubhe endows idealism, self-confidence, boldness, and pride. This star grants intelligence, articulate speech, and persuasive expression. Although you are probably adventurous, at times you may feel insecure and let suspicious and mistrustful thoughts cause you worry.

Linked to your Sun's degree, Dubhe bestows determination to succeed and to overcome obstacles. Love of learning and a desire to achieve may direct you toward higher studies, astrology, law, or the military. In turn, this may also reveal a flair for writing and philosophy. This star warns against becoming overly materialistic and suggests channeling your power positively lest it become destructive.

- *Positive:* higher learning, artistic talents, beautiful voice
- *Negative:* worry, insecurity, lack of imagination, inclination to materialism

MERAK

Star's name: Merak
Degree position: 18°29'–19°34' Leo between the years 1930 and 2000
Magnitude: 2
Strength: ★★★★★★★
Orb: 2°10'
Constellation: Alpha Ursa Major
Applicable days: August 10, 11, 12, 13, 14
Star qualities: Mars
Description: a white giant star located on the side of the Great Bear

Merak imparts a love of command and leadership abilities, although it may also indicate an inclination to be overly dominant. Your determination means that you are likely to achieve much in life and succeed where others may fail.

Linked to your Sun's degree, this star bestows courage, assertiveness, and hot-blooded vitality. The power of attainment that is associated with this star ensures that your life will be full of activity. Merak's influence carries opportunities and possible fame and honors.

- *Positive:* love of life, active and creative, ambition, courage
- *Negative:* hastiness, stubbornness, overstrain

AL GENUBI

Star's name: Al Genubi, also called Asad Australis
Degree position: 19°44'–20°43' Leo between the years 1930 and 2000
Magnitude: 3
Strength: ★★★★★
Orb: 1°40'
Constellation: Epsilon Leo
Applicable days: August 12, 13, 14, 15
Star qualities: Saturn/Mars
Description: a yellow star located in the Lion's mouth

Al Genubi's influence imparts endurance, artistic talent, and the power of expression. This star also suggests that you possess a bold and daring personality.

Linked to your Sun's degree, Al Genubi endows determination, a need to be productive, and natural executive abilities. Your good organizational skills usually gain you positions of authority. Your need for self-expression and creativity may direct you toward the arts and more glamorous professions. This star warns that if you do not find ways to express yourself in a constructive manner, you may behave destructively.

- *Positive:* resilient, creative, artistic, vitality, personal magnetism
- *Negative:* domineering, proud, arrogant, cruel

ALPHARD

Star's name: Alphard
Degree position: 26°17'–27°8' Leo, between the years 1930–2000
Magnitude: 2
Strength: ★★★★★★★
Orb: 2°10'
Constellation: Alpha Hydrae
Applicable days: August 19, 20, 21, 22
Star qualities: varied interpretations: Saturn/Venus and Sun/Jupiter
Description: a giant orange star located in the neck of the Hydra

Alphard's influence bestows natural wisdom and a deep understanding of human nature. You appreciate the arts and have keen ambitions and a sensitive nature. Alphard warns against overindulgence, intemperance, and lack of self-control. This star suggests turbulence and at times upheaval. Alphard also warns against all forms of poisoning and infections.

Linked to your Sun's degree, this star bestows executive abilities, positions of authority, and great opportunities for advancement. You tend to seek prominent positions and to be in the limelight. Nevertheless, you must always be fair and just, otherwise others will push you out. This applies also to work and relationships, where jealousy can creep in, although often you attempt to hide it.

- *Positive:* confidence, can make a name for yourself, fame
- *Negative:* legal entanglement and disputes, loss of self-control, jealousy

ADHAFERA

Star's name: Adhafera, also called Al-Serpha
Degree position: 26°35'–27°34' Leo between the years 1930 and 2000
Magnitude: 3.5–4
Strength: ★★★★
Orb: 1°30'
Constellation: Zeta Leo
Applicable days: August 19, 20, 21, 22

Star qualities: Saturn/Mercury

Description: a double yellow star in the Lion's mane

Adhafera imparts depth of thought, love of order, good practical skills, and an ability to focus on the job or problem at hand. You are industrious and have the ability to concentrate on large projects. This star warns against the use of unorthodox methods and suggests avoiding anti-establishment activities.

Linked to your Sun's degree, this star endows a quick mind, a love of learning, and a pragmatic approach. Adhafera also bestows determination, endurance, and excellent skills in problem solving.

- *Positive:* practical skills, good mental focus, concentration
- *Negative:* obstinate, unyielding, pessimism

AL JABHAH

Star's name: Al Jabhah, also called the Forehead

Degree position: 26°55'–27°52' Leo between the years 1930 and 2000

Magnitude: 3.5

Strength: ★★★★★

Orb: 1°30'

Constellation: Eta Leo

Applicable days: August 19, 20, 21, 22

Star qualities: Mercury/Saturn

Description: a star located in the Lion's mane

Al Jabhah bestows ambition and a great potential for success and achievement at work. You frequently possess good judgment and the determination to achieve wealth and success. This star warns that anxious moments and periods of instability can occur if you are self-seeking and opportunistic.

Linked to your Sun's degree, this star imparts a competitive nature, executive abilities, and the ability to concentrate on creative projects through the application of method. This star warns against being overly confident and of rebellious actions, which you might later regret.

- *Positive:* endurance, determination, good structure, creativity
- *Negative:* foolhardiness, rashness, hasty decisions

REGULUS

Star's name: Regulus, also called the Lion's Heart

Degree position: 28°51'–29°48' Leo between the years 1930 and 2000

Magnitude: 1

Strength: ★★★★★★★★★★

Orb: 2°30'

Constellation: Alpha Leonis

Applicable days: August 21, 22, 23, 24, 25, 26

Star qualities: Mars/Jupiter

Description: a brilliant white and blue triple star located on the body of the Lion

Regulus is a royal star that takes a leading role among a nearly infinite cast of stars. Regulus imparts nobility, high honors, great charisma, and the power to project dignified personality. This star bestows a natural ability to make quick decisions and cope with demanding situations. It also imparts a desire for power and an ability to lead and command others. You have strong willpower and a love of enterprise, which often lead to a desire for freedom and independence. Regulus warns that these great benefits are not necessarily long-lasting.

Linked to your Sun's degree, this star imparts ambition, power, and authority, and opportunities to rise to high positions in government and large corporations. If you do not have a position of prominence, you probably have influential friends. This star suggests that you should be kind to others on your way up, as you are likely to meet them on your way down.

- *Positive:* high-spirited, frankness, courage, honor and riches, rise to prominent positions, authority
- *Negative:* stubborn, unruly, domineering, greatness but also great failures (especially through dishonesty), fleeting success and fame

---

PHECDA

Star's name: Phecda or Phachd

Degree position: 29°41' Leo–0°9' Virgo between the years 1930 and 2000

Magnitude: 3

Strength: ★★★★★★

Orb: 2°

Constellation: Gamma Ursa Major

Applicable days: August 22, 23, 24, 25

Star qualities: varied interpretations: Mars/Jupiter or Venus

Description: the third largest star of the Greater Bear

Phecda bestows an enterprising spirit, love of luxury, and a charismatic personality. Often this star is associated with enthusiasm and a need for constant expansion and creativity. This star bestows ambition and an ability to make decisions quickly. Phecda also imparts a love of the good life but warns against becoming lazy or self-indulgent.

Linked to your Sun's degree, this star can impart popularity, an attractive personality, and good social skills. Phecda often indicates creative talent and a potential for writing. Alternatively, it may stimulate you to be successful in business as a result of the desire for a more luxurious lifestyle.

- *Positive:* social skills, popularity, influential friends, the spirit of enterprise
- *Negative:* exaggeration, arrogant, opportunist, vanity, pride, overly confident

Virgo

ALIOTH

Star's Name: Alioth
Degree position: 7°52'–8°52' Virgo between the years 1930 and 2000
Magnitude: 2
Strength: ★★★★★★★★
Orb: 2°10'
Constellation: Epsilon Ursa Major
Applicable days: August 29, 30, 31, September 1, 2, 3
Star qualities: Mars
Description: a blue-white star located in the tail of the Great Bear

Alioth endows good judgment, a zest for life, and love of ease and comfort. Often you are broad-minded and inclined toward liberalism. This star imparts ambition to win, a competitive nature, and a constant need for activity. Alioth also imparts a talent for criticism and suggests that it should be used constructively.

Linked to your Sun's degree, Alioth's influence indicates an aptitude for business, sport, government posts, and dealing with the public. It can also stimulate thoroughness and the ability to exploit every situation, but warns against irritability and overconfidence.

• *Positive:* genuine, frank, endurance can overcome disappointment
• *Negative:* ruthlessness, egoism, destructiveness, obstinacy, overcritical

ZOSMA

Star's name: Zosma
Degree position: 10°19'–11°14' Virgo between the years 1930 and 2000
Magnitude: 2.5
Strength: ★★★★★★★
Orb: 2°10'
Constellation: Delta Leo
Applicable days: September 2, 3, 4, 5, 6
Star qualities: Saturn/Venus
Description: a white, pale yellow, and blue-violet triple star located on the Lion's back

Zosma bestows a serious and responsible nature and an alert mind, but also warns against becoming overserious or selfish. You may experience changeable circumstances but should guard against unwarranted fears and anxieties. Positively, Zosma can impart a liberal attitude, charm, and a positive approach as well as unexpected success and advancement.

Linked to your Sun's degree, this star can help you gain power and convince others with your opinions. You can become influential and rise socially, as Zosma bestows friendliness and popularity. Although you can appear extroverted and gregarious, usually your nature is somewhat reserved. This star warns that only in time of need will you find out who are your true friends.

• *Positive:* loyal, dutiful, thoroughness
• *Negative:* shamelessness, egotistical, false friends, overseriousness

MIZAR

Star's name: Mizar
Degree position: 14°36'–15°37' Virgo between the years 1930 and 2000
Magnitude: 2.5
Strength: ★★★★★★
Orb: 2°10'
Constellation: Zeta Ursa Major
Applicable days: September 6, 7, 8, 9, 10, 11
Star qualities: Mars and Saturn/Venus
Description: a white and pale emerald star located on the tail of the Great Bear

Mizar imparts ambition, a pragmatic nature, creativity, and artistic talents. This star, however, can also indicate disharmony and involvement in controversial issues.

Linked to your Sun's degree, this star indicates a prominence in writing and business and success in dealing with the general public. Mizar warns against being too critical and suggests using your mental powers in creative and positive ways.

• *Positive:* serious, responsible, creative
• *Negative:* rebellious, disharmonious, selfish

DENEBOLA

Star's name: Denebola
Degree position: 20°38'–21°31' Virgo between the years 1930 and 2000
Magnitude: 2
Strength: ★★★★★★★★
Orb: 2°10'
Constellation: Beta Leo
Applicable days: September 12, 13, 14, 15, 16
Star qualities: varied influences: Saturn/Venus/Mercury and Mars
Description: a blue star located in the Lion's tail

Denebola bestows good judgment, daring, courage, and a noble, generous nature. This star's influence can bring about exciting events and opportunities for advancement. You may have a natural talent for clear thinking and good values, accompanied by swift action. This star also indicates that you will be responsible and active on behalf of others. Denebola, however, also carries a reminder that benefits may not necessarily be long-lasting, and it warns against tendencies to get angry or anxious, which can spoil relationships.

Linked to your Sun's degree, this star imparts ingenuity and determination to acquire special skills. Rewards and honor through work are also indicated, and you may become a renowned specialist in your chosen field. Often gains and success come from work in the community and fulfilling public duties. Denebola may also impart restlessness and warns against hasty decisions that you might later regret.

- *Positive:* self-control, generous, inventive, responsible, honorable
- *Negative:* rashness, lack of responsibility, impatience

COPULA

Star's name: Copula
Degree position: 24°4'–24°47' Virgo between the years 1930 and 2000
Magnitude: 4
Strength: ★★★★
Orb: 1°
Constellation: M51 Canes Venatici
Applicable days: September 16, 17, 18
Star qualities: Venus/Moon
Description: a star or a spiral nebula located under the tail of the Great Bear

Copula's influence bestows strong passion, deep and intense feelings, and emotional sensitivity. You are often caring and sympathetic, with a tender heart. This star imparts love of music and an artistic appreciation, which may help you find modes of self-expression. Copula advises that care should be taken to ensure good eyesight.

Linked to your Sun's degree, Copula imparts a flair for dealing with the public, and you are likely to seek work in public office or be involved in legal affairs and matters concerning the law. This star warns against being put off by minor obstacles or setbacks and suggests that staying emotionally calm and exercising patience can be of great advantage.

- *Positive:* harmonious nature, happiness, cheerful disposition, learning to overcome minor setbacks
- *Negative:* irritability, moodiness, conflicts in love

LABRUM

Star's name: Labrum, also called the Holy Grail
Degree position: 25°41'–26°21' Virgo between the years 1930 and 2000
Magnitude: 4
Strength: ★★★★
Orb: 1°30'
Constellation: Delta Crateris
Applicable days: September 17, 18, 19
Star qualities: Venus/Mercury
Description: a small yellow star located in the Cup

Labrum bestows intelligence and often imparts a creative and receptive nature with intuitive and psychic powers. This star also suggests that you have cosmopolitan views, a liberal outlook, and ecclesiastical inclinations. Frequently you will find an interest in history, philosophy, or religion and develop natural writing talents, which can lead to honor and wealth.

Linked to your Sun's degree, this star bestows determination and opportunities for success in dealing with the public. You may seek to express yourself through creative pursuits such as the performing arts, writing, presenting, communications, and the media. This star also points to a love of comfort and pleasure and warns against overindulgence and avoiding responsibility.

- *Positive:* creativity, education, artistic success, writing
- *Negative:* vanity and conceit, lack of drive, indulgence

ZAVIJAVA

Star's name: Zavijava, also called Al Araph
Degree position: 26°10'–27°4' Virgo between the years 1930 and 2000
Magnitude: 3.5
Strength: ★★★★★
Orb: 1°30'
Constellation: Beta Virgo
Applicable days: September 18, 19, 20, 21
Star qualities: Mars/Mercury
Description: a pale yellow star located below the head of Virgo

Zavijava imparts a strong and dynamic character. You are intelligent and inclined toward education and scientific research or the legal profession. Alternatively, the world of publishing, news, and media may lure you. Zavijava imparts an ability to overcome obstacles and get ahead.

Linked to your Sun's degree, this star bestows a fine mind with the ability to concentrate and pay attention to detail. You prefer specialist work and may even become a leading figure in your field. You might be a researcher, surveyor, system refiner, statistics analyst, engineer, or computer expert.

- *Positive:* quick actions, skill and dexterity, decisiveness, frank and outspoken, impressive speech, quickness at repartee
- *Negative:* rashness, critical, argumentative

AL KAID

Star's name: Al Kaid, also called Benetnash
Degree position: 25°51'–26°50' Virgo between the years 1930 and 2000
Magnitude: 2
Strength: ★★★★★★★★
Orb: 2°10'
Constellation: Eta Ursa Major

Applicable days: September 18, 19, 20, 21, 22
Star qualities: Moon/Mercury
Description: a blue star located in the Great Bear

Al Kaid imparts an active mind, a need for creative expression, intuitiveness, and an ability to adapt easily to new situations. You probably enjoy exchanging thoughts and ideas but may have a tendency to change your mind easily. This star indicates an aptitude for business and a fondness for power, and may grant opportunities for success, luck, and wealth.

Linked to your Sun's degree, Al Kaid's influence imparts a talent for business and points to success in dealing with the general public. You are inclined toward dealing with data, research, or exacting work that requires attention to detail. Al Kaid also tends to make you restless and ambitious and, at times, ruthless in your desire to reach the top. This star also gives a talent for criticism, which should be used in a positive way.

• *Positive:* active mind, good grasp or perception, sympathetic, kind, work with children

• *Negative:* criticism, gossip, worry, sensitive, nerves, propensity for lying, impatience, moody, overcritical

MARKEB

Star's name: Markeb
Degree position: 27°53'–28°25' Virgo between the years 1930 and 2000
Magnitude: 2.5
Strength: ★★★★★★
Orb: 1°40'
Constellation: Kappa Velorum
Applicable days: September 19, 20, 21, 22
Star qualities: Jupiter/Saturn
Description: a small star located in the buckler of the Ship

Markeb bestows devotion and piety, love of knowledge, and an ability to gain general knowledge on a wide range of topics. This star imparts a need for, and an interest in, education, as well as a natural talent for philosophy. The influence of this star denotes that patience must be cultivated in order to achieve success. Long voyages and work in foreign lands are also under the effect of this star.

Linked to your Sun's degree, Markeb endows you with a talent for writing, business, and detailed research work. If you have this star you often appear to others as a storehouse of information and knowledge.

• *Positive:* keen mind, concentration, attention to detail
• *Negative:* collect useless information, interest in trivial matters and gossip

ZANIAH

Star's name: Zaniah
Degree position: 3°51'–4°43' Libra between the years 1930 and 2000
Magnitude: 4
Strength: ★★★★
Orb: 1°30'
Constellation: Eta Virgo
Applicable days: September 26, 27, 28, 29
Star qualities: Mercury/Venus
Description: a variable white star located on the southern wing of Virgo

Zaniah's influence bestows refinement, congeniality, and a love of harmony and orderliness. Usually you possess a kind nature, with a charming personality, and probably have many friends. This star imparts popularity, honor, and success through social contacts.

Linked to your Sun's degree, Zaniah favors education, intellectual learning, and a natural talent for research and literature. With the help of this star, you may become a specialist in your subject of interest. You enjoy good working relationships with co-workers and make a good marriage partner. This star suggests that you have a very agreeable nature unless aroused.

• *Positive:* visionary, mentally keen, refiner, ability to handle detailed work
• *Negative:* vanity, conceit, lack of drive, squandering, looking for easy options

VINDEMIATRIX

Star's name: Vindemiatrix, also known as Vindemiator or the Grapes Gatherer
Degree position: 8°57'–9°57' Libra between the years 1930 and 2000
Magnitude: 3
Strength: ★★★★★★
Orb: 1°40'
Constellation: Epsilon Virgo
Applicable days: October 1, 2, 3, 4
Star qualities: varied interpretations: Mercury/Saturn and Saturn/Venus/Mercury
Description: a bright yellow star located on the right wing of Virgo

Vindemiatrix's influence indicates that although you possess a quick mind, at times you are impulsive or indiscreet. This star bestows concentration, logical thinking, and the ability to come straight to the point. You tend to approach problems methodically and persist until you resolve them. Vindemiatrix, however, also suggests that you can be obstinate or unyielding.

Linked to your Sun's degree, this star imparts leadership

ability, pride, and a drive to accomplish and be recognized. You often conceal your cleverness and have a tendency to make insubstantial statements. This star also indicates that success comes mainly after effort, and it suggests a tendency to worry over money and failure even when there is no need to.

• *Positive:* reserved, clever, consistency, patience, methodical
• *Negative:* depression, worry, losses if not careful with monetary matters

---

CAPHIR

Star's name: Caphir, also called Porrima
Degree position: 9°9'–10°3' Libra between the years 1930 and 2000
Magnitude: 3
Strength: ★★★★★★
Orb: 1°40'
Constellation: Gamma Virgo
Applicable days: October 1, 2, 3, 4
Star qualities: Mercury/Venus and Venus/Mars
Description: a variable yellow and white binary star located on the left arm of Virgo

Caphir's influence endows an agreeable and lovable personality and bestows idealism, refined taste, and a diplomatic and courteous manner. This star can increase your popularity and provides opportunities for advancement through social contacts.

Linked to your Sun's degree, Caphir imparts a talent for writing, astrology, social sciences, and philosophy. A strong need to communicate with others makes you ideal for dealing with the public. With an innate inner drive for success and recognition, you eventually get the acclaim you deserve. Caphir suggests that trusting your instincts develops self-confidence.

• *Positive:* educated, intuitive, refined, good taste, creative, friendly
• *Negative:* involvement in questionable situations, doubts

ALGORAB

Star's name: Algorab, also called Al Ghirab or the Crow
Degree position: 12°28'–13°22' Libra between the years 1930 and 2000
Magnitude: 3
Strength: ★★★★★★
Orb: 1°30'
Constellation: Delta Corvi
Applicable days: October 5, 6, 7, 8
Star qualities: Mars/Saturn
Description: a pale yellow and purple binary star, located on the right wing of the Crow

Algorab imparts a flair for business and enterprise and bestows determination and power to overcome challenges with charm

and grace. This star indicates a reserved and studious nature, with ambition for recognition and success. Algorab also warns against destructiveness and deception from others.

Linked to your Sun's degree, this star imparts a talent for making a good impression and success in dealing with the public and in getting support or promotion from others. If in the public view, you can gain fame and popularity, although you must guard against scandals that can lose you your position.

• *Positive:* persistence, big enterprises, popularity, military honor
• *Negative:* unorthodox methods, working against the establishment

---

SEGINUS

Star's name: Seginus
Degree position: 16°38'–17°20' Libra between the years 1930 and 2000
Magnitude: 3
Strength: ★★★★★★
Orb: 1°40'
Constellation: Gamma Bootes
Applicable days: October 9, 10, 11, 12
Star qualities: Mercury/Saturn
Description: a small yellow and white star located on the left shoulder of Bootes

Seginus's influence imparts a quick and keen mentality, many contacts, and popularity. This star indicates that you are versatile and a quick learner, but warns against an inclination to be inconsistent and make too many sudden changes.

Linked to your Sun's degree, Seginus bestows success in business, a natural aptitude for astrology and philosophy, or an inclination toward unusual interests. Sociable and friendly, you have many friends who will come to your aid when they are needed.

• *Positive:* cooperative, popularity, versatility
• *Negative:* losses through friendships and partnerships

FORAMEN

Star's name: Foramen
Degree position: 21°12'–22°18' Libra between the years 1930 and 2000
Magnitude: 4
Strength: ★★★★
Orb: 1°30'
Constellation: Eta Carina
Applicable days: October 14, 15, 16, 17
Star qualities: Saturn/Jupiter
Description: a variable reddish star located in the stern of the Ship Argos and surrounded by a keyhole nebula

Foramen's influence bestows an intuitive, charming, and broad-minded personality, with leadership abilities. Although you are friendly and unassuming, you nevertheless possess a strong character. With dignity and dedication, success and prosperity can be achieved.

Linked to your Sun's degree, Foramen imparts natural diplomatic skills and an agreeable and sympathetic nature that is socially inclined. You are able to conceive of and see two or more points of view simultaneously; you are therefore ideally suited to act as a mediator in disputes.

• *Positive:* sociable, understanding, congenial, patience

• *Negative:* indecisiveness, lack of direction, easily fooled, acquisitiveness

SPICA

Star's name: Spica, also called Ishtar or Arista
Degree position: 22°51'–23°46' Libra between the years 1930 and 2000
Magnitude: 1
Strength: ★★★★★★★★★
Orb: 2°30'
Constellation: Alpha Virgo
Applicable days: October 14, 15, 16, 17, 18
Star qualities: varied: Venus/Mars or Venus/Jupiter/Mercury
Description: a brilliant white binary star located in the head of wheat in Virgo

Spica is one of the predominant stars in the sky and it is of great importance. This star bestows good judgment and unexpected turns of good fortune. Spica also suggests refinement, interest in science, and love of culture and art. Honors and riches increase after your education is completed. Spica can also bring success in foreign lands, long voyages, and trading in imports and exports.

Linked to your Sun's degree, Spica offers eminent position, good social connections, success in business undertakings, and an ability to gain from new ideas and inventions. You have good concentration, are intuitive, and possess psychic abilities. Associations with intellectual activities and big organizations can bring success. You enjoy dealing with the public and can acquire immense wealth, especially from commercial enterprises.

• *Positive:* economical, pragmatic focused goals

• *Negative:* too extravagant, constantly changing direction, unsettled mind

ARCTURUS

Star's name: Arcturus, also called the Bear Watcher, Alchameth, or Al Simak
Degree position: 23°15'–24°2' Libra between the years 1930 and 2000
Magnitude: 1
Strength: ★★★★★★★★★
Orb: 2°30'
Constellation: Alpha Bootes
Applicable days: October 16, 17, 18, 19, 20

Star qualities: Mars/Jupiter and Venus/Jupiter
Description: a golden orange and yellow star located on the left knee of Bootes

Arcturus imparts artistic talent and success in the world of fine arts. This star can bestow riches, honors, and acclaim and bring prosperity. Arcturus may also bring success in foreign lands and through long journeys. This star warns against restlessness and anxious moments, which create instability in your life.

Linked to your Sun's degree, Arcturus imparts wealth and a good reputation. This star brings success after early setbacks and grants intuitive, psychic, or healing abilities. An inclination toward the legal profession or public office may bring success. Alternatively, you may find an interest in writing on philosophical, spiritual, or religious subjects. This star suggests guarding against becoming too apprehensive and discontented by learning to accept calmly the ups and downs of life and staying detached.

• *Positive:* religious contacts, good judgment, long voyages, glamorous

• *Negative:* overindulgence, overly enthusiastic, laziness, negligence

Scorpio

PRINCEPS

Star's name: Princeps, also called Tsieh Kung
Degree position: 2°8'–2°50' Scorpio between the years 1930 and 2000
Magnitude: 3.5
Strength: ★★★★★
Orb: 1°30'
Constellation: Delta Bootes
Applicable days: October 26, 27, 28, 29
Star qualities: Mercury/Saturn
Description: a pale yellow giant star located in the spear shaft of Bootes

Princeps suggests a keen mentality and a studious and profound mind, with a depth of understanding that favors research. This star bestows determination, resourcefulness, and a conservative outlook.

Linked to your Sun's degree, this star imparts prominence in education, science, or legal and government affairs. You have a competitive nature and a daring personality. Your subtle assertiveness and resourceful attitude help you to undertake and succeed with new or untried ideas. You have a reserved nature and will not commit yourself until you are sure where you stand. When you are convinced of the facts, you can be quite outspoken and are unafraid to be direct and stand your ground, as you prefer to be in control.

- *Positive:* relentless, strong-willed, hardworking, ambitious
- *Negative:* stubborn, unorthodox methods, create your own problems, too controlling

KHAMBALIA

Star's name: Khambalia, also called Khamblia
Degree position: 5°53'–6°49' Scorpio between the years 1930 and 2000
Magnitude: 4
Strength: ★★★★
Orb: 1°30'
Constellation: Lambda Virgo
Applicable days: October 30, 31, November 1
Star qualities: Mercury/Mars
Description: a small white star located on the left foot of Virgo

Khambalia imparts a quick mind and good debating skills. This star indicates changing circumstances, which might include unexpected gains. Khambalia's influence suggests that you have a pragmatic outlook and an inclination toward higher learning and education. Although friendly and sociable, often you may appear impersonal.

Linked to your Sun's degree, Khambalia offers success in business or politics and public office. You may become a specialist with unique abilities in your chosen profession. Occasionally this star can also bestow some unusual and outstanding talents that can bring changes in work and employment.

- *Positive:* dedication, higher learning, polished logic, power of thought
- *Negative:* argumentative, restlessness, unreliability

ACRUX

Star's name: Acrux
Degree position: 10°54'–11°50' Scorpio between the years 1930 and 2000
Magnitude: 1
Strength: ★★★★★★★★★
Orb: 2°30'
Constellation: Alpha Crux
Applicable days: November 2, 3, 4, 5, 6, 7
Star qualities: Jupiter
Description: a blue-white triple star, the brightest star in the Southern Cross

Acrux bestows a love of knowledge, harmony, and justice. This star imparts an interest in philosophy, metaphysics, and astrology as well as granting psychic abilities. You have an inquisitive mind and probably an insatiable appetite for books or a desire to travel. Acrux may lead you toward research and education, the social sciences, philosophy, and religion.

Linked to your Sun's degree, Acrux suggests a sensitive and

sentimental nature. This star imparts broad-minded humanitarian beliefs, and you may be a seeker of justice. You may become a leader in your profession and can excel or gain a high position in affairs that concern humankind.

- *Positive:* justice, love toward your fellow man, compassion
- *Negative:* revenge, injustice, lack of feelings

ALPHECCA

Star's name: Alphecca
Degree position: 11°16'–12°0' Scorpio between the years 1930 and 2000
Magnitude: 2.5
Strength: ★★★★★★
Orb: 2°10'
Constellation: Alpha Corona Borealis
Applicable days: November 4, 5, 6, 7
Star qualities: Venus/Mercury and Mars/Mercury
Description: a brilliant white star located in the knot of the Ribbon

Alphecca imparts dignity, leadership ability, healing powers, and a talent for higher learning of esoteric subjects such as astrology. This star also bestows artistic abilities and a flair for music and poetry. You are decisive and able to achieve a position of authority. Alphecca also suggests beneficial legacies.

Linked to your Sun's degree, this star denotes an active mind with brilliant intellectual abilities, talent for writing, and work with the public. If your Sun is linked to this star, you may well turn to the performing arts and can become a showman or a public figure. If trouble arises, it does not affect your position. Through education, you can enhance what is already an active and creative mind.

- *Positive:* clever, creative, writing talent, education, knowledge
- *Negative:* indecision, cunning, unlucky

AL GENUBI

Star's name: Al Genubi, also called South Scale or the South Claw
Degree position: 14°6'–15°4' Scorpio between the years 1930 and 2000
Magnitude: 3
Strength: ★★★★★★
Orb: 1°40'
Constellation: Alpha Libra
Applicable days: November 6, 7, 8, 9
Star qualities: varied interpretations: Jupiter/Mars/Saturn/Venus
Description: a pale yellow and white-gray binary star located in the southern scale of the Balance

Al Genubi suggests that you may encounter changes and times of instability throughout life. This star also warns that you may need to follow orthodox ways or stay on the right side of the track. Success and accomplishment may be achieved through learning to overcome obstacles.

Linked to your Sun's degree, this star imparts the ability to focus on goals and objectives and thus overcome obstacles and disappointments. You may, however, need to avoid mental anxiety by learning that favors carry a price tag.

• *Positive:* learn to forgive, patience, perseverance
• *Negative:* unforgiving, dealing with unsavory characters, some legal problems

AL SCHEMALI

Star's name: Al Schemali, also called North Scale or the North Claw
Degree position: 18°23'–19°19' Scorpio between the years
1930 and 2000
Magnitude: 2.5
Strength: ★★★★★★
Orb: 1°30'
Constellation: Beta Libra
Applicable days: November 11, 12, 13
Star qualities: varied interpretations: Mercury/Jupiter and Jupiter/Mars
Description: a blue-white, sometimes pale emerald star located in the northern scale of the Balance

Al Schemali offers opportunities for good fortune. You have a sound intellect and a flair for science or esoteric subjects, which highlights your intuitive and psychic abilities. This star may bestow honors, wealth, and riches and may also bring long-lasting happiness.

Linked to your Sun's degree, Al Schemali imparts a strong character, leadership abilities, and executive skills. With the help of this star's influence, you may enjoy promotion to a high position in your career and achieve success after initial difficulties. This star warns that you should avoid legal entanglements and questionable situations. On the other hand, trouble does not last long and good fortune returns if the correct choices are made.

• *Positive:* sound common sense, wealth of ideas, optimism, organizational abilities
• *Negative:* exaggeration, conceit, arrogance

UNUKALHAI

Star's name: Unukalhai
Degree position: 21°3'–21°54' Scorpio between the years 1930 and 2000
Magnitude: 2.5
Strength: ★★★★★
Orb: 1°40'
Constellation: Alpha Serpentis
Applicable days: November 13, 14, 15, 16
Star qualities: Saturn/Mars
Description: a pale orange-yellow star located on the neck of the Serpent

Unukalhai imparts a bold and daring nature, determination, and endurance, which can help you overcome difficulties. This star also warns against keeping unsuitable company and suggests that although learning to do the right thing might be hard, it is also very rewarding.

Linked to your Sun's degree, Unukalhai imparts success in writing, politics, and affairs dealing with the public. This star bestows a good sense of structure and determination, although you may be obstinate. Unukalhai's influence also suggests that family matters need to be settled in a fair and just way and warns against involvement in feuds and legal battles.

• *Positive:* determination, endurance, power of resistance, overcoming challenges
• *Negative:* rebelliousness and quarrels, breaking the law, antiestablishment

AGENA

Star's name: Agena
Degree position: 22°48'–23°45' Scorpio between the years
1930 and 2000
Magnitude: 1
Strength: ★★★★★★★★★
Orb: 2°30'
Constellation: Beta Centuris
Applicable days: November 14, 15, 16, 17, 18
Star qualities: varied influences: Venus/Jupiter or Mars/Mercury
Description: a small white star located on the right foreleg of the Centaur

Agena bestows achievement and the rise to a high position. This star also imparts vitality and good health. Often you are refined and possess a high moral code, which may in turn bring friendship, success, and honors.

Linked to your Sun's degree, Agena bestows ambition and success. You are probably well connected or have prominent friends and associates. This star provides good social skills and the ability to attract wide popularity, which in turn brings opportunities. Agena encourages mental activity and quick, outspoken responses; however, it also suggests that speaking out of turn or being indiscreet can be costly.

• *Positive:* assertive, clever, stamina, popularity, good morals
• *Negative:* rashness, indecision, lack of honor

BUNGULA

Star's name: Bungula, also called Tolliman
Degree position: 28°36'–29°35' Scorpio between the years
1930 and 2000
Magnitude: 1
Strength: ★★★★★★★★★
Orb: 2°30'

Constellation: Alpha Centauri
Applicable days: November 20, 21, 22, 23, 24
Star qualities: Venus/Jupiter
Description: a brilliant white and yellow binary star located on the left foot of the Centaur

Bungula bestows a passionate yet refined nature and beneficial social contacts. If you seek help, this star grants friends who will assist you when you need help most. It also imparts opportunities and positions of honor or power. Bungula nevertheless warns against extremist behavior and a fatalistic attitude.

Linked to your Sun's degree, this star indicates an ambitious nature, and the consistency and determination to achieve steady progress. It also warns of rivalry, envy, or self-centeredness.

• *Positive:* self-reliant, learn to share, generosity, popularity
• *Negative:* overly sensitive, falling out with other people, alienating yourself from others

Sagittarius

YED PRIOR

Star's name: Yed Prior
Degree position: 1°19'–2°13' Sagittarius between the years 1930 and 2000
Magnitude: 3
Strength: ★★★★★
Orb: 1°40'
Constellation: Delta Ophiuchi
Applicable days: November 23, 24, 25, 26
Star qualities: Saturn/Venus
Description: a deep yellow star located on the left hand of Ophiuchus

Yed Prior's influence imparts a frank and direct nature with a serious demeanor. Usually you are ambitious and determined with good social skills.

Linked to your Sun's degree, this star bestows charm and a pleasant personality as well as ambition and success. Yed Prior also grants success in writing and achievement in education and higher learning, and indicates a special interest in astrology, philosophy, and religion. Alternatively, you may pursue a career in the legal profession or politics. You are admired and liked by colleagues and employers.

• *Positive:* popularity, focus at all times
• *Negative:* verbose, immorality, shamelessness, revolutionary

ISIDIS

Star's name: Isidis, also called Dshubba
Degree position: 1°33'–2°29' Sagittarius between the years 1930 and 2000

Magnitude: 2.5
Strength: ★★★★★★
Orb: 1°40'
Constellation: Delta Scorpio
Applicable days: November 24, 25, 26
Star qualities: Mars/Saturn
Description: a bright star located near the right claw of the Scorpion

Isidis imparts a liberal attitude, pride, and high aims. This star's influence grants ambition; you are competitive, with daring and unconventional views. Isidis warns against being impatient and also suggests guarding against keeping unreliable company.

Linked to your Sun's degree, this star encourages good education and an inclination toward higher learning in fields such as law, politics, philosophy, religion, metaphysics, and astrology. You are probably outgoing and enjoy popularity, many friends, and lasting partnerships. You may need to exercise discretion.

• *Positive:* outspoken and frank, educated, worldly
• *Negative:* indiscreet, opportunist, overly optimistic

GRAFFIAS

Star's name: Graffias, also called Acrab or Frons Scorpi
Degree position: 2°12'–3°13' Sagittarius between the years 1930 and 2000
Magnitude: 3
Strength: ★★★★★★
Orb: 1°40'
Constellation: Beta Scorpio
Applicable days: November 24, 25, 26, 27
Star qualities: Saturn/Mars
Description: a pale white and lilac triple star located on the head of the Scorpion

Graffias bestows good business sense, wealth, and material power. Often this star grants an active mind and the desire to take risks. Graffias also indicates that success is achieved after many difficulties; therefore endurance and determination are the keys to achieving your goals. This star warns that benefits may not necessarily be long-lasting and suggests that too much activity may cause stress and bad health.

Linked to your Sun's degree, Graffias bestows success in politics and prominence in education, religion, and work linked to the public. This star suggests that high honors are often gained through hard work and service. You may possess the power to wish and get what you desire, but not always have the ability to enjoy fully the rewards of your hard-earned success.

• *Positive:* endurance, hardworking, dedication
• *Negative:* changes and turbulence, materialistic inclinations

HAN

Star's name: Han
Degree position: 8°15'–9°13' Sagittarius between the years
1930 and 2000
Magnitude: 3
Strength: ★★★★★
Orb: 1°40'
Constellation: Zeta Ophiuchi
Applicable days: November 30 and December 1, 2, 3
Star qualities: Saturn/Venus
Description: a small blue-white star located near the left
knee of Ophiuchus

Han imparts opportunities for success, lucky breaks, and honor; however, it also warns against self-destructive behavior and misconduct in affairs.

Linked to your Sun's degree, Han grants a charismatic personality and an ability to make a good impression. You often receive help from others and can achieve quick promotion, at times with little effort and not always justly deserved. This star also imparts accomplishment in writing and work for the public and warns against being involved in questionable situations that might cause you unnecessary anxiety and stress.

• *Positive:* committed, responsible, serious
• *Negative:* detached from feeling, denial

ANTARES

Star's name: Antares, also called Anti Aries or the Rival of Mars
Degree position: 8°48'–9°49' Sagittarius between the years
1930 and 2000
Magnitude: 1
Strength: ★★★★★★★★★★
Orb: 2°30'
Constellation: Alpha Scorpio
Applicable days: November 30, December 1, 2, 3, 4, 5
Star qualities: Mars/Jupiter, also Jupiter/Venus
Description: a binary star, fiery red and emerald green, located in the
body of the Scorpion

Antares is one of the four royal stars and therefore is of great importance. This star imparts an adventurous nature, keen mentality, broad-minded outlook, and liberal attitude. It also indicates unexpected events, lucky breaks, and numerous opportunities for travel to foreign lands. Antares bestows courage, strong convictions, and a daring character. However, it also warns against rashness, destructive behavior, obstinacy, and vengeful acts.

Linked to your Sun's degree, Antares imparts an interest in education, politics, or business dealing with the public. You are probably idealistic, optimistic, and willing to fight for just

causes. Antares also bestows a talent for writing and a religious outlook that seeks knowledge and wisdom. Although Antares bestows honor and riches, these are not necessarily long-lasting. With Antares's influence, unforeseen circumstances can change situations suddenly for good or bad.

• *Positive:* courageous, worldly, travel to foreign lands, higher education
• *Negative:* hot temper, outspoken, rebellious, destructive behavior

RASTABAN

Star's name: Rastaban
Degree position: 10°49'–11°42' Sagittarius between the years
1930 and 2000
Magnitude: 2.5
Strength: ★★★★★★
Orb: 1°40'
Constellation: Beta Draconis
Applicable days: December 3, 4, 5, 6
Star qualities: Saturn/Mars
Description: an irregular, variable, giant red and blue-yellow binary
star, located in the head of the Dragon

Rastaban imparts strong convictions, determination, and success in dealing with the general public. This star may also indicate opportunities for unusual discoveries and inventions as well as changes and unexpected turns of fortune. Rastaban bestows great courage, daring, and an ambitious nature. Often, through the help of others, you may gain power and fame.

Linked to your Sun's degree, Rastaban imparts executive abilities, an ambitious nature, and persistence. This may eventually lead to high positions in careers such as education, religion, science, and innovative research.

Horses are also associated with this star, and working with them may be a desired career.

• *Positive:* endurance, patience, pragmatic outlook
• *Negative:* rebellious and antiestablishment, lack of drive

SABIK

Star's name: Sabik
Degree position: 16°58'–17°59' Sagittarius between the years
1930 and 2000
Magnitude: 2.5
Strength: ★★★★★★
Orb: 1°40'
Constellation: Eta Ophiuchi
Applicable days: December 8, 9, 10, 11
Star qualities: varied influences: Saturn/Venus and Jupiter/Venus
Description: a pale yellow star located on the left knee of Ophiuchus

Sabik's influence suggests honesty and moral courage. This star also urges you to remain true to your nature and to avoid dishonesty and wastefulness. It suggests that it may be necessary to exercise judgment and avoid underhanded dealings, no matter how lucrative they may seem.

Linked to your Sun's degree, Sabik bestows sincerity, honorable conduct, and a love of justice. You may seek spiritual wisdom and have inclinations toward philosophical studies as well as unconventional or controversial subjects. This star grants changes for the better, and undesirable situations often end up being blessings in disguise. It also indicates that no matter what the circumstances, good morals and convictions will see you through difficult times.

- *Positive:* morals and courage, overcoming obstacles
- *Negative:* wastefulness, dishonesty, deception, lack of morals

RASALHAGUE

Star's name: Rasalhague, also called the Serpent Charmer
Degree position: 21°28'–22°26' Sagittarius between the years 1930 and 2000
Magnitude: 2
Strength: ★★★★★★★★
Orb: 2°10'
Constellation: Alpha Ophiuchi
Applicable days: December 13, 14, 15, 16
Star qualities: Saturn/Venus
Description: a bright white and blue sapphire star located on the head of Ophiuchus

Rasalhague imparts a desire for knowledge and education, humanitarianism, and a broad-minded or liberal perspective. You may also be interested in philosophy and religion and have a gift for visualization.

Linked to your Sun's degree, Rasalhague suggests a reserved yet thoughtful nature. This star may indicate success in business through the ability to concentrate on large projects or think in worldly terms. Often this star suggests great individual achievement or that you will be ahead of your time. Rasalhague can also make you suspicious, and it implies that learning to trust others may bring popularity and widen your circle of friends.

- *Positive:* connected with large enterprises, involvement in sports, good income
- *Negative:* suspicious, scattered energies, overly serious

LESUTH

Star's name: Lesuth, also called the Sting
Degree position: 23°2'–24°0' Sagittarius between the years 1930 and 2000
Magnitude: 3

Strength: ★★★★★★
Orb: 1°40'
Constellation: Nu Scorpio
Applicable days: December 15, 16, 17, 18
Star qualities: Mercury/Mars
Description: a small quadruple-star system surrounded by a nebula, located on the stinger of the Scorpion

Lesuth imparts a quick and keen mind, assertiveness, and self-motivation. You are probably ambitious, with sound judgment and a sociable nature. This star bestows creativity, inventiveness, and opportunities to work on new discoveries or enjoy unexpected benefits and good fortune.

Linked to your Sun's degree, Lesuth indicates success in public affairs, a flair for writing, or an inclination toward education and higher learning. You are probably inventive and inquisitive and contribute to society through your discoveries. You make a good detective or investigator because of your quick and active mind. You are outspoken, hardworking, and full of vitality, with swift actions. Nevertheless, you must learn to channel all your energy into worthwhile projects and avoid activities that could bring danger or legal entanglements.

- *Positive:* shrewd, creative, determination, common sense
- *Negative:* tendency to exaggeration, turbulence

ACULEUS

Star's name: Aculeus
Degree position: 24°49'–25°57' Sagittarius between the years 1930 and 2000
Magnitude: 4.5
Strength: ★★★
Orb: 1°
Constellation: 6M Scorpio
Applicable days: December 17, 18, 19
Star qualities: Mars/Moon
Description: this star is located a little above the stinger of Scorpio in a cluster together with the star Acumen

Aculeus imparts great energy, determination, and leadership and executive abilities. You are active but restless and may be prone to changing moods. This suggests that cultivating patience will increase opportunities for success.

Linked to your Sun's degree, Aculeus bestows success in public affairs, if you are willing to work hard and apply yourself to the job at hand. This star carries a warning that suggests that care must taken of the eyes.

- *Positive:* quick mind, intuition, assertive, ambitious
- *Negative:* impatience, irritability, fluctuating moods

ETAMIN

Star's name: Etamin
Degree position: 26°55'–27°57' Sagittarius between the years
1930 and 2000
Magnitude: 2.5–3
Strength: ★★★★★★
Orb: 1°40'
Constellation: Gamma Draconis
Applicable days: December 19, 20, 21
Star qualities: Mars/Moon
Description: a red giant binary star located in the Dragon's eye

Etamin bestows a keen mentality, enthusiasm, individuality, and a pioneering spirit. Often you are self-assured but at times overconfident, which results in hasty actions that lead to loss of position.

Linked to your Sun's degree, this star encourages you to pursue a career in higher education, writing, publishing, or the legal profession. Usually Etamin imparts an assertive and determined nature with an interest in unusual subjects, ideas, and issues.

• *Positive:* willpower, fighting spirit, ambition, sincerity
• *Negative:* impulsive actions, quarrels, irritability, moodiness

ACUMEN

Star's name: Acumen
Degree position: 27°45'–28°54' Sagittarius between the years
1930 and 2000
Magnitude: 4.5
Strength: ★★★
Orb: 1°
Constellation: 7M Scorpio
Applicable days: December 20, 21, 22
Star qualities: Mars/Moon
Description: this star cluster is located with the star Aculeus just above the stinger of Scorpio

Acumen bestows leadership abilities, energy, assertiveness, and a need to get ahead. It also imparts strong willpower, inner tensions, and impulsive tendencies. Frequently, these emotional intensities and a tendency to become overly excited may lead to confusion, misunderstandings, or even quarrels. Acumen indicates success in business and love of country life and a large family.

Linked to your Sun's degree, this star bestows enthusiasm and a get-up-and-go attitude. You like to demonstrate what you can achieve, and winning is your main objective. Acumen endows vitality, and you can often initiate ideas or be enterprising and work with the public. However, you need the support and

love of family and home. Acumen also warns that care must be taken of eyesight.

• *Positive:* independent, emotional, popular, ambitious
• *Negative:* overly sensitive, fluctuating moods, impatience, inner tension

SINISTRA

Star's name: Sinistra
Degree position: 28°46'–29°44' Sagittarius between the years
1930 and 2000
Magnitude: 3
Strength: ★★★★★★
Orb: 1°40'
Constellation: Nu Ophiuchi
Applicable days: December 21, 22, 23
Star qualities: Venus/Saturn
Description: a dwarf orange star located in the left hand of Ophiuchus

Sinistra bestows success in business enterprises, good executive abilities, leadership potential, and an independent or original personality. This star, however, also imparts restlessness and a constant need for change, which may result in fluctuating circumstances. Often you seek powerful and influential positions.

Linked to your Sun's degree, Sinistra bestows high aspirations and a daring and original yet contentious nature. Achievements in business, the legal profession, government, or dealing with the public are all indicated by the influence of this star. Alternatively, you may have aspirations for higher learning, religion, and philosophy. There are also opportunities to make a name for yourself and achieve fame or notoriety.

• *Positive:* high position in public life
• *Negative:* domineering, unfeeling, overserious

SPICULUM

Star's name: Spiculum, also called Trifid Nebulae
Degree position: 29°41' Sagittarius–0°39' Capricorn between the years
1930 and 2000
Magnitude: 5
Strength: ★★
Orb: 1°
Constellation: 20M, 21M Sagittarius
Applicable days: December 21, 22, 23
Star qualities: Moon/Mars
Description: two clusters and a nebula located on the arrowhead of Sagittarius

Spiculum imparts ambition, assertiveness, great courage, and strong convictions. This star indicates that you are socially inclined and enjoy group gatherings. This star suggests that you may also be prone to moodiness and restlessness and are likely to make unpredictable decisions or behave in a peculiar manner.

Linked to your Sun's degree, Spiculum imparts intense emotions, aspirations, ambition, courage, and strong convictions. This star indicates that you are gregarious and enjoy social events and have many friends, especially women. Spiculum also warns that hastiness or premature action often result in regrettable conduct.

- *Positive:* willpower, fighting spirit, vigor
- *Negative:* moodiness, irritability, restlessness, quarrels, regrettable decisions

Capricorn

POLIS

Star's name: Polis
Degree position: 2°15'–3°14' Capricorn between the years
1930 and 2000
Magnitude: 4
Strength: ★★★★
Orb: 1°30'
Constellation: Mu Sagittarius
Applicable days: December 23, 24, 25, 26
Star qualities: Jupiter/Mars
Description: a blue and white triple star located in the upper part of the bow of the Archer

Polis bestows keen perception and the power to focus upon a particular goal. This star encourages you to search for success and good fortune and grants the determination to rise to high positions. The ability to make quick and fortunate decisions imparts leadership abilities. This star also warns against a tendency to be rebellious and domineering.

Linked to your Sun's degree, Polis imparts a pioneering and courageous nature, many opportunities, endurance, and high ambitions. You are proud and seek to make a name for yourself, whether it results in fame or notoriety. This star can also impart success in higher education, with special interests in spirituality. Polis also warns against a tendency to dominate situations and take the lead unless you are the initiator of the enterprise.

- *Positive:* concentration, competitive nature
- *Negative:* rebelliousness, restlessness, lack of endurance, overly optimistic

KAUS BOREALIS

Star's name: Kaus Borealis
Degree position: 5°20'–6°19' Capricorn between the years
1930 and 2000

Magnitude: 3
Strength: ★★★★★
Orb: 1°40'
Constellation: Lambda Sagittarius
Applicable days: December 27, 28, 29
Star qualities: Mercury/Mars
Description: a giant orange star located in the northern part of the bow of the Archer

Kaus Borealis imparts intelligence, a keen mentality, energetic and impressive speech, and good communication skills. A love of discussion and debate is also indicated by this star; however, at times you appear aggressive or argumentative. Frequently this star bestows ability at repartee, humanitarian tendencies, and an idealistic nature with a keen sense of justice. This star may also force changes on you and challenge your obstinacy.

Linked to your Sun's degree, Kaus Borealis imparts resoluteness and an inner driving force to achieve positions of influence. Your leadership ability and ingenuity are often recognized by others and lead to accomplishment or promotion. Nevertheless, an inner restlessness and a continual need to forge ahead may suggest discontent.

- *Positive:* versatile, determined, knowledgeable, outspoken
- *Negative:* lack of satisfaction, extremist, opinionated

FACIES

Star's name: Facies
Degree position: 7°12'–8°24' Capricorn between the years
1930 and 2000
Magnitude: 5
Strength: ★★
Orb: 1°
Constellation: M22 Sagittarius
Applicable days: December 29, 30, 31
Star qualities: Sun/Mars
Description: a bright open star cluster and nebula located in the bow of the Archer

Facies imparts assertiveness, a fighting spirit, and a fearless nature. You are full of vitality and vigor, and usually you wish to exercise power and have the necessary leadership qualities. Facies grants the ability to make decisions quickly, and you are a good strategist who can enjoy competitive activities and win.

Linked to your Sun's degree, this star bestows success in business and dealing with the public as well as strong willpower, inner drive, and a competitive spirit. This star also warns that the constant need to be number one may involve some risks, and suggests avoiding underhanded dealings and dangerous situations.

- *Positive:* will to live, active life, power of attainment, decisiveness
- *Negative:* overstrain, obstinacy, inclination to quarrel

PELAGUS

Star's name: Pelagus, also called Nunki
Degree position: 11°15'–12°21' Capricorn between the years
1930 and 2000
Magnitude: 2
Strength: ★★★★★★★
Orb: 2°10'
Constellation: Sigma Sagittarius
Applicable days: January 1, 2, 3, 4, 5
Star qualities: Mercury/Jupiter
Description: a star located on the vane of the arrow at the Archer's hand

Pelagus's influence bestows a love of truthfulness, a strong character, and a direct and assertive manner. This star imparts determination to achieve success and sound common sense. Pelagus urges the individual toward education and higher learning, especially in science, philosophy, history, and spirituality. This star also indicates an outspoken personality and strong convictions.

Linked to your Sun's degree, Pelagus bestows creativity and a wealth of ideas, a rise to influential public position, and favorable conditions at home and with family matters. You can make a name for yourself, and even though you sometimes become involved in complex situations, you usually come out unscathed.
- *Positive:* higher learning, sound common sense, love of truth
- *Negative:* controversial, failure through dishonesty

ASCELLA

Star's name: Ascella
Degree position: 12°39'–13°37' Capricorn between the years
1930 and 2000
Applicable days: January 3, 4, 5, 6
Magnitude: 3
Strength: ★★★★★★
Orb: 1°40'
Constellation: Zeta Sagittarius
Star qualities: Jupiter/Mercury
Description: a binary star located in the armpit of the Archer

Ascella bestows a wealth of ideas, good judgment, and an inclination for spirituality and philosophy. This star indicates that wealth and good fortune can be achieved through being enterprising and combining your ability to think big with your pragmatic nature.

Linked to your Sun's degree, Ascella imparts ambition, moral courage, and sound judgment. You probably have strong beliefs or convictions. This star suggests that influential friends and employers will aid you when you need it most. Ascella's influence also implies that your executive abilities together with your social nature will provide you with many opportunities, good luck, and happiness.

- *Positive:* gregarious, sociable and friendly, strong convictions
- *Negative:* disagreeable, argumentative

MANUBRIUM

Star's name: Manubrium
Degree position: 14°01'–15°03' Capricorn between the years
1930 and 2000
Magnitude: 4
Strength: ★★★★
Orb: 1°30'
Constellation: Omicron Sagittarius
Applicable days: January 5, 6, 7
Star qualities: Sun/Mars
Description: a star, part of a cluster located in the face of the Archer

Manubrium's influence suggests that you have courage or a daring and dynamic personality. This star also implies that you are capable of great heroism or acts of defiance. You probably possess a hot temper and are capable of being impatient.

Linked to your Sun's degree, this star bestows vitality and vigor and a strong desire for leadership positions. Manubrium suggests that you are proud and pioneering and often enjoy sport and competition. It may also indicate that you often desire to dominate a situation.
- *Positive:* vigor, power of attainment, courage, ambition
- *Negative:* stubborn, restless, inclination to quarrel

WEGA

Star's name: Wega, also called Vulture
Degree position: 14°20'–15°19' Capricorn between the years
1930 and 2000
Magnitude: 1
Strength: ★★★★★★★★★
Orb: 2°30'
Constellation: Alpha Lyra
Star qualities: varied interpretations: Venus/Mercury, also
Jupiter/Saturn
Description: a bright white and blue sapphire star located in the lower part of the Lyre

Wega bestows leadership ability and a sociable and outgoing personality. Usually you possess an idealistic and optimistic outlook and have creative abilities and a talent for writing. This star, however, also implies that changeable circumstances can bring about fluctuating periods of success and suggests that only with determination can you ensure stability.

Linked to your Sun's degree, Wega imparts success and opportunities to rise to high positions. This star may bring you into contact with influential people, and this might lead to honor and popularity. Wega's influence also suggests that changeable circumstances may cause success to be short-lived. You probably enjoy work in a governmental position or dealing with the general public. This star also warns against being too critical or abrupt.

- *Positive:* refinement, hope, serious, responsible
- *Negative:* misuse of power, overly reserved, critical, abrupt, hidden enemies

DENEB

Star's name: Deneb, also called Al Danab
Degree position: 18°49'–19°55' Capricorn between the years 1930 and 2000
Magnitude: 3
Strength: ★★★★★
Orb: 1°40'
Constellation: Zeta Aquila
Applicable days: January 9, 10, 11, 12
Star qualities: Mars/Jupiter
Description: a green star located in the eye of the Eagle

Deneb imparts leadership abilities and bestows a liberal attitude and a broad-minded nature. Optimistic, enterprising, and daring, you are enthusiastic and ambitious, with sound common sense and an ability to act assertively.

Linked to your Sun's degree, this star bestows success in dealing with the public and an inclination toward business and the legal profession. You probably possess leadership and executive skills, a strong will, and the ability to instruct others. This star imparts an independent and dynamic personality or true individuality, which gives you opportunities for advancement through courage and enthusiasm.

- *Positive:* enterprising spirit, competitive, ambitious
- *Negative:* hastiness, impatience, dishonesty, negligence

TEREBELLUM

Star's name: Terebellum
Degree position: 24°52'–25°55' Capricorn between the years 1930 and 2000
Magnitude: 5
Strength: ★★
Orb: 1°
Constellation: Omega Sagittarius
Applicable days: January 15, 16, 17
Star qualities: Venus/Saturn
Description: an orange-red star in the four-sided figure in the tail of the Archer

Terebellum imparts a clear and pragmatic outlook, with an ambitious and determined personality. Often you succeed after

overcoming difficulties. This star indicates that you are responsible and dutiful and can endure hardship and struggle. This star may also suggest that you can experience doubts and inner conflicts between personal desires and duties to others.

Linked to your Sun's degree, this star bestows cleverness and ambition to rise to prominent positions. Terebellum, however, warns that you may nevertheless be crafty and suggests guarding against mischief and wrongdoing. This star indicates that good fortune and success can be achieved, but often at considerable expense or sacrifice.

- *Positive:* ambitious, devotion, sentimental, clever
- *Negative:* mercenary, ruthlessness, crafty, self-seeking

Aquarius

ALBIREO

Star's name: Albireo
Degree position: 0°17'–1°16' Aquarius between the years 1930 and 2000
Magnitude: 3
Strength: ★★★★★
Orb: 1°40'
Constellation: Beta Cygnus
Applicable days: January 20, 21, 22, 23
Star qualities: Mercury/Venus
Description: a topaz yellow and sapphire blue binary star located on the head of the Swan

Albireo's influence bestows a refined and gentle nature and often indicates an elegant or handsome appearance. This star suggests that you prefer neatness, have a lovable character, and enjoy popularity. If you seek help from others, you usually find it when it is most needed.

Linked to your Sun's degree, this star imparts a sociable, likable, and easygoing personality that enables you to make friends easily and succeed in dealing with the public. Albireo can impart a talent for writing, especially on humanitarian or social subjects. This star also indicates that you are likely to choose unusual occupations and may possess some eccentric habits, and warns against becoming too radical or extremist.

- *Positive:* communicative, liberal, creative ideas, inventive
- *Negative:* rebellious, too radical, eccentric and unfriendly

ALTAIR

Star's name: Altair, also called Al Tair or the Eagle
Degree position: Aquarius 0°47'–1°43' between the years 1930 and 2000
Magnitude: 1
Strength: ★★★★★★★★★
Orb: 2°30'

Constellation: Alpha Aquila
Applicable days: January 20, 21, 22, 23, 24
Star qualities: Mars/Jupiter, Uranus, Mercury
Description: a white and yellow star in the neck of the Eagle

Altair bestows strong desires, confidence, ambition, and a liberal attitude, yet an unyielding nature as well. This star indicates that although you can be radical and rebellious or sometimes cause trouble by throwing a monkey wrench in the works, your originality, eccentricity, and ingenious ideas often compensate for your misbehavior. Altair also bestows sudden bursts of wealth or success through new inventions but warns that fluctuating circumstances can frequently endanger positions of authority.

Linked to your Sun's degree, this star imparts originality, popularity, and adventurous tendencies. Altair also urges you to seek knowledge and reveals a talent for writing and education. Often ambitious and daring, you seek a change of fortune and may enjoy unexpected gains or other benefits. Group-oriented, you can make friends and influence people.

- *Positive:* original, inventive, individual, humanitarian, creative
- *Negative:* rebellious, antagonistic, unpredictable

GIEDI

Star's name: Giedi, also called Al Jady
Degree position: 2°50'–3°48' Aquarius between the years 1930 and 2000
Magnitude: 4
Strength: ★★★★
Orb: 1°40'
Constellation: Alpha Capricorn
Applicable days: January 23, 24, 25
Star qualities: varied influences: Venus/Mars and Venus/Mercury
Description: a yellow, ash, and lilac binary star located on the south horn of the Goat

Giedi bestows an eventful life full of unexpected events, twists and turns, good luck or sudden success, and unusual associations. It also suggests that you will experience periods of instability and changing circumstances, so, although you may enjoy good fortune now, Giedi suggests that you should learn to expect the unexpected.

Linked to your Sun's degree, Giedi imparts energy, vitality, and a dynamic personality. Through creative talents, including writing, this star may impart success and popularity with the general public. You may have influential friends who can support you and grant favors. Giedi also warns against criticism and suggests avoiding underhand dealings.

- *Positive:* creative talents, popularity, unusual associations, favors from others
- *Negative:* instability, eccentricity, critical

DABIH

Star's name: Dabih
Degree position: 3°4'–4°3' Aquarius between the years 1930 and 2000
Magnitude: 3
Strength: ★★★★★★
Orb: 1°40'
Constellation: Beta Capricorn
Applicable days: January 23, 24, 25, 26
Star qualities: Saturn/Venus and Saturn/Uranus
Description: a binary orange-yellow and blue star located in the left eye of the Goat

Dabih imparts positions of trust and authority, and bestows a responsible nature that may gain you public recognition. Dabih also suggests that you may have a reserved nature and a tendency to be mistrustful. It warns against unsavory associations or losses through friends.

Linked to your Sun's degree, this star imparts determination and success through steady progress and hard work. Dabih also suggests that you should proceed cautiously and use conventional methods to gain opportunities for promotion.

- *Positive:* hard work, dedication, perseverance
- *Negative:* overly suspicious, mistrustful

OCULUS

Star's name: Oculus
Degree position: 3°44'–4°44' Aquarius between the years 1930 and 2000
Magnitude: 5
Strength: ★★
Orb: 1°
Constellation: Pi Capricorn
Applicable days: January 24, 25, 26
Star qualities: Venus/Saturn
Description: a small white-yellow star located in the right eye of the Goat

Oculus imparts a keen intellect, a sense of duty, and a pragmatic outlook. Although you have good social skills and many friends and acquaintances, your somber demeanor gives the impression of detachment. This star, however, bestows loyal friends who will assist you and may help you gain success.

Linked to your Sun's degree, this star imparts charm and a friendly personality. Oculus also bestows popularity and success in dealing with the general public.

- *Positive:* social, friendly, group-oriented
- *Negative:* isolated, uncaring, overly serious

Star's name: Bos
Degree position: 4°11'–5°1' Aquarius between the years 1930 and 2000
Magnitude: 5
Strength: ★★
Orb: 1°
Constellation: Rho Capricorn
Applicable days: January 25, 26
Star qualities: Venus/Saturn
Description: a small white star located in the Goat's face

Bos bestows discernment, talent for artistic expression, and a piercing intellect. This star also imparts a strong sense of duty and urges you to be industrious and hardworking. When you have determination and strong convictions, this star will grant success and good fortune.

Linked to your Sun's degree, this star imparts strong character and convictions, individuality, and a sense of purpose. Bos also indicates that you may have peculiar areas of interest and should avoid a tendency to be too radical or extreme.

• *Positive:* good mind, self-control, ambition, success through industry
• *Negative:* overly serious, self-torment, separations

Star's name: Armus
Degree position: 11°45'–12°45' Aquarius between the years 1930 and 2000
Magnitude: 5
Strength: ★★
Orb: 1°
Constellation: Eta Capricorn
Applicable days: February 1, 2, 3
Star qualities: Mars/Mercury
Description: a small orange and red star located in the heart of the Goat

Armus imparts originality, inventiveness, and a contentious nature, along with a quick mind and the ability to impress others. Armus bestows a special talent for speech and quick repartee. This star also warns against being argumentative or disagreeable, and against an inner restlessness that can cause instability.

Linked to your Sun's degree, this star imparts independence, quick action, and an alert mind. You are probably socially inclined and achieve success through dealing with the general public.

• *Positive:* common sense, ability to judge, skill, impressive speech
• *Negative:* irritability, mental tension, nervousness, quarrelsome

Star's name: Dorsum
Degree position: 12°51'–13°50' Aquarius between the years 1930 and 2000
Magnitude: 4
Strength: ★★★★
Orb: 1°30'
Constellation: Theta Capricorn
Applicable days: February 2, 3, 4
Star qualities: Jupiter/Saturn
Description: a small white-blue star located on the back of the Goat

Dorsum bestows an ability to attain far-reaching objectives through perseverance and patience. Often industrious, you can achieve success in dealing with public affairs.

Linked to your Sun's degree, this star imparts slow but steady advancement, and progress is usually linked to responsibility. Dorsum encourages you to explore and develop your writing skills.

• *Positive:* sense of duty, diplomatic, willingness to serve
• *Negative:* tension, discontent, lack of patience

Star's name: Castra
Degree position: 19°30'–20°12' Aquarius between the years 1930 and 2000
Magnitude: 4
Strength: ★★★★
Orb: 1°30'
Constellation: Epsilon Capricorn
Applicable days: February 8, 9, 10
Star qualities: Jupiter/Saturn
Description: a small yellow-orange star located in the belly of the Goat

Castra imparts leadership ability, assertiveness, and prominence in public office. This star also suggests that patience and hard work lead to success but that destructive behavior may result in failure.

Linked to your Sun's degree, Castra can bestow honors in writing and achievement in higher education. You may well have an interest in philosophy or astrology. This star may also grant you intuitive and psychic abilities.

• *Positive:* perseverance, ambition, philosophical thinking
• *Negative:* lack of self-confidence, pessimism

Star's name: Nashira, often called the Bringer of Good Tidings
Degree position: 20°48'–21°45' Aquarius between the years 1930 and 2000

Magnitude: 4
Strength: ★★★★
Orb: 1°30'
Constellation: Gamma Capricorn
Applicable days: February 10, 11, 12, 13
Star qualities: Saturn/Jupiter
Description: a small star located in the tail of the Goat

Nashira bestows success and the ability to overcome setbacks and other challenges. Often this star imparts a cautious nature and suggests that patience is rewarded, while success comes after difficulties.

Linked to your Sun's degree, Nashira may impart writing skills, managerial and executive abilities, and successful employment in dealing with the public. Although this star may indicate struggle, once success is achieved it is often long-lasting, with possibilities for a distinguished position in later life.

• *Positive:* endurance, patience, cautious
• *Negative:* tense feelings, dissatisfaction, irritability

SAD AL SUUD

Star's name: Sad Al Suud
Degree position: 22°24'–23°20' Aquarius between the years 1930 and 2000
Magnitude: 3
Strength: ★★★★★
Orb: 1°30'
Constellation: Beta Aquarius
Applicable days: February 11, 12, 13, 14
Star qualities: varied influences: Mercury/Saturn and Sun/Uranus
Description: a pale yellow star located on the left shoulder of Aquarius

Sad Al Suud's influence suggests creativity, imagination, intuition, and psychic abilities. You may find interest in astrology and metaphysical studies. Usually you are domestically inclined and love your home. This star also bestows a happy family life and gains through marriage.

Linked to your Sun's degree, this star indicates originality, success dealing with the public, and interest in astrology, philosophy, or spirituality. You are probably competitive, original, and inventive. This star also suggests the occurrence of some strange or unexpected events.

• *Positive:* originality, creativity, lucky changes, new opportunities
• *Negative:* scandals, hasty action that can backfire

DENEB ALGEDI

Star's name: Deneb Algedi
Degree position: 22°23'–23°39' Aquarius between the years 1930 and 2000

Magnitude: 3
Strength: ★★★★★
Orb: 1°40'
Constellation: Delta Capricorn
Applicable days: February 11, 12, 13, 14
Star qualities: Jupiter/Saturn
Description: a small star located in the tail of the Goat

Deneb Algedi's influence imparts success, fame, and wealth, and the ability to turn difficult and unprofitable situations into successful ones. A good business sense and assertive personality can encourage leadership and executive abilities. Usually you are a good strategist and like to think big. With the influence of Deneb Algedi you can rise to high positions, although you may have to exercise discretion and be selective of the company you keep.

Linked to your Sun's degree, this star bestows high preferment for work in legal or government posts and steady but sure progress. This star also indicates a tendency to be impatient or irritable over minor problems that needs to be overcome.

• *Positive:* persuasive, perceptive, ambitious, shrewd
• *Negative:* destructive behavior, missed opportunities

Pisces

SAD AL MELIK

Star's name: Sad Al Melik
Degree position: 2°21'–3°16' Pisces between the years 1930 and 2000
Magnitude: 3
Strength: ★★★★★
Orb: 1°30'
Constellation: Alpha Aquarius
Applicable days: February 19, 20, 21, 23
Star qualities: varied influences: Saturn/Mercury and Saturn/Jupiter
Description: a giant pale yellow star located on the right shoulder of Aquarius

Sad Al Melik's influence imparts an imaginative and conservative nature. It also bestows psychic abilities and interest in metaphysics and astrology.

Linked to your Sun's degree, this star grants you opportunities for work in large enterprises and to gain success through big corporations. It also suggests a tendency to be acquisitive, industrious, and materialistic. Sad Al Melik often indicates that success comes after failure, and a great deal depends on how much effort you exert.

• *Positive:* practical, patience, sensitive, hard-working
• *Negative:* distrust, unrealistic, confused

FOM AL HAUT

Star's name: Fom Al Haut
Degree position: 2°51'–3°51' Pisces between the years 1930 and 2000
Magnitude: 1
Strength: ★★★★★★★★★
Orb: 2°30'
Constellation: Alpha Piscis Australis
Applicable days: February 19, 20, 21, 22, 23, 24, 25
Star qualities: Venus/Mercury
Description: a reddish white star located in the mouth of
the southern Fish

Fom Al Haut is one of the four royal stars and marks the winter solstice. Fom Al Haut is an especially powerful star and thus bestows good fortune, success, and a keen mentality. This star may also indicate a need to change from a material view to a more spiritual one.

Linked to your Sun's degree, this star imparts good rhythm, receptivity, and a tendency to go with the current. Easily influenced by your environment, you are self-seeking and may need to find creative self-expression. This star also suggests that legacies and inheritance can be expected, but warns against squandering or spending them quickly.

- *Positive:* learn to budget, idealistic, imaginative, creative
- *Negative:* costly legal matters, lack of insight, carelessness

DENEB ADIGE

Star's name: Deneb Adige, also called Al Dhanab
Degree position: 4°19'–4°55' Pisces between the years 1930 and 2000
Magnitude: 1
Strength: ★★★★★★★★★
Orb: 2°30'
Constellation: Alpha Cygnus
Applicable days: February 22, 23, 24, 25, 26, 27
Star qualities: Venus/Mercury
Description: a brilliant white star located in the tail of the Swan

Deneb Adige's influence bestows intelligence and the capability to grasp information quickly. This star imparts versatility and idealism as well as psychic abilities. Friendly and likable, you may need to be careful in your choice of friends.

Linked to your Sun's degree, this star imparts a talent for writing, a love of literature, and a possible interest in astrology. Deneb Adige can bring popularity and success in dealing with the public. This star can also indicate some difficulties in childhood that leave a strong impression.

- *Positive:* articulate, imaginative, astute mind, good intellect
- *Negative:* lack of tact, undermining of relationships

SKAT

Star's name: Skat
Degree position: 7°51'–8°40' Pisces between the years 1930 and 2000
Magnitude: 3.5–4
Strength: ★★★★
Orb: 1°30'
Constellation: Delta Aquarius
Applicable days: February 26, 27, 28, 29
Star qualities: varied interpretations: Saturn/Jupiter or
Uranus/Venus/Mercury
Description: a small star located on the right leg of Aquarius

Skat's influence bestows idealism, artistic flair, and a receptive mind. This star indicates that you often have a romantic nature, good fortune, success, and lasting happiness.

Linked to your Sun's degree, this star imparts sensitivity, idealism, and psychic ability, and offers success in dealing with the general public. You probably enjoy popularity and gain help from friends in times of need. This star, however, warns against being overemotional and suggests that you may need to overcome a tendency to overreact to criticism.

- *Positive:* creativity, rhythm, sensitivity, patience
- *Negative:* inconstancy, moodiness, nervousness

ACHERNAR

Star's name: Achernar
Degree position: 14°17'–15°11' Pisces between the years 1930 and 2000
Magnitude: 1
Strength: ★★★★★★★★★
Orb: 2°30'
Constellation: Alpha Eridanus
Applicable days: March 3, 4, 5, 6, 7, 8
Star qualities: Jupiter
Description: a blue-white star located at the mouth of the river Eridani

Achernar's influence stimulates expanded vision and the ability to see the whole. You are likely to have an optimistic outlook, a love of justice, and high aspirations. This star bestows success and a flair for dealing with the general public. Achernar may also direct you toward philosophy and religion.

Linked to your Sun's degree, this star bestows a generous, patient, and optimistic nature. This star gives prominence in higher education and a talent for writing. Rewards for outstanding work may be indicated. Achernar suggests that you can achieve success in business and dealing with the general public. If you gain fame, it is often long-lasting.

- *Positive:* justice, social sense, aspirations
- *Negative:* impressionability, escapism, speculation, misunderstandings

Star's name: Markab
Degree position: 22°29'–23°22' Pisces between the years 1930 and 2000
Magnitude: 2.5–3
Strength: ★★★★★★★★
Orb: 1°40'
Constellation: Alpha Pegasus
Applicable days: March 12, 13, 14, 15, 16
Star qualities: Mars/Mercury
Description: a bright white star located on the wing of Pegasus

Markab's influence bestows a spirit of enterprise, powers of resolution, and a determined mind. This star imparts a love of discussion or argument, good judgment, practical skills and dexterity, and quickness at repartee. You probably have the ability to retaliate in the right manner with impressive speech and can utilize situations to your advantage.

Linked to your Sun's degree, Markab bestows love of travel, creative and artistic talents, and success in dealing with the public. This star brings an aptitude for business and material gain, which may be achieved through the ability to think and act quickly and intuitively. You may feel stimulated to pursue an interest in higher education, spirituality, philosophy, or writing. Markab also warns against complacency and a lack of enthusiasm, which you may need to overcome.

• *Positive:* energetic, creative, enterprising
• *Negative:* fault-finding, willfulness, irritability, rashness and premature actions

Star's name: Scheat
Degree position: 28°14'–29°6' Pisces between the years 1930 and 2000
Magnitude: 2
Strength: ★★★★★★★★
Orb: 2°10'
Constellation: Beta Pegasus
Applicable days: March 16, 17, 18, 19, 20, 21
Star qualities: Mars/Mercury or Saturn/Mercury
Description: a giant deep orange-yellow star located on the left leg of Pegasus

Scheat's influence imparts determination but also stubbornness. This star suggests that you are a dreamer and an idealist, with an enterprising nature. You probably have many friends and enjoy a good social life in which you have a sense of belonging.

Linked to your Sun's degree, Scheat bestows success in dealing with the general public, as well as a talent for metaphysics, astrology, and esoteric subjects. You probably possess psychic or intuitive ability and a strong imagination. This star also indicates that success is not necessarily long-lasting and suggests a need to exercise caution in your choice of friends, acquaintances, or business colleagues.

• *Positive:* resolution, common sense, discussion, enterprise, determination
• *Negative:* danger by water, rashness, obstinate

About the Authors

GERALDINE SULLIVAN, B.Sc., born June 4, is a professional astrologer with twenty years of experience. She is an international lecturer and has appeared on television talk shows in the United States. She runs a successful astrology practice, gives workshops, and teaches adult education classes in London. Her science degree combined astrology and psychology and included research into the unconscious, dreams, and mystical experience.

SAFFI CRAWFORD, M.A., born May 28, is a professional numerologist and astrologer with thirteen years of experience. She runs a successful astrological counselling practice in London, teaches, and gives workshops in astrology and numerology. Her M.A. in social sciences combined the history and philosophy of Western civilization and included research into the history of astrology, hermeneutics, and reflexivity.

The authors welcome any inquiries and comments about the material in the book.

For further information on your complete fixed star listing and personal horoscope, you can contact the authors at

http://members.aol.com/AstroNum   http://members.aol.com/SunAstNum

or send a self-addressed stamped envelope (or international stamp coupon) to

BSN
P.O. Box 95
Barnet EN5 5ZT
England